W9-AXJ-754

DINOSAURS
THE ENCYCLOPEDIA
Supplement 4

DINOSAURS
THE ENCYCLOPEDIA
Supplement 4

by Donald F. Glut

Foreword by PETER J. MAKOVICKY, PH.D.

McFarland & Company, Inc., Publishers
Jefferson, North Carolina, and London

To Luis M. Chiappe,
who took me under his wing and
taught me about the birds

Front cover art: *Ornitholestes hermanni* (Berislav Krzic).

LIBRARY OF CONGRESS CATALOGUING-IN-PUBLICATION DATA

Glut, Donald F.
Dinosaurs: the encyclopedia : supplement four / by Donald F. Glut :
foreword by Peter J. Makovicky, Ph.D.
p.   cm.
Includes bibliographical references and index.

ISBN-13: 978-0-7864-2295-1
(library binding : 50# alkaline paper) ∞

1. Dinosaurs — Encyclopedia.   I. Title.
QE862.D5G652   2006
567.9'1'03 — dc20   95-47668

British Library cataloguing data are available

Manufactured in the United States of America

*McFarland & Company, Inc., Publishers
Box 611, Jefferson, North Carolina 28640
www.mcfarlandpub.com*

Acknowledgments

The author thanks the following vertebrate paleontologists for their critical review of selected sections of the manuscript, for their invaluable criticisms, suggestions, and other comments, and for generally helping me to improve the text:

(For primitive saurischians and theropods) Ralph E. Molnar, Museum of Northern Arizona, Flagstaff; (basal sauropodomorphs and prosauropods) Peter M. Galton, College of Naturopathic Medicine, University of Bridgeport, Bridgeport, Connecticut; (sauropods) John S. McIntosh, Wesleyan University, Middletown, Connecticut; (thyreophorans) Kenneth Carpenter, Denver Museum of Nature and Science, Denver, Colorado; and (primitive ornithischians, pachycephalosaurs, iguanodontians and hadrosaurs) Michael K. Brett-Surman, National Museum of Natural History, Smithsonian Institution, Washington, D.C., also my chief scientific advisor, who reviewed the entire work and made myriad suggestions for improving the overall manuscript; (pachycephalosaurians and more primitive marginocephalians) Robert M. Sullivan, State Museum of Pennsylvania; (ceratopsians) Peter Dodson, School of Veterinary Medicine, University of Pennsylvania, Philadelphia; (pterosaurs) S. Christopher Bennett, College of Chiropractic, University of Bridgeport; and (birds) Luis M. Chiappe, Natural History Museum of Los Angeles County.

Thanks to the following vertebrate paleontologists, who sent me reprints of articles, copies of journals, photographs, slides, illustrations, personal communications, advice, or otherwise contributed directly in some way to the production of this volume: Lawrence G. Barnes, Doug Goodreau, Gerald Grellet-Tinner, John M. Harris, Gary Takeuchi, Howell W. Thomas, and Xiaoming Wang, Natural History Museum of Los Angeles County; James M. Clark, Department of Biological Sciences, George Washington University; Laura Codorniú, Departmento de Geologia, Universidad Nacional de San Luis; Rodolfo A. Coria, Museo Municipal Carmen Funes; Philip J. Currie, Smithsonian Institution; Darren Tanke, Royal Tyrrell Museum of Palaeontology; Fabio M. Dalla Vecchia, Museo Paleontologico Cittadino; Michael J. Everhart, Sternberg Museum of Natural History, Fort Hays State University; Ursula Goehlich, Institut für Paläontologie und Historische Geologie; Jerald D. Harris, Department of Earth and Environmental Science, University of Pennsylvania; Brenda J. Chinnery-Allgeier and John R. Horner, Museum of the Rockies, University of Montana; Takuya Konishi; Giuseppe Leonardi; Peter L. Larson, Neal L. Larson, and Larry Shaffer, Black Hills Institute of Geological Research, Inc.; Robert A. Long, Kevin Padian, and Mathew J. Wedel, Museum, University of California Museum of Paleontology; Peter J. Makovicky and William F. Simpson, The Field Museum; Ruben D. Martínez, Laboratorio de Paleontologia de Vertebrados, Universidad Nacional de la Patagonia; Darren Naish, University of Portsmouth; Angela C. Milner, The Natural History Museum, London; Mark A. Norell, American Museum of Natural History; J. Michael Parrish, Department of Biological Sciences, Northern Illinois University; Gregory S. Paul; Raymond R. Rogers, Geology Department, Macalester College; Hans Jakob ("Kirby") Siber, Sauriermuseum Aathal; Daniela Schwarz, Naturhistorisches Museum Basel; Joshua B. Smith, Washington University; Kent A. Stevens, University of Oregon; Hans-Dieter Sues, National Museum of Natural History; David B. Weishampel, Department of Cell Biology and Anatomy, Johns Hopkins University School of Medicine; and Lawrence M. Witmer, Department of Biomedical Sciences, Ohio University.

Also thanks to the "paleo-artists" who contributed dinosaur illustrations (and who retain all copyrights and any other rights to their respective illustrations, whether explicitly stated or not) to this volume. These include Mark Hallett, Katy Hargrove, Berislav Krzic, Todd Marshall, and Gregory S. Paul.

Finally, thanks to Howard Allen, *Alberta Palaeontological Society Bulletin*; Stephen A. and Sylvia J. Czerkas, the Dinosaur Museum; Nina Cummings, library, and Jerice Barrios, photography department, The Field Museum; Allen A. Debus and Diane E. Debus, Hell Creek Creations; Dave Elhert and Michael Triebold, Triebold Paleontology, Inc.; Mick Ellison, American Museum of Natural History; Tracy L. Ford ("Dino Hunter"); Mike Fredericks, *Prehistoric Times*; my mother, Julia Glut; Roy Kempa; Karen A. Kennelly, The Children's Museum of Indianapolis; Dan Lagiovane and Mindy McNaugher, Carnegie Museum of Natural History; Gerhard Maier; Cathy McNassor, Library, Natural History Museum of Los Angeles County; Clark J. Miles and Clifford A. Miles, Western Paleontological Laboratories and North American Museum of Ancient Life; Urs Möckli, Sauriermuseum Aathal; George Olshevsky, Publications Requiring Research, San Diego; David Peters; Society of Vertebrate

Acknowledgments

Paleontology (SVP); Adam Spektor, Spektor Manor; Thomas Thornbury; Pete Von Sholly, Fossil Records; and Bill Warren.

I apologize to anyone and any institution I may have missed.

Once again, I have done my best to credit all illustrations and to obtain permissions for their use in this book, if permissions are so required. Copyrights for photographs (except for those privately taken, such as the ones shot by the author) of specimens, whether stated or not, are assumed to be held by the institution housing those specimens or by the publications in which those pictures initially appeared.

Foreword

Even the most casual observer of dinosaur paleontology could not fail to notice that ours is a rapidly expanding field.

The number of new dinosaurian taxa being named annually has increased twofold over the last decade, with no hint of a slow-down in this prolific rate of discovery. Much of the new diversity is accounted for by the growing sample of very small dinosaurs from China and Mongolia, sometimes preserved with soft tissues such as skin and even stomach contents in place, or found in life poses capturing instances of behaviors such as sleep or parental care.

Despite their recent appearance, these discoveries have already profoundly altered public perceptions of dinosaurs, and feathered theropods have, for example, become the norm in depictions of these animals gracing everything from book covers to Chinese liquor bottles. But beyond China, discoveries of dinosaurs of all sizes are occurring on almost all continents, with even the hallowed stomping grounds of the western United States yielding new species of sauropods, stegosaurs, and even theropods.

The myriad taxonomic and descriptive contributions to dinosaur paleontology — prompted by this "Age of Discovery" — is matched, if not overshadowed, by a voluminous literature on the evolution and biology of dinosaurs. The ever-increasing diversity of dinosaurs is being compiled into progressively more detailed phylogenies, and the discrepancies among these are the topics of yet more research. On the paleobiological front, a revolution in integrative approaches is taking place. New discoveries are approached with cutting-edge technological and computational methods and combined with better understanding of the biology of living animals to "flesh out" our knowledge of how dinosaurs lived, reproduced and died.

An unexpected result of current paleobiological approaches is that the need to develop a biomechanical foundation from which to extrapolate the abilities of dinosaurs, has served as an impetus to study poorly understood aspects of locomotion and other functions in living animals. In this deluge of new information, it requires an almost superhuman effort to keep abreast of current developments in dinosaur science.

In spite of his career as a film-maker, his active pursuit of many varied interests, and volunteering his time at two natural history museums, Donald Glut has amazingly managed to keep in stride with the burgeoning literature as he has updated his *Dinosaurs: The Encyclopedia* with ever longer supplements. Whereas, the first supplement was some 400 pages long, the last two supplements have exceeded 600 and 700 pages, respectively. This new installment is truly gargantuan, rivaling the original volume, which covered all of dinosaur knowledge from Robert Plot to the present, in size. To crown his latest achievement, Don has not only updated the dinosaurs, but added whole new sections on pterosaurs and Mesozoic birds.

Don's *Dinosaurs: The Encyclopedia* and its supplements have appeared in a time replete with new dinosaur books. Indiana University Press, for example, has produced a series of books covering both systematic and biological topics within dinosaur paleontology, and second editions of staples such as *The Dinosauria* and *The Complete Dinosaur* are also just out or nearing publication.

Nevertheless, in this cornucopia of literary offerings on dinosaurs, Don's *Encyclopedia* represents a unique contribution. More detailed than any other work on the market, and heavily illustrated, his are the volumes that many professionals and laymen alike reach for first to get the basic facts for a poorly known dinosaur taxon, or to hunt down an obscure literature source. Don's detailed taxonomic and thematic entries are often sufficient to answer most questions, and in cases that require more detailed literature searches, the appropriate sources are conveniently listed at the end of each entry.

Dinosaurs: The Encyclopedia is an invaluable literary tool for which the community as a whole owes Don a debt of gratitude. Ironically, our payment will probably be to keep him ever more busy in the years to come.

PETER J. MAKOVICKY, PH.D.
Geology Department
The Field Museum

Table of Contents

Cast of the holotype skeleton (MUCPvCH-1) of the giant abelisaurid theropod dinosaur *Giganotosaurus carolini*, mounted under Rodolfo Anibal Coria's direction at the Museo Municipal Carmen Funes in Neuquén Province, Patagonia, Argentina. Established by municipal disposition in 1984, this roadside museum has recently expanded its dinosaur displays to include a number of mounted skeletons (see "Introduction"). Photograph by Gary Takeuchi, courtesy Museo Municipal Carmen Funes.

Preface

This is the fourth supplement in the present writer's unofficial and open-ended "series" of reference books that began in the fall of 1997, with the publication by McFarland & Company of *Dinosaurs: The Encyclopedia*. (That book is referred to in this text as *D:TE*; the previous three supplementary volumes are referred to herein as *S1*, *S2*, and *S3*).

As in the previous supplements, the author's intent is to keep the subject of dinosaur paleontology reasonably current (the term "dinosaur" generally referring to "non-avian dinosaurs," taxa traditionally accepted as dinosaurs; for information pertaining specifically to "avian dinosaurs," *i.e.*, birds, see "Appendix Two"). This supplement, like those preceding it, largely presents new information based upon the more recent research of vertebrate paleontologists; also, it corrects or emends "old information" that was either incorrect originally or is no longer regarded as correct.

This book, like the previous supplements, builds upon the foundation established in *D:TE*. The purpose of that original tome was to make available, between two covers, a more or less tidy compendium of dinosaur-related information based upon the original work of vertebrate paleontologists. The intent of following *D:TE* with a number of supplementary volumes was and is an attempt to keep the subject of dinosaur paleontology current.

Like the original volume and its first three supplements, this book's intent is to serve as a handy reference tool useful to both the professional scientist and student, while also offering a fair amount of less technical information of interest to the more casual dinosaur enthusiast. As the author has stated before, this book is not a substitute for the original paleontological literature, nor has it been used for formal taxonomic purposes. Again, the present writer encourages those readers lacking a more technical background in the subject matter to consult this book's glossary as an aide in understanding the more difficult passages in the text. Also, I again suggest that the reader utilize the bibliography in the back of the book and seek out the cited original publications.

The vast majority of information in this volume was based on the original research of vertebrate paleontologists, the results of their work having been published and made available to the present writer in time for inclusion. Generally speaking, these studies appeared as peer-reviewed technical articles published in scientific journals.

Some of this information was originally published as "abstracts" — *i.e.*, short, concise, and often preliminary summaries of works-in-progress — that were also presented as talks at a scientific conference or symposium, the final detailed results (sometimes differing in content from what is stated in the abstract) of which may later appear in the form of a fully realized article. However, caution should be exercised when considering the information presented in these short publications. Abstracts are not peer reviewed; therefore, their content should not be given the same weight as a reviewed article published in an accredited journal.

Once more, it must be stressed that none of the volumes in this "encyclopedia" series is intended to substitute for the original paleontological literature, and also that the reader is always encouraged to seek out and read the cited original sources.

The science of paleontology depends upon the collection, preparation, then study and analysis of fossil materials housed in institutions certified by the American Association of Museums. Our knowledge of dinosaurs (and other extinct organisms) is in direct proportion to the number of fossils representing these animals and to the completeness and preservational quality of those specimens. Fortunately — thanks in no small way to modern and improved prospecting and collecting methods — new discoveries of dinosaur specimens continue to be made on a global basis. Such discoveries often lead to the naming of new dinosaurian genera and species and also to the reinterpretation of already named taxa. Thus, the present supplement offers a host of new dinosaurian generic and specific names, as well as supplying additional information regarding taxa that have appeared in previous volumes.

As stated already in those volumes, the present writer asks the reader to be tolerant in dealing with a multi-volume book containing so many words. Spelling and other errors (blame them on the "paleo-gremlins") can enter the text regardless of the number of human eyes and computer spell-checks scrutinizing the manuscript and proofs prior to the publisher sending off the final materials to the printer. I ask, then, that you kindly direct any and all corrections to me in care of McFarland, or via email (dinosaur@frontlinefilms.com), so that the author can deal with them accordingly in a future volume. Some of those past errors have been noted and corrected in various places within the present text.

As always, I welcome any and all articles, photographs of specimens, artwork, and so forth that the reader might send me for possible use in preparing the next supplement.

Following the style of the previous supplements and to keep these books at a manageable size, I have avoided as much as possible repeating material (*e.g.,* background data, definitions of taxa above the level of genus level, illustrations, *etc.*) already appearing in the earlier volumes. Needless to add, the content of the text is restricted to information that has published in the paleontological literature before this volume went to press. Consequently, information and illustrations acquired by the author beyond the cut-off date (February 28, 2005) imposed by the publisher must await the next supplement for inclusion. Because a book of this size, nature, and complexity requires many months of editorial and production work, some of this new information will undoubtedly find its way to the public (*e.g.,* newspapers, fan magazine such as *Prehistoric Times*, websites, Internet chatrooms, *etc.*) before appearing in this series.

As always, life restorations of dinosaurs featured in the "genera" section of this book are included *only* if, in my estimation, they portray taxa known from fossil remains sufficient enough to produce a reasonably accurate restoration.

DONALD F. GLUT
Burbank, California USA
2005

I: Introduction

More dinosaur specimens continue to be collected, resulting in the naming and describing of new dinosaurian taxa, and the way in which paleontologists view previously described taxa. Among this new fossil material, since the publication of the last supplement in this series of books, some unexpected dinosaur discoveries—discussed in the current volume—have appeared in the paleontological literature. These include the first tyrannosauroid documented as possessing "protofeathers" (*Dilong*), a troodontid preserved in a bird-like sleeping posture (*Mei*), a "beaked" sauropod (*Bonitasaura*), and what appears to be the first record of a meat-eating ornithischian (see *Protecovasaurus* entry).

Indeed, dinosaurs remain a continuing source of interest in both the realms of science and the public. Consequently, museum dinosaur collections continue to grow, while new display specimens are placed on view for the benefit of both the scientist and nonscientist, and more museums update their exhibit halls.

Traditionally, the Vertebrate Paleontology Department of the Natural History Museum of Los Angeles County—an institution (then named the Los Angeles County Museum of History, Science and Art) that opened to the public on November 6, 1913—has focused its attention on the fossils of Pleistocene mammals and birds recovered from the famous "tar pits" at Rancho La Brea. The department was initiated during the 1930s by paleontologist Chester Stock, who supervised the extensive excavations at La Brea, and who, in 1949, would become Head of the Science Division at the museum.

Over the years, the Natural History Museum of Los Angeles County's main attention, regarding collecting of fossils and paleontological research, increased to include mainly birds, fishes, and marine mammals of Cenozoic age. Indeed, the museum's collection of fossil cetaceans is currently the finest collection of extinct dolphins and whales in the world. In 1977, the vast majority of the Pleistocene La Brea specimens were moved to their own facility, the site-specific George C. Page Museum of La Brea Discoveries.

However, the Natural History Museum of Los Angeles County has not been bereft of dinosaur research. In 1957, largely through the efforts of staff paleontologist Hildegarde Howard and colleagues, the museum acquired the vertebrate paleontology collections of California Institute of Technology, among these being a partial hadrosaur skeleton, collected by Stock for the Institute, probably referrable to the genus *Saurolophus* (see Morris 1973).

During the 1960s, museum field expeditions brought back to the institution a considerable amount of fine dinosaur material, including specimens that would be designated holotypes. Most of the dinosaur specimens acquired during this time were recovered under the direction of freelance fossil collector Harley G. Garbani. Among these treasures were the then largest known reasonably complete skull of *Tyrannosaurus*, a couple of skulls of the horned dinosaur *Triceratops*, remains of the small ornithopod *Thescelosaurus*, and a skull (a rare specimen, as it preserves the beak) and postcranial remains of *Edmontosaurus*, all of this material recovered from the famous Hell Creek Formation of Montana.

In the middle 1960s, the first dinosaur skeletons to be exhibited at the Los Angeles museum—the carnivorous *Allosaurus* posed as if confronting the herbivorous *Camptosaurus*, dramatically mounted without external supports by the museum's chief preparator, Leonard Bessem—greeted visitors in the foyer. During this decade, William J. Morris, a visiting paleon-

Reconstructed skull (LACM 7244/23844) of the giant carnivorous dinosaur *Tyrannosaurus rex*, collected by Harley G. Garbani. When discovered, this was the largest known reasonably complete skull of this dinosaur.

Photograph by the author, courtesy Natural History Museum of Los Angeles County.

Skeletons of *Allosaurus fragilis* (LACM 3729/ 46030) and *Camptosaurus dispar* (LACM 3729/46031) mounted by chief preparator Leonard Bessem, these specimens on display from the middle 1960s through late 1990s in the foyer of the Natural History Museum of Los Angeles County.

tologist based at Occidental College and specializing in hadrosaurs, headed museum field expeditions to the El Gallo Formation of Baja California that yielded specimens that would eventually be designated holotypes. These include a partial skeleton with skin impressions representing a new hadrosaur species probably belonging to the genus *Lambeosaurus* (see *D:TE*), plus a partial skull of the theropod *Labocania*. An expedition led by Garbani to the Hell Creek Formation of Montana recovered dinosaur specimens including the juvenile partial skull of the so-called "Jordan theropod" (see *Aublysodon* entry, *D:TE*; *Stygivenator* entry, *S2*; *Tyrannosaurus* entry, *S3*). Also during this period, skeletons of the plated dinosaur *Stegosaurus* and juveniles of the duckbilled dinosaurs *Corythosaurus* (see photograph, section on hadrosaurs, below), collected decades earlier by Charles M. Sternberg, and *Edmontosaurus* (see photograph, *S2*), collected by Garbani, were mounted for exhibit.

By the 1980s and into the 1990s, the Natural History Museum of Los Angeles County offered to visitors an actual dinosaur hall featuring an impressive array of mounted skeletons, comprising both real fos-

sil bone and also cast elements (*e.g.*, *Dilophosaurus*, *Mamenchisaurus*, *Tsintaosaurus*, *Carnotaurus*) from other institutions (see *D:TE*, *S1*, *S2*, and *S3* for photographs of most of the above-mentioned specimens). Additionally, during these two decades, the museum was host to a number of traveling exhibits featuring dinosaur specimens from China, Russia, and other areas of the globe. Also during these decades, several dinosaur-related art exhibitions made their debuts at the Natural History Museum of Los Angeles County. These included "Dinosaurs, Mammoths and Cavemen: The Art of Charles R. Knight" (1982), featuring paintings, drawings, sculptures, and personal items pertaining to that great pioneer paleontological artist, and "Dinosaurs Past and Present" (1986), the latter including a symposium, and displaying original pieces by the best paleontological artists from the 19th through 20th centuries. Both of these exhibits were organized by Sylvia Czerkas and both were accompanied by books of the same title (see Czerkas and Glut 1982; Czerkas and Olson 1987).

While most of the Natural History Museum of Los Angeles County's "behind the scenes" fossil

Skeletal cast (based on holotype MACN-CH 894) of *Carnotaurus sastrei.*

vertebrates activity, over the decades, continued to center around animals other than dinosaurs, the public's interest in the institution's dinosaur exhibits (and that of visiting scientists in the museum's dinosaur collections) remained strong. More dinosaur-minded visitors were no doubt lured inside with the addition in 1998 to the museum's grounds of life-sized bronze restorations of *Tyrannosaurus* and *Triceratops* (see *S1, S2, S3,* also photograph, section on extinctions, below), bringing a semblance of life to the "Dueling Dinosaurs" skeletal display to be viewed in the foyer (see *S2*; also, see photograph below, section on extinction) and which, two years earlier, replaced the relocated *Allosaurus/Camptosaurus* mounts.

More recently, professional interest at the Natural History Museum has considerably expanded to include dinosaurs, thanks to the appointment in 1999 of dinosaur and fossil bird specialist Luis M. Chiappe, formerly of New York's American Museum of Natural History, as Chair of the Vertebrate Paleontology Department. During the years under Chiappe's direction, summer field expeditions to the Laramie Formation of Niobrara County, Wyoming (2002), and to the Hell Creek Formation of Carter County, Montana (2003), brought back a wealth of dinosaur material including, respectively, a specimen of either *Triceratops* or *Torosaurus* and also a nearly complete skeleton of *Tyrannosaurus* (see entry), bringing the museum's collection of significant *Tyrannosaurus* (see entry) original specimens up to represent at least five individuals.

Most importantly, Chiappe's 2000–2002 expeditions to the Upper Cretaceous Auca Mahuevo locality, Anacleto Formation, of Patagonia, Argentina, resulted in the collection of a new abelisaurid theropod *Aucasaurus* (see *S3*), now mounted in the museum's dinosaur hall, and the spectacular discovery of several nest structures containing thousands of "titanosaurid" sauropod egg clutches, fossil embryos, and also preserved impressions of sauropod skin. Casts of the eggs were deposited at the museum (see section on sauropods, below). These eggs became a focal point of a traveling exhibit — "The Tiniest Giants: Discovering Dinosaur Eggs" — which premiered at the Los Angeles museum in 2001.

In summer, 2004, a field expedition under

Introduction

Left: Full-scale sculpture by Stephen A. Czerkas and Sylvia J. Czerkas of *Carnotaurus sastrei* (see *S1*) made during the mid–1980s for the Natural History Museum of Los Angeles County dinosaur hall to accompany a mounted cast skeleton of this theropod. *Right:* The "Dueling Dinosaurs" exhibit — the horned *Triceratops horridus* (LACM 7107/118118, cast of LACM 7207/59049) and the carnivorous *Tyrannosaurus rex* (skull LACM 7244/23844, most of postcrania cast from TMP 81.6.1, "Black Beauty").

Chiappe's direction returned to the Montana locality where an uncrushed *Triceratops* skull and associated limb were collected, in addition to more of the *Tyrannosaurus* skeleton. (At present, as pointed out by Carr and Williamson 2004, the Natural History Museum of Los Angeles County is distinguished as the only museum that houses a growth series of *Tyrannosaurus rex*— ranging from small juvenile [LACM 238471] to subadult [LACM 23845] to old adult [LACM 23844]; see *Tyrannosaurus* entry.)

To date of this writing, employees and volunteers at the museum vertebrate paleontology laboratory, under the supervision of Senior Paleontological Preparator Howell W. Thomas and Paleontological Preparator Doug Goodreau, have completed preparing or are preparing previously unopened "jackets" containing dinosaur material, including a *Triceratops* pelvis collected decades earlier by Garbani, and the *Tyrannosaurus* specimen collected by Chiappe's field crew during the summers of 2003 and 2004. When

fully prepared, these and other recently recovered dinosaur specimens will either be put on exhibit for the benefit of the public, or stored in the museum's research collections.

Also, Chiappe is currently encouraging more outside researchers to utilize the museum's dinosaur and other fossil collections, and is also promoting a program whereby casts of the museum's dinosaur and other fossil specimens can be exchanged with cast and original material from other institutions. In summer of 2004, a field team from the Natural History Museum of Los Angeles County returned to the Montana site, collecting, among other fossil material, more of the same *Tyrannosaurus* specimen, and also a beautifully preserved, noncrushed *Triceratops* skull, discovered by Thomas Thornbury. Also in 2004, the museum, through Chiappe's efforts, acquired from the Carnegie Museum of Natural History (see below) a large block from the Ghost Ranch quarry in New Mexico, containing numerous remains of the

Life-sized figures of *Tyrannosaurus rex* and *Triceratops
horridus*, based upon the
"Dueling Dinosaurs" (see
S1) skeletal exhibit in the
Natural History Museum of
Los Angeles County foyer
(which replaced the former
Allosaurus/Camptosaurus
skeletons display) see *S1*),
weighing five tons and rendered in bronze by Douglas
Van Howd of Sierra Sculp-
ture.

Field workers at the Pedro's
Site collecting a partial
skeleton (LACM 150076) of
a horned dinosaur, either
Triceratops or *Torosaurus*,
during the 2002 expedition
of the Natural History Museum of Los Angeles County
to the Laramie Formation of
Niobrara County, Wyoming.
The expedition was led by
paleontologist Luis M.
Chiappe.

Introduction

Top, left: In situ dorsal vertebra (LACM 150076) belonging either to *Triceratops* or *Torosaurus* as found at Pedro's Site in the Laramie Formation of Niobrara County, Wyoming. *Top, right:* Fossil preparator Doug Goodreau with a femur and tibia (jacketed) belonging to a specimen (LACM 150076) of *Triceratops* or *Torosaurus* collected by the Natural History Museum of Los Angeles County in 2002 under the leadership of Luis M. Chiappe. *Bottom, left:* Volunteer fossil collector Dan Goodreau with the partially jacketed right femur (LACM 150167) of *Tyrannosaurus rex* (see *Tyrannosaurus* entry), found in 2003 by Bob Curry in the Hell Creek Formation of Carter County, Montana, and nicknamed "Thomas" after Curry's brother. *Bottom, right: In situ* skull (LACM 150167) of *Tyrannosaurus rex* before collection by the Natural History Museum of Los Angeles County field expedition to Montana led by Luis M. Chiappe.

carnivorous dinosaur *Coelophysis* (see *D:TE*), these constituting the first Triassic vertebrate fossils to be housed in the institution's collections.

Another museum that has recently made dinosaurs more accessible to both researchers and the public, and which has a connection with Chiappe's discoveries at Auca Muevo, is the Museo Principal Carmen Funes, located on Plaza Huincul in Neuquén Province, Patagonia, Argentina. This roadside museum was established by municipal disposition in 1984 as a kind of eclectic exhibition of historical regional artefacts. Today, under the direction of paleontologist Rodolfo Anibal Coria, the museum offers primarily

two kinds of exhibits, showcasing both paleontology and local history.

The paleontological exhibit mainly focuses upon the research projects undertaken by the institution, *i.e.*, those dedicated to explore and seek out dinosaur and other Cretaceous vertebrate specimens in the surrounding areas. At present, the Museum Carmen Funes bears the most important collection of these fossils yet recovered from northwestern Patagonia.

Through Coria's efforts, the museum has, in recent years, presented a number of fine dinosaur-related exhibits that attract much public interest. These displays include such standard displays as dioramas

Above: Paleontologist Luis M. Chiappe in the Hell Creek Formation of Carter County, Montana, collecting a tooth (LACM 150167) of *Tyrannosaurus rex,* now on display at the Natural History Museum of Los Angeles County (see *Tyrannosaurus* entry). *Top, right:* Fossil preparator Doug Goodreau with an isolated tibia (LACM 150024) belonging to a hadrosaurid dinosaur, recovered during the 2002 field expedition of the Natural History Museum of Los Angeles County to the Laramie Formation of Niobrara County, Wyoming. *Bottom, right:* Thomas Thornbury in Montana's Hell Creek Formation in 2004 with a recently discovered *Triceratops* skull and scapula. The California businessman funded that year's field expedition of the Natural History Museum of Los Angeles County. Preparation of the skull began the next year at the museum's vertebrate paleontoogy laboratory.

and factual videos, but, most importantly, the mounted bones of dinosaurs indigenous to Patagonia. Although a small museum, the institution offers visitors an up close look at some of the largest known members of various dinosaurian groups. Exhibits at the Museo Principal Carmen Funes include the holotype bones of *Argentinosaurus huenculensis,* possibly the largest of all known sauropods, the mounted skeleton of *Gigan-*

Frankie Jackson (left), Luis M. Chiappe (middle) and Nancy Rufenacht (right) working on a fossil "titanosaurid" nest at the Auca Mahuevo locality in Argentina.

Luis M. Chiappe collecting fossil "titanosaurid" egg fragments at the Auca Mahuevo locality, Argentina.

otosaurus carolini, a theropod reportedly as large as or even larger than *Tyrannosaurus rex,* and the skeleton of *Aucasaurus garridoi,* a large theropod recently described in 2002 by Coria, Chiappe and Lowell Dingus (see *Aucasaurus* entry, *S3* and this volume). The

museum also houses the only example of embryonic sauropod skin, another treasure retrieved by Chiappe's Natural History Museum of Los Angeles county expedition to Auca Mahuevo.

Among the jewels of vertebrate fossil displays has

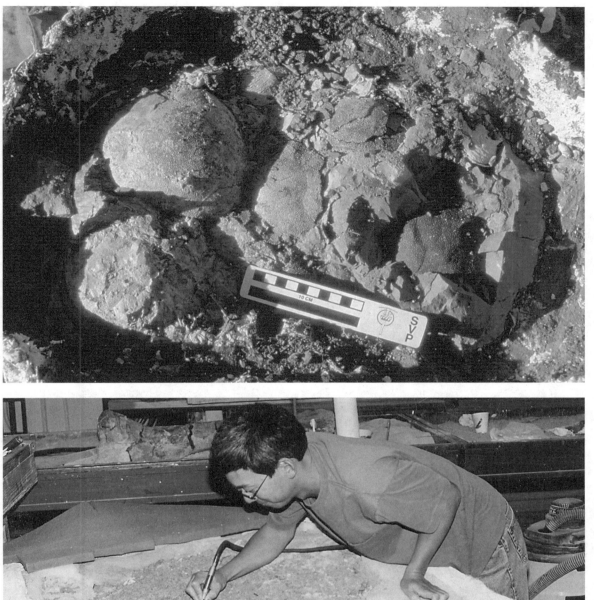

Photograph by Gary Takeuchi, courtesy Natural History Museum of Los Angeles County.

Nest of "titanosaurid" eggs *in situ* at the Auca Mahuevo fossil locality, Argentina.

Photograph by the author, courtesy Natural History Museum of Los Angeles County.

Gary Takeuchi, in the vertebrate paleontology laboratory of the Natural History Museum of Los Angeles County in October, 2004, working on the preparation of the museum's recently acquired block containing *Coelophysis bauri* specimens collected at Ghost Ranch, New Mexico. This block was attained from the Carnegie Museum of Natural History of Luis M. Chiappe.

long been the Dinosaur Hall at the Carnegie Museum of Natural History in Pittsburgh, Pennsylvania. The museum (belonging to the Carnegie Institute and Carnegie Museums of Pittsburgh), named for its benefactor, industrialist and philanthropist Andrew Carnegie, opened on November 5, 1895. The museum's Department of Vertebrate Paleontology was established years later. Largely due to Andrew Carnegie's interest in dinosaurs and his resultant financial backing, the Carnegie Museum amassed, over the

Introduction

Photograph by Luis M. Chiappe, courtesy Museo Municipal Carmen Funes.

Cast of reconstructed holotype skeleton (PVPH-1) of *Argentinosaurus huenculensis* mounted under the direction of Rodolfo A. Coria, at the Museo Municipal Carmen Funes in Neuquén Province, Patagonia, Argentina. Most of this skeleton was reconstructed based upon proportions of other, better known titanosaurs.

Photograph by Gary Takeuchi, courtesy Museo Municipal Carmen Funes.

Cast of holotype skeleton (MUCPvCH-1) of the giant theropod *Giganotosaurus carolini* mounted under the direction of Rodolfo Anibal Coria at the Museo Municipal Carmen Funes in Neuquén Province, Patagonia, Argentina.

succeeding years, a vast collection of original dinosaur material, much of it excavated over a 13-year period under the direction of Earl Douglass at a single quarry that would eventually be designated Dinosaur National Monument, located on a flank of the Uinta Mountains in northeastern Utah (for more details on the history of the Carnegie Museum of Natural History and its fossil vertebrates collections, see the book *Carnegie's Dinosaurs*, by Helen J. Mcginnis 1982).

The Carnegie Museum of Natural History's original Dinosaur Hall opened to the public in 1907, built as an expansion of the museum building to accommodate displaying the mounted skeleton of *Diplodocus carnegie* (nicknamed "Dippy"; see *D:TE*), a then new species of the giant sauropod named in honor of Andrew Carnegie. In the years following, many fine skeletons collected at Dinosaur National Monument were mounted in Dinosaur Hall, including those of such "classic" dinosaurs as *Apatosaurus louisae*, *Camarasaurus lentus*, *Allosaurus fragilis*, *Dryosaurus altus*, and *Stegosaurus ungulatus*. In 1941, the institution acquired from the American Museum of Natural History in New York the holotype skeleton (originally AMNH 973; now CM 9380) of *Tyrannosaurus rex* (see *D:TE*), which, the following year, was added to the displays in Carnegie's Dinosaur Hall. Another *T. rex* specimen, nicknamed "Samson"— reportedly representing the largest *Tyrannosaurus* yet recovered (see *Tyrannosaurus* entry, "Notes")— became part of the museum's dinosaur fossils collection in 2004.

For approximately a century, the museum's Dinosaur Hall remained virtually unaltered in regards displaying its dinosaur fossils. Skeletons stayed mounted in the traditional yet "old fashioned" ways, with tails dragging behind them. On April 11, 2002, the Carnegie Museum announced plans to expand dramatically its Dinosaur Hall in a group of dynamic exhibits — reflecting modern paleontological knowledge and theories — collectively called "Dinosaurs in Their World." The plan of this renovation, having an estimated cost of $37 million, is to integrate, for the first time (according to the Carnegie Museum's Media Relations Manager Dan Lagiovane) "dinosaurs into the environments of their respective time periods."

As Carnegie Museum of Natural History director Bill R. DeWalt stated, "Our collection of dinosaurs — many of which have never been seen by the public — is truly a world treasure, and we are committed to using that collection to become the best place in the world to see and learn about dinosaurs. This is a project 200 million years in the making, and it will attract dinosaur enthusiasts from around the world."

"Dinosaurs in Their World" will focus upon the

Photograph by Mindy McNaugher, courtesy Carnegie Museum of Natural History.

Dinosaur Hall as it exists today (and as it has been seen for decades) at the Carnegie Museum of Natural History. Included in this photograph are holotype mounted skeletons of (left to right) *Diplodocus carnegie* (CM 84, mount supplemented by referred specimens CM 94 and 307, and skull cast of USNM 2673), (background) *Tyrannosaurus rex* (CM 9380), and *Apatosaurus louisae* (CM 11162, with probable referred skull CM 3018).

Fossil preparators work on the skull (see in caudal view) of "Samson," a specimen of *Tyrannosaurus rex* recently collected by the Carnegie Museum of Natural History (see *Tyrannosaurus* entry). A temporary "prep" workshop has been set up in the museum's Dinosaur Hall for the benefit of visitors.

Photograph by Mindy McNaugher, courtesy Carnegie Museum of Natural History.

Jurassic and Cretaceous periods, with the current Dinosaur Hall being transformed into a Jurassic Hall (and including "Dippy," the Carnegie Museum's first collected dinosaur). An adjacent Cretaceous Hall is being built within an atrium — an expansion into a connecting courtyard in the middle of the museum — that "will become the core of Carnegie Museum of Natural History and reinforce the basic themes of the museum, including biodiversity, ecology, and evolution." Both halls are to include state-of-the-art interactive displays and also classrooms. Currently exhibited dinosaur skeletons, to be remounted in scientifically accurate and active poses, will share display space with new specimens never exhibited before. Among the new exhibits featured in this hall will be a skeletal tableau portraying *Allosaurus fragilis* in pursuit of *Diplodocus carnegie* and an adult and juvenile *Apatosaurus louisae*; and two *Tyrannosaurus rex* having a dispute over a dead hadrosaur.

An opening date for this renovation has not yet been announced.

A major event in dinosaur paleontology was the publication of the long-awaited second edition of *The Dinosauria*, once again edited by vertebrate paleontologists David B. Weishampel, Peter Dodson, and Halszka Osmólska (2004). Conceived in 1984, the original book of that title was published in 1990, a time during which there was little in the way of reference books on dinosaur paleontology available both to the public as well as to professional paleontologists. As stated by the editors in their introduction to the second edition, that first book — a massive tome that proved to be a benchmark work on the subject — was intended "to provide the first comprehensive, critical, and authoritative review of the taxonomy, phylogeny, biogeography, paleobiology, and stratigraphic distribution of all dinosaurs and to explore topics ranging from dinosaur origins and interrelationships to dinosaur energetics, behavior, and extinction." Authors of the various chapters of *The Dinosauria* consisted of world-reknowned authorities in the various areas of dinosaur science.

However, the almost decade and a half elapsing after the release of the first *Dinosauria* saw a veritable explosion of dinosaur studies, many of them saliently affecting or even negating portions of the original text. For example, as the editors pointed out in their introduction, in 1990 fewer than 300 dinosaurian genera were accepted as valid since dinosaurs were first recognized for what they are during the early 1800s. By 2004, over 200 additional genera had been named and described, constituting an almost 70-percent increase since the first *Dinosauria* debuted. Moreover, the now standard use of cladistics has accelerated the pace of dinosaur studies, calling into question some of the most basic tenets of the science.

As with the original *Dinosauria*, the second edition comprises a collection of articles newly authored by a select grouping of specialists in specific areas of dinosaur science, most of them returning from the first book, others newly recruited, "reflecting the dynamic fields of dinosaur systematics, extinction, physiology, taphonomy, and paleoecology, as well as [the editors'] efforts to keep each chapter vibrant and current." The book was basically organized in accordance with the plan of the first edition, with the noteworthy addition of a chapter devoted to basal birds (see below and "Appendix Two"), a topic that was mentioned only in passing in the original book.

(The second edition of *The Dinosauria* followed recently issued similar volumes on Mesozoic birds and pterosaurs; see, respectively, Chiappe and Witmer 2002; Buffetaut and Mazin 2003.)

Photograph by the author.

Photograph by the author.

Photograph by the author.

Left: **Restored head of the giant theropod dinosaur** *Carcharodontosaurus saharicus*, **sculpted by Garfield Minott, part of the "Giants: African Dinosaurs" temporary exhibit at the Garfield Park Conservatory, Chicago. The exhibit was created and developed by paleontologists Paul C. Sereno and Gabrielle Lyon.** *Top, right:* **Skeletal casts (prepared by the PAST (Prehistoric Animals Structures) Company of the Late Jurassic dinosaurs** *Afrovenator abokensis* **(foreground) and** *Jobaria tiguidensis* **(background), components of the "Giants: African Dinosaurs" exhibit that debuted on December 20, 2003, and ran until September 6, 2004, at Chicago's Garfield Park Conservatory. The exhibit presents casts representing various African dinosaurs placed in a natural setting of living plants.** *Bottom, right:* **Full scale model by Gary Staab of an as yet unnamed Late Jurassic pterosaur from Niger. The model, with a wingspan of about 16 feet, is part of the "Giants: African Dinosaurs" exhibit (see "Appendix One" for more on pterosaurs).**

The Mesozoic Era

Non-avian dinosaurs constituted the dominant terrestrial vertebrate group from approximately 228 to 65.5 million years ago, during an expanse of geologic time that has been named the Mesozoic (meaning "middle life") Era and which began approximately 251 million years ago. The Mesozoic Era was preceded by the Paleozoic Era, dominated by more primitive vertebrate forms, and followed by the Cenozoic Era, dominated by mammals and birds.

The Mesozoic Era, sometimes referred to as the "Age of Reptiles," is subdivided into three "periods": the Triassic, the latter part of which saw the emergence of the earliest dinosaurs known from unequivocal fossil evidence; the Jurassic, a kind of "golden age" of dinosaurian diversity; and the Cretaceous, the very latter part of which witnessed the extinction of all then-existing non-avian dinosaurs.

Each Mesozoic period is subdivided into various chronostratigraphic "stages," designated by such (al-

ways capitalized) adjectives as "Early," "Middle," and "Late" (*e.g.*, Early Jurassic or Late Cretaceous), with further modifications in lower case (*e.g.*, early Late Jurassic or latest Late Cretaceous). Lithostratigraphic levels (having geological as opposed to chronal meaning) of the three periods are designated by capitalized terms such as "Lower" and "Upper" (*e.g.*, Upper Triassic). (Note: Not all workers have adopted the Middle Cretaceous stage used in the present volume, a term proposed by Ratkevich 1998, see *S2*; *e.g.*, see *The*

Life restoration by Berislav Krzic of *Monolophosaurus jiangi*, a Middle Jurassic theropod from China.

Life-sized sculpture by Stephen A. Czerkas of the Late Triassic (middle Carnian) saurischian dinosaur *Herrerasaurus ischigualastensis*.

Photograph by the author, courtesy The Field Museum.

Dinosauria, edited by Weishample, Dodson and Os-mólka 2004, and authors therein.)

Every stage is then further divided into various "ages" (*e.g.*, "Hettangian" and "Campanian"), which can also be further modified by such (noncapitalized) adjectives as "early" and "late." (See *D:TE* for additional information regarding the Mesozoic Era and its subdivisions.) Dinosaurs are known from skeletal remains ranging from the Carnian to the Maastrichtian.

Following is a breakdown of the Mesozoic Era and its three periods. These periods, and then the stages and ages contained therein, are arranged in chronologically descending order, starting with the most recent (Late Cretaceous; Maastrichtian). Numerical values for the foregoing periods and ages are subject to change (see *D:TE* and past supplements). The following datings are from the "International Stratigraphic Chart," published in 2003 by the International Commission on Stratigraphy, incorporating numerical ages taken from *A Geologic Time Scale 2004* (Gradstein, Ogg, Smith *et al.* 2004):

Cretaceous

LATE
MAASTRICHTIAN (70.6 ± 0.6 to 65.5 ± 0.3 million years ago)
CAMPANIAN (83.5 ± 0.7 to 70.6 ± 0.6 million years ago)
SANTONIAN (85.8 ± 0.7 to 83.5 ± 0.7 million years ago)
CONIACIAN (89.3 ± 1.0 to 85.8 ± 0.7 million years ago)
TURONIAN (93.5 ± 0.8 to 89.3 ± 1.0 million years)

MIDDLE
CENOMANIAN (99.6 ± 0.9 to 93.5 ± 0.8 million years ago)
ALBIAN (112.0 ± 1.0 to 99.6 ± 0.9 million years ago)

EARLY
APTIAN (125.0 ± 1.0 to 112.0 ± 1.0 million years ago)
BARREMIAN (130.0 ± 1.5 to 125.0 ± 1.0 million years ago)
HAUTERIVIAN (136.4 ± 2.0 to 130.0 ± 1.5 million years ago)
VALANGINIAN (140.2 ± 3.0 to 136.4 ± 2.0 million years ago)
BERRIASIAN (145.5 ± 4.0 to 140.2 ± 3.0 million years ago)

Jurassic

LATE
TITHONIAN (150.8 ± 4.0 to 145.5 ± 4.0 million years ago)
KIMMERIDGIAN (155.0 ± 4.0 to 150.8 ± 4.0 million years ago)
OXFORDIAN (161.2 ± 4.0 to 155.0 ± 4.0 million years ago)

MIDDLE
CALLOVIAN (164.7 ± 4.0 to 161.2 ± 4.0 million years ago)
BATHONIAN (167.7 ± 3.5 to 164.7 ± 4.0 million years ago)
BAJOCIAN (171.6 ± 3.0 to 167.7 ± 3.5 million years ago)
AALENIAN (175.6 ± 2.0 to 171.6 ± 2.0 million years ago)

EARLY
TOARCIAN (183.0 ± 1.5 to 175.6 ± 2.0 million years ago)
PLIENSBACHIAN (189.6 ± 1.5 to 183.0 ± 1.5 million years ago)
SINEMURIAN (196.5 ± 1.0 to 189.6 ± 1.5 million years ago)
HETTANGIAN (199.6 ± 0.6 to 196.5 ± 1.0 million years ago)

Triassic

LATE
"RHAETIAN" (203.6 ± 1.5 to 199.6 ± 0.6 million years ago)
NORIAN (216.5 ± 2.0 to 203.6 ± 1.5 million years ago)
CARNIAN (228.0 ± 2.0 to 216.5 ± 2.0 million years ago)

MIDDLE
LADINIAN (237.0 ± 2.0 to 228.0 ± 2.0 million years ago)
ANISIAN (245.0 ± 1.5 to 237/0 ± 2.0 million years ago)

EARLY
OLENEKIAN (249.7 ± 0.7 to 245.0 ± 1.5 million years ago)
INDUAN (251.0 ± 0.4 to 249.7 ± 0.7 million years ago)

Copyright © Berislav Krzic.

Life restoration by Berislav Krzic of *Ornitholestes hermanni,* a Late Jurassic (Kimmeridgian–Tithonian) North American theropod.

Copyright © Todd Marshall.

Life restoration of the Late Jurassic (early Tithonian) bird *Archaeopteryx lithographica* (see "Appendix Two") by artist Todd Marshall.

Top: Early to Middle Cretaceous (Valanginian–Albian) scene by artist Todd Marshall depicting a family of *Iguanodon bernissartensis*. *Bottom:* An Early to Middle Cretaceous African (Aptian–Albian) scene by artist Todd Marshall depicting the giant crocodile *Sarcosuchus imperator* (see *S3*) attacking the sauropod *Nigersaurus taqueti*.

A scene by artist Todd Marshall of Late Cretaceous (?Campanian) Madagascar. At the right is the "domed" theropod *Majungatholus atopus.*

A Late Cretaceous (?late Campanian–early Maastrichtian) riverbed in China with three *Tarbosaurus bataar* individuals. Artwork by Todd Marshall.

Life restoration by Todd Marshall of the Late Cretaceous (Maastrichtian), recently described theropod *Rajasaurus narmadensis*.

New Discoveries, Ideas and Studies

Since the discovery of dinosaurs during the nineteenth century, most of what is known about this group of animals has resulted from studies made of their fossil bones. Other materials, however, such as teeth, have also yielded important data concerning dinosaurs.

Until recently, the study of the tooth enamel of dinosaurs (as well as nondinosaurian reptiles) has been largely neglected, while that of both extinct and extant mammals has been given extensive study. The reason for this, as pointed out by Hwang (2003) in an abstract, is that mammal teeth are generally characterized by distinctive prismatic enamel viewable in thin sections under polarized light. The teeth of most reptiles, however, have nonprismatic enamel whose individual crystallites can only be differentiated utilizing a scanning electron microscope. Hwang pointed out that, because of the small number of individuals sampled and lack of precise identification of the studied taxa, "phylogenetic patterns of enamel microstructure within different dinosaur groups have probably not been adequately discerned."

Hwang's preliminary survey of teeth from both carnivorous saurischians (*e.g.*, *Byronosaurus*, *Tarbo-*

saurus, *Velociraptor*) and herbivorous ornithischians (*e.g.*, *Psittacosaurus*, *Protoceratops*) revealed different patterns in enamel microstructure among these dinosaurian groups. Troodontids, for example, were found to be characterized by very thin parallel crystallite enamel having strong incremental lines, and ceratopsians by very thick columnar enamel containing numerous enamel tubules. Because most studied teeth belonged to specimens known at least at the generic level, the observed patterns are representative of the studied taxa. Knowing the general enamel structure within a higher-order taxonomic dinosaurian group, Hwang concluded, "means that isolated dinosaur teeth can be identified more specifically, contributing to taxonomic diversity data for a locality."

Sipla, Georgi and Forster (2004), in an abstract, reported briefly on the semicircular canals — "vestibular organs which register changes in angular acceleration experienced by the head"— in the inner ear of dinosaurs, as assessed via computed tomography. As these authors explained, rotation detected by these organs "are integrated at the neurophysiological level with somatosensory and proprioceptive systems, resulting in reflex stabilization of the head and visual field."

From this study, Sipla *et al.* observed in dinosaurs a correlation between enlargement of the rostral semicircular canal and locomotor preference. The authors found that bipedal dinosaurs, including such diverse taxa as the theropod *Tyrannosaurus* and ceratopsian *Psittacosaurus*, possess vertical enlargement of this semicircular canal relative to the caudal canal. Contrarily, in quadrupedal dinosaurian taxa ranging from the ankylosaur *Euoplocephalus* to the ceratopsian *Chasmosaurus*, enlargement of the rostral and caudal canal dimensions is less pronounced. Additionally, in derived theropods such as *Dromaeosaurus*, Sipla *et al.* observed a vertical hyper-elongation of the furculus, a structure of the brain responsible for the integration and modulation of both vestibular signals and position of the eye, a pattern consistently seen in ground-dwelling birds.

From this study, Sipla *et al.* postulated that, in dinosaurs, the expansion of the rostral semicircular canal is associated with both the sensory and coordination necessities of bipedal locomotion, the rostral canal being most sensitive to detecting "nose-down, vertex-up rotation in the sagittal plane," as could occur when the hindlimbs touch the ground. Moreover, the authors suggested, removing the forelimbs from locomotion could "subject the head to higher-amplitude pitch rotations," as reflected by enhanced sensitivity of the rostral semicircular canal and also "resultant improvements in motor integration."

Among extant vertebrates, as explained by Curry Rogers, Erickson and Norell (2003) in a published

Skeleton (BHI-3033) of *Tyrannosaurus rex* ("Stan"), to date the second largest and second most complete skeleton yet recovered belonging to this species, found in the Hell Creek Formation of Harding County, South Dakota, and prepared, mounted, and displayed at the Black Hills Museum of Natural History. Justin Sipla, Justin Georgi and Catherine Forster (2004) performed a study relating the inner ear's semicircular canal to motor capabilities in bipedal dinosaurs such as *T. rex*.

abstract, comparisons of whole-body growth rates and life history strategies are usually achieved via "comparisons of regressions of exponential stage growth standardized to body mass," Similar quantified data, the authors noted, are required for comparing whole-body patterns between dinosaurs and extant taxa. Moreover, the recent combining "of traditional bone histological analysis with scaling principles in a method termed Developmental Mass Extrapolation (DME) has provided the requisite tools and data to assess how dinosaurs really grew."

Performing an analysis of the Dinosauria spanning the phylogenetic and size diversity of this clade, Curry Rogers *et al.* discovered the following: Sigmoidal equations correctly describing ontogenetic data for six diverse dinosaurian taxa; somatic maturity beginning between the ages of three and 13 years, values corre-

lating with increased body size; and all dinosaurs growing more rapidly than extant reptiles, at rates below, equal to, or above those of extant mammals, yet not at the extremely rapid rates attained by modern altricial birds.

Curry Rogers *et al.* suggested that, while birds clearly acquired a portion of their elevated growth rates from their non-avian dinosaurian precursors, how and when they achieved such rates remains obscured. However, Curry Rogers *et al.*'s study indicated that small maniraptoran non-avian theropods grew from to to seven times slower than extant precocial birds, and that the very rapid growth rates of birds may have evolved following the origin of Aves.

Kozisek and Derstler (2004), in a published abstract, briefly reported on the scapular facets on the dorsal vertebrae of both sauropods and neoceratopsians, two very different groups of dinosaurs representing both the Saurischia and Ornithischia, respectively. These flattened areas, the authors noted—one facet per rib, and found in different positions on the second through fourth, and ?fifth dorsal ribs—are in alignment, forming a tract that climbs caudally when the torsos of these dinosaurs are assembled.

As Kozisek and Derstler observed, this zone in the sauropod genera *Apatosaurus*, *Diplodocus*, and *Camarasaurus* "ascends from midshaft on the second dorsal rib to a progressively higher position on the third and fourth ribs," this facet zone in sauropods describing a 20- to 25-degree angle from the horizontal. In the neoceratopsian genus *Triceratops*, this "zone occupies the second through fifth dorsal ribs and appears to have a slightly steeper path across the torso." The facet positions in both Sauropoda and Neoceratopsia are consistent with the postures of scapulae seen in articulated specimens, the authors noted. This suggests "that the rib facets record the resident position of the scapula upon the rib cage," an observation having "significant implications for pectoral assembly and forelimb motion in the Dinosauria."

In an abstract for a poster, Hengst (2004) reported on the gravitational stresses that would have been imposed on large bipedal dinosaurs. As that author noted, the only things that prevented "this anatomical beam from sagging were the combination of bone morphology, connective tissue, and muscle." Moreover, during locomotion vertical stresses would have increased these already considerable stresses. Typically, Hengst pointed out, the vertebrae of theropod dinosaurs have broad neural spines bearing prominent scars where intraspinous ligaments invested the bone. Hengst's study consisted of an examination of "how much of the total vertebral support load was carried by the connective tissues in bipedal dinosaurs and how much would be required of muscles, which have the potential to tire over the coarse of a day."

Hengst measured intraspinous ligament and intervertebral disk attachment points for all regions of the vertebral column "in specimens of *Tyrannosaurus rex*, *Gorgosaurus libratus*, and *Maiasaura peeblesorum*" in The Field Museum and The Childrens Museum of Indianapolis, with ligament length and cross-sectional

Peter L. Larson and Leon Thiesen within the ribcage of the nicknamed "Kelsey," a *Triceratops horridus* skeleton (TCM 2001.93.1) discovered in 1998 by Leonard Zerbst in the Lance Formation of Niobrara County, Wyoming, and collected that same year by the Black Hills Institute of Geological Research.

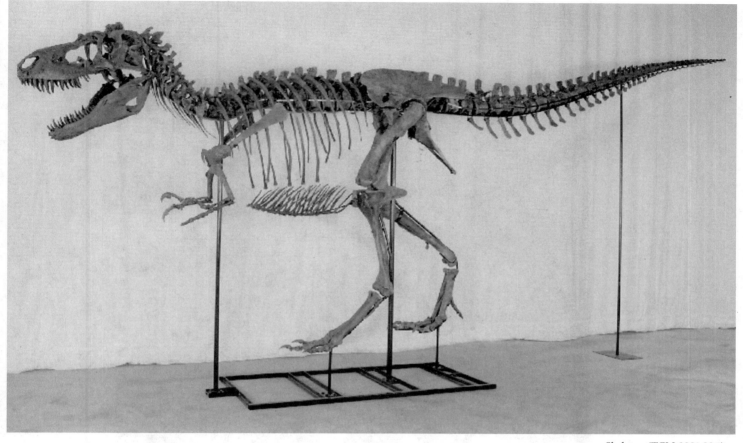

Skeleton (TCM 2001.89.1) of *Gorgosaurus libratus* prepared and mounted by the Hills Institute of Geological Research for display at The Children's Museum of Indianapolis. Richard A. Hengst (2004) performed a study on the gravitational stresses that would have been imposed on such large bipedal dinosaurs.

areas determined for representative sites within each region of the column, and body mass determined from museum-reconstructed dimensions. Hengst's study concluded that, in theropods, ligaments were sufficient for normal posture, support values being "consistent with those known for load bearing tendons and ligaments in living animals, with the tail somewhat stiffer than the body." In the hadrosaur *Maiasaura*, however, slender neural spines having little attachment area "implies greater dependence on muscle support during bipedal activities." Additionally, that author stated, the ossified tendons often associated with hadrosaurid specimens "may have been a means of reducing muscular effort necessary for bipedal activities.

In a published abstract, Wings (2003) reassessed the role of gastroliths in dinosaurs, mostly associated with sauropod remains from Jurassic and Cretaceous formations in the United States, but also known in a few theropods. These stones have been generally interpreted as — when swallowed by the animals — having constituted an internal grinding mill to aid in the processing of food (see *D:TE, S1, S3*). Wings, however, questioned whether the mere presence of these so-called "gizzard stones" is sufficient evidence to warrant such an interpretation.

In an attempt to answer this question, Wings undertook a comprehensive survey of gastroliths in the ostrich *Struthio camelus*, the largest living bird, put into a phylogenetic context relative to other extant birds. Analyzing the stomach contents of over 300 free-ranging ostriches from farms in Germany and South Africa, that author found that gastroliths comprise from 20 to 50 percent of the stomach contents by weight and make up approximately one percent of the body mass.

Examining in several *in vivo* experiments the abrasion rate of different stones, Wings discovered that most of the stones disintegrated in the gizzard within several days to weeks, with only vein quartz more resistant and, consequently, accumulating in the gizzard. Thus, due to the ongoing grinding action and high abrasion rates, most of the examined ostriches' gastroliths proved to be dull, having almost never developed surface polish. In this respect, the ostrich gastroliths differ from the polished stones attributed to sauropods.

As Wings reported, a survey of the literature of 19 extant avian species — Anseriformes, Galliformes, Columbiformes, and Passerifores — showed a mean gastrolith mass of 0.5 percent of the body mass, these

Introduction

Skeleton (cast) of *Allosaurus fragilis* mounted in the outmoded "upright" posture.

Top: Peter L. Larson and Aaron Gunter with a skeleton of *Maiasaura peeblesorum*, discovered and collected by Cliff and Sandy Lynster, from the Two Medicine Formation of Teton County, Montana, prepared by the Black Hills Institute of Geological Research for exhibition at The Children's Museum of Minneapolis. This species was part of the recent study by Richard A. Hengst (2004) on large bipedal dinosaurs. *Bottom:* Skeleton (TCM 2001.90.1) of *Tyrannosaurus rex*, nicknamed "Bucky," mounted by the Black Hills Institute of Geological Research for The Children's Museum of Indianapolis. This giant theropod was the main focus of Richard A. Hengst's (2004) recent study on bipedal dinosaurs.

values agreeing with those for several theropod dinosaurs (*e.g.*, ornithomimids, *Caudipteryx*), "suggesting that the extensive use of stones in digestion is not an autapomorphy of the crown group birds, but rather evolved much earlier along the avian stem lineage." However, in all confirmed examples of gastroliths associated with sauropod skeletal material, the stones weigh significantly less than 0.1 percent of the estimated body mass of these animals. Therefore, Wings concluded, the role of these rocks in the processing of sauropod food must have been minimized or was not analogous to that in extant birds.

In a subsequent abstract for a poster, Wings (2004) noted that when only some specimens of a certain taxon include small amounts of gastroliths, it is plausible to hypothesize that the stones were swallowed accidentally; however, when higher numbers of gastroliths are associated with particular taxa (*e.g.*, the theropods *Sinornithomimus* and *Caudipteryx*), it is reasonable to assume that such stones provided a grinding function similar to that found in living birds (*e.g.*, Galliformes).

Saurischians

Claessons (2004) discussed in detail the origin, morphology, and function of gastralia — dermal ossifications located in the ventral abdominal area of an animal's body — in two groups of saurischian — *i.e.*, "lizard-hipped" — dinosaurs (that author noting that no gastralia have yet been identified in the Ornithischia).

As Claessens pointed out, gastralia have not been adequately understood for a number of reasons: Their occurrence in extant vertebrates is limited, being found only in modern crocodilians and the tuatara

(*Sphenodon*), and possibly as part of the plastron in chelonians; these "floating bones" possess no solid connection to the rest of the skeleton and are, consequently, rarely preserved with an associated skeleton; and they are often confused with other skeletal elements found in the ventral abdominal region.

It was Claessen's opinion that the gastralia in both theropods and prosauropods were attached to the pubic bones and sternum, similar to the condition seen in extant crocodilians; gastralia in prosauropods were imbedded in the M. rectus abdominis in a fashion similar to that seen in extant crocodilians and *Sphenodon*; and, as theropods as opposed to extant crocodilians have a comparatively narrow body profile, the area of attachment on the gastralia of the M. obliqui abdomini and M. transversus abdominis was greater than in modern crocodilians.

Claessens stated that, contrary to previously published studies, "a similar structural configuration of the gastralia is shared throughout prosauropods and (nonornithurine) theropods." These bones, Claessens noted, are slender and rodlike, set in metametric rows within the abdominal wall between the sternum and pubis. The number of these rows range from about eight in smaller species to about 21 in larger species. Each row comprises four individual bones — a lateral and medial gastralium on each side of the midline, the lateral gastralia articulating with contralateral gastralia along the ventral midline, the medial gastralia imbricating with contralateral gastralia along the ventral midline to produce a zig-zag articulation pattern. The most cranial and caudal gastralial rows sometimes coalesce, forming a single median gastralium resembling a chevron. Therefore, all gastralia connect with one another, operating as a single functioning unit.

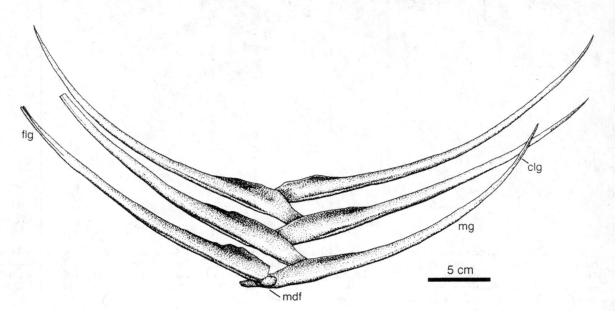

In situ imbricating articulation of gastralia (TMP 91.36.500) in a subadult *Gorgosaurus libratus* specimen (dorsal view). (After Claessens 2004.)

In earlier reports (*e.g.*, Romer 1956; Holtz and Brett-Surman 1997), gastralia in basal tetrapods and also dinosaurs have been interpreted as bones utilized in the protection and support of viscera, as in other nondinosaurian animals possessing gastralia. More recently, Perry (1983) had suggested that gastralia may have functioned as a passive component during respiration, preventing — by stiffening the belly wall — the encroachment of viscera into the lung space upon inspiration.

Claessens, however, observed that gastralia in theropods — as opposed to the reduced gastralia in other amniote groups — show elaborate modification, the anatomy of the gastralial system in these dinosaurs, therefore, suggesting a more active function than simply abdominal support or protection. It was Claessens' conclusion that gastralia in theropods could have affected the shape and volume of the trunk. Also, evaluation by Claessens (2001, 2004) of the morphology of these gastralia and muscle scars, while also considering comparative and experimental examination of living vertebrates, indicate that the system of gastralia could actively expand or compress the abdominal cavity in both theropods and birds, the gastralia thereby functioning as an accessory breathing mechanism operating in concert with the sternocostal aspiration pump. Additionally, if the caudal area of the theropod lung had differentiated to form abdominal air sacs, the gastralia would have been ideally positioned to ventilate these air sacs. "Gastralial aspiration may have been linked to the generation of small pressure differences between potential cranial and caudal lung diverticula," Claessens (2004) concluded, "which may have been important for the evolution of the unidirectional airflow lung of birds."

According to Claessens (2004), bones previously identified as gastralia in sauropod dinosaurs (*e.g.*, Filla and Redman 1994), are most likely sternal elements (see *Apatosaurus* entry, this volume and *D:TE*).

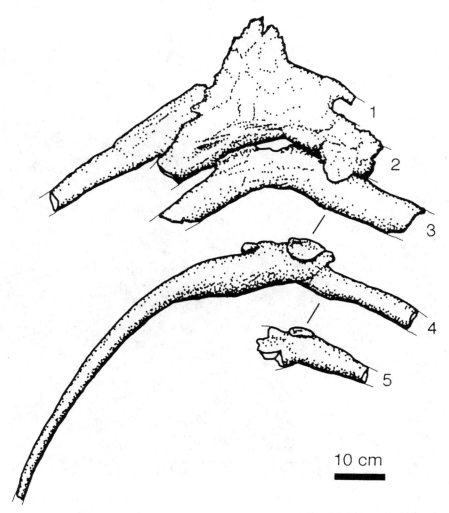

Cranial chevron-shaped gastralia (FMNH PR 2081) in *Tyrannosaurus rex*, individual diapophyses marked 1 through 5 (dorsal view). (After Claessens 2004.)

In an abstract, Padian, Horner and Dhaliwal (2004) questioned previously offered hypotheses attempting to explain the evolution of various bizarre cranial structures and postcranial armor in some Mesozoic dinosaurs. Padian *et al.* recounted that, in the majority of these studies, two general explanations

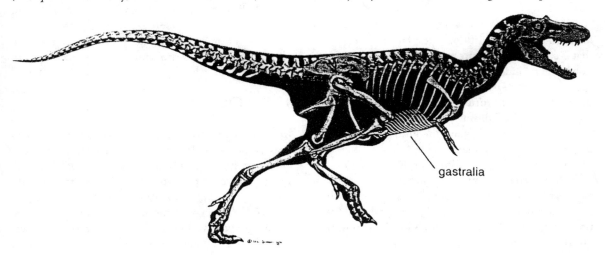

gastralia

The position of the gastralia in a subadult *Gorgosaurus libratus* (TMP 91.36.500), as reconstructed by Donna Sloan, Royal Tyrrell Museum of Palaeontology. (After Claessens 2004.)

Male (left) and female (right) morphs of *Cryolophosaurus elliotti* as envisioned by artist Todd Marshall, the male bearing an ornate cranial crest.

have generally been proposed for the development of such structures — 1. function and 2. display. As the authors noted, functional explanations (as well as certain display explanations) pertain to natural selection, while most display explanations involve sexual selection, with the display explanation further dividing into intraspecific (*e.g.*, attracting mates, intimidating rivals, *etc.*) and interspecific (*e.g.*, intimidating predators, *etc.*) regimes.

However, as Padian *et al.* pointed out, variations of these structures within a clade fail to fit a pattern that is consistent with any explanation regarding function; rather, "individual dinosaurs have generally been interpreted in *ad hoc* terms that do not extend evolutionarily to related forms." Furthermore, the authors noted, sexual dimorphism — where it has been demonstrated — rarely goes beyond the kind of size disparities observed between males and females of extant reptiles (*e.g.*, crocodiles, monitor lizards) and mammals, wherein which such unusual structures do not generally participate in either agonistic display·or combat.

Based upon phylogenetic, histological, and functional evidence, Padian *et al.* found that the observed bizarre cranial and postcranial structures in dinosaurs can be more generally explained by the phenomenon of species recognition, which is supported both by fossil and also recent evidence. The expected morphological patterns of diversification in species "differ sharply between the causes of selection (whether natural or sexual) and species recognition," the former generally resulting in linear trends, the second evincing but one pattern (*i.e.*, differentiation). This second pattern, Padian *et al.* noted, can be observed in extant ungulates also. The inference of this pattern in dinosaurs "is most strongly supported when several closely related species are sympatrically present, or can be shown to have been recently present as ghost taxa."

THEROPODS

Theropods, a diverse group of mostly carnivorous dinosaurs, have often been portrayed in so-called "paleoart" — and also in such popular media as novels, short stories, dramatic radio and television programs, comic strips and books, and motion pictures (see, for example, Glut 1980) — "engaged in mortal combat," either with others of their species or, more frequently, with various kinds of herbivorous taxa (see, for example, Debus 2003). However, as theropod

The giant theropod *Spinosaurus aegyptiacus* portrayed by artist Todd Marshall with a dorsal "sail" (for a different interpretation, see *SI*). According to a study by Thomas R. Holtz, Jr. (2003), the crocodile-like skulls of such dinosaurs, with their elongate snouts and numerous thick, conical teeth, were well adapted to a piscivorous diet.

specialist Thomas R. Holtz, Jr. (2003) recently pointed out, "direct evidence of these hypothesized interactions is difficult to find in the fossil record."

Holtz listed various factors that contribute to the difficulty in establishing the interaction among dinosaurs (and large-bodied vertebrates in general) of predators and prey compared to similar associations regarding marine invertebrates — "the differences between sedimentary styles and modes in terrestrial rather than marine realm; the larger body size (and hence greater difficulty in preservation) of dinosaurs

relative to marine invertebrates; the much greater number of hard parts in the vertebrate versus invertebrate skeleton; the vastly greater abundance of invertebrate than vertebrate fossils; and the difficulty in distinguishing predation versus scavenging events."

While there is evidence in the fossil record suggesting theropod-prey interaction, Holtz cautioned that establishing such direct evidence is compounded by numerous factors. Among these, it is difficult to demonstrate that a specific fossil represents a predation rather than a scavenging event; also, as some carnivorous dinosaurs constitute the largest fully terrestrial meat-eating animals in the Earth's history, depositional environments (unlike those preserving much smaller-bodied invertebrate remains) are not likely to record actual events of dinosaur predation.

Among the documented cases in the fossil record of probable predator-prey activity, discussed by Holtz (see paper for additional examples and references), is the pair of skeletons commonly referred to as the "fighting dinosaurs." Found in the Upper Cretaceous Djadokhta Formation of Mongolia, these fossils represent the skeletons of the herbivorous, primitive horned dinosaur *Protoceratops andrewsi* preserved as if engaged in its last moments of life locked in combat with the carnivorous *Velociraptor mongoliensis*, these individuals apparently having been trapped by the collapse of a sand dune collapse struggling against each other (see Kielan-Jaworoska and Barsbold 1972; Osmólska 1993; Carpenter 2000 for differing interpretations of this find; see also *D:TE* and *S1* for details and photographs). As Holtz commented, however, while these skeletons are generally interpreted to be "a predation event trapped in time," there are also other possible explanations for this association of taxa — *e.g.*, "the *Velociraptor* may have been defending itself against the *Protoceratops* individual, rather than trying to kill the herbivore for food."

While, as Holtz had stated, direct evidence of predation and predatory modes in theropod fossils is quite limited, some speculation can be presented based upon the morphology of theropods and, especially, "of their primary implements of prey acquisition and dispatch: skulls and teeth, forelimbs, and hindlimbs."

Regarding the generalized body plan of carnivorous dinosaurs, Holtz noted the following:

From the Late Triassic through the Late Cretaceous, theropods retained the ancestral dinosaurian condition of obligate bipedality. The forelimbs of theropods, which in other groups of vertebrates would have been used both as organs of locomotion and implements to acquire prey, could then specialize exclusively for the latter mode. Consequently, theropods evolved grasping forelimbs with trenchant claws.

Moreover, theropods demonstrate fully upright hindlimbs resulting in a digitigrade stance, indicative of animals that were striding cursors (see Farlow, Gatesy, Holtz, Hutchinson and Robinson 2000).

Additionally, Holtz pointed out that the theropod jaw apparatus is distinguished in part by an intramandibular joint. "The tooth-bearing dentary is hinged with the postdentary bones, allowing for some flexion in several bones," apparently working "as a shock-absorber to dampen the forces generated by the acquisition, manipulation, and/or consumption of large prey."

Based on the above observations, Holtz offered some general trends concerning the possible predatory behavior of carnivorous dinosaurs. From the cursorial nature of their limbs, theropods seem to have been rather swift animals for their size, probably utilizing this speed, either in pursuit or ambush. Theropods probably incorporated both the skull and forelimbs in acquiring prey, although the theropod skull ancestrally "would have been less resistant to the additional torsional forces associated with struggling prey, and so (unlike living carnivoran mammals or crocodylians) most theropods probably did not bite and hold throughout the kill," instead (as suggested by Rayfield, Norman, Horner, Horner, Smith, Thomason and Upchurch 2001 for the carnosaur *Allosaurus*; see *S3*) more typically using "strike-and-tear" bite to produce fatal wounds. Holtz further speculated that the theropod may have used its grasping forelimbs and trenchant claws to maintain a purchase of its prey, dispatching the victim by a combination of bites and claw wounds, then feeding on the soft tissues.

As Holtz noted, theropods comprise a diverse dinosaurian group, some taxa possessing specializations that indicate a deviation from the stereotyped mode of predation as suggested above. Holtz presented a brief survey of some of those derived taxa — *i.e.*, Coelophysidea, Ceratosauria (=Ceratosauridae and Abelisauroidea), Tyrannosauridae, Spinosauridae, and Dromaeosauridae (excluding taxa for which evidence for nonpredation exists, *e.g.*, ornithomimosaurs — and their adaptations, plus "speculations as to their particular variation on feeding habits (see also Paul, 1988)":

Coelophysids — characterized by small skull size, suggesting possible typical predation on smaller-sized animals than other theropods having the same body size.

Ceratosaurids and abelisauroids — having forelimbs with greatly reduced manual phalanges (see Gilmore 1920; Bonaparte, Novas and Coria 1990), strongly suggesting a reliance more on the skull and less (if at all) on the forelimbs in the acquisition, dispatch, and manipulation of prey.

Tyrannosaurids — skulls more solidly constructed than in the genralized theropod condition, teeth thickened, reduced forelimbs proportionally shorter than in most "nonceratosaur" theropod clades, hindlimbs elongate relative to other similar-sized theropods and to herbivorous dinosaurs, possessing the shock-absorbing "arctometatarsalian" condition (see Holtz 1994; Farlow *et al.* 2000; see also Kobayashi and Lü 2003, "Systematics" chapter), suggesting a capability to run at faster speeds than other large dinosaurs; the reinforced skull and thickened teeth indicating a capability to withstand the torsional forces associated with holding onto struggling prey and absorbing the forces created by tooth-on-bone contact, the forelimbs, if used during predation, possibly bracing the victim's body while the skull was employed in killing and dismembering.

Spinosaurids — crocodile-like skulls with elongate snouts, large number of thick, conical, crocodile-like teeth that are stronger in torsional stresses than more primitive teeth, their remains routinely found in sediments containing the remains of fish up to three meters long; apparent adaptations for stalking fish (for at least part of their diets; Sereno, Beck, Dutheil, Gado, Larsson, Lyon, Marcot, Rauhut, Sadleir, Sidor, Varricchio, Wilson and Wilson 1998), traveling from one water source to another, "striking down vertically and grasping the larger fish with their pincer-like terminal rosettes" (see also Holtz 1998).

Dromaeosaurids — greatly elongated forearms, sickle "killer" claw on hyperextensible second pedal digit, tails strengthened by caudal prezygapophyses and chevrons resulting in a tail apparently serving as a dynamic stabilizer for balance or rapid turns (see Ostrom 1969a), a suite of adaptations suggesting "a more felid-like predatory mode than in typical carnivorous dinosaurs": an ambush during which the predator could make rapid turns, followed by a quick forelimb strick to acquire prey, then a combination of strike and tear bites and strikes by the "killer claw" to dispatch the victim.

To defend themselves against theropods, some potential prey evolved various defenses throughout the Cretaceous, Holtz (2003a) noted, these including osteoderm scutes (thyreophorans and at least some titanosaurian sauropods), active defense weapons such as horns (ceratopsians) and tail clubs (ankylosaurids), herding behavior (sauropods and some ornithischians), and enhanced cursorial ability (nonpredatory theropods including ornithomimosaurs and troodontids) (see Holtz 1994).

Concluding, Holtz (2003a) stated that non-avian theropod dinosaurs were the dominant group of land-dwelling predators during the Late Jurassic through Late Cretaceous. With the extinction of these forms at the Cretaceous–Tertiary boundary, however, "the generalized theropod ecomorphotype has vanished ... the striding cursorial bipedal carnivores with grasping hands and serrated teeth [having] never again evolved in Earth's history."

Therrien, Henderson and Ruff (2003), in a published abstract, reported on their biomechanical approach, using solid models of theropod mandibles, in assessing the feeding behavior in this group of dinosaurs. As these authors explained, "the bite force applied at any given point along the mandible should be proportional to the external dimensions of the mandible at that point"; consequently, varying patterns in these dimensions reflect jaw adaptations to particular loads related to the method of killing prey. In conducting this study, Therrien et al. compared beam models of various theropods to models of two extant species of varanid lizards having distinct behaviors of feeding.

Among the species of the varanid Varanus, Therrien et al. noted, Varanus komodoensis employs ambush predator behavior incorporating a slashing bite, while V. niloticus feeds on molluscs. Theropods, however, were found to "exhibit an extremely high diversity of feeding behaviors," just a few kinds of these dinosaurs showing such behaviors similar to that of V. komodoensis.

Therrien et al. identified the following feeding

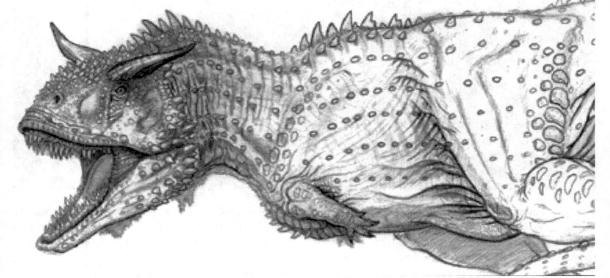

Life restoration by artist of Todd Marshall of *Carnotaurus sastrei*. According to a 2003 study by Francois Therrien, Donald M. Henderson, and Christopher B. Ruff (2003), features of the mandible suggest that this theropod employed slashing bites during feeding similar to those of species of *Varanus*, the extant Komodo dragon lizard.

Life restoration by Todd Marshall of *Majungatholus atopus*. According to a 2003 study by Francois Therrien, Donald M. Henderson, and Christopher B. Ruff (2003), such dinosaurs could have employed "slashing bites" in feeding.

characters among the theropod dinosaurs studied: 1. *Majungatholus atopus*, *Carnotaurus sastrei*, and "*Antrodemus valens*" [the authors possibly meaning *Allosaurus fragilis*, a *nomen dubium* known only from a partial caudal centrum, regarded by some workers as conspecific with the latter taxon; see *S2*) sharing mandibular properties of *V. komoedensis*, suggesting that they too employed slashing bites; 2. dromaeosaurids having mandibular properties similar to *V. komoedensis* for slashing bites, differences between

dromaeosaurines and velociraptorines, however, indicating that dromaeosaurines had a stronger bite than velociraptorines, probably using it against prey; 3. *Baryonyx* (=*Suchomimus* of the authors' usage; see *S3*) *tenerensis* and *Dilophosaurus wetherilli* with mandibular adaptations related to bite-and-hold strategy, *D. wetherilli* probably using slashing bites to finish off prey; 4. *Ceratosaurus nasicornis*, *Allosaurus fragilis*, *Acrocanthosaurus atokensis*, and *Giganotosaurus carolinii* with adaptations of rostal end of mandible for capture of prey and delivery of powerful bites to bring down or finish off prey; and 5. tyrannosaurids uniquely demonstrating mandibular adaptations for resisting high torsial stresses at rostral end of mandible (related to prey capture and bone-crushing abilities; see also Buckley 2003, *Tyrannosaurus* entry).

In a follow up abstract for a poster, Weishampel, Therrien, Henderson and Ruff (2004) concluded the following: Velociraptorines having bite forces close to *Varanus*, but bite of dromaeosaurine *Dromaeosaurus* three times stronger than that of velociraptorines (perhaps reflecting greater reliance on bite in killing prey); *Dilophosaurus*, despite similar mandibular length, apparently having slightly weaker bite than *Alligator* and "*Antrodemus*," suggesting preference for hunting small prey; "*Suchomimus*," *Ceratosaurus*, *Allosaurus*, and "*Antrodemus*" seemingly capable of exerting bite forces near that of *Alligator*, bite force of *Majungatholus* and *Carnotaurus* doubly powerful; *Acrocanthosaurus* and *Giganotosaurus* with bite force respectively almost four and five times that of *Alligator*, exceeded only by tyrannosaurids; *Daspletosaurus* having bite force seven times greater than *Alligator*, average *Tyrannosaurus* with bite force almost 16 times higher, the values for tyrannosaurids being consistent with published values indicative of bone-cracking capabilities.

In a survey review of dinosaur teeth collected from the Upper Triassic ("Rhaetian") Habay-la-Vielle locality in southern Belgium, Godefroit and Knoll (2003; see also below) described various shed teeth that "strongly resemble those of theropod dinosaurs," being caniniform, recurved backwards, with serrated carinae (although, the authors cautioned, such a dental morphology is also found in several independent Late Triassic archosauriform lineages; see Godefroit and Cuny 1997). The largest and best preserved specimen in this series (IRSNB R213) has a caniniform crown, is curved backwards, and strongly compressed labio-lingually. Such teeth resemble closely those of the coelophysoid *Liliensternus liliensterni*, but also those of other ceratosaurs as well as the above-mentioned nondinosaurian archosauriforms. However, two specimens differ substantially from the typical *Liliensternus* morphotype, described by Godefroit and Knoll as more slender, less labio-lingually compressed,

and less backwardly recurved, with minute serrations on the distal carinae and no trace of serrations on the well-developed mesial carinae.

Maisch and Matzke (2003) described a number of fragmentary theropod remains, mostly teeth, collected at two localities (see below) from the Middle Jurassic (?Bathonian–Callovian), upper part of the upper Toutunhe Formation of the southern Jungga Basin (Xinjiang Uygur Autonomous Region), at Liuhongou, Southwest Urumqi, Xinjiang, northwestern China. Represented by these specimens are two different kinds of theropod dinosaurs.

Life restoration by Todd Marshall of *Acrocanthosaurus atokensis*. According to a 2003 study by Francois Therrien, Donald M. Henderson, and Christopher B. Ruff (2003), the skulls of such dinosaurs could were designed for capturing prey and delivering powerful bites in bringing down and finishing off prey.

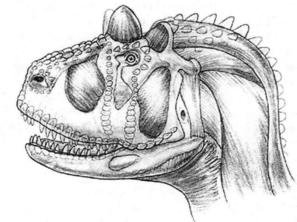

Life restoration by Mark Hallett of the abelisaurid *Carnotaurus sastrei*, one of the taxa figuring into the study of theropod feeding behavior published by Francois Therrien, Donald M. Henderson, and Christopher B. Ruff (2003).

Life restoration by Todd Marshall of *Allosaurus fragilis*. According to a study by David B. Weishampel, Francois Therrien, Donald M. Henderson, and Christopher Ruff (2004), this theropod had a bite force comparable to that of an alligator.

The recovered material — currently housed at the Institut und Museum für Geologie und Paläontologie, Tübingen — includes an uncomplete tooth crown (specimen number SGP 2001/5) from the considerably older Dinosaur Hill locality, and the possibly referrable distal end of a hollow left fibula (SGP 2000/2) from the TAAA ("turtle-archosaur-amphibian assemblage") locality, representing a small theropod (estimated total length of three meters) possibly belonging to the Coelophysoidea. The tooth is remarkable, the authors noted, for its bifurcated mesial carina, a condition possibly explained as a "genetically induced abnormality." As Maisch and Matzke observed, this tooth resembles teeth of the North American, Late Triassic species *Coelophysis bauri*, while the limb bone resembles its counterpart in *Sarcosaurus*, from the Lower Jurassic of England, and *Syntarsus* from the Lower Jurassic of Africa and North America.

Four tooth crowns (SGP 2001/4) from the Dinosaur Hill locality and one (SGP 2000/1) from the TAAA locality represent a large carnosaur with an estimated total length of from six to eight meters. This material, according to Maisch and Matzke, may or may not be referrable to *Monolophosaurus*, a crested theropod from the roughly equivalent Wucaiwan Formation of the Kelameili area of the Junggar Basin.

In another study based upon an analysis of dinosaur teeth, particularly shed teeth recovered from the latest Jurassic Morrison Formation at Como Bluff, Wyoming, Bakker and Bir (2004) attempted "to map out the feeding habits of large theropods across a wide habitat mosaic of dry floodplains, wet floodplains, swamp and lake margins."

As Bakker and Bir explained, the Como Bluff theropods can be arranged in a sequence from least birdlike predators, that are close to a Late Triassic form (in general, possessing long, sinuous bodies, short hindlimbs, and flexible ankles), to the most birdlike genera, the latter approaching the conditions seen in the Cretaceous tyrannosaurids and dromaeosaurids (having stiff torso and tail, long limbs, and long, compressed ankles). This arrangement can basically be broken down into three theropod groups — ceratosaurids, represented by *Ceratosaurus*, exhibiting many features in common with the "dilophosaurs" and *Coelophysis*-like Late Triassic and Early Jurassic

Acrocanthosaurus atokensis, an Early Cretaceous theropod portrayed by artist Todd Marshall as a striding runner.

Life restoration by Todd Marshall of *Giganotosaurus carolini*, another theropod—according to a study by David B. Weishampel, Francois Therrien, Donald M. Henderson, and Christopher Ruff (2004)—having a bite force comparable to that of an alligator.

forms, essentially "living fossils" possessing a very archaic body plan (*e.g.*, shins and ankles relatively short, metatarsal III less constricted, scalpular blade wide, torso long and flexible, tail long and flexible); megalosaurids, represented by *Torvosaurus*, resembling some older Middle Jurassic forms, unique among Jurassic theropods in having short forearm and metacarpal elements, sharing various features with ceratosaurids (*e.g.*, subdued neck curvature, wide scapular blades, short and wide metatarsals, long, low torsos,

Photograph by the author, courtesy North American Museum of Ancient Life.

The giant theropod *Tyrannosaurus rex* depicted by artist Berislav Krzic as an aggressive combatant, here encountering the ceratopsian *Triceratops horridus*. In a 2003 study, Thomas R. Holtz, Jr. found little direct evidence in the fossil record to substantiate such envisioned dinosaurian battles.

Combat between two *Tyrannosaurus rex* individuals (casts of the specimen nicknamed "Stan").

Predator-prey interaction as depicted in this hypothetical scene by artist Todd Marshall — the large, European theropod *Megalosaurus bucklandii* versus the small North American ornithopod *Othnielia rex*.

sinuous tails) and also the more advanced allosaurids (*e.g.*, manual claws very large); allosaurids, represented by *Allosaurus*, having the most birdlike shape (*e.g.*, comparatively shortest, stiffest torso, neck sharply bent, distal tail stiffened with elongated prezygapophyses, scapular blade thin, hind legs long relative to body, metatarsals relatively long, metatarsal III somewhat constricted).

Considering the above-mentioned body forms — ranging "from low and sinuous to compact, long-legged and birdlike" — Bakker and Bir speculated as to how the spectrum of these plans may have controlled the choices and hunting styles of these different kinds of theropods. Based upon the authors' observations of these forms, ceratosaurids and megalosaurids

appeared to be better designed "for snaking through dense forest and underbrush," while allosaurids seemed to be the "best adapted for running in open terrain." Noting that allosaurs survived beyond the extinction of the ceratosaurids and megalosaurids at the top of the Morrison Formation at Como Bluff, the authors also questioned whether the more birdlike allosaur body design was superior to the other two plans.

Bakker and Bir's performed an extensive taphonomic investigation (see paper for details) focusing primarily upon numerous shed theropod teeth collected from a Morrison outcrop with "crime scene integrity" — *i.e.*, one at which the association between bones and shed teeth had not been disturbed by an

earlier collection of shred crowns from the surface. In order to determine if allosaur social behavior was more like that of a giant ground hawk than a crocodile, Bakker and Bir included in their analysis comparisons between the allosaur shed teeth and those of *Goniopholis* sp., the common aquatic crocodile found at Como Bluff, which the authors assumed to have had a sociobiology close to that of extant crocodiles. Among the other factors included in this study were the skeletal remains of various kinds of herbivorous dinosaurs.

Bakker and Bir's analysis concluded with a number of deductions, the most important being the following:

1. Shed teeth record life activities (*i.e.*, feeding sites) not necessarily corresponding to burial sites of the same species (*e.g.*, megalosaurid skeletons found in habitats bereft of shed megalosaur teeth, ceratosaurid and megalosaurid shed teeth very abundant in swampy facies bereft of their skeletal remains).

2. Shed teeth of *Goniopholis* sp. are distributed over environments expected in an extant crocodile of comparable head and tooth design, with hatchling teeth common only in secluded, shallow, near-shore habitats including small fish, crowns from large adults most common in deep, wide, open waters including large lungfish. Most young died at from two to three years old, just a small percentage surviving to adulthood. Crocodile teeth are rare in dry floodplain habitats. The gapfree distribution of such teeth suggest year-round residence of the crocodile population.

3. Large herbivorous dinosaurs (*e.g.*, sauropods, stegosaurs, and camptosaurs) were not resident in the Como Bluff area during Morrison times, the abundance of their skeletons and the rarity of their shed teeth indicating migration through the area without lingering to feed, with some individuals suffering sporadic mass deaths.

4. Ceratosaurids and megalosaurids fed mostly in and around permanent watercourses, mostly preying on large lungfish, crocodiles, and turtles, with ceratosaurids sometimes feeding on sauropods in dry and wet floodplains, megalosaurids very occasionally on sauropods on wet floodplains.

5. *Ceratosaurus* had the strongest swimming ability among the theropods found at Como Bluff, megalosaurids being stronger swimmers than allosaurids.

Among the relatively small number of documented cases in the fossil record apparently indicating dinosaurian predator-prey activity is the famous "fighting dinosaurs" specimen comprising skeletons of *Velociraptor mongoliensis* and *Protoceratops andrewsi* locked together as if in battle (see *D:TE* and *SI*). Artist Todd Marshall has envisioned this possible moment from that battle.

Introduction

Institut und Museum für Geologie und Paläontologie collection, SGP 2001/5, small theropod incomplete tooth crown in 1. labial, 2. lingual, and 3. mesial views. Scale = 5 mm. (After Maisch and Matzke 2003.)

Institut und Museum für Geologie und Paläontologie collection, SGP 2001/2, maxillary or middle dentary carnosaur tooth, in 1. labial, 2. lingual, and 3. mesial views. Scale = 30 mm. (After Maisch and Matzke 2003.)

6. Allosaurids were the fastest yet least maneuverable of the three groups of Como Bluff theropods, and overwhelmingly dominated the dry floodplain feeding sites preserving sauropod remains.

7. Allosaurids are the most common large predators found in and around water habitats, probably having shifted their feeding sites from dry floodplains (feeding mostly on sauropods) to lake margins and alkaline swamps (feeding on aquatic vertebrates), the latter shift probably imposed by seasonal disappearance of migrating herbivore herds.

8. Allosaur hatchlings fed on huge prey carcasses with their parents and older siblings, allosaurids remaining in a family group until achieving maturity.

9. Ceratosaurids and megalosaurids were supplanted by theropods having a more birdlike shape, allosaurids and, later, tyrannosaurids (a long-term trend repeated in the Cenozoic, with short-limbed creodonts with spread-

ing feet progressively replacing longer-limbed and more digitigrade dogs, hyaenas, and cats), this shift to longer and stiffer limbs being possibly associated with a more complex social behavior.

In a published abstract, Novas and Canale (2004) briefly reported on an as yet unnamed basal theropod collected from the Upper Triassic (Carnian) Ischigualasto Formation of San Juan Province, Argentina. Recovered material belonging to this new taxon includes the basicranium, cervical, dorsal, sacral, and caudal vertebrae, fragments of both ilia and ischia, and fragments of a femur, fibula, and metatarsals.

Novas and Canale referred this material to the Saurischia based on the presence of a hyposphene-hypantrum in the dorsal vertebrae; and to the Theropoda based upon cervical vertebrae having prominent, sharply pointed epipophysis.

Comparing the new taxon with other basal theropods, the authors noted the following: Differs from *Eoraptor* in having ilium with extended postacetabular process, femur with trochanteric shelf, cranial trochanter subvertical and conical; proximal end of femur suggesting condition in gracile members of Coelophysoidea, distal femur also exhibiting features in common with coelophysoids; differing from [the basal saurischians; see "Systematics" chapter] *Herrerasaurus* and *Eoraptor* by strong fibular furrow; absence of pleurocoels in cervical and dorsal vertebrae plesiomorphic, precluding referral to clade "Eutheropoda" (defined by Calvo and Canale as "Ceratosauria" plus Tetanurae; see "Systematics" chapter).

According to Novas and Canale, this new taxon partially fills a morphological gap between primitive dinosaurs and basal "eutheropods" (*i.e.*, Coelophysoidea), at the same time enriching our knowledge of the Ischigyalasto fauna.

Dal Sasso (2003), in a survey paper on the dinosaurs of Italy, offered more information regarding the theropod known, as of this writing, only by the popular name of "*Saltriosaurus*" (see Dalla Vecchia 2001*a* for a preliminary report).

As chronicled by Dal Sasso, the discovery of this theropod — to date, the largest and also most ancient (Sinemurian, approximately 200 million years ago; see Sacchi Vialli 1964, date supported by "a hundred species of marine invertebrates," including index fossils comprising 19 ammonites) large theropod known from skeletal remains found in Italy — was made in summer 1996, when a quarry (known since the fifteenth century for its fine marble) in the Alpine foothills, at the Swiss-Italian border near Saltrio, north of Milan (Varese Province, Lombardy) yielded some large bones.

Discovery of these bones was made by Angelo

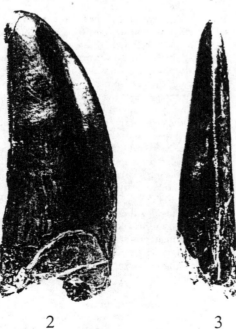

Zanella, an amateur fossil collector and a collaborator of the Museo di Storia Naturale di Milano, who was accustomed to searching for ammonites and other invertebrate fossils in the quarry blocks. Zanella reported his discovery to the museum which made arrangements to collect the specimen. Recovery proved difficult, however, as dynamite utilized in industrial quarrying had severely damaged the fossil-bearing layer.

As Dal Sasso related, the specimen, following its retrieval from the quarry, was exposed in 1999 at the Milan museum, following 1,800 hours of chemical preparation. The work resulted in a fragmentary specimen (MSNM V3664) comprising 199 elements including ribs and 21 limb bones. The material represents a large theropod, preliminary examination finding it to be morphometrically comparable with a skeleton of *Allosaurus* mounted at the Museum of Natural Sciences in Bergamo. In life, Dal Sasso estimated, the Saltrio theropod—the largest theropod known from Italy—would have measured approximately 8 meters (more than 27 feet) long and weighed about 1.5 metric tonnes (over 1.7 tons).

Dal Sasso noted that, while ceratosaurs have generally been regarded as the dominant Sinemurian-age theropods, the form from Saltrio presents anatomical features typical of more advanced forms (*i.e.*, Tetanurae), including an apparently three-fingered manus (four fingers in ceratosaurs) and a true furcula (apparently absent in ceratosaurs). Another tetanuran feature is the low degree of supination of the phalanges of the manus, comparable to the condition in *Allosaurus*.

Conversely, according to Dal Sasso, other features of the Italian theropod are reminiscent of the more primitive ceratosaurs, these including the very short first phalanx of the central digit; and others are suggestive of megalosaurs, such as the moderately stout, nonsigmoidal form of the humerus.

According to Dal Sasso, the Saltrio dinosaur constitutes a very important specimen regarding theropod evolution, possibly representing a transitional form between Ceratosauria and Tetanurae, a basal member of the Tetanurae, or even the most ancient known member of the Carnosauria. For the present, this specimen establishes "that large, meat-eating dinosaurs with three-fingered hands (possibly forerunners of the allosauroid kin) already existed 200 Myr ago."

Hunt and Chure (2003), in a published abstract for a poster, reported on remains of a theropod right pes that had been recovered in 1972 in the Lower Cretaceous Trinity Group of southwestern Arkansas, these constituting the only dinosaur fossils yet discovered in that state. While these remains have not yet been adequately described, Hunt and Chure stated that they

Photograph by the author, courtesy Riverside Municipal Museum.

are "Characterized by differential pedal unguals and a laterally compressed third metatarsal." According to the authors, this new and as yet unnamed theropod seems to be closely related both to the ceratosaur *Elaphrosaurus* and the possible maniraptoran *Nedcolbertia*, both from the Early Cretaceous.

Carabajal, Coria and Currie (2004), in an abstract, reported the first discovery of an abelisauroid theropod in the Upper Cretaceous (?Turonian) Lisandro Formation of Neuquén Province, Argentina, at a site near Plaza Huincul previously known for yielding remains of the iguanodontian ornithopod *Anabisetia saldiviai*. The specimen (MCF-PVPH-409), as reported

Cast of elements of *Allosaurus fragilis*, a large theropod, remains of which have been found in the Morrison Formation at Como Bluff, Wyoming. Robert T. Bakker and Gary Bir (2004) utilized "crime scene investigation" techniques in their taphonomic study of shed *Allosaurus* and other theropod teeth to determine the possible feeding habits of the carnivorous dinosaurs found at Como Bluff.

Introduction

Skeleton (cast from DINO-LAB) of *Stegosaurus ungulatus* mounted during the 1980s at Rick Halbrooks' DinoStore's Prehistoric Museum in Birmingham, Alabama. According to a study by Robert T. Bakker and Gary Bir (2004), stegosaurs numbered among the Morrison Formation herbivorous dinosaurs that migrated through the Como Bluff area.

by Carabajal *et al.*, includes a caudal dorsal vertebra, the first three sacral vertebrae, the incomplete right ilium, both pubes missing their distal extremities, and fragments of the right ischium. It pertains to a rather small animal, seemingly either an adult or subadult, given the fusion of the neural arches with the vertebral centra.

As Carabajal *et al.* noted, the specimen exhibits a number or features identifying it as an abelisaur, including the following: Dorsal vertebrae with cranioventral processes in prezygapophyses, centra of second and third sacral vertebrae very transversely compressed; iliac blade having very marked longitudinal, dorsal crest; pubis having obturator foramen.

To date, no detailed descriptions had been published about abelisaurid teeth. Offering "the first detailed information about the tooth's structure of a member of this theropod clade, Bittencourt and Kellner (2002) described several of nine incomplete isolated teeth (no jaw elements found with the material), discovered in association with an incomplete skeleton (DGM 859-R; first reported by Kellner and Campos 2000*a*) which they referred to the "Abelisauria" [of

their usage, apparently meaning Abelisauroidea or Abelisauridae] (including hind-limb, pelvic, and caudal vertebral elements) collected from continental Cretaceous deposits in Mato Grosso State, Brazil.

As described by Bittencourt and Kellner, four of these teeth are fragmentary, essentially comprising the root, while the others, while better preserved, lack several portions of the enamel. The most complete tooth includes the root and crown, but lacks most of the distal region and part of the lingual facet. Included in their description of these teeth, the authors noted the following details: Strong lateral compression; eliptic transverse cross section; root long; length of best preserved tooth 84.3 millimeters (crown 49.7 millimeters, root 34.6 millimeters); denticles chisellike, with from two (base) to eight (top) denticles per millimeter.

Notably, these teeth differ from other described theropod teeth, especially from those of spinosaurids (subcircular transverse cross section, some lacking serrations, as in *Irritator* [see Kellner and Campos 1996 for "*Angaturama*"], or finely serrated, as in *Baryonyx* [see Charig and Milner 1997; Sereno, Beck, Dutheil, Gado,

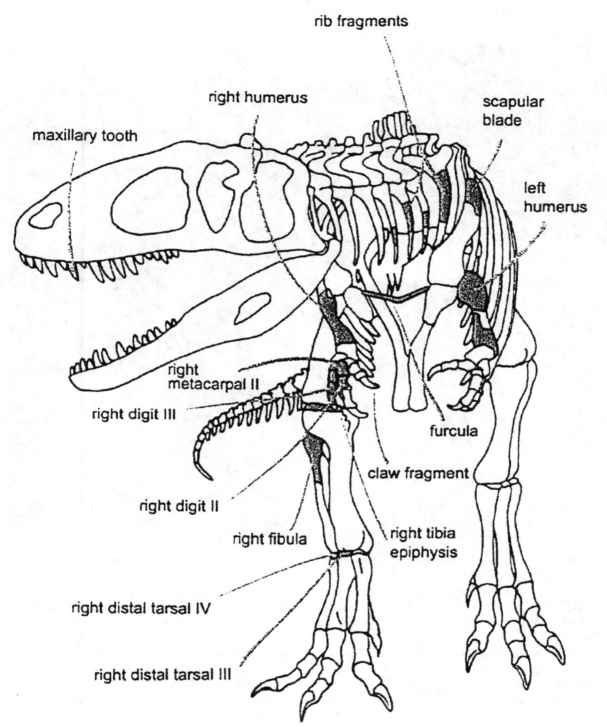

rib fragments

right humerus

scapular blade

maxillary tooth

left humerus

right metacarpal II

right digit III

furcula

claw fragment

right digit II

right fibula

right tibia epiphysis

right distal tarsal IV

right distal tarsal III

Skeletal reconstruction of the theropod from Saltrio, Italy, currently known by the popular name of "Saltriosaurus." Less than 10 percent of this skeleton has been recovered. (After Dal Sasso 2003.)

Larsson, Lyon, Marcot, Rauhut, Sadlier, Sidor, Varricchio, Wilson and Wilson 1998, for "*Suchomimus*"; Taquet and Russell 1998 for "*Cristatusaurus*"]); dromaeosaurids (*Dromaeosaurus albertensis*— smaller, slightly curved denticles, blood grooves oriented perpendicularly to longitudinal axis; see Currie, Rigby and Sloan 1990; *Saurornitholestes langstoni*— denticles sharply pointed, strongly curved towards apex of tooth, anterior carinae finely denticulate, with seven denticles per millimeter; see Sues 1978); tyrannosaurids (D-shaped in cross section, sharp ridges along denticles; see Currie, Sloan and Rigby; sharing with tyrannosaurids approximate length, two denticles per millimeter in both carinae); and other abelisaurid taxa (teeth from Serra da Galga, Minas Gerais State [figured by Kellner and Campos 2000*b*] and from Morro do Cambambe, Morro

Allosaurus fragilis, a theropod that probably used both its skull and forelimbs to bring down prey. Illustration by artist Todd Marshall.

Grosso State, tentatively attributed to the Patagonian *Giganotosaurus* or the Moroccan *Carcharodontosaurus*—transverse wrinkles on enamel; see, respectively, Kellner and Campos 2000*b*; Sereno, Beck, Dutheil, Iarochene, Larsson, Lyon, Magwene, Sidor, Varricchio and Wilson 1996).

Furthermore, Bittencourt and Kellner observed that DGM 859-R differ (*e.g.*, in size, number and form or denticles, comparative length of blood grooves) from most isolated theropod teeth in Brazil, but display some similarities (*e.g.*, straight, chisellike denticles, distal curvature of mesial margin) with one (KM-1) of six morphotypes reported by Kellner (1995*a*, 1996) from Cretaceous layers outcropping in Peirópolis (Minas Gerais State).

Veralli and Calvo (2004), in an abstract, reported the collection or more than 70 theropod teeth from the Futalognko quarry, in outcrops of the Upper Cretaceous (late Turonian) Portezuelo Formation, on the northern coast of Barreales lake, northwest of Neuquén city, Neuqué Province, Argentina.

The authors described five of these teeth thusly: Caudal rim marked by curved winkles, mesial to serrations, on lingual and labial sides (character diagnostic for Carcharodontosauridae); short banding on labial and lingual sides (similar to banding in carcharodontosaurids *Carchardontosaurus* and *Giganotosaurus*); sampled teeth ranging from 22 to 45 millimeters in height; denticles varying from 11 to 13 per five millimeters; distinctive character of upwardly curved wrinkles only on distal rim (otherwise only found in tooth from Upper Cretaceous [Turonian–Santonian] Baurú Group of Brazil, wrinkles present in both mesial and distal carina in other known carcharodontosaurids).

The first theropod remains reported from the yellowish-white sandstone of the Tacuarembó Formation (Late Jurassic–Early Cretaceous, based on the presence of the hybodontid shark *Priohybodus*; see, for example, Cappetta 1987) of Uruguay were described by Ubilla and Rojas (2003). Recently, a number of

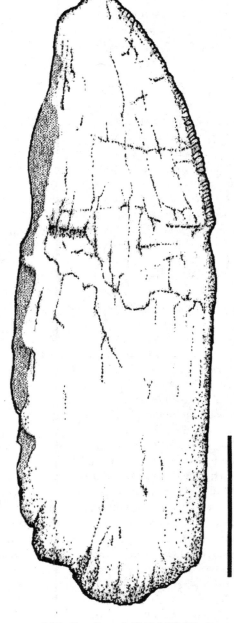

Best-preserved "abelisaur" tooth (DGM 859-R) of a specimen collected from Cretaceous rocks of Mato Grosso State, Brazil. Scale = 10 mm. (After Bittencourt and Kellner 2002.)

isolated theropod teeth were recovered from the lower part of the formation, Tacuarembó Department, distinguishing them as the oldest dinosaurian remains yet found in Uruguay. The most abundant of these teeth were discovered in a bonebed near the town of Martinote.

Two of the tooth crowns (MGCT-142, collected at Los Rosanos, near Valle Edén, and FC-DPV, near Martinote, east of Batovhills) were identified by Ubilla and Rojas as from probably either the left maxilla or right dentary. In describing these specimens, the au-

thors observed that they are of medium size (approximately 35 millimeters in crown height, 16 millimeters in length, and 11.5 millimeters in width at the crown base), smooth, mesially curved, and sharp and straight distally. The authors were unable to refer these specimens to any particular theropod subgroup.

Additionally, Ubilla and Rojas described five tooth crowns (FC-DPV 1000, 1047, 1048, 1140, and 1223), noting that they are curved, serrated, of medium size (the best preserved being about 28 millimeters high, 10.5 millimeters long, and six millimeters wide at the crown base), and have somewhat fine denticles (averaging four to five per millimeter) on both the mesial and distal carinae, with smaller denticles at the proximal and distal ends of the carinae. Although these teeth resemble those of the dromaeosaurid *Dromaeosaurus albertensis* and exhibit features (*e.g.*, mesial carina close to midline near tip, twisting toward linqual surface basally) unknown in

Indeterminate theropod tooth (MGCT-142) from the Tacuarembó Formation of Uruguay, in A. labial and B. mesial views. Scale = 5 mm. (After Ubilla and Rojas 2003.)

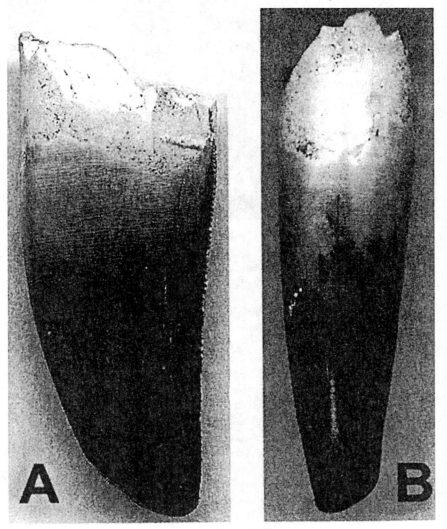

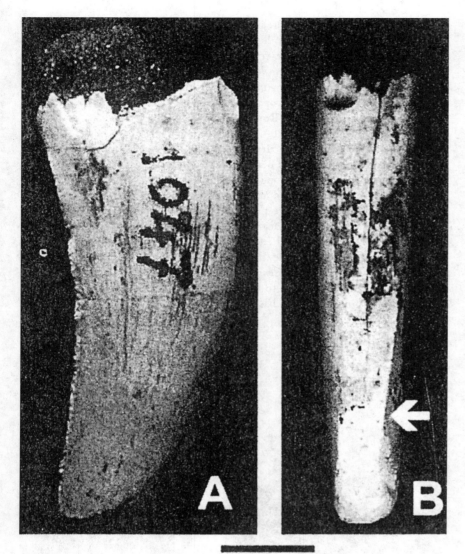

Possible coelurosaurian theropod tooth (FC=DPV-1047) from the Tacuarembó Formation of Uruguay, in A. labial and B. mesial views. Scale = 5 mm. (After Ubilla and Rojas 2003.)

4. maintaining contact with metatarsal II distally and proximally, all three metatarsals thereby forming a wedge-and-buttress morphology, the buttressing surfaces of the outer metatarsals overhanging and contacting the distal surfaces of the wedgelike third metatarsal.

Snively *et al.* utilized three methods (see paper for details) in their study — quantitative descriptive analysis (using published data, photographs and measurements of specimens, and so forth), principal component analysis (determining shape variation independent of size), and thin-plate spline analysis (computer imagery). These analyses were used to test three hypotheses of variation among theropod third metatarsals —1. metatarsals classified as arctometatarsalian share a significantly greater degree of proximal metatarsal III constriction, regardless of size, than do those of other theropods; 2. arctometatarsalian metatarsal III can be phylogenetically differentiated based on their degree of relative constriction; and 3. Tyrannosauridae, Troodontidae, and Ornithomimidae differed in modes of footfall energy transmission. Snively *et al.*'s analyses confirmed the segregation of the arctometatarsus from the pedal morphologies of other kinds of theropods, while also revealing variation within phylogenetic and functional coelurosaurian subgroups of metatarsi.

Quantitative descriptive analysis was employed in describing the third metatarsals of exemplars of terminal coelurosaurian taxa, then exploring notable variations within more diverse subclades:

First, Snively *et al.* noted that, in general, theropod third metatarsals usually have in common such features as follows: Deep subcircular ligament fossae (for collateral ligaments between metatarsal and first phalanx; see Ostrom 1969*b*) on disto-lateral and disto-medial surfaces; proximally, articular surfaces for metatarsals II and IV rugosely striated in tyrannosaurids, other large theropods, and *Deinonychus*; complimentary surfaces of metarsals II and IV similarly striated (probably indicative of intermetatarsal ligaments; see Snively and Russell 2003).

This method of analysis also revealed to Snively *et al* both variations and similarities in the morphology of third metatarsals in a number of theropod groups:

TYRANNOSAURIDAE — (*Tyrannosaurus rex*) metatarsal III hook-shaped in proximal cross section, outline of hook running craniocaudally near plantar surface, with sharp lateral bend cranially; discrete ligament scars marking articular surfaces where metatarsal III is constrained cranially by metatarsal II, caudally by IV; metatarsal narrowing to splint distal to those articulations, then reexpanding asymmetrically

other theropods (see Currie, Rigby and Sloan 1990; Currie 1995), Ubilla and Rojas suspected that the similarities are examples of convergence and "insufficient to establish more precise systematics conclusions."

Snivley, Russell and Powell (2004) published their study on the evolutionary morphology of the arctometatarsus in coelurosaurian dinosaurs. Introduced by Holtz in 1994, the "arctometatarsalian condition" constitutes an unusual pes morphology that evolved several times among various groups (*i.e.*, Tyrannosauridae, Ornithomimidae, and Troodontidae). According to that author, four characteristics define this condition —1. proximal constriction of metatarsal III (relative to the condition in other Theropoda); 2. metatarsal III triangular in distal transverse cross section, consequently restricted towards plantar surface; 3. outer, weight-bearing metatarsals (II and IV) encroaching towards midsagittal plane of metatarsal III, where III is constricted, in cranial aspect, strong convex curvature medially; cross section in this region asymmetrically triangular, apex towards plantar surface, offset laterally; surfaces exposed in plantar aspect distal articular facets with metatarsals II and IV; scar for metatarsal II wider, extremely rugose; phalangeal articular surface proximodistally extensive, with primarily medially inclined proximal edge, deep, medially inclined reniform indentation (*i.e.*, oblique ligament fossa) proximal to that edge; (other tyrannosaurids) metatarsal III less robust, with lighter scarring on articular facet of II (some elements of *Albertosaurus* specimens more gracile than in similar-length *Daspletosaurus*, *Gorgosaurus*, and *Tarbosaurus*).

ORNITHOMIMIDAE — Metatarsal III craniocaudally expanded in lateral or proximal aspect; faceted articular surfaces for metatarsals II and IV in this area; distally very similar to tyrannosaurid condition, although symmetrical mediolaterally in cranial aspect, with sharp edges along lateral and medial sides, lack of rugosity on distal articular facets; caudal edge of plantar constriction sharp edge; very shallow oblique ligament fossa proximal to phalangeal articular surface, (as in tyrannosaurids) more proximal edge of surface inclining medially.

TROODONTIDAE — (*Troodon formosus*) metatarsal III expanding proximally, forming triangular cross section, apex towards cranial (dorsal) surface; proximal splint strikingly narrow mediolaterally and long relative to distal expansion, in cranial aspect; distal articular surface with metatarsal IV medially inclined in cranial aspect, straight with II; caudal edge of plantar constriction more medially deflected than in other arctometatarsalians, forming sharp ridge (as in ornithomimids); cranially, phalangeal articular surfaces more asymmetrical than in tyrannosaurids and ornithomimids, surface extending father proximally in caudal aspect.

OVIRAPTOROSAURIA — (*Elmisaurus* sp.) metatarsal III narrower at proximal point cranially (as in troodontids), but not triangular, this condition persisting farther distally along proximal splint; fused near mesotarsal joint to metatarsals II and IV; metatarsals II, III and IV grading together in caudal aspect; metatarsal III expanding distally in cranial aspect (as in tyrannosaurids, ornithomimids, and troodontids), never triangular in cross section; phalangeal articular surface having medially and laterally expansive trochlear ridges; (*Chirostenotes pergracilis* and *Rinchenia mongoliensis*) metatarsal III constricted proximally, entire element more triangular in cranial aspect than in *Elmisaurus*, lacking discrete proximal

splint; (*Ingenia yanshini*) metatarsal III robust, with slight craniocaudal expansion proximally, rectangular in cranial aspect.

DROMAEOSAURIDAE — (*Deinonychus antirrhopus*) metatarsal III craniocaudally expanded near mesotarsal articular surface, lightly striated along articular facets for metatarsals II and IV; shaft rectangular in cranial aspect; large distal articular facet for metatarsal II, slightly inclined towards caudal (plantar) surface; phalangeal articular surface spool-shaped, inclined proximomedially.

CARNOSAURIA/BASAL TETANURAE — (*Allosaurus fragilis*) metatarsal III completely expanded proximally, wider towards plantar surface, with overall craniolateral inclination; proximal articular surface for metatarsal II strongly inclined craniolaterally in proximal aspect, that for IV more sagittal; both surfaces with longitudinal striations; shaft slightly curved medially, with poorly defined, unstriated distal extension of metatarsal II articular surface (Snively and Russell); phalangeal articular surface low in cranial aspect, variably symmetrical among specimens; (*Sinraptor dongi*) metatarsal III more gracile, distal articular extension for metatarsal II better defined, slightly rugose; carcharodontosaurid specimen having discrete roughened scar (presumably for ligamentous articulation with metatarsal II); (*Torvosaurus tanneri*) metatarsal III elements very similar to those of robust *Allosaurus*.

Results of Snively *et al.*'s principal component analysis showed that the arctometatarsalian metatarsus III differs in proximo-distal shape from nonarctometatarsalian metatarsi independent of overall size, this indicating to the authors that allometric differences among the studied taxa resulted in this divergence in metatarsus III morphology. In Troodontidae (*Troodon*), Ornithomimidae, Tyrannosauridae, and Caenagnathidae (*Elmisaurus*, *Chirostenotes*), a subclade of Oviraptorosauria, the morphology of metatarsal III is affected by taxon-specific allometry more so than in other coelurosaurian groups — *e.g.*, Oviraptoridae (*Ingenia*), Therizinosauridae (*Segnosaurus*), Dromaeosauridae (*Bambiraptor*, *Deinonychus*), *Ornitholestes*, and *Sinosauropteryx* (Compsognathidae) — while some of the more gracile taxa approach the arctometatarsalian distribution. According to Snively *et al.*, "robust arctometatarsalians do not overlap robust nonarctometatarsalians in this regard, nor do most gracile arctometatarsalians overlap with gracile nonarctometatarsalians"; moreover, robust nonarctometatarsalian forms (*e.g.*, the carnosaurs *Torvosaurus* and *Fukuiraptor*) are strongly separated from the gracile nonarctometatarsalian forms by variation in the proximo-distal shape of the third metatarsal, although this is largely not true of gracile and robust arctometatarsalian taxa.

Thin-plate spline analysis by Snively *et al.* revealed substantial footfall force from metatarsals II to III in Ornithomimidae and Tyrannosauridae (ridge of plantar constriction shifting from inclining proximomedially) and from IV to III in Troodontidae (ridge of plantar constriction shifting to proximolaterally), indicating a larger distal metatarsal III–IV contact in Troodontidae than in the other two clades. This analysis further indicated a more marked morphological shift from Troodontidae to Tyrannosauridae than between Troodontidae and Ornithomimidae, and also proportionally much larger distal intermetatarsal articulations in Tyrannosauridae than in the other two groups.

A phylogeny proposed by Snively *et al.*, showing distribution of the arctometatarsus among Theropoda and the observed ligament correlates on theropod metatarsals, indicated that homoplasy of the arctometatarsalian condition was extensive, this structure having evolved independently along multiple evolutionary courses (*i.e.*, in Tyrannosauridae, Ornithomimidae, and Troodontidae); that proximal constriction of metatarsal III may have evolved before plantar constriction (the latter condition not present in the primitive ornithomimosaur *Garudimimus*); and that arctometatarsalian-like morphologies evolved independently in other theropod clades (*e.g.*, Caenagnathidae, Alvarezsauridae, and [Deinonychosauria: Microraptoria] *Sinorithosaurus millenii* [see Xu, Wang and Wu 1999]).

As noted by Snively *et al.*, intermetatarsal ligaments seem to have been distributed generally among Theropoda, these attached to the proximal metatarsal heads. The specialized arctometatarsalian metatarsus III, however, would also have required strengthening by strong and expansive deep distal ligaments not present in nonarctometatarsalian theropod metatarsi, these ligaments serving to bind the metatarsals at the place of their distal plantar angulation, without strong ligamental development in the area between proximal and distal ligaments. It was the authors' postulation that proximal intermetatarsal ligaments were a precursor to the acquisition of these distal intermetatarsal ligaments.

Snively *et al.* further postulated that the arctometatarsalian metatarsus III may have originally evolved as an innovation related to enhanced locomotor agility in these theropods. Moreover, if that hypothesis is correct, the increased agility was probably related to the predatory performance of these carnivorous dinosaurs, with the biological roles associated with intraspecific and interspecific competition and escape most likely at various stages in the life history of the animal.

Snively and Henderson (2004), in an abstract, briefly reported on the nasal fusion that reinforced the rostrum in the skulls of tyrannosauroids throughout the phylogenetic history and ontogenetic size range of this clade of thereopods. Computed tomographic (CT) scans, by the authors, of several tyrannosauroid specimens of different sizes confirmed "that the fusion extends fully through the nasals, rather than being isolated to ornamental fusion of the dorsal suture." Contrarily, CT scans of a number of different-sized *Allosaurus* skulls confirmed "no tendency towards fusion."

As Snively and Henderson explained, this ankylosis in the nasals of tyrannosauroid proceeded ontogenetically, both caudally and rostrally, starting at the region above the largest maxillary teeth. Calculations by the authors of bending, and torsional and compressional strengths, demonstrate "that nasal fusion and thickening, and a staircase-style naso-maxillary joint in giant individuals, contributed to reinforcement of the snout." From their observations, Snively and Henderson postulated that nasal fusions in this theropod clade "was part of a correlated progression towards crushing bone, and reducing prey by vigorous lateral flexion of the head and neck." The authors noted that nasal fusion had also evolved independently in spinosaurids and abelisaurs, indicating "the utility of mechanical reinforcement in the skulls of large theropods."

Currie (2003*a*) published a study of allometric growth in tyrannosaurid theropods from the Upper Cretaceous of North America and Asia. As noted by Currie, tyrannosaurids are known from numerous skeletons collected in the United States, Canada, and Mongolia, while juvenile specimens are also known for these taxa.

For a period of over 10 years, Currie measured more than 250 catalogued tyrannosaurid specimens, some consisting of isolated bones, but more than half of these being partial to almost complete skeletons. These specimens represent five tyrannosaurid genera—*Albertosaurus*, *Gorgosaurus*, *Daspletosaurus*, *Tyrannosaurus*, and *Tarbosaurus*—belonging to two distinct clades within a monophyletic Tyrannosauridae, the Albertosaurinae clade (alluded to by Holtz 2001; including *Albertosaurus sarcophagus* and *Gorgosaurus libratus*, *Albertosaurus* and *Gorgosaurus*, now generally considered to be distinct genera, yet currently regarded as congeneric by Carr 2003) and the Tyrannosaurinae (including *Daspletosaurus torosus*, a new unnamed *Daspletosaurus* (see entry) species, *Tarbosaurus bataar*, *Tyrannosaurus rex*, and "*Nanotyrannus*

Photograph by the author, courtesy North American Museum of Ancient Life.

Skeleton of *Tyrannosaurus rex* (cast of BHI-3033, the specimen known as "Stan"). Philip J. Currie (2003*a*) recently published a major 10-year study on allometric growth in such tyrannosaurid theropods, based upon at least 250 specimens.

Introduction

Group of small tyrannosaurids based by artist Todd Marshall on the skull (CMNH 7541) regarded by most theropod workers as belonging to a juvenile *Tyrannosaurus rex* (see entry), although others consider it to represent a distinct genus and species, *Nanotyrannus lancensis*. Philip J. Currie (2003*a*), who, with co-authors Robert T. Bakker and Michael Williams, named and described this taxon in 1988, has recently suggested that CMNH 7541 may be distinct at the species level.

lancensis" [regarded by most workers as a juvenile *T. rex*, *e.g.*, Carpenter 1992, Carr 1999, see *S1* and *S2*; considered by Currie as possibly "distinct at the species level"; see Currie 2003*b*; see also *Tyrannosaurus* entry]; *Tarbosaurus* and *Tyrannosaurus* considered to be congeneric by Carr 2003). Both subfamilies have now been formally defined based upon morphological differences (see Currie, Hurum and Sabath 2003; see also "Systematics" chapter).

For this study, Currie regarded *Tyrannosaurus* and *Tarbosaurus* as distinct genera (see *Tarbosaurus* entries, *S3*, this volume); regarded as junior synonyms of *Tyrannosaurus rex* LACM 28345 (designated *Albertosaurus megacracilis* by Paul 1988, renamed *Dinotyrannus megagracilis* by Olshevsky, Ford and Yamamoto 1995*a*, 1995*b*; see *S2*), LACM 28471 (named *Aublysodon molnari* by Paul, referred to *Aublysodon* cf. *A. mirandi* by Molnar and Carpenter 1989, and renamed *Stygivenator molnari* by Olshevsky *et al.*) as well as, by implication, Leidy's (1868) tooth genus *Aublysodon*. Currie, following Currie and Dong 2001, also regarded *Shanshanosaurus* as a juvenile of *Tarbosaurus bataar*. Given this reassignment of *Aublysodon* to *T. rex* and *Shanshanosaurus* to *T. bataar*, Currie removed the subfamily Aublysodontinae from the Tyrannosauridae (see "Systematics" chapter). Because of insufficient information, Currie excluded from his study *Alectrosaurus olseni*, a possible albertosaurine (see Paul), and also *Alioramus remotus*, a probable close relative of *Tarbosaurus* (Currie, in press).

Currie (2003*a*) made 85 bivariate comparisons, most of them utilizing femur length (in theropods and many other animals, the femur having one of the least variable lengths of the body, *e.g.*, see Russell 1970; Currie and Zhao 1993; Holtz 1994; also, femoral length in extant mammals is also correlated highly with body mass, see Christainsen 1999) as the standard against which measurements of other bones were made. As some tyrannosaurid specimens consist only of skulls or lack the femur, Currie (2003*a*) also used skull length and maxillary tooth row length, both being isometric with femur length, as elements for comparison with other bones and dimensions. Considering that few of the catalogued 250 specimens are complete skeletons, and that crushing, distortion, and other factors affected taking accurate measurements, the net result of Currie's (2003*a*) study was that less than 10 percent of the specimens were suitable for bivariate comparisons (see Currie 2003*a* for precise methods of evaluating measurements). This study reached a number of conclusions including the following:

Allometric changes in the size of skeletons of the relatively conservative family Tyrannosauridae are similar in trends to those seen in most other terrestrial vertebrate groups.

The Tyrannosauridae may be divided into two subfamilies, the Albertosaurinae and the Tyrannosaurinae. However, a number of tyrannosaurid taxa were founded largely on the basis of proportional differences that, when analyzed by Currie (2003*a*), proved to reflect ontogenetic trends rather than present diagnostic features. Consequently, such proposed genera as *Maleevosaurus*, *Jenghizhkan*, and *Shanshanosaurus* were assessed by Currie (2003*a*) as representing probable junior synonyms of *Tarbosaurus*, with *Dinotyrannus*, *Stygivenator*, and perhaps *Nanotyrannus* representing growth stages of *Tyrannosaurus* (see entry). *Contra* Olshevsky *et al.*, Currie (2003*a*) found the long, low, narrow skulls of "aublysodontines" to be expected in small tyrannosaurids, becoming relatively short and broad in maturity. The long and narrow frontals cited by Olshevsky *et al.* in "*Stygivenator*" and "*Dinotyrannus*" represent "statistically immature stages of the short broad frontals of *Tyrannosaurus*." The slenderness of the dentaries "(presumably referring to the height)" used by Olshevsky *et al.* to separate "*Jenghizkhan*" from *Tyrannosaurus* is not a useful character in diagnosing genera (see also Carr 1999). Furthermore, Currie (2003*a*) stated that at least one of the characters (*i.e.*, relatively tall anterior maxillary and dentary teeth, height of longest maxillary tooth exceeding depth of dentary) used to diagnose "*Stygivenator*" (Molnar 1978; Molnar and Carpenter; Olshevsky *et al.*) cannot be used as such, as "the dentaries are always lower than the longest teeth in small individuals (Currie and Dong 2001)," the teeth increasing in size at a lower rate than the height of the dentary.

As demonstrated earlier by Currie (1978), differences in ontogenetic size do not scale the same way as do interspecific size differences; also, tyrannosaurid species grow to different adult sizes. Based on skull length, Currie (2001) noted, adult *Albertosaurus* (TMP 81.10.1, 0.98 meters long) and *Gorgosaurus* (AMNH 5458, 0.99 meters long) individuals are about the same size, a mature *Daspletosaurus* (FMNH PR308, 1.12 meters long) is approximately 10 percent larger, *Tarbosaurus* (PIN 551-1. 1.35 meters long) is larger still, and *Tyrannosaurus* (FMNH PR2081, "Sue," 1.53 meters is the largest of all. These skull lengths are consistent in that limb bones produce virtually the same relationships. For example, a mature *Albertosaurus* (ROM 807) has a femur measuring 1.02 meters in length, *Daspletosaurus* (TMP 85.62.1) a femur length of 1.02 meters, and *Gorgosaurus* (CMN 2120) one of 1.04 meters, all slightly smaller than *Tarbosaurus* (GIN 107/2), having a femur length of 1.12 meters, while that of *Tyrannosaurus rex* (BHI 3033) is 1.34 meters.

Currie (2003*a*) found allometric differences among specimens representing mature specimens of different species to be trivial in comparison with those relating to growth (see also Currie 1978, 2003*b*). This was not surprising, as "tyrannosaurids increase in linear dimensions by more than 1000% during their lifetimes, whereas the largest mature tyrannosaurid is only 30% larger than the smallest." Still, that author noted (see also Paul), "albertosaurines tend to be more lightly built than tyrannosaurines in dimensions associated with weight bearing (such as the diameters of hind

limb bones)." Moreover, albertosaurines having the same absolute size of a tyrannosaurine possessed "slightly shorter, lower skulls, shorter ilia, longer tibiae, longer metatarsals, and longer toes;" generally both albertosaurines and tyrannosaurines are of the same relative size, having forelimbs of comparatively the same length, although *Tarbosaurus* has shorter front-limb elements (see Holtz 2001); and tooth counts exhibit some individual and intraspecific variation, but no evidence was found indicating that the number of teeth are affected by size or age.

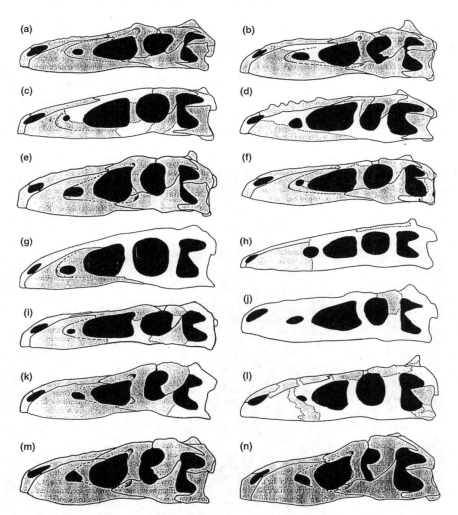

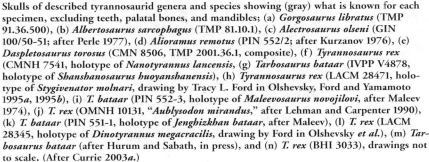

Skulls of described tyrannosaurid genera and species showing (gray) what is known for each specimen, excluding teeth, palatal bones, and mandibles; (a) *Gorgosaurus libratus* (TMP 91.36.500), (b) *Albertosaurus sarcophagus* (TMP 81.10.1), (c) *Alectrosaurus olseni* (GIN 100/50-51; after Perle 1977), (d) *Alioramus remotus* (PIN 552/2; after Kurzanov 1976), (e) *Daspletosaurus torosus* (CMN 8506, TMP 2001.36.1, composite), (f) *Tyrannosaurus rex* (CMNH 7541, holotype of *Nanotyrannus lancensis*, (g) *Tarbosaurus bataar* (IVPP V4878, holotype of *Shanshanosaurus huoyanshanensis*), (h) *Tyrannosaurus rex* (LACM 28471, holotype of *Stygivenator molnari*, drawing by Tracy L. Ford in Olshevsky, Ford and Yamamoto 1995*a*, 1995*b*), (i) *T. bataar* (PIN 552-3, holotype of *Maleevosaurus novojilovi*, after Maleev 1974), (j) *T. rex* (OMNH 10131, "*Aublysodon mirandus*," after Lehman and Carpenter 1990), (k) *T. bataar* (PIN 551-1, holotype of *Jenghizkhan bataar*, after Maleev), (l) *T. rex* (LACM 28345, holotype of *Dinotyrannus megacracilis*, drawing by Ford in Olshevsky *et al.*), (m) *Tarbosaurus bataar* (after Hurum and Sabath, in press), and (n) *T. rex* (BHI 3033), drawings not to scale. (After Currie 2003*a*.)

Introduction

Left maxilla and jugal (TMP 81.10.1) of *Albertosaurus sarcophagous* in A. lateral and B. medial views, the complete specimen comprising a skeleton with skull recovered from the Horseshoe Canyon Formation, Red Deer River, Alberta, Canada. (After Currie 2003*b*.)

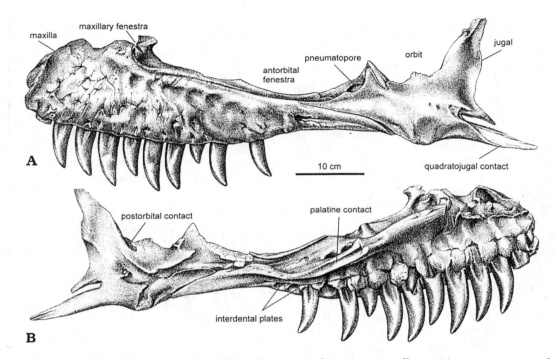

In a subsequently published study, Currie (2003*b*) described in detail the cranial anatomy of the tyrannosaurid dinosaurs known from the Late Cretaceous of Alberta, Canada, well-preserved tyrannosaurid specimens from this area offering "the greatest range of information because it includes the most taxa and most ontogenetic stages in a relatively restricted geographic range." Moreover, Currie (2003*b*) pointed out, the

Skull (cast of FMNH PR308) of *Daspletosaurus torosus* in the Geology Department laboratory of The Field Museum.

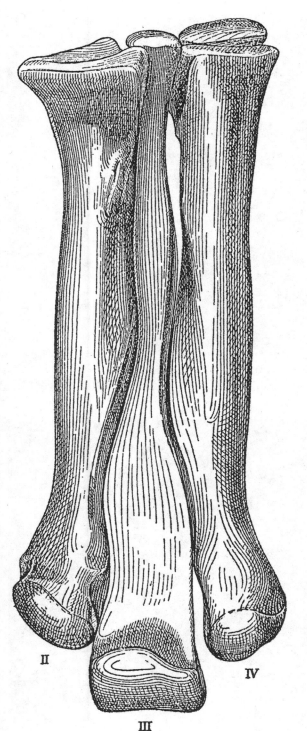

Metatarsus (part of ROM 807, the holotype of the tyrannosaurid theropod *Albertosaurus arctunguis*) of *Albertosaurus sarcophagus*. This metatarsus exhibits the typical arctometatarsalian condition (proximally pinched metatarsal III, consequently obscured from view cranially, and reduced or excluded from contact with the tibiotarsus). (After Parks 1928).

global influx of new specimens at last permits the solution of some long-standing taxonomic problems regarding this theropod group.

Currie (2003*b*) cautioned, however, that while the generic and specific identification of complete adult tyrannosaurid skeletons is possible, identifying partial skeletons and juvenile specimens remains difficult, there being enough overlapping variability among isolated bones and incomplete skeletons to introduce uncertainty as to generic or specific identification. Juvenile specimens are particularly difficult to identify, Currie (2003*b*) pointed out, as some features do not become generically distinct until maturity. Currie (2003*b*) explained that the maxillary fenestrae in albertosaurines are smaller and more caudally located than in adult tyrannosaurines, similar to those in juvenile tyrannosaurines. Furthermore, the postorbital of the tyrannosaurine *Daspletosaurus* lacked a suborbital process during all ontogenetic stages of the animal, while in other tyrannosaurids only the juveniles lack this process.

Moreover, individual variation can also confuse the identity of adult specimens. As Currie (2003*b*) pointed out, "albertosaurines and tyrannosaurines are generally different at the base of the postorbital process of the jugal." In adult tyrannosaurines, this area is craniocaudally wide at the base and externally concave; in most adult albertosaurines, it is a narrow process having a slightly convex lateral surface. In the largest albertosaurine individuals, however, this process can be identical to that in tyrannosaurines. Also, in juvenile tyrannosaurines the external surface of this process is flat or slightly convex, as seen in albertosaurines.

Generally, albertosaurines and tyrannosaurines can largely be identified based upon the diagnostic postorbital process of the jugal (see "Systematics" chapter). However, Currie (2003*b*) cautioned, "The degree of allometric (including ontogenetic), individual and interspecific variability introduces considerable uncertainty in both identifications and phylogenetic analyses," the variability being "such that it is recommended that multiple characters are necessary to identify most tyrannosaurid fossils to generic level."

Currie's (2003*b*) study reaffirmed his position that *Albertosaurus* and *Gorgosaurus* are distinct at the generic level (at present, most reliably separated by characters of the braincase), as are *Tarbosaurus* (see entry) and *Tyrannosaurus*; found that some of the characteristics used by Kurzanov (1976) to distinguish the Asian *Alioramus* (see *D:TE*, also entry, this volume) do not have diagnostic significance; found *Daspletosaurus* (see entry) to be more closely related to the Asian *Tarbosaurus* than is *Tyrannosaurus*; and suggested that "*Nanotyrannus*" could be a valid genus or at least a valid species (see *Tyrannosaurus* entry).

Introduction

Gastralia belonging to *Tyrannosaurus rex* (FMNH PR2081), among the material used in the study of growth in tyrannosaurids published by Gregory M. Erickson, Peter J. Makovicky, Philip J. Currie, Mark A. Norell, Scott Yerby and Christopher A. Brochu (2004).

Skeleton (FMNH PR2081) of the *Tyrannosaurus rex* called "Sue" on the day of its public unveiling (May 17, 2000) at The Field Museum in Chicago. The skull on this mount is a cast due to its weight, the original being exhibited elsewhere in the museum. Some of the postcranial elements of this specimen were used by Gregory M. Erickson, Peter J. Makovicky, Philip J. Currie, Mark A. Norell, Scott Yerby and Christopher A. Brochu (2004) in their study on tyrannosaurid growth.

Life restoration by artist Todd Marshall of the giant tyrannosaurid *Daspletosaurus torosus.*

How did tyrannosaurids grow so large, what evolutionary changes occurred in their body size, and what was the average lifespan of such dinosaurs? These and related questions were confronted in a study by Erickson, Makovicky, Currie, Norell, Yerby and Brochu (2004) of the life-history parameters and the evolution of gigantism in such North American tyrannosaurids as *Tyrannosaurus rex* (this species attaining a mass of up to 5,654 kilograms, achieving a size at least 15 times greater than that of the largest extant terrestrial carnivore).

Erickson *et al.*'s study was based upon numerous substantially complete specimens, representing various ontogenetic stages, of *T. rex* (including juvenile specimens regarded by some workers as "dwarf" and distinct species; see *Tyrannosaurus* entry, *S3*) and its close and somewhat smaller North American tyrannosaurid relatives *Gorgosaurus libratus, Albertosaurus sarcophagus,* and *Daspletosaurus torosus.* Specimens studied in this investigation, representing adolescent, juvenile, subadult, and adult animals, included the following: *T. rex* (FMNH PR 2081, TMP 81.12.1, TMP 81.6.1, ICM 2001.90.1, LACM 23845, LACM 28471, and AMNH 30564), *G. libratus* (TMP 94.12.802, TMP 73.30.1, TMP99.33.1, TMP 86.144.1, and FMNH PR

2211), *A. sarcophagus* (TMP 81.10.1, TMP 2002.45.46, TMP 86.64.01, USNM 12814/AMNH 5428, and AMNH 5432), *D. torosus* (FMNH PR 308, AMNH 5438, and TMP 94.143.1). Preliminary analyses by the authors of this material revealed that a number of nonweight-bearing bones (*e.g.*, pubes, fibulae, ribs, gastralia, postorbitals) in these dinosaurs "did not develop hollow medullar cavities and showed negligible intracortical remodeling during their entire life history" (see Erickson *et al.* for details on the methods used in their investigation).

Among the conclusions of Erickson *et al.* (2004) are the following: *T. rex* grew at a maximum rate of 2.07 kilograms per day, reached skeletal maturity in two decades beginning at about 18.5 years of age with maximum exponential rates maintained for approximately four years, and had a maximum average life span of up to 28 years. Except for some exceptionally large individuals, the usually smaller-sized *G. libratus, A. sarcophagus,* and *D. torosus* (averaging from 50.3 to 1,791 kilograms) also grew at a rate of from 0.31 to 0.48 kilograms per day, reached maturity at between 14 and 16 years with maximum exponential rates maintained for about four years, and had maximum average life spans of about 24 years. Optimization of

Introduction

Ed Gerken with the "exploded" skull of the *Tyrannosaurus rex* specimen (BHI-3033) popularly known as "Stan."

these growth rates onto current phylogenetic hypotheses of tyrannosaurid relationships indicated to Erickson *et al.* that a 1.5 acceleration of maximum growth rate could constitute a diagnostic feature for the tyrannosaurid clade Tyrannosaurinae, while a second substantial increase in growth rate in *Tyran-*

nosaurus optimizes as a physiological autapomorphy for that genus regardless of phylogenetic hypothesis and optimization criterion.

Regarding the question of how *T. rex* attained such gigantic size, Erickson *et al.* found it "most parsimonious to conclude that *T. rex* acquired the

majority of its giant proportions after diverging from the common ancestor of itself and *D. torosus*, a species with an optimized body mass of about 1,800 kilograms." Comparing directly the tyrannosaurid growth curves revealed to the authors that the transition to exponential and stationary phases of development took place in *Tyrannosaurus rex* about two to four years later than in the smaller taxa; this temporal placement, however, "had little to do with the evolution of its gigantism because the exponential stage, during which most body size is accrued, was not extended beyond the ancestral, 4-year condition observed in other tyrannosaurids." Instead, Erickson *et al.* postulated, "the key developmental modification that propelled *T. rex* to giant proportions was primarily through evolutionary acceleration in the exponential stage growth rate and the transition zones bounding it."

As Erickson *et al.* noted, the data garnered from their study also allows for a more comprehensive understanding of tyrannosaurid biology. For example,

the presence of thin, tightly packed growth lines late in the development of these animals indicates that tyrannosaurids — possibly all dinosaurs — had determinate growth, not gaining an appreciably greater size than the largest of the studied specimens, and would have spent almost 30 percent of their lives as fully grown adults.

Maximal growth rates for these tyrannosaurids "are only 33–35% of the rates expected for non-avian dinosaurs of their size when compared with the more broadly sampled data of [Erickson, Curry-Rogers and Yerby 2001]," this constituting the first evidence indicating major differences in whole body growth rates among a subclade of non-avian dinosaurs.

The findings of Erickson *et al.* also relate to the biomechanical abilities of tyrannosaurids. Upon attaining a body mass of approximately 1,000 kilograms, the capacity of *T. rex* for "fast running" was not feasible (see Hutchinson and Garcia 2002), this corresponding to a 13-year-old juvenile-sized animal based upon

Skull and cervical vertebrae (BHI-3033) of *Tyrannosaurus rex*. The jaws and teeth of this giant carnivorous dinosaur were designed for crushing bone.

the authors' longevity data and comparative body-mass estimates. Assuming the same relationship for *G. libratus*, *A. sarcophagus*, and *D. torosus*, "such locomotory limitations would not have emerged until these animals were much closer to adult size."

Finally, these authors' findings afforded "a glimpse into the potential population age structure for a dinosaur." Based upon femoral lengths, it is now possible to estimate the age and developmental stage of an individual animal. Applying this method to a catastrophic death assemblage comprising eight or nine *A. sarcophagus* individuals (see Currie 1998), Erickson *et al.* identified two or three older adults (at least 21 years old), one young adult (about 17 years old), four sub-adults (about 12 to 17 years old) undergoing exponential growth rates at the time of death, and two juveniles (about two and 10 years old, respectively), suggesting that groups of this species, whether temporary or permanent, could have comprised "individuals spanning the age spectrum from adolescents to very old, senescent adult, a finding consistent with trackway evidence for other theropod dinosaurs" (Currie 1998).

Wegweiser, Breithaupt and Chapman (2004), in an abstract for a poster, briefly described an adult hadrosaur specimen apparently constituting evidence of tyrannosaurid [perhaps *Tyrannosaurus*] hunting behavior. The element studied—a rib belonging to a lambeosaurine skeleton nicknamed "Lucky," collected from the This Side of Hell Quarry in northern Wyoming—exhibits extensive osteosis around a large theropod tooth impression. As interpreted by Wegweiser *et al.*, the tooth "shaved" the rib as it slid along, permanently twisting the rib out of shape by the torque and the crushing force imparted to the living tissue during the bite. Although the tooth embedded itself in the rib in an obvious attempt to tear the bone from the rest of the hadrosaur's body, the attack presumably failed, with the rib being torn almost subparallel to its long axis. Subsequently, the bone "healed around a hole that provides an outline of a tooth, leaving a permanent gape with an arching bridge." Closely fitting this bite outline are teeth belonging to adult tyrannosaurids.

As Wegweiser *et al.* reported, the above specimen is currently being analyzed utilizing three-dimensional scanning and rapid prototyping. Additionally, adjacent ribs display evidence of suppuration, implying that the hadrosaur survived a massive infection subsequent to the attack. Based on studies of extant animals, from one to two years may have been required for the wound to heal entirely. This further suggested to the authors that the hadrosaur died a number of years after the alleged attack occurred.

While numerous papers discussing dinosaurian coprolites have been published, only one (Bertrand 1903), until recently, had reported traces of muscle tissue in the fossilized dung of a carnivorous dinosaur. In 2003, Chin, Eberth, Schweitzer, Rando, Sloboda and Horner described a tyrannosaurid coprolite found *in situ* in the middle of the Campanian Lethbridge Coal Zone near Onefour, a 20-meter-thick transgressive succession forming the top of the Dinosaur Park Formation, in southern Alberta, Canada (see Eberth and Hamblin 1993). Three tyrannosaurid taxa are known from this formation—*Gorgosaurus*, *Daspletosaurus*, and "*Aublysodon*" [=*Tyrannosaurus*; see entry] (see Eberth, Currie, Brinkman, Ryan, Braman, Gardner, Lam, Spivak and Newman 2001)—although only the former two genera are of Campanian age.

As described by Chin *et al.*, this large, oblong comprolitic mass (TMP 98.102.7) measures approximately 64 centimeters in length by up to 17 centimeters in width. "It is quite remarkable because it bears morphological and organic evidence of undigested soft tissues." Electron-microscopic examination in thin section of the specimen revealed cordlike structures, the morphology of which indicates "that they are the fossilized remains of muscle cells, connective tissues, and possible capillary fragments." As Chin *et al.* pointed out, these tissues—perhaps representing a pachycephalosaurid—constitute the major components of animal flesh, the surprising quality of their preservation revealing clues pertaining to their digestive and diagenetic history.

In their analysis of this specimen, Chin *et al.* reached a number of conclusions such as the following: The ingested flesh seems to have been poorly comminuted or passed relatively rapidly through the gut of the tyrannosaurid, perhaps representing a digestive pattern typical for this group of theropods. As evidenced by the exceptional preservation of the soft tissues, the fecal matters seemingly lithified somewhat quickly, with phosphatization most likely facilitated by quick burial (probably by a flood event) and chemical reactions generated by bacteria, and with the absence of significant recrystallization over time preventing subsequent destruction of the morphology of the phosphatized tissues.

Ksepka and Norell (2004) described a well-preserved ornithomimosaur remains collected as a surface find in 1998 during the Mongolian Academy of Sciences-American Museum of Natural History Paleontological Expedition to the Xanadu sublocality at Uhkaa Tolgod (Upper Cretaceous; ?Campanian), Omnogov, Mongolia. The specimen (IGM 100/1245), comprising the rostral portion of the snout, rostral portion of the mandible, and some vertebral

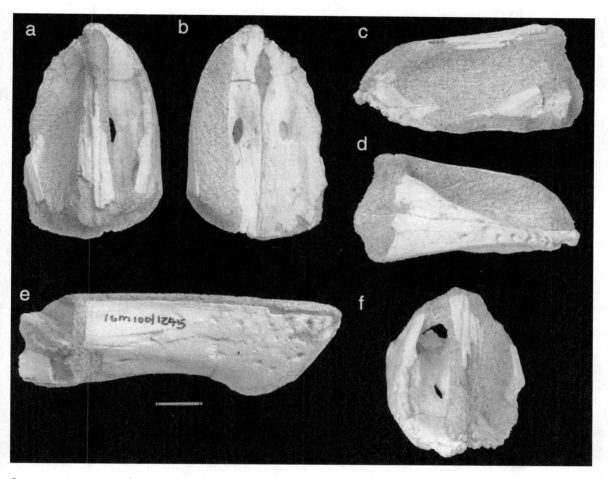

IGM 100/1245, ornithomimosaurian remains from the "Xanadu" sublocality of Ukhaa Tolgod, Mongolia: Premaxilla and nasals in a. dorsal, b. ventral, c. left lateral, d. right lateral, and f. rostral oblique views, e. right dentary in lateral view. Scale = 1 cm. (After Ksepka and Norell 2004.)

fragments, represents the second ornithomimosaur to be found at Ukhaa Tolgod (see Dashveg, Novacek, Norell, Clark, Chiappe, Davidson, McKenna, Dingus, Swisher and Perle 1995).

IGM 100/1245, as described by Ksepka and Norell, resembled the Asian ornithomimosaurs *Gallimimus*, *Garudimimus*, and *Sinornithosaurus*, in that the tip of the snout is U-shaped in dorsal profile.

In comparing IGM 100/1245 to other Mongolian ornithomimosaurian genera, Ksepka and Norell could not refer the specimen to any known Mongolian taxon. Differences in the shape of the mandible and also age disparity make referral either to *Gallimimus* (Maastrichtian) or *Garudimimus* (Cenomanian–Turonian) unlikely. Differences in the shape of the mandible preclude referral of IGM 100/1245 from the Late Cretaceous Chinese genus *Sinornithomimus* (see entry), while lack of skull remains belonging to the Mongolian *Archaeornithomimus* (?Campanian) and *Anserimimus* (Maastrichtian) prevent comparisons with those genera.

Comparing IGM100/1245 with a contemporaneous ornithomimosaur braincase (IGM 100/987) from the Ankylosaur Flats sublocality at Ukhaa Tolgod (see Makovicky and Norell 1998; see S2), Ksepka

and Norell noted that the lack of shared preserved elements precludes direct comparison of these specimens. IGM 100/987, however, is significantly smaller than the Xanadu specimen. While the authors could not rule out the possibility that one of these specimens represents a smaller individual of a single taxon, they pointed out that the degree of fusion of IGM 100/987 indicates that the this individual was near somatic maturity at the time of death.

Hwang, Norell, Ji and Gao (2004*b*), in an abstract, reported on a new and as yet unnamed specimen (CAGS-IG01-004) of troodontid theropod collected recently from the lower, sandy portion of the Lower Cretaceous Yixian Formation of China. The nearly complete skeleton had been preserved in a three-dimensional state, thereby enhancing its value in regards yielding scientific information.

Briefly, Hwang *et al.* described this specimen as follows: Skull having unusually small teeth, constricted between root and crown (as in other troodontids), yet lacking serrations (as in *Byronosaurus*; see entry, S2 and this volume); very slender dorsal and ventral rami of maxilla and ventral process of lacrimal; no apparent articulation point for postorbital on frontal; laterodorsal process of squamosal contacting directly fronto-parietal suture, lateroventral process quite long.

Although the jugal and quadratojugal is missing from the specimen, comparison by Hwang *et al.* with two different as yet undescribed taxa from the Upper Cretaceous Djadokhta Formation of Ukhaa Tolgod, Mongolia, "suggests that these taxa and CAGS-IG01-004 do not have a postorbital, and that the squamosal, jugal, and quadratojugal are rearranged to compensate."

Moreover, in these two Mongolian taxa, Hwang *et al.* noted the following details: In IGM 100/1323, lateroventral process quite long, probably having articulated with junction of quadrate and quadratojugal (as in other troodontids); in the other taxon, laterodorsal process of squamosal contacting fronto-parietal suture; in both taxa, dorsal process of jugal contacting quadrate instead of postorbital. Apparently,

the authors suggested, in all three of the above taxa the caudal part of the orbit was not closed, but open, as in birds. Also, there is evidence that both CAGS-IG01-004 and the second Mongolian taxon possess "an avialan-like quadratojugal that does not contact the squamosal." As Hwang *et al.* pointed out, the skull of IGM 100/1323 is most similar to CAGS-IG01-004, including morphology and number of teeth. Considering these similarities, all three taxa may form a monophyletic troodontid clade more closely related to birds than any theropods yet discovered (see "Systematics" chapter for contradictory opinions).

In a paper on troodontid eggs found in the Upper Cretaceous of China, Zhao (2003) speculated upon the possible nesting behavior of these birdlike dinosaurs.

As reported by Zhao, these eggs — referred to the oogenus *Prismatoolithus*; see *S3*, "Appendix" — were preserved in siltstone, suggesting that the egg-layers selected lakeside or riverine sands in which to nest. Each clutch found contained from six to seven eggs (Horner 1984 reported up to 24 per nest in *Troodon*, a troodontid genus from Montana).

The eggs were preserved standing up on the nest with their pointed ends facing downwards, looking "as if they had been stuck in the ground when they were laid." As Zhao explained, such vertically oriented eggs can withstand external pressures from four to five times better than eggs laid in a horizontal position. Thus, the author found it reasonable that the troodontid had to arrange its eggs vertically or rather obliquely in the ground while nesting "in order to prevent the eggshell from being crushed by the external pressure during the incubation."

Zhao also inferred that, upon selecting this nesting site, the troodontid first loosened the sands, squatted down with the body vertically oriented, subsequently laying from six to eight eggs, after manipulating one or more of the slippery eggs, finally covering the entire clutch with sediment. Zhao found it likely that the Chinese troodontid likewise laid as many as 24 eggs, separating them into several clutches. "Under the circumstances," that author stated, "the troodontids could hardly construct a special nest more than one meter in diameter for laying and putting [the eggs] vertically into the sands."

In an abstract published on a study of the neck of non-avian maniraptorans, Tsuihiji (2004) asked the question: "How birdlike was the cervical musculature of the 'birdlike' theropods?" As that author pointed out, among the distinguishing features of the avian neck is a highly complex musculature. Tsuihiji's study involved the identification of osteological correlates of the axial muscles in the necks of several non-

Nesting behavior of a Chinese troodontid ("they probably had feathers"), as hypothesized by Zhao Zi-Kui: A. building the nest, and B. laying eggs. (After Zhao 2003.)

avian maniraptoran taxa to infer phylogenetically when such features evolved.

Tsuihiji observed both plesiomorphic archosaurian and derived avian conditions present in dromaeosaurid theropods and also in the bird *Archaeopteryx*.

The Munich *Archaeopteryx* specimen, for example, exhibits a thin, rodlike element (a probable atlas rib) not retained as a free element in extant birds. Consequently, Tsuihiji pointed out, while that genus is generally regarded as the oldest "bird," its neck is not yet entirely avian in that feature. Moreover, the presence of such an element seemingly represents a primitive archosaurian condition found also in more basal dinosaurs (*e.g.*, the sauropod *Camarasaurus* and some ornithopods), and also in various "pseudosuchians" (*e.g.*, phytosaurs). In modern crocodylians, Tsuihiji explained, a long, robust atlast rib constitutes the origin for the m. rectus capitis lateralis; in birds, that muscle arises from the centra of the cranial cervical vertebrae; the origin for that muscle in dinosaurs, however, may have changed as the atlas rib became reduced, the condition in *Archaeopteryx* perhaps representing a traditional stage.

Contrarily in the dromaeosaurid *Velociraptor*, Tsuihiji observed, the prezygapophyses of several caudal cervical vertebrae possess a laterally projecting process, this probably constituting a homologue to the avian tuberculum ansae, the latter being the origin of m. ascendens cervicalis. This condition suggested to Tsuihiji that this muscle could have been already well developed in the caudal cervical area of this non-avian theropod.

As suggested by Tsuihiji, more derived Mesozoic birds like *Ichthyornis* and *Hesperornis* (see "Appendix Two") may have already acquired the avian-like m. ascendens cervicalis along their entire necks, while still lacking prominent cristae lateralis, this suggesting that the well-developed, interdigitating tendinous system of mm. intertransversarii found in modern birds may have not been present in these two genera. In conclusion, Tsuihiji suggested "that the derived avian conditions arose in a step-wise fashion in basal members of Maniraptora."

Lü and Zhang (2003), in a published abstract for a poster, briefly described a new and as yet unnamed oviraptorid theropod collected in 1995 by the Beijing Natural History Museum from red beds of the Upper Cretaceous Nanxiong Group of Luyuan, Shixin County, Nanxiong Basin, Guangdong Province, in southern China (these beds apparently geologically younger in Nanxiong Basin than in the nearby Heyuan Basin, where another oviraptorid, *Heyuannia*, was found; see *S3*).

According to Lü and Zhang, this new form is distinguished by characters including the following: Preacetabular process of ilium relatively short compared to postacetabular process; ilium with great height to length ratio; ventral margins of preacetabular and postacetabular processes higher than dorsal margin of acetabulum; unique presence of large ?pneumatic opening (transverse diameter of about half diameter of shaft) on craniolateral surface of proximal end of femur.

Lü and Zhang speculated that the above-mentioned opening might "have contained a complex of smaller foramina and bony struts, similar to that of modern birds," although such delicate struts are not visible in the oviraptorid material. Possibly, the authors further speculated, this opening was "the entrance for the air sac diverticula as in birds." Lü and Zhang concluded that the possible pneumatic hindlimb bones in this new oviraptorid indicate that it is derived and further strengthens support for the avian adaptation of oviraptorosaurs (see section on "Dinosaurs and Birds," below).

Zanno and Sampson (2003), in an abstract for a poster, reported briefly on a new, small, and partial caenagnathid skeleton, collected in Grand Staircase-Escalante National Monument in southern Utah, this specimen preserving an almost complete, articulated left manus, an articulated pedal phalanx and ungual, and a series of associated yet damaged pedal elements and distal metatarsals. Comparing this specimen with the caenagnathid *Chirostenotes pergracilis*, the authors noted "numerous diagnostic characters including unguals that display an extremely pronounced dorsal lip." As Zanno and Sampson observed, the proportional length of metacarpals I, II, and III are identical to those of *C. pergracilis*, although the third metacarpal of the new specimen is markedly longer and more robust than in specimens of the other taxon. Consequently, Zanno and Sampson found the new specimen different enough from *C. pergracilis* to preclude referral to that taxon. However, because "no other definitively caenagnathid taxa preserve manual elements, and only one other taxon preserves pedal phalanges, a more specific taxonomic assignment is unwarranted at this time."

As pointed out by Zanno and Sampson, previous authors had proposed two discrete, latitudinally arrayed faunal provinces — northern and southern — in the Late Cretaceous Western Interior of North America. Southern Utah's Kaiparowits Formation helps to remedy the paleontological and geographical gaps between these inferred faunas that have clouded biogeographic reconstructions during this interval, the presence of a caenagnathid theropod in this formation suggesting that at least a portion of Utah's dinosaurian diversity reveals affiliation with the fauna of the northern province. Moreover, this evidence, in combination with that of vertebrate taxa from the southern province, is showing the integrated and transitional nature of the Late Cretaceous Utah ecosystems. Most importantly, Zanno and Sampson concluded, this newly collected caenagnathid "vastly expands the southernmost extent of this formerly localized clade, nearly doubling the previously documented range of North American caenagnathids."

In an abstract, Kirkland, Zanno, Deblieux, Smith and Sampson (2004) reported the recent discovery of abundant remains pertaining to a new, primitive therizinosauroid theropod in the Crystal Geyser Quarry (sedimentologic, taphonomic, and rare earth geochemical analyses suggesting for this site "a reworked or time-averaged fossil accumulation"; see abstract for a poster by Suarez, Suarez, Grandstaff, Terry and Kirkland 2004), at the base of the Cedar Mountain Formation (Lower Cretaceous, Barremian), in beds directly overlying the Morrison Formation (Upper Jurassic), in east-central Utah. The quarry constitutes a paucispecific bonebed that spans almost two acres, with densities of more than 100 elements per cubic meter. Kirkland *et al.* predicted that the theropod excavated from this site "will likely be the best represented therizinosauroid and one of the most thoroughly documented maniraptorans based on the abundance of well-preserved elements which represent multiple growth stages."

Therizinosauroid characters recognized by Kirkland *et al.* in the collected material include the following: Edentulous rostral end of dentary; elongate cervical vertebrae having continuous deep ventral depressions; well-developed, angular internal tuberosity on proximal humerus; ilium with laterally diverging preacetabular process; fibula with solid medial face; retaining (as in *Beipiaosaurus*) primitive tridactyl pes. Derived therizinosauroid characters noted by Kirkland *et al.* in this new taxon include: Dentary with dorsolateral shelf; teeth increasing in size mesially; basisphenoid ventrally inflated; loss of fossa for m. cupedicus; metatarsals abbreviated; astragalus having reduced articular surface. Both the semilunate and unfused conditions of the first two distal carpals were recognized by the authors.

Performing a phylogenetic analysis, Kirkland *et al.* found this new taxon to be a basal member of Therizinosauroidea. Comparison by the authors of the Crystal Geyser theropod cervical vertebrae with the partial cervical vertebra described for the European genus "*Thecocoelurus* indicates the presence of an unrecognized therizinosauroid in the upper Wealden Group of Britain." Along with the Lower Cretaceous Asian therizinosauroid *Beipiaosaurus*, the above evidence indicated to Kirkland *et al.* "a pan–Laurasian

distribution of therizinosauroids prior to the development of a Beringean migration corridor between North America and Asia.

In a related abstract, Smith, Kirkland, Sanders, Zanno and Deblieux (2004) made a comparison of the partial braincases belonging to the new therizinosauroid currently being collected from the Crystal Geyser Quarry (see above) and those of other, more derived forms (*e.g.*, *Nothronychus*, from the Turonian of New Mexico.

Smith *et al.* noted the following differences between the braincases of these taxa: Crystal Geyser braincase having more elongate, caudoventrally oriented paroccipital process (dorsoventrally inflated, laterally oriented in *Nothronychus* and other more derived therizinosauroids); Crystal Geyser braincase conservative in retention of open basisphenoidal recess and distinct basal tubera and basipterygoid process, as in other theropods (ventrally hyperexpanded basisphenoid obscuring latter structures in derived therizinosauroids); (as revealed by CT scanning) *Nothronychus* having more foreshortened braincase, with respect to middle ear, than in Crystal Geyser taxon).

As the Crystal Geyser form exhibits the primitive condition for the Therizinosauroidea, "its morphology can be used to suggest a developmental pathway for some of the more unusual structures observed in more derived taxa." As the authors pointed out, the development of basicranium pneumaticity in the Therizinosauroidea is generally striking, although this character is developed only incompletely in the Crystal Geyser species. Moreover, while (above the basisphenoidal recess) the basisphenoid, prootic, and opisthotic are much pneumaticized in the Cryustal Geyser species as well as in other therizinosauroids, the new taxon retains an open basisphenoidal recess. Smith *et al.* postulated that the enclosure of the latter could possibly be explained by "ossification of the ventral epithelium under the base of the recess, resulting in the large pneumatic chamber observed in derived therizinosaurs" (see also Zanno 2004, "Systematics" chapter).

Kundrát, Cruickshank, Manning, Nudds, Joysey and Ji (2004), in an abstract, reported briefly on the skeletal and dental development of some unusually well-preserved "and exceptionally prepared in ovo" therizinosauroid embryos collected from the Upper Cretaceous of China. As the authors pointed out, these embryos, which died during their final third of development, allow "the first in-depth insight into morphogenetic processes of an extinct amniote."

The following details were observed in the embryos by Kundrát *et al.*: Advanced ossification patterns of axial and appendicular skeleton; fused neural arches and vertebral centra, coossified tibia-fibula complexes, well-developed cristae and tuberosities, small epiphyses of long bones (these features suggesting higher level of precocity than suggested for oviraptorid embryos [IGM 100/971; see *Citipati* entry, *S3*] from Upper Cretaceous of Mongolia; hyaline cartilage of small epiphysis caps fossilized, showing hypertrophied chondrocytes with calcified interstitial matrix; advanced development of bones (increasing their taxonomic value, allowing comparisons with poorly preserved therizinosauroids and also oviraptorosaurs); unique documentation of odontogenetic shift between generations of erupted teeth, each having different crown morphologies; crown transformed from primitive archosaur to advanced patterns (indicating omnivorous diet for hatchlings); rapid *in ovo* transformation of teeth (possibly indicating appearance of odontogenetic shift quite early in evolution of therizinosauroids).

In an abstract, Novas, Canale and Isasi (2004) reported on a new giant (about six meters or more than 20 feet in length) yet gracile deinonychosaurian theropod—known from several cranial and postcranial elements—found recently in the Upper Cretaceous (Campanian–Maastrichtian) Allen Formation of Bajo de Santa Rosa, Río Negro Province, Patagonia, Argentina, "a productive fossil locality" that has also yielded remains of fishes, turtles, and other kinds of dinosaurs (*e.g.*, hadrosaurs, ankylosaurs, titanosaurian sauropods, and the abelisaurid theropod *Quilmesaurus curriei*).

Novas *et al.* briefly described this specimen as follows: Frontal resembling that of *Troodon* and *Sinornithosaurus*, being triangular in dorsal view, defining with postorbital wide, rounded orbital cavity; jaws elongate, low, dentary with 25 tooth alveoli; centra of cervical vertebrae with cranial articular surface nearly at same plane as ventral surface (as in other deinonychosaurians); neural spine of dorsal vertebrae transversely enlarged at distal end; manual ungual phalanges strongly curved, extensor tubercle prominent; second phalanx of pedal digit II having constricted "neck" between both proximal and distal articular surfaces, caudoventrally projected "heel."

Furthermore, Novas *et al.* noted "Bizarre traits" regarding the morphology of this new taxon's teeth, "which are conical and circular in cross-section, and devoid of serrations and carinae." Concerning the postcrania, the authors cited "a notable disparity in transverse width of pedal phalanges 2.2 and 1.4," features suggesting to them a marked assymetry in the construction of the pes.

In conclusion, Novas *et al.* noted that the discovery of this new deinonychosaurian—along with other Patagonian theropods (*i.e.*, *Patagonykus*, *Al-*

Velociraptorine tooth crown (BMNH R 16510) from the Wessex Formation of the Isle of Wight, southern England, in (left) lingual view and (right) basal profile. Scale = 5 mm. (After Sweetman 2004.)

varezsaurus, and *Unenlagia*, and also the Malgalasy bird *Rahonavis*—"support the interpretation that an important adaptive radiation of derived coelurosaurians took place in Gondwana at least from Turonian through Maastrichtian times."

Sweetman (2004) reported the first record of a velociraptorine dromaeosaurid from the Wealden of southern England (also the second record of the Dromaeosauridae in Great Britain and the first record of this family from British Wealden Group strata). The velociraptorine material comprises five large, almost complete teeth (IWCMS 2002.1 through 2002.4, and BMNH R 16510) collected from the Early Cretaceous (Barremian) Wessex Formation, Isle of Wight.

None of these teeth preserve more than just a vestige of the root, this, coupled with tooth tip and denticle wear, suggesting that these are shed teeth. In describing these teeth, Sweetman observed that each tooth is "strongly labiolingually compressed and moderately to strongly mesiodistally recurved," with denticles (where not removed by wear) "present along the entire length of distal carinae."

In 1995, Rauhut and Werner refined a method—based upon previous work by Currie, Rigby and Sloane (1990)—whereby the morphology of theropod teeth can be reliably utilized for taxonomic purposes, determining identity at the family level and sometimes higher levels. Following Rauhut and Werner, Sweetman calculated the denticle size difference index (DDS) of these teeth, concluding that they could only be assigned to the dromaeosaurid subfamily Velociraptorinae. Sweetman found that two of these Wessex teeth, IWCMS 2002.1 and BMNH R 16510, belong to the same taxon. However, sufficient differences between these and the other Wessex teeth "warrant caution in referring all to the same taxon." Furthermore, differences in dental morphology and orientation preclude referring any of these specimens to *Nuthetes*, a velociraptorine from the Berriasian of mainland England, or to any continental European velociraptorines.

Sweetman noted also that the Wessex Formation teeth are relatively large by dromaeosaurid standards, indicating animals perhaps comparable in size to the North American *Utahraptor*.

SAUROPODOMORPHS

Prosauropods

Prosauropod dinosaurs — the first very large dinosaurs to appear during the Late Triassic — are poorly represented in the Upper Triassic of North America. Susan K. Harris, Andrew B. Heckert, Spencer G. Lucas and Adrian P. Hunt (2002) described an isolated prosauropod tooth (NMMNH P-26400) collected recently by those authors from channel- to point-bar deposits ("dark reddish-brown, clay- and siltstone-pebble conglomerate overlain by a very fine-grained, light greenish-gray to pale yellowish-brown micaceous sublitharenite") of a microvertebrate locality in the lower part of the Tecovas Formation, above the base of the Chinle Group, in Crosby County, near Kalgary, Texas.

Dated by Harris *et al.* as of Late Triassic/latest Carnian ("Adamanian"; based on the co-occurrence of the phytosaur *Rutiodon* and aetosaur *Stagonolepis*; e.g., Lucas 1998), this fossil represents the oldest North American prosauropod yet discovered.

Harris *et al.* described NMMNH P-26400 as laterally compressed and spatulate in form, measuring 6 millimeters in height, with a basal labio-lingual crown width of one millimeter. Harris *et al.* observed the following prosauropod dental synapomorphies

Photograph (A) and interpretative drawing (B) of NMMNH P-26400, indeterminate prosauropod tooth from the Tecovas Formation of West Texas, labial view. Scale = 2 mm. (After Harris, Heckert, Lucas and Hunt 2002.)

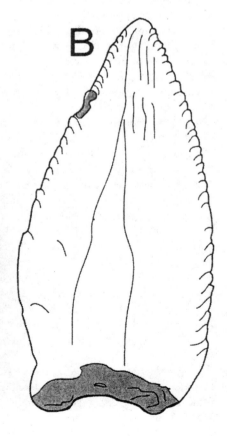

(see Galton 1990; Hunt and Lucas 1994) in this specimen: Shape spatulate; crown symmetrical; numerous, obliquely angled marginal serrations; "neck" poorly developed; straight, narrow shape in mesiodistal aspects. The tooth is similar to teeth referred to *Plateosaurus*, particularly, in the slender, conical shape of its denticles, to teeth from the mesial (following the dental nomenclature proposed by Smith and Dodson 2003) positions of the dentition of *Plateosaurus gracilis* (=*Sellosaurus* of their usage; see *Plateosaurus* entry), and also in comparable size.

As Harris *et al.* pointed out, this specimen is significant in constituting the only body fossil yet discovered offering evidence for pre–Norian North American prosauropods. Moreover, the addition of this tooth to other recent late Carnian prosauropod discoveries from Brazil and Madagascar "indicates a Pangea-wide distribution for prosauropods near their oldest occurrences."

Godefroit and Knoll (2003), in their survey of dinosaur teeth from the Upper Triassic ("Rhaetian") Habay-la-Vielle locality in southern Belgium, described the crown (IRSNB R212) of an indeterminate prosauropod as labio-lingually compressed, higher than long, and slightly recurved backwards and inwards, with carinae bearing 15 coarse denticles set at approximately 45 degrees to the edges. As the authors observed, these teeth resemble those of a number of other prosauropods including *Plateosaurus*. Also, Godefroit and Knoll described the tooth (IRSNB R211) of an indeterminate eusauropod sauropod (see below), the root being rounded in cross section, separated from the crown by a slight constriction, the crown typically spatulate, rather mesio-distally expanded, with convex labial and slightly concave lingual sides. These teeth, the authors noted, confirm the coexistence of both prosauropods and sauropods at the end of the Triassic.

Martinez, Alcober, Fernandez, Trotteyn, Colombi and Heredia (2004), in an abstract, briefly described a new prosauropod specimen collected from braided paleochanel deposits of the Quebrada del Barro Formation of the Marayes Basin, in northwestern Argentina. The well-preserved specimen includes a complete skull with articulated lower jaw, the first seven cervical vertebrae, the left scapula and coracoid, proximal ischia, left metatarsals III to V, and distal tarsals III and IV.

The authors described this new form as "a plateosaurid [=massosponylid] closely related to *Massospondylus*," yet different in the following details: Maxilla having caudally oriented dorsal process and well-developed medial lamina; larger orbital fenestra; wider external naris; and very elongate cervical vertebrae.

Based upon its affinities with *Massospondylus*, Martinez *et al.* considered this new prosauropod as from Late Triassic to Early Jurassic in age, thereby "questioning the previous assigned age to the Quebrada del Barro Formation, usually considered as strictly Upper Triassic."

Sauropods

Mathew J. Wedel (2003*a*, 2003*b*) continued to publish his studies of vertebral pneumaticity in sauropods (see *S3* for Wedel's 2001 preliminary report)—a group of very large to gigantic, long-necked dinosaurs—also commenting upon a number of earlier works based on this same topic (*e.g.*, Cope 1877; Marsh 1877*b*; Longman 1933; Janensch 1947; Britt 1993, 1997; Wilson 1999*b*).

Wedel (2003*a*, 2003*b*) pointed out that sauropod vertebrae are characterized by a complex architecture that involves laminae, fossae, and various-sized and shaped internal chambers, these structures, Wedel (2003*b*) stated, "interpreted as osteological correlates of an intricate system of air sacs and pneumatic diverticula similar to that of birds" (for a contrary opinion on this topic, see Ruben, Jones and Geist 2003, below).

Wedel's (2003*b*) detailed description of the vertebral pneumaticity of sauropod dinosaurs did not center upon all known sauropods or "track down every published description of pneumatic morphology in sauropods," but rather focused on taxa occupying key phylogenetic positions, thereby being the most useful in "determining the probable distribution and evolution of pneumatic characters in sauropod phylogeny." That author's current study primarily dealt with "vertebral internal structures (camera and camellae) and their external correlates (fossae and foraminae)."

Describing taxa in approximate phylogenetic order and utilizing the phylogeny of the Sauropoda proposed by Wilson and Sereno (1998), Wedel (2003*b*) determined the following:

In such basal members of the Sauropoda as *Vulcanodon*, a genus from Africa, and *Isanosaurus*, from Thailand, pneumatic features are limited to fossae. In the Indian *Barapasaurus*, which has been classified as either a basal eusauropod (Selgado, Coria and Calvo 1997; Wilson and Sereno) or the sister taxon to Eusauropoda (Upchurch 1998), the presacral vertebrae have fossae on the lateral faces of their centra, while several dorsal vertebrae possess hollow neural spines, their chambers communicating directly with the neural canal (see Jain, Kutty, Roy-Chowdhury and Chatterjee 1979; Britt 1993). Among sauropods lying outside the radiation of Neosauropoda (*e.g.*, the Chinese *Mamenchisaurus* and African *Jobaria*), the species *Mamenchisaurus hochuanensis* has small elliptical fossae on the lateral faces of the cervical and dorsal centra, and is honeycombed internally by numerous small cavities (see Yang [Young] and Zhao 1972); in *M. sinocanadorum*, the internal structure of a cervical vertebra has been described as resembling a honeycomb (Russell and Zheng 1993). In *Jobaria*, apparently the

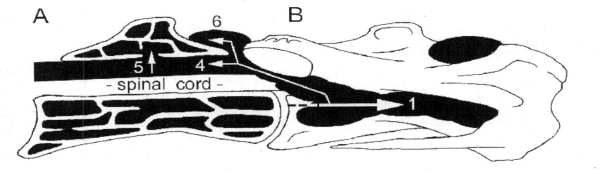

Pneumatization of the cervical series in the ostrich, vertebrae illustrated in A. midsagittal section, B. right lateral view, and C. horizontal section. Cranial direction is towards the right. White arrows indicate development of pneumatic diverticula and camellae. (After Wedel 2003*b*.)

Introduction

CT sections through the neck of an ostrich, air shown as black, bone white, and soft tissue gray: A. basically camellate external diverticula, forming aggregates of narrow tubes rather than large, simple sacs; B. supramedullary airway comprising three diverticula separated by thin membranes; and C. cervical ribs, appearing ventrolateral to the centrum on either side. Scale = 10 cm. (After Wedel 2003*b*.)

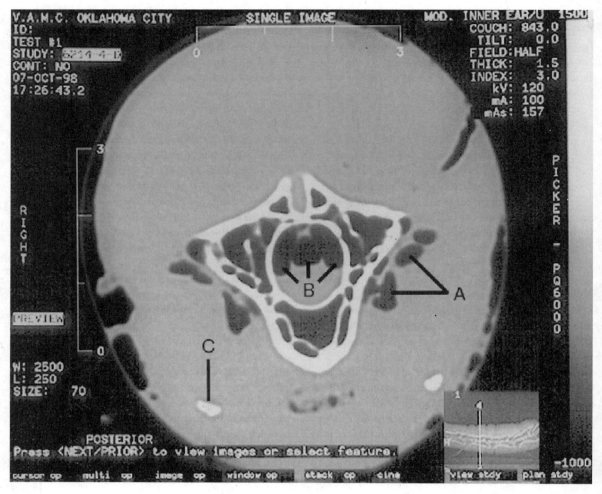

sister taxon to Neosauropoda, pneumatic fossae are present in the centra of each postatlantal cervical vertebra (atlas unknown in this genus), the condyles of some vertebrae are excavated by cranial extensions of lateral fossae, and, in the dorsal series, pneumatic fossae are found in the center of cranial vertebrae (see Sereno, Beck, Dutheil, Larsson, Lyon, Moussa, Sadleir, Sidor, Varrichio, Wilson, and Wilson 1999).

In Neosauropoda and some Chinese taxa (see below), camerae and camellae are internalized pneumatic chambers that were acquired independently. Among Diplodocidae, the vertebrae of the North American *Apatosaurus* are polycamerate, displaying a branching pattern of successively smaller camerae (see Wedel, Cifelli and Sanders 2000*a*). In very immature specimens, the vertebrae are characterized by large lateral fossae resembling those of the North American *Pleurocoelus*, these fossae developing into camerae during ontogeny (see below; see also the abstract by Sander 2003, wherein the author notes that, because of shape and size differences, sauropod bones of a single skeleton grow at different rates, producing different histologies — *e.g.*, growth marks well expressed in

comparatively slow-growing cortex, such as scapula, but absent in femur; femur preserving larger growth rate due to less remodeling). Vertebrae of the North American *Diplodocus* are also characterized by a camerate internal structure exceeding the complexity found in less derived taxa. The pneumatic features of this genus are extensive, with laminae and pneumatic foramina extending well into the caudal series (see Osborn 1899).

Among Macronaria, the North American *Haplocanthosaurus* — either the sister taxon to Neosauropoda (see Upchurch) or a basal neosauropod united with Camarasauromorpha (a macronarian group comprising camarasaurs, brachiosaurs, and titanosaurs; see Wilson and Sereno) — pneumatization is limited to large, simple fossae, essentially deep depressions, in the cervical and dorsal vertebrae, the latter in the same area as the foramina of truly camerate vertebrae. In the North American and African species of *Brachiosaurus*, the most basal titanosauriform (see Selgado *et al.*; Wilson and Sereno), both cervical and dorsal vertebrae possess large foramina that open into large camera (see Janensch 1950) that do not, however, occupy the

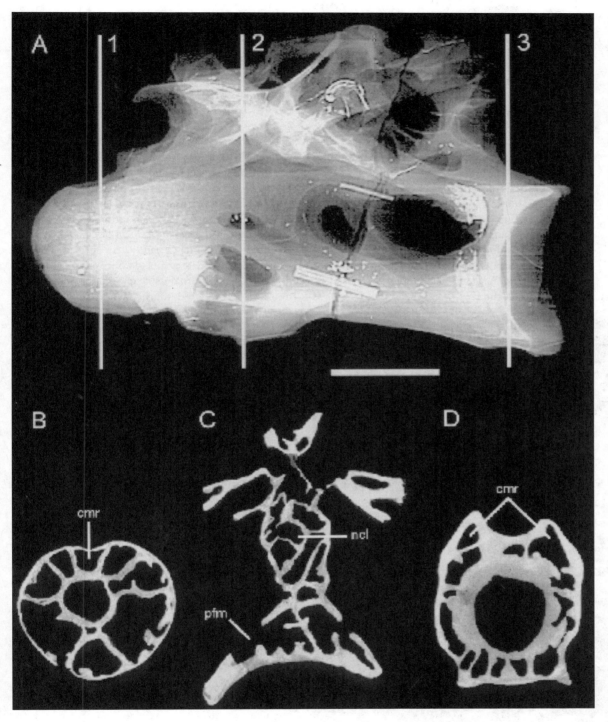

CT sections through a cervical vertebra (OMNH 01094) of the sauropod *Apatosaurus* in A. left lateral view, showing location of sections, B. section through the condyle, showing large, radially arranged camerae, C. section through the midcentrum, showing irregular and opportunistic development of camerae within the centrum, and D. section through the cotyle, showing small camerae arranged radial around the cotyle rim. Scale = 10 cm. (After Wedel 2003*b*.)

entire internal structure. Furthermore, the condyles, cotyles, and zygapophyses of *Brachiosaurus* are filled with camellae (see Wedel *et al.*; Janensch 1950). As Wedel (2003) observed, the latter are larger and simpler than those found in the North American *Sauroposeiden* or more derived titanosaurians, and can be distinguished from small camerae based upon "their thin walls, irregular occurrence, and lack of branching pattern." In *Sauroposeiden*, a genus linked to *Bra-*

chiosaurus by several synapomorphies, the "lateral faces of the centra and neural spines are occupied by pneumatic fossae that are larger, deeper, and more elaborate than those of basal sauropods," the vertebrae being internally filled completely by small pneumatic camellae (see Wedel *et al.*).

In *Pleurocoelus*—a ?brachiosaurid genus for which the type and referred vertebrae from the Arundel Clay pertain to juvenile individuals only—the

Introduction

cervical, dorsal, and sacral vertebrae have large lateral fossae penetrating into a median septum. Considering the lack of adult material, however, this absence of internalized pneumatic chambers may have ontogenetic rather than phylogenetic significance. (As Wedel 2003*b* later discussed in detail, large pneumatic fossae are typical of sauropod juveniles regardless of phylogenetic affinities, vertebrae of *Pleurocoelus* not differing significantly from juveniles of other taxa, *e.g.*, *Apatosaurus* and *Camarasaurus*; see, for example, Wedel *et al.*).

A sauropod from the Jones Ranch Quarry in the Twin Mountains Formation (Aptian–Albian) of Texas (see Winkler, Jacobs and Murry 1997) may, based upon a preliminary study, lies within Titanosauriformes, yet outside Somophospondyli (Gomani, Jacobs and Winkler 1999). As Wedel (2003*b*) observed, the cervical vertebra of a Jones Ranch Quarry sauropod, exhibited at the Fort Worth Museum of Science

and History, is very similar to cervicals of the Chinese *Euhelopus* (see Wiman 1929) and also to an unnamed "titanosaurid" (this group of sauropods no longer recognized as valid; see "Systematics" chapter) from Peirópolis, Brazil (Powell 1987). According to Wedel (2003*b*), however, the Jones Ranch form differs the latter two forms in having large foramina on the lateral faces of the centrum, these being more similar to those of camerate than camellate taxa and consistent with the lack of camellae noted by Gomani *et al.*

Among Somphospondyli, *Euhelopus*— belonging to the Euhelopodidae, a monophyletic and endemic family of Chinese forms (see Upchurch 1995, 1998) closely related to the basal eusauropods *Shunosaurus*, *Omeisaurus*, and *Mamenchisaurus* (see Heathcote and Upchurch 2003 and *Cetiosauriscus* entry, with Euhelopodidae regarded as a clade outside of Neosauropoda and, hence, also outside of Somphospondyli); or more closely related to the Titanosauria than to *Omeisaurus*, with *Euhelopus* the sister taxon to Titanosauria (Wilson and Sereno)— has entirely camellate presacral vertebrae, with the laminae of the cervical and cranial dorsal vertebrae more poorly developed than in other sauropods.

In Titanosauria, the South American "*Gondwanatitan* [=*Aeolosaurus*]," a form more derived than the basal South American titanosaurians *Andesaurus* and *Malawisaurus* and less so than saltasaurines, a recovered partial cervical vertebra displays a few, comparatively large pneumatic chambers, the thick cortical bone and distinct median septum, Wedel noted (2003*b*), suggesting that these are camerate rather than camellate chambers. In *Alamosaurus*, a North American titanosaur closely related to the Mongolian *Opisthocoelicaudia* and South American saltasaurines (see Selgado *et al.* Upchurch 1998; Wilson and Sereno), a broken neural spine (TMM 41398-1) reveals an entirely camellate internal structure, Wedel (2003*b*) observed, while the laminar structure of this spine is poorly developed. Also, a poorly preserved, fragmentary cervical vertebra (WL 362) belonging to *Alamosaurus* reveals small and irregular camellae. In the South American *Saltasaurus*, generally considered to be the most derived titanosaurid yet known (Salgado *et al.*; Upchurch 1998; Wilson and Sereno), the presacral, sacral, and proximal caudal vertebrae are entirely camellate, fully camellate vertebrae constituting a synapomorphy of Saltasaurinae. Moreover, Sanz, Powell, Le Loeuff, Martínez and Pereda Suberbiola (1999) had described the ilium of this genus as possessing a "cancellous inner structure." As Sanz *et al.* also described the camellate vertebrae of this genus as having a "cancellous inner structure," making no distinction between these structures as pertaining to the ilium and vertebrae, Wedel (2003*b*) consequently

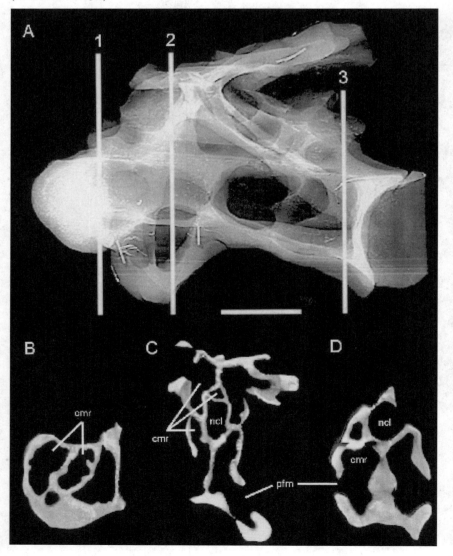

assumed that the authors may have been "actually reporting the presence of camellae in the ilium of *Saltasaurus*." If accurate, this interpretation is extremely important, Wedel (2003*b*) stated, constituting the only record of appendicular pneumaticity in a sauropod dinosaur. Wedel (2003*b*) cautioned, however, that Sanz *et al.* did not discuss this cancellous structure as pneumatic, and could have "meant the apneumatic medullary bone typical for most vertebrates of the pneumatic camellate bone typical of derived sauropods and birds"; nor did Powell (1992) mention the possibility of ilial camellae in his monograph on the osteology of *Saltasaurus*.

Following Upchurch's (1998) phylogeny, with *Haplocanthosaurus* positioned outside Neosauropoda and *Euhelopus* grouped with an endemic radiation of Chinese taxa, Wedel (2003*b*) proposed that camerae must have evolved twice, once in either of these groupings, with camerae thereby being synapomorphic for Neosauropoda. Also, camellae evolved at least twice, once among the Chinese taxa and at least once in Titanosauriformes, although some titanosauriforms seem to lack a camellate internal structure (*e.g.*, the Jones Ranch form). However, as all known brachiosaurids, as well as such derived titanosaurs as *Alamosaurus* and *Saltasaurus*, have camellae, the latter may be synapomorphic for Titanosauriformes, according to Wedel (2003*b*), with the camerate taxa perhaps representing numerous reversals. An alternative hypothesis is that camellae may have evolved independently within both Brachiosauridae and "Titanosauridae" (see "Systematics" chapter), while more basal titanosauriforms could have been primitively camerate.

Following Wilson and Sereno's phylogeny, in which *Haplocanthosaurus* is regarded as a basal macronarian more closely allied with Titanosauriformes than Diplodocoidea, Wedel (2003*b*) noted that the procamerate morphology of that genus suggests that camerae are not synapomorphic for Neosauropoda and instead evolved independently among the Chinese sauropods, Diplodocoidea, and Macronaria. Furthermore, accepting Wilson and Sereno's grouping of the camellate *Euhelopus* included in the Titanosauria, the latter clade including camerate forms, it can be stated with certainty that the evolution of camellae among titanosauriforms was complex, with that condition in basal members of the Titanosauriformes "best regarded as equivocal for the present."

According to Wedel (2003*b*), both camerae and camellae clearly evolved more than once in Sauropoda, regardless of which of the above phylogenies is adopted. As the Chinese forms, derived diplodocoids, brachiosaurids, and some titanosaurians all possessed

necks of exceptional length (see Powell 1986; Wilson and Sereno), Wedel (2003*b*) proposed that the presence of such complex polycamerate and camellate internal structures may correlate with the development of large body size and very long necks.

As Wedel (2003*b*) observed, the pattern of vertebral pneumatization in the evolution of the Sauropoda is similar to that observed during the ontogeny of birds, allowing speculation as to the nature and extent of the thoracoabdominal air sac system. In such basal sauropod taxa as *Jobaria*, pneumatic fossae are observed only in the cervical and cranial thoracic vertebrae (see Sereno *et al.*), while in most neosauropods pneumatization also occurs in the distal thoracic and sacral vertebrae. Furthermore, pneumatized caudal vertebrae also developed independently in diplodocoids and titanosaurians (see Britt 1993; Sanz *et al.*). Wedel (2003*b*) noted that "This caudal progression of vertebral pneumaticity in sauropod phylogeny is mirrored in avian ontogeny" — in extant birds, cervical and cranial thoracic vertebrae being pneumatized first, by way of diverticula from the cervical air sacs (see, for example, Hogg 1984), with diverticula of the abdominal air sacs pneumatizing the caudal thoracic vertebrae and synsacrum during later ontogeny.

Wedel (2003*b*) concluded that all sauropods likely possessed cervical air sacs, while most neosauropods probably had abdominal air sacs (a similar caudad progression of pneumatized vertebrae, and consequently, air sacs, having also been suggested for theropod evolution; see Britt 1993). According to Wedel (2003*a*, 2003*b*), extant birds are the most appropriate models for comprehending the ontogenetic and phylogenetic development of postcranial skeletal pneumatization in these dinosaurs. A pulmonary air sac system, albeit one less complex and extensive than in birds, was most likely present in sauropods, the irregular distribution of postcranial skeletal pneumatization among Archosauria suggesting that air sac evolution may have involved considerable parallelism. Wedel (2003*a*) found it probable that air sac systems evolved in Ornithodira primarily for lung ventilation, this adaptation possibly being one of the factors in the group's success. "The potential benefits of a pulmonary air sac system," Wedel (2003*a*) stated, "include mass reduction, thermoregulation, and most importantly, efficient lung ventilation."

Referring to Wedel *et al.* (2000*b*), Tsuihji (2004*a* published a study describing the ligament system in the neck of the large extant flightless bird, *Rhea amaricana*, and its implications relative to the bifurcated neural spines found in the cervical and dorsal vertebrae of various sauropod dinosaurs (including diplodocids, dicraeosaurids, *Camarasaurus*, and

Reconstructed skeleton (cast by the PAST Company) of a subadult *Jobaria tiguidensis*, a basal sauropod having pneumatic cervical vertebrae, part of the "Giants: African Dinosaurs" exhibit (December 20, 2003 to September 6, 2004) at Garfield Park Conservatory.

Euhelopus; *e.g.*, see McIntosh 1990; Upchurch 1998; Wilson and Sereno 1998).

In a related study published as an abstract, Wedel (2004) used CT scan analysis of cross sections of sauropod and theropod bone to determine the amount of mass conserved (*i.e.*, air space proportion) in saurischian dinosaurs, including sauropods, via skeletal pneumatics. From this study (see abstract for further details), Wedel (2004) calculated the air space proportions of a large sampling of sauropod and theropod vertebrae to range from 0.32 to 0.89, with a mean of 6.0—*i.e.*, air, on average, occupying over half the volume of pneumatic saurischian vertebrae. Wedel (2004) found three other features worthy of mention: Above values quite similar to range and mean of air space proportions for pneumatic long bones of extant birds; brachiosaurid sauropod *Sauroposeidon* having highest air space proportion values (up to 0.89; an autapomorphy of this genus, probably having evolved to lighten the neck); air space proportion apparently independent of internal complexity of vertebrae.

Excepting *Sauroposeiden*, Wedel (2004) calculated the mean values for the studied saurischian verebrae (whether camerate or camellate) to fall between 0.50 and 0.60, indicating that the evolution of such complex internal structures from simple structures included a redistribution of bony tissue, not a reduction, within the vertebrae. Wedel's (2004) study showed that pneumatization of the skeletons of the sauropod *Diplodocus* and theropod *Tyrannosaurus* lightened the mass of these dinosaurs by from seven to 10 percent,

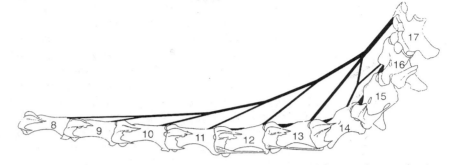

this figure not including extraskeletal diverticula, pulmonary air sacs, lungs, and trachea. With the latter all taken into account, the specific gravities of these two genera come to 0.80 and 0.82, respectively, these values being higher than those published for birds, but lower than those recorded for crocodilians and squamates.

Tsuihji applied the rigorous method proposed by Bryant and Russell (1992) and Witmer (1995) to infer unpreserved attributes such as soft tissues "in fossil taxa based on the phylogenetic distributions of such attributes in their extant sister (bracketing) taxa." According to that method, if a soft tissue and its osteological correlate exist in the first two extant outgroups of a fossil taxon, and if that correlate also exists in the fossil taxon, then the presence of that tissue can be inferred in the fossil taxon, parsimoniously and with a modicum of speculation.

As explained by Tsuihji, a median ligament—the ligamentum nuchae—extends, in extant birds and non-avian diapsids, along the tips of the neural spines,

Schematic diagram showing configuration of ligamentum elasticum interspinale (black line) and ligamentum elasticum interlaminare between adjacent vertebrae in middle to caudal cervical regions, left lateral view. (After Tsuihiji 2004, modified from Boas 1929.)

Computer-generated sauropod skeletal reconstruction by Kent A. Stevens showing (middle) the brachiosaurid *Brachiosaurus* with neck in "neutral" orientation, and the diplodocids (background) *Diplodocus* and (foreground) *Apatosaurus* with neck raised to maximum height.

Introduction

attaching to them in the cervical region, thereby "enabling a parsimonious inference that a homologous ligament would also have attached to the same sites in extinct diapsids, including sauropods." In order to identify the soft tissues associated with bifurcated neural spines in *R. americana*, Tsuihji dissected three specimens of this ratite—two adults (just the cervical region) and a nearly hatched embryo. Tsuihji also examined two *Rhea* skeletons (YPM 564 and 6503) for osteological features associated with ligament attachments and neck muscles; and dissected several specimens of *Alligator mississipiensis* and *Iguana iguana* to identify the attachment sites of ligamentum interspinale and ligamentum supraspinale in non-avian diapsids. Data from these studies were then compared with putative attachment sites for muscles and ligaments in the cervical and cranial dorsal vertebrae of *Apatosaurus ajax* (YPM 1860), *Apatosaurus* sp. (OMNH 1095, 1326, 1344, 1404, 1421, and 1423), *Camarasaurus grandis* (YPM 1905), and *Camarasaurus* sp. (OMNH 1383).

As described by Tsuihji, "lig. nuchea" in *R. americana* splits ventrally into halves as the neural spines divide in the caudal cervical vertebrae, thereby maintaining the connection of this ligament to the tips of each bifurcated spine. This illustrates "the conservative nature of connection between 'lig. nuchae' and its osteological correlate." Moreover, this ligament and the notches of the divided spines enclose another ligament, "lig. elasticum interspinale," that arises from the undivided neural spine of the caudalmost "cervico-dorsal," giving off branches inserting on the caudal surfaces of the spines of the middle to caudal cervical vertebrae. Tsuihji postulated that this ligament is "a good modern analog to the structure occupying the notches of the bifurcated neural spines of sauropods."

Using *Camarasaurus* and *Apatosaurus* as examples, Tsuihji offered a hypothetical reconstruction of the proposed ligament system in the sauropod neck based entirely on the system observed in *Rhea*; therefore, this inference was not predicted based upon phylogenetic data. Tsuihji noted that, although the presence of ligament associated with the notches of the

bifurcated neural spines in sauropod dinosaurs is strongly supported by osteological and phylogenetic data, its morphology is proposed in his study "only as a working hypothesis that will need to be tested in the future."

According to Tsuihji, the tensional force of this hypothesized ligament would most effectively work with the neck tilting downward, with the insertions of the ligament below the level of its origin. Following the computer-generated reconstructions by Stevens and Parrish (1999; see S2) of the necks of *Apatosaurus* and *Diplodocus*, in which the neck extended almost straight forward with a downwards slope, Tsuihji suggested that his proposed ligament would have been taut in such a position "and would have exerted a stronger tensional force that it would in a more erect neck posture." Additionally, that author stated, the insertion of this proposed ligament "on scars at the bases of the cleft between the metapophyses, rather than on the top of the neural spine, would have increased the leverage of the tensional force of the ligament by lowering the positions of its insertion, thereby making this ligament a more effective bracing device."

In a related study, published as an abstract for a poster, Christian (2004) noted that the habitual neck postures of various sauropods, as well as other vertebrates, can be reconstructed "based on the comparison of the distribution of compressive forces along the neck with the distribution of the cross-sectional areas of the intervertebral discs," this method having already been tested successfully among such extant long-necked vertebrates as camels and giraffes.

As Christian noted, compressive forces in habitual postures "tend to be proportional to the cross-sectional areas of the intervertebral joints resulting in approximately constant stress in the joint cartilage along the neck." Applying this method to sauropod dinosaurs, Christian found a considerable degree of neck-posture variation among different taxa, with the neck of *Brachiosaurus* "kept nearly vertically" and that of *Diplodocus* "much more horizontally." Such contrasts in neck posture, that author noted, is reflected in the overall design of the body, particularly in the length of the tail and limbs.

As summarized by Bonnan (2003*a*) in a study on the evolution of sauropod manus shape, the manus in these giant dinosaurs is unique in being both digitigrade and semitubular, with five robust metacarpals forming a vertical, U-shaped colonade (*e.g.*, see Upchurch 1995, 1998; Wilson and Sereno 1998). The triangular and wedge-shaped proximal articular surfaces of the metacarpals are appressed tightly against each other, their distal ends not splaying apart. Indeed, the U-shaped manus prints preserved in most known

Hypothetical reconstruction of the ligament system in the neck of *Camarasaurus grandis*, using as a modern analog the neck of the ratite *Rhea americana*, black line representing ligament analogous to ligamentum elasticum interspinale as if dorsally stretched out, gray areas representing ligamentum elasticum, interlaminare/ligamentum interspinale, profile of vertebrae modified from Gilmore (1925). (After Tsuihiji 2004.)

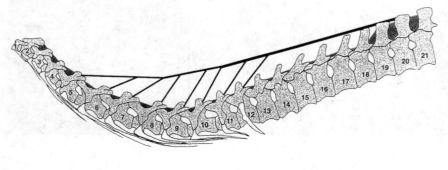

sauropod trackways confirm that this configuration was maintained during locomotion (*e.g.*, Farlow, Pittman and Hawthorne 1989; Lockley 1991). This odd shape of the sauropod metacarpus, differing from other saurischian dinosaurs, has been interpreted as a synapomorphy uniting most members of the Sauropoda (*e.g.*, Upchurch 1995, 1998, for Eusauropoda; Wilson and Sereno, for Neosauropoda).

As Bonnan pointed out, "The vertical orientation and semitubular arrangement of the metacarpals suggest that the sauropod manus improved the mechanical ability of the forelimb to support great weight." Taking into consideration the columnar limb posture in these dinosaurs, it is reasonable to interpret the morphology of the sauropod manus as simply a graviportal adaptation for reducing and redistributing tensile and shearing forces during locomotion. Bonnan's study, however, constituted the first major investigation into the possible "evolutionary mechanism responsible for modifying the relatively flat metacarpus of basal saurischians into [the sauropod] semitubular arrangement."

In many kinds of mammals, Bonnan noted, the manus can be rotated so that the palmar surface faces cranially during supination or caudally in pronantion, this action being facilitated by a rounded radial head pivoting in a facet on the proximal and lateral aspect of the ulna (Hildebrand 1995), permitting the distal end of the radius to rotate about the ulnar shaft, thereby changing the orientation of the manus. Contrarily in elephants, the radial head is angular and locked in a triangular fossa on the cranial and lateral ulnar face, serving to immobilize the forearm, preventing supination of the front foot during locomotion. Moreover, the distal half of the radial shaft is quite S-shaped, entirely crossing over the ulna to lie internally in the forearm (see Sikes 1971), producing a "permanent pronation that allows the manus to function like the pes by flexing and extending anteroposteriorly."

Bonnan noted that in saurischian dinosaurs active manus pronation was either precluded or very poorly developed because the oblong morphology of the radial head prevents the rotation of the radius about the ulna into a cross-over condition. In theropods and prosauropods, complete pronation of the manus was not likely because the radius in these dinosaurs lies lateral and cranial to the ulna at the elbow, and the radial shaft is cranial, not medial, to the ulna distally, resulting in an incomplete crossover of radius and ulna. However, sauropod trackway evidence indicates that manus pronation was indeed well developed in sauropods (*e.g.*, Lockley), more so, in fact, than in other saurischian dinosaurs, although not as developed as in proboscidean (see Wilson and

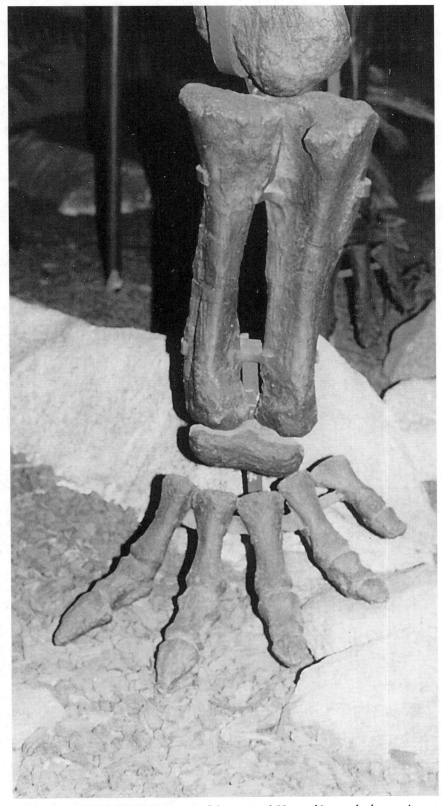

Left forelimb (LACM 5166/125972; cast) of the sauropod *Mamenchisaurus hochuanensis* showing the internally shifted radius, relative to the ulna, and the pronated manus (see 2003 study by Matthew F. Bonnan).

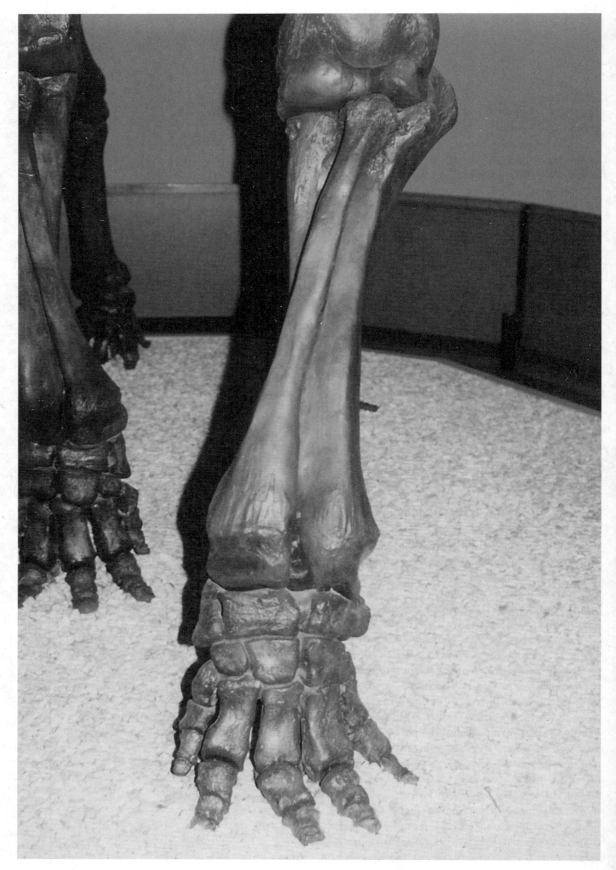

Forelimb (LACMHC 240) of the proboscidian *Mammuthus columbi* showing the radius crossing over the ulna (see study 2003 study by Matthew F. Bonnan).

Sereno). Reconciling sauropod manus print orientation with forelimb osteology has been difficult, however, because the radius and ulna in these dinosaurs do not completely cross.

Bonnan examined — incorporating articulation and manipulation of the various elements, either the original material or casts — the forelimb and manus of several North American neosauropod taxa (*e.g.*, primarily *Apatosaurus, Camarasaurus, Diplodocus*) in 15 collections (see paper for list), and also examining other taxa (*e.g.*, the basal saurischian *Herrerasaurus*, basal theropod *Allosaurus*, prosauropod *Plateosaurus*, the sauropods *Barosaurus lentus, Pleurocoelus, Alamosaurus sanjuanensis*, and "*Pelorosaurus*" *becklesii*, and also the African (*Loxodon africanus*) and Indian (*Elephas maximus*) elephants. Other skeletal materials and also a ¹⁄₁₂th scale model of the skeleton of *Apatosaurus louisae* (based on Gilmore's 1936*a* osteology of *Apatosaurus*) were also used in this study.

It was Bonnan's assessment that the unique shape of the semitubular sauropod manus was intimately and temporally linked with the posture of the forelimbs. As the sauropod ancestor gradually reverted from a bipedal to a quadrupedal posture, the column-like orientation of the forelimb and the need for manus pronation altered the primitively cranial and lateral position of the radius proximally, shifting the radius internally relative to the position of the ulna. With both radius and ulna then oriented somewhat parallel to each other, the sauropod forelimb was, consequently, augmented to reduce shear stress during the support phase. Bonnan pointed out that, had the radius crossed over the ulna (as in elephants), its angled orientation could have subjected the radial shaft to shear forces great enough to damage the radius. By internally shifting that bone, however, its shaft "would be loaded such that tensile and shear stresses were reduced, perhaps providing a more structurally stable configuration for bearing weight."

The internal shift of the radius, Bonanan concluded, constituted the mechanism that transformed the relatively flat basal dinosaurian manus of the sauropod ancestor into a digitigrade, semitubular structure, subsequently altering the shape of the digital arch. Consequently, while the shape of the sauropod manus probably served as an ideal tension and shear-reducing structure, its evolution may have been a "fortuitous side effect or exaptation that arose out of the constraints imposed by the saurischian forelimb, a columnar limb posture, and the necessity of manus pronation." While the evolution of this manus morphology was ideal for the supporting of great weight, its initial development, according to Bonnan, was more likely "the result of achieving pronation within the historical constraints of the saurischian

forelimb." Perhaps, Bonnan further proposed, a semitubular manus and a parallel radius and ulna may functionally have contributed to a greater number of mechanisms that inevitably resulted in gigantism in this dinosaurian group.

If the hypothesis that manus shape and radius position in sauropods relate to quadrupedalism is correct, Bonnan noted, then the following characters collectively form an integrated functional suite: Obligatory quadrupedal posture with columnar limbs (see Wilson and Sereno); proximal end of ulna triradiate, with deep radial fossa (Wilson and Sereno); radial distal condyle subrectangular, flat posterior margin for ulna (Wilson and Sereno); and proximal ends of metacarpals subtriangular, composite articular surface U-shaped (McIntosh 1990; Upchurch 1995, 1998; Wilson and Sereno). Bonnan noted that, while some of the above characters have been suggested as synapomorphies for clades beyond the basal sauropods, "each has functional and osteological correlations with other characters that suggest they were present in the earliest sauropods instead — *e.g.*, *Vulcanodon* (a basal sauropod for which the manus is poorly known) having a proximally triradiate ulna suggesting, by comparison with other sauropods, a semitubular manus. While a phylogeentic analysis of the suggested distribution of these characters was not within the scope of Bonnan's study, that author proposed that "the apparent correlation between quadrupedal posture and the presence of specific morphological features in the ulna, radius, and manus offer compelling evidence that manus orientation, manus shape, and forelimb posture are linked in sauropods," this hypothesis predicting that the complete manus of a basal sauropod, if ever found, will be semitubular.

In a somewhat related report, Bonnan (2004*a*) performed morphometric analyses of sauropod limbs, noting that the potential of such studies to shed light upon functional aspects of the locomotion and paleobiology of these dinosaurs. However, that author pointed out, analyses of the dimensions of sauropod limb bones typically reveal but few discernible morphological trends, due to the large size differences among the individual specimens in a sample. Therefore, combined analyses incorporating both limb size and shape may be more advantageous in performing such studies.

Bonnan's (2004*a*) analyses were based on his examination of thin-plates taken from numerous humeri and femora from the well-known Morrison Formation genera *Apatosaurus, Diplodocus*, and *Camarasaurus*, preserved in 14 North American collections, these specimens offering "an opportunity to explore and compare limb morphology in contemporaneous, sympatric sauropods." The intents of this study were to 1.

determine if humerus and femur shape differed significantly among these genera, 2. determine where changes in shape occurred, and 3. infer the basic functional implications of morphological differences utilizing an Extant Phylogenetic Bracket approach.

Using both traditional morphometric and thin-plate analyses, Bonnan (2004a) achieved results largely correlating with earlier studies of sauropod limb dimensions, detecting but few differences between the three taxa, with most of the paleobiological trends revealed being related to size. Basic shape of the studied limbs remained almost the same in both adult and juvenile individuals (contrasting with the condition seen in prosauropods, non-avian theropods, crocodilians, and birds). Perhaps most significantly, analysis of the linear measurement variables showed an underlying isometric or near-isometric relationship between most measurement variables and bone size.

However, thin-plate analyses did reveal a number of significant morphological differences in the humeri and femora of *Apatosaurus, Diplodocus,* and *Camarasaurus,* including the following: *Apatosaurus* humeri and femora most robust, having expanded regions for muscle insertion and more distally located deltopectoral and caudofemoral landmarks; *Diplodocus* humeri and femora gracile, landmarks of muscular insertion more proximally located; *Camarasaurus* humeri "surprisingly gracile," deltopectoral crest less extensive, femora more robust, similar to those of *Apatosaurus.* These important differences, Bonnan (2004a) suggested, "may be correlated with differences in locomotor functional morphology," although future exploration and qualification of the sauropod appendicular skeleton is required before the paleobiological and paleoecological picture of these dinosaurs can be completed.

In a related report published as an abstract, Bonnan (2004b), after comparing the findings from his analyses with earlier histological studies, suggested that isometric or near-isometric limb growth in sauropods could be "explained by predominantly appositional, periosteal growth and reduced endosteal and metaphyseal remodeling," resulting in these giant dinosaurs maintaining "simplified limb morphologies into adulthood characterized by greatly expanded proximal and distal articular surfaces and a relatively solid interior." Perhaps, that author suggested, these features could have more effectively distributed compressive stresses through the humerus and femur, across their joints, and across the pectoral and pelvic girdles. Bonnan (2004b) concluded that limited remodeling of the humeri and femora in these dinosaurs also suggests a limited axial rotation of these bones, with parasagittal limb movements being predominant; consequently, "a simplified locomotor repertoire and

the retention of juvenilized limbs may have exapted sauropods for gigantism."

Rothschild, Molnar and Helbling (2003) discussed, in a published abstract, the behavioral implications of stress fractures in sauropod bones (see also the abstract by Rothschild and Panza 2004, discussing osteoarthritis in *Apatosaurus,* as well as in nonsauropod dinosaurs and birds). Their paleopathologic study, testing the hypothesis that sauropods were able to rear up on their hind legs, was stimulated by the skeleton of the gigantic *Barosaurus lentus,* mounted at the American Museum of natural history in a tripodal posture (see *D:TE* for photograph). As Rothschild *et al.* pointed out, resuming a normal quadrupedal posture from this stance would have exerted enormous forces on the thoracic and lumbar verebrae and metacarpals or forefoot phalanges (routinely seen in ballet dancers), as demonstrated by stress fractures.

Rotschild *et al.* macroscopically examined for surface abnormalities sauropod thoracic and lumbar vertebrae, phalanges, and metapodials. Stress fractures were radiologically identified by the authors "as oblique radiolucent knife-slicelike clefts with smudged (indistinct) periosteal overgrowth forming a surface hump."

This study revealed the following in the examined sauropod material: Absence of stress fractures in forefeet (221 metacarpals and 121 manual phalanges) and 1222 lumbar or thoracic vertebrae; pronounced anterior bulges (characteristic of stress fractures) seen in six percent of metatarsals, frequency indistinguishable among genera —*i.e.,* metatarsal I of *Apatosaurus* and *Camarasaurus,* II of *Diplodocus,* IV of *Apatosaurus* and *Brachiosaurus,* V of *Apatosaurus,* and proximal pedal phalanges of *Apatosaurus* and *Nurosaurus.*

According to Rothschild *et al.,* the articulatory joints of sauropods had sufficient range of motion to permit rearing up to a tripodal posture; however, the lack of manual stress fractures indicates that they did not assume such a stance. This, the authors noted, "contrasts with relatively frequent notation of pedal stress fractures" and suggests that the sauropod pes "provided much of the propulsive thrust of ambulation, perhaps with dry land habitat implications."

Wilson and Fisher (2003), in a published abstract, briefly discussed the various "manus-only" and "manus-dominated" sauropod trackways, exlusively or preferentially showing impressions of the forefeet, preserved in Middle to Lower Jurassic rocks in many countries. For approximately 60 years, these tracks have been generally interpreted as direct evidence for swimming behavior in this dinosaurian group, the lack of hindfoot impressions being explained as a partially buoyant animal making its way through the water via action of the forelimbs. A more recent interpretation of these tracks, these authors noted, suggests that the manus-only tracks are, in fact, "undertracks," made by a walking sauropod whose comparatively small forefeet sank through an exposed substrate that deformed the underlying layers of sediment.

Noting that neither of the above scenarios is consistent with the caudally positioned center of mass implied by the osteology of these giant dinosaurs, Wilson and Fisher proposed a new interpretation of the "manus-only" footprints, their interpretation involving "a partially submerged, but otherwise typical sauropod trackmaker." As the authors explained, a sauropod shoulder-deep in water would, by the shape of its body, experience a forward shift in its center of mass, this permitting the submergence of the tail while its neck and head remained held out of water. While partial submersion effectively lessens the animal's weight, a considerably larger proportion of the load is carried by the manus. In all sauropods, Wilson and Fisher pointed out, the manus has less than half the surface area of the pes. Moreover, measurements of partially submerged sauropod scale models confirm that the forefoot experienced over twice the pressures experienced by the hindfoot, this possibly resulting in the manus leaving impressions where the pes did not, an effect most pronounced in *Brachiosaurus*, which has the most forwardly position center of mass among all known sauropods. Furthermore, the authors pointed out that asymmetry or forefoot prints and occasional preservation of hindfoot prints can also be explained in other ways, *e.g.*, changes in water level, substrate consistency, and carriage of neck and tail. While not implying that sauropods could neither swim nor create undertracks, results of Wilson and Fisher's study did imply that those earlier proposals "do not best explain the manus-only sauropod trackway patterns."

In another study involving sauropod footprints, Lingham-Soliar (2003*a*) described an excellently preserved left pes track from the Chewore area of Zimbabwe as showing a deep ridge (apparently recorded for the first time) on the pavement surrounding the impression. This ridge, that author noted, "includes stress cracks, a probable consequence of the animal's great weight and displacement of the substrate as the trackmaker's foot cut into it." As Lingham-Soliar reported, slight traces of a similar ridge can be seen along the cranial edge of other sauropod tracks, including those preserved along the Paluxy River near Glen Rose, Texas (see Kuban 1989), this feature having been interpreted as the forward-shifting of the dinosaur's weight during locomotion. A computer-generated topographical image of the track revealed that

the greatest pressure was on the midcranial inner and cranial surface of the foot. From an analysis of the Zimbabwe track based upon the topographical picture, plus an analysis of a section of the Paluxy River trackway, Lingham-Soliar deduced that a waddling gait was unlikely for these animals, and that the trackmaker's footfall pattern was in diagonal cranio-caudal pairs (see Lingham-Soliar's paper for further details).

Engelmann, Chure and Fiorillo (2004) published on the implications of a dry climate for the paleoecology of the fauna of the Morrison Formation (Upper Jurassic), their study largely focusing upon the giant sauropod dinosaurs preserved in Morrison rocks. As Engelmann *et al.* noted, diverse geological evidence (see paper for details and references) "indicates a seasonal, semiarid climate for the time of deposition of the Morrison Formation." Such generalized environmental conditions may, therefore, be assumed "for the purpose of reconstructing the ancient ecosystem." The author interpreted wet Morrison environments preserving plant fossils, invertebrates, and small vertebrates (including small dinosaurs) "as representing local conditions limited in space and/or time," these elements most likely being restricted to those wetland areas during times of environmental stress."

Regarding sauropods, Engelmann *et al.* noted that the Morrison Formation includes a diverse fauna of giant sauropods — mainly the diplodocid *Diplodocus*, the camarasaurid *Camarasaurus*, and more rarely, the brachiosaurid *Brachiosaurus*— each displaying differences in body form and dentition that suggest some degree of resource partitioning concerning food and other resources (*e.g.*, see Fiorillo 1998 for an examination and comparison of wear facets on teeth of *Diplodocus* and *Camarasaurus*, the two most common Morrison sauropods; also, see S1). Such feeding strategies possibly included the vertical stratifications of browsing levels, with the rarer brachiosaurs probably being high browsers, the more common camarasaurs browsing on course vegetation at intermediate height, and diplodocids browsing on low-level herbaceous plants.

Although the concept of such large plant-eating animals may seem inconsistent with environments that are sometimes arid and offer sparse resources, Engelmann *et al.* noted the following: Being very large does, in fact, offer certain physiological advantages conducive to such averse conditions. The scaling effect of large size makes large plant-eating animals very efficient relative to their size, most likely requiring proportionately less food and food of poorer quality than do smaller herbivores (see McGowan 1991). Also, very large herbivores such as sauropods can survive starvation longer than smaller plant-eating animals

Introduction

Caudal vertebrae (BHI 6200) *in situ* of *Camarasaurus* cf. *supremus*, this specimen popularly known as "Elaine," being collected by the Black Hills Institute of Geological Research at the Waugh Ranch, in the Morrison Formation, near Hullett, Wyoming. George F. Engelmann, Daniel J. Chure and Anthony R. Fiorillo (2004) reported on the effects of dry climate on such Morrison dinosaurs.

addressed the question of why most dinosaur remains are known from low-latitude to marginally midlatitude regions where plant fossils are usually sparse and evaporites common, while few are known from mid- to high latitudes having higher floral diversities and abundant coals. The authors attributed this "obvious geographic mismatch between known dinosaur distributions and their primary food source" to possible taphonomic bias.)

Buffetaut (2003), in an abstract, reported briefly on a primitive sauropod specimen exhibiting features reminiscent of prosauropod dinosaur. The specimen, an incomplete right dentary in the care of Didier Descouens, was collected from Middle Jurassic rocks of the Majunga Basin in Madagascar. As Buffetaut observed, the specimen is typically sauropod in form, *i.e.*, its height increases significantly and regularly caudally to rostrally, as opposed to the prosauropod condition, *i.e.*, the dentary being deeper caudally than rostrally. However, the teeth closely resemble those of prosauropods (*e.g.*, *Plateosaurus*), being leaf-shaped, with large serrations along the edges.

To date, this dentary is distinguished as the only sauropod specimen exhibiting such a mosaic of sauropod and prosauropod features. Probably representing a new taxon, this specimen suggested to Buffetaut "that mosaic evolution was involved in the early history of sauropods, with the dentary evolving faster than the teeth towards the consition seen in Late Jurassic and later forms."

In recent years, various phylogenetic studies of the Sauropoda have been published, most of which focused upon the more advanced sauropod clades (see "Systematics" chapters, *D:TE*, *1*, *S2*, *S3*, and this volume). However, the phylogenetic relationships of more basal taxa—genera from the Late Triassic and early Jurassic periods have largely not been given such rigorous treatment. Recently, Gillette (2003) published a study concerning the geographic and phylogenetic position of such basal sauropods, focusing primarily upon *Barapasaurus tagorei* and *Kotasaurus yamanpalliensis*, taxa from the probably Lower Jurassic Kota Formation of the Pranhita-Godavari Basin of India.

As Gillette pointed out, phylogenetic analyses have placed both *Barapasaurus* and *Kotasaurus* at or near the ancestry of the Sauropoda. Their origin, however, as well as the history of Indian sauropods, continues to be enigmatic. However, recent studies have pushed sauropod origins back even further, the occurrence of the earliest known sauropod *Isanosaurus attavipachi* (see *S2*), from the Late (possibly Middle; Norian–"Rhaetian") Triassic of Thailand, described by Buffetaut, Suteethorn, Cuny, Tong, Le Loeuff, Khansubha and Jongautchariyakul (2000), having

(*e.g.*, see McGowan 1991, 1994), and also reach widely separated resource patches with greater energy efficiency than can smaller animals (Alexander 1989; McGowan 1991, 1994). These size-related advantages would, Engelmann *et al.* pointed out, apply only to subadult and adult sauropods of a certain size, the juveniles having to face the same environmental restrictions faced encountered by other small herbivorous animals.

(See also the somewhat related recent paper by Rees, Noto, Parrish and Parrish 2004, relating the Late Jurassic climates and vegetation of the Morrison Formation and the East African Tendaguru Formation to dinosaur distributions. In this study, the authors

Black Hills Institute of Geological Research preparator Deb Christie with the still-jacketed skull (BHI 6200) of *Camarasaurus* cf. *supremus* ("Elaine").

placed the Sauropoda in Laurasia before the Early Jurassic expansion of this clade through Asia and some of the southern continents. Additionally, recently described sauropod taxa from China, Morocco, and Germany have verified the geographic distribution of this dinosaurian group in Asia and Europe.

Gillette reviewed a number of basal sauropod taxa, noting the following: *Isanosaurus attavipachi* resembles *Barapasaurus* and *Kotasaurus* in the proximal position of the fourth trochanter of the femur (see Buffetaut *et al.*). *Kotasaurus yamanpalliensis* is distinguished from *Barapasaurus tagorei* based on such osteological features as simple dorsal vertebrae and a low iliac blade, while other characteristics—*e.g.*, less ex-

panded humerus with slight twist at both ends, lacking craniocaudal expansion in dorsal end, retention of lesser trochanter of femur, osteology of astragalus—resemble those of prosauropods and *Vulcanodon* (see Yadagiri 2001). *Vulcanodon karibaensis*, from the Early Jurassic (?Hettangian) of Zimbabwe, generally regarded as older than the Kota Formation taxa, displays features (*e.g.*, four fused sacral vertebrae, broadly articulated pubes and ischia, pubes having prominent distal "apron," ilium having long pubic peduncle and short ischiac peduncle) suggesting an apparent close relationship with *Barapasaurus* (see Cooper 1984). The Early Jurassic Chinese taxa *Zizhongosaurus chuanchengensis*, *Gongxianosaurus shibeinsis*, and *Yunnano-*

saurus robustus (generally classified as a prosauropod, but regarded by Gillette and also Barrett 1999 as a primitive sauropod; see *S2*) were deemed by Gillette as insufficient for phylogenetic analysis, their taxonomic status and placement questionable. *Ohmdenosaurus liasicus*, from the late Early Jurassic (Toracian) of Germany, is about the same age as the Kota Formation taxa and is less derived in some features than *Vulcanodon*, *Barapasaurus*, and *Kotasaurus* (see McIntosh 1990).

As *Barapasaurus* and *Kotasaurus* are known from almost complete skeletons, their osteology and stratigraphic positions are critical to an understanding of the origin and evolution of the Sauropoda. As mentioned above, *Isanosaurus*, *Barapasaurus*, *Kotasaurus*, and *Vulcanodon* all retain certain features indicating their relationship with the Prosauropoda, a clade with which these sauropods were contemporaneous. However, Gillette pointed out, no cladistic analysis of the Sauropoda yet published has included *Isanosaurus*; consequently, the phylogenetic relationships between that genus, *Vulcanodon*, and the two Kota Formation taxa remain unresolved.

According to Gillette, the occurrence of *Isanosaurus* in the Late Triassic of Thailand suggests that the Sauropoda may have originated as early as the Middle Triassic (see Wilson and Sereno 1998), although, considering the rich global record of Late Triassic dinosaurian faunas, the sole occurrence of that genus is problematical. Gillette offered that "the simplest explanation of this obvious rarity is that Late Triassic sauropod populations were restricted to a small geographic area and had not yet diversified."

As noted above, the Gondwanan genera *Barapasaurus*, *Kotasaurus*, and *Vulcanodon* appear to be closely related to the Laurasian genus *Isanosaurus*, all four of which have been classified as basal sauropods. Moreover, these early sauropods occur in middle rather than higher latitudes (see Smith, Smith and Funnell 1994).

According to Gillette, this distribution suggests "certain limitations, perhaps physiological constraints, which precluded global expansion into the American continents and other southern landmasses until the Middle and Late Jurassic," with sauropod populations expanding into Late Jurassic Australia and South America preceding the introduction of this clade into North America (no Middle Jurassic North American sauropods have yet been reported; see, for example, McIntosh; Gillette 1996a, 1996b) during the Late Jurassic. By that time, limitations denying sauropods widespread distribution during the Early Jurassic were either lost or overcome, possibly "as a consequence of the post–Toarcian global regression of sea level (earliest Middle Jurassic)."

Gillette's study found that the early evolution and paleogeography of the Sauropoda involve at least four stages through the end of the Jurassic period: 1. Origin of sauropods during the Middle or Late Triassic, with first geographic distribution limited to southeastern Asia; 2. expanded distribution and increased diversity through southern Laurasia and eastern Gondwana during the Early Jurassic, with such gigantic forms as *Barapasaurus*, *Kotasaurus*, and *Vulcanodon* demonstrating that an early achievement of gigantism (*contra* Monbaron, Russell and Taquet 1999; see *Atlasaurus* entry, *S2*); 3. continued Middle Jurassic geographic expansion to include Australia and South but not North America, including derived sauropods achieving yet greater size; and 4. Late Jurassic expansion into North America, some forms (*e.g.*, *Brachiosaurus*, *Supersaurus*, *Seismosaurus*) achieving exceptionally large size.

The first sauropod remains reported from the Jurassic of the Nequén Basin, in Patagonia, Argentina, were recently described by Garcia, Salgado and Coria (2003). The fragmentary specimen (MCF-PHV-379) consists of the distal end of a left femur and the proximal end of a left tibia and fibula, collected in 1980 by Alberto Gutiérrez and Carlos Gulisano from Upper Jurassic (Kimmeridgian) Tordillo Formation (see Muñoz, Gulisano and Conti Persino 1984).

As Garcia *et al.* noted, MCF-PHV-379 offers few features by which to refer it to any particular sauropod group. The proximal end of the tibia is subcircular, this feature being one of the criteria by which Wilson and Sereno (1998) diagnosed the clade Neosauropoda. Other features however, are suggestive of basal members of Eusauropoda, such as *Barapasaurus* and *Patagosaurus*. According to Garcia *et al.*, discovery of this specimen is significant in establishing the occurrence of possible basal eusauropods in the Late Jurassic of Patagonia.

Given the fragmentary nature of this specimen, Garcia *et al.* could only regard it as representing indeterminate sauropod.

Fowler, Simmonds, Green and Stevens (2003), in an abstract for a poster, briefly reported on two small, conspecific, possibly diplodocid sauropods — represented by three forelimbs, measuring 1.2 meters in length — found recently preserved in life position, facing south and four meters apart, in the Lower Cretaceous Wessex Formation of the Isle of Wight, England. According to the authors, the vertical orientation of these specimens, the lack of other preserved elements, and also their preservation in smectite-rich paleovertisols (mottled/red marls) strongly suggests a miring event. Furthermore, a shed theropod tooth associated with these specimens supports the postulation that the mired carcasses of these dinosaurs were

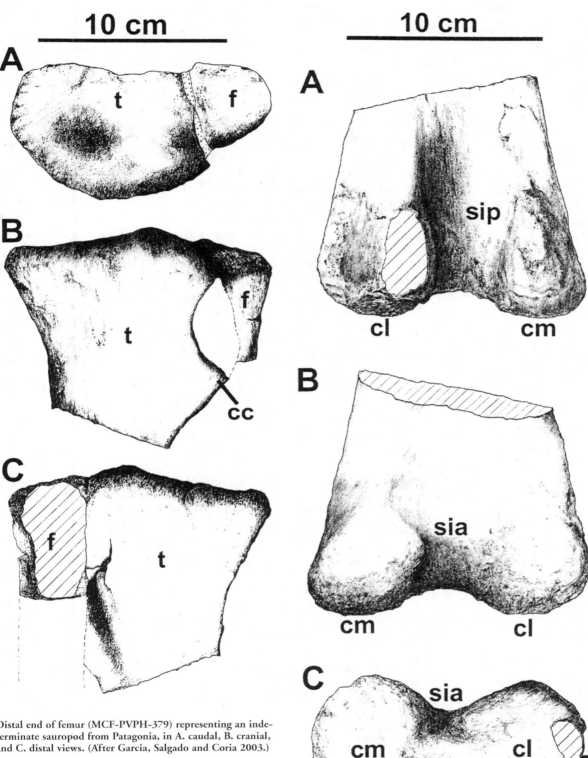

Distal end of tibia and fibula (MCF-PVPH-379) representing an indeterminate sauropod from Patagonia, in A. proximal, B. craniomedia, and C. caudolateral views. (After Garcia, Salgado and Coria 2003.)

Distal end of femur (MCF-PVPH-379) representing an indeterminate sauropod from Patagonia, in A. caudal, B. cranial, and C. distal views. (After Garcia, Salgado and Coria 2003.)

then scavenged, leaving only the embedded limbs for preservation.

As noted by Fowler *et al.*, tentative evidence lends support "to the hypothesis of taxon preservation bias between different facies," with sauropods comprising a greater percentage of the megafauna preserved "within red and purple marls (medium to well-drained oxidised sediment) than other facies." (Other plant-debris beds, the authors pointed out, tend to preserve other groupings of dinosaurs —*e.g.*, *Iguanodon* [waterlogged reduced sediment formed by flood-fire associations], juvenile/subadult *Hypsilophodon* [mottled sand/mud facies, mudflows]), suggesting that such morphologically dissimilar taxa were probably susceptible to different preservational biases.)

Among the rarest and least understood of sauropod material is that belonging to the skull. Vietti and Hartman (2004), in an abstract for a poster, reported briefly on a recently discovered well-preserved sauropod braincase (WDC-BB 1188), missing the parietals, collected in summer, 2002, from a large polytypic bonebed of the Upper Jurassic (Tithonian) Morrison Formation of north-western Wyoming. The authors assigned this specimen to the family Diplodocidae based upon the following features: Parasphenoid rostrum slender, elongate; well-developed fossa between basipterygoid processes; nonspherical occipital condyle. Accepting the subfamilies of "Apatosaurinae" and "Diplodocinae," Vietti and Hartman noted that the new braincase displays synapomorphies of both —*e.g.*, ("apatosaurines") flattened, slightly concave dorsal margin of occipital condyle, relatively reduced, robust basipterygoids, and occipital condyle axis oriented to angle greater than 90 degrees from long axis of skull; ("diplodocines") fossa on ventral side of paroccipital processes, constriction of paroccipital processes. Autapomorphic characters noted in WDC-BB 1188 include: Rostrodorsal tapering of supraoccipital; elongate paroccipital processes. Based upon these observations, the authors classified this specimen as Diplodocidae *incertae sedis*, at the same time anticipating that study of postcranial remains from the same bonebed will eventually permit a more precise diagnosis.

Chevrons are small bones of the caudal vertebrae that protect the hemal arch and offer attachments for the M. caudofemoralis longus and the M. ischiocaudalis. In 1901, John Bell Hatcher published his osteology of the diplodocid sauropod dinosaur *Diplodocus*. Hatcher, in that classic publication, was the first worker to speculate that the presence of proximodistally chevrons (also seen in the Chinese sauropods *Shunosaurus*, *Omeisaurus*, and *Mamenchisaurus*, as well as in the stegosaurid *Kentrosaurus*, both nodosaurids and ankylosaurids, and a few theropods including *Tyrannosaurus*) constituted evidence that such giant terrestrial herbivores engaged in tripodal rearing. According to that author, these "sled-shaped" bones could have served to better protect the hemal canal when the dinosaur was standing up on its hind legs, its great weight supported on the tail.

In the succeeding years, various other workers have followed Hatcher's idea (*e.g.*, Bakker 1986; Paul 1987), with the notion that diplodocids sometimes reared up into a tripodal position commonly accepted. While some researchers have challenged this proposal in recent years, Wilhite (2002) questioned whether the presence of these elongate chevrons in diplodocids is actually indicative of tripodality, his paper dealing only with chevron function and the possible role of chevrons in tripodal rearing.

Performing dissections of the tail musculature of an extant archosaur, the crocodilian *Alligator mississippiensis*, Wilhite found that, contrary to previously offered publications, the M. caudofemoralis longus originates primarily from the bodies of the proximal chevrons. In extant crocodilians, that author noted, the chevrons also serve as points of attachment for the M. ischiocaudalis, a complex segmented muscle that facilitates lateral and possibly ventral movement of the tail during swimming or when the tail functions as a defensive weapon.

Three kinds of chevron morphology are present in both saurischian and ornithischian dinosaurs, Wilhite noted — two (common to most taxa) involving proximodistal elongation of the chevron in the middle and distal parts of the tail, the third being the modified proximodistally elongate form found in diplodocids (and other taxa noted above). Notably, almost all taxa having these modified chevrons — the exceptions being a few theropods, including *Tyrannosaurus*, and also possibly diplodocids — also possess some kind of tail weapon. It was apparent to Wilhite that the presence of such modified chevrons "is related to increasing the lateral mobility of the tail," the most likely purpose for these chevrons in diplodocids, consequently, being "some specialized function of the tail involving lateral motion [*e.g.*, using the long, tapering 'whiplash' as a weapon] and not for supporting the body during tripodal rearing."

Martinez, Casal, Luna, Ibiricu, Cardozo and Lamanna (2004), in an abstract for a poster, reported on recently collected associated remains pertaining to "the youngest and most austral indisputable diplodocoid" sauropod yet recorded. The material — discovered in the Upper Cretaceous Bajo Barreal Formation of northern Santa Cruz Province, central Patagonia, Argentina — includes one cranial and two caudal dorsal vertebrae, four proximal caudal vertebrae (three articulated), left scapula, ribs, plus other yet to be recovered remains.

Briefly, Martinez *et al.* described this material as follows: Cranial dorsal vertebra having forked neural spine, caudal dorsals unforked spines; dorsal centra pleurocoelous; proximalmost caudal vertebrae with winglike transverse processes, high neural spines progressively widening dorsally; distal end of scapula well expanded, width less than twice minimum width of blade. As the authors noted, several of these features permit referral of this specimen to the Diplodocoidea, distinguishing the unnamed taxon as the first non-rebbachisaurid diplodocoid to be documented from the Upper Cretaceous.

Martinez *et al.* recognized two distinct Bajo Barreal faunas — the older (Cenomanian–Turonian) fauna includes a minimum of two sauropod lineages, the Diplodocoidea and the Titanosauria; the younger (?Campanian–Maastrichtian) fauna including the titanosaurian *Aeolosaurus* sp. As the authors pointed out, the bed that yielded the new diplodocoid taxon overlies the older, dinosaur-bearing levels of the Bajo Barreal Formation, yet is older than the ?Campanian–Maastrichtian bed. Consequently, the new diplodocoid can be no younger than of Turonian age.

As Martinez *et al.* noted, discovery "of this ancient sauropod lineage in Upper Cretaceous Patagonian continental assemblages dominated by titanosaurians could shed light on the last surviving diplodocoids," a group that "may have been relicts of a former Pangaean distribution that ended their long and successful history in geographically remote central Patagonia."

Bonde and Christiansen (2003*a*) described in detail a sauropod tooth recently collected from the Early Cretaceous (late Berriasian of "Ryazanian") sediments of the small Baltic island of Bornholm. The tooth was recovered from the same gravel pit at Robbedale that yielded the theropod *Dromaeosauroides bornholmensis* (see *Dromaeosauroides* entry).

The sauropod tooth, as described by Bonde and Christiansen, is represented by a worn and eroded crown that is, as are other sauropod teeth, elongate, slender, and rather subrectangular in cross section. As preserved, the total height of the crown is 14.5 millimeters.

As Bonde and Christiansen observed, the tooth resembles the slender, apomorphic teeth of derived sauropods (*e.g.*, diplodocoids and titanosaurians). However, the authors excluded the present tooth from the Diplodocoidea as, unlike the condition in diplodocoids, it seems to have possessed a serrated carina. More likely, Bonde and Christiansen noted, the affinities of this tooth lie with the Titanosauria, plesiomorphic titanosaurs having serrated carinae, this assessment also being in accord with the specimen's Early Cretaceous age. Furthermore, tooth-to-tooth contact in titanosaurs usually resulted in terminal wear facets, just such a facet being apparently present in the Bornholm tooth. Accepting that this tooth belongs to the Sauropoda, Bonde and Christiansen provisionally assigned it to the Titanosauriformes.

Pereda Suberbiola, Bardet, Iarochène, Bouya and

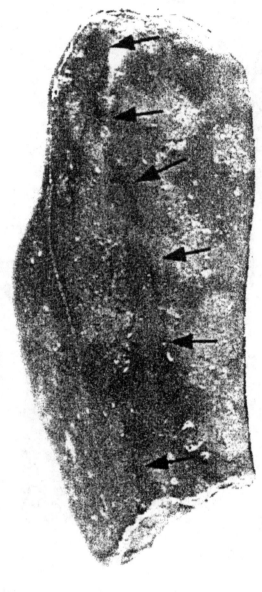

?Titanosauriform sauropod (labial view) tooth from the island of Bornholm. Scale = 5 mm. (After Bonde and Christiansen 2003.)

Amaghzaz (2004) announced the first sauropod record from the Late Cretaceous phosphates of central Morocco. The specimen (OCP DEK/GE 31), still partly in the matrix at the date of publication, consists of the partial right hindlimb comprising the femur (approximately one meter in length), tibia, and fibula representing a relatively small sauropod. Recently collected from the late Maastrichtian phosphatic deposits near Khouribga, this discovery is the result of active collaboration between the Office Chérifien des Phosphates and the Centre National de la Recherche Scientifique et Technologique in the Oulad Abdoun Basin. As the specimen was found associated with a basically marine fauna (mostly selachian, actinopterygian fishes, turtles, plesiosaurs, and mosasaurs), the authors deduced that the sauropod specimen may constitute a remnant of a floating carcass.

Introduction

Indeterminate titanosauriform partial hindlimb (OCP DEK/GE 31) comprising A. femur (caudal view), B. tibia (caudal view), and C. fibula (medial view). Scale = 100 mm. (Pereda Suberbiola, Bardet, Iarochène, Bouya and Amaghzaz 2004.)

(A) (B) (C)

In describing this material, Pereda Suberbiola *et al.* noted that the proximal third of the femur displays a prominent lateral bulge, a feature diagnostic of the Titanosauriformes (*e.g.*, see McIntosh 1990). Moreover, the femur lacks synapomorphies of the Titanosauria and other more inclusive groups (*i.e.*, distal end of tibia expanded transversely to twice breadth of midshaft [Wilson 2002*a*]; distal condyles of femur angled dorsomedially relative to shaft [*e.g.*, Wilson and Carrano 1999; Wilson). Consequently, Pereda Suberbiola could identify this sauropod only as an indeterminate basal member of Titanosauriformes.

As Pereda Suberbiola *et al.* pointed out, discovery of this sauropod is significant in being one of the few dinosaurs recorded from the uppermost Cretaceous formations of northern Africa, in confirming the wide geographical distribution of the Titanosauri-

formes in Late Cretaceous times, and in supporting the survival of this clade into the late Maastrichtian of Africa. While the latter was not unexpected, the authors found the present discovery significant because nontitanosaur titanosauriforms are not well known, occurring preferentially in the Lower Cretaceous formations. Pereda Suberbiola also found it interesting that "the Moroccan specimen, one of the youngest sauropod records worldwide, demonstrates the survival of Titanosauriformes into the Late Maastrichtian of northern Africa."

In an abstract for a poster, Rose (2004) reported on an as yet unnamed, primitive titanosauriform from the Lower Cretaceous Twin Mountains Formation of central Texas, this sample representing "one of the richest accumulations of sauropod bones in North America of its age," and occurring near sauropod trackways dating to approximately 112 million years ago.

Rose briefly described this sauropod noting the following autapomorphic characters: Neural arches of proximal and middle caudal vertebrae having prominent spinoprezygapophyseal and spinopostzygapophyseal laminae restricted to proximal and distal aspects of neural arch, respectively, not extending onto lateral surface of neural spine; proximal and middle caudal neural arches having intraprezygapophyseal lamina forming, with spinoprezygapophyseal and spinopostzygapophyseal laminae, prespinal fossa above neural canal; proximal and middle caudal transverse processes relatively long, dorsoventrally compressed, broad proximodistally; accessory neural arch lamination on cranial dorsal vertebrae; ischial distal shafts meeting, forming broad angle in cross section intermediate between primitive (acute angle) and derived (coplanar) conditions; plesiomorphic character retained in lack of prespinal and postspinal laminae on proximal caudal neural spines.

Performing a cladistic analysis, Rose found this new sauropod as positioned "firmly within Titanosauriformes and either as a sister taxon to Somphospondyli or *Brachiosaurus*." Although this taxon does not share the derived characters that diagnose Somphospondyli, it does display characters (*e.g.*, proximodistally compressed shaft of femur, crescent-shaped sternal plates, iliac preacetabular process perpendicular to body of axis) used to diagnose the more derived clade Titanosauria, these interpreted by Rose "as independently derived conditions."

What seems to be a German "dwarf" among sauropod giants was described briefly in an abstract by Mateus, Laven and Knotschke (2004). Remains of several Late Jurassic (middle Kimmeridgian) sauropods — including the first sauropod skull known from Europe — were discovered in a quarry at Oker, near

Goslar, in Lower Saxony, Germany. As documented by Mateus *et al.*, the first sauropod bone from this quarry was found in 1998 by Holger Ludkte. Since that original discovery, the quarry has yielded fossil material representing at least 10 sauropod individuals.

According to Mateus *et al.*, the skull and other sauropod material collected at Oker belong to a new macronarian genus closely related to brachiosaurids. Unlike typical members of this clade, however, these sauropods are comparatively small, with body lengths (extrapolated from *Camarasaurus grandis*) estimated as varying between 1.8 and 6.2 meters approximately six to 22 feet), one of the smallest individuals having a tibia measuring only 119 millimeters in length.

Mateus *et al.* briefly described this as yet unnamed taxon as follows: Skull having premaxilla with short muzzle; nares large; jugal having important role in lower rim of skull. Histological studies by Mateus *et al.* revealed adult development of the bones despite their comparatively small size, the authors' conclusion having been deduced by sampling seven long bones.

Over 650 well-preserved cranial and postcranial bones belonging to this single species of sauropod have, to date, been recovered from this site, implying gregarious behavior to Mateus *et al.*, this species possibly having lived in herds. Moreover, the assumption that the death and body accumulation represented at this site resulted from one event isolated in time proposed "that sauropods formed multi-aged gregarious groups."

In another abstract, Sander, Laven, Mateus and Knotschke (2004) noted that this new sauropod—possibly representing an island dwarf—may have reached maturity in from only two to three years. Possibly, the authors suggested, such dwarfing among dinosaurs "evolved by reduction of growth rate and shortening of ontogeny" (see also *Zalmoxes* entry).

Coulson, Barrick, Straight, Decherd and Bird (2004) briefly reported, in an abstract, upon multiple elements belonging to an unnamed brachiosaurid titanosauriform discovered in the Price River II Quarry, close to the top of the Ruby Ranch Member of the Cedar Mountain Formation, southeast of Wellington, Utah. The quarry, which opened in 1997, has thus far yielded disarticulated elements belonging to at least seven individuals and representing an allometric range of from young adults to mature adults. To date of the authors' report, specimens already prepared include a dozen teeth, vertebrae (two cervicals, 14 dorsals, and 36 caudals), multiple partial ribs, two partial sacra, and multiple pieces of limb and girdle elements (except sternals). Although morphological comparison of these elements suggested to Coulson *et al.* a single taxon, the nondiagnostic nature of some sauropod bones make possible the presence of other taxa.

As Coulson *et al.* observed, brachiosaurid affinities of this new sauropod are based upon the following traits: Metacarpals long, straight; distal shaft of ilium oriented 80 degrees down from horizontal; metatarsal I with laterodistal process. Despite these features, however, the new taxon differs in some ways from other known brachiosaurids (*e.g.*, lacking pubic apron found in *Brachiosaurus*; caudal vertebrae distinct from those of *Pleurocoelous*, *Cedarosaurus*, *Sonorosaurus*, and *Venenosaurus*).

Coulson *et al.* identified three autapmorphies potentially distinguishing this taxon as a new species—*i.e.*, coracoid foramen open to border of scapulocoracoid, even in mature individuals; prespinodiapophyseal lamina parallel to spinodiapophyseal lamina in cranial to middorsal vertebrae; postspinal lamina on neural spines of midcervical. As the authors pointed out, the first two of these traits are currently unknown in other sauropods and the latter only in the recently described taxon *Isisaurus colberti* (see *Isisaurus* entry).

A brachiosaurid specimen (previously figured by Martill and Naish 2001) belonging to what could represent the largest dinosaur yet found in Europe was described by Naish, Martill, Cooper and Stevens (2004). The specimen (MIWG.7306) consists of a partial cervical vertebra (possibly the sixth) collected by Gavin Leng in 1992 from the Lower Cretaceous

MIWG.7306, partial cervical vertebra in A. right lateral view, B. right prezygapophysis in dorsal view. This specimen, recently described by Darren Naish, David M. Martill, David Cooper, and Kent A. Stevens, may represent the largest known European dinosaur. Scale = 100 millimeters. (After Naish, Martill, Cooper and Stevens 2004.)

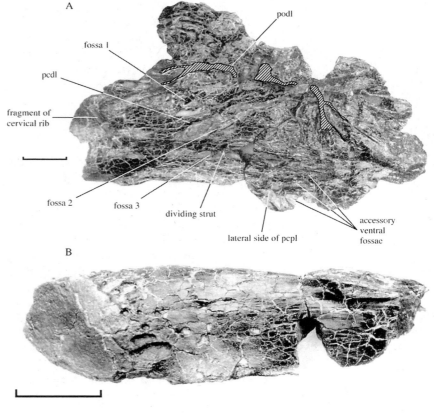

(Barremian) Wessex Formation on the foreshore between Chilton Chine and Sudmoor Point, on the Isle of Wight in southern England. Obliquely crushed, the specimen is relatively complete, missing most of its cranial condyle, the left prezygapophysis, right diapophysis, most laminae associated with the neural arch, and most left caudal centroparapophyseal lamina. Possibly a fragment of neural spine has also been preserved, although this element cannot be attached to the specimen.

As measured by Naish *et al.*, the specimen is 745 millimeters in length, suggesting an animal with a total length of more than 20 meters (almost 70 feet). According to these authors, the specimen is close in size to the cervical vertebrae of the Late Jurassic Tanzanian species *Brachiosaurus brancai*. As Naish *et al.* observed, MIWG.7306 shares various salient morphological characters—*e.g.*, extensive lateral fossae; well-developed caudal centroparapophyseal lamina—with the Early to Middle Cretaceous North American species *Sauroposeiden proteles*, indicating that this sauropod belongs to a *Brachiosaurus-Sauroposeiden* clade. Moreover, in some characters—*e.g.*, caudal centroparapophyseal lamina beginning ventral to caudal half of centrum (beginning in relatively caudoventral position in *S. proteles*)—the Isle of Wight brachiosaurid may be intermediate between *Brachiosaurus* and *Sauroposeiden*. As various characters (*e.g.*, elongate cervical centra and ribs; prezygapophyses extensively overhanging condyle; transition point in neural spine height of midcervical vertebrae (see Wedel, Cifelli and Sanders 2000*a*, 2000*b*) shared by *B. brancai* and *S. proteles* are not observed in other members of Titanosauriformes "traditionally regarded as brachiosaurids" (*e.g.*, *Cedarosaurus*, *Eucamerotus*, *Ornithopsis*, *Pelorosaurus*, and *Sonorasaurus*; see "Systematics" chapter), Naish *et al.* recognized a monophyletic Brachiosauridae for *Brachiosaurus* (*B. altithorax* and *B. brancai*) and *Sauroposeiden*.

Due "to the complexities of Isle of Wight sauropod taxonomy," Naish *et al.* could not attribute MIWG.7306 (currently on exhibit at the Dinosaur Isle Visitor Centre, Sandown, Isle of Wight) to any single taxon.

What appears to be one of the oldest members of the Titanosauria yet discovered was described by O'Leary, Roberts, Head, Sissoko and Bouare (2004). As reported by these authors, remains of this indeterminate titanosaurian genus and species were collected by a joint expedition of the Centre Nationale de la Recherche Scientifique et Technologique, Bamako, and Stony Brook University in 1999, from pre–Cenomanian "Continental Intercalaire" sediments on the northern side of the Adrar des Iforas Mountains in northeastern Mali. Recovered remains of this dinosaur include three very much abraded caudal vertebrae (CNRST-SUNY-197, proximal; CNRST-SUNY-196, middle; and CNRST-SUNY-195, distal).

O'Leary *et al.* described these vertebrae as being gently procoelous, thereby validating their referral to the Titanosauria, a clade that survived into and became abundant during the Late Cretaceous (see Wilson, Martinez and Alcober 1999). Furthermore, O'Leary *et al.* stressed, the early diversification of the Titanosauria remains poorly understood. Moreover, with the added knowledge gleaned from such fragmentary material as the specimens from Mali, "it becomes increasingly clear that we do not understand this clade well enough yet to use these taxa as index fossils for the Late Cretaceous" (see also Sullivan and Lucas 2000).

Lacovara, Harris, Lamanna, Novas, Martinez and Ambrosio (2004), in an abstract, reported the discovery of an enormous titanosaurian sauropod represented by a femur (MPM-PV-39) collected from the (Upper Cretaceous, Maastrichtian, based on microfaunal assemblages) Pari Aike Formation of westcentral Santa Cruz Province, in southernmost Patagonia.

As briefly described by Lacovara *et al.*, this femur is exceptionally robust and measures 2.22 meters in length. Based upon the minimum shaft circumference (990 millimeters) of this specimen, the authors estimated the total mass of this dinosaur to have totaled approximately 58 metric tons (about 60.5 tons). The head of the femur "is 'squared' and sharply angled dorsomedially, reminiscent of other titanosaurians," this derived feature indicating that the dinosaur had "a 'wide-guage' stance." Moreover, Lacovara *et al.* noted, the proximolateral margin of this femur shows a lateral bulge, a titanosauriforme diagnostic character.

The discovery of MPM-PV-39 documents the survival of enormous dinosaurs until the end of the Cretaceous, Lacovara *et al.* stated, enervating "arguments for a general reduction in the size of the largest sauropods through the Late Cretaceous"; moreover, the occurrence of this dinosaur "is consistent with paleogeographic reconstructions of southern Patagonia as an areally restricted landmass isolated from other regions by epeiric seas."

Apesteguía and Gallina (2004), in an abstract, briefly described a new and as yet unnamed "nonsaltasaurine titanosaur," known from a lower jaw with slender, chisel-like teeth, one cervical vertebra, six dorsal vertebrae, eight articulated midcaudal vertebrae, a humerus, femur, tibia, and some metatarsals (Museo de la Plata collection), recovered from 'Rancho de Avila' (Río Negro), in the upper levels of the Bajo de la Carpa Formation, at the boundary with

Anacleto, Argentina. The authors observed the following about the new titanosaur: More robust than *Laplatasaurus* and *Antarctosaurus* (titanosaurs from close stratigraphical levels); characterized by long, well-developed prezygodiapophyseal laminae, absence of prezygoparapophyseal laminae in dorsal vertebrae; differing from other known titanosaurs in possession of cranial dorsal neural spines with remarkably robust diagonal bases, bulging spine summits. Lack of a ventral keel in the caudal vertebrae preclude assignment of this new taxon to the Saltisaurinae, Apesteguía and Gallina noted.

The earliest known North American "titanosaurid" (see Britt, Stadtman, Scheetz and McIntosh 1998) — an unnamed form from the Dalton Wells Dinosaur Quarry in the Cedar Mountain Formation (?Barremian–Aptian) of Utah (see Britt *et al.*; also Britt, Scheetz, McIntosh and Stadtman 1998), a taxon excluded from Wedel's (2003*b*) phylogenetic analysis — is unusual in that its vertebrae are camerate and seemingly lack camellae, this fully camerate condition being thus far unique among described "titanosaurids."

Trotta, Campos and Kellner (2002) described an incomplete series of eight titanosaur caudal vertebrae (DGM 497-R) collected in 1957 at the "Mombuca" site in the continental Upper Cretaceous Baurú Group, Peirópolis, Minas Gerais state, Baurú Basin, Brazil.

These vertebrae, the authors noted, decrease in gradually size distally and, therefore, pertain to the distal part of the tail. Moreover, their centra present some unusual morphologies. The first vertebra is amphicoelous, the second biconvex, and the remaining vertebrae are procoelous. Thus far unique for all members of the "Titanosauridae" (see "Systematics" chapter) described to date, this combination of vertebral types "demonstrates that those conditions can be preserved in a single individual and therefore not necessarily represent distinct species." Because of lack of sufficient materials, Trott *et al.* could not state whether or not this combination of caudal vertebrae with different centra was a common feature of "titanosaurid" tails, especially in the distal region. Furthermore, the incompleteness of the newly described material precluded the authors' assignment of these vertebrae to a genus or species.

Trotta *et al.* further commented that these vertebrae are extremely light, indicating poor mineralization, this kind of preservation being very rare, and recorded for the first time from Baurú deposits. Furthermore, this preservation exhibits the great taphonomic diversity of fossils from the continental Cretaceous layers of the Baurú group.

Kellner, Azevedo, Carvalho, Henriques, Costa

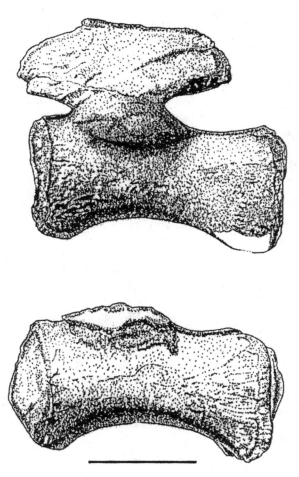

DGM 497-R, preserved titanosaur vertebrae numbers one and two from the Upper Cretaceous Bauru Group, Peirópolis, Brazil. The first vertebra is amphicoelous, the second is biconvex, and the remaining vertebrae (not figured) are procoelous, a condition unique among known "titanosaurids" (see "Systematics" chapter). Scale = 50 mm. (After Trotta, Campos and Kellner 2002.)

and Campos (2004), in an abstract, reported the recent discovery of sauropod bones in a new quarry near the Confusao creek at Mato Grosso, Brazil, the outcrop having been formed by conglomerates and sandstones correlated with lithographic units of the Upper Cretaceous (Santonian–Maastrichtian) Baurú Group. Two distinct fossiliferous layers were found at this site, the stratigraphically higher layer comprising mostly sandstones yielding several fragmentary bones and teeth, the second and approximately 50 centimeters deeper section comprising essentially conglomerates yielding the majority of specimens. To date of the abstract, approximately 100 bones, and also 40 sauropod and theropod teeth, had been recovered from the quarry.

As Kellner *et al.* reported, the recovered sauropod remains include a sequence of dorsal and caudal vertebrae found associated with some (as yet unprepared) long bones. Briefly, the authors described some of the collected sauropod material as follows: Some proximal caudal vertebrae unfused, showing low, anteroposteriorly elongated neural spines; caudals procoelic (as in Titanosauria); caudal centrum dorsoventrally depressed (not showing "heart-shaped" condition seen in *"Gondwanatitan* [=*Aeolosaurus*]); neural spine reduced in size, this combined with marked lateral depression proximal to postzygapophyses on basal portion of spine and its particular anteroposterior elongation differing from all other known sauropod caudals from Brazil; dorsal vertebrae showing large, well-developed lateral prominence (diagnostic of Titanosauriformes); small yet marked lateral concavity (unknown in other sauropods) above lateral prominence.

Although the work being done on this material is still in its early stages, Kellner *et al.* predicted that "the anatomical features of the titanosaurid sauropod collected at this site suggest that they belong to new taxa."

Calvo and Grill (2004), in an abstract, briefly reported on "titanosaurid" teeth recently collected from the Futalognko quarry — a stite that has yielded "an extraordinary associated fauna and flora," including remains of sauropod, theropod (see *Megaraptor* entry), and ornithopod dinosaurs, turtles, crocodiles, pterosaurs, and fishes — in the Late Cretaceous (upper Turonian–lower Coniacian) Portezuelo Formation on the north coast of Barreales Lake, in Neuquén Province, Patagonia, Argentina. To date of their writing, 11 sauropod teeth had been collected, which were described by the authors as follows: Crowns of larger teeth 10 millimeters labiolingually, 11 millimeters mesiocaudally, medium-sized teeth six to seven millimeters labiolingually, eight to nine millimeters labiolingually; apical portion convex, worn surface inclined 80 degrees with that of horizontal on concave side (typical of "Titanosauridae"); worn surface oval, main axis directed 55 degrees relative to tooth row; small, elongated lateral worn surface; crowns flattened at tip labiolingually, forming sharp corner on contact between lingual and labial sides; smaller teeth more flattened labiolingually; oval worn surface with axis at right angle to tooth row; two thin lateral worn surfaces showing side by side contact between upper and lower teeth.

Based on their size and morphology, Calvo and Grill suggested that these teeth represent at least two different "titanosaurid" individuals.

Following a succession of brief reports on the "titanosaurid" eggs and nests found at the Auca Mahuevo site in the Upper Cretaceous Anacleto Formation of Patagonia (see *S2*, *S3*; for additional details on these discoveries, see also the book *Walking on Eggshells: The Astonishing Discovery of Dinosaur Eggs in the Badlands of Patagonia*, by Luis M. Chiappe and Lowell Dingus, published in 2000), Chiappe, Schmitt, Jackson, Garrido, Dingus and Grellet-Tinner published a detailed paper on the structure of these nests. Six egg-filled depressions at this locality were interpreted by Chiappe *et al.* as dinosaur nests, these offering the first and only known evidence of "titanosaurid" nest construction.

Chiappe *et al.* described these depressions as sub-circular to sub-elliptical to kidney-shaped, consisting of "well-cemented, medium- to fine-grained, pinkish-gray sandstone." Each depression truncates primary stratification of the host substrate and is encircled by a massive sandstone rim. The depressions range in size from about 100 to 140 centimeters across their greatest planview axes and in depth from about 10 to 18 centimeters. Eggs of varying condition had been distributed randomly in the nests. As Chiappe *et al.* noted, the eggs found in these depressions are consistent in size, shape, ornamentation, and shell microstructure to eggs from the same locality preserving "titanosaurid" embryos (see Chiappe, Salgado and Coria 2001). Analysis of these nests indicated to Chiappe *et al.* (2004) that the "titanosaurid" adults did not bury their eggs within sediment; rather, these animals excavated open nests into which they deposited their eggs.

Additionally, Chiappe *et al.* (2004) proposed the following criteria, in the order of decreasing importance, for the reliable recognition of nesting trace fossils excavated by an adult dinosaur: Presence of depression that truncates stratification within host substrate; within that depression, complete or significant portions of eggs or articulated juvenile skeletons showing no evidence of transport; evidence of elevated ridge of massive sediment surrounding perimeter of depression containing eggs lithologically distinct (*i.e.*, grain size, shape, sorting, fabric, sedimentary structures) from laterally adjacent and overlying sediment; and sediment fill within depression differing from host substrate in grain shape, size, sorting, fabric, sedimentary structures, or mineralogic and chemical composition.

In a subsequent paper, Salgado, Coria and Chiappe (2005) published an osteology of the Auca Mahuevo titanosaurian embryos, describing in detail the following specimens: MCF-PVPH-263 (almost complete skull, narial region partially damaged; MCF-PVPH-272 — almost complete, partially deformed skull, broken in supraorbital and rostral areas; MCF-PVPH-250 — premaxillae, maxillae, articulated nasals, two series of sclerotic rings (each belonging to different orbit, one comprising at least five plates, the other at least three), incomplete frontal, complete right parietal, postorbital, ?squamosal, incomplete mandible, ?dentary, more than 30 variably preserved, scattered teeth, numerous unidentified appendicular bones; MCP-PVPH-113a — partial nasal, ?prefrontal, lacrimal, frontals fused after death by diagenetic processes, unidentified long bones; MCP-PVPH-113b — ?left premaxilla and maxilla, partial left jugal, ?squamosal articulated to ?left quadrate, possible fragments of right squamosal and quadrate, possibly parts of

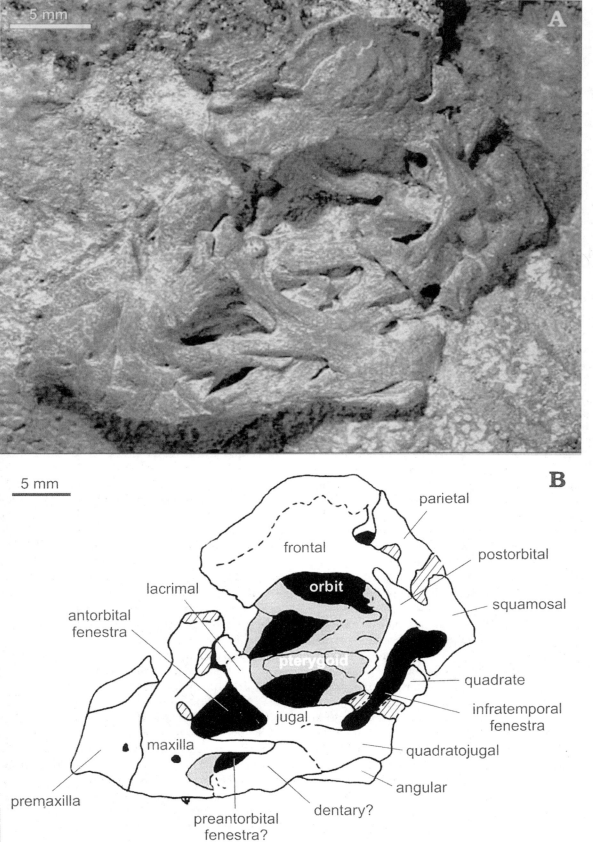

MCF-PVPH-263, indeterminate titanosaurian embryo, A. photograph and B. interpretive drawing (left lateral view). (After Salgado, Coria and Chiappe, 2005.)

parietal and postorbital; MCF-PVPH-264 — maxillae (left maxilla articulated to corresponding premaxilla), frontals, partial parietal, jugals, articular, unidentified bones; MCF-PVPH-262 — right premaxilla, fragmentary maxillae (one with at least four teeth implanted), nasals, frontal, ?postorbital, right jugal, squamosal, unidentified bones; and MCF-PVPH-147 — somewhat deformed complete skull.

As noted by Salgado *et al.*, the morphology of the premaxillae, maxillae, nasals, parietals, postorbitals, and jugals represented in more than one of these specimens is essentially constant, with minor differences among these elements attributed to differing degrees of preservation. The cranial morphologies of MCF-PVPH-147, 263, and 272 are basically identical, "having the same proportions and similarly oriented fenestrae delimited by the same elements," and probably represent a single sauropod species. Moreover, Salgado *et al.* noted, all of the studied embryos offer the same degree of ontogenetic development.

In describing these embryos, Salgado *et al.* observed a mosaic of juvenile features and adult features (the latter synapomorphic for groups of varying degrees of inclusiveness), these characters ordered as follows (see, for example, Salgado and Calvo 1997; Upchurch 1999; Wilson and Sereno 1998; Wilson 2002*a*): Juvenile characters — parietal fenestra; relatively large orbit; incomplete ossification of periosteum; character absent in adult Sauropodomorpha — jugal participation in rim of antorbital fenestra; synapomorpies of Eusauropoda — jugal process of postorbital much longer than rostrocaudal extent of its dorsal end; snout having stepped rostral margin; absence of squamosal-quadratojugal contact; rostral ramus of quadratojugal elongate, distally expanded; absence of antorbital fossa; characters absent in adult Eusauropoda (plesiomorphic for this clade) — extensive participation of frontal in orbital rim; nonretracted external nares; absence of external narial fossa; subcircular orbital margin; quadratojugal not contacting maxilla; synapomorphies of Neosauropoda — absence of tooth crown denticles; preantorbital fenestra; ventral process of postorbital broader mediolaterally than rostrocaudally; long axis of supratemporal fenestra oriented transversely; character absent in adult Neosauropoda (plesiomorphic for this clade) — mandible having short articular glenoid; synapomorphies of Titanosauria — skull proportionally wide caudally; mandible low; characters absent in adult Titanosauria (plesiomorphic for this clade) — well-developed supratemporal fenestra; tooth row caudally surpassing rostral margin of antorbital fenestra.

Comparisons by Salgado *et al.* between the Auca Mahuevo embryonic skulls and the best-preserved adult sauropod skulls showing titanosaurian similarities (*e.g.*, *Nemegtosauru*, *Rapetosaurus*) revealed dramatic transformations that occurred during early ontogeny, the most significant of these centering upon the infraorbital and narial regions: Frontals and parietals greatly reduced in relative size, migrating dorsally to caudodorsal region of orbit; orbit becoming constricted ventrally, adopting tear-shaped contour; rostrum becoming substantially enlarged, most likely resulting from maxillary expansion; maxilla expanding caudally, establishing connection with quadratojugal, maxilla thereby excluding jugal from ventral margin of skull, perhaps enclosing preantorbital; external naris probably expanding in size, migrating caudodorsally to position dorsal to orbits. However, as in other sauropods, the temporal cranial region underwent less profound changes.

From this study, Salgado *et al.* deduced "that the skull changes taking place during the early ontogeny of titanosaurians do not exactly reflect the transformations that seem to have occurred during the evolution of the clade." Moreover, the mosaic of characters observed by the authors in these embryos is otherwise unknown in adult eusauropods, this difference probably resulting from different developmental rates for different areas of the skull.

In conclusion, Salgado *et al.* postulated that the exclusion of the jugal from the ventral margin of the skull constitutes a two-fold transformation — the first step of this change most likely involving expansion of the maxilla and premaxilla, the second shown by subsequent expansion of the caudal process of the maxilla enclosing and sometimes obliterating the preantorbital fenestra in adults. As the authors suggested, this transformation probably occurred during early ontogeny. Not evident when taking into conderation a series of successive adult-sauropodomorph sister taxa (*e.g.*, *Plateosaurus*, *Shunosaurus*, *Omeisaurus*, *Camarasaurus*), these changes may have occurred in a neosauropod ancestor, as "a rudimentary, almost obliterated preantorbital fenestra became characteristic of the adult neosauropod skull" (see Wilson 1001*a*).

Preserved trackways made by sauropod dinosaurs are fairly common in the fossil record (*e.g.*, see Farlow 1994; see also *S3*, "Appendix"). Such trackways have been broadly classified either as "wide guage" — *i.e.*, hind foot impressions relatively far from the midline of the trackway — or "narrow guage" — *i.e.*, footprints near or overlapping the trackway's midline. As pointed out by Wilson and Carrano (1999), narrow-guage sauropod trackways are have mostly been found in Jurassic rocks; wide guage trackways were most common during the Cretaceous; however, roughly similar abundances of both types of trackways are known from the Middle Jurassic through the earliest Cretaceous.

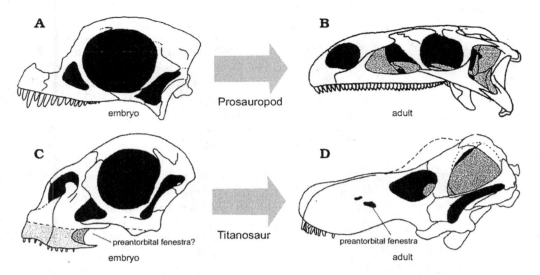

A

embryo

Prosauropod

adult

B

C

preantorbital fenestra?

embryo

Titanosaur

preantorbital fenestra

adult

D

Ontogenetic evolution of the sauropodomorph skull, the prosauropod skull based on A. the embryo of *Mussaurus* and B. the adult *Plateosaurus*, the titanosaurian skulls based on C. embryonic specimens from Auca Mahuevo and D. the adult *Nemegtosaurus*. The drawing depicts the ventral expansion of the premaxilla and maxilla of the titanosaurian embryo (shaded area), then enclosing the preantorbital fenestra in the adult. (After Salgado, Coria and Chiappe 2005.)

Farlow had suggested that the narrow-guage trackways were made by sauropods with medially inclined limbs, while the wide-guage types were made by sauropods having vertically held limbs. A detailed analysis by Wilson and Carrano of titanosaur hind limbs and pelvic girdles strongly suggested that these Cretaceous forms were osteologically capable of making the wide-guage type of trackway. However, as noted by Henderson (2003*a*), in an abstract relating sauropod body shapes to these different kinds of trackways, a biomechanical/functional explanation for these two trackway guages has remained elusive (see Farlow).

Henderson (2003*a*) postulated "that the narrow- and wide-guage trackways attributed to sauropod dinosaurs are a consequence of the relative position of the centres of mass (CM) of different body forms. Henderson (2003*a*) utilized three-dimensional, trackway-producing computer models to test this hypothesis, moving modeled limbs and bodies "under the control of systems of coupled differential equations," with possible gaits "subject to a CM-based stability constraint at all stages of a simulated cycle step."

Two computer models were generated by Henderson (2003*a*)—one of the brachiosaurid *Brachiosaurus brancai*, the other of the diplodocid *Diplodocus carnegii*. The *Brachiosaurus* model, with a center of mass calculated as being about midway between the hips and shoulders, was stable, possessing a wide margin when a wide-guage trackway was replicated; the *Diplodocus* model, having its CM located just cranial to the hips, was most stable when a narrow-guage trackway was replicated. However, when forced to use gaits producing opposite-guage trackways, "both models experienced tipping at various points during their step cycles, in addition to other problems."

(In a related study published as an abstract, Henderson 2003*b*, again using computer models compared with trackways, studied the biomechanics of bipedalism in both theropod [*Coelophysis bauri*, *Allosaurus fragilis*, and *Tyrannosaurus rex*] and ornithopod [*Hypsilophodon foxii*, *Iguanodon bernissartensis*, and *Edmontosaurus regalis*] dinosaurs. As that author noted, combining trackways with knowing the exact hip-height value of a given trackmaking model offers "a means to test predictions of hip heights made for dinosaurs based solely on observed trackways and different formulae"; see abstract for more details.)

Identifying a trend in larger sauropods to have more cranially positioned centers of mass, Henderson (2003*a*) proposed that such gigantic forms as *Brachiosaurus*, regardless of clade, were restricted to producing narrow-guage trackways, while less massive forms such as *Diplodocus* were the narrow-guage trackmakers.

In another abstract, Henderson (2003*c*) investigated the long-standing hypotheses concerning sauropod buoyancy and aquatic habits, topics that have been largely ignored by paleontologists as outmoded in more recent years. As that author related, a general-purpose, three-dimensional mathematical and computational model was produced to examine the buoyancy and stability of both extant and extinct tetrapods immersed in water. This model determined "the downward weight force, the upward buoyant force, and the torques associated with these forces that would act to rotate the body." Beginning with an arbitrary initial orientation and depth in the water, the model was "brought to equilibrium by an iterative process so that all vertical forces and turning moments" were balanced. It incorporated an axial body having variable density, a hollow lung cavity, and all limbs. (Henderson 2003*c* noted that an alligator model can replicate the depth of immersion and body inclinations of a live alligator that had reached stable equilibrium while floating at the surface of the water.)

Introduction

Three-dimensional, computer generated, body and bone model of *Brachiosaurus brancai*, the "plus" sign indicating the position of the body's center of mass. This model, prepared by Donald M. Henderson, proved to be consistent with the wide-guage type of trackway. Scale = 4 m. (After Henderson 2003*a*.)

Photograph by Urs Möckli, copyright © and courtesy Sauriermuseum Aathal.

In using models to analyze *Apatosaurus, Diplodocus, Brachiosaurus,* and *Camarasaurus,* Henderson (2003*c*) found that all four genera, despite their great body masses, could float at the water surface. Buoyancy would have been enhanced, that author noted, by the highly pneumatized skeletons of these giant dinosaurs (see Wedel, 2003*a*, 2003*b*, above). However, Henderson (2003*c*) found irrelevant the problem of sauropods being able to breathe while walking on the bottom of a deep late, stating that "they would have been unable to walk on the bottom in the first place." Also determined by Henderson's (2003*c*) study were the maximum water depths at which floating could commence for each of these sauropod genera, that depth found to be about equal to the tops of the ilia.

Henderson (2003*c*) found that the diplodocids *Apatosaurus* and *Diplodocus* floated with the body tilted upwards, with the hind feet submerged deeper than the forefeet. Contrarily, the macronarians *Brachiosaurus* and *Camarasaurus* floated with their bodies tilted downwards, forefeet deeper than hind feet. Moreover, that author found, while it was apparently "impossible for diplodocids to have produced manus-only trackways while floating, the macronarians could have done so."

Until recently, most of the descriptions of sauropod braincases have been of Late Jurassic forms, and no Cretaceous sauropod braincases from North America had been described. The first braincase pertaining

Skeleton of *Diplodocus* mounted in a bipedal posture. Sauropods, as noted by Donald M. Henderson (2003*a*) in a study on sauropod body shapes and trackways, having descended from bipedal ancestors. This juvenile specimen (including original vertebrae and a skull cast) was collected in 1991 from the Howe Stephens Quarry, at Howe Ranch, in northern Wyoming. Six partial *Diplodocus* skeletons, plus a number of individual bones, were collected at this quarry during the 1990s by the Sauriermuseum Aathal under the direction of paleontologist Hans Jakob "Kirby" Siber.

Life restoration by Todd Marshall of *Iguanodon bernissartensis*. According to a study by Denver Fowler, Keith Simmonds, Mick Green, and Kent A. Stevens (2003), preservation of *Iguanodon* remains is often related to waterlogged reduced sediment formed by flood-fire associations.

to an Early Cretaceous North American sauropod was described in 2003 by Tidwell and Carpenter. As the authors pointed out, sauropod braincases had not received much attention in the past, "in part because they are either hidden by outer skull bones or are heavily damaged." Furthermore, the difficulty of cleaning out the brain cavity has resulted in little information regarding sauropod endocasts.

The specimen (TMM 40435) described for the first time by Tidwell and Carpenter consists of a well-preserved, partial braincase collected from the Early or Middle (upper Aptian or lower Albian; see Winkler, Jacobs, Lee and Murry 1995) Glen Rose Formation of Texas. It was first mentioned, but neither described nor named, by Langston (1974). As observed by Tidwell and Carpenter, the specimen includes the supraoccipital, exoccipital-opisthotic complex (incomplete paroccipital processes), basioccipital, basiosphenoid (minus basioccipital processes), and the prootic.

The specimen is small, measuring just 62 millimeters from caudal edge of occipital condyle to hypospheal fenestra, and 91 millimeters from basitubera to supraoccipital apex. Nevertheless, the firm fusion of the elements, with almost no trace of sutures and the lack of any juvenile characters, suggest that, despite its size, TMM 40435 represents an adult individual no more, as Langston proposed, six meters (slightly more than 20 feet) in overall length.

Diagnostic characters noted by Tidwell and

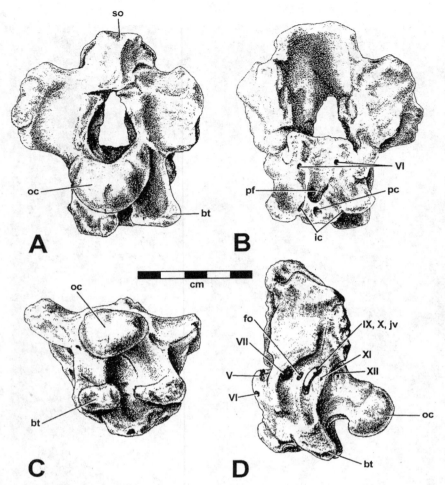

A. **B.**

C. **D.**

TMM 40435, titanosauriform sauropod braincase in A. caudal, B. rostral, C. ventral, and D. lateral views. Scale = 5 cm. (After Tidwell and Carpenter 2003.)

An endocast prepared from by Tidwell and Carpenter from the endocranial cavity of TMM 40435 revealed that, as in other sauropods, the midbrain was the widest part of the brain, the narrowest part being between the optic capsules. Similarities and differences were observed between the endocast made from this specimen and those of *Brachiosaurus, Camarasaurus,* and *Diplodocus* (*e.g.*, exit for trigeminal nerve [V] located just above caudal edge of pituitary fossa, slightly more cranial than in those three genera; small root of facial nerve [VII] caudal to trigeminal, in *Brachiosaurus* relatively larger and very close to trigeminal root; flexure between endocranium floor and pituitary region rounded as in *Camarasaurus*, deeply notched in *Brachiosaurus*; large nub dorsal to trigeminal, possibly representing middle cerebral vein, similar to that in *Brachiosaurus*, apparently not occurring in *Camarasaurus* or *Diplodocus* [see Hopson 1979]; hypoglossal nerve [XII] present, unlike that in *Diplodocus* [see Hopson]).

Ornithischians

Fricke (2003), in a study published as an abstract, based upon teeth of ornithischians —*i.e.*, "bird-hipped," herbivorous — dinosaurs, reported on his use of carbon isotope ratios of tooth enamel and associated sedimentary organic matter to ellucidate the nature of dinosaurian ecology and behavior. Especially, that author noted, this approach could be used in investigating such topics as "(1) dinosaur diet, (2) environmental differences between regions, (3) photosynthetic pathways of ingested plants, and (4) ecological niche partioning among herbivorous dinosaurs."

This study incorporated data from the Upper Cretaceous Judith River Formation of Montana with additional information including that gleaned from the paleontological literature, global-scale data pertaining to dinosaur eggshells, data concerning modern plants and associated fossil plants from the Judith River Formation, and also other information sources. Results of Fricke's study indicated that, among the herbivorous dinosaurs studied, at least four kinds were almost exclusively eating aquatic C3 plants or a mixture of those and C4 plants, the latter offering evidence that plants using C4 photosynthetic pathways could have played a significant role in some terrestrial ecosystems. Additionally, at least in the Judith River Formation of Montana, there existed nich partitioning between different kinds of herbivorous taxa living in the same area, the diet of ankylosaurs comprising a mixture of aquatic C3 and C4 plants, that of hadrosaurs consisting of salt-stressed C3 plants. (For a related study, see the abstract by see Steele, Fricke and Rogers 2003, who present carbon isotope evidence

Carpenter in this specimen include the following: Supraoccipital crest prominent, with distinct median ridge extending almost to foramen magnum; basitubera short, ventrally directed, divided by deep groove extending to basipterygoid; single foramen for cranial nerve XII; accessory foramen for cranial nerve XI.

Comparing TMM 40435 with the crania of other sauropods, Tidwell and Carpenter found that the specimen most closely resembles that of *Brachiosaurus*, both taxa sharing various features (*e.g.*, medial crest of supraoccipital prominently displayed, bearing strong sagittal ridge; relatively short, individually divergent, ventrally directed basitubera). These taxa differ, however, in the comparative lengths of their occipital condyles (relatively shorter in *Brachiosaurus*).

While TMM 40435 shares the greatest number of characters with *Brachiosaurus*, Tidwell and Carpenter were not able to place it with confidence phylogenetically, as "key regions of the specimen are missing, and because of the limited amount of sauropod specimens available for comparison." Tidwell and Carpenter concluded that TM 40435 represents a titanosauriform sauropod, similar both to brachiosaurids and titanosaurs.

for ecological niche partitioning among Hadrosauridae and Ankylosauria from Montana's Judith River Formation).

THYREOPHORANS

In their survey review of dinosaur teeth from the Upper Triassic ("Rhaetian") Habay-la-Vielle locality in southern Belgium, Godefroit and Knoll (2003) described various recently collected specimens belonging to primitive ornithischians. One tooth (IRSNB R208), the authors observed, resembles closely teeth described by Thulborn (1973) as the distal premaxillary teeth of the indeterminate thyreophoran armored dinosaurian type species *Alocodon kuehnei* (a taxon Godefroit and Knoll regarded as a *nomen dubium*), its crown leaf-shaped in labial and lingual views, somewhat higher than long, its labial side regularly smooth and convex, lingual side less convex and ornamented, with strong vertical ridges. Another tooth (IRSNB R209) resembles teeth described by Thulborn as caudal cheek teeth of *A. kuehnei*, being much mesio-distally longer than high and somewhat thick labio-lingually. An indeterminate third tooth (IRSNB R210) is triangular in outline, slightly higher than long, and quite narrow, the labial side more convex than the lingual side.

Ankylosaurs

Garner (2004), in an abstract for a poster, reported briefly on the origins of the dorsal skull armor — armor that is thoroughly fused to the cranium — in the thyreophoran clade Ankylosauria (armored dinosaurs). Considering two previous hypotheses for the evolution of this armor (*i.e.*, osteoderms developed first in the skin, then coossified with the skull; skull surfaces was remodeled, forming armor), and also examining histological thin sections of ankylosaurian skulls and various osteoderms of ankylosaurs and extant reptiles, revealed to Garner the following: Ankylosaurian skull armor is not the result of coossification of osteoderms, but, instead, mostly remodeled bone. However, a small number of ankylosaurs (*e.g.*, *Minmi*) show small, thin sheets of osteoderms that are attached to the surface of the skull. Consequently, "both methods appear to have been utilized, although remodeled bone surface dominates."

In an abstract, Attila (2002) reported on two partial skeletons belonging to the ankylosaurian family Nodosauridae, found in the Upper Cretaceous (Santonian, based upon palynological data) Csehbánya Formation, in the Bakony Mountains of Western Hungary. The first specimen comprises a cervical vertebra, cervical rib, six dorsal ribs, and five dermal plates; the second, more complete and disarticulated, comprising skull elements, vertebrae (two cervicals, four dorsals, and three caudals), several cervical and dorsal ribs, a right scapula, the preacetabular part of a left ilium, a left ischium, ?left fibula with four metatarsals, three chevrons, and more than 100 dermal plates and spikes. Regarding the second specimen, skull elements include a premaxilla, ?prevomer, right postorbital and jugal, right quadrate, a pterygoid, occipital condyle, and nine isolated teeth.

Attila briefly described this material as follows: Caudal portion of the premaxilla bearing teeth; quadrate wide mediolaterally, quadrate condyle rhomboidal, more robust than in *Struthiosaurus*; suture between quadrate and quadratojugal not visible (as opposed to the condition in *Struthiosaurus*); pterygoid having interpterygoid vacuity, as in *Pawpawsaurus campbelli*; jugal and postorbital with dermal plates, jugal wider dorsoventrally than in *Struthiosaurus transylvanicus*; centra of cervical vertebrae more wide than long; caudal cervical vertebrae strongly opisthocoelous, cranial face higher than caudal face; neural arches of dorsal vertebrae not so high and without deep cavity towards centrum as in *S. transylvanicus*; caudal vertebrae similar to those in *Struthiosaurus*; dorsal ribs T-shaped in cross section; pseudoacromial process more caudal on scapula than in *Struthiosaurus*; preacetabular portion of left ilium developed similar to that of *S. austriacus*; body of left ilium long, laterally compressed, slightly curved, cranially concave, distinct flexion of trachia (characteristic of Nodosauridae) not visible; fibula straight in side and cranial views; four metatarsals; distal and proximal ends of metatarsals strongly divergent.

Based upon the condition and measurements of the elements, Attila deduced that the second specimen represents a mature individual ranging in length from about three to four meters (more than 10 to almost 14 feet). Furthermore, features of the skull, the wider than long cervical vertebrae, and strongly opisthocoelous caudal cervical vertebra suggested to Atilla that these remains represent a new nodosaurid taxon more primitive than *Struthiosaurus*.

The first major comparative survey of the complex histology of ankylosaurian postcranial dermal-armor osteoderms was published by Scheyer and Sander (2004), this study including material pertaining to the ankylosaurian *Polacanthus foxii*, the ankylosaurids *Gastonia* sp., *Saichania chulsanensis*, *Pinacosaurus grangeri*, an indeterminate ankylosaurid, the possible nodosaurid *Struthiosaurus austriacus*, and an indeterminate nodosaurid (these authors regarding *Polacanthus* and *Gastonia* as "polacanthids"; however, see "Systematics" chapter for revisions in ankylosaurian subclades). Samples of outgroups bearing osteoderms (*e.g.*, *Scelidosaurus harrisoni*, phytosaurs, and

Introduction

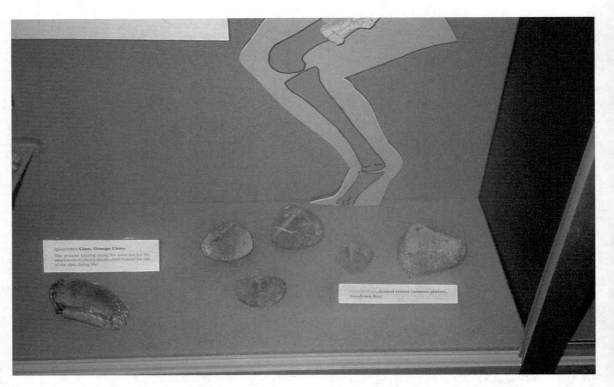

(Right) osteoderms referred to the armored dinosaur *Polacanthus.*

crocodilians as well as literature pertaining to the plates and tail spikes of the stegosaur *Stegosaurus stenops*) were also utilized in this study.

According to Scheyer and Sander, the histology of ankylosaurian osteoderms seems to have phylogenetic value, the sectioned osteoderms falling into one of three distinctive groups: 1. "polacanthid"—diverse shapes including small spiked, ridged, or flat specimens; histology relatively generalized and primitive (somewhat like that in such outgroup taxa as phytosaurs, crocodilians, *Scelidosaurus*, and *Stegosaurus*), with well-developed, thickened, uniformed cortex on all surfaces entirely surrounding trabecular bone; some specimens having woven pattern of ordered collagen fibers on margins and basal surfaces; 2. nodosaurid—osteoderms approximately symmetrical, unique among ankylosaurs in having external cortex, much thicker underlying internal spongiosa forming somewhat flat base; and 3. ankykosaurid—osteoderms diverse in shape, but very thin (sampled specimens being from 0.5 to 1.0 centimeters thick), specimens with ride, keel, or apex having deeply concave base; osteoderms considerably strengthened by incorporation of structural collagen fiber bundles (somewhat like, but not identical, to Sharpey's fibers) into thin cortex and (uniquely) secondary bone tissue.

Scheyer and Sander noted that abundant "structural fibers" also occur in "polacanthids" and nodosaurids, although their arrangement and occurrence are significantly different among the anklosaurian groups (*i.e.*, randomly crossing the well-developed cortex and inner bone trabeculae in "polanthids"; highly ordered in nodosaurids; random in ankylosaurids).

Additionally, the cortex in nodosaurids has two sets of three-dimensional orthogonal fibers rotated to 45 degrees of one another, the combination of much strengthened external cortex covering a thick cushion of cancellous bone having served to resist local breakage and penetration (*e.g.*, by predator teeth). In ankylosaurids, the thin osteoderms contain an inner area of Haversian bone surrounded by a thin cortex, with numerous structural fibers incorporated in a chipboard arrangement of secondary osteons for strengthening the osteoderms. Therefore, Scheyer and Sander concluded, both nodosaurid and ankylosaurid osteoderms were "highly optimized towards a resistant yet light-weight armor."

The first finds of armored dinosaurs from the Upper Cretaceous (early Maastrichtian) Arkharinskii District, Amur Region of Russia were reported by Tumanova, Bolotsky and Alifanov (2004). The material was collected in 1991 by a paleontological team from the Amur Complex Research Institute of the Amur Scientific Center, Far East Division, Russian Academy of Sciences. The fossils were found at the Kundur locality in the Udurchukan (lowermost part of the Tsagayan) Formation, a locality rich in vertebrate fossils (including hadrosaurine and lambeosaurine hadrosaurs, tyrannosaurid and dromaeosaurid theropods, plus crocodilians and chelonians). They include (AEHM 2/1) a jaw ("cheek") tooth having a slightly damaged mesial edge, worn labial crown surface, and broken off root; (AEHM 2/2) incomplete jaw tooth with basal part of crown and root base; (AEHM 2/16) conical osteodermal scute.

In describing these specimens, Tumanova *et al.* noted that it was not yet possible to diagnose the material on a generic level. However, taking into account the structure and large size of the osteoderm (*i.e.*, thick-walled, base with pear-shaped projection, surface texture dense) and teeth (cingulum clearly formed, asymmetrical), the material is more likely referrable to the Nodosauridae than the Ankylosauridae. Interpreted thusly, these remains are significant as the first Asian report of that ankylosaurian family.

ORNITHOPODS

Dinosaur fossils are rare finds in Japan. In a recently published abstract for a poster, Ohashi (2004) reported upon the somewhat disarticulated partial skull of a primitive ornithopod dinosaur recovered from apparently "inter-channel deposits of floodplain origin" of the Lower Cretaceous ("Neocomian" or Hauterivian) Kuwajima Formation, Tetori Group, of Ishikawa Prefecture, Japan.

According to Ohashi, the specimen seems to belong to a single individual, as indicated by the arrangement of the preserved elements, suggesting their original placement, and by the lack of matching elements. The cranium is approximately 40 percent complete, the left half of the skull being the best preserved, the length of the skull measuring approximately 10 centimeters (about 3.8 inches).

Ohashi identified this specimen "as a hypsilophodontian-grade ornithopod" by such characters as the following: Crescentic paroccipital process and cingulum at base of maxillary and dentary tooth crowns; dentary with laterally projecting ridge extending along long axis (corresponding ridge absent from maxilla); dentary teeth having deep, concave occlusal wear facets; maxillary teeth with occlusal wear, wear surface approximately half width observed in dentary teeth.

According to Ohashi, the above mentioned differences between the maxilla and dentary in this ornithopod indicate "a developed pleurokinetic system usually associated with more derived ornithopods" (*e.g.*, hadrosaurs).

This find is significant, Ohashi explained, as "the first associated example of such an animal from Japan." Prior to the recent discovery of this specimen, "hypsilophodontian-grade ornithopods" were only represented in the Tetori Group by fragments (mostly teeth).

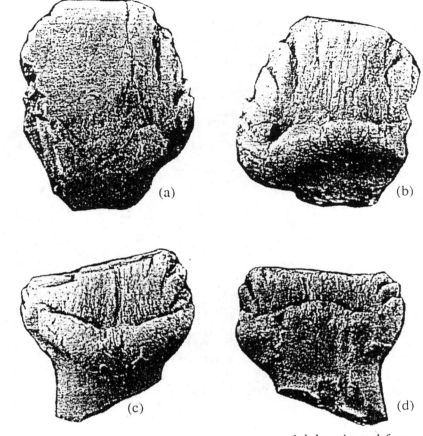

Iguanodontians

Calvo and Porfiri (2004), in an abstract, reported on a number of iguanodontian specimens collected in February, 2003, by a team from the National University of Comahue, from the Canaan quarry, north of the Barreales Lake Paleontological Center, in Neuquén Province, Patagonia, Argentina. The recovered material includes femora (three proximal left and four proximal right, two distal left and one distal right), the distal end of a humerus, several vertebral centra, and some fragments, these remains representing a minimum of five individuals.

Briefly, Calvo and Porfiri described these specimens as follows: Femora with partially fused lesser and greater trochanter; cleft, observed in lateral view, as in dryomorph [=euiguanodontian of their usage] *Anabistia saldiviai* and ?"hypsilophodontid" *Notohypsilophodon comodoroensis*, in medial view, cleft absent by fusion, as in euornithopod *Gasparinisaura cincosaltensis* (this character possibly autapomorphic for Canaan quarry taxon); distal end of femur with cranial intercondylar groove, as in Iguanodontia, but absent in *Gasparinisaura* [genus regarded by Calvo and Porfiri as iguanodontian]; condylid in medial position, as in other iguanodontians, absent in *Gasparinisaura*.

Ankylosaurian teeth from the Kundur locality of Russia, AEIM 2/1in a. labial and b. lingual views, AEIM 2/2 in c. labial and d. lingual views. Scale = .5 cm. (After Tumanova, Bolotsky and Alifanov 2004.)

Introduction

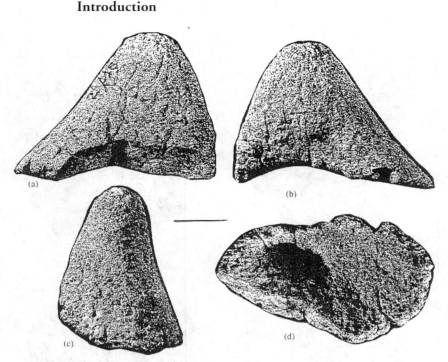

Ankylosaurian osteodermal scute (AEIM 2/16) from the Kundur locality of Russia in a.–b. lateral, c. caudal, and d. ventral views. Scale = .4 cm. (After Tumanova, Bolotsky and Alifanov 2003.)

Calvo and Porfiri suggested that the above specimens, as well as a complete juvenile femur from the Futalognko quarry in Patagonia — exhibiting the same morphology as the above specimens and coming from the same levels as those of the Canaan quarry — pertain to the same species.

Hadrosaurs

Adams and Organ (2003), in a published abstract, reported on ontogenetic development of ossified tendons — commonly preserved along the axial column of most ornithischians, these structures representing fossilized portions of muscle-tendon units — in hadrosaurian or "duckbilled" dinosaurs. As these authors pointed out, a knowledge of tendon development is required in understanding the presence and function of these structures, as "the metaplastic alteration of tendon can occur as a response to various types of stress, disease, injury, and aging, as well as through normal developmental processes."

Noting that in many avian groups tendons ossify as part of the normal process of growth, Adams and Organ performed histologic examination on hadrosaurian and avian ossified tendon samples representing different ontogenetic stages. This examination resulted in the authors recognizing numerous similarities between normally ossifying bird and dinosaur tendons. Adams and Organ's study concluded that hadrosaurian tendons "ossified as part of their normal developmental process and not as a response to abnormal stress." Moreover, intratendinous ossification begins much earlier in hadrosaurians than in avians.

Tendon ossification in hadrosaurs apparently proceeds in a manner similar to that on tendon metaplasia in birds, although ossifying more extensively at earlier allometric stages. According to Adams and Organ, knowledge of how and when the axial column becomes more ridgid, due to the ossification of tendons, "may be instrumental in determining the changes in locomotor strategies throughout the hadrosaur life span."

Rothschild, Tanke, Helbling and Martin (2003), performing an epidemiologic study of tumors in dinosaurs, utilizing X-rays, computerized tomography (CT scans), and cross sections, examined over 10,000 dinosaurian specimens. Surprisingly, of the myriad specimens studied, only the bones of hadrosaurids revealed the presence of tumors, these including hemangiomas and metastatic cancer (known previously in dinosaurs, the latter the rarest, found in only one percent of *Edmontosaurus* vertebrae studied), desmoplastic fibroma, and osteoblastoma. As suggested by Rothschild *et al.*, the epidemiology of such tumors in this one clade of dinosaurs apparently reflects a familial pattern, possibly the result of a genetic propensity or environmental mutagens.

The authors speculated that the occurrence of tumors in just this one group of dinosaurs may be related to diet or physiology. Stomach contents associated with hadrosaurid specimens including the celebrated duckbill "mummies" have included conifers, a diet possibly being unique to this dinosaurian clade (see Barrett and Upchurch 2001). Furthermore, the physiology of hadrosaurids could be different from that of other kinds of dinosaurs, the bone structure of hadrosaurids, unlike that of most other dinosaurs (*e.g.*, theropods) apparently suggestive of endothermic metabolism (see Chinsamy 1994; Chinsamy and Dodson 1995). (Examination by the authors of a theropod humerus [BYUVP 5009, either pertaining to *Allosaurus* or *Torvosaurus*] with a cauliflower-like growth, reported on in a popular article [Taylor 1992], revealed no evidence of cancer and was seemingly the result of a malaligned infected fracture.)

Main and Fiorillo (2003), in a published abstract for a poster, briefly reported on a newly collected hadrosaurian postcranial skeleton from the Upper Cretaceous (Cenomanian) Woodbine Formation, along the shores of Lake Grapevine, in southern Denton County, north-central Texas, a locality where well-preserved dinosaur fossils are rare. This relatively well-preserved specimen includes a cervical centrum, proximal radius, metacarpal, femoral condyle, proximal fibula, complete tibia and fibula, and caudal centra. The authors identified the remains as belonging to a hadrosaur based upon their relative morphology and size. As Main and Fiorillo noted, this discovery is

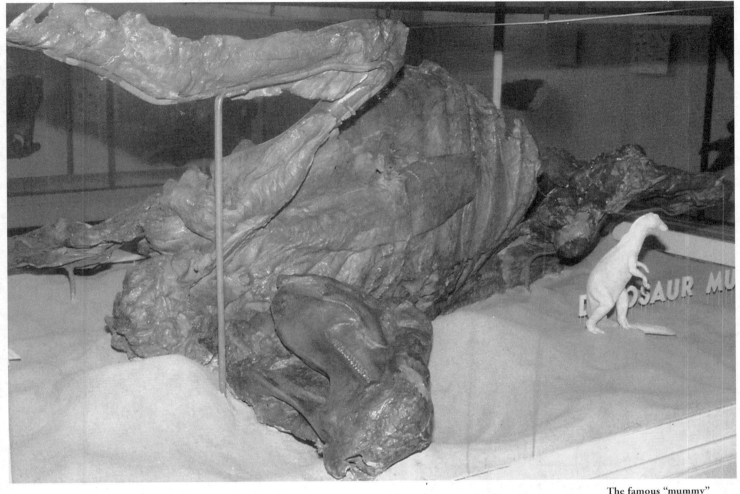

The famous "mummy" (AMNH 5060) of *Edmontosaurus annectens*, found in 1908 by Charles M. Sternberg in Niobrara County, Kansas. In 2003, Bruce M. Rothschild, Darren H. Tanke, Mark Helbling and Larry D. Martin published a study suggesting that tumors found in some hadrosaur specimens may be related to the diet (including conifers, preserved as stomach contents in such "mummies") of this group of dinosaurs.

important in expanding our knowledge of the postcranial morphology of North American, Cenomanian hadrosaurs.

Heckert, Lucas and Krzyzanowski (2003) reported an indeterminate hadrosaurid specimen (ASDM 920) recovered from the Late Cretaceous (late Campanian/"Judithian"; see Heckert *et al.* for reasons for this dating), lower "shale member" of the Fort Crittenden Formation, in Adobe Canyon, Santa Rita Mountains, southeastern Arizona. The specimen, a relatively large distal femur, has a greatest width of 210 millimeters. As preserved, the condyles are about 280 millimeters long. The specimen was identified as hadrosaurid (but not to the subfamily level) based on its left condyle being larger than the right and, cranially, the very deep groove between the condyles (see Lull and Wright 1942; Brett-Surman 1975; Weishampel and Horner 1990). Other hadrosaurid material from this formation reported by Heckert *at al.* include an associated complete vertebra (ASDM 919) and a centrum (ASDM 922), both weakly amphicoelous. As the authors noted, hadrosaurs seem to be the most common large dinosaurs from the Fort Crittenden Formation, this group, to date, mostly represented by teeth and bone fragments (see Stoyanow 1949; Miller 1964).

Jagt, Mulder, Schulp, Dortangs and Fraaije (2003), in a survey report on dinosaur remains collected from the Maastrichtian of southeastern Netherlands and northeastern Belgium, described several specimens recently recognized as dinosaurian. These include the proximal portion of a right hadrosaurid tibia (NHMM 2002067) collected from the upper Nekum Member or lower Meerssen Member of the Maastricht Formation of southern Limburg, The Netherlands (exact locality information lacking). As preserved, this specimen, comprising about two-thirds of the original bone, measures 263 millimeters in length. The greatest diameters of the spongeous core and compact bone are, respectively, 36 millimeters and 62 millimeters. As these measurements differ significantly from those (25 and approximately 60 millimeters) of MND K 21.04.004 (a fragmentary left tibia found in September 1967 in the former Curfs

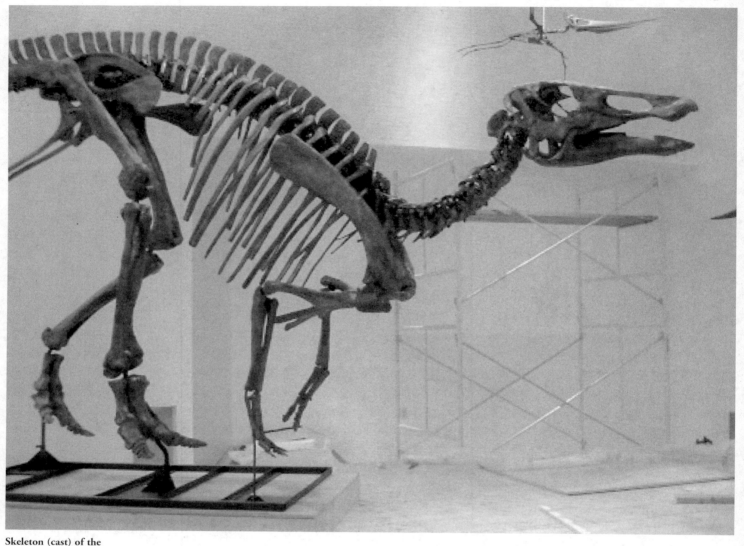

Skeleton (cast) of the hadrosaurid *Edmontosaurus annectens*. A study by Henry Fricke (2003) utilized carbon isotope ratios of tooth enamel and associated sedimentary organic matter to ellucidate the nature of ecology and behavior of such dinosaurs.

quarry [now Ankerpoort-Curfs; Geulhem, The Netherlands]), Jagt *et al.* found it most likely that these specimens do not represent conspecific taxa, this suggesting the existence of more than one hadrosaurid species in this area.

(Other recently recognized dinosaurian specimens, unidentified but described by Jagt *et al.*, include NHMM RN 28, a fragmentary, very abraded ?right dentary from the former Blom quarry at Berg en Terblijt, southern Limburg, The Netherlands; OGP 2111, a poorly preserved fragment from the Geulhem area [possibly the Ankerpoort-Curfs quarry]; and OGP 0196, a fragment of femoral shaft. Although the precise stratigraphic provenance of the latter two specimens is not known, the authors assumed that they were recovered from the upper Nekum Member or lower Meersen Member of the Maastricht Formation, southern Limburg. OGP 0196 is particularly interesting, Jagt *et al.* noted, "in showing numerous bivalve

borings of the *Gastropchaenolites* ichnogenus type," indicating that the specimen had been reworked or stayed on the seafloor for a relatively long time.)

Manabe, Hasegawa and Takahashi (2003) described an isolated, almost complete, indeterminate hadrosaurid vertebra (IMCF 1124), recovered in 1989 by the Kairyu-no-sato Fossil Study Group, led by Toshinobu Takahashi, from the Upper Cretaceous (Coniacian) Obisagawa Member of the marine Ashizawa Formation (Futuba Group), in the Tsurubo area, Iwaki City, Fukushima, Japan. (The outcrop that yielded this specimen has subsequently been incorporated into an on-site exhibition.) Originally this specimen was tentatively identified by Takahashi as a hadrosaurid cervical vertebra. As Manabe *et al.* reported, additional comparisons revealed it to be more likely a first dorsal vertebra.

In describing this specimen, Manabe *et al.* observed that its morphology closely resembles that of the cranial-most dorsal vertebrae (NSM PV 20376, 20377, and 20378) of *Hypacrosaurus* sp. Furthermore, its size "lies within the range of a subadult *Hypacrosaurus* (NSM PV 20377 and 20378)." As noted by these authors, the vertebra displays strongly upturned diapophyses with relatively short neural spines, features suggesting that it belongs to the Hadrosaurinae (see González Riga and Casadio 2000). However, these character states can also be found in such lambeosaurines as *Hypacrosaurus* sp., bringing into question the usefulness of these features in the classification of hadrosaurs.

As pointed out by Manabe *et al.*, the identification of IMCF 1124 as a hadrosaurid of Coniasian age distinguishes the specimen as one of the oldest fossil records of the Hadrosauridae in Asia and certainly the oldest in Japan.

Hernandez, Kirkland, Paul, Serrano, Garcia and Pasac (2003), in an abstract for a poster, reported on the 2001 discovery by Juan Pablo Garcia of a large hadrosaurine dinosaur in an excavation in the Upper Cretaceous (latest Campanian) San Miguel Formation, near the town of Sabinas, in Coahuila, Mexico. Recovered material includes dentaries, a maxilla, quadratojugal, quadrates, braincase, postorbital, other skull bones, the entire vertebral column, a partial ilium, pubis, ischium, femur, tibia, fibula, scapula, and coracoids. All of these elements having been identified at the Geological Institute in Mexico City as belonging to a single individual, the specimen is believed to be the most complete dinosaur individual yet found in that country.

In their preliminary description of this as yet unnamed taxon, Hernandez *et al.* observed that the ischium is distinctive, being dorsally recurved (as in *Hadrosaurus foulkii*). Relative proportions of the pre-

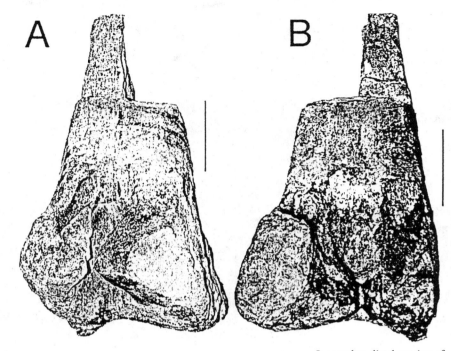

Incomplete distal portion of hadrosaurid femur (ASDM 920) from the Fort Crittenden Formation of southeastern Arizona. Scale = 100 mm. (After Heckert, Lucas and Krzyzanowski 2003.)

served parts of the skull suggest that the specimen is most comparable to *Kritosaurus navajovius*; however, the new specimen is approximately 20 percent larger than the holotype of *K. navajovius*.

Based upon a femur length of 1.3 meters, Hernandez *et al.* estimated the total length of this dinosaur to be about 11 meters (approximately 38 feet), with a weight of about four tons. The authors also noted that a second specimen of this new taxon, collected from the Parras Basin near Presa de San Antonio, and represented by the rostral part of the skull, shows that the muzzle was deep (as in *Gryposaurus*). Reconstruction of a nasal belonging to the type

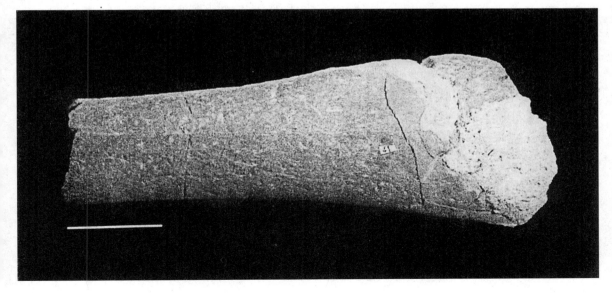

NHMM 2002067, proximal portion of right tibia of a hadrosaurid dinosaur from the Maastricht Formation of southern Limburg, The Netherlands. Scale = 50 mm. (After Jagt, Mulder, Schulp, Dortangs and Fraaije 2003.)

Introduction

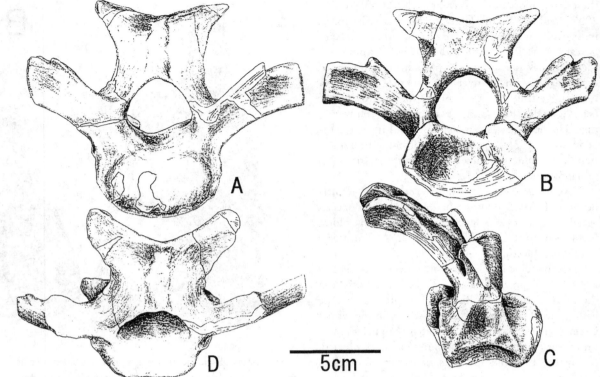

5cm

specimen (AMNH 5799) of *Kritosaurus* indicated to Hernandez *et al.* "that the circumnarial was pulled back to the rear of the nasals as in *Parasaurolophus* and supports the synonymy of *Kritosaurus* and *Naashoibitosaurus*."

Godefroit and Bolotsky (2002), in an abstract, reported briefly on the complete skeleton of a "remarkable new hollow-crested hadrosaurid dinosaur" collected in 2000 and 2001 from Upper Cretaceous ("middle" to late Maastrichtian, based upon palynological evidence) rocks at Kundur, in Far East Russia, distinguished as the first lamebeosaurine specimen from outside western North America preserving the supracranial crest. (This site has also yielded numerous bones and teeth representing hadrosaurine hadrosaurid, ankylosaurian, and theropod dinosaurs; also crocodiles, chelonians, and multituburculate mammals.)

As briefly described by Godefroit and Bolotsky, this lambeosaurine "is remarkable by the unusual shape of its hollow crest, by the important elongation of its neck (18 cervical vertebrae) and by an additional articulation between adjacent neural spines that rigidified the proximal third of the tail."

Performing a phylogenetic analysis, Godefroit and Bolotsky found this taxon to constitute the sister group to the North American, Campanian-age lambeosaurines *Corythosaurus* and *Hypacrosaurus*. Furthermore, their cladogram indicated that lambeosau-

rines originated in Asia, the most basal taxa being, successively, *Tsintaosaurus spinorhinus*, *Jaxartosaurus aralensis*, and *Amurosaurus riabinini*, and that this clade migrated to North America before or at the beginning of the Campanian.

As these authors noted, lambeosaurines comprised the dominant plant-eating dinosaurs in the latest Cretaceous Amur Region localities, represented by three taxa (as currently known) — the new form from Kundur, *A. riabinini* from Blagoveschensk, and *Charonosaurus jiayinensis* from Jiayin along the banks of the Amur River.

The most distinguishing feature of many hadrosaurid taxa is the cranial crest, with the crests of hadrosaurines (*e.g.*, *Prosaurolophus*) and lambeosaurines (*e.g.*, *Corythosaurus*) parsimoniously regarded as homologous. As recounted in an abstract by Wagner (2004), suture-mapping shows that phylogenetic transition to the morphology of the crest in Lambeosaurinae "involved facial rotation, transposition of the dorsal rostrum to the skull roof accompanied by rotation of the nasal capsule," this transformation being somewhat restated during lambeosaurine ontogeny.

Regarding the more spectacular crests found in Lambeosaurinae, Wagner noted the following: Enrolled premaxillary tubes and lateral diverticulum representing ossification around circumnarial space, defined ancestrally by circumnarial fossa (see Hopson

Mounted skeleton (LACM 5167/125973; cast of IVP AS V251) of the lambeosaurine hadrosaurid *Tsintaosaurus spinorhinus*, with the narrow, vertically oriented "crest" depicted in earlier mounts (see *Tsintaosaurus* entry, *D:TE*) brought down to a horizontal orientation and reinterpreted as a nasal. According to a study by Pascal Godefroit and Yuri L. Bolotsky (2002), this species is one of the most basal members of the Lambeosaurinae.

1975); internal surfaces of lateral diverticulum and tubes homologous to circumnarial space fossa; passage from lateral diverticulum to common median chamber of crest homologous to osseous narial foramen; external naris neomorphic; common median chamber partly homologous to ancestral space between narial foramina; bulk of nasal capsule proper beneath crest.

Lambeosaurines reportedly lack both a maxillary rostrodorsal process (probably flooring the nasal cavity in ancestral Dinosauria), and an expanded bill and reflected lip on the premaxilla (indicating invasion by the common median chamber), these features, Wagner suggested, being perhaps attributable to facial rotation. The s-loops—curving "around a region homologous to paired premaxillary (vomeronasal?) cavities that open to the palate in other ornithopods"—found in lambeosaurine crests may echo structures of ancestral soft tissue. Lambeosaurine palates lack foramina due to a displacement of these cavities, Wagner noted. In ancestral hadrosaurs, "Large maxillary foramina conducted neurovasculature rostrally deep to the premaxillae"; in lambeosaurines, however, "these openings are oriented dor-

sally," the premaxillary foramen dorsal to them most likely having "passed this neuromusculature into the narial region."

In all hadrosaurids, Wagner pointed out, the circumnarial fossa is on the lateral surface of the nasal (this arrangement hidden within the crest in lambeosaurines). Moreover, fontanelles in the lambeosaurine crests "represent failure of the crest walls to completely enclose the [circumnarial fossa]," the walls possibly homologous to the circumnarial fossa margins found in some hadrosaurines.

Wegweiser, Breithaupt, Babcock and Skinner (2003), in a published abstract, briefly reported on fossilized skin and possible muscle tissue, preserved by authigenic pyrolusite, associated with lambeosaurine skeletal remains recovered from the This Side of Hell Quarry, in the Upper Cretaceous (Maastrichtian) Konservat-Lagerstätte in the Lance Formation of Park County, Wyoming. According to these authors, pyrolusite seems to have "replaced the soft tissue by forming a coating in bentonite sandstone while it was a sediment encasing the dinosaur carcass," resulting "in finely detailed preservation of small (1–2 mm) to

Introduction

Photograph by the author, courtesy Academy of Natural Sciences of Philadelphia.

Skull (cast of ROM 776, originally GSC 8676, first referred to the now abandoned species *Corythosaurus excavatus*) of the high-crested lambeosaurine *Corythosaurus casuarius*, in the preparation laboratory (1983) of the Academy of Natural Sciences of Philadelphia. The crests of such duckbilled dinosaurs was the focus of a study by Jonathan Wagner (2004).

Photograph by the author, courtesy Natural History Museum of Los Angeles County.

Fossilized skin impressions in the pelvic area of a subadult skeleton (LACM 3743/126137) of *Corythosaurus casuarius*.

large (5–20 mm) diameter pentagonal and hexagonal nonoverlapping scales," grooves between these scales ranging from one to four millimeters deep. To date of their writing, skin has been recovered only from the region of the quarry preserving the scapula, ribs, and upper portion of the humerus. Analyses of these soft materials were conducted at The Ohio State University using a scanning electron microscope combined with energy dispertive X-ray analysis. Chemical analyses were performed on the rock matrix at this site.

According to Wegweiser *et al.*, this lambeosaurine perished in "an inferred marginal-marine setting including distal stream to shallow intermedial environments." The presence of pyrosite, the authors speculated, is probably related to this dinosaur being buried in saltine pore water-saturated sediments, salinity of the pore waters possibly having "inhibited scavenging and some bacterial breakdown of soft tissues."

In an abstract for a poster, Williams and Wegweiser (2003) briefly described an associated and almost complete half-rack of lamebeosaurine ribs, discovered in 2001, also in the This Side of Hell Quarry. As the authors noted, these ribs offer "an opportunity to study morphological characters that may lead to a better understanding of the paleoecology of hadrosaurs." According to Williams and Wegweiser, detailed examination of these ribs are useful in phenetically distinguishing between the two major hadrosaurid clades, Hadrosaurinae and Lambeosaurinae.

In this, the first detailed examination of the morphological characters differentiating these two clade, Williams and Wegweiser measured ribs from four major landmarks—*i.e.*, the turberculum, capitulum, distal end of the shaft, and minimum width of the shaft, measurements being taken from tuberculum to capitular facet, capitular facet to distal tip, curvature of entire rib, and circumference of rib shaft at its least thickest.

Williams and Wegweiser's collected data (details presumably to be published at some later date) support their "original hypothesis that hadrosaur ribs were specific at the tribal level," their research offering a new definitive postcranial character for separating the two hadrosaurid subfamilies. Furthermore, this conclusion "suggests that the concept of tribal specific ribs could be applied elsewhere to revive dinosaur systematics based on characters that could be symplesiomorphic."

MARGINOCEPHALIANS

Tsuihiji (2003), in a published abstract, presented a brief report on a study of evolutionary changes of the axial musculature in the occipital region in the Marginocephalia, the ornithischian clade including all pachycephalosaurian ("bone-headed") and ceratopsian ("horned") dinosaurs, that author's reconstruction of this musculature being made after several studies and "with a view to its functional implications."

According to Tsuihiji, most earlier studies have focused upon just one reptilian clade, usually Squamata, and lack phylogenetic justification. Tsuihiji's reconstructions, however, were tested via dissections of various extant diapsid reptiles, then comparing osteological correlates of their muscles with those found in marginocephalians.

Tsuihiji's study showed the following: Conditions unique to Lepidosauria/Squamata within Diapsida—*e.g.*, subvertebral muscle inserts on basal tubera in lepidosaurs—are found in some muscles. In Archosauria (including Marginocephalia), however, innervation patterns show a division of this muscle into two parts, inserting on both the basal tubera and distal end of paroccipital process. Proximal to the insertion of this vertebral muscle on the basal tubera in Archosauria is the M. transversalis cervicis, this relationship being reversed in Squamata. In the rhyncocephalian reptile *Sphenodon*, the condition is similar to that in Archosauria, the subvertebral muscle partially surrounding the M. transversalis cervicis, this indicating "that the squamate condition is unique to that clade within Diapsida." Consequently, Tsuihiji pointed out, previous reconstructions simply superimposing the squamate condition onto the marginocephalian occiput cannot be phylogenetically justified.

According to Tsuihiji, evolutionary changes in the suboccipital muscles of marginocephalians "can be inferred by tracing changes in their osteological correlates"—*e.g.*, ceratopsids having a longitudinally elongated neural spine/neural arch of the atlas-axis and two pairs of large depressions in the excoccipital, these respectively constituting the putative origin and insertion of the M. rectus capitis posterior and suggesting the massive development of this muscle. As Tsuihiji observed, the pachycephalosaurian *Stygimoloch* likewise possesses a deep depression as the postulated insertion for the M. rectus capitis, "suggesting its convergent hypertrophy in derived pachycephalosaurians and ceratopsians to support a heavy skull." Also in pachycephalosaurians and ceratopsians, the attachments of other muscles are enlarged, correlated with an expansion of the parietosquamosal shelf in derived members of the Marginocephalia.

Pachycephalosaurs

Pachycephalosaurian or "bone-headed" dinosaurs were so named because of the thickened domes—consisting of the fused frontal and parietal bones (see Brown and Schlaikjer 1943)—that distinguish the skulls of members of this marginocephalian group.

The function of these domes has long been a topic for speculation. Colbert (1955) was the first author to speculate that such domes could have constituted a battering ramlike adaptation for head-butting in behavior analogous to that seen in the bighorn sheep *Ovis canadensis*. This notion of head-butting pachycephalosaurs, sometimes depicted in detailed life restorations of two such dinosaurs colliding head-on, would persist in the paleontological literature and also in popular writings about dinosaurs for decades (*e.g.*, see *Stegoceras* entry, *D:TE*).

Within the frontoparietal dome are structures of bone that Galton (1970) first described as "a radiating series of trabeculae or bony fibers, each of which is perpendicular to the outer surface of the dome." Some authors (*e.g.*, Alexander 1997) have suggested that the spongy texture of these structures provided "cushioning" to protect the head during the alleged head-butting activity. Others workers (*e.g.*, Rigby, Rice and Currie 1987) have argued that these structures indicate that the dome is better interpreted as a thermoregulatory than a head-butting organ.

Only in more recent years has the head-butting hypothesis been seriously challenged (*e.g.*, see Horner and Goodwin 1998, *S2*). In order further to test both hypotheses, Goodwin and Horner (2004) subsequently applied high resolution images of histologically thin samples taken from a nonconspecific, ontogenetic series of North American pachycephalosaurid frontoparietal domes. Materials studied in these authors' analysis consisted of thin sections cut — utilizing an ultra-thin diamond blade saw, resulting in the loss of minimal fossil material — from seven nonconspecific pachycephalosaurid frontoparietal domes.

These specimens comprise the following: (Judith River Formation) UCMP 130049 (low-domed, fused frontoparietal dome), *Stegoceras* sp., MOR 295 (unfused frontals), *Stegoceras validum*, and MOR 1179 (dome), *S. validum*; (Hell Creek Formation) UCMP 134979 (dome), indeterminate pachycephalosaurid, UCMP 128383, *Stygimoloch spinifer*, and VRD 13 (partial skull), *Pachycephalosaurus wyomingensis* (*sensu* Sues and Galton 1987); and (Two Medicine Formation) MOR 453, indeterminate pachycephalosaur.

Required for this study was the assignment of a relative ontogenetic stage — juvenile, subadult, or adult — to each of the above specimens. As Goodwin and Horner (2004) explained, these specimens represent "a size gradient among phylogenetically closely related taxa." As stated, all of these specimens were recovered from Upper Cretaceous fossil-bearing sediments, either the coeval Judith River Formation and Two Medicine Formation or the younger Hell Creek Formation. The ontogenetic stage of each specimen was determined according to its phylogenetic relationships, the entire length and inflation of the dome, and sutural morphology. Following that determination, the authors placed the seven specimens in a presumed successive allometric sequence.

Based on the above-mentioned criteria, Goodwin and Horner (2004) postulated the following: UCMP 130049 (the starting point in the authors' proposed growth series), juvenile *Stegoceras*, based on its incipient doming and braincase being large relative to frontoparietal length; MOR 295 and MOR 1179, juvenile *Stegoceras*, based on their size, sutural contacts, and the deeply sculptured dorsal surface of the domes; UCMP 134979, UCMP 128383, and MOR 453, subadults, domes of intermediate size, UCMP 134979 comparing favorably with some *Pachycephalosaurus* specimens (*e.g.*, CM 3180; see Gilmore 1936*b*); UCMP 12838, subadult *Stygimoloch spinifer*, based on size, and cranial postcranial morphpology; and VDR 13 (the endpoint in this growth series), the largest specimen sampled, adult *Pachycephalosaurus wyomingensis* based upon relative size, the full development of the dome, and the possession of parietosquamosal ornamentation.

Furthermore, Goodwin and Horner (2004) identified three distinct and ontogenetically mapped zones within the unique architecture of the pachycephalo-

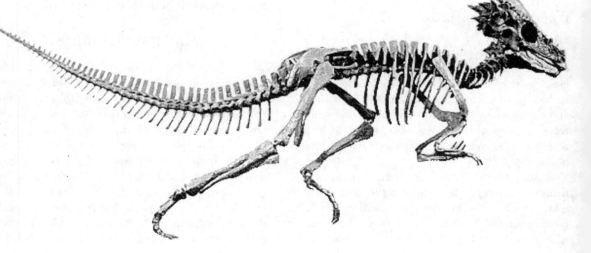

Skeleton (cast) of the Late Cretaceous dinosaur *Pachycephalosaurus wyomingensis*, original specimen (nicknamed "Sandy") collected from the Sandy Site Quarry, Hell Creek Formation of South Dakota (see *D:TE*, *S1* and *S2*). In the past, such dinosaurs were believed to have engaged in head-butting behavior, a notion that has been refuted in more recent studies.

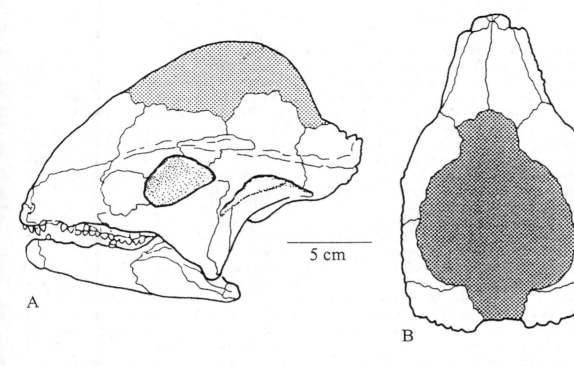

5 cm

A

B

Skull (UA 2) of the pachycephalosaurid *Stegoceras validum* in A. left lateral and B. dorsal views, stippled portion indicating the frontoparietal bone. A recent paper coauthored by Mark B. Goodwin and John R. Horner refutes earlier studies wherein head-butting behavior was attributed to such "bone-headed" dinosaurs. (After Goodwin and Horner 2004.)

saurid dome: Zone I—"a blend of deformed, stretched-out, and ropey-looking primary and secondary osteons," the histological features and thickness of this zone remaining relatively constant throughout ontogeny, no matter the height of the overlying bone; Zone II—the highly variable vascular portion of the dome, its thickness diminishing during ontogeny, the radiating structures associated with this zone transitory with growth, increasing allometrically, Sharpey's fibers (when this zone is extensive) anchoring some external covering over the dome; and Zone III—"a relatively dense, sparsely vascularized layer of bone sandwiched between the vascular bone of Zone II and the exterior, periosteal surface of the frontoparietal bone," the dense layer of Sharpey's fibers found on the outer margin of this zone showing that the dome possessed an outer covering during life, these fibers precluding any determination of the ultimate shape of the skull.

Goodwin and Horner's (2004) study showed that the spongy, highly vascular bone structures or "radiating trabeculae"—used by previous researchers as evidence to support both the head-butting and heat-exchange scenarios—"are fundamentally an ephemeral ontogenetic stage of dome growth." Moreover, these structures tend to diminish in specimens representing mature individuals and are almost absent in adults, the ontogenetic stage at which the behavior of butting heads is presumed to have occurred. Consequently, this new and "unexpected" interpretation of the pachycephalosaurid dome effectively disputes both the head-butting and thermoregulatory scenarios, the authors stated.

As Goodwin and Horner explained, North American pachycephalosaurid taxa can be differentiated from one another by the relative size and shape of their domes and such accompanying skull ornamentation as nodes, tubercles, and horns (*e.g.*, see Maryańska 1990). Therefore, their domes possibly served "as a communication system that was primarily visual within species, analogous to the crests, horns, and frills of ceratopsid dinosaurs (Sampson and Forster 2001)."

Determining sexual dimorphism in bone-headed dinosaurs is difficult, Goodwin and Horner (2004) explained. Earlier studies attempting to differentiate male from female pachycephalosaurid specimens (*e.g.*, Chapman, Galton, Sepkowski and Wall 1981; see *Stegoceras* entry, *D:TE*) were based primarily on sexually immature juvenile and subadult material. Consequently, the former identification of males as individuals possessing larger and thick domes cannot be substantiated. Based on their own observations, Goodwin and Horner proposed "that cranial display in support of species recognition and communication is a more parsimonious interpretation of the function of the pachycephalosaurid dome." Moreover, if the pachycephalosaurid frontoparietal dome were, in fact, a component of sexual display in these dinosaurs, then such behavior was most likely secondary considering "the apparent late ontogenetic development of the frontoparietal dome and absence of sexual dimorphism expressed in the group so far."

Ceratopsians

Ceratopsians, or "horned dinosaurs," are well known mostly for the anatomy of their heads. Indeed, the taxonomy of this group of small to large Late Cretaceous dinosaurs has been based almost entirely on cranial characters, with most past anatomical studies of ceratopsians having focused upon their skulls. Comparatively few such published studies having been devoted to ceratopsian postcranial anatomy.

Recently, however, Chinnery (2004*b*) offered a detailed morphometric analysis of evolutionary trends in the ceratopsian postcranial skeleton research that would, in fact, yield information applicable to the long-standing debate over the forelimb posture of ceratopsian dinosaurs. To study the morphological differences among ceratopsian postcranial elements and to compare evolutionary patterns, Chinnery employed multivariate (Principal Components Analysis) and bivariate methods to analyze linear measurement information. Also, that author applied various shape methods—*i.e.*, Resistant-Fit Theta-Rho Analysis (RFTRA), Least-Squares Theta-Rho Analysis (LSTRA), and Euclidean Distance Matrix Analysis (EDMA)—to biological landmark data.

Incorporated into Chinnery's data set were isolated specimens as well as materials yielded by bonebeds, her primary data base comprising elements found directly associated with diagnostic cranial material. Chinnery's data base consisted of girdle and limb bones, with all measurements taken directly from the original specimens (no casts or photographs were used), and all of the elements utilized, to decrease the potential for error, were nondeformed and almost complete. All bones studied were oriented in identical positions (allowing for comparable results), then measured and photographed.

Chinnery's analyses of the materials revealed the following: Size is the primary change through the evolution of the ceratopsian skeleton, with the girdle and limb elements increasing in robustness through the Neoceratopsia and within the Psittacosauridae. Most measurements increased with positive allometry compared to their length; reflecting this increase most are the ventral scapulocoracoid, the distal humerus, the proximal ulna, both ends of the radius, the prepubic process, the distal femur, the distal tibia, and both ends of the fibula. However, some measurements (*e.g.*, length of rim of sigmoid fossa of ulna distally, length of postacetabular process of ilium, height measurements of ilium, height of articular portion of pubis) increased with negative allometry, although still showing increasing robustness. Moreover, some measurements assumed to show allometric trends (*e.g.*, maximum height of scapula, length of deltopectoral crest of humerus, width of femoral shaft being 75 percent of length) change almost isometrically with increasing length.

According to Chinnery's analyses, bipediality in the primitive ceratopsian *Psittacosaurus* is a plesiomorphic condition supported by comparisons of shapes, indicators of bipediality and possible alternate forelimb use in this genus (but not in Neoceratopsia) including "a more mobile radial head, reduced manus digits, and modifications of the pelvis [*e.g.*, ilium not as tall, pubic and ischiadic process smaller] that support more weight cranially." Moreover, the forelimb elements, being more robust than those seen in basal neoceratopsians, and increased mobility suggest that *Psittacosaurus* used its forelimbs to manipulate its environment in some way.

Chinnery found a shift to quadrupedalism in basal Neoceratopsia "verified by the change in orientation of the [smaller] deltopectoral crest on the [less robust] humerus, the more compact manus, and the shift in the pelvis elements to support more weight centrally." Furthermore, the increase in size from basal Neoceratopsia to Ceratopsidae is indicated by "a change of stance from the more upright one of the basal neoceratopsians to a more sprawling posture, especially in the forelimbs." Chinnery also observed in the Ceratopsidae the more horizontal orientation of the deltopectoral crest, the larger olecranon process of the ulna, and the more developed lateral condyle of the femur and lateral side of the distal tibia.

Chinnery and Horner (2003), in an abstract for a poster, briefly described a new and as yet unnamed basal neoceratopsian ceratopsian genus recently collected from the lower Two Medicine Formation of Montana. This new taxon, the authors noted, is distinguished by a unique combination of characters, some of which have only been observed previously in Asian basal neoceratopsian forms. Moreover, referral to this new genus of various specimens identified as *Leptoceratops* sp., in the National Museum of Natural History collections, adds to this mosaic of characters.

The authors noted the following characters exhibited by this new taxon: Fenestrated frill and premaxillary teeth (known only in Asian basal neoceratopsians, unknown in any North American taxa); additionally, absence of large gap between basisphenoid processes and basiosphenoid contributing to basioccipital tubera, maxilla with short, ventrally angled edentulous portion (these characters also unknown in North American forms). Characters of the new genus similar to those of other North American taxa include: Everted bascioccipital tubera; crest-shaped epijugals; (most significantly) tooth wear pattern with both vertical shear and horizontal shelf or notch.

As Chinnery and Horner pointed out, previous

Life restoration by artist Todd Marshall of the bipedal primitive ceratopsian *Psittacosaurus.*

cladistic analyses have failed to demonstrate the monopholy of basal Neoceratopsia. However, "with the addition of this taxon as well as another new North American genus the current cladistic analysis of basal Neoceratopsia includes a strong Protoceratopsidae consisting of all basal taxa except for *Asiaceratops* (most likely due to lack of material) and *Archaeoceratops.*" The latter clade, the authors noted, is supported by at least 10 characters. Based upon Chinnery and Horner's cladistic analysis, the new genus is the sister taxon to the Leptoceratopsinae, a group including three other North American forms and the Asian genus *Udanoceratops.* (Full details of this study will presumably be published at a later date; see "Systematics" chapter.)

Varriale (2004), in an abstract, researched the jaw mechanics of ceratopsid dinosaurs, this study centering on the well known genera *Triceratops* and *Chasmosaurus.* As Varriale pointed out, ceratopsids are unique among plant-eating tetrapods in having "a vertically oriented occlusal surface that committed these dinosaurs to a vertical shearing jaw mechanism." This current and traditional model of mastication "involves an isognathous orthal power stroke produced by a scissor-like adduction of the mandible," this inter-

pretation primarily arising from observing "that the rostroventrally-oriented quadrate, and rostral convergence of the dental rows, negates the possibility of palinal (retraction) and proall (protraction) power strokes respectively."

A different approach was taken in Varriale's study, one focusing upon dental microwear in these two ceratopsid genera. As that author explained, microwear on teeth is produced by the direction and magnitude of the power stroke. Consequently, dental wear patterns can be used in testing models of chewing in these dinosaurs. The vertical slicing model, Varriale noted, predicts that the dominant microwear feature on ceratopsid teeth will be scratching; moreover, such scratches should be unimodally oriented, their long axes vertically directed.

In examining dental microwear in *Triceratops* and *Chasmosaurus*, Varriale observed a pattern differing from the above-stated prediction, thereby refuting the traditional hypothesis of ceratopsid mastication. Varriale discovered, rather, both bimodal and polymodal striations with long axes oriented about 90 degrees to each other.

After exploring several possible motions to explain this pattern, Varriale found only the following

Introduction

Photograph by the author, courtesy University of Kansas Natural History Museum.

Skull of *Triceratops horridus*. Frank Varriale (2004) has used dental wear morphology as a criterion in a study of the jaw mechanics in such large horned dinosaurs.

to fit with the observed microwear: All teeth coming into occlusion with elevation of mandible, power stroke producing vertical striations; rostral convergence of upper and lower teeth preventing jaw protraction, eliminating microwear possibility; isognathous retraction, with lower dentition pulled caudally, releasing dentary teeth from occlusion with maxillary, producing no microwear; asymmetric mandibular reaction, with upper and lower dentitions unilaterally kept in occlusion during power stroke, consistent with skull morphology, explaining observed microwear pattern. Based upon these notations, Varriale hypothesized "that, in addition to the current interpretation of vertical slicing, ceratopsids also engaged in an anisognathous palinal power stroke."

Among the intriguing aspects of ceratopsian paleobiology is the occurrence of fenestrae or openings with the frill and also other areas of the skull. This feature is usually found in chasmosaurines (excluding *Avaceratops* and *Triceratops*), wherein the parietal part of the frill is pierced by large fenestrae. Some ceratopsian individuals, Tanke and Farke (2003) noted in an abstract, also possess the puzzling feature of

"extra" openings in the squamosals, these being "similarly positioned across a variety of specimens, with both unilateral and bilateral occurrences known."

For more than a century, paleontologists have been speculating as to the origins of these openings, including that they may have taxonomical rather than pathological significance (see Wiman 1930), or that they could represent wounds created by intraspecific horn thrusts (Lull 1933; Molnar 1977; Rothschild and Tanke 1997).

Also observed in ceratopsian skulls is the anomaly of crater-like pits affecting the horns in both chasmosaurine and centrosaurine ceratopsians, these having been interpreted as "punched out" lesions of uncertain origins. Only recently have these features been addressed using a critical and systematic approach (see Tanke and Farke 2002).

Taking a survey of ceratopsian skull material from paucispecific bonebeds archived in numerous North American museums, especially the wealth of specimens housed at the Royal Tyrrell Museum of Palaeontology, Tanke and Farke (2003) observed the following:

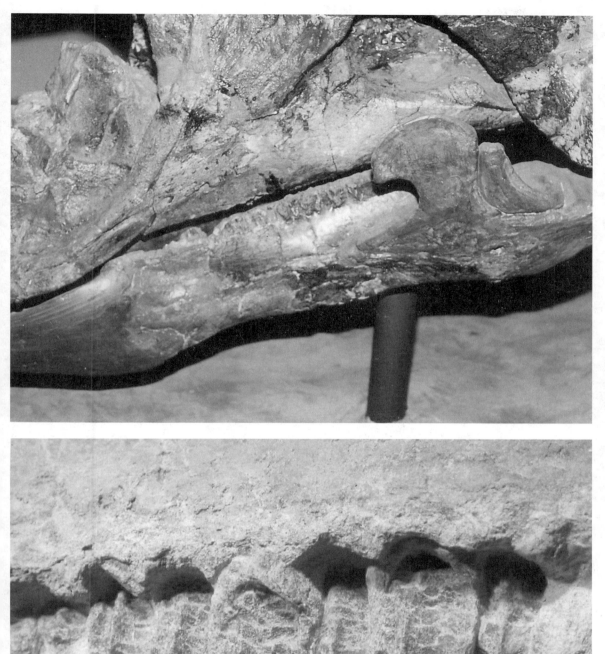

Detail of the jaws of a skull (LACM 7207/59049) of the ceratopsid *Triceratops horridus*. Frank Varriale (2004) proposed a new model for mastication in ceratopsid dinosaurs, based upon microwear of their teeth.

Maxillary teeth of the *Triceratops horridus* specimen (TCM 2001.93.1) nicknamed "Kelsey, collected by the Black Hills Institute of Geological Research from the Lance Formation of Wyoming.

Introduction

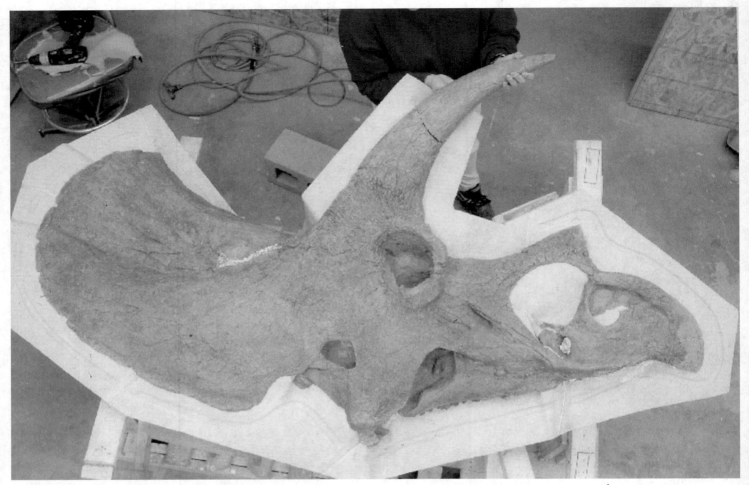

Skull of the *Triceratops horridus* specimen (TCM 2001.93.1) known as "Kelsey" undergoing preparation at the Black Hills Institute of Geological Research. A recent study by Andrew Farke (2003) concluded that ceratopsians such as *Triceratops* and *Chasmosaurus* were incapable of using their horns in bovid-like intraspecific contests.

1. *Extra fenestrae*— Chasmosaurines most affected by these openings; holes piercing the squamosal, circular to oval in outline, with no associated fracture callus, bone disruption, or subsequent infection in most specimens; holes appearing to be "fresh," but apparently a long-standing condition; hole margins mostly smooth, some showing well-developed vascular impressions up to edge of hole; extra fontanelles apparently related to bone resorption of thin part of squamosal; squamosal opening in chasmosaurines sometimes associated with pathology.

2. *Resorption pits*— Mostly found in centrosaurines, occurring on external hight points of skull (*e.g.*, the postorbital horn in *Centrosaurus*, the nasal boss in "pachyrhinosaurids"); pit appearing as small, rounded depression having finely pitted floor texture; pitting generally bilateral in centrosaurines (where both postorbital horns are preserved); pitting progressively affecting brow horn with advancing ontogeny, horn core eventually lost completely; flat-topped boss (in "pachyrhinosaurids") with appearance of having collapsed or folded down into caudal pocket of "folded frontal complex" with associated smoothing or normally rugose texture of bone, similar pitting less frequently seen on nasal horn core, epijugal, and epoccipitals around margin of frill; pitting appearing age-related, not pathological.

3. *Punched-out lesions (POLs)*— Occurring on both internal and external bone surfaces, hemispherical in shape; bones of frill most commonly affected, but lesions also seen on some facial bones; late-stage POLs sometimes penetrating flat platy bone, then expanding equally in all directions, creating large holes simulating horn thrust injury; seemingly representing desease process of uncertain origin.

4. *Puckered lesions*— Rare, presently only observed in centrosaurines; similar to POLs, consisting of very shallow, circular to oval lesions with series of low ridges radiating out from center, giving "puckered" appearance; some with tiny, centrally located hole that can full pierce bone (Tanke has also observed similar patterns, but without the centrally located hole, in tyrannosaurid jaw elements).

As Tanke and Farke (2003) pointed out, only adult-sized individuals were affected in the above categories, even in bonebed deposits were juvenile and subadult individuals were well represented.

While the problem of "extra" fenestrae and pitting in the skulls of horned dinosaurs is complex, Tanke and Farke (2003) concluded the following:

Centrosaurines, with advanced ontogeny, develop resorption pitting on the high points of the skull, the postorbital horn core and nasal boss being most strongly affected, this pitting over time eventually increasing to the point that the horncore or boss are entirely lost. These additional openings thus far observed seem to be related to disease (POL or infection).

In chasmosaurines, the squamosal openings, when present, are generally similarly located high up, in areas where the bone is thinnest. These fenestrae are apparently nonpathological, probably resulting from bone resorption "possibly related to age, calcium required for egg production, removal of structurally unnecessary bone or other unknown factor."

Only centrosaurine specimens have exhibited "puckered" lesions, while both Centrosaurinae and Chasmosaurinae show examples of POL development. While ceratopsian dinosaurs may have engaged in combative behavior that sometimes resulted in penetrating horn thrust skull injuries, "none of the fossil evidence at hand is compelling enough to support this suggestion."

Heckert, Lucas and Krzyzanowski (2003) reported an indeterminate ceratopsian specimen (NMMNH P-34906) collected from the Late Cretaceous (late Campanian/"Judithian"; see paper details), lower "shale member" of the Fort Crittenden Formation, in Adobe Canyon, Santa Rita Mountains, southeastern Arizona. Ceratopsian material has, the authors noted, been historically limited to isolated teeth and fragmentary postcranial remains (see Miller 1964). NMMNH P-34906, discovered recently by Stan E. Krzyzanowski, includes a partial lower jaw (originally misidentified by the authors as a right nasal; see paper for details), a left squamosal, plus vertebral, rib, and appendicular bone fragments. As observed by the authors, the general shape of the squamosal, being rectangular rather than elongate, suggests affinities with the Centrosaurinae (see Dodson and Currie 1990). Other ceratopsian material reported by Heckert *et al.* from this locality includes an incomplete vertebra (ASDM 940) measuring, as preserved, about 87 millimeters long, more than 140 millimeters wide, and 135 millimeters tall.

For almost a century, the phalangeal formula of the pes in centrosaurine ceratopsian dinosaurs has been listed as 2-3-4-5-0. However, as reported by Noriega (2003) in a published abstract, recent examination of a complete and entirely articulated pes ("down to the unguals of each digit") exhibited at the Dinosaur Provincial Park field station of the Royal Tyrell Museum or Palaeontology in Alberta, Canada, offers evidence demonstrating that this phalangeal formula is not correct. According to Noriega, the phalangeal formula of this foot is 4-4-3-3-0. This drastically altered phalangeal formula, Noriega noted, "may have serious implications regarding not only the

posture, but ultimately the locomotion of the centrosaurines specifically and the neoceratopsians in general."

Farke (2003), in an abstract, addressed the more than century-long practice of comparing ceratopsid dinosaurs with bovid mammals, mostly due to the common presence of horns in both groups of animals. However, as that author pointed out, while "This 'bovid paradigm' has colored interpretations of ceratopsid behavior, sexual dimorphism, systematics, functional morphology, and pathology," a critical comparison of horn morphology in these groups had never been undertaken.

Farke observed the following: Ceratopsid postorbital horns typically pointing rostrally and dorsally, bovid horns caudally or laterally; cornual sinus within ceratopsid postorbital horns consisting of simple tube extending for no more than one third length of horn, cornual sinuses in bovid horns internally strutted, frequently extensive.

These differences, Farke noted, have significant implications regarding the behavior of ceratopsids, especially regarding the postulation that at least some taxa engaged in intraspecific combat. Utilizing scale models of ceratopsid skulls, that author was able to explore various fighting modes possibly employed by these dinosaurs. In many bovids, Farke pointed out, skull roof contact, in addition to horn locking, plays an important role in intraspecific combat. In some ceratopsid taxa (*e.g.*, *Triceratops*), however, such contact was impossible both because of the near-vertical orientation of the brow horns and also limitations in skull mobility. Additionally, "this horn orientation would have made frontal charges and head butting (as in *Bison* or *Capra*) nearly impossible to execute without great risk of injury." Furthermore, the nasal horn present in many ceratopsid taxa further complicates such behavioral comparisons with bovids.

According to Farke, the wide range of horn morphologies among ceratopsid dinosaurs ultimately shows the difficulties of inferring the behavior and evolution of these extinct animals from modern analogies. As an example, Farke proposed that some centrosaurine genera, such as *Pachyrhinosaurus*, possibly "evolved flank butting from a 'jousting' fighting style," this postulation countering "previously proposed bovid-based models of ceratopsid horn evolution, in which flank butting behavior is hypothesized to evolve inevitably into jousting and horn locking."

Getty, Roberts and Loewen (2003), in a published abstract for a poster, reported on the first associated ceratopsian skeleton known from the Upper Cretaceous of Utah. The specimen, belonging to a chasmosaurine, was excavated between 2000 and 2002 by the Utah Museum of Natural History from

Introduction

Photograph by the author, courtesy Natural History Museum of Los Angeles County.

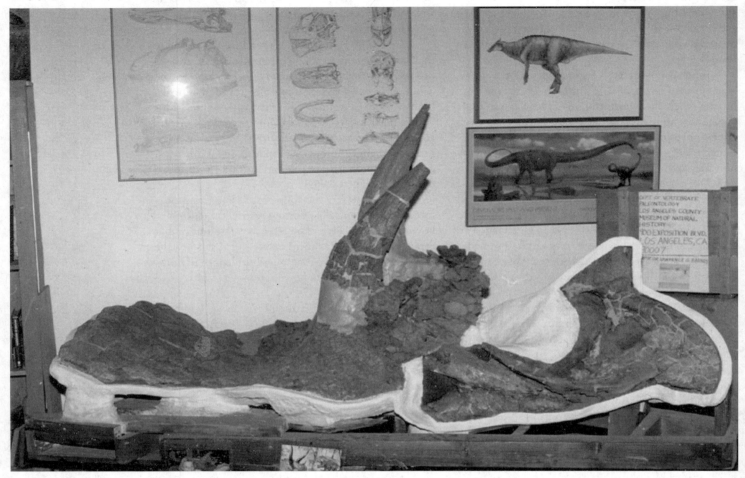

Incomplete skull (LACM 7202/27428) of *Triceratops* currently displayed in a recreation of a vertebrate paleontology laboratory at the Natural History Museum of Los Angeles County. This specimen was collected in 1965 by Harley G. Garbani.

the Kaiparowits Formation (apparently late Campanian, based upon palynomorph and mammalian data; see the abstract by Imhof and Albright 2003 for a preliminary magnetostratigraphic analysis of this formation) within the Grand Staircase-Escalante National Monument in the southern part of the state. Recovered were over 300 individual elements and fragments representing more than half of the entire skeleton, these remains including an approximately 80-percent complete disarticulated skull.

According to Getty *et al.*, morphological cranial characters verify that this specimen, currently under systematic study, represents a chasmosaurine (see below).

Performing a detailed taphonomic analysis of the quarry that yielded this specimen, Getty *et al.* noted the following: Quarry characterized by three-meter thick fining-upwards sequence of muddy, fine-grained sandstone grading to mollusc-rich silty mudstone, bones concentrated in lower 0.8 meters; carcass having been subject to weathering, insect modification, scavenging, and trampeling before burial; small skeletal elements poorly represented; carcass apparently

having been sub-aerially exposed on dry floodplain, there being subjected before burial to disarticulation and physical and biological weathering.

Getty *et al.* speculated following their taphonomic analysis that "A relatively low-energy overbank flooding event resulted in the development of an ephemeral floodplain pond, which subsequently led to the burial and preservation of the carcass," this flooding possibly having "caused minor winnowing of distal limb elements." Consequently, a complex, multi-event taphonomic history resulted in the unusual preservation of this disarticulated and fragmented specimen.

In a subsequently published related abstract, Smith, Sampson, Roberts and Getty (2004) reported that, to date of their writing, three partial skeletons of this new chasmosaurine taxon had been excavated, including the above mentioned specimen that preserves about 48 percent of the postcranium.

Chasmosaurine synapomorphies observed by Smith *et al.* in the specimens include: Facial skeleton elongate; predentary having subhorizontal cutting surface; squamosal relatively elongate, triangular.

Smith *et al.* diagnosed this new taxon by a suite of autapomorphies including the following: Supraorbital horncores projecting dorsolaterally (this being the new species' most distinctive feature, the conformation of these horns unique among known ceratopsids); horncores abbreviated, rostrocaudally compressed, with overall oblate morphology; epijugals D-shaped; orbits elliptical, long axis vertically inclined.

As determined by Smith *et al.*, this as yet unnamed genus occupies a relatively basal position within the Chasmosaurinae, sharing various characters with *Pentaceratops* (*e.g.*, hypertrophied, caudally directed epijugal; subrectangular parietosquamosal frill; rostrodorsally curved P1 [medialmost] epoccipital).

Smith *et al.* pointed out that the new chasmosaurine occurs in the lower to middle part of the Kaiparowits Formation (approximately 76 to 75 million years ago, dated by new radiometric evidence based upon multiple ash layers), while *Pentaceratops* occurs in the uppermost Fruitland Formation and Kirkland Formation (about 74.5 to 74.1 million years ago), these dates suggesting "that the Kaiparowits taxon immediately preceded *Pentaceratops* temporally."

The Continuing Ectothermy/Endothermy Debate

During the 1970s and 1980s, following the dawning of the so-called "Dinosaur Renaissance," it became fashionable to envision all or most dinosaurs as very active — even hyperactive — endothermic animals, as opposed to the earlier portrayal of slow and sluggish reptiles. Although most workers seem to have gravitated towards hypotheses suggesting that dinosaurs lived lives with metabolisms more comparable to those of mammals and birds than to extant reptiles, the concept of "warm blooded dinosaur" continues to have its detractors, such as the report that follows.

In 2003, John A. Ruben, Terry D. Jones, and Nicholas R. Geist — who have numbered among the most vocal detractors from the postulation hypothesis that dinosaurs were endothermic — published a detailed paper focusing on the respiratory and reproductive paleophysiology of dinosaurs and early birds. As Ruben *et al.* pointed out, while these highly successful animals are known only from their fossils, "a variety of attributes of these taxa can be inferred by identification of shared anatomical structures whose presence is usually linked to specialized functions in living reptiles, birds, and mammals."

Ruben *et al.* discussed — and then dismissed — as evidence supporting the idea of an avian-style respiratory system, various features found in the skeletons of different kinds of dinosaurs (see Ruben *et al.* for complete references). For example, ossified sternal ribs preserved with some sauropod (*e.g.*, Marsh 1883) and theropod (*e.g.*, Clark, Norell and Chiappe 1999) specimens, in all instances "lack the thickened lateral border and the transversely oriented articulations for the sternal ribs that characterize the sterna of all extant birds." Birdlike uncinate processes, observed in some oviraptorids (*e.g.*, Clark *et al.*) and dromaeosaurids (*e.g.*, Norell and Makovicky 1999), in birds seem "to function primarily in strengthening the rib cage and stabilizing the shoulder musculature," with no particular role in sternocostal ventilation of the lungs. Avian-like pneumatized vertebrae (*e.g.*, Bakker 1986), found in sauropods and some theropods yet apparently lacking the diverticuli of the cervical air sacs possessed by birds, "cannot be regarded as indicative of an extensive air sac system (see Wedel 2003*a*, 2003*b*, above). Gastralia, postulated as generating negative abdominal pressure during inhalation to facilitate expansion of caudal, birdlike air sacs (*e.g.*, Carrier and Farmer 2000), "perform no known role for active generation of either negative or positive abdominal pressure during lung ventilation" in extant crocodilians and rhynchocephalians.

Also, Ruben *et al.* posited that, contrary to earlier proposals by various authors (see *S1, S2*), dinosaurs and early birds lack respiratory turbinates (RTs), indicating that these taxa most likely maintained ectothermic (reptile-like) metabolic rates while at rest or routine, metabolic, and lung ventilation rates. Nevertheless, these authors suggested, some of these extinct taxa "may have possessed the capacity for sustained activity that might have approached that in some endotherms."

According to Ruben *et al.*, various data (*e.g.*, the absence of air sacs in the preserved viscera of the theropods *Sinosauropteryx* and *Scipionyx*; the axial skeletal features and distinct organization of viscera in *Scipionyx*) are consistent with the presence in theropods of crocodilian-like hepatic piston, diaphragm-breathing (see *S1, S2*, and *S3* for pro and con opinions on this topic). Indeed, the expansion of lung ventilatory capacity via this specialized diaphragm could have allowed multicameral, septate lungs in dinosaurs to have attained rates of oxygen to carbon dioxide exchange possibly approaching those of a few mammals having relatively low aerobic scopes. Consequently, the presence of diaphragm-assisted lung ventilation in these dinosaurs "might indicate that,

Tyrannosaurus rex adult and feathered hatchling, as portrayed by artist Todd Marshall. Such altricial behavior among Dinosauria was largely denied by John A. Ruben, Terry D. Jones, and Nicholas R. Geist in a study published in 2003.

although these dinosaurs maintained ectotherm-like routine metabolic rates, they were, nevertheless, uniquely capable of sustaining active oxygen consumption rates and activity levels beyond those of the most active living reptiles."

Therefore, Ruben *et al.* suggested, theropods (also early crocodylomorphs and possibly pterosaurs) may have been afforded "the low maintenance cost of ectothermy combined with enhanced endurance similar to that in some modern endotherms." This strategy, the authors noted, possibly operated best "in the relatively mild, equable climatic regimes of most of the Mesozoic Era, where chronic maintenance of ectothermic homeothermy would have been possible" (as in some extant large tropical-latitude lizards, such as the Komodo dragon, *Varanus komodoensis*; *e.g.*, see McNab and Auffenberg 1876). Like these giant lizards, theropods may very well have maintained significant home ranges and actively hunted and killed large prey.

In the same paper, Ruben *et al.* challenged suggestions that some kinds of dinosaurs brooded their eggs and some cared for their young in the nest (*e.g.*, see Norell, Clark, Chiappe and Dashzeveg 1995; Dong and Currie 1996; Clark, Norell and Barsbold 2001). As these authors explained, most extant birds incubate their eggs by brooding (*e.g.*, see Welty and Baptista 1988). Consequently, birds are likely to disturb their eggs while brooding, further disturbing them when turning and redistributing the eggs in the nest to ensure the equal distribution of temperature (Drent 1972). Also, egg turning ensures against "premature adhesion of the chorioallantois to the inner shell membranes, which would disrupt the albumen uptake by the embryo and prevent the embryo from assuming the tucking position essential for hatching (Drent 1972; Gill 1994)." On the other hand, such manipulation or rotation for reptilian eggs is generally fatal (see Grenard 1991).

Regarding dinosaurs as most likely ectothermic animals, Ruben *et al.* found it "unlikely that any dinosaur brooded its eggs in a birdlike manner," pointing out that all known *in situ* dinosaur clutches "contain at least partially buried eggs whose placement within the nest indicates that postdepositional manipulation was unlikely" (*e.g.*, see Seymour 1979). Furthermore, even partial burial of the eggs would have resulted in an inefficient transfer of body heat from the mother to the eggs (Varricchio, Jackson, Borkowski and Horner 1997).

According to Ruben *et al.*, finds of adult *Oviraptor* and *Troodon* (see entry) individuals atop their nests do not necessarily imply brooding, as similar behavior is also widely known among extant reptilian groups. Moreover, while the "folded under" posture of these theropods' limbs has been interpreted as more avian than crocodilian (Norell and Clark 1996), Ruben *et al.* found this to be a function of the relative length of the limbs rather than the avian-like nature of these animals.

Ruben *et al.* also found unconvincing the argument of Horner, Padian and de Ricqlès' (2001) "that the supposed high proportion of calcified cartilage to endochondral bone in some dinosaurs is indicative of hatchling altriciality at eclosion," pointing out that "it has been demonstrated that it is not possible to separate altricial, semialtricial, semiprecocial, and precocial hatchlings according to the degree or pattern of ossification of their skeletons (Starck 1996)." Ruben *et al.* agreed with Norell and Clark, who found pre-

cocity to be expected in dinosaur young because hatchling crocodilians and ratite birds (the basal sister group to all extant birds) are precocial.

Various earlier studies have used as evidence supporting endothermy in dinosaurs the fact that many dinosaurian taxa, especially the larger ones (and also large pterosaurs), typically achieved adult size relatively rapidly. The long bone cortex in such animals, being almost always mainly composed of well-vascularized fibro-lammellar bone, are indicative of rapid rates of growth (*e.g.*, see Ricqlès 1980; Ricqlès, Meunier, Castanet and Francillon-Viellot 1991; Reid 1996, 1997; see also *D:TE* and supplements). As noted by Padian, Horner and Ricqlès (2004; see also Horner, Padian and Ricqlès 1999, *S2*, for a preliminary report) in a study of growth in small dinosaurs and pterosaurs and the evolution of archosaurian growth strategies, similar tissues are also found in large mammals (*e.g.*, horses, cows, elk) and in very large birds; they are not necessarily, however, seen in small birds, dinosaurs (*i.e.*, dinosaurs having a total adult length of no more than 1.5 meters or slightly over five feet), and pterosaurs. Asking the question "why do tissues vary among dinosaur and pterosaur bones?," the authors proceeded with their investigation by placing known dinosaurian and pterosaurian osteohistological information within the context of both phylogeny and ontogeny.

Padian *et al.*'s study was based upon these authors' descriptions of transverse and longitudinal thin-sections of the cortical bone taken from the midshaft regions of well-preserved long bones of the following taxa: The Early Jurassic basal thyreophoran *Scutellosaurus* (UCMP 130580 and UCMP 170829, these specimens having been previously described by Rosenbaum and Padian 2000, collected by James M. Clark in 1993 from the Kayenta Formation of northern Arizona; see *S2*); the Late Cretaceous ornithopod *Orodromeus* (see Ricqlès, Horner and Padian, in press, for a summary of the histology of this genus); the Early Cretaceous basal ceratopsian *Psittacosaurus*; the large, Late Cretaceous hadrosaurid *Maiasaura* (reaching an adult length of seven meters in approximately seven years, this genus used to contrast its histology with the histologies of smaller taxa, and using only a very young—*i.e.*, few months old hatchling [MOR GS400]—ontogenetic stage); the Late Triassic primitive neotheropod *Coelophysis* (UCMP 129618, an adult possibly reaching a length of 1.7 meters or almost six feet; see Padian 1986*b*); the Early Cretaceous basal bird *Confuciusornis* (MOR 1063, an ostensibly adult specimen representing an individual about the size of a small crow; see "Appendix Two"); and the small pterosaurs *Eudimorphodon* (MGUH VP 3393, a Late Triassic basal pterosaur), *Dimorphodon* (YPM

Introduction

Oviraptor depicted by artist Berislav Krzic sitting on its nest. Such hypothesized brooding behavior, as evidenced by recent fossil finds, was questioned by John A. Ruben, Terry D. Jones, and Nicholas R. Geist in their 2003 study.

350 and the smaller YPM 9182, an Early Jurassic form), *Rhamphorhynchus* (CM 11433 and the larger Raymond Alf Museum of Paleontology specimen V97017/258, cortical bone tissues of this Middle to Late Jurassic genus described for the first time by Padian *et al.*), and *Pterodactylus* (CM 11430, cortical bone tissues described for the first time in this Late Jurassic genus also) (see "Appendix One").

For purposes of comparison, Padian *et al.* also described the cortical tissues of various members of the Crocodylia, these including the Late Cretaceous–Early Tertiary crocodile *Leidyosuchus* (MOR 266), the Late Triassic or Early Jurassic crocodylomorph *Terrestrisuchus*, and a three-year-old laboratory-raised modern taxon, *Alligator mississippiensis*.

Long-bone tissues of the above-mentioned nonavian dinosaurian, avian, and pterosaurian taxa revealed histological features suggesting comparatively lower growth rates for most (but not all) such small taxa than the rates seen in larger "typical dinosaurs" (*e.g.*, hadrosaurs such as *Maiasaura* and *Hypacrosaurus*, various sauropods, and large theropods such as *Allosaurus*). Conversely, the growth rates of the examined smaller taxa are more similar to — although generally somewhat faster than — those of young, rapidly growing crocodiles (as well as other typical reptiles). Nevertheless, the authors pointed out, such superficial similarities to the bone growth of crocodilians "belie some important differences, which are most usefully interpreted in phylogenetic and ontogenetic contexts."

As Padian *et al.* noted, large size in several dinosaurian and pterosaurian lineages evolved secondarily, this larger size hypothesized by the authors as having resulted "from rapid growth strategies that are reflected by characteristic highly vascularized fibrolamellar bone tissues that comprise most of the cortex." Attaining such large size as fast as possible, the authors suggested, may have been a strategy employed by these animals for avoiding predation during ontogeny. As do other tetrapods, Padian *et al.* noted, dinosaurs and pterosaurs generally grew more rapidly during their early ontogeny, and then more slowly as they approached adulthood, with small taxa perhaps growing at slower rates or for shorter lengths of time than larger taxa.

Padian *et al.* agreed with Erickson, Rogers and Yerby (2001) that both dinosaurs and pterosaurs most likely achieved their high growth rates in their common ancestor during the Middle or early Late Triassic, possibly as early as the separation of these two ornithosuchian groups from the clade "Pseudosuchia" (see Padian, Ricqlès and Horner 2001). Moreover, according to the phylogenetic distribution of bone tissue patterns in Archosauria, most "pseudosuchians" seem to have maintained lower rates of growth subsequent to their divergence from Ornithosuchia (Ricqlès, Padian and Horner 2003). Such high, "typically dinosaurian" growth rates seem to have evolved several times in large dinosaurs and pterosaurs, the authors stated. Padian *et al.* (2004) also proposed an alternative hypothesis that moderately high to high rates of growth may be "plesiomorphic for Archosauria, with secondary reversals to lower rates in some clades of small size as well as throughout Pseudosuchia (with some exceptions)."

However, Padian *et al.* (2004) cautioned that, by themselves, low vascularity and any inferred low growth rates are not good indicators of thermometabolic regime in small dinosaurs and pterosaurs considering their strong correlation with size. Possibly they "reflect mechanical exigencies of small size rather than especially lower growth rates, tied to the process of deposition of particular kinds of bone tissue."

Dinosaurs and Birds

In past volumes in this series of books, a major debate among researchers has concerned whether or not theropod dinosaurs directly gave way to birds (see "Appendix Two"), with numerous published articles offering various lines of evidence intended to support either side of this once highly controversial issue. More recently, however, the number of such articles — whether supporting the dinosaur-to-bird scenario or attempting to refute it — has noticeably dwindled, with the vast amount of the collective evidence reinforcing the scenario that birds did in fact descend directly from a line of non-avian theropods. Moreover, more feathered non-avian theropod taxa continue to be named and described (e.g., see *Yixianosaurus* entry), adding yet more weight to arguments favoring a close relationship between dinosaurs and birds. Among such more recent discoveries are theropod specimens with associated feather-like structures pertaining to taxa more remotely related to birds or occurring farther back in time (see Kundra 2004b for a recent report on filamentous impressions associated with locomotive theropod fossil footprints from the Lower Jurassic Turners Falls Formation of western Massachusetts, evidence supporting an earlier origin for feathers than previously documented; see also *Dilong* and *Coelophysis* entries).

Nevertheless, both thought-provoking pro and con studies, some of them controversial, continue to appear in the literature.

Various authors (e.g., Elźanowski 1999; Maryańska, Osmólska and Wolson 2002; Czerkas, Zhang, Li and Li 2002), in recent years, have postulated that certain maniraptoran clades (e.g., Oviraptorosauria, Dromaeosauridae, etc.; see S2 and S3), traditionally classified as non-avian theropods, are actually secondarily flightless taxa more closely related to modern birds than is the primitive bird *Archaeopteryx lithographica*.

In a published abstract for a poster, Paul (2003), in agreement with the above hypothesis, opined that "Conventional but obsolete phylogenetics continue to place the most birdlike avepod theropods basal to the *Archaeopteryx*-modern bird clade, even though Cretaceous dromaeosaurs, troodontids, oviraptorosaurs and therizinosaurs had advanced flight-related characters absent in *Archaeopteryx*, and became even less avian as they evolved; classic indicators of loss of flight more advanced than that of the Ürvogel."

According to Paul, such obvious flight adaptations as oversized sternal plates, folding arms, and birdlike to pterosaur-like tails are generally explained away as exaptations, while pennaceous feathers have been explained as having developed prior to flight. However, the recent discovery of "sinornithosaurs" (informally defined by Paul as "microraptors and cryptovalians") having fully developed forearm and hindlimb wings confirms "that basal dromaeosaurs were aerial as the neoflightless hypothesis predicts." Interpreting "sinornithosaurs" as "glider protofliers," Paul found these theropods to be, in all respects, as adapted for flight as was *Archaeopteryx*, perhaps more

Copyright © Berislav Krzic.

A hatchling *Tyrannosaurus rex* portrayed by artist Berislav Krzic with an insulating covering of downy feather-like integument. Recent studies by such workers as Chuong Cheng-Ming, Ping Wu, Fu-Cheng Zhang, Xing Xu, Minke Yu, Randall B. Widelitz, Ting-Xin Jiang and Lianhai Hou (2003), and by and Thomas P. Hopp and Mark J. Orsen (2004), have endeavored to trace the evolution of modern feathers from such structures.

A depiction by artist Mark Hallett of the "ground up" hypothesis for the origin of flight, with the primitive bird *Archaeopteryx* fleeing from a pursuing carnosaur.

so, possessing a much larger sternum, ossified sternal ribs, ossified uncinate processes, a strongly bowed outer metacarpal, a flattened central finger anchoring relatively longer outer primaries, alula feathers, and a body-streamlining, caudally directed distal pubis.

Paul deduced the flight performance of "sinornithosaurs" to be intermediate between that of *Ar-*

chaeopteryx and *"Jeholornis"* [=*Shenzhouraptor*], with a similar phylogenetic position probably applying to long-tailed dromaeosaurs and troodontids, and with short-tailed oviraptorosaurs near to or a little more derived than the bird *Confuciusornis*. Various features (*e.g.*, large heads, serrated and bladed teeth, raptorial fingers, sickel pedal claws) indicate that "sinornithosaurs were arch predators." Additionally, that author suggested, the spherical heads of the femora of these dinosaurs "allowed the hindwing to be held horizontal; it could not strongly flap and may have been folded during normal powered flight, being deployed for soaring and/or for extra lift and drag during final approach to prey." While it was unclear to Paul whether or not dromaeosaur hindwings constitute the basal avian condition or an independent adaptation, he noted that "the dromaeosaur-like jeholornid tail suggests that pterosaur-like tails were the basal avian norm" (see also Padian 2003, *Microraptor* entry).

In a contradictory report published as an abstract, Carney (2003) pointed out that "no phylogenetic framework or methodology has yet been applied to [the] evolutionary scenario" that these maniraptoran groups are secondarily flightless and closer to modern birds than *Archaeopteryx lithographica*. Carney's study, therefore, tested this hypothesis via analyzing, in a phylogenetic context, the appearance required for flight.

Utilizing a methodological framework for testing functional hypotheses plylonetically, Carney "structurally and functionally defined the key adaptation central to the origin of avian flight, which is the origin of the flight stroke itself." Carney then described (details presumably to be published in a forthcoming paper) and divided the relevant flight characters into two tiers — those required for active flight (present in *Archaeopteryx*), and those (*e.g.*, alula, elongate coracoid) required for advanced flight. Following defining relative taxa (again, details presumably to be published later), that author analyzed the sequence of appearance of those flight-requiring characters in birds and outgroups based upon recent theropod phylogenies, then tested this sequence against the original hypothesis.

Results of Carney's analysis — while "many so-called 'avian' features" (*e.g.*, aerodynamic, or asymmetrical, pennaceous feathers) did, in fact, evolve prior to *Archaeopteryx*— resulted in no evidence supporting the postulation that non-avian theropod dinosaurs were secondarily flightless. Moreover, that author stated, "evolutionary convergence and exaptations for flight within this clade of dinosaurs seem to have been previously misinterpreted as evidence for secondary flightlessness due to an 'anachronistic' fossil record and an absence of phylogenetic framework and methodology."

The nature of the filamentous integumentary structures described as "protofeathers" in the Chinese non-avian theropods *Sinornithosaurus* (see *S2, S3*) and *Sinosauropteryx* (see *D:TE, S1, S2, S3*) came into question in a study by Lingham-Soliar (2003*b*), with the debate as to whether or not birds descended from di-

nosaurs being "not pertinent to the study." As recounted by Lingham-Soliar, the past decade has seen the featuring "in high-profile journals" published articles on "feathered dinosaurs," "non-avian theropods," and "dromaeosaurs with integumental structures," many of these discoveries being "so highly sensationalized that it is difficult to separate fact from fiction." However, this topic requires that the suggested presence in dinosaurs of so-called protofeathers must either "be proven or rejected based on incontrovertible evidence," especially considering the fact that similar structures have also been reported in other groups of fossilized vertebrates, including pterosaurs (Wang, Zhou, Zhang and Xu 2002), ichthyosaurs (Lingham-Soliar 2001), and mammoths (Kukhareva and Ileragimov 1981).

Hopp and Orsen (2004) formally published their paper concerning dinosaur brooding and its relationship to the origin of flight feathers (see Hopp and Orsen 2001, *S3*; see also "Introduction," section on dinosaurs and birds, this volume). As Hopp and Orsen explained (2004), the origin of birds within Theropoda "has been controversial because it is difficult to understand how wing feathers evolved through short intermediate stages before becoming long enough to generate adequate power and lift for flight." According to these authors, the postulation that flight originated from the "ground up" (*e.g.*, Ostrom 1973) can be criticized, as no apparent selective pressure has yet been proposed for driving the process of lengthening a feather through its earliest stages. Yet, while a number of proposed feather functions (*e.g.*, hunting, insect trapping, display) have been proposed, none of them require the length and shape of the feather found in *Archaeopteryx*.

As Hopp and Orsen (2004) pointed out, proponents of both the "ground up" and "trees down" scenarios for the origin flight have neglect one of the most significant aspects of life in birds — brooding. However, while many extant birds are known to utilize their wing feathers in nesting and in the raising of chicks, no previous authors have proposed that brooding may have constituted a critically important selective pressure in evolving flight feathers. It was Hopp and Orsen's (2004) hypothesis that dinosaurian nesting and hatchling care "could have been responsible for the development of long feathers on the forelimbs and tails of pre-avian theropod dinosaurs."

To date, Hopp and Orsen (2004) noted, a number of fossil discoveries have been made implying that at least one group of cursorial theropod dinosaurs (*i.e.*, oviraptorids) may have incubated their eggs much in the fashion of modern birds (*e.g.*, Norell and Clark 1996; Dong and Currie 1996; Clark, Norell and Barsbold 2001). Unfortunately, Hopp and Orsen (2004) pointed out, while the posture of these nesting oviraptorids is quite similar to that seen in avian incubation, the lack of feather evidence in these described specimens preclude verification as to whether feathers may have been utilized in such incubations.

The position of the forelimb of these nesting oviraptorids, however, suggested to Hopp and Orsen (2004) "a selective mechanism for the elongation of wing feathers." In the most complete of the described specimens (see Norell and Clark), the oviraptorid lies with breast, belly, and feet contacting the eggs. As the authors pointed out, this position is "strikingly similar to that of many modern birds" (*e.g.*, the ostrich; see Sauer and Sauer 1966). Gaps in the oviraptorid's coverage of their eggs were great enough to allow detrimental solar-heating, wind-cooling, or rain-wetting effects on the exposed eggs, the authors noted. However, a covering comprising enlarged wing feathers and tail feathers would improve greatly an oviraptorid's ability to shield its eggs from such conditions and also to offer protection for hatchlings. Comparisons by Hopp and Orsen (2004) to modern birds showed that these gaps could have been covered in life by such wing and tail feathers.

According to Hopp and Orsen (2004), the requirements for brooding in oviraptorids could very well have led to the modern flight feather, whether feathers evolved from scales or from some downy, filamentous, or contour type of feather. The authors envisioned the feathered brooding forelimb in these dinosaurs as evolving "as an integrated unit, shaped by the need to shelter chicks and to carry the sheltering structure compactly when not in use." This evolutionary process would have offered brooding advantages at every stage in the lengthening of feathers, with even the comparatively shortest feathers providing additional protection for the young.

In order to determine whether or not brooding feathers could have evolved among early non-avian dinosaurs, Hopp and Orsen (2004) compared the skeletal anatomy of various primitive dinosaurs with extinct and extant birds, emphasizing avian nesting and brooding postures. Hopp and Orsen (2004) cited the trait of forelimb lengthing seen among more primitive non-avian theropods, this trend progressing more or less continuously from *Coelophysis* to *Ornitholestes*, to dromaeosaurs, and to *Archaeopteryx* (see Dingus and Rowe 1998). It was Hopp and Orsen's (2004) opinion that brooding may have been the driving force not only in lengthening of feathers in these dinosaurs, but also in the lengthing of the forearms to accommodate such feathers.

In the yet more primitive, Late Triassic *Herrerasaurus*, the wrist and elbow joints were far less flexible than in maniraptoran theropods and *Archaeo-*

pteryx; nevertheless, they suggest the beginnings of the folding characteristics of avian wings (see Paul 1988). Sereno (1993) had observed in this primitive saurischian moderate flexion capacity, including some sideways wrist flexion (*i.e.*, eversion). Hopp and Orsen (2004) particularly noted that the ulnare of this dinosaur and its wide articulation surface on the ulna, as described by Sereno, "suggest a primitive form of birdlike wrist eversion," this implying that *Herrerasaurus* could already have possessed lengthened primary feathers, as "this eversion is required for folding such feathers."

Therefore, Hopp and Orsen (2004) concluded that the utilization of long forelimb and tail feathers could have existed among early non-avian theropod dinosaurs. Moreover, because these early theropods were designed for brooding but not flying, it was reasonable to suggest that "forelimb and tail quill feathers may have evolved in these animals to the sizes and shapes seen in *Archaeopteryx* in the absence of flight, whereupon they were subsequently co-opted by *Archaeopteryx* or a similar creature for the additional purpose of flying."

Assuming that *Archaopteryx* arose from a small, cursorial, nonflying theropod ancestor, and using the modern roadrunner as a model, Hopp and Orsen (2004) envisioned an animal very similar to *Archaeopteryx*, possessing long feathers and the bone structure to maintain the orientation of those feathers. An animal such as this would have benefited from brief forelimb flapping which could lengthen the distance or increase the duration of leaps when hunting or fleeing predators. The authors noted that such brief flight maneuvers begin from the folded wing position, returning to it after landing, offering "an explanation for the unique geometry of the flight stroke, which includes a close approach to the folded position during recovery before the next stroke begins (Ostrom 1997).

Hopp and Orsen (2004) proposed the following sequence of events in the evolution of avian flight: 1. Long quill feathers having modern flight architecture developed on forelimbs of nonflying non-avian theropods for brooding purposed; 2. (arising subsequently or concurrently) ability to fold forelimb to streamline animal and protect feathers; and 3. subsequent development of flapping maneuvers, starting from folded posture, evolving into flight stroke.

From their model for the origin of flight, Hopp and Orsen (2004) found it most parsimonious to regard wing-brooding as a basal instead of a repeatedly derived trait that existed in the common ancestor of both palaeognath and neognath birds, which diverged during Late Cretaceous times (see Chiappe 1995*b*). This, the authors noted, pushes the origin of wing feather brooding back to a time almost contemporaneous with *Oviraptor*, and suggests that, if oviraptorids did have brooding feathers, the point of divergence "would revert to an even earlier common ancestor with *Archaeopteryx*, one that must have predated the Jurassic appearance of the latter."

In conclusion, Hopp and Orsen (2004) found such recently described feathered theropods as *Caudipteryx*, *Protarchaeopteryx*, and *Sinornithosaurus* to be consistent with their proposed scenario, noting that the forelimb feathers in these genera, while insufficient for flight, "are large enough and distributed appropriately along the forelimb to have functioned in brooding." Other recently proposed models, Hopp and Orsen (2004), are also consistent with the one offered by them —*e.g.*, that proposed by Prum (1999), based upon the ontogeny of feather forms, and that proposed by Ostrom, Poore and Goslow (1999), concerned with limb-bone flexibility in the evolution of the flight stroke.

Chuong, Wu, Zhang, Xu, Yu, Widelitz, Jiang and Hou (2003) utilized experimental evidence from molecular laboratories in a detailed study of Mesozoic feathers that included a review of various feathered non-avian theropods (*e.g.*, *Sinosauropteryx*, *Sinornithosaurus* (see entry), *Caudipteryx*, *Microraptor "gui"* [=*M. zhaoianus*]) and birds (*e.g.*, *Confusciusornis*) belonging to the Jehol Biota of China. Chuong *et al.* questioned the long-accepted view that the feather — "the centerpiece of bird flight"—evolved from an elongation of protective scales. According to this hypothesis, the scale subdivided over time, forming pennaceous, then plumulaceous feathers (see Regal 1975), the order of formation being from scalelike plates, to partial pennaceous vanes with emerging rachies, to bilaterally symmetric feathers, to plumulaceous barbs, and finally to radially symmetric downy feathers.

As related by Chuong *et al.*, this by now traditional view has been shaken during the past decade by two major advances: 1. The discovery of various fossils representing intermediate feather forms or feather-like appendages found on specimens of China's Jehol Biota; and developmental biological experiments using chicken integuments for the model, whereby "Feather forms can be modulated using retrovirus mediated gene mis-expression that mimics those found in nature today and in the evolutionary past."

From the evidence of their study, Chuong *et al.* recognized "that not all organisms with feathers are birds, and that not all skin appendages with hierarchical branches are feathers."

Moreover, the authors developed the following set of criteria for defining true avian feathers: "1) possessing actively proliferating cells in the proximal follicle for proximo-distal growth mode; 2) forming hierarchical branches of rachis, barbs, and barbules, with barbs formed by differential cell death and bilaterally or radially symmetric; 3) having a follicle structure, with mesenchyme core during development; 4) when mature, consisting of epithelia without mesenchyme core and with two sides of the vane facing the previous basal and supra-basal layers, respectively; and 5) having stem cells and dermal papilla in the follicle and hence the ability to molt and regenerate."

Based on this study, Chuong *et al.* proposed the following evolutionary sequence: Feather filaments splitting to form primitive barbs lacking barbules, to radially symmetric downy feathers having plumulaceous barbs, to bilaterally symmetric plumulaceous feathers, to bilaterally symmetric pennaceous vanes, to bilaterally asymmetric vanes. According to Chuong *et al.*, this order takes place in development (molecular pathways identified in the molecular biology laboratory), and probably also occurred in evolution, with, in the broad view, ontogeny repeating phylogeny, each of the above-mentioned transition points most likely representing a single evolutionary novelty (*e.g.*, Prum 1999).

As Chuong *et al.* pointed out, integument and integumentary appendages all consist of ectodermal cells and share ectodermal stem cells. In fact, "all the diverse appendages can be viewed on top of a common theme" (see Chuong 1998). Via experimental manipulation of molecular pathways, the authors stated, feather forms can now be modulated one to another, and, likewise, appendage phenotypes can be converted one to another. Consequently, feather morphogenesis offers a suitable paradigm with fossil evidence, theoretical models (*e.g.*, see Prum and Dyck 2003), and experimental possibilities (*e.g.*, Sawyer and Knapp 2003). "We are positioned to identify more molecular bases of evolutionary novelties," Chuong *et al.* predicted, "that eventually adapt the birds to the sky."

Holtz (2003*b*), in an abstract, noted that the recent discovery of wing-assisted incline running behavior (WAIR) in primitive modern avians (see the work of behavioral ecologist Kenneth P. Dial 2003, *S3*; 2004 [WAIR, "the only origin-of-avian-flight thesis that has been investigated experimentally," elucidating "a mechanical explanation for half a wing"]; see also Bundle and Dial 2003) "represents an important behavioral 'missing link' between cursorial and fully arboreal forms," permitting "a synthesis of 'ground up' and 'trees down' models of the origin of avian aerial flight." However, Holtz (2003*b*) pointed out, anatomical evidence suggests that such behavior also characterizes a more inclusive clade than Aves, thereby allowing some potential insight into the ecology of these coelurosaurian groups.

According to Holtz (2003*b*), the functional

correlates with WAIR seem to be as follows: Hindlimb adapted to running; elongated forelimb capable of lateral and forward excursions (not necessarily vertical power stroke); feathers. These traits, that author noted, characterize not only birds, but the group Maniraptora as a whole, being present in oviraptorosaurs and therizinosaurs.

Holtz (2003*b*) stated that the ability to escape predators by fleeing to high places would have been beneficial to nonaerial fliers (*e.g.*, all juvenile and small-bodied adult maniraptorans). Moreover, the size of non-avian dinosaur egg clutches suggest that mortality levels among these animals were higher than for modern birds or placental mammals.

Addressing the arguments of some workers that the above mentioned anatomical features constitute evidence for secondary flightlessness in oviraptorosaurs and therizinosaurs (see above), Holtz (2003*b*) suggested that these traits could rather be indicative of WAIR.

In conclusion, Holtz (2003*b*) suggested that the reduction in forelimb length found in some maniratoran clades (*e.g.*, *Caudipteryx*, Alvarezsauridae, advanced Troodontidae [positioned by some workers outside of Maniraptora; see Senter, Barsbold, Britt

and Burnham 2004, "Systematics" chapter]) could be a sign that these groups abandoned the behavior of wing-assisted incline running (as in modern ratite birds).

The "trees down" scenario of the origin of flight was addressed again by Chatterjee and Templin (2004), who contended that this hypothesis, based upon ecological and aerodynamic constraints, is more parsimonious than the "ground up" idea. According to these authors, recent discoveries of various feathered coelurosaurs (*e.g.*, *Sinosauropteryx*, *Caudipteryx*, and *Protarchaeopteryx*) from the Early Cretaceous of China provides "a rare glimpse of the transitional stages of avian flight and reinforces the arboreal theory."

Chatterjee and Templin explained that the evolution of flight in early birds was key to their success during the Mesozoic Era, the ability to fly enabling them to escape predators, exploit new resources, find mates, and migrate rapidly and cheaply to more favorable habitats. The most important adaptation of this purpose lies in the modification of forelimbs into wings, the latter providing upward lift against gravity and also forward propulsion through the air, with lift and thrust provided, respectively, by the proximal

Photograph courtesy and copyright © Triebold Paleontology, Inc.

Composite skeleton (cast) of an as yet unnamed giant North American oviraptorosaurian theropod from the Hell Creek Formation of South Dakota (see *S2* for more information). According to Thomas R. Holtz, Jr. (2003*b*), the fore- and hindlimbs of oviraptorosaurs and also therizinosaurs show traits comparable to those in birds.

and distal wings. Avian flight combines three independent wing movements to exchange energy from the air — dorsoventral flapping about gleno-humeral joint; rotation of wing about its long axis; and complex wrist movement that shortens wing stroke during downstroke (*e.g.*, see Rayner 1991). Feather evolution, Chatterjee and Templin further explained, "is linked closely to the insulation and aerodynamics of protobirds." Moreover, flight is a complex adaptation that must have evolved "in a sequence of small stages, over many generations, with each stage in the development of wings and feathers becoming functional and adaptative," with each level contingent on the preceding one (*e.g.*, Bock 1986, 2000).

As Chatterjee and Templin noted, the argument for an arboreal rather than strictly cursorial ancestor of birds "seems obvious" considering that virtually all modern gliding and flying animals live or move in trees. The authors greed that "Arboreal life is key to the origin of feathers, elongated forelimbs, enlargement of the brain, three-dimensional perceptual control, and the evolution of the flight stroke (Chatterjee 1997*b*; Bock 1986, 2000)." Furthermore, Chatterjee and Templin stated, the arboreal theory is supported by the fact that the acceleration of gravity accommodates the process of flight (see Norberg 1990; Rayner). This scenario used gravity to create an energy efficient airflow over body surfaces (see Tarsitano, Russell, Horne, Plummer and Millerchip 2000), while also providing "a complete series of plausible transitional stages of adaptations, from preflight to flapping flight, as is evident from the Chinese feathered coelurosaurs."

Small, ancestral, cursorial, terrestrial coelurosaurs probably climbed trees to escape predators, thereby invading arboreal habitats, Chatterjee and Templin speculated. Climbing, consequently, put new demands on the forelimbs, which became slowly and progressively longer to facilitate climbing and, therefore, more conducive to flight. Life in the trees, according to the authors, brought the added third dimension of height into these animals' lives, thus promoting the enlargement of the brain and increased acuity of vision. At the same time, the authors speculated, downy feathers or protofeathers evolved (as in *Sinosauropteryx*), both for insulating the body in the cooler arboreal environment and for streamlining the body for leaping.

From the ancestral coelurosaurian stage, the authors postulated the following sequence of stages of these dinosaurs in an arboreal environment leading to powered flight: 1. *leaping* from branch to branch, with outstretched forelimbs facilitating balance, coordination, and control of the body (*Sinosauropteryx*); 2. *parachuting*, with symmetrical contour feathers appearing in the remiges, offering a large lifting surface

(*Caudipteryx* and *Protarchaeopteryx*); 3. *gliding*, with modification of the shoulder and pelvic girdles, further elongation of the forelimbs, and the development of a swivel wrist joint and rigid tail enhancing climbing, with the sequence of a strong and synchronized forelimb cycle (up-and-forward, down-and-backward) during climbing as a precursor to the flight stroke, and with the achievement of a wing folding mechanism (*Sinornithosaurus*); and 4. *flapping flight*, following the appearance of large, asymmetrical contour feathers, with increased wing area and reduced wing loading, and with the tail becoming shorter for controlling pitch and increasing lift (*Archaeopteryx*).

Chatterjee and Templin stated that heterochrony — "the mechanism by which a species gives rise to a descendant species through changes in the timing or rate of developmental events relative to the ancestral condition" (see McKinney and McNamara 1991) — may have been the primary factor in the evolution of feathers (see Brush 2000). As shown earlier by Lucas and Stettenheim (1972), different kinds of feathers develop in successive generations in a hierarchal fashion, *i.e.*, natal down appearing during embryonic life, followed by second-generation adult down, then by pulmaceous feathers, and finally by contour feathers. Six stages of feather development were reconstructed by Chatterjee and Templin based on ontogeny and phylogeny, beginning with the most primitive protofeather structure: 1. simple, conical filament (as in *Sinosauropteryx* and *Beipiaosaurus*); 2. stage corresponding to natal down, this being first generation of feathers in ontogeny (*Sinornithosaurus*); 3. stage resembling adult down, with developed rachis and barbs (*Caudipteryx, Sinornithosaurus, Protarchaeopteryx*); 4. formation of a central shaft, as in bristle, semiplume, and filoplume with plumose barbs, with rachis longer than barbs (*Sinornithosaurus*); 5. development of symmetrical contour feathers, having vanes fully formed with an interlocking mechanism (*Caudipteryx, Protarchaeopteryx*); and 6. development of asymmetrical vane, with robust rachis in rectrices, and remiges for aerodynamic function (*Archaeopteryx, Confusciousornis*, other Chinese fossil birds).

In 1999, Wagner and Gauthier (see *S2*) proposed their "frame-shift" theory to explain the controversial question of how a theropod manus (possessing digits I, II, and III) devolved into an avian manus (with DII, DIII, and DIV) (see *S1*). The authors' theory proposed that, in the lineage of theropods following the secondary reductions of DV and then DIV, a deletion of condensation CI took place, eliminating redundancy in the condensations of digits, this forcing a homeotic shift in digital identity so that condensation CII developed into DI, CIII into DII, CIV into

DIII, with CV not differentiating. Smith (2003), however, in a published abstract for a poster, noted that "Recent embryological data have revealed a pentadactyl arrangement of prechondrogenic digital anlagen in the avian manus, suggesting a highly conserved pentadactyl ground state for the avian hand," thus making it seem "unlikely that redundancy in condensations was the impetus behind digital reduction."

In Smith's estimation, it could be more parsimonious to postulate that "frame shift" took place earlier in the lineage of the Theropoda, and via an evolutionary process other than the one proposed by Wagner and Gauthier.

Smith's alternate scenario hypothesized that the "loss of the digital development pathway of condensation CI" occurred before the appearance of Neotheropoda, at the same time as took place "a homeotic shift in the developmental identity of the initial digital condensations such that condensation CII develops into digit DI, CIII develops into DII, CIV develops into DIII, and CV develops into DIV." This considerably earlier homeotic shift, Smith explained, is more parsimonious, taking into account the numbers of elements that would be lost or reevolved under Wagner and Gauthier's scenario. Additionally, Smith suggested, this new scenario "would reconcile the pattern of digital reduction in the theropod manus with an apparently highly conserved pattern of digital reduction amniotes," perhaps also explaining "why advanced development of CV relative to CI is observed in chick embryos." Finally, the rearrangement of wrist elements in Neotheropoda could also relate to the "initial loss of the digital development pathway of CI."

Smith cautioned, however, that the above hypothesis could be refuted by the putative presence of a fifth manual digit in some specimens of the primitive neotheropod *Coelophysis*.

Grellet-Tinner and Chiappe (2004) approached the origins of birds topic from another perspective. Their study was based upon descriptions that have been published in the literature of the egg morphology (*e.g.*, shape, superficial attributes, and eggshell microstructure) and nesting behaviors of hard-shelled turtles, crocodilians (*Alligator mississippiensis*), and various kinds of dinosaurs—*i.e.*, hadrosaurids (*Hypacrosaurus stebingeri* and *Maiasaura peeblesorum*), titanosaurs (unidentified forms represented by eggs and embryos from the Auca Mahuevo locality in Patagonia; see above), troodontids (*Troodon formosus*; see *Troodon* entry), and oviraptorids (see *D:TE, S1, S2,* and *S3* for discussions on parental care in Dinosauria). These descriptions were then compared with the egg morphologies and nesting behaviors of various kinds of extant birds, including members of Neognathidae (*Meleagris gallopavo*, wild turkey; *Anser anser*, greylag goose) and Paleognathae (*Struthio camelus*, ostrich; *Rhea americana*, greater rhea; *Dromaius novahollandiae*, emu).

As Grellet-Tinner and Chiappe reiterated, only three among the many formerly proposed hypotheses regarding the origins of birds are currently held—1. the hypothesis identifying crocodilians as the closest relatives of birds (*e.g.*, Martin, Stewart and Whetstone, 1980); 2. that supporting a relationship between birds and basal Archosauromorpha (*e.g.*, Feduccia and Wild 1993); and 3. the most agreed-upon postulation that birds descended directly from non-avian theropod dinosaurs (*e.g.*, Ostrom 1976*a*). Because no oological information is currently known for any extinct basal archosauromorphs, the nest morphologies and nest attendances described in Grellet-Tinner and Chiappe's study could only contrast two of these hypotheses.

Grellet-Tinner and Chiappe found birds to be clustered within Archosauria based upon the following: Clacitic eggshell mineralogy; and presence of parental nest attendance. Birds nested within Theropoda based upon the following: Two eggshell layers; aprismatic condition among eggshell layers; eggs asymmetrical; brooding behavior; and monautochronic ovulation. Grellet-Tinner and Chiappe's analysis further supported a sister-taxa relationship between Troodontidae and Aves [see "Systematics" chapter for a contrary view], this node diagnosed by presence of shell units having blade-shaped crystals. Aves was unambiguously diagnosed by these authors "by the presence of three or more eggshell layers ... and one functioning ovary."

Based upon the descriptions offered in their study, Grellet-Tinner and Chiappe found both egg morphology and parental nesting strategies to possess distinct attributes useful for phylogenetic inference. Regarding the hypothesis relating birds to crocodilians, Grellet-Tinner and Chiappe identified but one similarity—*i.e.*, calcitic composition of eggshell—uniting these two groups; furthermore, the nest attendance strategies between these groups were found not to go beyond basic parental care behavior.

According to Grellet-Tinner and Chiappe's analysis, seven additional steps—and the future discovery of seven more unambiguous synapomorphies—would be needed to support a sister-taxon relationship between Crocodylia and Aves. Contrarily, however, their present "study documents how egg and nesting behavior attributes of living birds can be seen as transformations of those found in non-avian theropod dinosaurs, hence adding support to the hypothesis that birds are evolutionarily nested within Theropoda."

In a published abstract, Padian (2004*a*) addressed the origin of the avian body plan. Padian pointed out that members of the avian crown group Neornithes substantially differ from Mesozoic birds. As Padian noted, such basal members of Aves as *Archaeopteryx* (and more derived forms) essentially resemble their small contemporaneous non-avian theropod relatives, although their feathered wings and tail allowed for flight. Flight, according to that author, was instrumental in shaping much but not all of the evolution of birds.

Padian's scenario for the origin of the avian body plan is as follows: The forelimbs of non-avian relatives of birds were already capable of producing the flight stroke, although this movement was employed in the capture of prey rather than in flying. It was in this context that the wishbone also evolved. Prior to the evolution of flight, some non-avian theropods evolved feathers for various behaviours, including insulation and color. As flight evolved, locomotor emphasis shifted — *i.e.*, the tail module differentiating from the hindlimb module, the forelimb module gradually achieving dominance. Flight evolved as avian ancestors reduced their body size — accomplished by shortening their otherwise rapid growth at juveniles stages — thereby allowing their already feathered limbs to become aerodynamically effective. "Basal stem-group birds," Padian concluded, "fused some skeletal elements, reduced the tail, lost teeth, expanded the respiratory adaptations, and evolved the alula."

Life restoration by Todd Marshall of the duckbilled dinosaur *Maiasaura peeblesorum*. In 2004, Gerald Grellet-Tinner and Luis M. Chiappe published a study relating dinosaurs to birds, based upon published descriptions of eggs and embryos of this and other dinosaurian taxa. In the background of this illustration are two individuals of *Albertosaurus sarcophagus*, a Canadian theropod.

Dinosaur Extinctions

Theories and debates concerning the extinction of the last dinosaurs at the end of the Cretaceous period continue to be published, although (as with the dinosaur-birds issue) seemingly not with the frequency or abundance of previous years. As before, most of these pertain to the popular scenario of a giant asteroid impact being the culprit responsible for the final demise of the dinosaurs (see *D:TE*, *S1*, *S2*, and *S3*).

Kozisek (2003), in a published abstract, took a new approach to this topic based upon the persistence of extant tropical honeybees. As that author pointed out, tropical honeybees enjoyed widespread distribution during Late Cretaceous (Maastrichtian), among these being the oldest known species, *Trigona prisca*), found in latest Cretaceous (Maastrichtian) amber of New Jersey.

It had been estimated that the "nuclear winter" type conditions resulting from the asteroid impact would have globally reduced tropical temperatures to a temperate climate of from seven to 12 degrees centigrade. However, as explained by Kozisek, studies have demonstrated that honeybees have an optimal temperature range of from 26 to 36 degrees centigrade, freeze at zero degrees, become immobilized at 11 degrees, and die below 28 degrees. To have survived through the K-T event, these insects would require access all year round to flowering plants. Therefore, Kozisek noted, tropical conditions must have continued through the K-T boundary, this persistence placing limitations upon the maximal effect of the asteroid impact theory of dinosaurian extinction.

Witzke (2003), in a published abstract, reassessed the much published claims "that dinosaur diversity was gradually and inexorably declining through the Late Cretaceous (especially Campanian–Maastrichtian)." That author evaluated these claims by tabulating all published North American dinosaur occurrences, noting preservational categories (*i.e.*, articulated skeletons to bone scraps) for each geographic and

Skeletal casts of the Late Cretaceous dinosaurs *Edmontosaurus annectens* (left, foreground) and *Albertosaurus sarcophagus* (center), displayed at Triebold Paleontology's "Savage Ancient World: The Last American Dinosaurs" traveling exhibit, which premiered at the Westin Crown Center in Kansas City, Missouri, in 2002.

Photograph courtesy and copyright © Triebold Paleontology, Inc.

stratigraphic occurrence. Witzke's lists for all dinosaurian taxa for each age/stage resulted in both "conservative and liberal tallies of fossil diversity through time," conservative tabulations considering only taxa regarded as valid by most workers, liberal tabulations adding controversial taxa and those not yet fully documented.

According to Witzke, both tallies exhibited "similar trends over time," although "each produced significantly different absolute numbers of genera and species," Judithian and Lancian tabulations showing the greatest number of taxa. Witzke also observed a general relationship between the number of dinosaurian taxa and that of dinosaur-bearing formations for each age/stage.

As Witzke pointed out, Alberta's Dinosaur Park Formation "has become the standard of reference against which other dinosaur-bearing formations are compared," although the exceptional preservation and diversity in this formation renders such comparisons unclear; without this formation, the Hell Creek For-

mation would offer the most diverse fauna known for the Cretaceous. Moreover, according to that author, supposed patterns of diversity are apparently "more closely related to the distribution of dinosaur-bearing strata and taphonomic issues associated with each dinosaur-bearing lithofacies."

Witzke concluded that, given the general scarcity of well-preserved dinosaur faunas in the fossil record, it seems unlikely that the dinosaurian record is adequate to say much about the biodiversity of these animals through time, particularly on a global scale; moreover, "Faunal compilations for North America do not seem to provide any clear basis for waning dinosaur diversity through the Campanian–Maastrichtian."

In a somewhat related study, Fastovsky, Huang, Hsu, Martin-McNaughton, Sheehan and Weishampel (2004) utilized a new global database, based upon 1,266 positively identified body fossils, and also data from ichnotaxa, ootaxa, and coprolites (culled from the database of Weishampel, Barrett, Coria, Le Loeuff,

Skeleton (cast) of an unnamed oviraptorosaur from the Hell Creek Formation of South Dakota. This composite skeletal reconstruction is part of Triebold Paleontology's "Savage Ancient World: The Last American Dinosaurs."

Skeletons (casts) of the "bone headed" dinosaur *Pachycephalosaurus wyomingensis*, mounted for the "Savage Ancient World: The Last American Dinosaurs" traveling exhibit.

Xu, Zhao, Sahni, Gomani and Noto 2004), to examine the generic "richness" of the Dinosauria during the Mesozoic Era. Fastovsky *et al.*'s study showed that dinosaurs steadily increased their rate of diversity throughout the Mesozoic, this pattern attributable, at least in part, "to the development of new innovations driving an increasing variety of behavioral strategies."

Fastovsky *et al.* presented their data "at three levels of temporal resolution"—1. Late Triassic to Late Cretaceous (by epoch); 2. Late Cretaceous (by stage), and 3. Campanian to Maastrichtian (by substage)— illustrating two richness metrics at each level (*i.e.*, "absolute generic richness," or a compilation of genera, and "total generic richness," using repeat sample counts derived from a number of geographic localities).

From the Late Triassic through Late Cretaceous, Fastovsky *et al.* found a steady increase in both absolute generic richness and total generic richness during that span of time, with dinosaur diversity culminating during the Late Cretaceous, the latter containing 44 percent of all dinosaurian genera (nearly totalling all earlier dinosaur-bearing epochs combined). This database is dominated by genera from Asia and North America, accounting for 67 percent of the absolute Mesozoic generic richness and 80 percent of that of the Late Cretaceous.

Regarding the Late Cretaceous (the only interval for which substages were recognized), Fastovsky *et al.* found the Campanian stage to represent a stunning (almost 90 percent) increase in richness from the Cenomanian through Santonian levels, apparently suggesting "that the Campanian was the high water mark for dinosaur richness in the Mesozoic."

Examination of the Campanian through Maastrichtian intervals by substage (*i.e.*, Early Campanian–Late Maastrichtian), the authors, with a 95-percent confidence level, found the late Campania to have "had at least 13.8 and at most 22.1 more dinosaur genera than the late Maastrichtian when rarefied to the late Campanian level."

No evidence (*contra*, for example, Marsh 1882; Bakker 1986; Dodson 1996; Russell and Dodson 1997)

Skeleton (cast) of the duck-billed dinosaur *Edmontosaurus annectens* on display with the "Savage Ancient World: The Last American Dinosaurs" traveling exhibit.

was found by Fastovsky *et al.* suggesting that dinosaurs were decreasing in richness over the approximate 10 million-year timescales at the termination of the Cretaceous. The authors concluded that, in attempting to resolve extinction rates at the Cretaceous–Tertiary boundary, refinement of dating dinosaur-bearing units supercedes in effectiveness the collection of more dinosaur specimens.

Retallack (2004) proposed another scenario in which acid rain might explain why non-avian dinosaurs became extinct at the end of the Cretaceous period while birds, as well as other kinds of animals (*e.g.*, mammals), survived—the proposal that acid generated by a massive asteroid impact at the end of the Cretaceous resulted in differential extinctions.

As Retallack explained, "Acid would have been a consequence of catastrophic events postulated for the Cretaceous–Tertiary boundary: nitric acid from atmospheric shock by bollides and from burning trees; sulfuric acid from volcanic aerosol and from impact vaporizations of evaporites; hydrochloric acid from volcanic aerosols; and carbonic acid from carbon dioxide of volanoes, fires, and methane-hydrate release." Such acid, that author noted, would have left records in paleosols (pedoassay), boundary beds (chemoassay), and also the differential extinction of acid-sensitive organisms (bioassay).

Retallack's analyses (see paper for details) were based primarily upon assays of materials found at various Cretaceous–Tertiary sites in the badlands of Montana. Pedoassays, chemoassays, and biassays performed by Retallack indicated that acid rain was indeed "a consequence of the latest Cretaceous asteroid impact in Yucatan," and that this seems to have constituted a selective extinction mechanism among various taxa (*e.g.*, allowing, in Montana, the survival of amphibians and fish, but not nonmarine molluscs). Toxic acid rain could also have resulted in heavy extinctions among green angiosperms, a major food source for plant-eating dinosaurs. Consequently, browsing on such vegetation would have been difficult for such animals, yet "less problematic for small

Introduction

Skeletal cast of one of the last — if not *the* last — dinosaurs to become extinct, *Triceratops horridus*. Measuring about six meters (21 feet) long, the original specimen was collected in 1992 from the Hell Creek Formation of South Dakota.

Life restoration by Berislav Krzic of *Triceratops horridus*, one of the last Late Cretaceous dinosaurs to become extinct.

insectivorous and detritivorous mammals and birds." In conclusion, Retallack proposed that "the fatal component of end–Cretaceous events for dinosaurs and other creatures was browsing on leaves and other transient destruction of primary productivity by impact-induced acid rain."

All nonavian dinosaurs are generally believed to have gone extinct by the end of the Cretaceous period, some 65 million years ago. Nevertheless, infrequent reports of some dinosaurian taxa possibly persisting into the later Tertiary Era continue to be investigated. If this hypothesis were proven to be correct, it would follow that various theories relating to the final extinction of the dinosaurs — especially such theories as the bollide-impact scenario — would be seriously challenged. Among the areas postulated for the alleged survival of "Tertiary dinosaurs" is the Nanxiong basin in China (*e.g.*, see Sloan 1987).

The possibility of dinosaurs surviving into the post–Cretaceous period Paleocene of the Nanxiong basin was recently investigated by Buck, Hanson, Hengst and Hu (2004). As noted by these authors, the uppermost Nanxiong Formation and lowermost

Shanghu Formation of southeastern China span the K-T boundary interval. Earlier studies placed this boundary at the Nanxiong/Shangu formational contact. Both formations preserve an important paleontological record that includes both dinosaur eggshell fragments and Tertiary fossils, this seemingly anchronistic combination of fossils having been previously interpreted as evidence for "Tertiary dinosaurs." Until Buck *et al.*'s study, however, "no one has presented evidence refuting the presence of Tertiary dinosaurs in the Nanxiong basin."

Buck *et al.*'s study focused upon data Naxiong basin data relating to sedimentology, examining evidence of climatic conditions preserved in strata spanning the well-preserved K-T boundary. The authors measured a 1,258-meter section across the boundary, and documented and sampled lithological units (see paper for details). Among the conclusions of Buck *et al.* are the following:

The uppermost (101 meters) interval of the Nan-xiong Formation is of Tertiary age. Both the Nanxiong and Shanghu formations were deposited in comparable alluvial fan/playa mudflat environments having a highly seasonal, semiarid climate. This climate was basically consistent throughout the time that these sediments were deposited, the authors finding no evidence indicating a climate-related link between extinctions at the K-T border in the Nanxiong Basin. Mixing Cretaceous and Tertiary assemblages in the uppermost (and most controversial) interval of the Nanxiong Formation and lowermost interval (76 meters) of the Shanghu Formation can be explained as "the result of reworked Cretaceous fossils that were redeposited in previously unrecognized Paleocene debris flows and mudflows." Earlier studies (*e.g.*, Liu and Wang 1990; Rigby, Sneel, Unruh, Harlan, Guan, Li, Rigby and Kowalis 1993) seemingly had neglected to recognize the extent of the debris flow deposits occurring in the controversial intervals.

II: Dinosaurian Systematics

The following arrangement of the Dinosauria has been erected based upon similar breakdowns that have appeared in *D:TE* and its succeeding supplements, and also upon various more recently proposed phylogenies as cited below. Again, as in the previous volumes in the "series," this arrangement is the present writer's conservative attempt to organize the various taxa above the level of genus into a convenient and usable system, based upon the published data. Some of this writer's choices in following certain phylogenies to follow were subjective, based upon opinions formed after weighing the published evidence. As always, much of what is presented here is subject to future change. (For definitions, diagnoses, and other pertinent information concerning these taxa — *e.g.*, age and geographic distribution — consult previous volumes.)

Again, the present writer is not proposing or sanctioning any "official" organization of the higher dinosaurian taxa. Pending a more complete fossil record, it is not now possible to produce an entirely stable classification of the Dinosauria. As in the earlier books in this series, cladograms are not included, and the following attempt at organizing a phylogeny of the Dinosauria is, at best, tentative and subject to change.

Well-known published monotypic taxa above level of genus (*e.g.*, the family Dryptosauridae, which currently includes but one genus, *Dryptosaurus*, thereby rendering the family name redundant) are listed according to the name of the higher taxon, although many systematists list only the genus in their phylogenies. The terms "family," "subfamily," and "superfamily" have been retained, although many workers have abandoned these designations; such familiar terms as "suborder," "infraorder," and others, formerly used in Linnaen classification, have been mostly eliminated in this text. Family names can be identified by the suffix "-idae," subfamily names by "-inae," and superfamily names by "oidea."

Taxa preceded by a question mark (?) — *e.g.,* the genus *Eoraptor* (see below) or the clade Oviraptorosauria (see "Introduction," section on birds) — are regarded as valid, although their phylogenetic position is currently uncertain or under question. The validity of taxa set flagged by quotation marks ("_____") are in some kind of dispute, under discussion, or for some reason may inevitably prove to be invalid.

Following taxa above the genus level (*e.g.*, the level of family), listed alphabetically, are genera that are at present believed to belong to those higher-level groups. Genera, the placements of which are currently uncertain in those more clades, are designated as *incertae sedis*. Genera regarded in this document as junior synonyms of other genera (*e.g.*, *Morosaurus*, a junior synonym of *Camarasaurus*), exclusive of preoccupied names (*e.g.*, the preoccupied *Walkeria*, replaced by *Alwalkeria*), follow the generally accepted valid name, flagged in parentheses or brackets, and preceded by an equal sign (=).

Retained below are genera that have been designated as *nomina dubia* (singular, *nomen dubium*), such as the poorly known ceratopsian *Agathaumas*, which is probably a synonym of *Triceratops*. These taxa have dubious validity and are often based on meager fossil material. Some of these doubtful genera may be referrable to other better known taxa, such as *Antrodemus*, which could be referrable to *Allosaurus*, yet also to some other large Morrison Formation theropod. Also included herein are genera currently regarded as *nomina nuda* (singular, *nomen nudum*), *e.g.*, the possible saurischian *Nyasasaurus*. Note, however, that junior synonyms designated as either a *nomen dubium* and *nomen nudum* are not identified as such within the parentheses or brackets.

DINOSAURIA (*incertae sedis*: ?*Aliwalia, Alwalkeria,* ?*Macrodontophion* [*nomen dubium*], *Sanpasaurus* [*nomen dubium*], *Teyuwasu* [*nomen dubium*], *Tichosteus* [*nomen dubium*], *Yaverlandia*)

   I. SAURISCHIA (*incertae sedis*: *Chindesaurus,* ?*Nyasaurus* [*nomen nudum*])
      HERRERASAURIA
        HERRERASAURIDAE (?*Agnostiphys* [*nomen dubium*], *Herrerasaurus* [=*Frenguellisaurus, Ischisaurus*], ?*Spondylosoma, Staurikosaurus*)
      [unnamed clade]
        Eoraptor
      EUSAURISCHIA
        THEROPODA (*incertae sedis*: *Asiamerica, Calamosaurus* [*nomen dubium*], *Calamospondylus* [*nomen dubium*], ?*Chuandongocoelurus* [*nomen dubium*], *Dandakosaurus* [*nomen dubium*], *Deinocheirus, Embasaurus* [*nomen dubium*], *Huaxiasaurus* [*nomen nudum*], *Inosaurus* [*nomen dubium*], *Itemirus, Lukousaurus, Prodeinodon, Protoavis, Rapator* [*nomen dubium*], *Sinocoelurus* [*nomen dubium*], *Sinosaurus* [*nomen dubium*], *Teinurosaurus* [=*Caudocoelous*] [*nomen dubium*], *Thecospondylus* [*nomen dubium*], ?*Velocipes* [*nomen dubium*], *Wyleia* [*nomen dubium*]

THEROPODA (cont.)

?GUAIBISAURIDAE (*Guaiisaurus*)

NEOTHEROPODA

CERATOSAURIA

COELOPHYSOIDEA (*incertae sedis*: *Camposaurus, Dolicosuchus* [*nomen dubium*], ?*Halticosaurus* [*nomen dubium*], *Podokesaurus*, ?*Pterospondylus* [*nomen dubium*], ?*Sarcosaurus* [*nomen dubium*]）

Liliensternus

?*Segisaurus*

COELOPHYSIDAE (*Coelophysis* [=*Longosaurus, Rioarribosaurus*], ?*Eucoelophysis* [*nomen dubium*], ?*Gojirasaurus, Syntarsus* [=*Megapnosaurus*]

DILOPHOSAURIDAE (*Dilophosaurus*)

NEOCERATOSAURIA (*incertae sedis*: ?*Betasuchus* [=*Ornithomimidorum*] [*nomen dubium*], *Genusaurus, Ligabueino*)

Elaphrosaurus

CERATOSAURIDAE (*Ceratosaurus*, ?*Genyodectes, Spinostropheus*)

ABELISAUROIDEA (*incertae sedis*: *Coeluroides* [*nomen dubium*], *Dryptosauroides* [*nomen dubium*], ?*Ilokelesia, Jubbulpuria* [*nomen dubium*], *Ornithomimoides* [*nomen dubium*], ?*Quilmesaurus*, ?*Tarascosaurus, Xenotarsosaurus*)

NOASAURIDAE (*Deltadromeus, Laevisuchus* [*nomen dubium*], *Masiakasaurus, Noasaurus, Santanaraptor, Velocisaurus*)

ABELISAURIDAE (*Abelisaurus, Rugops*; *incerae sedis*: *Compsosuchus* [*nomen dubium*]), ?*Pycnonemosaurus*

CARNOTAURINAE (*Aucasaurus, Carnotaurus*, ?*Indosaurus*, ?*Indosuchus, Majungatholus* [=*Majungasaurus*], *Rajasaurus*)

TETANURAE (*incertae sedis*: *Bruhathkayosaurus, Chilantaisaurus, Condorraptor, Iliosuchus, Kaijiangosaurus, Kelmayisaurus* [*nomen dubium*], *Labocania, Orthogoniosaurus* [*nomen dubium*], *Walgettosuchus* [*nomen dubium*], *Zupaysaurus*)

"*Szechuanosaurus*" *zigongensis*

[unnamed clade]

Xuanhanosaurus

[unnamed clade]

SPINOSAUROIDEA (*incertae sedis*: ?*Poekilopleuron*)

MEGALOSAURIDAE

MEGALOSAURINAE (*Altispinax* [*nomen dubium*], *Magnosaurus, Megalosaurus* [=*Avalonianus, Picrodon*], *Piveteausaurus, Torvosaurus* [=*Edmarka*], ?*Wakinosaurus* [*nomen dubium*]）

EUSTREPTOSPONDYLINAE (*Afrovenator, Eustreptospondylus;* *Piatnitzkysaurus, Streptospondylus*)

SPINOSAURIDAE (*incertae sedis*: *Siamosaurus*)

BARYONYCHINAE (*Baryonyx* [=*Cristatusaurus, Suchomimus*]）

SPINOSAURINAE (*Irritator* [=*Angaturama*], *Spinosaurus*)

AVETHEROPODA (*incertae sedis*: *Antrodemus* [*nomen dubium*], *Bahariasaurus, Bradycneme* [*nomen dubium*], *Gasosaurus, Ozraptor, Valdoraptor*)

CARNOSAURIA (*incertae sedis*: ?*Cryolophosaurus, Lourinhanosaurus*, ?*Fukuiraptor*, ?*Siamotyrannus*)

Monolophosaurus

ALLOSAUROIDEA (?*Becklespinax, Megaraptor*, ?*Szechuanosaurus* [*nomen dubium*]; *incertae sedis*: *Erectopus*, ?*Metriacanthosaurus*)

SINRAPTORIDAE (*Sinraptor, Yangchuanosaurus*)

[unnamed clade]

ALLOSAURIDAE (*Allosaurus*, [=*Apatodon, Creosaurus*, ?*Epanterias, Hypsirophus* in part, *Labrosaurus*], *Saurophaganax* [=?*Epanterias*]）

CARCHARODONTOSAURIDAE

Acrocanthosaurus

[unnamed clade]

[unnamed clade] (cont.)
    (*Carcharodontosaurus* [=*Sigilmassaurus*],
      Giganotosaurus)
    Neovenator
COELUROSAURIA (*incertae sedis*: *Archaeornithoides*, ?*Diplotomodon* [*nomen dubium*], *Kakuru*, ?*Marshosaurus*, *Ngexisaurus* [*nomen nudum*], *Richardoestesia* [=*Paronychodon*, *Tripriodon*, *Zapsalis*], *Shanyangosaurus*, *Tanycolagreus* [*nomen dubium*], *Tugulusauruns* [*nomen dubium*])
    COMPSOGNATHIDAE (*Aristosuchus* [*nomen dubium*], *Compsognathus*, *Huaxiagnathus*, *Mirischia*, *Sinosauropteryx*)
    [unnamed clade]
      Nedcolbertia
      Scipionyx
      [unnamed clade]
        ?*Ornitholestes*
        Proceratosaurus
        Nqwebasaurus
      TYRANNORAPTORA
        Coelurus
        TYRANNOSAUROIDEA
          Aviatyrannis
          ?*Bagaraatan*
          [unnamed clade]
            Dilong
            Stokesosaurus
            DRYPTOSAURIDAE (*Dryptosaurus*)
            [unnamed clade]
              ?*Eotyrannus*
              TYRANNOSAURIDAE (*incertae sedis*: *Alectrosaurus*, *Shayangosaurus*)
                ALBERTOSAURINAE
                  Albertosaurus
                  Gorgosaurus
                TYRANNOSAURINAE (*incertae sedis*: ?*Chingkankousaurus*, ?*Deinodon* [*nomen dubium*])
                  Daspletosaurus
                  ?*Alioramus*
                  [unnamed clade]
                    Tarbosaurus [=*Jenghiskhan*, *Maleevosaurus*, *Shanshanosaurus*]
                    Tyrannosaurus [=*Aublysodon*, *Clevelanotyrannus*, *Dinotyrannus*, *Dynamosaurus*, *Manospondylus*, *Nanotyrannus*, *Stygivenator*])
      MANIRAPTORIFORMES
      ORNITHOMIMOSAURIA
        Pelecanimimus
        Shenzhousaurus
        HARPYMIMIDAE (*Harpymimus*)
        GARUDIMIMIDAE (*Garudimimus*)
        ORNITHOMIMIDAE (*Anserimimus*, *Archaeornithomimus*, *Gallimimus*, *Ornithomimus*, [=*Coelosaurus*, *Dromiceiomimus*], *Sinornithomimus*, *Struthiomimus*, *Timimus* [*nomen*

ORNITHOMIMIDAE (cont.)
dubium])
TROODONTIDAE (*incertae sedis: Borogovia, ?Elopteryx*
[*nomen dubium*], *Koparian* [*nomen dubium*], *Mei, ?Ornithodesmus, Sinusonasus, Tochisaurus*)
[unnamed clade] (*Byronosaurus, Sinornithoides*)
[unnamed clade] (*Saurornithoides, Troodon* [=*Pectinodon, Polyodontosaurus, Stenonychosaurus*])
MANIRAPTORA (*incertae sedis: ?Scansoriopteryx*) [*Epidendrosaurus*], *Yixianosaurus*)
THERIZINOSAUROIDEA (*incertae sedis: Erliansaurus, Nothronychus*)
Beipiaosaurus
?Eshanosaurus
[unnamed clade]
ALXASAURIDAE (*Alxasaurus*)
Enigmosaurus
THERIZINOSAURIDAE (*Erlikosaurus, Nanshiungosaurus, Neimongosaurus, Segnosaurus, Therizinosaurus*)
METORNITHES (*Protarchaeopteryx* [=*Incisivosaurus*])
Unquillosaurus
OVIRAPTOROSAURIA (*incertae sedis: ?Microvenator*)
AVIMIMIDAE (*Avimimus*)
[unnamed clade]
CAUDIPTERYGIDAE (*Caudipteryx, Heyuannia*)
CAENAGNATHOIDEA
CAENAGNATHIDAE (*Caenagnathasia, Chirostenotes* [=*Caenagnathus, Macrophalangia*], *Elmisaurus, ?Euryonychodon* [*nomen dubium*], *?Nomingia, ?Thecocoelurus* [*nomen dubium*])
OVIRAPTORIDAE
OVIRAPTORINAE (*?Citipati, Conchoraptor, ?Khaan, Oviraptor, Rinchenia*)
INGENIINAE (*Ingenia*)

PARAVES
ALVAREZSAURIDAE (*Alvarezsaurus, Patagonykus; incertae sedis: Heptasteornis* [*nomen dubium*]
MONONYKINAE (*Mononykus, Parvicursor, Shuvuuia*)
EUMANIRAPTORA
DEINONYCHOSAURIA (*incertae sedis: ?Variraptor* [*nomen dubium*])
Hulsanpes

Hulsanpes (cont.)
Pyroraptor
?Sinovenator
Unenlagia
MICRORAPTORIA
Bambiraptor
Microraptor (=*Archaeo-raptor, Cryptovolans*)
Sinornithosaurus
DROMAEOSAURIDAE
(*incertae sedis: Graciliraptor, ?Nuthetes* [*nomen dubium*], *?Phaedrolosaurus* [*nomen dubium*])
DROMAEOSAURI-NAE (*?Achillobator, ?Adasaurus, ?Atroci-raptor, Deinonychus, Dromaeosauroides, Dromaeosaurus, Saur-ornitholestes, Utah-raptor*)
VELOCIRAPTORI-NAE (*?Ichabondran-iosaurus* [*nomen nu-dum*], *?Koreanosau-rus* [*nomen nudum*], *Velociraptor* [=*Ovo-raptor*])
AVES [see "Appendix Two: Birds:]
SAUROPODOMORPHA (*incertae sedis: Dachungosaurus* [*nomen nudum*], *Efraasia* (=*Palaeosauriscus*), *?Thotobolosaurus* [*nomen nudum*])
PROSAUROPODA (*incertae sedis: Fulengia* [*nomen dubium*], *Ruehleia, Tawasaurus* [*nomen dubium*], *Yimeno-saurus*)
?Saturnalia
?THECODONTOSAURIDAE (*Thecodontosaurus* [=*Agrosaurus*])
ANCHISAURIA
ANCHISAURIDAE (*Ammosaurus, Anchisaurus,* [=*Yaleosaurus*])
MELANOROSAURIDAE
Riojasaurus (=*Strenusaurus*)
[unnamed clade] (*Melanorosaurus*)
[unnamed clade] (*Camelotia, Lessemsaurus*)
PLATEOSAURIA (*Jingshanosaurus*)
MASSOSPONDYLIDAE (*Massospondylus* [=*Aetonyx, Aristosaurus, Dromicosaurus, Gryponyx, Hortalo-tarsus, Leptospondylus, Pachyspondylus*])
YUNNANOSAURIDAE (*Yunnanosaurus*)
PLATEOSAURIDAE (*incertae sedis: Mussaurus*)
[unnamed clade] (*Coloradisaurus*)
[unnamed clade] (*Lufengosaurus*)
[unnamed clade] (*Euskelosaurus* [=*Eucnemesaurus, Gigantoscelus, Orinosaurus, Orosaurus, Plateo-sauravus*])
[unnamed clade] (*Plateosaurus* [=*Dimodosaurus, Gresslyosaurus, Pachysauriscus, Sellosaurus*])
SAUROPODA (*incertae sedis: Aepisaurus* [*nomen dubium*], *Algoasaurus* [*nomen dubium*], *Atlantosaurus* [*nomen du-bium*], *Cardiodon* [*nomen dubium*], *Chinshakiangosaurus* [*nomen nudum*], *Chuanjiesaurus, Damalasaurus* [*nomen nudum*], *Datousaurus* [=*Lancangosaurus*], *Dystrophaeus* [*nomen dubium*], *Kotasaurus, Lancanjiangosaurus* [*nomen*

SAUROPODA (cont.)

    nudum], *Microdontosaurus* [*nomen nudum*], *Mongolosaurus* [*nomen dubium*], *Oplosaurus* [*nomen dubium*], *Qin-
lingosaurus* [*nomen dubium*], *Tendaguria*, *Ultrasaurus* [*nomen dubium*], *Volkheimeria*)

    ?*Gongxianosaurus*

    ?BLIKANASAURIDAE (*Blikanasaurus*)

    VULCANODONTIDAE (?*Ohmdenosaurus*, *Vulcanodon*)

    ?*Isanosaurus*

    EUSAUROPODA (*incertae sedis*: *Amygdalodon* [*nomen dubium*], ?*Aragosaurus*, *Asiatosaurus* [*nomen dubium*],
Hudiesaurus, ?*Klamelisaurus*, ?*Rhoetosaurus*)

        CETIOSAURIDAE (*incertae sedis*: ?*Protognathosaurus* [*nomen dubium*])

            Barapasaurus

            Cetiosaurus

            Patagosaurus

       "EUHELOPODIDAE" (*incertae sedis*: *Pukyongosaurus* [*nomen dubium*])

           SHUNOSAURINAE (*Kunmingosaurus* [*nomen nudum*], *Shunosaurus* [=*Shuosaurus*], *Zizhon-
gosaurus* [*nomen dubium*])

           EUHELOPODINAE (*Euhelopus* [=*Tienshanosaurus*], *Mamenchisaurus* [=*Zigongosaurus*], *Omei-
saurus*, *Tehuelchesaurus*)

    Lourinhasaurus

    NEOSAUROPODA (*incertae sedis*: *Ferganasaurus*)

        DIPLODOCOIDEA (*incertae sedis*: *Amphicoelias* [*nomen dubium*], ?*Cetiosauriscus*, *Histriasaurus*,
[*nomen dubium*], *Losillasaurus*)

           REBBACHISAURIDAE (*Limayasaurus*, *Nigersaurus*, *Rayososaurus*, *Rebbachisaurus*)

           ?*Dinheirosaurus*

           FLAGELLICAUDATA (*incertae sedis*: *Suuwassea*)

               Amazonsaurus

               DICRAEOSAURIDAE (*Amargasaurus*, *Dicraeosaurus*, *Dyslocosaurus*)

               DIPLODOCIDAE (*Apatosaurus* [=*Brontosaurus*], *Barosaurus*, *Diplodocus*, *Mega-
cervixosaurus* [*nomen nudum*], *Seismosaurus*, *Supersaurus* [=*Dystylosaurus*, *Ultra-
sauros*], *Tornieria*)

      MACRONARIA (*incertae sedis*: *Abrosaurus*)

      [unnamed clade] (*Atlasaurus*, *Bellusaurus*, *Jobaria*)

        CAMARASAUROMORPHA

           ?HAPLOCANTHOSAURIDAE (*Haplocanthosaurus* [=*Elosaurus*])

           CAMARASAURIDAE (*Camarasaurus* [=*Cathetosaurus*], *Caulodon*, *Morosaurus*,
Uintasaurus], *Eobrontosaurus*, ?*Neosodon* [*nomen dubium*], *Nurosaurus* [*nomen
nudum*])

           TITANOSAURIFORMES (*incertae sedis*: *Chiayüsaurus* [*nomen dubium*], *Eucamero-
tus* [*nomen dubium*], *Lapparentosaurus*, ?*Ornithopsis* [*nomen dubium*], *Pelorosaurus*
[=*Dinodocus*], ?*Pleurocoelus*)

               BRACHIOSAURIDAE (*incertae sedis*: ?*Astrodon* ?[*nomen dubium*], *Bothrio-
spondylus* [*nomen dubium*], ?*Chondrosteosaurus* [*nomen dubium*], ?*Gigantosaurus* [*nomen dubium*], ?*Ischyrosaurus* [*nomen dubium*], ?*Lusotitan*, ?*Mori-
nosaurus* [*nomen dubium*], *Sauroposeidon*, ?*Sonorasaurus* [*nomen dubium*])

                  [unnamed clade]

                     Brachiosaurus (=*Giraffatitan*)

                     Cedarosaurus

             TITANOSAURIA (*incertae sedis*: *Aegyptosaurus*, *Agustinia*, *Andesaurus*, *Ar-
gentinosaurus*, *Clasmodosaurus* [*nomen dubium*], *Gobititan*, ?*Huabeisaurus*,
Iuticosaurus [*nomen dubium*], *Macrurosaurus* [*nomen dubium*], *Tangvayosaurus*, *Venenosaurus*)

               Phuwiangosaurus

               Janenschia

               Epachthosaurus (=*Pellegrinisaurus*)

               LITHOSTROTIA (*Alamosaurus*, *Ampelosaurus*, *Antarctosaurus*, ?*Austro-*

LITHOSTROTIA (cont.)
saurus, *Chubutisaurus*, *Hypselosaurus* [*nomen dubium*], *Jainosaurus*, *?Jiangshanosaurus*, *Laplatasaurus*, *Lirainosaurus*, *Magyarosaurus*, *Malawisaurus*, *Mendozasaurus*, *Paralititan*, *Rapetosaurus*, *Rocasaurus*, *Titanosaurus* [*nomen dubium*])

[unnamed clade] (*Aeolosaurus* [=*Eolosaurus*, *Gondwanatitan*], *Rinconsaurus*)

?NEMEGTOSAURIDAE (?*Bonitasaura*, *Nemegtosaurus*, *Quaesitosaurus*)

Isisaurus

SALTASAURIDAE

SALTASAURINAE (*Argyrosaurus*, ?*Campylodoniscus* [*nomen dubium*], *Loricosaurus*, ?*Microcoelus* [*nomen dubium*], *Neuquensaurus*, *Saltasaurus*)

OPISTHOCOELICAUDINAE (*Alamosaurus*, ?*Borealosaurus*, *Opisthocoelicaudia*)

II. ORNITHISCHIA (*incertae sedis*: *Crosbysaurus* [*nomen nudum*], *Galtonia*, *Lucianosaurus* [*nomen dubium*], *Notoceratops* [*nomen dubium*], *Pekinosaurus* [*nomen dubium*], *Protecovasaurus* [*nomen nudum*], *Revueltosaurus* [*nomen dubium*], ?*Silesaurus* [*nomen nudum*], ?*Taveirosaurus* [*nomen dubium*], *Technosaurus*, *Tecovasaurus*, *Xiaosaurus* [*nomen dubium*])

Lesothosaurus

PREDENTATA

FABROSAURIDAE (*Fabrosaurus* [*nomen dubium*], *Gongbusaurus* [*nomen dubium*])

GENASAURIA (*incertae sedis*: *Onychosaurus* [*nomen dubium*]), ?*Pisanosaurus*

THYREOPHORA (*incertae sedis*: *Bienosaurus*, ?*Alocodon* [*nomen dubium*], *Lusitanosaurus* [*nomen dubium*], *Tatisaurus*)

Scutellosaurus

[unnamed clade]

Emausaurus

THYREOPHOROIDEA

SCELIDOSAURIDAE (*Scelidosaurus*)

EURYPODA

STEGOSAURIA (*incertae sedis*: *Craterosaurus* [*nomen dubium*], ?*Dravidosaurus*, *Monkonosaurus*, *Paranthodon*)

HUAYANGOSAURIDAE (*Huayangosaurus*, *Regnosaurus* [*nomen dubium*])

STEGOSAURIDAE (*incertae sedis*: *Changdusaurus* [*nomen nudum*], *Yingshanosaurus* [*nomen nudum*])

Dacentrurus

STEGOSAURINAE (*Chialingosaurus*, ?*Chungkingosaurus*, *Hespersaurus*, *Kentrosaurus*, [=*Doryphosaurus*, *Kentrurosaurus*], *Lexovisaurus*, *Stegosaurus* [=*Diracodon*, *Hypsirophus*, in part], *Tuojiangosaurus*, *Wuerhosaurus*)

ANKYLOSAURIA (*incertae sedis*: ?*Amtosaurus*, ?*Anoplosaurus* [*nomen dubium*], *Brachypodosaurus* [*nomen dubium*], *Crichtonsaurus*, *Chritonsaurus*, *Dracopelta*, *Hanwulosaurus* [*nomen nudum*], *Hoplitosaurus*, *Hylaeosaurus*, *Liaoningosaurus*, *Mymooropelta*, *Niobrarasaurus*, *Nodosaurus*, ?*Peishansaurus* [*nomen dubium*], *Polacanthus* [=*Polacanthoides*, *Vectensia*], *Sarcolestes*, *Sauroplites*, [*nomen dubium*], *Stegopelta*, *Stegosaurides* [*nomen dubium*])

ANKYLOSAURIDAE (*incertae sedis*: *Aletopelta* [*nomen dubium*], *Heishansaurus* [*nomen dubium*], *Maleevus*, *Tianchiasaurus* [*nomen dubium*])

Gargoyleosaurus

[unnamed clade]

Minmi

[unnamed clade]

Gastonia

[unnamed clade]

Gobisaurus

Shamosaurus

Shamosaurus (cont.)

ANKYLOSAURINAE (*incertae sedis*: ?*Nodocephalosaurus*)

    Tsagantegia

    [unnamed clade]

        Tarchia

        [unnamed clade] (*Pinacosaurus* [=*Syrmosaurus*], *Shanxia* [*nomen dubium*], *Saichania, Talarurus, Tianzhenosaurus*)

        [unnamed clade] (*Ankylosaurus, Euoplocephalus* [=*Anodontosaurus, Dyoplosaurus, Scolosaurus, Stereocephalus*])

NODOSAURIDAE (*incertae sedis*: *Acanthopholis* [=*Eucersaurus*] [*nomen dubium*], ?*Animantarx, Crataeomus* [*nomen dubium*], ?*Cryptodraco* [*nomen dubium*], *Glyptodontopelta* [*nomen dubium*], *Hierosaurus* [*nomen dubium*], ?*Lametasaurus* [*nomen dubium*], *Palaeoscincus* [*nomen dubium*], ?*Priconodon* [*nomen dubium*], *Priodontognathus* [*nomen dubium*], *Rhodanosaurus* [*nomen dubium*], ?*Struthiosaurus* [=*Craetomus, Danubiosaurus, Hoplosaurus, Leipsanosaurus, Pleuropeltus*])

    Cedarpelta

    [unnamed clade] (*Pawpawsaurus, Sauropelta, Silvisaurus*)

    [unnamed clade] (*Panplosaurus, Edmontonia* [*Denversaurus*])

CERAPODA

  ORNITHOPODA (*incertae sedis*: *Laosaurus* [*nomen dubium*], *Loncosaurus* [*nomen dubium*], ?*Nanosaurus* [*nomen dubium*], *Phyllodon* [*nomen dubium*], *Qantassaurus*, ?*Siluosaurus* [*nomen dubium*], *Syngonosaurus* [*nomen dubium*])

    EUORNITHOPODA (*incertae sedis*: *Drinker, Fulgurotherium, Leaellynsaura*, ?*Notohypsilophodon, Yandusaurus*)

      Agilisaurus

      [unnamed clade]

        Othnielia

        Orodromeus

        "HYPSILOPHODONTIDAE"

          Hypsilophodon

          Zephyrosaurus

      [unnamed clade]

        Gasparinisaura

        ?*Atlascoposaurus*

        THESCELOSAURIDAE (*incertae sedis*: *Bugenasaura*)

          Parksosaurus

          Thescelosaurus

        IGUANODONTIA (*incertae sedis*: *Callovosaurus* [*nomen dubium*], *Craspedodon* [*nomen dubium*])

          Tenontosaurus

          Muttaburrasaurus

          RHABDODONTIDAE (?*Mochlodon* [*nomen dubium*], *Rhabdodon* [=*Oligosaurus, Ornithomerus*], *Zalmoxes*)

          DRYOMORPHA (*incertae sedis*: *Anabisetia, Talenkauen*)

            DRYOSAURIDAE (*Dryosaurus* [=*Dysalotosaurus*], *Kangnasaurus* [*nomen dubium*], *Valdosaurus*)

          ANKYLOPOLLEXIA

            CAMPTOSAURIDAE

              (*Camptosaurus* [=*Brachyrophus, Camptonotus, Cumnoria, Symphyrophus*], *Draconyx*)

            STYRACOSTERNA

              Lurdusaurus

              Equijubus

              IGUANODONTOIDEA

IGUANODONTOIDEA (cont.)

    IGUANODONTIDAE (*Bihariosaurus, Iguanodon* [=*Heterosaurus, Hikanodon, Procercosaurus, Sphenospondylus, Therosaurus, Vectisaurus*], ?*Planicoxa*)

Ouranosaurus

?*Fukuisaurus*

[unnamed clade]

    Jinzhousaurus

    Probactrosaurus

    Nanyangosaurus

[unnamed clade]

    Altirhinus

    Protohadros

    Eolambia

HADROSAUROIDEA (*incertae sedis: Gilmoreosaurus, Claosaurus, Heilonjiangosaurus* [*nomen nudum*], *Secernosaurus, Tanius*)

?*Bactrosaurus*

Shuangmiaosaurus

HADROSAURIDAE (*incertae sedis: Cionodon* [*nomen dubium*], *Diclonius* [*nomen dubium*], *Hypsibema* [=*Parrosaurus*] [*nomen dubium*], *Mandschurosaurus* [*nomen dubium*], *Microhadrosaurus* [*nomen dubium*], *Ornithotarsus* [*nomen dubium*], ?*Orthomerus* [*nomen dubium*], *Thespesius* [*nomen dubium*])

    Pararhabdodon

    Telmatosaurus

    EUHADROSAURIA

        HADROSAURINAE (*incertae sedis: Aralosaurus*)

            Lophorhothon

            EDMONTOSAURINI (*Brachylophosaurus, Edmontosaurus* [=*Anatosaurus, Anatotitan*], *Hadrosaurus, Kritosaurus* [=*Anasazisaurus, Maiasaura, Prosaurolophus, Shantungosaurus*)

            SAUROLOPHINI (*Saurolophus, Gryposaurus, Kerberosaurus, Naashoibitosaurus*)

        LAMBEOSAURINAE (*incertae sedis: Amurosaurus, Barsboldia, Jaxartosaurus*)

            Tsintaosaurus

            PARASAUROLOPHINI (*Charonosaurus, Parasaurolophus*)

            CORYTHOSAURINI (*Corythosaurus* [=*Procheneosaurus,* in part, *Pteropelyx*], *Hypacrosaurus* [=*Cheneosaurus, Procheneosaurus,* in part], *Lambeosaurus* [=*Didanodon, Procheneosaurus,* in part, *Stephanosaurus, Tetragonosaurus,* in part], *Nipponosaurus, Olorititan*)

CHASMATOPIA

    ?HETERODONTOSAURIDAE

        Abrictosaurus

        Dianchungosaurus (*nomen dubium*)

        Echinodon

        Geranosaurus (*nomen dubium*)

        Heterodontosaurus

        Lanasaurus

        Lycorhinus

        ?*Oshanosaurus* (*nomen nudum*)

        ?*Trimucrodon* (*nomen dubium*)

    MARGINOCEPHALIA

MARGINOCEPHALIA (cont.)
    PACHYCEPHALOSAURIA (*incertae sedis: Micropachycephalosaurus, ?Tianchungosaurus* [=*Teinchisaurus* [*nomen dubium*], *Tenchisaurus* [*nomen dubium*]
        Stenopelix
        GOYOCEPHALA
            ?Wannanosaurus
            Goyocephale
            HOMALOCEPHALOIDEA
                Homalocephale
                PACHYCEPHALOSAURIDAE (*incertae sedis: Ferganocephale*)
                    Stegoceras (=*Ornatotholus*)
                    PACHYCEPHALOSAURINAE (*Gravitholus* [*nomen dubium*], *Prenocephale* [=*Sphaerotholus*], *Tylocephale*)
                        [unnamed clade] (*Colepiocephale, Hanssuesia*)
                        PACHYCEPHALOSAURINI (*Pachycephalosaurus, ?Stygimoloch* [=*Stenotholus*])
CERATOPSIA (*incertae sedis: Claorhynchus* [*nomen dubium*], *Trachodon* [*nomen dubium*])
    PSITTACOSAURIDAE (*Hongshanosaurus, Luanpingosaurus* [*nomen dubium*], *Psittacosaurus* [*Protiguanodon*])
    NEOCERATOPSIA (*incertae sedis: Arstanosaurus* [*nomen dubium*], *Kulceratops* [*nomen dubium*])
        [unnamed clade] (*Asiaceratops* [*nomen dubium*], *Chaoyangsaurus* [=*Chaoyoungosaurus*])
        Liaoceratops
        Microceratops [*nomen dubium*]
        ARCHAEOCERTOPSIDAE (*Archaeoceratops*)
        CORONOSAURIA
            PROTOCERATOPSIDAE (*Bagaceratops* [=*Breviceratops*], *Bainoceratops, Graciliceratops, Magnirostris, Protoceratops*)
            CERATOPSOIDEA
                LEPTOCERATOPSIDAE
                    Montanoceratops
                    LEPTOCERATOPSINAE (*Leptoceratops, Prenoceratops, Udanoceratops*)
                [unnamed clade]
                    Zuniceratops
                    CERATOPSIDAE (*incertae sedis: Dysganus* [*nomen dubium*])
                      ?Turanoceratops [*nomen dubium*]
                      CENTROSAURINAE (*incertae sedis: ?Avaceratops*)
                        [unnamed clade]
                          Achelousaurus
                          Pachyrhinosaurus
                      Einiosaurus
                      [unnamed clade] (*incertae sedis: Brachyceratops, Monoclonius ?*[*nomen dubium*])
                      Centrosaurus [=*Eucentrosaurus*]
                      Styracosaurus
                    CHASMOSAURINAE (*incertae sedis: Agathaumas* [*nomen dubium*], *Ceratops* [=*Proceratops*] [*nomen dubium*]), *Polyonax* [*nomen dubium*])
                      [unnamed clade]
                        Chasmosaurus [=*Eoceratops*]
                        Pentaceratops
                        [unnamed clade]
                          Arrhinoceratops
                          Anchiceratops
                          [unnamed clade]
                          Triceratops [=*Ugrosaurus, Sterrholophus*]

Saurischia

New or emended definitions and diagnoses continue to be proposed in the paleontological literature for the dinosaurian clades above the level of genus. Among these recent offerings, numerous earlier published phylogenies have again been reassessed and revised — by systematists specializing in particular dinosaurian groups — in the second edition of *The Dinosauria* (see Weishampel, Dodson and Osmólska 2004), wherein most participants are presumably in agreement as to current dinosaurian systematics.

Benton (2004), in a chapter of that tome on the origin and relationships of Dinosauria, discussed the apomorphy-based clade Archosauria — a group included in the larger vertebrate clade Diapsida — noting that phylogenetic studies of dinosaurs in their context within Archosauria have resulted in the following generally accepted conclusions: 1. Monophyly of Archosauria; 2. Archosauria including basal Triassic forms regarded as sister taxa to Avesuchia, the latter including two lines, one leading to crococilians and the other to birds; 3. Crurotarsi, the crocodilian line comprising the problematically related clades Phytosauridae, Ornithosuchidae, Prestosuchidae, Rauisuchidae, Poposauridae, and Crocodylophorpha; 4. Avematarsalia consisting of *Sclermochlus*, Pterosauria, and Dinosauromorpha; 5. monophyly of Dinosauria; 6. Dinosauria including two clades, Saurischia and Ornithischia; 7. Saurischia comprising several basal taxa, Theropoda, and Sauropodomorpha; and 8. Ornithischia comprising several basal taxa, Thyreophora, and Cerapoda.

Sereno (1991*b*), Benton noted, had given the more inclusive group Dinosauromorpha the node-based definition of the clade including the basal taxa *Lagerpeton chanarensis*, *Marasuchus talampayensis*, *Pseudolagosuchus major*, the Dinosauria, plus all descendants of their common ancestor; within Dinosauromorpha, the less inclusive clade Dinosauriformes was node-defined by Novas (1992) as the clade including the most recent common ancestor of *Marasuchus* [=*Lagosuchus* of his terminology], Dinosauria, and all taxa descended from it (see Benton for diagnoses of these and other nondinosaurian clades).

Benton defined and diagnosed Dinosauria as follows (see Benton for definitions and diagnoses of more encompassing and also related clades):

DINOSAURIA

Node-based definition: *Triceratops*, Neornithes [Late Cretaceous to modern birds; see "Appendix Two"], their most common ancestor, and all descendants (Benton 2004).

Diagnosis: Loss of postfrontal; humerus with elongate deltopectoral crest, apex at point corresponding to over 38 percent down length of humerus; brevis shelf on ventral surface of postacetabular part of ilium; acetabulum extensively perforated; tibia having transversely expanded, subrectangular distal end; tibia with caudolateral flange, receiving depression on dorsal aspect of astragalus; astragular ascending process on cranial face of tibia (Benton 2004).

Within Dinosauria, Benton accepted the two traditional major subgroups of that clade, Saurischia and Ornithischia, the former group defined and diagnosed as follows:

SAURISCHIA

Stem-based definition: Dinosaurs more closely related to *Tyrannosaurus* than to *Triceratops* (Holtz and Osmólska 2004).

Partial skeleton (FMNH P25112) of *Apatosaurus excelsus*, a member of the Saurischia, the clade of so-called "lizard-hipped" dinosaurs.

Courtesy The Field Museum, negative number GN79248.

Skeleton (cast) of *Edmontosaurus annectens*, a representative of the Ornithischia, the clade of so-called "bird-hipped" dinosaurs.

Reconstructed skeleton (including casts of PVSJ 407, 53, and 373) and life-sized sculpture (by Stephen A. Czerkas) of *Herrerasaurus ischigualastensis*, currently classified as a basal saurischian, although some workers regard this species as a primitive theropod.

Diagnosis: Narial fossa expanded in rostroventral corner of naris; subnarial foramen; lacrimal folding over caudal and/or dorsocaudal part of antorbital fenestra; articular facet for atlas in axial intercentrum concave, lateral borders upturned; neural arch of cranial cervical vertebra having marked concavity between postxygapophyses and caudodorsal corner of centrum (caudal conos); centra of postaxial cranial cervical vertebrae three to five) longer than that of axis; epipophyses on caudal cervical vertebrae six to nine; dorsal vertebrae with hyposphene-hypantrum articulation; expanded transverse process of sacral ver-

tebrae roofing space between adjacent ribs; absence of fifth distal carpal; first phalanx of manual digit I twisted, longest manual nonungual phalanx; well-developed supraacetabular crest, accounting for over 0.3 of iliac acetabulum depth; medioventral lamina restricted to proximal third of ischium (Langer 2004).

In concert with other authors in *The Dinosauria*, Langer, in a review of basal Saurischia, regarded such primitive dinosaurian genera as *Eoraptor*, *Herrerasaurus*, and *Staurikosaurus*—classified in some past and recent studies as basal theropods (see below)—as basal saurischians outside of Theropoda. Performing a cladistic analysis including 107 anatomical characters, with an ingroup including *Eoraptor lunensis*, *Guaibasaurus candelariensis*, *Herrerasaurus ischigualastensis*, and *Staurikosaurus pricei*, as well as the oldest well-known ornithischian, *Pisanosaurus mertii*, plus all other members of Ornithischia, Langer found a monophyletic Saurischia to comprise two main groups. The first of these groups is Herrerasauria (a clade introduced by Galton 1985*a*, and including the family Herrerasauridae); the second, an unnamed clade including *Eoraptor*, *Guaibasaurus*, *Saturnalia* (having been regarded as a basal prosauropod, a sauropodomorph outside of Prosauropoda, and also a primitive saurischian outside of Sauropodomorpha; see *Saturnalia* entries, *S2* and this volume), Theropoda, and Sauropodomorpha (Langer 2004).

Langer accepted the Eusaurischia, a monophyletic clade introduced by Padian, Hutchinson and Holtz (1999; see *S3*) to unite the two major groups Theropoda and Sauropodomorpha exclusive of Herrerasauridae and *Eoraptor*; within Eusaurischia, the genus *Saturnalia* representing the sister taxon of Sauropoda; and *Guaibasaurus* either a sister taxon of Theropoda or the most basal of known theropods (see *Guaibasaurus* entry). Additionally, Langer regarded the primitive type species *Agnosphitys cromhallensis* and *Teyuwasu barberenai* as *nomina dubia* (these and other such taxa not having been so designated in *D:TE*, *S1*, *S2*, or *S3*).

Langer offered the following definitions and diagnoses of the basal saurischian clades:

HERRERASAURIA

Node-based definition: All dinosaurs sharing a more recent common ancestor with *Herrerasaurus* than with *Liliensternus* and *Plateosaurus* (Langer 2004).

HERRERASAURIDAE

Node-based definition: *Herrerasaurus*, *Staurikosaurus*, plus all descendants of their most recent common ancestor (Novas 1992; 1997*b*).

[Unnamed clade comprising *Eoraptor* plus EUSAURISCHIA]

Diagnosis: Metacarpal stouter; (shared with Theropoda only) supraacetabular ridge continuous with lateral border of brevis fossa; caudally expanded ischial peduncle (Langer 2004).

EUSAURISCHIA

Node-based definition: Least inclusive saurischian clade containing *Cetiosaurus* and Neornithes (Langer 2004).

Theropoda

Among all the recent revisions of the Dinosauria, most of them have dealt with the Theropoda, the large saurischian clade embracing numerous diverse clades of mostly bipedal and carnivorous taxa.

The breakdown of the Theropoda presented by the present author at the beginning of this chapter basically follows the cladogram of Holtz and Osmólska (2004) in their review of the Saurischia. Holtz and Osmólska found Theropoda to include Tetanurae, which in turn includes the clades Spinosauroidea and Avetheropoda (the clade Ceratosauria being currently under question); Avetheropoda (introduced by Paul 1988) comprising the large clades Carnosauria and Coelurosauria, the latter including, among many other taxa, Sereno's (1999*b*) Tyrannoraptora, a clade including Tyrannosauroidea plus Maniraptoriformes; Maniraptoriformes uniting *Ornithomimus velox* with *Passer domesticus*; Maniraptora including *P. domesticus* plus all taxa nearer to *O. velox*, almost all recent cladistic analyses including in this clade the Oviraptorosauria, Therizinosauroidea, Dromaeosauridae, Troodontidae, and Aves; Paraves consisting of *P. domesticus* plus all taxa closer to it than to *Oviraptor philoceratops*; and Eumaniraptora comprising Deinonychosauria and Avialae (see below).

Holtz and Osmólska offered the following:

THEROPODA

Stem-based definition: All taxa closer to [the extant European house sparrow] *Passer domesticus* than to *Cetiosaurus oxoniensis* (Maryańska, Osmólska and Wolson 2002, emended after Padian and May 1993).

For the past 15 or more years, phylogenies of the Theropoda have mostly focused upon the large clade Coelurosauria, leaving the relationships of noncoelurosaurian taxa poorly understood. Ironically, as pointed out by Carrano and Sampson (2003) in an abstract, coelurosaurian phylogenies often include the most fragmentary taxa, those dealing with more basal forms often relying on well-known or species or those of particular interest, this resulting in "an inability to place many incomplete but geographically and temporally important forms." Furthermore, the authors noted, this practice has hindered attempts at analyzing fully evolutionary patterns within this diverse clade of dinosaurs.

Carrano and Sampson, after a three-year systematic study of basal theropods based upon first-hand examination of nearly all taxa worldwide, utilizing a matrix incorporating approximately 350 characters and almost 70 taxa, and despite the inclusion of significantly fragmentary forms, reached the following conclusions: The recovery of most major clades (*i.e.*, Coelophysoidea, Ceratosauria, Spinosauroidea, Allosauroidea, and Coelurosauria), with some (*e.g.*, Coelophysoidea) "surprisingly poor"; Herrerasaurididae and *Eoraptor* supported as primitive theropods (see above for a contrary opinion), the latter weakly so; also the resolution of more than a dozen taxa as spinosauroids (including a megalosaur clade) and over 15 ceratosaurians.

According to Cerrano and Sampson, this phylogenetic pattern (full details of these authors' analysis which will presumably be published at a later date) will clarify many aspects of theropod evolution worthy of additional study, including "(1) convergent evolution of several trophic and locomotory features; (2) repeated size increases and decreases throughout the group; (3) complex patterns in the evolution of pneumatic characters; and (4) few robust biogeographic patterns among these basal forms."

Carrano and Sampson stressed that their results underscore the importance of incorporating into such analyses taxa based upon fragmentary material (particularly for biogeographic hypotheses), verifying the published observations of other authors, and examining material that has not been named or described.

In a paper by Wilson, Sereno, Srivastava, Bhatt, Khosla and Sahni (2003) naming and describing the new abelisaurid genus *Rajasaurus* (see entry), the authors cited Sereno *et al.* (in review), who will offer a new phylogenetic analysis of basal neotheropods. This analysis accepts as valid the clade Ceratosauria (=Neoceratosauria; see *S2*), although excluding from it the

Life restoration by artist Mark Hallett of the abelisaurid theropod *Abelisaurus comahuensis*.

Coelophysoidea, a group traditionally regarded as a clade of primitive ceratosaurs, and with the ceratosaurian taxa *Ceratosaurus* and Abelusauroidea sharing a more recent ancestry with Tetanurae than with forms such as the coelophysoid *Coelophysis* (*e.g.*, see Carrano and Sampson 1999). *Elaphrosaurus*, *Ceratosaurus*, and the then unnamed "Niger taxon 1" [=*Spinostropheus*; see entry] were recognized as successive outgroups to Abelisauroidea (the latter including the families Noasauridae and Abelisauridae), and with the relationships of the genera *Ilokelesia* and *Genusaurus* unresolved within Abelisauroidea. Carnotaurines are restricted to India, Madagascar, and South America, their successive outgroups found in Africa.

As Wilson *et al.* pointed out, recent attempts "to stabilize the phylogenetic taxonomy of the Theropoda have arranged and evaluated clade names in the context of a monophyletic Ceratosauria that included *Ceratosaurus* and *Coelophysis*" (*e.g.*, see Sereno 1998; Padian, Hutchinson and Holtz 1999). However, the recent hypothesis, which places *Ceratosaurus*-like theropods closer to Tetanurae than to *Coelophysis*-like forms, presents important taxonomic consequence. The revision by Wilson *et al.* focused upon giving taxon names to six, currently ambiguously defined clades, this proposed taxonomy attempting "to provide stability of constituency and Linnean rank agreement while preserving priority of definition and original intent where possible."

Giving detailed summaries of these six clades, including their taxonomic histories (see Wilson *et al.* for details), the authors proposed that the following node- and stem-based definitions be adopted:

NEOTHEROPODA

Node-based definition: Least inclusive clade containing *Coelophysis bauri* and Neornithes (Sereno 1998).

TETANURAE

Node-based definition: Most inclusive clade containing Neornithes, but not *Ceratosaurus nasicornis* (Padian, Hutchinson and Holtz 1999).

CERATOSAURIA

Node-based definition: Most inclusive clade containing *Ceratosaurus nasicornis*, but not Neornithes (Padian, Hutchinson and Holtz 1999),

ABELISAUROIDEA

Node-based definition: Most inclusive clade containing *Carnotaurus sastrei* and *Noasaurus leali* (Wilson, Sereno, Srivastava, Bhatt, Khosla and Sahni (2003).

ABELISAURIDAE

Node-based definition: Most inclusive clade containing *Carnotaurus sastrei*, but not *Noasaurus leali* (Wilson, Sereno, Srivastava, Bhatt, Khosla and Sahni (2003).

NOASAURIDAE

Node-based definition: Most inclusive clade containing *Noasaurus leali*, but not *Carnotaurus sastrei* (Wilson, Sereno, Srivastava, Bhatt, Khosla and Sahni (2003).

In a published abstract, Tykoski (2004) focused upon the basal theropod group Ceratosauria, recently considered by some workers to be paraphyletic. Tykoski criticized such analyses for not taking into account the ontogenetic stages of various pertinent coelophysoid specimens utilized in scoring characters, pointing out that all included taxa were instead treated as if known from adult specimens, and that some of the incorporated characters had been selectively deleted *a priori* from the analyses if regarded as too ontogenetically variable.

Tykoski's analysis employed a method ("suitable for any clade of closely related taxa likely to share similar ontogenetic pathways") of estimating the ontogenetic stage of individual specimens of numerous coelophysoid taxa, creating a character-specimen matrix to determine "the most parsimonious hierarchy of specimens based upon shared ontogenetic transformations." That author's resultant "ontogram depicts the degree of specimens' ontogenetic development relative to other specimens of their own and closely related taxa," with juvenile, subadult, and adult stages of the specimens recognized by natural breaks on the

ontogram, and sequences of ontogenetic transformations mapped relative to each other.

Tykoski included both previously examined and also new coelophysoid specimens in an analysis of basal theropods, applying the results of the ontogenetic analysis to character coding. Resulting from this analysis was a hypothesis supporting the inclusion of Coelophysoidea within Ceratosauria; however, by removing the late ontogeny-dependent characters the Coelophysoidea was excluded from Ceratosauria. Consequently, Tykoski suggested "that accurate assessment of a specimen's ontogenetic stage is vital to phylogeny reconstruction, and *a priori* deletion of ontogeny-dependent characters is detrimental to obtaining accurate phylogenetic hypotheses."

In a review of the Ceratosauria, a phylogenetic analysis performed by Tykoski and Rowe (2004) found this clade — contrary to some other recent studies — to be monophyletic and including two major sister groups, the Coelophysoidea and Neoceratosauria. Tykoski and Rowe offered the following definitions and diagnoses for the Ceratosauria and its subclades:

CERATOSAURIA

Stem-based definition: All theropods more closely

related to *Ceratosaurus nasicornis* than to birds (Rowe 1989).

Diagnosis: Unambiguous apomorphies comprising the following: axial neural spine extending cranially beyond prezygapophyses; dorsoventrally low postaxial neural spines; transverse processes of dorsal vertebrae caudally backswept, triangular in dorsal

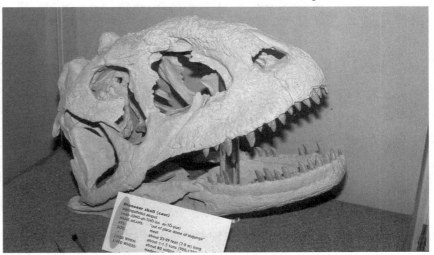

Mounted holotype skeleton (MACN-CH 894) of the carnotaurine abelisaurid *Carnotaurus sastrei*.

Skull (cast of FMNH PR2100) of the carnotaurine abelisaurid *Majungatholus atopus*.

Photograph by the author, courtesy The Field Museum.

Life restoration of the carnotaurine abelisaurid *Majungatholus atopus* by artist Todd Marshall.

of craniodorsal half of acetabulum in lateral aspect; pubic-shaft axis bowing cranially; dimorphism in femoral cranial trochanter; femur with well-developed, crestlike medial epicondyle; tibiofibular crest of distal end of femur sharply separated from fibular condyle; astragalus and calcaneum fused, forming astragalocalcaneum (in adults); fourth distal tarsal with large rectangular notch in caudolateral margin; two pleurocoels in proximal cervical and cranial dorsal vertebrae (Tykoski and Rowe 2004).

NEOCERATOSAURIA

Diagnosis: Unambiguous apomorphies comprising the following: six sacral vertebrae by addition of either second dorsosacral or third caudosacral vertebra; centra of midsacral vertebrae strongly reduced in size; ventral margin of sacrum arching dorsally; distal end of ischium expanded into ischial "foot"; cnemial crest of tibia craniocaudally as long as or longer than articular condyles, crest hooking sharply laterally, rising well above proximal condyles; ambiguous apomorphies (missing in *Elaphrosaurus*, present for Neoceratosauria under ACCTRAN optimization; most diagnostic of a *Ceratosaurus* plus Abelisauroid clade under DELTRAM) including the following: skull length less than three times height of caudal skull height; premaxilla dorsoventrally taller than it is rostrocaudally short, permitting significant contribution of maxilla with external naris; nasal contributing to antorbital cavity; lacrimal antorbital recess with single opening; frontals fused; frontals and parietals fused; infratemporal fenestra approximately twice size of

aspect; sacral ribs fused with ilia; ilium with broad M. caudofemoralis brevis fossa; supraacetabular crest of ilium flaring laterally and ventrally, overhaning much

Life restoration of the
carnotaurine abelisaurid
Rajasaurus narmadensis by
artist Todd Marshall.

orbit in lateral aspect; quadrate and quadratojugal fused; absence of quadrate foramen; quadrate dorsal ramus taller than orbit; pronounced, sharply defined median ridge on supraoccipital; interdental plates fused to one another; pleurocoel in cranial end of axis; pneumatic foramen or foramina in axis neural arch caudodorsal to diapophysis; sacral centra fused to extreme degree, sutures difficult to discern, only swellings marking articular surfaces of centrum; cranial to middorsal centra with two pairs of pleurocoels; cranial margin of sapulocoracoid smoothly curved, uninterrupted by notch at scapulocoracoid contact; proximal head of humerous bulbous; distal humeral condyles flattened; deltopectoral crest greater than 45 degrees length of humerus; deltopectoral crest oriented obliquely on humeral shaft; proximal end of metacarpal I loosely appressed to II; iliac postacetabular process with concave caudal margin; peg-in-socket ilium-pubis articulation; ischial peduncle of ilium oriented ventrally; distal end of pubis terminating in caudally expanded "foot"; craniocaudal length of pubic "foot" 10 to 30 percent length of pubic shaft; ischial antitrochanter large or markedly developed; shallow extensor groove on cranial surface of distal femur; tibia expanded caudal to fibula; pedal

digits having two lateral grooves (Tykoski and Rowe 2004).

COELOPHYSOIDEA

Diagnosis: Unambiguous apomorphies consisting of the following: Craniocaudal length of internal antorbital fenestra greater than 25 percent of maximum skull length; premaxilla nasal process forming half or less of rostrodorsal narial border; maxillary process of premaxilla loosely overlapping that of maxilla, resulting in flexible articulation; subnarial diastema in tooth row at contact of premaxilla and maxilla; maxilla alveolar border sharply upcurved rostrally, resulting in rostroventral orientation of first maxillary tooth; rostral end of dentary dorsally raised over length of first three to four alveoli; serrations reduced or absent on premaxillary teeth; mesial premaxillary teeth subcircular to circular in cross section, straight or just slightly recurved (nearly conical); premaxillary tooth row not extending distally below external naris; most mesial dentary teeth almost straight, subcircular in cross section, serrations reduced or absent; lacrimal rostral ramus longer than ventral ramus; absence of axial diapophysis; reduced axial parapophysis; largest sacral rib articulating with first caudosacral vertebra; distal end of scapular blade expanding relative to base of blade; humerus sigmoid in lateral aspect; iliac-pubic articulation smaller than iliac-ischial articulation; distal end of iliac-pubic articulation with distinct cranial and ventral articular faces separated by sharp angle; distal end of pubis terminating with small expansion, or "knob"; femoral head ligament (ligamentum capitus femoralis) sulcus on caudal surface of proximal femur deep, giving femur caudally hooked profile in proximal aspect; medial flange on distal fibula partly overlapping ascending process of astragalus; ambiguous apomorphies comprising the following: skull longer than three times caudal skull height; absence of subnarial foramen; low ridges along lateral margins of nasals; single opening for trigeminal nerve; mesial premaxillary teeth circular to subcircular in cross section, straight or just slightly recurved; postaxial cervical and cranial dorsal pleurocoels deep ovoid pockets or well-defined fossae excavated into lateral surfaces of centra; length of midcervical centra approximately twice diameter of cranial face; cervical ribs long, extremely thin, four or five times centrum length; sharp ventral groove on at least proximal caudal centra; pubic shafts separated by short rectangular notch in pubic apron at distal extremity; distal ischial shaft terminating in small knob; proximal femur transversely elongate and wedge-shaped in proximal aspect; distal tibia not expanded caudal to fibula; distal third tarsal fused to metatarsal III (Tykoski and Rowe 2004).

Tykoski and Rowe regarded the type species *Camposaurus arizonensis* and *Podokesaurus holyokensis*, previously phylogenetically located elsewhere, as Coelophysoidea *incertae sedis*; *Genusaurus sisteronis*, *Indosaurus matleyi*, *Indosuchus raptorius* (the latter two species currently regarded as abelisaurids; see *Indosaurus* and *Indosuchus* entries), and *Ligabueino andesi* as Neoceratosauria *incertae sedis*; and *Sarcosaurus woodi* (see *Sarcosaurus* entry) as Ceratosauria *incertae sedis*. In addition to taxa already regarded as *nomina dubia*, the authors considered the type species *Eucoelophysis baldwini*, *Genyodectes serus*, and *Halticosaurus longotarsus*—which are or have been classified as ceratosaurs—to be of doubtful validity.

Holtz, Molnar and Currie (2004), in a review of basal Tetanuranae (including Spinosauroidea, Carnosauria, and basal members of Coelurosauria), performed a cladistic analysis of this clade incorporating 75 terminal taxa as the ingroup and 638 characters. This analysis found the problematic taxa "*Szechuanosaurus*" *zigongensis* and *Xuanhanosaurus* (see *Szechuanosaurus* and *Xuanhanosaurus* entries) to be basal tetanurans, with the former taxon the most basal member of the Tetanurae; *Xuanhanosaurus*, spin-

osauroids, carnosaurs, and coelurosaurs to be united based upon a suite of features; Spinosauroidea to include the families Megalosauridae (including the subfamilies Megalosaurinae, embracing more robust genera, plus Eustreptosponylinae) and Spinosauridae (including the subfamilies Baryonychinae plus Spinosaurinae); and Avetheropoda, the second major tetanuran clade and the sister group to Spinosauroidea, including the two large clades Carnosauria (including Allosauroidea and its families Sinraptoridae, Allosauridae, and Carcharodontosauridae) and Coelurosauria (including Compsognathidae, the sister group to all remaining coelurosaurs including two major subclades, the Tyrannoraptora and a generalized grouping of *Proceratosaurus*, *Ornitholestes*, and *Nqwebisaurus*; see below).

Holtz *et al.* offered the following definitions and diagnoses for Tetanurae and its inclusive clades:

TETANURAE

Node-based definition: *Passer domesticus* plus all taxa sharing a more common ancestor with that species than with *Ceratosaurus nasicornis* (Maryańska, Osmólska and Wolson 2002; also see Gauthier 1986).

Diagnosis: Apomorphies comprising the following: Shallow margin formed by low ridge demarcating maxillary antorbital fossa (sharp rim possibly present rostral to premaxillary fenestra); spine table on axis (not present in spinosaurids); craniocaudally reduced, rodlike axial spinous process; scapula with prominent acromion process; loss of digits of metacarpal IV; metacarpal II greater than 180 percent metacarpal I length; metacarpal III midshaft width less than 50 percent that of II; base of metacarpal III set on palmar surface of II; triangular proximal articulation of metacarpal III; femoral trochanteric shelf reduced; prominent femoral intercondylar groove on cranial distal femur; most proximal point of cranial trochanter of femur above distal margin of femoral head; fibular condyle on proximal tibia strongly offset from cnemial crest; metatarsal I broadly triangular, attached to distal part of II; (distribution of additional synapomorphies at base of Tetanurae uncertain because of lack of preservation of appropriate elements in basalmost taxa or ambiguous distribution among Spinosauroidea and basal Carnosauria) (Holtz, Molnar and Currie 2004).

Unnamed clade comprising *Xuanosaurus*, SPINOSAUROIDEA, CARNOSAURIA, and COELUROSAURIA

Diagnosis: Enlarged distal carpal (possibly resulting from fusion with second distal carpal) that is trochlear and rectangular (as opposed to semilunate) in palmar view, overlapping articular surface of metacarpal II ventrally (not dorsally); metacarpal I just one-half to one-third length of II, articular surface between them extending well into diapophysis of metacarpal I; first phalanx of manual digit I more than 1.5 times length of metacarpal I (Holtz, Molnar and Currie 2004).

Unnamed clade comprising SPINOSAUROIDEA plus AVETHEROPODA

Diagnosis: Derived characters consisting of the following: scapulocoracoid dorsal margin having pronounced notch between acromial process and coracoid; ventral coracoid process well developed; medial ridges on pubes and ischia (for attachment of puboischial membrane; see Hutchinson 2001); distal end of tibia expanded to contact calcaneum; fibula closely appressed to tibia throughout main shaft (Holtz, Molnar and Currie 2004).

SPINOSAUROIDEA

Stem-based definition: *Spinosaurus aegyptiacus* and all taxa sharing a more recent common ancestor with *Passer domesticus* (Holtz, Molnar and Currie 2004).

Diagnosis: Premaxillary body rostral to external nares longer than portion of body ventral to nares; angle between rostral margin and alveolar margin less than 70 degrees; rostral ramus of maxilla present, rostrocaudally as long as or longer than dorsoventrally; lacrimal rostral ramus dorsoventrally pinched, narrow; deltopectoral crest greater than 45 percent humeral length, well developed; well-developed olecranon fossa on caudal face of distal end of humerus (Holtz, Molnar and Currie 2004).

MEGALOSAURIDAE (=TORVOSAURIDAE of some authors)

Node-based definition: *Megalosaurus bucklandii* plus all taxa sharing a more recent common ancestor with it than with *Passer domesticus* (Holtz, Molnar and Currie 2004).

Diagnosis: Jugal process of postorbital broader transversely than rostrocaudally, cross section U-shaped; axial vertebral centrum lacking pleurocoel (Holtz, Molnar and Currie 2004).

MEGALOSAURINAE

Stem-based definition: *Megalosaurus bucklandii* plus all taxa sharing a more recent common ancestor than with *Eustreptospondylus oxoniensis*.

Diagnosis (provisional, based on reversals): Dorsal margin of scapulocoracoid lacking notch between acromial process and coracoid; coracoid without ventral process (Holtz, Molnar and Currie 2004).

EUSTREPTOSPONYLINAE

Node-based definition: *Eustreptospondylus ox-*

oniensis plus all taxa sharing a more recent common ancestors with it than with *Megalosaurus bucklandii* (Holtz, Molnar and Currie 2004).

Diagnosis: Maxillary fenestra (unknown in spinosauroids and nontetanuran theropods, present in Avetheropoda); distal ischial tubercle (see Hutchinson 2001, also in allosauroids); reversion to lack of deep groove on medial side of proximal fibula (Holtz, Molnar and Currie 2004).

SPINOSAURIDAE

Node-based definition: *Spinosaurus aegyptiacus* plus all taxa sharing a more recent common ancestor with it than with *Passer domesticus*, *Megalosaurus bucklandii*, or *Allosaurus fragilis* (Holtz, Molnar and Currie 2004).

Diagnosis: Synapomorphies including the following: Preorbital skull over 2.5 times as long as tall (also in *Afrovenator* and *"Poekilopleuron" valesdunensis*; see S3), rostrum at least three times length of internal antorbital fenestra; premaxilla having seven teeth (also in basal ornithomimosaur *Pelecanimimus*; see Pérez-Moreno, Sanz, Buscalloni, Moratalla, Ortéga and Rasskin-Gutman 1994); premaxillary and dentary terminal rosettes (lateral expansions) supporting elongate rostral teeth; premaxillary-maxillary articulations having interlocking (rather than scarf) joint; dorsal and ventral ramus of lacrimal meeting at 45-degree angle (Holtz, Molnar and Currie 2004).

BARYONYCHINAE

Node-based definition: *Baryonyx walkeri* plus all taxa sharing a more recent common ancestor with it than with *Spinosaurus aegyptiacus* (Holtz, Molnar and Currie 2004).

Diagnosis: Dentary tooth count approximately 30 (about 15 inb spinosaurines, less in other spinosauroids); head of quadrate subrectangular (rather than oval); caudal dorsal spinous processes with basal webbing and accessory laminae connecting costal fovea and ventral body; humeri (unknown in Spinosaurinae) distinguished from other spinosauroids by lateral (rather than cranial) orientation of apex of deltopectoral crest, extremely well-developed internal tuberosity (Holtz, Molnar and Currie 2004).

SPINOSAURINAE

Node-based definition: *Spinosaurus aegyptiacus* plus all taxa sharing a more recent common ancestor with it than with *Baryonyx walkeri* (Holtz, Molnar and Currie 2004).

Diagnosis: Lack of serrations along dental carinae (very fine serrations in Baryonychinae); fluted surfaces along lateral surfaces of teeth; also (Sereno 1998), wider spacing between dentary teeth than in other theropods (Holtz, Molnar and Currie 2004).

AVETHEROPODA (=NEOTETANURAE of some workers)

Node-based definition: Clade consisting of *Allosaurus fragilis*, *Passer domesticus*, their most recent common ancestor, plus all of its descendants (Holtz, Molnar and Currie 2004).

Diagnosis (provisional due to incompleteness of material pertaining to basal members of immediate outgroups, *i.e.*, Spinosauroidea, *Xhuanshanosaurus*, and "*Szechuanosaurus*" *zigongensis*): Maxillary fenestra (also in eustreptospondyline megalosaurids); broad contact between dorsal ramus of quadrojugal and ventrolateral ramus of squamosal; palatine recesses; ectopterygoid expanded, deep ventral groove excavated into body on medial side; notch on caudal margin of splenial (for internal mandibular fenestra; also in "*Poekilopleuron*" *valesdunensis*); attachment of M. depressor mandibulae on retroarticular process facing caudodorsally; zygapophyses of cervical vertebrae displaced laterally away from vertebral centrum in dorsal aspect; costolateral eminences in caudalmost dorsal vertebrae distinctly below transverse processes; transition point in proximal half of tail; L-shaped hemal arches in at least distal half of tail; iliac preacetabular fossa for M. iliofemoralis internus, large, narrow; ventral floor of pelvic canal widely open as pelvic fenestra (see Hutchinson 2001); obturator process separate from pubic plate, located on proximal third of ischium; ischial obturator notch with subparallel sides; head of femur medially oriented; insertion on proximal lateral femur for M. pubo-ischio-femoralis internus on accessory trochanter (Hutchinson); distal condyles of astragalus oriented cranioventrally; metatarsal III wedge-shaped at midshaft in cross section (Holtz, Molnar and Currie 2004).

CARNOSAURIA

Node-based definition: *Allosaurus fragilis*, *Sinraptor dongi*, their most recent common ancestor, and all of its descendants (Padian, Hutchinson and Holtz 1999).

Diagnosis: Synapomorphines including the following: long axis of naris more than half length of long axis of orbit; lateral surface of nasal participating in antorbital cavity, forming nasal antorbital fossa; nasal recesses; prefrontal excluded from rostral rim of orbit in lateral aspect, displaced caudally and/or medially, ventral process absent; supraorbital notch between paroccipital processes directed strongly ventrolaterally from occiput, distal end below level of foramen magnum; notch between caudoventral limit of exoccipital-opisthotic-basisphenoid complex and basal tubera; basipterygoid processes short, not fused to pterygoids; depths of occiputs subequal above and below foramen magnum; articular having pendant medial process; length of midcervical vertebral centrum less than twice diameter of cranial articular surface; cranial margin of spinous processes of proximal midcaudal vertebrae with distinct kink, dorsal part of margin more strongly inclined caudally than ventral part; cranial spur along cranial margin of spinous processes of midcaudal vertebrae (Holtz, Molnar and Currie 2004).

Life restoration of two individuals of the possible carnosaur *Cryolophosaurus elliotti* by artist Todd Marshall.

The analysis of Holtz *et al.* found that within Carnosauria most taxa belong to the Allosauroidea, with *Monolophosaurus*, lacking allosauroid synapomorphies, falling outside that clade as a primitive carnosaur (*e.g.*, see Sereno, Beck, Dutheil, Iarochene, Larsson, Lyon, Magwene, Sidor, Varracchio and Wilson 1996; Currie and Carpenter 2000); *Lourinhanosaurus*, *Fukuiraptor*, and *Siamotyrannus* having variable positions either outside or inside of Allosauroidea (see *Fukuiraptor* and *Siamotyrannus* entries); within Carcharodontosauridae, *Acrocanthosaurus* united with a clade comprising the Gondwanan genera *Giganotosaurus* and *Carcharodontosaurus*, and with the smaller and older *Neovenator* as sister group to those taxa.

Holtz *et al.* further offered the following definitions and diagnoses:

ALLOSAUROIDEA

Node-based definition: *Allosaurus fragilis, Sinraptor dongi*, their most recent common ancestor, and all of its descendents (Holtz, Molnar and Currie 2004).

Diagnosis: Paired narial ridges along lateral edges of nasals, lacrimal ridges continuous with raised surface of lateral edges of nasals; lacrimal recesses; postorbital dorsal surface with enlarged bump (also in Tyrannosauridae); quadratojugal having broad, short caudal process wrapping around ventrolateral edge of quadrate (also in Coelurosauria); quadrate with well-developed articular flange for quadratojugal; paired palatines contacting medially; jugal process of palatine expanded distally; palatine having flange-shaped articular process for lacrimal; lateral transverse nuchal crest height rising dorsal to parietal crest (also in Tyrannosauridae); paroccipital processes oriented strongly caudolaterally, extending well beyond caudalmost point of occipital condyle (also in ceratosaur *Ceratosaurus*); pneumatic fossa around opening for internal carotid artery; horizontal shelf on lateral surface of surangular rostral and ventral to mandibular condyle, prominent, pendant; premaxillary tooth crowns asymmetrical — strongly convex labially, flattened lingually (also in Coelurosauria); spinous processes of cervical vertebrae at least twice as long as vertebral centrum; spinous process of caudal dorsal vertebra oriented cranially; pubic boot having cranially expanded wedge shape; distal ischial tubercle (also in Eustreptospondylinae) (Holtz, Molnar and Currie 2004).

SINRAPTORIDAE

Node-based definition: *Sinraptor dongi* plus all taxa sharing a more recent common ancestor with it than with *Allosaurus fragilis* or *Carcharodontosaurus saharicus* (Holtz, Molnar and Currie 2004).

Diagnosis: Caudal margin of external nares markedly inset; loss of rostral ramus of maxilla; promaxillary fenestra much larger than maxillary fenestra (latter reduced to small pore or lost); squamosal flange covering quadrate head in lateral aspect (Holtz, Molnar and Currie 2004).

Unnamed clade uniting ALLOSAURIDAE and CARCHARODONTOSAURIDAE

Sinraptor

Life restoration by Berislav Krzic of the sinraptorid carnosaur *Sinraptor dongi*.

Photograph by the author, courtesy Earth Science Museum, Brigham Young University.

Skeleton (cast) of the allosaurid carnosaur *Allosaurus fragilis* mounted by Kenneth L. Stadtman under the direction of James A. Jenson at the Earth Science Museum, Brigham Young University.

Diagnosis: Rostral ramus of surangular deep, much more than half height of postdentary mandible; retroarticular process of articular broadened with groove caudally for M. depressor mandibulae; hatchet-shaped hemal arches (distal portion longer craniocaudally than proximal portion, margin ventrally convex) in distal third of tail; caudal expansion of scapular blade reduced or absent; metacarpal I stout, approximately as broad as long, blocklike; obturator foramen on pubis open ventrally, forming obturator notch; pubic boot 30 to 50 percent length of pubic shaft; puboischial contact only along narrow region; proximolateral (fibular) condyle of tibia conspicuously narrowing between body of condyle and main body of tibia when viewed from articular surface (these uniting characters not present in other carnosaurs including Sinraptoridae, but present in Coelurosauria) (Holtz, Molnar and Currie 2004).

ALLOSAURIDAE

Node-based definition: *Allosaurus fragilis* plus all taxa sharing a more recent common ancestor with it

Photograph by the author.

Reconstructed skull cast (including cast of SGM-Din 1, restored under the direction of Paul C. Sereno) of the carcharodontosaurid allosauroid *Carcharodontosaurus saharicus*, displayed in the temporary "Giants: African Dinosaurs" exhibit at Chicago's Garfield Park Conservatory.

Life restoration by Todd Marshall of the carcharodontosaurid allosauroid *Carcharodontosaurus saharicus*.

than with *Sinraptor dongi* or *Carcharodontosaurus saharicus* (Holtz, Molnar and Currie 2004).

Diagnosis: Long, cranially directed lamina extending from obturator process of ischium cranially to level of pubioischial contact; large, mediolaterally compressed, dorsally projecting cornual process of lacrimal (similar to that of *Ceratosaurus*); fenestrate dorsal wall of maxillary antrum; spindle-shaped foramen on lateral surface of fourth sacral vertebral centrum (Chure, in press, *see in* Holtz, Molnar and Currie 2004).

CARCHARODONTOSAURIDAE

Node-based definition: *Carcharodontosaurus saharicus* plus all taxa sharing a more recent common ancestor with it than with *Allosaurus fragilis* or *Sinraptor dongi* (Holtz, Molnar and Currie 2004).

Diagnosis: Ilium having pre- and postacetabular blades of subequal length; pubic peduncle with ventral flange; pubic boot more than half length of pubic shaft (convergent with largest Tyrannosauridae); loss of ventral notch on distal portion ischial obturator notch (also in derived Coelurosauria); pronounced medial epicondyle, extending at least one-fourth length of femoral shaft (Holtz, Molnar and Currie 2004).

Unnamed clade comprising *Acrocanthosaurus* plus Gondwanan CARCHARODONTOSAURIDAE

Diagnosis: Length of long axis of naris reduced to less than half length of long axis of orbit (reveral to noncarnosaurian condition); lateral margins of nasals subparallel throughout length (as in Spinosauroidea and Coelurosauria); lacrimal suborbital bar; wide contact between lacrimals and postorbitals, forming thick brow above orbits (as in largest Tyrannosauridae), suborbital notch lost; fusion of frontal-frontal contact; postorbital surface having rostrally projecting rugosity; postorbital suborbital flange; sacral vertebrae procoelous (Holtz, Molnar and Currie 2004).

Unnamed clade comprising *Giganotosaurus* plus *Carcharodontosaurus*

Diagnosis: Facial bones having external sculpturing; loss of narial ridges characterizing other carnosaurs; rugose nasal dorsal surfaces; supratemporal fossa rostromedial corner roofed over by shelf of frontals and parietals; infratemporal fenestra approximately twice as large as area of orbit in lateral aspect (also in *Ceratosaurus* and Sinraptoridae); lateral surfaces of teeth with wrinkles in enamel internal to serrations; reduced curvature of tooth crown; cranial and

Photograph by Gary Takeuchi, courtesy
Museo Municipal Carmen Funes.

Cast of the holotype skeleton (MUCPvCH-1) of the
carcharodontosaurid al-
losauroid *Giganotosaurus
carolini.*

Photograph by the author, courtesy Museum of Isle of Wight Geology.

Skull and cervical vertebrae (cast) of the carcharodontosaurid carnosaur *Neovenator salerii*.

midcervical centra wider than high; absence of elevation of articular face of midcervical centra (Holtz, Molnar and Currie 2004).

The second major clade within Tetanurae is Coelurosauria, a large and very diverse group of more derived theropods (including extant birds). As Holtz *et al.* noted, the Coelurosauria comprises two basic

The carcharodontosaurid carnosaur *Neovenator salerii* pursues a group of the euronithopod *Hypsilophodon foxii*, in this painting by Todd Marshall.

clades — the family Compsognathidae, sister group to a clade comprising Tyrannoraptora (including Tyrannosauroidea, Orithomimosauria, *Coelurus*, and Maniraptora), and a generalized group including *Proceratosaurus*, *Ornitholestes*, and *Nqwebasaurus*.

Holtz *et al.* offered the following definitions and diagnoses for Coelurosauria and some of its more primitive subclades:

COELUROSAURIA

Node-based definition: *Passer domesticus* and all taxa sharing a more recent common ancestor with it than with *Allosaurus fragilis* (Holtz, Molnar and Currie 2004).

Diagnosis (provisional, pending inclusion of certain basal taxa): Synapomorphies including: maxillary antorbital fossa greater than 40 percent rostrocaudal length of antorbital cavity; quadratojugal having broad, short caudal process wrapping around ventrolateral edge of quadrate (also in Allosauroidea); caudalmost extent of jaw joint rostral to caudalmost point of occipital condyle; rostral ramus of surangular deep, much more than half height of predentary mandible; articular surfaces of cervical vertebral centrum amphiplatyan; caudal transverse processes only on caudal vertebrae 1–15 or fewer; elongate prezygapophyses on caudal vertebrae 15 and beyond; boat-shaped hemal arches (with cranial and caudal projections, more than twice as long craniocaudally as tall dorsoventrally) in distal third or more of tail; medial side of metacarpal II not expanded proximally; metacarpal III shorter than II; ilium with pre- and postacetabular blades of subequal length (also in Carcharodontosauridae); obturator foramen on pubis open ventrally, forming obturator notch (also in Allosauroidea); puboischial contact only along narrow region (also in Allosauroidea); craniocaudal length of proximal end of fibula at least 75 percent craniocaudal length of proximal end of tibia; ascending process of astragalus arising from complete breadth of astragalar condyles; metatarsal I plantar to medial side of II; simple filamentous branching integument (if not true feathers) at least in some forms (Holtz, Molnar and Currie 2004).

COMPSOGNATHIDAE

Node-based definition: *Compsognathus longipes* plus all taxa sharing a more recent common ancestor with it than with *Passer domesticus* (Holtz, Molnar and Currie 2004).

Diagnosis: Short ventral process at caudal end of premaxillary body; nasal excluded from external antorbital fenestra; fan-shaped dorsal spinous processes (also in basal dinosauromorph *Marasuchus* and basal deinonychosaur [see below] *Sinovenator*); dorsal transverse processes short, wide, just slightly inclined; cranial and dorsal pleurocoels lacking; more than 60 caudal vertebrae; medial gastral elements shorter than lateral segments; digit I longest in manus (also in Alvarezsauridae); phalanx I of first digit longer than metacarpal II, wider than radius; ungual of manual digit I more than two-thirds length of radius; absence of cranial portion of pubic boot; ischium less than 66 percent length of pubis (also in Maniraptora); ischial shaft slenderer that pubic shaft (also in Tyrannosauroidea); most proximal point of cranial trochanter extending above proximal margin of femoral head (as in some derived Coelurosauria) (Holtz, Molnar and Currie 2004).

Unnamed clade comprising *Nedcolbertia*, *Scipionyx*, plus all remaining COELUROSAURIA

Diagnosis: Loss of ventral notch on distal portion of ischial obturator notch (as in Carcharodontosauridae); incisura tibialis occupying more than 66 percent of medial surface of proximal tibia; proximolateral (fibular) condyle of tibia with conspicuous narrowing between body of condyle and main body of tibia when viewed from articulaer surface (Holtz, Molnar and Currie 2004).

Unnamed clade including *Ornitholestes*, *Proceratosaurus*, and *Nqwebasaurus*

Diagnosis: Rostral ramus of maxilla rostrocaudally at least as long as dorsoventrally (also in many basal noncoelurosaurian Tetanurae); prezygapophyses of cervical vertebrae flexed; combined humeral and radial length greater than femoral length; medial side of metacarpal II expanded proximally (reversal of condition of basal Coelurosauria); caudal projection of pubic boot round knob (reversal).

Unnamed clade comprising "ornitholestian" clade plus TYRANNORAPTORA

Diagnosis: Loss of contribution of nasals to antorbital cavity; 44 or less caudal vertebrae; "I"-shaped hemal arches (subvertical proximal portion, dramatic bend, and caudally directed distal portion) in distal third of tail; hatchet-shaped hemal arches in proximal third of tail; loss of notch on dorsal margin of scapulocoracoid between acromial process and coracoid; pubic peduncle of ilium craniocaudally elongate and narrow (also in some Carnosauria); absence of ischial foot (reversal in Ornithomimosauria) (Holtz, Molnar and Currie 2004).

TYRANNORAPTORA

Node-based definition: *Tyrannosaurus rex*, *Passer domesticus*, their most recent common ancestor, and all of its descendents (Sereno 1999*b*).

Diagnosis: Medial alae from maxillae meeting in front of vomers; maxillae oriented subparallel to each other (rather than acutely angled) in dorsal aspect (convergent with Carcharodontosauridae and Spinosauridae); prefrontal excluded from rostral rim of orbit in lateral aspect, displaced caudally and/or medially, ventral process absent; ectopterygoid excavated by foramen leading from medial side laterally into body of ectopterygoid; basipterygoid process significantly elongate rostrocaudally (longer than wide); caudal end of dentary straight of only slightly forked (convergent with derived Allosauroidea); internal mandibular fenestra reduced to narrow slit or absent; cranial projection of pubic boot ending in tapered point; ischial obturator notch having divergent sides; bracing for ascending process of astragalus on cranial side of distal tibia flat; pronounced groove offsetting ascending process of astragalus offset from astragalar body; calcaneum distal articular width 10 percent maximum transverse width of astragalus; metatarsal cross section deeper craniocaudally than mediolaterally at midshaft; dorsal surface area of metatarsal III smaller than those of II and IV (Holtz, Molnar and Currie 2004).

The study by Holtz *et al.* also regarded the type species *Nedcolbertia justinhofmanni*, *Scipionyx samniticus*, *Proceratosaurus bradleyi*, *Ornitholestes hermanni*, *Nqwebasaurus thwazi*, *Coelurus agilis*, *Archaeornithoides deinosauriscus*, *Deltadromeus agilis* (now regarded as a noasaurid; see *Deltadromeus* entry), *Richardostesia gilmorei*, *Shanyangosaurus niupanggouensis*, and *Tugulusaurus faciles* as Coelurosauria *incertae sedis*; and *Bahariasaurus ingens*, *Gasosaurus constructus*, *Marshosaurus bicentesimus Ozraptor subotaii*, *Quilmesaurus currieri*, *Shangyangosaurus niupanggouensis*, and *Valdoraptor oweni* as Avetheropoda *incertae sedis*. In addition to other taxa already regarded as *nomina dubia*, Holtz *et al.* found the type species *Nuthetes destructor Phaedrolosaurus ilikensis*, *Prodeinodon mongoliensis*, *Siamosaurus suteethorni* (however, see *Siamosaurus* entry), and *Wakinosaurus satoi* to be of dubius validity.

Currie, Hurum and Sabath (2003), in their study on the skull structure and evolution in tyrannosaurid theropods, performed a phylogenetic analysis of the Tyrannosauridae including seven tyrannosaurid genera (*Albertosaurus*, *Alioramus*, *Daspletosaurus*, *Gorgosaurus*, "*Nanotyrannus*" [which these authors treated as a possibly valid genus, but also noted that it could be congeneric with *Tyrannosaurus*; *e.g.*, see Carr 1999; Holtz 2001], *Tarbosaurus*, and *Tyrannosaurus*), with the carnosaur *Allosaurus* as the outgroup, and incorporating data gleaned from the recent examination of more that 200 original catalogued specimens of the

North American *Albertosaurus*, *Daspletosaurus*, *Gorgosaurus*, and *Tyrannosaurus* (see Currie), and the Asian *Tarbosaurus* (see Hurum and Sabath 2003).

Rejecting the weakly supported subfamily Aublysodontinae, which had been based upon morphologically and allometrically immature characters (the genus *Aublysodon* now generally accepted as representing a juvenile *Tyrannosaurus rex*; see *Tyrannosaurus* entry, *S3*; and *Shanshanosaurus* now regarded as a juvenile *Tarbosaurus*; see *Tarbosaurus* entry), Currie (2003*a*) and Currie *et al.* subdivided the Tyrannosauridae into two distinct clades, the more primitive Albertosaurinae and the more derived Tyrannosaurinae.

Currie *et al.* noted that albertosaurines were quantifiably more lightly built and most likely faster animals than the known tyrannosaurines. The authors included in the Albertosaurinae the genera *Albertosaurus* and *Tyrannosaurus*. To the Tyrannosaurinae, Currie *et al.* referred *Alioramus*, *Daspletosaurus*, "*Nanotyrannus*," *Tarbosaurus*, and *Tyrannosaurus*. Within this subfamily, the authors found *Daspletosaurus* to be more closely related to *Tarbosaurus* (see entry) than *Tyrannosaurus*, this contradicting previous studies (*e.g.*, Paul 1988; Carr; Holtz 2001) suggesting a sister taxon or congeneric relationship between *Tarbosaurus* and *Tyrannosaurus*. Moreover, *Tarbosaurus* has comparatively shorter arms than all other known tyrannosaurid genera, this suggesting the unlikelihood of the Asian genus being ancestral either to *Daspletosaurus* or *Tyrannosaurus*.

Concerning *Alioramus* and *Tarbosaurus*, Currie *et al.* pointed out that these Asian genera, used informally as a tyrannosaurine subgroup by Hurum and Sabath (see *Tarbosaurus* entry), display but one cranial synapomorphy (*i.e.*, regarding contact amongst lacrimal, maxilla, and nasal, lacrimal process of nasal is lost, contact of maxilla and lacrimal dominating). Currie *et al.* stated that "in the near future" they will revise the postcranial skeleton of *Tarbosaurus* and "describe the group formally." Concerning another Asian taxon, *Alectrosaurus olseni*, Currie *et al.* posited that, pending the more detailed study of cranial material, "this species cannot be assigned to either subfamily."

Holtz (2004), in a revision of the Tyrannosauroidea, accepted the monophyletic clade Tyrannosauridae and its two subfamilies, Albertosaurinae and Tyrannosaurinae (as did Currie; Currie *et al.*, above). Furthermore, Holtz's analysis found within Tyrannosauroidea a clade comprising *Stokesosaurus*, *Dryptosaurus*, plus a clade uniting *Eotyrannus* and Tyrannosauridae; the problematic Asian taxa *Alectrosaurus* and *Alioramus* to place in more than one phylogenetic position near the base of the Tyrannosauridae —*Alectrosaurus* as the sister taxon to Tyrannosauridae, a basal

Life restoration by artist Todd Marshall of the primitive tyrannosauroid *Eotyrannus lengi*.

TYRANNOSAUROIDEA

Node-based definition: *Tyrannosaurus rex* plus all taxa sharing a more recent common ancestor with *T. rex* than with *Ornithomimus velox*, *Deinonychus antirrhopus*, or *Allosaurus fragilis* (Holtz 2004).

Diagnosis: Main body of premaxilla taller dorsoventrally than long rostrocaudally (also in Abelisauridae); prominent, laterally extending horizontal shelf on lateral surface of surangular, rostral and ventral to mandibular condyle; large opening for caudal surangular foramen; reduced retroarticular process; dorsal surface of iliac blades converging closely on midline (also in Ornithomimosauria and Mononykinae); dorsal portion of cranial margin of preacetabular blade of ilium concave cranially, ventral portion convex; accessory broad, ventral hooklike projection from preacetabular blade of ilium; straight supraacetabular crest on lateral margin of ilium in dorsal view (also in various Maniraptora); median vertical ridge on external surface of ilium; ventral flange on puboischial peduncle; concave cranial margin of pubic peduncle; pubis shaft with marked concave curvature cranially (convergent with some Oviraptorosauria); ishial shaft much more slender than pubic shaft; semicircular scar on caudolateral surface of ischium, just distal to iliac process (also in Ornithomimosauria); bone sheet extending from obturator process, continuing down at least half length of ischium; fibular cranial tubercle distal to cranial expansion comprising two longitudinal ridges; metatarsals elongate relative to those of other theropods with femora of same length (also in ceratosaur *Elaphrosaurus*, Ornithomimosauria, and Troodontidae); proximal surface of metatarsal III crescentic, limited to plantar half of proximal surface of metatarsus (Holtz 2004).

Unnamed clade comprising *Stokesosaurus*, *Dryptosaurus*, and a clade including *Eotyrannus* plus TYRANNOSAURIDAE

Diagnosis: Derived features including the following: premaxillary tooth row arcade oriented more transversely than rostrodorsally; nasals fused, their dorsal surface rugose; premaxillary teeth "D"- or "U"-shaped, carinae along same plane perpendicular to long axis of skull; premaxillary teeth much smaller than maxillary teeth; caudal dorsal vertebrae pleurocoelous; ends of humerus little expanded; ulna facet for radius transversely expanded, concave (also in some Maniraptora) (Holtz 2004).

TYRANNOSAURIDAE

Stem-based definition: Theropods more closely related to *Tyrannosaurus rex* than to *Eotyrannus lengi* (Holtz 2004).

Diagnosis: Synapomorphies including the fol-

albertosaurine, or a basal tyrannosaurine; *Alioramus* as the sister taxon to Tyrannosauridae, or as a tyrannosaurine closer to *Tarbosaurus* and *Tyrannosaurus* than to *Daspletosaurus*.

Holtz offered the following definitions and diagnoses for Tyrannosauroidea and its related clades:

lowing: Surface of nasals contacting maxillae facing ventrally; supratemporal fossae occupying caudolateral half of frontal; frontal edge notched in region of lacrimal suture; supratemporal fenestrae confluent over parietals, forming sagittal parietal crest; squamosal recess (also in Ornithomimosauria); jugal pneumatized by foramen in caudal rim of jugal antorbital fossa; squamosal-quadratojugal flange constricting infratemporal fenestra; prominent muscular fossae on dorsal surface of palatines; palatine foramen on dorsal surface of palatine recess; transverse nuchal crest at least twice as tall as foramen magnum, rising well above parietal crest, with transverse width more than twice height; pair of tablike processes on supraoccipital wedge; caudal tympanic recess extending into opisthotic caudodorsal to fenestra ovalis, confluent with this fenestra; deep basisphenoid sphenoidal sinus with large foramina; basisphenoid with well-developed subcondylar recess (also in Ornithomimosauria); supraoccipital excluded from foramen magnum; tripartite supraoccipital sinus; coronoid and supradentary fused (see Hurum and Currie 2000; this apparent synapomorphy — also seen in Allosauroidea and Dromaeosauridae; see Holtz et al. — possibly due to better preservation of tyrannosaurid skulls compared with those of other toothed theropods); retroarticular process further reduced to broad, shallow, concave semicircular plate; vertical ridge on distal surface of premaxillary teeth strongly developed; maxillary and dentary incrassate (in adults, cross section greater than 60 percent as wide labiolingually as long mesiodistally); carina of dentary teeth asymmetrical, long axis of dentary (also in Allosauroidea and carcharodontosaurid *Acrocanthosaurus*); small ventral projections on ventral sides of cranial cervical vertebral centra; dorsal vertebral series subequal to length of femur; midcaudal vertebrae cranial zygapophyses extending more than half but less than one centrum length (also in Ornithomimosauria and Coelophysidae); distal caudal spinous processes axially elongate; cranialmost gastralia fused into platelike mass (possibly more widespread among large-bodied Tetanurae; see Holtz et al.); scapula contributing more than half to glenoid; coracoid dorsoventral length at least five times diameter of coracoid glenoid; femur-humerus ratio more than 2.6; distal articular surface of ulna expanded transversely; distal radius flattened craniocaudally; metacarpal III lacking phalanges; ilium craniocaudal length subequal to or greater than femur length; pubic tubercle crestlike, pointing cranially; ischial tuberosity expanded into proximal dorsal ischial process; most proximal point of cranial trochanter extending above proximal margin of femoral head; pronounced, rugose, cranially facing proximal tuberosity on metatarsal V; metatarsals II and IV contacting at midshaft on plantar surface; arctometatarsus; short contact between metacarpals II and IV on dorsal surface of proximal end of metatarsals (also in Ornithomimidae) (Holtz 2004).

ALBERTOSAURINAE

Diagnosis: Antorbital cavity reaching nasomaxillary suture; lateral surface of nasal excluded from antorbital cavity; triangular cornual process on lacrimal, oriented dorsally, rostral to descending ramus of lacrimal (Holtz 2004).

TYRANNOSAURINAE

Diagnosis: Extent of ventral curvature of maxilla at least length of crown of tallest premaxillary teeth; promaxillary fenestra rostrally oriented; maxillary fenestra expanded, one-half to two thirds of area of eyeball-bearing portion of orbit; cranial margin of maxillary fenestra terminating along cranial margin of antorbital fossa; internal antorbital fenestra at least as tall as long; caudal portion of nasals pinched between lacrimals, thinnest point approximately half transverse width of thickest point or less; margin of external antorbital fenestra on craniolateral surface of descending ramus of lacrimal flattening out, not continued on surface of jugal; palatine foramen on dorsal surface of palatine recess large; ectopterygoid internal sinus enlarged, resulting in inflated appearance of ectopterygoid body; centra of midcervical vertebrae less than half as long as height of vertical face (neck much shorter than dorsal series); craniocaudal length of ilium greater than femoral length; pubic boot greater than 60 percent length of pubic shaft (some of these features possibly allometric) (Holtz 2004).

Unnamed clade comprising *Tarbosaurus* plus *Tyrannosaurus*

Courtesy and copyright © Triebold Paleontology, Inc.

Mounted skeleton (cast) of the albertosaurine tyrannosaurid *Albertosaurus sarcophagus*, original material discovered in 1998 in the Two Medicine Formation of Teton County, Montana. The 40-percent complete specimen measures nearly six meters (20 feet) in length, with an almost 2.75-meter (three-foot-long) skull.

The original skeleton (BHI-3033) of the *Tyrannosaurus rex* known as "Stan," the second largest and second most complete specimen of this species yet recovered, on display at the Black Hills Museum of Natural History.

Diagnosis: Pronounced ventral curvature of maxilla, ventral deflection of curvature at least length of crown of largest premaxillary teeth; lateral lamina of maxilla obscuring large shelf overlapping rostral part of maxillary antrum in lateral aspect; lateral projections of caudal suture of nasal extending farther caudally than medial projections; dorsal ramus of lacrimal with inflated appearance; lacrimal recess with multiple openings; main body of frontal rectangular, only small triangular rostral prong remaining; supratemporal fossa occupying most of caudal portion of frontal, latter meeting along midline, forming large rugose boss in adults; postorbital suborbital prong, prominent in adults; palatines trapezoidal; two foramina on lateral surface of palatines (also in Canadian albertosaurines); transverse nuchal crest rostrocaudally thick, dorsal margin rugose; basal tubera reduced, smaller than ventral ends of basipterygoid processes; occipital region caudoventrally directed; dorsoventral depth of caudal end of dentary greater than 200 percent depth of dentary symphysis; ratio of metacarpal II to I 170 percent or less; manual ungual with blunted distal tips, reduced curvature (Holtz 2004).

Makovicky, Kobayashi and Currie (2004), in a review of the Ornithomimosauria (including the families Garudimimidae, Harpymimidae, and Ornithomimidae), performed a cladistic analysis of this inclusive clade, resulting in the following:

ORNITHOMIOSAURIA

Node-based definition: The last common ancestor of the clade including *Ornithomimus edmontonicus* and *Pelecanimimus polyodon* (Padian, Hutchinson and Holtz 1999).

Diagnosis: Inflated cultriform process forming bulbous, hollow structure (bulla); premaxilla with long, tapering subnarial ramus separating maxilla and nasal for distance caudal to naris; dentary elongate and subrectangular in lateral aspect; surangular bearing dorsolateral flange for articulation with lateral extension of lateral quadrate condyle; radius and ulna adhering tightly distally; (potentially diagnostic [problematic due to combinations of homoplasy and missing data among Ornithomimosauria and nearest outgroups] including the following) metacarpal I subequal in length to II and III (absent in *Harpymimus*

Photograph by the author, courtesy North American Museum of Ancient Life.

Skeleton of the tyrannosaurid theropod *Tyrannosaurus rex* (cast of BHI-3033, the specimen known as "Stan").

and *Shenzhousaurus*); subcondylar and subotic pneumatic recesses on side of basicranium (not known for *Pelecanimimus*, *Harpymimus*, and *Archaeornithomimus*) (Makovicky, Kobayashi and Currie 2004).

Additionally, Makovicky *et al.*'s study found the type species *Timimus hermani* to be a *nomen dubium*.

In describing the new genus *Sinornithomimus* (see entry), Kobayashi and Lü (2003) performed a phylogenetic analysis incorporating 17 cranial and 21 postcranial characters, 10 ornithomimosaurian ingroup taxa, and two outgroups (*Allosaurus* and Tyrannosauroidea. The resulting cladogram found *Pelecanimimus* to be a basal ornithomimosaur outside of Ornithomimidae. Contrary to earlier analyses (*e.g.*, Barsbold and Osmólska 1990*a*), Kobayashi and Lü found the monophyly of the Ornithomimidae to be supported by just one unambiguous synapomorphy — *i.e.*, arctometatarsalian condition (see also Norell, Clark and Makovicky 2001) — with other characters previously used to diagnose this clade plesiomorphic. Consequently, Kobayashi and Lü suggested that the so-called arctometatarsalian condition, proposed by Holtz (1994, 2000) as a synapomorphy of the clade "Arctometatarsalia" (see Xu, Norell, Kuang, Zhao and Jia 2004 and *Dilong* entry for comments on the validity of this group), was in fact "derived convergently within Ornithomimosauria and is an important character for the clade of Ornithomimosauria."

Kobayashi and Lü's analysis further suggested that the Ornithomimidae includes two clades for Late Cretaceous ornithomimids, one for Asian forms (*Anserimimus* plus *Gallimimus*), the other North American forms (*Struthiomimus* plus a clade comprising "*Dromicieomimus*" [=*Ornithomimus*; see entry] plus *Ornithomimus*). These authors found monophyly of the Asian clade supported by two characters (*i.e.*, arrangements of biceps tubercle and glenoid in scapula and coracoid), and monophyly of the North American taxa also by two (*i.e.*, ventral expansion of pubic boot and presence of series of maxillary neurovascular foramina). This analysis also implies that the shape of the rhamphotheca in North American ornithomimids may have differed significantly from that in the Asiatic forms. The rostral ends of the premaxillae in North American taxa are acute, while those of Asian taxa are U-shaped in dorsal aspect (see Makovicky *et al.*), this possibly demonstrating real differences in beak morphology and, consequently, also suggesting different feeding or display adaptations (see Kobayashi and Barsbold 2003; also, *Harpymimus* entry).

An analysis by Makovicky, Norell, Clark and Rowe (2003) found the Alvarezsauridae to lie outside of Ornithomimosauria, having a close relationship with Dromaeosauridae and Troodontidae (see also Chiappe and Coria 2003, *Patagonykus* entry; Ji, Norell, Makovicky, Gao, Ji and Yuan 2003, *Shenzhousaurus* entry, with the Alvarezsauridae found to be the sister taxon to all other maniraptorans excluding *Ornitholestes*).

In their review of the Troodontidae, Makovicky and Norell (2004) found the Troodontidae to be a monophyletic clade well supported by numerous unambiguous characters, comprising the type species *Sinovenator changi* plus a clade including all other troodontids; Troodontidae the sister taxon to Deinonychosauria (see below for an alternate assessment), which is, in turn, the sister group to Avialae; and a clade comprising *Byronosaurus jaffei*, *Sinornithoides youngi*, and a more exclusive clade (including the large-bodied taxa *Troodon formosus*, *Saurornithoides mongoliensis*, and *Saurornithoides junior*).

Makovicky and Norell provided the following definition and diagnoses for these clades:

TROODONTIDAE

Stem-based definition: All taxa closer to *Troodon formosus* than to *Velociraptor mongoliensis* (Makovicky and Norell 2004).

Diagnosis: Dentary nutrient foramina in horizontal groove on labial face of dentary; pneumatic quadrate having pneumatopore on posterior face; absence of basisphenoid recess; absence of basisphenoid recess; internarial bar dorsoventrally flattened; closely packed rostral dentition in symphyseal region of dentary; depression on ventral surface of postorbital process of laterosphenoid; basal tubera reduced, directly ventral to occipital condyle; large number of teeth; transverse processes long, slender; subotic recess on side of braincase ventral to middle ear; (where tail is known) distal caudal vertebrae with sulcus on dorsal midline in place of neural spine (unknown in *Sinovenator* [see below]); metatarsus asymmetrical (as in [microraptorans; see below] *Microraptor zhaoianus* and *Sinornithosaurus milleni*, more symmetrical in most Theropoda), metatarsal II slender, markedly shorter than III and IV, metatarsal IV robust (Makovicky and Norell 2004).

Unnamed clade comprising all TROODONTIDAE except *Sinovenator changii*

Diagnosis: Otosphenoidal crest; teeth with enlarged, apically hooked serrations (secondarily lost in *Byronosaurus jaffei*).

Unnamed clade including *Troodon formosus* plus *Saurornithoides mongoliensis* and *S. junior*

Diagnosis: Medially deflected symphysis on dentary; secondary loss of dorsal tympanic recess (Makovicky and Norell 2004).

Makovicky and Norell regarded as *nomina dubia*, among other taxa, the following type species that are sometimes regarded as belonging to Troodontidae: *Bradycneme draculae*, *Elopteryx nopscai*, *Heptasteornis andrewsi*, and *Koparian douglassi* (see *Elopteryx* and *Heptasteornis* entries).

(For an alternate interpretation of *Sinovenator* and Troodotidae, see Senter, Barsbold, Britt and Burnham 2004, below, who found *Sinovenator* to be a basal deinonychosaur, placing troodontids closer to ornithomimids than to deinonychosaurs).

Zanno (2004), in one of several related abstract relating to a new therizinosauroid taxon from the Crystal Geyser Quarry in Utah (see "Introduction"), briefly described the pectoral girdle and forelimb of this taxon, noting that their description offers the "basis for the first species-level phylogenetic investigation of this enigmatic group to include derived members." Zanno's analysis, comprising 32 characters as distributed amongst 13 taxa, revealed the Crystal Geyser Quarry form to be the most basal known member of the maniraptoran clade Therizinosauroidea. It further supported the monophyly of the clade based upon seven unambiguous synapomorphies, at the same time suggesting, *contra* previous studies, "that Therizinosauroidea is more appropriately defined as the derived clade including *Nothronychus*, *Therizinosaurus*, and *Segnosaurus*, with equally strong support recovered for a clade comprising five genera plus "*Alectrosaurus*" and *Erliansaurus*.

As Zanno noted, the sequence of character developments in the pectoral girdle and forelimb throughout the evolution of the Therizinosauroidea demonstrates various "structural modifications likely corresponding to the loss of predatory function in derived members of the clade." Moreover, the morphology of primitive therizinosauroids (characterized by the Crystal Geyser genera *Alxasaurus* and *Beipiaosaurus*) "suggest that Early Cretaceous taxa already exhibited the beginnings of a trend toward increased robustness and range of motion, together with a decrease in the grasping abilities of the manus." Such trends, Zanno proposed, greatly elaborated in later and more derived taxa, probably relate to a total "loss of predatory function by the Late Cretaceous, associated with the advent of exclusively herbivorous habit among these aberrant theropods."

Clark, Maryańska and Barsbold (2004), in their review of the Therizinosauroidea, found *Beipiaosaurus inexpectus* to be a basal member of this clade; *Alxasaurus*, *Enigmosaurus*, and Therizinosauridae comprising an unnamed clade; and *Eshanosaurus deguchiianus* tentatively belonging to this clade, based on the following shared features: Lateral shelf on dentary; dentary teeth becoming larger mesially; teeth mediolaterally compressed, symmetrical, roots cylindrical.

These authors offered the following definitions and diagnoses for these clades:

THERIZINOSAUROIDEA

Node-based definition (problematic, as it excludes *Eshanosaurus*): Least inclusive clade containing *Therizinosaurus* and *Beipiaosaurus* (Clark, Maryańska and Barsbold 2004).

Diagnosis: Premaxilla edentulous, with sharp, ventrally projecting rim (also in many Avialae); external naris very elongate, bordered caudoventrally by maxilla (also in Troodontidae); antorbital fossa surrounded by well-developed rim except caudally (also, to lesser extent, in some Oviraptoridae); palate having greatly elongate vomers, rostrally reduced pterygoids; greatly enlarged, pneumatized basicranium constricting external acoustic meatus ventrally (possibly homologous with expanded parasphenoid of Troodontidae and Ornithomimidae, although not strictly comparable); rim on lateral surface of dentary, forming horizontal shelf; size of dentary teeth increasing rostrally; maxillary and distal dentary teeth laterally compressed, symmetrical in lateral aspect, serrations coarse (except in *Eshanosaurus*), roots cylindrical; humerus having strongly expanded proximal and distal ends, distal condyles on cranial surface (convergent with birds and Alvarezsauridae), sharply pointed tubercle on caudomedial surface midshaft; two large distal carpals capping metacarpals I and II, medial carpal semilunate; ilium with long, deep preacetabular process, cranioventral extremity pointed, flaring outward at right angle to sagittal plane; long obturator process of astragalus contacting pubis; ascending process of astragalus covering only part of distal end of tibia; short, broad metatarsals; (possibly diagnostic, depending upon group relationships) premaxilla edentulous (also in Ornithomimosauria, Oviraptorosauria, and Neornithes); maxilla dorsal to palatal surface, facing ventrolaterally (also in Oviraptoridae); large prefrontal (reduced in all Coelurosauria except Ornithomimosauria and possibly Alvarezsauridae); mesial end of dentary downturned (also in Ornithomimosauria and some Troodontidae); absence of coronoid (much reduced in Oviraptorosauria, absent in Avialae); deltopectoral crest at least one-third length of humerus (also in Oviraptorosauria); opisthopubic condition of pelvis (also in Dromaeosauridae and Avialae); (possibly diagnostic, pending collection of more complete material) skull and mandible small relative to postcranial skeleton (Clark, Maryańska and Barsbold 2004).

Unnamed clade comprising *Alxasaurus, Enigmosaurus,* and THERIZINOSAURIDAE

Diagnosis: Preacetabular portion of ilium ventrally expanded, longer than postacetabular portion; ischial shaft mediolaterally compressed (not in *Enigmosaurus*) (Clark, Maryańska and Barsbold 2004).

THERIZINOSAURIDAE

Node-based definition: Least inclusive clade including *Therizinosaurus* and *Erlikosaurus* (Clark, Maryańska and Barsbold 2004).

Osmólska, Currie and Barsbold (2004), in a review of the Oviraptorosauria, found this group to divide into an unnamed clade comprising Avimimidae and an unnamed clade including all other ovitap-

torosaurian clades; the latter unnamed group breaking down into Caudipterygidae (emended) plus Caenagnathoidea (see Sereno 1999*b*); Caenagnathoidea including *Chirostenotes* plus the family Oviraptoridae; and Oviraptoridae splitting into the subfamilies Oviraptorinae and Ingeniinae.

Osmólska *et al.* presented the following definitions and diagnoses for these clades:

OVIRAPTOROSAURIA

Stem-based definition: All maniraptorans closer to *Oviraptor philoceratops* than to *Passer domesticus* (Sereno 1998; Maryańska, Osmólska and Wolson 2002, emended).

Diagnosis: Unequivocal synapomorphies including the following: Premaxilla with crenulated ventral margin; parietal at leas as long as frontal; ascending process of quadratojugal bordering more than three-fourths infratemporal fenestra; U-shaped mandibular symphysis; dentary edentulous; cranial process of pubic foot longer than caudal process (Osmólska, Currie and Barsbold 2004).

Unnamed clade comprising AVIMIMIDAE plus CAENAGNATHOIDEA

Stem-based definition: All Oviraptora closer to *Caudipteryx zoui* than to *Avimimus portentus* (Osmólska, Currie and Barsbold 2004).

Diagnosis: Synapomorphies comprising the following: ratio of preorbital length to basal skull length 0.5 or less; ratio of lateral maxillary length to basal skull length approximately 0.3; antorbital fossa bordered rostrally by premaxilla; cotyle-like incision on ventrolateral margin of squamosal; ascending process of quadratojugal bordering ventral two-thirds or more of infratemporal fenestra; ratio of length of external mandibular fenestra to total mandibular length at least 0.25; caudoventral process of dentary extending caudally at least to caudal border of external mandibular fenestra; splenoid straplike, shallow, not approaching dorsal mandibular margin; absence of maxillary teeth (Osmólska, Currie and Barsbold 2004).

CAENAGNATHOIDEA

Node-based definition: Least inclusive clade containing *Oviraptor philoceratops* and "*Caenagnathus collinsi*" [=*Chirostenotes pergracilis*] (Maryańska, Osmólska and Wolsan 2002).

Diagnosis: Unambiguous synapomorphies comprising the following: palatal shelf on maxilla with two longitudinal ridges, toothlike ventral process; depression in periotic region; jaw joint close to midline of skull; mandibular symphysis having extended symphyseal shelf; mandibular rami bowed at midlength in dorsal aspect; concave rostrodorsal margin of dentary;

mandibular articular facet for quadrate composed exclusively of articular; mandibular articular facet for quadrate convex in lateral aspect, transversal wide; articular facet for quadrate elevated above level of adjoining part of mandibular ramus; rostral portion of preacetabular shallow, straplike, not approaching dorsal mandibular margin; mandibular adductor fossa rostrally and dorsally extended, not delimited rostrally; sacral centra with pleurocoels; caudal centra with pleurocoels (Osmólska, Currie and Barsbold 2004).

CAENAGNATHIDAE

Stem-based definition: Most inclusive clade containing "*Caenagnathus collinsi*" [=*Chirostenotes pergracilis*] but not *Oviraptor philoceratops* (Maryańska, Osmólska and Wolsan 2002, emended after Sereno 1998).

Diagnosis: Unambiguous synapomorphy of fused mandibular symphysis (Osmólska, Currie and Barsbold 2004).

OVIRAPTORIDAE

Stem-based definition: Most inclusive clade containing *Oviraptor philoceratops* but not "*Caenagnathus collinsi*" [=*Chirostenotes pergracilis*] (Maryańska, Osmólska and Wolsan 2002).

Diagnosis: Synapomorphies consisting of the following: ratio of snout width to its length 0.3–0.4; ratio of length of tomial edge of premaxilla to height of premaxilla below naris 0.7 or less; premaxilla pneumatized; subantorbital portion of maxilla inset medially; ventral margin of maxilla sloping retroventrally, longitudinal axis at approximately 20-degree angle to longitudinal axis of jugal; nasals fused; external naris overlapping most of antorbital fossa rostrodorsally; medial portion of lacrimal shaft projecting laterally, forming flattened transverse bar in front of eye; skull roof bones pneumatized; infratemporal fenestra large, subquadrate, rostrocaudal length comparable to orbital length; otic process of quadrate articulating with squamosal and lateral wall of braincase; quadrate pneumatized; accessory lateral process on distal end of quadrate (for articulation with quadratojugal); lateral cotyle on quadrate (for quadratojugal); nuchal transverse crest not pronounced; basisphenoid pneumatized extensively; absence of basipterygoid process; parasphenoid rostrum sloping rostroventrally; periotic region pneumatized extensively; quadrate ramus of pterygoid overlapping braincase laterally; pterygoid with basal process (for contacting basisphenoid); ectopterygoid rostral to pterygoid; ectopterygoid contacting maxilla and lacrimal; ectopterygoid elongate, shaped like Viking ship, without lateral hooklike process; pterygoid and ectopterygoid forming massive longitudinal bar; palate extending below cheek margin; palatines developed in horizontal, vertical, and transverse planes perpendicular to each other; pterygoid ramus of palatine ventral to pterygoid; vomer approaching or contacting parasphenoid rostrum; suborbital fenestra reduced or closed; mandibular symphysis tightly sutured; ratio of maximum manibular height to mandibular length 0.3–0.4; ratio of height of external mandibular fenestra to length 0.7–1.0; absence of premaxillary teeth; centra of cranial cervical vertebrae extending caudally beyond corresponding neural arches; combined length of manual phalanges III-1 and III-2 less than or equal to length of phalanx III-3; dorsal margins of opposite iliac processes near or contacting each other along their medial sections; pubic shaft cranially concave; well-developed adductor fossa and associated craniomedial crest on distal femur (Osmólska, Currie and Barsbold 2004).

OVIRAPTORINAE

Node-based definition: *Oviraptor philoceratops*, *Citipati osmolskae*, their most recent common ancestor, and all descendants (Osmólska, Currie and Barsbold 2004).

Diagnosis: Synapomorphies consisting of: pneumatized crestlike prominence along skull roof; rostroventral margin of premaxilla inclined rostrodorsally relative to horizontally positioned jugal; premaxilla projecting slightly ventrally below ventrolateral margin of maxilla; postorbital process of jugal perpendicular to ventral ramus of jugal (Osmólska, Currie and Barsbold 2004).

INGENIINAE

Node-based definition: *Conchoraptor gracilis*, *Ingenia yanshini*, their most recent common ancestor, and all descendants (Osmólska, Currie and Barsbold 2004).

Diagnosis: Putative synaporphies (recognized under both DELTRAN and ACCTRAN optimizations) comprising the following: synsacrum including seven to eight vertebrae; deltopectoral crest extending for approximately 40–50 percent proximal length of humerus; distal end of postacetabular process of ilium truncated (Osmólska, Currie and Barsbold 2004).

Norell and Makovicky (2004), in a review of the Dromaeosauridae, performed a phylogenetic analysis of this clade based on 220 characters and 50 taxa and rooted on the carnosaurian genus *Allosaurus*. This analysis found Dromaeosauridae to be a monophyletic clade and sister taxon to Troodontidae, these clades comprising the larger monotypic group Deinonychosauria, the latter being the sister taxon to Avialae;

within Dromaeosauridae, *Microraptor* and *Sinornithosaurus* constituting sequential sister taxa relative to an unresolved polytomy of other dromaeosaurids (see below for a different assessment).

Norell and Makovicky (2004) offered the following definitions and diagnoses:

DROMAEOSAURIDAE

Node-based definition: All descendants of the most recent common ancestor of *Microraptor zhaoianus*, *Sinornithosaurus milleni*, and *Velociraptor mongoliensis* (Norell and Makovicky 2004).

Diagnosis: Frontal short, "T"-shaped, sinusoidal edge demarcating rostral boundary of supratemporal fenestra; squamosal with caudolateral overhanging shelf; lateral process of quadrate contacting quadratojugal dorsally above enlarged quadrate foramen; dorsal vertebrae having raised, stalklike parapophyses; coracoid with subglenoid fossa; (in some dromaeosaurids) reduction of cuppedicus fossa of ilium; postorbital ramus of jugal broad, platelike (Norell and Makovicky 2004).

Unnamed clade comprising all DROMAEOSAURIDAE excluding *Microraptor*

Diagnosis: Secondary loss of constriction between tooth roots and crowns (Norell and Makovicky 2004).

A major new and somewhat different phylogeny of the Coelurosauria was introduced by Senter, Barsbold, Britt and Burnham (2004) in order to elucidate relationships within the Dromaeosauridae, their analyses contradicting in various ways most recently published assessments of the Dromaeosauridae and its subfamilies (see Senter *et al.* for references; Norell and Makovicky, above; also, *D:TE, S1, S2,* and *S3*). The analysis of Senter *et al.* included 101 osteological characters for 32 coelurosaurian taxa, with *Allosaurus frag-*

Skull (cast of AMNH 5356, restored) of the dromaeosaurine dromaeosaurid *Dromaeosaurus albertensis.*

Photograph by the author, courtesy Royal Tyrrell Museum/Alberta Community Development.

ilis constituting the outgroup, and *Protarchaeopteryx* the only supraspecific taxon used.

Senter *et al.*'s analyses (see below for definitions and synapomorphies) found the Dromaeosauridae to comprise the monotypic subfamily Velociraptorinae (including only *Velociraptor mongoliensis*) plus the subfamily Dromaeosaurinae (including *Adasaurus, Saurornitholestes, Deinonychus, Achillobator,* and *Utahraptor* [but not *Atrociraptor*, a genus recently described by Currie and Varricchio 2004 as a velociraptorine; see entry], these taxa being successively more closely related to the dromaeosaurine *Dromaeosaurus.*) As sister group to Dromaeosauridae, Senter *et al.* introduced the new clade Microraptoria (see below), embracing *Bambiraptor, Sinornithosaurus* (including specimen NGMC 91; see *Sinornithosaurus* entry), these forms being more closely related to *Microraptor zhaoianus* (see *Microraptor* entry for synonymies of *M. gui* and *Cryptovalens pauli* with *M. zhaoianus*). *Bambiraptor, Sinornithosaurus,* and *Microraptor* had earlier been classified as dromaeosaurids.

These analyses found *Sinovenator* (see entry), previously regarded as belonging to the Troodontidae, to be a basal member of Deinonychosauria; Aves to be the sister group to *Sinovenator* plus (Microraptoria plus Dromaeosauridae); and the Troodontidae, here excluded from Deinonychosauria (as defined by Padian, Hutchinson and Holtz 1999; *contra*, for example, Sereno 1998; Makovicky *et al.* 2003, above; Holtz 2003*b*), to be more closely related to Ornithomimidae than to Deinonychosauria (see also, for example, Snively, Russell and Powell 2004). In regards Troodontidae, the authors pointed out that the pairing of *Sinovenator* with Troodontidae in previous analyses can be partly explained by the use in those studies of 10 characters, only two of which (*i.e.*, slender second and robust fourth metatarsals; maxilla and dentary having moderate number of small teeth) were included in Senter *et al.*'s analyses.

Citing the various putative synapomorphies that had been used to unite *Sinovenator* with the Troodontidae, Senter *et al.* noted that at least two of these (*i.e.*, moderate number of small maxillary and dentary teeth; flat internarial bar) are shared with ornithomimosaurs, thereby providing additional support for a close relationship between the Ornithomimosaur and Troodontidae.

Also, Senter *et al.*'s analyses confirmed the nonavian deinonychosaurian status of *Unenlagia comahuensis* (see entry), *Hulsanpes perlei*, and *Pyroraptor olympius*, but could neither confirm nor falsify that status for *Variraptor mechinorum*.

Senter *et al.* offered the following definitions and suites of character states for the nodes in their analyses:

COELUROSAURIA

Stem-based definition: All neotetanurans more closely related to Neornithes than to *Allosaurus* (Sereno 1998).

ACCTRAN and DELTRAN: Caudal tympanic recess; metatarsal V less than half length of IV (Senter, Barsbold, Britt and Burnham 2004).

ACCTRAN: Paroccipital processes not strongly downturned; length of preorbital region of cranium less than twice height at rostral margin of preorbital bar; manual phalanx II-2 1.3 times length of II-1; manual ungual I shorter than manual phalanx I-1 (Senter, Barsbold, Britt and Burnham 2004)

Ornitholestes plus (*Sinosauropteryx* plus MANI-RAPTORIFORMES)

ACCTRAN and DELTRAN: Internal antorbital fenestra smaller than orbit; transverse width of foramen magnum subequal to that of occipital condyle; frontal process of postorbital vertically oriented; length of dorsal centra subequal to or greater than height; caudal neural spines of dorsal vertebrae less than 1.5 times taller than cranioposteriorly long; caudal dorsal parapophyses not set on stalks (nonpedunculate); total length of pedal phalanx II-1 equal to or greater than length of distal condylar eminence; absence of prominent lateral flange at proximal end of metatarsal IV (Senter, Barsbold, Britt and Burnham 2004).

ACCTRAN: Cranial length equal to or less than 0.8 times length of femur; postorbital process of frontal not sharply demarcated; premaxillary teeth without denticles; denticles absent on mesial keels of distal teeth; length of humeral shaft between deltopectoral crest and distal condyles equal to or greater than three times diameter of shaft (Senter, Barsbold, Britt and Burnham 2004).

Sinosauropteryx plus MANIRAPTORIFORMES

ACCTRAN and DELTRAN: Length of maxillary process of jugal greater than four times height; neural spines of cervical vertebrae low; metatarsus length greater than four times proximal transverse width; tibia longer than femur (Senter, Barsbold, Britt and Burnham 2004).

ACCTRAN: Length of preorbital region of cranium equal to or greater than twice height at rostral edge of preorbital bar; dorsal vertebrae without pneumatopores; length of ischium less than 0.7 times that of pubis (Senter, Barsbold, Britt and Burnham 2004).

DELTRAN: Postorbital process of frontal not sharply demarcated; premaxillary teeth without denticles; denticles absent on mesial keels of distal teeth; manual phalanx II-2 1.3 times length of II-1 (Senter, Barsbold, Britt and Burnham 2004).

MANIRAPTORIFORMES

Node-based definition: All taxa phylogenetically bracketed by *Ornithomimus* and birds (Holtz 1996).

ACCTRAN and DELTRAN: Teeth constricted between root and crown; distal keels of distal teeth lacking denticles; length of bony tail less than 1.2 times hindlimb length, greater than length of presacral series of vertebrae; length of manual phalanx I-1 greater than five times diameter (Senter, Barsbold, Britt and Burnham 2004).

ACCTRAN: Articular glenoid ventrally displaced; pectoral glenoid facing laterally; distal carpals one and two having semilunate shape; greater and cranial trochanters fused into trochanteric crest; metatarsal I distally displaced.

"ARCTOMETATARSALIA" [For explanation of quotation marks, see Xu, Norell, Kuang, Wang, Zhao and Jia 2004 and *Dilong* entry.]

Stem-based definition: All taxa more closely related to *Ornitholestes* than to birds (Holtz 1996).

ACCTRAN and DELTRAN: Maxillary fenestra enlarged, craniocaudally elongate; parasphenoid base bulbous; length of preorbital region of cranium equal to or greater than three times height at rostral border of preorbital bar; dentary with more than 30 teeth; centra of cervical vertebrae significantly longer than dorsal centra; cervical centra length equal to or greater than three times height; cranioproximal contact between metatarsals II and IV; length of pedal phalanx II-2 equal to or less than six times length of II-1; total length of pedal phalanx II-2 equal to or less than twice length of distal condylar eminence (Senter, Barsbold, Britt and Burnham 2004).

DELTRAN: Cranial length less than 0.8 times that of femur; dorsal vertebrae without pneumatopores (Senter, Barsbold, Britt and Burnham 2004).

Pelecanimimus plus *Struthiomimus*

ACCTRAN and DELTRAN: Craniomandibular joint suborbital; metacarpal I greater than 0.8 times length of II (Senter, Barsbold, Britt and Burnham 2004).

ACCTRAN: Distal carpals one and two lunar in shape (Senter, Barsbold, Britt and Burnham 2004).

DELTRAN: Paroccipital processes not strongly downturned; articular glenoid ventrally displaced (Senter, Barsbold, Britt and Burnham 2004).

TROODONTIDAE

Stem-based definition: All taxa more closely related to *Troodon* than to *Ornithomimus, Mononykus, Therizinosaurus, Velociraptor, Oviraptor,* or Aves (Senter, Barsbold, Britt and Burnham 2004).

ACCTRAN and DELTRAN: Maxilla contacting

external naris; caudoventral "lip" on pedal phalanx II-2 (Senter, Barsbold, Britt and Burnham 2004).

ACCTRAN: Articular glenoid not ventrally displaced; loss of elongate extension of ischial shaft distal to obturator process; enlarged pedal ungual II (Senter, Barsbold, Britt and Burnham 2004).

Saurornithoides youngi plus (*Troodon* plus *Saurornithoides mongoliensis* plus *S. junior*)

ACCTRAN and DELTRAN: Denticles on distal keels of distal teeth, apically pointed (Senter, Barsbold, Britt and Burnham 2004).

DELTRAN: Distal carpals one and two with semilunate shape; greater and cranial trochanters fused into trochanteric crest; metatarsal I distally displaced; enlarged pedal ungual II (Senter, Barsbold, Britt and Burnham 2004).

Troodon plus *Saurornithoides mongoliensis* plus *S. junior*

ACCTRAN and DELTRAN: Premaxillary teeth having denticles; denticles on mesial keels of distal teeth, more denticles per five millimeters than on distal keels (Senter, Barsbold, Britt and Burnham 2004).

MANIRAPTORA

Stem-based definition: All coelurosaurs more closely related to birds than to Ornithomimidae (Gauthier 1986).

ACCTRAN and DELTRAN: Transverse width of foramen magnum greater than that of occipital condyle; angle between acromion process and scapular blade greater than 160 degrees; overhang of acromion process cranial to cranial margin of scapulocoracoidal suture; proximodorsal "lip" on manual digit II; tip of manual ungual level with flexor tubercle; obturator process distally displaced (Senter, Barsbold, Britt and Burnham 2004).

ACCTRAN: Rostral border of premaxilla slanted caudally at 50 to 70 degrees; paroccipital processes strongly downturned; dorsal vertebrae with pneumatopores (Senter, Barsbold, Britt and Burnham 2004).

DELTRAN: Distal carpals one and two having semilunate shape; ischial length less than 0.7 pubic length; greater and cranial trochanters fused into trochanteric crest (Senter, Barsbold, Britt and Burnham 2004).

OVIRAPTOROSAURIA

Stem-based definition: All maniraptorans more closely related to *Oviraptor* than to Neornithes (Sereno 1998).

ACCTRAN and DELTRAN: Length of preorbital region of cranium less than twice height at rostral margin of preorbital bar; length of bony tail less than that of presacral vertebral series; shaft of ischium strongly concave caudally (Senter, Barsbold, Britt and Burnham 2004).

ACCTRAN: Metatarsal I not distally displaced (Senter, Barsbold, Britt and Burnham 2004).

DELTRAN: Cranial length less than 0.8 times that of femur; rostral border of premaxilla slanted caudally at 50 to 70 degrees; articular glenoid ventrally displaced.

Caudipteryx plus *Khaan*

ACCTRAN and DELTRAN: Parietals longer than frontals; dentary edentulous; manual phalanx II-2 less than 1.3 times length of II-1 (Senter, Barsbold, Britt and Burnham 2004).

PARAVES

Stem-based definition: All maniraptorans more closely related to Neornithes than to *Oviraptor* (Sereno 1998).

ACCTRAN and DELTRAN: Proximal hemal arches of caudal vertebrae less than 1.5 times length of associated vertebrae; proximalmost distally expanded hemal arch proximal to ninth caudal vertebra; humerus longer than scapula; cranioventral corner of iliac blade caudally displaced; retropuby; absence of cranial portion of pubic boot; loss of elongate extension of ischial shaft distal to obturator process; caudal end of iliac blade pointed; ischial peduncle of ilium reduced in height relative to pubic peduncle; metatarsal III distally ginglymoid (Senter, Barsbold, Britt and Burnham 2004).

ACCTRAN: Cranial length equal to or greater than 0.9 times femoral length; metacarpal II subequal in length to I plus manual phalanx I-1 (Senter, Barsbold, Britt and Burnham 2004).

AVES [see "Appendix Two"]

Node-based definition: All taxa phylogenetically bracketed by *Archaeopteryx* and Ornithurae (Sereno 1997).

ACCTRAN and DELTRAN: Rostral border of premaxilla slanted caudally equal to or less than 45 degrees; maxilla contacting external naris; cervical vertebrae markedly longer than dorsals; cervical centra longer than tall; humerus longer than femur; manus length equal to or more than 1.25 femoral length; length of ilium cranial to midacetabulum markedly longer than length of ilium caudal to midacetabulum; iliac blade rounded cranially; hallux retroverted; pedal phalanx II-2 equal to or greater in length than II-1; pedal phalanx IV-4 longer than UV-3 (Senter, Barsbold, Britt and Burnham 2004).

DELTRAN: Articular glenoid ventrally displaced;

metatarsal I distally displaced (Senter, Barsbold, Britt and Burnham 2004).

ORNITHURAE

Stem-based definition: All taxa more closely related to extant birds than to *Archaeopteryx* (Gauthier 1986).

ACCTRAN and DELTRAN: Radius markedly longer than femur; coracoid proximally constricted; metacarpal II longer than I plus manual phalanx I-1; manual phalanx III-2 less than 1.3 times length of III-1; craniodorsal "lip" absent on manual ungual II; diameter of manual phalanx II-1 enlarged by caudal flange; humeral diameter equal to or greater than that of femur; ischium having strong proximal, caudodorsal process; metatarsal II distally ginglymoid (Senter, Barsbold, Britt and Burnham 2004).

ORNITHORACES

Node-based definition: All taxa phylogenetically bracketed by *Sinornis* and Neornithes (Sereno 1998).

ACCTRAN and DELTRAN: Craniomandibular joint suborbital; ischium greater than 0.7 times pubic length; fibula not reaching tarsus (Senter, Barsbold, Britt and Burnham 2004).

DELTRAN: Sacrum with eight or more vertebrae (Senter, Barsbold, Britt and Burnham 2004).

DEINONYCHOSAURIA

Stem-based definition: All taxa more closely related to *Deinonychus* than to Neornithes (Padian, Hutchinson and Holtz 1999).

ACCTRAN and DELTRAN: Cranial articular surfaces of cervical centra facing largely ventrally; caudoventral "lip" on pedal phalanx II-2; pedal ungual 2 enlarged (Senter, Barsbold, Britt and Burnham 2004).

ACCTRAN: Articular glendoid not ventrally displaced; distal caudal zygapophyses longer than centrum; total length of pedal phalanx II-1 less than three times length of distal condylar eminence; pedal phalanx II-1 shorter than IV-1 (Senter, Barsbold, Britt and Burnham 2004).

MICRORAPTORIA plus DROMAEOSAURIDAE

ACCTRAN and DELTRAN: Maxillary fenestra dorsally displaced; caudal tympanic recess displaced onto paroccipital process; denticles on mesial keels of distal teeth, more denticles per millimeter than on distal keels; loss of constriction between tooth crown and root, at least for mesial teeth; denticles on distal keels of distal teeth, apically pointed; dentary bowed (concave dorsally); cervical neural spines high; distal dorsal parapophyses set on stalks; metatarsal II distally; total length of pedal phalanx II-2 equal to or less than twice length of distal condylar eminence (Senter, Barsbold, Britt and Burnham 2004).

ACCTRAN: Nasals upturned rostrally; premaxillary teeth with denticles; caudal dorsal neural spines equal to or greater than 1.5 times higher than craniocaudally long (Senter, Barsbold, Britt and Burnham 2004).

DELTRAN: Rostral border of premaxilla slanted caudally at 50 to 70 degrees; distal caudal prezygapophyses longer than centrum; pedal phalanx II-1 shorter than IV-1 (Senter, Barsbold, Britt and Burnham 2004).

MICRORAPTORIA

Stem-based definition: All taxa more closely related to *Microraptor* than to *Velociraptor* and *Dromaeosaurus* (Senter, Barsbold, Britt and Burnham 2004).

ACCTRAN and DELTRAN: Coracoid constricted proximally; manual phalanx III-1 equal to or greater than twice length of III-2; manual phalanx I-1 bowed (concave ventrally); metatarsal V equal to or greater than 0.5 times length of IV (Senter, Barsbold, Britt and Burnham 2004).

DELTRAN: Nasals upturned rostrally; metacarpal II subequal in length to I plus manual phalanx I-1; metatarsal I distally displaced (Senter, Barsbold, Britt and Burnham 2004).

Sinornithosaurus plus (NGMC 91 [=*Sinornithosaurus*]) plus (*Microraptor zhaoianus* plus "*M. gui*" plus "*Cryptovolans*" [=*M. zhaoianus*])

ACCTRAN and DELTRAN: Diameter of radius less than 0.5 times than of ulna; manual phalanx II-2 less than 1.3 times that of II-1; diameter of manual phalanx II-1 increased by caudal flange; tip of obturator process forming strongly acute angle; pubic shaft kinked caudally at midlength; caudal part of pubic boot lost; pedal phalanx II-2 equal to or greater than length of II-1; pedal phalanx IV-4 longer than IV-3 (Senter, Barsbold, Britt and Burnham 2004).

ACCTRAN: Loss of denticles on premaxillary teeth; dorsal neural spines less than 1.5 times higher than craniocaudally long; total length of pedal phalanx II-2 greater than twice length of distal condylar eminence (Senter, Barsbold, Britt and Burnham 2004).

NGMC 91 plus (*Microraptor zhaoianus* plus "*M. gui*" plus "*Cryptovolans*" [see above])

ACCTRAN: Mesial keels of distal teeth without denticles; dentary with midlength height increase (Senter, Barsbold, Britt and Burnham 2004).

Microraptor zhaoianus plus "*M. gui*" plus "*Cryptovolans*" (see above)

ACCTRAN and DELTRAN: Length of bony

tail greater than 1.2 times that of hindlimb; diameter of humerus almost equal to or greater than that of femur; length of pedal ungual IV subequal to that of III; tibia bowed (Senter, Barsbold, Britt and Burnham 2004).

DROMAEOSAURIDAE

Node-based definition: All taxa phylogenetically bracketed by *Dromaeosaurus* and *Velociraptor* (Padian, Hutchinson and Holtz 1999).

ACCTRAN and DELTRAN: Maxillary proxess of jugal length less than four times height; postorbital process of frontal sharply demarcated, jutting out at 90 degrees; paroccipital processes not strongly downturned; transverse width of foramen magnum subequal to that of occipital condyle; caudal surangular foramen enlarged; acromion overhang lost; manual ungual I longer than manual phalanx I-1; dorsal margin of manual ungual II arching high over dorsal extremity of proximal articular facet; cranial portion of pubic boot an elongate ridge; elongate extension of ischium distal to obturator process; length of metatarsus less than four times proximal transverse width (Senter, Barsbold, Britt and Burnham 2004).

ACCTRAN: Metacarpal II less than length of I plus manual I-1; metatarsal I not distally displaced (Senter, Barsbold, Britt and Burnham 2004).

DELTRAN: Premaxillary teeth with denticles; dorsal neural spines equal to or greater than 1.5 times smaller than craniocaudally long; total length of pedal phalanx II-2 equal to or less than twice length of distal condylar eminence (Senter, Barsbold, Britt and Burnham 2004).

DROMAEOSAURINAE

Stem-based definition: All dromaeosaurids more closely related to *Dromaeosaurus* than to *Velociraptor* (Sereno 1998).

ACCTRAN and DELTRAN: Metatarsal IV having prominent lateral flange at proximal extremity (Senter, Barsbold, Britt and Burnham 2004).

ACCTRAN: Manual phalanx I-1 length less than five times diameter (Senter, Barsbold, Britt and Burnham 2004).

Saurornitholestes plus (*Deinonychus* plus (*Achillobator* plus (*Dromaeosaurus* plus *Utahraptor*)))

ACCTRAN and DELTRAN: Caudal dorsal centra equal to or greater than 1.2 times taller than long (Senter, Barsbold, Britt and Burnham 2004).

Deinonychus plus (*Achillobator* plus (*Dromaeosaurus* plus *Utahraptor*))

ACCTRAN and DELTRAN: Dentary straight (Senter, Barsbold, Britt and Burnham 2004).

DELTRAN: Length of manual phalanx I-1 less than five times diameter (Senter, Barsbold, Britt and Burnham 2004).

Achillobator plus (*Dromaeosaurus* plus *Utahraptor*)

ACCTRAN and DELTRAN: Jugal process of maxilla dorsoventrally deep ventral to external antorbital fenestra; caudal dorsal vertebrae having pair of pneumatopores on each side; obturator process not distally displaced; femur longer than tibia (Senter, Barsbold, Britt and Burnham 2004).

Dromaeosaurus plus *Utahraptor*

ACCTRAN and DELTRAN: Mesial and distal keels of distal teeth with equal number of denticles per millimeter (Senter, Barsbold, Britt and Burnham 2004).

DELTRAN: Denticles gently rounded, not apically pointed

AVES [see "Appendix Two"]

Diagnosis: Rostral border of premaxilla slanted caudally equal to or less than 45 degrees; maxilla contacting external naris; cervical vertebrae markedly longer than dorsals; cervical centra longer than tall; humerus longer than femur; manus length equal to or more than 1.25 femoral length; length of ilium cranial to midacetabulum markedly longer than length of ilium caudal to midacetabulum; iliac blade rounded cranially; hallux retroverted; pedal phalanx II-2 equal to or greater in length than II-1; pedal phalanx IV-4 longer than UV-3 (Senter, Barsbold, Britt and Burnham 2004).

Addressing recent propositions that dromaeosaurids are not non-avian theropods but rather secondarily flightless, terrestrial birds descended from flying, arboreal ancestors (Czerkas, Zhang, Li and Li 2002; Paul 2002), Senter *et al.* found the Dromaeosauridae not to be nestled within Aves, although "this alone does not preclude the possibility that their ancestors were volant or arboreal." Rather, Senter *et al.* proposed that the distribution of various character states (see paper for details) relating to arboreality and flight arose independently in both non-avian maniraptoran theropods and birds.

Sauropodomorpha

Among the most radical of recent revisions of the Sauropodomorpha — the clade including both Prosauropoda and Sauropoda — were those proposed by Adam M. Yates in 2003 and 2004. In the first of these two studies, Yates (2003*b*), following various brief earlier reports by that author (see Yates 2001, 2003*a*, 2004; see also *S3*, and *Anchisaurus, Antetonitrus, Plateosaurus,* and *Thecodontosaurus* entries), published his detailed formal phylogenetic analysis of the Sauropodomorpha. In the past, most workers (*e.g.*, Pisani, Yates and Langer 2001) have accepted the traditional assessment of both Prosauropoda and Sauropoda as constituting monophyletic groups within Sauropodomorpha.

The analysis by Yates (2003*b*), however, resulted in a conflicting conclusion. As that author noted, the presumed monophyly of the Prosauropoda has largely been based upon a single derived character—a reduced pedal digit V, generally considered by prosauropod workers to be irreversable. Indeed, Yates (2003*b*) found it unlikely that so complicated a structure could have been required again, following its loss (the genes coding for its construction being deleted or degraded); however, the reenlargement of such a structure is not impossible. Yates (2003*b*) cited the manual claws of the hoatzin (see Parker 1891), a bird, and the large hallux of therizinosauroids (*e.g.*, see Perle 1979; Barsbold and Maryańska 1990*b*; Russell and Dong 1993) as "two good examples of this phenomenon within the Dinosauria." In Yates (2003*b*) opinion, therefore, "The atrophy of pedal digit V is, by itself, extraordinarily weak evidence for the monophyly of 'prosauropods' with respect to Sauropoda."

Yates (2003*b*) found the Saurischia to be a monophyletic group, with the Herrerasauridae (regarded by some workers as a clade of basal theropods; *e.g.*, see Pisani, *et al.*, "Systematics" chapter, *S3*; see also Carrano and Sampson 2003; Langer 2004, above) and Neotheropoda placed as serially closer outgroups to the Sauroporomorpha. Within Sauropodomorpha, the taxa *Saturnalia tubpiniquim* (see entry and above) and *Thecodontosaurus* (traditionally classified as a primitive prosauropod; see Galton and Upchurch 2004*a*, below) were assessed by Yates (2003*b*) to be basal to all other members of Sauropodomorpha (see also Leal and Azevedo 2003, below).

Yates' (2003*b*) analysis also concluded the following: All sauropodomorphs more derived than *Thecodontosaurus* forming a well-supported clade, with *Efraasia* and *Plateosaurus* forming serial outgroups to a trichotomy involving *Anchisaurus* (see entry), *Riojasaurus*, and a clade comprising all remaining sauropodomorphs; a basal polytomy within the latter clade, comprising *Lufengosaurus, Coloradisaurus,* a clade consisting of *Massospondylus* plus *Yunnanosaurus* (a genus regarded by some workers as a primitive sauropod), and the "near-sauropod sauropodomorphs"; within the latter clade, *Euskelosaurus, Melanorosaurus,* and *Blikanasaurus* [Blikanasauridae, regarded by various workers as either a member of the Prosauropoda or the

earliest known member of the Sauropoda; see Yates 2004, below; Galton and Upchurch 2004*a*] forming serially closer outgroups to Sauropoda (*Vulcanodon* plus Eusauropoda).

However, Yates (2003*b*)—following a method described by Wilkinson (1994) that resulted in a reduced cladistic consensus tree—found that the simple removal of *Coloradisaurus* from his analysis resulted first in the resolution of *Lufengosaurus* as the sister taxon to the clade of *Massospondylus* plus *Yunnanosaurus*, and second in five unstable terminal taxa (*i.e., Riojasaurus, Anchisaurus, Coloradisaurus, Yunnanosaurus,* and *Euskelosaurus*.

Of the latter, *Euskelosaurus, Riojasaurus,* and *Anchisaurus* were found to be particularly unstable, able to fall any place on the Sauropodomorpha stem between *Thecodontosaurus* and *Massospondylus* with but minimal loss of parsimony. Yates (2003*b*) explained the instability of *Coloradisaurus* and *Euskelosaurus* as the result of a paucity of codable data for these taxa, and that of the other more completely known taxa as resulting from incongruence in the distribution of character states.

Deletion of the above unstable terminals resulted in a single most parsimonious tree identical to the previous tree, in which the unstable terminals had been simply pruned from the original source trees. Consequently, Yates (2003*b*) concluded "that the unstable terminals exert no influence over the final topology and we can be confident that removing them does not produce an inaccurate result." Within this restricted analysis, however, the robustness of the nodes is "remarkably good, with the exception of the *Massospondylus* + *Lufengosaurus* clade."

According to Yates (2003*b*), support for the paraphyly of early sauropodomorphs significantly arises from both the basal (*Saturnalia* and *Thecodontosaurus*) and derived (*Euskelosaurus, Melanorosaurus,* and *Blikanasaurus*) taxa. The first of these supports paraphyly "by combining some of the putative synapomorphies of Prosauropoda with plesiomorphies that strongly indicate that the taxa are basal to the *Plateosaurus*-Sauropoda dichotomy. Therefore, such putative synapomorphies—*e.g.*, inset first dentary tooth; strap-shaped ventral ramus of squamosal; strongly asymmetrical distal condyles of first metacarpal; strongly twisted first phalanx of first manual digit—are really symplesiomorphies diagnostic of the Sauropodomorpha. The second group illustrates the development of characters shared with the Sauropoda—*e.g.*, tall dorsal neural spines; four sacral vertebrae; craniodistally compressed proximal caudal centra; broad blade of scapula—in otherwise prosauropod-like dinosaurs.

Removing both sets of these terminal taxa from

the analysis results in a monophyletic Prosauropoda, while including just one of them "will cause the Prosauropoda to fragment into a paraphyletic array of basal sauropodomorphs on the sauropod stem." Yates (2003*b*) concluded, therefore, "that paraphyly of the 'prosauropods' is a significantly better explanation of the present data than is monophyly." (Yates' 2003*b* results have not yet been adopted by the majority of other prosauropod researchers.)

Yates (2003*b*) proposed the following lists of unambiguous synapomorphies, as applied to his reduced cladistic consensus:

SAURISCHIA

Diagnosis: Lacrimal exposed on dorsal skull roof; axial postzygapophyses set further from midline than axial postzygapophyses; cervical vertebrae three to six longer than axis; presacral vertebrae with hyposphene-hypantra articulations; dorsal neural arches laminated; manus more than 45 percent of humerus plus radius; first phalanx of manual digit I longer than metacarpal I; phalangeal formula of manual digits IV and V reduced to two and one, respectively; ilium with prominent supra-acetabular buttress; ischium having proximal obturator plate (Yates 2003*b*).

NEOTHEROPODA plus SAUROPODOMORPHA

Diagnosis: Loss of premaxilla-nasal suture below naris; large subnarial foramen within or on border of narial fossa; lacrimal erect, inverted "L"-shaped; cervical vertebrae seven to nine longer than axis; radius less than 80 percent of humerus; distal carpal I at least 120 percent wider than II; manual digit I at least length of ungual of II; manual digit II longer than III; caudal margin of postacetabular blade of ilium square-shaped in lateral aspect; large distal expansion of ishium; dorsolateral groove on proximal ischial shaft (Yates 2003*b*).

SAUROPODOMORPHA

Diagnosis: Skull less than 50 percent length of femur; narrow, star-shaped quadraojugal ramus of squamosal; teeth having constriction between root and crown; cervical vertebrae three to eight without diapo-postzygapophyseal lamina; cranial and middle dorsal vertebrae without diapo-postzygapophyseal lamina; forelimb at least 50 percent length of hindlimb; distal humerus more than three times width of midshaft of humerus; hindlimb no longer than trunk; tibia no longer than femur (Yates 2003*b*).

Thecodontosaurus plus more derived SAUROPODOMORPHA

Diagnosis: First dentary tooth inset from dentary tip; maxillary and dentary teeth having coarse serrations angled at 45 degrees from tooth margins; all tooth crowns lacking recurvature; cranial cervical vertebrae lacking ventral keels; reversal to absence of supra-acetabular-preacetabular buttress; pubic peduncle of ilium greater than twice length of pubic articular surface; supra-acetabular crest at widest above base of pubic peduncle; proximal metatarsal II with concave medial margin for reception of I; proximal end of metatarsal V transversely flared (Yates 2003*b*).

Thecodontosaurus
Diagnosis: Platelike epipophyses on cervical vertebrae, with planar dorsal surface (Yates 2003*b*).

Efraasia plus (*Plateosaurus* plus (*Anchisaurus, Riojasaurus* plus (*Lufengosaurus* plus (*Massospondylus* plus *Yunnanosaurus*)) plus (*Euskelosaurus* plus (*Melanorosaurus* plus (*Blikanasaurus* plus Sauropoda)))))
DIAGNOSIS: Maxilla with enlarged caudal vascular foramen; jaw joint below alveolar margin of dentary; dentary with caudolateral shelf; absence of pointed medial process of articular; retroarticular process exceeding length of glenoid; centrum of third cervical vertebra 2.5 times longer than high; three sacral vertebrae; centra of middle caudal vertebrae less than twice as long as high; proximal width of metacarpal I over 65 percent length; reversal to three and two phalanges on manual digits IV and V, respectively; reversal to absence of trochanteric shelf and associated muscle scar on femur (Yates 2003*b*).

Plateosaurus plus (*Anchisaurus, Riojasaurus* plus ((*Luffengosaurus* plus *Massospondylus*) plus (*Euskelosaurus* plus (*Melanorosaurus* plus *Blikanasaurus* plus Sauropoda)))))
Diagnosis: Deeply cleft basal tubera; five premaxillary alveoli; reversal of first phalanx of manual digit I that is shorter than metacarpal I; manual ungual II less than 75 percent of I in all linear dimensions; acetabulum fully open; distal demur with extensor depression (Yates 2003*b*).

Anchisaurus plus *Riojasaurus* plus ((*Lufengosaurus* plus *Massospondylus*) plus (*Euskelosaurus* plus (*Melanorosaurus* plus (*Blikanasaurus* plus Sauropoda)))
Diagnosis: Reversal to manus less than 45 percent length of humerus plus radius; loss of laterally projecting ambiens process on proximal pubis; femur straight in cranial aspect; lesser trochanter of femur a proximodistally elongated ridge; long axis of femoral head parallel with transverse axis of distal femoral condyles; fourth trochanter on medial margin of femoral head in caudal aspect (Yates 2003*b*).

Lufengosaurus plus ((*Massospondylus* plus *Yunnanosaurus*) plus (*Euskelosaurus* plus (*Melanorosaurus* plus (*Blikanasaurus* plus Sauropoda))))

Diagnosis: Reversal to loss of exposure of lacrimal in dorsal skull roof; caudodorsally short lacrimal head with triangular antorbital fossa; jugal excluded from margin of antorbital fenestra by contact of lacrimal and maxilla; reversal to four premaxillary alveoli; serrations restricted to upper half of tooth crowns; digit I longest in manus; nonterminal phalanges of manual digits II and III as wide as long, or wider; craniocaudal expansion of distal pubes; pedal ungual I longer than II (Yates 2003*b*).

Lufengosaurus plus (*Massospondylus* plus *Yunnanosaurus*)

Diagnosis: Prefrontal with enlarged caudal process; distal carpal I overlapping II; metacarpal I inset into manus; distal carpal II less than one-third width of I, failing to cover all of proximal surface of metacarpal II; metacarpal I as wide as long; transverse axis through distal condyles of first phalanx of manual digit I twisted 60 degrees ventrolaterally relative to transverse axis of proximal facet (Yates 2003*b*).

Massospondylus plus *Yunnanosaurus*

Diagnosis: Distally tapering obturator plate of ischium reaching 50 percent length of ischium; reversal to femur sinuous in cranial aspect; reversal to fourth trochanter inset from medial margin of femoral shaft in caudal aspect (Yates 2003*b*).

Euskelosaurus plus (*Melanorosaurus* plus (*Blikanasaurus* plus SAUROPODA))

Diagnosis: Height of caudal dorsal neural spines greater than craniocaudal length; first caudal centrum higher than long; reversal to shallow, narrow, poorly defined brevis shelf (Yates 2003*b*).

Melanorosaurus plus (*Blikanasaurus* plus SAUROPODA)

Diagnosis: Deltopectoral crest low, ridgelike; medial radial fossa on proximal ulna; ulna without olecranon process; shaft of femur craniocaudally flattened; distal end of fourth trochanter at distal half of femur (Yates 2003*b*).

Blikanasaurus plus SAUROPODA

Diagnosis: Ascending process of astragalus widening laterally; caudal margin of astragalus convex in dorsal aspect (Yates 2003*b*).

SAUROPODA

Diagnosis: Distal tarsals not ossified; proximal end of metatarsal I broader than II; reversal to absence of concave lateral margin to proximal end of metatarsal II; pedal unguals deep, narrow; pedal digit IV having three or less phalanges; weight-bearing pedal digit V (Yates 2003*b*).

Yates (2004), in a subsequent study wherein that author reassessed the phylogenetic standing of the genus *Anchisaurus* (see entry), proposed a new cladogram (incorporating 205 characters and 17 ingroup taxa) for the Sauropodomorpha that differed in various significant ways from that author's (Yates 2003*b*) earlier conclusions.

In this later analysis, Yates (2004) coded superspecific taxa by examining several members from each basal branch of their respective clades, supplemented with especially well-represented taxa. *"Rayososaurus"* [=*Limayasaurus*] *tessonei*, *Apatosaurus* spp., *Camarasaurus* spp., and *Brachiosaurus brancai* as the main taxa to code the Neosauropoda, and *Liliensterus liliensterni*, *Dilophosaurus wetherilli*, *Elaphrosaurus bambergi*, *Sinraptor dongi*, and *Allosaurus fragilis* to code the Theropoda. *Herrerasaurus ischiagualastensis* (regarded by Yates 2004) as a nontheropod saurischian) and Theropoda were selected as outgroups.

As Yates (2004) pointed out, previous authors have generally found the Prosauropoda either to be very paraphyletic (*e.g.*, Huene 1932; Romer 1956; Gauthier 1986; Benton 1990 Yates 2003*b*) or monophyletic (*e.g.*, Cooper 1984; Galton 1990; Upchurch 1995; Sereno 1999*a*; Benton, Juul, Storrs and Galton 2000; Galton and Upchurch 2004*a*, see below). However, Yates' (2004) more recent analysis resulted in "an intermediate hypothesis with a moderately diverse prosauropod clade." This analysis produced two most parsimonious trees, differing "only in the placement of *Efraasia minor*, which is either the sister group to all other prosauropods or the sister group to Prosauropoda + Sauropoda." Excluded from the Prosauropoda in this analysis were a number of taxa traditionally regarded as members of that group (see below).

Contrary to most earlier studies, *Anchisaurus polyzelus*, traditionally regarded as a prosauropod, was found by Yates (2004) to be nested at the base of Sauropoda. As in Yates (2003*b*) earlier analysis, *Saturnalia* and the two species of *Thecodontosaurus* (*T. antiquus* and *T. caducus*) were found to be basal sauropodomorphs. *Efraasia*, as mentioned above, placed either as a nonprosauropod sauropodomorph or a basal member of the Prosauropoda. This analysis split the Prosauropoda into two sister taxa, the first constituting the genus *Riojasaurus*, and the second the Plateosauria (see below), a clade comprising *Plateosaurus* [Plateosauridae] plus Massospondylidae, the latter family dividing into the genus *Coloradisaurus* plus a clade comprising the genera *Massospondylus* plus *Lufengosaurus*. In addition to *Anchisaurus*, the genera *Melanorosaurus* [Melanorosauridae, generally regarded as a prosauropod family], *Blikanasaurus*, and *Kotasaurus* placed as primitive sauropod taxa lying outside of Eusauropoda.

As Yates (2004) observed via his analysis, the lineage leading to the Neosauropoda exhibits "a fairly continual increase in body size after the last common ancestor shared with *Saturnalia tupinquim*." Also, while such offshoots of this lineage (*e.g.*, *Thecodontosaurus*, see Kermack 1984) were probably omnivorous (omnivory possibly being a basal condition for this lineage; see Barrett 2000), this lineage — exclusive of Massospondylidae, *Anchisaurus polyzelus*, and *Blikanasaurus cromptoni*, which display trends toward decreasing body size — shows a number of specializations towards herbivory, such as the general increasing of body size coupled with an increased commitment to herbivory (see Farlow 1987; Barrett). As Yates (2004) stated, this coupling could exemplify "'correlated progression' whereby a positive feedback loop drives changes in multiple features of an organism towards increased specialization (Lee 1996)." Regarding the lineages to Neosauropoda, an increase in the diet of plant matter would necessitate an increase in body side and slower locomotion, this, in turn, leading "to an increased vulnerability to predation, as a positive pressure to further increase size for protection is produced, which reduces the amount of nonplant material that an organism can procure," the evolution of this lineage thereby becoming "channeled towards the niche of gigantic, graviportal herbivores."

Yates' (2003*b*, 2004) reorganization of the Sauropodomorpha, particularly his referral of traditional prosauropoda taxa to the Sauropoda, has not been adopted.

In a reassessment of the Prosauropoda, presented in an abstract heralding a more detailed report to be published at a later date, Barrett, Zhou and Wang (2003), focused primarily on the prosauropod dinosaurs from the Lower Lufeng Formation (Lower Jurassic) of China. As Barrett *et al.* noted, prosauropod remains comprise the most abundant elements recovered from this fauna rich in Early Jurassic terrestrial vertebrates, some genera including more than one species and based upon nearly complete skeletons. Prosauropod genera listed in this fauna include *Lufengosaurus*, "*Gyposaurus*" [usually considered to be a junior synonym of *Lufengosaurus*], and *Yunnanosaurus*.

While some of this prosauropod material has been neglected for almost 60 years, it has recently become a research project of Barrett *et al.* It was the authors' intent first to redescribe this material. Second,

noting the importance of this material's age, provenance, and completeness, Barrett *et al.* used the new information gleaned from their study to address such issues as sauropodomorph phylogeny, prosauropod taxonomy, paleobiology, and paleobiogeography, and also Early Jurassic paleoecology.

Reexamination by Barrett *et al.* of the type specimens of *Lufengosaurus* and *Yunnanosaurus* reconfirmed their generic distinction, with revised diagnoses, based mostly on cranial autapomorphies, to be proposed for both genera. Most specimens referred to "*Gyposaurus*" are fragmentary and nondiagnostic, probably representing juvenile *Lufengosaurus* individuals; however, a nearly complete specimen, characterized by various postcranial autapomorphies, "probably represents a new taxon." Furthermore, first-hand examination by Barrett *et al.* of this material allowed them "to correct many errors in the original descriptions of these taxa and has provided the first accurate character-codings for these animals." A new phylogenetic analysis by Barrett *et al.*, incorporating these new data, "confirms prosauropod monophyly and addresses the relationships of these previously enigmatic taxa."

In an abstract for a poster, Leal and Azevedo (2003) published their own preliminary phylogeny of the Prosauropoda, noting that most comprehensive cladistic analyses including this group have been inconclusive, and that some "competing hypotheses not only diverge in the relationships of the supposed major prosauropod clades, but also use different taxa in their analyses, restricting direct comparisons." According to Leal and Azevedo, three Brazillian taxa closely related to basal sauropodomorphs — *Saturnalia tupiniquim* and *Guaibasaurus candelariensis* (see above, and *Saturnalia* and *Guaibasaurus* entries for different opinions), considered by those authors to be stem-lineage sauropodomorphs (see breakdown, above), and also the unpublished Brazilian prosauropod UFSM11069 — complete the prosauropod crown group. Moreover, the same features (*e.g.*, rostral portion of dentary; angle of tooth serration; robustness of pes; length of deltopectoral crest of humerus) excluding *S. tupiniquim* from the Prosauropoda include UFSM11069 in that clade.

The analysis of Leal and Azevedo found *G. candelariensis* (formerly considered to be a possible theropod) to be a member of the Sauropodomorpha based upon its type specimen (regarded by the authors as pertaining to a juvenile animal) exhibition of the following sauropodomorph synapomorphies: Total length of tibia, ascending process of astragalus; total length of ungual of pedal digit I.

Leal and Azevedo's analysis included 18 sauropodomorph taxa (*Saturnalia*, *Guaibasaurus*, UFSM

11069, and *Thecodontosaurus* [see Yates 2003*b*, above; see also *Thecodontosaurus* entry], and the prosauropods *Plateosaurus, Massospondylus, Anchisaurus,* "*Sellosaurus*" [=*Plateosaurus*; see entry], *Melanorosaurus, Riojasaurus, Coloradisaurus, Lufengosaurus,* and *Yunnanosaurus*) and four members of the Sauropoda (*Vulcanodon, Barapasaurus* [regarded by some workers as a prosauropod], *Shunosaurus,* and *Brachiosaurus*). This analysis was scored for 65 characters, with the herrerasaurids *Herrerasaurus* and *Staurikosaurus* used as an outgroup to Sauropodomorpha. Preliminary results of this analysis indicate that the Sauropodomorpha comprises a stem group (*S. tupiniquim* and *G. candelariensis*) and two monophyletic clades (Prosauropoda plus Sauropoda), the Prosauropoda comprising "an unresolved clade in a strict consensus approach, probably due to incomplete studies and noncomparable material among the South American prosauropods."

Galton and Upchurch (2004*a*), in their a review of the Prosauropoda, found this clade to be monophyletic, embracing a number of clades both named and unnamed. Regarding the named clades, the newly introduced clade Anchisauria includes the families Anchisauridae and Melanorosauridae; and a reinstated Plateosauria Tornier 1913 includes the family Plateosauridae, and, currently in interchangeable order leading to plateosaurids (because of uncertain prosauropod relationships), *Massospondylus* [=Massospondylidae] and *Yunnanosaurus* [=Yunnaosauridae]

(see above breakdown for higher taxa to which Galton and Upchurch assigned the various prosauropod genera).

Galton and Upchurch provided the following definitions and diagnoses for these clades:

PROSAUROPODA

Stem-based definition: All taxa more closely related to *Plateosaurus* than to Sauropoda (Galton and Upchurch 2004*a*).

Diagnosis: Maxilla with lateral lamina; squamosal with straplike ventral process; ridge on lateral surface of dentary; caudally inset first dentary tooth; centra of caudal dorsal vertebrae elongate (length-height ratio greater than 1.0, this character variable, possibly size-related); absence of prezygapophyseal lamina on caudal dorsal vertebrae; deltopectoral crest oriented at right angles to long axis through distal humeral condyles (reversed in "*Gyposaurus*" *sinensis* [=*Lufengosaurus hueni*], *Jingshanosaurus,* and *Melanorosaurus*); transverse width of distal carpal I greater than width of metacarpal 1 (reversed in "*Sellosaurus*" [=*Plateosaurus*]); phalanx I on manual digit I with proximal "heel"; phalanx I of manual digit I with long axes of proximal and distal articular surface twisted at 45 degrees to each other; large pubic obturator foramen (multiple reversals) (Galton and Upchurch 2004*a*).

[unnamed node-based clade including *Saturnalia*]

Life restoration by Todd Marshall of the tetanuran theropod *Kaijiangosaurus lini* being warded off by the shunosaurine sauropod *Shunosaurus lii*. At least some shunosaurines possessed "tail clubs" that may have been used as defensive weapons.

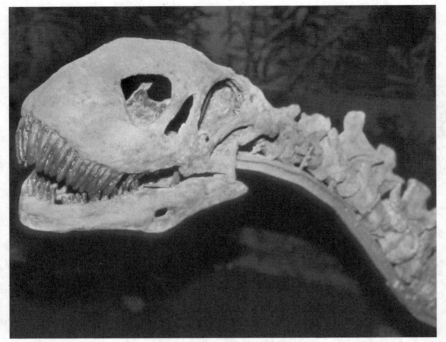

Referred skull of the shunosaurine sauropod *Shunosaurus lii.*

Diagnosis: Medially and distally located teeth lanceolate or unrecurved (alternately synapomorphic for Sauropoda, reversed in *Thecodontosaurus*); deltopectoral crest of humerus terminating at or below midlength of humerus (reversed in *"Gyposaurus" sinensis* [=*Lufengosaurus hueni*]); distal end of ischium expanded dorsoventrally (synapomorphic for Sauropoda, reversed in *Anchisaurus* and *Thecodontosaurus*) (Galton and Upchurch 2004a).

ANCHISAURIA

Node-based definition: *Anchisaurus* and *Melanorosaurus*, their common ancestor, and all its descendants (Galton and Upchurch 2004a).

Diagnosis: Prefrontal subequal in length to frontal; at least five teeth in premaxilla; ratio of forelimb length to hindlimb length greater than 0.60; pubic foramen completely visible in cranial aspect of pubis; femoral shaft straight in cranial or caudal view; proximal end of metatarsal II hourglass-shaped (Galton and Upchurch 2004a).

ANCHISAURIDAE

Stem-based definition: All taxa more closely related to *Anchisaurus* than to *Melanorosaurus* (Galton and Upchurch 2004a).

Diagnosis: Synapomorphies including the following: length to height ratio of longest postaxial cervical centrum at least 3.01; deltopectoral crest terminating in front of distal tip of pubic process in lateral aspect; angle between preacetabular and pubic pro-

cesses of ilium acute in lateral aspect (Galton and Upchurch 2004a).

MELANOROSAURIDAE

Stem-based definition: All taxa more closely related to *Melanorosaurus* than to *Anchisaurus* (Galton and Upchurch 2004a).

Diagnosis: Apomorphies including: Dorsosacral added to sacrum; dorsal margin of ilium with steplike sigmoid profile in lateral aspect; cranial trochanter developing into prominent sheetlike structure; proximal and lateral margins of femur meeting at abrupt right angle in cranial aspect; distal end of fourth trochanter at or below femoral midlength; femoral shaft transversely wide, craniocaudally compressed (Galton and Upchurch 2004a).

Unnamed clade including *Melanorosaurus readi* and *M. thabanensis*

Diagnosis: Prezygadiapophyseal lamina absent on cranial dorsal vertebrae; central of proximal caudal vertebrae high relative to their axial length; at least some pedal phalanges (excluding unguals) broader transversely than long proximodistally (Galton and Upchurch 2004a).

Unnamed clade including *Camelotia borealis* and *Lessemsaurus sauropoides*

Diagnosis: Length-height ratio for centra of caudal dorsal vertebrae less than 1.0 (Galton and Upchurch 2004a).

PLATEOSAURIA

Node-based definition: *Jingshanosaurus*, *Plateosaurus*, their most recent common ancestor, and all of its descendants (Galton and Upchurch 2004a).

Diagnosis: Long retroarticular process; length-height ratio of longest postaxial cervical centrum at least 3.0; one caudosacral vertebra lost; dorsosacral vertebra added to sacrum; proximal carpals ossified; large obturator foramen of pubis (Galton and Upchurch 2004a).

PLATEOSAURIDAE

Stem-based definition: All taxa more closely related to *Plateosaurus* than to *Yunnanosaurus* or *Massospondylus* (Galton and Upchurch 2004a).

Diagnosis: Infratemporal fenestra not extending ventrally beneath orbit (Galton and Upchurch 2004a).

Unnamed clade including *Coloradisaurus brevis*

Diagnosis: Apomorphies comprising horizontal caudal half of premaxillary ascending process; supratemporal fenestra obscured laterally by upper temporal bar; parasphenoid rostrum below level of occipital condyle; jaw articulation below tooth row (Galton and Upchurch 2004*a*).

Unnamed clade including *Lufengosaurus hueni* and "*Gyposaurus*" *sinensis* (=*L. hueni*)

Diagnosis: Transverse processes of cranial dorsal vertebrae directed dorsolaterally; proximal carpals absent of failing to ossify; lateral margin of pubis concave in cranial aspect; pubic obturator foramen entirely visible in cranial aspect; femoral shaft straight in cranial aspect; ungual one of pedal digit I subequal in length to or longer than other pedal phalanges (Galton and Upchurch 2004*a*).

Unnamed clade including *Euskelosaurus browni*

Diagnosis: Loss of dorsosacral vertebra; addition of caudosacral vertebra (Galton and Upchurch 2004*a*).

Unnamed clade including *Plateosaurus "longiceps"* (=*P. engelhardti*), *P. engelhardti*, and "*Sellosaurus*" (=*Plateosaurus*) *gracilis*

Diagnosis: Maxilla excluded from external narial margin by contact between premaxilla and nasal; frontal excluded from margin of supratemporal fossa; proximal end of cranial trochanter terminating below level of femoral head (Galton and Upchurch 2004*a*).

Furthermore, Galton and Upchurch's analysis found the genera *Ruehleia*, and *Yimenosaurus*, previously classified as plateosaurids, as Prosauropoda *incertae sedis*.

Concerning the Sauropoda, Allain, Aquesbi, Dejax, Meyer, Monbaron, Montenat, Richir, Rochdy, Russell and Taquet (2004), in a paper describing the new primitive sauropod *Tazoudasaurus*, referred that genus to the family Vulcanodontidae, which they redefined as all sauropods closer *Vulcanodon* than to Eusauropoda, including in that clade as sister taxa the genera *Tazoudasaurus* and *Vulcanodon*, while excluding such primitive taxa as *Barapasaurus*, *Kotasaurus*, and *Shunosaurus*. The phylogenetic analysis by Allain *et al.* (see *Tazoudasaurus* entry for more details) also found *Atlasaurus imlakei* to be a the sister taxon to the Neosauropoda, as had been previously proposed by Wilson (2002).

Harris and Dodson (2004), in a paper in which they described the new sauropod *Suuwassea* (see entry), introduced the new diplodocoid clade Flagellicaudata, including that genus and various other sauropods (*e.g.*, *Apatosaurus*, *Diplodocus*, and *Barosaurus*) possessing "whiplash" tails (their analysis excluding the clade Rebbachisauridae):

FLAGELLICAUDATA

Node-based definition: Clade consisting of the most recent common ancestor of *Dicraeosaurus* and *Diplodocus* and all of its descendants (=the clade 'Dicraeosauridae + Diplodocidae' of other authors) (Harris and Dodson 2004).

Diagnosis: Atlantal intercentrum having cranioventrally expanded occipital fossa; cranial cervical and cranial dorsal neural spines bifid; distal condyle of metatarsal I having caudolateral projection (Harris and Dodson 2004, after Wilson 2002*a*).

Parrish (2003), in a published abstract focusing upon ecomorphs, briefly discussed a study mapping locomotor patterns, neck types, and skull and tooth shape onto an updated version of Upchurch's (1998) phylogeny of the Sauropoda, and yielding the following observations:

1. Most ecomorphic discriminators can be found in different sauropod lineages (*e.g.*, ventral inclination of skull relative to occiput in Diplodocidae and Brachiosauridae; extreme cervical elongation, with increased vertebral count, in Diplodocidae, Brachiosauridae, and Euhelopodidae).

2. Distributions of some ecomorphic discriminators do not always overlap (*e.g.*, elongate, sloping skulls in "Titanosauroidea" [of Upchurch 1999; =Titanosauria, see below] and Diplodocidae, correlating with varying degrees of cervical elongation, each clade also exhibiting distinct tooth morphologies and dental battery configurations).

3. Some ecomorphic discriminators recur in more than one lineage having disjunct geographical distribution (*e.g.*, long, horizontally inclined necks in Asian Euhelopodidae and primarily North American/European/African Diplodocidae).

As Parrish pointed out, sauropods exhibit considerable ecological diversity despite the constraints of a highly distinctive body plan, this not clearly reflecting the group's overall phylogenetic or biogeographic history; rather, "sauropods reflect a complex mosaic of ecomorphs which is a classic, albeit morphologically canalized example of an adaptive radiation." Parrish further commented that the "Titanosauroidea," despite the incomplete fossil record of this primarily Cretaceous clade, seems to have undergone its own ecomorphic radiation after the other sauropod groups had become extinct.

Recently, the validity of the sauropod genus *Titanosaurus* (see entry) and, by inference, the traditional family Titanosauridae and its subfamily Titanosaurinae—clades grouping together a large number of Late Jurassic to Late Cretaceous titanosaurian members of the Sauropoda — have been questioned (see, for example, Wilson 2002*b*). Thus, in the previous volume (*S3*) in this series of books, the present writer began setting such terms as "Titanosauridae" in quotation marks.

Questions regarding the validity of the "Titanosauridae" were recently addressed by Jaime Eduardo Powell, a paleontologist who for almost 20 years has been specializing in this sauropod group. In 1986, Powell's PhD dissertation offered his own revision of the "Titanosauridae" of South America. This document, however, long remained unpublished, its data not being accessible to many researchers of sauropods. While, over the years, Powell (*e.g.*, 1987, 1992) continued to publish papers focusing on various topics relating to "titanosaurid" dinosaurs, it was not until 2003 that that author's long awaited and much anticipated thorough revision of South American titanosaurids was finally issued, his monograph taking into account the paleobiological, paleobiogeographical, and phylogenetic aspects of this sauropod group. Powell's (2003) study, while based largely upon his 1986 dissertation, also took into account the markedly increased Cretaceous sauropod fossil record and other recent related studies. Powell's (2003) work also included a detailed history of South American "titanosaurid" discoveries, plus sections on biomechanics, feeding behavior, and other aspects pertaining to this sauropod group.

Powell (2003) accepted *Titanosaurus* as a valid, diagnosable genus and that titanosaurs comprise a monophyletic group having the rank of family ("Titanosauridae," the present writer's quotation marks), as first proposed by Lydekker (1893) for a group of Indian and Argentinian sauropods possessing procoelous caudal vertebrae, and subsequently by Huene (1929, 1956). This was "justified by traditional use, and with the aim of avoiding the creation of new names" and somewhat concordant with some earlier proposed classification schemes (Berman and McIntosh 1978; McIntosh 1981, 1990; Bonaparte 1996). The "Titanosauridae," Powell (2003) noted, comprise a well-represented South American group that played "an important role in the Late Cretaceous ecosystem as gigantic herbivores, an adaptive zone which evidently they alone occupied for the greater part of that period."

"TITANOSAURIDAE"

Diagnosis: Quadrupedal herbivorous dinosaurs, medium to gigantic size; skull having very long, recurved paroccipital processes; teeth cylindrical, roots open, teeth slightly spatulate when unworn (except in *Ampelosaurus*); basipterygoid processes short; 13 cervical vertebrae, probably 12 dorsals, six sacrals, more than 30 caudals; opisthocoelous presacral vertebrae having cancellous structure in centra and bulky parts of neural arch (neural arch peduncles, ends of neurapophyses and diapophyses); dorsal vertebrae without hyposphene-hypantrum (except in primitive *Epachthosaurus*); sacral vertebrae completely fused; sacral ribs T-shaped in cross section, participating in conformation of acetabular articular surface; first caudal vertebra biconvex or procoelous; remaining caudals having distal articular condyle, occasional amphicoelic elements on distal part of tail; neural arches joined to anterior portion of centrum in middle and distal caudal vertebrae; hemapophyses open proximally; scapula with glenoid articular facet oriented forward, down, inwards; quadrangular coracoids; sternal plates long, relatively broad, lateral margin concave; forelimbs shorter than hind limbs; femur straight, somewhat flattened anteroposteriorly; fibula having marked lateral process; astragalus relatively narrow (Powell 2003).

Powell regarded the "Titanosauridae" as the only valid titanosaurian family, including in it such taxa as *Saltasaurus*, which had previously been referred to its own family Saltasauridae (see *S3*). (Various other authors have regarded "saltasaurs" as a distinct family or subfamily, *e.g.*, Powell 1986, 2003; Wilson, Martinez and Alcober 1999.)

Basically following Upchurch (1995) and Sanz, Powell, Le Loeuff, Martinez and Pereda-Suberbiola (1999), Powell's (2003) phylogenetic analysis of "titanosaurid" and related sauropod dinosaurs reached the following conclusions:

According to Powell, an unnamed and fairly inclusive sauropod clade can be diagnosed by a number of synapomorphies:

Unnamed sauropod clade

Diagnosis: Developed, clearly defined pleurocoelous cavity in medial and caudal dorsal vertebrae, slightly developed opisthocoelous in caudal dorsal vertebrae (reversed in *Argyrosaurus*); spinodiapophyseal lamina in caudal dorsal vertebrae; acuminate pleurocoelic outline in cranial and middorsals; poorly developed basal branching of prespinal lamina on mid- and caudal dorsals (reversed in *"Titanosaurus"* [=*Isisaurus*] *colberti*); hemapophyseal ridges in midcaudal vertebrae; anteromedial coracoid outline straight; coracoidal foramen situated away from scapulocoracoidal suture (Powell 2003).

Within the above group, Powell (2003) included two clades. The first of these groups comprises the genera *Haplocanthosaurus* and *Andesaurus* (the latter usually classified as a titanosaur); the second of these clades is the "Titanosauroidea" (*sensu* Upchurch; see below): within Titanosauroidea, the genus *Opisthocoelicaudia* as the nearest sister taxon to the Titanosauria; within Titanosauria, the genus *Epachthosaurus* (see entry; see also Sanz *et al.*), diagnosed by the following—absence of hyposphene-hypanrum articulation in caudal dorsal vertebrae; femur having reduced fourth trochanter; osteoderms (documented in Argentina, Brazil, Spain, France, and Madagascar), and the Eutitanosauria (Sanz *et al.*); Eutitanosauria splitting into two basic clades, the first group joining the genera *Alamosaurus, Lirainasaurus*, and the unnamed "Peirópolis titanosaur" (see *S3*), the second including *Aeolosaurus* plus other taxa included in succeeding clades (the latter clade including a weakly supported clade comprising *Argyrosaurus* plus taxa included in the succeeding clade]); within the latter, a clade comprising *"Titanosaurus"* [=*Isisaurus*] *colberti* plus *Ampelosaurus*)]. Powell (2003) diagnosed these clades as follows:

Unnamed clade comprising *Haplocanthosaurus* plus *Andesaurus*
Diagnosis: Axial keel in centrum of dorsal vertebrae (character paralleled in *Lirainosaurus*) (Yates 2003*b*).

TITANOSAUROIDEA

Diagnosis: Prespinal and postspinal lamina in proximal caudal vertebrae (reversed in *Saltasaurus*); ilium expanded craniolaterally (reversed in *Ampelosaurus*); femur with lateroproximal buttress; strongly developed opisthocoely in caudal dorsal vertebrae (reversed in *Argyrosaurus*) (Powell 2003).

TITANOSAURIA

Diagnosis: Flat horizontal surface at end of diapophysis on caudal dorsal vertebrae (paralleled in *Haplocanthosaurus*); developed posterior condyles in centra of proximal caudal vertebrae; sternal plate having anteroventral ridge (Powell 2003).

EUTITANOSAURIA

Definition: All derived forms traditionally regarded as "titanosaurids" (Powell 2003).

Unnamed clade comprising *Alamosaurus* plus *Lirainasaurus* plus "Peirópolis titanosaur"
Diagnosis: Almost perpendicular angle between planes including greatest proximal dimensions of tibia and distal region (Powell 2003).

Unnamed clade comprising *Aeolosaurus* plus taxa in succeeding clades
Diagnosis: (Reversions) high neurapophysis in dorsal vertebrae; absence of anteroventral ridge of sternal plate (Powell 2003).

Unnamed clade comprising *Argyrosaurus* plus taxa included in the succeeding clade
Diagnosis: (Reversion) incipient prespinal and postspinal laminae in proximal caudal vertebrae (Powell 2003).

Unnamed clade comprising *"Titanosaurus"* [=Isisaurus] *colberti* plus *Ampelosaurus*
Diagnosis: Nonprojected spinal postzygapophyseal structure in distal caudal vertebrae (Powell 2003).

Another recent paper accepting the "Titanosauridae" as a valid family was that of Calvo and González Riga (2003), in which these authors described the new titanosaurian form *Rinconsaurus* (see entry for details).

The same year that saw the release of Powell's (2003) revision of this sauropod assemblage, a major revision of the genus *Titanosaurus* (see entry), co-authored by sauropod specialists Jeffrey A. Wilson and Paul Upchurch (2003), was published. In reevaluating *Titanosaurus* and its numerous species, finding (*contra* Powell) that genus to be invalid based upon "obsolescent characters" (*i.e.*, those once regarded as diagnostic, but which are now known to have broader taxonomic applications), Wilson and Upchurch also addressed the validity of the various rank taxa that had been based upon that genus, *i.e.*, the subfamily "Titanosaurinae," the family "Titanosauridae," and the superfamily "Titanosauroidea."

As pointed out by Wilson and Upchurch, when accepting that *Titanosaurus* is an invalid genus, it follows that "co-ordinate supragenetic Linnean taxa must likewise be abandoned." Citing Gilmore (1946*b*), the authors noted that "'Titanosauridae' has served as little more than a receptacle for indeterminate Cretaceous sauropods," its "broad, featureless definition … combined with partially and nonoverlapping taxa referred to the ill-defined genus '*Titanosaurus*' [having] abetted the inertial state of titanosaur systematics over the last half century."

However, the clade Titanosauria, not being a ranked taxon, was adopted by Wilson and Upchurch. Moreover, the more generally used term Titanosauria ("the most diverse and geographically wide-spread clade of sauropod dinosaurs, represented by more than 30 genera that have been recorded from all continental landmasses except Antarctica during the Cretaceous"; *e.g.*, see Weishampel 1990) was used in favor of the equivalent "Titanosauroidea," which Upchurch had proposed in 1998 because he believed that "a set of taxonomic categories of superfamily rank will bring greater consistency and stability to sauropod classification." Furthermore, although Wilson and Sereno (1998) had proposed a stem-based definition for Titanosauria ("Titanosauriforms more closely related to

Saltasaurus than to either *Brachiosaurus* or *Euhelopus*"), Wilson and Upchurch opted to use the node-based definition ("the most recent common ancestor of *Andesaurus delgadoi* and Titanosauridae and all of its descendants") of Salgado, Coria and Calvo (1997), which has priority, and also closely follows the traditional definition offered by Bonaparte and Coria in 1993.

As explained by Wilson and Upchurch, Salgado *et al.* and Upchurch had used the term "Titanosauridae," the former applying the name to *Malawisaurus* and the more derived titanosaurs, the latter to titanosaurs more derived than *Malawisaurus*. Wilson had used the term Saltasauridae for a clade equivalent to the "Titanosauridae" of Upchurch and the Saltisaurinae of Curry Rogers and Forster (2001). The new clade Eutitanosauria was introduced by Sanz *et al.* "for the most recent common ancestor of *Saltasaurus, Argyrosaurus, Lirainosaurus*, plus the Peirópolis titanosaur and all its descendants," this group as defined, Wilson and Upchurch noted, possibly synonymous with either Saltasauridae or Saltasaurinae.

Wilson and Upchurch accepted Upchurch, Barrett and Dodson's (2004; see below) Lithostrortia, a new node-based clade including *Malawisaurus* plus more derived titanosaurs sharing the feature of dermal armor, defined as *Mawalisaurus dixeyi, Saltasaurus loricatus*, their most recent common ancestor and all descendants. This new group, the authors noted, should "help discriminate between basal members of the titanosaur radiation." Wilson and Upchurch also accepted Sereno's (1998) Saltasauridae (*Opisthocoelicaudia skarzynskii, S. loricatus*, their most recent common ancestor and all descendants) and that family's constuent subgroups, the Saltasaurinae (all saltasaurids more closely related to *S. loricatus* than to *O. skarzynskii*) and Opisthocoelicaudinae (all saltasaurids more closely related to *O. skarzynskii* than to *S. loricatus*).

More recently, in their review of the inclusive clade Sauropoda, Upchurch *et al.* (2004) performed a phylogenetic analysis incorporating 309 characters pertaining solely to variation with this clade. This study reevaluated a number of sauropod genera, some of its conclusions following: *Chuanjiesaurus*—provisionally valid, its description by Fang, Pang, Lu, Zhang, Pan, Wang, Li and Cheng (2000) insufficient for determining its relationships or taxonomic status; *Cetiosaurus*—part of a monophyletic group including *Patagosaurus* and *Barapasaurus*, suggesting the use of Cetiosauridae to include those taxa more closely related to *Cetiosaurus* than to Neosauropoda; *Euhelopus*—placing outside of Neosauropoda; *Klamelisaurus*—broad spatulate teeth, 16 cervical vertebrae, five sacral vertebrae, and forked chevrons suggesting resemblance to *Omeisaurus* and status as a nonneosauropod eusauropod; *Oplosaurus*—holotype tooth distinctive in

several details from those of other broad-toothed sauropods, possibly valid; *Rhoetosaurus*—opisthocoelous dorsal vertebrae having well-developed pleurocoels suggesting relationship closer to Neosauropoda than to cetiosaurids (regarded as a valid clade by Upchurch, Barrett and Dodson 2004; see below) and basal eusauropods; *Haplocanthosaurus*—a derived macronarian closer to Titanosauriformes than to *Camarasaurus*; *Tendaguria*—apparent absence of accessory laminae in infrapostzygapophyseal cavity suggesting primitive sauropod, large pleurocoels suggestive of neosauropod affinities, best regarded as Sauropoda *incertae sedis*; *Volkheimeria*—regarded by McIntosh (1990) as brachiosaurid without cladistic analysis, status presently unresolved; *Lourinhasaurus*—"the closest known relative of Neosauropoda"; *Amygdalodon*, a *nomen dubium* based on inadequate material, and possibly *Aragosaurus*, requiring further cladistic analysis—Eusauropoda *incertae sedis*; *Hudiesaurus*—type material identifiable only as belonging to an indeterminate eusauropod; *Amphicoelias*, possibly *Cetiosauriscus, Dinheirosaurus*, and *Losillasaurus*—Diplodocidae *incertae sedis*; *Nigersaurus*—a possible rebbachisaurid (following the analysis by Sereno, Beck, Dutheil, Larrson, Lyon, Moussa, Sadleir, Sidor, Varrichio, Wilson and Wilson (1999); *Dyslocosaurus*—a diplodocid (see entry); *Abrosaurus, Atlasaurus* (see entries), *Bellusaurus*, and *Jobaria*—basal, noncamarasauromorph members of Macronaria; *Lapparentosaurus*, probably *Ornithopsis* (see entry), *Eucamerotus* (see entry), *Pelorosaurus*, and *Pleurocoelus*—Titanosauriformes *incertae sedis*, the described material assigned to these taxa insufficient for purposes of diagnosis; *Aegyptosaurus, Andesaurus, Agustinia, Argentinosaurus, Tangvayosaurus*, and *Venenosaurus*—basal titanosaurians outside of Lithostrotia, a new clade introduced by Upchurch *et al.* (see below).

Contrary to a number of recent studies (*e.g.*, Salgado and Calvo 1997; Wilson 1997; Wilson and Sereno 1998; Curry Rogers and Forster 2001), which placed Nemegtosauridae within the clade Titanosauria, Upchurch *et al.* found Nemegtosauridae to be nestled, as various earlier analyses had indicated, within Diplodocoidea; and *Aeolosaurus, Alamosaurus, Ampelosaurus, Antarctosaurus, Paralititan*, "*Pelligrinisaurus*" [=*Epachthosaurus*; see entry], *Rapetosaurus, Rocasaurus*, and *Titanosaurus* to be members of Lithostrotia.

Upchurch *et al.* offered the following definitions and diagnoses for Sauropoda and its included clades:

SAUROPODA

Stem-based definition: Sauropodomorphs more closely related to *Saltasaurus* than to *Plateosaurus* (Wilson and Sereno 1998).

Diagnosis: Centrodiapophyseal lamina system on cranial and midcervical vertebrae; ratio of forelimb length to hindlimb length greater than 0.60; proximal end of ulna triradiate; distal radius subrectangular in outline, caudal margin flattened; ratio of metacarpal V length to metacarpal III length greater than 0.90; triangular striated ligament attachment area on proximal parts of metacarpal shafts; distal ischial shaft compressed, maximum width at least three times minimum width; femoral cranial trochanter reduced to low ridge; middle and distal portions of femoral shaft straight in cranial view; femoral shaft elliptical in horizontal cross section, long axis directed transversely; ratio of tibia length to femur length less than 0.70; tibial cnemial crest reduced to low ridge; base of cranial face of ascending process of astragalus lacking depression and nutritive foramen; ratio of metatarsal III length to tibia length less than 0.40; proximal end surfaces of metatarsals I and V larger than those of II, III, and IV; ratio of metatarsal III length to V length at least 0.85 (Upchurch, Barrett and Dodson 2004).

BLIKANASAURIDAE (=*Blikanasaurus* of Upchurch *et al.*'s usage]

Diagnosis: Apomorphy of distal end of fibula facing strongly ventromedially (Upchurch, Barrett and Dodson 2004).

EUSAUROPODA

Node-based definition (differing from the stem-based definition of Wilson and Sereno 1998): Most recent common ancestor of *Shunosaurus* and *Saltasaurus* and all descendants of that ancestor (Upchurch 1995).

Diagnosis: Snout broadly rounded in dorsal aspect; caudal margin of external naris behind caudal margin of antorbital fenestra; lateral plate on premaxillae, maxillae, and dentaries; contact between dorsal ends of maxilla and lacrimal at caudodorsal margin of antorbital fenestra; platelike flange of bone at base of ascending process of maxilla; rostral process of quadratojugal at least twice length of dorsal process; quadratojugal rostral process expanded dorsoventrally at its tip; absence of prefrontal rostral process; transverse width of frontals greater than rostrocaudal length; rostral tip of maxillary process of palatine expanded transversely; ectopterygoid process of pterygoid below rostral rim of orbit; diameter of external mandibular fenestra less than 10 percent length of mandible; wrinkled tooth crown enamel; caudalmost tooth beneath antorbital fenestra; at least 12 cervical vertebrae; height of midcervical neural arches greater than diameter of centrum; caudal margins of caudal cervical neural spines sloping strongly forward in lateral aspect; dorsal surfaces of sacral plates level with dorsal margin of ilium; lamina linking first caudal rib linked to neural arch; carpals blocklike; metacarpals arranged in "U"-shaped colonnade; manual phalanges (apart from unguals) wider transversely than proximodistally; manual unguals II–IV with two or less phalanges; dorsal margin of ilium strongly convex in lateral aspect; ischial peduncle of ilium reduced, long axis of blade sloping craniodorsally in lateral aspect; middle and distal portions of pubis in same plane as proximal part; absence of femoral cranial trochanter; medial malleolus of tibia reduced, exposing caudal fossa of astragalus in caudal aspect; lateral muscle scar at midlength on fibula; metatarsals II–IV diverging from each other distally; ratio of length to proximal transverse width for metatarsal I 1.5 or less; pedal digit IV having three phalanges; pedal phalanges lacking collateral ligament pits; nonungual pedal phalanges wider transversely than proximodistally; pedal digits II–IV with rudimentary penultimate phalanges; ratio of ungual length to metatarsal length for pedal digit I greater than 1.0; unguals for pedal digits II and III with transversely compressed proximal articular ends (Upchurch, Barrett and Dodson 2004).

CETIOSAURIDAE

Stem-based definition: Sauropods more closely related to *Cetiosaurus* than to *Saltasaurus* (Upchurch, Barrett and Dodson 2004).

Diagnosis: Pleurocoels of cervical vertebrae deep excavations lacking accessory laminae; presence of neural cavity opening to exterior of neural arch through lateral foramen in at least caudal dorsal vertebrae (uncertain in *Cetiosaurus*); cranial dorsal vertebrae having deep lateral excavation on either side of neural arch, immediately below base of transverse process, leaving just thin bone septum on midline (Upchurch, Barrett and Dodson 2004).

NEOSAUROPODA

Node-based definition: Most recent common ancestor of *Diplodocus* and *Saltasaurus* and all descendants of that ancestor (Wilson and Sereno 1999).

Diagnosis: Dorsally facing subnarial foramen on premaxilla-maxilla suture; platelike projections at base of maxillary ascending processes meeting on midline; canal or preantorbital fenestra in base of maxillary ascending process; rostral process of quadratojugal contacting caudal end of maxilla; rostroventral corner of infratemporal fenestra terminating level with or rostral to rostral rim of orbit; lateral end of ectopterygoid contacting medial surface of maxilla; ascending process of astragalus terminating level with caudal edge of astragalus; pedal digit IV with two or less phalanges (Upchurch, Barrett and Dodson 2004).

DIPLODOCOIDEA

Stem-based definition: Neosauropoda more closely related to *Diplodocus* than to *Saltasaurus* (Wilson and Sereno 1998).

Diagnosis: Snout subrectangular in dorsal aspect; external nares fully retracted, cranial rim behind rostral margin of orbit; subnarial foramen elongate, length at least twice maximum width; premaxilla losing distinction between heavy ventral main body and slender ascending process; angle between midline and premaxilla-maxilla suture reduced in dorsal aspect to 20 degrees or less; rostrocaudal diameter of supratemporal fenestra reduced to less than 10 percent occipital width (possibly convergent with some advanced lithostrotians); caudalmost tooth rostral to antorbital fenestra (Upchurch, Barrett and Dodson 2004).

NEMEGTOSAURIDAE

Stem-based definition: Diplodocoidea more closely related to *Nemegtosaurus* than to *Diplodocus* (Upchurch, Barrett and Dodson 2004, *contra* Wilson and Sereno 1998).

Diagnosis: Quadratojugal rostral process with steplike bend in lateral aspect; squamosal excluded from dorsal margin of supratemporal fenestra by parietal-postorbital contact (Upchurch, Barrett and Dodson 2004).

REBBACHISAURIDAE

Stem-based definition: Diplodocoidea more closely related to *Rebbachisaurus* than to *Diplodocus* (Upchurch, Barrett and Dodson 2004).

Diagnosis: Scapular blade expanding at distal end, wide as proximal end, outline paddle-like in lateral aspect (Upchurch, Barrett and Dodson 2004).

DICRAEOSAURIDAE

Stem-based definition: Diplodocoidea more closely related to *Dicraeosaurus* than to *Diplodocus* (Upchurch, Barrett and Dodson 2004).

Diagnosis: Frontals coossified along their midline contact; postparietal fenestra; lead-shaped, dorsolaterally directed processes on crista prootica; basipterygoid processes diverging at 20-degree angle; deep pit between bases of basipterygoid processes; extreme elongation of presacral neural spines (Upchurch, Barrett and Dodson 2004).

DIPLODOCIDAE

Stem-based definition: Diplodocoidea more closely related to *Diplodocus* than to *Dicraeosaurus* (Upchurch, Barrett and Dodson 2004).

Diagnosis: Dorsally facing external nares; absence of internarial bar; jugal forming substantial part of caudoventral margin of antorbital fenestra; 130-degree angle between rostral and dorsal quadratojugal

Photograph by Mindy McNaugher, courtesy Carnegie Museum of Natural History.

(Right) holotype skeleton (CM 3018, with probable skull CM 11162; see *D:TE*) of *Apatosaurus louisae*, mounted in the Dinosaur Hall at the Carnegie Museum of Natural History (see "Introduction"). This skeleton, collected from the Morrison Formation of Utah, measures 23 meters (76.5 feet) in length and 5.5 meters (18 feet) tall at the hips. Also seen in this photograph are skeletons of (left) *Stegosaurus ungulatus* (CM 1134) and (center background) *Diplodocus carnegie* (including holotype CM 84 and referred specimens CM 94 and 307, and cast of skull USNM 2673), the latter a sauropod closely related to *A. louisae*.

Photograph by Urs Möckl, copyright © and courtesy Sauriermuseum Aathal.

Skull of the diplodocid sauropod *Diplodocus*. This specimen was collected during the 1990s from the Howe Stephens Quarry at Howe Ranch, in northern Wyoming.

process; distal end of paroccipital process rounded, tonguelike; parasphenoid rostrum laterally compressed, thin spike lacking longitudinal dorsal groove; ectopterygoid process of pterygoid below antorbital fenestra; ectopterygoid process of pterygoid reduced, not visible below ventral margin of skull in lateral aspect; breadth of main body pterygoid at least 33 per- cent pterygoid length; at least five or six replacement teeth per alveolus (as in *Nigersaurus*); no more than 10 dorsal vertebrae; 70 to 80 caudal vertebrae; proxi- moventral margin of pedal phalanx I-1 drawn out into thin plate or heel underlying distal end of metatarsal I; pedal phalanx II-2 reduced in craniocaudal length, shape irregular (Upchurch, Barrett and Dodson 2004).

Reconstructed skeletal cast of the diplococid sauropod *Seismosaurus halorum* exhibited at Dinofest (2000–2001), Navy Pier, Chicago, this display having been prepared by Dinosauria International, Inc., based upon the holotype material and also specimens of *Diplodocus*.

Photograph by the author.

Skull (cast by the PAST Company) of an adult *Jobaria tiguidensis*, a basal macronarian sauropod, part of the "Giants: African Dinosaurs" exhibit at Garfield Park Conservatory.

MACRONARIA

Stem-based definition: Neosauropoda more closely related to *Saltasaurus* than to *Diplodocus* (Wilson and Sereno 1998).

Diagnosis: Greatest diameter of external naris exceeding that of orbit; subnarial foramen within external narial fossa (Upchurch, Barrett and Dodson 2004).

CAMARASAUROMORPHA

Node-based definition: Most recent common ancestor of *Camarasaurus* and *Saltasaurus* and all descendants of that ancestor (Upchurch, Barrett and Dodson 2004).

Diagnosis: Premaxillary ascending process directed dorsally most of its length; rostral end of splenial reaching mandibular symphysis; pleurocoels in cranial dorsal vertebrae having acute caudal ends; metacarpal I longer than IV; length of longest metacarpal 40 percent that of radius (Upchurch, Barrett and Dodson 2004).

TITANOSAURIFORMES

Node-based definition: Most recent common ancestor of *Brachiosaurus* and *Saltasaurus* and all the descendants of that ancestor (Wilson and Sereno 1998).

Diagnosis: Neural arches of middle caudal vertebrae on cranial half of centrum; cranial lobe of ilium rounded in lateral aspect (also in Chinese Eusauropoda, *e.g.*, *Mamenchisaurus* and *Euhelopus*); presacral vertebrae with coarse cancellar structure (also in some Chinese eusauropods, *e.g.*, *Mamenchisaurus*) (Upchurch, Barrett and Dodson 2004).

BRACHIOSAURIDAE

Stem-based definition: Titanosauriformes more closely related to *Brachiosaurus* than to *Saltasaurus* (Wilson and Sereno 1998).

Diagnosis: Humerus with enlarged deltopectoral crest (reversal); ratio of humerus length to femur close to 1.0 (Upchurch, Barrett and Dodson 2004).

TITANOSAURIA

Stem-based definition: Titanosauriformes more closely related to *Saltasaurus* than to *Brachiosaurus* (Upchurch, Barrett and Dodson 2004).

Diagnosis: Caudal end of sternal plate having prominent caudolateral expansion; radius and ulna extremely robust (*e.g.*, proximal width of radius at least 3.3 percent radius length) (Upchurch, Barrett and Dodson 2004).

LITHOSTROTIA

Node-based definition: Most recent common ancestor of *Malawisaurus* and *Saltasaurus* and all descendants of that ancestor (Upchurch, Barrett and Dodson 2004).

Diagnosis: Caudal vertebrae having strongly procoelous proximal centra (convergent with *Mamenchisaurus*); strong procoely in all but most distal caudal vertebrae (Upchurch, Barrett and Dodson 2004).

Skeleton of a juvenile individual of the camarasaurid *Camarasaurus*, collected at Howe Ranch, Wyoming.

SALTASAURIDAE

Node-based definition: Least inclusive clade containing *Opisthocoelicaudia* and *Saltasaurus* (Sereno 1998).

Diagnosis: Caudal dorsal vertebre with parapophysis directly below diapophysis; proximal caudal vertebrae with broad, deep fossae on ventral suture of centra; neural spines of proximal caudal vertebrae wider transversely than axially, lamination complex; prominent, rounded process at junction of proximal and lateral surfaces of humerus (Upchurch, Barrett and Dodson 2004).

Upchurch *et al.* regarded the type species *Cardiodon rugulosus*, *Chuanjiesaurus anaensis*, *Datousaurus bashanensis*, *Dystrophaeus viaemale*, *Klamelisaurus gobiensis*, *Oplosaurus armatus*, *Rhoetosaurus brownei*, *Tendaguria tanzaniensis*, and *Volkeimeria chubutensis*, previously phylogentically placed elsewhere, as Sauropoda *incertae sedis*; and *Aragosaurus ischiaticus* as Eusauropoda *incertae sedis*. Furthermore, Upchurch *et al.* found among other taxa the following type species, which are or have been referred to the Sauropoda, to be *nomina dubia*: *Algoasaurus bauri*, *Astrodon johnstoni* (see *Astrodon* entry for a contradicting opinion), *Bothriospondylus suffosus*, *Chinshakiangosaurus chungshoensis*, *Histriasaurus boscarollii*, *Protognathosaurus oxyodon*, *Pukyongosaurus millenniumi*, *Qinlingosaurus luonanensis*, *Sanpasaurus yaoi*, *Sonorosaurus thompsoni*, and *Zizhongosaurus chuanchengensis*.

More recently, in a paper introducing the new rebbachisaurid genus *Limayasaurus* (see entry), Sal-

gado, Garrido, Cocca and Cocca (2004) performed a cladistic analysis that concluded the following: *Limayasaurus*, *Nigersaurus*, and *Rebbachisaurus* comprising the clade Rebbachisauridae, a clade of Cretaceous basal diplodocoids (see Wilson 2002*a*); and *Amazonsaurus* placing as the sister taxon to Dicraeosauridae plus Diplodocidae.

REBBACHISAURIDAE

Diagnosis: Frontal rostrocaudally elongate; rounded orbital ventral margin; postorbital without rostral process; supratemporal fenestra reduced or absent; absences of hyposphene-hypantrum articulations; proximal and middle caudal vertebrae quadrangular, flat ventrally and laterally; scapular blade "racquet"-shaped (only this character verified in *Limayasaurus*, *Nigersaurus*, and *Rebbachisaurus*); ischial shaft flat, twisted almost 90 degrees with respect to proximal ischial expansion (Salgado, Garrido, Cocca and Cocca 2004).

Salgado *et al.* proposed a scenario whereby two major sauropod clades, the Titanosauriformes and "Diplodocimorpha," coexisted in Patagonia during Early to Middle (Cenomanian) times. Diplodocoids, represented in Patagonia only by rebbachisaurids, became extinct globally by the middle of the Cenomanian, their extinction possibly facilitating the expansion and diversification of derived titanosauriformes (see Salgado 2003).

As Salgado *et al.* speculated, the titanosaurs and rebbachisaurids apparently occupied well-differentiated niches. Titanosaurs, these authors noted, have comparatively longer forelimbs than rebbachisaurids, the humeri in the latter being considerably shorter than their femora (see Calvo and Salgado 1995). Additionally, the teeth of titanosaurs are relatively broad, while those in diplodocoids are cylindrical (see Wilson 2002a). These differences may have suggest different feeding habits for these two sauropod groups.

Ornithischia

Buchholz (2002) published a detailed revision of basal Ornithischia [excluding Hadrosauroidea]—Ornithischia being the very large clade of herbivorous dinosaurs (see S3 for his preliminary report)—"perhaps the most diverse clade within Dinosauria, incorporating a tremendous number of bauplan modifications, where quadrupedal locomotion evolved at least three times (Thyreophora, Ceratopia, Iguanodontoidea), numerous cranial display structures evolved (Ankylosauria, Marginocephalia, *Zephyrosaurus* + *Orodromeus* [see below], Hadrosauridae), and increasingly complex mastication processes evolved within Cerapoda." As Buchholz pointed out, most recent phylogenetic analyses have centered around saurischian dinosaurs, particularly theropods, while previous analyses of the Ornithischia "have suffered by rather unrefined methodology," *i.e.*, "by treating various operational taxonomic units (OTUs) as monophyletic without testing this beforehand, using animals that are very derived (such as *Heterodontosaurus* as outgroups, and only testing the positions of major groups rather than single taxa" (see Norman, Sues, Witmer and Coria 2004, below, for another, more recent opinion regarding the phylogeny of basal Ornithopoda).

The phylogeneny proposed by Buchholz was based upon both previously published analyses and original research involving specimens. Buchholz's analysis included 20 ornithischian taxa and 97 ordered characters (38 cranial, six mandibular, 16 dental, and 36 postcranial) (see paper for complete lists of taxa and characters).

A number of well-known taxa were eliminated from Buchholz's study, being either too fragmentary or not sufficiently described, these including the following: *Pisanosaurus mertii*, generally regarded as the most basal member of Ornithischia known from skeletal remains (see, for example, Sereno 1991a); *Jeholosaurus shangyuanensis*, a basal ornithopod requiring additional postcranial material to clarify its placement; *Yandusaurus hongheensis*, Peng's (1972) referral of this species to *Agilisaurus multidens* being rejected by Buchholz for lack of any nonplesiomorphic characters linking these taxa, its assignment to the juve-

nile (see Carpenter 1994) "*Yandusaurus*" *multidens* also doubtful based on the very different form of the skull bones and teeth; *Thescelosaurus neglectus*, found to be the most basal member of Iguanodontia, although much important skull data yet needs to be published; *Muttaburrasaurus langdoni*, a basal iguanodontian sharing some "peculiar characters" (*e.g.*, rhomboid orbid) with *Tenontosaurus*, additional material being required for further understanding its relationships (and also forming a more complete scenario of the biogeography of Gondwanan dinosaurs); and also such "interesting but fragmentary, or poorly described" forms as *Notohypsilophodon comodorensis*, *Leaellynnasaura amicagraphica*, *Bugenasaura infernalis*, and *Valdosaurus*, more complete remains of which are needed to clarify further the evolutionary relationships of the Ornithopoda and the biogeographical origins of this clade. Bucholz reinstated the ornithischian subgroup Predentata Marsh 1881, a clade including Genasauria, the latter including Thyreophora and Cerapoda (including and also the new clade Chasmatopia (see below):

ORNITHISCHIA

Node-based definition: Most inclusive clade containing *Triceratops horridus*, but not [the Andean condor] *Vulture gryphus* (Buchholz 2002).

PREDENTATA

Node-based definition: Least inclusive clade containing both *Lesothosaurus diagnosticus* and *Triceratops horridus* (the least inclusive group in which the predentary bone can clearly be demonstrated on the mandible).

GENASAURIA

Node-based definition: Least inclusive clade containing both *Ankylosaurus magniventris* and *Triceratops horridus* (Buchholz 2002).

THYREOPHORA

Node-based definition: Most inclusive clade containing Stegosauria and Ankylosauria, exclusive of other ornithischians (Buchholz 2002).

CERAPODA (=Neornithischia Cooper 1981)

Node-based definition: Most inclusive clade containing *Iguanodon bernissartensis*, but not *Ankylosaurus magniventris* (Buchholz 2002).

ORNITHOPODA

Node-based definition: Most inclusive clade containing *Iguanodon bernissartensis*, but not *Triceratops horridus* (Buchholz 2002).

Within Ornithopoda, Buchholz included an unnamed clade (supported in some but not all of the most parsimonious trees) comprising the taxa *Othnielia rex* plus "*Yandusaurus*" *multidens* (supported by dorsally curved distal pubis; no denticle ridges over most of surface of teeth); an unnamed clade (supported in some most parsimonious trees) comprising *Zephyrosaurus schaffi* plus *Orodromeus makelai* (supported by elongate acromion process of scapula; jugal boss); and Euornithopoda Sereno 1986, one of the best supported ornithopod clades, defined by Buchholz "as the least inclusive clade containing both *Hypsilophodon foxii* and *Iguanodon bernissartensis*," supported by numerous characters (*e.g.*, dentary teeth with primary ridge; antorbital fenestra more circular than triangular).

Buchholz included within Euornithopoda the clades "Hypsilophodontidae" and Iguanodontia. Traditionally, the "Hypsilophodontidae" (currently including but one taxon, *Hypsilophodon foxii*) has been regarded as a monophyletic family comprising numerous taxa of small ornithopods retaining premaxillary teeth. Contrarily, Buchholz found this group to constitute a paraphyletic assemblage united only by plesiomorphic characters, with *Agilisaurus*, *Othnielia*, *Orodromeus*, *Hypsilophodon*, and other taxa forming serial outgroups to Iguanodontia (including Euiguanodontia, and within that clade, the new family Parksosauridae and Dryomorpha):

"HYPSILOPHODONTIDAE"

Node-based definition: Most inclusive clade containing *Hypsilophodon foxii*, but not *Parasaurolophus walkeri* (Buchholz 2002).

IGUANODONTIA

Node-based definition: Most inclusive clade containing *Iguanodon bernissartensis*, but not *Hypsilophodon foxii* (Buchholz 2002).

EUIGIANODONTIA

Node-based definition: Most inclusive clade containing *Gasparinisaura cincosaltensis*, but not *Iguanodon bernissartensis* (Buchholz 2002).

PARKSOSAURIDAE

Node-based definition: Most inclusive clade containing *Parksosaurus warreni*, but not *Hypsilophodon foxii*, *Dryosaurus altus*, or *Iguanodon bernissartensis* (Buchholz 2002).

Diagnosis: Ramus of jugal reduced or absent; quadratojugal with long, thin rostral ramus; somewhat large, somewhat tongue-shaped descending process of quadratojugal, overlying quadrate laterally) (Buchholz 2002; for a contrary opinion, see Weishampel, Jianu, Csiki and Norman 2003, below).

DRYOMORPHA

Node-based definition: Least inclusive clade containing *Dryosaurus altus* and *Iguanodon bernissartensis* (Buchholz 2002).

Within Parksosauridae, Buchholz included *Parksosaurus* and *Gasparinisaura*, further noting that *Parksosaurus* also seems to have hemal arches (see Parks 1926) with caudal expansions on their distal ends similar to those described (Coria and Salgado 1996) for the latter genus. While noting that the ornithopod *Notohypsilophodon comodorensis* displays some femoral features similar to those seen in *Parksosaurus*, Buchholz found the former taxon too fragmentary for inclusion in his analysis. Within the more inclusive genasaurian clade Cerapoda, Buchholz also included Chasmatopia:

CHASMATOPIA

Node-based definition: Most inclusive clade containing *Triceratops horridus*, but not *Iguanodon bernissartensis* (Buchholz 2002).

Chasmatopia, Buchholz noted, comprises ornithischians having "the arched diastemata between the maxillae and premaxillae seen in heterodontosaurids, pachycephalosaurs, and possibly basal ceratopians." Therefore, as had a relatively small number of previous authors (see S3; also see *Hongshanosaurus* entry and You, Xu and Wang 2003, below), Buchholz found the Heterodontosauridae—*Heterodontosaurus* traditionally classified as the most basal ornithopod (*e.g.*, Sereno 1986, 1999*a*; Weishampel and Witmer 1990)—to be the sister group to Marginocephalia, with numerous synapomorphies, many pertaining to facial structures, supporting this placement.

As observed by Buchholz, chasmatopian premaxillary teeth are very distinctive, being reduced to three in number, caniniform, and increasing caudally in length, a condition seen in heterodontosaurids, pachycephalosaurs, and the basal ceratopsian *Liaoceratops*. (In primitive ornithischians there are six premaxillary teeth which are subequal in size, shaped like thickened blades.) Also, heterodontosaurids, pachycephalosaurs, and perhaps in the ceratopsian *Chaoyangsaurus* have an arched distema between premaxillae and maxillae for inserting the dentary fang (when present). Buchholz noted that all known chasmatopians have an enlarged jugal boss that may be hornlike (*e.g.*, heterodontosaurids and psittacosaurs) or simply a large boss that is lateral to the mandibular articulation (*e.g.*, pachycephalosaurs and ceratopsids). Furthermore, all known members of this clade "have widened caudal pelves in dorsoventral aspect, as well as the loss of the obturator process of the ischium."

In an abstract for a poster, Liu (2004) proposed another revision of the Ornithischia (details of this analysis not given in the abstract), incorporating 44 species and 326 characters. Liu's study corroborated the long recognized statuses of the clades Stegosauria, Ankylosauria, Iguanodontia, Marginocephalia, and Ceratopsia, but found Fabrosauridae and "Hypsilophodontidae" to be polyphyletic. Surprising to that author, *Lesothosaurus* was found to be the sister taxon of Thyreophora, *Agilisaurus* a basal member of a clade "Neornithischia," and the monophyletic Marginocephalia clustering with Iguanodontia.

The above results suggested to Liu "that the degree of missing data should not be used as an inclusion or exclusion criterion for taxa." Liu suggested that, in analyzing the phylogenetic relationships of higher taxa, the method be used of including more primitive species of higher monophyletic groups, accompanied by "another more complex taxon when the percent of missing characters [is] high in primitive species."

Liu's study predicted the most basal members of Ornithischia to possess a maxillary shelf, cheek teeth having a distinct root and crown, subtriangular tooth crowns, and marginal denticles, the appearance of all of these characters in the most basal ornithischians indicating that these dinosaurs "adapted to herbivorous diets from the earliest known records."

Weishampel (2004), in his chapter on the Ornithischia written for the second edition of *The Dinosauria*, reaffirmed the rather traditional basal split of this clade "into *Lesothosaurus diagnosticus* (and possibly *Pisanosaurus mertii*) ... and Genasauria," the latter, in turn, dividing into the large sister clades Thyreophora (including Stegosauria and Ankylosauria) and Cerapoda (including Ornithopoda and Marginocephalia, the latter comprising Pachycephalosauria plus Ceratopsia). Weishampel's definitions for Thyreophora and Cerapoda were essentially the same as those offered by Bucholz (see above):

ORNITHISCHIA

Stem-based definition: All dinosaurs more closely related to *Triceratops* than o *Tyrannosaurus* (Weishampel 2004).

Diagnosis: Distinctive opisthopubic pelvis; neomorphic predentary bone; toothless (at least width of one or more edentulous positions) and roughened tip of snout; shallow, broad premaxillary palate; long premaxillary caudolateral process; palpebral, subtriangular maxillary and dentary crowns, mesial and distal margins denticulate; elevated coronoid process; jaw joint below maxillary tooth row level; cheek teeth hav-

ing low, triangular crowns; at least five sacral vertebrae; loss of gastralia; ossified tendons at least above sacral region, probably also farther along vertebral column; pubic symphysis restricted to distal ends of pubic shaft; puboischial symphysis; loss of phalanges for pedal digit V (Weishampel 2004).

GENASAURA

Diagnosis: Derived characters including the following: buccal emargination of tooth rows; elevation of dentary coronoid process to at least 50 percent depth of dentary at midlength; tapering of distal end of pubic peduncle of ilium (Weishampel 2004).

THYREOPHORA

Diagnosis: Postorbital process of jugal broadened transversely; parallel rows of keeled dermal scutes on dorsum of body (Weishampel 2004).

CERAPODA

Diagnosis: Diastema between premaxillary and maxillary teeth; asymmetrical enamel on crowns of maxillary and dentary teeth; fingerlike cranial trochanter; (other unstated derived characters) (Weishampel 2004).

MARGINOCEPHALIA

Node-based definition: Most recent common ancestor of *Pachycephalosaurus* and *Triceratops*, plus all descendants of that common ancestor (Weishampel 2004).

Diagnosis: Shelf formed from both parietal and squamosals, extending over back of skull; reduced contribution of premaxilla to palate; pubis short, without symphysis with its partner (Weishampel 2004).

In their review of basal Ornithischia, Norman, Witmer and Weishampel (1984*a*) performed a cladistic analysis which determined the following: *Lesothosaurus diagnosticus* (previously regarded as a fabrosaurid; see *S3*)—excluded from higher position within Ornithischia, retaining as it does a large external mandibular fenestra, considered here to be the sister taxon to Genasauria; *Pisanosaurus mertii*—extremely problematic (due to poor preservation and loss of data as to the original association of the material), possibly a basal ornithischian (see *Pisanosaurus* entry); and *Technosaurus smalli* (also other primitive taxa based on nondiagnostic remains, *e.g., Xiaosaurus dashanpensis, Revueltosaurus callenderi, Galtonia gibbidens,* and *Lucianosaurus wildi*)—Ornithischia *incertae sedis*. In addition to other taxa ornithischian already listed as *nomina dubia, Lucianosaurus wildi, Pekinosaurus olseni,* and *Revueltosaurus callenderi* were regarded by Norman *et al.* as of dubious validity.

Thyreophora

Herrmann (2003), in a published abstract, criticized recently published phylogenetic analyses of the Thyreophora — this group including basal thyreophorans, Stegosauria, and Ankylosauria — because they have mostly focused only upon one group of these armored dinosaurs and just included supraspecific taxa as terminals. In order to investigate more thoroughly the interrelationships among the Thyreophora, Herrmann incorporated into her analysis 113 cranial and 73 postcranial skeletal characters from specimens and the paleontological literature for four basal thyreophoran species, nine stegosaurian species, 44 ankylosaurian species, and the outgoing *Lesothosaurus diagnosticus*, this data being analyzed simultaneously using maximum parsimony methods.

Herrmann's analysis recovered the clades Thyreophora, Eurypoda, Stegosauria, and Ankylosauria, each of them supported by at least eight synapomorphies. Within Stegosauria, both families Huayangosauridae and Stegosauridae were recovered, although the Ankylosauria broke down into several groups. The Ankylosauridae was recovered as a monophyletic clade, but the Middle Jurassic species "*Tianchiasaurus*" [=*Shanxia*] *nedegoapeferima* fell outside that group as the sister taxon to *Polacanthus* spp. The Nodasauridae was found to be a paraphyletic assemblage of species including two new, fully resolved clades.

Also, Norman, Witmer and Weishampel (2004) reviewed basal Thyreophora, performing a phylogenetic analysis of the clade based on 21 characters, with Cerapoda and *Lesothosaurus diagnosticus* the successive outgroups. This analysis revealed Thyreophora to include the genera *Scutellosaurus*, *Emausaurus*, and *Scelidosaurus* (previously referred by Dong 2001 to the Ankylosauria, and by Carpenter 2001*b* to the now redundant clade Ankylosauromorpha; see *S3*) to be basal thyreophorans, representing "successive taxa on the stem lineage leading to Eurypoda"; *Scutellosaurus lawleri* the sister group to a clade consisting of *Emausaurus* plus *Scelidosaurus* plus Eurypoda; and *Scelidosaurus harrisonii* the sister taxon to Eurypoda, these two taxa combining to form the clade Thyreophoroidea (*sensu* Sereno 1986).

Norman *et al.* offered the following definitions and diagnoses for the above clades:

THYREOPHORA

Stem-based definition: Genasauria more closely related to *Ankylosaurus* than to *Triceratops* (Sereno 1999*a*).

Diagnosis: Jugal having transversely broad postorbital process; at least one supraorbital incorporated into orbital margin (uncertain in *Scuttelosaurus law-* *leri*); median palatal keel (uncertain in *S. lawleri*); elongate trunk region compared with hindlimb length; ilium elongate relative to femur length; several pairs of parasagittal rows of low, conical scutes on dorsum of body (uncertain in *Emausaurus*); one or more rows of low-keeled scutes on flanks of body (probable but unconfirmed in *Emausaurus*); differentiation of high- and low-keeled scutes, and ventrally excavated scutes (Norman, Witmer and Weishampel 2004*b*).

Unnamed clade comprising *Emausaurus* plus *Scelidosaurus* plus EURYPODA

Diagnosis: Ventral deflection of mesial dentary teeth; high root to crown ratio; horizontal ledge on external surface of surangular; tightly sutured postorbital-jugal; shape of jugal-quadratojugal suture (Norman, Witmer and Weishampel 2004*b*).

THYREOPHOROIDEA

Diagnosis: Reduction of antorbital fossa; infratemporal fenestra narrowing; complete suturing of supraorbital to dorsal orbital margin (Norman, Witmer and Weishampel 2004*b*).

Norman *et al.* regarded as Thyreophora *incertae sedis* the type species *Tatisaurus oehleri* (synonymized by Lucas 1996 with *Scelidosaurus harrisoni*; see *S1*), noting that this species is too poorly known to determine for it a more precise position, and also *Bienosaurus lufengensis*, which Dong (2001) had placed with *Scelidosaurus* in the thyreophoran subclade Scelidosauridae (see *S3*), as Thyreophora *incertae sedis*.

In their review of the Stegosauria, Galton and Upchurch (2004*b*) performed a cladistic analysis based on 55 characters (24 of them being parsimony uninformative) for 11 stegosaur genera. This analysis resulting in the generally accepted split of that clade into two clades, *Huayangosaurus* (*i.e.*, the family Huayangosauridae) plus a polytomy comprising all other stegosaurs (*i.e.*, Stegosauridae); Stegosauridae dividing into *Dacentrurus* plus the subfamily Stegosaurinae; and regarded the type species *Craterosaurus pottonensis*, *Dravidosaurus blandfordi*, *Monkonosaurus lawulacus*, and *Paranthodon africanus* as Stegosauria *incertae sedis* (see *Craterosaurus*, *Dravidosaurus*, and *Paranthodon* entries).

Galton and Upchurch offered the following definitions and diagnoses of these clades:

STEGOSAURIA

Stem-based definition: All taxa more closely related to *Stegosaurus* than to Ankylosauria (Sereno 1998, 1999*a*).

Diagnosis: Synapomorphies comprising the following: ?flattened dorsal surface of parietals; quadrate

Skeletal reconstruction of the stegosaurine stegosaur *Hesperosaurus mjosi* including cast of holotype HMNH 001.

having transversely compressed proximal head; neural canals of cranial dorsal vertebrae with diameter greater than half that of centra; dorsal neural arches at least 1.5 times height of dorsal centra; middorsal transverse processes oriented at 50 degrees to horizontal or more steeply; dorsal portions of neural spines of proximal caudal vertebrae transversely widened, axially compressed; length:width ratio of distal caudal vertebral centra 1.2 or less; proximal scapular plate with larger surface than coracoid; prominent triceps tuburcle and descending ridge caudolateral to deltopectoral crest of humerus; dorsoventral thickness of carpal elements exceeding 10 percent humeral length; ulnare and intermedium fused in adults; proximal carpals block-shaped in cranial aspect; distal carpals absent or failing to ossify; preacetabular process of ilium directed outward at 35 degrees to sagittal plane; acetabular portion of pubis cup-shaped, facing laterally; prepubis pubic shaft length ratio higher than 0.4; pubic shaft length divided by acetabular diameter at least 2.0; loss of pedal digit I; pedal digit III with no more than three phalanges; pedal digit IV with no more than three phalanges; parasagittal rows of plates or spines; loss of ossified epaxial tendons (Galton and Upchurch 2004*b*).

HUAYANGOSAURIDAE

Stem-based definition: Stegosauria more closely related to *Huayangosaurus* than to *Stegosaurus* (Galton and Upchurch 2004*b*).

Diagnosis: Autapomorphies including the following: Oval lateral depression between maxilla and premaxilla; small process on postorbital; high maxillary tooth count (25 to 30 in adults); cranial dorsal ribs having intercostal flanges, flared distal ends; all proximal carpals coossified, forming subsylindrical block (Sereno and Dong 1992).

STEGOSAURIDAE

Stem-based definition: Stegosauria more closely related to *Stegosaurus* than to *Huayangosaurus* (Sereno 1998, 1999*a*).

Diagnosis: Synapomorphies comprising the following: sacral ribs "T"-shaped in parasagittal cross section; proximal ends of proximal caudal transverse processes having dorsal processes; dorsal portions of neural spines of proximal caudal vertebrae strongly expanded transversely relative to rest of spine; transverse width of distal end of radius at least 38 percent radius length; enlarged supraacetabular process

Photograph by the author, courtesy
Natural History Museum of Los Angeles County.

Reconstructed mounted
skeleton (LACM 3719/
16440; other elements cast)
of the stegosaurine stegosaur *Stegosaurus ungulatus.*

("antitrochanter") on ilium; prepubis:pubic shaft length ratio higher than 0.50; femur:humerus length ratio higher than 1.40 (Galton and Upchurch 2004*b*)

STEGOSAURINAE

Stem-based definition: All taxa more closely related to *Stegosaurus* than to *Dacentrurus* (Galton and Upchurch 2004*b*).

Diagnosis: Synapomorphies including the following: Middle and caudal dorsal vertebrae with fused prezygapophyses and fused postzygapophyses; neural spines of proximal caudal vertebrae at least twice height of centrum; transverse width of distal end of humerus at least 40 percent humeral length; ulna robust; femur:humerus length ratio at least 1.5 (Galton and Upchurch 2004*b*).

Hill, Witmer and Norell (2003), in a paper describing a juvenile skull of the ankylosaurid *Pinacosaurus grangeri* (see *Pinacosaurus* entry), also performed a new phylogenetic analysis of the Ankylosauria, taking into account data gleaned from that specimen, examination of fossil material and casts of numerous other armored-dinosaur specimens (see original paper for list), plus original published descriptions of other thyreophoran taxa.

The results of Hill *et al.*'s analysis differed considerably from various recently published analyses of the Ankylosauria (*e.g.*, Carpenter, Miles and Cloward 1998; Kirkland 1998*a*; Hill 1999; Sereno 1999*a*; Carpenter 2001*a*; Vickaryous, Russell and Currie 2001), especially concerning relationships among the Ankylosauridae. The analysis of Hill *et al.* recovered Ankylosauria as a monophyletic clade united by 10 unambiguous synapomorphies:

Life restoration by Berislav Krzic of *Gobisaurus domoculus*. Robert V. Hill, Lawrence M. Witmer and Mark A. Norell (2003) interpreted this taxon as a primitive member of the Ankylosauridae.

ANKYLOSAURIA

Diagnosis: Maxillary tooth row deeply inset from lateral edge of skull; antorbital fenestra closed; dorsoventrally narrow pterygoid ramus of quadrate; shaft of quadrate angled strongly rostroventrally; occiput rectangular, wider than high; supratemporal fenestra closed; obliteration of cranial sutures in adults, involving fusion and dermal sculpturing of outer surface of most of dermal skull roof; secondary dermal ossification, projecting ventrolaterally from quadratojugal region; external mandibular fenestra closed; elongate osteoderm fused to ventrolateral aspect of mandible in adults (Hill, Witmer and Norell 2003).

As had Coombs (1978*a*), in his benchmark paper on the families of Ankylosauria, Hill *et al.* found this clade to include only two major monophyletic divisions (see below), the Ankylosauridae and Nodosauridae, diagnosed by Hill *et al.* by a number of unambiguous synapomorphies:

ANKYLOSAURIDAE

Diagnosis: Rostral edge of premaxilla having broad, ventrally concave notch in rostral view; secondary dermal ossification, projecting caudolaterally from region of squamosals (Hill, Witmer and Norell 2003).

NODOSAURIDAE

Diagnosis: Occipital condyle set off from ventral braincase by distinct neck; rostrocaudally narrow dermal ossification along posterior border of skull roof; median dermal ossification overlying dorsum of nasal region); also, these ambiguous synapomorphies: maxillary tooth rows deeply concave laterally, outlining hourglass shape; occipital condyle formed exclusively by basioccipital; sinuous ventral margin of mandible, paralleling sinuosity of dorsal margin in lateral aspect (Hill, Witmer and Norell 2003).

Recent analyses have introduced the taxa Polacanthinae, as a subfamily of Ankylosauridae (see Kirkland), and Polacanthidae, as a sister taxon to Ankylosauridae (see Carpenter). However, Hill *et al.* found these clades to be paraphyletic assemblages. The authors cautioned, however, that their analysis had been based strictly upon cranial characters. As both Polacanthidae and Polacanthinae were diagnosed also based upon postcranial characters, the inclusion of the latter could affect the results of their analysis. Nevertheless, based solely on cranial information, *Gastonia* and *Gargoleosaurus*, North American "polacanthid" genera for which both excellent skull and postcranial material is known, were found by Hill *et al.* to "represent two successively more distant sister taxa to the remaining ankylosaurids" (see Vickaryous, Maryańska and Weishampel 2004, below).

Hill *et al.* found the Asian genus *Gobisaurus* to be a primitive ankylosaurid, although (*contra* Vickaryous *et al.*) one not sharing a sister-taxon relationship with the Asian *Shamosaurus* (see *Gobisaurus* entry, *S3*); *Nodocephalosaurus* as a highly derived ankylosaurid (see Sullivan 1999), but (*contra* Sullivan, who proposed a close relationship between this North American genus and the Asian *Saichania* and *Tarchia*), based upon currently available data, one for which further resolution as to its phylogenetic position cannot be determined; and *Minmi*, the only known Australian ankylosaur, as an ankylosaurid, based on several synapomorphies (*e.g.*, relatively wide skull; quadrate with vertically oriented mandibular ramus; development of secondary dermal ossifications overlying quadratojugals).

In another phylogenetic analysis of the Ankylosauria, preliminary results of which were published in an abstract, Parish (2003) criticized recently published cladograms, noting that they all differ in their topologies, present "little consensus on the interrelationships of several taxa and the monophyly (or otherwise) of several ankylosaurian ingroups," and contain only a limited number of taxa, most of which have been coded from the paleontological literature and often considering just a small selection of the available character data (*e.g.*, only cranial material).

Parish's analysis included all valid ankylosaurian taxa, most of which the author examined firsthand, and based this study on characters of the skull, postcranium, and dermal armor. A reduced consensus study was performed to prune unstable taxa, followed by decay and double decay analyses. The results of this study indicated the following: Polacanthidae weakly supported; *Minmi* positioned outside of the clades Ankylosauridae plus Nodosauridae; *Scelidosaurus* a basal ornithischian and sister taxon to Ankylosauria; *Cedarpelta* located outside Ankylosauridae plus Nodosauridae (probably due to immature nature of specimens and paucity of significant data).

Parish examined the resulting trees to assess the phylogenetic distribution and evolution of various character states (*e.g.*, appearance and arrangement of dermal armor, form of scapulocoracoid) and to comment upon the paleogeography of the clades within Ankylosauria. As that author observed from this study, ankylosaurids appear to have originated in Asia, followed by a Middle Cretaceous dispersal into North America. Presumably full details concerning Parish's analysis will be published at a later date.

Vickaryous *et al.*, in their review of the Ankylosauria for the second edition of *The Dinosauria*, performed a cladistic analysis, selecting "21 of the best-

known ankylosaur taxa" for the ingroup, and basing this analysis on 63 (44 cranial, three dental, and 16 postcranial) characters. This study divided the Ankylosauria into its two traditional families, the Ankylosauridae plus Nodosauridae, the former group further splitting into the subfamily Ankylosaurinae.

Contrary to other recent studies, that of Vickaryous *et al.* also concluded the following: *Minmi*—ankylosaurid rather than possible nodosaurid; *Gargoyleosaurus parkpinorum* and *Gastonia burgei*—ankylosaurids rather than "polacanthids," the former clustering as the sister taxon to all other Ankylosauridae; *Shamosaurus scutatus* and *Gobisaurus domoculus*—sister taxa within Ankylosaurinae; *Tsagantegia longicranialis*—clustering with Ankylosaurinae as the sister taxon to all other ankylosaurines; *Tarchia gigantea*—an ankylosaurine close to *Tsagantegia*, the former close to two subclades, one comprising Late Cretaceous Asian forms, the other Late Cretaceous North American forms; *Saichania chulsanensis*, *Tianzhenosaurus youngi*, *Shanxia tianzhenensis*, and *Pinacosaurus*—included among the Asian ankylosaurine clade, with *Tianzhenosaurus* (see entry) accepted as a valid taxon and *Shanxia* considered a *nomen dubium*; *Ankylosaurus* and *Euoplocephalus*—sister taxa included in the North American ankylosaurine clade; *Nodocephalosaurus* (see entry)—possibly ankylosaurine, having skull-ornamentation pattern similar to *Tarchia* and *Saichania*; *Cedarpelta bilbeyhallorum*—the most basal known member of Nodosauridae; *Sauropelta edwardsorum*, *Silvisaurus condrayi*, and *Pawpawsaurus campbelli*—forming a basal polytomy within Nodosauridae, deep to *Cedarpelta*; *Panoplosaurus* and *Edmontonia*—comprising a clade within Nodosauridae; *Animantarx ramaljonesi* and species of *Struthiosaurus* (*S. austriacus*, *S. languedocensis*, and *S. transylvanicus*)—tentatively referred to Nodosauridae (*Animantrax* on the basis "of rounded supraorbital bosses and a knoblike acromion," *Struthiosaurus* based on "a knoblike acromion" in the species *S. austriacus* and *S. transylvanicus*); and *Sarcolestes leedsi*, *Dracopelta zbyszewskii*, and *Mymoorrapelta maysi*, *Hylaeosaurus armatus*, *Polacanthus foxii* and *P. rudgwickensis*, *Texasetes pleurohalio*, *Hoplitosaurus marshii*, *Nodosaurus textilis*, *Stegopelta landerensis*, *Niobrarasaurus coeleii*, and possibly *Liaoningosaurus paradoxus*, *Amtosaurus magnus* and *A. archibaldi*, and *Anoplosaurus curtonotus*—Ankylosauria *incertae sedis*. Neither Polacanthidae nor Polacanthinae were accepted as valid ankylosaurian clades by Vickaryous *et al.*

The following definitions and diagnoses of these clades were offered by Vickaryous *et al.*:

ANKYLOSAURIA

Stem-based definition: All eurypods close to *Ankylosaurus* than to *Stegosaurus* (Sereno 1998).

Diagnosis: Unambiguous synapomorphies as

Copyright © Berislav Krzic.

Reconstructed skeleton (cast) of the ankylosaurid ankylosaur, *Gargoyleosaurus parkpinorum*.

follows: cranial ornamentation across rostral region of skull and lateral surface of angular; no antorbital, supratemporal, or external mandibular fenestrae; maxillary tooth row inset from lateral edge of maxilla; multiple parasagittal rows of osteoderms across dor-

sal surface of neck and postcervical region of body; imperforate acetabulum; synsacrum comprising coossified dorsal, sacral, and caudal vertebrae (Vickaryous, Maryańska and Weishampel 2004).

ANKYLOSAURIDAE

Stem-based definition: Ankylosauria more closely related to *Ankylosaurus* than to *Panoplosaurus* (Sereno 1998).

Diagnosis: Unambiguous features comprising the following: squamosal boss pyramidal protuberance; raised nuchal sculpturing; premaxillary plate wider than long; premaxillary notch; rostrolaterally oriented mandibular ramus or pterygoid; ambiguous features as follows: quadratojugal boss deltoid protuberance; rostral face of pterygoid directed vertically or rostrally; postocular shelf; tail club; vertical border of coracoid straight in profile (Vickaryous, Maryańska and Weishampel 2004).

Unnamed clade comprising *Shamosaurus* plus *Gobisaurus*

Diagnosis: Deltoid dorsal profile having narrow rostrum, rounded squamosal, and quadratojugal

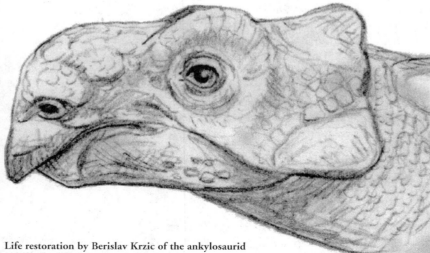

Life restoration by Berislav Krzic of the ankylosaurid ankylosaur *Shamosaurus scutatus*.

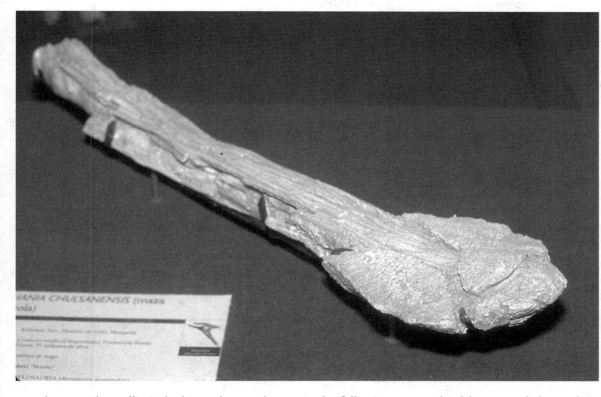

Photograph by the author, courtesy Mesa Southwest Museum.

Tail club of the ankylosaurine ankylosaur *Saichania chulsanensis*, this specimen from the Gobi Desert, People's Republic of Mongolia part, of the traveling "Great Russian Dinosaurs Exhibition."

protuberences; large elliptical orbits and external nares (Vicaryous 2001); caudolaterally directed paroccipital processes (Vickaryous, Maryańska and Weishampel 2004).

ANKYLOSAURINAE

Stem-based definition: All ankylosaurs closer to *Ankylosaurus* than to *Shamosaurus* (Vickaryous, Maryańska and Weishampel 2004, modified from Sereno 1998).

Diagnosis: Unambiguous synapomorphies comprising the following: nuchal shelf obscuring occiput in dorsal aspect; quadrate condyle obscured laterally by quadratojugal boss; ambiguous feature of strongly concave buccal emargination (Vickaryous, Maryańska and Weishampel 2004).

Unnamed ankylosaurine clade comprising Late Cretaceous North American taxa

Diagnosis: Unambiguous synapomorphies comprising the following: dorsal surface of rostral region of skull convexly domed; maxillary and dentary teeth without cingulum; caudal margin of pterygoid transversely aligned with ventral margin of pterygoid process of quadrate; acromion crestlike, restricted to cranial margin of scapula (Vickaryous, Maryańska and Weishampel 2004).

NODOSAURIDAE

Diagnosis: Unambiguous characters comprising

the following: supraorbital boss rounded protuberance; occipital condyle derived only from basioccipital; ornamentation on premaxilla (Vickaryous, Maryańska and Weishampel 2004).

Unnamed clade comprising *Panoplosaurus* plus *Edmontonia*

Diagnosis: Lack of premaxillary teeth; well-developed rostrodorsal component to osseous secondary palate (Vickaryous, Maryańska and Weishampel 2004).

Vickaryous regarded the type species *Crichtonsaurus bohlini* and *Stegopelta landerensis* and provisionally *Amtosaurus magnus*, *Anoplosaurus curtonotus*, and *Liaonigosaurus paradoxus* as Ankylosauria *incertae sedis*; and *Nodocephalosaurus kirtlandensis* as Ankylosaurinae *incertae sedis*. Vickaryous *et al.* also considered the following type species as *nomina dubia*, among other taxa already so regarded: *Aletopelta coombsi*, *Sauroplites scutiger*, and *Tianchiasaurus nedegoaperferima*

Ornithopoda

Weishampel, Jianu, Csiki and Norman (2003), in describing the new ornithopod genus *Zalmoxes* (see entry), performed a phylogenetic analysis in which they introduced the new family Rhabdodontidae, placed by the authors as the sister taxon of Iguanodontia (however, see Norman 2004, below), and within that group a new unnamed clade comprising these taxa:

RHABDODONTIDAE

Node-based definition: Including the most recent common ancestor of *Zalmoxes robustus* and *Rhabdodon priscus* and all the descendants of this common ancestor (Weishampel, Jianu, Csiki and Norman (2003).

Diagnosis: (Unambiguous synapomorphies) more than 12 sharp ridges on lingual side of dentary tooth crowns; straight to slightly convex dorsal margin of ilium in lateral aspect; preacetabular process of ilium strongly twisted; ilium with narrow, poorly defined acetabular margin; femur distinctly bowed in cranial aspect; and absence of metatarsal V (Weishampel, Jianu, Csiki and Norman (2003).

RHABDONDONTIDAE plus IGUANODONTIA

Diagnosis: Rectangular lower margin of orbit; widening of frontals; predentary broadly rounded; dentary having parallel dorsal and ventral margins; shrouding of distal dentition by coranoid process; absence of premaxillary teeth; maxillary crowns 50 percent or higher than mesiodistally wide, no appreciable difference in diameter or root; dentary crowns asymmetrical, more than 50 percent or more higher mesiodistally wide, no appreciable difference in diameter of root; at least 10 cervical vertebrae; at least six sacral vertebrae; partial ossification of sternal rib segments; deltopectoral crest angular; first phalanx of manual digits II–IV over twice length of second; manual digit III having only three phalanges; ischial shaft ovoid to cylindrical in cross section; prepubic process long, flat; femur relatively longer than femur; anterior intercondylar groove; inflation of medial condyle of femur (Weishampel, Jianu, Csiki and Norman (2003).

Weishampel *et al.*, as have other recent workers (*e.g.*, Buchholz, above), found the "Hypsilophodontidae" to be a paraplyletic grouping of taxa. Weishampel *et al.* found sibling relationships with *Gasparinisaura cincosaltensis*, *Hypsilophodon foxii*, and "*Agilisaurus*" *multidens*. Coria and Salgado (1996) originally regarded *G. cincosaltensis* as a basal iguanodontian (see Buchholz, above), most closely related to Dryomorpha.

However, as Weishampel *et al.* pointed out, this assessment was based on the assumption that the "Hypsilophodontidae" was a monophyletic clade. According to Weishampel *et al.*'s analyses, "the dissolution of Hypsilophodontidae has a cascading effect on the position of *G. cincosaltensis*," consistently identifying that taxon as the sister-species to a clade comprising *Thescelosaurus*, *Parksosaurus*, and higher members of the Euornithopoda, based upon 10 synapomorphies:

Thescelosaurus plus *Parksosaurus* plus higher taxa within EURONITHOPODA

Diagnosis: External opening of antorbital fossa small, subcircular; separation of quadratojugal from jaw articulation; predentary broadly rounded; bilobate ventral process of predentary; coronoid process of dentary distinctly elevated; absence of premaxillary teeth; at least 16 dorsal vertebrae; between six and nine sacral vertebrae; high neural spines on proximal caudal vertebrae; sinuous dorsal iliac margin (Weishampel, Jianu, Csiki and Norman (2003).

Based upon the above reevaluation, Weishampel *et al.* found *Gasparinisaura cincosaltensis* to be "positioned within a plexus of basal euornithopods, as the sibling species of the Iguanodontia + *Thescelosaurus neglectus* clade."

Norman, Sues, Witmer and Coria (2004), in their recent review of basal Ornithopoda, performed a cladistic analysis based upon 54 characters, with outgroup comparisons made utilizing "Marginocephalia and the theoretical ancestor outgroup." As in other recent analyses, that of Norman *et al.* "confirmed the challenge to the monophyly of Hypsilophodontidae." Furthermore, this analysis found both Ornithopoda and the subgroup Euornithopoda to be robust clades, with the affinities of Heterodontosauridae (traditionally nestled within Ornithopoda, but reassessed by some recent workers as the sister group to Marginocephalia; see *S3*, also below) uncertain. Within Euornithopoda, the authors found a clade comprising *Gasparinisaura cincosaltensis*, *Thescelosaurus neglectus*, and *Parksosaurus warreni*.

Regarding Heterodontosauridae, Norman *et al.* — while stating that the phylogenetic position of this clade is not certain, and acknowledging opinions that its affinities could lie with the Marginocephalia — pointed out that Heterodontosauridae shares a number of unique features with Euornithopoda, *e.g.*, paroccipital process unusually deep; quadrate tall, making occipital profile taller than wide (depressing jaw joint far below tooth row level); caudolateral process of premaxilla elongate (contacting lacrimal, covering contact of nasal and maxilla); cheek teeth with high crowns, when abraded chisel-shaped, with denticles on mesial and distal margins restricted to apical third of crowns. Moreover, Norman *et al.* further affirmed the monophyly of this clade by possession of "the caniniform tooth in both the premaxilla and dentary and perhaps by the low-angle tooth wear on the dentary teeth."

Norman *et al.* reviewed various basal orinthopod

taxa as follows: *Agilisaurus louderbacki*— the most basal known member of Euornithopoda; *Orodromeus makelai* and *Othnielia rex*— closely related within Euronithopoda; *Hypsilophodon foxii* and *Zephyrosaurus schaffi*— closely related, more derived than *O. makelai* and *O. rex*, all four taxa united by a suite of features (see below); *Gasparinisaurus cincosaltensis*— the sister taxon to a clade comprising *Thescelosaurus neglectus* and *Parksosaurus warreni*, the latter two taxa representing the most derived of known euornithopods; (the following poorly known euornithopod taxa not included in Norman *et al.*'s analysis) *Bugenasaurus infernalis*— placing in an unresolved relationship with *Thescelosaurus* and *Parksosaurus*; *Atlascoposaurus loadsi*— basal euornithopod, possibly at the same level as *Gasparinisaura*, based on various features (see entry); *Drinker nisti, Leaellynasaura amicagraphica,* and *Fulgurotherium australe*— basal euornithopods, their relationships unresolved; *Qantassaurus intrepidus*— too poorly known for specific placement, but bearing a superficial resemblance to material referred to *Zalmoxes robustus*; and *Notohypsilophodon comodorensis*— possibly a basal euornithopod, too fragmentary for placement within that clade.

The following clade definitions and diagnoses were offered by Norman *et al.*:

ORNITHOPODA

Stem-based definition: All cerapodans more closely related to *Edmontosaurus* than to *Triceratops* (Norman, Sues, Witmer and Coria 2004).

Diagnosis: Ventral offset of premaxillary occlusal margin relative to maxillary tooth row; crescentic paroccipital process; jaw articulation offset ventral to maxillary tooth row; premaxilla contacting with lacrimal on external surface of snout (Norman, Sues, Witmer and Coria 2004).

EURONITHOPODA

Diagnosis: Scarflike suture between postorbital and jugal; limited edge on orbital margin of postorbital; ilium with deep postacetabular blade; brevis shelf well developed; laterally swollen ischial peduncle; elongate, narrow prepubic process; ischial shaft with tablike obturator process; deep pit on femoral shaft, adjacent to fourth trochanter; less consistent features including the following: angle subtended by floor of braincase and ventral edges of occipital condyle and basipterygoid processes; jugal participating in antorbital fenestra; position of paraquadrate foramen (Norman, Sues, Witmer and Coria 2004).

Unnamed clade comprising *Gasparinisaura cincosaltensis* plus (*Thescelosaurus neglectus* plus *Parksosaurus warreni*)

Diagnosis: Distinguished from more basal taxa by the following: quadraojugal restricted, having migrated away from lower jaw articulation; sinous curvature to dorsal margin of ilium (Norman, Sues, Witmer and Coria 2004).

Unnamed clade comprising *Othnielia rex, Orodromeus makelai* plus (*Hypsilophodon foxii* plus *Zephyrosaurus schaffi*)

Diagnosis: Subcircular external antorbital fenestra; distal offset to apex of maxillar crowns; tendency to shift palpebral articulation to prefrontal alone; strongly constricted neck to scapular blade; ossification of sternal ribs; hypaxial ossified tendons in tail; obturator process near midshaft of ischium (Norman, Sues, Witmer and Coria 2004).

Unnamed clade comprising *Thescelosaurus neglectus* plus *Parksosaurus warreni*

Diagnosis: Elongate skull (reflected by flattening of frontals, forming flattened instead of arching plates, assuming Galton's [1973a] reconstruction of *Parksosaurus* is correct); elevation in maxillary and dentary tooth counts; considerably more robust hindlimb (reflected by structure of femur) (Norman, Sues, Witmer and Coria 2004).

In addition to taxa already considered to be of dubious validity, Norman *et al.* regarded the type species *Phyllodon henkeli* and *Siluosaurus zhangqiani* as *nomina dubia*.

Norman (2004), in a review of basal Iguanodontia, performed a cladistic analysis of this inclusive clade based on 67 characters and incorporating 21 taxa, with the genera *Lesothosaurus* and *Hypsilophodon* used as outgroups. Norman's analysis determined the following: *Gasparinasaura*— basal to *Tenontosaurus; Tenontosaurus (T. tilletti* and *T. dossi*)— the most basal known member of Iguanodontia; *Zalmoxes robustus* and *Rhabdodon priscus*—(*contra* Weishampel *et al.* 2003, above) basal iguanodontians; *Muttaburrasaurus langdoni*— iguanodontian close to *Tenontosaurus* and the next most derived form, *Z. robustus; Zalmoxes robustus* and *Rhabdodon priscus*— combining to form a clade basal to Dryomorpha (including the clades Dryosauridae and Ankylopollexia, the latter including *Camptosaurus dispar* and Styracosterna, the latter including Iguanodontoidea (=Hadrosauriformes of some authors); *Equijubus normani*— preliminary analysis placing this taxon between *Lurdosaurus* and *Iguanodon* within Styracosterna; *Ouranosaurus nigeriensis*— iguanodontoid close to *Iguanodon* spp., basal to more derived nonhadrosaurid iguanodontians (*e.g.*, *Probactrosaurus, Eolambia, Protohadros,* and *Altirhinus*); *Altirhinus kurzanovi* and *Eolambia caroljonesa*—

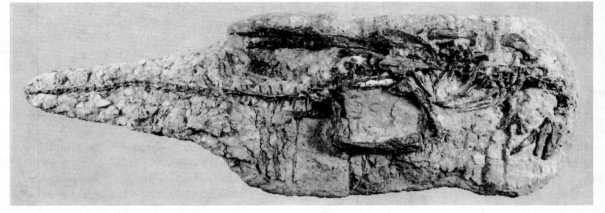

One of two skeletons referred to the primitive ornithopod *Othnielia rex* collected during the late 1990s at Howe Ranch, in the Morrison Formation of northern Wyoming.

sister taxa to a clade basal to the successively more derived *Protohadros*, *Probactrosaurus*, and Hadrosauridae.

Norman presented the following definitions and diagnoses for Iguanodontia and its subclades:

IGUANODONTIA

Stem-based definition: Euornithopoda more closely related to *Edmontosaurus* than to *Thescelosaurus* (Norman 2004).

Diagnosis: Premaxilla having expanded and edentulous margin; predentary having smoothly convex rostral margin in dorsal aspect; dentary ramus deep, dorsal and ventral borders parallel; no evidence of sternal rib ossification; one phalanx lost on manual digit III; prepubic process compressed, blade-shaped (Norman 2004).

Unnamed clade comprising *Zalmoxes robustus* and *Rhabdodon priscus*

Diagnosis: Bifurcated ventral process developed on predentary; thickened lateral flange on dorsal margin of ilium; ischial shaft with rounded (rather than

Skull of the primitive ornithopod *Othnielia rex* collected at Howe Ranch, in the Morrison Formation of northern Wyoming. This skull (specimen nicknamed "Barbara") belongs to a skeleton found at that site in 1995.

flattened) cross section; arched (rather than straight) ischium (Norman 2004).

DRYOMORPHA

Stem-based definition: *Dryosaurus* (*D. altus* and *D. lettowvorbecki*) plus all more derived iguanodontians (Norman 2004).

Diagnosis: Lateral process of premaxilla elongated, contacting lacrimal-prefrontal; distinct primary ridge developed on maxillary tooth crowns; enclosure of paraquadrate foramen between quadratojugal and quadrate embayment; development of forwardly projecting acromial process on scapula; obturator process positioned close to acetabular margin (instead of nearer midshaft); ischium with booted distal tip; distinctive extensor (cranial intercondylar) groove on distal end of femur (Norman 2004).

STYRACOSTERNA

Stem-based definition (emended): *Lurdosaurus arenatus* plus all more derived iguanodontians (Norman 2004).

Diagnosis: Hatchet-shaped sternal bones; flattened manual unguals; structure of pelvis (Norman 2004).

IGUANODONTOIDEA

Stem-based definition: Species of *Iguanodon* plus all more derived iguanodontians (Sereno 1997, 1998, 1999a).

Diagnosis: Strong offset of premaxillary margin relative to maxilla; peg-in-socket type articulation between maxilla and jugal; pronounced diastema developed between beak and mesial teeth; mammillations on marginal denticles of teeth; maxillary tooth crowns narrower, more lanceolate than dentary crowns; metacarpals II–IV closely appressed; prepubic process deep, laterally flattened; fourth trochanter triangular; deep, nearly tubular extensor (cranial intercondylar) groove; blunt pedal ungual phalanges (Norman 2004).

In performing a phylogenetic analysis of *Kerberosaurus* (see entry), a new genus of hadrosaurine hadrosaurid from Russia, Bolotsky and Godefroit (2004) found this genus to be the sister taxon to a clade comprising the genera *Prosaurolophus* and *Saurolophus*. This latter group, referred to by these authors as simply "the sauroloph clade (*Prosaurolophus* and *Saurolophus*, named after Chapman and Brett-Surman" [in 1990])," is essentially identical to the taxon Saurolophini, introduced along with other hadrosaurine and also lambeosaurine tribes (the term "tribe" being rarely used by cladists) by Michael K. Brett-Surman in his 1989 PhD dissertation (see *D:TE*) but not subsequently adopted by most workers (see, for example, the phylogeny by Horner, Weishampel and Forster 2004, below).

Brett-Surman (personal communication, 2004) supplied the following definitions for the two hadrosaurid subfamilies and the tribes contained with as follows:

HADROSAURINAE

Stem-based definition: All taxa closer to *Edmontosaurus* than to Corythosaurus.

EDMONTOSAURINI

Stem-based definition: All taxa closer to *Edmontosaurus* than to *Kritosaurus* (="*Gryposaurus*").

KRITOSAURINI

Stem-based definition: All taxa closer to *Kritosaurus* (="*Gryposaurus*") than to *Saurolophus*.

SAUROLOPHINI

Stem-based definition: All taxa closer to *Saurolophus* than to *Kritosaurus* (="*Gryposaurus*").

LAMBEOSAURINAE

Stem-based definition: All taxa closer to *Lambeosaurus* than to *Edmontosaurus*.

CORYTHOSAURINI

Stem-based definition: All taxa closer to *Corythosaurus* than to *Parasaurolophus*.

PARASAUROLOPHINI

Stem-based definition: All taxa closer to *Parasaurolophus* than to *Corythosaurus*.

Skeleton (cast) of the thescelosaurid euornithopod *Thescelosaurus neglectus*, original specimen (nicknamed "Peep"), measuring almost three meters (10 feet) in length, collected in 2000 from the Hell Creek Formation of South Dakota.

Bolotsky and Godefroit characterized the "edmontosaur clade (*Edmontosaurus* and '*Anatotitan*' [=*Edmontosaurus*; see Horner, Weishampel and Forster 2004])," essentially Brett-Surman's Edmontosaurini, mainly by the massive jugal. This clade, according to Bolotsky and Godefroit, forms a monophyletic

Life restoration by Berislav Krzic of the thescelosaurid euornithopod *Thescelosaurus neglectus*.

Life restoration by Berislav Krzic of the iguanodontid iguanodontian *Iguanodon bernissartensis*.

group with *Kerberosaurus* plus the "saurolophs," all three clades sharing the following synapomorphies: Rostral process of jugal asymmetrically strongly upturned; caudal border of circumnarial depression marked by well-developed ridge. Also, the "edmontosaur" and "sauroloph" clades share the following synapomorphies (elements not preserved in *Kerberosaurus*): Elongate mandibular diastema; corresponding premaxillary extension (see Weishampel and Horner 1990).

Bolotsky and Godefroit regarded as basally hadrosaurine the clade (essentially Brett-Surman's Kritosaurini tribe) including *Barchylophosaurus* and *Maiasaura*, lacking a significant feature (*i.e.*, extension of supraoccipital/exoccipital shelf above foramen magnum) found in more derived hadrosaurines. As noted by these authors, *Brachylophosaurus* and *Maiasaura* share several synapomorphies: Isosceles-triangle-shaped rostral process of jugal; ventral projecting boss on jugal; and broad, solid crest.

Bolotsky and Godefroit diagnosed "the sauroloph clade" by two characters (*i.e.*, development of narrow solid crest; caudal extension of circumnarial depression above or caudal to rostral margin of orbit).

Gryposaurus, contrary to previous analyses (*e.g.*, Weishampel and Horner), was found to be the sister taxon of the monophyletic clade comprising "*Kerberosaurus* + sauroloph clade + edmontosaur clade," Bolotsky and Godefroit regarding the characters formerly considered to be synapomorphic for *Gryposaurus* and the "brachylophosaur clade" to be "either of doubtful polarity, or too variable and difficult to delineate to be really useful for phylogenetic purposes."

Considering other Asian hadrosaurine dinosaurs, Bolotsky and Godefroit noted that *Gilmoreosaurus mongoliensis*, a Mongolian species known only from fragmentary remains, displays some hadrosaurine apomorphies (*e.g.*, maxilla symmetrical in lateral aspect; dentary straight; see Weishampel and Horner 1986). However, the rostral process of the jugal of this species is not dorsoventrally expanded, as in Hadrosauridae; and the distal end of the quadrate is slightly expanded, morphologically intermediate between that of more basal and typical members of this group. Consequently (following Weishampel and Horner 1990; Head 1998), Bolotsky and Godefroit regarded *Gilmoresaurus* as Hadrosauroidea *incertae sedis*.

According to Bolotsky and Godefroit, *Aralosaurus tuberiferus*, a species from Kazakhstan most often (because of its apparently arched nasal) regarded as a close relative to "gryposaur" hadrosaurines, seems to lack a feature (*i.e.*, elongated supraoccipital/exocipital shelf) characteristic of derived hadrosaurines; therefore, the authors regarded for the present this taxon as Hadrosaurinae *incertae sedis*.

Bolotsky and Godefroit agreed with previous workers (*e.g.*, Weishampel and Horner 1990; Brett-Surman 1989) that the huge Chinese form *Shantungosaurus giganteus* is most likely closely related to "*Anatotitan*" [=*Edmontosaurus*] and *Edmontosaurus*. (G. Nelms, personal communication to M. K. Brett-Surman 1996, believed *hantungosaurus* to be a very large individual of *Edmontosaurus*.)

Horner, Weishampel and Forster (2004), in their review of the Hadrosauridae, performed a cladistic analysis of this group of duckbilled dinosaurs, scoring 19 ingroup taxa for 105 cranial, dental, and postcranial characters, with outgroup comparison using *Iguanodon* and *Camptosaurus*. As in numerous earlier analyses, the family Hadrosauridae was found to be monophyletic, basically splitting split into the major subfamilies Hadrosaurinae and Lambeosaurinae.

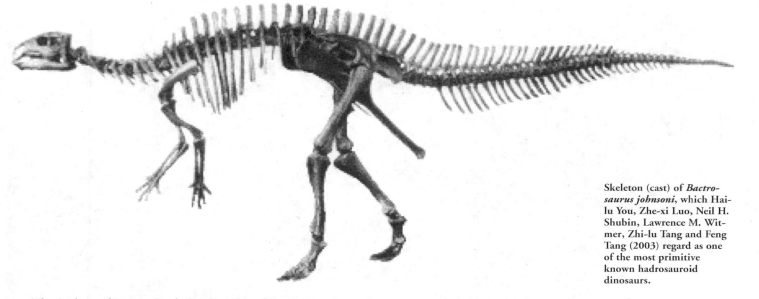

Skeleton (cast) of *Bactrosaurus johnsoni*, which Hai-lu You, Zhe-xi Luo, Neil H. Shubin, Lawrence M. Witmer, Zhi-lu Tang and Feng Tang (2003) regard as one of the most primitive known hadrosauroid dinosaurs.

The analysis of Horner *et al.* also determined the following: *Telmatosaurus*— a basal hadrosaurid and the sister taxon of Euhadrosauria (Hadrosaurinae plus Lambeosaurinae); *Eolambia caroljonesa* and *Protohadros byrdi*— placing outside of Hadrosauridae, yet retaining the primitive state in various hadrosaurid derived characters (*e.g.*, *Protohadros* retaining surangular foramen, jugal process on maxilla, just slightly expanded coronoid process; *Eolambia* retaining seven sacral vertebrae, coarse denticles of dentary teeth, weakly expanded coronoid process); *Lophorhothon*— belonging to Hadrosaurinae as the sister taxon to all other hadrosaurines; *Naasoibitosaurus*, "*Kritosaurus*" *australis*, and *Saurolophus*, and then *Brachylophosaurus*, *Maiasaura*, *Edmontosaurus*, *Gryposaurus*, and *Prosaurolophus*— two clades, respectively, of non–*Lophorhothon* hadrosaurines; *Tsintaosaurus*— a lambeosaurine and sister taxon to all remaining lambeosaurines; and

Life restoration of the hadrosaurine hadrosaurid *Saurolophus angustirostris* by Berislav Krzic.

Black Hills Institute of Geological Research preparator Larry Shaffer assembling a skull of the hadrosaurine hadrosaurid *Maiasaura peeblesorum* for The Children's Museum of Indianapolis.

Parasaurolophus, *Corythosaurus*, *Hypacrosaurus*, and *Lambeosaurus*— higher lambeosaurines forming an additional clade; *Parasaurolophus*— united with the remaining lambeosaurines (*Corythosaurus*, *Hypacrosaurus*, and *Lambeosaurus*) in an unresolved trichotomy.

HADROSAURIDAE

Node-based definition (slightly emended): Clade including the most recent common ancestor of *Telmatosaurus* and *Parasaurolophus* plus all descendants of that common ancestor (Horner, Weishampel and Forster 2004).

Diagnosis: At least three replacement teeth per tooth family; distal extension of dentary tooth row terminating caudal to apex of coronoid process; caudalmost termination of dentary well behind coronoid process; absence of surangular foramen; absence of contact between ectopterygoid and jugal; absence of supraorbital or its fusion to orbital rim; elevation of cervical zygapophyseal peduncles on neural arches, extending well above level of neural canal; long, dorsally arched postzygapophyses; coronoid having long cranioventral process extending well below glenoid; dorsoventrally narrow proximal scapula, acromion process projecting horizontally; notched cranioventral corner; reduced area for coracoid articulation; deep intercondylar extensor groove on femur, edges meeting or near meeting to enclose extensor tunnel (Horner, Weishampel and Forster 2004).

EUHADROSAURIA

Diagnosis: Ambiguous characters comprising the following: small, dorsoventrally narrow angular, exposed only in medial aspect; absence of coronoid bone; almost entire expanded apex of coronoid process formed by dentary, surangular reduced to thin sliver along caudal margin (latter also not reaching distal end of coronoic process); premaxillary oral margin with "double-layer" morphology comprising denticle-bearing external layer and internal palatal layer set back slightly from oral margin, separated from denticulate layer by deep sulcus-bearing vascular foramina; deep, near vertical face formed by squamosals seen in caudal aspect; triangular occiput exposed in caudal aspect, quadrate splayed distinctly laterally;

Mounted holotype skeleton of the hadrosaurine "gryposaur" originally named "*Kritosaurus*" *australis.*

Courtesy Fernando E. Novas and Museo Argentino de Ciencias Naturales.

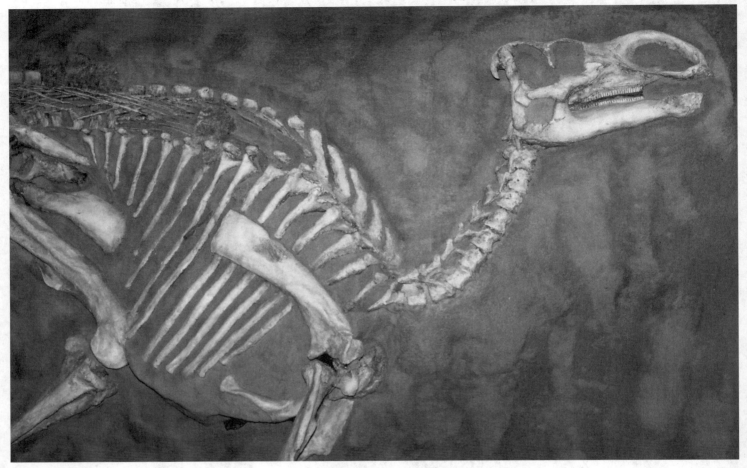

Cast of holotype skeleton (ROM 4614) of *Kritosaurus invcurvimanus*, a hadrosaurine "gryposaur."

acute angle between postorbital and jugal bars along ventral margin of infratemporal fenestra; at least eight sacral vertebrae; carpus reduced to two small elements; penultimate phalanges of digits II and III wedge-shaped; pubic peduncle short; pubic obturator foramen entirely open; ilium distinctly depressed over supraacetabular process, dorsally bowed over base of preacetabular process; absence of distal tarsals II and III (Horner, Weishampel and Forster 2004).

HADOSAURINAE

Diagnosis: Unambiguous synapomorphy of caudal margin on circumnarial fossa (Horner, Weishampel and Forster 2004).

Unnamed clade comprising *Lophorhothon* plus all remaining HADROSAURINAE
Diagnosis: Unambiguous synapomorphy of outer narial fossa demarcated from circumnarial fossa by strong ridge (Horner, Weishampel and Forster 2004).

LAMBEOSAURINAE

Diagnosis: Maxilla lacking rostral process, but developing sloping rostrodorsal shelf underlying pre-maxilla; groove on caudolateral process of premaxilla, communicating with maxillary foramen on maxilla-premaxilla contact surface and with lateral fontanelle of crest; low maxillary apex (dorsal process of maxilla, gently rounded in lateral aspect); parietal crest less than half length of supratemporal fenestrae (Horner, Weishampel and Forster 2004).

Unnamed clade comprising LAMBEOSAURI-NAE above *Tsintaosaurus*
Diagnosis: Unambiguous characters consisting of: elongate premaxillary process joining behind external opening of narial passages to exclude nasals and completely enclose vestibule of nasal cavity, lying in supracranial position; caudally retracted nasals lying over braincase in adults, resulting in convoluted, complex narial passage and hollow crest with enlarged *cavum nasi proprii*; parietal sagittal crest strongly downwarped to below level of postorbital-squamosal bar; dorsal (caudal) and sacral neural spines elongate to more than three times height of centrum (Horner, Weishampel and Forster 2004).

Unnamed clade comprising *Parasaurolophus* plus remaining LAMBEOSAURINAE

Photograph by the author, courtesy Natural History Museum of Los Angeles County.

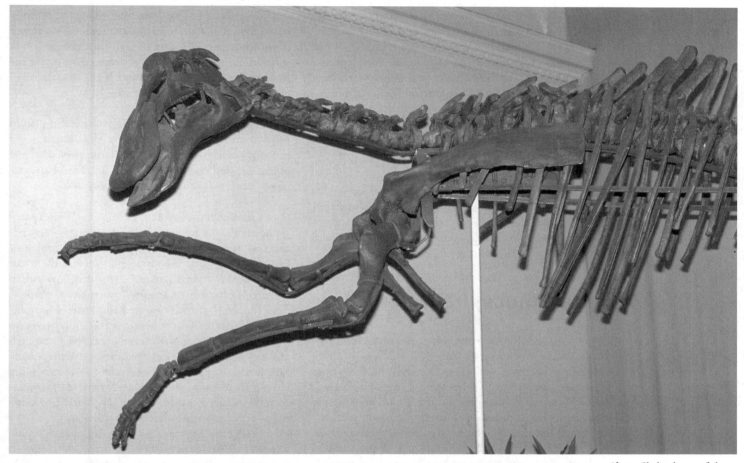

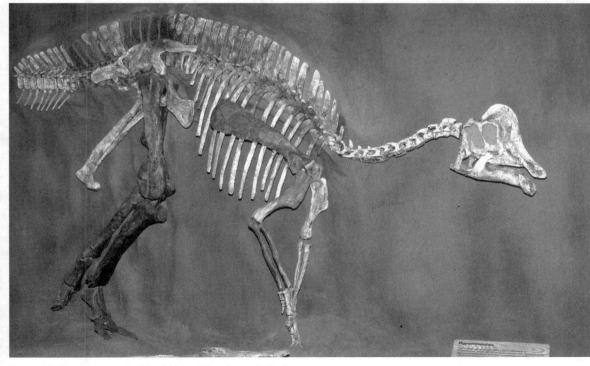

Above: Skeletal cast of the basal lambeosaurine hadrosaurid *Tsintaosaurus spinorhinus*, skull reconstructed without the traditional vertically-oriented crest.

Skeleton (cast) of the lambeosaurine hadrosaurid *Hypacrosaurus altispinus.*

Photograph by the author, courtesy Royal Tyrrell Museum/Alberta Community Development.

Diagnosis: Unambiguous synapomorphies consisting of: premaxilla and nasal meeting in complex "W"-shaped interdigitating suture on side of hollow nasal crest (reversed in *Lambeosaurus*); caudal lobe of caudal caudolateral process higher than rostral lobe on hollow nasal crest (reversed in *Corythosaurus*); hollow nasal crest raised into large vertical fan; caudal margin of hollow nasal crest composed mainly of nasal (condition reversed in *Lambeosaurus*); rostral jugal truncated to smoothly rounded margin (Horner, Weishampel and Forster 2004).

In addition to taxa already regarded as *nomina dubia*, Horner *et al.* regarded the following type species that are or have been classified as hadrosaurs — *Hypsibema crassicauda*, *Kritosaurus navajovius*, and *Sanpasaurus yaoi*— also as of doubtful validity.

Marginocephalia

In describing the new psittacosaurid genus *Hongshanosaurus* (see entry), You, Xu and Wang (2003) also performed a phylogenetic analysis on the groups within and related to the Marginocephalia, a clade including all pachycephalosaurian (bone-headed) and ceratopsian (horned) dinosaurs. This study reconfirmed the monophyletic status of Marginocephalia, Ceratopsia, and Neoceratopsia, all of these clades being diagnosed by the authors by cranial features:

MARGINOCEPHALIA
Diagnosis: Parietosquamosal shelf; caudally reduced quadratojugal; and caudodorsally sloped quadrate (You, Xu and Wang 2003).

CERATOPSIA
Diagnosis: Rostral bone; flat margin separating narial fossa and ventral margin of premaxilla; absence of antorbital fenestra; and wide dorsoventral width of infraorbital ramus of jugal at least equal to its infratemporal ramus (You, Xu and Wang 2003).

NEOCERATOPSIA
Diagnosis: Derived features including solid jugal-postorbital joint; caudally positioned jugal process; parietal-dominated parietosquamosal shelf; pointed rostral end of predentary; and biolobate, enlarged predentary (You, Xu and Wang 2003).

Like Buchholz (see above), You *et al.* found Marginocephalia to be the sister group to *Heterodontosaurus*, this relationship supported by a number of features (*e.g.*, short preorbital portion less than half length of skull, jugal laterally expanded, fewer than five premaxillary teeth; see also "Systematics" chapter, *S3*). You *et al.* further pointed out that *Heterodontosaurus* lacks many of the key ornithopod features observed in *Hypsilophodon* and more derived taxa such as *Camptosaurus* (*e.g.*, enlarged external naris; quadrate foramen; premaxilla ventrally located; maxilla having rostral process; rostrally elongated lacrimal; rostrally reduced quadratojugal; crescentic paroccipital process; enlarged biolobate predentary).

With *Heterodontosaurus* and Marginocephalia interpreted as sister taxa, You *et al.* found the origin of "Neornithopoda" (a clade including Marginocephalia, proposed by Cooper in 1985) to be based in the Early Jurassic, with *Hypsilophodon*, the earliest known member of Euornithopoda, to be of Middle Jurassic age, neither "Neornithopoda" nor Euornithopoda originating later than the Early Jurassic.

Robert M. Sullivan (2003), a specialist in pachy-

Life restoration by Berislav Krzic of the primitive pachycephalosaur *Goyocephale lattimorei*.

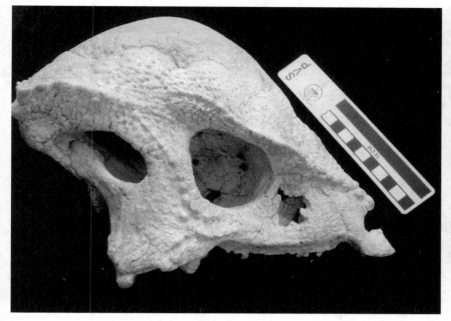

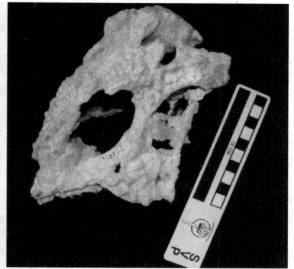

Holotype skull (ZPAL MgD-I/104) of *Prenocephale prenes*, a pachycephalosaurine pachycephalosaurid, in right lateral view.

Holotype partial skull (ZPAL MgD-I/105) of *Tylocephale gilmorei*, a pachycephalosaurine pachycephalosaurid, in left lateral view. According to pachycephalosaur specialist, Robert M. Sullivan, this taxon could be synonymous with *Prenocephale prene*.

cephalosaurs, recently performed a new analysis of the Pachycephalosauria. Sullivan's analysis found two sister groups to exist within Pachycephalosauria — one comprising the Asian taxa *Tylocephale gilmorei* and *Prenocephale prene*, taxa which may inevitably prove to be synonymous; the other, a monophyletic clade including the North American taxa ("*Prenocephale*" [=*Stegoceras*] "*edmontonensis*" plus "*P. brevis*" [=*Stegoceras breve*]; see *Prenocephale* entry) plus *P. goodwini*. These groups, Sullivan noted, "are united by the lack of minute clusters of nodes and retention of a linear row of nodes." *Hanssuesia sternbergi* and *Colepiocephale lambei* form their own clade comprising the sister group to the Pachycephalosaurini, a new clade introduced by Sullivan:

PACHYCEPHALOSAURINI

Diagnosis: Pachycephalosaurids having nodes in large clusters on squamosals (hypernoded forms) and nasals (Sullivan 2003).

Sullivan included within this monophyletic group the type species *Stygimoloch spinifer* and *Pachycephalosaurus wyomingensis*.

Maryańska, Chapman and Weishampel (2004), in their review of Pachycephalosauria — presumably written before the publication of Sullivan's (2003) study that introduced *Hanssuesia sternbergi* and *Colepiocephale lambei*) — performed their own phylogenetic analysis of this clade. Including 10 terminal members of the clade, the analysis by Maryańska *et al.*

yielded results somewhat different from those published by Sullivan.

Maryańska *et al.* found *Stenopelix* to be most basal known member of Pachycephalosauria; Homalocephalidae not a monophyletic clade at the base of the pachycephalosaur tree (*contra* earliest studies); a serial arrangement of terminal taxa with evercloser relationships identified from *Wannanosaurus* to an unresolved clade comprising *Tylocephale*, *Prenocephale*, and *Pachycephalosaurus*; the internal clade Goyocephala (see Sereno 1986) including the clade Homalocephaloidea, that, in turn, comprising two unnamed clades (the first including "*Ornatotholus*" [=*Stegoceras*; see entry], *Stygimoloch*, *Stegoceras*, *Tylocephale*, *Prenocephale*, and *Pachycephalosaurus*, the second including all of these taxa except "*Ornatotholus*"); an unresolved relationship among *Stegoceras* plus the clade Pachycephalosaurdae (=Tholocephalidae of Sereno 1986), the latter comprising *Tylocephale*, *Prenoephale*, and *Pachycephalosaurus*; and *Tylocephale*, *Prenocephale*, and *Pachycephalosaurus* forming an unresolved clade possibly equivalent to Sereno's (1986) Domocephalinae.

Moreover, while noting that *Stygimoloch* could possibly be a pachycephalosaurid, Maryańska *et al.* found this genus (*contra* previous studies, *e.g.*, Goodwin, Buchholtz and Johnson 1998; Sereno 1999*a*, 2000; Sullivan 2003) to place lower on the pachycephalosaurian tree, lacking documentation of features (*e.g.*, inclusion of nasal and medial portion of postorbital into dome, presence of distinct supraorbital) used by the authors to diagnose Pachycephalosauridae.

Maryańska *et al.* offered the following definitions

Holotype partial skull cap (TMP 87.113.3) of *Sphaerotholus buchholtzae* [=*Stegoceras edmontonensis*] in dorsal view.

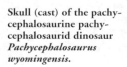

Skull (cast) of the pachycephalosaurine pachycephalosaurid dinosaur *Pachycephalosaurus wyomingensis*.

and diagnoses for the Pachycephalosauria and the clade included therein:

PACHYCEPHALOSAURIA

Stem-based definition: All taxa more closely related to *Pachycephalosaurus wyomingensis* than to *Triceratops horridus* (Sereno 1997).

Diagnosis: Synapomorphies comprising the following: skull roof thickened; frontal excluded from orbital margin; flat, broad dorsal surface of postorbital bar; parietal without caudolateral wings; tubercles on caudolateral margin of squamosal; thin, platelike basal tubera; prootic-basiphenoid plate contacting pterygoid-prootic plate; double ridge-and-groove articulation on dorsal vertebrae; elongate sacral ribs; caudal basket of fusiform ossified tendons; ilium having sigmoidal border; medial process on iliac blade; pubis almost excluded from acetabulum; tubercles on squamosal; broad expansion squamosal onto occiput; jugal and quadrate eliminating free ventral margin of quadratojugal (Maryańska, Chapman and Weishampel 2004).

GOYOCEPHALA

Node-based definition: Most recent common ancestor of *Goyocephale* and *Pachycephalosaurus* plus all descendants of this common ancestor (Maryańska, Chapman and Weishampel 2004).

Diagnosis: Supratemporal fenestrae reduced (reversed in "*Ornatotholus*" [=*Stegoceras*]; exclusion of frontal from supratemporal fenestra by parietal-jugal joint; tubercles on angular and surangular; rectangular postacetabular process on ilium; (possibly other features not preserved in *Wannanosaurus* (Maryańska, Chapman and Weishampel 2004).

HOMALOCEPHALOIDEA

Node-based definition: Most recent common ancestor of *Homalocephale* and *Pachycephalosaurus* plus all of its descendants (Maryańska, Chapman and Weishampel 2004).

Diagnosis: Broad parietal between supratemporal fenestrae; broad medial process on ilium; possibly lack of participation of quadratojugal in ventral margin of lower temporal arch (Maryańska, Chapman and Weishampel 2004).

Unnamed clade including "*Ornathotholus*" [=*Stegoceras*], *Stygimoloch, Stegoceras, Tylocephale, Prenocephale*, and *Pachycephalosaurus*
Diagnosis: Doming of skull roof (Maryańska, Chapman and Weishampel 2004).

Unnamed clade including *Stygimoloch, Stegoceras, Tylocephale, Prenocephale*, and *Pachycephalosaurus*
Diagnosis: Obliteration of interfrontal and frontal-parietal sutures; full closure of supratemporal fenestrae (Maryańska, Chapman and Weishampel 2004).

PACHYCEPHALOSAURIDAE

Diagnosis: Nasals and medial process of postorbitals included into dome; possible ornamentation of quadratojugal (Maryańska, Chapman and Weishampel 2004).

Unnamed clade comprising *Tylocephale, Prenocephale*, and *Pachycephalosaurus*
Diagnosis: Loss of lateral and caudal shelves; inclusion of frontals, parietals, postorbitals, and squamosals in dome (Maryańska, Chapman and Weishampel 2004).

New analyses have also been performed on the Ceratopsia, the second major clade within Marginocephalia.

In redescribing the basal neoceratopsian genus *Archaeoceratops* (see entry), You and Dodson (2003) performed a phylogenetic analysis for 12 taxa and 148 characters, excluding from their study various genera (*i.e.*, *Graciliceratops, Udanoceratops, Asiaceratops*, and *Turanoceratops*) known only from poorly preserved specimens. Agreeing with earlier analyses, You and Dodson's study found *Liaoceratops* and *Archaeoceratops* to be successive outgroups to the Coronosauria (*sensu* Sereno 1998); reaffirmed the sister-taxa relationship of *Protoceratops* and *Bagaceratops*; supported *Chaoyangsaurus* as the most basal member of Neoceratopsia (Sereno 2000), and also the sister-taxa relationship of *Montanoceratops* and *Leptoceratops* (Makovicky 2001). Their analysis differed from earlier studies, however, in finding the Leptoceratopsidae (rather than the Protoceratopsidae) to be the sister

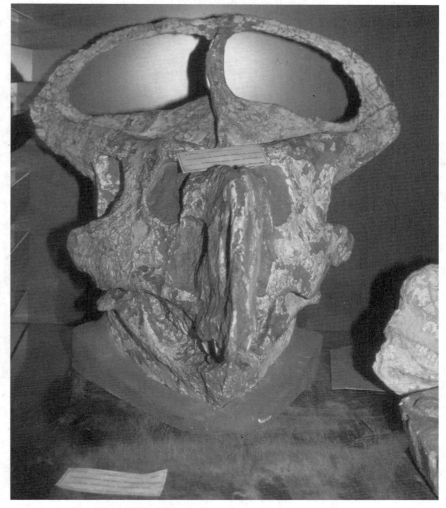

Photograph by the author, courtesy The Field Museum.

Skull (FMNH P14045; formerly AMNH collection) of the protoceratopsid ceratopsian *Protoceratops andrewsi*.

group to the Ceratopsidae, this result having "profound significance for reinterpreting the paleobiogeographical pattern and evolutionary progression of horned dinosaurs" (see below; see also Chinnery and Horner 2003).

Subsequent to the publication of You and Dodson's paper, Chinnery (2004*a*), in a study offering a preliminary description of the new ceratopsian type genus *Prenoceratops*, performed a cladistic analysis that found the primitive genus *Chaoyangosaurus* to be a member of the Neoceratopsia, and the families Leptoceratopsidae and Ceratopsidae to be strongly supported, with the family Protoceratopsidae embracing only Asian genera (see *Prenoceratops* entry for more details). (See also the abstract by Makovicky 2004, in which he discusses the problems involved in assessing the relationships of basal ceratopsians, and mentions two new undescribed basal species of Ceratopsia from China and Mongolia.)

You and Dodson (2004), in their subsequently published, more expansive review of basal Ceratopsia,

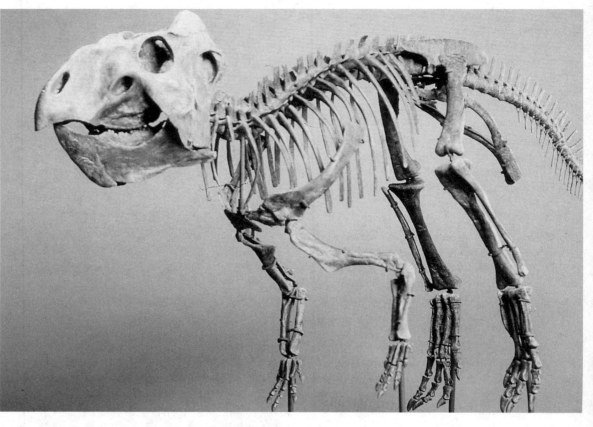

Composite skeleton (ICM collection) of the leptosaurine ceratopsian *Prenoceratops pieganensis* on display at The Children's Museum of Indianapolis, in Indianapolis, Indiana.

performed a cladistic analysis of the Ceratopsia based upon 11 taxa and 148 characters, with *Hypsilophodon foxii* (representing Ornithopoda) and *Stegoceras validum* (representing Pachycephalosauria) selected as outgroups, and with ingroups including *Psittacosaurus mongoliensis*, *Chaoyangsaurus youngi*, five nonceratopsid neoceratopsians (*Archaeoceratops oshimai*, *Leptoceratops gracilis*, *Bagaceratops rozhdestvensky*, *Protoceratops andrewsi*, and *Montanoceratops cerorhynchus*) and two ceratopsid neoceratopsians (*Centrosaurus apertus* and *Triceratops horridus*). Within Ceratopsia, You and Dodson (2004) found *Psittacosaurus* (*i.e.*, Psittacosauridae) to be the sister taxon to Neoceratopsia; *Chaoyangsaurus* (see also You and Dodson 2003) the most basal neoceratopsian (see Sereno 2000; *contra* Makovicky 2001); *Archaeoceratops* the sister taxon of Coronosauria; *Protoceratops* and *Bagaceratops* closely related members of Protoceratopsidae; *Leptoceratops* the sister taxon to *Montanoceratops*, these together forming the ceratopsoid clade Leptoceratopsidae; and *Zuniceratops* the sister taxon to Ceratopsidae.

Chaoyangsaurus, You and Dodson (2004) noted, the most primitive known member of Neoceratopsia, lacks the features typical of the later horned dinosaurs. Different from the closely related pachycephalosaurs and psittacosaurus, this genus evolved such features common to later neoceratopsians as a relatively large skull, keeled predentary with a narrow caudoventral process, and a reduced retroarticular process.

Liaoceratops (see Xu, Makovicky, Wang, Norell and You 2002), the sister taxon to *Archaeoceratops* and all other neoceratopsians, evolved a keeled rostrum, pointed ventrally along the rostral margin (You and Dodson 2004, personal observation), and a caudolateral process along the buccal edge. You and Dodson (2004) also observed the following features of this genus: Premaxilla longer than tall; maxillary tooth ovate in lateral aspect; median primary ridge on labial side of maxillary teeth; last caudal dentary tooth coincident with apex of pronounced coronoid process.

In *Archaeoceratops*, the sister taxon to all currently known Late Cretaceous neoceratopsians (*i.e.*, the Coronosauria; see below), You and Dodson (2004) observed the following features: Short infratemporal bar (less than half supratemporal bar); edentulous portion along rostral maxilla occupying four or five tooth spaces; epijugal; quadratojugal transversely expanded and triangular in coronal section; predentary having round, beveled buccal edge; prominent primary ridge of maxillary tooth crown.

You and Dodson's (2004) analysis found the clade Coronosauria to split into two clades — Protoceratopsidae (*Protoceratops* plus *Bagaceratops*) and Ceratopsoidea (Leptoceratopsidae plus Ceratopsidae).

According to You and Dodson (2004), proto-

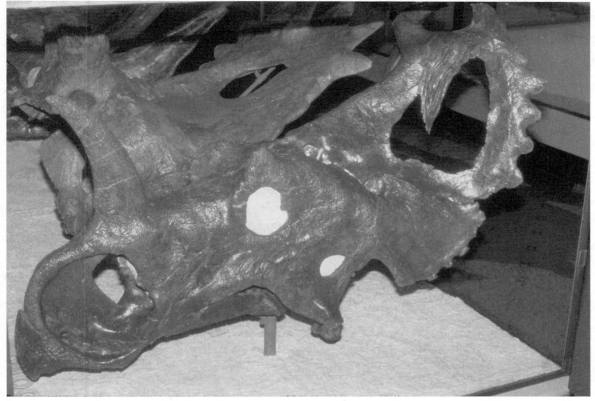

Photograph by the author, courtesy American Museum of Natural History.

Skull (AMNH 5239) of the centrosaurine ceratopsian *Centrosaurus apertus.*

ceratopsids are known only in Asia (however, see Chinnery and Horner, who regard American forms like *Leptoceratops* and the Asian *Udanoceratops* as members of the Leptoceratopsinae, a subfamily of Protoceratopsidae), while ceratopsoids are known only in North America, this recognition indicating "a biogeographic coherence that has not been apparent previously (You 2002)." Thus, the divergence between these groups most likely took place in the early Late Cretaceous, with the Ceratopsidae probably originating in North America, as the complete fossil record of that group and the Leptoceratopsidae are currently known only on that continent.

You and Dodson (2004) offered the following definitions and diagnoses for Ceratopsia and its basal subclades:

CERATOPSIA

Stem-based definition: All Marginocephalia closer to *Triceratops* than to *Pachycephalosaurus* (You and Dodson 2004).

Diagnosis: Autapomorphies including the following: High external naris separated from ventral border of premaxilla by flat area; rostral bone; enlarged; enlarged premaxilla; well-developed lateral flaring of jugal; wide dorsoventral length of infraorbital ramus of jugal; contact of palatal extensions of maxillae rostral to choana (You and Dodson 2004).

PSITTACOSAURIDAE

Diagnosis: Short preorbital portion (less than 40 percent of basal length of skull); elevated external naris; lack of antorbital fossa and fenestra; extremely broad caudolateral premaxillary process; long rostral process of nasal extending below external naris; convergence of premaxilla, maxilla, lacrimal, and jugal sutures to point on snout; eminence on rim of buccal emargination of maxilla near junction with jugal; unossified gap in wall of lacrimal canal; well-developed jugal process from midsection of jugal; postorbital with elongate jugal and squamosal processes; dentary crown having bulbous primary ridge; manual digit IV having just one simplified phalanx; manual digit V absent (You and Dodson 2004).

NEOCERATOPSIA

Stem-based definition: All ceratopsians more closely related to *Triceratops* than to *Psittacosaurus* (You and Dodson 2004).

Diagnosis: Head enlarged relative to body; keeled rostral end of rostral bone; postorbital with short jugal process; quadratojugal much reduced; basioccipital excluded from formation of foramen magnum; coronoid process covering distal tooth row in lateral aspect; primary ridge on maxillary teeth; caudal process on coracoid; development of humeral head; ischium dently decurved (You and Dodson 2004).

CORONOSAURIA

Diagnosis: Antorbital fossa oval, rather than triangular; parietal much wider than dorsal skull roof; basioccipital excluded from foramen magnum; broad, moderately deep coronoid process of dentary; dentary tooth crowns becoming ovate in lateral aspect, median primary ridge developed on lingual side; atlas intercentrum fused to odontid; atlas neuropophyses fused to intercentrum and odontid; syncervical developed, elements of atlas, axis, and several proximal cervical vertebrae fused together, supporting enlarged head; mutual contact among neural spines (You and Dodson 2004).

PROTOCERATOPSIDAE

Diagnosis: Premaxilla higher than long; development of small nasal horn; quadratojugal triangular in coronal section; slender rostral prong articulating with jugal; caudal end of frill straight or wavy; palatine having elongate parasagittal process; occipital condyle reduced in size; rostral end of predentary pointed rostrodorsally; surangular with long ventral process overlapping angular; surangular-dentary and surangular-angular sutures forming acute angle on lateral face of mandible (You and Dodson 2004).

CERATOPSOIDEA

Diagnosis: (Facial region of skull) external naris round; caudolateral process of rostral elongated; ventral margin of premaxilla convex, premaxilla-maxilla suture caudal to it; (caudal region) lateral expansion of jugal projecting more ventrally than laterally; quadratojugal obscured in lateral aspect; exoccipital contacting quadrate; supraoccipital in same plane as caudal face of basioccipital (rather than inclined rostrally). You and Dodson further noted that the manus of *Leptoceratops* is stouter than in *Protoceratops* and more similar to that in ceratopsids, its nonungual phalanges being wider than long (You and Dodson 2004).

You and Dodson (2004) regarded as *nomina dubia*, among other taxa, the type species *Asiaceratops salsopaludalis*, *Kulceratops kulensis*, *Microceratops gobiensis*, and *Turanoceratops tardabilis*.

In their review of the Ceratopsidae, Dodson, Forster and Sampson (2004) performed a cladistic analysis based on 12 ingroup taxa (*Achelousaurus*, *Anchiceratops*, *Arrhinoceratops*, *Centrosaurus*, *Chasmosaurus*, *Diceratops*, *Einiosaurus*, *Pachyrhinosaurus*, *Pentaceratops*, *Styracosaurus*, *Torosaurus*, and *Triceratops*, with *Protoceratops* and *Zuniceratops* used as outgroups, and including 73 cranial and postcranial characters.

Dodson *et al.*'s analysis nearly completely resolved all valid ceratopsid genera. This analysis found *Zuniceratops* to be the sister taxon to Ceratopsidae; confirmed the traditional split of this family into two

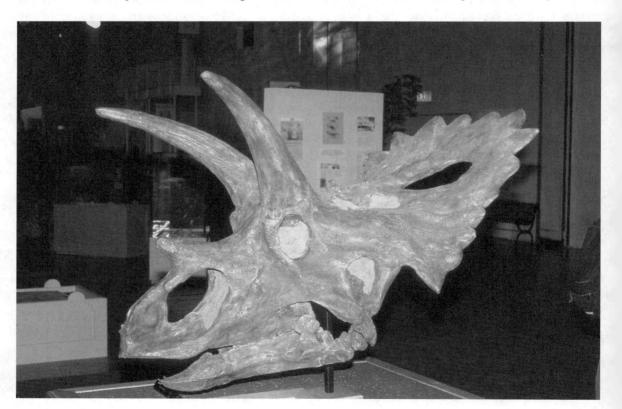

Much reconstructed skull (cast) of the chasmosaurine ceratopsian *Anchiceratops ornatus*.

Photograph by the author, courtesy
Natural History Museum of Los Angeles County.

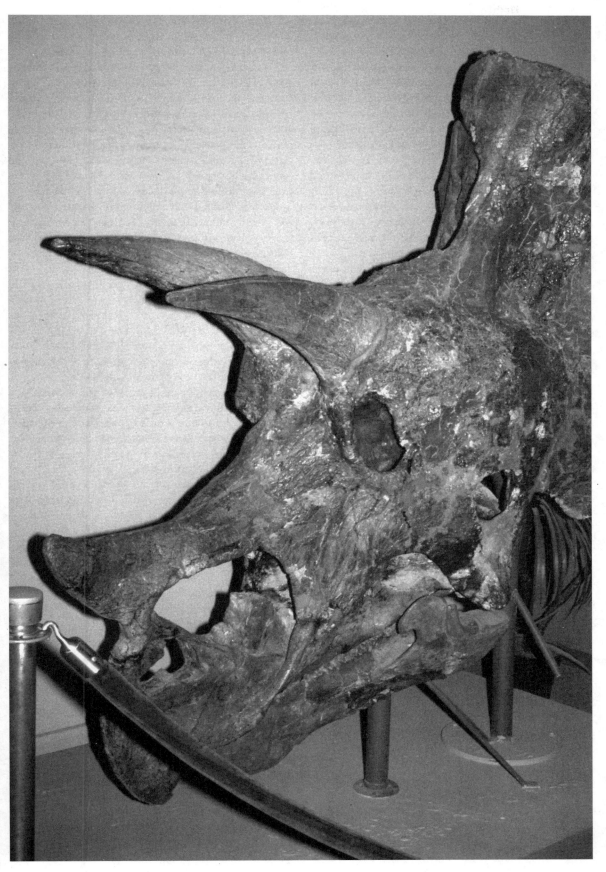

Skull (LACM 7207/59049) of the chamosaurine ceratopsian *Triceratops horridus.*

subfamilies, the Centrosaurinae and Chasmosaurinae; and found within Chasmosaurinae two unnamed clades, one comprising *Triceratops* (*Diceratops* plus *Torosaurus*) plus *Anchiceratops-Arrhinoceratops*, another comprising *Chasmosaurus-Pentaceratops*. Eliminated from Dodson *et al.*'s analysis was *Avaceratops* because of its subadult status, although its placement within Centrosaurinae was supported by a number of characters (*e.g.*, morphology and length of squamosal; morphology of premaxilla). The controversial type species *Monoclonius crassus* (see *D:TE*, *S3*), regarded by some authors (*e.g.*, Tumarkin and Dodson 1998) as a valid type species and others (*e.g.*, Sampson, Ryan and Tanke 1997) as a *nomen dubium*, was provisionally included among the ceratopsid taxa accepted as valid in this study.

Dodson *et al.* offered the following definitions and diagnoses for the Ceratopsidae and its clades:

Unnamed clade comprising *Zuniceratops* plus CERATOPSIDAE

Diagnosis: Supraorbital ornamentation; craniocaudally expanded distal coronoid process (Dodson, Forster and Sampson 2004).

CERATOPSIDAE

Node-based definition: *Centrosaurus* and *Triceratops* plus their most recent common ancestor and all of its descendants (Dodson, Forster and Sampson 2004).

Diagnosis: External naris greatly enlarged; prominent premaxillar septum; antorbital fenestra greatly reduced in size; nasal horncore; reduced lacrimal; frontal eliminated from orbital margin; dentary articulation set well below alveolar margin; basioccipital excluded from foramen magnum; supraoccipital eliminated from foramen magnum; marginal undulations on frill augmented by epoccipital processes; tooth row extending caudal to coronoid process; quadrate-quadratojugal laterally stacked; shallow supracranial cavity complex; elongate groove on squamosal to receive quadrate; largest dimension of parietal fenestra axially oriented; olfactory tract exiting for c.nn. X, XI, XII reduced to two; more than two replacement teeth in each vertical series; loss of subsidiary ridges on teeth; teeth having two roots; atlantal neural arch steeply inclined caudally; at least 10 sacral vertebrae; sternum short, broad; laterally everted shelf on dorsal rim of ilium; supraacetabular process ("antitrochanter"); ischium gently to greatly decurved; greater and cranial trochanters of femur fused together; femur longer than tibia; pedal ungual hook-like (Dodson, Forster and Sampson 2004).

CENTROSAURINAE

Stem-based definition: All Ceratopsidae more closely related to *Centrosaurus* than to *Triceratops*.

Diagnosis: (Unambiguous characters) Premaxillary oral margin extending below alveolar margin; postorbital horns less than 15 percent basal skull length; jugal infratemporal flange; parietal marginal imbrication; squamosal much shorter than parietal; squamosal rostromedial lamina; pattern of epoccipital fusion from caudal to rostral; six to eight parietal epoccipitals per side; parietal epoccipital at locus two medially directed; predentary triturating surface inclined steeply laterally; (ambiguous characters) caudoventral premaxillary process inserting into nasal; short parietosquamosal frill (0.70 or less than basal skull length); wide median bar; epoccipital crossing parietal-squamosal joint; parietal epoccipital at locus three modified into large horn (Dodson, Forster and Sampson 2004).

CHASMOSAURINAE

Stem-based definition: All Ceratopsidae more closely related to *Triceratops* than to *Centrosaurus*. (Dodson, Forster and Sampson 2004).

Diagnosis: (Unambiguous characters) rostral enlarged, caudal margin deeply concave, dorsal and ventral processes hypertrophied; premaxillary septum; premaxillary narial strut; interpremaxillary fossa; rostrally elongate premaxillary narial process; keyhole-shaped fontanelle; triangular squamosal epoccipitals; rounded ventral sacrum (sulcus absent); cross section of ischium laterally compressed, dorsal margin blade-like; ischial shaft decurved broadly and continuously (Dodson, Forster and Sampson 2004).

Unnamed *Triceratops* (*Diceratops* plus *Torosaurus*) plus *Anchiceratops-Arrhinoceratops* clade

Diagnosis: (ambiguous character) caudoventral premaxillary process inverting into nasal; (unambiguous) nasal ornamentation over dorsal or rostrodorsal naris; postorbital ornamentation arising caudodorsal or caudal to orbit; (ambiguous) postorbital horns straight or rostrally curved; supracranial cavity deep, complex; frontal fontanelle round to oval; wide parietal median bar (Dodson, Forster and Sampson 2004).

Unnamed *Triceratops* (*Diceratops* plus *Torosaurus*) clade

Diagnosis: (Unambiguous characters) nasal ornamentation over dorsal or rostrodorsal naris; postorbital ornamentation arising caudodorsal or caudal to orbit; supracranial cavity deep, complex; frontal fontanelle round to oval; (ambiguous characters) caudoventral premaxillary process inserting into nasal; postorbital horns straight or rostrally curved; wide parietal median bar (Dodson, Forster and Sampson 2004).

Unnamed *Triceratops* (*Diceratops* plus *Torosaurus*) clade

Diagnosis: Unambiguous synapomorphies comprising the following: recess in ventral premaxillary septum; large, deep recess in premaxillary septum; recess in premaxillary narial process (Dodson, Forster and Sampson 2004).

Unnamed *Chasmosaurus-Pentaceratops* clade

Diagnosis: (Unambiguous characters) bony flange along caudal margin of narial strut; forked distal end of premaxillary caudoventral process; large parietal fenestra (at least 45 percent total parietal length); (ambiguous) parietal epoccipital at locus I caudally directed (Dodson, Forster and Sampson 2004).

Unnamed *Triceratops* (*Diceratops* plus *Torosaurus* clade

Diagnosis: (Unambiguous synapomorphies) recess in ventral premaxillary septum; large, deep recess in premaxillary septum; recess in premaxillary narial process (Dodson, Forster and Sampson 2004).

Unnamed *Chasmosaurus-Pentaceratops* clade

Diagnosis: (Unambiguous characters) bony flange along caudal margin of narial strut; forked distal end of premaxillary caudoventral process; large parietal fenestrae (at least 45 percent total length of parietal); (ambiguous character) caudally directed parietal epoccipital at locus one (Dodson, Forster and Sampson 2004).

III: Dinosaurian Genera

The following section consists of a compilation of dinosaurian genera, arranged in alphabetical order, including information about the genus and its species. Some of these entries are new to the current volume; others pertain to entries previously published in the original *Dinosaurs: The Encyclopedia* (*D:TE*), *Dinosaurs: The Encyclopedia, Supplement 1* (*S1*), *Supplement 2* (*S2*), and *Supplement 3* (*S3*).

Entries (*e.g., Cardiodon*) marked with a dagger (†) identify those which appeared in the earlier volumes, but in this book offer new, revised, or corrected data, new species, or new, or updated, or otherwise different illustrations. Within each dagger-marked entry, basic introductory information (*e.g.*, that relating to classification, age, diagnosis, *etc.*) is usually included only when it is new or has been revised. Information offered in this volume that conflicts with information appearing in *D:TE* or its already issued supplements replaces the earlier published information. Most photographs and drawings of type specimens and referred fossil material, and also life restorations relevant to dagger-marked entries, can be found in the previous books.

Revised or new diagnoses, definitions, and generalized descriptions and explanations of higher taxa, having broader applications to each genus or species, can be found in the preceding "Systematics" chapter; unchanged data relevant to those topics can be found in *D:TE*, *S1*, *S2*, or *S3*.

The following genera have their own entries which are new to this volume:

Amazonsaurus, Antetonitrus, Atrociraptor, Aviatyrannis, Bainoceratops, Bonitasaura, Colepiocephale, Dilong, Dromaeosauroides, Equijubus, Fukuisaurus, Graciliraptor, Hanssuesia, Hongshanosaurus, Huaxiagnathus, Isisaurus, Kerberosaurus, Limayasaurus, Lusotitan, Magnirostris, Mei, Mendozasaurus, Mirischia, Olorotitan, Prenoceratops, Rajasaurus, Rinchenia, Rinconsaurus, Rugops, Shenzhousaurus, Sinornithomimus, Sinusonasus, Spinostropheus, Suuwassea, Talenkauen, Tazoudasaurus, Unenlagia, Yixianosaurus, and *Zalmoxes, Zupaysaurus.*

The following genera (excluding taxa currently regarded as junior synonyms, *e.g., Sellosaurus*), had their own entries in the previous books, but also have entries in this volume:

Abrosaurus, Adasaurus, Aeolosaurus, Afrovenator, Agustinia, Alamosaurus, Albertosaurus, Alioramus, Allosaurus, Alwalkeria, Amargasaurus, Ammosaurus, Ampelosaurus, Amphicoelias, Amurosaurus, Anchiceratops, Anchisaurus, Andesaurus, Antarctosaurus, Apatosaurus, Archaeoceratops, Argentinosaurus, Argyrosaurus, Astrodon, Atlasaurus, Atlascoposaurus, Aucasaurus, Avimimus, Bagaraatan, Bambiraptor, Barapasaurus, Barosaurus, Baryonyx, Becklespinax, Beipiaosaurus,

Blikanasaurus, Borogovia, Brachiosaurus, Brachylophosaurus, Byronosaurus, Caenagnathasia, Camarasaurus, Camelotia, Campylodoniscus, Cardiodon, Caudipteryx, Cedarosaurus, Cedarpelta, Centrosaurus, Ceratosaurus, Cetiosauriscus, Cetiosaurus, Chasmosaurus, Chialingosaurus, Chindesaurus, Chirostenotes, Chungkingosaurus, Citipati, Clasmodosaurus, Coelophysis, Coeluroides, Coloradisaurus, Compsognathus, Compsosuchus, Corythosaurus, Craterosaurus, Dacentrurus, Daspletosaurus, Deinonychus, Deltadromeus, Dicraeosaurus, Dilophosaurus, Diplodocus, Dravidosaurus, Dromaeosaurus, Dryptosauroides, Dyslocosaurus, Edmontosaurus, Efraasia, Elopteryx, Enigmosaurus, Eobrontosaurus, Epachthosaurus, Erectopus, Erlikosaurus, Eshanosaurus, Eucamerotus, Euoplocephalus, Euskelosaurus, Eustreptospondylus, Ferganasaurus, Fukuiraptor, Garudimimus, Gastonia, Genyodectes, Gobititan, Gongxianosaurus, Gorgosaurus, Gravitholus, Guaibasaurus, Hadrosaurus, Haplocanthosaurus, Harpymimus, Heptasteornis, Hesperosaurus, Huabeisaurus, Hudiesaurus, Hylaeosaurus, Iguanodon, Indosaurus, Indosuchus, Ingenia, Isanosaurus, Iuticosaurus, Janenschia, Jaxartosaurus, Jiangshanosaurus, Jingshanosaurus, Jubbulpuria, Kakuru, Kentrosaurus, Klamelisaurus, Kotasaurus, Labocania, Laevisuchus, Lambeosaurus, Laplatasaurus, Lapparentosaurus, Lessemsaurus, Lexovisaurus, Liaoningosaurus, Liliensternus, Lirainosaurus, Lourinhasaurus, Lufengosaurus, Magyarosaurus, Majungatholus, Malawisaurus, Mamenchisaurus, Masiakasaurus, Massospondylus, Megaraptor, Melanorosaurus, Microcoelus, Microraptor, Microvenator, Mochlodon, Mononykus, Nemegtosaurus, Neuquensaurus, Niobrarasaurus, Nipponosaurus, Noasaurus, Nodocephalosaurus, Nomingia, Nothronychus, Ohmdenosaurus, Opisthocoelicaudia, Oplosaurus, Ornithomimoides, Ornithomimus, Ornithopsis, Orodromeus, Oviraptor, Ozraptor, Pachyrhinosaurus, Panoplosaurus, Paralititan, Paranthodon, Patagonykus, Patagosaurus, Pawpawsaurus, Pelecanimimus, Pelorosaurus, Pentaceratops, Phuwiangosaurus, Piatnitzkysaurus, Pinacosaurus, Pisanosaurus, Plateosaurus, Prenocephale, Probactrosaurus, Psittacosaurus, Rapetosaurus, Rayososaurus, Revueltosaurus, Rhabdodon, Riojasaurus, Rocasaurus, Ruehlei, Saltasaurus, Saturnalia, Sauropelta, Saurophaganax, Sauroposeidon, Saurornithoides, Saurornitholestes, Scipionyx, Segnosaurus, Seismosaurus, Shuangmiaosaurus, Siamosaurus, Siamotyrannus, Sinovenator, Sinraptor, Staurikosaurus, Stegoceras, Stegosaurus, Struthiosaurus, Stygimoloch, Styracosaurus, Supersaurus, Syngonosaurus, Syntarsus, Szechuanosaurus, Tarascosaurus, Tarbosaurus, Tarchia, Tehuelchesaurus, Tendaguria, Tenontosaurus, Thecodontosaurus, Therizinosaurus, Tianzhenosaurus, Titanosaurus, Tochisaurus, Tornieria, Torvosaurus, Triceratops, Troodon, Tsagantegia, Tuojiangosaurus, Tyrannosaurus, Unquillosaurus, Utahraptor, Velociraptor, Venenosaurus,

Volkheimeria, Wuerhosaurus, Xuanhanosaurus, Yandusaurus, Yaverlandia, Yimenosaurus, Yunnanosaurus, Zephyrosaurus, and *Zuniceratops.*

†ABROSAURUS

Saurischia: Eusaurischia: Sauropodomorpha: Sauropoda: Eusauropoda: Neosauropoda: Macronaria *incertae sedis.*

Diagnosis of genus (as for type species): Parietals narrow, supratemporal fenestrae separated by only short distance; extremely elongate ascending process of maxilla, length nearly three-quarters that of maxillary ramus; exceptionally large antorbital, external narial, and infratemporal openings, larger than in other known sauropods (Upchurch, Barrett and Dodson 2004).

Comments: In 1996, Zhang Yihong and Chen Wei described the sauropod type species *Abrosaurus donpoensis,* established on a well-preserved skull and mandible from the Lower Shaximiao Formation of Sichuan, China, the authors regarding it as a camarasaurid (see *S1*).

More recently, in a review of Sauropoda, Upchurch, Barrett and Dodson (2004) reassessed this genus, noting the following "interesting combination of characters" exhibited by the skull of *Abrosaurus*: (Eusauropoda) external nares rostrodorsal to antorbital fossa; loss of bone sheet from medial margin of antorbital fossa; (Neosauropoda) extension of infratemporal opening beneath orbit (neosauropod features absent including contact between maxilla and quadratojugal); (Macronaria) diameter of external nares greater than diameter of orbit; tall, straight ascending premaxillary process; surangular dorsoventral height at least twice that of angular.

While more information is required before a definite referral is possible, Upchurch *et al.* currently regarded *Abrosaurus* as a basal macronarian, noting also that the previous referral by Zhang and Chen to the Camarasauridae is not possible based upon the published character data.

Key references: Upchurch, Barrett and Dodson (2004); Zhang and Chen (1996).

†ADASAURUS

Saurischia: Eusaurischia: Eusaurischia: Theropoda: Neotheropoda: Tetanurae: Avetheropoda: Coelurosauria: Tyrannoraptora: Maniraptoriformes: Maniraptora: Metornithes: Paraves: Deinonychosauria: Dromaeosauridae: Dromaeosaurinae.

Diagnosis of genus (as for type species): Differing from all other known dromaeosaurids in having ilium with indented cranial margin, extremely robust hindlimbs, pedal digit II with reduced raptorial ungual (Norell and Makovicky 2004).

Comment: In their review of the Dromaeosauridae, Norell and Makovicky (2004) rediagnosed the type species *Adasaurus mongoliensis* (see *D:TE*).

Key reference: Norell and Makovicky (2004).

†AEOLOSAURUS

Saurischia: Eusaurischia: Sauropodomorpha: Sauropoda: Eusauropoda: Neosauropoda: Macronaria: Titanosauriformes: Titanosauria: Lithostrotia.

Diagnosis of genus (as for type species): Middle caudal vertebrae with forwardly projecting craniocaudal corner of neural spine, overhanging cranial face of centrum; humerus with prominent knoblike process on deltopectoral crest (Upchurch, Barrett and Dodson 2004).

Comments: The type species *Aeolosaurus rionegrinus* was named and described in Jaime Eduardo Powell's (1986) unpublished Ph.D dissertation on the "titanosaurid" dinosaurs of South America, after which this taxon, as it had already been officially published, was discussed in various publications (*e.g.*, Salgado and Coria 1993*b*; see *D:TE, S2*).

In 2003, Powell finally published a somewhat revised version of his original 1986 study, presenting *Aeolosaurus rionegrinus* as a new genus and species of "late titanosaurid found in association with Late Senonian South American hadrosaurs." Powell (2003) offered an emended version of his original diagnosis of the type species (see *D:TE*) and also described in detail the material assigned to this taxon.

Powell diagnosed the type species *Aeolosaurus rionegrinus* as follows: Caudal vertebrae having compressed centra, with high lateral walls, narrow ventral face, from third to fourth caudal; prexygapophysis longer than in other known "titanosaurids," projecting forward and upward on proximal caudal vertebrae, slightly forward on fourth caudal; neural arch inclined somewhat forward; neurapophysis slightly inclined forward, located on proximal half of centrum; facets of postzygapophyses more inclined than in *Saltasaurus,* almost paralleling sagittal plane in proximal caudals, located on proximal half of centrum; hemapophyses having separated articular ends; articular facets of hemapophysis divided into two angled surfaces; scapular lamina wide, expanded distally; prominence for muscular attachment upon internal face near upper margin of scapula (as in *Saltasaurus loricatus*); humerus robust, having prominent apex on deltoid crest (for insertion of pectoral muscle); metacarpals relatively short and stout (as in *S. loricatus*); pubis having wide distal end of pubic lamina.

As noted by Powell (2003), *A. rionegrinus* exhibits "a mixture of peculiar features of very different titanosaurids" (*e.g.*, *Saltasaurus, Neuquensaurus, Titanosaurus*).

The caudal centra of *Aeolosaurus* resemble those of *Titanosaurus* in the following features — ventral face of centrum quite narrow; lateral walls of the former inclined somewhat downward; neural spine laterally compressed, facets of postzygapophyses laterally oriented. They differ from *Titanosaurus*, however, in the following features — prezygapophyses significantly longer, articular surfaces having greater diameter; neural spine and facets of postzygapophyses located farther forward relative to centra.

Aeolosaurus resembles both *Saltasaurus* and *Neuquensaurus* in the following features — limb bones stout; scapula with similar prominence on medial face for muscle attachment. The humerus is robust (as in *Saltasaurus* and *Argyrosaurus*); and the ischium is similar to that of *Alamosaurus sanjuanensis* (see Gilmore 1922), the latter differing only in possessing a longer, wider ischiaotic lamina and shorter pubic peduncle.

Powell (2003) tentatively referred to *A. rionegrinus* a series of partially articulated caudal vertebrae comprising 15 elements, collected from Late Cretaceous (Campanian–Maastrichtian; see Bonaparte, Franchi, Powell and Sepúlveda 1984) Los Alamitos Formation at Estancia Los Alamitos, southeast of Cona Niyeu, southeast region of Río Negro Province, near the border of Chubut Province. As that author observed, these vertebrae resemble those of *A. rionegrinus* in the morphology of the centrum (*e.g.*, prox-imal centrum ventrally broad, relatively short, ventral face short and concave), features of the neural arch (*e.g.*, located on proximal part of centrum, slightly inclined forward), the considerable length and forward and upward position of the prezygapophysis, and the postzygapophyseal facets' position at the bases of the neural spines.

According to Powell (2003), the most significant feature in this material is an amphicoelic vertebra, a feature previously described by Huene (1929) in vertebrae he referred to the European sauropod *Macrurosaurus* (see *D:TE*).

Key references: Bonaparte, Franchi, Powell and Sepúlveda (1984); Gilmore (1922); Huene (1929); Powell (1986, 2003); Salgado and Coria (1993*b*); Upchurch, Barrett and Dodson (2004).

†AFROVENATOR

Saurischia: Eusaurischia: Theropoda: Neotheropoda: Tetanurae: Spinosauroidea: Megalosauridae: Eustreptospondylinae.

Comment: In their review of basal tetanuran theropods, Holtz, Molnar and Currie (2004) performed a cladistic analysis that found *Afrovenator abakensis* to be a member of the megalosaurid subfamily Eustreptospondylinae, sharing with other members of this clade the following synapomorphies:

Reconstructed skeleton of the theropod *Afrovenator abokensis* approaching the partial skeletal carcass of the sauropod *Jobaria tiguidensis* (casts by the PAST Company), displayed in 2003 in the "Giants: African Dinosaurs" exhibit at Garfield Park Conservatory.

Photograph by the author.

Life restoration by Berislav Krzic of *Afrovenator abakensis*.

Maxillary fenestra (not known in Spinosauridae or non-tetanuran theropods, but present in Avetheropoda); distal ischial tubercle (see Hutchinson 2001; also found in allosauroid carnosaurs); reversion to lack of deep groove on medial side of proximal end of fibula.

Key reference: Holtz, Molnar and Currie (2004).

†AGUSTINIA

Saurischia: Eusaurischia: Sauropodomorpha: Sauropoda: Eusauropoda: Neosauropoda: Macronaria: Titanosauriformes: Titanosauria *incertae sedis*.

Diagnosis of genus (as for type species): Three unique kinds of osteoderms: 1. elongate, dorsoventrally projecting flattened or cylindrical; 2. subrhomboidal or leaf-shaped; 3. large, flat, transversely expanded, with lateral projections (Upchurch, Barrett and Dodson 2004).

Comment: In their review of the Sauropoda, Upchurch, Barrett and Dodson (2004) rediagnosed the type species *Agustinia ligabuei* (see *S2*).

Key reference: Upchurch, Barrett and Dodson (2004).

†ALAMOSAURUS

Saurischia: Eusaurischia: Sauropodomorpha: Sauropoda: Eusauropoda: Neosauropoda: Macronaria: Titanosauriformes: Titanosauria: Lithostrotia.

Diagnosis of genus (as for type species): Absence of caudal ribs from caudal vertebrae nine and beyond; acute (rather than broad) craniolateral process of sternal plate (Upchurch, Barrett and Dodson 2004).

Comment: In their review of the Sauropoda, Upchurch, Barrett and Dodson (2004) rediagnosed the type species *Alamosaurus sanjuanensis* (see *D:TE*).

Key reference: Upchurch, Barrett and Dodson (2004).

†ALBERTOSAURUS

Saurischia: Eusaurischia: Theropoda: Neotheropoda: Tetanurae: Avetheropoda: Coelurosauria: Tyrannoraptora: Maniraptoriformes: Tyrannoraptora: Tyrannosauroidea: Tyrannosauridae: Albertosaurinae.

Diagnosis of genus (as for type species): Lacrimal horns dorsally oriented (also in *Daspletosaurus*); occipital region caudoventrally oriented, basal tubera

Skull (cast) of *Albertosaurus sarcophagus*, the original specimen having been collected from the Two Medicine Formation, Teton County, Montana.

reduced, at least two foramina on lateral surface of palatine (also in *Tyrannosaurus* and *Tarbosaurus*); scapula caudally expanded, deltopectoral crest large (as in *Tyrannosaurus*); basisphenoid within distinct fossa; rostral margin of postorbital suborbital prong jagged (rather than smooth, suggesting tendinous sheet beneath orbit homologous to fully ossified condition in *Gorgosaurus* (Holtz 2004).

Comment: Holtz (2004), in his review of the Tyrannosauroidea, rediagnosed the type species *Albertosaurus sarcophagous*.

Key reference: Holtz (2004).

†ALIORAMUS — (=? *Tarbosaurus*)
Saurischia: Eusaurischia: Eusaurischia: Theropoda: Neotheropoda: Tetanurae: Avetheropoda: Coelurosauria: Tyrannoraptora: Maniraptoriformes: Tyrannoraptora: Tyrannosauroidea: Tyrannosauridae: ?Tyrannosaurinae.

Comments: In a study on the cranial anatomy of tyrannosaurid dinosaurs from Alberta, Canada, Currie (2003*b*) addressed the Mongolian type species *Alioramus remotus*, which Sergei M. [Mikhailovich] Kurzanov had described in 1976*b*, based on a partial, presumably (see below) juvenile skull and skeleton (PIN 3142/1) from Nogon-Taav in Mongolia (see *D:TE*).

Two characteristics cited by Kurzanov — pair of conspicuous rows of foramina on outer surface of maxilla; position and contacts of laterosphenoid — were noted by Currie as characters shared by all tyrannosaurids. The low skull is due to the small size of the type specimen, while the "greatly elongated jaws" are typical for all similarly-sized tyrannosaurid individuals. Currie also noted that other characters of this type species — *e.g.*, smoothness of postorbital; mediolateral

Life restoration by Berislav Krzic of *Alioramus remotus*.

compression of teeth — are to be expected in any small tyrannosaurid; the location of the maxillary fenestra falls within the variability range for tyrannosaurines such as *Tarbosaurus*; and the pronounced nasal "hornlets" are comparable in number and location to the lower bumps found in some *Tarbosaurus* and *Daspletosaurus* specimens.

Moreover, Kurzanov had described the prootic as surrounding the trigeminal foramen; examination of PIN 3142/1 by Currie, however, found that interpretation to be probably incorrect, the cranial border of trigeminal being almost certainly formed, in the conventional way, by the laterosphenoid.

As Currie observed, the shape and orientation of the basisphenoid recess in *A. remotus* is quite similar to those of *Daspletosaurus*, "*Nanotyrannus* [= *Tyrannosaurus*]," *Tarbosaurus*, and *Tyrannosaurus*, while proportions of the skull suggest that this species could represent an immature ontogentic stage of *Tarbosaurus*. However, other features — *e.g.*, higher number of teeth (16 or 17 maxillary, 18 dentary), prominence

Undescribed skull of *Alioramus remotus* before its appearance at the Arizona Mineral and Fossil Show (2005), in Tucson.

of osseous excrescences on nasal — also suggest the generic distinction of PIN 3142/1.

(As commented by R. E. Molnar, personal communication 2004, the number, development, and location of the "hornlets" on the *Alioramus* holotype — taking into consideration that such ornamentation in modern tetrapods [*e.g.*, the horns of stags] only appears in sexually mature adults — suggest that this theropod is an adult, and, therefore, probably generically distinct from *Tarbosaurus*.)

Hurum and Sabath (2003) suggested a possible sister-taxon relationship between *Alioramus* and the better known genus *Tarbosaurus* (see entry), while Hurum (personal communication to Holtz, 2004) suggested that both taxa could form a clade to the exclusion of North American Tyrannosauridae. Holtz, in his review of tyrannosauroids, found *Alioramus* to be either the sister taxon of Tyrannosauridae, or a tyrannosaurine closer to *Tarbosaurus* and *Tyranno-*

saurus than to *Daspletosaurus* (see "Systematics" chapter).

Key references: Currie (2003*b*); Holtz (2004); Hurum and Sabath (2003); Kurzanov (1976*b*).

†**ALLOSAURUS**—(=*Apatodon, Creosaurus, Hypsirophus* [in part], *Labroaurus*; =?*Epanterias, Saurophaganax*)
Saurischia: Eusaurischia: Eusaurischia: Theropoda: Neotheropoda: Tetanurae: Avetheropoda: Carnosauria: Allosauroidea: Allosauridae.

Diagnosis of genus: Long, cranially directed lamina extending from obturator process of ischium cranially to level of pubioischial contact; large, mediolaterally compressed, dorsally projecting cornual process of lacrimal; fenestrate dorsal wall of maxillary antrum; spindle-shaped foramen on lateral surface of fourth sacral vertebra centrum (Chure, in press, *see in* Holtz, Molnar and Currie 2004).

Photograph by Urs Möckli, copyright © and courtesy Sauriermuseum Aathal.

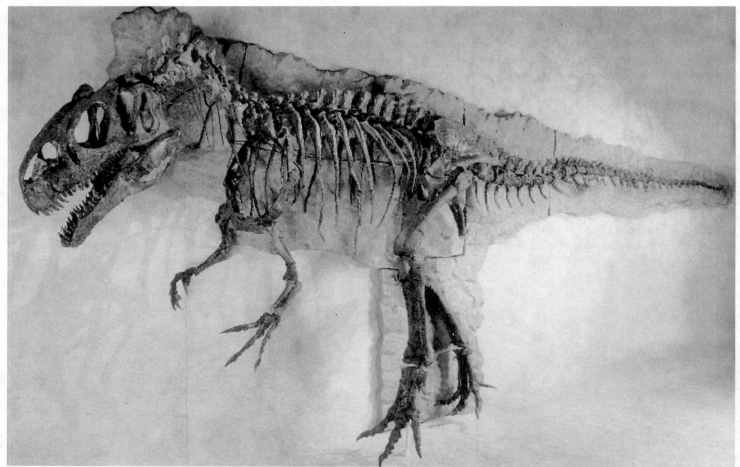

Skeleton of *Allosaurus fragilis* mounted at the Sauriermuseum Aathal in Switzerland. Nicknamed "Big Al Two," this specimen was found in 1996 in the Howe Stephens Quarry, at Howe Ranch, located in the Morrison Formation of northern Wyoming. Prepared by Ben Pabst, the skeleton measures 7.6 meters (about 25 feet) long and 2.5 meters (almost 8.5 feet) tall. The skull, too heavy for the mount, has been replaced by a cast and is displayed separately. Hailed as the best preserved *Allosaurus* specimen yet found, the skeleton is missing only "one claw and about ten small bones." Skin impressions are preserved near the base of the tail. Healed fracturing of the scapula, ribs, neck, and tail indicate that this individual survived some kind of an attack, perhaps from the whiplash tail of a *Diplodocus* or the tail spikes of a *Stegosaurus* (see Ayer 1999).

Skull of the *Allosaurus fragilis* specimen informally referred to as "Big Al Two."

Diagnosis of *A. fragilis*: Two large pneumatic recesses at base of lacrimal cornual process; ventral margin of jugal deflected ventrally at midlength, that margin not straight; metacarpal I proportionately shorter than in "*A. jimmadseni*" (Chure, in press, *see in* Holtz, Molnar and Currie 2004).

Diagnosis of "*A. jimmadseni*": Row of neurovas-cular foramina piercing that part of maxilla, forming medioventral wall of maxillary antorbital fossal in lateral aspect; axial intercentrum rotated dorsally, rim flared; obturator notch of pubis craniocaudally long, with cranially directed triangular process arising from its caudal and medioventral corner; spinous processes of proximal caudal vertebrae with accessory ossifications along their cranial and caudal margins, giving spines rectangular outline on lateral view, obscuring beveled cranial margin of spine; elongate proximolateral corner on pedal phalanx III-2 (Chure, in press, *see in* Holtz, Molnar and Currie 2004).

Comments: The type species *Allosaurus fragilis* is celebrated as the most abundant and best known of all Late Jurassic theropods; however, as noted in an abstract by Loewen, Sampson, Carrano and Chure (2003), the composition of this genus — to which 16 species have been referred over the past century and a quarter — has long been a topic of debate.

As related by Loewen *et al.*, the Cleveland-Lloyd Dinosaur Quarry (the bone accumulation at this site probably recording "more than one drought season," as determined by facies, taphonomy, and rare earth

Skeleton (cast) of *Allosaurus fragilis* mounted at the Earth Science Museum by Kenneth L. Stadtman under the direction of James A. Jenson.

Life restoration by artist Todd Marshall of the juvenile specimen to be named "Allosaurus jimmadseni."

Snout (BYU 2028) of *Allosaurus fragilis* in left lateral view, this specimen including a nasal having an ornamented crest and expanded pneumatic cavities, features unique to this specimen. Scale = 10 cm. (After Smith and Lisak 2001.)

element geochemistry analyses; see abstract for a poster by Suarez and Suarez 2004; see also Suarez 2004 for a report on the taphonomy and preservation of *A. fragilis* and *Stegosaurus* sp. at this quarry) in central Utah has preserved at least 47 individuals (comprising the largest sample yet collected pertaining to a large theropod species) of the type species *Allosaurus fragilis*. This material represents an ontogenetic series ranging from juvenile (body length less than one meter or approximately 3.4 feet) to adult (body length greater than 11 meters or about 37 feet), thereby offering unique insights pertaining to individual variation within this species. Most bones from this quarry

exhibit minor variation explained as ontogenetic and individual differences, while some cranial elements typically linked with sexual dimorphism or species variation display considerable variation. Considering this evidence, the authors pointed out, intraspecific variation must be taken into account when establishing taxonomic boundaries based on these elements.

Analysis by Loewen *et al.* of the Cleveland-Lloyd material, combined with variation data, suggested to them "that there are only two valid species of Allosaurus from the Morrison Formation," distinguished upon the basis of several characters (*e.g.*, morphology of jugal; that of *A. fragilis*, best represented by UUVP 6000 [see *D:TE* for photograph], jugal having strongly sigmoid ventral margin; that of *Allosaurus* sp. 2, best represented by DINO 11541 and NOR 693, jugal having relatively straight margin).

Also, Loewen *et al.* pointed out, the stratigraphic distribution of *Allosaurus* specimens supports the concept of two species being included in this genus, with A. sp. 2 occurring in the Salt Wash Member and later equivalents in the lower Morrison Formation, and *A. fragilis* restricted to the overlying Brushy Basin Member of that formation. The evidence, these authors concluded, "strongly suggests that these taxa are temporally, as well as morphologically, distinct."

Loewen *et al.* regarded the type species *Saurophaganax maximus*, considered by some paleontologists (*e.g.*, *Allosaurus* specialist David K. Smith 1998; see *SI*) to be referrable to *Allosaurus* as the species *A. maximus*, as belonging to its own distinct genus (see *Saurophaganax* entry).

In a later abstract for a poster, Baziak and Loewen (2004)—following the measurement and analysis of *A. fragilis* elements from the Cleveland-Lloyd Dinosaur Quarry, including the premaxilla, maxilla, dentary, nasal, lacrimal, and jugal—reconstructed the overall skull morphology of this taxon at different sizes, their study addressing the range of variation within the species and also tracking ontogenetic changes in proportions of the skull.

As suggested by Baziak and Loewen, dramatic changes in *A. fragilis* skull shape and width (observed in dorsal view) may reflect "structural changes in response to increased stress and loading associated with feeding," especially changes in the caudal region of the skull, which significantly increased more in width during ontogeny than did the rostal area. Possibly also linked to feeding stresses with increased size, the authors noted, are an increase in the size of the interdental plates. Furthermore, Baziak and Loewn suggested that the proportions and sizes of the orbit and the lateral temporal fenestra perhaps also contributed to strengthening the skull during growth.

Noting changes during ontogeny in all of the

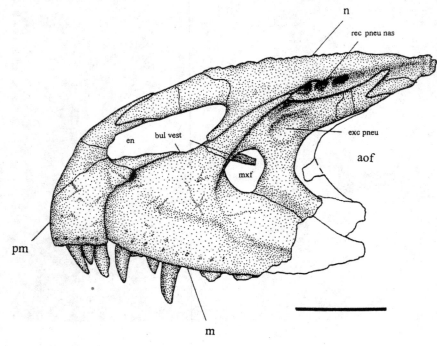

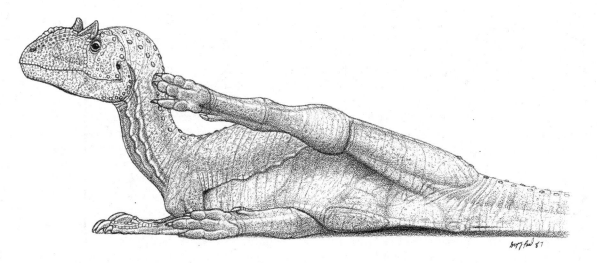

Life restoration by Gregory S. Paul of *Allosaurus fragilis* reclining.

studied elements, Baziak and Loewen found the height of the skull apparently increasing more dramatically than the width (as seen in other theropods). Also, pneumatic features of various skull elements (*e.g.*, maxilla, nasal, and lacrimal) "are quite variable in the pattern and size of pneumaticity" in the Cleveland-Lloyd sample, suggesting that changes in these features should not be regarded as entirely reliable criteria for taxonomic identification.

Pinegar, Loewen, Cloward, Hunter and Weege (2003), in an abstract for a poster, briefly described other theropod specimens that could represent a distinct species of *Allosaurus* other than *A. fragilis*. The recently excavated specimens — a large adult and a smaller individual interpreted as a conspecific juvenile — were yielded by the Meilyn Quarry in the Morrison Formation, near Medicine Bow, Wyoming. The fossils were recovered from a fine-grained sandstone showing depositional features indicating a fluvial system. The high degree of articulation of the juvenile specimen, plus preserved skin impressions, suggest that it was subjected to little or no fluvial transport when buried.

As Pinegar *et al.* reported, the juvenile specimen includes the following elements: Disarticulated skull remains including dentaries, surangulars, prearticulars, splenials, hyoids, jugals, quadratojugals, quadrates, squamosals, and pterygoids, right articular, maxilla, palatine, and vomer, left postorbital and prefrontal, and partial braincase; postcrania including most of vertebral column (missing axis and some midcaudal vertebrae), ribs, gastralia, shoulder girdles, forelimbs, right hindlimb; left side of body preserving skin impressions comprising small scales two to three millimeters in diameter (suggesting that allosaur juveniles possessed scaly integument, this being the most derived tetanuran specimen known to retain this character, otherwise present in more basal taxa, *e.g.*, *Carnotaurus*).

Pinegar *et al.* estimated the total length of this specimen to be approximately four meters (nearly 14 feet), with a height at the hips of one meter (about 3.4 feet) and skull length of 36 centimeters (almost 14 inches), these dimensions suggesting a juvenile individual. This interpretation is also supported by various size-independent morphological characters (*e.g.*, open cranial and postcranial sutures, proportions of forelimbs and hindlimbs, and juvenile bone surface texture).

Comparing this specimen with both juvenile and adult specimens collected from the Cleveland-Lloyd Dinosaur Quarry and also with the recently collected DINO 11541 (see above), Pinegar postulated that the Wyoming form is not *A. fragilis*, this assessment based mostly on the possession "of a relatively flat ventral jugal margin, and the shape of the caudal neural spines." Moreover, the above characters combined with another on the adult specimen — *i.e.*, pubis having wide obturator notch — are consistent with characters seen on DINO 11541, suggesting that these specimens "belong to a distinct species of *Allosaurus*.

A vertebrate paleontologist specializing in *Allosaurus* is David K. Smith. In 2001, Smith and co-author Francis J. Lisak reported on an unusual specimen (BYU 2028) of *Allosaurus*. As recounted by Smith and Lisak, this moderate-sized partial skull was discovered during the mid–1970s by Gene Day of the United States Bureau of Land Management in a conglomeratic boulder in the Mill Creek Dinosaur Trail region (see Lisak 1980) in the Salt Valley of the Paradox Basin, near Moab, Utah. The specimen was collected by James A. Jensen and Kenneth L. Stadtman of Brigham Young University from what they determined to be the upper part of the Brushy Basin Member of the Morrison Formation (K. Stadtman, personal communication to Smith and Lisak 2001).

BYU 2028 was later described by Lisak in his 1980 masters thesis, a document wherein Lisak referred the specimen to *Allosaurus* cf. *fragilis*. The preserved cranium includes the premaxillae, maxillae, nasals, vomer, and fragmentary lacrimals; the preserved mandibular parts comprise the dentary, surangular, prearticular, splenial, coronoid, and intercoronoid (*i.e.*, supradentary).

As Smith and Lisak observed, the majority of elements preserved in BYU 2028 are typical of the type species *Allosaurus fragilis* (see Madsen 1976). However, this specimen also presents some unusual characters "that increase the range of morphological variation for the species," these characters primarily concerning the nasal.

As described by Smith and Lisak, the nasal is long and has a narrow dorsal surface distinct from the part that contributes to the antorbital fenestra. The nasal is dorsally concave, this condition resulting from the presence of an ornamented ridge — similar to but less pronounced than that described for the tyrannosaurid *Alioramus* (see Kurzanov 1976*b*) — spanning the lacrimal to the rostral portion of the nasal. Also, the nasal pneumatic recess is expanded, invading the wall of the nasal and visible externally in a development similar to that described by the sinraptorid *Sinraptor* (see Currie and Zhao 1993).

Characters observed for the first time in BYU 2028 were utilized by Smith and Lisak — with a basis for comparison previous descriptions of *Allosaurus* and *Sinraptor* published by Madsen and Currie and Zhao, respectively — to document more fully some of the range of morphological and paranasal pneumatic variation in the skull of the genus *Allosaurus*. As the paranasal pneumatic system and nasal crest in BYU 2028 are more extensively developed than in other collected *Allosaurus* specimens, while most of the elements of that specimen are quite similar to those considered typical for the genus, the authors regarded that specimen as representing an adult *A. fragilis* individual.

Smith and Lisak concluded that BYU 2028 demonstrates "an increase in the amount of morphological and pneumatic variation seen within this taxon," thereby reinforcing the relative amount of variation to be found in different parts of the skull of the genus. Morphological variation may include the degree of development and ornamentation of cranial crests. Also, pneumatic cavities may vary from specimen to specimen, even from side to side in a single specimen (D. Chure, personal communication to Smith 1999). Smith and Lisak concluded that, as variation in pneumatic openings seem not to be related to ontogeny, the expanded openings in BYU 2028 must be associated with individual variation.

Later, Smith (2003), in a published abstract for a poster, further showed that a considerable amount of variation, not related to size, exists within some of the skull bones of *A. fragilis*. Smith (2003) documented this variation by comparing a number specimens recovered from the Dry Mesa Dinosaur Quarry, Cleveland-Lloyd Dinosaur Quarry, Como Bluff, Dinosaur National Monument, and an isolated site in eastern Utah. Material utilized in this study include a bisected specimen and a prepared endocranium from Cleveland-Lloyd, and also CT scans or a larger specimen from Dry Mesa. As Smith pointed out, the Cleveland-Lloyd braincases (as are other elements) are generally smaller than those recovered at other sites.

The following cranial differences in these specimens were observed by Smith (2003): Changes in orientation of paroccipital processes; arrangement of bones comprising basisphenoid recesses; allometric variation in pneumatic recesses in wall of basisphenoid (previously reported); differences in supraoccipital and parietal making up nuchal and parietal crests. Smith (2003) noted that the prootic, laterosphenoid, and opisthotic remain somewhat conservative. Although the information is limited, there seems to be but little nonsize-related endocranial variation.

According to Smith (2003), the variation noted in these specimens "is not a function of the geographic location, stratigraphic position, or size of the animal"; rather, these results reflect both functional and systematic implications. Moreover, a caudal deflection of the paroccipital processes would limit the lateral movement of the skull, at the same time allowing dorso-ventral movement at the occipital condyle.

Smith (2003) regarded all of the above mentioned material "as being derived from a single variable species, *Allosaurus fragilis*."

Rayfield (2004), in a published abstract, continued her research using finite element analysis (FEA; see *S3*) "to investigate the mechanical significance of sutures and regions of intracranial flexibility in [the] skulls" of large carnivorous dinosaurs such as *Allosaurus*. By means of a skull model illustrating the stress response to feeding, Rayfield was able to "compare the axis of distortion and orientation of stress and strain in the model to the degree of movement at actual sutural contacts in the real skull." This line of research allowed for constructing and later testing hypotheses detailing the effect of introducing patency or flexibility on mechanical performance.

Rayfield's study investigated "the correlation between stress environment, cranial strength, and sutural morphology and mobility" in the skull of *A. fragilis*. As Rayfield pointed out, the skulls of this and also other large theropods, while massive and capable of generating extremely powerful bite forces, have obvious sutures between many of the facial bones. Rayfield's analysis discovered that these sutures in

Allosaurus were seemingly "capable of accommodating stress and strain patterns generated during biting, although a dual-feeding regime may have been present."

As explained by Foster (2003) in an abstract for a poster, simplified models of ecosystems having "a fixed number of herbivorous species and a fixed amount of biomass transfer from prey to predator species" make possible several end-member patterns, the main variables of these patterns being "predator diversity, abundance, and specialization." These variables can take such patterns as "low predator diversity with equal abundance and low specialization, high diversity with equal abundance and high specialization, and high diversity with unequal abundance and mixed specialization."

Foster noted that in a more complex model, including approximate Morrison Formation predator-prey diversity ratios and within-group proportions of abundance for both predators and prey, the last of the above models best matches the situation in Late Jurassic North America. Morrison Formation theropods are relatively diverse, including 10 known genera as compared to a dozen herbivorous genera. *Allosaurus* accounts for almost two thirds of collected theropod specimens.

In both the simplified and more complex models, Foster stated, *Allosaurus*, the most common theropod of this fauna, must feed upon more prey species types than other theropods for "the modeled abundances to match those observed in the Morrison Formation." Both models suggested the Foster that this genus "was a generalized predator," while other theropod taxa were more specialized. Moreover, while such large forms as *Torvosaurus* and *Ceratosaurus* may have overlapped to some extent with *Allosaurus* in targeting prey species, smaller theropods such as *Ornitholestes* and *Coelurus* most likely sought out small, possibly nondinosaurian prey.

In a publicized abstract for a poster, Jennings (2004) reported on paleoenvironmental and taphonomic applications of geospacial technology at a new carbonate-mudstone dinosaur quarry, located on the Warm Spring Ranch, in the Morrison Formation, Thermopolis, Wyoming. Among the fossils recently yielded by this site are "dozens of shed *Allosaurus* teeth," plus a number of sauropod bones. The combination of dinosaur teeth, bones and footprints "led paleontologists to interpret the site as a record of predation activity," Jennings stated, "behavior not well documented in the literature."

Goodchild (2004), in another abstract for a poster, reported briefly on a specimen (WDC-TYA collection)—referred to *Allosaurus* sp.—being excavated, at the date of his writing, from a calcerous mudstone quarry in the Morrison Formation of north-central Wyoming. Remnants of small shells at this site, that author pointed out, indicate a lacustrian environment. Fragmentary material suggests also a smaller individual preserved at this site.

As reported by Goodchild, collected and prepared material to date includes a left premaxilla, scapulae, right fibula, dorsal vertebrae, a caudal vertebra, 2:1 left pes, and 1:1 and 1:2 right manus. Material currently remaining in the field includes a right dentary, left maxilla, and unidentified pedal elements.

According to Goodchild's estimates, this specimen would have a total length of eight meters (almost 28 feet). However, based upon the unfused zygapophysis of the preserved dorsal vertebra, this specimen, despite its large size, seemingly represents a subadult animal.

Goodchild noted that she allosaur teeth found near theropod rib fragments suggests cannibalism. Moreover, tooth marks are apparently present on the right scapula (WDC-TYA 58, this specimen having "a pathological surface on the glenoid fossa"); these could "be responsible for mechanical removal of the acromial process."

Note: The theropod skeleton showing in the photograph on page 32 of *S3* has been identified by paleontologist Brooks B. Britt as a juvenile of the not yet formally named new species "Allosaurus jimmadseni" (C. A. Miles, personal communication 2003).

Key references: Baziak and Loewen (2004); Currie and Zhao (1993); Foster (2003); Holtz, Molnar and Currie (2004); Jennings (2004); Kurzanov (1976*b*); Lisak (1980); Loewen, Sampson, Carrano and Chure (2003); Pinegar, Loewen, Cloward, Hunter and Weege (2003); Rayfield (2004); Smith (1998, 2003); Smith and Lisak (2001); Suarez (2004); Suarez and Suarez (2004).

†ALWALKERIA

Erratum: In 1987, Sankar Chattegee named and described the dinosaurian type species *Walkeria maleriensis* (see *D:TE*, in which the publication date was incorrectly given as 1986). Neglected, however, was the fact Chatterjee and Creisler (1994), after discovering that the name *Walkeria* was preoccupied (Fleming 1823) for a genus of bryozoan "moss animal," renamed this dinosaur *Alwalkeria*.

Key references: Chatterjee (1987); Chatterjee and Creisler (1994); Fleming (1823).

†AMARGASAURUS

Saurischia: Eusaurischia: Sauropodomorpha: Sauropoda: Eusauropoda: Neosauropoda: Diplodocoidea; Dicraeosauridae.

Life restoration by Berislav Krzic of the dicraeosaurid diplodocoid *Amargasaurus cazaui*.

Diagnosis of genus (as for type species): Cranial cervical vertebrae having extremely long, caudally curving neural spines, distal ends of neural spines lying dorsal to successive cervical vertebra; presacral vertebral count reduced to 11 cervicals, 11 dorsals (Upchurch, Barrett and Dodson 2004).

Comment: In their review of the Sauropoda, Upchurch, Barrett and Dodson (2004) rediagnosed the type species *Amargasaurus cazaui* (see *D:TE*).

Key reference: Upchurch, Barrett and Dodson (2004).

AMAZONSAURUS de Souza Carvalho, Avilla and Salgado 2003

Saurischia: Eusaurischia: Sauropodomorpha: Sauropoda: Eusauropoda: Neosauropoda: Diplodocoidea.

Name derivation: "[Brazilian] Amazon [Region]" + Greek *sauros* = "lizard."

Type species: *A. maranhensis* de Souza Carvalho, Avilla and Salgado 2003.

Other species: [None.]

Occurrence: Itapecuru Formation, Maranhão State, Brazil.

Age: Early to Middle Cretaceous (Aptian–Albian).

Known material/holotype: MN 4558-V and UFRJ-DG 58-R/9, two neural spines of dorsal vertebrae, MN 4559-V and MN s/no-V, two dorsal centra, UFRJ-DG 58-R/7, neural spine of proximal caudal vertebra, MN 4555-V, midcaudal vertebra, MN 4560-V, middistal caudal vertebra, MN 4556-V and UFRJ-DG 58-R/10, distal caudal vertebrae, UFRJ-DG 58-R/2, 58-R/3, 58-R/4, 58-R/5, and MN 4564-V, eight chevrons, UFRJ-DG 58-R/1, ilium, MN s/no-V, partial pubis, MN 4562-V, three ribs.

Diagnosis of genus (as for type species): Small sauropod characterized by straight and distally inclined

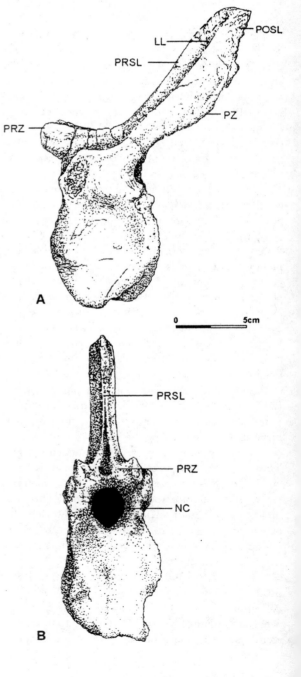

Amazonsaurus maranhensis, MN 4555-V, holotype midcaudal vertebra in A. left lateral and B. proximal views. (After de Souza Carvalho, Avilla and Salgado 2003.)

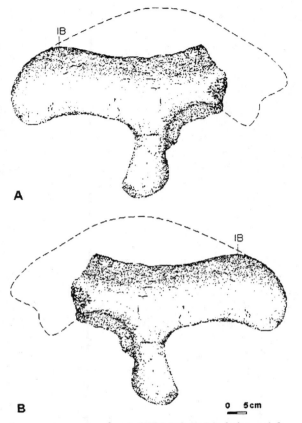

A

B

Amazonsaurus maranhensis, UFRJ-DG 58-R/1, holotype left ilium in A. lateral and B. medial views. (After de Souza Carvalho, Avilla and Salgado 2003.)

caudal neural spines, "lateral" laminae formed by spinoprezygapophyseal and postzygapophyseal lamina that, at least in proximalmost ones, bend proximally so that proximal surface of lamina is concave, distal surface convex (de Souza Carvalho, Avilla and Salgado 2003).

Comments: The type species *Amazonsaurus maranhensis* was founded upon various postcranial el-

ements (MN and UFRJ-DG collections; see above) recovered from the Itapecuru Formation, Itapecuru-Mirim County, Maranhão State, Parnaiba Basin (see Rossetti, Goe's and Truckenbrodt 2001), northern Brazil. It is significant as constituting the first sauropod dinosaur known from the Brazillian Lower Cretaceous (de Souza Carvalho, Avilla and Salgado (2003).

De Souza Carvalho *et al.* interpreted several features as autapomorphies of this taxon, including the following: Proximal caudal vertebrae having lateral laminae formed by coalescence of spinoprezygapophgyseal, postzygapophyseal, and (to a lesser extent) postzygodiapophyseal laminae.

This species was referred by the authors to the Diplodocoidea on the basis of numerous diplodocoid synapomorphies, including the following: High caudal neural arches (*e.g.*, see Calvo and Salgado 1995; Wilson and Sereno 1998); proximal caudal neural arches having spinoprezygapophyseal laminae on lateral aspect of neural spines. The open hemal canals, the authors noted, suggest that *Amazonsaurus* occupies a basal position within Diplodocoidea (*e.g.*, Calvo and Salgado; Upchurch 1998; Wilson 2002*a*).

As de Souza Carvalho *et al.* noted, the occurrence of this basal diplodocoid in the Aptian–Albian of northern Brazil constitutes evidence supporting the hypothesis of a South American–African dinosaur community including basal diplodocoids and titanosaurs (among sauropods), and carcharodontosaurids and spinosaurids (among theropods) (*e.g.*, see Calvo 1999).

Key references: Calvo (1999); Calvo and Salgado (1995); de Souza Carvalho, Avilla and Salgado (2003); Upchurch (1998); Wilson (2002*a*); Wilson and Sereno (1998).

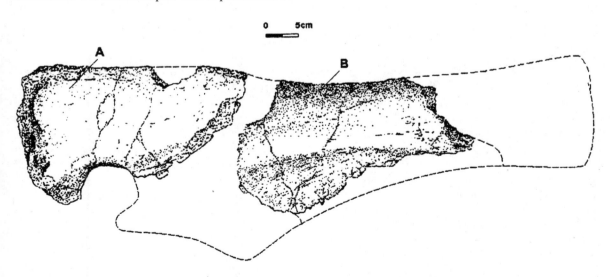

Amazonsaurus maranhensis, MN s/n°-V, holotype (reconstructed) pubis. (After de Souza Carvalho, Avilla and Salgado 2003.)

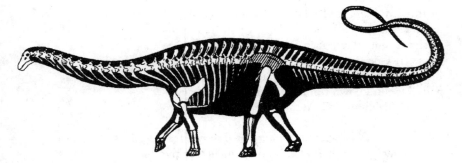

Amazonsaurus maranhensis, reconstructed skeleton based upon holotype material, oblique parallel lines indicating the preserved elements. (After de Souza Carvalho, Avilla and Salgado 2003.)

†AMMOSAURUS—(=?*Anchisaurus*)

Saurischia: Eusaurischia: Sauropodomorpha: Sauropoda: Prosauropoda: Anchisauria: Anchisauridae.

Diagnosis of genus (as for type species): Autapomorphies including the following: distal separation of transverse process and rib of caudosacral vertebra; ventral margin emargination of proximal portion of ischium (Galton and Upchurch 2004*a*).

Comments: In 1976, prosauropod specialist Peter M. Galton considered valid *Ammosaurus major*, a medium-sized (about four meters) type species erected by Othniel Charles Marsh (1891) on a partial skeleton (YPM 208) collected from a quarry near Manchester, Connecticut. Marsh (1889) originally referred this specimen to the genus *Anchisaurus*, the most complete referred skeleton (YPM 1883) of which had been excavated at the same site (see *D:TE*).

Although most subsequent authors have adopted Galton's acceptance of *Ammosaurus major* as a valid taxon, Yates (2004) recently challenged the validity of *A. major* in his recent reassessment of the genus *Anchisaurus* (see entry; see also, for example, Sereno 1999*a*). Yates, after reexamination of the holotypes of both *A. major* and the type species *Anchisaurus polyzelus*, observed that both specimens share a number of apomorphies that are not found in other closely related Sauropodomorpha (*e.g.*, foramen opening ventrally at base of second sacral rib; ilium having elongate preacetabular blade, twice as long as it is deep at base [also in *Kotasaurus yamanpalliensis*; see Yadagiri 2001]; pubic obturator fenestrae occupying most of obturator plate; flattened coplanar ischial shafts [also in many neosauropods; see Wilson and Sereno 1998; also in AM 41/109 and YPM 209, the latter juvenile individual referred to *A. major* by Galton 1986].

Yates (2004) found Galton's (1976) main reason for separating these genera to be the broader pes of *Ammosaurus*, noting that the ratios of proximal width to total length of the metatarsi of YPM 208, YPM 1883, and YPM 209 (measured as maximum dimension across all five metatarsals) are very close (0.66, 0.62, and 0.60, respectively). Yates attributed their differences to size between specimens, explaining other differences noted by Galton (1976) (*e.g.*, longer laterodistal groove on tibia of YPM 208; pubis of YPM 1883 with open obturator notch) as probably resulting from, respectively, severe craniocaudal crushing and the loss after death of the thin caudomedial rim of the obturator fenestra.

In their review of the Prosauropoda, Galton and Upchurch (2004*a*) addressed the issue of the possible synonymy of *Ammosaurus* with *Anchisaurus*, acknowledging that the allometry-related differences between *Anchisaurus* and *Ammosaurus* could suggest that they are congeneric. However, other nonage-related differences (*e.g.*, emarginated proximal portion of pubis in *Anchisaurus*, not *Ammosaurus*; reduced ungual on first pedal digit in *Anchisaurus*, not in *Ammosaurus*) suggested that it is premature to regard these taxa as congeneric, with "*Ammosaurus*" the adult stage. Additionally, the metatarsus in a one-meter long juvenile specimen of *A. major* is broad; that of the larger *Anchisaurus* is small (see Galton 1976).

Note: In a published abstract for a poster, Fedak 2004 stated that recently discovered basal sauropodomorph specimens from the earliest Jurassic McCoy Brook Formation sandstones in Nova Scotia, previously referred to *Ammosaurus* cf.— representing yearling, subadult, and adult ontogenetic stages — actually seem to represent a new taxon.

Key references: Fedak (2004); Galton (1976, 1986); Galton and Upchurch (2004*a*); Marsh (1889, 1891); Sereno (1999*a*); Wilson and Sereno (1998); Yadagiri (2001); Yates (2004).

†AMPELOSAURUS

Saurischia: Eusaurischia: Sauropodomorpha: Sauropoda: Eusauropoda: Neosauropoda: Macronaria: Titanosauriformes: Titanosauria: Lithostrotia.

Diagnosis of genus (as for type species): Dorsal vertebrae with neural arches and neural spines directed strongly caudodorsally at angle of almost 45 degrees to vertical (Upchurch, Barrett and Dodson 2004).

Comments: In their review of the Sauropoda, Upchurch, Barrett and Dodson (2004) rediagnosed the type species *Ampelosaurus atacis* (see *D:TE*).

Although this taxon has not yet been subjected to a cladistic analysis, Upchurch *et al.* noted that "The strongly procoelous centra throughout the caudal series, as well as several other derived characters, suggests that this form is a member of the advanced lithostrotian clade."

Key reference: Upchurch, Barrett and Dodson (2004).

Life restoration by Berislav Krzic of *Ampelosaurus atacis.*

†AMPHICOELIAS

Saurischia: Eusaurischia: Sauropodomorpha: Sauropoda: Eusauropoda: Neosauropoda: Diplodocoidea.

Diagnosis of genus (as for type species): Basal tubera having pendant lateral processes; pleurocoels of cervical vertebrae surrounded by well-marked fossa; neural spines of caudal dorsal vertebrae directed caudodorsally (unusual condition for Diplodocoidea); femur circular (rather than craniocaudally) compressed in cross section (Upchurch, Barrett and Dodson 2004).

Comment: In their review of the Sauropoda, Upchurch, Barrett and Dodson (2004) rediagnosed the type species *Amphicoelias altus* (see *D:TE*).

Key reference: Upchurch, Barrett and Dodson (2004).

†AMUROSAURUS

Ornithischia: Predentata: Genasauria: Cerapoda: Ornithopoda: Euornithopoda: Iguanodontia: Dryomorpha: Ankylopollexia: Styracosterna: Iguanodontoidea: Hadrosauroidea: Euhadrosauria: Hadrosauridae: Lambeosaurinae *incertae sedis.*

Type species: *A. riabinini* Godefroit and Kurzanov 1991.

Occurrence: Udurchukan Formation, Amur Region, Russia.

Age: Late Cretaceous (?"middle" to ?late Maastrichtian).

Holotype: AENM 1/12, associated left maxilla and dentary.

Diagnosis of genus (as for type species): Lambeosaurine characterized by the following autapomorphies: prominent median process between basipterygoid processes; sagittal crest particularly elevated on caudal portion of parietal, forming high, triangular, deeply excavated triangular process on occipital aspect of skull; crest separating squamosals separated along their entire height; caudal process of postorbital especially elongated, narrow, regularly convex upwardly; prefrontal forming at least half width of floor for supracranial crest; ulna and radius sigmoidal in lateral and cranial aspects (Godefroit, Bolotsky and Van Itterbeeck 2004).

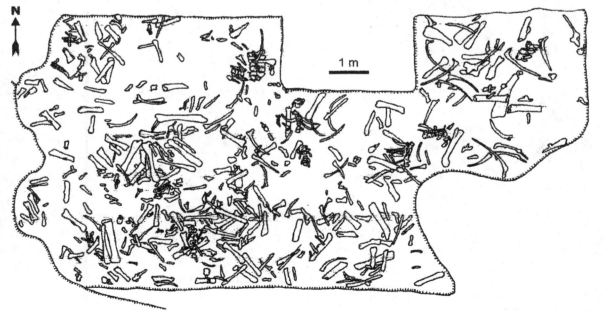

Sketch of bonebed at Blagoveschensk dinosaur locality showing remains, as discovered, of *Amurosaurus riabinini.* (After Godefroit, Bolotsky and Itterbeeck 2004.)

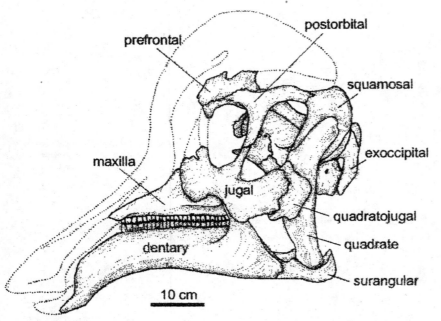

Amurosaurus riabinini, reconstructed skull including holotype AENM 1/12. (After Godefroit, Bolotsky and Itterbeeck 2004.)

Comments: In, Pascal Godefroit and Sergei M. [Mikhailovich] Kurzanov named and briefly described, in an abstract, *Amurosaurus riabini*, a large lambeosaurine type species established on a left maxilla and dentary (AENM 1/12) recovered from the Amur region of far eastern Russia (see *S2*).

More recently, Godefroit, Bolotsky and Van Vitterbeeck (2004) fully described *A. riabinini* based

upon numerous disarticulated bones collected from an Upper Cretaceous (apparently "middle" to late Maastrichtian, based on the presence of the angiosperm palynomorph *Wodehouseia spinata*; see Markevich and Bugdaeva 1997) bonebed at Blagoveschensk, in the Udurchukan Formation (Tasgayan Group; Markevich and Bugdaeva), Amur-Zeya Basin, Far Eastern Russia, this material collectively distinguishing Amurosaurus as "the most abundantly known dinosaur ever discovered on the Russian territory."

Godefroit *et al.* performed a cladistic analysis of *Amurosaurus* based upon 40 cranial, dental, and postcranial characters and 11 hadrosauroid taxa, and the nonhadrosaurid hadrosauroid *Bactrosaurus johnsoni* (revised by Godefroit, Dong, Bultynck, Li and Feng 1998; see *S1*) chosen for the outgroup. This analysis confirmed the monophyly of the Hadrosauridae and Hadrosaurinae. *Amurosaurus* was confirmed as a lambeosaurine, the genus exhibiting the following nine unambiguous synapomorphies of that subfamily: Length/minimal width ratio of parietal greater than 2 (1); hollow supracranial crest; frontal excluded from participation in orbital rim by postorbital-prefrontal joint; caudal portion of prefrontal horizontally oriented; rostral border of jugal angular straight; maxillary shelf developed; median carina of dentary teeth sinuous; deltopectoral crest of humerus strongly developed, extending down below midshaft; distal end of ilium tapering distally.

As shown by Godefroit *et al.*'s analysis, *Amurosaurus* occupies a comparatively basal position within the Lambeosaurinae, while sharing a sister-taxon relationship with a monophyletic clade comprising the "parasauroloph and corythosaur clade" (*i.e.*, the clades Parasaurolophini and Corythosaurini; see Brett-Surman 1989; Chapman and Brett-Surman 1990; also, see Horner, Weishampel and Forster (2004), "Systematics" chapter).

Moreover, Godefroit *et al.*'s cladogram demonstrated that the Lambeosaurinae originated in Asia, this group dominating late Maastrichtian dinosaur localities in eastern Asia, while apparently no longer being represented in western North American synchronous localities. However, as these authors pointed out, their analysis was based on the assumption of a late Maastrichtian age for the Blagoveschensk locality, a hypothesis requiring corroboration by further palynological analyses. Consequently, the observed differences between the Amur region (?late Maastrichtian) dinosaur faunas and the western North American "Lancian" (late Campanian to early Maastrichtian) faunas "may reflect temporal ambiguity rather than spacial differentiation."

Erratum: In *S2*, the species name for *Amurosaurus riabinini* was misspelled as *A.* "*riabini*."

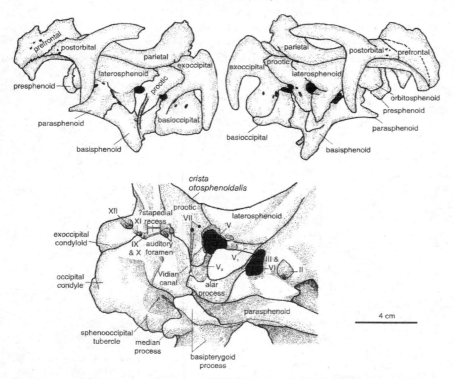

Amurosaurus riabinini, referred braincase (AENM 1/232) in (left) left and (right) right lateral views, (bottom) detail of right side. (After Godefroit, Bolotsky and Itterbeeck 2004.)

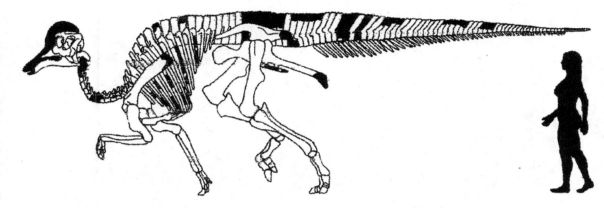

Amurosaurus riabinini, reconstructed skeleton including holotype skull (AENM 1/12). (After Godefroit, Bolotsky and Itterbeeck 2004.)

Life restoration of *Amurosaurus riabinini* drawn by Berislav Krzic, crest reconstructed following Godefroit, Bolotsky and Itterbeeck.

Key references: Brett-Surman (1989); Chapman and Brett-Surman (1990); Godefroit, Bolotsky and Van Vitterbeeck (2004); Godefroit, Dong, Bultynck, Li and Feng (1998); Horner, Weishampel and Forster (2004); Markevich and Bugdaeva (1997).

†ANATOTITAN—(See *Edmontosaurus*.)

†ANCHICERATOPS

Ornithischia: Predentata: Genusauria: Cerapoda: Chasmatopia: Marginocephalia: Ceratopsia: Neoceratopsia: Coronosauria: Ceratopsoidea: Ceratopsidae: Chasmosaurinae.

Notes: Farke (2004) reported on a chasmosaurine partial skull that had been collected in 1937 during the American Museum of Natural History–Sinclair Oil Company joint expedition to the Upper Cretaceous

(Campanian and early Maastrichtian) Almond Formation (Mesaverde Group) of the Rock Springs Uplift, in southwestern Wyoming. As Farke recounted, American Museum Paleontologist Barnum Brown (1938), in a popular article about this expedition, reported the discovery during this expedition of two ceratopsid skulls, of particular interest to him being one that was "fairly complete" [missing the frill] and "undoubtedly a new species—the first of its kind from this horizon." However, Brown never formally described this skull, nor did he assign it an AMNH catalogue number.

A search of the American Museum of Natural History vertebrate paleontology collections eventually located its only partial ceratopsid skull, AMNH 3652, which Farke posited is almost certainly the one mentioned by Brown. Later, Carpenter (1992*b*) tentatively referred this skull to *Anchiceratops* sp. based upon similarities perceived by that author between AMNH 3652 and recovered skulls of *Anchiceratops*. As Farke pointed out, however, Carpenter, not having access to the actual specimen, had to base his interpretation of AMNH 3652 on an archival field photograph that had been taken at an angle. Consequently, Farke noted, a number of discrepancies — "particularly in snout length, horn size, and other cranial proportions"—exist between the specimen and the drawing of it that Carpenter executed and published in his paper.

Farke published the first full and accurate description of AMNH 3652, which includes the partial skull (lacking the frill and parts of the right facial side, associated with indeterminate cranial and postcranial fragments), and also AMNH 3656, the second ceratopsid specimen mentioned by Brown, consisting of a fragmentary frill.

Farke referred AMNH 3652 to the ceratopsid subfamily Chasmosaurinae primarily based upon its possession of a premaxillary fossa (see Lehman 1990). Because it lacks the important diagnostic feature of the frill, Farke was not able to identity the specimen at either the generic or specific level. Farke ruled out

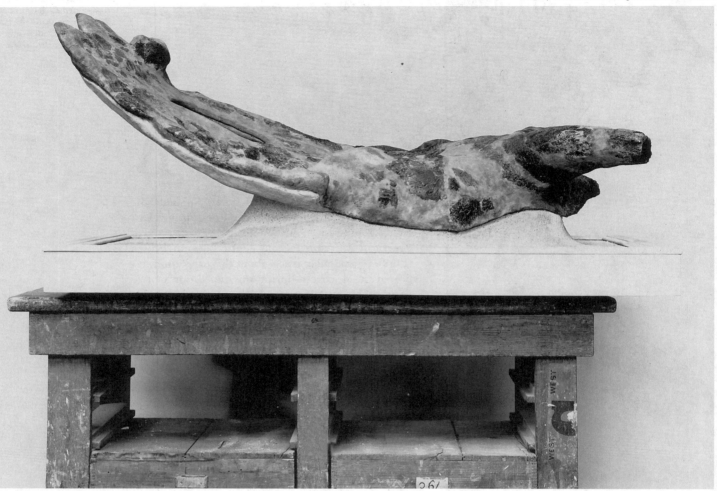

Frill and supraorbital horn-cores (FMNH P15004) of *Anchiceratops ornatus* (right lateral view).

Chasmosaurus as a potential generic candidate for AMNH 3652, as the former has relatively slender, re-curved brow horns (those of the latter being robust and procurved); both *Chasmosaurus* and *Pentaceratops* possess a premaxillary septal flange (lacking or possibly not preserved in AMNH 3652), thereby possibly also excluding *Pentaceratops*; also, the caudally positioned nasal horn (relative to caudal borders of external nares) of AMNH 3652 separates the specimen from both *Triceratops* and *Torosaurus*, leaving *Anchiceratops* and *Arrhinoceratops* as possible chasnosaurine candidates.

As Farke observed, the depth of the snout of AMNH 3652 is reminiscent of the holotype (ROM 796; see *D:TE* for photographs) of *Arrhinoceratops brachyops*. While the fragmentary condition of AMNH 3656 precludes positive identification of the specimen, "its prominent triangular marginal processes are most similar to morphology observed in some specimens of *Anchiceratops*." Moreover, the range of thickness of the parietal in the epoccipitals area of the *Anchiceratops ornatus* holotype (AMNH 5251) is up to

49 millimeters, while that around the squamosal epoc-cipitals are between 32 and 40 millimeters, these

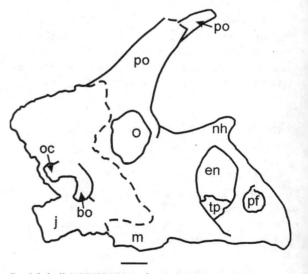

Partial skull (AMNH 3652) of an indeterminate chasmosaurine ceratopsian dinosaur, possibly referrable to *Anchiceratops*. Scale = 10 cm. (After Farke 2004.)

dimensions falling within the thickness range (40 to 62 millimeters) of AMNH 3565.

The belief of Brown that AMNH 3652 could represent a new taxon cannot be demonstrated, Farke stated, lacking as it does more complete material.

Farke concluded that, as AMNH 3652 and AMNH 3656 were found some 10 kilometers apart, they probably represent two individuals; moreover, as no elements common to both specimen were collected, "it cannot be determined if the specimens represent the same species."

Key references: Brown (1938); Carpenter (1992); Farke (2004); Lehman (1990).

†ANCHISAURUS — (=*Amphisaurus, Megadactylus, Yaleosaurus*; =?*Ammosaurus*)

Saurischia: Eusaurischia: Sauropodomorpha: Sauropoda: Prosauropoda: Anchisauria: Anchisauridae.

Diagnosis of genus (as for type species): Basal sauropod distinguished by the following autapomorphies: ventrally facing foramen for internal carotid artery situated in deep lateral notch of parabasisphenoid plate; distance between short basipterygoid processes less than width of basal tubera (Galton 1985*b*, 1985*c*); lateral pit on distal quadrate, just above articular condyle; large surangular foramen (dorsoventral diameter approximately 30 percent of dorsoven-

tral height of surangular) below apex of coronoid process; foramen opening ventrally at base of second sacral rib (first primordial sacral); large fenestra piercing third sacral (second primordial sacral); preacetabular blade of ilium long, narrow, at least twice as long as high at base; ischium with ventrally emarginate obturator plate; ischial blades flat, coplanar, obturator foramen occupying most of obturator plate of pubis (Yates 2004).

Comments: In 1865, Edward Hitchcock, Jr. established the new genus and species *Megadactylus polyzelus*, based on a partial postcranial skeleton (AC 41/109) from the Lower Jurassic Portland Formation, Newark Supergroup, Hartford Basin, Springfield, Massachusetts. As the generic name *Megadactylus* was preoccupied (Fitzinger 1843), Marsh (1885) later renamed referred this species to the new genus *Anchisaurus* (see *D:TE* for details and a photograph of the holotype).

Traditionally, this long-familiar taxon — a rather small and slender, facultatively bipedal (see Galton 1976) saurischian dinosaur — has been regarded by most workers (*e.g.,* Huene 1932; Romer 1956; Steel 1970; Galton 1976, 1990; Upchurch 1995; Sereno 1999*a*; Benton, Juul, Storrs and Galton 2000) as a member of the Prosauropoda. The placement of this genus within Prosauropoda has varied over the years, ranging from its interpretation as a basal prosauropod

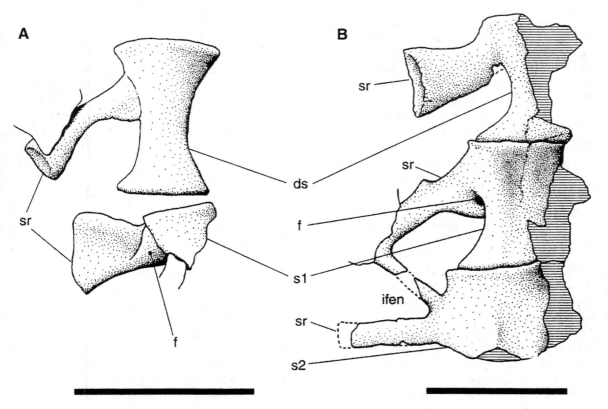

Referred sacra (ventral views) of *Anchisaurus polyzelsus,* A. YPM 1883 and B. YPM 208. Although this type species has traditionally been classified as a prosauropod, the phylogenetic analysis by Adam M. Yates (2004) found it to be the most basal known sauropod. Scale = 50 mm. (After Yates 2004).

Anchisaurus

Referred left postorbital bar (YPM 1883) of *Anchisaurus polyzelsus* in A. lateral and B. caudal views. According to Adam M. Yates, number 28.1 indicates derived character state that is a synapomorphy of Sauropoda (transverse width of ventral ramus of postorbital greater than its rostrocaudal width at midshaft; Wilson and Sereno 1998). Scale = 10 mm. (After Yates 2004).

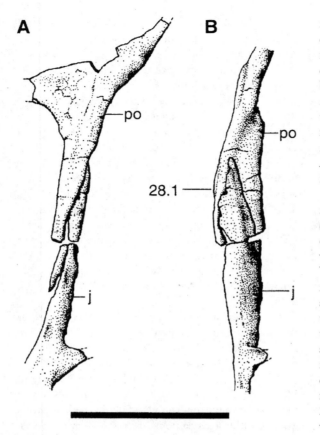

(Upchurch), to a sister taxon to the Melanorosauridae (Benton *et al.*, to the sister taxon of the Plateosauridae (Sereno).

A radically different view of *Anchisaurus*— one having somewhat severe implications for the clades Sauropodomorpha, Prosauropoda, and Sauropoda (see below)— was recently offered by Yates (2003*b*), in a recent paper wherein he described a new species of the prosauropod *Thecodontosaurus* (see entry). In that paper, Yates performed a phylogenetic analysis that found the Prosauropoda to be a paraphyletic assemblage of taxa. In Yates' study, *Anchisaurus polyzelus* fell somewhere in the middle of that array of taxa, its precise location differing among a number of most-parsimonious trees (see below).

Yates (2004) subsequently, in a reevaluation of *Anchisaurus*, also reassessed the validity of the type species *Ammosaurus major* (see *D:TE*), a type species founded by Marsh (1889) on a partial skeleton (YPM 208; see Galton 1976) collected from the same site— the Manchester Quarry— that yielded YPM 1883, thus far the most complete referred specimen of *A. polyzelus* yet recovered. Although most workers (following Galton 1976) have regarded Ammosaurus as a valid genus, others (*e.g.*, Sereno) have considered *A. polyzelus* and *A. major* to be conspecific.

In reexamining both type species, Yates (2004) observed that both YPM 1883 and YPM 208 share a number of apomorphies that are not found in other closely related sauropodomorphs, these including the following: Foramen opening ventrally at base of second sacral rib; ilium having elongate preacetabular blade, twice as long as it is deep at base (also in *Kotasaurus yamanpalliensis*; see Yadagiri 2001); pubic obturator fenestrae occupying most of obturator plate; flattened coplanar ischial shafts (found in many neosauropods; see Wilson and Sereno 1998; also in AM 41/109 and YPM 209, the latter a juvenile specimen referred by Galton 1986 to *A. major*).

According to Yates (2004), Galton's (1976) primary criterion for separating *Ammosaurus* from *Anchisaurus* was the broader pes of the former genus. According to Yates (2004), however, ratios of proximal width to total length of the metatarsi of YPM 208, YPM 1883, and YPM 209, "measured as the maximum dimension across all five metatarsals," are actually quite close (0.66, 0.62, and 0.60, respectively), their differences attributable to size differences between these specimens (metatarsal III in the three specimens measuring, respectively, 120, 98, and 48 millimeters in length). Noting two other differences cited by Galton (1976), Yates (2004) stated that the first— longer laterodistal groove on tibia of YPM 208— can be explained as probably the result of severe craniocaudal crushing, and the second— pubis of YPM 1883 having open obturator notch— probably by "the postmortem loss of the thin, caudomedial rim of the obturator fenestra."

Therefore, Yates (2004) concluded that "all sauropodomorph specimens from the Manchester Quarry, as well as the holotype of *Anchisaurus polyzelus* from Springfield, Massachusetts, represent different sized individuals of a single species," *A. major* being consequently regarded by that author as a junior synonym of *A. polyzelus* (however, see Galton and Upchurch 2004*a*, below).

As Yates (2004) pointed out, *Anchisaurus polyzelus* had been previously placed within the Prosauropoda based upon a number of characters (*e.g.*, narrow, straplike ventral process of squamosal, ventrolateral rotation of distal condyles of first phalanx of manual digit I; see Sereno). However, the derived states for these characters are also found in basal sauropodomorphs (*i.e.*, *Saturnalia tupiniquim* and *Thecodontosaurus* spp.) that seemingly diverged before the Prosauropoda–Sauropoda dichotomy.

In reexamining the material referred to *Anchisaurus polyzelus*, Yates (2004) found that this species shares the following derived (and previously unrecognized) characteristics with the Sauropoda: Tooth enamel having wrinkled surface (see Wilson and Sereno; Wilson 2002*a*), not previously recognized in *A. polyzelus*, most of the exposed enamel apparently

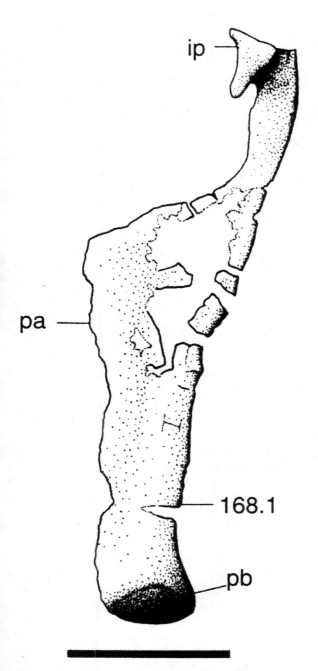

ip

pa

168.1

pb

Referred right pubis (YPM 1883) of *Anchisaurus polyzelsus* in caudal view. According to Andrew M. Yates (2004), number 168.1 indicates derived character state that is a synapomorphy of Sauropoda (minimum transverse width of pubic apron less than 40 percent of width across iliac peduncles of ilium). Scale = 50 mm. (After Yates 2004).

1998; Wilson and Sereno; Wilson); exclusion of frontal from supratemporal fossa (Gauthier; Upchurch 1998; Wilson and Sereno; Wilson); absence of quadrate foramen; ventral margin of braincase V-shaped, with lowered basal tubera and raised parasphenoid rostrum; deep U-shaped fossa opening caudally between basal tubera; transverse notch bounded by unfinished, spongy bone between basioccipital and basisphenoid components of each basal tuber; loss of well-defined fossa on distal flexor surface of humerus; manus shortened relative to rest of forelimb, comprising less than 40 percent of humerus plus radius (polarity reversed from Sereno, Forster, Rogers and Monetta 1993); pubic apron narrowed relative to pubic basin; flattened ischial blades (Wilson and Sereno; Wilson); caudolateral process of distal tibia failing to extend lateral to craniolateral corner of distal tibia; calcaneum reduced relative to astragalus.

Performing a cladistic analysis in which *Anchisaurus* placed as the most basal known member of Sauropoda, Yates (2004) also found that a number of other taxa traditionally regarded as prosauropods lie outside of Prosauropoda, either as more basal members of Sauropodomorpha or as members of Sauropoda (see "Systematics" chapter; also Yates 2003*b*).

That author noted, however, that YPM 1883, the smaller of the above mentioned Manchester Quarry specimens (femur 211 millimeters in length) possesses trunk vertebrae with closed neurocentral sutures, indicating that the individual was either mature or approaching maturity when it died (see Brochu 1996). Therefore, the larger animal represented by YPM 208 is most likely an adult. "Thus, despite its basal position," Yates (2004) stated, "the species is almost half the size that is estimated for the common ancestor it shared with all other sauropods." Yates' (2004) reassignment of Anchisaurus to the Sauropoda and his revision of Sauropodomorpha have not, however, been accepted by other sauropodomorph workers (*e.g.*, P. M. Galton, personal communication 2004).

In their 2004 review of the Prosauropoda, Galton and Upchurch reaffirmed the prosauropod status of *Anchisaurus*, referring the family Anchisauridae to a new and more encompassing clade, the Anchisauria (see "Systematics" chapter). At the same time, these authors at least tentatively preferred retaining *Ammosaurus* (see entry) as a genus distinct from *Anchisaurus*.

Fedak (2003), in an abstract, briefly reported on a new reconstruction and description of the braincase of *A. polyzelus* (YPM 1883, collected in 1883), based upon comparisons with the braincases of the prosauropods *Thecodontosaurus* (2192), "*Sellosaurus*" [=*Plateosaurus*; see entry] (SNMS 12667), and *Plateosaurus* (AMNH 6810) (full details of this study presumably to be published at a later date).

having been lost in preparation; procumbent maxillary and dentary teeth (Gauthier 1986; Upchurch 1998); loss of antorbital fossa from rostroventral corner of lacrimal (modified from Upchurch 1998; Wilson and Sereno; Wilson); transversely expanded ventral ramus of postorbital (Wilson and Sereno; Wilson); lower temporal fenestra extending under orbit for more than 25 percent of its length (Upchurch 1995,

As chronicled by Fedak (who, as do most workers, regards *Anchisaurus* as a prosauropod), the skull of *A. polyzelus* seems to have been separated into several pieces shortly after its recovery, a transverse fracture separating the caudal fourth from the rest of the skull. The skull was subsequently repaired, the two major pieces being attached along the dorsal elements of the skull, although a ventral wedge of bone rostral to this fracture was not reattached (current whereabouts unknown). However, this wedge "affects the majority of the basisphenoid and the posterior area of the left mandibular ramus." Fedak also noted that (*contra* earlier reports) the basipterygoid processes have not been preserved in this skull; consequently, "the often-cited 'small basipterygoid processes' cannot be reliably demonstrated."

Incorporating the above-cited new data, Fedak observed that the preserved braincase elements of *A. polyzelus* are apparently similar to those seen in other well-known "prosauropod" taxa. That author further noted that, while many visible sutures suggest that YPM 1883 represents a juvenile animal, it will require histological analysis to determine definitive ontogenetic age assessment of the specimen.

As Fedak concluded, the above observations have important implications regarding Sauropodomorph phylogenetic hypotheses. Removal of a feature formerly regarded as a major apomorphy of *Anchisaurus* implies that the validity of this genus necessitates clarification in future work. Moreover, the condition of this braincase offers "important comparative material for the upcoming description of new prosauropod material from Nova Scotia and future studies of *Ammosaurus* or *Massospondylus*, the other prosauropod genera previously reported from North American deposits."

Key references: Benton, Juul, Storrs and Galton (2000); Brochu (1996); Fedak (2003); Galton (1976, 1985*b*, 1985*c*, 1990); Galton and Upchurch (2004*a*); Gauthier (1986); Hitchcock (1865); Huene (1932); Marsh (1885, 1889); Romer (1956); Sereno (1999*a*); Steel (1970); Upchurch (1995, 1998); Wilson (2002*a*); Wilson and Sereno (1998); Sereno, Forster, Rogers and Monetta (1993); Yadagiri (2001); Yates (2003*b*, 2004).

†ANDESAURUS

Saurischia: Eusaurischia: Sauropodomorpha: Sauropoda: Eusauropoda: Neosauropoda: Macronaria: Titanosauriformes: Titanosauria *incertae sedis*.

Diagnosis of genus (as for type species): Autapomorphy of caudal neural spines twice height of their centra (Upchurch, Barrett and Dodson 2004).

Comment: In their review of the Sauropoda, Upchurch, Barrett and Dodson (2004) rediagnosed the basal titanosaurian type species, *Andesaurus delgadoi* (see *D:TE*).

As Upchurch *et al.* pointed out, it is very unusual among Sauropoda for titanosaurians to find caudal dorsal, sacral, or proximal caudal neural spines having lengths of more than 1.5 times the height of the centrum height.

Key reference: Upchurch, Barrett and Dodson (2004).

†ANKYLOSAURUS

Ornithischia: Predentata: Genasauria: Thyreophora: Thyreophoroidea: Eurypoda: Ankylosauria: Ankylosauridae: Ankylosaurinae.

Diagnosis: Largest known ankylosaurid, up to 6.25 meters (about 22 feet) in length; premaxillae expanded laterally by internal sinuses, crowding external nares to lateral sides; maximum width of maxillary tooth rows equal to width of premaxillary beak; external nares opposite first maxillary tooth; large, triangula osteoderm fused to postorbital and squamosal, caudodorsolaterally directed; large triangulat osteoderm fused to jugal and quadratojugal, caudoventrolaterally directed; cranial ornamentation of large, flat polygons (including large, diamond-shaped internatial); sharp supraorbital osteoderms continuous with squamosal osteoderm; greatest number of cheek teeth of all ankylosaurids (34-35/35-36); quadrate process of pterygoid laterally (not caudolaterally) directed; cervical half-ring comprising three keeled plates, outermost with laterally projecting keel; body armor including relatively smooth textured plates, sharp edge or lower keel along one margin (Carpenter 2004).

Comments: *Ankylosaurus*, among the largest of known ankylosaurs, has long been one of the more commonly depicted armored dinosaurs in popular books about these extinct animals. Barnum Brown named the type species *Ankylosaurus magniventris* in 1908 and described its armor, not much of which had been preserved (see *D:TE*).

Recently, Ford (2002) reexamined the armor of *A. magniventris* in an attempt to produce a more accurate life restoration of this long established dinosaur, using as a basis the holotype specimen (AMNH 5859; see below), Brown's original description, and also as comparative references (to "fill in the gaps in the missing armor of *Ankylosaurus*") the more completely known armor of related taxa having similar armor (*e.g.*, *Euoplocephalus tutus*).

Ford's new life restoration of *Ankylosaurus*, including "corrections and additions to Brown's account," resulted in the following details of the armor: Two cervical rings with three sets of scutes; large, flat

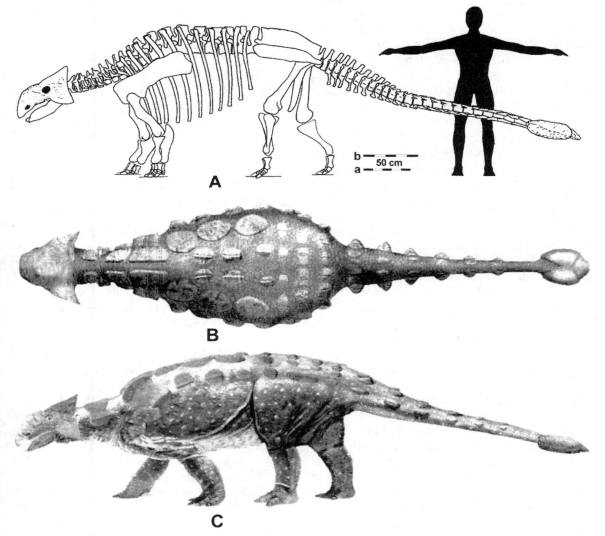

Skeletal reconstruction (A) and life restoration, in (B) dorsal and (C) left lateral; views), of *Ankylosaurus magniventris* by Kenneth Carpenter. (For larger specimen CMN 8880, use scale bar a., for AMNH 5214 scale bar b.) (After Carpenter 1984).

medial and primary scutes, ridge facing dorsally toward midline of body; large, triangular secondary scute; pectoral region having similar large, flat scutes with larger, longer secondary or lower tertiary scute over foreleg; body scutes suboval oval, ridge near middle of scute; pelvic shield possibly covering pelvis, as in "Polacanthidae" (a group no longer considered valid see "Systematics" chapter) as "pelvis forms a stiff unmoving area"; smaller scutes similar to large pectoral secondary/lower tertiary scute continuing along side of body and onto tail; medial caudal scutes possibly oval, continuing to tail club.

Subsequent to the publication of Ford's new restoration, ankylosaur specialist Kenneth Carpenter (2004) published a thorough redescription of *Ankylosaurus magniventris* based upon the following specimens: AMNH 5895 (holotype), the dorsal part of the skull, vertebrae (five cervicals, 11 dorsals, and three caudals), the right scapulodcoracoid, ribs, and dermal armor, recovered in 1906 by Peter Kaisen, a collector

for Brown, from badlands in the Hell Creek Formation of Garfield County, Montana (see *D:TE*); AMNH 5214, a complete and mostly uncrushed skull including both mandibles, six ribs, seven caudal vertebrae with associated tail club (known only in this specimen), humeri, the left ischium, left femur, right fibula, and dermal armor, collected in 1910 by Brown and Kaisen from the Scollard Formation of Alberta, Canada; AMNH 5866, 77 dermal plates and smaller osteoderms, from the Lance Formation of Niobrara County, Wyoming; CCM V03, a section of fused caudal vertebrae, from high the Hell Creek Formation, Powder River County, Montana; and CMN (formerly NMC) 8880, a poorly preserved and distorted skull (the largest skull yet referred to *Ankylosaurus*) with left mandible, collected in 1947 by Charles M. Sternberg and T. P. Channey from the Scollard Formation of Alberta.

Describing this taxon, Carpenter noted that *Ankylosaurus* has a "long, low skull having very prominent cranial 'horns' that project laterally or dorsolaterally," possessing body armor including "a large half-ring that sat across the base of the neck and shoulders and a large, low tail club."

Carpenter described the armor of *Ankykosaurus* as follows: Osteoderms (present in AMNH 5895 and AMNH 5866), compared with those of *Euoplocephalus*, having "remarkably smooth texture"; left cervical-scapular half-ring (in AMNH 5895) comprising three plates fused along their margins, smallest plate fused medially, largest laterally; all plates keeled, most prominent of these projecting laterally from largest plate; no evidence for underlying bone band (as found in *Saichania*; see Maryańska 1977); all traces of sutures obliterated by fusion; assumed cranial edge of armor belt comparatively straight, caudal side angled; when paired, wide, inverted V-shaped gap (probably filled with small ossicles for allowing neck movement) created dorsally on caudal side of shoulders; armor belt wider than half width of skull (suggesting it is equivalent to second cervical ring of other ankylosaurids), width considerably greater than can be accommodated by only neck (suggesting position at base of neck and onto shoulders); large body plates, unusually flat but with sharp edge or keel along one side, unique, probably occurring on back; dorsoventrally compressed pointed plates resembling plates along sides of tail in *Saichania*, probably similarly distributed; oval keeled plates possibly on dorsal surface of tail and sides of limbs; variety of small, irregular osteoderms and ossicles probably occurring around and among larger plates.

The preserved tail club in AMNH 5214 (see Coombs 1978a; S2) is a quite large structure. However, taking into account the considerable variety in know shape in the tail clubs of the ankylosaurid *Euoplocephalus* (Coombs 1995), Carpenter found no reason to assume that the tail club belonging to AMNH 5214 is typical for the genus *Ankylosaurus*. As Carpenter noted, the preserved knob of *Ankylosaurus* comprises "a pair of major plates laterally, a midline row of minor plates ventrally, and a terminal pair of minor plates," with the knob belonging to Coombs' (1995) "oval-round category," resembling most closely a specimen housed at the Royal Tyrrell Museum of Palaeontology. Consequently, the considerable knob shape variety seen in *Euplocephalus* and presumably *Ankylosaurus* "makes the head-mimicry hypothesis for the tail club by Thulborn (1993) very doubtful."

Published with Carpenter's redescription of *A. magniventris* was his own revised skeleton reconstruction and life restoration of this species (differing in various details from Ford's), based upon the above mentioned specimens.

Key references: Brown (1908); Carpenter (2004); Coombs (1978a, 1995); Ford (2002); Maryańska (1977); Thulborn (1993).

†ANTARCTOSAURUS—(=?*Campylodoniscus*)

Saurischia: Eusaurischia: Sauropodomorpha: Sauropoda: Eusauropoda: Neosauropoda: Macronaria: Titanosauriformes: Titanosauria: Lithostrotia.

Age: Late Cretaceous (late Coniacian–early Santonian).

Holotype of *A. wichmannianus*: MACN 6904, incomplete cranium and mandible, rib fragments, left scapula, incomplete right humerus, two fragments of distal radius, fragment of proximal end of ulna, seven metacarpals (two incomplete), phalanx, fragment of ilium, almost complete right ischium, part of left ilium, fragment of pubis, left femur, left fibula, five left metacarpals, pedal phalanges.

Diagnosis of genus (provisional): Femur straight, slim, cranial articulation vaulted, fourth trochanter somewhat above middle of bone (Powell 2003).

Diagnosis of *A. wichmannianus*: Skull high caudally, orbits large, muzzle wide, straight and broad symphyseal region perpendicular to mandibular rami; broad, short parietal and frontal; upper temporal fenestra reduced, partially open towards dorsal side; triangular basipresphenpoid complex wide, short; foramen for nerves IX to XI separated from fenestra ovalis; basipterygoid process long, in form of bar, very divergent; basioccipital tuberosities separated; paroccipital processes long and recurved (as in *Saltasaurus*); scapular blade narrow; supraglenoid regions wide; axis of lamina nearly perpendicular to major axis of supraglenoid part of scapula; ischiadic lamina narrow, expanded distally; pubic peduncle well developed; tibia having stout articular ends; fibula with lateral tuberosity formed by two parallel rugosities parallel to long axis of the bone (Powell 2003).

Diagnosis of *A. giganteus*: Femur much longer than in other known "titanosaurids," more slender than in *A. wichmannianus*; caudal expansion of femur relatively narrow; prominent fourth trochanter, located near middle of bone; caudal vertebrae short, having broad, convex ventral surface (Powell 2003).

Comments: In his monograph on the "titanosaurids" of South America, Jaime Eduardo Powell (2003) related how the type species *Antarctosaurus wichmannianus* was founded upon cranial and postcranial remains (MACN 6904) discovered and collected in 1912 by Dr. R. Wichmann in the Río Colorado Formation (possibly Anacleto Member), Neuquén Group (see Bonaparte and Gasparini 1979; see also see Leanza, Apesteguía, Novas and Fuente 2004, for a review of the Cretaceous terrestrial beds from the Neuquén basin and their tetrapod assemblages), on the south bank of the Río Negro, southwest of the city of General Roca, El Cuy Department, Rio Negro Province, Argentina. Wichman, who published on this material in 1916, gave the material (comprising "numerous bones of a dinosaur represented by a cranium, bones of the limbs, vertebrae and ribs") to General Roca, after which many other elements were found relating to this species. Following the transfer of most of these remains to the collections of the Director General of Mines, Museo Argentino de Ciencias Naturales "B" Rivadavia (Argentine Museum of Natural Sciences Bernardino Rivadavia), they were studied and described by Friedrich von Huene (1929).

As told by Powell, no plans of notes pertaining to the discovery site were found that might offer information as to the condition of the material or the degree of association of these remains; consequently, it is not possible to verify which postcranial elements referred by Huene to *A. wichmannianus* actually belong to the skull allocated to that species.

Powell pointed out that the locality where *Antarctosaurus* was discovered is historically important, being the leading site in this region that has yielded dinosaur fossils. As early as 1882, A. Doering published a mention of "a fragment of gigantic bone and other different things originating on the first lower terrace" of the south bank of the Río Negro, near Fresno Menocó. The next year, these specimens were given to Captain Jorge Rohde, most likely during the 1879 campaign of General Roca in the Desert. While not identified as such, these bones were probably of dinosaurian origin, Powell pointed out, "because geographic, geomorphologic and lithologic data presented by Doering" suggest that these specimens are of Late Cretaceous age and came from the same area. Captain Rohde gave a number of boxes, containing some of the fossils collected at "Fuerta Roca," to Argentinian naturalist, paleontologist, and anthropologist Florentino Ameghino, among them "some pieces of a gigantic dinosaur."

Although sauropod specialist Paul Upchurch (1999) found the affinities of *Antarctosaurus* to lie more with the Nemegtosauridae than the "Titanosauridae" (that author regarding the Nemegtosauridae as a family nestled within Diplodocoidea rather than Titanosauria; see "Systematics" chapter and *Antarctosaurus* entry, S2; see also Wilson and Upchurch 2003; Upchurch, Barrett and Dodson 2004), Powell retained this genus in its traditional titanosaurid classification.

Powell justified this assessment in noting that the cranium of *Anarctosaurus* is similar to that of *Saltasaurus* (e.g., both genera sharing long paroccipital processes, a unique character among all other saurischians). However, important differences between

A. wichmannianus and *Saltasaurus loricatus*, and probably also *Neuquensaurus australis*, seemingly indicate that the former species is a more primitive "titanosaurid." For example, the basipterygoid processes in *A. wichmannianus* are in the form of cylindrical bars, this being a common feature among the Sauropoda. Consequently, the L-shaped laminar processes found in *S. loricatus* may be interpreted as a derived character.

Also in *W. wichmannianus*, the incoming foramen of the internal carotid is located lateral and caudal to the pterygoid process, similar to *Diplodocus* (see Berman and McIntosh 1987), but different from *Saltasaurus*, the latter exhibiting the more derived condition; the basipresphenoidal complex differs from that in *Saltasaurus*; and the supratemporal opening is upwardly directed (the derived condition of being dorsally closed in *Saltasaurus*).

In redescribing *A. wichmannianus*, Powell observed that this species differs from such titanosaurs as *Argyrosaurus*, *Saltasaurus*, *Neuquensaurus*, and *Laplatasaurus* [=*Titanosaurus* of his usage] *araukanicus* in having a relatively narrow scapular blade relative to a well-developed proximal expansion of the scapula, the two comprising a right angle. In lacking a medial muscular attachment to the most narrow part of the scapula and on its inner face near the craniodorsal edge (present in *Saltasaurus*), *A. wichmannianus* resembles *Argyrosaurus* and *L. araukanicus*. In having its tuberosity formed by two parallel rugosities, the fibula of *A. wichmannianus* is morphologically similar to that of *Argyrosaurus*.

As Powell pointed out, the long bones of the forelimb in *A. wichmannianus* are poorly preserved and very incomplete, making them useless for comparison or diagnosis. Therefore, that author considered it inappropriate "to assign to this genus specimens based solely on isolated elements such as the humerus" (e.g., the fragmentary specimens referred to this species by Casamiquela, Corbalan and Franquesa 1969). Furthermore, Powell regarded Huene's referral of an astragalus and calcaneum to *A. wichmannianus* as doubtful, noting that the calcaneum has not yet been documented, and the element identified as such by Huene could also be an astragalus belonging to a smaller individual. Likewise, Powell stated, the astragalus assigned to the holotype of *A. wichmannianus* seems to be much too small relative to the tibia.

Powell also reevaluated two other species that have been referred to *Antarctosaurus—Antarctosaurus giganteus*, established by Huene (1929) on two femora, two fragments of a pubis, the distal end of a tibia, two incomplete caudal vertebrae, and some indeterminable fragments (MLP 26-316), collected from the then Plottier Member (see Pascual, Bondesio, Schillaro

Yane, Vucetich and Gasparini 1978) of the Upper Cretaceous [now Plottier Formation, belonging to the Rio Neuquén Formation (now Subgroup), dated as of late Coniacian–early Santonian age; see Leanza, Apesteguía, Novas and Fuente 2004], Aguada del Caño, north of China Muerta, Department of Confluencia, Neuquén Province, Argentina; and *Antarctosaurus brasiliensis*, established by Arid and Vizotto (1971) on an incomplete though well-preserved left femur (FFCL GP-RN 2) from the Baurú Formation, Ruta Estatal Barretos-São Jose do Río Preto, Brazil, with a well-preserved, incomplete right humerus and incomplete dorsal vertebra (FFCL GP-RD3 and 4, respectively) referred to this species.

A. giganteus, characterized by its great size, was regarded by Van Valen (1969) as simply a larger ontogenetic stage of *A. wichmannianus*, an evaluation rejected by Bonaparte and Gasparini based upon both morphological differences and also the different stratigraphic units from which these species came. Powell also regarded *A. giganteus* as a valid species, noting that superficial resemblances to other titanosaurids could be the result of convergence, at the same time suggesting that it could represent a new genus.

Powell found the material referred to *A. brasiliensis* to be insufficient either in establishing a new species or referring it confidently to *Antarctosaurus* or any other "titanosaurid genus," that author pointing out that no dorsal vertebrae are known either for *A. wichmannianus* or *A. giganteus*. Moreover, the morphological features of the humerus are not, in that author's opinion, diagnostic. Therefore, Powell regarded this species as a *nomen dubium* (as did Upchurch *et al.*).

In a paper describing *Bonitasaura* (see entry), a titanosaur having what appears to be a high, keratinous "beak," Apesteguía (2004) addressed the idea proposed by Upchurch that the skull referred to *Antarctosaurus* is either a chimera comprising elements from different sauropod lineages, or belongs to a diplodocid that had acquired mostly convergently a postcranium resembling that of derived titanosaurs (see *S2*). As suggested by Apesteguía, the presence in *Antarctosaurus* of an extensive edentulous area—yet one not possessing a tall "beak"—suggests "that incipient guillotine-like structures could have developed in other titanosaurs." Additionally, the discovery of *Bonitasaura* sheds "light on the systematic affinities of *Antarctosaurus*, showing that its bizarre lower jaw features are not unusual in advanced titanosaurs, which can bear a squared snout convergent to that of diplodocids, as originally proposed" (*e.g.*, Huene; Calvo 1994; Salgado 2001).

Key references: Apesteguía (2004); Arid and Vizotto (1971); Berman and McIntosh (1978); Bonaparte and Gasparini (1979); Casamiquela, Corbalan and

Franquesa (1969); Doering (1882); Huene (1929); Pascual, Bondesio, Schillaro Yane, Vucetich and Gasparini (1978); Powell (2003); Uliana and Dellapa Upchurch (1999); Upchurch (1999); Van Valen (1969); Wichmann (1916); Wilson and Upchurch (2003); Upchurch, Barrett and Dodson (2004).

ANTETONITRUS Yates and Kitching 2003
Saurischia: Eusaurischia: Sauropodomorpha: Sauropoda.
Name derivation: Latin *ante* = "before" + Latin *tonitrus* = "thunder" [meaning "before *Brontosaurus*," or "before the thunder lizard"].
Type species: *A. ingenipes* Yates and Kitching 2003.
Other species: [None.]
Occurrence: Lower Elliot Formation, South Africa.
Age: Late Triassic (Norian).
Known material: Partial postcrania apparently belonging to two individuals.
Holotype: BP/1/4952, partial postcranial skeleton including cervical centrum, four dorsal vertebrae, sacral vertebra, caudal vertebrae, dorsal ribs, chevrons, scapulae, right humerus, ulnae, left radius, left metacarpal I, left and right metacarpals II, left manual phalanx I1, two ?manual unguals, left pubis, left femur, left tibia, left fibula, left metatarsal I, right metatarsal II, left metatarsal III, right metatarsal V, two pedal phalanges, right pedal ungual I, right pedal ungual ?III.

Diagnosis of genus (as for type species): Primitive sauropod distinguished by the following autapomorphies: neural spines of dorsal vertebrae flared transversely at distal ends; dorsal vertebrae having broad, triangular hyposphenes (in caudal aspect); ventral ridge on hyposphenes of caudal vertebrae; deep sulcus adjacent to lateral distal margin of deltopectoral crest; metacarpal I extremely short, broad (Yates and Kitching 2003).

Comments: Distinguished as the earliest sauropod dinosaur known to date, the genus *Antetonitrus* was founded upon a partial disarticulated (but closely associated *in situ*) skeleton (BP 1/4952) collected from the Lower Elliot Formation (well-supported for being of late Norian age, based primarily on the domination of the prosauropod *Euskelosaurus*, fossil prosauropod footprint correlations (*i.e.*, *Pseudotetrasauropus*), and stratigraphical continuity with the Early Jurassic Upper Elliot Formation; see Knoll 2003 for details and additional references), in the Landybrand District, Free State, South Africa (for a photograph of the excavation site, see Kitching and Raath 1984). These remains were assumed to belong to a single individual, as all form a large (for the Triassic) and robust sauropodomorph representing most skeletal

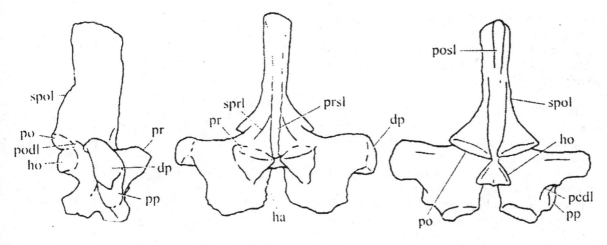

Antetonitrus ingenipes, BP/1/4952, holotype neural arch of dorsal vertebrae in (left) cranial, (middle) left lateral, and (right) caudal views. (After Yates and Kitching 2003.)

regions with no duplication of elements. Referred to the type species, *A. ingenipes*, was a specimen (BO/1/4952b) found at the same site, comprising a right scapula, right humerus (with deep sulcus on lateral margin of deltopectoral crest), left ulna, left fibula, and right metatarsal II), representing an approximately 20-percent smaller individual (Yates and Kitching 2003.)

Originally, Kitching and Raath referred BP/1/4952 to the Prosauropoda, identifying the specimen as *Euskelosaurus* sp. As Yates and Kitching pointed out, however, the type species *Euskelosaurus browni* is probably a *nomen dubium*, presenting "no derived characters or unique combination of characters that allow it to be distinguished from several early sauropodomorphs." Regardless of the validity of *E. browni*, Yates and Kitching noted, the holotype of that taxon reveals "a subcircular cross-section of the femoral midshaft and a low ridgelike lesser trochanter that is not shifted towards the lateral margin of the femoral shaft (Van Heerden 1979) that distinguish it from *A. ingenipes*." Hence, Yates and Kitching referred this material to its own new genus.

In describing *Antetonitrus*, Yates and Kitching noted that the skeleton is that of a small, robustly built sauropod, having an estimated total length of approximately eight to 10 meters (about 27 to 34 feet) and a height at the hips of 1.5 to two meters (over five to almost eight feet), and with exceptionally long fore-limbs. Moreover, the open neurocentral sutures of the cervical and dorsal vertebrae suggest that the individual represented by the holotype specimen was immature when it died.

Performing a cladistic analysis, Yates and Kitching referred *Antetonitrus* to the Sauropoda based upon the following synapomorphies: Suprapostzygapophyseal laminae on dorsal vertebrae; humerus more than 80 percent length of femur; long cranial process on proximal ulna; femur having elliptical cross section; metatarsal III less than 40 percent tibial length; midshaft of metatarsal I broader than other metatarsals; pedal ungual I longer than metatarsal I.

The authors found *A. ingenipes* to represent an important intermediate form between gracile, basal (and presumably facultativel bipedal) sauropodomorphs (see Van Heerden) and the specialized graviportal, obligate quadrupeds characterizing sauropods. Noting that *Anchisaurus* (regarded by Yates 2004 as a primitive sauropod rather than a prosauropod; see *Anchisaurus* entry) retains the primitive body form, Yates and Kitching postulated that "the characteristic body form of eurosauropods must have started to evolve some time after the initial diversification of the Sauropoda," an evolution that, given the early occurrence of *Antetonitrus*, was probably quite rapid. Furthermore, the authors also regarded both *Blikanasaurus cromptoni* and *Melanorosaurus radii* as primitive sauropods, considering these taxa along with *Ante-*

Antetonitrus ingenipes, skeletal reconstruction based on holotype partial skeleton BP/1/4952. Scale = 1 m. (After Yates and Kitching 2003.)

tonitrus to represent the oldest known members of the Sauropoda,

Key references: Kitching and Raath (1984); Knoll (2003); Van Heerden (1979); Yates (2004); Yates and Kitching (2003).

†APATOSAURUS

Saurischia: Eusaurischia: Sauropodomorpha: Sauropoda: Eusauropoda: Neosauropoda: Diplodocoidea: Diplodocidae.

Diagnosis of genus (as for type species): Marked flaring of distal end of basipterygoid process; 60-degree angle between basipterygoid processes in palatal aspect (40 to 45 degrees in most Sauropoda); cervical ribs short, robust, with rounded processes projecting from dorsal margin immediately caudal to tuberculum; lateral surfaces of centra of proximal caudal vertebrae converging ventrally, forming narrow midline ridge (Upchurch, Barrett and Dodson 2004).

Comment: In their review of the Sauropoda, Upchurch, Barrett and Dodson (2004) rediagnosed the genus *Apatosaurus* (see *D:TE*).

Key reference: Upchurch, Barrett and Dodson (2004).

†ARCHAEOCERATOPS

Ornithischia: Predentata: Genusauria: Cerapoda: Chasmatopia: Marginocephalia: Ceratopsia: Neoceratopsia: Archaeoceratopsidae.

Age: Middle Cretaceous (?Albian).

Diagnosis of genus (as for type species): Rostral keeled, pointing ventrally along its rostral margin; caudolateral process along ventral edge of rostral; lateral expansion of jugal at caudal end; prominent crest de-

Skeleton of *Apatosaurus* collected at Howe Ranch, located in the Morrison Formation of northern Wyoming. Nicknamed "Max," this specimen is distinguished as one of the most complete skeletons with associated skull (exhibited separately from this mount) yet recovered. Belonging to a modest-sized, probably subadult individual, this skeleton measures 17 meters (about 57 feet) in length.

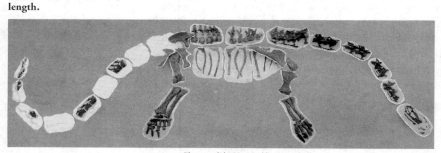

Photograph by Urs Möckli, copyright © and courtesy Sauriermuseum Aathal.

Skull of *Apatosaurus* on display at the Sauriermuseum Aathal in Switzerland.

Photograph by Urs Möckli, copyright © and courtesy Sauriermuseum Aathal.

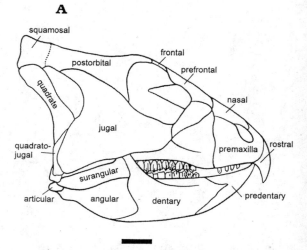

Archaeoceratops oshimai, A. IVPP V 11114, holotype skull in right lateral view, and B. life restoration. Scale = 2 cm. (After You and Dodson 2003.)

veloped along lateral surface of jugal; prominent primary ridge of maxillary tooth crown, located caudal to midline; last dentary tooth beside or caudal to apex of pronounced coronoid process (You and Dodson 2004).

Comments: In 1997, Dong Zhiming and Yoichi Azuma named and briefly described *Archaeoceratops oshimai*, the type species of a primitive horned dinosaur founded upon a well-preserved, almost complete skull with jaws, a partial vertebral column, and partial pelvis (IVPP V 11114), collected from the Mazongshan area (probably Albian age; see Tang, Luo, Zhou, You, Georgi, Tang and Wang 2001) of Gansu Province in northwestern China. A paratype specimen (IVPP V 11115), belonging to a smaller individual and recovered from the same locality, includes an almost complete tail, a partial pelvis, fragmentary hind limb, and complete pes. Both specimens were collected in 1992 by the Sino-Japanese Silk Road Dinosaur Expedition. Dong and Azuma referred *Archaeoceratops* to its own neoceratiosian family, the Archaeoceratopsidae, while other workers classified the genus as a protoceratopsid (see *S1*).

You and Dodson (2003) later redescribed the above specimens in detail. In performing a new cladistic analysis based upon data gleaned from their description of *A. oshimai*, these authors found *Archaeoceratops* to be the sister taxon to all currently known Late Cretaceous Neoceratopsia (see "Systematics" chapter for more results of this analysis).

Key references: Dong and Azuma (1997); Tang, Luo, Zhou, You, Georgi, Tang and Wang (2001); You and Dodson (2003).

†ARGENTINOSAURUS

Saurischia: Eusaurischia: Sauropodomorpha: Sauro-

poda: Eusauropoda: Neosauropoda: Macronaria: Titanosauriformes: Titanosauria *incertae sedis*.

Diagnosis of genus (as for type species): Dorsal vertebrae with additional articular areas ventrolateral to hyposphene (also in *Epachthosaurus*); tubular cylindrical dorsal ribs; (possibly) proximal end of tibia rising to peak at caudal margin in medial aspect (Upchurch, Barrett and Dodson 2004).

Comment: In their review of the Sauropoda, Upchurch, Barrett and Dodson (2004) rediagnosed the type species *Argentinosaurus huinculensis* (see *D:TE*).

Key reference: Upchurch, Barrett and Dodson (2004).

†ARGYROSAURUS

Saurischia: Eusaurischia: Sauropodomorpha: Sauropoda: Eusauropoda: Neosauropoda: Macronaria: Titanosauriformes: Titanosauria: Lithostrotia: Saltasauridae: Saltasaurinae.

Diagnosis of genus (as for type species): Neural arches of proximal caudal vertebrae craniocaudally short, dorsoventerally tall (Upchurch, Barrett and Dodson 2004).

Comments: In 1893, Richard Lydekker named and described the type species *Argyrosaurus superbus* (see *D:TE*), established on an anterior left forelimb (MLP 77-V-29-1) comprising a humerus, radius, ulna, carpals, and five metacarpals, collected from Upper Cretaceous (probably "Senonian") of possibly the Bajo Barreal Formation, Chubut Group (see Bonaparte and Gasparini 1979), on the left bank of the Río Chico, near Pampa Pelada, northwest of Lake Colhue Huapi (Huene 1929), Chubut Province, Argentina. Additional material recovered from the San Jorge Basin has been referred to *Argyrosaurus* and doubtfully to the type species.

In his monograph on South American "titanosaurids," Powell (2003) rediagnosed *A. superbus* as follows: Huge "titanosaurid"; humerus stout, proximal end broad, straight upper edge (margin) perpendicular to long axis of bone; insertion area for pectoral muscle far more prominent, projected forward and medially; ulna having extremely robust proximal end showing prominent edges delimiting markedly concave facets; metacarpals stout, about one-third length of humerus.

In redescribing this species, Powell noted the following: *Argyrosaurus superbus* is a very large sauropod, with *Antarctosaurus giganteus* and *Alamosaurus sanjuanensis* among the only known "titanosaurids" of comparable size. Both *Argyrosaurus* and *Saltasaurus* have a stout humerus, although the former genus has a smaller gait and robustness index of the radius and ulna.

Powell described a disarticulated specimen (PVL 4628) consisting of three dorsal and three caudal vertebrae, a left scapula, a humerus, radius, right ulna, left ulna, right pubis, incomplete left tibia, and various rib fragments, all of these elements representing a single individual, collected from the lower part of the Upper Cretaceous (?"Senonian") Laguna Palacio Formation (Bonaparte and Gasparini), on the right bank of Río Senguerr, southeast of the southernmost part of the Sierra San Bernardo du Chubut Province, Argentina. Referred by Bonaparte and Gasparini to *Argyrosaurus* sp., this specimen is important, Powell

Holotype dorsal vertebrae (PVPH-1) of the gigantic titanosaurian sauropod *Argentinosaurus huenculensis* on display at the Museo Municipal Carmen Funes in Neuquén Province, Patagonia, Argentina.

noted, in comprising elements belonging to a single individual. The material upon which *A. superbus* was based, however, only allowed Powell a tentative referral to that species.

Also, Powell described several specimens described by Huene—two right femora (FMNH-P 13018, assigned by Huene to *A. superbus*, and 13019, assigned by Huene to *Antarctosaurus wichmannianus*), and a left tibia (FMNH-FP 13020) (see *D:TE* for photographs)—from an indeterminable Upper Cretaceous formation (possibly the San Jorge Formation) in the Chubut Group, Sierra de San Bernardo, west of the Sarmiento locality, Chubut Province. Due to similarities of these specimens to the femur and tibia of *A. superbus*, and because they come from the same region and most likely near or at the same stratigraphic position that yielded *A. superbus*, yet also owing to the lack of positive diagnostic features (excluding robustness and proportions) displayed by this material, Powell referred these specimens to cf. *Argyrosaurus* sp.

Key references: Bonaparte and Gasparini (1979); Huene (1929); Lydekker (1893); Powell (2003); Upchurch, Barrett and Dodson (2004).

†ASTRODON   ?[*nomen dubium*]

Saurischia: Eusaurischia: Sauropodomorpha: Sauropoda: Eusauropoda: Neosauropoda: Macronaria: Titanosauriformes: ?Brachiosauridae.

Type species: *A. johnstoni* Leidy 1865 ?[*nomen dubium*].

Comments: Celebrated as "America's first sauropod" and the largest dinosaur known from the East Coast, the type species *Astrodon johnstoni* was established on two sauropod teeth (YPM 798) discovered in November, 1858, in an open pit iron mine belonging to John D. Latchford, located in the Lower Cretaceous Arundel Formation of Prince George's County, Maryland. Leidy formally described these fossils in 1865. In the years following that discovery, YPM 798 has generally been regarded as pertaining to the better represented type species *Pleurocoelus nanus*, which had been founded by Marsh (1888*a*) on vertebrae (USNM 4968) representing a juvenile sauropod, also recovered from the Arundel Formation of Maryland. While regarded as a junior synonym of *Pleurocoelus*, the genus *Astrodon* itself has mostly come to be considered a *nomen dubium* (see Krantz 1996, 1998; Upchurch, Barrett and Dodson 2004; also *D:TE, S2*).

While the location of the site that yielded YPM 798 had never been given, an investigation by Peter M. Krantz apparently found the former Lanchford property, now adjacent to a quarry that, since 1989, has yielded hundreds of dinosaur bones and teeth (for details, see Krantz 1996, 2004). In a recent paper again

chronicling in detail the history of the discovery of the *Astrodon* teeth, Krantz (2004) also addressed the questionable validity of this genus. As Krantz (2004) related, sauropod remains (including a very large femur, perhaps some two meters in length when complete), presumably belonging to *Astrodon*, number among the dinosaurian specimens collected from this site during the past approximately half decade. Some of these, that author noted, as well as material yet to be collected, can be regarded as potential lectotypes for *Astrodon johnstoni*.

Consequently, Krantz (2004) suggested, *A. johnstoni* is not a dubious taxon; moreover, if proven to be synonymous with *Pleurocoelus*, the name *Astrodon* would have priority.

Note: On October 1, 1998, *Astrodon* became the official State Fossil of Maryland.

Key references: Kranz (1998, 2004); Leidy (1865); Marsh (1888*a*); Upchurch, Barrett and Dodson (2004).

†ATLASAURUS

Saurischia: Eusaurischia: Sauropodomorpha: Sauropoda: Eusauropoda: Neosauropoda: Macronaria.

Diagnosis of genus (as for type species, *A. imelakei*): Supratemporal fenestra not visible in lateral aspect (Upchurch, Barrett and Dodson 2004).

Comments: In 1999, Michel Monbaron, Dale A. Russell, and Philippe Taquet described the genus *Atlasaurus*, founded on an almost complete partial skeleton with skull elements (Musée des sciences de la Terre de Rabat collection) from the Tilougguit Formation of Morocco. Monbaron *et al.* originally referred this genus to the Camarasauromorpha, with a close relationship to *Brachiosaurus* (see *S2*).

More recently, in their review of Sauropoda, Upchurch, Barrett and Dodson (2004) noted that most of the supposed autapomorphies used by Monbaron *et al.* to diagnose this genus (*e.g.*, supratemporal fenestra twice as wide as long; combined width of paroccipital processes 50 percent of estimated mandibular length) are not unique derived characters.

A cladistic analysis by Upchurch *et al.* found *Atlasaurus* to be a basal, noncamarasauromorph macronarian in a clade shared by *Bellusaurus* and *Jobaria*.

Key references: Monbaron, Russell and Taquet (1999; Upchurch, Barrett and Dodson (2004).

†ATLASCOPOSAURUS

Ornithischia: Predentata: Genasauria: Cerapoda: Ornithopoda: Euornithopoda.

Comments: In a review of basal ornithopoda, Norman, Sues, Witmer and Coria (2004) interpreted the type species *Atlascoposaurus loadsi* (see *D:TE*) as a basal member of Euornithopoda, possibly at the same phylogenetic level as *Gasparinisaura*, based upon the following: Prominent primary ridge on buccal and lingual surfaces of maxillary and dentary teeth, respectively; well-developed subsidiary ridges also traversing crown surfaces; apparently low tooth count; gracile form of associated femur.

Key reference: Norman, Sues, Witmer and Coria (2004).

ATROCIRAPTOR   Currie and Varricchio 2004
Saurischia: Eusaurischia: Eusaurischia: Theropoda: Neotheropoda: Tetanurae: Avetheropoda: Coelurosauria: Tyrannoraptora: Maniraptoriformes: Maniraptora: Metornithes: Paraves: Deinonychosauria: Dromaeosauridae: Velociraptorinae.

Name derivation: Latin *atroci* = "savage" + Latin *raptor* = "thief."

Type species: *A. marshalli* Currie and Varricchio 2004.

Other species: [None.]

Occurrence: Horseshoe Canyon Formation, Alberta, Canada.

Age: Late Cretaceous (late Campanian or early Maastrichtian).

Known material/holotype: TMP 95.166.1, partial skull including premaxillae, right maxilla, right dentary, portions of left dentary, teeth, numerous bone fragments, juvenile.

Diagnosis of genus (as for type species): Small velociraptorine, dromaeosaurid differing from *Saurornitholestes* and *Velociraptor* in having shorter, deeper face; subnarial body of premaxilla taller than rostrocaudal length (as in *Deinonychus* and possibly *Dromaeosaurus*); internarial and maxillary process of premaxilla subparallel, oriented more dorsally than caudally; maxillary fenestra directly above promaxillary fenestra (rather than well behind it, as in all other known dromaeosaurids); maxillary teeth more strongly inclined toward throat than in all other known dromaeosaurids except *Bambiraptor* [see Burnham, Senter, Barsbold and Britt 2004, "Systematics" chapter, for a conflicting new assessment of this genus] and *Deinonychus*; maxillary teeth dentition essentially isodont (Currie and Varricchio 2004).

Comments: The type species *Atrociraptor marshalli* was based upon a partial skull with teeth, plus numerous fragments of bone (TMP 95.166.1), discovered in 1995 in a relatively hard, isolated block of sandstone in the Horseshoe Canyon Formation, about five kilometers west of the Royal Tyrrell Museum of Palaeontology, in Drumheller, Alberta, Canada (Currie and Varricchio 2004).

Atrociraptor was identified by Currie and Varricchio as a dromaeosaurid, and distinguished from

Courtesy Philip J. Currie.

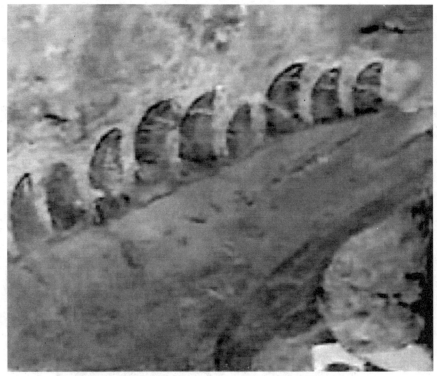

Atrociraptor marshalli, TMP 95.166.1, holotype right maxilla in lateral view.

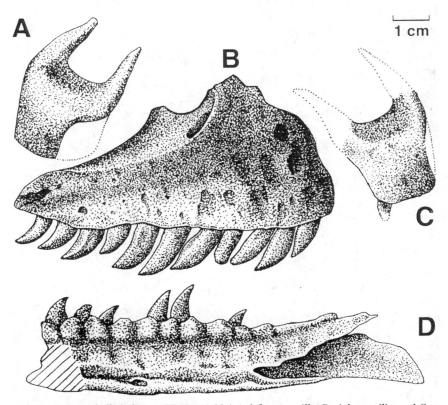

Atrociraptor marshalli, holotype (TMP 95.166.1) A. left premaxilla, B. right maxilla, and C. right premaxilla, lateral views, and D. left dentary, medial view. (After Currie and Varricchio 2004.)

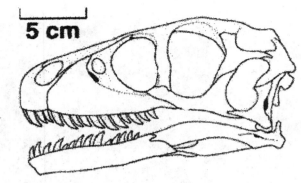

Atrociraptor marshalli, reconstruction of holotype partial skull (TMP 95.166.1), missing parts restored after Dromaeosaurus and Velociraptor. (After Currie and Varricchio 2004.)

Copyright © Berislav Krzic.

Holotype (MCF-PVPH-236) hind feet of Aucasaurus garridoi.

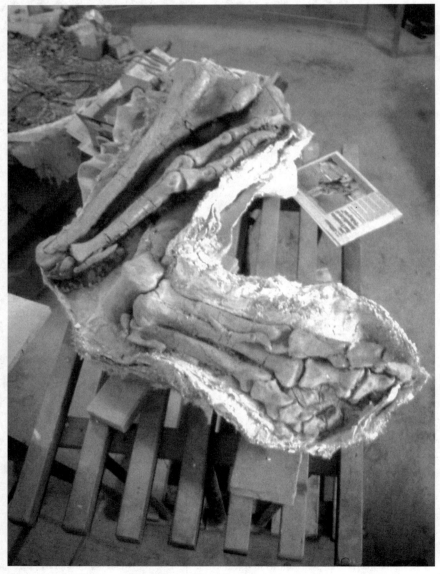

Photograph by Gary Takeuchi, courtesy Museo Municipal Carmen Funes.

contemporary tyrannosaurids and troodontids, by such collective evidence as the following: Relatively small size; sizes and positions of antorbital and maxillary fenestrae; subnarial-maxillary process on pre-

Life restoration of Atrociraptor marshalli, drawn by Berislav Krzic.

maxilla, extending caudally to wedge between maxilla and nasal; subparallel dorsal and ventral margins of dentary; labiolingually thick dentary; fusion of interdental plates; and bladelike teeth. As these authors observed, the short, deep snout of Atrociraptor readily distinguishes this genus from other members of the Dromaeosauridae.

Currie and Varricchio identified Atrociraptor as a member of the Velociraptorinae by the following: Denticles on mesial carinae significantly smaller than distal serration in maxillary and most dentary teeth. Additionally, the largest premaxillary tooth in this genus is the second alveolus, as in other known velociraptorines, but not in the dromaeosaurine Dromaeosaurus (see Currie 1995).

Currie and Varricchio performed a cladistic analysis based on 42 parsimony-informative cranial characters, 12 of which were coded for Atrociraptor, with Coelophysis and Allosaurus used as successively proximal outgroups, and Troodontidae included "because of their purported relationship with dromaeosaurids." The resulting singlemost parsimonious tree showed Atrociraptor sorting "most strongly with Deinonychus ... and secondarily with Bambiraptor."

Key references: Burnham, Senter, Barsbold and Britt (2004); Currie (1995); Currie and Varricchio (2004).

†AUBLYSODON Leidy 1868 [nomen dubium]—
(See Tyrannosaurus.)
Type species: A. mirandus Leidy 1868 [nomen dubium].

†AUCASAURUS
Saurischia: Eusaurischia: Eusaurischia: Theropoda: Neotheropoda: Ceratosauria: Abelisauroidea: Abelisauridae: Carnotaurinae.
Erratum: In S3, the photograph on page 248 of the foot of Aucasaurus garridoi was inadvertently reversed.

AVIATYRANNIS Rauhut 2003

Saurischia: Eusaurischia: Theropoda: Neotheropoda: Tetanurae: Avetheropoda: Coelurosauria: Tyrannoraptora: Maniraptoriformes: Tyrannoraptora: Tyrannosauroidea.

Name derivation: Latin *avia* = "grandmother" + Latin *tyrannis* = "tyrant [genitive form of *tyrannus*]."

Type species: *T. jurassica* Rauhut 2003.

Other species: [None.]

Occurrence: Guimarota locality, Alcobaca Formation, Portugal.

Age: Late Jurassic (Kimmeridgian).

Known material: Pelvic elements, teeth.

Holotype: IPFUB Gui Th 1, nearly complete right ilium.

Diagnosis of genus (as for type species): Small tyrannosauroid; ilium low, elongate, with well-developed vertical, hollow ridge above acetabulum; dorsal half of cranial margin of preacetabular blade shallowly concave, that part set off from dorsal rim by smaller, craniodorsally facing concavity; differing from most other theropods in presence of strongly developed ridge above acetabulum and dorsally concave part of cranial rim; from *Piatnitzkysaurus* and specimen (OUM J 13560) referred to *Megalosaurus* in more elongate shape of ilium, relatively longer preacetabular blade, relatively narrower pubic peduncle, and more clearly defined vertical ridge; from *Iliosuchus* (BMNH R 83) in lack of bulge of dorsal rim above acetabular part, ridge not inclined caudally, and caudally expanding, relatively broader brevis fossa; from *Stokesosaurus* in more elongate shape, ridge not in-

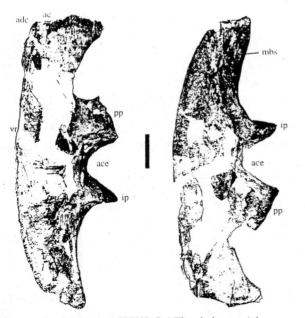

Aviatyrannis jurassicus, IPFUB Gui Th 1, holotype right ilium in (left) lateral and (right) medial views. Scale = 10 mm. (After Rauhut 2003.)

clined caudally, and overall shape; from *Siamotyrannus* in more elongate shape of ilium, relatively longer preacetabular blade, comparatively narrower pubic peduncle, just one vertical ridge, and dorsal concavity in cranial rim; and from later tyrannosaurids in being relatively lower, more elongate, and lacking very strongly ventrally expanded cranial hook (Rauhut 2003a).

Comments: One of the earliest known tyrannosauroids, the genus *Aviatyrannis* was founded upon a partial right ilium (IPFUB Gui Th 1) collected at the Guimarota coal mine from a lignitic coal layer within the Alcobaca Formation, near Leiria, in central Portugal. Additional remains referred to the type species, *T. jurassica* include a fragmentary ilium (IPFUB Gui Th 2), a partial right ischium (IPFUB Gui Th 3), and several previously reported premaxillary teeth (see Zinke 1998; Rauhut 2000) recovered from the same locality (Rauhut 2003a).

Rauhut (2003a) referred this material to the Tyrannosauroidea based upon the following characters: Ilium having strongly developed, well-defined vertical ridge above acetabulum; concave dorsal part of cranial margin of preacetabular blade; distal flange on ischium extending from obturator process to at least halfway along ischial shaft.

As shown by Rauhut (2003a), *Aviatyrannis* and the North American (Morrison Formation) *Stokesosaurus* comprise the only tyrannosauroids currently known from the Jurassic period. However, that author deduced, given the poor fossil record of Middle Jurassic theropods, the origin of the Tyrannosauroidea might be pushed back further, pending new discoveries. Moreover, the small, Middle Jurassic theropod *Iliosuchus*, the referred ilium (OUM 29871) of which also displays a well-developed ridge above the acetabulum, could be a yet earlier representative of this lineage.

Rauhut (2003a) further noted that the presence of basal tyrannosauroids in both the Kimmeridgian of Portugal and the Morrison Formation (Kimmeridgian–Tithonian) of North America (see Madsen 1974; Foster and Chure 2001) strengthens the relationships between these areas during the Late Jurassic.

As Rauhut (2003a) pointed out, the oldest probable Late Cretaceous tyrannosauroid record consists of isolated teeth collected from the Cenomanian of Utah (see Kirkland and Parrish 1995), the oldest skeletal record probably being the genus *Alectrosaurus* from the Iren Dabasu Formation of central Asia (see Mader and Bradley 1989; Currie and Eberth 1993), with tyrannosaurids already widely distributed in both Asia and North America towards the end of the Late Cretaceous (Carpenter 1992a). Consequently, the available data suggest "a Euro-North American origin of

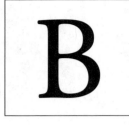

tyrannosauroids and a probable subsequent Asian diversification of this group," although testing this hypothesis depends upon the collection of more material, especially that pertaining to small Middle and Late Jurassic forms.

Rauhut (2003*a*) concluded that the material referred to this new genus and species demonstrate that early tyrannosauroids were relatively small animals, this group mainly attaining giant size during the Late Cretaceous (see Manabe 1999), although some early tyrannosaurs (*e.g.*, *Eotyrannus*, from the Barremian of England; see Hutt, Naish, Martill, Barker and Newbery 2001, *S3*) had already attained large size by the Early Cretaceous.

Key references: Carpenter (1992*a*); Currie and Eberth (1993); Ford and Chure (2001); Foster and Chure (2000); Hutt, Naish, Martill, Barker and Newbery (2001); Kirkland and Parrish (1995); Mader and Bradley (1989); Madsen (1974, 1976); Manabe (1999); Rauhut (2000, 2003*a*); Zinke (1998).

†AVIMIMUS

Saurischia: Eusaurischia: Eusaurischia: Theropoda: Neotheropoda: Tetanurae: Avetheropoda: Coelurosauria: Tyrannoraptora: Maniraptoriformes: Maniraptora: ?Metornithes: Oviraptorosauria *incertae sedis*.

Diagnosis of genus (as for type species): Premaxilla with teeth; bones of caudal part of skull entirely fused; parietofrontal part of skull roof convex; posttemporal part of skull strongly shortened; infratemporal fenestra confluent with orbit due to absence of postorbital process of jugal; neck long, at least 12 cervical vertebrae; cervical ribs fused with vertebrae; synsacrum with seven vertebrae; scapula with laterally everted acromion; length of forelimb (excluding manus) equal to approximately one-third hindlimb length; manus (incomplete) with metacarpals I–III fused with one another and with distal carpals; ilium strongly inclined dorsomedially along medial part; preacetabular process entirely lacking cranioventral process; tibiotarsus about 30 percent longer than femur; pes arctometatarsal, metatarsals II–IV fused proximally with each other and with distal carpals; upturned caudolateral corner of fourth tarsal (Osmólska, Currie and Barsbold 2004).

Note: Trace-fossil evidence could reflect gregarious behavior in the small, birdlike type species *Avimimus portentosus*.

Ishigaki, Watabe, Tsogtbaatar and Barsbold (2004), in an abstract, reported briefly on more than 13,000 fossil dinosaur footprints found in 1995 during the Hayashibara Museum of Natural Sciences–

Mongolian Paleontological Center Paleontological Expedition in Shar Tsav, South Gobi Imag, Mongolia. Most of these ichnites, the authors noted, are those of various-sized theropod dinosaurs, the prints ranging in length from six to 70 centimeters. Included in this suite of ichnites are nine groups of parallel theropod trackways, the tracks within each group being "similar in size, morphology, stride, direction, and substrate conditions."

As interpreted by Ishigaki *et al.*, these tracks seem to have been imprinted at the same time by animals of similar body size and foot shape (most likely belonging to one species), the trackmakers having "formed a pack moving together at a similar speed." This find, the authors noted, constitutes the first footprint evidence of gregarious behavior in "large" theropods (*i.e.*, footprint length of more than 35 centimeters).

Ishigaki *et al.* found at least five pieces of evidence of gregarious behavior in small-sized footprints (*i.e.*, eight to 12 centimeters in length) and at least four in middle-sized prints (*i.e.*, 22 to 34 centimeters in length). Packs of the smaller forms seem to have comprised from five to 80 individuals and those of the middle-sized forms two to 21 individuals.

Regarding the former, Ishigaki *et al.* suggested that over 80 animals ran together, changing their direction from north to east-northeast as if in a stampede. Furthermore, the size and shape of these smaller tracks are consistent with the pes of the birdlike theropod *Avimimus*, whose body fossils have been found in the same locality (see *D:TE*, *S2*, and *S3*).

Key reference: Ishigaki, Watabe, Tsogtbaatar and Barsbold (2004).

†BAGARAATAN

Saurischia: Eusaurischia: Eusaurischia: Theropoda: Neotheropoda: Tetanurae: Avetheropoda: Coelurosauria: Tyrannoraptora: Maniraptoriformes: Tyrannoraptora: ?Tyrannosauroidea.

Diagnosis of genus (as for type species): Apomorphies including the following: two caudal surangular foramina; stout hyposphene-hypantrum articulations in first 16 caudal vertebrae (Holtz 2004).

Comment: Holtz (2004), in his review of the Tyrannosauroidea, found the Late Cretaceous Mongolian type species *Bagaraatan ostromi*— originally described by Halszka Osmólska (1996) as an avetheropod (see *S1*)— possibly to be a basal tyrannosauroid and also close to related taxa, based upon the following features: Prominent, laterally extending horizontal shelf on lateral surface of surangular, rostral and ventral to mandibular condyle; retroarticular process reduced, broadened; ischial peduncle of pubis having ventral flange.

However, Holtz cautioned that given the fragmentary nature of this taxon and the paucity of data available for *B. ostromi*, the above-determined "position is not particularly secure and is likely to change with new information."

Key references: Holtz (2004); Osmólska (1996).

BAINOCERATOPS Tereschenko and Alifanov 2003

Ornithischia: Predentata: Genusauria: Cerapoda: Chasmatopia: Marginocephalia: Ceratopsia: Neoceratopsia: Coronosauria: Protoceratopsidae.

Name derivation: "Bain[-Dzak locality]" + Greek *keratos* = "horn" + Greek *ops* = "face."

Type species: *B. efremovi* Tereschenko and Alifanov 2003.

Other species: [None.]

Occurrence: Djadokhta Formation, South Gobi, Mongolia.

Age: Late Cretaceous (?"Senonian" to Campanian).

Known material/holotype: PIN 614–33, series of vertebrae including cervical numbers six, seven, and nine, dorsal numbers one, five, and seven, sacral number eight, and caudal numbers one to three, ?10 and 11, ?18 and 19.

Diagnosis of genus (as for type species): Medium-sized protoceratopsid, body length up to 2.5 meters (approximately 8.4 feet); centra of presacral vertebrae short, of medium depth; cranial surface of presacral vertebrae moderately concave, caudal surface flat; (cervical vertebrae) ventral crest of numbers six and seven well-pronounced, oval in cross section, extending beyond proximal edge of centrum; parapophyseal facets dorsolaterally oriented; diapophyses of number seven with narrow bases, oriented dorsolaterally at angle of 40 degrees to horizontal plane; prezygapophyseal facet of this vertebra projecting for about one-third length, extending lateroproximally at 80-degree angle to longitudinal axis of vertebra; absence of ventral crest on corpus of number nine; (dorsals) prezygapophyses of numbers nine and 10 drawn together, two infraparapophyseal crests; in number nine, lateral edge of prezygapophyseal facet curving inward, short, round in cross section, diapophyses inclining caudolaterally at approximately 35 degrees to longitudinal vertebral axis; distalmost (?13) with centrum extended dorsoventrally, prezygapophyses short, facets oriented in transverse plane at angle less than 20 degrees to horizontal, small process on spino-postzygapophyseal crest above postzygapophyseal facet; synapophyses relatively short, projecting laterally, facet clearly outlined, extended, included at about 45 degrees; crest extending across middle of long axis of synapophyseal facet; poorly pronounced postzygapophyseal crest; short caudosynapophyseal crest; neurapophysis at more than 90 degrees to vertebral column; (sacrals) transverse process of caudalmost

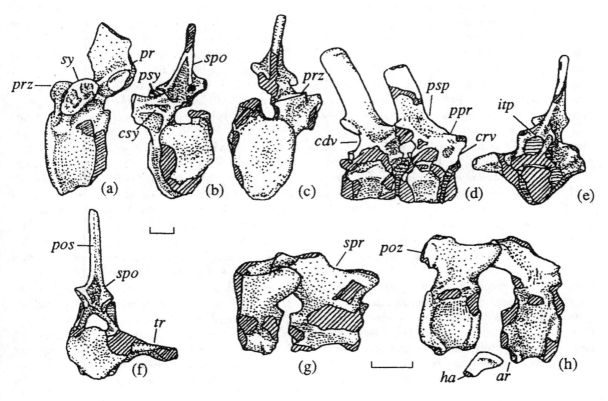

Bainoceratops efromovi, PIN 614-33, holotype cervical vertebrae, in (a, c, f, h, j, l, n) lateral, (b, d, i, k, m) cranial, (g) ventral, (o) caudal views, (a, f, h, n) right lateral and (c, l) left lateral views. Scale = 1 cm. (After Tereschenko and Alifanov 2003.)

Bainoceratops efromovi, PIN 614-33, holotype vertebrae, (a, b, c) 13th dorsal vertebra, (d) eighth sacral-first dorsal, (e) eighth sacral, (f) first caudal, (g) caudals ?10–11, and (h) caudals ?18–19), in (a, d, g, h) lateral, (c, e) cranial, (b, f,) caudal views, (a) left lateral and (d, g, h) right lateral views. Scale = 1 cm. (After Tereschenko and Alifanov 2003.)

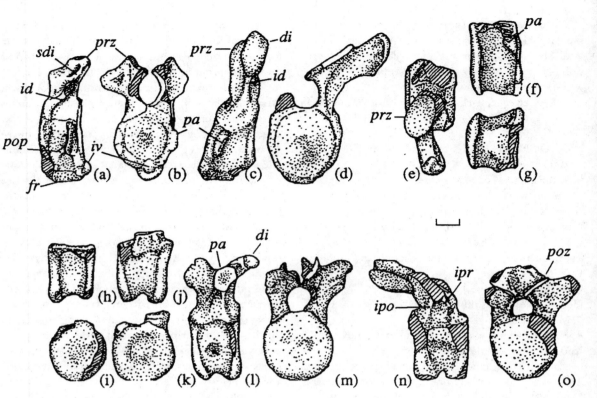

sacral vertebra protecting laterally, bases round in cross section; zygapophyses spaced widely, postprezygapophyseal crest weakly pronounced; concave prezygapophyseal facet; prespinal crest passing onto neural arch, level with dorsal surface of postzygapophyses and at midlength of vertebral centrum; (caudals) base of first two or three spinous processes of caudal vertebrae about half as long as centrum; proximal vertebral incisure smaller than distal incisure; postzygapophyses not ventrally contacting each other; transverse processes of first caudal projecting laterodistally, prespinal crest wedging in between relatively poorly pronounced spinoprezygapophyseal crests; spinous processes of number two distally inclined at angle less than 60 degrees to horizontal, transverse processes projecting caudolaterally at about 70 degree; in ?10 to 11 and ?18 to 19, facets for connection with hemapophyses (chevrons) notably concave; flat proximal and distal caudal surfaces of centra of ?18 to 19, prezygapophyses at angle approximately 20 degrees to horizontal (Tereschenko and Alifanov 2003).

Comments: Most ceratopsian genera and species have been named and described based upon features of their very diagnostic skulls. *Bainoceratops efromvi,* however, was founded solely upon postcranial remains collected from the Bain-Dzak locality in the Upper Cretaceous Djadokhta Formation, South Gobi, Mongolia, during the Mongolian Paleontological Expedition of the Academy of Sciences of the USSR (1946–1949).

Tereschenko and Alifanov (2003), who described this new type species, recounted their realization that they had discovered a new taxon: While revising the collections of the Mongolian Paleontological Expedition, one specimen — PIN 614–33, a series of sacral and caudal vertebrae that had originally been tentatively referred to *Protoceratops andrewsi,* the most commonly known Central Asian ceratopsian dinosaur — particularly attracted their attention. A cursory inspection by the authors "revealed some peculiar features" of PIN 614–33, prompting them to reassess all of the available specimens recovered by the Mongolian Paleontological Expedition of the Academy of Sciences of the USSR and also the Joint Soviet-Mongolian Paleontological Expedition (from 1969 to the present).

Tereschenko and Alifanov included in their study the following material: PIN 614–30, cranial part of vertebral column, PIN 614–31, middle dorsal and sacral vertebrae, PIN 614–32, caudal region; PIN 614–35, caudal cervical and dorsal vertebrae, and PIN 614–61, cranial dorsal vertebrae from Bain-Dzak; PIN 3143–4, 3143–5, 3143–7, 3143–9, skeletons, 3143-12, distal dorsal, sacral, and proximal caudal vertebrae, 3143-16, dorsal, sacral, and proximal caudal vertebrae, from the Tugrikiin-Shire; referred to cf. *Bagaceratops* sp., PIN 3143-11, caudal vertebrae numbers five to 20, PIN 614–29, vertebral column lacking cervicals one through four, sacrals three through six, caudals two through ?10, ?15, and subsequent distal caudals, PIN

614–34, neural arch of fifth cervical, dorsals number one, three through seven, centra of first to seventh sacrals, caudals number one through three and ?10, PIN 614–53, sacral vertebrae, caudals one through seven (or eight), several caudals from middle region, PIN 614–62, two distal dorsal vertebrae, and PIN 4550–3, first cervical through ninth dorsal vertebrae, from Gilbentu-2, southeast of Gilbentu locality (see Efremov 1962); PIN 3907-11, *Udanoceratops tschizhovi* skeleton, from Udan-Sair locality; and PIN collection, cast of *Leptoceratops gracilis* skeleton (CMN [formerly NMC] 8887 (Brown 1914). Also analyzed was various published data (*e.g.*, Brown; Brown and Schlaikjer 1940, 1942; Sternberg 1951; Chinnery and Weishampel 1998).

In studying PIN 614–33, Tereschenko and Alifanov considered the possibility that the specimen exhibits the intraspecific variability characteristic of the Protoceratopsidae (see Brown and Schlaikjer 1940; Rozhdestvensky 1965; Kurzanov 1972; Maryańska and Osmólska 1975; Dodson 1976), including allometric variations (see Brown and Schlaikjer; Sternberg; Chinnery and Weishampel; Tereschenko 2001) and sexual dimorphism (*e.g.*, see Tereschenko 1991, 1997, 2001). However, as PIN 614–33 "differs appreciably from *Protoceratops andrewsi* and other protoceratopsids with known postcranial morphology, the authors interpreted the specimen as representing a new genus and species.

Comparing *Bainoceratops* to other protoceratopsids, Tereschenko and Alifanov found the morphology of the new form to be more similar to *Leptoceratops* and *Udanoceratops* than to *Protoceratops* and cf. *Bagaceratops* sp.

Bainoceratops resembles *Leptoceratops* in the following: Length, width, and depth of presacral vertebrae, with concave cranial flat caudal surfaces; and less indented edge of elongated symphyseal facet.

The new genus is similar to *Udanoceratops* in the following features: Weakly projecting prezygapophyses, transversely elongated facets in cervical vertebra number seven; dorsal curvature of lateral edge of cervical number nine's prezygapophyseal facets; just slightly projecting synapophyses of caudalmost dorsal vertebra; zygapophyses widely spaced; prezygapophyseal facet of caudalmost dorsal vertebra inclining and transversely expanding; prespinal crest extended between spinoprezygapophyseal crests, almost to edge of interzygapophyseal incisure in first caudal; wider disconnection of inferior edges of postzygapophyseal facets in proximal caudals; and deep concave articular surfaces for chevrons on caudals ?10 to 11 and ?18 to 19.

According to Tereschenko and Alifanov, *Bainoceratops* differs from *Protoceratops* and *Bagaceratops* in

the following: Centra of presacral vertebrae short, with concave cranial and flat caudal surfaces (cranial surface in *Udanoceratops* more concaved than in caudal surface); diapophyses on ninth dorsal vertebra almost circular in cross section; narrow interprezygapophyseal space in dorsals nine and 10; and sculptured synapophyseal face of caudalmost dorsal vertebra.

Tereschenko and Alifanov pointed out that 11 protoceratopsid forms (*Protoceratops andrewsi*, *Microceratops gobiensis*, *Bagaceratops rhozdestvenskyi*, *Bagaceratops* sp., "*Breviceratops kozlowskii*" [=*Bagaceratops*]; see S3), *Asiaceratops salsopaludalis*, *Udanoceratops tschizovi*, *Kulceratops kulensis*, *Archaeoceratops oshimai*, *Graciliceratops mongoliensis*, and *Bainoceratops efremovi*) are currently known from the Cretaceous of Asia, with four of these — *U. tschizhovi*, *B. efremovi*, *P. andrewsi*, and *Bagaceratops* sp. — occurring in Djadokhta deposits, the latter two having been found in the same locality. Consequently, the authors found it "reasonable to suppose that the Djadokhta Time was the golden age in the evolution of Asian protoceratopsids," the presence of several species in Bain-Dzak requesting the revision of taxonomic diversity of the Protoceratopsidae from Mongolia's Djadokhta localities.

Note: In 2004, Tereschenko published a study in which that author described the vertebrae of various kinds of protoceratopsid dinosaurs, including the specimens cited by Tereschenko and Alifanov (see above), and the type specimen of *Bainoceratops efremovi*. As Tereschenko (2004) observed, the centra of four or five proximal caudal vertebrae in protoceratopsids are heterocoelous or "saddle shaped" (see Tereschenko and Alifanov), resembling the state in avian cervical vertebrae. The hererocoelous state in the vertebrae of birds, as defined by Borkhvardt (1982), is a combination of the procoelous pattern in the frontal plane with the opisthocoelous pattern in the sagittal plane. However, Tereschenko (2004) pointed out, when applying this definition to protoceratopsid dinosaurs, the heterocoelous centra are actually opposite in shape to those of birds (*i.e.*, procoelous in vertical plane, opisthocoelous in sagittal plane).

As Tereschenko (2004) explained, the heterocoelous shape of such vertebral centra — having proximally concave cranial and caudal articular surfaces in ventral aspect, distally concave in lateral aspect — permits neighboring vertebrae to move relative to each other in both horizontal and ventral planes (see Dzerzhinsky 1998) while preventing torsion (see Dementiev 1940).

In the past various authors have speculated that protoceratopsids were aquatic (*e.g.*, Kurzanov 1972) or at least semiaquatic (Barsbold 1974) animals.

Tereschenko (2004) further postulated that the heterocoelous caudal vertebrae on protoceratopsids, allowing these vertebrae to move in horizontal and vertical planes without torsion, may have developed as an adaptation to swimming in these dinosaurs. Unlike the situation with birds, however, the prohibition of torsion in the proximal caudals of protoceratopsids would have been particularly important while the animals were moving on dry land, and the caudofemoral muscles—in dinosaurs as in extant reptiles connecting the femur to the first 10 or 11 caudal vertebrae (see Hamley 1990)—functioned actively. As Tereschenko (2004) noted, contraction of these muscles would have resulted "in a torsional force that is especially strong at the caudal base."

Key references: Barsbold (1974); Borkhvardt (1982); Brown (1914); Brown and Schlaikjer (1940, 1942); Chinnery and Weishampel (1998); Dementiev (1940); Dodson (1976); Dzerzhinsky (1998); Efremov (1962); Hamley (1990); Kurzanov (1972); Maryańska and Osmólska (1975); Rozhdestvensky (1965); Sternberg (1951); Tereschenko (1991, 1997, 2001, 2004); Tereschenko and Alifanov (2003).

†**BAMBIRAPTOR** (=?*Saurornitholestes*)
Saurischia: Eusaurischia: Eusaurischia: Theropoda: Neotheropoda: Tetanurae: Avetheropoda: Coelurosauria: Tyrannoraptora: Maniraptoriformes: Maniraptora: Metornithes: Paraves: Deinonychosauria: Microraptoria.
Holotype: AMNH 001, virtually complete partially articulated skeleton, subadult.

Comments: In 2000, David A. Burnham, Philip J. Currie, Robert T. Bakker, Zhonghe Zhou, and John H. Ostrom briefly described the new type species *Bambiraptor feinbergi*, a very small and birdlike dinosaur based upon remains of three individuals—including the holotype (AMNH 001), a subadult, almost complete skeleton with skull (AMNH 001)—recovered from the Two Medicine Formation of Montana (see *S1*; also see *S3* for photograph of mounted skeletal cast).

Subsequently, Burhnam (2004) described the skull and postcranial skeleton of *B. feinbergi* in greater detail, noting such previously unreported features as the following: Scapula not fused with coracoid, scapula having pronounced acromion for contact with furcula, glenoid caudolaterally oriented (condition similar to that in the deinonychosaur *Unenlagia* [see entry], the velociraptorine *Deinonychus* and the bird *Archaeopteryx*); coracoid articulating with relatively large sternal plate; humerus having limited range of cranial motion and wider range of dorsal-ventral movement, capable of being folded back against body, but incapable of being brought forward much beyond ventral plane passing through glenoid; manual digits II and III usually working in concert as functional unit; arm-to-leg ratio of 0.69, one of the highest among known non-avian theropods (comparable to proportions in extant running birds, indicative of cursoriality; see Coombs 1978*b*); pelvis opisthopubic, pubis having well-developed pubic boot; pes functionally didactylous, supporting large, strongly curved raptorial claw (as in dromaeosaurids).

An endocast taken from the type specimen proved sufficiently detailed to show vascular imprints on the ventral surface of the skull roof, suggesting that the brain of the living animal occupied the entire cavity of the braincase, and that *Bambiraptor* possessed one of the largest dinosaurian brains known. From this endocast, Burnham noted such details as the large optic lobes large which, coupled with the large eyes and possibly overlapping fields of vision, probably indicate good vision (see Allman 1999) in this dinosaur.

Burnham identified the holotype of *B. feinbergi* as representing an immature individual based upon a number of observations. Among the specimens collected from the same site referred to *B. feinbergi*, the femur in AMNH 001 is 69 percent and tibia 74 percent as long as the largest femur and longest tibia, respectively, the latter belonging to a specimen presumably representing a more mature individual of the same species. Also, the bones of the braincase in AMNH 001 are separate, indicating immaturity. However, the presence of sternal plates and fusion of some bones reveal that the holotype is not that of a hatchling. While it was not yet possible to determine the age of the holotype at death, Burnham noted that its small size, and the relatively large brain and orbits "may be at least partially attributable to immaturity."

As noted by Burnham, the combination of small size, the comparatively large brain, the overlapping fields of vision, and the elongate front limbs could indicate that *Bambiraptor* was arboreal. The complex environment of an arboreal animal could have resulted in the evolution of a large brain (see Bock 1985); however, Burnham pointed out, increased brain size may also have been a consequence of hunting complex prey items (see Radinsky 1974).

In describing the new velociraptorine *Atrociraptor* (see entry), Currie and Varricchio also described two isolated specimens identified by those authors as velociraptorine maxillae, these being utilized for comparison purposes in their diagnosis of that genus. The first of these specimens (TMP 94.12.844), collected from the Dinosaur Park Formation of Alberta, Canada, was referred by those authors to *Saurornitholestes langstoni*, having been found in the same

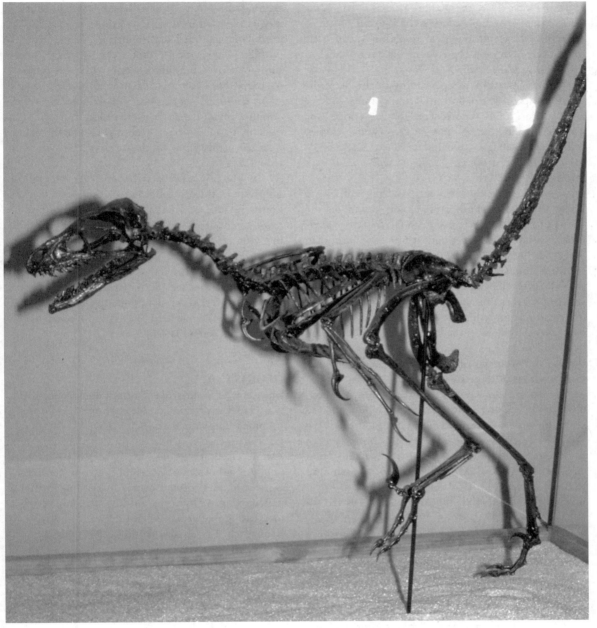

Photograph by the author, courtesy
North American Museum of Ancient
Life.

Mounted skeleton including
cast of holotype FIP 001 of
Bambiraptor feinbergi.

formation as, and less than five kilometers from where, the holotype of that type species was found. The second specimen (MOR 5535–7.30.91.274), from the Two Medicine Formation of Montana, morphologically similar to *B. feinbergi*, was referred by Currie and Varricchio to cf. *Bambiraptor feinbergi*. Contrary to the original description of *B. feinbergi* by Burnham *et al.*, Currie and Varricchio noted that the holotype of *B. feinbergi* has 12 rather than 10 maxillary tooth positions, as does MOR 5535–7.30.91.274.

Although *Bambiraptor* was originally described as a dromaeosaurid, Burnham, Senter, Barsbold and Britt (2004), in an abstract for a poster presenting a new phylogenetic analysis of the Dromaeosauridae (see "Systematics" chapter), referred this genus to the new deinonychosaurian clade Microraptoria.

In their review of the Dromaeosauridae, presumably written before the above study by Burnham *et al.*, Norell and Makovicky (2004) stated that *Bambiraptor* "is obviously a dromaeosaurid, as it shares with other taxa elongate caudal vertebral prezygapophyses and chevrons, a T-shaped lacrimal, and a modified second pedal digit."

Additionally, Norell and Makovicky pointed out that *Bambiraptor* "differs from [the dromaeosaurid] *Saurornitholestes* only in the amount of frontal participation in the orbit," this character probably being influenced by the juvenile nature of the skeleton of *B.*

feinbergi. Therefore, the possibility exists that *Bambiraptor* may inevitably prove to be a juvenile form of *Saurornitholestes*, although the resolving of this issue must await "a more complete analysis of unpublished *Saurornitholestes* remains."

Note: Sternal plates pertaining to theropod dinosaurs, especially small forms, are very rare. Godfrey and Currie (2004) reported on an incomplete (approximately three quarters preserved) yet well-preserved velociraptorine right sternal plate (TMP 92.36.333), collected in 1992 from sandstone in the Dinosaur Park Formation of Alberta.

In describing this element, Godfrey and Currie noted that the sternum most closely resembles the sterna of *Bambiraptor feinbergi* and *Velociraptor mongoliensis*. Birdlike features described by the authors in TMP 92.36.333 include the following: Length of sternum equal to or greater than width of paired sternal plates (elongation of the sternum possibly constituting the only feature rendering sternum in Dromaeosauridae more birdlike than that in Oviraptoridae; wide, well-developed coracoidal sulcus along nearly all of its cranial margin; clustering of at least three costal processes on craniolateral half of element (for reception of three sternal ribs).

Primitive (non-avian) features of the specimen, observed by Godfrey and Currie, "include its paired structure with no development of a sternal keel."

Key references: Allman (1999); Bock (1985); Burnham (2004); Burnham, Currie, Bakker, Zhou and Ostrom (2000); Coombs (1978*b*); Currie and Varricchio (2004); Godfrey and Currie (2004); Radinsky (1974); Norell and Makovicky (2004).

†BARAPASAURUS

Saurischia: Eusaurischia: Sauropodomorpha: Sauropoda: Eusauropoda: Cetiosauridae.

Comments: *Barapasaurus*, from the Kota Formation (Early Jurassic, Hettangian to Pleinsbachian) of eastern India, is one of the earliest known sauropod genera. As pointed out in an abstract by Bandyopadhyay, Saswati and Gillette (2003), the dentition of such primitive forms, while poorly known, may offer important phylogenetic information.

Bandyopadhyay *et al.* described the teeth of *Barapasaurus* as follows: Spoon-shaped, some having coarse denticles on distal carina; largest, probably right upper tooth typical, being slightly curved in mesial aspect, straight in lingual and labial aspects, crown having slight asymmetrical bulge; root tapered, elliptical in cross section, slightly constricted at junction with crown, latter also constricted and subcircular at base; most crown enamel weakly crenulated; labial surface of crown convex; lingual surface weakly

sigmoid, producing spoon-shaped profile in lateral or medial aspect; three coarse tubercles on distal carina producing scalloped, asymmetrical outline, proximal profile shallow, apical profile steep; three other teeth similar in overall anatomy, one with two tubercles on distal carina, others lacking tubercles; smaller tooth having elongate root and reduced crown, resembling mammalian incisor; bulbous crown truncated by beveled surface, seemingly lingually inclined wear facet (this probably the tooth of a juvenile individual).

As the authors observed, these teeth resemble descriptions of those belonging to *Vulcanodon*, from the Lower Jurassic of Zimbabwe, but not those of *Kotasaurus*, also from the lower Kota Formation of India, the latter being short and having a curved apex.

In their review of Sauropoda, Upchurch, Barrett and Dodson (2004) referred *Barapasaurus* to the family Cetiosauridae (see "Systematics" chapter).

Key references: Bandyopadhyay, Saswati and Gillette (2003); Upchurch, Barrett and Dodson (2004); Wilson and Sereno (1998).

†BAROSAURUS

Saurischia: Eusaurischia: Sauropodomorpha: Sauropoda: Eusauropoda: Neosauropoda: Diplodocoidea: Diplodocidae.

Diagnosis of genus (as for type species): Nine dorsal vertebrae; second dorsal vertebra with parapophysis at bottom of vertebral centrum; ventral fossae in proximal caudal centra increasing in prominence from cranial to middle caudal vertebrae (decreasing in *Diplodocus* and derived lithostrotians) (Upchurch, Barrett and Dodson 2004).

Comment: In their review of the Sauropoda, Upchurch, Barrett and Dodson (2004) rediagnosed the type species *Barosaurus lentus* (see *D:TE*).

Key reference: Upchurch, Barrett and Dodson (2004).

†BARYONYX

Saurischia: Eusaurischia: Eusaurischia: Theropoda: Neotheropoda: Tetanurae: Spinosauroidea: Spinosauridae: Baryonychinae.

Note: Hutt and Newbery (2004), in an abstract for a poster, reported the finding "of a remarkable vertebra" on the southwest coast of the Isle of Wight. Upon comparing this specimen with the holotype skeleton of *Baryonyx walkeri*, these authors found the former to be closely related both to that type species and also to the North African species *B. tenerensis*, the latter having originally been described by Sereno, Beck, Dutheil, Gado, Larsson, Lyon, Marcot, Rauhut,

Skeletal cast (by the PAST Company) of *Baryonyx tenerensis*, this mount being one of the attractions of the "Giants: African Dinosaurs" exhibit here debuting in December, 2003, at Chicago's Garfield Park Conservatory.

Life restoration by Berislav Krzic of a *Baryonyx walkeri*. In the background are a group of *Iguanodon*.

Sadleir, Sidor, Varricchio, Wilson and Wilson (1998) as belonging to a new genus, *Suchomimus* (see *S2*).

Based in part upon "the information derived from this important fossil," Hutt and Newbery concluded that "*Suchomimus*" indeed represents a second species of *Baryonyx* (as previously suggested by Sues, Frey, Martill and Scott 2002).

Erratum: In *S3*, it was incorrectly stated that the huge theropod claw from the Isle of Wight, discussed by Naish (2002), measures two meters in length. The correct length of this specimen — in the collection of Martin Simpson — is two centimeters. The estimated complete length of this claw, according to Naish, would have been approximately 30 centimeters along the dorsal margin.

Key references: Hutt (2004); Naish (2002); Sereno, Beck, Dutheil, Gado, Larsson, Lyon, Marcot, Rauhut, Sadleir, Sidor, Varricchio, Wilson and Wilson (1998); Sues, Frey, Martill and Scott (2002).

†BECKLESPINAX

Saurischia: Eusaurischia: Eusaurischia: Theropoda: Neotheropoda: Tetanurae: Avetheropoda: ?Carnosauria: ?Allosauroidea.

Comment: Holtz, Molnar and Currie (2004), in their review of basal Tetanurae, commented that the holotype and only specimen (BMNH R1828, three massive dorsal vertebrae with unusually tall neural spines from the Wealden of Hanover, Germany) of the type species *Becklespinax altispinax* (see *D:TE*) displays no particular derived feature other than their atypical height (neural spines five times as high as vertebral centrum), which may suggest a relationship with spinosaurids.

Previously, Stovall and Langston (1950) had suggested a possible relationship between these vertebrae and the North American allosauroid *Acrocanthosaurus*. Later, George Olshevsky (1991), in proposing the new genus *Becklespinax* for these vertebrae, implied a possible affinity of *B. altispinax* with the South American spinosauroid (?megalosaurid) *Piatnitzkysaurus*. As pointed out by Holtz *et al.*, however, "the relationship of this taxon remains problematic (see "Note," below).

Note: Naish (2003) described a partial proximal right tibia (HASMG G.378; previously mentioned by Benton and Spencer 1995 as HASMG GG98) belonging to a definitive allosauroid and which might be referrable to *Becklespinax* (see below; see also *D:TE*).

As Naish related, this specimen was discovered in the Samuel Husbands Beckles collection of the Hastings Museum and Art Gallery in Hastings, East Sussex, southern England. It was collected by Beckles between 1814 and 1890, presumably from the Lower Cretaceous (Berriasian-Valanginian) Hastings Group and from the Hastings area of East Sussex. Although the formation and exact location from which the specimen was collected is unknown, the lack of evidence for beach roll suggests an inland recovery site.

In describing HASMG G.378, Naish estimated that the tibia, if complete, would measure approximately 550 millimeters in length, indicating a large theropod.

Naish identified HASMG G.378 as belonging to the Theropoda by the form of its cnemial crest (*i.e.*, squared off in lateral profile, projecting dorsocranially with apex significantly taller than proximal articular surface).

Furthermore, Naish noted that the following derived character states confirm referral of HASMG G.378 to the Allosauroidea: Notch between proximal articular condyles (comparable to the notch in *Allosaurus* and *Neovenator salerii*) (see Chure 2003); well-developed incisura tibialis (the "fibular fossa" of Sereno, Beck, Dutheil, Iarochene, Larsson, Lyon, Magwene, Sidor, Varricchio and Wilson 1996); relative craniocaudal elogantion of proximal end (width to length ratio or proximal tibia similar to that of *Allosaurus* and *N. salerii*); and form of lateral condyle, with "conspicuous waisting between body of condyle and main body of tibia [with] small, triangular prominence anteriorly, sometimes with low ridge extending to crista fibularis" [as in allosauroids other than sinraptorids], see Azuma and Currie 2000).

Naish observed that HASMG G.378 resembles the proximal tibiae of the allosauroids *Allosaurus* and *N. salerii* (the latter being the only well-known Wealden member of the Allosauroidea). However, the specimen is more robust than the tibia of *N. salerii*; also, the tibiae of these taxa differ in the forms of the cnemial crest (mediolaterally broader in *N. salerii*), fibular crest (extending farther proximally in HASMG G.378), and proximal articular condyles (projecting further laterally in *N. salerii*).

The above-mentioned differences suggested to Naish that HASMG G.378 is not referrable to *Neovenator*, but rather to a related allosauroid possessing more robust limb bones. Naish considered *Becklespinax altixpinax*, based upon three caudal dorsal vertebrae, to be "an allosauroid (pending future work)," noting that the depth of the centra and the craniocaudal and mediolateral dimensions of the neural spines of that type species "imply that it was a robust animal that would have had tibiae of less gracile morphology than those seen in *N. salerii*." Positive referral of HASMG G.378 to *B. altispinax* cannot be made, however, until better material of the latter is known.

Key references: Azuma and Currie (2000); Benton and Spencer (1995); Chure (2003); Holtz, Molnar and Currie (2004); Naish (2003); Olshevsky (1991); Sereno, Beck, Dutheil, Iarochene, Larsson,

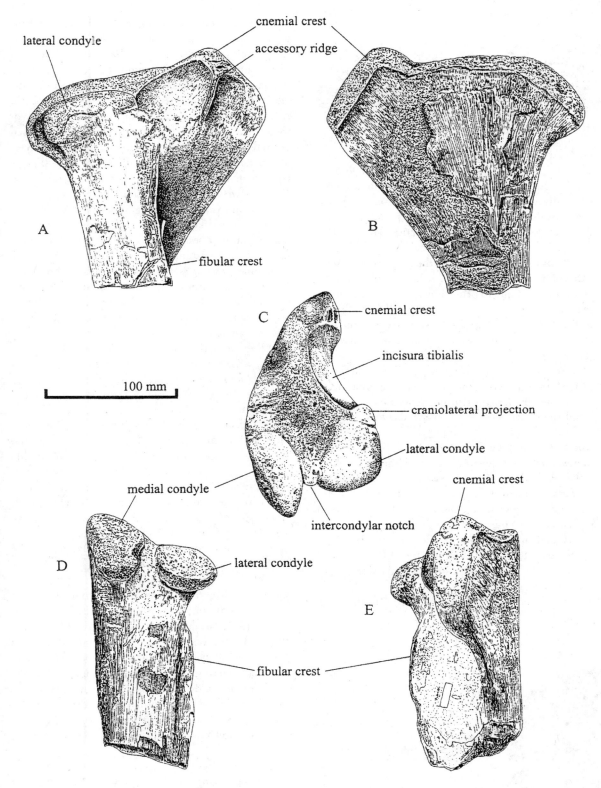

A lateral condyle · cnemial crest · accessory ridge · fibular crest

B

C cnemial crest · incisura tibialis · craniolateral projection · lateral condyle · intercondylar notch · medial condyle

100 mm

D lateral condyle · medial condyle · fibular crest

E cnemial crest · fibular crest

HASMG G.378, proximal right tibia of an allosauroid from East Sussex, in A. lateral, B. medial, C. proximal, D. caudal, and E. cranial views. This specimen could be referrable to *Becklespinax altispinax*. (After Naish 2003.)

Lyon, Magwene, Sidor, Varricchio and Wilson (1996); Stovall and Langston (1950).

†BEIPIAOSAURUS

Saurischia: Eusaurischia: Eusaurischia: Theropoda: Neotheropoda: Tetanurae: Avetheropoda: Coelurosauria: Tyrannoraptora: Maniraptoriformes: Maniraptora: Metornithes: Therizinosauroidea.

Diagnosis of genus (as for type species): Dentary longer than in other know therizinosauroids; preac-

Beipiaosaurus

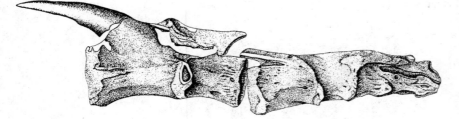

etabular and postacetabular parts of pelvis comparatively smaller; preacetabular part of pelvis expanded; ischial shaft cylindrical; first metatarsal mediolaterally compressed proximally; proximal part of metatarsals II and III compressed; (possibly also) teeth more bulbous (Clark, Maryańska and Barsbold 2004).

Comments: In the past, the pygostyle (a structure comprising fused caudal vertebrae) was regarded as a feature unique to ornithoracine birds and used to maneuver the feathers of the avian tail (see Chiappe 1997). Only in recent years has this character been also recognized in non-avian theropod dinosaurs (*e.g.*, the oviraptorosaurian *Nomingia*; see *S2*).

Yet more recently, Xu, Cheng, Wang and Chang (2003), in considering the phylogentic significance of the feathered therizinosauroid *Beipiaosaurus*, reexcavated the quarry — at the Lower Cretaceous Sihetun locality of Beipiao, Liaoning Province, China — from which the holotype of the type species *Beipiaosaurus inexspectus* was recovered (see Xu, Tang and Wang 1999). Among the material collected at that time was a nearly complete ilium, two incomplete ischia, and vertebrae (two sacrals and 30 caudals) (IVPP V11559), preserved in a single slab.

Of surprise to Xu *et al.* (2003) was a pygostyle observed on the almost complete tail of IVPP V11559. Additionally, filamentous integuments were found preserved on the tail.

As described by Xu *et al.* (2003), the well-

articulated distal tail comprises 11 caudal vertebrae having "a steady distal reduction in dimensions and no pathological structures." The sixth and seventh distal caudal vertebrae are completely fused together, the neural arch and centrum of the seventh distal caudal being entirely co-ossified with those of the sixth. A well-developed tubercle is on the lateral border of these vertebrae. The terminal five caudals are fused entirely into a pygostyle-like bone. This pygostyle-like structure is relatively straight, having a slightly concave distal margin, slightly convex dorsal margin, and somewhat blunt distal end.

As Xu *et al.* (2003) suggested, it is possible that this pygostyle-like structure — poorly understood in non-avian theropods, yet observed in both therizinosauroids and oviraptorosaurs — could constitute a synapomorphy for a more inclusive theropod clade. However, the authors cautioned that such structures must be documented in other theropod taxa and their phylogenetic implications need to be determined via cladistic analysis.

Regarding the possible function of this structure in non-aviant theropods, Xu *et al.* (2003) noted that no evidence for retrices at the end of the tail was found with the *Beipiaosaurus* material, and that such retrices may not have been present when the animal was alive. Considering the possibility that an absence of such retrices might be explained by preservational bias, the authors pointed out that filamentous integument is otherwise well and densely preserved along the tail of this dinosaur. Moreover, reported retrices, to date, have always been present along with other types of feathers or feather-like structures having the morphology of modern feathers (as found in specimens of *Protarchaeopteryx* and *Caudipteryx*, the latter genus lacking a pygostyle).

In *Beipiaosaurus*, the preserved integuments display little distinctive features of modern feathers, this absence conflicting with the presence of retrices in this genus. Consequently, it was the opinion of Xu *et al.* (2003) that the pygostyle-like structure may have "evolved initially for some unknown function(s), other than maneuvering tail feathers," this line of thought offering more evidence that some features previously thought to be unique to birds (*e.g.*, birdlike shoulder girdle, feathers) "have a wide distribution and initial function unrelated to birds and their flight" (see Feduccia 1999).

Key references: Chiappe (1997); Feduccia (1999); Xu, Cheng, Wang and Chang (2003); Xu, Tang and Wang (1999).

†BLIKANASAURUS

Saurischia: Eusaurischia: Sauropodomorpha: ?Sauropoda: Blikanasaurus.

Diagnosis of genus (as for type species): Apomorphy of distal end of fibula facing strongly ventromedially (Upchurch, Barrett and Dodson 2004).

Comment: In their review of the Sauropoda, Upchurch, Barrett and Dodson (2004) *Blikanasaurus cromptoni* (see *D:TE*), a type species regarded by them as a possible member of Sauropoda and, if that assessment is correct, a basal member of that clade.

Key reference: Upchurch, Barrett and Dodson (2004).

BONITASAURA   Apesteguía 2004

Saurischia: Eusaurischia: Sauropodomorpha: Sauropoda: Eusauropoda: Neosauropoda: Macronaria: Titanosauriformes: Titanosauria: ?Nemegtosauridae.

Name derivation: "[La] Bonita [quarry] + Greek *sauras* = "[female] lizard."

Type species: *B. salgadoi* Apesteguía 2004.

Other species: [None.]

Occurrence: Bajo de la Carpa Formation, Río Negro Province, Patagonia, Argentina.

Age: Late Cretaceous (Santonian).

Known material/holotype: MPCA 300, partially articulated skeleton including left frontal, left parietal, right dentary with 15 teeth (lacking at least three or four alveoli distal to symphysis), vertebrae (two cervicals, six dorsals, and 12 caudals), two chevrons, several cervical and dorsal ribs, humerus, radius, two metacarpals, femur, tibia, two metatarsals, subadult.

Diagnosis of genus (as for type species): Differing from all other known titanosaurs in following combination of features: dentary alveoli reduced in number (three in main ramus, one in angle, up to seven in mesial region); middle and distal region of dentary edentulous, forming sharp dorsal edge, lateral side profusely vascularized; very robust, diagonal neural arch pillars and bulging neural spine summits on cranial dorsal vertebrae; (more diagnostic characters perhaps to emerge subsequent to the complete preparation of the postcranial material) (Apesteguía 2004).

Comments: Distinguished as the first sauropod found to possess a "beak," the type species *Bonitasaura salgadoi* was erected upon an incomplete, partially articulated subadult skeleton (MPCA 300) collected from the "La Bonita" hill fossil quarry, in a fluvial

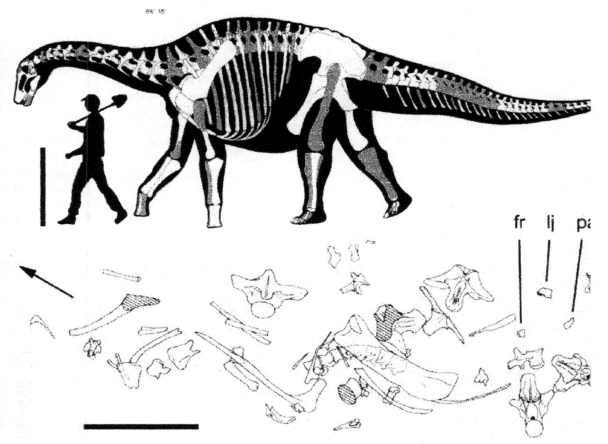

Bonitasaura salgadoi, MPCA 300, holotype skeleton (above) reconstruction, preserved bones indicated by dashed lines, and (below) quarry map, arrow pointing north. Scale = 1 meter. (After Apesteguía 2004.)

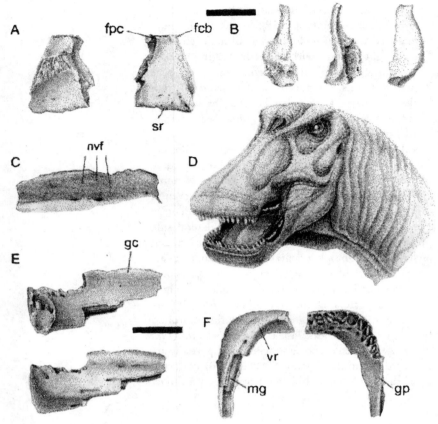

A fpc fcb B
sr
nvf
C D
gc
E
F vr
mg gp

**Bonitasaura salgadoi,
MPCA 300, holotype A.
right frontal (ventral and
dorsal views), B. left parietal (rostral, dorsal, and
caudal views), C. cutting
mandibular crest on caudal
dentary (labial view), D.
restoration of head showing
position of "guillotine-like"
mandibular crest or "beak,"
E. right dentary (lingual
and labial views), and F.
dentary (ventral and dorsal
views). Scale = 50 mm
(A–B, E–F) and 30 mm (C).
(After Apesteguía 2004.)**

sandstone of the uppermost layers of the Santonian
(Hugo and Leanza 1999) Bajo de la Carpa Formation,
Cerro Policia, Río Negro Province, in northwestern
Patagonia (Apesteguía 2004).

As measured by Apesteguía, the holotype skeleton of *B. salgadoi* is 9 meters (about 30 feet) in length.

In describing *B. salgadoi*, Apesteguía emphasized
the unusual morphology of the skull. The lower jaw
is rectangular and possesses narrow, mesially restricted
teeth such as those seen in derived titanosaurs (*e.g.,
Rapetosaurus*; see entry). A striking feature of the skull,
however, is evidence of a sharp, keratinous sheath over
the nondentigerous region, described by Apesteguía as
a crest or "beak" (analogous to the beaks reported previously in various Laurasian ornithischian taxa, particularly hadrosaurs) that could have functioned like
a guillotine to cut plant material. This novel (for
sauropods) adaptation, that author speculated, "would
have permitted effective slicing of tougher vegetation
and minimized tooth wear." According to Apesteguía,
the similarities in mouth configurations and body mobility (*i.e.*, loss of hyposphene-hypantrum complex)
in both the diplodocoid clade Rebbachisauridae and
in derived titanosaurs such as *Bonitasaura* "suggest
probable constraints on sauropod morphology that
conditioned them to take advantage of a determinate
resource," these constraints possibly "related to ge-

netical or morphological limitations, environmental
stasis, or the dominance of a particular vegetational
food source."

Although it was beyond the scope of Apesteguía's
initial study of this dinosaur to present a detailed character analysis of the new taxon, that author stated that
the available data suggest that *Bonitasaura* is closely related to three other known Late Cretaceous sauropods,
the Malagasy titanosaur *Rapetosaurus*, and the Mongolian nemegtosaurids *Nemegtosaurus* and *Quaesitosaurus*. All four of these taxa "share sculptured
frontal borders, a dentary symphysis that is almost
perpendicular to the mandibular rami, and narrow,
pencil-chisel-like teeth that are cylindrical in cross-
section and mostly restricted to the anteriormost portion of the lower jaw," a suite of characters suggesting
to Apesteguía that *Bonitasaura* could be closely related to the Nemegtosauridae (a family sometimes
classified with Titanosauria, but more recently assessed
by Upchurch, Barrett and Dodson 2004 as belonging
to Diplodocoidea; see "Systematics" chapter).

In comparing *Bonitasaura* to other titanosaurs,
Apesteguía noted that the new genus differs from
Antarctosaurus (see entry) in its possession of the "guillotine crest," a straight angle of symphysis, and a parietal having a somewhat flat sinuous caudal surface.
Moreover, the presence in *Antarctosaurus* of an extensive edentulous region and in *Rapetosaurus* of a
short rugose postalveolar ridge and unusual post-
dentigerous corner of the maxilla, suggest that such
guillotine-like structures could have developed also
in other members of the Titanosauria.

As pointed out by Apesteguía, Late Cretaceous,
southern hemisphere sauropods seem to have entered
an adaptive zone previously believed to have been the
exclusive domain of ornithischian dinosaurs (see Powell 2003). However, both titanosaurs and rebbachisaurids exhibit unusual features suggesting that some
Late Cretaceous sauropod taxa "acquired a disparate
morphological diversity." Moreover, the several known
contemporaneous ornithischian lineages were limited
to rare and small-sized forms, unlike the large forms
found in other regions. This panorama would not
change until the late Campanian arrival in South
America of ornithischians from North America. Perhaps, Apesteguía concluded, the morphological diversity and adaptive capabilities of these sauropods
can "help to explain their persistence into the latest
Cretaceous."

Key references: Apesteguía (2004); Hugo and
Leanza (1999); Powell (2003); Upchurch, Barrett and
Dodson (2004).

BOREALOSAURUS You, Ji, Lamanna, Li and Li
2004

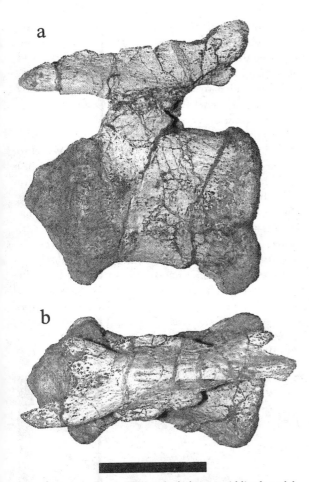

Borealosaurus wimani, LPM 0167, holotype middistal caudal vertebra in a. left lateral and b. dorsal views. Scale = 5 cm. (After You, Qiang, Lamanna, Li and Li 2004.)

Saurischia: Eusaurischia: Sauropodomorpha: Sauropoda: Eusauropoda: Neosauropoda: Macronaia: Titanosauriformes: Titanosauria: Lithostrotia: Saltasauridae: ?Opisthocoelicaudinae.

Name derivation: Greek *borealis* = "northern (referring to northern Chinese fossil locality and Northern Hemisphere)" + Greek *sauros* = "lizard."

Type species: *B. wimani* You, Ji, Lamanna, Li and Li 2004.

Other species: [None.]

Occurrence: Sunjiawan Formation, Liaoning Province, China.

Age: Early Late Cretaceous.

Known material: Caudal vertebrae, tooth crown, right humerus.

Holotype: LPM 0167, middistal caudal vertebra.

Diagnosis of genus (as for type species): Distinguished from all other sauropods by opisthocoelous middistal caudal vertebrae (You, Ji, Lamanna, Li and Li 2004).

Comments: The genus *Borealosaurus* was founded upon an isolated and "unusual" middistal caudal ver-

tebra (LPM 0167) collected near the Shuangmiao village of Beipiao, in the early Late Cretaceous (*e.g.,* Dong 2002) Sunjiawan Formation of Liaoning, northern China. Specimens possibly referrable to the type species, *Borealosaurus wimani,* comprise an isolated tooth crown (LPM 0169), a middle caudal vertebra (LPM 0168), and a right humerus (LPM 0170), collected from the same locality; association of these specimens to the holotype or to each other, however, cannot be determined (You, Ji, Lamanna, Li and Li 2004).

In performing a cladistic analysis, You *et al.* referred *Borealosaurus* to the Titanosauriformes based upon the proximal placement of the neural arch in LPM 0176 (see Salgado, Coria and Calvo 1997; Upchurch 1998); and tentatively to the Opisthocoelicaudinae based upon the opisthocoelous caudal vertebrae, a condition otherwise known only in *Opisthocoelicaudia* (Borsuk-Bialynicka 1977).

Regarding the specimens provisionally referred to *Borealosaurus,* You cited the following features consistent with titanosaurian relationships: LPM 0169 — enamel wrinkled (synapomorphy of Eusauropoda), lacking denticles (referrable to Neosauropoda), cylindrical cross section indicating affinities with titanosaurians more derived than *Malawisaurus* or with diplodocoids (see Wilson 2002*a*); LPM 0168 — proximally placed neural arch, as in holotype, permitting referral to the Titanosauriformes (see Salgado *et al.*; Upchurch); LPM 0170 — deltopectoral crest mediolaterally expanded, indicating referral to the Titanosauria and possibly to Saltisauridae (see Wilson).

As You *et al.* concluded, the presence of opisthocoelous caudal vertebrae in both *Borealosaurus* and *Opisthocoelicaudia* could indicate that both genera belong to an as-yet unrecognized titanosaurian subclade endemic to the Cretaceous of Asia.

Key references: Borsuk-Bialynicka (1977); Dong (2002); You, Ji, Lamanna, Li and Li (2004); Salgado, Coria and Calvo (1997); Upchurch (1998); Wilson (2002*a*).

†BOROGOVIA

Saurischia: Eusaurischia: Eusaurischia: Theropoda: Neotheropoda: Tetanurae: Avetheropoda: Coelurosauria: Tyrannoraptora: Maniraporiformes: Troodontidae.

Diagnosis of genus (as for type species): Distinguished from other troodontids by straight, weakly developed ungual on pedal digit II, and by phalanges of digit III slender, shorter and thinner than IV; preserved portion of arctometatarsal metatarsus asymmetrical, metatarsal II short, IV robust (the latter possibly belonging to *Saurornithoides junior* because of its size; see Barsbold and Osmólska 1990) (Makovicky and Norell 2004).

Comment: In their review of the Troodontidae, Makovicky and Norell (2004) rediagnosed the type species *Borogovia gracilicrus* (see *D:TE*).

Key references: Barsbold and Osmólska (1990); Makovicky and Norell (2004).

†BRACHIOSAURUS

Saurischia: Eusaurischia: Sauropodomorpha: Sauropoda: Eusauropoda: Neosauropoda: Macronaria: Titanosauriformes: Brachiosauridae.

Diagnosis of genus: Excavation behind articular facets of prezygapophyses of cervical vertebrae, between spinoprezygapophyseal and prezygodiapophyseal laminae; midcervical spinopostzygapophyseal laminae producing thin medial laminae meeting on midline immediately caudal to summit of spine, producing smooth troughlike area; ungual of manual digit I reduced, subequal in length to first phalanx of manual digit I (Upchurch, Barrett and Dodson 2004).

Comments: Among the rarest of Late Jurassic North American sauropods, *Brachiosaurus* has been reported on that continent from Colorado, Utah, and Wyoming. Recently, the provenance of this genus has been expanded to Oklahoma with the reporting by Bonnan and Wedel (2004) of *Brachiosaurus* remains from the Kenton Pit 1 site, in the Upper Jurassic Morrison Formation of the Oklahoma panhandle.

The specimen referred by Bonnan and Wedel to *Brachiosaurus* consists of a metacarpal (OMNH 01138) that the authors identified as a left metacarpal II. In describing this specimen, the authors noted that it is longer and more slender than metacarpals of diplodocids (*Apatosaurus* and *Diplodocus*) and *Camarasaurus* also recovered at the Kenton site. Moreover, the specimen, in its size and proportions, most closely resembles the elongate metacarpals described for the brachiosaurids *Brachiosaurus brancai*, *Brachiosaurus* sp. (see Jensen 1987), the Middle Cretaceous genus *Sonorasaurus* (Ratkevitch 1998), and the Early Cretaceous *Cedarosaurus* (Tidwell, Carpenter and Brooks 1999).

Life restoration by artist Todd Marshall of *Brachiosaurus altithorax*.

Reconstructed skeletal cast of the brachiosaurid titanosauriform **Brachiosaurus altithorax** (including cast of holotype FMNH PR25107) mounted by the PAST company outside The Field Museum.

Because *Brachiosaurus* is the only member of the Brachiosauridae currently known from North America during the Late Jurassic, Bonnan and Wedel referred OMNH 01138 to *Brachiosaurus* sp.

As Bonnan and Wedel noted, the Kenton quarry is unusual in having yielded the remains of several juvenile sauropods (*e.g.*, baby specimens — rare in the Morrison Formation — of *Apatosaurus* and *Camarasaurus*; see Carpenter and McIntosh 1994). Therefore, the many juvenile sauropod specimens recovered at this site "indicate that the absence of small-bodied dinosaur taxa from the quarry is probably not a result of taphonomic bias."

While the above find constitutes the first official report of the genus from Oklahoma, Bonnan and Wedel proposed that "some anomalously long cervical centra in the OMNH collection may also pertain to *Brachiosaurus*."

Key reference: Bonnan and Wedel (2004); Carpenter and McIntosh (1994); Jensen (1987); Ratkevitch (1998); Tidwell, Carpenter and Brooks (1999); Upchurch, Barrett and Dodson (2004).

†BRACHYLOPHOSAURUS

Ornithischia: Predentata: Genasauria: Cerapoda: Ornithopoda: Euornithopoda: Iguanodontia: Dryomorpha: Ankylopollexia: Styracosterna: Iguanodontoidea: Hadrosauroidea: Euhadrosauria: Hadrosauridae: Hadrosaurinae: Edmontosaurini.

Comments: Bergeron and Schweitzer (2003), in an abstract, briefly reported on a bonebed — containing more than 300 elements belonging to the solid-crested duckbilled dinosaur *Brachylophosaurus*— deposited in a distributary channel of the Judith River Formation, near Malta, Montana.

As described by Bergeron and Schweitzer, the exterior of these bones is unusually well preserved, exhibiting minor or no sediment infilling. The quality and extent of bone preservation depends upon "the biological, chemical, and physical environment of deposition and diagenesis of the bone and surrounding sandstones." Petrographic analysis by Bergeron and Schweitzer of the sandstones at this site "revealed varying geochemical environments that affect the quality of preservation": The exceptionally well-preserved bones had been surrounded by early calcite-cemented concretions containing floating grains, spherulitic and euhedral calcite; the less well-preserved elements by clay and iron oxide-cemented sandstones with long grain contacts.

In another abstract, Hartman (2004) briefly discussed recently collected specimens of the type species *Brachylophosaurus canadensis*, two of which, because of their "Exquisite preservation," offer evidence pertaining to the probable stance and walking mode of this dinosaur (locality not given in this report).

Hartman observed the following in this material: (Three specimens) scapulae preserved at approximately 45 degrees from horizontal, almost entire blade overlapping ribcage; (all specimens) cranial thoracic ribs swept strongly caudally, glenoid fossa consequently cranial to ribcage, precluding contact between ribs and proximal humerus despite degree of humeral eversion; glenoid orientation suggesting nongraviportal upright stance, with 10 to 20 degrees of humeral eversion from vertical; ulna and radius not strongly crossing; proximal carpal (in articulation)

Life restoration by Berislav Krzic of *Brachylophosaurus canadensis*.

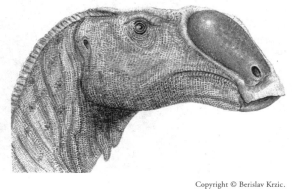

sitting firmly between distal ends of ulna and radius, preventing rotation about long axis; distal carpal protruding distally beyond forearm; distal carpal (when manus is extended) forming peg and socket joint, notch in metacarpal packet formed by raised proximal ends of metacarpals 2 and 4, wrist and elbow therefore limited during extension to movement in parasagittal plane; weight-bearing metacarpals (2–4) tightly bound, effectively transmitting (because of reduced carpus) ground forces directly to ulna and radius.

The forelimb specialization in *Brachylophosaurus* "to reduce the range of movement of the distal elements to within a parasagiital plane" reminded Hartman of the forelimb in ungulate mammals, "which have a similar reduction in degrees of freedom of joint rotation." This, combined with the elongate distal forelimb bones and tightly bound metacarpals, suggested to Hartman that this genus of dinosaur "spent much of its time in a quadrupedal stance, perhaps even engaging in rapid quadrupedal locomotion."

Key references: Bergeron and Schweitzer (2003); Hartman (2004).

Locality (looking north) where the holotype (IGM 100/983) of *Byronosaurus jaffei* was discovered, arrow showing the point of discovery. (After Makovicky, Norell, Clark and Rowe 2003.)

†BYRONOSAURUS

Saurischia: Eusaurischia: Eusaurischia: Theropoda:
    Neotheropoda: Tetanurae: Avetheropoda: Coeluro-

Photograph by Mick Ellison, courtesy American Museum of Natural History.

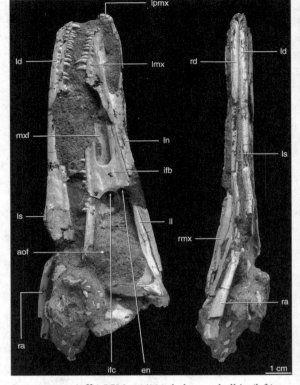

Byronosaurus jaffei, IGM 100/983, holotype skull in (left) right lateral and (right) dorsal views. (After Makovicky, Norell, Clark and Rowe 2003.)

Photograph by Mick Ellison, courtesy American Museum of Natural History.

Photograph by Mick Ellison, courtesy American Museum of Natural History.)

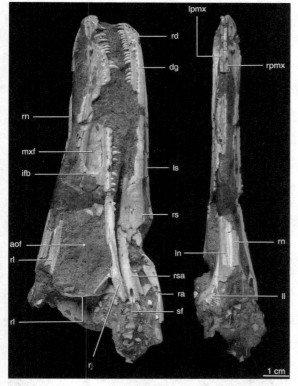

Byronosaurus jaffei, IGM 100/983, holotype skull in (left) left lateral and (right) ventral views. (After Makovicky, Norell, Clark and Rowe 2003.)

sauria: Tyrannoraptora: Maniraptoriformes: Troodontidae.

Diagnosis: Teeth lacking serrations; interfernestral bar separating antorbital fenestra from accessory not inset from lateral surface of skull (these features unique among described Troodontidae) (Makovicky and Norell 2004).

Comments: In 2000, Mark A. Norell, Peter J. Makovicky and James M. Clark named and described the new type species *Byronosaurus jaffei*, based on two specimens, including well-preserved skull and fragmentary postcranial material (holotype IGM 100/983 and referred specimen IGM 100/987), recovered from adjacent localities in the Nemegt basin, Önögov Aimag, Mongolia (see *S2*). During a later examination of these materials, elements (now catalogued as IGM 100/987) belonging to a second and significantly larger animal were discovered intermixed with the holotype elements. Lacking any troodontid apomorphies, this specimen has been identified as belonging to the Ornithomimidae (see Makovicky and Norell 1998).

Subsequently, in their published detailed osteology of *B. jaffei*, Makovicky, Norell, Clark and Rowe (2003) noted that the holotype was recovered from the "Ankylosaur Flats" sublocality in 1993 by American Museum of Natural History paleontologist Michael Novacek during the museum's 1994–98 field seasons. The very fragmentary referred specimen, a rostrum in six pieces collected on July 15, 1996 at the "Bolor's Hill" locality, west of the main Ukhaa Tolgod exposure, preserves some salient features not preserved in the holotype. It was referred to *B. jaffei*

Byronosaurus jaffei, detail of the narial region of holotype IGM 100/983, in left lateral view. (After Makovicky, Norell, Clark and Rowe 2003.)

Photograph by Mick Ellison, courtesy American Museum of Natural History.)

Byronosaurus

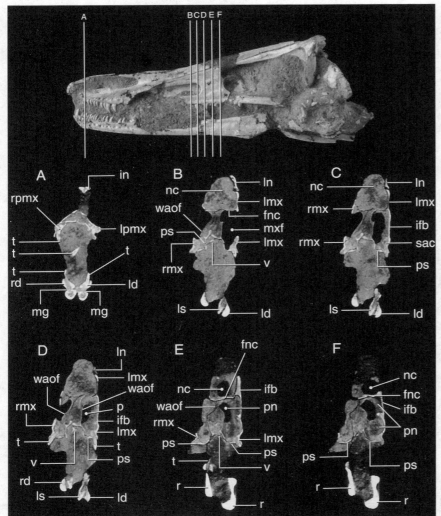

Byronosaurus jaffei, scans of the rostrum of holotype IGM 100/983. "Notice the osseous floor of the nasal cavity (fnc) as it extends through the interfenestral bar in C, D, E, and F." (After Makovicky, Norell, Clark and Rowe 2003.)

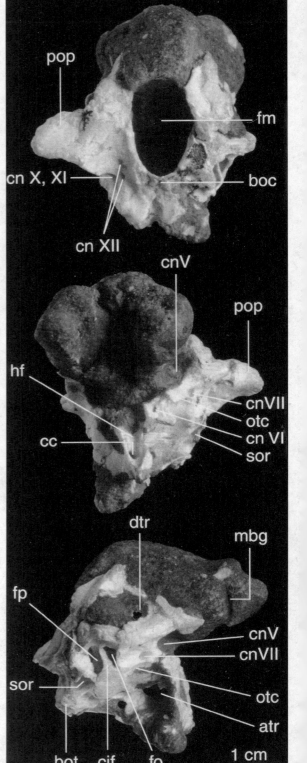

Byronosaurus jaffei, braincase of holotype IGM 100/983, in (top) caudal, (middle) rostral, and (bottom) right lateral views. (After Makovicky, Norell, Clark and Rowe 2003.)

based upon the following features: Supernumery teeth lacking serrations; distinctive lacrimals having lateral shelf overhanging anterodorsal corner of orbit; and pair of passages through interfenestral bar, not recessed from plane of rostrum.

As Makovicky *et al.* pointed out, *B. jaffei* is, to date, one of the best preserved troodontid dinosaurs known, extending of knowledge on the diversity of these Late Cretaceous theropods, and also revealing a number of important characters (*e.g.,* extensive secondary palate, opening interpreted as subnarial foramen, connection between antorbital and accessory fenestrae). Atypically of Troodontidae, the teeth are not serrated.

B. jaffei, Makovicky *et al.* noted, also offers the first data on the anatomy of the rostral part of the troodontid palate. For example, the palate is formed rostrally by the premaxilla and more caudally by the palatal shelves, the latter being flat rostrally, becoming more vaulted caudally. An unusual feature of this

Photograph by Mick Ellison, courtesy American Museum of Natural History.)

ln

lpmx

lf

lpo

lq

ll

lj

lqj

lmx

lsa

lan

rd

la

3 cm

C

Byronosaurus jaffei, exploded view of holotype skull (IGM 100/983). (After Makovicky, Norell, Clark and Rowe 2003.)

species, found also in the alvarezsaurid *Shuvuuia deserti*, is "a small tubular foramen on the maxilla just dorsal to the tooth row on the ventral border of the narial fossa," this interpreted by Makovicky *et al.* "as homologous to the subnarial foramen, which typically lies in the premaxillary-maxillary suture and level with the supraalveolar canal in theropods."

According to Makovicky *et al.*, the teeth of *B. jaffei*, being unserrated unlike the serrated teeth of other known troodontids, present important implications concerning understanding the phylogenetic position of the Troodontidae. In some previous analyses, Troodontidae and Therizinosauroidea (and the toothless Oviraptorosauria) have been grouped, in part, based on the enlarged, atypically hooked tooth serration found in bother groups. However, the small tooth serrations observed in the sinraptorid allosauroid *Sinovenator* (see Xu, Norell, Wang, Makovicky and Wu 2002) and absence of them in *B. jaffei* demonstrate "that large denticles can no longer be regarded as plesiomorphic within Troodontidae, and are diagnostic of a more exclusive clade within Troodontidae" (see "Systematics" chapter).

Key references: Makovicky and Norell (1998); Makovicky, Norell, Clark and Rowe (2003); Makovicky and Norell (2004); Norell, Makovicky and Clark (2000); Xu, Norell, Wang, Makovicky and Wu (2002).

†CAENAGNATHASIA

Saurischia: Eusaurischia: Theropoda: Neotheropoda: Tetanurae: Avetheropoda: Coelurosauria: Tyrannoraptora: Maniraptoriformes: Maniraptora: Metornithes: Oviraptorosauria: Caenagnathoidea: Caenagnathidae.

Diagnosis of genus (as for type species): Smallest known caenagnathid; dentary with nearly straight dorsal margin, lacking toothlike projections; fluting of occlusal edge less distinct than in other caenagnathids (Osmólska, Currie and Barsbold 2004).

Comment: In their review of the Oviraptorosauria, Osmólska, Currie and Barsbold (2004) rediagnosed the type species *Caenagnathasia matinsoni* (see *D:TE*).

Key reference: Osmólska, Currie and Barsbold (2004).

†CAMARASAURUS—(=?*Cathesaurus*, *Caulodon*, *Morosaurus*, *Uintasaurus*; =?*Eobrontosaurus*)

Saurischia: Eusaurischia: Sauropodomorpha: Sauropoda: Eusauropoda: Neosauropoda: Macronaria: Camarsauromorpha: Camarasauridae.

Comments: During field seasons of 1997 and 1998, teams from the University of Kansas collected vertebrate fossils from a dinosaur quarry, comprising fluvial quartz sandstones and mudstones, in the upper Morrison Formation in the Black Hills of northeastern Wyoming. Bader (2003), in an abstract, briefly

Skeleton of a baby (estimated age of six months) *Camarasaurus* mounted at the Sauriermuseum Aathal. This specimen, nicknamed "Toni," was collected at Howe Ranch in the Morrison Formation of northern Wyoming. The specimen measures 1.5 meters (about five feet) in length. The skull has been restored.

Photograph by Urs Möckli, copyright © and courtesy Sauriermuseum Aathal.

Camarasaurus

Skull of *Camarasaurus* belonging to a virtually complete skeleton discovered in 1993 in the Howe Stephens Quarry at Howe Ranch, in the Morrison Formation of northern Wyoming. This perfectly preserved skull, nicknamed "E.T.," measures 54 cm (about 21 inches) in length. Skin impressions have been preserved (light color) on the lower jaw. The entire skeleton, missing just a few caudal vertebrae, measures approximately 10 meters (about 37 feet) long (see Ayer 1999).

pod genus to be recovered at this site since the original diggings began) was excavated.

(Bader further reported that other material recently collected from this site includes a probably brachiosaur skeleton; large and small theropod teeth, crocodile teeth, and shell fragments belonging to the freshwater turtle *Glyptos plicatalus* [all associated with the *Camarasaurus* specimen]; a juvenile *Allosaurus* specimen; in a zone below the dinosaurian remains, abundant fish bones and scales; also, rare gynosperm leaf and more abundant seed fossils, the most common being *Araucaria*.)

Ikejiri (2003), in a published abstract for a poster, discussed determination of the sequence of closure of neurocentral sutures in the vertebrae of a series of *Camarasaurus* specimens representing different ontogenetic stages. As noted by that author, the centra and neural arches of the middle and distal caudal vertebrae in juveniles of the genus are highly fused without sutures. All presacral, sacral, and proximal (from number one to approximately number six) caudal vertebrae are unfused, with suture lines seen between the centra and proximal caudal ribs from juvenile to subadult stages. The time of closure for these sutures probably varies among *Camarasaurus* individuals, although Ikejiri observed the following typical

reported on the university's return to that site in the summer of 2002, during which a subadult *Camarasaurus* skeleton (the fourth specimen of this sauro-

Detail of teeth belonging to a skull (BHI 6200) of *Camarasaurus* cf. *supremus* (nicknamed "Elaine").

Life restoration by artist Todd Marshall depicting a group of "*Allosaurus jimmadseni*" bringing down a juvenile *Camarasaurus lentus*.

sequence: 1. Middle to distal caudal vertebrae; 2. ribs of proximal caudals; 3. neural arch of proximal caudals; 4. cervical vertebrae (from cranial ones) or sacrum (neural arch and sacral ribs); and 5. dorsal vertebrae. Ikejiri noted the same or similar pattern in other archosauromorphs (*e.g.*, *Alligator*, *Crocodilus*).

Ikejiri also noted the following: The timing of vertebral suture closer is relatively late in some theropods (*e.g.*, *Coelophysis*, *Gojirasaurus* [="*Godzillasaurus*" of Ikejiri's usage]); in extant birds these sutures are already closed before hatching; some large-bodied turtles (*e.g.*, chelids and chelonids) have sutures between the neural arches and centra in adult stages, while juveniles of some small-bodied forms (*e.g.*, emydids) have closed sutures; such sutures were not observed in *Sphenodon* or Squamata, including juveniles and large-bodied forms (*e.g.*, pythons, Komodo dragons, mosasaurs). Ikejiri concluded that the pattern and tempo of closure of these sutures seems to be due to phylogenetic position in Reptilia in addition to body size, not merely a consequence of ontogeny.

In a subsequently published and related abstract for a poster, Ikejiri (2004) compared growth patterns in juvenile through adult *Camarasaurus* individuals, with data acquired from 10 articulated or reasonably complete skeletons including six specimens of *Camarasaurus lentus*, three of *C. grandis*, and one referred to *Camarasaurus* sp. (see abstract for details on methods used in that author's calculations). Ikejiri (2004)

found no significant difference in the relative growth between the measured specimens, indicating that *C. lentus* and *C. grandis* shared similar growth patterns. Moreover, Ikejiri (2004) observed that overall skull size in these species remains proportionally the same from juvenile to adult stages, this "suggesting that cranial development occurs in the embryonic or hatchling stage."

Ikejiri (2004)'s study concluded the following regarding *Camarasaurus*: Four growth stages, based upon patterns of bone fusion and degree of ossified tendon (enthesis) of vertebrae, and on rugosity of limb articular surfaces; up to 72 percent of body size attained by end of subadult stage; fusion of scapulocoracoids and vertebrae not occurring during juvenile stage (approximately 60 percent body size), even in juvenile sauropods thought to exhibit faster growth rate during life cycle.

Key references: Bader (2003); Ikejiri (2003, 2004).

†CAMELOTIA

Saurischia: Eusaurischia: Sauropodomorpha: Sauropoda: Prosauropoda: Anchisauria: Melanorosauridae.

Diagnosis of genus (as for type species): Autapomorphy of large, sheetlike cranial trochanter (Galton and Upchurch 2004*a*).

Comment: In their review of the Prosauropoda,

Galton and Upchurch (2004a) rediagnosed the type species *Camelotia borealis* (see *D:TE*).

Key reference: Galton and Upchurch (2004a).

†**CAMPYLODONISCUS** [*nomen dubium*]—(=?*Antarctosaurus*)

Saurischia: Eusaurischia: Sauropodomorpha: Sauropoda: Eusauropoda: Neosauropoda: Macronaria: Titanosauriformes: Titanosauria *incertae sedis*.

Comments: In his monograph on the "titanosaurids" of South America, Powell (2003) reassessed the type species *Campylodoniscus ameghinoi* Kuhn 1961 (see also Steel 1970), based on an incomplete left maxilla with seven alveoli, one functional tooth, and an isolated broken replacement tooth crown (MACN A-IOR63), collected from an Upper Cretaceous (?Senonian) unknown formation of the Chubut Group, on the western flank (see Huene 1929) of the Sierra de San Bernardo, west of Lake Musters, in Chubut, Argentina, this material originally described by Huene as *Campylodon ameghinoi* (see *D:TE*).

According to Powell, MACN A-IOR63 cannot be compared with other "titanosaurids," as there is no knowledge of maxillaries among all known members of the "Titanosauridae" with the exception of *Antarctosaurus wichmannianus*, the latter species having comparatively small teeth in adults. However, detailed examination of the teeth of *C. ameghinoi* shows a structural similarity (*i.e.*, clear differentiation between crown and root by presence of enamel, possession of backwards-curved edge, bulbous nature of labial face, and transverse surface concavity parallel to mesial and distal edges of tooth) between it and *Camarasaurus*. Contrarily, Powell noted, other known "titanosaurid" teeth have a straight edge, are largely symmetrical, the enamel face either smooth or just slightly rugose, the lateral face not having a bulbous expansion. Therefore, *Campylodoniscus* has a "camarasauroid" rather than the apparently typical "diplodocoid" (as seen in *A. wichmannianus*) kind of morphology.

According to Powell, *C. ameghinoi* could be synonymous with *A. wichmannianus* or represent a distinct form; however, it is not possible at present to resolve this question, and is "therefore convient to consider *Campylodoniscus ameghinoi* as a *nomen dubium*, according to the definition in the [International] Code of Zoological Nomenclature."

Powell further commented that Huene and Matley (1933) had described a short and tall maxilla that had been found along with *Antarctosaurus* remains recovered at Bara Simla, Jabalpur, India. Another cranium, however, collected at Arroyo Morterito, Department of Candelaria, Salta Province, Argentina,

has a short, tall premaxilla that is certainly not of the "diplodocoid" form. According to Powell, this evidence strongly suggests that, among the forms now classified as "titanosaurids," "there exist two groups with markedly different cranial structure."

Key references: Huene (1929); Huene and Matley (1933); Kuhn (1961); Powell (2003); Steel (1970).

†**CARDIODON**

Saurischia: Eusaurischia: Sauropodomorpha: Sauropoda: Eusauropoda *incertae sedis*.

Comments: In 1841, Richard Owen named the genus *Cardiodon*, based only on a tooth collected from the Middle Jurassic Forest Marble of Bradford-On-Avon, Wiltshire. Owen neither illustrated this specimen nor assigned to it a specific name (see *D:TE*), and the whereabouts of this tooth are currently unknown.

Recently, sauropod specialists Paul Upchurch and John Martin (2003) addressed this infrequently discussed taxon in their revision of the genus *Cetiosaurus*, recounting the somewhat entangled taxonomic history of *Cardiodon*: Owen (1844) subsequently added the specific name *rugulosus* to the genus, as the combination *Cardiodon rugulosus*.

Additional isolated teeth were later discovered at various Oxfordshire localities. One of these teeth (OUM J13597), lacking its root and damaged along its ?distal margin, was found at Bletchingdon Station, a site that had yielded several partial skeletons of *Cetiosaurus oxoniensis* (see entry). For that reason, Phillips (1871) referred these teeth to *Cetiosaurus*.

Based on similarities between the teeth of *Cardiodon* and *Cetiosaurus*, various workers (*e.g.*, Owen 1875; Marsh 1888b) suggested that these genera could be synonymous. Lydekker (1890) referred to *Cardiodon* an apparently similar tooth (BMNH R1527) collected from the Great Oolite near Cirencester, Gloucestershire. At the same time, Lydekker, also believing that the two forms were congeneric, referred all material assigned to *C. oxoniensis* to the genus *Cardiodon*. This synonymy was mostly either ignored by subsequent authors, or adopted, although they opted to retain the better known name *Cetiosaurus* over *Cardiodon*. Consequently, Steel (1970) erected the new combination *Cetiosaurus rugulosus* upon the type specimen of *Cardiodon*.

However, Upchurch and Martin pointed out that, before *Cardiodon* can become a senior synonym of the more widely known *Cetiosaurus*, several criteria must first be met: "(1) the teeth assigned to *Cetiosaurus* must genuinely belong to that genus; (2) the teeth assigned to *Cardiodon* and *Cetiosaurus* must share autapomorphic features; and (3) *Cardiodon* must have priority over *Cetiosaurus* (the latter condition controversial [see Bush 1903; Steel], but obviated by considering the first two conditions).

As Upchurch and Martin noted, Philips' association of the Bletchingdon tooth and partial skeletons can only be supported by the following: 1. No other sauropod taxa have been found at Bletchingdon; and 2. OUMNH J13597 is morphologically similar to teeth of *Patagosaurus* (see Bonaparte 1986*a*), which may occupy the same phylogenetic position as *Cetiosaurus*.

Assuming that the Bletchingdon tooth and partial skeletal remains are associated presents problems. In the past, Upchurch and Martin noted, utilizing such circumstantial evidence as same locality and horizon has resulted in numerous taxonomic problems (see, for example, McIntosh 1990). Therefore, "although the Bletchingdon tooth could belong to *Cetiosaurus*, the evidence supporting this view is weak."

In describing the tooth of *Cardiodon*, Upchurch and Martin observed that the tooth is spatulate, curving somewhat lingually towards its apex, its labial surface being strongly convex mesiodistally and bearing a shallow groove that extends parallel to its distal margin. However, unlike other known spatulate teeth, its lingual surface is also convex, albeit less convex than the labial surface. There are no serrations along the margins of the crown, and the surface of the enamel is finely wrinkled, warranting referral of the specimen to the Eusauropoda (see Wilson and Sereno 1998). The Bletchingdon tooth generally resembles, in most respects, that of *Cardiodon*, although the former "has the conventional concave lingual surface (bearing a vertical midline ridge) that is observed in basal sauropods and *Camarasaurus* (Upchurch 1995, 1998)." Therefore, these two types of teeth do not share any autapomorphies. Furthermore, the lack of a lingual cavity in the *Cardiodon* tooth "suggests that it may have come from a different taxon from that which produced the '*Cetiosaurus*' tooth."

Upchurch and Martin concluded there is no supporting evidence for a synonymy of *Cetiosaurus* with *Cardiodon*. Furthermore, the available morphological data, in fact, argue against synonymy. Thus, the authors provisionally retained *Cardiodon rugulosus* as a valid taxon, being the only known spoon-shaped sauropod tooth also having a convex lingual surface.

Upchurch and Martin regarded *Cardiodon rugulosus* as Eusauropoda *incertae sedis*, its type specimen potentially lost, its referred material only barely diagnostic, and with *Cetiosaurus rugulosus* considered to be a junior objective synonym of the genus *Cardiodon*.

In their review of the Sauropoda, Upchurch, Barrett and Dodson (2004) reiterated that the referred tooth crown of *C. rugulosus* cannot be characterized by true autapomorphies, although it does present the following unique combination of characters characteristic of Eusauropoda: Outline broadly spatulate; enamel wrinkled; groove on labial surface near distal margins.

Key references: Bonaparte (1986*a*); Bush (1903); Lydekker (1890); Marsh (1888*b*); McIntosh (1990); Owen (1841*b*, 1844, 1875); Phillips (1871); Steel (1970); Upchurch (1995, 1998); Upchurch, Barrett and Dodson (2004); Upchurch and Martin (2003); Wilson and Sereno (1998).

†CAUDIPTERYX

Saurischia: Eusaurischia: Theropoda: Neotheropoda: Tetanurae: Avetheropoda: Coelurosauria: Tyrannoraptora: Maniraptoriformes: Maniraptora: Metornithes: Oviraptorosauria: Caudipterygidae.

Diagnosis of genus: Skull short due to shortening of antorbital region (Ji, Currie, Norell and Ji 1998); premaxilla short, dorsomedial region convex, nasal and maxillary processes short; four long, thin, recurved premaxillary teeth, constricted at base; narial opening large, elliptical; nasals separate, short, wide; mandibular symphysis unfused, external mandibular fenestra long, undivided; 12 cervical, nine dorsal, and 22 caudal vertebrae; scapula and coracoid joining at approximately 90-degree angle; forelimb slender, less than half hindlimb length; three metacarpals, length of metacarpal I only about 40 percent length of II; third digit thin, including only two phalanges, lacking ungual; manual unguals curved; ilium with straight dorsal margin, preacetabular process distinctly longer than postacetabular process; cranioventral process dorsoventrally longer than ischial process; hindlimb long, slender, metatarsus elongate; hallux at least partially reversed (Maryańska, Currie and Barsbold 2004).

Comments: The phylogenetic status of *Caudipteryx*—as a non-avian theropod dinosaur or a bird—has been debated since this Early Cretaceous Chinese genus was first described in 1998 by Ji Qiang, Philip J. Currie, Mark A. Norell and Ji Shu-An (see *S1*).

Among the recently published studies advocating the avian status of *Caudipteryx* was that of Jones, Farlow, Ruben, Henderson and Hillenius (2002), who concluded—based upon their own quantitative analysis of hind limb and body proportions—that the center of mass in this genus is more similar to that of modern "ground dwelling" birds than to non-avian theropods (see *S2*). However, subsequent to the publication of their study, the findings of Jones *et al.* have been challenged by other workers.

As pointed out by Christainsen and Bonde (2002), among the anatomical features characterizing non-avian theropod dinosaurs is a considerably vertically

Caudipteryx

Life restoration by artist
Katy Hargrove of
Caudipteryx dongi.

oriented femur, along with femoral kinetics and, consequently, a loading pattern more similar to that of fast-running mammals than to birds (*e.g.*, see Gatesy 1991, 1995; Carrano 1998, 1999; Hutchinson and Gatesy 2000). Birds, however, have a cranially located center of gravity, mostly due to the near absence of a tail, a more craniocaudally constricted torso, and proportionally greater mass in the cranial chest area; also, a subsequent almost-horizontal femur required to position the feet below the center of gravity.

Jones *et al.* had argued that *Caudipteryx* possessed a cranially located center of gravity, and that its exceptionally long hindlimbs relative to trunk length were indicative of cursorial birds. Thus, according to those authors, *Caudipteryx* walked like a bird rather than a theropod dinosaur. Jones *et al.* further proposed that, based upon the results of their study, the phylogenetic placement of this genus should be reassessed; additionally, that *Caudipteryx* could actually be a secondarily flightless bird more closely related to Aves than *Archaeopteryx.*

In response, Christiansen and Bonde set out to expand upon the arguments of Jones *et al.*, noting that "following traditional methods for phylogenetic reconstruction would simply dismiss the allegedly avian characteristics in *Caudipteryx* as convergences." Christiansen and Bonde criticized Jones *et al.* for not stat-

ing how their model of *Caudipteryx* was constructed; moreover, their model was "not based on measurements of the fossils but rather on published colour reconstructions of the animal and a too portly and inaccurate three-dimensional model" (D. M. Henderson, personal communication to Christiansen and Bonde, 2001). This model was subsequently tested utilizing computer software to compute mass and center of mass (see Henderson 1999).

To produce their "more accurate model," Christiansen and Bonde computed volumes, centers of gravity, and surface areas utilizing graphic double integration (*e.g.*, see Henderson), and also illustrations by Gregory S. Paul (1988) published in his book *Predatory Dinosaurs of the World*, the authors checking the latter for accuracy against morphometric data gleaned by Per Christiansen directly from mounted skeletons (see Christiansen 1998, 1999*b*).

From analysis of their model, Christiansen and Bonde concluded that the center of gravity in *Caudipteryx* is not as cranially located as suggested by Jones *et al.*; in fact, it is located no further cranially than seen in other non-avian theropod taxa. Moreover, the supposedly very long hindlimbs of this genus — limb/trunk ratios in *Caudipteryx* being 2:2.13, data taken from five specimens — are not unusually long. In fact, the hindlimb to trunk ratio in *Caudipteryx* is slightly lower than that offered by Jones *et al.* While Christiansen and Bonde's ratio is indeed among the highest yet verified from a non-avian dinosaur, it is not particularly atypical, as the hindlimb/trunk ratios of several other smaller, long-limbed bipedal dinosaurs fall quite close to or within this ratio range as found in birds. Such ratios, Christiansen and Bonde noted, "are clearly influenced by both size and phylogeny position," with smaller theropods generally having longer limbs than large forms, this being also evident from the allometric patterns of the long bones (see Christiansen 1999*b*). Moreover, evolving proportionally shorter limbs with size is apparently a means of adapting mechanically, at large body size, to faster locomotion, as seen in parasagittal, terrestrial mammals (see Christiansen 1998, 1999*b*). Christiansen and Bonde further pointed out that more plesiomorphic theropods possess proportionally shorter limbs than more derived, comparably sized forms, this condition "to be expected if enhanced locomotor performance was a driving force in theropod evolution."

Regarding possible avian limb kinematics in *Caudiperyx*, Christiansen and Bonde agreed that the tibia to femur ratio of this genus, and also that of the birdlike theropod *Protarchaeopteryx*, do not significantly differ from those of birds; nor do they, however, differ from those ratios in other small to medium-sized, gracile theropods (*e.g.*, *Compsognathus*, *Ingenia*,

Elaphrosaurus, ornithomimids, and *Oviraptor*). Moreover, all non-avian theropods — including *Caudipteryx* and *Protarchaeopteryx*— have substantially longer femora compared to tibiae than ground birds, this corroborating previous conclusions (see Gatesy 1990, 1991; Carrano; Christiansen 1998) that no non-avian theropod dinosaur possessed avianlike limb kinematics and loading patterns.

Christiansen and Bonde further pointed out that birds possess proportionally short, thick femora compared to those of non-avian theropods and mammals (see Alexander 1983; Alexander, Maloiy, Njau and Jayes 1979; Gatesy; Carrano 1998; Christiansen 1998, 1999). Not sharing these proportions, *Caudipteryx* and *Protarchaeopteryx* group with other theropods, according to the authors. As Christiansen and Bonde explained, the tibiotarsus in birds has a loading platform more comparable both to the femora and tibiae of non-avian theropods and parasagittal mammals, and is considerably weaker than the avian femur (*e.g.*, see Alexander *et al.*; Alexander; Gatesy 1991; Carrano 1998; Christiansen 1988, 1999*b*). As the femora and tibia in non-avian theropods and parasagittal mammals do not exhibit this great difference in bone strength (Christiansen 1998), the regression lines of tibial length to circumference found in 23 non-avian theropod taxa (see Christiansen 1999) and 19 species of large ground birds were found not to be statistically different. This data, therefore, showed the loading pattern of the femora of *Caudipteryx* and *Protarchaeopteryx* to be similar to those of other non-avian theropods and different from those of birds, biomechanically arguing "against their having been able to walk like birds, with sub-horizontal femora."

Finally, Christiansen and Bonde criticized Jones *et al.*'s systematic approach for a phylogenetic position for *Caudipteryx* as an avian more advanced than *Archaeopteryx*. In Christiansen and Bonde's opinion, the functionally anatomical characters (*e.g.*, hindlimb/trunk ratios, position of center of gravity) cited by Jones *et al.*, even if that had been correct, are not avian synapomorphies (*e.g.*, Gauthier 1986; Sereno 1999*a*), thereby indicating that these features are convergences unless they are given a much higher weight. Cladists generally regard the function of anatomical features as irrelevant as criteria for phylogenetic analyses (*e.g.*, Cracraft 1981), this practice inevitably leading to confusion of analogy (*i.e.*, convergence) and homology (*i.e.*, synapomorphy).

Because Jones *et al.* noted several convergent traits common both to secondarily flightless birds, the supposed similarities between *Caudipteryx* and those birds cannot be regarded as indicating that that genus is a bird more advanced than *Archaeopteryx*, unless, Christiansen and Bonde noted, "those similarities can be shown to be restricted to *Caudipteryx* and some specific group of ground birds." Consequently, as the latter cannot be demonstrated, it is invalid to use these characters to identify this genus as a secondarily flightless bird.

In conclusion, Christiansen and Bonde found it ironic that, according to the more traditional, functional and adaptational models for the origin of birds (*e.g.*, Geist and Feduccia 2000), an approach favored by Ruben and Jones (2000), the body proportions of *Caudipteryx* would effectively preclude any avian status for this genus.

More recently in a related study, Dyke and Norell (2005) addressed the conclusions reached by Jones *et al.*, at the same time reviewing the evidence offered by those authors:

Jones *et al.* concluded that the hind limb structure of *Caudipteryx* constitutes evidence that the locomotor strategy employed by this taxon was similar to that seen in secondarily flightless neoornithine birds, thereby implying that because non-avian theropod dinosaurs and neornithines had different locomotor strategies, indicated by body shapes and limb proportions, the two groups are probably not related. Dyke and Norell argued, however, that just because two groups employ different locomotor strategies, it does not necessarily follow that these groups are not related. Moreover, many groups of closely related modern birds hop while on the ground while other run (see Barker, Cibois, Shickler, Feinstein and Cracraft 2000).

According to Dyke and Norell, Jones *et al.*, in offering their two linear regression analyses, had produced their first graph including regression calculations made with the *a priori* assumption that *Caudipteryx* is a bird, thereby contradicting "the available skeletal evidence uniting *Caudipteryx* with Oviraptoridae." Consequently, Jones *et al.*'s second graph (plotting effective hind limb lengths of terrestrial [neoornithine] birds, non-avian theropods, and ornithopods against total body length), only included measurements for the distal hind limb segments, with *Caudipteryx* plotting out with the birds only because "data from these taxa were included in the analysis."

Dyke and Norell found very problematic additional comparisons made by Jones *et al.* between hind limb proportions and estimated trunk length. As Dyke and Norell pointed out, total trunk length is no longer seriously regarded as a proxy for overall body size, in part due to the variance in the number of dorsal vertebrae observed among both non-avian theropods and neornithine birds, and also because of serious problems involving measurement of this quantity in many of the specimens (*e.g.*, some affected by differential preservation) used in Jones *et al.*' study.

Also, Dyke and Norell that the hind limb and trunk measurements offered by Jones *et al.* in a variety of dinosaurian taxa "are extremely hard to reconcile with the actual specimens from which they were taken"; first, because to measure trunk length accurately various assumptions must first be made concerning the length of the vertebral discs, and second, because of the problem in correctly identifying the number of (sometimes smashed) dorsal relative to thoracic vertebrae preserved in many specimens. According to Dyke and Norell, the measurement sample offered by Jones *et al.* "cannot be considered to be an unbiased tabulation of non-avian theropod taxa," notable deletions including *Archaeopteryx* and *Sinornithoides*. Furthermore, Dyke and Norell cited "severe difficulties with measurements of trunk lengths reported by Jones *et al.* (2000) for three specimens of *Caudipteryx*," these measurements being imprecise at best (one of the authors, Norell, having "spent significant time studying these specimens").

Additionally, as Dyke and Norell (regarding *Caudipteryx* as an oviraptorid; see "Systematics" chapter) pointed out, Jones *et al.* included but one oviraptorid (*Ingenia*, for which most of the dorsal vertebrae are unknown) in their study, despite numerous analyses (*e.g.*, Currie, Norell and Ji 1998; Clark, Norell and Chiappe 1999; Sereno; Holtz 2000; Norell, Clark and Makovicky 2001) that have supported placing *Caudipteryx* within the Oviraptoridae. Moreover, measurements taken by Dyke and Norell of two exceptionally well-preserved articulated specimens (IGM 100/1002 and IGM 100/973) of the oviraptorid *Khaan* revealed "differences in up to 20 percent when trunk length was measured based on the total extent of the dorsal vertebral series compared to taking individual measurements from each vertebral centrum," thereby rendering unclear the accuracy of Jones *et al.*'s measurements.

Finally, Dyke and Norell Jones *et al.*'s claim that the hind limbs of *Caudipteryx* differ significantly from those of non-avian theropods and are more like those of terrestrial birds, finding *Caudipteryx* to cluster, rather, with a number of small non-avian theropods.

Based upon their assessment of the study by Jones *et al.* and also their own analysis (including much additional measurement information and incorporating phylogenetic control), Dyke and Norell found no reason to conclude that the genus *Caudipteryx* is anything but a small non-avian theropod.

Key references: Alexander (1983); Alexander, Maloiy, Njau and Jayes (1979); Barker, Cibois, Shickler, Feinstein and Cracraft (2004); Carrano (1998; 1999); Christiansen (1998, 1999*b*); Christiansen and Bonde (2002); Clark, Norell and Chiappe (1999); Cracraft (1981); Dyke and Norell (2005); Gatesy (1990, 1991, 1995); Gauthier (1986); Geist and Feduccia (2000); Henderson (1999); Holtz (2000); Hutchinson and Gatesy (2000); Ji, Currie, Norell and Ji (1998); Jones, Farlow, Ruben, Henderson and Hillenius (2000); Makovicky and Sues (1998); Maryańska, Currie and Barsbold (2004); Norell, Clark and Makovicky (2001); Ruben and Jones (2000); Sereno (1999*a*).

†CEDAROSAURUS

Saurischia: Eusaurischia: Sauropodomorpha: Sauropoda: Eusauropoda: Neosauropoda: Macronaria: Titanosauriformes: ?Brachiosauridae.

Diagnosis of genus (as for type species): Caudal articular faces of proximal caudal vertebrae deeply concave (?autapomorphy; also found in several other sauropods); ridge on lateral margin radius terminating in prominent rugosity at distal end; distal articular surface of radius flat (mildly convex in all other known Sauropoda) (Upchurch, Barrett and Dodson 2004).

Comment: In their review of the Sauropoda, Upchurch, Barrett and Dodson (2004) rediagnosed the type species *Cedarosaurus weiskopfae* (see S2).

Performing a cladistic analysis (see "Systematics" chapter), Upchurch found *Cedarosaurus* to be a brachiosaurid sharing a sister-taxon relationship with *Brachiosaurus*.

Key reference: Upchurch, Barrett and Dodson (2004).

†CEDARPELTA

Ornithischia: Predentata: Genasauria: Thyreophora: Thyreophoroidea: Eurypoda: Ankylosauria: Nodosauridae.

Diagnosis of genus (as for type species): Premaxilla having six conical teeth; pterygoid rostrocaudally elongate, with caudolaterally oriented, trochlear-like process; unpaired parietal element; ischium straight (Vickaryous, Maryańska and Weishampel 2004).

Comments: In their review of the Ankylosauria, Vickaryous, Maryańska and Weishampel (2004) rediagnosed the type species *Cedarpelta bilbeyhallorum*.

Originally referred by Carpenter, Kirkland, Burge and Bird (2001) to the Ankylosauridae, this taxon was reassessed by Vickaryous *et al.*, who assigned it to the Nodosauridae

Key references: Carpenter, Kirkland, Burge and Bird (2001); Vickaryous, Maryańska and Weishampel (2004).

Life restoration by Berislav Krzic of *Cedarpelta bilbeyhallorum*.

†CENTROSAURUS

Ornithischia: Predentata: Genusauria: Cerapoda: Chasmatopia: Marginocephalia: Ceratopsia: Neoceratopsia: Coronosauria: Ceratopsoidea: Ceratopsidae: Centrosaurinae.

Comments: Ryan and Russell (2003), in a published abstract for a poster, announced the discovery of new centrosaurine material, including a new and as yet unnamed species of *Centrosaurus* from the uppermost Oldman Formation of Alberta, Canada, and another taxon from the coeval Judith River Formation of Montana. According to these authors, the former is distinguished from the type species, *Centrosaurus apertus*, by the unique dermal ossifications that are part of its parietal ornamentation, and by the strong lateral inflection of the unmodified brow horns. (The latter new taxon — the oldest centrosaurine known and the sister taxon to all other Centrosaurinae — possesses a mosaic of characters unique to the clade, *e.g.*, large, robust chasmosaurine-like brow horncores, pair of large, pachyostotic hooks projecting from caudolateral margins of parietal).

Skeleton (cast) of *Centrosaurus apertus* on display at the Royal Tyrrell Museum of Palaeontology.

Photograph by the author, courtesy Royal Tyrrell Museum/Alberta Community Development.

Examination by Ryan and Russell of the geographic and stratigraphic distributions of Late Cretaceous centroaurine ceratopsians of the Western Interior Basin confirmed the restricted ranges, with apparently a modicum of overlap, of the Canadian and Montana faunas. The known geographic ranges of the best known taxa from Alberta—*Centrosaurus apertus* and *Styracosaurus albertensis*—are essentially congruent with the outcrop limits of the Dinosaur Park Formation, the increasing abundances of these species towards the northern limits of their ranges and their patter of geographic overlap suggesting "the temporal replacements of *Centrosaurus* by *Styracosaurus*, in association with the transgression of the inland sea during the late Campanian." Moreover, morphological and stratigraphical evidence, rather than supporting an earlier postulation of anagenetic change within a lineage of late Campanian centrosaurines, indicates "a hierarchal pattern of sister group relationships." Furthermore, the authors noted, the coeval stratigraphic replacement patterns of some taxa (*e.g.*, centrosaurines, chasmosaurines, hadrosaurs) in the Dinosaur Park Formation of Alberta's Dinosaur Provincial Park, suggest that a partial turnover of fauna took place within this area over an approximate 250,000-year timespan.

In another abstract for a poster, Lee (2004) studied the ontogenetic histology of *Centrosaurus*, addressing the relationship between limb bone form and function. As Lee pointed out, quadrupedalism evolved independently four times within Dinosauria. The forelimb bones of basal members of Sauropodomorpha, Thyreophora, Ornithopoda, and Ceratopsia are relatively gracile, while those of derived members of those clade are relatively robust and elephantine. Less clear, that author noted, is if weight-bearing adaptations occur also at the microscostructural bone level, "particularly because mechanics is only one of the factors responsible for bone microstructural variation" that "is also a product of ontogeny and phylogeny."

In limb bones of *Centrosaurus*, Lee observed the following: Occurrence of primary fibrolamellar bony tissue; radially oriented vascular canals deposited during ontogeny, particularly in humerus; vascular canals oriented circumferentially later during ontogeny; medullary cavity not produced during ontogeny (although cortical thickness generally decreases); cancellous bone occurring internal to cortical shell; secondary remodeling becoming prominent only during late ontogeny; limb bone microstructure suggesting sustained and rapid growth to fore- and hindlimbs during ontogeny.

Preliminary comparisons by Lee between the limb bone microstructure of *Centrosaurus* and that of bipedal theropods suggested "that phylogenetic differences in limb growth strategy might account for much of the variation in microstructure."

Key references: Lee (2004); Ryan and Russell (2003).

†CERATOSAURUS

Saurischia: Eusaurischia: Eusaurischia: Theropoda: Neotheropoda: Ceratosauria: Ceratosauridae.

Comments: Britt, Scheetz, Stadtman and Chure (2003) described broad osseous bands preserved along the lateral surfaces of sacral neural spines of recently collected specimens of the horned theropod *Ceratosaurus*.

As Britt *et al.* observed, these bands consist of ossified tendons of epaxial muscles. Tendon fascia originate low on the spine, then extend cranially and slightly dorsally before they merge with the main bundle of tendons extending caudocranially as a band alongside of the spines (contrasting with the crisscrossed pattern of rod-shaped ossified tendons common in ornithischian dinosaurs). The authors noted that unusual muscle and tendon scars on the dorsal vertebrae suggest ossified tendons may also have attached to those vertebrae.

Thin sections of a nearly complete *Ceratosaurus* pelvis (BYU 17550) revealed to Britt *et al.* fibrous bands grading into immature Haversian bone. Longitudinal sections of the dark bands showed pinnate structures having parallel rows of lacunae, the latter representing tendonoblasts that (as in modern ossified tendons) increase in size towards entirely ossified bone, marking the area of active tendon mineralization. A waveform pattern seen in one fascicle indicates that it was relaxed (unloaded) when fossilization occurred. Transverse sections of the dark bands revealed nested bundles possibly representing collagen fibers.

According to Britt *et al.*, tendon ossification in *Ceratosaurus* occurred comparatively late during ontogeny, no evidence of this condition being found in a specimen (NAMAL 2002–02–28) belonging to a three-quarters grown animal. Moreover, the tendon of subadult BYU 17550 was in the process of being replaced by Haversian bone when the animal died, while the tendon is completely ossified in BYU 12893, representing a large individual.

Britt *et al.* also reported that well-preserved fungi, with hyphae penetrating the bones, have been preserved in calcite-filled nutrient canals of the Haversian bone; that fungal mycelia seem to follow the canals, obtaining nutrients from organic components of the bone; and that fungal fragments occur also in unossified tendons.

Key reference: Britt, Scheetz, Stadtman and Chure (2003).

Skeleton (cast) of an as yet undescribed juvenile *Ceratosaurus nasicornis.*

†CETIOSAURISCUS

Saurischia: Eusaurischia: Sauropodomorpha: Sauropoda: Eusauropoda: ?Neosauropoda: ?Diplodocoidea *incertae sedis.*

Diagnosis of genus: Neural spines of proximal and middle caudal vertebrae having axially concave summits (Upchurch, Barrett and Dodson 2004).

Comments: In 1898, a partial postcranial sauropod skeleton (BMNH R3078) was collected from the Middle Jurassic (Callovian) marine Oxford Clay of St. Peterborough, in easter England. This skeleton, the type specimen of *Cetiosauriscus stewarti,* as related in an abstract by Heathcote and Upchurch, is distinguished as one of the most complete sauropods yet found in the United Kingdom (see *D:TE*).

In the past, Heathcote and Upchurch pointed out, *Cetiosauriscus* has been referred to the Diplodocoidea or Diplodocidae, based primarily on the presence of high sacral neural spines, forked chevrons, and an apparent "whiplash" distal tail sequence. However, no rigorous phylogenetic testing had ever been applied to this sauropod.

Heathcote and Upchurch performed a cladistic analysis utilizing recently published data matrices (*e.g.,* Upchurch 1998; Wilson 1998), with character information obtained directly from holotype material, and the distal "whiplash" ignored as no evidence supports this feature's association with *Cetiosauriscus.* Applying reduced consensus methods, Heathcote and Upchurch produced six trees, each placing *Cetiosauriscus* as the sister taxon to *Tehuelchesaurus,* with these together forming a clade with *Omeisaurus, Mamenchisaurus,* and *Euhelopus.* In another analysis based upon Wilson's data set, Heathcote and Upchurch again found *Cetiosauriscus* to cluster with *Omeisaurus,* both analyses indicating that "*Cetiosauriscus* lies outside of the neosauropod clade and is therefore not a basal diplodocoid."

However, in a more recently published cladistic analysis by Upchurch, Barrett and Dodson (2004), *Cetiosauriscus* was found to have affinities with diplodocoids, based upon several derived characters (*e.g.,* tall neural spines; winglike ribs on proximal caudal vertebrae; procoelous proximal caudal vertebrae; shortened forelimb). For the present, therefore, these authors provisionally classified this genus as Diplodocoidea *incertae sedis.*

Key references: Heathcote and Upchurch (2003); Upchurch (1998); Upchurch, Barrett and Dodson (2004); Wilson (1998).

†CETIOSAURUS

Saurischia: Eusaurischia: Sauropodomorpha: Sauropoda: Eusauropoda: Cetiosauridae.

Type species: *C. oxoniensis* Phillips 1871.

Other species: ?*C. epioolithicus* Owen 1842 [*nomen nudum*], ?*C. hypoolithicus* Owen 1842 [*nomen nudum*], ?*C. longus* Owen 1842 [*nomen nudum*]; ?*C. medius* Owen 1842 [*nomen dubium*], ?*C. giganteus* Owen in Phillips in Huxley 1870 [*nomen nudum*].

Known material: Various specimens, mostly postcranial remains.

Lectotype specimen: OUMNH J13605-13613, J13615-13616, J13619-13688, and J13899, partial postcranial skeleton.

Diagnosis of genus (as for type species): Neural spines of caudal cervical and cranial dorsal vertebrae pyramidal, cranial, lateral, and caudal faces excavated; 12th cervical vertebra with cranially directed rounded process projecting from dorsal part of neural spine; middle and cranial dorsal vertebrae with deep, excavated areas on either side of neural arches; dorsal vertebrae without spinodiapophyseal lamina; neural canal extending extended cranially and caudally, above centrum articular surface, by short tonguelike process in distal caudal vertebrae; proximal hemal arches with proximodistally compressed distal shafts not tapering to form transversely narrow and axially elongate blade; triangular pit bounded dorsally by craniocaudally oriented ridge at dorsal end of lateral surface of iliac pubic process (Upchurch, Barrett and Dodson 2004.

Comments: As sauropod specialists Paul Upchurch and John Martin (2003) pointed out in their detailed review of the genus *Cetiosaurus*, this taxon is significant, both historically (being one of the first sauropods to be named; see McIntosh 1990) and for its potential phylogenetic relationships. However, the anatomy and taxonomy of *Cetiosaurus* have been "poorly understood because inadequate diagnoses have allowed the proliferation of species and the referral of very fragmentary specimens." Indeed, *Cetiosaurus* represents a kind of "wastebasket" taxon to which has been referred a large quantity of sauropod remains from England and also other countries (see *D:TE, 3*).

Upchurch and Martin detailed the complex taxonomic history of *Cetiosaurus* and the many species that, over more than a century, had been referred to it, at the same time commenting upon the validity of each of these species:

The new genus *Cetiosaurus* was founded by Richard Owen in 1841 on very incomplete specimens from various places in England, including Tilgate Forest in Sussex, from Buckingham, Oxford, and the Isle of Wight. Owen believed these remains to represent a gigantic strictly aquatic crocodilian. Collectively Owen named these remains *Cetiosaurus* without assigning a specific name. The following year, Owen (1842*b*) erected the type species *Cetiosaurus medius* (see below), which he originally intended to call *C. hypoolothicus* (see below), a name that has generally come to be accepted as the type species (*e.g.*, Steel 1970; McIntosh; see *D:TE* for more details).

Three decades after Owen's naming of the genus, following the discovery of additional *Cetiosaurus* remains, John Phillips (1871), in his book *Geology of Oxford and the Valley of the Thames*, was able to identify this genus correctly as a gigantic, land-dwelling herbivorous dinosaur. Phillips referred this new material to a new species *Cetiosaurus oxoniensis* (see *D:TE*).

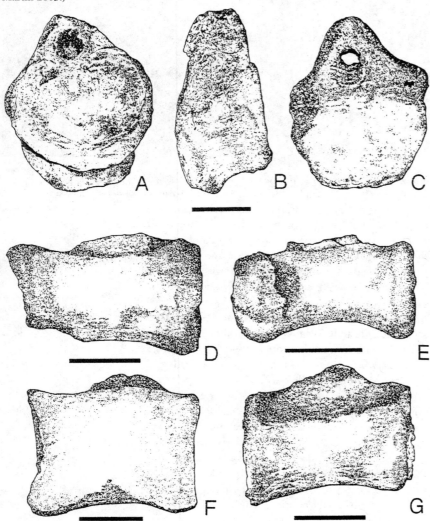

?*Cetiosaurus medius*, A–C. OUMNH J13693, D. OUMNH J13700, E. OUMNH J13702, F. OUMNH J13697, and G. OUMNH J13698, caudal centra forming part of type series, in A. proximal, B. and D–G. right lateral, and C. distal views. Scale = 50 mm, A–C. drawn to same size. (After Upchurch and Martin 2003.)

Cetiosaurus oxoniensis, lectotype presacral vertebrae, A. portion of cervical centrum (OUMNH J13660), in left lateral view; B. portion of proximal dorsal neural spine and right transverse process (OUMNH J13646), proximal view; C. as for B., distal view; D. middorsal vertebra (OUMNH J13644/2), proximal view; E.–F. as for D., right lateral and distal views, respectively. Scale = 50 mm. (After Upchurch and Martin 2003.)

The species name *C. hypoolithicus* Owen 1842*a* had first been published in an 1842 anonymous report of an 1841 lecture by Owen at a meeting of the British Association for the Advancement of Science. An unspecified number of vertebrae and limb elements from the "Inferior Oolite" of Chipping Norton, Oxfordshire, this material most likely represents the John Kingdon collection upon which Owen first described *Cetiosaurus*. As the only anatomical characters noted in the anonymous report (*i.e.*, biconcave vertebral

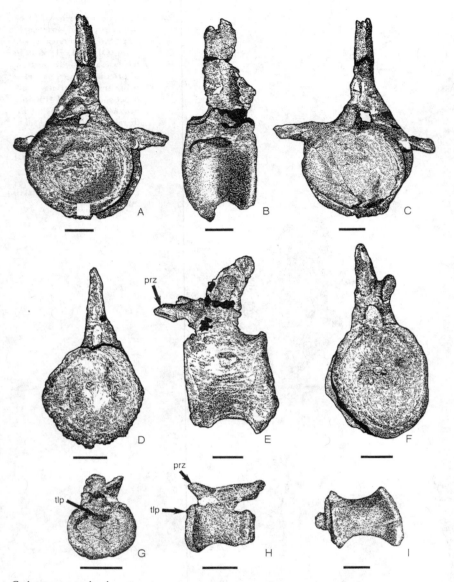

Cetiosaurus oxoniensis, (OUMNH J13634) lectotype selected caudal vertebrae, A.–C. proximal caudal (in A. proximal, B. right lateral, and C. distal views), D.–F. proximal midcaudal (in D. proximal, E. left lateral, and F. distal views), and G.–I. middle-distal caudal (in G. proximal, H. left lateral, and I. ventral views). Scale = 50 mm. (After Upchurch and Martin 2003.)

centra; absence of central cavity in limb bones) are features listed by own characteristics of the genus *Cetiosaurus,* this species cannot be distinguished from *C. epioolithicus* (see below). Published without an adequate description or figure, this species was regarded by Upchurch and Martin as both a *nomen dubium* and a *nomen nudum.*

C. epioolithicus, named by Owen (1842*a*), was founded upon an unspecified number of vertebrae and metatarsals from White Nab, West Yorkshire, and subsequently included by Owen (1842*b*) in the type series of *C. longus* (see below). Published without figures or description (save for width and height measurements for a single vertebral centrum), this species also was regarded by Upchurch and Martin as a *nomen dubium* and a *nomen nudum.*

C. brevis was founded by Owen (1842*b*) on several vertebrae (BMNH R10390?) from Sandown Bay

and Culver Cliff (Barremian; see Rawson, Curry, Dilley, Hancock, Kenedy, Neale, Wood, and Worssam 1978) and other specimens (BMNH R2133, R2115, R2544–2550) from the Hastings Beds (Valanginian; see Rawson *et al.*) of Cuckfield, Sussex. This species, with the exception of BMNH R2544–2550, was referred by Steel to the genus *Iguanodon;* BMNH R2544–2550, belonging to a sauropod, had previously been referred by Melville (1849) to a new species of *Cetiosaurus,* which he named *C. conybeari.* As Upchurch and Martin pointed out, however, because part of the type series of *C. brevis* remained following the removal of the *Iguanodon* elements, *C. conybeari*—according to the rules of the International Commission for Zoological Nomenclature (ICZN)—is effectively a junior objective synonym of *C. brevis.* This retained material exhibits features implying affinities with the Brachiosauridae (*e.g.,* caudal vertebrae with lateral ridge extending along proximodorsal margin to its distal end, expanding forward forming overhanging "shelf"). Furthermore, this species has long been accepted as belonging to the brachiosaurid genus *Pelorosaurus* (see Mantell 1850; see also *D:TE*) as the species *P. conybeari.*

C. brachyrus, described by Owen (1842*b*), was based on dorsal and caudal centra (probably BMNH collection) from the "Wealden" (Hastings Beds) of Tetham, Kent, and later referred by Melville and Steel to *Iguanodon.* As Upchurch and Martin noted, these vertebrae, even if belonging to a sauropod, lack any diagnostic features, yet lie within the range expected for the caudal end of the dorsal series in *Iguanodon* and the distal end of a eusauropod tail. Upchurch and Martin concurred that this species is a junior synonym of *Iguanodon.*

C. medius, which was described by Owen (1842*b*), was founded upon a type series of remains including 11 caudal centra (OUMNH J13693-13703), some sacral ribs and a metatarsal (OUMNH J13704-13712), one metacarpal (OUMNH J13748; figured by Sir Charles Lyell in his book *Elements of Geology,* 1838), an ungual (OUMNH J13721), partial dorsal centrum (OUMNH J13877), all of these remains collected by John Kingdon, and also additional material recovered at Oxfordshire, Northamptonshire, and Buckinghamshire. As Upchurch and Martin pointed out, the lack of sufficient locality information makes dubious the degree of association of these various specimens, while there are also questions regarding the identification of some elements (see Upchurch and Martin for details). In summary, Upchurch and Martin stated that, among the material referred to *C. medius,* the sacral ribs, a metacarpal, and a metatarsal resemble equivalent elements in other sauropods, yet cannot be identified more precisely. Consequently, the authors regarded the material assigned to *C. medius* as representing an indeterminate sauropod, the discovery that the accepted type species of this genus was founded upon undiagnostic remains thereby creating problems in nomenclature (see below).

Owen (1842*b*) also described *C. longus*, the type series including single dorsal and caudal centra from the Portland Stone (Kimmeridgian; see Cope, Duff, Parsons, Torrens, Wimbledon and Wright 1980) of Garsington, near Oxford Thame, Oxon. McIntosh referred this species to the genus *Cetiosauriscus* as the new combination *Cetiosauriscus longus*. However, as Upchurch and Martin noted, the Garsington specimens could not be identified in the OUMNH collections. Based on Owen's (1842*b*) descriptions, Upchurch and Martin found the material assigned to this species to be undiagnostic and therefore a *nomen dubium*. Furthermore, they stated that it cannot be demonstrated that this taxon possesses any autapomorphies found in *Cetiosauriscus*.

C. giganteus, "attributed to Owen by Phillips in a letter published by Huxley" (1870), was apparently based by Owen on a left femur (OUMNH J13617) from the Gibraltar quarry (see, for example, anonymous 1848), near Bletchingdon Station. Lacking any description or illustration, this species was regarded by Upchurch and Martin as a *nomen nudum*.

C. oxoniensis was described by Phillips who, while not specifying a type specimen, listed a large series of remains that incorporated Owen's (1842*b*) original type elements for *C. medius*, the partial remains of three individuals from Bletchingdon Station, plus several fragmentary specimens from Buckinghamshire and Oxfordshire. Upchurch and Martin would use the largest Bletchingdon specimen for their revised diagnosis (see above) and detailed description of the genus *Cetiosaurus*.

C. glymptonensis, also named and described by Phillips, was established on nine middle-distal caudal centra (OUMNH J13750-13758) from Glympton, Oxon, differing from specimens referred to *C. oxoniensis* only in their relative length (typical length in height ratios in *C. oxoniensis* being 1.0 to 1.5; in *C. glymptonensis*, from 1.33 in larger more proximal specimens to 2.17 in more distal elements). McIntosh referred this species to *Cetiosauriscus* as the new combination *Cetiosauriscus glymptonensis*. As Upchurch and Martin observed, this species possesses the autapomorphy of a lower ridge and could represent a distinct genus, although the type material is barely sufficient for this purpose; furthermore, the authors noted, this species does not exhibit any of the autapomorphies of *Cetiosauriscus*, and is therefore a junior objective synonym of "*Cetiosaurus glymptonensis*." Moreover, it displays features (*e.g.*, elongate middle caudal vertebrae)

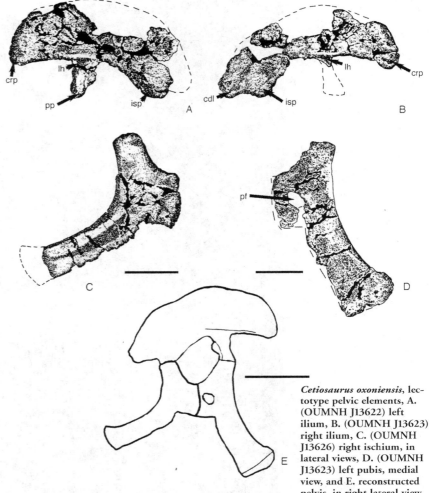

Cetiosaurus oxoniensis, lectotype pelvic elements, A. (OUMNH J13622) left ilium, B. (OUMNH J13623) right ilium, C. (OUMNH J13626) right ischium, in lateral views, D. (OUMNH J13623) left pubis, medial view, and E. reconstructed pelvis, in right lateral view. Scale = 500 mm for A., B., and E., 250 mm for C. and D. (After Upchurch and Martin 2003.)

that suggest this species could be an early diplodocid.

C. humerocristatus was described by Hulke (1874), founded on a left humerus (BMNH R44635) recovered from the Kimmeridge Clay (Kimmeridgian), near Weymouth, in Dorset. Lydekker (1888) subsequently referred to this species the proximal end of a pubis (BMNH R49165), obtained from the same horizon and locality. According to Upchurch and Martin, this pubis is undiagnostic; however, the humerus is potentially distinctive. Hulke distinguished the latter from *C. oxoniensis* by its more prominent deltopectoral crest (a possible synapomorphy of the Brachiosauridae; see Wilson and Sereno 1998). Also, Upchurch and Martin pointed out, this humerus is

Isolated tooth (OUMNH J13597), referred to *Cetiosaurus*, from the Bletchingdon quarry (labial view). Scale = 10 mm. (After Upchurch and Martin 2003.)

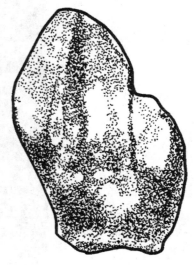

Cetiosaurus

Photograph by the author, courtesy Oxford University Museum of Natural History.

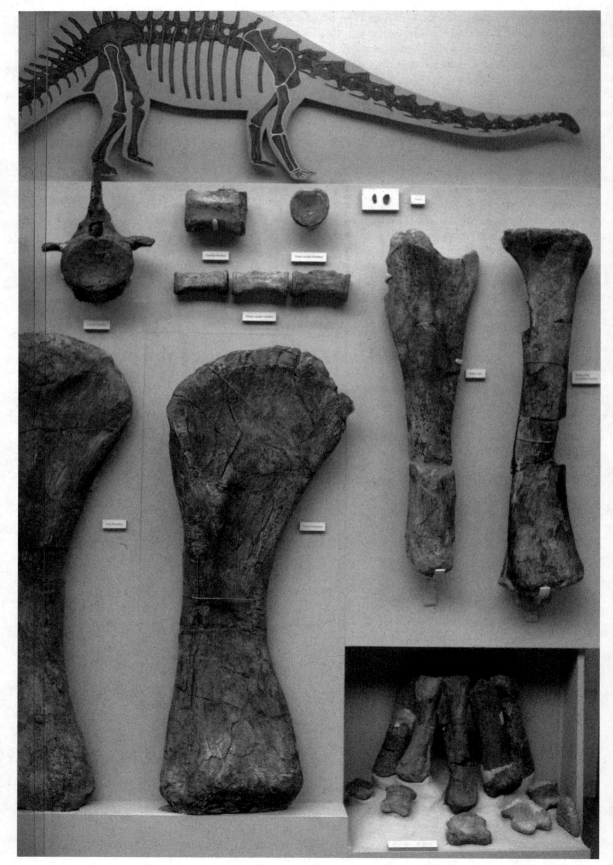

Part of the original holotype (OUMNH collection) of *Cetiosaurus oxoniensis* on exhibit at the Oxford University Museum of Natural History.

relatively long. Taken separately, these features, according to Upchurch and Martin, do not constitute autaporphies; taken together, however, they make this bone humerus unique. For the present, those authors regarded BMNH R44635 as an as yet unnamed taxon belonging to the Brachiosauridae.

C. leedsi was described by Woodward (1905), founded upon fragmentary remains (BMNH R1984-1988) collected from the Oxford Clay (Callovian; see Cope *et al.*), near Peterborough, Cambridgeshire. According to Upchurch and Martin, no autapomorphic features can be seen in any of the material referred to this species. However, the ischia referred to *C. leedsi* have broad, strongly downward-directed distal shafts as found in brachiosaurids. Therefore, this taxon was regarded by these authors as representing an indeterminate brachiosaurid, the name a *nomen dubium*.

Finally, *C. rugulosus* was a new species of *Cetiosaurus* erected by Steel based on a tooth from the Middle Jurassic Forest Marble of Bradford-On-Avon, Wiltshire, which Owen (1841*b*) had, without species, referred to a new genus, *Cardiodon*, Owen (1844) subsequently adding the species name *rugulosus*. As Upchurch and Martin noted, however, there is no evidence supporting the synonymy of *Cetiosaurus* and *Cardiodon* (see entry for more details).

In summary, after reviewing the 13 species that had been referred to *Cetiosaurus*, Upchurch and Martin concluded the following:

1. *C. hypoolithicus, C. epioolithicus,* and *C. giganteus*—are *nomina nuda*.

2. *C. bracyhyurus, C. medius, C. longus,* and *C. leedsi* are *nomina dubia*, based upon undiagnostic remains.

3. *C. brevis, C. oxoniensis, C. glymptonensis,* and *C. humerocristatus* can be recognized by autapomorphies or unique combinations of character states that suggest they cannot all be retained in a single genus.

4. *C. brevis*, the only valid species of the genus first published by Owen (1842*b*), under strict interpretation of ICZN rules (Article 67[g]), should be regarded as the type species, thereby excluding *C. oxoniensis*, which would, consequently, be placed within a new genus.

In this matter of nomenclature, Upchurch and Martin found a strict application of ICZN rules inadvisable, pointing out that the type material of *C. brevis* has been known in the literature as *Pelorosaurus conybeari* for most of the twentieth century, and that the name *Cetiosaurus* has been most closely linked with the sauropod material from the Middle Jurassic of Great Britain, particularly the specimens of *C. oxoniensis* from Bletchingdon. Consequently, "restriction of the name *Cetiosaurus* to the Lower Cretaceous titanosauriform material, and the creation of a new generic name for the Middle Jurassic specimens from near Oxford, would inevitably change current nomenclatural usage and generate considerable confusion."

For the present, Upchurch and Martin proposed two alternative treatments to this situation: 1. Strictly applying ICZN rules, with *C. brevis* becoming the correct name for *Pelorosaurus conybeari*, with *Cetiosaurus oxoniensis* given a new generic name; or 2. conserving both the names *Pelorosaurus conybeari* and *Cetiosaurus oxoniensis*, suppressing *C. brevis*, an option that would also adhere to ICZN rules (under article 79, which allows the rules to be suspended to promote nomenclatural stability and avoid confusion).

Preferring the latter option, and stating that they would submit a case for the conservation of the name *Cetiosaurus* according to its current usage, Upchurch and Martin continued in their paper to refer by that name to the Middle Jurassic basal sauropod from Oxfordshire, while also cautioning "that such a treatment has no formal standing until ratified by the ICZN."

Because no worker had yet designated the type material of *C. oxoniensis*, Upchurch and Martin proposed that the lectotype be recognized as a partial skeleton (OUMNH J13605-J13613, J13615-J13616, J13619-J13688, and J13899) collected from a quarry near Bletchingdon (old Kirtlington) Station, near Enslow Bridge, Oxon, this material including fragmentary dorsal and sacral elements, portions of thoracic ribs, about 30 proximal and middle caudal centra (some having arches and processes), seven damaged hemal arches from the proximal and middle part of the tail, scapulae, damaged corocoids, a left sternal plate, humeri, ulnae, portions of metacarpal, ilia, left pubis, right ischium, femora, left tibia and fibula. Paralectotype specimens include (OUMNH J13614) a portion of ?sternal plate, a left humerus, and a femur; (OUMNH J13617-J13618) scapula, femur, tibia, and fibula representing a small individual; and, from the same locality and horizon as the lectotype, (OUMNH J13596) the dorsal half of a braincase, possibly belonging to the lectotype but, for the present, considered to be another paralectotype specimen.

As noted by Upchurch and Martin, the Bletchingdon Station sauropod material "potentially represents one of the best preserved sauropods from the Jurassic of Europe." In March 1868, the authors recounted, quarry workers found a right sauropod femur measuring approximately 1,600 millimeters in length. Additional remains, comprising a large number of bones scattered over a relatively small area, were subsequently discovered at the quarry from March 1869 to June 1870.

Phillips had assessed these remains as belonging to three different-sized individuals — a large animal represented by the partial skeleton; a medium-sized animal known only from a portion of apparent sternal plate, a humerus, and femur; and a small individual known just from a scapula, femur, tibia, and fibula. The accuracy of Phillips' distinguishing these three individuals takes into account the following:

1. The relative completeness of the large individual may question why the other two were so poorly represented. Phillips noted, however, that most of the remains of the smaller forms had been destroyed by quarrying before they could be salvaged.

2. The large individual preserves paired limb elements of virtually identical size and proportions, the relative proportions between elements being consistent with their interpretation of belonging to a single individual.

3. The large specimen includes fragmentary dorsal and sacral vertebrae, the proximal half of the tail, limb girdle elements, and the more proximal limb bones, this type of preservation being common among sauropods, as "their body shape and size facilitates loss of distal elements such as the skull, manus, pedes and distal end of the tail."

As Upchurch and Martin related, Owen (1841, 1842b) had originally diagnosed *Cetiosaurus* as follows: Centra of dorsal vertebrae broad, with subcircular articular faces; dorsal centra constricted in middle portions; vertebral centra displaying unequal excavation of anterior and posterior articular faces; caudal neurapophyses short anteroposteriorly, "anchylosed" to anterior part of centrum; caudal vertebrae having long prezygapophyses that project beyond anterior end of centrum; caudal vertebrae with reduced postzygapophyses represented by facets at base of neural spine; internal texture of vertebral centra "spongy." Later, Owen (1875) supplemented his diagnosis with the following characters: Chevron facets paired, chevrons articulating intervertebrally; subquadrangular coracoid having rounded edges.

Upchurch and Martin (2003) pointed out, however, that all of the characters listed in the above diagnosis have a much wider phylogenetic distribution among the Sauropoda and, therefore, are not useful in providing an adequate differential diagnosis for this genus. Moreover, Upchurch and Martin proposed a new diagnosis of the genus *Cetiosaurus* (and the species *C. oxoniensis*), based largely on the lectotype and paralectotype material, and described in detail these specimens.

Backed by their revised diagnosis of *Cetiosaurus*, Upchurch and Martin also offered a preliminary assessment of *Cetiosaurus mogrebiensis* Lapparent 1955, based on three cotype partial skeletons collected from three separate localities in Morocco. Lapparent had referred these specimens to *Cetiosaurus* based upon the following shared characters: Pleurocoels in dorsal vertebrae in elevated position; proximal chevrons strongly developed; middle caudal vertebrae robust; reduced curvature of scapula; similarly shaped humeri; shaft of ulna triangular in cross section; radius differing from that of *Bothriospondylus*; ischium elongate, with expanded shaft; pubis robust, strongly expanded proximally; and similarly shaped femur.

According to Upchurch and Martin, most of the above features are only vaguely defined or can also be found in various other sauropod genera, none of them identifying with autapomorphies identified by those authors in their 2003 study. Upchurch and Martine found it "difficult to justify Lapparent's referral of the Moroccon specimens to *Cetiosaurus* because the former are damaged in key areas such as the cervical and dorsal neural spines." Furthermore, various differences between the English and Moroccan materials — *e.g.*, presence of more extensive dorsal pleurocoels in the latter — suggest that these forms are not congeneric.

According to the research of Upchurch and Martin, there is currently only one species of *Cetiosaurus* that should be accepted as valid — *C. oxoniensis*.

Key references: [Anonymous] (1848); Cope, Duff, Parsons, Torrens, Wimbledon and Wright (1980); Hulke (1874); Huxley (1870); Lapparent (1955); Lydekker (1888); Lyell (1838); Mantell (1850); McIntosh (1990); Melville (1849); Owen (1841, 1842a, 1842b, 1844); Phillips (1871); Rawson, Curry, Dilley, Hancock, Kenedy, Neale, Wood and Worssam (1978); Steel (1970); Upchurch, Barrett and Dodson (2004); Upchurch and Martin (2002, 2003); Wilson and Sereno (1998); Woodward (1905).

†CHASMOSAURUS

Ornithischia: Predentata: Genusauria: Cerapoda: Chasmatopia: Marginocephalia: Ceratopsia: Neoceratopsia: Coronosauria: Ceratopsoidea: Ceratopsidae: Chasmosaurinae.

Comments: In 1929, fossil hunter George F. Sternberg collected a small chasmosaurine skull and associated dentary fragment (UALVP 40) near Sand Creek, on the Red Deer River, in Alberta, Canada. The specimen was originally described by Gilmore (1923), who tentatively referred it to the type species genus "*Eoceratops*" *canadensis* (=*Chasmosaurus belli*; see Godfrey and Holmes 1995 and S2 for the most recent assignment of this skull) as the second specimen assigned to that now abandoned taxon. The skull was rather unusual for a chasmosaurine in possessing long postorbital horncores. Due to incomplete preparation, only the left side of the specimen had been described.

More recently, as reported by Konishi (2004) in an abstract for a poster, UALVP 40 has at last been completely prepared, allowing for a description of the entire morphology of specimen, new observations by that author showing "that there are some substantial differences in the cranial features between the right and left side of the skull, adding new information previously unknown to the specimen." According to Konishi, these observed details suggest that the specimen, contrary to the conclusion of the earlier study, probably represents an immature chasmosaurine individual. Moreover, some of the newly revealed features of the right side of the specimen "seriously contradict some of the previous interpretations made on the specimen based only on the data from the left side of the skull."

Konishi noted that UALVP 40 is currently assigned to *Chasmosaurus* sp. However, comparisons of this skull with other Canadian chasmosaur specimens having long brow horns apparently suggest assignment to the currently abandoned (juvenile) species *Chasmosaurus canadensis* Lehman 1989 (=*C. belli*; see *D:TE*), "from ontogenetic as well as ecological points of view."

Key references: Gilmore (1923); Godfrey and Holmes (1995); Konishi (2004); Lehman (1989).

†CHIALINGOSAURUS

Ornithischia: Predentata: Genasauria: Thyreophora: Thyreophoroidea: Eurypoda: Stegosauria: Stegosauridae: Stegosaurinae.

Diagnosis of genus (as for type species): Humerus and ulna slender; femur having broad-base triangular cranial trochanter and pendant fourth trochanter; small platelike spine (Galton and Upchurch 2004*b*).

Comment: In their review of the Stegosauria, Galton and Upchurch (2004*b*) rediagnosed the type species *Chialingosaurus kuani* (see *D:TE*).

Key reference: Galton and Upchurch (2004*b*).

†CHINDESAURUS—(=*Caseosaurus*)
Saurischia *incertae sedis*.

Comments: In a review of basal saurischians, Langer reassessed the phylogenetic position of the primitive dinosaur *Chindesaurus*, which had generally been regarded as possibly belonging to the family Herrerasauridae, or, as Hunt (1996) had proposed, could represent a nonherrerasaurid member of the Herrerasauria (see *D:TE, S2*).

According to Langer, the proposition of Hunt could be correct, as this genus lacks the derived eusaurischian feature of elongate cervical vertebrae. However, Langer cited a number of features (*i.e.*, femur having fourth trochanter in downward posi-

tion of shaft, as in Sauropodomorpha; distal end of tibia narrower laterally than medially, descending process partially overlapping fibula, as in some basal Saurischia but not Herrerasauridae). Accordingly, Langer considered it best, for the present, to regard *Chindesaurus* as Saurischia *incertae sedis*, at the same time noting that "its high nesting within any of the major saurischian groups (Herrerasauridae, Theropoda, and Sauropodomorpha) can be dismissed."

Langer considered the type species *Caseosaurus crosbyensis* (see *S2*) to be a junior synonym of the type species *Chindesaurus bryansmalli*.

Key references: Hunt (1996); Langer (2004).

†CHIROSTENOTES
Saurischia: Eusaurischia: Theropoda: Neotheropoda: Tetanurae: Avetheropoda: Coelurosauria: Tyrannoraptora: Maniraptoriformes: Maniraptora: Metornithes: Oviraptorosauria: Caenagnathoidea: Caenagnathidae.

Diagnosis of genus (as for type species): Maxilla with long tomial edge; vertical basicranial region, basal tubera poorly developed and placed near basipterygoid processes; mandible long, shallow, symphysis fused, symphyseal shelf long, low undivided external mandibular fenestra; dentary concave in lateral aspect, occlusal edge sharp; (laterally) lingual surface of edge fluted with occlusal grooves and toothlike apical projections; (rostrally) edge turned up along symphysis; convex lingual ridge extending medially to occlusal groove; surangular fused with articular; ilium with uniformly arched dorsal margin, deepest above acetabulum; postacetabular process pointed caudally, shorter than preacetabular process; distal portion of ischial shaft caudoventrally directed, its axis at approximately 135-degree angle to axis of proximal portion; obturator process of ischium with strong, dorsoventrally short, well-demarcated process; pes arctometatarsal, metatarsus long, constituting 22 percent total hindlimb length (excluding digits) (Osmólska, Currie and Barsbold 2004).

Comment: In their review of the Oviraptorosauria, Osmólska, Currie and Barsbold (2004) rediagnosed the type species *Chirostenotes pergracilis* (see *D:TE*).

Key reference: Osmólska, Currie and Barsbold (2004).

†CHUNGKINGOSAURUS
Ornithischia: Predentata: Genasauria: Thyreophora: Thyreophoroidea: Eurypoda: Stegosauria: Stegosauridae; ?Stegosaurinae.

Diagnosis of genus (as for type species): Humerus

Chirostenotes pergracilis pair being pursued by *Tyrannosaurus rex*, as depicted by artist Todd Marshall.

primitive in retention of proximal deltopectoral crest, derived in having broad ends; derived feature of four pairs of terminal tail spines (Dong 1990, 1992); dermal plates large, thick, many morphologically intermediate between plates and spines (Galton and Upchurch 2004*b*).

Comment: In their review of the Stegosauria, Galton and Upchurch (2004*b*) rediagnosed the type species *Chungkingosaurus jianbeiensis* (see *D:TE*).

Key references: Dong (1990, 1992); Galton and Upchurch (2004*b*).

†CITIPATI

Saurischia: Eusaurischia: Eusaurischia: Theropoda: Neotheropoda: Tetanurae: Avetheropoda: Coelurosauria: Tyrannoraptora: Maniraptoriformes: Maniraptora: Metornithes: Oviraptorosauria: Oviraptoridae: Oviraptorinae.

Diagnosis of genus (as for type species): Large oviraptorid with crested skull (Clark, Norell and Barsbold 2001); occiput and quadrate sloping rostrodorsally (with jugal-quadratojugal bar placed horizontally); postorbital process of jugal perpendicular to ventral ramus of jugal; external naris large, "teardrop" shaped (Osmólska, Currie and Barsbold 2004).

Comment: In their review of the Oviraptorosauria, Osmólska, Currie and Barsbold (2004) rediagnosed the type species *Citipati osmolskae* (see *S3*).

Key references: Clark, Norell and Barsbold (2001); Osmólska, Currie and Barsbold (2004).

†CLASMODOSAURUS [*nomen dubium*]

Saurischia: Eusaurischia: Sauropodomorpha: Sauropoda: Eusauropoda: Neosauropoda: Macronaria: Titanosauriformes: Titanosauria *incertae sedis*.

Comments: In 1989, Florentino Ameghino based the type species *Clasmodosaurus spatula* upon three incomplete teeth (Ameghino personal collection) recovered from (Upper Cretaceous) Río Sehuen, Santa Cruz Province, Argentina (see *D:TE*).

Recently, in his review of the "titanosaurid" sauropods of South America, Jaime Eduardo Powell (2003) reassessed this taxon. As that author observed, these teeth are of the "diplodociform" (Diplodociforma of Calvo and Salgado 1995, generally regarded as belonging to the Diplodocoidea, *e.g.*, Wilson and Sereno 1998; see "Systematics" chapter, *S1*) type, comparable to the known teeth of the diplodocid *Diplodocus*, of the "titanosaurids" *Antarctosaurus*, and *Alamosaurus sanjuanensis*, and of various indeterminate "titanosaurids" described by Powell (see *Titanosaurus* entry, "Note"). However, the teeth of *C. spatula* differ from the others in having longitudinal grooves in both labial and lingual faces.

Powell accepted Ameghino's interpretation of

these teeth as being those of a sauropod dinosaur. Furthermore, based upon their geographic and stratigraphic context, Powell included them in the "Titanosauridae." However, because dinosaurian dental morphology cannot by itself be used as a reliable diagnostic character, Powell considered *C. spatula* to be a *nomen dubium.*

Key references: Ameghino (1898); Powell (2003).

†COELOPHYSIS

Saurischia: Eusaurischia: Eusaurischia: Theropoda: Neotheropoda: Ceratosauria: Coelophysoidea: Coelophysidae.

Comments: In 1989, Edwin H. Colbert reported on four or five partially articulated sclerotic ossicles that he had observed in a specimen (MCZ 4327) of the small Late Triassic theropod *Coelophysis bauri* in the collections of Harvard University. From this specimen, Colbert estimated a total of 20 such ossicles, predicting that they were arranged with dorsal and ventral elements outermost among a series of four sequentially overlapping plates, these proceeding rostrally and caudally, overlapping the nasal and temporal ossicles from the top and bottom.

Rinehart, Heckert, Lucas and Hunt (2004), in an abstract for a poster, reported and described the first complete sclerotic ring ever found in a gracile-morph specimen (NMMNH P-42200) of *C. bauri*, preserved in a block recovered from the Whitaker Quarry in the Apachean Rock Point Formation, Chinle Group, at Ghost Ranch, north-central New Mexico. The 123-millimeter length of the skull, the authors noted, places the specimen in the range of large juvenile or small gracile adult. The orbit of the skull has a mean diameter of 31 millimeters.

Preserved in a ring within the orbit of this specimen are 20 articulated ossicles. The caudal portions of the orbit and the ring are slightly elongated caudally; otherwise, they are not distorted. The ring has an outside diameter of 21 millimeters and an inside diameter of 12 millimeters. The ring, as preserved, occludes 63 percent of the orbit

Rinehart *et al.* described the ossicles as follows: Sub-trapezoidal to sub-triangular, except for more elongate oval nasal and temporal ossicles; ossicles measuring approximately seven millimeters in width circumferentially, five millimeters high radially, wider bases bounding corneal aperture; nasal and temporal ossicles about 10 to 12 millimeters in length, five millimeters high.

As Rinehart *et al.* pointed out, their discovery shows that the extrapolations of Colbert were essentially correct.

Comparing their findings with the morphology of the sclerotic rings and orbits of extant reptiles and birds, Rinehart *et al.* concluded "that *Coelophysis* was a diurnal, visually oriented predator."

In a subsequent and related abstract for a poster, Rinehart, Lucas, Heckert and Hunt (2004) further reported on above (probably female) specimen, relating that they "corrected the skull, orbit, and sclerotic ring for slight taphonomic distortion, reconstructed the ring, and allometrically projected the specimen to

Skeletons of adult (DMNH 14729, including 25 percent original fossil material) and juvenile (DMNH 22702, 50 percent original material) *Coelophysis bauri* mounted to suggest playful activity. This exhibit — adult mounted by paleontologist Kenneth Carpenter with an aetosaur tail dangling from its mouth, juvenile by Karen Alf under Carpenter's direction — is celebrated as the first free-mounting of skeletons of this dinosaur.

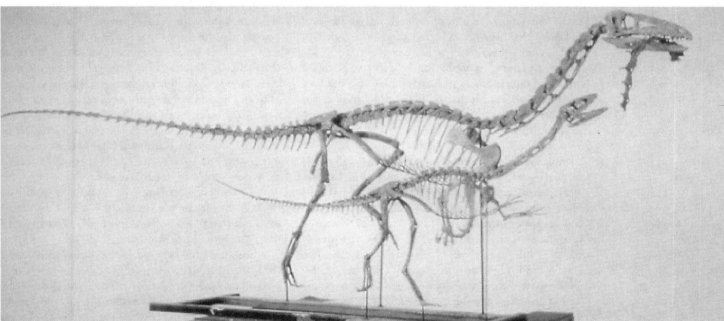

Courtesy Denver Museum of Nature and Science.

Coelophysis

adult size." Rinehart *et al.* (2004) analyzed the morphology of the sclerotic ring and orbit, comparing these to extant lizard and bird outgroups and also to the primitive ornithischian *Hypsilophodon foxii* and basal avian *Archaeopteryx*. The avian outgroup included 18 species representing 10 orders; the lizard outgroup nine species and six families. Orbit size versus skull size was plotted by the authors in order to estimate the relative importance of vision to the taxa studied.

Rinehart *et al.*'s (2004) study found *Coelophysis* to rank with most of the studied birds and well above most lizards. Eye morphology in this dinosaur was evaluated by the authors in two ways—ring area as opposed to orbit area, and cross-sectional shape of the ring (indicating eye shape)—that were then compared to the outgroups. Rinehart *et al.* (2004) discovered that, in both cases, the eyes of *Coelophysis* seem to be closest to those of falconiform birds (*e.g.*, hawks, eagles), wherein the eye is globe-shaped and accommodation power is quite high. In comparing cornea size to orbit size, the authors found *Coelophysis* as showing poor night vision capability (about on a par with

that of most lizards and nonraptorial birds, with night vision in *Hypsilophodon* and *Archaeopteryx* rating about on a par with Falconiformes), this further suggesting that the *Coelophysis* eye probably had a round rather than slit pupil. Moreover, skull and orbit measurements by Rinehart *et al.* (2004) of P-42200 indicated an overlap of both right and left fields of vision of from a minimum of 26 to maximum of 40 degrees, depending on cornea shape. From this study, the authors concluded "that *Coelophysis* was a diurnal, visually oriented predator and that high power of accommodation and good frontal binocular vision is extremely probable" for this genus.

Notes: For details on the rotation of a six-ton *Coelophysis* block excavated from the Whitaker Quarry, see the abstract for a poster published by Pierce, Rinehart, Heckert, Lucas and Hunt (2004).

Kundrát (2004*b*) described a dinosaur footprint (PMNH-EHC 1/7) with pubic imprint and associated filamenous impressions, collected during the nineteenth century by Edward Hitchcock from Lower Jurassic deposits of the Lily Pond Quarry, in the Lower Jurassic (?Hettangian; P. E. Olsen, personal communication to Kundrát) Turners Falls Formation of western Massachusetts. Originally described by Edward Hitchcock, Jr. (1865) as *Anomoepus major*, the track "was made by a *Coelophysis*-like ceratosaur," Kundrát concluded. Its pubic imprint, that author noted, found between the right metapodial and caudalmost abdominal impressions, "suggests a Lower Jurassic theropod trackmaker with a posteriorly expanded distal pubis: a character shared by both tetanuran and neoceratosaurian theropods" (see Weishampel, Dodson and Osmólska 1990). The feather-like impressions, made while the animal was in a sitting position, demonstrate that the origin of feathers in Theropoda dates much earlier than generally presumed.

Key references: Colbert (1989); Kundrát (2004*b*); Pierce, Rinehart, Heckert, Lucas and Hunt (2004); Rinehart, Heckert, Lucas and Hunt (2004); Rinehart, Lucas, Heckert and Hunt (2004); Weishampel, Dodson and Osmólska (1990).

†**COELUROIDES**—(=?*Indosuchus*, ?*Jubblpuria*)
Saurischia: Eusaurischia: Eusaurischia: Theropoda: Neotheropoda: Ceratosauria: Abelisauroidea *incertae sedis*.

Comments: In 1932, Friedrich von Huene named and described the new theropod *Coeluroides largus*, based on several isolated vertebrae (GSI K27/562, GSI K27/574, and GSI K27/595) recovered from the Lameta Formation of India. The following year, Huene, in an extensive report on the dinosaurs of India co-authored with Charles Alfred Matley, described these specimens as dorsal vertebrae (see *D:TE*), although they were correctly identified by subsequent workers (*e.g.*, Welles 1980; Molnar 1990) as belonging to the caudal region.

More recently, in a review of the theropods discussed in Huene and Matley's report, Novas, Agnolin and Bandyopadhyay (2004) observed that GSI K27/595 resembles closely proximal caudal vertebrae of *Majungatholus* (Novas *et al.*, personal observation) and those of *Ornithomimoides* (see entry).

However, Novas *et al.* noted, GSI K27/562 and GSI K27/574 also display various distinctive features. For example, GSI K27562 is distinguished by wide, nearly horizontal, well-separated prezygapophyses and postzygapophyses. In dorsal view, the transverse processes are expanded and triangular, their dorsal surface deeply excavated, the proximal margins of the transverse process, therefore, being raised. Also, the preserved base of the neural spine is robust and axially extended.

The above-described morphology, Novas *et al.* noted, can also be seen in a caudal vertebra (AMNH 1957)—also having a low, elongate apneumatic centrum—referred to *Indosuchus raptorius* (see *Indosuchus* entry). Furthermore, GSI K27/562 and AMNH 1957 closely resemble (*e.g.*, triangular, dorsally excavated, extensive transverse processes) GSI K20/612, a fragmentary caudal vertebra referred to *Jubbulpuria* (see entry). Novas *et al.* found interesting the fact that all three of these specimens "share a similar set of features that contrasts with the caudal morphology of *Majungatholus*, *Carnotaurus*, *Ilokelesia*, and *Aucasaurus*, as well as other abelisaurid caudal vertebrae of the Indian collections (GSI K27/595, GSI K20/610, GSI K20/614B, GSI K27/614, GSI K27/586, GSI K27/597, GSI K27/600)." Importantly, Novas *et al.* pointed out, midcaudal vertebra AMNH 1957 differs morphologically from proximal caudal AMNH 1960 (referred to *I. raptorius*) and is also much larger, thereby "indicating that they do not belong to a same individual (and presumably pertain to different species)."

Coeluroides largus could represent a valid although indeterminate abelisauroid taxon, Novas *et al.* stated, or be conspecific with *Jubbulpuria tenuis*, although the evidence is not strong enough to demonstrate their synonymy. Possibly the caudal vertebrae of *C. largus* and *J. tenuis* represent theropod lineages distinct from the Abelisauroidea, the authors suggested, the above-noted similarities between the distal caudals of *J. tenuis* and the abelisauroid *Ligabuieno andesi* (see Bonaparte 1996; see *SI*) arguing "in favor that other caudals with delta-shaped transverse processes (*e.g.*, *Coeluroides largus*, AMNH 1957) also belong to Abelisauroidea."

Key references: Bonaparte (1996); Huene (1932); Huene and Matley (1933); Molnar (1990); Novas, Agnolin and Bandyopadhyay (2004); Welles (1984).

CÓLEPIOCEPHALE Sullivan 2003
Ornithischia: Predentata: Genusauria: Cerapoda: Chasmatopia: Marginocephalia: Pachycephalosauria: Goyocephala: Homalocephaloidea: Pachycephalosauridae: Pachycephalosaurinae.
Name derivation: Latin *colepium* = "knuckle" + Greek *cephale* = "head."
Type species: *C. lambei* (Sternberg 1945).
Other species: [None.]
Occurrence: Foremost Formation, Alberta, Canada.
Age: Late Cretaceous (Campanian).
Known material: Numerous incomplete frontoparietal domes, other cranial remains, some fragmentary.
Holotype: CMN 8818, almost complete frontoparietal bone with peripheral skull elements.

Diagnosis of genus (as for type species): Almost fully-domed pachycephalosaur; differing from all other known pachycephalosaurs in the following features: lack of lateral (caudal supraorbital and postorbital)

Colepiocephale

Colepiocephale lambei, CMN 8818, holotype frontoparietal dome of *Stegoceras lambei,* dorsal view.

the Foremost Formation (formerly "Oldman" Formation, in part; D. A. Eberth, personal communication to R. M. Sullivan 2000), on the South Saskatchewam River, below Bow Island ferry, in Alberta, Canada. (This specimen was originally described by Sternberg 1945 as a new species of *Stegoceras*, which Sternberg named *Stegoceras lambei*.)

Sullivan also referred to this type species the following specimens, all of which were collected from the Foremost Formation: CMN 29419, almost complete frontoparietal dome; CMN 29420, skull fragment; CMN 29421, incomplete frontoparietal; ROM 3632, almost complete frontoparietal dome; TMP 70.2.1, nearly complete frontoparietal dome; TMP 86.146.1, incomplete frontoparietal dome with fused prefrontals; TMP 86.146.2, incomplete frontoparietal dome with complete right prefrontal; TMP 92.88.1, almost complete frontoparietal dome with fused prefrontals; TMP 97.99.2, nearly complete frontoparietal dome with prefrontals; TMP 97.99.3, incomplete frontoparietal dome; TMP 2000.57.1, nearly complete frontoparietal; UALVP-349, incomplete frontoparietal; and UALVP-31471, almost complete frontoparietal.

Also, Sullivan (2003) referred to cf. *Colepiocephale lambei* the following very fragmentary specimens from the Foremost Formation, all of which, while too incomplete for precise identification, conform to *C. lambei*: CMN 9952, incomplete frontoparietal; CMN 29420, incomplete ?parietal fragment; CMN 29421, left side (medial section) of frontoparietal with three fragments, postorbital, prefrontal; TMP 80.20.1, incomplete parietal; TMP 86.146.3, caudal portion of frontoparietal dome; TMP 86.145.4, fragmentary frontoparietal dome; TMP 86.146.5, fragmentary right side of frontoparietal dome; TMP 86.146.6, caudal medial fragment with down-turned part of parietal (ventral-supraoccipital); TMP 87.7.7, rostral part of left frontal; TMP 97.99.2, incomplete frontoparietal; TMP 99.31.1, ?left side of frontoparietal; and TMP 99.31.2, fragmentary frontoparietal.

and caudal squamosal shelf; squamosals restricted to lateral sides, much reduced, with only hint of their margins lying ventrally under parietal; parietal strongly down-turned, forming steeply inclined border across entire caudal breadth of skull; occiput reduced; frontoparietal mass thick and broad caudally, medial frontal lobe high, relatively narrow; lateral frontal lobes recessed caudally; frontoparietal dome having pronounced constriction at contact of postorbital and caudal supraorbital (in dorsal aspect); peripheral elements (postorbital, caudal supraorbital, rostral supraorbital, prefrontal) reduced, situated low along frontoparietal; differing further from *Stegoceras validum* in lacking supratemporal fossae; differing from "*Prenocephale edmontonense*" [=*Stegoceras edmontonensis*] in having incipient rostral supraorbitals, not incorporated into rostrolateral (frontal) part of dome (Sullivan 2003).

Comments: The oldest diagnostic North American dome-headed dinosaur, *Colepiocephale lambei*, a new genus and species named by pachycephalosaur specialist Robert M. Sullivan in 2003, was founded upon a nearly complete frontoparietal dome with peripheral skull elements (CMN 8818) collected from

Life restoration of *Colepiocephale lambei* by artist Denver Fowler, prepared under the direction of Robert M. Sullivan.

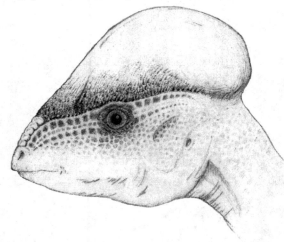

Life restoration of *Colepiocephale lambei* by artist Denver Fowler (detail of head) prepared under the direction of Robert M. Sullivan.

Sullivan (2003) found the parietal and squamosal of this taxon to be of particular interest. In one particularly well-preserved specimen (TMP 92.88.1), the parietal, in ventral aspect, wraps around the caudal margin of the skull. The right side of the skull shows remnants of two vestigial, somewhat flattened, spade-shaped nodes reminiscent of the well-developed squamosal nodes found in some specimens of *Stegoceras validum* and "*Prenocephale edmontonensis*" [=*S. edmontonensis*] (see Sullivan 2000a). This interpretation implies "the presence of a much reduced squamosal (on each side of the skull). The lack of evidence for squamosals and any associated vestigial ornamentation in the holotype suggested to Sullivan (2003) that the squamosals may be lost in larger and more mature individuals.

In studying the pachycephalosaur specimens housed at the Canadian Museum of Nature, the Royal Ontario Museum, the Royal Tyrrell Museum of Palaeontology, and the University of Alberta Laboratory of Vertebrate Paleontology, Sullivan (2003) verified that all specimens belowing to *C. lambei* are from the Foremost Formation, while no other pachycephalosaurian species are known from this stratigraphic interval (stratigraphic occurrences of this material verified with Eberth, personal communication to Sullivan). Consequently, *C. lambei*, based upon its distinct morphology and restricted stratigraphic occurrence, seems to have some biostratigraphic utility.

As Sullivan (2003) pointed out, the unique morphology (*e.g.*, loss of squamosals, much reduced lateral elements) suggests a derived condition in this species, one antedating the appreance of more primitive taxa such as *Stegoceras*, *Homalocephale*, and possibly *Prenocephale* and other related forms.

Interpreting the frontoparietal dome to be a derived feature, Sullivan (2003) found significant the fact that such fully domed pachycephalosaurs as *C. lambei* predate the geologically younger yet more primitive *Stegoceras* in western North America (middle Campanian) and also *Homalocephale calathocercos* in Asia (early Maastrichtian). Thus, that author noted, the premise that many Late Cretaceous dinosaurs migrated to North America from Asia (see Russell 1993) does not seem to apply to pachycephalosaurs.

Key references: Russell (1993); Sternberg (1945); Sullivan (2000a, 2003).

†COLORADISAURUS

Saurischia: Eusaurischia: Sauropodomorpha: Sauropoda: Prosauropoda: Plateosauria: Plateosauridae.

Diagnosis of genus (as for type species): Autapomorphies including the following: Wide dorsal process; large medial lamina to maxilla; large medial lamina to lacrimal (Galton and Upchurch 2004a).

Comment: In their review of the Prosauropoda, Galton and Upchurch (2004a) rediagnosed the type species *Coloradisaurus brevis* (see *D:TE*).

Key reference: Galton and Upchurch (2004a).

†COMPSOGNATHUS   Wagner 1861

Saurischia: Eusaurischia: Eusaurischia: Theropoda: Neotheropoda: Tetanurae: Avetheropoda: Coelurosauria: Compsognathidae.

Type species: *C. longipes* Wagner 1861.

Other species: *C. corallestris* Bidar, Demay and Thomel 1972.

Comments: In a published abstract, Peyer (2003) reported on her reexamination of *Compsognathus corallestris*, a referred species of the very small genus *Compsognathus*, founded by Bidar, Demay and Thomel (1972) on a skeleton from the Portlandian limestones of the Tithonian of southern France, but later referred by Ostrom (1978) to the Bavarian type species, *C. longipes* (see *D:TE*). This specimen, Peyer noted, offers both additional cranial and postcranial data that permits a new interpretation of the genus.

Peyer briefly described this specimen as follows: Skull long, slender, reconstructed maximal length of 100 millimeters comprising 22 percent length of presacral vertebral column; 23 presacral, five sacral, and 31 caudal vertebrae (preserved *in situ*); pubis slightly longer than femur, pubic boot showing no cranial extension but pronounced caudal extension; ilium characterized by large obturator process, expanded distally into small foot on ilium; ilium slightly convex dorsally, cranial iliac process seemingly shorter than caudal one.

As Peyer observed, the manus of this specimen

Group of *Compsognathus longipes* as restored by artist Todd Marshall. The feathers are conjectural. (For an argument against the presence of feathers in this genus, see John H. Ostrom's paper on the osteology of *Compsognathus*, published in 1978; see also *D:TE.*)

has three functional digits (most manual elements being fragmentary, just the proximal halves of right metacarpals I-3 and proximal end of phalanx I-1 of the left manus having been preserved; metacarpal I-3 of the right and left manus, plus five additional phalanges, known only from impressions in calcareous matrix).

Peyer also observed the following details: Elements of metacarpal I-3 comparable to those in various other theropods (*e.g.*, *Ornitholestes*, *Deinonychus*, *Archaeopteryx*), in having a short, stout metacarpal I, long II, and slender, long, and somewhat curved III; right carpus preserving radiale, distal first carpal, and distal second carpal, the latter two not forming semilunate carpal, as well-defined suture separates these elements from one another.

According to Peyer, anatomical and morphological characters of the Bavarian species are almost identical to those in the species described from France, the differences between them attributable to different ontogenetic stages; consequently, "this study supports the idea that *C. corallestris* is a junior synonym of *C. longipes.*"

In a subsequently published abstract for a poster, Peyer (2004) offered a contrary opinion regarding the French species, stating that the genus *Compsognathus* currently "includes *C. longipes* and *C. corallestris.*" Peyer (2004) further noted that previous phylogenetic analyses of the Coelurosauria had included only the well-known Bavarian specimen, although a reevaluation of the French taxon provides "new cranial and postcranial information crucial for a better understanding of the genus *Compsognathus* and the phylogenetic assessment of basal Maniraptoriformes and Compsognathidae."

Performing a phylogenetic analysis, based upon previously published data and also her own observations — including 30 terminal taxa and 350 characters, with rooting done by outgroup comparisons with *Herrerasaurus* and *Coelophysis*— Peyer (2004) found the family Compsognathidae to be a monophyletic clade comprising five genera (see "Systematics" chapter) and six species. Compsognathidae placed near the base of Maniraptoriformes, with the coelurosaur *Scipionyx* falling out of the base of Compsognathidae, with *Sinosauropteryx*, *Huaxiaognathus*, and SMNK

2349 PAL [=the holotype of *Mirischia*; see entry] following, the latter having a sister-taxon relationship to a clade comprising both *Compsognathus* species.

Erratum: In *D:TE* the date of Wagner's publication of the name *Compsognathus longipes* was incorrectly given as 1859.

Key references: Bidar, Deman and Thomel (1972); Ostrom (1978); Peyer (2003, 2004); Wagner (1861).

†**COMPSOSUCHUS**—(=?*Dryptosauroides*, ?*Indosaurus*, ?*Indosuchus*, ?*Jubbulporia*, ?*Ornithomimoides*)

Saurischia: Eusaurischia: Eusaurischia: Theropoda: Neotheropoda: Ceratosauria: Abelisauroidea: Abelisauridae *incertae sedis*.

Comments: In a review of the theropod specimens from India described by Friedrich von Huene, in a paper co-authored with Charles Alfred Matley in 1933, Novas, Agnolin and Bandyopadhyay (2004) reassessed the type species *Compsosuchus solus* Huene 1932. Based on a single axis with fused atlantal intercentrum (GSI K27/578) from India's Lameta Formation, this taxon was later regarded by Molnar, Kurzanov and Dong (1990), in a review of "Carnosauria," as a possible allosaurid (see *D:TE*).

Novas *et al.* more recently observed, however, that GSI K27/578 resembles a carnotaurine abelisaurid in the following features: Pneumatic pore caudoventrally to diapophysis; at least one large pleurocoel on centrum of axis; proportionally small, rodlike diapophyses; sharp lamina extending obliquely from diapophysis to postzygapophysis; neural arch expanded laterally, triangular in dorsal aspect.

As Novas *et al.* further observed, the type specimen of *Compsosuchus solus* resembles closely the axis of ISI R91/1 that Chatterjee and Rudra (1996) had referred to the genus *Indosaurus* (according to Novas *et al.*, a possibly synonym of *Indosuchus*; see entry). Acknowledging that the general morphology of GSI 27/578 indicates that it belongs to an abelisaurid, Novas *et al.* found no substantial differences between it and ISI R91/1; nor did they recognize any autapomorphies in GSI 27/578. Consequently, Novas *et al.* considered *Compsosuchus* to be a *nomen dubium*.

According to Novas *et al.*, the elements referred to the genera *Compsosuchus*, *Dryptosauroides*, *Jubbulpuria*, and *Ornithomimoides* (see entries) all pertain to different portions of the neck and tail, intimating that some or all of these taxa may be congeneric.

Key references: Chatterjee and Rudra (1996); Huene and Matley (1933); Molnar, Kurzanov and Dong (1990); Novas, Agnolin and Bandyopadhyay (2004).

CONDORRAPTOR Rauhut 2005

Saurischia: Eusaurischia: Theropoda: Neotheropoda: Tetanurae *incertae sedis*.

Name derivation: "[Village of Cerro] Cóndor" + Latin *raptor* = "robber, snatcher."

Type species: *C. currumili* Rauhut 2005.

Other species: [None.]

Occurrence: Cañadón Asfalto Formation, Patagonia, Argentina.

Age: Middle Jurassic (Callovian).

Known material: Teeth, partial fragmentary postcrania including vertebrae, rib fragments, partial pubic elements, partial femora, tibia, pedal elements.

Holotype: MPEF-PV 1672, incomplete left tibia.

Diagnosis of genus (as for type species): Autapomorphies including the following: absence of caudal incision between fibular condyle and medial part of proximal tibia; large, shallow depression laterally on base of cnemial crest; apomorphic characters, based upon referred specimens, including: pleurocoel in caudal cervical vertebrae behind caudoventral corner of parapophyses; large nutrient foramina on lateral side ischial peduncle of ilium; metatarsal IV having distinct step dorsally between shaft and distal articular facet (Rauhut 2005).

Comments: The genus *Condorraptor* was established upon a left tibia (MPEF-PV 1672) missing its distal end, collected from a series of lacustrine clays, tuffs, and limestones at Las Chacritas (locality discovered by landowner Hipólito Currumil), west of the village of Cerro Cóndor, in the upper Middle Jurassic Cañadón Asfalto Formation of Patagonia, Argentina. Material referred to the type species, *Condorraptor currumili*, recovered from the same locality, includes two teeth (MPEF-PV 1694–1695), three cervical vertebrae (MPEF-PV 1673–1675), seven dorsal vertebrae (all missing at least part of their neural arch) and vertebral fragments (MPEF-PV 1676–1680, 1697, 1700, and 1705), four sacral vertebrae (MPEF-PV 1681

Condorraptor currumili, MPEF-PV 1672, holotype left tibia in J. lateral (stereopair), B. cranial (stereopair), C. medial, and D. caudal (stereopair) views. Scale = 100 mm. (After Rauhut 2005.)

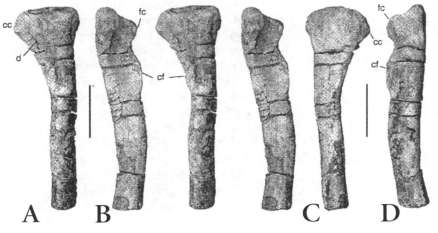

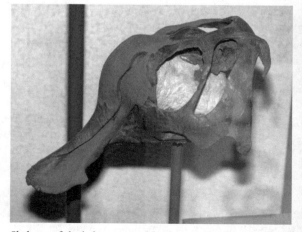

and 1701), three caudal (proximal, proximal midcaudal, and distal) vertebrae (MPEF-PV 1682–1683 and 1702), rib fragments and a partial chevron (MPEF-PV 1684–1685 and 1703), a partial ilium, pubes, and ischium (MPEF-PV 1686–1689 and 1704), and partial incomplete femora, metatarsal IV, and pedal unguals (MPEF-PV 1690–1693). As all of these remains (including the teeth) are of matching size with no element duplicated, and all elements are of matching preservation, they probably belong to the same individual animal as represented by the holotype (Rauhut 2005).

In describing this new taxon, Rauhut noted that *Condorraptor currumili* is currently the second most completely known (after *Piatnitzkysaurus floresi*) Middle Jurassic Gondwanan theropod.

Performing a cladistic analysis, Rauhut found *Condorraptor* to be a member of the Tetanurae based upon the following characters: Cervical vertebrae having pair of pleurocoels (see Rauhut 2003*c*); prezygapophyses of cranial cervical vertebrae entirely lateral to neural canal (Rauhut 2003*c*); cranial dorsal vertebrae with pronounced ventral keel (Rauhut 2003*c*); supraacetabular crest of ilium shelflike (Carrano, Sampson and Forster 2002); iliac-ischial articulation smaller than iliac-pubic articulation (Holtz 2000); pubic peduncle of ilium more developed craniocaudally than mediolaterally (Holtz); lateral ridge for contact with fibula on tibia offset from proximal end of tibia (Rauhut 2003*c*).

Observing no synapomorphies of more derived clades (*e.g.*, Coelurosauria, Allosauroidea, Spinosauroidea; see Holtz; Rauhut 2003*c*) in *Condorraptor currumili*, while also citing various plesiomorphic characters (*e.g.*, amphi-platycoelous cervical vertebrae; ventral keel in cervical vertebrae; obturator foramen entirely enclosed in bone), Rauhut (2005) assessed this species to be a basal member of Tetanurae "as might be expected for a Middle Jurassic" member of that clade. *Condorraptor* differs from most basal tetanurans, that author noted, in the rectangular shape and craniocaudal orientation of the cnemial crest of the tibia. Furthermore, the presence in the upper Middle Jurassic of Argentina of at least two basal tetanurans, *Condorraptor* and *Piatnitzkysaurus*, apparently not more closely related to each other than to Laura-

sian taxa, demonstrates the global diversification of the Tetanurae during the Middle Jurassic, with no evidence of differentiation between the fauna of the Northern and Southern Hemisphere. Therefore, both *Condorraptor* and *Piatnitzkysaurus* are seemingly "part of a global theropod fauna that was dominated by basal tetanurans during the late Middle Jurassic."

Key references: Carrano, Sampson and Forster (2002); Holtz (2000); Rauhut (2003*c*, 2005).

†CORYTHOSAURUS

Ornithischia: Predentata: Genasauria: Cerapoda: Ornithopoda: Euornithopoda: Iguanodontia: Dryomorpha: Ankylopollexia: Styracosterna: Iguanodontoidea: Hadrosauroidea: Euhadrosauria: Hadrosauridae: Lambeosaurinae: Corythosaurini.

Comments: The "helmut crested" duckbilled dinosaur *Corythosaurus* is known from the Dinosaur Park Formation of Alberta, Canada, from more than 20 articulated skulls. As reported by Evans (2003) in a published abstract, these specimens reflect an almost complete postnatal growth series, from small juveniles to large adults, although juvenile skull material is comparatively rare. However, several recently recovered juvenile skulls allowed Evans to reassess in depth cranial growth and variation in this genus.

As Evans pointed out, the taxonomically significant bones forming the lambeosaurine cranial crest pass through morphologically similar stages of growth, complicating the correct taxonomic identification of juveniles. To confirm the identity of the studied skulls, Evans examined remains representing each of the four known Dinosaur Park Formation lambeosaurines, establishing "discrete, ontogeny-independent cranial

Skeleton of the helmut-crested lambeosaurine, *Corythosaurus casuarius*, the crest of of this juvenile specimen not yet fully developed.

Photograph by the author, courtesy Royal Tyrrell Museum of Palaeontology/Alberta Community Development.

Skeleton of a subadult *Corythosaurus casuarius.*

characters that distinguish genera." Evans pointed out that the nature of the articulation between component bones of the crest is the most diagnostic of these characters among lambeosaurine genera. As that author observed, the genus *Corythosaurus* can be identified at all ontogenetic stages "by a distinctly bifurcated anterior projection on the nasal that overlaps the dorsal premaxillary process of the anterior region of the crest."

Investigating cranial growth in *Corythosaurus* using quantitative and qualitative approaches, Evans concluded the following: Most facial bones not significantly changing shape during ontogeny; crest a late-maturing feature, changing drastically through ontogeny; crest shape showing considerable intrageneric variation, with two comparatively distinct adult morphotypes suggesting sexual dimorphism (putative female with differential dorsal and caudoventral growth of nasal leading to characteristic indentation along caudal crest margin; putative male with more uniform peripheral nasal growth, resulting in relatively smooth outward curvature of crest margin. The premaxilla-nasal fontanelle, Evans noted,

prominent late into ontogeny, "subsequently closes in morph-related patterns."

Notes: A long debated topic regarding hadrosaurine dinosaurs has been the function and evolution of the hypertrophied nasal passages within the cranial crest. In a subsequently published and related abstract, Evans (2004) — addressing the possibility that the crest served to enhance the lambeosaurine sense of smell — posited that determining homologies between the nasal cavity of lambeosaurines and extant archosaurs is a prerequisite for making functional inferences regarding the crest. In order to test hypotheses of homology within a phylogenetic framework, Evans (2004) reconstructed various anatomical aspects (*e.g.*, the neural olfactory system) of the lambeosaurine nasal capsule.

New information gleaned from lambeosaurine presphenoid bone osteology and forebrain endocast morphology suggested to Evans (2004) the following: Olfactory bulbs housed within ossified braincase rather than within cavity of crest; robust afferent olfactory nerve bundles joining bulb in diffuse manner, from rostrolateral and rostroventral directions; latter,

Life restoration by artist Gregory S. Paul of *Corythosaurus casuarius*, based directly on the holotype complete skeleton with preserved integument (AMNH 5240; see *D:TE* for photograph of specimen).

combined with position of choana, orientation of nasolacrimal duct, and inferred path of ramus medialis nasi (VI) indicating nasal cavity proper extended ventrally to level of palate (not confined to common median crest chamber, as previously thought).

Moreover, Evans (2004) noted that the nasopharyngeal duct was short, and that all information now available suggests that the olfactory nerve did not proliferate within the cavity of the crest; consequently, "the hypothesis that the crest evolved to increase olfactory capability can be definitely rejected."

See also Heathcote (2004) for a recent brief report, published as an abstract, on applying geometric morphometric analysis to the skulls of ornithopod dinosaurs, particularly lambeosaurine hadrosaurs with their elaborate ornamentation, such mapping permitting "the assessment of a number of taxa currently believed to be juvenile lambeosaurines," and also "an interpolation between existing taxa, thus facilitating an estimation of the shape of the skull in hypothetical ancestors."

Errata: On page 104 of *S3*, the photograph was incorrectly identified as the skeleton of the juvenile *Corythosaurus casuarius* on display at the Natural History Museum of Los Angeles County. The skeleton shown in the photograph (reversed) is not that specimen, but rather one on exhibit at the Royal Tyrrell Museum of Palaeontology. Also, there may have been confusion regarding the genus *Procheneosaurus* in the *Corythosaurus* and *Lambeosaurus* entries of *D:TE*. To clarify (see *D:TE* for additional details).

Procheneosaurus was named (no species given) by William Diller Matthew (1920) in a popular article on Canadian dinosaurs published in *Natural History* magazine, the genus having been founded upon a partial skeleton and skull with jaws (ROM 758; originally GSC 3579; see *Lambeosaurus* entry, *D:TE* for figure) from the Oldman Formation of Alberta, Canada. Matthews briefly and informally described *Procheneosaurus* as a small form having a short, rounded skull and small bill.

Parks (1931), later noting Matthew's lack of a specific name and that his description was insufficient, referred the specimen to the new genus and species *Tetragonosaurus praeceps*, at the same time erecting a referred species from the Oldman Formation of Alberta, *T. erectofrons*, based on a skull with jaws (ROM 759; originally GSC 3578). Subsequently, Sternberg (1935) described another new species of *Tetragonosaurus*, *T. cranibrevis*, based on an incomplete skull with jaws (CMN [formerly GSC] 8633) from Alberta's Oldman Formation (see *D:TE*, *Corythosaurus* entry for photographs of both holotype skulls). The skulls of all three species of *Tetragonosaurus* are short and possess incipient crests.

In 1942, Lull and Wright, in their classic monograph on North American hadrosaurs, accepted the original name *Procheneosaurus* as valid for the specimens assigned to *Tetragonosaurus*, noting the priority of that name and features that they opined defined the genus. Lull and Wright designated *Procheneosaurus praeceps* as the type species of the genus. At the same time, these authors tentatively referred to *Procheneosaurus* the species *Trachodon altidens* [*nomen dubium*], also from Alberta, which Lambe (1902) had based on a left maxilla with teeth (CMN 1092).

Decades later, Dodson (1975), following a study of all the above and additional material, determined that all of the specimens referred to the genus *Procheneosaurus* represented, in fact, juvenile morphs of known adult hadrosaurine genera. Dodson referred *P. erectofrons* to *Corythosaurus casuarius*, *P. praeceps* and *?P. altidens* to *Lambeosaurus lambei*, and material belonging to *P. cranibrevis* both to *C. casuarius* and *L. lambei*.

AMNH 5461 (specimen currently on loan to the Museum of the Rockies), an incomplete skeleton with skull referred to *P. erectofrons*, collected from the Two Medicine Formation of Montana, may be a subadult of *Hypacrosaurus stebingeri* (J. R. Horner, personal communication 2003). The tentative species *?P. convincens* (Rozhdestvensky 1968) was referred by Brett-Surman (1989) to *Jaxartosaurus aralensis*.

Key reference: Brett-Surman (1989); Dodson (1975); Evans (2003, 2004); Lambe (1902); Lull and Wright (1942); Matthew (1920); Parks (1931); Rozhdestvensky (1968); Sternberg (1935).

†CRATEROSAURUS

Ornithischia: Predentata: Genasauria: Thyreophora: Thyreophoroidea: Eurypoda: Stegosauria *incertae sedis*.

Diagnosis of genus (as for type species): Unique deep excavation immediately caudal to prezygapophyses (Galton and Upchurch 2004*b*).

Comment: In their review of the Stegosauria, Galton and Upchurch (2004*b*) rediagnosed the type species *Craterosaurus pottonensis* (see *D:TE*), regarding this taxon as Stegosauria *incertae sedis*.

Key reference: Galton and Upchurch (2004*b*).

CROSBYSAURUS   Heckert 2004

Ornithischia *incertae sedis*.
Name derivation: "Crosby [County, Texas]"
Type species: *C. harrisae* Heckert 2004.
Other species: [None.]
Occurrence: Tecovas Formation, Texas, United States.
Age: Late Triassic (Carnian).
Known material: Teeth.
Holotype: NMMNH P-34200, tooth.

Diagnosis of genus (as for type species): Basal ornithischian distinguished by possession of compound or "graduated" denticles, each of several larger mesial or distal denticles bearing smaller yet similar denticles (Heckert 2004).

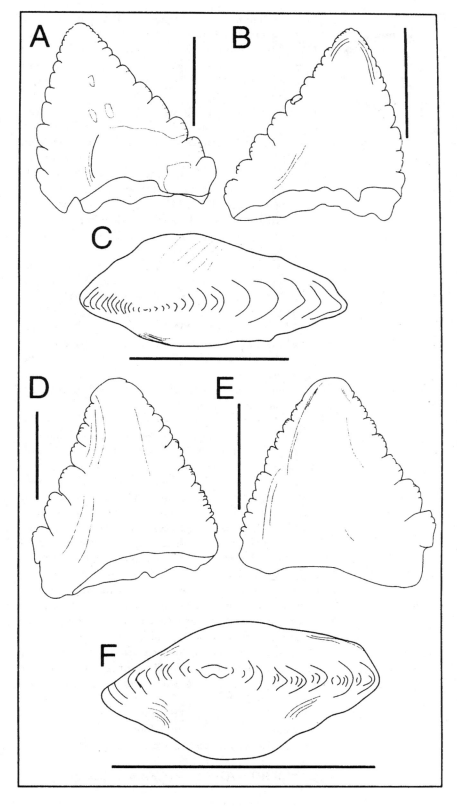

Crosbysaurus harrisae, interpretive sketches of teeth: A.–C. NMMNH P-34200, holotype tooth in A. lingual, B. labial, and C. occlusal views; D.–F. NMMNH P-34201, paratype tooth in D. labial, E. lingual, and F. occlusal views. Scale bars = 1 mm. (After Heckert 2004.)

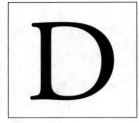

Comments: A "highly unusual ornithischian," the genus *Crosbysaurus* (first mentioned by Heckert 2002*b*, although considered then to be a *nomen nudum*) was founded upon an almost complete tooth crown (NMMNH P-34200) from the lower Kalgary locality (Upper Triassic: Carnian ["Otischalkian–Adamanian"]) in the lowermost Tecovas Formation (Chinle Group) of Crosby County, west Texas. Dental specimens referred to the type species, *P. lucasi*, collected from the same locality (and therefore regarded as paratypes), include a crown (NMMNH P-34201), three crowns (NMMNH P-34319), a worn crown (NMMNH P-34320), nearly complete crown (NMMNH P-34261), teeth (NMMNH P-34262, P-34394, and P-34397), and a small incomplete tooth (NMMNH P-34393); from other lowermost Tecovas Formation localities of Crosby County, numerous fragments of graduated ornithischian teeth (NMMNH P-36496), a worn incomplete crown (NMMNH P-34408) having a root very similar to NMMNH P-34404, teeth (NMMNH P-34409, P-18402, and PEFO 20336), plus various fragments; possibly a conical tooth (NMMNH P-34347); and from the upper Kalgary locality of the Tecovas Formation, Crosby County, nine incomplete crowns possibly referrable to *C. harrisae* (Heckert 2004).

Heckert acknowledged that the fact that no other known ornithischian possesses completely denticled teeth resembling those of NMMNH P-34200 could raise the criticism that they do not really represent members of this clade. That author found this possibility, however, to be unlikely "because these teeth possess all the classic ornithischian teeth synapomorphies" (*i.e.*, expanded basally, moderately low; subtriangular in lateral aspect; asymmetrical in occlusal aspect; denticles oblique to tooth margin).

Also, Heckert addressed the possibility that *Crosbysaurus* could be synonymous with *Protecovasaurus* (see entry), another genus based upon teeth and described by that author. However, Heckert pointed out, the level of heterodonty exhibited by the teeth in these genera is atypical of Triassic tetrapods. Consequently, that author was "reasonably confident that the type specimens of both taxa represent unique tooth morphologies," finding it "highly unlikely that a single taxon would include both tooth morphologies" (*i.e.*, recurved in *Protecovasaurus*, foreswept in *Crosbysaurus*).

Key references: Heckert (2002*b*, 2004).

†**CRYPTOVOLANS**—(See *Microraptor*.)

†**DACENTRURUS**
Ornithischia: Predentata: Genasauria: Thyreophora: Thyreophoroidea: Eurypoda: Stegosauria: Stegosauridae.

Diagnosis of genus (as for type species): Derived characters including the following: fusion of cervical ribs to cervical vertebrae; dorsal vertebrae having massive centra, centra wider than long, with prominent lateral depressions; pubis with deep prepubic process; dermal tail spines long, lateral and medial edges sharp (Galton and Upchurch 2004*b*).

Comments: In their review of the Stegosauria, Galton and Upchurch (2004*b*) rediagnosed the type species *Dacentrurus armatus* (see *D:TE*).

According to the analysis by Galton and Upchurch, *Dacentrurus* is either the sister taxon to the remaining Stegosauridae, or the sister taxon of Stegosaurinae, depending upon the phylogenetic placement of *Chungkingosaurus*.

Key reference: Galton and Upchurch (2004*b*).

†**DASPLETOSAURUS**
Saurischia: Eusaurischia: Eusaurischia: Theropoda: Neotheropoda: Tetanurae: Avetheropoda: Coelurosauria: Tyrannoraptora: Maniraptoriformes: Tyrannoraptora: Tyrannosauroidea: Tyrannosauridae: Tyrannosaurinae.

Diagnosis of genus (as for type species): Dorsolateral surface of postorbital with convex tablike process (Holtz 2004).

Comments: The giant theropod *Daspletosaurus*—a genus known from a number of skulls and skeletons collected from the Oldman Formation and the younger Dinosaur Park Formation of Alberta, Canada, and also from a skull (MOR 590) discovered in Montana—was reassessed by Currie (2003*b*) in his study of the cranial anatomy of tyrannosaurid dinosaurs from the Late Cretaceous of Alberta.

Until recently, this genus has only been known from a single species, *Daspletosaurus torosus*. Based on Currie's study, however, this taxon seems to be represented by multiple species spanning extensive geographic, ecological, and temporal ranges.

As Currie reported, the cranial morphology of all of the Dinosaur Park Formation specimens suggests that these represent a species distinct from the type species (Currie and Bakker, in preparation). The Montana specimen seems to represent yet a third species, distinguished from the others by the possession of a relatively high, triangular lacrimal horn (see Horner, Varricchio and Goodwin 1992). Additionally, the skeleton (OMNH 10131; see *Aublysodon* entry, *D:TE*) described by Lehman and Carpenter (1990) as "*Aublysodon*" could, based upon differences in skull morphology (Carr and Williamson 2000), could represent yet a third new undescribed *Daspletosaurus* species. For the present, Currie referred to these new and as yet unnamed taxa to *Daspletosaurus* sp.

A

B

6

18

5 cm

Right dentary (TMP 94.143.1) currently referred to *Daspletosaurus* sp. in A. right lateral and B. medial views. The entire specimen consists of a skeleton with skull collected from the Dinosaur Park Formation of Alberta, Canada. (After Currie 2003*b*.)

While in the past *Daspletosaurus* has sometimes been regarded as congeneric with *Tyrannosaurus* (*e.g.*, see Paul 1988), Currie posited that the recognition of three or more distinct *Daspletosaurus* forms justifies the generic separation of *Daspletosaurus* and *Tyrannosaurus*.

Currie also noted that while there has, in the past, been a tendency to regard *Daspletosaurus* as the sister taxon to *Tarbosaurus* plus *Tyrannosaurus*, such an assessment is not justified, lacking a full phylogenetic analysis. Moreover, such a recent analysis by Currie, Hurum and Sabath (2003), albeit one based upon relatively few characters, found *Tarbosaurus* to be the sister taxon to *Daspletosaurus* plus *Tyrannosaurus*. Furthermore, Currie stated, "the geographic and stratigraphic occurrences of these animals suggest the most parsimonious *a priori* interpretation is that *Daspletosaurus* and *Tyrannosaurus* are probably more closely related to each other than either is to *Tarbosaurus*."

Although *Daspletosaurus* shares numerous derived characters with other members of the Tyrannosaurinae, this genus can clearly be distinguished from *Tarbosaurus* and *Tyrannosaurus* by postorbitals lacking a suborbital process (see Currie *et al.*). Furthermore, the premaxilla and nasal contact one another beneath the external naris (*contra* Russell 1970; Holtz 2001).

Key references: Carr and Williamson (2000); Currie (2003*b*); Currie, Hurum and Sabath (2003); Holtz (2001, 2004); Horner, Varricchio and Goodwin (1992); Lehman and Carpenter (1990); Paul (1988); Russell (1970).

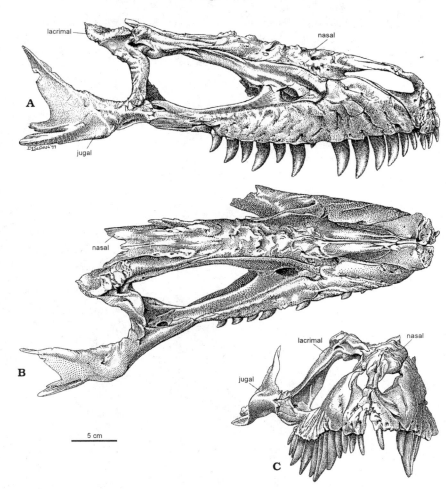

A

lacrimal

nasal

jugal

B

nasal

5 cm

lacrimal

nasal

jugal

C

. Front of skull (TMP 94.143.1) currently referred to *Daspletosaurus* sp. but apparently representing a new and as yet unnamed species, in A. right lateral, B. dorsal, and C. rostral views. (After Currie 2003*b*.)

Skull (FMNH PR308; originally referred to *Gorgosaurus libratus*; see *D:TE*, *S1*, and *S2*) of *Daspletosaurus torosus*, in 1956, during the mounting of the reconstructed skeleton at The Field Museum (then the Chicago Natural History Museum).

From *Predatory Dinosaurs of the World* (1988), copyright © Gregory S. Paul.

Life restoration by Gregory S. Paul of two *Daspletosaurus torosus* engaging in intraspecific combat.

†**DEINONYCHUS**

Saurischia: Eusaurischia: Eusaurischia: Theropoda: Neotheropoda: Tetanurae: Avetheropoda: Coelurosauria: Tyrannoraptora: Maniraptoriformes: Maniraptora: Metornithes: Paraves: Deinonychosauria: Dromaeosauridae: Dromaeosaurinae.

Comments: Parsons and Parsons (2003), in a published abstract, briefly described a recently collected small specimen (MOR 1178) of the type species *Deinonychus antirrhopus* from the Early–Middle (Aptian–Albian) Cloverly Formation of central Montana.

The fragmentary specimen includes the following elements: Dentary fragment; squamosal fragment; partial tooth; left coracoid; right scapula; middle portion of humerus; middle portion and distal end of femur; left semilunate carpal; left manual digit I-2; proximal right fibula; tarsal; proximal end of right metatarsal II; fragment of coossified sacral neural arches with remnant of neural spine lamina; several partial vertebrae (axis, cervico-dorsal, ?sixth cervical, proximal caudal, two midcaudals, distal caudal); ?sternal plate fragment; fragments of ilium; other (as of yet unidentified) fragments.

Based upon the unfused nature of the neural arch of a cervical vertebrae, Parsons and Parsons deduced

Life restoration of a group
of *Deinonychus antirrhopus*
by artist Todd Marshall.

that MOR 1178 represents a subadult individual. Comparing this specimen to more mature *D. antirrhopus* specimens (*e.g.*, AMNH, YPM, and MCZ collections), the authors observed a considerable degree of size variation among certain elements. The limb morphology of MOR 1178, especially, reveals a pattern of growth development possibly differing from that seen in OMNH 50268, and also from that seen in the ontogentic stages of other theropods. According to Parsons and Parsons, the derived character of the curvature of the manual II-3 ungual and also the configuration of the forelimb morphology could "indicate some unique aspects to the possible juvenile behavior of this genus."

Understanding the function of maniraptoran forelimbs is important in understanding the origin of avian flight. In a published abstract, Gishlick and Carney (2003) reported on their use of three-dimension digital scanning and modeling to reconstruct the bones and muscles of such a theropod limb, thereby eschewing the limitations of actualistic modeling utilizing original fossil material or casts. To test, via digital reconstruction of its limb function, the

flight stroke capabilities of non-avian maniraptorans, the authors selected the type species *Deinonychus antirrhopus* because of "its relative completeness, high quality of preservation, and phylogenetic closeness to the avian stem."

Gishlick and Carney's study was based upon high quality molds and casts were generated from a number of *Deinonychus* specimens, including type specimen left manual elements (YPM 5208 and 6206), left radius, left ulna, and right ulna (YPM 5220), right metacarpal II (YPM 5270), proximal left ulna, left humerus (MCZ 4371), and left coracoid (YPM 5236). Following scanning and the importing into a computer of three-dimensional data, the resulting virtual forelimb was articulated and the range of motion about each joint reconstructed incorporating motion-limiting perameters. Muscle scars and phylogenetic bracketing then determined the positions of dynamic musculature, with inverse kinetic constrains applied for analyzing the elevation, depression, protraction, and retraction of the *Deinonychus* arm.

This remodeling revealed to Gishlick and Carney "that *Deinonychus* was capable of a coordinated, automatic extension and flexion of the arms of a rudimentary form of an avian flight stroke," this constituting strong support for the hypothesis that non-avian maniraptors already "possessed flight stroke capabilities and that they could have made use of their forelimbs in flight adaptive behaviors such as wing-assisted inclined running."

Senter, Barsbold, Britt and Burnham (2004), in a major reevaluation of the Dromaeosauridae, considered the genera *Deinonychus* and *Saurornitholestes*, both previously regarded as velociraptorines, as belonging to the subfamily Dromaeosaurinae (see "Systematics" chapter).

Key reference: Gishlick and Carney (2003); Parsons and Parsons (2003); Senter, Barsbold, Britt and Burnham (2004).

†**DELTADROMEUS**—(=?*Bahariasaurus*)

Saurischia: Eusaurischia: Theropoda: Neotheropoda: Ceratosauria: Abelisauroidea: Noasauridae.

Comments: In 1996, Sereno, Beck, Dutheil, Iarochene, Larsson, Lyon, Magwene, Sidor, Varric-chio and Wilson described *Deltadromeus agilis*—a type species from Morocco (see *D:TE*)—as a basal coelurosaurian. More recently, Sereno, Wilson and Conrad (2004) reinterpreted *D. agilis* "as a basal noasaurid," this taxon as well as the smaller Malagasy genus *Majungatholus* being the only known non-avian theropods having fourth metatarsals with strongly reduced distal condyles.

Note: Sereno *et al.* (2004) also reported partial noasaurid and abelisaurid skeletons recently collected from Middle Cretaceous (Aptian–Albian) in Gadoudaoua, Niger Republic. The former small (one meter in length) skeleton exhibits such abelisauroid and noasaurid synapomorphies as pneumatized presacral and sacral neural arches; proportionately long presacral centra, among other (see Carrano, Sampson and Forster 2002). The abelisaurid specimen includes a maxilla and pelvic girdle, the former bearing "the distinctive abelisaurid pit-and-groove texturing of the skull bones." These remains, the authors noted, "push back the basal divergence among abelisauroids deep into the Early Cretaceous … as had been foreshadowed by discovery of an abelisaurid jaw in the earliest

Reconstructed skeletal cast (by the PAST Company) of *Deltadromaeus agilis*, compared with the skeleton of *Homo sapiens*, part of the "Giants: African Dinosaurs" exhibit which debuted on December 20 at Chicago's Garfield Park Conservatory. This type species was referred by Sereno, Wilson and Conrad to the Noasauridae.

Photograph by the author.

Late [=Early] Cretaceous (Cenomanian) of Argentina (Lamanna *et al.* 2002)."

According to Sereno *et al.* (2004), the foregoing observations, plus a recently discovered maxilla from Morocco having a rugose external texture and subrectangular alveoli, reinforce the postulation that abelisaurids from the same horizon originated in Africa (see Russell 1996).

In their review of basal Tetanurae, Holtz, Molnar and Currie (2004) noted that the African *Bahariasaurus ingens* might, pending the discovery of new materials, be revealed to be senior synonym of *Deltadromeus agilis* or a junior synonym of *Carcharodontosaurus saharicus*.

Key references: Carrano, Sampson and Forster (2002); Holtz, Molnar and Currie (2004); Lamanna, Martinez and Smith (2002); Russell (1996); Sereno, Beck, Dutheil, Iarochene, Larsson, Lyon, Magwene, Sidor, Varricchio and Wilson (1996); Sereno, Wilson and Conrad (2004).

†DICRAEOSAURUS

Saurischia: Eusaurischia: Sauropodomorpha: Sauropoda: Eusauropoda: Neosauropoda: Diplodocoidea: Dicraeosauridae.

Diagnosis of genus: Middle and caudal cervical vertebrae with neural spines directed craniocaudally; cervical centra with prominent, platelike midline keel on cranial half of centrum (Upchurch, Barrett and Dodson 2004).

Comment: In their review of the Sauropoda, Upchurch, Barrett and Dodson (2004) rediagnosed the genus *Dicraeosaurus* (see *D:TE*).

Key reference: Upchurch, Barrett and Dodson (2004).

DILONG   Xu, Norell, Kuang, Zhao and Jia 2004

Saurischia: Eusaurischia: Theropoda: Neotheropoda: Tetanurae: Avetheropoda: Coelurosauria: Tyrannoraptora: Maniraptoriformes: Tyrannosauroidea.

Name derivation: Chinese *di* = "emperor" + Chinese *long* = "dragon."

Type species: *D. paradoxus* Xu, Norell, Kuang, Zhao and Jia 2004.

Other species: [?None.]

Occurrence: Yixian Formation, Liaoning Province, China.

Age: Early Cretaceous.

Known material: Skeleton with almost complete skull, almost complete skull with partial postcrania, partial skull (possibly representing a second species).

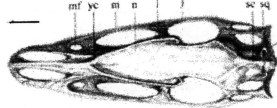

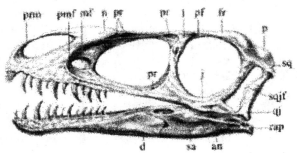

Dilong paradoxus, reconstruction of skull including holotype IVPP V14243, in (left) left lateral and (right) dorsal views. Scale = 2 cm. (After Xu, Norell, Kuang, Zhao and Jia 2004.)

Dilong paradoxus, skeletal reconstruction of IVPP V11579 showing preserved elements. Scale = 10 cm. (After Xu, Norell, Kuang, Zhao and Jia 2004.)

Dilong paradoxus, integumentary structures of IVPP V11579, preserved along dorsal edge of distal caudal vertebrae. (After Xu, Norell, Kuang, Zhao and Jia 2004.)

Holotype: IVPP V14243, semiarticulated skeleton with almost complete skull, juvenile.

Diagnosis of genus (as for type species): Small tyrannosauroid, distinguished from other tyrannosauroids by the following unique features: presence of two large pneumatic recesses dorsal to antorbital fossa on maxilla; Y-shaped crest formed by nasals and lacrimals; extremely long descending process of squamosal extending close to mandibular articulation of quadrate; lateral projection of basisphenoid rostral to basal tuber; cervical vertebrae with very deep, subcircular interspinous ligamentous fossae; scapula robust, distal end wide (about twice width of proximal scapular blade); hypertrophied coracoid (dorsoventral length approximately 70 percent of scapular width (Xu, Norell, Kuang, Zhao and Jia 2004).

Comments: The only tyrannosauroid genus found preserving protofeathers, *Dilong* was founded on a skeleton with a nearly complete skull (IVPP V14243), collected from the Yixian Formation, at Lujiatun, Beipiao, western Liaoning Province, China. Specimens referred to the type species *Dilong paradoxus* are an almost complete skull with associated presacral vertebrae (TNP01109), and also a partial skull (IVPP V11579), the latter, pending additional analysis, possibly representing a closely related second species of *Dilong* (Xu, Norell, Kuang, Zhao and Jia 2004).

In describing *D. paradox*, Xu *et al.* noted that the material represents a small tyrannosauroid, the largest specimen (IVPP V14243) having an estimated length of 1.6 meters (about 5.5 feet). The body is gracile and the arms are comparatively long, the hands three-fingered. Postcranially, the neck and trunk of *Dilong* are proportionally longer than in other tyrannosauroids, more similar, in fact, to those of basal coelurosaurians.

Regarding the ontogenetic stages of the specimens assigned to *Dilong*, Xu *et al.* noted that IVPP V14242 is smaller than IVPP V14243, the former therefore representing a younger animal, and also differing from the latter in the following features: Smaller external nares, more caudally located maxillary fenestrae, more expanded braincase, more slender ventral process of squamosal, less-developed and more caudally positioned lateral process of basisphenoid, longer retroarticular process, and lack of sagittal and nuchal crests.

Xu *et al.* referred the fragmentary IVPP V11579 — collected from about 125-million-year-old gray shale of the Zhangjiagou locality, in the Yixian Formation, at Beipiao — to *Dilong* based upon morphologies of most overlapping elements, including the squamosals, dentaries, splenials, teeth, vertebrae (cervical, dorsal, and caudal), and metatarsals. In addition, manual elements preserved in this specimen reveal the following: Manual digit II robust, metacarpal II and associated phalanges much more robust than I and corresponding phalanges (derived feature observed in other tyrannosauroids; see Brochu 2003*b*); manual digit III, though extremely slender, not reduced in phalangeal number or digit length (representing precursor to reduced manual digit III in more advanced tyrannosauroids; Holtz 2001); relatively long forearms having three-fingered hands conforming to predictions of current phylogenetic hypotheses regarding morphology of basal Tyrannosauroidea (Manabe 1999; Holtz 2000); distal end of ischium slightly expanded, cranially curved (unlike derived tyrannosauroids, similar to many basal coelurosaurians; Holtz 2000).

Most surprising, the tail of IVPP V11579 preserves "traces of filamentous integumentary structures" at an approximate 30- to 40-degree angle to the series of caudal vertebrae. Also preserved, near the caudal left mandible, is a small patch of such structures. As described by Xu *et al.*, the integumentary structures attached to the distal caudal vertebrae are branched and measure over 20 millimeters in length. Although their pattern was difficult to discern, these structures seem to comprise "a series of filaments joined at their bases along a central filament as in *Sinornithosaurus*" (Xu, Zhou and Prum 2001). Xu *et al.* (2004) interpreted these structures as protofeathers, noting that their discovery in IVPP V1159 offers "the first direct evidence showing that tyrannosauroids possessed protofeathers." Furthermore, the authors pointed out, these protofeathers are branched, as are those found preserved with other coelurosaurian specimens (Xu *et*

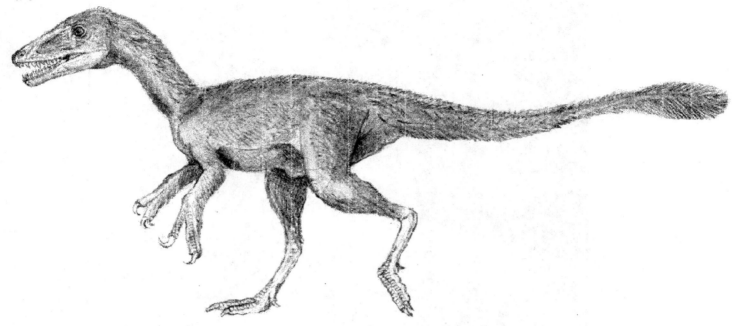

al. 2001), this distinctively modern feature "suggesting that this important modification occurred early in coelurosaurian evolution." As no such structures have yet been found in large tyrannosauroid taxa — some of which have been reported to have scaled skin (Martin and Czerkas 2000) — Xu *et al.* (2004) speculated that it could be possible, considering the diverse morphologies of integumentary structures in extant avians, "that non-avian theropods had different integumentary morphologies on different regions of the body, and derived, large tyrannosauroids might bear both scale-like and filamentous integumental appendages." Moreover, lack of such integumentary structures in derive tyrannosauroids can be "correlated with large size, as a physiological strategy also adopted by some mammals such as elephants, which lose most of their body hairs as they mature" (Spinage 1994), this, Xu *et al.* (2004) proposed, supporting "the hypothesis that the original function of protofeathers is correlated with thermoregulation."

According to Xu *et al.* (2004), the tyrannosauroids of Liaoning are similar to other known juvenile members of this clade, sharing features including the following: Snout and mandible long, with low proportions; teeth having different-sized mesial and distal serrations; cervical vertebrae with low neural spines; centra of dorsal vertebrae relatively low; dorsal centra much larger than cervical centra (Currie and Dong 2001; Carr 1999). As some of the foregoing have also been reported in other basal tyrannosauroids (*e.g.*, *Eotyrannus*; see Hutt, Naish, Martill, Barker and Newbery 2001), Xu *et al.* (2004) suggested that, pending an analysis using a more complete data set, "per-amorphosis might be important in tyrannosauroid evolution."

Some features of *D. paradoxus* are important, Xu *et al.* (2004) noted, for understanding the evolution of the Coelurosauria. Liaoning tyrannosauroids have a less pneumatic skeleton than the gigantic, derived taxa of the Late Cretaceous, the authors noted; this feature is also less developed in many small, basal, non-avian coelurosaurians. Additionally, the Liaoning tyrannosauroids do not have an arctometatarsalian pes — proposed by Holtz (1994) to diagnose the more inclusive clade "Arctometatarsalia" — a feature now known to be absent from small, basal members of most "arctometatarsalian" clades, suggesting strongly that this condition of the foot evolved independently within different coelurosaurian clades.

Key references: Brochu (2003*b*); Carr (1999); Currie and Dong (2001); Holtz (1994, 2000, 2001); Hutt, Naish, Martill, Barker and Newbery (2001); Manabe (1999); Martin and Czerkas (2000); Spinage (1994); Xu, Norell, Kuang, Zhao and Jia (2004); Xu, Zhou and Prum (2001).

†DILOPHOSAURUS

Saurischia: Eusaurischia: Theropoda: Neotheropoda: Ceratosauria: Coelophysoidea: Dilophosauridae.

Erratum: In *S3*, the photograph on page 305 of the skeletal cast of *Dilophosaurus wetherilli*, mounted at the Royal Tyrrell Museum of Palaeontology, was incorrectly identified with a Natural History Museum of Los Angeles County catalogue number.

Dilophosaurus

Dilophosaurus wetherilli skeleton (LACM 4462/118118, cast of holotype UCMP 37302).

A Double-crested Dinosaur

Dilophosaurus wetherilli
Early Jurassic Period, approximately 200 million years old
Kayenta Formation, Arizona

Dilophosaurus was a medium–size dinosaur that lived in North America and China during the early Jurassic Period. It is an early, distant relative of the meat eating dinosaurs, Allosaurus and Tyrannosaurus.

The name Dilophosaurus means "double crested lizard" and refers to the pair of thin bony crests on the top of its head, a unique feature of this dinosaur. This cast was made from the nearly complete skeleton of the first Dilophosaurus discovered, which was excavated in 1942.

LACM 4462/118118; CAST OF UCMP V4214/37302

Photograph by the author, courtesy Natural History Museum of Los Angeles County Museum.

†DINHEIROSAURUS

Saurischia: Eusaurischia: Sauropodomorpha: Sauropoda: Eusauropoda: Neosauropoda: Diplodocoidea.

Diagnosis of genus (as for type species): Lateral surface of neural spine of cervical vertebra 14 having elongate pneumatic fossa; robust horizontal lamina linking hyposphene with base of caudal centrodiapophyseal lamina (Upchurch, Barrett and Dodson 2004).

Comment: In their review of the Sauropoda, Upchurch, Barrett and Dodson (2004) rediagnosed the type species *Dinheirosaurus lourinhanensis* (see S2).

Key reference: Upchurch, Barrett and Dodson (2004).

†DIPLODOCUS

Saurischia: Eusaurischia: Sauropodomorpha: Sauropoda: Eusauropoda: Neosauropoda: Diplodocoidea: Flagellicaudata: Diplodocidae.

Diagnosis of genus: Ventral edge of maxilla forming thin bone sheet overlapping dorsal margin of mandible when jaws are fully closed; contact between postorbital and jugal short (not long, overlapping); caudal process of postorbital terminating before caudal margin of supratemporal fenestra; dorsal margin of mandible level throughout most of its length (no clear coronoid eminence); maxillary teeth substantially larger than dentary teeth (also in *Nigersaurus*); wear facets on labial tips of crowns in upper teeth (Upchurch, Barrett and Dodson 2004).

Comments: Myers (2003), in a published abstract, reported on the bones of either juvenile or subadult diplodocid sauropods (presumably the genus *Diplodocus*) found at the Mother's Day Site, in the Salt Wash Member of the Morrison Formation of south-central Montana. The bonebed (a site that has yielded much *Diplodocus* material) preserving these remains consists of a muddy, fine-grained sandstone that represents a levee or overbank deposit. The size of the recovered elements and lack of epiphyseal ossification identified these sauropods as immature individuals.

According to Myers' preliminary taphonomic analysis, this site is both monospecific and catastrophic. Three theropod teeth comprise the only nonsauropod remains found at this site, these probably having been reworked rather than associated with the sauropod remains. Furthermore, there is no evidence (*e.g.*, bite marks, weathering cracks) in the sampling of bones prepared to date indicating some interval of pre-burial exposure. Consequently, Myers deduced that "the assemblage represents a single, catastrophic mass mortality."

Myers stated the following regarding the Mother's Day Site: Long elements are oriented in a northwest/southeast direction, with a shallow northwesterly dip, this orientation and imbrication probably the result of a southeasterly flowing current; the weak orientation signal was probably caused by the partial decomposition and disarticulation of the carcasses when they were transported and buried; commonly found articulated elements include caudal vertebrae and complete pes units; and preserved skin impressions indicate relative rapid burial and demonstrate that the bodies were not remobilized following burial. Also, Myers noted, skin and other soft-tissue remnants "would have increased the buoyancy of the bone to which they were attached, explaining the hydraulic inequivalence of the larger elements with the relatively fine-grained sediment of the bonebed unit."

In a subsequent abstract, Myers (2004) described the *Diplodocus* assemblage represented at the Mother's Day Quarry "as an allochthonous, paucispecific accumulation resulting from a drought mortality of a herd group of sauropods." Myers (2004) noted the

Skeleton of a juvenile *Diplodocus* individual found during the 1990s in the Howe Stephens Quarry at Howe Ranch in northern Wyoming. Six partial skeletons belonging to this genus, plus numerous isolated bones, were recovered from the quarry during the 1990s by the Sauriermuseum Aathal under the direction of Hans Jakob ("Kirby") Siber (see Ayer 1999).

Photograph by Urs Möckli, copyright © and courtesy Sauriermuseum Aathal.

following details concerning this site: Time-average seemingly minimal; sauropod remains dominating collected material; transport from initial death location to point of final burial apparently turbulent, short in terms of distance and duration; sedimentary indicators suggesting mudflow as transport agent.

As Myers (2004) stressed, it is significant that all of the sauropod remains identified from the Mother's Day Site represent juvenile and subadult animals. If not the result of taphonomic bias, this lack of adult specimens in the assemblage suggests "segregation of sauropod herd groups on the basis of age." However, that author's taphonomic investigation the site — "involving analysis of bone modification features, element ratios, element position and orientation, and the depositional setting of the quarry" — found no evidence of any selective processes that could have significantly biased this assemblage. Myers (2004) concluded, therefore, that "the original herd group from which the death assemblage was derived must also have been devoid of adults, reflecting age segregation, a behavioral scenario previously postulated from trackway evidence, but never before noted in a taphonomically-constrained skeletal assemblage."

Schwarz (2004), in an abstract published for a poster, briefly discussed reconstructing air-sac systems and musculature in the neck of *Diplodocus*, based upon the internal cavities within the cervical vertebrae of this genus, aided by computer tomographic imagery. As noted by that author, the cervical vertebrae of *Diplodocus* juvenile specimens, unlike the complexly hollowed-out cervicals of adult specimens, are perforated by simpler and fewer cavities. Such differences also relate "to external pneumatic features and the amount of bifurcated *processus spinosi* (*i.e.*, neural spines) of the cervical vertebrae." However, each specimen of *Diplodocus* cervical vertebra examined by Schwarz had a neural canal connected closely both to internal and external pneumatic structures. Comparing the juvenile cervical vertebrae to those of the adults, Schwarz was able to reconstruct "an increase of the size, complexity and frequency of the pneumatic structures." Additionally, that author stated, the development of bifurcated neural spines in the cervical series "leads also to a change in the configuration of the dorsal cervical musculature and ligaments."

Key references: Myers (2003, 2004); Schwarz (2004); Upchurch, Barrett and Dodson (2004).

†DRAVIDOSAURUS

?Ornithischia: ?Predentata: ?Genasauria: ?Thyreophora: ?Thyreophoroidea: ?Eurypoda: ?Stegosauria *incertae sedis*.

Comments: Originally described in 1979 by Yadagiri and Ayyasami as a stegosaur (see *D:TE*), the type species *Dravidosaurus blandfordi* was subsequently reassessed to be a plesiosaur by Chatterjee and Ruda (1996; see *SI*), the latter authors noting that plesiosaurian fragments had been found at the same locality that yielded the holotype of *D. blandfordi* (see *SI*).

Galton and Upchurch (2004*b*), however, in their more recent review of the Stegosauria, posited that "the skull and plates of *Dravidosaurus* are certainly not plesiosaurian and consequently this material has to be redescribed." Galton and Upchurch regarded this taxon as Stegosauria *incertae sedis*.

Key references: Chatterjee and Ruda (1996). Galton and Upchurch (2004*b*); Yadagiri and Ayyasami (1979).

DROMAEOSAUROIDES Christainsen and Bonde 2003

Saurischia: Eusaurischia: Theropoda: Neotheropoda: Tetanurae: Avetheropoda: Coelurosauria: Tyrannoraptora: Maniraptoriformes: Maniraptora: Metornithes: Paraves: Deinonychosauria: Dromaeosauridae: Dromaeosaurinae.

Name derivation: Greek *dromaeos* = "fast running" + Greek *sauros* = "lizard" + Greek *oeides* = "form."

Type species: *D. bornholmensis* Christainsen and Bonde 2003.

Other species: [None.]

Occurrence: Jydegaard Formation, Isle of Bornholm, Denmark.

Age: Early Cretaceous (Berriasian–Valanginian).

Known material/holotype: MGUH collection [catalog number not yet assigned], rostral dentary tooth.

Diagnosis of genus (as for type species): Medium-sized dromaeosaurine; tooth crown recurved, not markedly bladelike, fore and aft basal length/basal width ratio of approximately 1.5; both mesial and distal carinae facing medially; both carinae finely serrate, around 31 denticles per five millimeters on mesial carina, around 30 per five millimeters on distal carina, denticle size difference index around one; denticles approximately 0.15 millimeters high, squarish, chisel-like in appearance, not rostrally hooked (Christainsen and Bonde 2003).

Comments: Distinguished as the first dinosaur of any kind to be found in Denmark, the type species *Dromaeosauroides bornholmensis* was based upon a single, isolated tooth (MGUH collection) collected in September, 2000, from the sandy layers of the basal part (lower two to three meters) of the Jydegaard Formation, Nyker Group, at the abandoned "Carl Nielsen's sandpit," a gravel pit in Robbedale, near the town

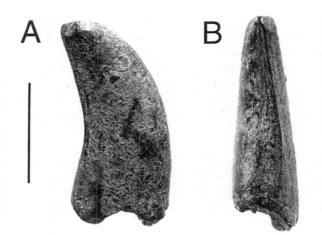

Dromaeosauroides bornholmensis, MGUH collection, holotype tooth in A. medial and B. distal views. Scale = 1 cm. (After Christainsen and Bonde 2003.)

of Ronne, Isle of Bornholm (Christainsen and Bonde 2003; see also Bonde and Christainsen for a review of dinosaurs from Denmark, including comments on *Dromaeosauroides*).

As Christainsen and Bonde pointed out, this new genus and species, having been found in rocks dated as approximately 140 million years ago, ranks among the oldest known dromaeosaurids yet discovered and the first and only verifiable member of the Dromaeosauridae to be described from the Lower Cretaceous of Europe (see "Note," below).

Christainsen and Bone noted that the holotype tooth of *Dromaeosauroides* resembles teeth of the North American dromaeosaurine *Dromaeosaurus*, after which the Danish genus was named. However, the authors pointed out, "the age and locality alone would indicate that it is unlikely that [*Dromaeosauroides*] is congeneric with *Dromaeosaurus*"; furthermore, "the larger size and distinctly smaller denticles would also suggest that this specimen is different from *Dromaeosaurus*."

Note: Christainsen and Bonde disagreed with the recent assessment of Milner [2002; cited by Christainsen and Bonde as 2000, in press] that a small jaw fragment and referred teeth and postcranial fragments referred to *Nuthetes destructor*, collected from the "Middle Purbeck (Barresian) Beds" of the Isle of Purbeck, England, share affinities with velociraptorine dromaeosaurids (see *Nuthetes* entry, S3). According to Christainsen and Bonde, after examining photographs of that material, the tooth denticles apparently differ from those of known velociraptorines, bearing a closer

Life restoration by artist Todd Marshall of the birdlike, North American theropod *Dromaeosaurus albertensis* with feathers. Although feathers and feather-like integuments have not yet been associated with fossils belonging to this dinosaurian species, they have been found associated with Chinese dromaeosaurid taxa.

resemblance to teeth of dromaeosaurines. However, the carinae of the Purbeck specimens are not placed asymmetrically on the crown and the bloodgrooves are indistinct. Furthermore, as the Purbeck teeth pertain to juvenile animals, their exact taxonomic position remains somewhat uncertain. Consequently, "the tooth from Bornholm should be regarded as the first certain Lower Cretaceous dromaeosaurid from Europe."

Key references: Bonde and Christianson (2003); Christainsen and Bonde (2003); Milner (2000).

†DROMAEOSAURUS

Saurischia: Eusaurischia: Eusaurischia: Theropoda: Neotheropoda: Tetanurae: Avetheropoda: Coeluro-

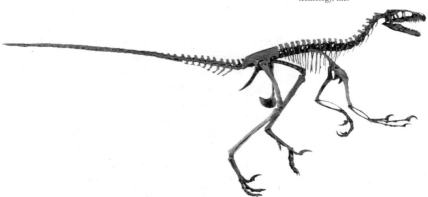

Skeletal cast of the dromaeosaurine dromaeosaurid *Dromaeosaurus albertensis*, reconstructed by Michael Triebold from material in the collections of the Royal Tyrrell Museum of Palaeontology and also remains from the Sandy Site Quarry, Hell Creek Formation, in South Dakota, with the vertebral column based largely upon *Deinonychus antirrhopus*.

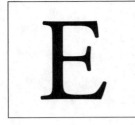

sauria: Tyrannoraptora: Maniraptoriformes: Maniraptora: Metornithes: Paraves: Deinonychosauria: Dromaeosauridae: Dromaeosaurinae.

Diagnosis of genus (as for type species): Braincase largely nonpneumatized except for caudal tympanic recess; premaxillary teeth "D"-shaped (also seen only in *Utahraptor* among Dromaeosauridae) (Norell and Makovicky 2004).

Comment: In their review of the Dromaeosauridae, Norell and Makovicky (2004) rediagnosed the type species *Dromaeosaurus albertensis* (see *D:TE*).

Key reference: Norell and Makovicky (2004).

†**DRYPTOSAUROIDES**—(=?*Compsosuchus*, ?*Indosaurus*, ?*Indosuchus*, ?*Jubbulpuria*, ?*Ornithomimoides*)

Saurischia: Eusaurischia: Theropoda: Neotheropoda: Ceratosauria: Abelisauroidea *incertae sedis*.

Comments: In 1932, Friedrich von Huene named and described the new theropod *Dryptosauroides grandis*, a large theropod type species founded upon six vertebrae (presumed to be dorsals)—GSI K20/334, K20/609, K27/549, K27/601, and K27/602)—collected from the Lameta Formation of India. The next year, Huene—in a paper jointly authored with Charles Alfred Matley discussing the dinosaurs of India—further described the material of *D. grandis*, at the same time referring to *D. grandis* a cervical vertebra (GSI K27/555) and a few dorsal ribs (GSI K20/615, K27/547, K27/623, K27/624, and K27/625) (see *D:TE*).

Recently, Novas, Agnolin and Bandyopadhyay (2004), in a detailed review of the theropods discussed in Huene and Matley (1933), correctly recognized the vertebrae assigned to *Dryptosauroides* as being from the caudal, not dorsal, region. Accessing but one of the above specimens (GSI K20/609), Novas *et al.* observed in it the same morphology as that of a caudal vertebra (GSI K20/610) referred to the abelisauroid *Ornithomimoides mobilis* (see *Ornithomimoides* entry); additionally, *Dryptosauroides* caudal vertebrae "match well with the proximal caudals of [the abelisaurid] *Majungatholus*" (Novas *et al.*, personal observation).

It was the conclusion of Novas *et al.*, therefore, that "the vertebrae of *Dryptosauroides* correspond to the proximal caudals of an indeterminate abelisauroid, and, following previous authors (*e.g.*, Molnar, Kurzanov and Dong 1990), that *D. grandis* be regarded as a *nomen dubium*.

As Novas *et al.* noted, the size of the caudal vertebrae referred to *Dryptosauroides* indicate that this genus was quite large, perhaps surpassing *Carnotaurus* in size.

Novas *et al.* pointed out that the elements referred to the genera *Dryptosauroides*, *Compsosuchus*, *Jubbulpuria*, and *Ornithomimoides* (see entries) correspond to different areas of the neck and tail, intimating that some or all of these taxa may be congeneric.

Key references: Huene (1932); Huene and Matley (1933); Molnar, Kurzanov and Dong (1990); Norman (1990); Novas, Agnolin and Bandyopadhyay (2004).

†**DYSLOCOSAURUS**

Saurischia: Eusaurischia: Sauropodomorpha: Sauropoda: Eusauropoda: Neosauropoda: Diplodocoidea: Flagellicaudata: Diplodocidae.

Diagnosis of genus (as for type species): Astragalus gracile (proximodistal width 50 percent transverse width, lower percentage than in other Diplodocoidea); metatarsals stout (greater circumference relative to width than in other Diplodocoidea); ungual phalanx on pedal digit IV (possibly also on V) (Upchurch, Barrett and Dodson 2004).

Comments: In 1992, John H. McIntosh, Walter P. Coombs, Jr. and Dale A. Russell described *Dyslocosaurus polyonychius*, a rather small sauropod type species based on fragmentary limb material collected from either the Morrison Formation or Lance Formation of Wyoming (see *D:TE*).

Formerly regarded as a dicraeosaurid, the diplodocid status of this taxon was affirmed by Upchurch, Barrett and Dodson 2004, in their review of Sauropods, based on the following suite of characters: Laterodistal process on metatarsal I; large rugosity on dorsolateral margin of metatarsal II, near distal end; prominent heel developed on caudoventral [plantar] margin of proximal articular surface of pedal phalanx I-1.

Key references: McIntosh, Coombs and Russell (1992); Upchurch, Barrett and Dodson (2004).

†**EDMARKA**—(See *Torvosaurus*.)

†**EDMONTOSAURUS**—(=*Anatosaurus*, *Anatotitan*)

Ornithischia: Predentata: Genasauria: Cerapoda: Ornithopoda: Euornithopoda: Iguanodontia: Dryomorpha: Ankylopollexia: Styracosterna: Iguanodontoidea: Hadrosauroidea: Euhadrosauria: Hadrosauridae: Hadrosaurinae: Edmontosaurini.

Comments: Boyd and Behlke (2003), in an abstract for a poster, tested the long held hypothesis that the presence of an entirely enclosed (rather than open) obturator foramen in the ischia of hadrosaurid dinosaurs indicates old age. The authors tested this postulation by examining 28 ischia belonging to the

Photograph by the author.

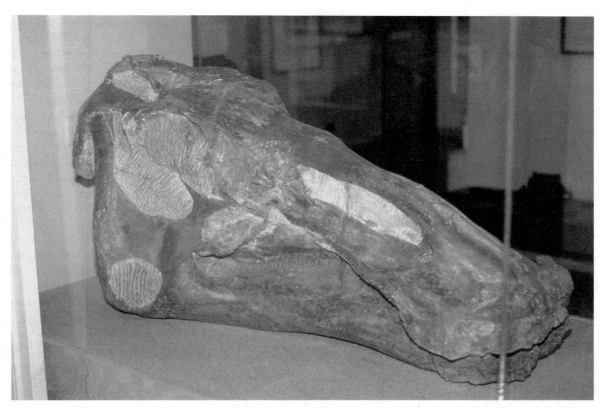

Skull of the classic "duck-billed dinosaur," *Edmontosaurus annectens*.

Skeleton (cast) of *Edmontosaurus annectens*.

classic duckbilled dinosaur, the type species *Edmontosaurus annectens*, collected from a single locality.

As Boyd and Behlke observed, a complete obturator foramen was present in only five of the examined ischia, two of them belonging to juvenile and subadult individuals. Of these, one ischium exhibits two obturator foramina — one of average size and location, the other smaller and located directly cranial to the first. The remaining 23 ischia displayed the more common elevated obturator notch.

Following cleaning of the materials, Boyd and Behlke discovered, on either side of each notch, the internal bone structure indicating that these areas had been damaged before burial; moreover, the "size, shape and common occurrence of this internal bone structure indicates that most if not all of these specimens had once displayed a completely enclosed obturator foramen." Additionally, the area surrounding the obturator foramen was found to be statistically the most probable one for the ischium to be damaged prior to deposition. Larger specimens belonging to older individuals, however, have thicker borders enclosing this foramen and, consequently, have generally

suffered less damage in this area; therefore, it is easier to recognize the obturator foramen in these ischia. This allometric thickening, the authors noted, and also the ensuing preservational bias, is the most likely explanation for the seeming presence of obturator foramina in hadrosaurid individuals of advanced age.

In conclusion, Boyd and Behlke proposed "that obturator foramina cannot be used to determine the relative age of a specimen"; also, the presence of an enclosed obturator foramen in juvenile hadrosaurine and lambeosaurine specimens, along with the high statistical probability of damage in the area around this foramen, "disqualifies its use as a taxonomic indicator."

Derstler (2003), in a published abstract, compared hadrosaur skin impressions, most of them associated with *Edmontosaurus*. Nine specimens were yielded by the Upper Cretaceous (Maastrichtian) Lance Formation of Wyoming and 12 (most occurring within point bar sands, one skeleton within a crevasse splay) by the laterally equivalent Hell Creek Formation of Montana and North and South Dakota. Also used in this comparison were three excellently preserved

Skull belonging to the skeleton (LACM 7233/23504) of a juvenile *Edmontosaurus annectens*, collected by Harley J. Garbani from the Hell Creek Formation, Garfield County, Montana.

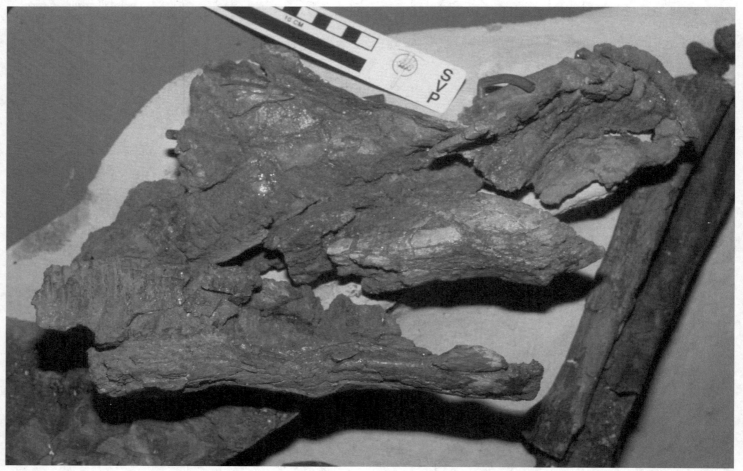

Photography by the author, courtesy Natural History Museum of Los Angeles County.

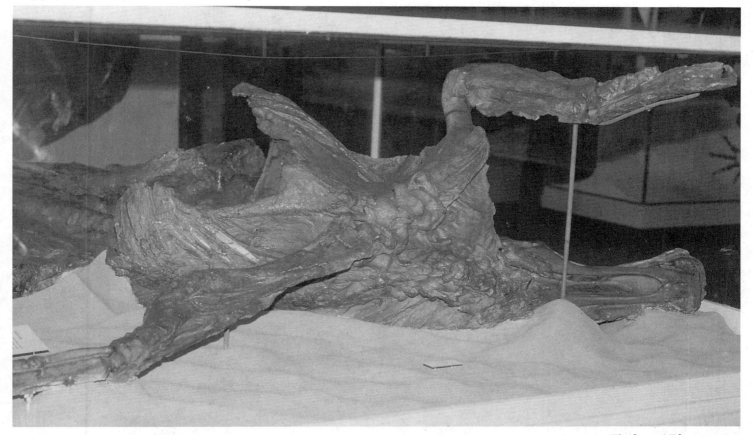

The famous *Edmontosaurus annectens* "mummy" (AMNH 5060), a skeleton preserved with impressions of skin and other soft tissues, collected in Niobrara County, Wyoming (see *D:TE*).

Brachylophosaurus skeletons in a small collecting area of the slightly older (Campanian), lower Judith River Formation of Montana. Comparison of these integumentary specimens revealed a single set of biostratinomic conditions, yet also "a modest range of diagenetic histories, as well as pronounced variation in the amount, quality, and preparability of skin."

As Derstler pointed out, skin impressions from all of the above formations are usually associated with well-preserved articulated skeletons, with most showing just a few patches of skin and preservation varying among individual specimens.

According to Derstler, these skin-bearing hadrosaurs offer a biostratinomic paradox: While both sets of carcasses show signs of dessication, all were buried in a humid environment by fastmoving water. A possible explanation for this paradox is the hypothesis of strong seasonality—*i.e.*, "a carcass is fortuitously mummified in open air during the dry season, then the toughened carcass gets transported and quickly buried during the early days of the rainy season." According to Derstler, a Lance Formation specimen buried in stages constitutes evidence supporting that hypothesis, the skeleton on later-buried portions being partly dessicated, with the bones abraded and the skin either poorly preserved or missing.

In a related abstract, Lyson, Hanks and Tremain (2003) reported on fossil skin impressions belonging to an individual of *E. annectens* collected from Slope County, North Dakota, this Upper Cretaceous site having yielded more than 40 well-preserved skin fragments, also cranial and postcranial bones identifying the specimen as a juvenile.

As described by Lyson *et al.*, this specimen includes skin impressions consistent with previously reported impressions, consisting of tuberculate scales ranging from one to five millimeters in diameter. However, the specimen also includes six types of skin structures previously unknown in this taxon, including "overlapping ovoid structures, a 9 cm. by 10 cm. trapezoidal horn-like structure, and grooved scales all recovered from the caudal section."

Gould, Larson and Nellermoe (2003), in an abstract for a poster, presented findings regarding their allometric study comparing *Edmontosaurus* second metatarsals collected from a low-diversity bonebed in Corson County, South Dakota, a site that has been worked from 1998 to their date of writing. Collected thus far were remains representing a population of *Edmontosaurus* of varying age and size (including juvenile, subadult, adult, and "super-adult" material). It was Gould *et al.*'s attempt to determine if there

Life restoration of *Edmontosaurus annectens* by artist Todd Marshall.

were significant differences in these specimens and, if so, if they might indicate sexual dimorphism.

As Gould *et al.* observed, two apparent morphs were present in this collection, a robust and a gracile form. A total sample of 40 left and right metatarsal IIs were utilized in their study, four of which "were in poor repair," 20 of which "had at least one measurement that could not be used." The authors measured the length, distal width, proximal length and width, and least circumference of these specimens, then ran multiple statistical analyses to determine if these measurements reflected sexual dimorphism.

Gould *et al.* observed the following allometric changes in the studied specimens: Significant variance between least circumference with increase of total length of metatarsal II, exhibiting robust and gracile forms; significant variance with greatest length compared with length of proximal end; no significant findings of that occurring in length and width of proximal end, nor in comparing greatest length to width of distal end. The authors did not, in their published abstract, state if these changes were indicative of sexual dimorphism.

In their review of the Hadrosauridae, Horner, Weishampel and Forster (2004) regarded *Anatotitan* (see *D:TE*), a genus erected by Brett-Surman *see in* Chapman and Brett-Surman (1990), as a senior synonym of *Edmontosaurus*, with the type species *Anatotitan copei* referred to *E. annectens*. Horner *et al.* were unable to find any unambiguous characters to warrant separation of these taxa. Moreover, these authors noted that the morphological skull differences used by Brett-Surman (1979) to separate these taxa are probably attributable to dorsoventral crushing of the skull of "*Anatotitan*."

Key references: Boyd and Behlke (2003); Brett-Surman (1979); Chapman and Brett-Surman (1990); Derstler (2003); Gould, Larson and Nellermoe (2003); Horner, Weishampel and Forster (2004); Lyson, Hanks and Tremain (2003).

†EFRAASIA

Saurischia: Eusaurischia: Sauropodomorpha *incertae sedis*.

Name derivation: "E[berhard] Fraas."

Type species: *E. minor* (Huene 1907–08).

Other species: [None.]

Occurrence: Löwenstein Formation, Pfaffenhofen, Ochsenbach, Stromberg region, Germany.

Age: Late Triassic (middle Norian).

Known material: Almost complete skeleton, partial skeleton, fragmentary remains, tooth.

Holotype: SMNS 11838, incomplete postcranium including dorsal vertebrae, sacral centrum, almost complete right manus, some left manual phalanges, pubes, right femur, right tibia, right fibula, partial right pes adult.

Diagnosis of genus (as for type species): Interbasipterygoid web having central tubercle and hypertrophied semilunate-shaped pubic tubercle projecting laterally from proximal pubis (Yates 2003*a*).

Comments: The genus now called *Efraasia*, a medium-sized ?prosauropod (see Yates 2004, "Systematics" chapter), has had a somewhat long and entangled history.

In 1836, Riley and Stutchbury named the new genus and species *Palaeosaurus platyodon*, based upon a single worn tooth (Bristol Museum collection) discovered in autumn, 1834, in the Magnesian Conglomerate of Durdham Down, near Bristol, England. At the same time, Riley and Sutuchbury named a second species, *P. cylindrodon*.

Huene (1907–08) then erected a new species of *Teratosaurus* (a genus now known to be a rauisuchian reptile rather than dinosaurian; see Galton 1985*a*; Benton 1986) which he named *Teratosaurus minor*, founded upon incomplete remains (SMNS 11838) comprising three dorsal vertebrae, the second sacral vertebra, pubes, and a right hindlimb, collected from the middle Löwenstein Formation at Weisser Steinbruch, Pfaffenhofen, Stromberg Region, Germany. Later, in the same paper, that author proposed the new genus and species *Sellosaurus gracilis*, based on an incomplete postcranial skeleton (SMNS 5175) from the ?lower Löwenstein Formation at Heslach in southwestern Germany. At the same time, Huene proposed the referred species *S. fraasi*, based on a caudal dorsal vertebra, second sacral vertebra, five caudal vertebrae, ribs, ilia, ischia, pubis, and a femur (SMNS 12188–92), recovered near Pfaffenhofen (for a detailed report on the taphonomy and feeding habits of *Sellosaurus*, see Hungerbüler 1998).

Later, Eberhard Fraas collected two additional specimens from the Burrerschen Quarry, near Pfaffenhofen — an almost complete skeleton (SMNS 12667) and a less complete skeleton (SMNS 12668). Fraas (1913) referred this material to a new species of *Thecodontosaurus*, which he named *T. diagnosticus*, but in failing to described this taxon he relegated it to *nomen nudum* status.

In 1932, Huene described Fraas' specimens, referring them to the genus *Palaeosaurus* as *Palaeosaurus diagnosticus*, with the more complete SMNS 12667 designated the holotype of this species. The generic name *Palaeosaurus*, however, inevitably proved to be preoccupied (Saint-Hilaire 1833); therefore, more than a century later, Kuhn (1959) proposed that this material be given the new generic name of *Palaeosauriscus* (this genus and its type species, *P. platyodon* now regarded as *nomina dubia*; see *D:TE*).

Efraasia minor, reconstructed skeleton (composite small adult based on SMNS 11838, holotype of *Teratosaurus minor*, SMNS 12354, holotype of *Palaeosaurus diagnosticus*, and SMNS 17928, and reconstruction of skull). Scale = 1 m. (After Yates 2003.)

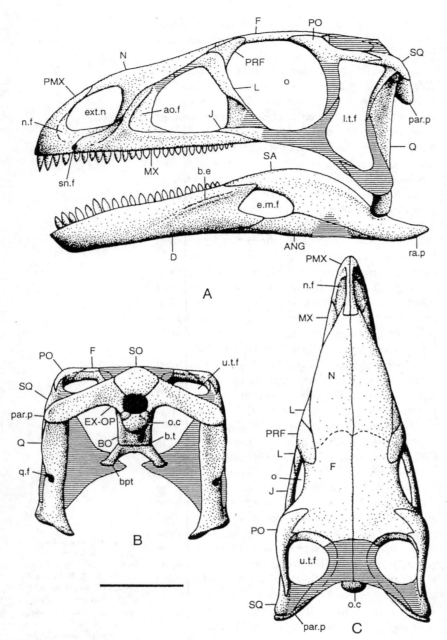

Efraasia minor, composite reconstruction of the skull (based on SMNS 12216, SMNS 12684, and SNMS 12667), in A. lateral, B. occipital, and C. dorsal views. Scale = 50 mm. (After Yates 2003).

codontosaurus hermannianus, based on a right maxilla (SMNS 4388) from Heslach (see *Plateosaurus* entry, "Notes"). In recent years, Galton continued publishing detailed papers on *Sellosaurus*, reevaluating the specimens and species that had been referred to this genus, the possibility of sexual dimorphism, and other topics (see *Sellosaurus* entries, *S2, S3* for details and references).

However, yet more recently, Yates (2003*a*) readdressed the species taxonomy of the sauropodomorph dinosaurs from the Löwenstein Formation of Germany. Yates noted a substantial amount of variation — in dentition, structure of the skull, the composition of the sacrum, and that of the caudal vertebrae and pelvis — in the current hypodigm of *Sellosaurus gracilis*. Performing a specimen-based parsimony analysis of the sauropodomorphs from the Löwenstein Formation, Yates found two discrete clades included in *Sellosaurus gracilis*, the second of which he referred to the genus *Plateosaurus* (see entry).

According to Yates's analysis, the first clade is diagnosed by two unambigious procranial apomorphies — hypertrophy of pubic tubercle, loss of craniocaudal swelling of distal pubic apron. Yates included the following specimens in this clade: SMNS 11838 (holotype of *Teratosaurus minor*), SMNS 1288–92 (holotype of *Sellosaurus fraasi*), SMNS 2354 (holotype of *Palaeosaurus diagnosticus*), SMNS 12654, SMNS 17928, and, tentatively, SMNS 12216, SMNS 12667, and SMNS 14881. All of these specimens, with the exception of SMNS 17928 (which is from the Goesel Quarry at Ochsenbach), are from the type locality at Pfaffenhofen (see Galton 1984).

As Yates pointed out, the oldest name assigned to species distinct from *S. gracilis* that can be referred to this taxon is *Teratosaurus minor*, a name having page priority over *Sellosaurus fraasi*. SMNS 11838, the holotype of the former species, displays the diagnostic enlarged, semilunate pubic tubercle; however, that species clearly does not belong to *Teratosaurus* (see above). As the next available generic name is *Efraasia*, and as its type species, *E. diagnostica*, has the diagnostic pubic turbercle of "*T.*" *minor*, differing only in juvenile characters, Yates proposed that *E. diagnostica* be regarded as a junior synonym of the type species *E. minor*.

Note: Chure and McIntosh (1989) listed both *P. platyodon* and the referred species *P. stricklandi* Davies 1881 as nondinosaurian.

Key references: Benton (1986); Chure and McIntosh (1989); Cope (1878); Fraas (1913); Galton (1973*b*, 1984, 1985*a*, 1985*b*, 1985*c*); Huene (1907–08; 1932); Hungerbühler (1998); Kuhn (1959); Riley and Stutchbury (1836); Saint-Hilaire (1833); Yates (2003*a*).

Galton (1973*b*; see *Sellosaurus* entry, *D:TE*), noting that teeth provide only little information in generic identification, removed *P. diagnosticus* from the tooth genus *Palaeosauriscus* and referred it to a new genus, *Efraasia* as the new combination *Efraasia diagnostica*. Galton (1985*a*) later regarded this taxon as synonymous with *Sellosaurus gracilis*, which he then accepted as a valid type species. Subsequently, Galton (1985*b*, 1985*c*) offered evidence supporting the juvenile status of material originally referred to *Efraasia*. To *S. gracilis*, Galton (1985*a*) referred the species *fraasi*; *T. minor, T. trossingensis*, based on postcranial remains (GPIT 18064) including an articulated tail and limb bones, collected at Trossingen, and also *The-*

†ELOPTERYX [*nomen dubium*]

Saurischia: Eusaurischia: Theropoda: Neotheropoda: Tetanurae: Avetheropoda: Coelurosauria: Tyrannoraptora: Maniraptoriformes: ?Troodontidae *incertae sedis*.

Type species: *E. nopcsai* Andrews 1913 [*nomen dubium*].

Comments: In 2004, Darren Naish, in a paper reidentifying the genus *Heptasteornis* (see entry) as an alvarezsaurid theropod, also reevaluated the fragmentary femora (including holotype BMNH A.1234 and referred specimen BMNH A1235) of *Elopteryx nopscai*, a type species, originally described in 1913 by Charles W. Andrews. Over the years this taxon has been classified with a number of non-avian theropod and avian groups, one of the most recent being its assignment by Csiki and Grigorescu (1998) to Maniraptora *incertae sedis* (see S2).

Among the observations Naish made concerning the femora referred to *E. nopscai* are the following: Lateral ridge (reduced structure also in ornithomorphan birds; see Hutchinson 2001), apparently comparable with that of pygostylian birds, less prominently also found in dromaeosaurid *Velociraptor mongoliensis* (see Norell and Makovicky 1999); prominent depression just proximal to lateral ridge (as in other "eumaniraptorans"), not as prominent in ridge described in enantiornithines (*e.g.*, Chiappe and Calvo 1994), suggesting exclusion from that clade; caudal trochanter not present, indicating exclusion from Alvarezsauridae.

Based upon the above features, Naish concluded that *E. nopscai* is apparently either a troodontid non-avian theropod or a nonornithuromorphan pygostylian (but not enantiornithine) bird. Inclusion in the former group, Naish pointed out, would be strengthened if troodontids were to be described possessing an oblique trochanteric crest as seen in this species. However, if *E. nopscai* is, in fact, a pygostylian bird, "its thick-walled bones suggest that it was a diver or a graviportal ratite-like form."

In their review of the Troodontidae, Makovicky and Norell (2004) regarded *Elopteryx nopcsai* as a *nomen dubium* (see "Systematics" chapter).

Key references: Andrews (1913); Csiki and Grigorescu (1998); Hutchinson (2001); Makovicky and Norell (2004); Naish (2004); Norell and Makovicky (1999).

†ENIGMOSAURUS—(=?*Erlikosaurus*)

Saurischia: Eusaurischia: Eusaurischia: Theropoda: Neotheropoda: Tetanurae: Avetheropoda: Coelurosauria: Tyrannoraptora: Maniraptoriformes: Maniraptora: Metornithes: Therizinosauroidea.

Diagnosis of genus (as for type species): Ischium having small, shallow obturator process; caudal process on pubic foot (Clark, Maryańska and Barsbold 2004).

Comments: In their review of the Therizinosauroidea, Clark, Maryańska and Barsbold (2004) rediagnosed the type species *Enigmosaurus mongoliensis* (see S3).

According to Clark *et al.*, the possible synonymy of *E. mongoliensis* with the type species "*Erlikosaurus andrewsi* cannot be ruled out until elements shared by both taxa are discovered."

Key reference: Clark, Maryańska and Barsbold (2004).

†EOBRONTOSAURUS—(=?*Camarasaurus*)

Saurischia: Eusaurischia: Sauropodomorpha: Sauropoda: Eusauropoda: Neosauropoda: Macronaria: Camarsauromorpha: Camarasauridae.

Comments: In 1998, Robert T. Bakker described the type species *Eobrontosaurus yahnalpin*, founded on an incomplete skeleton (TATE [also TM] 001), from the Morrison Formation of Wyoming, that James B. Filla and Pat D. Redman (1994) described as a new species of *Apatosaurus*. Bakker assigned this specimen and also some referred material to the diplodocoid family Diplodocidae (see S1).

More recently, Upchurch, Barrett and Dodson (2004), in their review of the Sauropoda, reassessed the validity of *Eobrontosaurus*, pointing out that the feature of long cervical ribs preclude referral of this genus to the Diplodocoidea; the distally flared scapular blade is distinct from the narrow-bladed scapulae seen in all known diplodocids; and that the features utilized by Filla and Redman, and Bakker, to diagnose this taxon have a wider range among the Sauropoda. Moreover, Upchurch *et al.* found the scapulocoracoid, humerus, and cervical vertebrae of *Eobrontosaurus* to be "almost indistinguishable from those of *Camarasaurus*, suggesting that the former is probably a junior synonym of the latter."

Among the material belonging to the holotype of *E. yahnahpin* are elements that Filla and Redman interpreted to be gastralia or "belly ribs" (see D:TE). This identification was subsequently accepted by various other authors (*e.g.*, McIntosh 1997; McIntosh, Brett-Surman and Farlow 1997; Makovicky 1997).

More recently Claessens (2004), in a detailed study of gastralia in theropod and prosauropod dinosaurs (see "Introduction"), reinterpreted these elements, questioning their identification as gastraila. As observed by that author, the supposed "gastralia" of this species are preserved in nine V-shaped rows with cranially pointed apices. The single rodlike bones of each body half in the ventral midline do not overlap. These bones vary in length, the caudalmost element being about five times smaller than the cranial elements. They are either rodlike or flattened strips, the shape of their cross sections varying considerably. The entire surface of these bones bear rugosities and knobby outgrowths.

As Claessens pointed out, Filla and Redman's identification of these elements was strongly influenced by "a body of literature that allowed a wide range of morphological structures to be designated as gastralia." However, what is currently known of gastralia morphology — contrary to the data found in that literature — shows "a remarkable consistency in the composition of the gastrialial apparatus in dinosaurs." According to Clasessens, the bones identified by Filla and Redman as sauropod gastralia lack several of the characteristics seen in a wide range of taxa that includes basal archosauromorphs, extant crocodilians, and the rhynchocephalian *Sphenodon*, as well as in theropod and prosauropod dinosaurs. In all of these groups, Classens noted, the gastralia comprise lateral and medial components, taper at lateral or both ends, and have grooves for articulation between medial and lateral gastralia. None of these characteristics appear in the elements described by Filla and Redman as sauropod gastralia.

Furthermore, prosauropods possess a range of about 14 to 16 individual gastrialial rows, while theropods have a range of from eight to 21. Only nine rows of alleged "gastralia" are present in *E.* [=*Apatosaurus* of his terminology] *yahnapin*; if indeed these elements are gastralia, the rows would, Classens stated, have been quite widely spaced given the size of the animal's abdomen.

According to Claessens, nearly all discrepancies could be resolved if such elements were instead interpreted as sternal ribs (as originally suggested for *Apatosaurus excelsus* by Marsh 1896; see also Osborn and Mook 1921), with the rugosities and knobby outgrowths possibly the result of the mineralization of cartilage. The low number of nine rows would precisely conform with the number of sternal ribs figured by Marsh in his reconstruction of *A. excelsus* specimen YPM 1980. Moreover, "the rarity of 'gastralia' in the relatively extensive sauropod fossil record would be more plausible considering the limited ossification or fossilization of cartilaginous structures such as sternal ribs."

Only one fact — the bones having been recovered in cranially directed, V-shaped rows near the pubic bones — oppose the identification of these elements as sternal ribs, Claessens stated. However, this discrepancy could be explained by the collapse of the thorax, which could have moved the sternal ribs to the position as that in which these alleged "gastralia" were found. Moreover, Claessens pointed out, the distal ends of the thoracic ribs — where the proximal sternal ribs articulate — were preserved adjacent to the proximal ends of these "gastralia."

According to Claessens, positive identification of these elements might eventually be determined through histological study. Gastralia are dermal bones, sternal ribs consist of calcified cartilage. If the sauropod sternal ribs had attained a degree of complete ossification, they may be histologically indistinguishable from gastralia. With neither the *E. yahnapin* or *A. excelsus* material currently available for study, Claessens found it most reasonable to accept the original interpretation of these sauropod elements as sternal ribs.

Key references: Bakker (1998); Claessens (2004); Filla and Redman (1994); Makovicky (1997); Marsh (1896); McIntosh (1997); McIntosh, Brett-Surman and Farlow (1997); Osborn and Mook (1921); Upchurch, Barrett and Dodson (2004).

†EORAPTOR
Saurischia.

Comments: In 1993, Paul C. Sereno, Catherine A. Forster, Raymond R. Rogers, and Alfredo M. Monetta described the type species *Eoraptor lunensis*, based upon the nearly complete articulated skeleton (PVSJ 512) from the Ischigualasto Formation of Argentina (see *D:TE*). Sereno *et al.*, as well as other authors (*e.g.*, Novas 1993, 1996*a*, 1997*b*; Rauhut 2003*c*; Sereno 1999*a*) regarded this very primitive saurischian dinosaur as a basal member of the Theropoda.

More recently, in a review of basal saurischian dinosaurs, Langer (2004) reassessed this taxon. According to Langer's analysis, *Eoraptor* is less basal in the tree of Dinosauria than Herrerasauridae. Moreover, Langer noted, *Eoraptor* shares with some basal sauropodomorphs or theropods (but not *Herrerasaurus*) the following features: Thin dorsocaudal premaxillary process (allowing maxilla to approach external naris); subnarial gap similar to that in Coelophysidae; maxilla having concave rostral margin, horizontal ridge on lateral surface; nasal forming dorsal border of antorbital fenestra, bearing caudolateral process enveloping part of rostal ramus of lacrimal; ramus of lacrimal long, subvertical; rostral ramus of jugal not reaching internal antorbital fenestra.

Key references: Langer (2004); Novas (1993, 1996*a*, 1997*b*); Rauhut (2003*c*); Sereno (1999*a*); Sereno, Forster, Rogers and Monetta (1993).

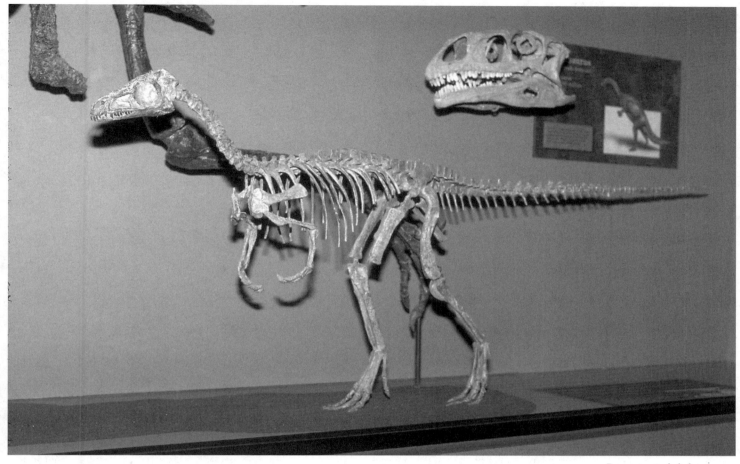

Life restoration by Berislav Krzic of *Eoraptor lunensis.*

Reconstructed skeleton (cast) of the primitive ?theropod *Eoraptor lunensis* and skull (cast) of the plateosaurid prosauropod *Plateosaurus engelhardti.*

†EPACHTHOSAURUS—(=*Pellegrinisaurus*)
Saurischia: Eusaurischia: Sauropodomorpha: Sauropoda: Eusauropoda: Neosauropoda: Macronaria: Titanosauriformes: Titanosauria.

Diagnosis of genus (as for type species): Medium-sized titanosaurian distinguished by the following autapomorphies: middle and caudal dorsal vertebrae with accessory articular processes extending ventrolaterally from hyposphene, strongly developed intraprezygapophyseal lamina, and aliform processes projecting laterally from dorsal portion of spinodiapophyseal lamina; hyposphene-hypantrum articulation in caudal vertebrae one to 14; pedal phalangeal formula (2–2–3–2–0) (Martínez, Gimènez, Rodríguez, Luna and Lamanna 2004).

Comments: In 1990, Jaime Eduardo Powell described *Epacthosaurus sciuttoi*, founded upon some incomplete caudal dorsal vertebrae (MACN-CH 1317) discovered in the Upper Cretaceous (late Cenomanian–early Turonian; *e.g.*, Archangelsky, Bellosi, Jalfin and Perrot 1994) Bajo Barreal Formation of Argentina (see *D:TE*). Later, Powell (2003), in his monograph on the "titanosaurids" of South America, rediagnosed and redescribed this type species, also commenting upon the materials referred to *E. sciuttoi* and also on this taxon's phylogenetic placement within Sauropoda.

As Powell (2003) reported, *E. sciuttoi* is also known from an articulated, nearly complete skeleton (UNPSJB-PV 920) missing the skull and some vertebrae (cervicals, four or five cranial dorsals, and extreme distal caudals; see Martínez, Gimènez, Rodríguez, Luna and Lamanna 2004) housed at the Universidad de La Patagonia "S. J. Bosco" (see Powell 1986); also a plaster cast (MACN 18689; see *D:TE*,

Epachthosaurus

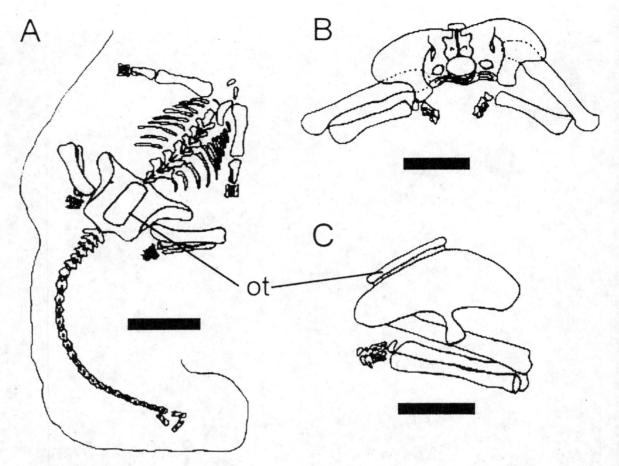

S1 for more details) of the paratype ("technical problems have impeded" recovering the original fossil material), comprising six articulated caudal dorsal vertebrae articulated with the incomplete sacrum and a fragment of the pubic peduncle of the ilium, molded at the site (J. F. Bonaparte, personal communication to Powell 2003).

Martínez *et al.* described in detail UNPSJB-PV 920, at the same time recounting the history of this specimen:

This well-preserved, articulated, partial postcranial skeleton ("one of the most complete titanosaurian skeletons known") was collected during excavations conducted as part of the project "Los vertebrados de la Formación Bajo Barreal, Provincia de Chubut, Patagonia, Argentina" by personnel from the Laboratorio de Paleontologia "San Juan Bosco." It was found at the Estancia "Ocho Hermanos" locality, Sierra de San Bernardo, west of Lago Musters, in south-central Chubut Province in central Patagonia.

The specimen was described briefly by Martínez, Giménez, Rodríguez and Luna (1988, 1989), who referred it to *Epachthosaurus*. Several features of this specimen—*e.g.*, six sacral vertebrae; procoelous first caudal vertebra; ossified ligament or tendon over neural spines of sacral vertebrae—suggest that it pertains to the Titanosauria (for remarks on titanosaurian sacra, see the recent abstract by Apesteguia and Salgado 2004).

As pointed out by Martínez *et al.* (2004), all of the characters used by Powell (1990) in his original diagnosis of *Epachthosaurus* are now known to be ambiguous or plesiomorphic (*e.g.*, see Salgado and Martínez 1993; Salgado 1996; Sanz, Powell, Le Loeuff, Martinez and Pereda Suberbiola 1999). Based upon characters used in his diagnosis, Powell (1990) had designated MACN-CH 18689 to be the "paraplastotype" of *Epachthosaurus*, although that assessment was subsequently challenged. Salgado found the referral of MACN-CH 18689 to *Epachthosaurus* to be without justification, noting that the characters used by Powell (1990) are not diagnostic, and because the caudal dorsal vertebrae of this specimen do not seem to possess an "interprezygapophyseal shelf." Bonaparte and Coria (1993) and Salgado argued that a feature not present in *Epachthosaurus*—*i.e.*, accessory articular processes extending ventrolaterally from hypotheses on caudal dorsal vertebrae—suggests that MACN-CH 18689 belongs to a distinct genus related to *Argentinosaurus*, another gigantic titanosaur, in the

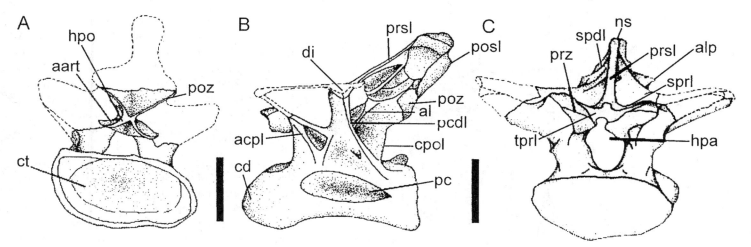

Epachthosaurus sciuttoi, UNPSJB-PV 920, middle dorsal vertebrae, A. fifth dorsal (caudal view), B. sixth (left lateral view), and C. sixth (cranial view). Scale = 10 cm. (After Martínez, Giménez. Rodríguez, Luna and Lamanna 2004.)

opinion of those authors (*contra* Salgado and Martínez; Sanz *et al.*), having dorsal vertebrae with accessory articulations. Martínez *et al.* (2004) found these accessory articulations of *Argentinosaurus* and MACNCH 18689 to be probably not homologous, the true affinities of MACN-CH 18689, therefore, yet to be determined.

Martínez *et al.* (2004) referred UNPSJB-PV 920 to *Epachthosaurus* based upon its possession of an automorphy previously determined for the genus — *i.e.*, middle and caudal dorsal vertebrae having strongly developed intraprezygapophyseal lamina ("interprezygapophyseal shelf"). Moreover, Martínez *et al.* (2004) noted, as in MACN-CH 18689, this specimen possesses accessory articular processes that extend ventrolaterally from the hyposphene on the caudal dorsal vertebrae. This feature, consequently, constitutes a synapomorphy of MACN-CH 18689 and UNPSJB-PV 920, thereby justifying Powell's (1990) original referral of the former specimen to *Epachthosaurus*.

Originally, Powell (1990) tentatively referred *Epacthosaurus* to the "Titanosauridae" (see *D:TE*). In his later study, however, Powell (2003), while also intimating that this genus is a "titanosaurid," determined through a phylogenetic analysis that *Epachthosaurus* lies outside of "Titanosauridae" and is rather the sister taxon to the more encompassing clade Eutitanosauria (see "Systematics" chapter).

According to Martínez *et al.*'s (2004) study, *Epachthosaurus* is clearly a member of the Titanosauria, possessing such proposed titanosaurian synapomorphies as the following: Caudal dorsal vertebrae having ventrally expanded distal centrodiapophyseal laminae; six sacral vertebrae; procoelous proximal, middle, and distal caudal centra having well-developed distal articular condyles; semilunar sternal plates having cranioventral ridges; humeri having squared proximolateral margins, proximolateral

processes; unossified carpals; strongly reduced manual phalanges; craniolaterally expanded, almost horizontal iliac preacetabular processes; pubes longer than ischia; and transversely expanded ischia (Giménez 1992; Salgado and Coria 1993*a*; Salgado, Coria and Calvo 1997; Upchurch 1995, 1998; Wilson 1999; Curry Rogers and Forster 2001).

Martinez *et al.* (2004) found *Epachthosaurus* most likely to be the basalmost known titanosaurian possessing the derived character of procoelous caudal vertebrae, occupying an intermediate phylogenetic position between *Andesaurus*, wherein all known caudal vertebrae are amphiplatyan, and most of the remaining known titanosaurians. The authors noted that a more accurate determination of the phylogenetic placement of *Epachthosaurus* should be included in a forthcoming cladistic analysis of the Titanosauria by Giménez (unpublished data).

As Martínez pointed out, *Epachthosaurus* currently numbers among the most complete of known titanosaurian genera, offering insight to several issues pertaining to the anatomy and evolutionary history of the Titanosauria. The sacral vertebrae of this genus are dorsally united by an ossified ligament or tendon, a character presently known otherwise only in an unnamed titanosaurian dinosaur from the Late Cretaceous of Brazil (see Powell 1987*a*; Campos and Kellner 1999), possibly indicating an affinity between these taxa or even a synapomorphy of a more inclusive titanosaurian subclade. Also, ossified ligaments or tendons most likely developed in more than one region of the titanosaurian skeleton, as they have been reported in different areas in a number of titanosaurian taxa (*e.g.*, Powell 1990; Martínez 1998; Jain and Bandyopadhyay 1997).

According to Martínez *et al.*, the dorsal, sacral, and proximal to middle caudal vertebrae of *Epachthosaurus* possess apomorphically developed hyposphene-hypantrum articulations, contrasting with the condition

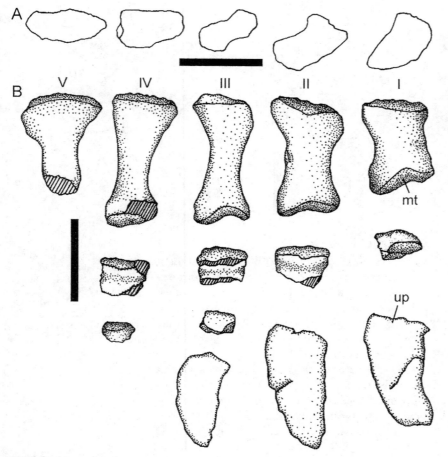

A

B

V IV III II I

mt

up

Epachthosaurus sciuttoi,
UNPSJB–PV 920, right pes,
in A. proximal and B. cra-
nial views. Scale = 10 cm.
(After Martínez, Giménez.
Rodríguez, Luna and
Lamanna 2004.)

in *Andesaurus*, in which such articulations are restricted to the dorsal vertebrae, and most remaining
known titanosaurians, wherein such structures are absent. These articulations, the authors noted, in con-
junction with the ossified ligaments or tendons associated with the caudal dorsal and sacral vertebrae,
could have greatly augmented the rigidity of the axial
skeleton of *Epachthosaurus* compared to that of other
sauropods.

As no osteoderms — these having been reported
in other titanosaurian dinosaurs — have yet been
found with any remains assigned to *Epachthosaurus*,
even in the largely complete UNPSJBPV 920, Martínez *et al.* (2004) deduced that this genus probably
lacked dermal armor. Possibly the possession of such
armor represents the retention of a plesiomorphic state
or is a reversal. Furthermore, the authors stated, the
lack of dermal armor plus the extreme development
of hyposohene-hypantrum articulations is consistent
with the postulation of Le Loeuff, Buffetaut, Cavin,
Martin, Martin and Tong (1994) that such ossifications "may have served to limit dorsal mobility in titanosaurians, most of which lack these articulations."

In 1996, Leonardo Salgado described the type
species *Pellegrinisaurus powelli*, founded upon the cen-

tra of four dorsal vertebrae, 26 incomplete caudal vertebrae, and an incomplete right femur (MPCA 1500)
from the lower member of the Upper Cretaceous
(early Maastrichtian; see Leanza, Apesteguía, Novas
and Fuente 2004) Allen Formation (Malargue Group),
in the Pala Mecánia quarry at the south margin of
Lago Pelligrini, General Roca Department, Río Negro
Province, Patagonia, Argentina. Salgado referred this
new taxon to the "Titanosauridae" (see *S1*).

Powell (2003) reevaluated this taxon and redescribed in detail its material, noting that the dorsal
vertebrae are similar to those of *E. sciuttoi* in the following features — centra broad; neural arches low; development of reinforcing lamina of apophysis and
pleurocoels. Some characters of the caudal vertebrae
(*e.g.*, morphology of centra) are similar to those in
the Saltasaurinae, while others (*e.g.*, neural spine laterally compressed, positioned vertically; long prezygapophyses) are similar to those in the Titanosaurinae. Based upon the strong similarities of these
vertebrae to those of *E. sciuttoi* and the fact that this
type of morphology is, to date, unknown in any "titanosaurids" where the dorsal vertebrae are known,
Powell (2003), pending the discovery of additional
material, identified the *P. powelli* type material as cf.
Epacthosaurus sp.

Contra Powell, Upchurch, Barrett and Dodson
(2004), in their review of Sauropoda, accepted *Pellegrinisaurus* as a valid genus of very large (estimated
body size of up to 25 meters, or over 65 feet) member of Lithostrotia, this genus diagnosed as follows:
Centra of caudal dorsal vertebrae compressed, transverse diameters being twice their dorsoventral heights;
middistal and distal caudal neural spines elongate axially, dorsally depressed, higher at cranial end than at
distal end. Upchurch *et al.* noted the fragmentary nature of the *Pellegrinisaurus* material; nor did they provide details explaining their referral of this taxon to
Lithostrotia.

Erratum: In *S1*, specimen MACN–CH 18689 was
given the incorrect number 13689.

Key references: Apesteguia and Salgado (2004);
Archangelsky, Bellosi, Jalfin and Perrot (1994); Bonaparte and Coria (1993); Campos and Kellner (1999);
Curry Rogers and Forster (2001); Gimènez (1992);
Jain and Bandyopadhyay (1999); Le Loeuff, Buffetaut,
Cavin, Martin, Martin and Tong (1994); Martínez
(1998); Martínez, Gimènez, Rodríguez and Luna
(1988, 1989); Martínez, Gimènez, Rodríguez, Luna
and Lammana (2004); Powell (1986, 1987*a*, 1990,
2003); Salgado (1996); Salgado and Coria (1993*a*);
Salgado, Coria and Calvo (1997); Salgado and
Martínez (1993); Sanz, Powell, Le Loeuff, Martinez
and Pereda Suberbiola (1999); Upchurch (1995, 1998);
Upchurch, Barrett and Dodson (2004); Wilson (1999).

EQUIJUBUS You, Luo, Shubin, Witmer, Tang and Tang 2003

Ornithischia: Predentata: Genasauria: Cerapoda: Ornithopoda: Euornithopoda: Iguanodontia: Dryomorpha: Ankylopollexia: Styracosterna.

Name derivation: Latin *equus* = "horse" + Latin *juba* = "mane" [after Ma Zong Mountain, "Ma Zong" meaning "Horse Mane" in Chinese].

Type species: *E. normani* You, Luo, Shubin, Witmer, Tang and Tang 2003.

Other species: [None.]

Occurrence: Xinminbao Group, Gansu Province, China.

Age: Late Early Cretaceous.

Known material/holotype: IVPP V 12534, complete skull with articulated lower jaw, incomplete postcranium.

Diagnosis of genus (as for type species): Characterized by unique, finger-like process extending dorsally from rostral process of jugal to lacrimal, and very large lower temporal fenestra; distinguished from nonhadrosaurid iguanodontians by long lacrimal with rostroventral process located above dorsal margin of maxilla; distinguished from other "hadrosauroids" [see Norman 2004, below] in lacking median primary ridge on crown of dentary teeth (You, Luo, Shubin, Witmer, Tang and Tang 2003).

Comments: Originally described as the most primitive hadrosauroid dinosaur yet discovered, the type species *Equijubus normani* was founded upon a skull (IVPP V 12534) collected from the Middle Grey Unit of the Xinminbao Group, Gongpoquan Basin, Mazongshan area, Gansu Province, in northwest China (You, Luo, Shubin, Witmer, Tang and Tang 2003).

Performing an initial phylogenetic analysis, You *et al.* found *Equijubus* to be a basal hadrosauroid closer to Hadrosauridae than to *Iguanodon*, in fact the most primitive member of the Hadrosauroidea, the discovery and basal position of this genus important in elucidating "the phylogenetic transformations in the origin of the feeding specializations of Late Cretaceous hadrosauroids." According to the authors, the highly developed feeding structures possessed by Late Cretaceous developed gradually over time in a clearly defined series of transformation, with some derived hadrosaurian features (*e.g.*, ventrally deflected and curved oral margin of premaxilla; long rostroventral process of lacrimal above maxilla) incipiently occurring in the common ancestor of *Equijubus* and all other members of the Hadrosauroidea.

Based on 15 taxa and 66 characters, You *et al.*'s analysis also showed (contradicting, in various ways, other recent analyses; see "Systematics" chapter) that the Iguanodontia, following this group's first appearance during the Early Cretaceous, split into three clades: Iguanodontidae (including primarily Early Cretaceous taxa such as *Iguanodon*, *Ouranosaurus*, and *Altirhinus*; Hadrosauroidea; and *Jinzhousaurus*, originally described as an iguanodontid (see Wang and Xu 2001, *S3*), but interpreted by them as a basal iguanodontian. According to their phylogeny, the diversification of the Iguanodontidae and Hadrosauroidea correlates "with differentiation in the maxillae and the consequent evolution of different masticatory mechanisms" — iguanodontids having rostrally

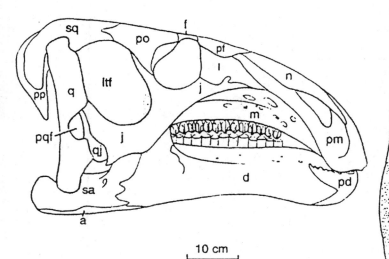

Equijubus normani, (left) reconstruction of holotype skull (IVPP V 12534) and (right) life restoration. (After You, Luo, Shubin, Witmer, Tang and Tang 2003.)

10 cm

elongate maxillae, with two processes inserting, respectfully, into the jugal and lacrimal; and hadrosauroids having comparatively smaller and shorter maxillae, their articulations with the jugal and lacrimal formed, respectively, by the rostral expansion of the jugal and elongation of the lacrimal. In hadrosauroids, You *et al.* noted, the maxilla has a simpler, more mobile, pleurokinetic articulation with the rostrum, forming a single, more efficient unit for masticating, this condition best developed in the Hadrosauridae, wherein the maxilla is less than half the preorbotal length of the skull and the premaxilla is enlarged and elongate.

You *et al.* pointed out that iguanodontids and hadrosauroids coexisted in Asia during the Early Cretaceous; that the basal iguanodontian *Jinzhousaurus* is known from the Early Cretaceous of China; and that the earliest and most primitive hadrosauroids (*e.g.*, *Equijubus*, *Probactrosaurus*, and *Bactrosaurus*) also originate in Asia. This suggested to You *et al.* "that hadrosauroids originated in Asia before the group diversified and dispersed to other continents" during the Late Cretaceous.

In a more recent preliminary cladistic analysis conducted in a review of basal Iguanodontia, Norman (2004) found *E. normani* to place between *Lurdusaurus* and *Iguanodon* within the clade Styracosterna (see "Systematics" chapter).

Key references: Norman (2004); Wang and Xu (2001); You, Luo, Shubin, Witmer, Tang and Tang (2003).

†ERECTOPUS

Saurischia: Eusaurischia: Theropoda: Neotheropoda: Tetanurae: Avetheropoda: Carnosauria: Allosauroidea incertae sedis.

Comments: In 1882, H. E. Sauvage referred some isolated teeth, bones, plus a partial skeleton (material apparently lost) from the Early Cretaceous Greensand ("Sables verts"), of the eastern Paris Basin, France, to the genus *Megalosaurus*, as the new species *Megalosaurus superbus*. The nondental remains were later referred by Huene (1923) to the new genus and species *Erectopus superbus* (see *D:TE*).

In an abstract, Buffetaut (2002) reported briefly on undescribed fragmentary dinosaur material from several "Sables vert" localities recently rediscovered in the collections of the Nancy Zoological Museum, in Lorraine, eastern France. Among this theropod material are three teeth pertaining to a medium-sized form, resembling the teeth originally described by Sauvage as *Megalosaurus superbus*; the distal end of a right tibia belonging to a large theropod, apparently "different from the tibia (erroneously identified as a radius)" which Sauvage had referred to *M. superbus*; and

a left metatarsal III (lacking its proximal end) of a large form the size of *Allosaurus*, this bone "remarkably slender (as was a metatarsal figured by Sauvage)."

As Buffetaut noted, among the most remarkable elements in this assemblage seems to be the remains of a rather large, yet slenderly constructed theropod. Moreover, the problem of how many theropod taxa are present in the "Sables verts" and also questions regarding the enigmatic *Erectopus* can now be reassessed in view of the rediscovered material.

Note: Also found among these specimens were two different-sized, amphicoelous caudal vertebrae representing somewhat small sauropods, this material constituting the first record of the Sauropoda from the "Sables verts": and the distal end of a humerus belonging to a nodosaurid ankylosaur, confirming the occurrence of the Ankylosauria in the "Sables verts."

Key references: Buffetaut (2002); Huene (1923); Sauvage (1882)

†ERLIKOSAURUS

Saurischia: Eusaurischia: Eusaurischia: Theropoda: Neotheropoda: Tetanurae: Avetheropoda: Coelurosauria: Tyrannoraptora: Maniraptoriformes: Maniraptora: Metornithes: Therizinosauroidea: Therizinosauridae.

Diagnosis of genus (as for type species): 31 small straight, and only slightly flattened mandibular teeth; coronoid process low; pedal claws strongly compressed transversely (Clark, Maryańska and Barsbold 2004).

Comment: In their review of the Therizinosauroidea, Clark, Maryańska and Barsbold (2004) rediagnosed the type species *Erlikosaurus andrewsi* (see *D:TE*).

Key reference: Clark, Maryańska and Barsbold (2004).

†ESHANOSAURUS

Saurischia: Eusaurischia: Eusaurischia: Theropoda: Neotheropoda: Tetanurae: Avetheropoda: Coelurosauria: Tyrannoraptora: Maniraptoriformes: Maniraptora: Metornithes: ?Therizinosauroidea.

Diagnosis of genus (as for type species): Teeth having smaller serrations; broader symphysial region (Clark, Maryańska and Barsbold 2004).

Comment: In their review of the Therizinosauroidea, Clark, Maryańska and Barsbold (2004) rediagnosed the type species *Eshanosaurus deguchiianus* (see *D:TE*).

Clark *et al.* tentatively referred this taxon to the Therizinosauroidea based upon the following synapomorphic features: Dentary having lateral shelf; dentary teeth becoming larger rostrally; teeth mediolaterally compressed, symmetrical, roots cylindrical.

Key reference: Clark, Maryańska and Barsbold (2004).

†EUCAMEROTUS   Hulke 1872 [*nomen dubium*]

Saurischia: Eusaurischia: Sauropodomorpha: Sauropoda: Eusauropoda: Neosauropoda: Macronaria: Titanosauriformes *incertae sedis*.

Name derivation: Greek eu = "good" + Greek *kamarotos* = "chamberedg."

Type species: *E.* [no specific name given] Hulke 1872 [*nomen dubium*].

Other species: [None.]

Occurrence: Wessex Formation, Isle of Wight, England.

Age: Early Cretaceous (Barremian).

Known material/holotype: Neural arch of dorsal vertebra.

Diagnosis of genus (as for type species): [None published.]

Comments: James A. Hulke, in 1872, described the new sauropod *Eucamerotus*, based on an incomplete dorsal vertebra collected from the Wessex Formation, Isle of Wight, England. Hulke did not assign this genus a specific name. Following the naming of this taxon, *Eucamerotus* has generally been regarded as a *nomen dubium* and also a junior synonym of either *Ornithopsis* (see entry) or the brachiosaurid *Chondrosteosaurus* (see *D:TE*).

More than a century later, Blows (1995), in reviewing this genus along with *Ornithopsis*, posited that *Eucamerotus* was indeed a valid genus founded upon diagnostic material. Additionally, Blows referred other fragmentary vertebrae and also a partial skeleton, to date of this writing undescribed, to *Eucamerotus*.

More recently, Upchurch, Barrett and Dodson (2004), in their review of the Sauropoda, pointed out that none of the characters cited by Blows are diagnostic, these authors finding *Eucamerotus* to be "an indeterminate titanosauriform sauropod of dubious validity."

Key references: Blows (1995); Hulke (1872); Upchurch, Barrett and Dodson (2004).

†EUOPLOCEPHALUS

Ornithischia: Predentata: Genasauria: Thyreophora: Thyreophoroidea: Eurypoda: Ankylosauria: Ankylosauridae: Ankylosaurinae.

Diagnosis of genus (as for type species): Unique pattern of cranial sculpturing across rostral region of skull; teeth small, fluting not corresponding to position of apical denticles; palprbral modified, articulating to occlude orbit; shallow nasal vestibule having vertically oriented internasal process of maxilla; pes tridactyl (Vickaryous, Maryańska and Weishampel 2004; based on Coombs and Maryańska 1990; Vickaryous and Russell 2003).

Comment: In their review of the Ankylosauria, Vickaryous, Maryańska and Weishampel (2004) rediagnosed the type species *Euoplocephalus tutus* (see *D:TE*).

Key references: Coombs and Maryańska (1990); Vickaryous, Maryańska and Weishampel (2004); Vickaryous and Russell (2003).

†EUSKELOSAURUS

Saurischia: Eusaurischia: Sauropodomorpha: Sauropoda: Prosauropoda: Plateosauria: Plateosauridae.

Diagnosis of genus (as for type species): Autapomorphies including the following: humerus with deltopectoral crest that is sigmoid in cranial aspect (Galton and Upchurch 2004a).

Comment: In their review of the Prosauropoda, Galton and Upchurch (2004a) rediagnosed the type species *Euskelosaurus browni* (see *D:TE*).

Key reference: Galton and Upchurch (2004a).

†EUSTREPTOSPONDYLUS

Saurischia: Eusaurischia: Theropoda: Neotheropoda: Tetanurae: Spinosauroidea: Megalosauridae: Megalosaurinae.

Comments: Sadleir, Barrett and Powell (2004), in an abstract, reassessed anatomy of the holotype skeleton (OUM J13558; "the most complete Middle Jurassic theropod specimen from Europe") of *Eustreptospondylus oxoniensis*, a rare primitive theropod from the Oxford Clay (Callovian) of Oxfordshire, United Kingdom (see *D:TE*), while at the same time reconsidering this taxon's phylogenetic position within Theropoda.

Incorporating a combination of both previously described details of the anatomy of *E. oxoniensis* (presumably to be published at a later date) plus new information into an existing detailed analysis of basal theropod phylogeny, Sadleir *et al.* concluded that *Eustreptospondylus* is a basal member of Spinosauroidea, exhibiting various anatomical features—*e.g.*, development of premaxillary/maxillary embayment—that seem to be incipient versions of the very specialized character states found in more derived spinosauroid taxa. Also, Sadleir *et al.*'s study suggested that the Spinosauroidea arose in Middle Jurassic Europe, its members subsequently dispersing into Gondwana.

Moreover, the authors pointed out that several previously unreported features support earlier published proposals that OUM J13558 represents a

Life restoration of *Euskelosaurus browni* by artist Todd Marshall.

juvenile or subadult animal, these highlighting "the potential utility of this specimen in understanding the developmental processes that underlie theropod character evolution."

Key reference: Sadleir, Barrett and Powell (2004).

†FERGANASAURUS

Saurischia: Eusaurischia: Sauropodomorpha: Sauropoda: Eusauropoda: Neosauropoda incertae sedis.

Comments: Although the text entry for the genus *Ferganasaurus* and type species *F. verzilini* — a very old and primitive, Middle Jurassic neosauropod from Fergana Valley, Kirghiza — was included in *S3*, the figures (Alifanov and Averianov 2003) of its remains were not available in time for their inclusion in that volume; therefore, the illustrations are reproduced herein.

Note: Averianov, Martin and Bakirov (2004) subsequently described various additional sauropod specimens — ZIN PH 6/42 (heavily worn tooth crown), ZIN PH 21/42 (apex of a tooth crown), ZIN PH 22/42 (left metatarsal), and ZIN PH 38/42 (right manual phalanx) — recovered in 2001 during a joint project of the Institut für Geologische Wissenschaften, Fachrichtung Paläontologie, Freie Universität and Zoological Institute of the Russian Academy of Sciences, and the Institute of Geology of the National

Academy of Sciences from the Balabansai Svita, in the northern Fergana Valley, Kyrgyzstan, in Central Asia.

One character observed by Averianov *et al.* in this material — absence of tooth denticles — was considered by Wilson and Sereno (1998) to be a synapomorphy of the Neosauropoda, although, denticles are present in such neosauropods as *Camarasaurus* and

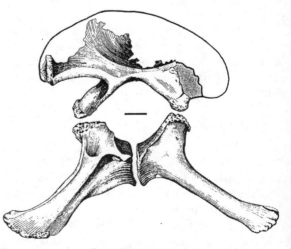

Ferganasaurus verzilini, PIN N 3042/1, holotype left pelvis in lateral view, ilium reconstructed from preserved part of right ilium. Scale = 10 cm. (After Alifanov and Averianov 2003.)

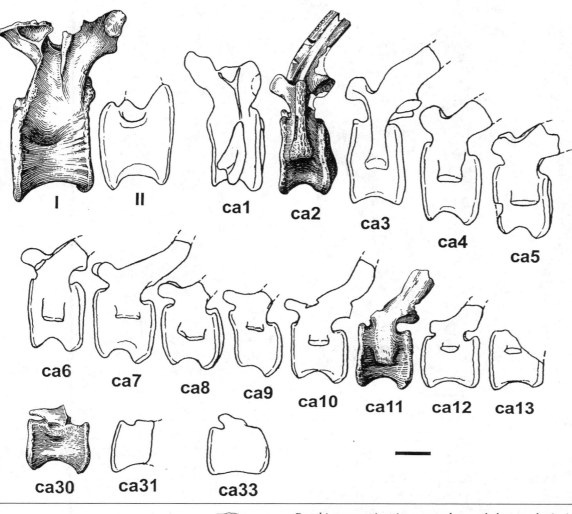

Ferganasaurus verzilini, PIN N 3042/1, holotype distal vertebrae (dorsals one and 11, caudals approximately one through 13, in left lateral view. Scale = 10 cm. (After Alifanov and Averianov 2003.)

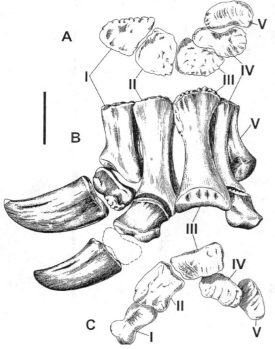

Brachiosaurus. Averianov *et al.* noted that teeth similar to ZIN PH 21/42 (*i.e.*, convex, corasely denticulate mesial margin, concave distal margin having finer, fewer denticles) are seen also in the primitive Middle to Late Jurassic eusauropods *Datousaurus*, *Omeisaurus*, and *Mamenchisaurus*, suggesting that this character may be primitive for Eusauropoda. Additionally, Averianov *et al.* noted, the proximal phalanx of manual digit V (ZIN PH 38/42) is very similar in size and proportions to that *Brachiosaurus brancai*.

While Averianov *et al.* were not, at the time, able to determine a more precise systematic position for this sauropod based upon the above-cited remains, these authors suggested that they could belong to *Ferganasaurus verzilini*.

Ferganasaurus verzilini, PIN N 3042/1, holotype left manus in A. proximal and B. cranial views, C. distal view of metacarpals I–IV. The figured ungual phalanges had been referred by Anatoly Konstantinovich Rozhdestvensky to manual digits I and II; however, according to Vladimir R. Alifanov and Alexander O. Averianov (2003), "at least one of these phalanges is actually a pedal claw, or these are right and left pollex unguals." Scale = 10 cm. (After Alifanov and Averianov 2003.)

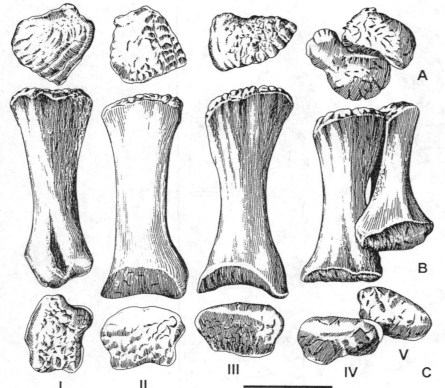

Ferganasaurus verzilini, PIN N 3042/1, holotype left metacarpals in A. proximal, B. cranial, and C. distal views. Scale = 10 cm. (After Alifanov and Averianov 2003.)

Key references: Alifanov and Averianov (2003); Averianov, Martin and Bakirov (2004); Rozhdestvensky (1968); Wilson and Sereno (1998).

FERGANOCEPHALE Averianov, Martin and Bakirov 2005

Ornithischia: Predentata: Genusauria: Cerapoda: Chasmatopia: Marginocephalia: Pachycephalosauria: Goyocephala: Homalocephaloidea: Pachycephalosauridae *incertae sedis*.

Name derivation: "Fergana [Valley]" + Greek *cephale* = "head."

Type species: *F. adenticulatum* Averianov, Martin and Bakirov 2005.

Other species: [None.]

Occurrence: Balabansai Svita, Fergana Valley, Kyrgyzstan.

Age: Middle Jurassic (Callovian).

Known material: Teeth, adult, ?juvenile.

Holotype: ZIN PH 34/42, tooth, adult.

Diagnosis of genus (as for type species): Differing from all other known pachycephalosaurians by the

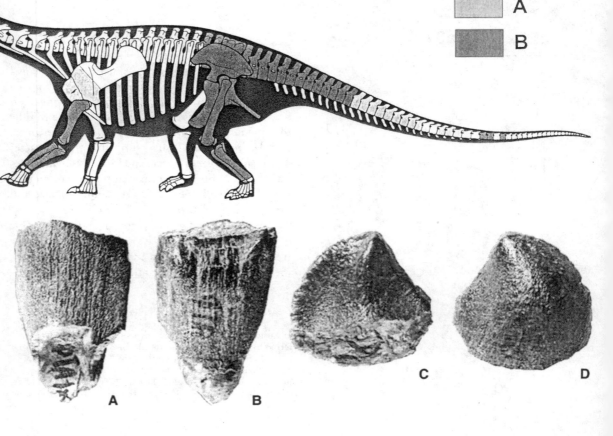

Ferganasaurus verzilini, reconstructed skeleton including holotype (PIN N 3042/1), A. excavated elements and B. those currently collected, A. based on sketch provided by S. M. Kurzanov and reported by A. K. Rhozdestvensky (1968), based in part on *Camarasaurus* (Wilson and Sereno 1998). (After Alifanov and Averianov 2003.)

Sauropod teeth (A–B, ZIN PH 6/24 and C–D, ZIN PH 21/42, all lateral views) from Balabansai Svita, Kyrgystan. According to Alexander O. Averianov, Thomas Martin and Aizek A. Bakirov (2004), these teeth may be referrable to *Ferganasaurus verzilini*. (After Averianov, Martin and Bakirov 2004.)

following autapomorphies: main tooth crown ridge poorly differentiated or not distinguishable; vertical crown ridges leading to marginal denticles very weak or absent; marginal crown denticles absent or very small (eliminated by slightest wear); basal crown cingulum interrupted at center of labial side in maxillary teeth, of lingual side in mandibular teeth; vertical wrinkled ornamentation possibly on less concave crown side, adjacent to basal cingulum interruption, at least in some teeth (Averianov, Martin and Bakirov 2005).

Comments: Distinguished as the oldest known pachycephalosaurian and marginocephalian genus, *Ferganocephale* was founded upon an unworn adult tooth (ZIN PH 34/42) collected in 2001 during a joint project of the Institut für Geologische Wissenschaften, Fachrichtung Paläontologies, Freie Universität, the Zoological Institute of the Russian Academy of Sciences, and the Institute of Geology of the National Academy of Sciences from the Balabansai Svita, in the northern Fergana Valley, Kyrgyzstan, Central Asia. Teeth collected from the same site and others in the Fergana Valley, referred to the type species *Ferganocephale adenticulatum*, include ZIN PH 5/42 (possibly juvenile), ZIN PH 4 [originally labeled by paleontologist Lev A. Nessov as stegosaurian], 30–33/42 (four isolated, adult), ZIN PH 35/42 (isolated, heavily worn, adult), and ZIN PH 36/42 (isolated, distal, adult) (Averianov, Martin and Bakirov 2005).

Averianov *et al.* noted that all of these teeth appear to be water-worn, although the authors found it more likely that—assuming that pachycephalosaurs, like many other kinds of plant-eating dinosaurs, often swallowed their teeth—they had been swallowed and then corroded when passing through the animals' digestive system.

In describing the teeth, Averianov *et al.* observed the following features of these teeth typical of Pachycephalosauria: Both lingual and labial crown sides covered by enamel (plesiomorphic); crowns asymmetrical in lateral aspect, one side (?mesial) more convex than opposite side; basal crown cingulum; basal cingulum more prominent on one crown side compared with its opposite side (lingual side in maxillary teeth, labial side in mandibular teeth); dentition monognathically heterodont, distal teeth with lower, more asymmetrical crowns than mesial teeth.

As Averianov *et al.* pointed out, the discovery of this primitive pachycephalosaur extends the known fossil record of the Marginocephalia by some 10 to 20 million years, depending upon the precise age (Late Jurassic or Early Cretaceous) for *Chaöyangsaurus*, a neoceratopsian previously regarded as the oldest known marginocephalian genus.

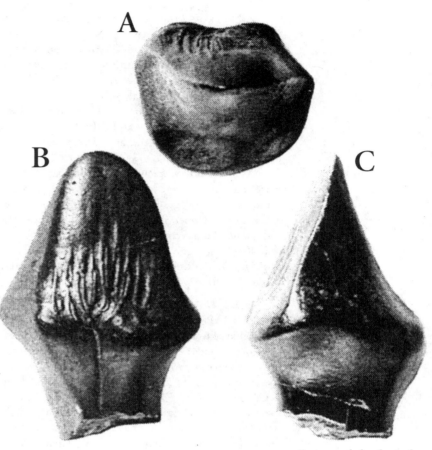

Ferganocephale adenticulatum, ZIN PH 34/42, holotype tooth in (top) occlusal, (bottom left) lateral (labial), and (bottom right) mesial or distal views. (After Averianov, Martin and Bakirov 2004.)

Note: Averianov *et al.* also described other isolated theropod, sauropod, and pterosaur material recovered during the same joint project at Balabansai Svita:

ZIN PH 7–20 and ZIN PH 26/42–29/42 (18 teeth), plus more than 20 uncatalogued teeth and tooth fragments, represents an indeterminate tetanuran theropod and possible dromaeosaurid. As described by Averianov *et al.*, the shape of these specimens "ranges from moderately laterally compressed to almost rounded in cross-section." Their most distinctive character, these authors noted, is the short mesial carina that extends only approximately half the height of the crown, an atypical character for large theropods (*e.g.*, carcharodontosaurids, allosaurids, tyrannosaurids) but found in Dromaeosauridae, more explicitly in Cretaceous velociraptorines (*e.g.*, in most teeth, mesial carina not lingually displaced; some teeth considerably laterally compressed; see Currie, Rigby and Sloan 1990). Moreover, the Balabansai specimens could "represent a morphotype that may be plesiomorphic compared with more derived Cretaceous dromaeosaurids, therefore belonging to a dromaeosaurid stem group that branched off before that clade's splitting into the Dromaeosaurinae and Velociraptorinae."

ZIN PH 6/42 (heavily worn tooth crown), ZIN PH 21/42 (apex of crown), ZIN PH 22/42 (left metatarsal), and ZIN PH 38/42 (right manual phalanx) belong to a basal neosauropod taxon, apparently a camarasaurid (see *Ferganasaurus* entry, "Note").

The pterosaur material—ZIN PH 1/42–3/42, ZIN PH 23/42, and ZIN PH 37/42 (five teeth of different sizes); ZIN PH 24 and ZIN PH 25/42 (two tooth fragments)—represents an indeterminate rhamphorhynchine.

As Averianov *et al.* noted, the Balabansai Svita vertebrate assemblage resembles most closely the Callovian assemblages from China's Qigu Formation and the older Upper Shaximiao Formation (see paper for detailed faunal comparisons).

Key references: Averianov, Martin and Bakirov (2005); Currie, Rigby and Sloan (1990); Wilson and Sereno (1998).

†FUKUIRAPTOR

Saurischia: Eusaurischia: Eusaurischia: Theropoda: Neotheropoda: Tetanurae: Avetheropoda: ?Carnosauria *incertae sedis*.

Comments: In 2000, Yoichi Azuma and Philip J. Currie described *Fukuiraptor kitadaniensis*, a type species founded upon a fragmentary skeleton (FPMN 97122) of an immature animal collected from the Kitadani Formation of Fukui Prefecture, Japan. Originally, those authors referred this taxon to the Dromaeosauridae (see *S3*).

More recently, Holtz, Molnar and Currie (2004), in a review of basal tetanurans, pointed out that, as in the possible carnosaur *Siamotyrannus* (see entry), the centra of the dorsal vertebrae of *Fukuiraptor* lack pneumatopores, this shared feature indicating a union between these two genera. However, as pneumatization of the theropod vertebral column proceeds caudally during ontogeny (*e.g.*, see Britt 1993), this possible synapomorphy could, the authors cautioned, simply reflect similar stages of growth.

Key references: Azuma and Currie (2000); Britt (1993); Holtz, Molnar and Currie (2004).

FUKUISAURUS   Kobayashi and Azuma 2003

Ornithischia: Predentata: Genasauria: Cerapoda: Ornithopoda: Euornithopoda: Iguanodontia: Dryomorpha: Ankylopollexia: Styracosterna: Iguanodontoidea.

Name derivation: "Fukui" [Prefecture, Japan] + Greek *sauros* = "lizard."

Type species: *F. tetoriensis*.

Other species: [None.]

Occurrence: Kitadani Formation, Fukui Prefecture, Japan.

Age: Early Cretaceous (late Hauterivian–Barremian).

Known material: Miscellaneous skull elements, teeth, sternal plate, subadult to adult.

Holotype: FPDM-V-40–1, right maxilla, FPDM-V-40–2, right jugal.

Diagnosis of genus (as for type species): Nonhadrosaurid iguanodontian differing from other known forms in having the following combination of characters: rostrum narrow, with caudally restricted primary palate, maxilla shallow with 20 alveoli, strong articular surface, vomer associated with horizontal ridges, grooves in rostral fourth of medial surface of maxilla, foramen on lateral surface of rostral process of jugal, straight caudal border of rostral process of jugal with squared caudoventral corner in lateral aspect, dentary deep with 19 alveoli and short coronoid process, rostroventrally projecting process extending from rostral edge of glenoid of surangular, sternal plate with straight lateral border (Kobayashi and Azuma 2003).

Comments: Dinosaur discoveries in Japan are rare. Among the more recent Japanese dinosaurian finds is *Fukuisaurus*, an iguanodontian genus represented by various disarticulated skull remains collected over a 50 square meter area in fluvial deposits of the bone-rich Kitadani Quarry, in the Lower Cretaceous (suggested as ranging from late Hauterivian to Barremian, based on an assemblage of freshwater molluscs; see Tashiro and Okuhira 1993) Kitadani Formation, upper part of the Akaiwa Subgroup, Tetori Group, Katsuyama City, Fukui Prefecture. (Fossil materials previously recovered from the Kitadani Quarry include remains pertaining to the theropod *Fukuiraptor kitadaniensis* [Azuma and Currie 2000; see *S2*], fish, turtles, a goniopholidid crocodyliform, and a sauropod [see Azuma and Tomida [1997]].)

The type species *Fukuisaurus tetoriensis* was founded upon a right maxilla (FPDM-V-40–1) and a right jugal (FPDM-V-402). Disarticulated skull paratype specimens from the Kitadani Quarry, referred by Kobayashi and Azuma to this species, include the following: FPDM-V-40–3 and FPDM-V-40–4, left and right premaxillae, respectively; FPDM-V-40–5, left maxilla; FPDM-V-40–6 and FPDM-V-40–7, left and right quadrates, respectively; FPDM-V-40–8, predentary; FPDM-V-40–9 and FPDM-V-40–10, left and right dentaries, respectively; FPDM-V-40–11 and FPDM-V-40–12, left and right surangulars, respectively; FPDM-V-40–13, isolated left maxillary tooth; FPDM-V-40–14 and FPDM-V-40–15, two isolated left dentary teeth; also FPDM-V-40–16, a right sternal plate.

As reported by Kobayashi and Azuma, the elements belonging to *Fukuisaurus* were found in a disarticulated state, making it difficult for the authors to

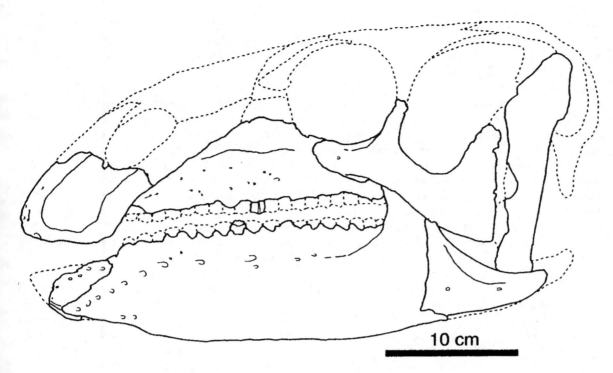

10 cm

determine the number of individual animals represented by the material they described. All of the elements most likely pertain to subadult to adult individuals. A composite skull of *F. tetoriensis* apparently represents at least two individuals and two different ontogenetic stages, as evidenced by the size difference in the maxillae (*e.g.*, left maxilla 90.7 percent the height of the right).

According to Kobayashi and Azuma, *Fukuisaurus*, suggested by two characters (*i.e.*, posterolateral process of sternum, distalmost dentary tooth positioned medial to coronoid process of dentary), is more derived than *Camptosaurus*, probably belonging to the "Styracosterna" (a monophyletic group proposed by Sereno 1999*b*, including *Probactrosaurus*, *Iguanodon*, *Ouranosaurus*, *Protohadros*, and Hadrosauridae). However, *Fukuisaurus* seems not to be a hadrosaurid, based upon a number of characters (*e.g.*, narrow rostrum, probable presence of paraquadratic foramen on quadratojugal, asymmetrical maxillary teeth, maxillary teeth not miniaturized; see Head 1998).

Based upon earlier phylogenetic analyses (*i.e.*, Kobayashi and Azuma 1999; Head and Kobayashi 2001), *Fukuisaurus* is basal to the clade of *Probactrosaurus*, *Eolambia*, *Protohadros*, and all higher iguanodontian taxa, while its relationships with *Iguanodon*, *Ouranosaurus*, and *Altihrinus* are uncertain.

A new phylogenetic analysis by Kobayashi and Azuma (2003), utilizing mostly cranial characters, was carried out mainly to resolve the relationships of *Fukuisaurus* with derived, nonhadrosaurid iguan-

odontians. As the authors noted, *Fukuiosaurus* shares with *Altirhinus* (see Norman 1998), *Ouranosaurus* (Taquet 1976), and *Eolambia* (2001) an accessory foramen on the surangular; with *Altirhinus*, *Iguanodon*, and *Ouranosaurus* (Norman) a paraquadratic foramen; tooth morphology resembling that of *Altirhinus*, especially in lacking secondary ridges in some maxillary teeth; with *Camptosaurus* and *Ouranosaurus*, premaxilla-maxilla sutural surface narrowing caudodorsally, but widening in *Iguanodon* (Weishampel 1984); *Fukuisaurus* lacking the iguanodontid character (see Norman) of a long caudolateral projection of the jugal process of the maxilla; *Fukuisaurus* sharing with *Protohadros* and higher taxa a possibly synampomorphic character (Head 1998) (*i.e.*, elevation of lacrimal process of maxilla, with medial displacement of antorbital fenestra).

This analysis showed *Fukuisaurus* to be a definitive derived nonhadrosaurid iguanodontian, closely related to yet apparently more derived than the clade of *Iguanodon* plus *Ouranosaurus*, and more basal to the clade comprising *Altirhinus*, *Probactrosaurus*, *Eolambia*, *Portohadros*, *Bactrosaurus*, *Telmatosaurus*, and Hadrosauridae.

Furthermore, as had already been suggested (see S3, "Systematics" chapter), Kobayashi and Azuma's (2003) analysis supports the interpretation of Iguanodontidae as a paraphyletic grouping, excluding *Altirhinus* (see Norman). Also, it supports a monophyletic relationship shared by *Iguanodon* and *Ouranosaurus*, and shows that all Early Cretaceous Asian taxa (*e.g.*, *Fukuisaurus*, *Altirhunus*, and *Probactrosaurus*)

have paraphyletic relationships, and are more derived than the *Iguanodon* plus *Ouranosaurus* clade and basal to the clade of *Eolambia* plus higher taxa.

The discovery of *Fukuisaurus* in Japan reveals a wider geographical distribution of the Iguanodontia in eastern Asia, also supporting a temporal extension of this clade in Japan. As shown by the topology of Kobayashi and Azuma's phylogenetic tree, derived, nonhadrosaurid iguanodontians established distribution in Laurasia, with either an independent dispersal (*Ouranosaurus*) to Africa or an origin in Africa, followed by a dispersal into Laurasia. Distribution of the Iguanodontia extended into eastern Asia during the Early to Middle Cretaceous for *Fukuisaurus* (late Hauterivian–Barremian), *Altirhinus* (late Albian–early Albian; see Norman), *Probactrosaurus* (Aptian–Albian; see Rozdestvensky 1967), the Mongolian *Iguanodon orientalis* (?Cenomanian; Rozdestvensky, 1952, 1967), with a dispersal into North America.

Pleurokinesis in the iguanodontian skull occurs in *Hypsilophodon*, *Iguanodon* and Hadrosauridae as an adaptation for more efficient mastication (see Norman). However, the skull of *Fukuisaurus* possesses a strong maxilla-vomer articulation. This condition, Kobayashi and Azuma (2003) pointed out, suggests that the skull of *Fukuisaurus* was uniquely nonpleurokinetic skull, despite similarities between this genus and other iguanodontians. Consequently, the authors suggested, given its absence in the more derived *Fukuisaurus*, the presence of a pleurokinetic skull may be a plesiomorphic state for the Iguanodontia.

Key references: Azuma and Currie (1990); Azuma and Tomida (1997); Head (1998, 2001); Head and Kobayashi (2001); Kobayashi and Azuma (1999, 2003); Norman (1998); Rozdestvensky (1952, 1967); Sereno (1999*b*); Taquet (1976); Tashiro and Okuhira (1993); Weishampel (1984).

†GARUDIMIMUS

Saurischia: Eusaurischia: Theropoda: Neotheropoda: Tetanurae: Avetheropoda: Coelurosauria: Tyrannoraptora: Maniraptoriformes: Ornithomimosauria: Garudimimidae.

Diagnosis of genus (as for type species): Jaw articulation caudally positioned; fossae at base of dorsal process of supraoccipital; proximal caudal vertebrae having paired depressions on neural spines; deep groove on lateral surface of pedal phalanx III-2 (Kobayashi and Barsbold 2004).

Comments: In 1981, Rinchen Barsbold named and briefly described *Garudimimus brevipes*, a new type species of primitive yet toothless "ostrich dinosaur," based upon a single specimen—(GIN 100/13, a well-preserved skull with associated incomplete postcrania—collected during the Joint Soviet-Mongolian Paleontogical Expedition from the Upper Cretaceous Bayanshiree Formation in southeastern Mongolia.

Recently, Kobayashi and Barsbold (2004), in an abstract for a poster, reassessed the holotype of *G. brevipes*, gleaning from it "a great deal of anatomical information, which allows us to revise the original diagnosis of this taxon and to make comparisons with other ornithomimosaur taxa to understand the evolution of the clade." Some of the characters used in Barsbold's original diagnosis (*i.e.*, short ilia; short metatarsals; exposure of proximal end of metatarsal III; pedal digit I; lack of pleurocoels) are actually not apomorphies of the genus, but rather diagnose larger clades, the authors stated.

In briefly describing the type specimen of *G. brevipes*, Kobayashi and Barsbold observed the following: Metatarsals displaying nonarctometatarsalian condition as in *Harpymimus okladnikovi* (see *Harpymimus* entry); metatarsal III intermediate in construction between *H. okladnikovi* and arctometatarsalian condition seen in *Gallimimus* sp. (GIN 100/14) and other derived forms (Ornithomimidae).

As Kobayashi and Barsbold pointed out, *G. brevipes* is distinguished as the only toothless, nonoviraptorid ornithomimosaur, its jaws probably having been covered by a rhamphotheca. This condition, according to the authors, combined with the development of a cutting edge in the dentary of this dinosaur "suggest the acquisition of feeding habits similar to ornithomimids."

Key references: Barsbold (1981); Kobayashi and Barsbold (2004).

†GASTONIA

Ornithischia: Predentata: Genasauria: Thyreophora: Thyreophoroidea: Eurypoda: Ankylosauria: Ankylosauridae.

Comments: Brill and Carpenter (2004), in an abstract for a poster, briefly described a large slab of articulated dermal armor belonging to the ankylosaur *Gastonia* (see *S1*, *S2*, and *S3*), collected at Lorrie's Bone Bed Site, a monospecific bonebed in the Lower Cretaceous Cedar Mountain Formation of east-central Utah.

The authors described this material as follows: Osteoderms arranged in "distinctive series of interconnecting rosettes comprising large osteoderms surrounded by rings of smaller osteoderms," fitting together closely "like tiles"; largest osteoderms (35 to 55 millimeters in diameter) roughly elliptical, peaks short, typically off-center; peaks asymmetrical, pitted; large osteoderms often with faint grooves radiating

Skeletal cast of *Gastonia burgei* mounted at the North American Museum of Ancient Life.

from peaks to margins; smaller osteoderms (six to 25 millimeters in diameter) irregularly shaped polygons having straight margins, there interfacing with neighboring element; smaller osteoderms with flat, parallel top, base surface having rough texture.

As Brill and Carpenter pointed out, the armor sheet was preserved with its external surface up and found in mudstone directly overlaying a hard concretion layer with a thickness of from approximately 20 to 30 centimeters. Also, "The sheet is undulating, conceivably indicating that the skin was flexible when deposited." Brill and Carpenter noted that cervical and dorsal ribs, fragments of vertebrae, ossified tendons, and one ulna were found adjacent to the armor sheet, suggesting — along with the absence of larger armor elements — that this skin was from the cranial region of the animal.

McWhinney, Matthias and Carpenter (2004), in an abstract for a poster, investigated corticated pressure erosions, or "pitting" — a pattern of pathologic depressions "clearly not associated with taphonomic alteration — in *Gastonia* osteodermal armor recovered from Lorrie's Bone Bed, this site having yielded to date at least 12 individuals of this genus. Also included in this study, for correlation purposes, was ankylosaurian osteodermal armor from other collections.

The following observation was noted by McWhinney *et al.*: Internal wall of each depression lined with cortical bone, indicating antermortem osteoblastic response to unknown disease process (this characteristic "useful in distinguishing this pathology from a nonpathologic, postmortem alteration as seen in exposed, eroded trabecular bone"). Based upon the cortical erosion seen in modern animal and human bone, McWhinney *et al.* suggested that probable differential etiologies in the ankylosaurian samples include "foreign body granuloma, intraosseous epidermoid inclusion cyst, fungal or bacterial infection, and glomus tumor." Aside from their cause, the authors suggested, these "pits" should better "be referred to as 'corticate pressure corosions.'"

In their review of the Ankylosauria, Vickaryous, Maryańska and Weishampel (2004) identified through cladistic analysis the type species *Gastonia burgei* as a member of the family Ankylosauridae (*contra* other previous assessments, *e.g.*, Kirkland 1998*a*, see S1).

Note: For a brief report on the taphonomy of the Dalton Wells Dinosaur Quarry in the Cedar Mountain Formation of Utah, a site that has already yielded the remains of from eight to nine *Gastonia* individuals, see the abstract by Britt, Eberth, Scheetz and Greengalgh (2004). See also the abstract by Greengalgh, Nolte, Lyman and Britt (2004) for a report on the integration of digital maps and data tables in facilitating the evaluation of the Dalton Wells Dinosaur Quarry.

Key references: Brill and Carpenter (2004); Britt, Eberth, Scheetz and Greenhalgh (2004); Greengalgh, Nolte, Lyman and Britt (2004); Kirkland (1998*a*); McWhinney, Matthias and Carpenter (2004); Vickaryous, Maryańska and Weishampel (2004).

†GENYODECTES

Saurischia: Eusaurischia: Eusaurischia: Theropoda: Neotheropoda: Ceratosauria: ?Ceratosauridae.

Diagnosis of genus (as for type species): Differing from all other theropods (with possible exception of *Ceratosaurus*) in premaxillary teeth being arranged in overlapping *en-echelon* pattern; and longest maxillary tooth crowns longer apicobasally than minimal dorsoventral mandibular depth; differing from *Ceratosaurus* in having four (rather than three) premaxillary teeth (Rauhut 2004*b*).

Comments: In 1901, Arthur Smith Woodward described the new genus and species *Genyodectes serus*, based on a fragmentary specimen (MLP 26–39) — a partial snout, including almost complete premaxillae, fragments of both maxillae, and dentaries (all with teeth), parts of both supradentaries, and fragments of the left splenial — collected from an unspecified geographic and stratigraphic provenance from Chubut Province, Argentina (for more information and illustrations, see *D:TE, S1*). The type material of this taxon is historically important, as noted more than a century later by Oliver W. M. Rauhut (2004*b*), being "the first unquestionable non-avian theropod dinosaur to be described from South America."

As Rauhut related, the type material of *G. serus* was recently prepared, following its removal from the artificial matrix in which it had been displayed at the Museo de La Plata. This preparation "revealed new information regarding the internal surfaces of the jaws, which were previously still largely covered in matrix." Rauhut redescribed the holotype in detail, taking into account "our much improved knowledge of South American theropods and theropods in general." Also, Rauhut deduced the probable geographic provenance — the lower part of the Cerro Barcino Formation (Chubut Group; Aptian–Albian), at Cañadón Grande, in central Chubut Province, Argentina (see paper for additional details) that yielded the type material.

As Rauhut noted, the phylogenetic placement and relationships of *Genyodectes* have been problematic. Over the decades since its original description by Woordward, this genus has been classified with the Megalosauridae (Huene 1929), the Tyrannosauridae (Huene 1932; ="Dinodontidae" of his usage), and possibly with the ceratosaurian clade Abelisauridae (Paul 1988), while some workers (*e.g.*, Tykoski and Rowe 2004; see "Systematics" chapter) have considered *Genyodectes serus* to be a *nomen dubium*.

Based upon he details gleaned from the prepared holotype, however, Rauhut found *Genyodectes* clearly differing from all other known South American theropods; moreover, based upon the characters presented in that author's diagnosis, this genus can now be considered a valid taxon, regardless of the poor preservation of its type material.

Although the extremely fragmentary nature of the holotype precluded a formal phylogenetic analysis of *Genyodectes* within Theropoda, Rauhut cited the following characters indicative of neoceratosaurian affinities and, more precisely, a relationship with the family Ceratosauridae: Fused interdental plates; maxillary and dentary teeth having pronounced flat or slightly concave area adjacent to serrated carinae; premaxillary teeth considerably shorter than maxillary teeth; strongly compressed, very long maxillary teeth.

In conclusion, Rauhut found this taxon significant in adding "a further lineage of neoceratosaurians to the already diverse South American record of the group." Furthermore, along with the ?abelisaur *Ligabueno* and also other fragmentary abelisaurid remains from the Barremian La Paloma member of the Cerro Barcino Formation (see Rauhut, Cladera, Vickers-Rich and Rich 2003), this record possibly suggests an early South American diversification of the Neoceratosauria well before the Late Cretaceous (see Lamanna, Martinez and Smith 2002).

Key references: Huene (1929, 1932); Lamanna, Martinez and Smith (2002); Paul (1988); Rauhut (2004*b*); Rauhut, Cladera, Vickers-Rich and Rich (2003); Tykoski and Rowe (2004); Woodward (1901).

†GOBITITAN   You, Tang and Luo 2003

Saurischia: Eusaurischia: Sauropodomorpha: Sauropoda: Eusauropoda: Neosauropoda: Macronaria: Titanosauriformes: Titanosauria *incertae sedis*.

Name derivation: "Gobi [geographical region of Mongolia and Inner Mongolia]" + Greek *Titan* [offspring of Uranus and Gaea, symbolic of brute strength and large size].

Type species: *G. shenzhouensis* You, Tang and Luo 2003.

Other species: [None.]

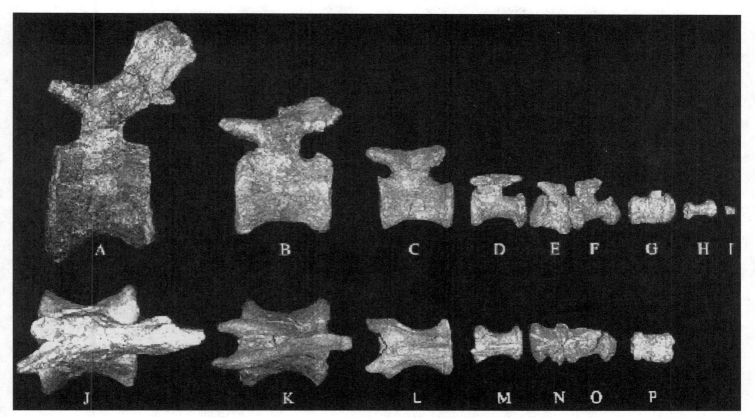

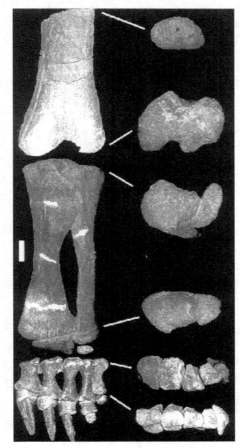

Occurrence: Xinminbao Group, Gongpoquan Basin, Gansu Province, China.

Age: Middle Cretaceous (Albian).

Known material/holotype: IVPP 12579, articulated series of 41 middle and distal caudal vertebrae, left hindlimb lacking proximal half of femur.

Diagnosis of genus (as for type species): Basal titanosaurian distinguished by higher proximal than distal centrum articular faces in middle caudal vertebrae, distal placement of neural arches on most proximal distal caudal vertebrae, relatively short and rodlike distalmost caudal vertebrae (You, Tang and Luo 2003).

Comments: Introduced and informally described by You (2002) in his unpublished Ph.D. dissertation on the Mazongshan dinosaur assemblage from "late Early" [=Middle] Cretaceous of northwest China (see S3), the type species *Gobititan shenzhouensis*, among the most basal members of Titanosauria, was founded upon caudal vertebrae and an almost complete hindlimb (IVPP 12579) from the Middle Gray Unit of the Xinminbao Group, Gongpoquan Basin, Mazongshan area, northwestern Gansu Province, China. The holotype of this type species was collected during summer, 1999, during explorations of the Sino-American Horse Mane Mountain (Ma-ZongShan) Dinosaur Project, comprising personnel from the Carnegie Museum of Natural History, the University

Above: Gobititan shenzhouensis, IVPP 12579, holotype caudal vertebrae 15 (A, J), 21 (B, K), (28) (C, L), 33 (D, M), 34 (E, N), 35 (F, O), 37 (G, P), 42 (H), and 53 (I). Scale = 5 cm. (After You, Tang and Luo 2003.)

Gobititan shenzhouensis, IVPP 12579, holotype left hindlimb. Scale = 10 cm. (After You, Tang and Luo 2003.)

of Pennsylvania, and the Institute of Vertebrate Paleontology and Paleoanthropology (You, Tang and Luo 2003).

As You *et al.* noted, the existence of three characters of the middle and distal caudal vertebrae and hindlimb — *i.e.*, proximally positioned neural arches in middle caudals (see Salgado, Coria and Calvo 1997; Upchurch 1998); simple, undivided chevron blades (Wilson 1999*a*; Curry Rogers and Forster 2001); backward and downward curved middle and distal chevron blades (Curry Rogers and Forster) — confirm the placement of *Gobititan* within the Titanosauriformes.

In comparing this new genus with various basal members of Titanosauria, You *et al.* observed the following: In the African genus *Malawisaurus*, the middle caudal vertebrae are slightly procoelous and have strongly proximally extended prezygapophyses, these derived titanosaurian characters not found in *Gobititan*; nor is the derived titanosaurian character of a very deep hemal canal, seen in the South American *Andesaurus*, present in *Gobititan*. In the Asian *Phuwiangosaurus*, the femur is more slender than in *Gobititan* and has a less pronounced distomedial process, and the proximal ends of the tibia and fibula do not expand transversely as in the new genus. In general shape, the tibia and fibula of the Asian genus *Tangvayosaurus* is closer to *Gobititan* than to *Phuwiangosaurus*, although the proximal end of the fibula in *Tangvayosaurus* is less expanded transversely as in *Gobititan*, and the middle caudal centrum possesses a distal higher than proximal articular surface (the opposite condition in *Gobititan*). Comparing two possible middle caudal vertebrae of Gobititan to those of the basal titanosaur *Jiangshanosaurus*, You *et al.* observed that the characteristic higher proximal than distal centrum articular faces of these vertebrae in the former genus do not exist in the latter. Consequently, *Gobititan* is most likely a basal member of the Titanosauria, closely related to *Tangvayosaurus*, less derived than *Malawisaurus* and *Andesaurus*, and more derived than *Phuwiangosaurus*.

As three very basal titanosaur genera (*i.e.*, *Gobititan*, *Phuwiangosaurus*, and *Tangvayosaurus*) are known from the Early to Middle Cretaceous (Aptian–Albian) of Asia, You *et al.* suggested the possibility of an Asian origin for the Titanosauria.

Key references: Curry Rogers and Forster (2001); Salgado, Coria and Calvo (1997); Upchurch (1998); Wilson (1999*a*); You (2002); You, Tang and Luo (2003).

†GONGXIANOSAURUS
Saurischia: Eusaurischia: Sauropodomorpha: ?Sauropoda.

Comment: In their review of the Sauropoda, Upchurch, Barrett and Dodson (2004) found the genus *Gongxianosaurus* (see *D:TE*) to be too poorly known to be diagnosed.

As these authors noted, the sauropod status of this genus cannot be confirmed, although it is a quite large animal (body length of 14 meters, or approximately 47 feet) for a prosauropod, its forelimbs are long, and it does present the following additional potential sauropod synapomorphies: Short pubis (subequal to ischial length); femur straight in lateral aspect, substantially longer than tibia.

Key reference: Upchurch, Barrett and Dodson (2004).

†GORGOSAURUS
Saurischia: Eusaurischia: Theropoda: Neotheropoda: Tetanurae: Avetheropoda: Coelurosauria: Tyrannoraptora: Maniraptoriformes: Tyrannoraptora: Tyrannosauroidea: Tyrannosauridae: Albertosaurinae.

Diagnosis of genus (as for type species): Autapomorphies consisting of the following: first maxillary tooth incisiform; palatine having slotlike articular surface for maxilla; articular surface of maxilla not reaching dorsal margin of maxillary ramus of palatine (Holtz 2004, following Carr, Williamson and Schwimmer, in press).

Comments: Currie (2003*b*), in a study of the cranial anatomy of tyrannosaurid theropods from the Late Cretaceous of Alberta, Canada (*i.e.*, *Gorgosaurus*, *Albertosaurus*, and *Daspletosaurus*), described in detail the skulls of all three genera. Included in this study was Currie's description of the cranial anatomy of the type species *Gorgosaurus libratus*, primarily based on the skull belonging to a virtually complete, presumably young adult skeleton (TMP.91.3.500) — to date, one of the finest specimens recovered belonging to this taxon — collected in 1991 from the badlands of Dinosaur Provincial Park (see Keiran 1999). As measured by Currie, this skeleton is 5.1 meters (almost 18 feet) in length.

In addition to describing these Canadian tyrannosaurid skulls, Currie again emphasized the generic separation (*contra* Carr 2003) between *Gorgosaurus* and the related yet geologically younger *Albertosaurus*.

As Currie related, Russell (1970), at a time when cladistic methodology was not the norm in paleontological classification, synonymized these two taxa because he could not find any salient differences between them. This was, however, "largely because the only cranial material of *Albertosaurus* that was available to study at that time consisted of several partial skulls that had 'not been satisfactorily characterized' (Gilmore

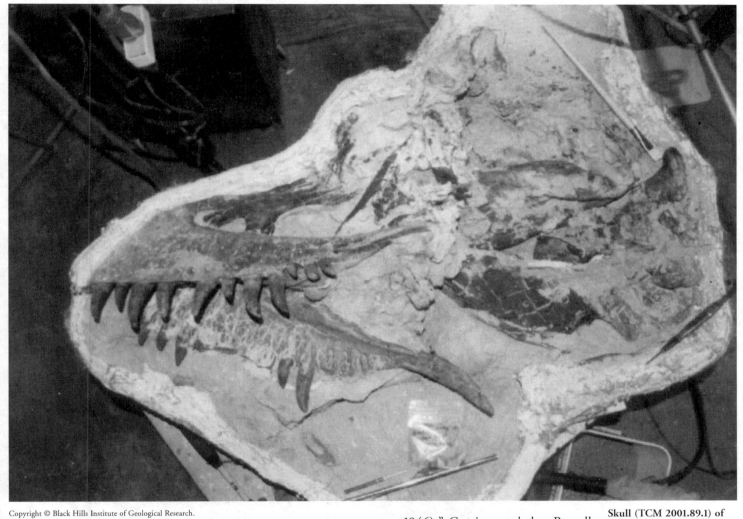

1946)." Currie noted that Russell primarily distinguished the type species *Albertosaurus sarcophagus* from *G. libratus* based upon the different times in which these animals lived, and also based on differences in relative lengths of the dentary tooth row (compared with metatarsal IV), the scapula (compared with femur length), and pubis plus astragalus (compared with femur length). Such proportional differences, however, are not very reliable, according to Currie, for taxa in which growth for most cranial and appendicular dimensions is allometric.

Based upon the subsequent

Skull (TCM 2001.89.1) of *Gorgosaurus* sp. being prepared at the Black Hills Institute of Geological Research for display at The Children's Museum of Indianapolis.

Skull (TCM 2001.89.1) of *Gorgosaurus* sp. following preparation by the Black Hills Institute of Geological Research.

Gorgosaurus

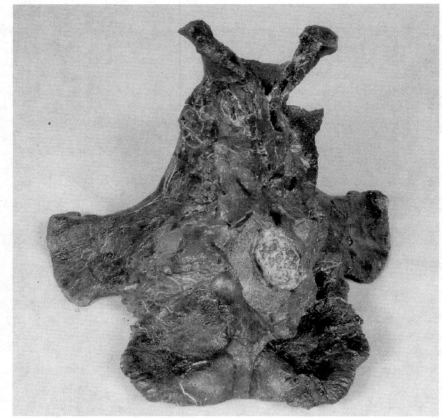

Braincase with tumor (TCM 2001.89.1) of *Gorgosaurus* sp. described by Dallas Evans and Peter L. Larson.

collection of additional specimens of these genera, Currie noted the following differences between *Gorgosaurus* and *Albertosaurus*: *Gorgosaurus* slightly smaller than Albertosaurus, with more robust adult specimens; most *Albertosaurus* specimens (compared with all other known tyrannosaurids) having more numerous, deeper pits in ventral surfaces of maxillary palatal shelves for accommodating tips of dentary teeth; occipital condyle more ventrally oriented in *Albertosaurus* than in *Gorgosaurus* (but not to degree in other tyrannosaurids); braincase box (Bakker, Williams and Currie 1988; see below) in *Albertosaurus* mediolaterally wide, opposite dimensions in *Gorgosaurus*; nasal-frontal suture more complex in *Albertosaurus*, paired midline processes of nasals expanding caudally (tapering in *Gorgosaurus*), extending farther backwards than caudolateral processes of nasal; prefrontal apparently having very limited dorsal exposure in *Albertosaurus*, lacrimal not plugging into socket in frontal, more similar to *Tyrannosaurus* than to *Gorgosaurus*; *Albertosaurus* differing from *Gorgosaurus* and all other known tyrannosaurids in having angular suture between exoccipital and basioccipital in occipital condyle.

Currie noted that among the most important studies supporting generic separation of *Gorgosaurus* and *Albertosaurus* was that of Bakker *et al.*, in which

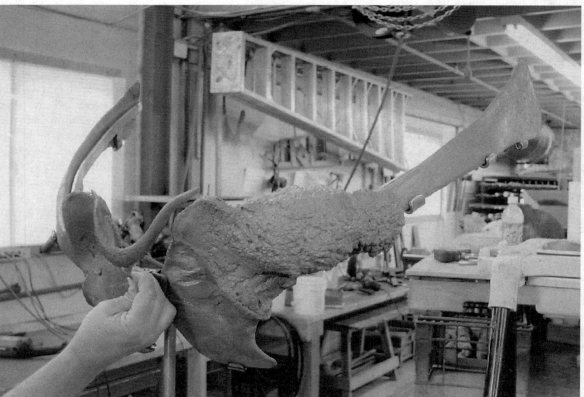

Pathological scapula and corocoid (TCM 2001.89.1) of *Gorgosaurus* sp.

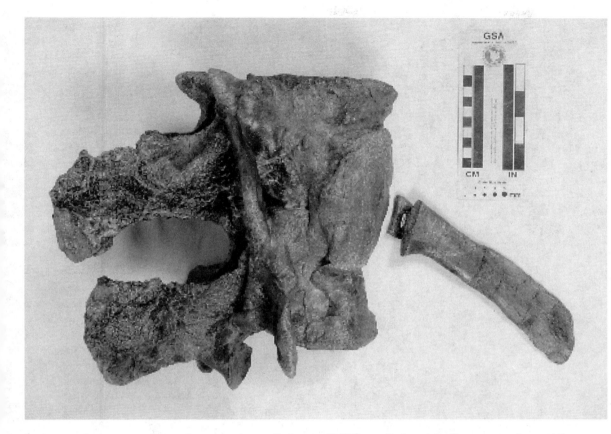

Fused fourth and fifth caudal vertebrae (TCM 2001.89.1) of *Gorgosaurus* sp.

braincase characters were used as criteria to distinguish various tyrannosaurid genera. In *Gorgosaurus*, the basal tubera of the braincase are wide and thick, while those in *Albertosaurus* are reduced and thin. seemingly reflecting a reduced size of attachments for tendonous muscles. Bakker *et al.* observed in *Albertosaurus* larger paired pneumatic foramina in the ceiling of the basisphenoid than in *Gorgosaurus*. Also (as stated above), the occipital condyle is more ventrally oriented. Currie also cited 14 characters listed by Holtz

(2001) to distinguish *Gorgosaurus* from *Albertosaurus*, two of them regarded by Holtz as unique in *Gorgosaurus* among all known tyrannosaurids (see S3).

In Currie's opinion, substantial morphological differences therefore distinguish *Gorgosaurus* from *Albertosaurus*, "although it is still an arbitrary decision as to whether the distinction is generic, specific or even subspecific." However, albertosaurine specimens currently being found to the south (New Mexico) and

Life restoration and skeletal reconstruction of an immature *Gorgosaurus libratus*, drawings based upon a complete skeleton (TMP 91.36.500) collected from the Dinosaur Park Formation of Alberta, Canada. (After Currie 2003*b*.)

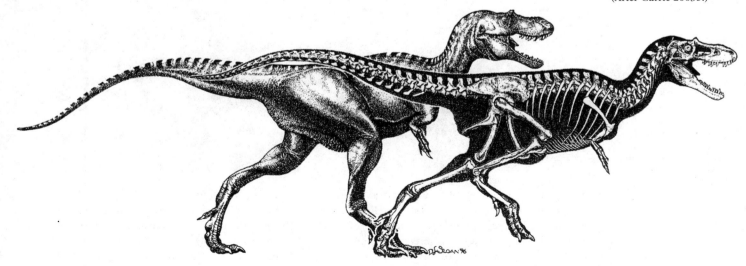

Skeleton (TCM 2001.89.1) of *Gorgosaurus* sp. mounted at the Black Hills Museum of Natural History.

north (Alaska) exhibit anatomical characters unknown in either of the Alberta taxa. Consequently, Currie suggested that more latitude is possible in assessing the relationships of these new specimens when maintaining the generic distinction of *Gorgosaurus* and *Alber-*tosaurus. Moreover, "there are as many anatomical differences between *Albertosaurus* and *Gorgosaurus* as there are between *Daspletosaurus*, *Tarbosaurus* and *Tyrannosaurus*"; therefore, based upon what is currently known of these dinosaurs, Currie found it

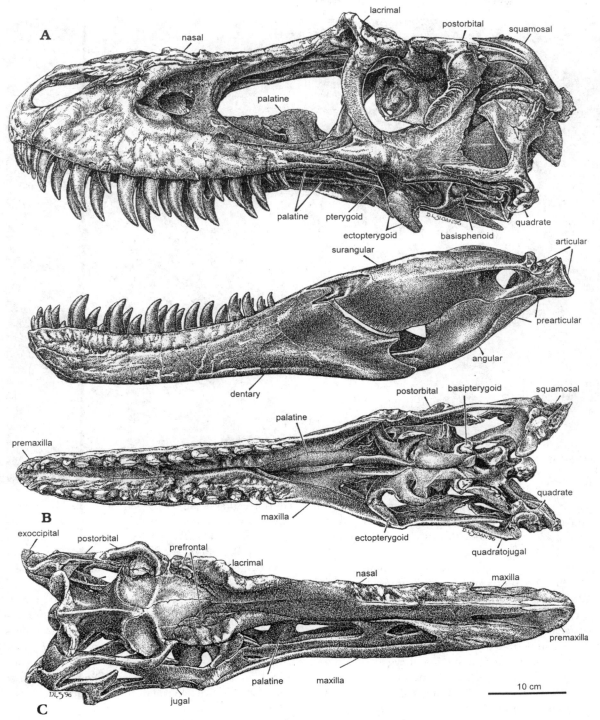

Skull (TMP 91.36.500) of an immature *Gorgosaurus libratus* individual in A. left lateral, B. palatal, and C. dorsal views. (After Currie 2003*b*.)

advisable to regard *Gorgosaurus* and *Albertosaurus* as generically distinct.

Evans and Larson (2003), in a published abstract, reported briefly on numerous pathologies found on a recently discovered robust (female morphotype) skeleton, referred to *Gorgosaurus* sp., from the Two Medicine Formation (Campanian) of Montana, these offering "insight into behavior, sexual dimorphism, and disease."

The pathologies found by these authors included the following: Calloused gastralia (fracture and calcified hematoma), bifurcated pedal ungual 1 (split claw sheath), remodelled scapulocoracoid (consistent with proliferative process and fracture), calloused, deformed right fibula (fracture and tendon retraction), detached greater trochanter of left femur, with bone remodeling and fistulous tracts (trauma, reattachment

Detail of maxillary teeth belonging to skeleton (TCM 2001.89.1) of *Gorgosaurus* sp. during its preparation at the Black Hills Institute of Geological Research.

and osteomyelitis), and calloused dentaries with fistulous tracts and subsequent loss of tooth positions (trauma and tooth root abscess with osteomyelitis).

According to Evans and Larson, two of these pathologies seemingly relate to sexual dimorphism — *i.e.*, fusion of centra and shared chevrons of fourth and fifth caudal vertebrae (presumably responding to stress created by "overload" of mounting male), collapse of articular surfaces of at least 11 caudal centra (probably resulting from decalcification due to skeletal stripping of calcium for production of eggs).

Also, Evans and Larson found a heterogenous, sphere-shaped mass occupying the caudal aspect of the braincase to be "consistent with the presence of a large tumor which could have caused the incapacitation and death of this individual."

Note: For almost nine decades, various paleontologists have noted wear surfaces on the sides of the teeth of tyrannosaurid theropods. Lambe (1917) first suggested that these wear surfaces — "of the inner surface of the upper teeth with the outer surface of the lower ones" — in such tyrannosaurid genera as *Gorgosaurus* were the result of tooth-to-tooth rubbing

during eating. Lambe's original interpretation of these worn surfaces was subsequently challenged, however, by subsequent workers (*e.g.*, Farlow and Brinkman 1994; Molnar 1998) suggesting that the shapes, placements, and incidents of the wear surfaces in tyrannosaurid teeth do not indicate tooth contact.

More recently, Schubert and Ungar (2005), in an attempt to resolve this issue, made a study of numerous lateral teeth belonging to indeterminate tyrannosaurid taxa — presumably either *Gorgosaurus* or *Daspletosaurus* — collected from the Upper Cretaceous (middle Campanian) Oldman and Dinosaur Park formations (Judith River Group) and housed at the Royal Tyrrell Museum of Paleontology. Observations by these authors of the wear surface shapes, locations, and wear patterning suggested "two different types of features, each with different etiologies," including spalled surfaces (*i.e.*, generally short, squat, proximal edges irregular or perpendicular to long axis of tooth) and occlusal facets (*i.e.*, generally elongated, elliptical, following long axis of tooth).

Consequently, Schubert and Ungar concluded that the wear surfaces found on these tyrannosaurid lateral teeth were probably the result of two independent factors — antemortem enamel spalling, followed by surface smoothing due to wear (*e.g.*, teeth chipping while the animal bit down on bones during eating); and attrition, resulting from regular contact between the lingual surfaces of the maxillary teeth and the labial surfaces of the dentary teeth (*e.g.*, postmortem repeated contact between these surfaces), similar to features seen in some herbivorous dinosaurs and mammals. As the latter surface feature was not observed on all of the tyrannosaurid specimens examined, and because no evidence for such wear was found in extant crocodilians or varanid lizards, Schubert and Ungar were unable to determine whether this contact of upper and lower tooth surfaces was adaptive or surrendipidous. However, the attritional wear facets as described by these authors are unusual for reptiles and perhaps a unique feature among Tyrannosauridae. Such "tooth–tooth contact may have allowed efficient slicing or perhaps even honing, whether fortuitous or the result of genetic adaptation."

Key reference: Bakker, Williams and Currie (1988); Carr (2003); Carr, Williamson and Schwimmer (in press); Currie (2003*b*); Evans and Larson (2003); Farlow and Brinkman (1994); Gilmore (1946*a*); Holtz (2001, 2004); Keiran (1999); Lambe (1917); Molnar (1998); Russell (1970); Schubert and Ungar (2005).

GRACILIRAPTOR Xu and Wang 2004

Saurischia: Eusaurischia: Theropoda: Neotheropoda: Tetanurae: Avetheropoda: Coelurosauria: Tyrannoraptora: Maniraptoriformes: Maniraptora: Metornithes: Paraves: Deinonychosauria: Dromaeosauridae *incertae sedis*.

Name derivation: Latin *gracilis* = "slender" + Latin *raptor* = "thief" ["commonly used for dromaeosaurid dinosaur names"]).

Type species: *G. lujiatunensis* Xu and Wang 2004.

Other species: [None.]

Occurrence: Yixian Formation, Liaoning Province, China.

Age: Early Cretaceous.

Known material/holotype: IVPP V 13474, fragmentary maxilla with some teeth, several caudal vertebrae, almost complete forelimbs, partial hindlimbs.

Diagnosis of genus (as for type species): Differing from all other known dromaeosaurid species based on the following derived features: laminar structure connecting postzygapophyses of midcaudal vertebrae; middle caudals extremely long and slender; ungual of manual digit I much smaller than that of II; proximal end of metacarpal III strongly expanded; tibiotarsus

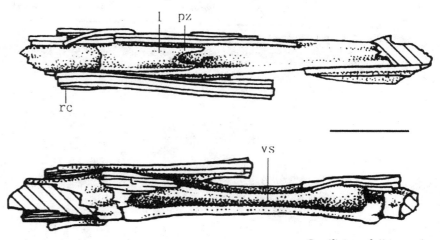

extremely slender; proximal tibiotarsal shaft rectangular in cross section; astragalar medial condyle significantly expanded caudally; metatarsal II distally wider than other metatarsals; pedal phalanx III-1 long, slender (Xu and Wang 2004).

Comments: Distinguished as the oldest definitive dromaeosaurid (at least three million years older than the fossil beds that yielded *Sinornithosaurus*; see Swisher, Wang, Zhou, Wang, Jin, Zhang, Xu, Zhang and Wang 2001), the genus *Graciliraptor* was based on a partial maxilla bearing some teeth, and some postcranial elements (IVPP V 13474) recovered from the lower part of the Yixian Formation, at Lujiatan, Beipiao City, in western Liaoning, China (Xu and Wang 2004).

Xu and Wang identified the following dromaeosaurid features in the holotype of *Graciliraptor lujiatunensis* (despite the incomplete nature of the

Graciliraptor lujiatunensis, IVPP V 13474, holotype midcaudal vertebrae in (above) dorsal and (below) ventral views. Scale = 1 cm. (After Xu and Wang 2004.)

Graciliraptor lujiatunensis, IVPP V 13474, holotype A. right and B. left forelimbs. Scale = 1 cm. (After Xu and Wang 2004.)

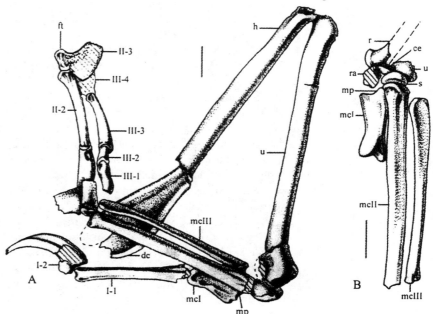

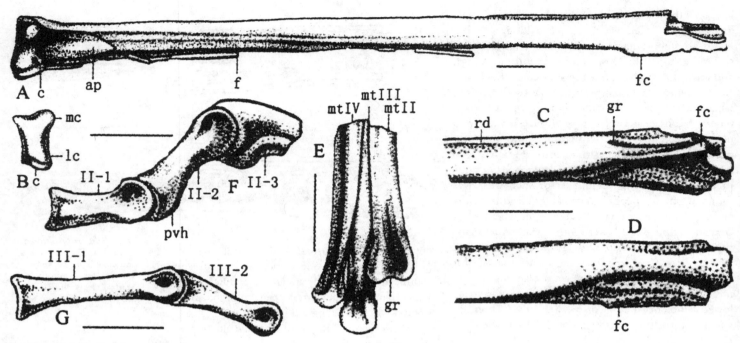

Graciliraptor lujiatunensis, IVPP V 13474, holotype A. left tibiotarsus and fibula (cranial view), B. left astragalus and calcaneum (distal view), C. right tibiotarsus (lateral view), D. right tibiotarsus (caudal view), E. left metatarsus (ventral view), F. left pedal digit II (medial view), and G. right pedal phalanges III-1 and III-2 (medial view). Scale = 1 cm. (After Xu and Wang 2004.)

specimen): Caudal vertebrae having extremely elongated prezygapophyses and chevrons (*e.g.*, see Ostrom 1990); significant size differences between mesial and distal denticles on maxillary teeth; significantly shortened manual phalanx III-2 (*e.g.*, see Ostrom 1969*a*).

Among other known members of the Dromaeosauridae, Xu and Wang found *Graciliraptor* to be most closely related to *Sinornithosaurus* and *Microraptor*, sharing with these Liaoning genera such features as the following: Radius significantly thinner than ulna; ungual of manual digit III much smaller than II; manual digit I significantly shortened; manual phalanx III-2 extremely short; manual phalanx III-2 with proximoventral heel.

Being the oldest known dromaeosaurid, *Graciliraptor lujiatunensis* provides new information important for understanding the early evolution of the Dromaeosauridae. As Xu and Wang noted, the holotype of this new species exhibits various features similar to those of basal avians (*e.g.*, significantly elongated caudal vertebrae; semilunate carpal small, primarily contacting metacarpal II; short manual digit II), thereby providing additional evidence for a close relationship between Dromaeosauridae and Aves. However, this species is also similar to Troodontidae in some respects (*e.g.*, middle caudal vertebrae lacking neural spines, bearing rather shallow groove on dorsal surface; middle caudals bearing deep sulcus ventrally). This combination of characters constituted to Xu and Wang additional evidence supporting a close relationship between the Dromaeosauridae, Troodontidae, and Aves.

The discovery of *G. lujiantunensis*, Xu and Wang noted, the fourth dromaeosaurid taxon named from the Jehol Biota, suggests that this theropod group diversified highly during the Early Cretaceous. Moreover, "The temporal distributions of the three paravian groups [see "Systematics" chapter for a contrary placement of Troodontidae] combined with character distributions among the basal dromaeosaurids and troodontids indicate that the basal deinonychosaur split might not be significantly earlier than Hauterivian, possibly in the earliest Cretaceous (Xu and Wang, in submission)."

Key references: Ostrom (1969*a*, 1990); Swisher, Wang, Zhou, Wang, Jin, Zhang, Xu, Zhang and Wang (2001); Xu and Wang (2004).

†**GRAVITHOLUS** [*nomen dubium*]

Ornithischia: Predentata: Genusauria: Cerapoda: Chasmatopia: Marginocephalia: Pachycephalosauria: Pachycephalosauridae: Pachycephalosaurinae.

Type species: *G. albertae* Wall and Galton 1979 [*nomen dubium*].

Comments: In 1979, William P. Wall and Peter M. Galton named and described *Gravitholus albertae*, a new genus and species of large, dome-headed dinosaur known from only one specimen, a frontoparietal dome (TMP [previously PMA] 72.27.1) from the Oldman Formation (verified by D. A. Eberth, personal communication to R. M. Sullivan, 2000) of Alberta, Canada (see *D:TE*).

Williamson and Carr (2003*a*) later suggested

that *G. albertae* is a *nomen dubium* and referred this taxon to *Stegoceras* sp. (see *Stegoceras* entry and *S3*).

More recently, in a revision of the genus *Stegoceras*, Sullivan also addressed the taxonomic status of *Gravitholus*. Considering the original diagnosis of the type species proposed by Wall and Galton (see *D:TE*), Sullivan pointed out that size, one of their criteria, is irrelevant as a character; and that the included large depression on the parietal and also the pitting are artifacts, the latter, also seen in other pachycephalosaurs, and are apparently related to dorsal surface wear. The only possible diagnostic character, Sullivan noted, in Wall and Galton's diagnosis — *i.e.*, small brain size relative to dome size — is ambiguous, the endocranial cavity in *G. albertae* comparing favorably in size with specimens of *Hanssuesia sternbergi*.

As Sullivan observed, the holotype of *G. albertae* resembles that of *Colepiocephale lambei* (see *Colepiocephale* entry) "in having incipiently developed postorbitals, caudal supraorbitals and rostral supraorbitals + prefrontals," but differs in retaining squamosals caudally. The specimen seems to have a broad medial nasal lobe of the frontal, resembling that of *H. sternbergi* (see *Hanssuesia* entry) and, to a lesser extent, *Stegoceras validum*, differing from the latter taxon in lacking a well-developed frontoparietal shelf.

According to Sullivan, the holotype of *G. albertae*, despite the assessment of Williamson and Carr, "cannot be assigned to the monotypic taxon *Stegoceras validum*." Additionally, *G. albertae* more favorably compares with *H. sternbergi* in its seeming possession of caudally positioned squamosals, these being separated by a medial, caudally directed extensions of the parietal. Contrary to *H. sternbergi*, however, the rostral lateral portions of the frontal are not inflated, a condition resulting in a somewhat odd, distinct appearance of the peripheral skull elements.

Sullivan interpreted the apparent fusion of the right caudal and rostral supraorbitals, along with the right prefrontal, and also the noninflated rostral part of the dome, to be aberrations (Maryańska 1990 believing the holotype to be pathologic, a position, based upon her examination of the specimen, also adopted by Sullivan). Lacking these features, Sullivan noted, *G. albertae* would be indistinguishable from *H. sternbergi*. Furthermore, the specimen appears to be slightly asymmetrical, a distortion possibly due to pathology and also postmortem deformation.

In conclusion, given that none of the preserved characters of TMP 72.27.1 are particularly diagnostic, plus the fact that the specimen is badly damaged and perhaps distorted, Sullivan, as had Williamson and Carr, regarded *Gravitholus albertae* as a *nomen dubium*, and found it impossible to synonymize this

Courtesy Robert M. Sullivan.

Gravitholus albertae, TMP 72.21.1, holotype frontoparietal dome.

taxon with any other pachycephalosaurian taxon due to the lack of diagnostic features.

Key references: Maryańska (1990); Sullivan (2003); Wall and Galton (1979); Williamson and Carr (2003*a*).

†GUAIBASAURUS

Saurischia: Eusaurischia: ?Theropoda: Guaibasauridae.

Comments: In 1999, Bonaparte, José F., Jorge Ferigolo, and Ana Maria Ribeiro named and described the primitive saurischian dinosaur *Guaibasaurus candelariai*, based on two partial skeletons (holotype MCN-PV 2355 and referred specimen MCN-PV 2356) recovered from the Caturrita Formation of Rio Grand du Sol, southern Brazil. Originally, Bonaparte *et al.* (see *S2*) referred this taxon to the Saurischia, placing closer to Sauropodomorpha than either to Theropoda or Herrerasauridae (see *S2*).

Langer (2004), however, in a reassessment of basal saurischians (see "Systematics" chapter), pointed out that Bonaparte *et al.* had linked *Guaibasaurus* to Sauropodomorpha based upon several characters (*e.g.*, well-developed ambiens process; unreduced metatarsal I) that are plesiomorphic for Dinosauria. As Langer noted, most basal dinosaurs possess a number of

characters found in *Guaibasaurus* (*e.g.*, femur straight in cranial aspect; cranial trochanter moderately developed; trochanter elongated, with medial depression [*i.e.*, insertion of M. caudofemoralis longus]; reduced metatarsal V). As shown by Bonaparte *et al.*, *Guaibasaurus* has features (*i.e.*, distal tibia with craniocaudally compressed lateral margin; calcaneum with reduced projections) apomorphic within Dinosauria, being found also in Theropoda and Ornithischia. Additionally, Langer pointed out, one character (*i.e.*, ischium massive, distally expanded, with long symphysis) is an apomorphy of the Eusaurischia.

It was Langer's conclusion that there is no strong evidence supporting a close relationship between *Guaibasaurus* and Sauropodomorpha. Rather, Langer's cladistic analysis placed *Guaibasaurus* as a basal member Theropoda, although, that author added, this postulation is weak, supported by only a few apomorphic features. For the present, then, Langer found the exact phylogenetic position of this genus to be uncertain, "although it is clearly more closely related to eusaurischians than to herrerasaurids"; and if a theropod, *Guaibasaurus* is currently the most basal known member of that clade, lacking as it does most synapomorphies of more derived members of the Theropoda.

Key references: Bonaparte, Ferigolo and Ribeiro (1999); Langer (2004).

†HADROSAURUS

Ornithischia: Predentata: Genasauria: Cerapoda: Ornithopoda: Euornithopoda: Iguanodontia: Dryomorpha: Ankylopollexia: Styracosterna: Iguanodontoidea: Hadrosauroidea: Euhadrosauria: Hadrosauridae: Hadrosaurinae: Edmontosaurini.

Diagnosis of genus (as for type species): Autapomorphies of ilium having hooklike preacetabular process that thins dorsoventrally, dorsal edge arching 180 degrees cranioventrally; and ischial shaft arching dorsocaudally, forming dorsally concave profile (Prieto-Marquez, Weishampel and Horner 2003).

Comments: The holotype (ANSP 10005) of the type species *Hadrosaurus foulkii*, the first North American dinosaur known from relatively complete fossil

Hadrosaurus foulkii, ANSP 10005, holotype left ilium. (After Leidy 1859.)

materials and by the first such remains to be mounted (see *D:TE*), was reexamined by Prieto-Marquez, Weishampel and Horner (2003) "to ascertain its systematic position and phylogenetic importance," their results being published in an abstract for a poster.

Performing a cladistic analysis, using 105 characters and including *H. foulkii* and 19 other ornithopod taxa (eight hadrosaurines, six lambeosaurines, and five nonhadrosaurid iguanodontians), Prieto-Marquez found *H. foulkii* to be "part of a large polytomy composed of euhadrosaurian taxa, with some internal differentiation into higher clades (*i.e.*, *Maiasaura*, *Brachylophosaurus*, *Lophorothon* and *Gryposaurus*)." The majority rule consensus tree, however, showed that *H. foulkii*, the unnamed gryposaur currently referred to as "*Kritosaurus*" *australis* (see *D:TE*), and Euhadrosauria share an unresolved relationship, but have a sister-group relationship with *Telmatosaurus* within the context of the Hadrosauridae.

Note: Spamer (2004), in a comprehensive article, chronicled such *Hadrosaurus*-related events as follows: The discovery by neighbors, ca. 1840, of the first recovered remains of *Hadrosaurus foulkii* from the greensand marl on John E. Hopkins' farm, in the Upper Cretaceous Woodbury Formation at Haddonfield, Pennsylvania; the loss of those fossils to history and the collection in 1858 of the remaining elements by the Academy of Natural Sciences of Philadelphia under the direction of Joseph Leidy of that institution, through the urging of Hopkins' friend and Academy member William Parker Foulke; the 1859 transfer of those bones, first to the University of Pennsylvania, and shortly afterwards to their permanent home in the Academy collections; Leidy's famous brief description the bones at a December 14, 1859 meeting at the Academy and his subsequent formal naming of *Hadrosaurus foulke* and describing of the material, that same year, in the *Proceedings of the Academy of Natural Sciences of Philadelphia*; the mounting in a bipedal pose of the original fossil material by sculptor Benjamin Waterhouse Hawkins, missing elements supplemented by casts, a scaled-up iguana skull used in place of the missing skull; the exhibition of that skeleton (described in a display label as "Remains of a Great Extinct Lizard") at the Academy; the repairs that were done over the years of the authentic bones incorporated into that mount; and the inevitable fates of the mount and the original fossils of *H. foulkii* at the Academy.

Included in Spamer's article were copies of all extant photographs of the bones of *H. foulkii* and also Hawkins' skeletal reconstruction as they were exhibited at the Academy of Natural Sciences of Philadelphia (for photographs of casts of this skeleton displayed at other museums, see *D:TE*, *S1*, *S2*, and *S3*).

Erratum: In *D:TE*, the figures of the ANSP 10005 elements published by Leidy in 1959 were incorrectly dated as 1858.

Key references: Leidy (1859); Prieto-Marquez, Weishampel and Horner (2003); Spamer (2004).

HANSSUESIA Sullivan 2003

Ornithischia: Predentata: Genusauria: Cerapoda: Chasmatopia: Marginocephalia: Pachycepalosauria: Goyocephala: Homalocephaloidea: Pachycephalosauridae: Pachycephalosaurinae.

Name derivation: "Hans[-Dieter] Sues."

Type species: *H. sternbergi* (Brown and Schlaikjer 1943).

Other species: [None.]

Occurrence: Dinosaur Park Formation or Oldman Formation, Alberta, Canada.

Age: Late Cretaceous (Campanian).

Known material: Numerous specimens representing parts of the frontoparietal dome.

Holotype: CMN 8817, almost complete frontoparietal dome.

Diagnosis of genus (as for type species): Differing from all other known pachycephalosaurs in having low, depressed parietal region of frontoparietal dome, rostral (frontal) and caudal (parietal) portions of fronto-

toparietal wide; nasal boss of frontal broad, with reduced, more inflated, lateral prefrontal lobes; parietosquamosal shelf reduced (Sullivan 2003*a*).

Comments: *Hanssuesia sternbergi*, a new genus and species of dome-headed dinosaur named by pachycephalosaur specialist Robert M. Sullivan in 2003, was founded upon a nearly complete frontoparietal dome (CMN 8817) collected from either the Dinosaur Park Formation ("Belly River Beds"), or less likely the Oldman Formation (D. A. Eberth, personal communication to Sullivan 2001), southeast of Steveville, Alberta, Canada, this specimen originally having been described by Brown and Schlaikjer (1943) as the new species *Troodon sternbergi*.

To *H. sternbergi* Sullivan (2003*a*) also referred a number of other partial frontoparietal specimens, including the following: CMN 192, 1953, 2379, 8945, and 9148; TMP 79.14.853, 87.36.363, 89.69.21, and 2000.26.01; and UALVP-3; to cf. *H. sternbergi*, from the Two Medicine Formation of Glacier County, Montana, Sullivan (2003*a*) referred MOR 453, a rather large frontoparietal dome, and MOR 480, an almost complete frontoparietal, based on the caudal sloping of the parietal portion of frontoparietal; also provisionally referred by Sullivan (2003*a*) to *H. sternbergi* were CMN 1075 and 8944; TMP 85.36.240 and 98.93.125; and UALVP-8502.

Hanssusia sternbergi, CMN 8817, holotype frontoparietal dome of *Troodon sternbergi*, dorsal view.

Courtesy Robert M. Sullivan.

As Sullivan related, this taxon has proved to be most difficult to categorize, as neither the holotype nor any of the referred specimens, with the exception of MOR 480 (if properly referred), have preserved the caudal medial part of the parietal intact. Goodwin (1990), however, had reported on a specimen (UCMP 130051) recovered from the Judith River Formation of Montana preserving all the peripheral elements of the skull. As noted by Sullivan (2003*a*) following his examination of a cast (MOR collection, unnumbered) of that specimen, UCMP 130051 conforms in dorsal view to *H. sternbergi*, the frontoparietal portion of its dome being wide both rostrally and caudally. The slope of the parietal conforms with some specimens of *H. sternbergi*, particularly the holotype. Additionally, the stratigraphic occurrence of UCMP 130051 is consistent with other specimens of *H. sternbergi* from the Campanian of Alberta. Consequently, Sullivan (2003*a*) referred UCMP 130051 to *H. sternbergi*, noting that "This referral is extremely significant because no other specimens of this taxon preserve the peripheral elements and their respective ornamentation.

Comparing *H. sternbergi* with another pachycephalosaurine described in the same paper, *Colepiocaphale lambei*, Sullivan (2003*a*) noted that the former is in part distinguished "by reduced sutural surfaces for the attachment of the left and right squamosals along the posterior edges of the frontoparietal dome" (in *C. lambei*, the parietal portion of the dome making up the entire caudal edge of the skull, the squamosals being restricted to the lateral sides).

Previously, Sullivan (2000*b*) had referred this species to the genus *Gravitholus* (see *S3*), a view no longer held by that author, as the material now named *H. sternbergi* significantly differs from *Gravitholus albertae* (*e.g.*, rostral expression of frontal portion of frontoparietal dome) and *Gravitholus* (see entry) is again regarded as a valid genus.

Note: In correcting the galleys for the original publication of this new genus and species, Sullivan saw that the generic name *Hanssuesia* was misspelled as *Hanssuessia*. Sullivan corrected this typographical error, but, nevertheless, the misspelled name appeared in the paper. The error was subsequently corrected formally by Sullivan (2003*b*).

Key references: Brown and Schlaikjer (1943); Goodwin (1990); Sullivan (2003*a*, 2003*b*).

†HAPLOCANTHOSAURUS

Saurischia: Eusaurischia: Sauropodomorpha: Sauropoda: Eusauropoda: Neosauropoda: Macronaria: Camarasauromorpha: Haplocanthosauridae.

Diagnosis of genus (as for type species): Dorsal vertebrae lacking cranial centrodiapophyseal laminae; elongate "infrapostzygapophyseal" laminae; dorsal vertebrae with dorsoventrally directed dorsal transverse processes approaching height of neural spines (autapomorphy within basal Macronaria, but not when considering full range of sauropod anatomical variation); distal end of scapular blade expanded dorsally, ventrally (Upchurch, Barrett and Dodson 2004).

Comment: In their review of the Sauropoda, Upchurch, Barrett and Dodson (2004) rediagnosed the type species *Haplocanthosaurus priscus* (see *D:TE*).

Key reference: Upchurch, Barrett and Dodson (2004).

†HARPYMIMUS

Saurischia: Eusaurischia: Theropoda: Neotheropoda: Tetanurae: Avetheropoda: Coelurosauria: Tyrannoraptora: Maniraptoriformes: Ornithomimosauria: Ornithomimidae.

Comments: In an abstract, Kobayashi and Barsbold (2003) reexamined the holotype partial skeleton (GIN 100/29) of the type species *Harpymimus okladnikovi*, a basal ornithomimosaur from the Early Cretaceous of Mongolia, selected elements of which were described by Barsbold and Perle in 1984 (see *D:TE*). According to Kobayashi and Barsbold, however, the relationship of *Harpymimus* to another basal ornithomimosaur, *Pelecanimimus*, is unclear, as *Harpymimus* has derived skull features but a more primitive manus morphology than *Pelecanimimus*.

Kobayashi and Barsbold compared the almost complete GIN 100/29 with all other known ornithomimosaur genera and also some undescribed specimens, testing the phylogenetic relationships within the clade Ornithomimosauria. The authors performed a cladistic analysis incorporating 95 characters for 10 taxa with just two outgroups, this study resulting in a single most parsimonious tree. Kobayashi and Barsbold's analysis confirmed that *Harpymimus* is more derived than *Pelecanimimus* (based upon loss of premaxillary and maxillary teeth) and is a sister taxon to a clade comprising *Garudimimus* plus Ornithomimidae.

According to Kobayashi and Barsbold, two scenarios could explain the evolution in manus structure in ornithomimosaurs — "reversal in *Harpymimus* or convergence in *Pelecanimimus*."

Kobayashi and Barsbold's analysis also resolved the following interrelationships within Ornithomimidae: Early Late Cretaceous forms (undescribed Chinese taxon plus *Archaeornithomimus*) forming stem group of Late Cretaceous clade; late Late Cretaceous Mongolian ornithomimids (*Anserimimus* plus *Gallimimus*) and North American (*Struthiomimus* plus

[*Ornithomimus* plus "*Dromicieomimus*"] [=*Ornithomimus*; see entry]) clades; congruence of ornithomimosaur tree topology with chronological appearance of its ingroups, suggesting European or eastern Asian origin of Ornithomimosauria during or before Barremian times, and dispersal of Ornithomimidae to North America during of before Late Cretaceous.

Key references: Barsbold and Perle (1984); Kobayashi and Barsbold (2003).

†HEPTASTEORNIS [*nomen dubium*]

Saurischia: Eusaurischia: Theropoda: Neotheropoda: Tetanurae: Avetheropoda: Coelurosauria: Tyrannoraptora: Maniraptoriformes: Maniraptora: Paraves: Alvarezsauridae.

Type species: *H. andrewsi* Harrison and Walker 1975 [*nomen dubium*].

Comments: In 1975, C. J. O. Harrison and Cyril A. Walker named and described the new type species *Heptasteornis andrewsi*, established on a well-preserved left, distal tibiotarsus (BMNH A4359) from Sinpetru (Upper Cretaceous), Hateg Basin, Romania. Although this taxon was referred by them to the Bradycnemidae, believed by the authors to comprise a group of Late Cretaceous owls within the avian clade Strigiformes, other workers subsequently assigned the species to various non-avian theropod clades, including an unspecified group (*e.g.*, see Brodkorb 1978), the Ornithomimidae (Martin 1983), Troodontidae (Paul 1988), Dromaeosauridae (Le Leouff, Buffetaut, Mechin and Mechin-Salessy 1992), as well as a non-maniraptoran theropod (Csiki and Grigorescu 1998; see *D:TE* for more details on this genus and its taxonomic history).

Heptasteornis was more recently reassessed by Naish (2004*b*), who posited that none of the above proposed referrals can be supported on the basis of derived characters. Although Naish did not describe BMNH A4359 (see Harrison and Walker for full description), that author observed that the specimen is nearly identical to that element in the alvarezsaurids *Patagonykus puertai*, *Shuvuuia deserti*, and *Mononykus olecranus*. Naish also noted the following details: Medial condyle projecting more cranially than lateral condyle (formed in part by calcaneum not fully fused to astragalus), also seen in *M. olecranus* and the alvarezsaurid *Parvicursor remotus* (see Perle, Chiappe, Barsbold, Clark and Norell 1994; Karhu and Rautian 1996), both condyles not projecting as far cranially as apparently in "eumaniraptorans" (including birds); pronounced notch excavating medial margin of ascending process of astragalus (regarded as a synapomorphy of the Alvarezsauridae by Novas 1996*b*, also present in *P. puertai*, *M. olecranus*, and *P. remotus*, but

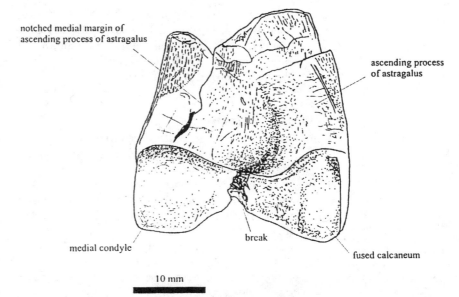

notched medial margin of ascending process of astragalus

ascending process of astragalus

medial condyle

break

fused calcaneum

10 mm

Heptasteornis andrewsi, BMNH A4359, holotype distal end of left tibiotarsus. (After Naish 2004.)

absent in *S. deserti*), this notch being just slightly developed in other theropods (see Welles and Long 1974) including birds.

According to Naish, despite the fragmentary nature of BMNH R4359, the strong overall similarity between this specimen and alvarezsaurids, in addition to a unique derived character, suggests referral of the specimen to the Alvarezsauridae. This identification is significant, Naish pointed out, as this first documentation of an alvarezsaurid in Europe extends the known paleogeographical range of the clade, while also having implications for its biogeography and time of origin. Assuming a dispersalist model, that author noted, the Alvarezsauridae "may have invaded eastern Europe prior to the Turonian as the Turgai Sea separated Asia from Europe by this time" (see Smith, Smith and Funnell 1994). Moreover, given that the oldest, stem-group members of Alvarezsauridae are of Coniacian to Santonian age (see Novas 1997*a* and references cited therein), this possibly suggests a "pre–Turonian dispersal and origin if it is assumed that the Turgai Sea was a permanent barrier." Assuming a vicariance model (Upchurch, Hunn and Norman 2002) suggests that alvarezsaurids arrived in Europe before the Early Cretaceous split of Gondwana and Laurasia, this further suggesting a pre–Albian origin for the Alvarezsauridae, and predicting the possible future discovery of alvarezsaurid remains in Africa.

Makovicky and Norell (2004), in reviewing the Troodontosauridae, considered *Heptasteornis andrewsi* to be a *nomen dubium* (see "Systematics" chapter).

Key references: Brodkorb (1978); Csiki and Grigorescu (1998); Harrison and Walker (1975); Karhu and Rautian (1996); Le Leouff, Buffetaut, Mechin and

Mechin-Salessy (1992); Martin (1983); Naish (2004*b*); Novas (1996*b*, 1997*a*); Paul (1988); Perle, Chiappe, Barsbold, Clark and Norell 1994); Smith, Smith and Funnell (1994); Upchurch, Hunn and Norman (2002); Welles and Long (1974).

†HESPEROSAURUS

Ornithischia: Predentata: Genasauria: Thyreophora: Thyreophoroidea: Eurypoda: Stegosauria: Stegosauridae: Stegosaurinae.

Diagnosis of genus (as for type species): Autapomorphies including the following: Broad maxillary shelf; cervical ribs having expanded blades distally; top of neural spines of proximal caudal vertebrae "teardrop"-shaped in cranial aspect; ossified tendons

Reconstructed mounted skeleton of *Hesperosaurus mjosi*, including cast of holotype HMNH 001.

Photograph by the author, courtesy North American Museum of Ancient Life.

in dorsal region; cervical plates low, oval (Galton and Upchurch 2004*b*).

Comment: In their review of the Stegosauria, Galton and Upchurch (2004*b*) rediagnosed the type species *Hesperosaurus mjosi* (see *D:TE*).

Key reference: Galton and Upchurch (2004*b*).

HONGSHANOSAURUS   You, Xu and Wang 2003
Ornithischia: Predentata: Genusauria: Cerapoda: Chasmatopia: Marginocephalia: Ceratopsia: Psittacosauridae.
Name derivation: Chinese *Hong Shan* = "red hill [for 'Red Hill Culture' that existed in western Liaoning about 6,000 years ago]" + Greek *sauros* = "lizard."
Type species: *H. houi* You, Xu and Wang 2003.
Other species: [None.]
Occurrence: Yixian Formation, Liaoning Province, China.
Age: Early Cretaceous (Hauterivian).
Known material/holotype: IVPP V 12704, almost complete skull with articulated jaw, probably juvenile.

Diagnosis of genus (as for type species): Psittacosaurid distinguished from *Psittacosaurus* by prominent jugal-quadratojugal caudoventral process below maxillary tooth row, and elliptical, caudodorsally oriented orbit (You, Xu and Wang 2003).

Comments: The genus *Hongshanosaurus* was established on a probably juvenile skull with lower jaw (IVPP V 12704) collected from the Lower Cretaceous (see Swisher, Wang, Zhou, Wang, Jin, Zhang, Xu, Zhang and Wang 2001) Yixian Formation, at Beipiao, Liaoning Province, northeastern China (You, Xu and Wang 2003).

In describing the holotype skull of the type species *Hongshanosaurus houi*, You *et al.* noted that it dorsoventrally compressed and nearly complete,

Copyright © Berislav Krzic.

Life restoration by Berislav Krzic of *Hongshanosaurus houi*.

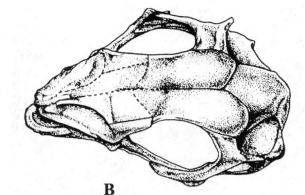

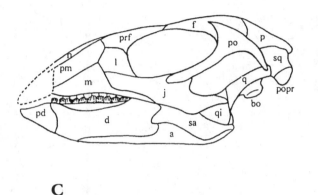

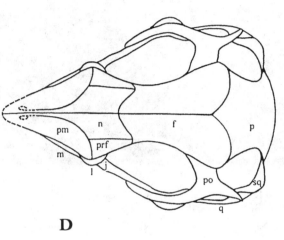

A

B

C

D

missing the rostral tip and right caudolateral corner. The specimen most likely belongs to a juvenile animal, as evidenced by the small size and large orbit.

As the authors pointed out, *Hongshanosaurus* shares with *Psittacosaurus* a number of features (*e.g.*, enlarged caudodorsal process of premaxilla; contact between premaxilla and maxilla; long rostral process of nasal; open canal on lateral surface of lacrimal; less than 10 maxillary teeth per ramus; see Coombs 1982; Sereno, Chao, Cheng and Rao 1988; Russell and Zhao 1996). While the its holotype skull seems to represent a juvenile individual, it nevertheless displays a number of differences separating it from the similarly sized skull of *Psittacosaurus* (see diagnosis, above; see also Coombs).

Key references: Coombs (1982); Russell and Zhao (1996); Sereno, Chao, Cheng and Rao (1988); Smith, Harris, Omar, Dodson and You (2001); You, Xu and Wang (2003).

†HUABEISAUERUS

Saurischia: Eusaurischia: Sauropodomorpha: Sauropoda: Eusauropoda: Neosauropoda: Macronaria: Titanosauriformes: ?Titanosauria *incertae sedis.*

Diagnosis of genus (as for type species): Blade of ilium extremely deep dorsoventrally (in lateral aspect) relative to that of other sauropods, reaching maximum dorsoventral depth just cranial to cranial termination of pubic peduncle; cranial iliac lobe strongly curved ventrally, cranial termination at lobe on same level as line drawn between ventral tips of ischial and pubic peduncles (Upchurch, Barrett and Dodson 2004).

Comment: In their review of the Sauropoda, Upchurch, Barrett and Dodson (2004) rediagnosed the type species *Huabeisaurus allocotus* (see *S2*).

According to Upchurch, various characters (*e.g.*, teeth peglike; dorsolateral bulge on femur; caudal vertebrae having cranially located neural arches; cranial iliac process with rounded cranial margin) suggest affinities of this taxon with Titanosauriformes and possibly Titanosauria.

Key reference: Upchurch, Barrett and Dodson (2004).

HUAXIAGNATHUS   Hwang, Norell, Ji and Gao 2004

Saurischia: Eusaurischia: Theropoda: Neotheropoda:

Huaxiagnathus orientalis, CAGS-IGO2-301, holotype almost complete subadult skeleton preserved on five slabs. (After Hwang, Norell, Ji and Gao 2004.)

Tetanurae: Avetheropoda: Coelurosauria: Compsognathidae.

Name derivation: Mandarin Hua Xia [ancient name for China] + Greek gnathos = "jaw."

Type species: *H. orientalis* Hwang, Norell, Ji and Gao 2004.

Other species: [None.]

Occurrence: Yixian Formation, Liaoning Province, China.

Age: Early Cretaceous (Hauterivian).

Known material: ?Two almost complete skeletons, subadult and ?adult.

Holotype: CAGS-IG02–301, almost complete skeleton lacking distal end of tail, subadult.

Diagnosis of genus (as for type species): Differing from other known compsognathids in having very long caudal process of premaxilla overlapping antorbital fossa, manus as long as combined lengths of radius and humerus, large manual unguals I and II subequal in length and 167 percent length of manual ungual III, first metacarpal with smaller proximal transverse width than second metacarpal, and ulna with reduced olecranon process (Hwang, Norell, Ji and Gao 2004a).

Comments: *Huaxiagnathus*, while a small dinosaur, is distinguished as the second largest theropod taxon yet collected from the Jehol Group (second only to therizinosauroid *Beipiaosaurus inexpectus*). The type species, *Huaxiagnathus orientalis*, was founded on a nearly complete skeleton (CAGS-IG02–301), pre-served on five large slabs with no preserved counterpart elements, collected from the Yixian Formation (Lower Cretaceous; see Swisher, Wang, Zhou, Wang, Jin, Zhang, Xu, Zhang and Wang 2001) deposits of Liaoning Province, China. The type specimen (first referred to in a poster by Hwang, Norell, Gao and Ji 2002 with the incorrect specimen number CAGS 30–2-035) was recovered by farmers from a quarry belonging to the village of Dabangou, in the Sihetun area, near the city of Beipiao. Tentatively referred to the type species was an unusually large "almost complete, poorly reconstructed and poorly prepared specimen" (see below) from the Sihetun area not suitable to be designated the holotype (Hwang, Norell, Ji and Gao 2004a).

Because of a number of recent fossil forgeries originating in China (*e.g.*, see *Microraptor* entry, *S2*), the holotype of *H. orientalis* was rigorously "searched for anomalous bits of matrix and protruding pieces of foreign bone that might have been added to 'complete' the skeleton," and "examined under ultraviolet light for any changes in fluorescence that might signal replacement parts." Hwang *et al.* (2004) found no signs of foreign skeletal material or matrix, or plaster, in the specimen, verifying that it was not a chimera.

As observed by Hwang *et al.* (2004), *Huaxiagnathus* superficially resembles a large *Compsognathus* or *Sinosauropteryx*, all three taxa having the same general skeletal proportions (*e.g.*, long tails, short forelimbs, comparatively large skulls, relatively short distal hindlimb proportions, all of which are characteristic of the Compsognathidae; see Gauthier 1986).

As Hwang *et al.* (2004) pointed out, compsognathids are relatively unspecialized coelurosaurians, difficult to diagnose based upon autapomorphies other than those characterizing them as compsognathids. While displaying some autapomorphic characters, *Huaxiagnathus* is most notable for two technically nondiagnostic features — relatively large size (approximately one half meter longer than the *Compsognathus* specimen from France and the largest *Sinosauropteryx* specimens) and primitive proportions.

The poor preservation and poor preparation of the slightly larger specimen NGMC 98–5-003 made its referral to *H. orientalis* somewhat problematic. As Hwang *et al.* (2004) noted, numerous mistakes were made in the reconstruction of this specimen (*e.g.*, placing the counterpart to the radius and ulna in the manus to mimic phalanges; addition of generous amounts of plaster to fill in the hindlimbs, with bone pieces stuck randomly into the plaster). However, despite the wanting condition of this specimen, both it and the holotype are of similar size and were discovered in identical facies of the Sihetun area. While size

Huaxiagnathus orientalis, photograph and drawing of holotype subadult skull (CAGS-IGO2-301), in right lateral view. (After Hwang, Norell, Ji and Gao 2004.)

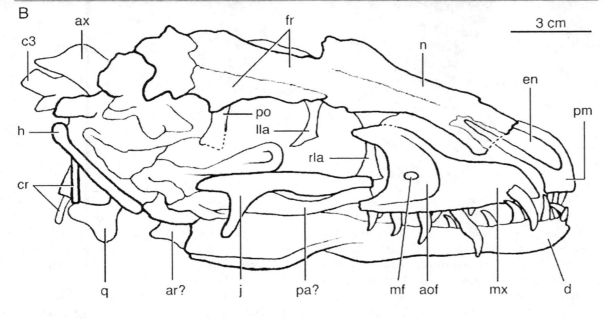

is not technically diagnostic, the small size of most theropod specimens recovered from this area distinguishes the comparatively large size of NGMC 98–5-003. Moreover, this specimen exhibits the same basic coelurosaurian body plan as the holotype of *H. orientalis*, with the bones preserved in their entirety in NGMC 98–5-003 having the same morphology as their counterparts in CAGS-IG02–301.

If both CAGS-IG02–301 and NGMC 98–5-003 do, in fact, belong to the same genus and species, then, Hwang *et al.* (2004) suggested, both specimens could represent different growth stages, with the holotype a subadult morph and the latter specimen possibly an adult. In the holotype, the carpals and tarsals are firmly coossified, although the skull is rather large relative to the rest of the body and the observable neural arches of the vertebrae are not fused to the cen-

tra. In the larger NGMC 98–5-003, although the general proportions are similar to those of CAGS-IG02–301, the skull is comparatively shorter (the extent of neural arch fusion unable to be determined). The authors could not, therefore, be certain whether or not NGMC 98–5-003 represents a fully adult individual.

The discovery of *Huaxiagnathus* yielded new data allowing for a reassessment of the family Compsognathidae and the latter's placement among other theropod groups. Performing a phylogenetic analysis, utilizing 222 characters and 55 taxa coded at the species level, *Huaxiagnathus orientalis* was found to fall out at the base of Compsognathidae, demonstrated by the species' comparatively longer and relatively unspecialized forearm, lacking the forearm adaptations seen in more derived compsognathids.

Life restoration of *Huaxiagnathus orientalis* by artist Berislav Krzic.

Moreover, *H. orientalis* was found to share a sister-taxon relationship to a clade comprising *Sinosauropteryx* [recently placed outside of Compsognathidae; see entry, *S3*] plus *Compsognathus*, the three taxa collectively forming a monophyletic Compsognathidae.

Compsognathidae — previously regarded as a maniraptoriform group outside of Maniraptora (see *S3*; also, see "Systematics" chapter) — was found by Huang *et al.* to occupy a position near the base of Maniraptora. In this same analysis, Alvarezsauridae, Paraves, and a monophyletic clade of Therizinosauroidea plus Oviraptorosauria were found to "fall out in an unresolved trichotomy in the strict consensus of our most parsimonious trees."

Key references: Gauthier (1986); Hwang, Norell, Gao and Ji (2002); Hwang, Norell, Ji and Gao (2004a); Swisher, Wang, Zhou, Wang, Jin, Zhang, Xu, Zhang and Wang (2001).

†HUDIESAURUS

Saurischia: Eusaurischia: Sauropodomorpha: Sauropoda: Eusauropoda incertae sedis.

Diagnosis of genus (as for type species): Transversely compressed process projecting cranially from front face of neural spine in cranial dorsal vertebrae (Upchurch, Barrett and Dodson 2004).

Comments: In their review of the Sauropoda, Upchurch, Barrett and Dodson (2004) rediagnosed the type species *Hudiesaurus sinojapanorum* (see *D:TE*).

According to Upchurch *et al.*, the teeth and forelimb (IVP V. 11121) referred by Dong (1997) to this taxon was not found in association with the holotype dorsal vertebra (IVPP V. 11120). As Upchurch *et al.* pointed out, there exists no anatomical overlap between these elements, while Dong's referral of the teeth and forelimb to *Hudiesaurus* was based only upon geographic and stratigraphic proximity. Consequently, Upchurch *et al.* rejected this referred material, restricting the genus *Hudiesaurus* only to the holotype, and provisionally regarding the teeth and forelimb as belonging to an indeterminate eusauropod.

Key references: Dong (1997); Upchurch, Barrett and Dodson (2004).

†HYLAEOSAURUS

Ornithischia: Predentata: Genasauria: Thyreophora: Thyreophoroidea: Eurypoda: Ankylosauria *incertae sedis*.

Comments: The armored dinosaur *Hylaeosaurus armatus* was the third dinosaur type species to be named and described (by Gideon Algernon Mantell in 1833). The holotype specimen (BMNH R 3376) had been discovered by Dr. Mantell the previous year, the caudal part of the animal having been preserved in numerous matrix blocks. As reported briefly in an abstract by Gray and Chapman (2004), and in an abstract for a poster by Chapman and Gray (2004), Mantell cemented these blocks together, producing the single slab often figured in the paleontological literature (see *D:TE* for illustration and additional information).

To date, however, this historically significant dinosaur has not been fully described, nor has its relationships among the Ankylosauria been resolved.

As reported by Gray and Chapman, the type specimen of *H. armatus* is currently undergoing full preparation at The Natural History Museum, Lon-

don. To date of their writing, "The bones have been exposed using a combination of chemical (acid) and mechanical (dental mallet, air-abrasive, *etc.*) methods where appropriate." First removed was the block containing the ?skull bones and axis, with preparation continuing until all the preserved remains have been extracted, along with any preserved molluscs and plants.

Key references: Chapman and Gray (2004); Gray and Chapman (2004); Mantell (1833).

†IGUANODON

Ornithischia: Predentata: Genasauria: Cerapoda: Ornithopoda: Euornithopoda: Iguanodontia: Dryomorpha: Ankylopollexia: nStyracosterna: Iguanodontoidea: Iguanodontidae.

Notes: A possible *Iguanodon* bonebed, discovered by Didier Néraudeau in December, 2000, was reported by Néraudeau, Allain, Perrichot, Videt, Broin, Guillocheau, Philippe, Rage and Vullo (2003). The Middle Cretaceous (early Cenomanian) bonebed is located on the tidal flat of the Fouras Peninsula,

Elements from Charente-Maritime, France, referred to *Iguanodon*? sp.: Right ulna in 1A. lateral and 1B. medial views, right tibia in 1C. cranial and 1D. caudal views. Scale = 4 centimeters. (After Néraudeau, Allain, Perrichot, Videt, Broin, Guillocheau, Philippe, Rage and Vullo 2003.)

Life restoration by artist Gregory S. Paul of *Iguanodon bernissartensis.*

Charente-Maritime, in southwestern France, a site also yielding the remains of pterosaurs, turtles, snakes, insects, plus amber and fossil wood.

The iguanodontid remains, referred by the authors to *Iguanodon*? sp., comprise approximately 50 bone fragments, only two of which are clearly determined — *i.e.*, a right ulna and the distal end of end of a right tibia. As Néraudeau *et al.* pointed out, the Fouras iguanodontid could constitute the latest record of the genus *Iguanodon*. Furthermore, the discovery is important because Cenomanian–Santonian-age dinosaur remains in Europe are very rare.

For about 120 years, the many skeletons of *Iguanodon bernissartensis* — collected from 1876–78 from a coal mine in Bernissart, in South-West Belgium (see *D:TE*) — have been on display at the Institut Royal des Sciences Naturelle de Belgique in Brussels. As these specimens were highly pyritized, however, curation of them under standard museum conditions has been

difficult. Ricqlès (2003), in an abstract, briefly reported on recently taken measures that could inevitably aid in the further preservation of these priceless specimens.

In 2003, as recounted by Ricqlès, a party of the Faculté Polytechnique de Mons, Belgium, organized a drilling campaign in order to localize better the limits of the local geological accident that caused the Lower Cretaceous (Wealden) clays containing these skeletons to collapse into the underlying coal measures (Carboniferous) strata. The drilling produced not only Wealden clays, but also odd structures found in the clay at depths of from -296.5 and -309 meters. Histological examination identified these structures — based upon the structure of bone and teeth materials and also on statistical probabilities — as *Iguanodon* bones yet *in situ*.

Ricqlès stated that these discoveries provide the opportunity to compare "fresh" *Iguanodon* specimens, barely submitted to atmospheric oxygen, to the "old" specimens housed at the museum. In progress physico-chemical and structural comparisons, that author noted, "will help to decipher how the pyrite oxydation causes fossil bone degradation at the micro- and macroscopical levels and hopefully devise efficient preservation strategies." According to Ricqlès, histological preservation of the "fresh" specimens is quite good. The "old" specimens, having for over a century oxydized and been in contact with the air at room temperature, exhibit generalized macroscopic breakage rather than any significant histological degradation.

In an abstract for a poster, Noè and Finney (2004) reported on the dismantling and cleaning of the *Iguanodon bernissartensis* plaster skeletal cast mounted at the Sedgwick Museum at the University of Cambridge. As these authors recounted, the skeleton was presented to the University in 1896 by King Leopold II of Belgium, remaining in its original posture and location, near the museum's entrance, for almost a century.

Improvements being made at the museum, including the removal of the floor, necessitated removal of the skeleton, also providing the "opportunity to dismantle, conserve, repaint and remount the skeleton, the first time in more than 30 years that this has been attempted." As Noè and Finney reported, the bones are being painted a dark brown, close to the color of the original fossil material, with a mixture of several different acrylic paints producing a "'life-like' three-dimensional effect."

Erratum: In *S3*, the paper by Ruiz-Omeñaca, Canudo and Cuenca-Bescós (1997) was incorrectly cited as 2001 in the Iguanodon entry, and in the bibliography as 1998. Key references: Néraudeau, Allain, Perrichot, Videt, Broin, Guillocheau, Philippe, Rage and Vullo (2003); Noè and Finney (2004); Ricqlès (2003).

†INCISIVOSAURUS—(See *Protarchaeopteryx*.)

†INDOSAURUS (=?*Coeluroides*; =?*Dryptosauroides*, ?*Compsosuchus*, ?*Indosuchus*, ?*Jubbulpuria*, ?*Ornithomimoides*)

Saurischia: Eusaurischia: Theropoda: Neotheropoda: Ceratosauria: Abelisauroidea: Abelisauridae: Carnotaurinae.

Holotype: GSI K27/565, partially damaged caudal part of skull, including right frontal, temporal region, area of articulation for postorbital (lost or misplaced).

Comments: In 1933, Friedrich von Huene, in a classic review of the dinosaurs of India co-authored with Charles Alfred Matley, named and described *Indosaurus matleyi*, a type species of large theropod founded on a braincase (GSI K27/565) from the Lameta Formation of India. Although Huene sensibly classified *Indosaurus* as a carnosaur closely related to *Allosaurus*, other workers (*e.g.*, Bonaparte and Novas 1985; Molnar 1990; Chatterjee and Rudra 1996) found its affinities to be with the Abelisauridae (see *D:TE, S1, S2*), a theropod group unknown in Huene's time.

More recently, Novas, Agnolin and Bandyopadhyay (2004), in a review of the Indian theropods discussed by Huene in Huene and Matley (1933), readdressed the holotype of *I. matleyi*. Accepting that *Indosaurus* belongs to the Abelisauridae, Novas *et al.* noted the following features that distinguish both that genus and another Indian genus, *Indosuchus* (see entry and below), from other known abelisaurids: Lack of prominent central dome on frontals (autapomorphic for the Malagasy *Majungatholus atopus*); lack of paired frontal horns (characterizing Argentinian *Carnotaurus sasteri*). In those features, the authors noted, the skull roof morphology of the two Indian genera is more conservative, being dorsoventrally thick and lacking prominences above the skull roof (as in the Argentinian *Abelisaurus*).

Novas *et al.* also questioned whether *Indosaurus* and *Indosuchus* are distinct taxa. As these authors recounted, some previous workers (*e.g.*, Huene and Matley; Chatterjee 1978; Chatterjee and Rudra) listed a number of anatomical features in the braincases supposedly separating these taxa, including the following: Differences in transverse width of parietal sagittal crest; presence or absence of "transverse crest" on dorsal surface of skull; dorsoventral thickness of frontals; contour of supratemporal fossa."

As Novas *et al.* pointed out, however, the above-cited distinctions are difficult to evaluate for a number of reasons, including the unavailability of specimens and also because of the specimens' poor preservations (*e.g.*, dorsal surface of GSI K27/565 eroded, with no features of frontal preserved; purported transverse crest above and behind orbit in *Indosaurus* not seen, thereby dismissing this feature's validity; preservation not demonstrating presence of hornlike tuberosities in *Indosaurus* or dorsally smooth postorbital in *Indosuchus*). Moreover, additional "distinctions" presumably separating these taxa — pertaining to skull roof thickness, rostrocaudal extension of supratemporal fossa, fusion of sutures, degree of development of cranial rugosities — possibly reflect individual variation.

Novas *et al.* pointed out that a considerable degree of variation has been reported in the frontal dome of specimens of *Majungatholus*, from being inflated (see Sues and Taqet) to only slightly developed (Sampson, Witmer, Forster, Krause, O'Connor, Dodson and Ravoavy 1998). Consequently, this possible case of individual variation in *Majungatholus* "serves as an alert when distinctions between the poorly preserved skulls of *Indosuchus* and *Indosaurus* are evaluated," Novas *et al.* concluding that "anatomical distinctions between *Indosuchus* and *Indosaurus* are doubtful, at least."

Note: Novas *et al.* also reassessed a number of skull bones belonging to Lameta Formation theropods described as "carnosaurian" in Huene and Matley. In describing the preserved parts of two basioccipitals (GSI K27/687 and GSI K27/628), Novas *et al.* observed the following: (GSI K27/687) exoccipitals presumably forming floor of foramen magnum; neck rostrocaudally elongate, with median ventral groove; caudal surface of basioccipital bearing double tubercle; basioccipital tubera apparently ventrally bifurcated; (GSI K27/628) exoccipitals excluded from floor of foramen magnum; neck rostrocaudally short. Chatterjee referred the former specimen to *Indosaurus* and the latter to *Indosuchus*, although Novas *et al.* found that referral untenable based upon current knowledge of these two genera. While recognizing that these basiocrania represent two distinct taxa and because other skull bones described in Huene and Matley pertain to the Abelisauridae, Novas *et al.* tentatively referred GSI K27/687 and GSI K27/628 to that clade.

Key references: Bonaparte and Novas (1985); Chatterjee (1978); Chatterjee and Rudra (1996); Huene and Matley (1933); Molnar (1990); Novas, Agnolin and Bandyopadhyay (2004); Sampson, Witmer, Forster, Krause, O'Connor, Dodson and Ravoavy (1998); Sues and Taquet (1979).

†**INDOSUCHUS**—(=?*Coeluroides*, ?*Dryptosauroides*, ?*Compsosuchus*, ?*Indosaurus*, ?*Jubbulpuria*, ?*Ornithomimoides*)

Saurischia: Eusaurischia: Theropoda: Neotheropoda: Ceratosauria: Abelisauroidea: Abelisauridae: ?Carnotaurinae.

Comments: In a review of theropod specimens from India, described by Friedrich von Huene in a 1933 report on Indian dinosaurs co-written with Charles Alfred Matley, Novas, Agnolin and Bandyopadhyay (2004) reassessed the three large basicrania (GSI K20/350, lectotype GSI K27/685, and GSI K27/690 from the so-called "Carnosaur bed" of the Lameta Formation, all of these specimens having been either lost or misplaced) that Huene had referred to the type species *Indosuchus raptorius* Huene 1932 (see *D:TE*).

Based on the drawings of these specimens published in Huene and Matley, Novas *et al.* noted that the braincase of *I. raptorius* exhibits various features quite similar to those of the abelisaurids *Abelisaurus comahuensis*, *Carnotaurus sasteri*, and *Majungatholus atopus*. However, Novas *et al.* also noted differences, including the following: (GSI K20/350) fronto-nasal suture apparently rostrally placed relative to lacrimals (in other known abelisaurids, more caudally placed, about at level of rostrolateral notch of frontals for articulation with lacrimals); (GSI K20/350) median suture on caudal half of braincase between frontals, clear fronto-parietal suture; (GSI K20/350) visible dorsal sutures agreeing with lack of fusion with parasphenoidal, exposing ventral furrow for olfactory canal (see Huene and Matley); (GSI K27/685) frontals and parasphenoid completely fused (also in *A. comahuensis*, *C. sastrei*, and (GSI K27/565) the type specimen of the Indian abelisaurid *Indosaurus matleyi*; see *D:TE*, *SI*; also, see below, and *Indosaurus* entry, this volume).

According to Novas *et al.*, the lack of ossification in the skull and braincase of *Indosuchus* may be the result of ontogenetic development, thereby having no phylogenetic importance. The remaining noted differences between *I. raptorius* and other cited taxa may, however, have autapomorphic significance for this taxon.

In 1932, Huene regarded GSI K27/685 and GSI K27/565 as pertaining to a single genus, *Indosuchus*, referring the latter specimen to the new genus *Indosaurus* in the 1933 paper. Although *Indosuchus* and *Indosaurus* have most often been regarded as valid and distinct genera, Novas *et al.* reevaluated the various differences perceived between these taxa (listed by Huene earlier in Huene and Matley, and later by Chatterjee 1978, and Chatterjee and Rudra 1996), *e.g.*, differences in transverse width of parietal sagittal crest, presence or absence of "transverse crest" on dorsal surface of skull, dorsoventral thickness of frontals, contour of supratemporal fossa.

However, Novas *et al.* found it difficult to evaluate the above-cited "distinctions," as the basicrania referred to *Indosuchus* were not available for the authors' examination, and "because the preservation of the skull is far from optimal." As an example of the latter consideration, Novas *et al.* pointed out that in GS 27/565, the holotype of *Indosaurus matleyi* (which the authors did examine), the dorsal surface of the braincase is eroded, with no features preserved of the frontals or sagittal parietal crest. Novas *et al.* were not able to see in that specimen any evidence for the transverse crest purported to have existed above and behind the orbit, thereby dismissing this feature as valid; nor did the preserved state of the specimens demonstrate the presence of any hornlike protuberances in

Indosaurus or a dorsally smooth postorbital in *Indosuchus*.

Novas *et al.* explained various other features cited by previous authors as possible differences between *Indosuchus* and *Indosaurus*—e.g., thickness of skull roof; rostrocaudal extension of supratemporal fossa; fusion of sutures; development degree of rugosities of skull bones — as possibly the result of individual variation.

Although Novas *et al.* could not unequivocally demonstrate a synonymy of *Indosuchus* and *Indosaurus*, they concluded that the anatomical distinctions between these taxa "are doubtful, at least." If these taxa do, in the future, prove to be congeneric, then *Indosuchus*, the name published a year earlier than *Indosaurus*, will have priority.

Notes: Novas *et al.* also described and reassessed a number of skull bones belonging to Lameta Formation theropods described in Huene and Matley as "carnosaurian":

Among these remains, Huene and Matley had described a right premaxilla (GSI K27/710), right premaxilla (GSI K20/619), and a pair of premaxillae (AMNH 1753). Chatterjee believed the latter to represent single individual of *Indosuchus*, although, as Novas *et al.* pointed out, premaxillae are not preserved in the holotype of *I. raptorius* for comparison. Consequently, Novas *et al.* regarded these specimens as belonging to an indeterminate abelisaurid.

Chatterjee referred to *Indosuchus* a reasonably complete maxilla (GSI K27/548) based on its considerable thickness, further utilizing this specimen as reference in referring another left maxilla (AMNH 1955) to *I. raptorius*. Because no maxilla has been preserved or identified for either *Indosuchus* or *Indosaurus*, Novas *et al.* (following Lamanna, Martinez and Smith 2002) regarded AMNH 1955 (and presumably GSI K27/548) as belonging to indeterminate genera and species of abelisaurid.

Also referred by Chatterjee to *Indosuchus* was a presumed postorbital (GSI K27/580), reidentified by Novas *et al.* as a portion of a right jugal. As observed by these authors, this specimen, as well as other Lameta Formation jugals (GSI K27/577, K27/535, K27/581 [the latter two not figured by Huene and Matley and not available to Novas *et al.*]), resemble their counterparts in *Carnotaurus* and *Majungatholus*.

Other Lameta Formation specimens reassessed by Novas *et al.*, regarded by them as belonging to indeterminate abelisauroids or abelisaurids, include the following:

(Specimens identified in Huene and Matley as "carnosaurian") right lacrimal (GSI K27/708) lacking the pattern of rigosities seen in *Carnotaurus* and *Majungatholus*; left quadrate (described in Huene and

Matley incorrectly as a right astragalus), with an almost flat rostral facet of the distal condyles (as in the abelisaurids *Ilokelesia*, *Majungatholus*, and *Carnotaurus*); dentaries (GSI K27/550, K27/709, K27/529, the latter incorrectly catalogued as K27/527, the authors pointed out, and AMNH 1960, the latter including a caudal vertebra; see below); and a left surangular (GSI K27/693, incorrectly identified in Huene and Matley as a left articular), resembling that of *Carnotaurus* "in the presence and position of a pair of foramina near the glenoid cavity."

(Specimens described in Huene and Matley as "allosaurid") dorsal vertebra (GSI K27/590; incorrectly identified as a cervical) resembling those in *Sinraptor*, *Carnotaurus*, and *Ceratosaurus*, thereby exhibiting neoceratosaurian features and having a morphology congruent with abelisaurids, identified as an indeterminate abelisauroid; large (16 centimeters tall) cervical vertebra (GSI K27/572), possibly an abelisauroid, although the specimen is lost, precluding first-hand observations; sacral vertebrae (GSI K27/554 [two pieces], K27/533 [two pieces], and K27/571), possibly belonging to more than one abelisauroid or abelisaurid taxon; proximal caudal vertebra (AMNH 1960), its general morphology congruent with that of *Carnotaurus* and *Majungatholus*; medium and distal caudal vertebrae (AMNH 1968, GSI K27/596, K27/532, K27/594, K27/589, K27/705, and K27/599), the latter specimen resembling that of noasaurid abelisauroid *Masiakasaurus*; hemal arches (GSI K27/672, K27/566, K27/676, K20/362, K27/764, and K27/680), all save GSI K27/680 being elongate and rodlike, lacking a distal expansion (as in Abelisauridae and *Ceratosaurus*), possessing proximally open hema canal (unlike *Carnotaurus*).

(Specimens described in Huene and Matley as either "allosaurid" or "coelurosaurian") two fragmentary ischia (GSI K27/686 and K27/546), smaller than in *Carnotaurus*; femora (stout forms GSI K27/558, K27/570, and K27/618; slender forms GSI K27/560, K27/563, K27/564, K27/569, K27/621, and K27/627), robust forms possibly belonging to a single taxon resembling those of the abelisauroid *Xenotarsosaurus* and of *Indosuchus*, slender femors resembling those of *Xenotarsosaurus* and *Carnotaurus*, all referrable to the Abelisauroidea; tibiae (GSI 27/568, K27/526, K27/670, K27/552, K27/556, K27/662, and K27/669, only the latter located by Novas *et al.*), GSI K27/526 and K27/669 apparently misidentified, and regarded by Novas *et al.* as indeterminate limb bones; incomplete left fibula (GSI K27/620) resembling fibulae in *Xenotarsosaurus* and the abelisaurid *Rajasaurus*, regarded as an that of an indeterminate abelisauroid; putative astragalus (GSI K27/684) and calcaneum (GSI K20/396), the former correctly identified by Novas *et al.* as a left quadrate, the latter an indeterminate bone; metatarsals (GSI K27/639, K27/658, K27/659, K27/665, K27/666, K27/667, K27/671, K27/681, K27/697, and K20/337C), all exhibiting abelisauroid features; pedal phalanges (GSI K27/651, K27/652, and K27/654 [only the latter figured by Huene and Matley, who mentioned a total of more than 40 such bones having been recovered), congruent with abelisauroid anatomy, suggesting an *Aucasaurus*-like foot (phalanges more robust) and *Velocisaurus*-like foot (phalanges slender); and pedal unguals with the same morphological pattern (*e.g.*, proximally bifurcated grooves; rounded bump on lateral side of ungual; ventral surface excavated or having narrow, deep furrow) seen in abelisauroids.

It was the conclusion of Novas *et al.* that all the theropod material found at the "Carnosaur bed pertain to the Abelisauroidea (see also *Indosaurus* entry, "Note").

Key references: Chatterjee (1978); Chatterjee and Rudra (1996); Huene (1932); Huene and Matley (1933); Lamanna, Martinez and Smith (2002); Novas, Agnolin and Bandyopadhyay (2004).

†INGENIA

Saurischia: Eusaurischia: Theropoda: Neotheropoda: Tetanurae: Avetheropoda: Coelurosauria: Tyrannoraptora: Maniraptoriformes: Maniraptora: Metornithes: Oviraptorosauria: Caenagnathoidea: Oviraptoridae: Ingeniinae.

Comments: A skull specimen (GIN 100/31; see below) of the type species *Ingenia yanshini* was the basis of a study by Osmólska (2004) to determine the relation of the brain to the endocranial cavity in oviraptorid theropods.

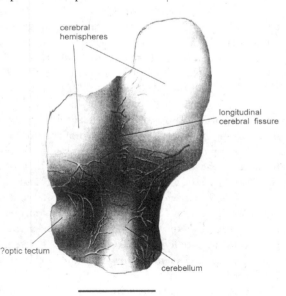

cerebral hemispheres

longitudinal cerebral fissure

?optic tectum

cerebellum

Schematized drawing of the endocast of *Ingenia yanshini* (GIN 100/3), pitting omitted, based upon latex cast of the undersurface of a frontoparietal fragment of the skull roof. Scale = 10 mm. (After Osmólska 2004.)

As Osmólska explained, the brain in extant tetrapods other than birds does not completely fill the brain cavity. In birds and mammals, the brain surface is closely appressed to the bones of the cranial roof, thereby leaving distinct impressions of the intercranial vascular channels on the underside of the bones in this area of the skull. Usually, however, the preserved braincases of dinosaurs do "not allow determination relating to how close walls of endocranial cavity lay to the surface of the brain."

Earlier, Hopson (1979) had cited endocasts of some theropod dinosaurs exhibiting a rather elaborate form and appearing quite brainlike, suggesting that the disparity between brain size and that of the cranial cavity was not great. The same observation has been made for troodontid and dromaeosaurid theropods, "which are well enough preserved to show ventrolateral displacement of the optic lobes, and often have shallow canals on the ventral surfaces of frontoparietals" (P. J. Currie, personal communication to Osmólska 2004). Until Osmólska's study, evidence among dinosaurs of direct contact between the brain surface and the skull-roof bones had previously only been reported in two maniraptoran clades, the Ornithomimidae ("*Dromiceiomimus brevitertius*" [=*Ornithomimus edmontonicus*; see Russell 1972; Makovicky, Kobayashi and Currie 2004; see also *Ornithomimus* entry) and seemingly in the Troodontidae (*Troodon inequalis*; see Russell 1969; Hopson).

The specimen (previously described briefly by Barsbold 1983 and in an abstract by Osmólska 2003) described in detail in Osmólska's (2004) study consists of a fragment of skull roof measuring 42 millimeters in length, collected from the Upper Cretaceous White Beds at the Hermiin Tsav locality (see Gradziński, Kielan-Jaworowska and Maryańska 1977), in Ömögov'aimag, Mongolia. In comparing GIN 100/31 with various complete adult oviraporid cranial specimens, Osmólska (2004) estimated that, if complete, this specimen would have a basal length of from 110 to 130 millimeters, this being an average length for an adult oviraptorid.

As observed by Osmólska (2004), a latex endocast taken from GIN 100/31 shows that the brain was appressed to the underside of surface of the cranial roof, leaving imprints of brain vascularization. These imprints, found on the underside of the frontals and parietals, comprise a number of arborizing grooves that cover the undersurface of the skull roof bones in the region of the cerebral hemispheres and the cerebellum. As Osmólska (2003) had previously noted, the density and regularity of vascularization of the brain surface in this genus compare favorably to the scarce and irregular ones described in "*Dromiceiomimus*" [=*Ornithomimus edmontonicus*]. This advanced state of the brain tightly filling the endocranial cavity—being now known in the maniraptoran clades Ornithomimosauria, Troodontidae, Dromaeosauridae, and Oviraptoridae—could very well constitute a synapomorphy of the Maniraptora.

Additionally, it was Osmólska's (2003) opinion that the present finding could offer additional evidence supporting the hypothesis for an avian status of the Oviraptoridae (*e.g.*, see Elżanowski 1999; Maryańska, Osmólska and Wolson 2002; see also *S2*, *S3*).

Note: Because the neurocranial region in oviraptorid skulls is overlapped laterally by expanded bones of the temporal region, little has been known about the detailed anatomy of this region. In a study related to the above and published as an abstract, Kudrát, Maryańska and Osmólska (2004) offered the following characters of an exposed neurocranial wall in an oviraptorid skull (ZPAL MgD-I/05) from Mongolia: Neurocranium highly pneumatized except orbitosphenoid (as in most other oviraptorid cranial bones); epipterygoid enclosing laterally passage for ophthalmic branch of trigeminal nerve; ventral to auricular nerve, two acoustic fossae hollowed into medial side of neurocramium; rostral one of latter comprising rostrally foramen for facial nerve; prominentia canalis semicircularis anterior et prominentia utriculosaccularis between otic region and quadrate, indicating projection of tympanic membrane at distal end of concave posteromedial edge of quadrate; metotic fissure divided into smaller upper and larger lower parts by caudal process of opisthotic; bilobically shaped external acoustic fossa opening rostral to fissure, communicating with superior tympanic recess, latter deepening rostrally.

Key references: Barsbold (1983); Elżanowski (1999); Gradziński, Kielan-Jaworowska and Maryańska (1977); Hopson (1979); Kudrát, Maryańska and Osmólska (2004); Makovicky, Kobayashi and Currie (2004); Maryańska, Osmólska and Wolson (2002); Osmólska (2003, 2004); Russell (1969; 1972).

†ISANOSAURUS

Saurischia: Eusaurischia: Sauropodomorpha: Sauropoda.

Diagnosis of genus (as for type species): Prominent process (?cranial trochanter) projecting from proximal end of femur, lateral margin of femoral shaft, therefore, strongly concave in cranial aspect; femur with large fourth trochanter having sigmoid curvature (Upchurch, Barrett and Dodson 2004).

Comment: In their review of the Sauropoda, Upchurch, Barrett and Dodson (2004) *Isanosaurus attavipachi* (see *S2*), a type species that these authors regarded as a basal (yet not necessarily the basalmost) member of the Sauropoda. Its membership in that clade, Upchurch *et al.* noted, is supported by characters including the following: Cervical vertebrae having opisthocoelous centra; shaft of femur straight, craniocaudally compressed.

Key reference: Upchurch, Barrett and Dodson (2004).

ISISAURUS   Wilson and Upchurch 2003

Saurischia: Eusaurischia: Sauropodomorpha: Sauropoda: Eusauropoda: Neosauropoda: Macronaria: Titanosauriformes: Titanosauria: Lithostrotia.

Name derivation: *Isi* [ISI, Indian Statistical Institute] + Greek *sauros* = "lizard."

Type species: *I. colberti* (Jain and Bandyopadhyay 1997).

Other species: [None.]

Occurrence: Lameta Formation, Maharashtra, India.

Age: Late Cretaceous (Maastrichtian).

Known material/holotype: ISI R335/1–65, partial associated skeleton including partial axial column, shoulder and pelvic girdles, forelimb lacking radius and manus.

Diagnosis of genus (as for type species): Medium-sized sauropod sharing with titanosaurs caudal dorsal vertebrae lacking hyposphene-hypantrum articulations, procoelous proximal caudal vertebrae, deep hemal canal, prominent olecranon process, and platelike ischia (Wilson 2002*a*; Upchurch, Barrett and Dodson, 2004); with more derived forms, sharing broad proximal caudal neural spines, proximal and middle caudal centra with ventral longitudinal hollow, procoelous (cone-shaped) middle and distal caudal centra, scapular blade deflected dorsally, stout ulnar proportions, iliac blades oriented perpendicular to body of axis, ischium shorter than pubis (Wilson); autapomorphies including the following: rostrocaudally elongate cervical parapophyses (Jain and Bandyopadhyay 1997), cervical neural arches having prespinal and postspinal laminae, rostralmost dorsal vertebra having pronounced coel between prezygapophyseal, centrozygapophyseal, and rostral centrodiapophyseal laminae, caudal dorsal neural arches having parapophyses positioned above level of prezygapophyses and proximodistally compressed distal caudal chevron blades (Wilson) (Wilson and Upchurch 2003).

Comments: The genus *Isisaurus* was founded upon a partial skeleton (ISI R335/1–65) representing a single individual, collected from the Upper Cretaceous (Maastrichtian; see Jain and Bandyopadhyay 1997) Lameta Formation, from a locality near Dongaragaon Hill, in the Chandrapur district, Maharashtra, central India. The specimen was originally

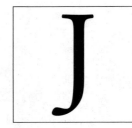

described by Jain and Bandyopadhyay (1997) as a new species of *Titanosaurus*, which they named *Titanosaurus colberti* (see *S1*).

More recently, Wilson and Upchurch (2003), in their reevaluation of the genus *Titanosaurus* (see entry) and its numerous species, designated the type species *Titanosaurus indicus* as a *nomen dubium*. These authors found *T. colberti* to be a valid species, its overlapping elements differing notably from the type caudal vertebrae of *T. indicus*. Unable to refer this species to the doubtful genus *Titanosaurus*, Wilson and Upchurch placed it into its own new genus, *Isisaurus*.

Recent cladistic studies (*e.g.*, Wilson; Upchurch, Barrett and Dodson, 2004) have placed *I. colberti* as a sister taxon to the titanosaurian family Saltasauridae.

Key references: Jain and Bandyopadhyay (1997); Upchurch, Barrett and Dodson, 2004); Wilson and Upchurch (2003).

†IUTICOSAURUS [*nomen dubium*]

Saurischia: Eusaurischia: Sauropodomorpha: Eusauropoda: Neosauropoda: Macronaria: Titanosauriformes: Titanosauria *incertae sedis*.

Type species: *I. valdensis* (Lydekker 1887) [*nomen dubium*].

Other species: ?*L. lydekkeri* (Huene 1888) [*nomen dubium*].

Occurrence: Wessex Formation (Wealden), ?Upper Greensand, Isle of Wight, England.

Known material/lectotypes: BMNH R146a and R151, caudal vertebrae.

Comments: In 1993, Jean Le Loeuff named and described the new genus *Iuticosaurus*, founded upon caudal vertebrae (BMNH R146a and R151) from the Wessex Formation on the Isle of Wight, this material originally having been described by Lydekker (1887) as *Titanosaurus valdensis*. Le Loeuff referred this new type species to the now defunct family "Titanosauridae," describing it as the oldest member of that clade known from Europe (see *D:TE*).

Subsequently, Le Loeuff's assessment of this material was questioned. Naish and Martill (2001), in a report on the dinosaurs of the Isle of Wight, did not accept the characters diagnosing this species to be valid and considered *I. valdensis* to be an indeterminate titanosaur.

More recently, Wilson and Upchurch (2003), in a thorough revision of the genus *Titanosaurus*, redescribed the type material of *I. valdensis*. In BMNH R146a, these authors found "no character states that indicate it belonged to a titanosaur" and regarded it as representing an indeterminate sauropod; moreover, the two autapomorphies (*i.e.*, "promontory" on lateral surface formed by ridge extending along ventral edge of neural spine onto neorocentral junction; neural spine terminating level with or beyond distal tip of centrum) found by Le Loeuff in BMNH R151 are also seen in other titanosaurs. Wilson and Upchurch (see also Upchurch, Barrett and Dodson 2004), therefore, also regarded *I. valdensis* as a *nomen dubium*.

Le Loeuff also referred to *Iuticosaurus* a proximal caudal centrum and partial neural arch (BMNH 32390) from the Upper Greensand (Cenomanian), Isle of Wight, originally described by Lydekker (1888) and named *Titanosaurus lydekkeri* by Huene (1929). Le Loeuff (also Naish and Martill; Wilson and Upchurch) regarded this second species as a *nomen dubium*. In redescribing this specimen, Wilson and Upchurch noted that, while apparently pertaining to a titanosaur, it displays no autapomorphic features to distinguish it at the generic level.

Key references: Huene (1888); Le Loeuff (1993); Lydekker (1887); Naish and Martill (2001); Upchurch, Barrett and Dodson (2004); Wilson and Upchurch (2003).

†JANENSCHIA

Saurischia: Eusaurischia: Sauropodomorpha: Sauropoda: Eusauropoda: Neosauropoda: Macronaria: Titanosauriformes: Titanosauria.

Diagnosis of genus (as for type species): Metatarsal V shorter than metatarsal I; ungual on pedal digit I longer than combined metacarpal I and phalanx I-1 (Upchurch, Barrett and Dodson 2004).

Comments: In their review of the Sauropoda, Upchurch, Barrett and Dodson (2004) rediagnosed the type species *Janenschia robusta* (see *D:TE*).

Although *Janenschia* had recently been reclassified as a possible camarsauromorph (Bonaparte, Heinrich and Wild 2000; see *S2*), the following titanosaurian synapomorphies were observed by Upchurch *et al.* (as previously noted by Upchurch 1995, 1998; Wilson and Sereno 1998) in this species: Radius and ulna robust; ulna having well-developed olecranon and concave area on articular surface of craniomedial process of proximal end. Upchurch *et al.* regarded *Janenschia* as representing "the earliest known osteological evidence for titanosaurians," these authors provisionally considering this genus to be "a basal titanosaurian pending its inclusion in a cladistic analysis."

Key references: Bonaparte, Heinrich and Wild (2000); Upchurch (1995, 1998); Upchurch, Barrett and Dodson (2004); Wilson and Sereno (1998).

†JAXARTOSAURUS

Ornithischia: Predentata: Genasauria: Cerapoda:

Ornithopoda: Euornithopoda: Iguanodontia: Dryomorpha: Ankylopollexia: Styracosterna: Iguanodontoidea: Hadrosauroidea: Euhadrosauria: Hadrosauridae: Lambeosaurinae *incertae sedis*.

Holotype: PIN 1/5009, caudal part of skull, juvenile.

Comments: Godefroit, Bolotsky and Van Itterbeeck (2004), in a paper focusing upon the Russian basal lambeosaurine *Amurosaurus* (see entry), also commented on *Jaxartosaurus aralensis* (see *D:TE*), a type species that Anatoly Nikolaenvice N. Riabinin had named and described in 1939, based on the caudal part of a skull (PIN 1/5009), and also a dentary and a few postcranial elements (these additional remains apparently having been lost; V. R. Alifanov, personal communication to Godefroit *et al.*, 2002).

According to Godefroit *et al.*, *J. aralensis* is positively a member of the Lambeosaurinae, displaying as it does the following lambeosaurine synapomorphies: Frontal-prefrontal region excavated, forming base for hollow crest; parietal short, having length/minimal width ratio of less than two; frontals forming well-developed median bulge (usually observed in juvenile lambeosaurines).

While various authors (*e.g.*, Maryańska and Osmólska 1981; Weishampel and Horner 1990) have regarded *J. aralensis* as a *nomen dubium*, Godefroit *et al.* considered the species to be "a valid taxon that cannot be synonymized with any other known lambeosaurine," displaying these autapomorphies: Lateral bar of supratemporal fenestra short, extremely robust; prootic process of laterosphenoid particularly thickened.

Godefroit *et al.* found *Jaxartosaurus* to occupy a basal position within Lambeosaurinae, based on the following features: Lateral border of squamosal not elevated above cotylus (as in "corythosaurs," "parasaurolophs," and *Amurosaurus*); excavated portion of frontal proportionally shorter and shallower than in other lambeosaurines except *Tsintaosaurus*. Based upon these considerations, Godefroit *et al.* determined that *Jaxartosaurus* is the sister taxon to a clade comprising Corythosaurini plus Parasaurolophini plus *Amurosaurus*, with *Tsintaosaurus* the sister taxon of the clade consisting of *Jaxartosaurus* plus the higher lambeosaurines (see also Horner, Weishampel and Forster 2004, "Systematics" chapter).

As Godefroit *et al.* recounted, Riabinin had referred to *J. aralensis* a fragmentary left humerus, a specimen now lost. This humerus, the authors noted, is especially narrow; nor does it exhibit an enlarged deltopectoral crest, a lambeosaurine synapomorphic feature observed in *Tsintaosaurus* (see Yang 1958). If this humerus was, in fact, associated with the holotype skull of *J. aralensis* rather than belonging to some contemporary hadrosaurine, then "*Jaxartosaurus, Tsintaosaurus,* and higher lambeosaurines form an unresolved trichotomy in the current state of our knowledge."

The authors further observed that the prefrontal in both *J. aralensis* and *Amurosaurus riabinini* contributes largely in the formation of the depressed base of the hollow crest. Given the assumption that *A. aralensis* is a basal member of the Lambeosaurinae, Godefroit *et al.* considered the possibility "that this condition is plesiomorphic in the Lambeosaurinae, and that the more or less complete exclusion of the prefrontal from the base of the crest (*e.g.*, as in *Corythosaurus*) is apomorphic, this hypothesis requiring further investigation to be demonstrated.

Key references: Godefroit, Bolotsky and Van Itterbeeck (2004); Horner, Weishampel and Forster (2004; Maryańska and Osmólska (1981); Riabinin (1939); Weishampel and Horner (1990); Yang (1958).

†JIANGSHANOSAURUS

Saurischia: Eusaurischia: Sauropodomorpha: Sauropoda: Eusauropoda: Neosauropoda: Macronaria: Titanosauriformes: Titanosauria: ?Lithostrotia.

Diagnosis of genus (as for type species): Scapula having large proximal expansion, resulting in "P"-shaped profile of scapula in lateral aspect; coracoid foramen at center of coracoid (coracoid foramen displaced forward or upward in some European Titanosauria) (Upchurch, Barrett and Dodson 2004).

Comments: In their review of the Sauropoda, Upchurch, Barrett and Dodson (2004) rediagnosed the type species *Jiangshanosaurus lixianensis* (see *S3*).

As noted by Upchurch *et al.*, evidence suggests that this taxon could "represent a derived titanosaur, perhaps a member of Lithostrotia" (*e.g.*, procoelous proximal caudal vertebrae persisting to at least middle of tail).

Key reference: Upchurch, Barrett and Dodson (2004).

†JINGSHANOSAURUS

Saurischia: Eusaurischia: Sauropodomorpha: Sauropoda: Prosauropoda: Plateosauria.

Diagnosis of genus (as for type species): Autapomorphies including the following: Small external mandibular fenestra; massive sacrocostal yoke (developed independently in Sauropoda); massive carpal block formed by fusion of second through fifth distal carpals (Galton and Upchurch 2004*a*).

Comment: In their review of the Prosauropoda, Galton and Upchurch (2004*a*) rediagnosed the type species *Jingshanosaurus xinwaensis* (see *S1*).

Key reference: Galton and Upchurch (2004*a*).

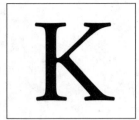

†JUBBULPURIA—(=?*Coeluroides*, ?*Dryptosauroides*, ?*Indosaurus*, ?*Indosuchus*, ?*Ornithomimoides*)

Saurischia: Eusaurischia: Theropoda: Neotheropoda: Ceratosauria: Abelisauroidea: Abelisauridae *incertae sedis*.

Comments: Friedrich von Huene, in 1932, named and described *Jubbulpuria tenuis*, a new theropod type species established upon two small vertebrae (presumed to be dorsals) (GSI K20/612 and GSI K27/614) from the Lameta Formation of India. The following year, Huene, in a report co-authored with Charles Alfred Matley, further described these remains in their review of Indian dinosaurs (see *D:TE*).

In a more recent review of the theropod material described by those authors, Novas, Agnolin and Bandyopadhyay (2004), in reevaluating the only available specimen (GSI K20/612) belonging to this taxon, recognized it as a distal caudal, not a dorsal, vertebra.

Novas *et al.* made the following observations concerning this specimen: Centrum low, elongate, with expanded and dorsally excavated transverse processes (as in abelisauroid *Coeluroides largus*; see *Coeluroides* entry), neural spine proximodistally extended; postzygapophyses facing laterally (as in distal caudal vertebrae of the abelisaurid *Majungatholus*, carnosaur *Allosaurus*, and coelurosaur *Tyrannosaurus*, and other theropods); transverse processes wing-shaped, appearing rather well developed for distal caudal, those of other abelisaurids (*e.g.*, *Majungatholus*, Novas *et al.*, personal observation) lacking well-developed transverse processes; dorsal surface excavated (dorsally flattened in Abelisauridae).

As the distal caudal vertebrae of the "Neocomian" [=Hauterivian] basal abelisauroid *Ligabueino andesi* (see *S1*) exhibits similarly developed transverse processes (see Bonaparte 1996), Novas *et al.* referred *Jubbulpuria* to the Abelisauroidea, also agreeing with Norman (1990) that this genus should be considered a *nomen dubium*.

The elements referred to *Jubbulpuria*, *Compsosuchus*, *Dryptosauroides*, and *Ornithomimoides* (see entries) pertain to different portions of the neck and tail, Novas *et al.* noted, intimating that some or all of these taxa may be congeneric.

Key references: Bonaparte (1996); Huene (1932); Huene and Matley (1933); Norman (1990); Novas, Agnolin and Bandyopadhyay (2004).

†KAKURU

Saurischia: Eusaurischia: Theropoda: Neotheropoda: Tetanurae: Avetheropoda: Coelurosauria *incertae sedis*.

Known material: Opalized fragmentary right tibia, opalized pedal phalanx.

Holotype: Fragmentary right tibia.

Comments: In 1980, Ralph E. Molnar and N. S. Pledge named and described a theropod type species, *Kakuru junani*, based on a partial opalized tibia and a referred opalized pedal phalanx, collected from the Marree Formation of South Australia. As the original fossil materials had been sold at auction in 1973, Molnar and Pledge had to described their new taxon based upon a "plastoholotype" (SAM 17926) cast of the original tibia and also a cast (SAM P18010) of the phalanx (see *D:TE*).

Recently, however, one of the above authors (R. E. Molnar, personal communication 2004) informed the present writer that "The specimen on which *Kakuru kujani* was based ... has reappeared and been donated to the South Australian Museum."

Key reference: Molnar and Pledge (1980).

†KENTROSAURUS

Ornithischia: Predentata: Genasauria: Thyreophora: Thyreophoroidea: Eurypoda: Stegosauria: Stegosauridae: Stegosaurinae.

Diagnosis of genus (as for type species): Autapomorphies including the following: Skull with prominent paraquadrate foramen; caudal vertebrae with cranially directed neural arches; neural spines of distal two-thirds of tail showing marked anticline; hemal arches "plough"-shaped; (probably apomorphic) cheek teeth simple, with only seven marginal denticles; dorsal armor comprising double series of small, paired plates (?15) and spines (Galton and Upchurch 2004*b*).

Comment: In their review of the Stegosauria, Galton and Upchurch (2004*b*) rediagnosed the type species *Kentrosaurus aethiopicus* (see *D:TE*).

Key reference: Galton and Upchurch (2004*b*).

KERBEROSAURUS   Bolotsky and Godefroit 2004

Ornithischia: Predentata: Genasauria: Cerapoda: Ornithopoda: Euornithopoda: Iguanodontia: Dryomorpha: Ankylopollexia: Styracosterna: Iguanodontoidea: Hadrosauroidea: Euhadrosauria: Hadrosauridae: Hadrosaurinae: Saurolophini.

Name derivation: *Kerberos* [in Greek mythology, the monstrous canine guardian of the Tartarus] + Greek *sauros* = "lizard."

Type species: *K. manakini* Bolotsky and Godefroit 2004.

Other species: [None.]

Occurrence: Tsagayan Formation, Amur Region, Russia.

Age: Late Cretaceous (?late Maastrichtian).

Known material: Partial cranium, several tentatively referred isolated cranial bones.

Holotype: AENM 1/319, caudal part of cranium.

Diagnosis of genus (as for type species): Autapomorphies including the following: basisphenoid processes of prootic deeply excavated by pocketlike depression; groove for ramus opthalmicus laterosphenoid; postotic foramina not restricted rostrally by prominent ridge; frontal particularly narrow mediolaterally; rostral margin of parietal depressed, circumnarial depressions limited by strong, wide, flattened crest on lateral side of nasal around external nares; maxilla having very prominent hooklike palatine process (Bolotsky and Godefroit 2004).

Comments: The hadrosaurine genus *Kerberosaurus* was founded upon a partial cranium (AENM 1/319) collected from a bonebed in the middle part of the Tsagayan Formation (see Bolotsky and Moiseyenko 1988), *Wodehouseia spinata-Aquilapollenites subtilis* palynozone (see Markevich and Bugdaeva 1997, 2001), near Blagoveschensk City, in the Amur-Zeya sedimentary Basin, Amur Region, Far Eastern Russia. Isolated remains from the same locality, tentatively referred to the type species *Kerberosaurus manakini*, include fused, paired exoccipitals (AENM 1/321), frontals (AENM 1/30, 1/31, 1/32, and 1/222), prefrontals (AENM 1/243 and 1/320), a jugal (AENM 1/200), nasals (AENM 1/318 and 1/324), a squamosal (AENM 1/36), quadrate (AENM 1/38), and maxillae (AENM 1/322 and 1/323). These latter remains were assumed to belong to *K. manakini*, as no evidence suggests that any other hadrosaurine taxa existed in this area during Maastrichtian time (Bolotsky and Godefroit 2004).

In performing a phylogenetic analyisis, incorporating 10 taxa and 21 cranial characters (only those directly observed by the authors in the remains referred to *K. manakini*), Bolotsky and Godefroit referred *Kerberosaurus* to the Hadrosauridae based upon the following synapomorphies (not found in the apparently nonhadrosaurid hadrosauroid *Bactrosaurus*): Rostral process of jugal dorsoventrally expanded; antorbital fenestra entirely surrounded by maxilla; ectopterygoid ridge strongly developed; distal head of quadrate dominated by large hemispherical lateral condyle; paraquadratic foramen absent.

Bolotsky and Godefroit further noted that *Kerberosaurus* lacks synapomorphies of the hadrosaurid subfamily Lambeosaurinae, but is characterized by various synapomorphies of the Hadrosaurinae: Circumnarial depression extending onto nasal; external naris enlarged (reversed in *Maiasaura*); maxilla roughly symmetrical in lateral aspect.

The authors further noted that, within Hadrosaurinae, various genera cluster together into lower-level clades (Bolotsky and Godefroit therefore mostly adopting the "tribes" introduced by Michael K. Brett-

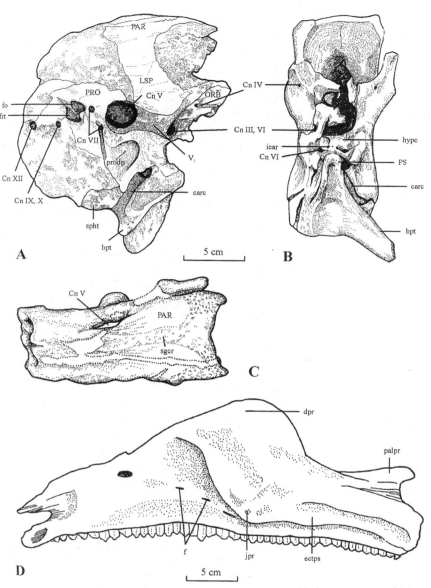

Surman in his 1989 unpublished PhD dissertation; see *D:TE*; see also Chapman and Brett-Surman 1991). Brett-Surman's clade Saurolophini is diagnosed by two characters: Development of narrow solid crest; and caudal extension of circumnarial depression above or caudal to rostral margin of orbit. Because in *Kerberosaurus* the frontal is excluded from the orbital rim (a character evolved convergently in the Lambeosaurinae), Bolotsky and Godefroit found this genus to be the sister taxon of the saurolph clade (see also Horner, Weishampel and Forster 2004, "Systematics" chapter).

According to Bolotsky and Godefroit, the autapomorphies — an original combination of primitive and derived characters — diagnosing *K. manalkini* show "that this taxon is not simply a new species of some already existing genus, but a new genus

Kerberosaurus manakini, AENM 1/319, holotype braincase in A. lateral, B. ventral, and C. dorsals views; D. composite reconstruction of left maxilla, in lateral view, based on AENM 1/32 and 1/323. (After Bolotsky and Godefroit 2004.)

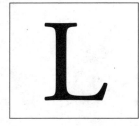

occupying an original position within the phylogenetic tree of Hadrosaurinae."

Considering *Kerberosaurus* to be the sister taxon to the sauroloph group, Bolotsky and Godefroit pointed out that the oldest known member of this group is the Campanian-age *Prosaurolophus*, from the Judith River Formation of Alberta and Montana and the Two Medicine Formation of Alberta. Therefore, *Kerberosaurus* can be assumed to be of middle to late Maastrichtian age, this implying that the lineage leading to this new genus branched off from "the sauroloph + edmontosaur clade no longer than the late Campanian, with a relatively long ghost lineage duration of 8 to 10 million years."

As explained by Bolotsky and Godefroit, an interior seaway divided North American into western Cordilleran and eastern shield regions during Late Cretaceous times. A land route probably opened across the Beringian isthmus (see Fiorilla 2005 for a brief report on Alaskan dinosaurs and the assembly of Beringia) during the Aptian–Albian, connecting Asia with Cordilleran North America, persisting into the Late Cretaceous. This land connection permitted numerous Asian vertebrate groups to migrate towards western North America by Campanian–Maastrichtian time, although no dinosaurian families had formerly been known to have then migrated from North America to Asia (see Jerzykiewicz and Russell 1989; Russell 1993). Study of the Amur dinosaur fauna (including *Kerberosaurus*, and the lambeosaurines *Amurosaurus riabini* and *Charonosaurus jiayinensis*), however, reveals that several hadrosaurid lineages probably also migrated from western North America into Asia. As Bolotsky and Godefroit noted, the common ancestor of both *Kerberosaurus* and the sauroloph clade probably lived in western North America before or at the start of the late Campanian, the ancestors of *Kerberosaurus* migrating to eastern Asia after this time and prior to the late Maastrichtian.

Furthermore, Bolotsky and Godefroit pointed out, the sister-taxon relationship (see Godefroit, Zan and Jin 2001) of late Maastrichtian, Chinese lambeosaurine *Charonosaurus jiayinensis* (see *2, S3*) with the late Campanian, North American lambeosaurine *Parasaurolophus* implies a pre–late Maastrichtian east to west migration. As the genus *Saurolophus* is known from both western Canada and Mongolia while its geologically older sister taxon *Prosaurolophus* is known only from western North America, the authors concluded that *Saurolophus* also probably migrated from North America into Asia in late Campanian or early Maastrichtian time. Consequently and despite the Beringian isthmus, numerous faunal exchanges between Asia and western North America occurred by Campanian–Maastrichtian time, both regions apparently merging from a biogeographical perspective.

As already pointed out by Godefroit *et al.* (2000, 2001), Maastrichtian Amur Region dinosaur faunas differ completely from potentially synchronous "Lancian" faunas from North America. This, according to Bolotsky and Godefroit, indicates the existence of some kind of geographical or paleoecological barrier separating these two regions during the late Maastrichtian.

Key references: Bolotsky and Godefroit (2004); Bolotsky and Moieseyenko 1988); Brett-Surman (1989); Chapman anbd Brett-Surman (1990); Godefroit, Zan and Jin (2000, 2001); Horner, Weishampel and Forster (2004); Jerzykiewicz and Russell (1989); Russell (1993).

†KLAMELISAURUS

Saurischia: Eusaurischia: Sauropodomorpha: Sauropoda: ?Eusauropod.

Diagnosis of genus (as for type species): Fusion of neural spines of three caudalmost cervical vertebrae (Upchurch, Barrett and Dodson 2004).

Comments: In their review of the Sauropoda, Upchurch, Barrett and Dodson (2004) rediagnosed the type species *Klamelisaurus gobiensis* (see *D:TE*).

As Upchurch *et al.* pointed out, some features of *Klamelisaurus* (*e.g.*, broad spatulate teeth; 16 cervical and five sacral vertebrae; forked chevrons of caudal vertebrae) suggest that this genus resembles *Omeisaurus* and could represent a nonneosauropodid member of the Eusauropoda.

Key reference: Upchurch, Barrett and Dodson (2004).

†KOTASAURUS

Saurischia: Eusaurischia: Sauropodomorpha: Sauropoda *incertae sedis*.

Diagnosis of genus (as for type species): Long, low preacetabular process of ilium maintaining dorsoventral width over its entire length (Upchurch, Barrett and Dodson 2004).

Comment: In their review of the Sauropoda, Upchurch, Barrett and Dodson (2004) rediagnosed the type species *K. yamanpalliensis* (see *D:TE*), regarded by these authors as a sauropod outside of Eusauropoda.

Key reference: Upchurch, Barrett and Dodson (2004).

†LABOCANIA

Saurischia: Eusaurischia: Theropoda: Neotheropoda: Tetanurae *incertae sedis*.

Diagnosis of genus (as for type species): Lateral surface of metatarsal II flattened (reminiscent of buttressing surfaces of tyrannosaurid arctometatarsi, also with general tetanuran condition of metatarsal III being slightly compressed within metatarsus, as in *Allosaurus* and *Sinraptor*); (as in Abelisauridae) frontals thick; quadrate apparently markedly angled caudoventrally (vertically in Tyrannosauridae); dorsal surface of frontal showing no sign of supratemporal muscle scar found in Tyrannosauridae; hemal process "L"-shaped, with longer distal than proximal extension (similar to those in end of proximal area of series in Tyrannosauridae, or middle of series in Carnosauria, unlike vertical, tapered hemal processes in Ceratosauria); maxillary teeth ziphodont (unlike in Tyrannosauridae); premaxillary teeth lacking "U"-shaped cross section of tyrannosaurids, more similar to teeth in carnosaurs, basal tetanurans, and ceratosaurs (Holtz 2004).

Comment: Holtz (2004), in his review of the Tyrannosauroidea, rediagnosed the type species *Labocania anomala* (see *D:TE*).

Key reference: Holtz (2004).

†LAEVISUCHUS

Saurischia: Eusaurischia: Theropoda: Neotheropoda: Ceratosauria: Abelisauroidea: Noasauridae.

Comments: In 1932, Friedrich von Huene named and described the new theropod *Laevisuchus indicus*, a type species founded upon four vertebrae—three cervicals (GSI K20/613, K20/614, and K20/696) and one dorsal (GSI K27/588)—recovered from the Lameta Formation of India. The following year, Huene—in a paper co-authored with Charles Alfred Matley on Indian dinosaurs—described a number of theropod specimens, including *L. indicus*.

More recently, in a review of the Indian theropods described in Huene and Matley (1933), Novas, Agnolin and Bandyopadhyay (2004) reassessed *L. indicus*, noting, unfortunately, that only GSI K27/696—presumably a fifth cervical vertebra—could be located for their examination.

Norman (1990), in a review of problematic "coelurosaurs," had perceived the vertebra of *L. indicus* as resembling that of the coelurosaur *Aristosuchus* [=*Calamospondylus* of Novas *et al.*'s usage; see *S3*]. *Contra* Norman, however, Novas *et al.* pointed out that the vertebrae of these taxa differ saliently in the following ways: Number of pleurocoels (one in *Aristosuchus*, two in *Laevisuchus*); cranial articular surface (convex in *Aristosuchus*, kidney-shaped in *Laevisuchus*); dorsal surface of neural arch (not transversally wide or well defined in *Aristosuchus*, transversely wide and well defined in *Laevisuchus*). These distinctions,

Novas *et al.* posited, preclude assignment of *Laevisuchus* to the Coelurosauria.

Contrarily, Novas *et al.* identified in the vertebra of *Laevisuchus* a number of features characteristic of the Abelisauroidea: Elongate epipophyses; pair of foramina on centrum; neural spines pyramidal, transversely thick.

In comparing *Laevisuchus* to abelisaurid abelisauroids, Novas *et al.* noted the following: Cervical vertebrae proportionally longer than in *Carnotaurus* and *Majungatholus*; cranial articular surface slightly concave (not convex as in *Carnotaurus*); articular surfaces of prezygapophyses craniocaudally wide (transversely expanded in *Carnotaurus* and *Majungatholus*); large pneumatic cavities below prezygapophyses (cavities smaller in diameter in *Carnotaurus* and *Majungatholus*).

Within the Abelisauroidea, Novas *et al.* found *Laevisuchus* to resemble more closely the noasaurids *Noasaurus* and *Masiakasaurus* (see the suggestion by Carrano, Sampson and Forster 2002 that all three genera belong in the family Noasauridae, sharing cervical vertebrae with cranially located neural spines, and caudally reduced cervical epipophyses). As Novas *et al.* pointed out, *Laevisuchus* and *Noasaurus* are further similar to one another in the following ways: Development of pneumatic cavities; cranial cervical vertebrae presumably lacking neural spines; position of prezygapophyses and postzygapophyses.

Laevisuchus differs from *Noasaurus*, Novas *et al.* noted, in exhibiting the following features: Shallower antediapophyseal, postdiapophyseal, and diapophyseal cavities; diapophyses wider, less ventrally directed; neural spine less extended craniocaudally; (in dorsal aspect) prezygapophyses shorter, postzygapophyses caudally rounded (acute in *Noasaurus*). Also, *Laevisuchus* differs from *Masiakasaurus* in the following: Region between postzygapophyses less excavated; prezygapophyses thinner; infrapostzygapophyseal and infraprezygapophyseal cavities shallower.

Key references: Carrano, Sampson and Forster (2002); Huene (1932); Huene and Matley (1933); Norman (1990); Novas, Agnolin and Bandyopadhyay (2004).

†LAMBEOSAURUS

Ornithischia: Predentata: Genasauria: Cerapoda: Ornithopoda: Euornithopoda: Iguanodontia: Dryomorpha: Ankylopollexia: Styracosterna: Iguanodontoidea: Hadrosauroidea: Euhadrosauria: Hadrosauridae: Lambeosaurinae: Corythosaurini.

Comments: To date, *Lambeosaurus magnicristatus*, the rare referred species of the high-crested genus *Lambeosaurus*, is known from only two definitive

Lambeosaurus

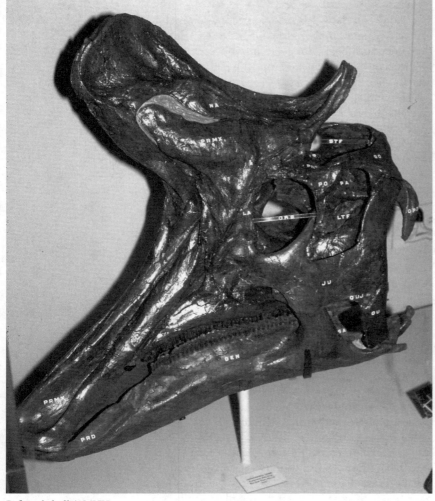

Referred skull (AMNH 5353) of the type species *Lambeosaurus lambei*, collected at Red Deer River in Alberta, Canada. This specimen measures almost one 0.9 meters (three feet) in length.

Referred skeleton (cast) of the lambeosaurine hadrosaurid *Lambeosaurus lambei*.

specimens — the holotype (CMN [formerly CGS and NMC] 8705), a poorly preserved skull and unprepared postcranial skeleton, and an articulated, almost complete referred skeleton with a well-preserved skull (TMP 66.04.01), the crest of which has an incomplete dorsal margin, and skin impressions (see *D:TE* for photographs). Both specimens were collected from the uppermost Upper Cretaceous (Campanian) Dinosaur Park Formation of Alberta, Canada, at a higher stratigraphic level than that which yielded all recorded specimens of the type species, *Lambeosaurus lambei*, and all other known lambeosarine specimens from that formation.

In a published abstract for a poster, Evans and Reisz (2004) briefly described of the referred skeleton, noting that this specimen offers new data regarding the braincase and postcranial skeleton of *L. magnicristatus*. Details observed by the authors in this specimen include the following: Dorsal process of premaxilla characteristically well developed rostrally and dorsally, forming acute angle to snout; incompleteness

of crest accounting for less full, dorsally excavated profile seen in CMN 8705; (as in *L. lambei*) laterosphenoid enclosing canal for ophtalmic nerve; position of rostroventral deflection of dentary more typical of other members of Lambeosaurinae than in

Life restoration by Berislav Krzic of *Lambeosaurus lambei*, the type species of the genus *Lambeosaurus*.

CMN 8705, consequently having doubtful taxonomic value; cervical series (complete) comprising 14 vertebrae including atlas-axis complex; forearm proportionately longer than humerus; fourth trochanter of femur large, symmetrical across horizontal plane (in lateral aspect); tibia 95 percent length of femur; skin impressions in regions of neck, upper arm, and crus.

Performing a preliminary cladistic analysis of the Lambeosaurinae, Evans and Reisz found *Lambeosaurus* to be a monophyletic taxon supported by at least six unambiguous cranial synapomorphies, with a remaining unresolved relationship between this genus, a monophyletic *Parasaurolophus*, and "corythosaurs."

Given biostratigraphic information and the incompleteness of the crest in the referred specimen, Evans and Reisz found evidence supported earlier published proposals of sexual dimorphism in *L. magnicristatus*.

Key reference: Evans and Reisz (2004).

†LAPLATASAURUS

Saurischia: Eusaurischia: Sauropodomorpha: Sauropoda: Eusauropoda: Neosauropoda: Macronaria: Titanosauriformes: Titanosauria: Lithostrotia *incertae sedis*.

Lectotype: MPL 26–306 [formerly cotypes MLP CS 1127 and 1128, respectively], right tibia and fibula.

Diagnosis of genus (as for type species); Tibia slender, cnemial crest longer than in *Antarctosaurus*, separated from axis of proximal end by clear depression on lateral face; distal end of tibia transversely wide; robustness index of tibia = 0.40; fibula slender, with prominent double lateral tuberosities, clearly defined depression on anteroproximal corner of external face (Powell 2003).

Comments: In 1929, Friederich von Huene named and described the new type species *Laplatasaurus araukanicus*, founded upon various postcranial remains from the Upper Cretaceous of Patagonia previously described by Lydekker (1893), in the latter's study on Pataginian dinosaurs, as *Titanosaurus*. Later, Powell (1986) reinterpreted *L. araukanicus* as belonging in the genus *Titanosaurus* as the species *T. araukanicus* (see *Titanosaurus* entry, S1).

In redescribing this species, Powell observed that the right fibula and right tibia of the lectotype are quite similar to elements described by Swinton (1947; see *Titanosaurus* entry) from the Chota Simla, near Jabalpur, India, in general proportions and morphology—especially in their slenderness, limited development of their distal articulations, and double lateral tuberosities on the proximal half of the fibula's external face. Nevertheless, differences between the South American and Indian species in the caudal vertebrae—in *Titanosaurus indicus*, centra relatively much longer and laterally compressed, with flattened, taller, vertically oriented walls—allow for their separation at the species level. Powell restricted reference to *L. araukanicus* the material collected from the lower level of the Allen Formation, from the Cinco Saltos and Lago Pellegrini localities, in Río Negro Province, Argentina.

More recently, Wilson and Upchurch, in their reevaluation of the genus *Titanosaurus* and the many species that have been referred to it, noted that Powell's referral decision was based upon similarities of the *L. araukanicus* material to remains that had been assigned without reliability to the type species *T. indicus* (see *Titanosaurus* entry, this volume). Consequently, the Patagonian material cannot be convincingly referred to *Titanosaurus*, a genus founded upon two dorsal vertebrae. Moreover, Wilson and Upchurch regarded "the hypertrophied fibular lateral trochanter to be diagnostic for a subgroup of Titanosauria" (see, for example, Wilson 2002; Upchurch, Barrett and Dodson 2004) and "aspects of the proportions and double lateral tuberosity of the fibula to be diagnostic at the generic level." It was Wilson and Upchurch's recommendation that *Laplatasaurus* be retained as a valid genus.

Key references: Huene (1929); Lydekker (1893); Powell (1986); Swinton (1947); Upchurch, Barrett and Dodson (2004); Wilson (2002*a*); Wilson and Upchurch (2003).

†LAPPARENTOSAURUS

Saurischia: Eusaurischia: Sauropodomorpha: Sauropoda: Eusauropoda: Neosauropoda: Macronaria: Titanosauriformes *incertae sedis*.

Diagnosis of genus (as for type species): Extremely shallow concave area at distal end of caudal surface of humerus; craniolateral surface of proximal end of femur with two distinct ridges extending ventrally and slightly medially across shaft of femur (Upchurch, Barrett and Dodson 2004).

Comment: In their review of the Sauropoda, Upchurch, Barrett and Dodson (2004) rediagnosed the type species *Lapparentosaurus madagascariensis* (see *D:TE*).

Key reference: Upchurch, Barrett and Dodson (2004).

†LESSEMSAURUS

Saurischia: Eusaurischia: Sauropodomorpha: Sauropoda: Prosauropoda: Anchisauria: Melanorosauridae.

Diagnosis of genus (as for type species): Autapomorphies including the following: Middle and caudal cervical vertebrae having tall neural arches with strong transverse infrapostzygapophyseal fossa; neural spines of middle and caudal dorsal vertebrae higher than wide (height to width ratio 1.5–2.1) (Galton and Upchurch 2004*a*).

Comment: In their review of the Prosauropoda, Galton and Upchurch (2004*a*) rediagnosed *Lessemsaurus sauropodies* (see *D:TE*), also noting that the vertebrae in this large (length nine meters) type species are more sauropodlike than those of any other known prosauropod.

Key reference: Galton and Upchurch (2004*a*).

†LEXOVISAURUS

Ornithischia: Predentata: Genasauria: Thyreophora: Thyreophoroidea: Eurypoda: Stegosauria: Stegosauridae: Stegosaurinae.

Diagnosis of genus (as for type species): Autapomorphies including the following: In proximal third of tail, centra of caudal vertebrae having large proximal chevron facet uniting with distal facet, giving "V"-shaped centrum in caudals seven through 11; midcaudal vertebrae having vertical neural spines; pubis with rugose central thickening; osteoderms including seven large, tall, thin plates, height more than twice axial length (Galton and Upchurch 2004*b*).

Comment: In their review of the Stegosauria, Galton and Upchurch (2004*b*) rediagnosed the type species *Lexovisaurus durobrivensis* (see *D:TE*).

Key reference: Galton and Upchurch (2004*b*).

†LIAONINGOSAURUS

Ornithischia: Predentata: Genasauria: Thyreophora: Thyreophoroidea: Eurypoda: Ankylosauria *incertae sedis*.

Diagnosis of genus (as for type species): Trapezoidal sternum with slendor, distally pointed posterolateral process and short medial articular margin; pes more than as long as manus; extremely large maxillary and dentary teeth; mosaic of osteoderms ventral to pelvis (Vickaryous, Maryańska and Weishampel 2004).

Comment: In their review of the Ankylosauria, Vickaryous, Maryańska and Weishampel (2004) rediagnosed the type species *Liaoningosaurus paradoxus* (see *S3*).

Key reference: Vickaryous, Maryańska and Weishampel (2004).

†LILIENSTERNUS

Saurischia: Eusaurischia: Eusaurischia: Theropoda: Neotheropoda: Ceratosauria: Coelophysoidea.

Type species: *L. liliensterni* (Huene 1934).
Other species: ?*L. airelensis* Cuny and Galton 1993 [*nomen dubium*].
Diagnosis of ?*L. airelensis*: Cervical vertebrae having dorsally narrow, craniocaudally elongated caudal pleurocoel; deep infradiapophseal fossa in cranial caudal vertebrae; cervical vertebrae with horizontal ridge at basis of neural spine; ilium having triangular lateral bulge above supraacetabular crest (Rauhut 2003*c*).

Comments: In reviewing the available coelophysoid material from the Early Jurassic of Europe, Carrano and Sampson (2004) reassessed the referred species *Liliensternus airelensis* (regarded by Tykoski and Rowe 2004, in their review of Ceratosauria, as a *nomen dubium*; see below).

In 1993, Gilles Cuny and Peter M. Galton Galton (1993) had based this species on vertebrae (five cervicals, two dorsals, four sacrals, and several caudals), parts of the pelvic girdle, and a tooth (Caen Museum specimen, no catalog number) collected from the Airel Quarry in the Upper Triassic–Lower Jurassic ("Rhaetian"–Hettangian) Moon-Airel Formation of Normandy France, this material having been originally referred by Larsonneur and Lappatent (1966) to the genus *Halticosaurus* as *Halticosaurus* sp. (see *D:TE*).

Carrano and Sampson noted that originally Cuny and Galton had described the sacrum of this species as including four vertebrae — two primordial sacrals, one dorsosacral, and one caudosacral — likening this pattern to the condition seen in the type species *Liliensternus liliensterni* and also in the coelophysoid *Dilophosaurus wetherilli*. While agreeing with that interpretation, Carrano and Sampson pointed out that most primitive neotheropods, the coelophysoids *Coelophysis* and *Syntarsus* included, possess sacra comprising five vertebrae, the fifth being drawn from the caudal dorsal series. Carrano and Sampson further noted that, if not sufficiently preserved, this dorsosacral vertebra can be difficult to identify, bearing as it does just slight modifications of the transverse process for contact with the ilium. As the caudal dorsal described by Cuny and Galton lacks its neural arch and was found attached to the first dorsosacral, Carrano and Sampson suggested that it could represent the second dorsosacral. If that interpretation is correct, then the sacrum of ?*L. airelensis* possessed five vertebrae.

Regarding the phylogenetic status of this species, Carrano and Sampson confirmed its identity as a member of the Coelophysoidea based on the following vertebral and pelvic synapomorphies: Distinct caudal "pleurocoel" in cervical vertebrae; cervical centra vertebrae craniocaudally long; sacral ribs fused to transverse processes; ilium having cranially facing pubic peduncle.

Carrano and Sampson also observed that the articulated right pubis and ischium of ?*L. airelensis* may not be truly fused, as evidenced by a suture between these elements, while the left pubis and ischium are not fused; that the presence of a pubic foramen or fenestra below the obturator foramen cannot be confirmed; and that various other features seen in ?*L. airelensis* (*e.g.*, subequally sized iliac peduncles, closed obturator foramen in proximal pubis, craniocaudally long dorsal centra) could be plesiomorphic, these being characteristic of most primitive theropods (see Sereno 1999*a*; Carrano, Sampson and Forster 2002; Rauhut 2003*c*).

Furthermore, Carrano and Sampson commented on Rauhut's proposal that a single synapomorphy (*i.e.*, cervical vertebrae with broad ridge extending from caudal diapophysis to ventral rim of caudal centrum) supported a sister-taxon relationship between the two species of *Liliensternus*. While agreeing that *L. liliensterna* and ?*L. airelensis* seem to be more closely related to each other than to other members of Coelophysoidea, Carrano and Sampson noted that the ridge cited by Rauhut is sometimes apparent in the cervicals of other coelophysoids, delineating the ventral edge of the postzygapophyseal fossa, and that it is obscured in many specimens having articulated cervical vertebrae (*e.g.*, in *Coelophysis bauri* and *Syntarsus rhodesiensis*) because the prezygapophysis of the succeeding vertebra generally lodges into this fossa. Consequently, "it may be that only the prominence of this structure characterizes *Liliensternus*."

Tykoski and Rowe noted that the material referred by Cuny and Galton to *Liliensternus* exhibits but one unambiguous ceratosaurian character (*i.e.*, two pairs of cervical pleurocoels) and also a coelophysoid feature (*i.e.*, well-defined fossae on lateral surface of centra). It was the opinion of Tykoski and Rowe that the material from France, possessing no diagnostic features, cannot be referred to *Liliensternus* and is best regarded as representing an indeterminate member of the Coelophysoidea.

Key references: Carrano and Sampson (2004); Carrano, Sampson and Forster (2002); Cuny and Galton (1993); Huene (1934); Larsonneur and Lapparent (1966); Rauhut (2003*c*); Sereno (1999*a*); Tykoski and Rowe (2004).

LIMAYASAURUS Salgado, Garrido, Cocca and Cocca 2004
Saurischia: Eusaurischia: Sauropodomorpha: Sauropoda: Eusauropoda: Neosauropoda: Diplodocoidea: Rebbachisauridae.

Name derivation: "[Rio] Limay + Greek *sauros* = "lizard.""
Type species: *L. tessonei* (Calvo and Salgado 1995).
Other species: [None.]
Occurrence: Río Limay Formation, Lohan Cura Formation, Neuquén Province, Patagonia, Argentina.
Age: Early to Middle Cretaceous (Aptian–Cenomanian).
Known material: Incomplete articulated skeleton, disarticulated elements, at least four individuals.
Holotype: MUCPv-205, articulated incomplete skeleton, including braincase, cervical vertebrae (disarticulated), vertebral column (caudal dorsals, all caudals), pectoral and pelvic girdles, almost complete fore- and hindlimbs (lacking manus), associated gastroliths.

Diagnosis of genus (as for type species): Lateral temporal fenestra extremely reduced; supraoccipital height less than that of foramen magnum; sheetlike basal tubera; neural arches of cervical vertebrae having accessory lamina extending from postzygodiapophyseal lamina craniodorsally; caudal centra with distal articular surfaces more concave than proximal counterparts; proximal caudal neural spines with distally thickened "lateral" laminae, terminating in robust bone; proximal caudal transverse processes comprising two laterodorsally projected osseous bars; pubis distally expanded; pubic shaft oval in cross section; ambiens process of pubis distal to level of obturator foramen; ischial shaft slender, twisted 90 degrees; distal end of ischium virtually unexpanded (Salgado, Garrido, Cocca and Cocca 2004).

Comments: The type species now called *Limayasaurus tessonei*— originally named *Rebbachisaurus tessonei* by Jorge Orlando Calvo and Leonardo Salgado (1995)—was founded upon an incomplete mostly articulated skeleton (MUCPv-205) recovered in the continental deposits (Albian–Cenomanian; see Calvo 1991) at the top of the Candeleros Member and the base of the Huincil Member of the Río Limay Formation (Neuquén Group), in Neuquén Province, Patagonia, Argentina.

Calvo and Salgado originally diagnosed this species as follows: "Diplodocimorph" displaying the following unique derived characters: basipterygoid very thin and short; absence of caudal process of postorbital; articular condyle of quadrate elongated craniocaudally; tuberas much reduced; paroccipital processes not expanded distally; neural spine in caudal cervical and dorsal vertebrae having accessory lamina connecting diapopopostzygapophyseal laminae and supraprezygapophyseal laminae; cranial dorsal vertebrae having both suprprezygapophyseal laminae contacting at top of spine; transverse process in proximal caudal vertebrae formed by dorsal and ventral bar directed upward; pubic shaft oval in cross section.

This species was subsequently transferred by Wilson and Sereno (1998) to the genus *Rayososaurus* (type species, *Rayososaurus agrioensis*) as the referred species *Rayososaurus tessonei* (see *S1* for details and illustrations).

More recently, Salgado, Garrido, Cocca and Cocca (2004) described in detail additional disarticulated skull and postcranial rebbachisaurid remains representing at least three individuals, recovered by José F. Bonaparte and assistants in 1996 and 1996 (J. F. Bonaparte, personal communication to Salgado, Garrido, Cocca and Cocca) and by Salgado, Alberto Garrido, Sergio E. Cocca, and Juan R. Cocca, from sandy siltstones of a single quarry at Cerro Aguado del León, in the Puesto Quiroga Member of the Lohan Cura Formation, La Picaza area of Neuquén Province, in south-central Patagonia, Argentina.

This material includes the following: A tooth (Pv-6718-MOZ), three partial dorsal vertebrae (Pv-6722-MOZ), an incomplete ?sacral vertebra (Pv-6741-MOZ), 11 caudal vertebrae, three proximal caudal centra (Pv-6734-MOZ, Pv-6760-MOZ, and Pv-6767-MOZ), a proximal midcaudal vertebra (Pv-6729-MOZ), six middistal caudal vertebrae (Pv-6729-MOZ, Pv-6738-MOZ, Pv-6753-MOZ, Pv-6759-MOZ, Pv-6759-MOZ, and Pv-6766-MOZ), three distal caudal vertebrae (Pv-6711-MOZ, Pv-6733-MOZ, and Pv-6734-MOZ), a hemal arch (Pv-6751-MOZ), a left coracoid (Pv-6763-MOZ), right humerus (Pv-6762-MOZ), pubes (Pv-6743-MOZ and Pv-6754-MOZ), the proximal portion of a right ischium (Pv-6713-MOZ), three right femora and one left femur, a proximal right tibia (Pv-6764-MOZ), and the proximal half of a fibula (Pv-6727-MOZ).

While agreeing with Wilson and Sereno's assessment that *Rebbachisaurus garasbae* (the type species of *Rebbachisaurus*) and the referred species *Rayososaurus tessonei* belong to separate genera, Salgado *et al.* rejected those authors' referral of the taxon described by Calvo and Salgado to the genus *Rayososaurus* on the following grounds:

First, there are no anatomical characters exclusive to *Rayososaurus agrioensis* and "*Rebbachisaurus tessonei*"; the alleged synapomorphy (*i.e.*, narrow acromion process forming "U"-shaped notch with long axis of scapula) of these species is not an autapomorphy of *Rayososaurus* (see Wilson 2002*a*). Also, a narrow acromial process is also seen in *Rebbachisaurus garasbae* (see Lavocat 1954), while a "U"-shaped acromial notch also occurs in *Nigersaurus* (Sereno, Beck, Dutheil, Larrson, Lyon, Moussa, Sadleir, Sidor, Varricchio, Wilson and Wilson 1999).

Second, the scapula of *Rayososaurus* is apparently unique (*i.e.*, possessing craniocaudally elongate, caudally directed acromial process; *e.g.*, see Bonaparte 1996; this process being relatively short, dorsally or caudodorsally oriented in other rebbachisaurids). Also, several scapula characters occurring in *R. agrioensis* seem to be plesiomorphic relative to other Rebbachisauridae (see Bonaparte 1997).

For the above reasons, Salgado *et al.* proposed the new generic name of *Limayasaurus* (originally used by Novas 1997*c*) but not a new specific name, the combination becoming *Limayasaurus tessonei* for the material first described by Calvo and Salgado in 1995, and *Limayasaurus* sp. for the remains from Cerro Aguada del León.

Salgado *et al.* referred *Limayasaurus* to the Rebbachisauridae based upon the following synapomorphies: Caudal vertebrae having distal articular surface more concave than proximal articular surfaces; pubis distally expanded; pubic shaft having oval cross section (see "Systematics" chapter).

Key references: Bonaparte (1996, 1997); Calvo (1991); Calvo and Salgado (1995); Lavocat (1954); Novas (1997*c*); Salgado, Garrido, Cocca and Cocca (2004); Sereno, Beck, Dutheil, Larrson, Lyon, Moussa, Sadleir, Sidor, Varricchio, Wilson and Wilson (1999); Wilson (2002*a*); Wilson and Sereno (1998).

†LIRAINOSAURUS

Saurischia: Eusaurischia: Sauropodomorpha: Sauropoda: Eusauropoda: Neosauropoda: Macronaria: Titanosauriformes: Titanosauria: Lithostrotia.

Diagnosis of genus (as for type species): Distal caudal vertebrae with restricted caudal articular condyle; distal caudal vertebrae having sagittal condylar groove on caudal articular condyle; proximal caudal vertebrae with lamina in interzygapophyseal fossa; spinopostzygapophyseal structure not caudally directed in distal caudal vertebrae; sternal plate having craniolateral process; ridge near ventral margin of medial surface of scapular blade (Upchurch, Barrett and Dodson 2004).

Comment: In their review of the Sauropoda, Upchurch, Barrett and Dodson (2004) rediagnosed the type species *Lirainosaurus astibiae* (see *S2*).

Key reference: Upchurch, Barrett and Dodson (2004).

†LOURINHASAURUS

Saurischia: Eusaurischia: Sauropodomorpha: Sauropoda: Eusauropoda.

Diagnosis of genus (as for type species): Spinodiapophyseal lamina greatly reduced; large postspinal lamina; strongly laterally expanded hyposphene; dorsal centra high compared to height of entire vertebra (Upchurch, Barrett and Dodson 2004).

Comments: In their review of the Sauropoda, Upchurch, Barrett and Dodson (2004) rediagnosed the type species *Lourinhasaurus alenquerensis* (see *S2*).

Cladistic analysis by Upchurch *et al.* found *Lourinhasaurus* to place "as the closest known relative of Neosauropoda."

Key reference: Upchurch, Barrett and Dodson (2004).

†LUFENGOSAURUS

Saurischia: Eusaurischia: Sauropodomorpha: Sauropoda: Prosauropoda: Plateosauria: Plateosauridae.

Diagnosis of genus (as for type species): Derived features including the following: Profrontals large; expanded top to dorsal process of maxilla; tibia to femur length ratio of 0.65 (Galton and Upchurch 2004*a*).

Comment: In their review of the Prosauropoda, Galton and Upchurch (2004*a*) rediagnosed the type species *Lufengosaurus huenei* (see *D:TE*).

Key reference: Galton and Upchurch (2004*a*).

LUSOTITAN   Antunes and Mateus 2003

Saurischia: Eusaurischia: Sauropodomorpha: Sauropoda: Eusauropoda: Neosauropoda: Macronaria: Titanosauriformes: ?Brachiosauridae.

Name derivation: *Luso* [inhabitant of Lusitania, ancient region corresponding in part to Portugal] + Greek *titan* [a mythological giant].

Type species: *L. atalaiensis* (Lapparent and Zbyszewski 1975).

Other species: [None.]

Occurrence: Peralta, Atalaia, Areia Branca, Portugal.

Age: Late Jurassic (Tithonian).

Known material: Several specimens including partial skeleton, isolated vertebrae, various postcranial remains.

Lectotype: MIGM 4798, 4801–10, 4938, 4944, 4950, 4952, 4958, 4964–6, 4981–2, 4985, 8807, 8793–4, partial skeleton including 28 vertebrae (two cranial cervicals, middorsal, two neural arches, two proximal caudal centra, proximal caudal, uninterrupted series of 18 caudals), 12 chevrons, fragmented ribs, ?scapula, distal epiphysis, humeri, proximal left ulna, radius, partial ilium, left ischium, left pubis, left tibia, proximal end of right fibula, right astragalus, ?sacral rib (previously identified as metacarpal II).

Diagnosis of genus (as for type species): Brachiosaurid, primarily due to characters of humerus and femur; middorsal vertebrae having very large

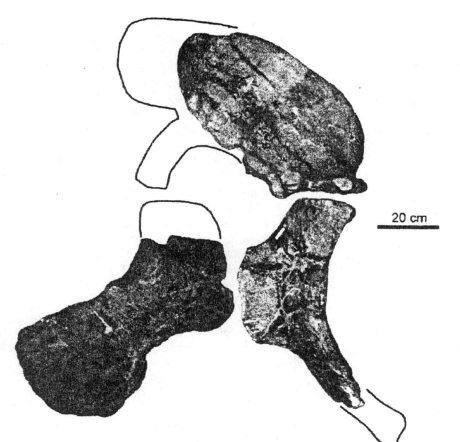

20 cm

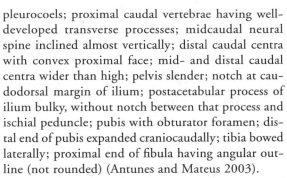

Lusotitan atalaiensis, lectotype pelvis (part of partial skeleton catalogued as MIGM 4798, 4801–10, 4938, 4944, 4950, 4952, 4958, 4964–6, 4981–2, 4985, 8807, and 8793–4) in left lateral view. (After Antunes and Mateus 2003.)

pleurocoels; proximal caudal vertebrae having well-developed transverse processes; midcaudal neural spine inclined almost vertically; distal caudal centra with convex proximal face; mid- and distal caudal centra wider than high; pelvis slender; notch at caudodorsal margin of ilium; postacetabular process of ilium bulky, without notch between that process and ischial peduncle; pubis with obturator foramen; distal end of pubis expanded craniocaudally; tibia bowed laterally; proximal end of fibula having angular outline (not rounded) (Antunes and Mateus 2003).

Comments: In 1957, Albert F. de Lapparent and Georges Zbyszewski described a new species of the genus *Brachiosaurus*, which they named *Brachiosaurus atalaiensis*, founded upon several specimens collected from various localities in west-central Portugal. These specimens included a partial skeleton from Atalaia and isolated vertebrae from Areia Branco, Porto Novo (Maceira), Alcobaca, Cambelas and Praia das Almoinhas, and a more complete postcranial specimen (MIGM 4798, 4801–10, 4938, 4944, 4950, 4952, 4958, 4964–6, 4981–2, 4985, 8807, and 8793–4) from Peralta, near Atalaia (Municipality of Lourinhã). However, Lapparent and Zbyszewski failed to designate any of the above material as the type specimen for their new taxon.

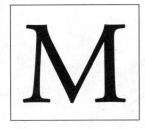

More than four decades later, Antunes and Mateus, in a paper surveying the dinosaurs of Portugal, recognized this species as representing also a new genus, which they named *Lusotitan atalaiensis*, at the same time designating the more complete specimen from Peralta as the lectotype and the other specimens as syntypes.

Antunes and Mateus referred *Lusotitan* to the Brachiosauridae based upon the vertebrae having low neural spines, the elongated humerus with its prominent deltopectoral crest, and the upward longitudinal axis of the ilium (however, see Naish, Martill, Cooper and Stevens 2004, "Introduction").

Key references: Antunes and Mateus (2003); Lapparent and Zbyszewski (1975); Naish, Martill, Cooper and Stevens (2004).

MAGNIROSTRIS   You and Dong 2003

Ornithischia: Predentata: Genusauria: Cerapoda: Chasmatopia: Marginocephalia: Ceratopsia: Neoceratopsia: Protoceratopsidae.

Name derivation: Latin *magnus* = "large" + Latin *rostrum* = "beak."

Type species: *M. dodsoni* You and Dong 2003.

Other species: [None.]

Occurrence: Bayan Mandahu redbeds, Bayan Mandahu, Inner Mongolia, China.

Age: Late Cretaceous (Campanian).

Known material/holotype: IVPP V 12513, nearly complete skull with articulated lower jaw (lacking squamosals, parietals, left jugal, postorbital, and quadrate).

Diagnosis of genus (as for type species): Distinguished from other protoceratopsids by possession of robust, elongate rostral bone and incipient orbital horncores (You and Dong 2003).

Comments: The genus *Magnirostris* was founded upon an almost complete skull (IVPP V 12513) collected by the Sino-Canadian Dinosaur Project from the Late Cretaceous (Campanian; (see Jerzykiewicz, Currie, Eberth, Johnson, Koster and Zheng 1993) Bayan Mandahu redbeds, at Bayan Mandahu, Inner Mongolia, China. Originally, this specimen was considered to belong to the genus *Protoceratops* and labeled as such at the Institute of Vertebrate Paleontology and Paleoanthropology of the Chinese Academy of Sciences, Bejing. Subsequent study of the specimen, however, revealed that it represents a new genus and species, which has been named *Magnirostris dodsoni* (You and Dong 2003).

As You and Dong noted, the pointed rostral and predentary bones of this specimen and the nature of the jugal flare (beginning near the caudal end of the jugals) exclude IVPP V 12513 from the Psittaco-

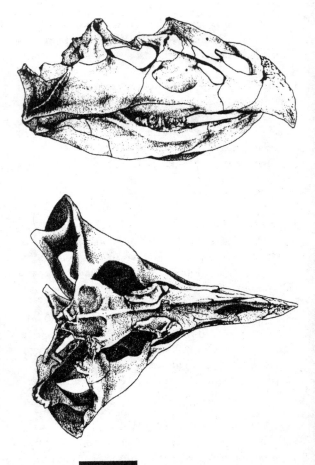

Magnirostris dongi, IVPP V 12513, holotype skull in (top) right lateral and (bottom) dorsal views. Scale = 8 cm. (After You and Dong 2003.)

sauridae, placing it instead with the Neoceratopsia. Moreover, the lack of prominent nasal and brow horn corse and the comparatively small external naris preclude its referral to the Ceratopsidae (see Dodson 1990).

In terms of geographical and stratigraphical distribution, *Magnirostris* is similar to both *Protoceratops* and *Bagaceratops*, all three protoceratopsid taxa occurring in the Campanian of the Gobi Desert (see Jerzykiewicz and Russell 1991; Jerzykiewicz *et al.*; Jerzykiewicz 2000). However, *Magnirostris* differs from *Protoceratops* in the former's comparatively longer and lower skull, relatively shorter preorbital portion of the skull, the lack of premaxillary teeth, and the less dorsoventrally high maxilla. *Magnirostris* shares with *Bagaceratops* an additional fenestra ventral to the external nares (this character not reported in any other ceratopsian) and is similar to that taxon in various other ways (*e.g.*, general appearance of skull, such as preorbital portion being approximately half basal skull length). It differs from *Bagaceratops*, however, in numerous features (*e.g.*, more robust rostral bone, length same as height in lateral aspect; maxilla contributing to rim of orbit; nasal horn pointed [blunt in *Bagaceratops*]; possession of incipient brow horn-cores).

Performing a cladistic analysis, You and Dong determined that *Magnirostris* and the Asian basal neoceratopsians *Protoceratops* and *Bagaceratops* (see Sereno 2000; Makovicky 2001; Xu, Makovicky, Wang, Norell and You 2002; You 2000), these genera comprising "the only definitive members of Protoceratopsidae."

Key references: Dodson (1990); Jerzykiewicz (2000); Jerzykiewicz, Currie, Eberth, Johnson, Koster and Zheng (1993); Jerzykiewicz and Russell (1991); Makovicky (2001); Sereno (2000); You and Dong (2003); Xu, Makovicky, Wang, Norell and You (2002); You (2002).

†MAGYAROSAURUS

Saurischia: Eusaurischia: Sauropodomorpha: Sauropoda: Eusauropoda: Neosauropoda: Macronaria: Titanosauriformes: Titanosauria: Lithostrotia.

Diagnosis of genus (as for type species): Proximal caudal vertebrae with pit on either side of midline, between bases of prezygapophyses; proximal caudal vertebrae with marked depression on lateral surface of neural arches at bases of prezygapophyses (Upchurch, Barrett and Dodson 2004).

Comments: In their review of the Sauropoda, Upchurch, Barrett and Dodson (2004) rediagnosed the type species *Magyarosaurus dacus* (see *D:TE*).

Although this taxon has not yet figured into any published cladistic analysis, Upchurch *et al.* noted that "the morphology of many of elements (*e.g.*, the dorsal and proximal vertebrae) indicate that it is probably an advanced lithostrotian."

Key reference: Upchurch, Barrett and Dodson (2004).

†MAJUNGATHOLUS

Saurischia: Eusaurischia: Theropoda: Neotheropoda: Abelisauroidea: Abelisauridae: Carnotaurinae.

Comments: Among extant carnivorous animals, cannibalism is a common ecological strategy. Until recently, however, reports of cannibalism in theropod dinosaurs have been rare and largely speculative (the most famous being the suggested cannibalism in the small theropod *Coelophysis bauri*; see Colbert 1989, 1995; see also *Rioarribasaurus* entry, *D:TE*; *Coelophysis* entry, *S3*).

Rogers, Krause and Curry Rogers (2003) reported on evidence strongly suggesting cannibalism in the type species *Majungatholus atopus*, a "dome-

Courtesy Raymond R. Rogers, Macalester College.

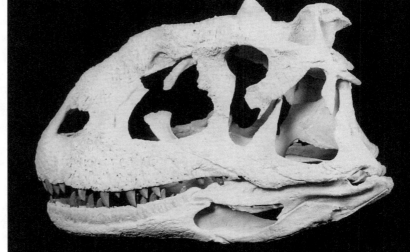

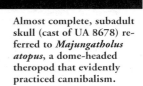

Almost complete, subadult skull (cast of UA 8678) referred to *Majungatholus atopus*, a dome-headed theropod that evidently practiced cannibalism.

headed" abelisaurid theropod mainly known from the Late Cretaceous (Campanian) of northwestern Magadascar (see below). Evidence of conspecific feeding was found on a subadult specimen (UA 8678) of this taxon — including disarticulated skull elements, left ilium, and most of the precaudal axial column — recovered from a bonebed at quarry MAD96–21, in the Anembalemba Member of Madagascar's Maevarano Formation, found in association with sauropod, turtle, frog, and crocodyliform remains.

As described by Rogers *et al.*, the bones of this individual are marked "by numerous conspicuous tooth marks," while at least nine *Majungatholus* elements found at this site offer "evidence of feeding by a fairly large and persistent vertebrate carnivore." Ribs, the authors observed, are the most frequently marked elements (although at least two neural arches also show tooth marks), two ribs revealing bite marks on both superficial and deep aspects of these bones. On one rib, multiple sets of drag marks accompany the tooth marks.

Rogers *et al.* compared tooth drag marks on *M. atopus* specimens FMNH PR2100 (see *S1*) and UA 8678 with 10 *Majungatholus* tooth crowns selected randomly from quarry MAD93–18, finding measurements taken from the modified bones and the teeth "definitely comparable." Parallel tooth marks on one specimen (96313–31D), spaced 1.0 to 1.7 centimeters apart, compare favorably with the tooth-bearing elements of FMNH PR2100, which was recovered from quarry MAD96–01. As Rogers *et al.* pointed out, *M. atopus* can exhibit an even pattern of tooth eruption, as exemplified by the right lower jaw of FMNH PR2100 and, which would be required in generating the marks on specimen 96313–31D as well as other bones in the sample.

Majungatholus

Physical evidence of cannibalism in the type species *Majungatholus atopus*: Tooth (left) and rib (UA 8678) (right), the chisel-like morphology and spacing of the denticles in the former matching drag marks on the latter. (After Rogers, Krause and Curry Rogers.)

Right dentary (FM PR2100) of *Majungatholus atopus* showing the even pattern of tooth eruption necessary for generating the marks found on several bones belonging to this species. (After Rogers, Krause and Curry Rogers.)

The above observations, the authors stated, "(with the caveats that tooth eruption varies among individuals, and intertooth spacing varies with ontogeny), make a compelling case for *Majungatholus* feeding on *Majungatholus* carrion at both quarries MAD96–01 and MAD96–21." Furthermore, the small size of *Masiakasaurus knopleri*, the only other theropod known from the Maevarano Formation, and the different tooth morphology of the contemporaneous crodocyliforms *Trematochampsa* and *Mahajangasuchus*, preclude their consideration as the perpetrators of these bite marks.

The authors did not speculate as to whether *Majugatholus* practiced intraspecific predation or opportunistically scavenged the remains of its own kind.

Smith and Krause (2003), in a published abstract, briefly reported on five apparent *M. atopus* tooth crowns (GSI 1991–1995) originally described by Mathur and Srivastava (1987) as ?*Megalosaurus* B, C, and D, from the Lameta Group (Upper Cretaceous: Maastrichtian) of Gujarat, India (see *SI*).

As Smith and Krause pointed out, these teeth closely resemble those of *M. atopus*, GSI 1991 and 1992 particularly, having "the distinctive morphology of *M. atopus* premaxillary teeth of triangular crown shapes with round labial faces, and denticulated carinae located lingually on the crowns." The authors further briefly described the Indian teeth, noting the following details: Teeth with basally curving interdenticular sulci, causing denticles seemingly to fan toward apices; crowns showing slight distal recurvature, recurvature profile curving smoothly toward apices.

Performing a stepwise discriminant function analysis (DFA) on the Lameta teeth, Smith and Krause's study found them to compare most favorably with those of *M. atopus*, concluding that "The morphological congruence of the Lameta teeth with *M. atopus* and the statistically robust DFA suggests this taxon existed in both Madagascar and India."

Witmer (2004), in an abstract, discussed new insights into the cephalic soft tissues of *Majungatholis*, gleaned from CT scanning and three-dimensional visualization of separate elements of a disarticulated skull of this genus from Madagascar. From this specimen that author extracted (segmented) and rendered in three dimensions various anatomical structures (including osseous labyrinth, cerebral endocast, and pneumatic sinuses), these datasets being subsequently registered with a three-dimensional surface model of an articulated cast of the skull, "allowing the segmented soft tissues to be viewed in place in the whole skull."

The resulting virtual endocast of *Majungatholus* revealed the following details: (as expected for basal member of Neotheropoda) brain not filling endocranial cavity, general organization of brain primitive; cerebral flocculus small; labyrinth of inner ear rather typical for noncoelurosaurian theropods; orientation of lateral semicircular canals suggesting alert head posture to have been basically horizontal (corresponding

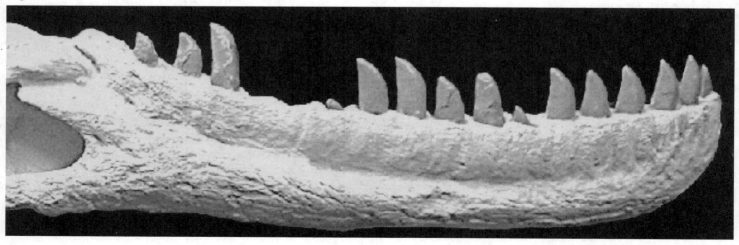

Life restoration by artist Mark Hallett of *Majungatholus atopus*.

to position of maximal binocular overlap); identification of anatomical domains (*e.g.*, adductor, tympanic, ocular, oropharyngeal), with comparisons to extant outgroups, clarifying soft-tissue reconstruction (*e.g.*, identification of epithelial inner ear sac boundaries, showing median phatympanic pneumatic system probably communicating with middle ear; absence of dorsal and caudal tympanic recesses found in many other theropods, rostral tympanic recess present, latter with unusual cranial expansion within braincase; frontals with sinus (possibly unique feature among Theropoda) of almost certain pneumatic origin, most likely probably from antorbital diverticulum in lacrimal; extent of frontal sinus variable (frontal almost absent in individual having largest cornual process); lacrimals and (especially) nasals extensively pneumatized by more typical antorbital diverticula, volume of antorbital sinus and its diverticula exceeding that of main nasal cavity.

Various recent studies have centered upon reconstructions of the pulmonary anatomy of non-avian dinosaurs and the possible physiological characteristics of different pulmonary designs, such as thermoregulatory capabilities. Some of these studies have proposed an avianlike pulmonary air-sac system (see "Introduction") for non-avian coelurosaurian (although not other clades) theropods. In an abstract,

O'Connor (2004) published a brief report on postcranial pneumaticity and pulmonary heterogeneity in Archosauria, his study focusing upon the evolution of the flow-through lung in a noncoelurosaurian theropod, *Majungatholus atopus*, and also in birds.

O'Connor's study was based upon examination of "the pulmonary air-sac system in extant birds, including pneumatic invasion of different portions of the postcranial skeleton," these data compared with site-specific pneumaticity in an almost complete, very well-preserved skeleton of *Majungatholus*. O'Connor found in this specimen "unequivocal evidence of pneumaticitic invasion of bone" (details presumably to be published at a later date), this specimen also offering "a glimpse into the higher-level organization of the pulmonary system in theropod dinosaurs." Throughout the precaudal vertebral system of *M. atopus*, O'Connor observed pneumatic features indicating the presence of both cervical and abdominal air sacs, this discovery highlighting "a fundamental similarity of air sac organization between extant birds and noncoelurosaurian theropods," and implying that the basic avian pulmonary bauplan existed also in theropod taxa more distantly related to birds and Maniraptora. Consequently, "The presence of both cranial and caudal components of an air sac system in noncoelurosaurian theropods indicates that the anatomical prerequisites of the avian flow-through lung had a lengthy history within the theropod lineage and were not limited to derived non-avian theropods and basal birds."

Note: For a report on new applications of CT scanning and 3D modeling for visualization of a disarticulated skull of *Majungatholus*, see the abstract published by Ridgely and Witmer (2004).

Key references: Colbert (1989, 1995); Mathur and Srivastava (1987); O'Connor (2004); Ridgely and Witmer (2004); Rogers, Krause and Curry Rogers (2003); Smith and Krause (2003); Witmer (2004).

†MALAWISAURUS

Saurischia: Eusaurischia: Sauropodomorpha: Sauropoda: Eusauropoda: Neosauropoda: Macronaria: Titanosauriformes: Titanosauria: Lithostrotia.

Diagnosis of genus (as for type species): Autapomorphy of premaxillary ascending process being vertical, located near extreme rostral tip of snout (Upchurch, Barrett and Dodson 2004).

Comment: In their review of the Sauropoda, Upchurch, Barrett and Dodson (2004) rediagnosed the type species *Malawisaurus dixeyi* (see *D:TE*).

Key reference: Upchurch, Barrett and Dodson (2004).

†MAMENCHISAURUS

Saurischia: Eusaurischia: Sauropodomorpha: Sauropoda: Eusauropoda: "Euhelopodidae": Euhelopodinae.

Diagnosis of genus: Cervical vertebrae with
greatly reduced pleurocoels retaining their division
into cranial and caudal portions by oblique lamina;
conical cranial process of cervical ribs lacking excavation on dorsomedial surface, curving slightly laterally
towards tip (Upchurch, Barrett and Dodson 2004).

Comment: In their review of the Sauropoda,
Upchurch, Barrett and Dodson (2004) rediagnosed
the genus *Mamenchisaurus* (see *D:TE*).

Key reference: Upchurch, Barrett and Dodson
(2004).

†MASIAKASAURUS

Saurischia: Eusaurischia: Theropoda: Neotheropoda:
Ceratosauria: Abelisauroidea: Noasauridae.

Comments: Carrano, Sampson and Loewen
(2004), in an abstract, briefly reported on new discoveries of materials referred to *Masiakasaurus
knopfleri*, an unusual theropod notable for its procumbent mesial dentary teeth (see *S3*). Collected from the
Upper Cretaceous Maevarano Formation of Madagascar, this material includes a postorbital, frontal,
quadrate, partial braincase, axis and intercentrum,
cervical and dorsal vertebrae, ischia, fibulae, phalanges, and unguals. As observed by these authors, the
newly recovered cranial elements confirm that the
skull of *Masiakasaurus* is relatively unornamented
compared to that of members of the Abelisauridae.
Additionally, the relatively complete pes of this genus
lacks a "raptorial" pedal ungual, suggesting to Carrano
et al. that the elements so identified in *Noasaurus* (see
entry; also, Agnolin, Apesteguía and Chiarelli 2004)
correctly belong to the manus.

According to Carrano *et al.*, these new materials
support a sister-group relationship between the
Noasauridae and Abelisauridae, resolving the once
ambiguous distribution of various derived characters.
Moreover, the diversification of the Noasauridae most
likely occurred before Albian times, offering "ample
opportunity for the clade to reach most Gondwanan
landmasses prior to their tectonic breakup."

Key reference: Agnolin, Apesteguía and Chiarelli
(2004); Carrano, Sampson and Loewen (2004).

†MASSOSPONDYLUS

Saurischia: Eusaurischia: Sauropodomorpha: Sauropoda: Prosauropoda: Plateosauria: Massospondylidae.

Diagnosis of genus (as for type species): Autapo-

morphies including the following: skull at least 10
percent wider than high, width of base of cultriform
process at least 20 percent length (Hinic 2002);
prominent muscle scar on lateral surface of fibula at
midlength (Galton and Upchurch 2004*a*).

Comment: In their review of the Prosauropoda,
Galton and Upchurch (2004*a*) rediagnosed the type
species *Massospondylus carinatus* (see *D:TE*).

Key references: Galton and Upchurch (2004*a*);
Hinic (2002).

†MEGALOSAURUS

Saurischia: Eusaurischia: Theropoda: Neotheropoda:
Tetanurae: Spinosauroidea: Megalosauridae: Megalosaurinae.

Comments: Although a considerable amount of
fossil material has been referred to the type species
Megalosaurus bucklandii, the lectotype specimen consists only of a partial right dentary (OUMNH
J13506). In 2002, Allain and Chure (2002) claimed
that various large theropod elements from the
Stonesfield Slate of Oxfordshire, England, generally
attributed to this species, in fact represents two distinct taxa based upon differences in the scapulocoracoids, ilia, and femora (see *S3*).

More recently, Day and Barrett (2004), as part
of an ongoing project to reevaluate the taxonomy and
systematics of Middle Jurassic British theropods, examined some of the material that had been referred to
M. bucklandii. Material studied by Day and Barrett
comprises the following:

Scapulocoracoids — OUMNH J.13574 (right,
largely complete, slightly restored); OUMNH
J.289879 (left, slightly broken, coracoid missing),
OUMNH J.29887a (right, proximal portion of
scapula only); OUMNH J.29888 (right, somewhat
broken, proximal portion of coracoid missing);
OUMNH J.29889 (left, badly damaged, most of
scapular blade and proximal coracoid missing);
BMNH 31810 (right, isolated, complete), and BMNH
R1099 (left, scapula broken distally, proximal plate
and coracoid somewhat restored).

Femora — OUMNH J.13561 (right, almost complete, partly restored, part of the syntype series of
Megalosaurus from Stonesfield described by Buckland
in 1824), OUMNH J.29753a (right, proximal third);
OUMNH J.29802 (right, almost complete, femoral
head and greater trochanter broken, apparently from
Stonesfield [H. P. Powell, personal communication to
Day and Barrett, 2000, *contra* Huene 1926]);
OUMNH J.29803 (right, damaged); BMNH 31804
(left, almost complete); BMNH 31806 (right, almost
complete); BMNH 31808 (left, almost complete,
slightly damaged); and MNHN 9630 (left, almost
complete, slightly damaged).

buckланди

Skull elements (casts) including holotype lower jaw (OUMNH J13506) of the megalosaurine megalosaurid *Megalosaurus bucklandii* on exhibit at the Oxford University Museum of Natural History, Oxford, England.

Photograph by the author, courtesy Oxford University Museum of Natural History.

• 391 •

Life restoration of *Megalosaurus bucklandii* by artist Todd Marshall.

ing taxonomical significance. Additionally, the irregular and unfinished articular surfaces of the latter isolated elements are indicative of poor preservation or over-preparation. Therefore, Day and Barrett found it impossible "to deduce whether they articulated with, or were fused to, the other part of the scapulocoracoid in life, rendering this potential difference ambiguous at present." Furthermore, the authors observed that one of these specimens, OUMNH J.29887a, is substantially larger and more robust than any other Stonesfield theropod scapulae, its very large size possibly suggesting that it belongs, rather, to a sauropod.

Day and Barrett noted that Allain and Chure recognized two femoral morphotypes attributed to *Megalosaurus*—one (based on OUMNH J.13561, noted by Owen 1842*b*) having an S-shaped shaft and craniomedially inclined femoral head; the other (based on OUMNH J.31806) having a straight shaft and a medially oriented head. As observed by Day and Barrett, specimens OUMNH J.29802, OUMNH J.29753a, BMNH 31804, BMNH 31806, and MNHN 9630 are straight in both cranial and caudal views, bowing very gently along their length in lateral view; however, OUMNH J.29803, OUMNH J.13561, and BMNH 31808 are nearly sigmoidal in outline, are slightly sigmoidal in lateral view, and bow first laterally and then medially. Day and Barrett described in detail both femoral morphotypes, referring to the "straight" femora as morphotype A and the S-shaped femora as morphotype B.

Also, Allain and Chure had recognized two morphotypes of ilia (based on comparisons between OUMNH J.13560, one of Buckland's syntypes for *Megalosaurus*, and BMNH 31811), stating that they clearly differed "in shape and proportions," while not offering descriptive data to support their conclusion. According to Day and Barrett, however, these specimens do, upon first inspection, appear to be rather different—*e.g.*, in BMNH 31811, cranial and caudal iliac lobes proportionally much shorter craniocaudally, relative to total length of height, than in OUMNH J.13560; in BMNH 31811, outline of cranial lobe subrectangular in lateral aspect, cranial margin nearly straight, meeting dorsal margin of ilium at abrupt, approximately 80-degree angle (much more rounded lobe in OUMNH J.13560, cranial and dorsal margins merging into each other along smoothly convex arc). However, as Day and Barrett pointed out, most of the cranial lobe and craniodorsal portion of BMNH 31811 had been reconstructed in plaster, with the reconstruction painted to resemble the original bone; also, a substantial portion of the caudal lobe of this ilium seems to be missing. Consequently, "any proportional or shape differences related to these areas of

Ilia—OUMNH J.13560 (right, part of Buckland's syntype series); OUMNH J.29881 (right), BMNH R1100 (left, *contra* Lydekker 1888), and BMNH R1101 (right), all complete; BMNH 31811 (right, *contra* Lydekker, incomplete and damaged, figured *contra* Allain and Chure as a coracoid by Owen 1857, noted by Lydekker as an ilium); and BMNH R283 (right, incomplete).

As Day and Barrett related, Allain and Chure agreed with Phillips (1871), who had noted that two distinct morphotypes of *Megalosaurus* pectoral girdles had been recovered from Stonesfield—one form, exemplified by a single individual, wherein the scapula and coracoid are separate from one another; and another form, found in several individuals, wherein these two elements are fused. Unfortunately, Day and Barrett were unable to locate the unfused elements mentioned by Phillips. However, most other pectoral girdle specimens (BMNH R1099, OUMNH J. 13574, OUMNH J.29888, and OUMNH J.29889) assigned to *Megalosaurus* display evidence of extensive fusion between scapula and coracoid, although an isolated coracoid (BMNH 31810) and proximal scapula (OUMNH J.29887a) show that fusion may not have occurred in some individuals, the latter possibly hav-

the ilium cannot be reliably determined in this specimen." Moreover, comparison of the preserved part of BMNH 31811 with any of the Stonesfield ilia reveals no significant differences, with the former specimen easily accommodated with OUMNH J.13560.

Day and Barrett concluded that, based upon differences in the morphology of the femur (and perhaps scapulocoracoid), two distinct morphs of large theropods are now known from the Stonesfield deposits, these morphs possibly representing distinct taxa (as suggested by Allain and Chure), "sexual dimorphs of a single taxon, or ontogenetic or individual variants." Regarding these, Day and Barrett found ontogenetic variation to be an unlikely explanation for the differences in these specimens, these authors pointing out that elements of both morphotypes occupy similar size ranges. Moreover, the morphological variation observed between the femora (and perhaps scapulo-coracoids) is consistent, implying either sexual dimorphism or taxonomically important differences. As Day and Barrett noted, some of the differences between the two morphs in the *Megalosaurus* sample are similar to those listed by Raath (1990) for the coelophysoid ceratosaur *Syntarsus rhodesiensis*. However, Day and Barrett suggested, sexual dimorphism cannot explain the differences seen in the Stonesfield *Megalosaurus* sampling, these authors pointing out that the femora of both male and female morphs of *Syntarsus* are gently sigmoidal along their lengths. Day and Barrett agreed with Allain and Chure, therefore, but for different reasons, that morphotypes A and B represent two distinct taxa. Pending a thorough taxonomic reevaluation of the genus *Megalosaurus*, Day and Barrett provisionally regarded OUMNH J.13561 and all other B type femora as referrable to *M. bucklandii*; and all A type femora, sharing no features with the type B femora, as not representative of *Megalosaurus*.

Regarding morphotype A, Day and Barrett noted that this kind of femur displays no unambiguous tetanuran synapomorphies and only one possible ceratosaurian feature (*i.e.*, groove present in crista tibiofibularis; see Sereno 1999; Holtz 2000; *contra* Rauhut 2003*c*). Therefore, Day and Barrett conservatively preferred regarding the morphotype B femora as representing an indeterminate theropod. Furthermore, these authors proposed that, given that two theropods are now known from the Stonesfield Slate, caution be exercised in the use of the various species of *Megalosaurus* as operational taxonomic units in phylogenetic analyses pending completion of a full reevaluation of this material.

Key references: Allain and Chure (2002); Buckland (1824); Day and Barrett (2004); Holtz (2000); Huene (1926); Lydekker (1888); Owen (1842*b*, 1857); Phillips (1871); Raath (1990); Rauhut (2003*c*); Sereno (1999).

†**MEGAPNOSAURUS**—(See *Syntarsus*.)

†**MEGARAPTOR**

Saurischia: Eusaurischia: Theropoda: Neotheropoda: Tetanurae: Avetheropoda: Carnosauria: Allosauroidea.

Comments: In 1998, Fernando E. Novas named and described *Megaraptor namumhuaquii*, a new type species of large predatory dinosaur, founded upon very incomplete material including manual and pedal elements (MCF-PVPH 79) collected from the Upper Cretaceous (Turonian–Coniacian) Río Neuquén Formation [now Subgroup] of Neuquén Province, in northern Patagonia, Argentina. Although Novas tentatively referred this taxon to the Coelurosauria, what that author described as a large pedal claw (apparently similar to the "killer claws" seen in Troodontidae and Dromaeosauridae; but see below) and also his use of the suffix (*i.e.*, "*raptor*," meaning "thief") in the generic name seem to have imparted a false impression that *Megaraptor* was, in fact, some kind of giant dromaeosaur (see *SI*), as a kind of scaled-up version of *Deinonychus* or *Velociraptor*.

Later, a second specimen—a partial skeleton including a cervical vertebra, two caudal vertebrae, hemal arches, scapula, coracoid, radius, ulna, complete manus, pubis, and fourth metatarsal—was discovered in June, 2002, at the Upper Cretaceous Futalognko paleontological site, on the north coast of Los Barreales Lake, Neuquén. This specimen was briefly described in an abstract by Calvo, Porfiri, Veralli and Novas (2002), who noted the following: Bladelike olecranon process on the proximal ulna and distal end of ulna, latter stout and triangular in distal view, are identical to those described for *Megaraptor*; digit I longest of manus, claw identical to that originally described by Novas for *Megaraptor* as pedal claw; digit II shorter than I, digit III shortest, vestigial digit IV represented by just metacarpal.

A preliminary cladistic analysis by Calvo *et al.* placed *Megaraptor* within the clade Tetanure, as evidenced by the following features: Centra of cervical vertebrae opisthocoelous; scapular blade long, slender, straplike, distal expansion of scapular reduced less than width of proximal end of scapula; metacarpal III clearly shorter than II, manual ungual length unusually long; neural spine surpassing level of epipophysis (as in *Piatnitzkysaurus* and *Allosaurus*; caudal centra with small pleurocoels (as in Carcharodontosauridae; coracoid with well-developed caudal process (as in other avetheropods [="neotetanurans" of Calvo *et al.*'s usage), distal end directed ventroposteriorly.

More recently, Lamanna, Martinez, Luna, Casa, Ibiricu and Ivany (2004), in an abstract, described two partial skeletons belonging to *Megaraptor*, recovered collected from the early Late Cretaceous (middle Cenomanian–Turonian) Lower Bajo Barreal Formation of Neuquén Province, central Patagonia. The smaller, possibly subadult specimen includes a cranial dorsal vertebra, two dorsal ribs, three incomplete proximal middle caudal vertebrae, manual phalanx ?II-2, fragments of a possible femur and fibula, distal end metatarsal II, and two fragmentary nonungual phalanges; the larger specimen comprises manual unguals I and III, fragmentary femur and fibula, almost complete fibula, distal end of metatarsal I, metatarsal II, several pedal phalanges, and some indeterminate bone fragments.

As noted by Lamanna *et al.*, these specimens preserve axial and appendicular elements previously not known in either the holotype or referred material of *Megaraptor*. A phylogenetic analysis (details not given in the abstract) by the authors found *Megaraptor* not to be a coelurosaur, but, instead, a basal tetanuran, placing as one of the youngest known members of the carnosaurian clade Allosauroidea, thereby representing the first occurrence of the genus outside of northern Patagonia.

Key references: Calvo, Porfiri, Veralli and Novas (2002); Lamanna, Martinez, Luna, Casa, Ibiricu and Ivany (2004).

MEI   Xu and Norell 2004

Saurischia: Eusaurischia: Theropoda: Neotheropoda: Tetanurae: Avetheropoda: Coelurosauria: Tyrannoraptora: Maniraptoriformes: Troodontidae *incertae sedis*.

Name derivation: Chinese *mei* = "to sleep soundly."

Type species: *M. long* Xu and Norell 2004.

Other species: [None.]

Occurrence: Yixian Formation, Liaoning Province, China.

Age: Early Cretaceous.

Known material/holotype: IVPP V12733, almost complete, fully articulated skeleton, subadult.

Diagnosis of genus (as for type species): Distinguished from all other know troodontids by extremely large nares extending caudally over one-half of maxillary tooth row; closely packed middle maxillary teeth; maxillary tooth row extending posteriorly to level of preorbital bar; furcula robust, sub–U-shaped; lateral process on distal tarsal IV; most proximal end of pubic shaft significantly compressed craniocaudally, extending laterally just ventral to atriculation with ilium (Xu and Norell 2004).

Comments: Among the more unusual of recent dinosaur discoveries (see below), the type species *Mei long* was founded upon a nearly complete skeleton collected from volcaniclastic beds of the Yixian Formation, at Lujiatun, Shangyuan, Beipiao City, western Liaoning Province, China (Xu and Norell 2004).

In describing the type specimen, Xu and Norell noted that several cranial sutures are unfused, and, although fused, sutures can still be seen between the neural arches and centra, these features indicating that IVPP V12733 does not belong to an adult animal. Additionally, caudal and sacral vertebral sutures cannot be seen, the parietal consists of a single element, and the astragalus and calcaneum are completely fused together, these features suggesting that the animal was approaching maturity when it died.

Xu and Norell measured the specimen to be approximately 53 centimeters (about 20 inches) long, comparable in length to the basal dromaeosaurid *Microraptor zhaoianus* and the basal bird *Archaeopteryx lithographica*.

As the authors observed, *Mei* has a proportionally small skull (approximately 69 percent as long as the femur), short trunk, and very long hindlimbs relative to the trunk, as in the deinonychosaur *Sinovenator* and basal dromaeosaurs (see Xu 2002). This latter feature—found also in *Sinovenator* (see Russell and Dong 1994) and the basal troodontid *Sinornithoides* (Currie and Dong 2001), in *Microraptor* (Xu), and the basal oviraptorosaurian *Caudipteryx* (Jones, Farlow, Ruben, Henderson and Hillenius 2000)—is "correlated with a knee-based avian running mechanism" (Jones *et al.*).

IVPP V12733 has preserved and clarifies several features previously unknown for troodontids, Xu and Norell noted, including the following: Cervical vertebrae incipiently heterocoelous (as in some dromaeosaurids); first and second dorsal vertebrae with prominent ventral processes on cranial half of distally ball-like centra; possibly sternal ribs present (as in other maniraptorans; *e.g.*, see Norell and Makovicky 1997), as represented by two small, flat bone fragments; large furcula loosely articulated with acromion process of scapula, robust and flat in cross section, with incipient hypocleidium and expanded distal articular ends, more U-shaped and robust (as in birds, not dromaeosaurids; see Xu; Hwang, Norell, Ji and Gao 2002); scapulocoracoid L-shaped, scapula close to neural spines of dorsal vertebrae, almost parallel to vertebral column (as in dromaeosaurids and birds); coracoid with large coracoid tubercle, subglenoid fossa, divided into craniodorsal and cranioventral surface by low ridge (as in many maniraptorans); humerus projecting laterally, forearm and

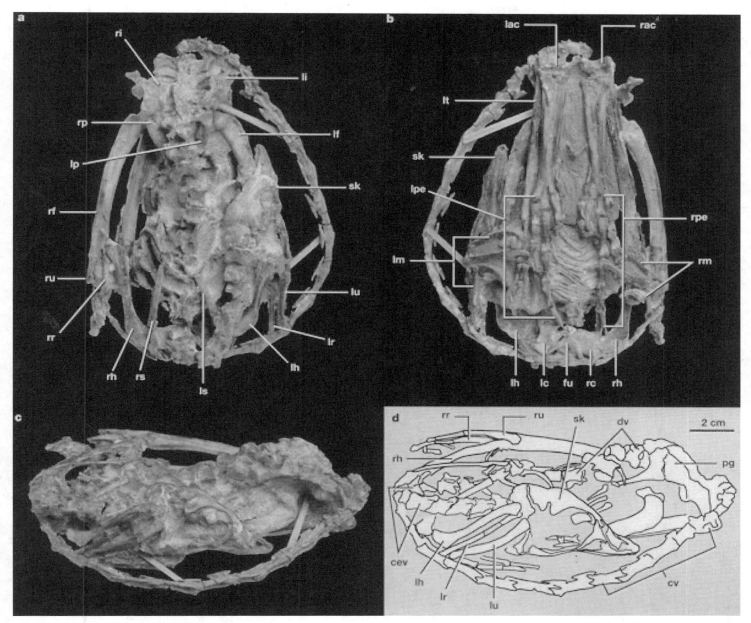

Mei long, IVPP V12733, holotype skeleton in a. dorsal, b. ventral, and c. lateral views, d. interpretive drawing. (After Xu and Norell 2004.)

many folding in avian mode (as in other maniraptorans).

As Xu and Norell recounted, several studies had hypothesized "that small size is crucial to the origin of flight and that miniaturization was responsible for many of the unique morphologies" found in birds (*e.g.*, see Sereno 1999*a*; Hwang *et al.*); consequently, the authors noted that *M. longus* offers additional evidence supporting that theory. Both *M. longus* and *Archaeopteryx* and possibly also dromaeosaurids (Xu; Chiappe, Ji, Ji and Norell 1999) lack jugal-postorbital and quadratojugal-squamosal contacts. In *M. longus* and perhaps basal dromaeosaurids the nasal-frontal articulation is weak. These features, according to Xu and Norell, also found in mononykines (see Chiappe,

Norell and Clark 1998), "suggest that some kind of cranial kinesis (probably prokinesis) evolved in the early evolution of eumaniraptorans."

Among the most stunning aspects of IVPP V12733 is its posture. As Xu and Norell observed, the specimen "is preserved in a remarkable life pose, capturing [a] tuck-in sleeping (or resting) posture" with limbs folded, a behavior otherwise known only in birds and some mammals. Birds, the authors explained, because of their long, very flexible necks, tuck their heads between one of their forelimbs and their torso. This tuck-in posture reduces area, thereby conserving heat when the animal is at rest or asleep. From the holotype of *M. long*, Xu and Norell discerned from a phylogenetic position that the tuck-in behavior

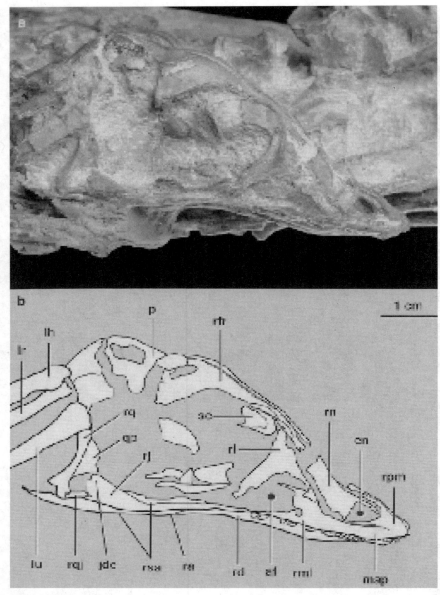

Mei long, IVPP V12733, holotype skeleton, detail of skull. (After Xu and Norell 2004.)

†MELANOROSAURUS

Saurischia: Eusaurischia: Sauropodomorpha: Sauropoda: Prosauropoda: Anchisauria: Melanorosauridae.

Diagnosis of genus (as for type species): Autapomorphy of incorporation of dorsal vertebra into sacrum as fourth sacral vertebra (with retention of caudosacral) (Galton and Upchurch 2004a).

Diagnosis of *M. thabanensis*: Autapomorphies including the following: Femur having oblique fourth trochanter far from lateral edge; skull characterized by wide basal fissure between basioccipital and basisphenoid of skull, and medially expanded retroarticular process (Welman 1999) (Galton and Upchurch 2004a).

Comment: In their review of the Prosauropoda, Galton and Upchurch (2004a) rediagnosed the type species *Melanorosaurus readi* and referred species *M. thabanensis* (see *D:TE*).

Key references: Galton and Upchurch (2004a); Welman (1999).

MENDOZASAURUS González Riga 2003

Saurischia: Eusaurischia: Sauropodomorpha: Sauropoda: Eusauropoda: Neosauropoda: Macronaria: Titanosauriformes: Titanosauria: Lithostrotia *incertae sedis*.

Name derivation: "Mendoza [Province]" + Greek *sauros* = "lizard."

Type species: *M. neguyelap* González Riga 2003.

Other species: [None.]

Occurrence: Río Neuquén Formation, Mendoza Province, Argentina.

Age: Late Cretaceous (later Turonian–late Coniacian).

Known material: Various postcranial elements including vertebrae, limb bones, and osteoderms, at least three individuals.

Holotype: IANIGLA-PV 065/1–24: 22 mostly articulated caudal vertebrae, two proximal chevrons.

Diagnosis of genus (as for type species): Large titanosaur (18 to 25 meters in length), characterized as follows: (autapomorphies: two subtriangular infrapostzygapophyseal fossae in cranial dorsal vertebrae; postzygapostspinal laminae parallel to plane of postzygapophyseal facets in cranial dorsal vertebrae; interzygapophyseal cavity dorsoventrally extended, limited by spinopostzygapophyseal and spinoprezygapopophyseal laminae in proximal caudal vertebrae; middle caudal vertebrae slightly procoelous, reduced distal condyles displaced dorsally; laminar middistal caudal neural spines having horizontal and straight dorsal border, proximodorsal corner forming right angle; large subconicspherical osteoderms lacking cingulum; (synapomorphies associated with the preceding autapomorphies) prespinal lamina extended until base

common to birds originated in their non-avian precursors. While it was not possible to measure this directly, Xu and Norell concluded that "the physiological/thermal implications of this and other fossil evidence (for example, brooding and feathers) are highly suggestive that these animals shared a homeothermic physiology with modern avians."

Note: To date, *Mei* is the shortest name published for a dinosaurian genus.

Key references: Chiappe, Ji, Ji and Norell (1999); Chiappe, Norell and Clark (1998); Currie and Dong (2001); Hwang, Norell, Ji and Gao (2002); Jones, Farlow, Ruben, Henderson and Hillenius (2000); Norell and Makovicky (1997); Russell and Dong (1994); Sereno (1999a); Xu (2002); Xu and Norell (2004).

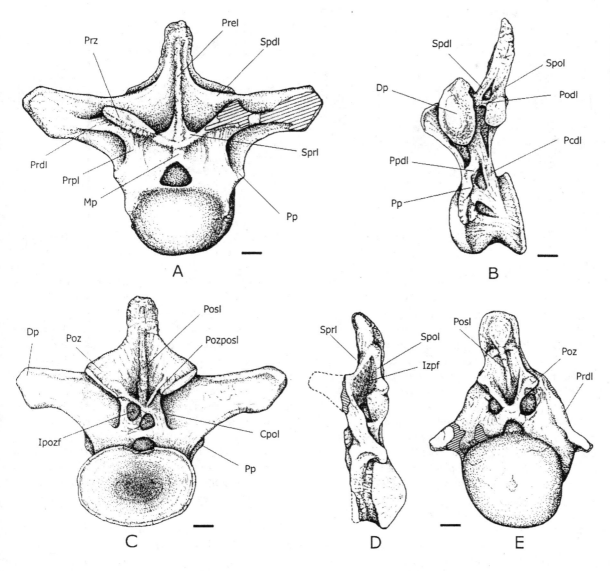

of neural spine in cranial dorsal vertebrae; absence of hyposphene-hypantrum articulation in cranial dorsal vertebrae; strongly procoelous proximal caudal vertebrae having prominent condyles; neural arches located proximally in middle and distal caudal centra; proximodorsal edge of neural spine located distally relative to proximal margin of midcaudal postzygapophyses; laminar and proximodistally elongated neural spines in middle caudal vertebrae; prezygapophyses relatively long in middle caudals, hemal arches articulations open proximally; semilunar sternal plates having relatively straight caudal border; cranial border of scapular blade concave in proximal section, straight in distal section; proximal border of humerus relatively straight and curved medially; metacarpals without distal articular facets; femur with large bulge below greater trochanter (González Riga 2003.)

Comments: The type species *Mendozosaurus neguyelap* was established upon 22 caudal vertebrae and two chevrons (IANIGLA-PV 065/1–24) collected during excavation of 1998 to 2001 from the Upper Cretaceous Río Neuquén Formation [now Río Neuquén Subgroup; see Leanza and Hugo 2001; Leanza, Apesteguía, Novas and Fuente 2004], in the southern region of Cerro Guillermo, Malargue Department, Mendoza Province, Argentina. Paratype disatriculated specimens associated with the holotype comprise the following: IANIGLA-PV 066, cranial dorsal vertebra; IANIGLA-PV 067, sternal plate; IANIGLA-PV 068, scapula; IANIGLA-PV 069, humerus; IANIGLA-PV 070/1–2, radius, ulna; IANIGLA-PV 071/1–4, metacarpals; IANIGLA-PV 072, fragment of pubis; IANIGLA-PV 073/1–2, femur, tibia; IANIGLA-PV 074/1–3, two tibiae, fibula; IANIGLA-PV 077/1–5, five metatarsals; IANIGLA-PV 078 and 079, two ungual phalanges; and IANIGLA-PV 080/1–2, 081/1–2, four osteoderms (González Riga 2003).

Mendozasaurus

Mendozasaurus neguyelap, A.–C., IANIGLA-PV 066, paratype osteoderms in A.–B. lateral and C. dorsal views. Scale = 10 cm. (After González Riga 2003).

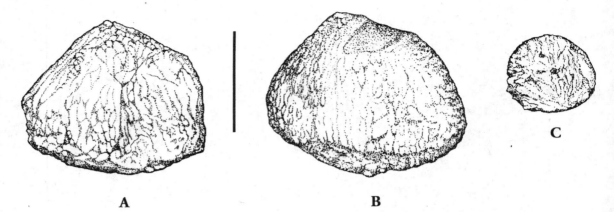

A **B** **C**

It was the opinion of González Riga that the holotype, the dorsal vertebrae (IANIGLA-PV 066), scapula (IANIGLA-PV 068), humerus (IANIGLA-PV 069), metacarpals (IANIGLA-PV 071), and the femur and tibia (IANIGLA-PV 073) could belong to a relatively slender adult specimen, while the sternal plate (IANIGLA-PV 067) and fibula and two tibiae (IANIGLA-PV 074/1–3) pertain to an approximately 15 percent larger individual. González Riga further stated that near the above specimens was "found fossils of an adult specimen of large size (IANIGLA-PV 084)."

M. neguyelap is unique among all known titanosaurs, González Riga noted, in its autapomorphies of slightly procoelous middle caudal vertebrae with reduced, dorsally displaced distal condyles, associated with typical strongly procoelous proximal caudal vertebrae.

That author also emphasized the possession by this taxon of large osteoderms. As described by González Riga, this armor, found in association with the caudal vertebrae of the holotype, is represented by two preserved forms — one small (81 millimeters in length, 44 millimeters high) osteoderm (IANIGLA-PV 081/1–2) presenting a "bulb morphology" (see Le Loeuff, Buffetaut, Cavin, Martin, Martin and Tong

1994), being ellipsoidal in lateral and dorsal aspects, with convex ventral and dorsal faces, and unlike the bone plates in *Saltasaurus* (see Powell 1980, 1986), lacking spines; and two large osteoderms. One of the latter (IANIGLA-PV 080/2) is subconical, its dorsal surface dominated by a 153-millimeter-high apex where grooves and fibers converge, with numerous acute nodules on one of the lateral faces, and with a slightly convex and irregular ventral surface and elliptical contour. The latter morph, González Riga noted, is similar to the smaller form, although it is more spherical and has a less pronounced dorsal apex. Furthermore, the larger osteoderms differ from those described for the South American titanosaurs *Saltasaurus* (Powell 1992) and *Aeolosaurus* (Salgado and Coria 1993*b*); although they resemble the plates described for *Ampelosaurus* (see Le Loeuff *et al.*; Le Loeuff 1995), they do not possess the cingulum found in that species.

Performing a phylogenetic analysis, González Riga found *Mendozasaurus* to be a basal member of the "Titanosauridae" (see "Systematics" chapter), sharing a sister-taxon relationship with *Malawisaurus*, having such features as the following — laminated, proximodistal elongated neural spine in midcaudal vertebrae, located on middle of centrum; development

Mendozasaurus neguyelap, skeletal reconstruction based up type holotype (IANIGLA-PV 065/1-24) and other preserved remains. Scale = 1 m. (After González Riga 2003).

of prezygapophyses relatively long; semilunar sternal plate with straight caudal border.

As González Riga stated, the discoveries of *Mendozasaurus* and other primitive titanosaurs, such as *Andesaurus* and *Malawisaurus*, illustrate "that the caudal procoely of this clade is a complex subject to analyze." Based upon recent cladistic analyses (*e.g.*, González Riga; Salgado, Coria and Calfo 1997), all titanosaurs lacking strongly procoelous middle caudal centra (*e.g.*, *Mendozasaurus*, *Andesaurus*, and *Malawisaurus*) may be regarded as basal taxa in respect to derived "titanosaurids" (*e.g.*, Saltasaurinae).

Key references: González Riga (2003); Le Loeuff (1995); Le Loeuff, Buffetaut, Cavin, Martin, Martin and Tong (1994); Leanza and Hugo (2001); Powell (1980, 1986, 1992); Salgado and Coria (1993b); Salgado, Coria and Calvo (1997).

†**MICROCOELUS** Lydekker 1893 [*nomen dubium*]—(=?*Neuquensaurus*, ?*Saltasaurus*)
Saurischia: Eusaurischia: Sauropodomorpha: Sauropoda: Eusauropoda: Neosauropoda: Macronaria: Titanosauriformes: Titanosauria: Lithostrotia: Saltasauridae: ?Saltasaurinae.
Name derivation: Greek *mikros* = "small" + Greek *koilos* = "hollow."
Type species: *M. patagonicus* Lydekker 1893 [*nomen dubium*].
Other species: [None.]
Occurrence: Río Colorado Formation, Neuquén Province, Argentina.
Age: Late Cretaceous (Campanian).
Known material/holotype: MLP Ly 23, incomplete cranial dorsal vertebra, including centrum and portion of neural arch.

Comments: In 1893, Richard Lydekker erected the new type species *Microcoelus patagonicus*, based upon an incomplete dorsal vertebra (MLP Ly 23) collected from the Upper Cretaceous [Campanian; see Uliana and Dellapa 1981] Río Colorado Formation (possibly Bajo de La Carpa Member), Neuquén Group, near the city of Neuquén, Patagonia, Argentina.

More than a century later, Jaime Eduardo Powell (2003), in a detailed review of South American "titanosaurids," described *M. patagonicus* as follows: Centrum small, probably belonging to first or second cranial dorsal vertebra; centrum broad in ventral aspect, lacking keel; parapophyses situated slightly cranial to and above pleurocoel.

Sauropod specialist John S. McIntosh (1990), in his review of the Sauropoda, tentatively referred this taxon to the type species *Saltasaurus loricatus* (see *D:TE*).

In Powell's assessment, however, the type and only specimen offers "no valid diagnostic features by which it can be referred to any known tyrannosaurid taxa." Consequently, Powell regarded *Microcoelus patagonicus* as a *nomen dubium*. However, in general morphology and proportions, that author noted, the specimen can be referred "with relative certainty to the Subfamily Saltasaurinae."

Powell further noted that the humerus referred by Lydekker to this species probably belongs to *Neuquensaurus australis* (see *Neuquensaurus* entry). Furthermore, Huene (1929) had referred MLP Ly 23 and also other material referred to *M. patagonicus* to "*Titanosaurus*" [=*Neuquensaurus*] *australis*, an assignment that Powell found to be "probably correct."

Key references: Huene (1929); Lydekker (1893); McIntosh (1990); Powell (2003); Uliana and Dellapa (1981).

†**MICRORAPTOR**—(=*Archaeoraptor*, *Cryptovolans*)
Saurischia: Eusaurischia: Theropoda: Neotheropoda: Tetanurae: Avetheropoda: Coelurosauria: Tyrannoraptora: Maniraptoriformes: Maniraptora: Metornithes: Paraves: Deinonychosauria: Microraptoria.
Type species: *M. zhaoianus* Xu, Zhou and Wang 2000.
Other species: [None.]

Comments: In a paper published in 2003, Xu Xing, Zhonghe Zhou, Xiaolin Wang, Xuewen Kuwang, Fucheng Zhang, and Xiangke Du described a second species of the very small and quite birdlike theropod genus *Microraptor* (regarded by those authors as a member of the Dromaeosauridae; see below). Named by these authors *Microraptor gui*, this species was considered to be most notable for the very long feathers that seem to be attached to the hindlimbs, as well as the forelimbs and tail. Xu *et al.* deduced that these feathers produced a "four-winged" gliding planiform interpreted as an incipient stage in the origin of avian flight, while also supporting the hypothesis that such flight began in the trees (see *S3*).

Subsequently, Kevin Padian (2003) criticized Xu *et al.*'s paper, noting that some of these authors' inferences are not yet convincing, that few scientists besides those authors have had the opportunity to see the specimens, and that there has not yet been the opportunity for extensive review and discussion regarding the authors' tantalizing inferences.

Padian noted that the following issues regarding *M. gui* have yet to be resolved:

1. There is insufficient evidence demonstrating that the feathers of *M. gui* were attached to the hind limbs. While Xu *et al.* mentioned that attachment can be seen in other specimens, this condition is not verifiable in the published photographs in their 2003

article. Indeed, there appears "to be a gap between the vaned area of feathers that are near the hind limbs and the bones of the hind limbs themselves." Therefore, lacking verification of such attachments, conclusions cannot be made regarding the transferral of bending moments to the skeletal frame; consequently, it cannot be assumed that the hind wings were carrying flight loads (J. Cunningham, personal communication to Padian).

2. Assuming that the feathers were attached to the hind limbs, it cannot be further assumed that the feathers were used as a gliding surface. Xu *et al.* did not establish how (or that) the feathers in *M. gui* could be arranged as an effective airfoil. If not organized into an airfoil with aerodynamic integrity, such feathers could slow descent, more like parachuting than gliding. Furthermore, there is no reason to assume that a gliding animal will evolve powered flight. As Padian pointed out, "Birds from *Archaeopteryx* onward have not used the hind limbs as airfoils and do not involve them in the flight stroke." Consequently, the feathers on the legs of *M. gui* have "nothing demonstrably to do with the evolution of the kind of flight that more derived birds use."

3. Xu *et al.* show, without comment, the hind limbs of *M. gui* oriented out to the side, a position, unknown in any bird or theropod, that would most likely dislocate the hip joint. Lacking evidence that the hip joint in this species function in a completely different way than in other theropods and birds, "it is difficult to see how the legs could be extended sideways so that the feathers could form a flight surface parallel to the wings." This begs a question — "if the 'hind wing' surface is not parallel to the wings, of what use is it in lift?" If, however, Xu *et al.* can demonstrate that this hip joint is unique among theropods and birds, then it would seemingly be irrelevant to the evolution of avian flight, as birds lack this feature and do not incorporate the hind limbs in flight, thereby rendering *M. gui* "a dead end in all senses."

4. Xu *et al.* described the tibia of *M. gui* as bowed, which would be a unique feature among all known animals, with no discernible use. Furthermore, being incapable of efficient terrestrial locomotion, as the authors maintain, would move this species yet farther from anything relating to the origin of birds.

5. The main issue concerning the evolution of flight is not whether it began in the trees or on the ground, but in the development of the flight stroke, without which flapping cannot be effective.

6. It cannot be convincingly argued that *Microraptor gui* is built like a glider.

Padian acknowledged that Xu *et al.* may be correct in some of their inferences, but added that additional questions need to be assessed. Moreover, *M.*

gui constitutes "an extraordinary find, and these specimens provide a lot of intriguing information about just how much equipment for flight was present in the small theropods that were closer to birds."

Subsequent to Padian's criticism, Xu, Zhou, Zhang, Wang and Kuang (2004), in an abstract, posited that the long, asymmetrical feathers of theropods such as *Microraptor* are not consistent with cursorial habits used to explain the origins of flight. Xu *et al.* (2004) proposed in their brief report that, during take-off, "the hind-limbs of basal dromaeosaurids were capable of stretching posteriorly and also defecting laterally in a position that the long penaceous feathers of the hind-limbs were placed in a subparallel position with respect to the tail." According to the authors, the leg and tail feathers in this posture combined to constitute a lifting surface. This posture, Xu *et al.* (2004) suggested, differs slightly from the parasagittal posture of other dinosaurs; also, it is consistent with the osteological pelvic and hind-limb features seen in "eumaniraptorans" (see *S2*).

As Xu *et al.* (2004) pointed out, in "eumaniraptorans" the caudolateral divergence of the iliac blades constitutes a significant modification, a design permitting a caudolateral orientation of the hind wings. Combined with the opsithopubic condition, this modification results in a flat caudal area of the pelvis. Furthermore, Xu *et al.* (2004) reported that recent reexamination of specimens of *Archaeopteryx* showed proportionately long pennaceous feathers along the tibia, this suggesting a small hind wing. From this evidence, Xu *et al.* (2004) proposed "that primitive eumaniraptorans developed two lift-generating airfoils" during the early evolution of birds —*i.e.*, front wings (and thrust generator), becoming the main airfoil, and hind wings (comprising hind limbs and tail), eventually losing their role in producing lift. *Microraptor gui*, the authors proposed, "represents an early stage in the evolution of flight with two large lift-generating surfaces; furthermore, the reduced leg feathers of *Archaeopteryx* were compensated for by a large feathered tail.

Although *Microraptor* was first described as a dromaeosaurid, that status was recently challenged, as were the species *M. gui* and the genus *Cryptovolans* (see *S3*). In a report proposing a new phylogeny of the Dromaeosauridae, Senter, Barsbold, Britt and Burnham (2004) removed *Microraptor* from the dromaeosauridae and referred it to the new clade Microraptoria (see "Systematics" chapter). At the same time, Senter *et al.* addressed the trichonomy of the taxa *Microraptor zhaoianus*, *Z. gui*, and *Cryptovolans pauli*, the latter a new type species named and described as a "flying dromaeosaur" by Czerkas, Zhang, Li and Li (2002) in the book *Feathered Dinosaurs* (see *S3*).

Senter *et al.* noted that the characters that had been used to diagnose these three species are also present or are unknown elements in each of the other taxa, as in the following examples: Manual phalangeal proportions originally regarded as diagnostic of *C. pauli* seen in *M. gui* and also dromaeosaurid *Sinornithosaurus milleni*, unknown in *M. zhoaianus*; fused sternal plates considered diagnostic of *C. pauli* also seen, albeit smaller (perhaps reflecting ontogeny) in *M. gui*; bowed tibia of *M. zhaoianus* also in *C. pauli*; length ratio of metacarpal I plus manual phalanx I-1 to humerus same (0.46) in *M. zhaoianus*, *M. gui*, and *C. pauli*; bent pubes in *C. pauli* and *S. milleni*; crural and pedal preserved feathers in both *M. gui* specimens and also *C. pauli* (not preserved in *M. zhaoianus*.

For the above reasons, Senter *et al.* recommended synonymizing both *M. gui* and *C. pauli* with *M. zhaoianus*.

Note: Sawyer and Knapp (2003), in a study focusing upon avian skin development and the evolutionary origin of feathers (see paper for details), commented that the discovery of a non-avian theropod feathered hindlimbs supports the interpretation that the ancestor of modern birds likewise possessed feathered hindlimbs.

Key references: Senter, Barsbold, Britt and Burnham (2004); Czerkas, Zhang, Li and Li (2002); Padian (2003); Sawyer and Knapp (2003); Xu, Zhou and Wang (2000); Xu, Zhou, Wang, Kuwang, Zhang and Du (2003); Xu, Zhou, Zhang, Wang and Kuang (2004).

†MICROVENATOR

Saurischia: Eusaurischia: Theropoda: Neotheropoda: Tetanurae: Avetheropoda: Coelurosauria: Tyrannoraptora: Maniraptoriformes: Maniraptora: Metornithes: ?Oviraptorosauria *incertae sedis*.

Diagnosis of genus (as for type species): Centra of dorsal and caudal vertebrae distinctly wide than high; femur having accessory crest at base of cranial trochanter (Osmólska, Currie and Barsbold 2004).

Comment: In their review of the Oviraptorosauria, Osmólska, Currie and Barsbold (2004) rediagnosed the type species *Microvenator celer* (see *D:TE*); at the same time, these authors found this taxon to be a probable oviraptorosaurian.

Key reference: Osmólska, Currie and Barsbold (2004).

MIRISCHIA Naish, Martill and Frey 2004

Saurischia: Eusaurischia: Theropoda: Neotheropoda:

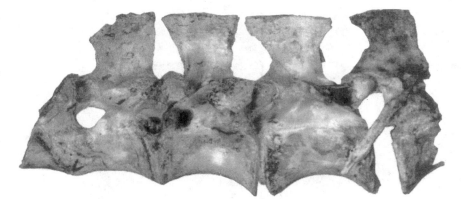

Mirischia asymmetrica, SMNK 2349 PAL, holotype articulated dorsal, dorsosacral, and cranial sacral vertebrae in right lateral view. (After Naish, Martill and Frey 2004.)

Tetanurae: Avetheropoda: Coelurosauria: Compsognathidae.

Name derivation: Latin *mir* = "wonderful" + Greek (pertaining to the pelvis, not just ischia).

Type species: *M. asymmetrica* Naish, Martill and Frey 2004.

Other species: [None.]

Occurrence: Santana Formation, Pernambuco, Brazil.

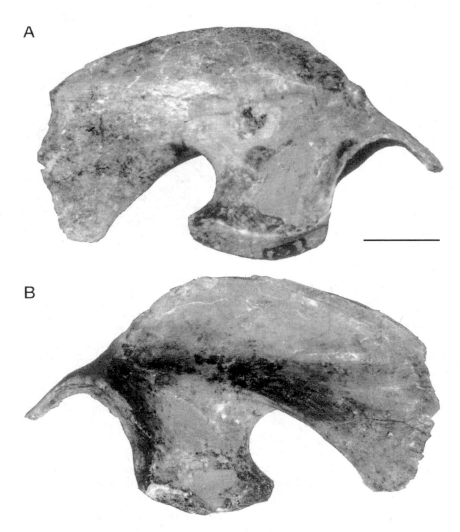

A

B

Mirischia asymmetrica, SMNK 2349 PAL, holotype fragment of right ilium, in A. medial and B. lateral views. Scale = 2 cm. (After Naish, Martill and Frey 2004.)

Mirischia asymmetrica, SMNK 2349 PAL, holotype pubis and ischium in right lateral view. Scale = approximately 2 cm. (After Naish, Martill and Frey 2004.)

Age: Middle Cretaceous (?late Albian).

Known material/holotype: SMNK 2349 PAL, dorsal vertebral centrum with part of neural arch, four sacral vertebra centra with parts of neural arches, several gastralia and lithified contents of terminal part of intestinal tract, articulated nearly complete pelvis and proximal parts of hind limbs (including partial ilia), left and right ossa pubis, (slightly damaged) ischia, partial femora, proximal end of right tibia, proximal end of right fibula.

Diagnosis of genus (as for type species): *Compsognathus*-like, adult body size probably larger than that of other compsognathids; pubic peduncle of ilium having concave cranial surface; pubic boot without cranial expansion; 32 percent length of pubis; pedicular fossae craniodorsal to neural canal on cau-

dal dorsal vertebrae; distal tips of neural spines between 63 and 67 percent longer than their bases; ventral surface of sacral centra with shallow median depressions at either end; all known elements having extremely thin bone walls (Naish, Martill and Frey 2004).

Comments: The small coelurosaurian genus *Mirischia* was founded upon a partial postcranial skeleton with preserved soft tissue (SMNK 2349 PAL) contained in a single calcium carbonate concretion, found in an unknown Middle Cretaceous (?late Albian; see Pons, Berthou and Campus 1990) locality in the Region of Araripina, Romualdo Member of the Santana Formation, Araripe Group, Chapada do Ariripe, Pernambuco, northeastern Brazil. The specimen was originally described, although not named, by Martill, Frey, Sues and Cruickshank in 2000 (see *S2*); nor did those authors discuss the specimen's paleoecological or phylogenetic significance (Naish, Martill and Frey 2004).

As noted by Naish *et al.,* SMNK 2349 PAL "clearly represents a new taxon," being distinct from previously described Santana Formation coelurosaurs. Moreover, the fine preservation of this specimen as well as its "intriguing osteology" make it integral to our understanding of theropod pelvic and hindlimb morphology, soft tissue biology and physiology, and in interpreting less complete specimens of similar taxa.

In describing *Mirischia,* Naish *et al.* observed its close resemblance to the compsognathids *Compsognathus,* from Europe, and *Sinosauropteryx,* from China. Like *Compsognathus,* the pubic boot in *Mirischia* lacks a cranial projection and is nearly flat ventrally. As in *Sinosauropteryx,* the neural spines of *Mirischia* are "fan-shaped," a feature also reported in ornithomimosaurs (see Makovicky 1995) and in *Sinraptor* (Xu, Norell, Wang, Makovicky and Wu 2002). A prominent pubic boot having only moderate cranial expansion is found in the compsognathids *Mirischia, Compsognathus, Sinosauropteryx,* and *Aristosuchus,* this feature perhaps constituting a derived character of the Compsognathidae, although, Naish *et al.* pointed out, similar morphologies have been described in other coelurosaurian groups (Currie and Chen 2001).

According to Naish *et al., Mirischia* is not synonymous with *Santanaraptor* (see *S2*), another small coelurosaur from the Santana Formation, the latter genus having a proportionally larger ischial obturator notch that entirely separates pubic peduncle from obturator process (see Kellner 1999), and a femur bearing a large suclus (not found in *Mirischia*).

As Naish *et al.* pointed out, mostly theropods — including spinosauroids (*Irritator*), compsognathids (*Mirischia*), ?manirapotoriforms (*Santanaraptor*), and oviraptorosaurs (sacrum of an unnamed form; see Frey and Martill 1995 — have thus far been reported from Brazil's Santana Formation. This high diversity of theropods in an assemblage where other kinds of dinosaurs are rare could, the authors suggested, be explained by a number of factors (*e.g.*, occurrence of intraguild predation, small carnivorous dinosaurs possibly subsisting in marginal environments, reliance on coastal resources).

Naish *et al.* noted that referral of *Mirischia* to the Compsognathidae has implications concerning the paleobiogeographic affinities of the Santana dinosaur faunas. Previously, all known compsognathids have been found in Eurasia. If the Compsognathidae originated as an endemic clade of Laurasia, it then follows that "*Mirischia* constitutes evidence of an interchange of dinosaurs between Europe and South America, probably via Africa, during the Early Cretaceous"; or, that the geographic distribution of this group could also reflect vicariances subsequent to the break-up of Pangaea. Furthermore, the presence in the Santana Formation of such diverse clades as the Spinosauroidea (represented in Africa and Europe), Compsognathidae, and Maniraptoriformes (globally represented) "casts further doubt on suggestions (Bonaparte, 1996) that Gondwana had a distinct tetrapod fauna during the Cretaceous" (although a study has not yet been published on the complete faunal composition of the South American theropods; R. E. Molnar, personal communication 2004).

Key references: Bonaparte (1996); Currie and Chen (2001); Frey and Martill (1995); Kellner (1999); Makovicky (1995); Martill, Frey, Sues and Cruickshank (2000); Naish, Martill and Frey (2004); Pons, Berthou and Campus (1990); Xu, Norell, Wang, Makovicky and Wu (2002).

†**MOCHLODON** [*nomen dubium*] — (=?*Rhabdodon*)
Ornithischia: Predentata: Genasauria: Cerapoda: Ornithopoda: Euornithopoda: Iguanodontia: ?Rhabdodontidae.
Type species: *M. suessi* (Bunzel 1881) [*nomen dubium*].
Other species: [None.]
Occurrence: Gosau Formation, Niederösterreich, Austria.
Age: Late Cretaceous (Campanian).
Known material/holotype: PIUW 2349/2, ramus of right dentary with teeth, also associated additional teeth (?belonging to same individual), parietal, proximal scapula.

Comments: For almost a century, the genus *Mocholodon* and its included species have been generally regarded as junior synonyms of the type species *Rhabdodon priscus*.

Collected from a coal mine in the Gosau Beds

[now Formation] (Campanian) near Muttmannsdorf, in Niederösterreich, Neu Welt, in eastern Austria, the type material — PIUW 2349/2, a well-preserved dentary with various associated remains — was originally referred by Emanuel Bunzel (1871) to the genus *Iguanodon* as the new (and somewhat smaller) species *Iguanodon suessi*.

Seeley (1881) later referred this species to a new genus, *Mochlodon*, as the type species *Mochlodon suessi*, noting that the parietal associated with the dentary (interpreted by Bunzel to be lacertilian) and the small incomplete scapula (with "somewhat Crocodilian characters") probably belonged to *Mochlodon*.

As observed by Seeley, the dentary "at first glance reproduces in miniature the characters of *Iguanodon* of the weald; but it differs in a character so remarkable that, had it occurred in a living animal, no hesitation would have been felt in relegating the jaw to a distinct genus. Anterior to the teeth, the symphysial extremity of every *Iguanodon*-jaw bends round so that the rami form a U-shaped curve; but this specimen is straight, and the anterior inward inflexion is scarcely appreciable, so that the snout was evidently sharply pointed, and therefore indicative of a new form of head."

In 1902, Nopcsa erected named and described a second species *Mochlodon robustum* (later emended to *M. robustus*), established on skull bones and much postcrania collected from various localities in the Hateg Basin, Transylvania, Hungary (now in Romania). Nopcsa distinguished this species as follows: Amount of joint excavation in squamosal to its length constant (a significant feature, as most of Nopcsa's mathematical operations for this species rest upon these data; D. B. Weishampel, personal communication 2004); quadrate coincidentally same length as tooth series (as in *Telmatosaurus* and *Iguanodon*); ontogenetic thickening of lower jaw; skull short, tall. Subsequently, Nopcsa (1915) synonymized *Mochlodon* and it species with *Rhabdodon*, a genus from southern France, that author believing that the differences between these genera could be explained by sexual dimorphism.

Until relatively recently, *Mochlodon* has generally been accepted as a junior synonym of *Rhabdodon* (*e.g.*, Romer 1933, 1956; Kuhn 1936, 1964; Steel 1969; see *Rhabdodon* entry). However, in 2003, Weishampel, Jianu, Csiki and Norman reassessed the genus *Mochlodon*, at the same time referring *M. robustus* to the new genus and species combination *Zalmoxes robustum* (see *Zalmoxes* entry), and erecting the new family Rhabdodontidae to include *Rhabdodon* and *Zalmoxes*. Weishampel *et al.* stated that the type material of *M. suessi* could also belong to this family.

As briefly described by Weishampel *et a.*, the dentary of *M. suessi* is comparatively straight (as opposed to the dentaries in juvenile and subadult

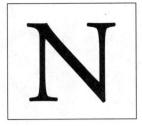

specimens of *Zalmoxes robustus*, in which the ventral surface tends to be convex). This, the authors noted, may constitute an apomorphy of *M. suessi* (see *Zalmoxes* entry). Also, the dentary has a distinct buccal platform rostral to the coronoid process (similar to the condition in *Z. shqiperorum*). However, the dentition in PIUW 2349/2 is indistinguishable from that in *R. priscus* and both species of *Zalmoxes*. Consequently, Weishampel *et al.* found it "likely that *M. suessi* is a distinct species (based on the shape of the dentary) that is positioned in an unresolved relationship within the Rhabdodontidae," this material currently being restudied and revised (S. Sachs, personal communication to Weishampel *et al.* 2001).

Key references: Bunzel (1881); Kuhn (1936, 1964); Nopcsa (1902, 1915); Romer (1933, 1956); Seeley (1881); Steel (1969); Weishampel, Jianu, Csiki and Norman (2003).

Mochlodon suessi, PIUW 2349/2, holotype partial dentary, (upper left) dorsal view, (middle) separate dentary tooth, in enlarged lingual view), and (right) tooth referred to the upper jaw, enlarged. (After Seeley 1881.)

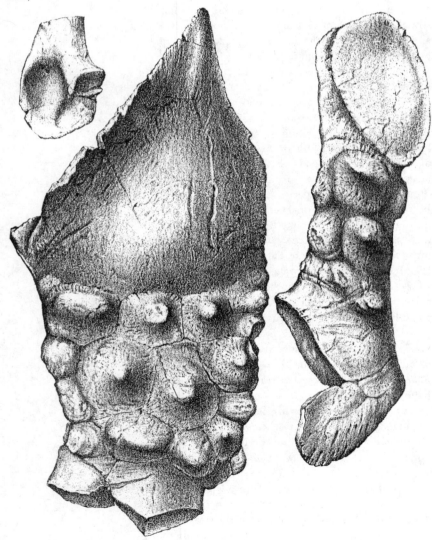

†MONONYKUS

Saurischia: Eusaurischia: Theropoda: Neotheropoda: Tetanurae: Avetheropoda: Coelurosauria: Tyrannoraptora: Maniraptoriformes: Maniraptora: Paraves: Alvarezsauridae: Mononykinae.

Comments: *Mononykus* is an unusual, very bird-like dinosaur distinguished by stunted forelimbs, with a manus possessing but one functional digit (see *S2*). The first study of the function of these forelimbs was presented by Senter (2004) in an abstract.

Senter's study — in which he manipulated casts of *Mononykus* forelimb bones to reveal the range of motion that constrains function — yielded surprising results. As that author pointed out, most theropod humeri hang vertically from the glenoid, with a large range of motion at the shoulders and elbows, hands with medially facing palms, and hands and fingers that move in a transverse plane. In *Mononykus*, however, the humeri sprawl laterally from the glenoid, this condition restricting the movement of the shoulders and elbows, with the palms permanently facing ventrally, and the hands and fingers moving in a subparasagittal plane. Also, "The metacarpophalangeal and interphalangeal joints of the pollex of *Mononykus* exhibit huge ranges of motion."

From his observations, Senter deduced that the forelimbs of *Mononykus* could not be employed in grasping prey, nor could the shoulders and elbows produce movements required for digging burrows. Rather, the forelimbs of this dinosaur are perfectly adapted for performing the motions that anteaters and pangolins employ in breaking into the tough nests of ants and termites (*i.e.*, facing the palms ventrally, then using the parasagittal movements of a single enlarged finger, having an enlarged ungual and great range of motion, to break into ant and termite mounds, vines, and twigs). Senter concluded that a diet of insects that make tough nests could also explain the unusual dental morphology of this theropod genus that "has lost the serrations, recurvature, and large dental size that are typical of the teeth of its carnivorous relatives."

Key reference: Senter (2004).

†NEMEGTOSAURUS

Saurischia: Eusaurischia: Sauropodomorpha: Sauropoda: Eusauropoda: Neosauropoda: ?Macronaria: ?Titanosauriformes: ?Titanosauria: Nemegtosauridae.

Diagnosis of genus (as for type species): Two preantorbital fenestrae; lacrimal expanding rostrocaudally, contributing to lateral margin of external naris; prominent parietal crest (Upchurch, Barrett and Dodson 2004).

Comments: In an abstract published in 2004,

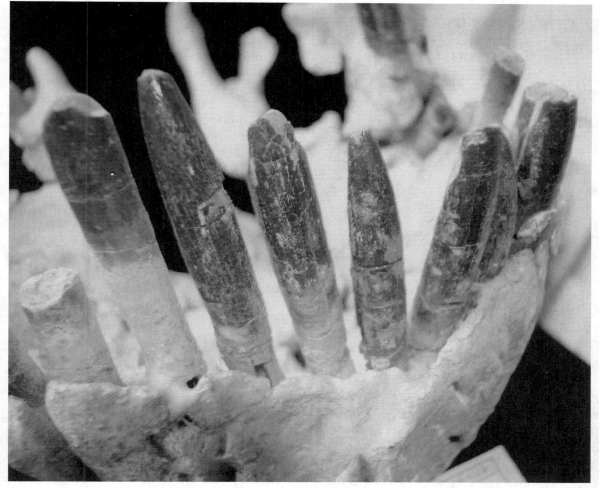

Nemegtosaurus mongoliensis, ZPAL MgD-I/9, holotype maxillary teeth.

sauropod specialist Jeffrey A. Wilson presented a brief report on his reassessment of the holotype skull (ZPAL MgD-I/9; see *S3* for additional photographs of the unreconstructed specimen) of *Nemegtosaurus mongoliensis*, a type species originally found in precladistic studies to belong to the Diplodocoidea (see *D:TE*). Wilson identified various cranial features apparently linking this Mongolian type species "and its closely related counterpart *Quaesitosaurus* to Titanosauria" (see below), the late-surviving sauropod clade that flourished into the late Maastrichtian on most continental land masses.

Titanosaurian synapomorphies observed by Wilson in the skull of *Nemegtosaurus* include: Quadrate fossa posterolaterally oriented; quadrate flange of pterygoid reduced; supraoccipital relatively short; novel basisphenoid contact.

Unique features observed by Wilson uniting *Nemegtosaurus* and *Quaesitosaurus* include the following: Symphyseal eminence on premaxillae; tooth-bearing part of maxilla highly vascularized; maxillary canal enclosed; orbital ornamentation on prefrontal and postorbital; squamosal excluded from supratemporal fenestra; dentary teeth smaller in diameter than premaxillary and maxillary teeth.

Considering the phylogenetic relationships of both of these Mongolian genera, taking into account the above-mention characters as well as others, Wilson concluded the following: All Cretaceous Asian sauropods belong to the Titanosauriformes; all Late Cretaceous Asian sauropods belong to the Titanosauria; and there is not yet any record of the Diplodocoidea in Asia. Consequently, Wilson noted the following: Uniformly nonneosauropod Jurassic Asian fauna supplanted by titanosauriforms by Early Cretaceous times; Middle Jurassic Titanosauriformes origin implied by wide-guage footprints, suggesting that clade originated outside Asia, later migrating to Asia; origin(s) of Asian titanosauriforms unknown despite occurrence of *Euhelopus*-like teeth and gobicondontid mammals in Early Cretaceous Spain suggesting communication between Europe and Asia.

As Wilson explained, titanosaurs constitute the major clade of latest Cretaceous sauropods virtually worldwide, their remains having been reported from all landmasses save Antarctica. Moreover, if connections

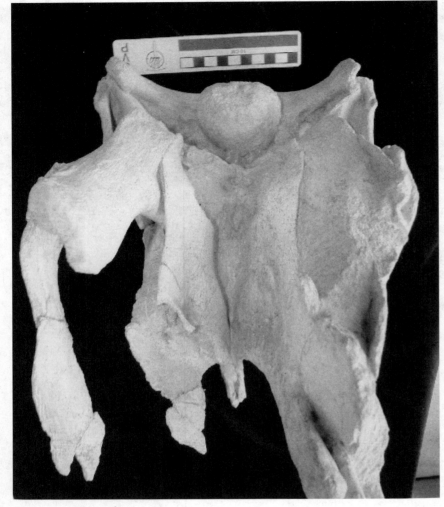

Nemegtosaurus mongoliensis, ZPAL MgD-I/9, holotype caudal part of skull (ventral view).

between the landmasses were severed by Cenomanian times, then the latest Cretaceous survival and predominance of the Titanosauria could have been independent of each landmass. "Confirmation of this pattern," Wilson stated, "will require further sampling of Cretaceous horizons, as well as a detailed framework of titanosaurian interrelationships to evaluate their paleobiogeography."

However, a contrary (and more "traditional") interpretation of the skull of *Nemegtosaurus* was offered by Upchurch, Barrett and Dodson (2004) in their more recently published review of the Sauropoda. According to these authors, citing Upchurch (1999), the skull of *Nemegtosaurus*, even allowing for postmortem distortion, presents a suite of derived characters that argue for the inclusion of this genus in Diplodocoidea. While acknowledging that nemegtosaurids could be ultimately shown to belong to Titanosauria or Diplodocoidea, the authors noted that "they remain an important clade since they either demonstrate the survival of diplodocids into the latest Cretaceous or

reinforce current suspicions that at least some titanosaurs convergently acquired diplodocoid-like skulls."

Key references: Upchurch (1999); Upchurch, Barrett and Dodson (2004); Wilson (2004).

†NEUQUENSAURUS—(=?*Microcoelus*)

Saurischia: Eusaurischia: Sauropodomorpha: Sauropoda: Eusauropoda: Neosauropoda: Macronaria: Titanosauriformes: Titanosauria: Lithostrotia: Saltasauridae: Saltasaurinae.

Type species: *N. australis* (Lydekker 1893).

Other species: *N. robustus* (Lydekker 1893) [*nomen dubium*].

Diagnosis of genus (as for type species): Centra of proximal caudal vertebrae having small, well-defined oval pleurocoel-like openings (also in Diplodocidae) (Upchurch, Barrett and Dodson 2004).

Comments: The type species *Neuquensaurus australis*—founded upon a caudal vertebra (MLP Ly 1/2/3/4/5/6) recovered from the Upper Cretaceous (early Maastrichtian; see Leanza, Apesteguía, Novas and Fuente 2004) rocks of the Allen Formation, on the bank of the Río Neuquén, near the city of Neuquén, Neuquén Province, Cinco Saltos and Lake Pellegrini, Río Negro Province, originally described by Lydekker (1893) as *Titanosaurus australis* (see *D:TE, SI*)—was redescribed by Powell (2003) in his study of the "titanosaurid" dinosaurs of South America.

Powell listed the following postcranial specimens that have been referred to *N. australis*:

Series Ly 1—MLP Ly D. 711A, 46, 19 (cervical vertebrae); MLP Ly 10, 23, D8 (dorsal vertebrae); MLP Ly 7 (sacral vertebrae); MLP 1–2, 5, 8–9, 48, 55–56, 58–59, 61–62, 68, 74, 79, 82–83 (caudal vertebrae).

Series Ly 2—MLP Ly 4, 6, 39, 42, 45, 49–50, 53, 57, 60, 64, 70–1, 73, 76–7, 80, 85, 90, 112 (caudals).

Series Ly 3—MLP Ly 8D, 40, 51, 75 (three vertebrae), 24, 98 (two caudals).

Series of Cinco Saltos 1—MLP CS 1311 (atlas-axis), 1147, 1360–2, 1359, 1366–7, 1372 (cervicals); MLP CS 1357, 1209, 1211–2, 1361, 1370, 1373, 1381, 1385–8 (dorsals); MLP CS 1390–1, 1394, 1404, 1408, 1412, 1416–8, 1419–20, 1422, 1424–6, 1428–9, 1432, 1440, 1443, 1447, 1449–1452 (caudals).

Series of Cinco Saltos 2—MLP CS 1139, 1165, 1378, 1406 (cervicals); MLP CS 1376, 1379, 1382–4 (dorsals); MLP CS 1389, 1392–3, 1399–1401, 1407, 1413 (caudals).

Series of Cinco Saltos 3—MLP CS 1142, 1374–5 (cervicals); MLP CS 1371, 1377 (dorsals); MLP CS 1320, 1395–7, 1408, 1410, 1421, 1423, 1427, 1430–1, 1433–4, 1436–9, 1442, 1444, 1446, 1465 (caudals).

Series of Cinco Saltos 4 — MLP CS 1207, 1321, 1323, 1398, 1411, 1415, 1441, 1622. 2000–1 (vertebrae); MLP CS 1096, 1129, MLP Ly 107, (711A) (scapulae); MLP CS 1096, MLP Ly 14, 95, 105 (coracoids); MLP CS 1019, 1051, 1091, 1099, 1100 (humeri), No. 124 (right humerus), MLP CS 1050, 1100, 1479, Nos. 25 and 89 (left humeri); MLP CS 1058, 1306, 2004 (left unlae), 1053, 1305 (right ulnae); MLP CS 1167, 1169 1172–3 (right radii), 1173–6 (left radii); MLP CS 1234 (carpals); (dubiously assigned) MLP CS 1186–7, 2003 (metacarpals); MLP CS 1261 (phalanges); MLP CS 1056, 1229, 1257–8, 1298, 2008 (ilia); MLP CS 1102, 1120, 1304, No. 109 (pubes); MLP CS 1021, 1101, 1107, 1118, 1120, 2005 (left femora); MLP CS 1093 (right tibia), 1103, 1123 (left tibiae); MLP CS 1098, No. 127 (fibulae); MLP CS 1216 (right astragalus); MLP CS 1179, 1185, 1199 (metatarsals II), 1137, 1177, 1193, 1236, 1238 (metatarsals III), 1178, 1197, 1201 (metatarsals IV), 1189–91, 1198 (metatarsals V), 1180–2, 1184, and 1195 (metatarsals).

According to Powell, a sacrum (MLP Ly 7) from the above hypodigm "should be considered as belonging to the same individual of the holotype"; two caudal centra (MLP Ly 66 and 48) articulate with holotype element MLP Ly 5; MLP Ly 6 should be removed from the holotype, as it belongs to another individual; also, MLP Ly 1 should be removed from the holotype, as it belongs to a different "titanosaurid" more closely related to *Titanosaurus*.

As Powell noted, *N. australis* is close to *Saltasaurus loricatus*, resembling that type species mostly in their comparative adult size, their morphological features, limb bone proportions, and the general characteristics of their vertebrae (see diagnosis, above). However, while the dorsal vertebrae of *N. australis* are not well preserved, they reveal differences from those of *S. loricatus*. The few preserved neural spines of *N. australis* show a different system of reinforcing the laminae, having a larger development of the prespinal laminae. The sacrum of *Neuquensaurus* is opisthocoeloues (in *Saltasaurus*, sacralization can be seen from the first biconvex vertebra, the sacrum biconvex). While the general form of the caudal vertebrae of *Neuquensaurus* closely resemble that in *S. loricatus*, the ventral face of the former is a wide, undivided, and deep depression (a narrower ventral depression, with a medial crest, usually seen in *S. loricatus*). Finally, the limb bones of *N. austrlis* are usually more slender than those in the other taxon.

A second and more robust species of *Neuquensaurus*, the appropriately named *Neuquensaurus robustus*, originally named *Titanosaurus robustus* by Bonaparte and Gasparini (1979), was founded upon a number of lectotype specimens — MLP CS 1095 (left and right ulnae), MLP CS 1171 (left radius), and MLP CS 1480 (left femur) from Cinco Saltos (see *D:TE*). Material (listed by Huene 1929) referred to this species include cervical vertebrae (MLP CS 1139/ 1165/1406/1378), dorsal vertebrae (MLP CS 1376/ 1379/1382 to 1834), a left sternal plate (MLP CS 1295), scapula (MLP Av 2064), humerus (MLP CS 1019), ulnae (MLP CS 1091/1094–1095/1052), a radius (MLP CS 1171), ilia (MLP Av 2068–2069/2083/ 2169), a pubis (MLP Av 2066), femora (MLP CS 1125/MACN "drawer 563"), a tibia (MLP CS 1264/ 1303/2064), and phalanges (MLP CS 1184/1179).

In Powell's opinion it is currently not possible to determine if the above specimens pertain to a single individual; furthermore, it is quite likely that many of these specimens belong to *N. australis*, the other belonging to yet other taxa. Furthermore, while some specimens arbitrarily assigned to *N. robustus* may appear to display differences possibly of taxonomic significance, many of these differences are merely "a matter of preservation of comparison with other genera," or reflect sexual dimorphism or individual variation. Powell concluded that, even without entirely ruling out the possibility of two contemporaneous species of similar size and morphology coexisting in the upper levels of the Neuquén Group and Malarque Group, *N. robustus* is best regarded as a *nomen dubium*.

Key references: Bonaparte and Gasparini (1979); Huene (1929); Leanza, Apesteguía, Novas and Fuente (2004); Lydekker (1893); Powell (2003); Upchurch, Barrett and Dodson (2004).

†NIOBRARASAURUS

Ornithischia: Predentata: Genasauria: Thyreophora: Thyreophoriodea: Eurypoda: Ankylosauria *incertae sedis*.

Comments: In 1995, Kenneth Carpenter, David Dilkes and David B. Weishampel, in a review of the dinosaurs of the Niobrara Chalk Formation of Kansas, named and described *Niobrarasaurus coleii*, a new type species of armored dinosaur founded upon a partial skeleton (MU 650 VP, original catalog number) found in 1930 by geologist Virgil Cole in southeastern Gove County (see *D:TE*).

As more recently pointed out by Hamm and Everhart (2001), the holotype of *N. coleii* to date constitutes the fourth of only six dinosaur specimens yet recovered from the Kansas Chalk.

In December 2002, the type specimen of this species was transferred to a new permanent home, the collections of the Fort Hays University's Sternberg Museum of Natural History in Hays, Kansas. As reported by Everhart (2004), the specimen — now catalogued as FHSM VP-14855 — comprises skull fragments, one tooth, cervical and dorsal vertebrae, almost

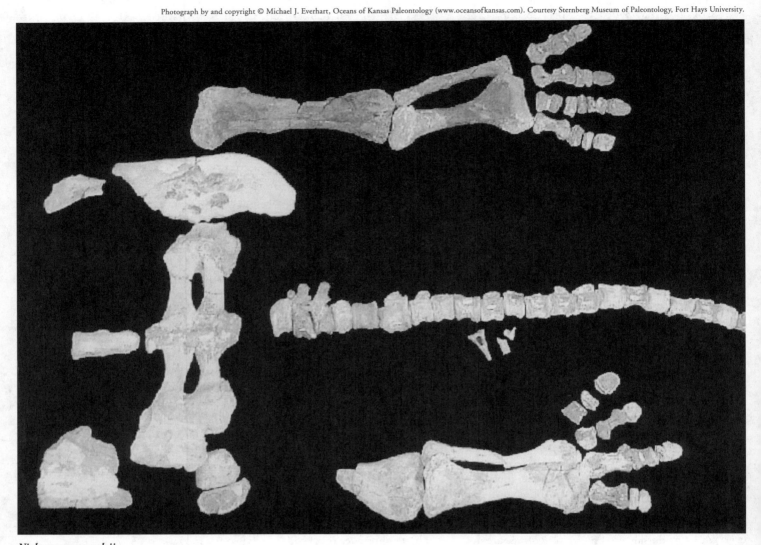

Niobrarasaurus coleii, FHSM VP-14855 (formerly MU 650 VP), holotype partial skeleton as now displayed in the Sternberg Museum of Natural History.

complete series of caudal vertebrae, rib fragments, almost complete right forelimb (minus the manus), partial pelvis, almost complete left forelimb, complete right forelimb, and numerous dermal scutes.

In May 2003, Michael J. Everhart, utilizing Cole's original notes and field sketches, returned to the Cove County site that yielded the *N. coleii* type material, recovering from it three metacarpals and one terminal phalange belonging to the missing right manus.

Key references: Carpenter, Dilkes and Weishampel (1995); Everhart (2004); Hamm and Everhart (2001).

†**NIPPONOSAURUS**—(=?*Hypacrosaurus*, ?*Jaxartosaurus*)

Ornithischia: Predentata: Genasauria: Cerapoda: Ornithopoda: Euornithopoda: Iguanodontia: Dryomorpha: Ankylopollexia: Styracosterna: Iguanodontoidea: Hadrosauroidea: Euhadrosauria: Hadrosauridae: Lambeosaurinae: Corythosaurini.

Age: Late Cretaceous (late Santonian–early Campanian).

Known material/holotype: UHR 6590, partial skeleton comprising left caudal part of skull including maxilla, dentary, parietal, and isolated cranial elements, plus cervical vertebrae, six dorsal centra, two sacral centra, almost complete series of caudal centra, left scapula, distal portions of humeri, remaining forelimbs, left ilium, ischia, almost complete hindlimbs, subadult.

Diagnosis: Robust coronoid process of surangular; slight development of neural spine of axis; strong deflection of lateral margin of first phalanx of pedal digit IV (Suzuki, Weishampel and Minoura 2004).

Comments: Once an enigmatic hadrosaurid genus, *Nipponosaurus* (see *D:TE*)—the first and one of the relatively few dinosaurs known from Japan—was named and first described in 1936 by Takumi Nagao, a professor at the Hokkaido Imperial University (now Hokkaido University). The type species

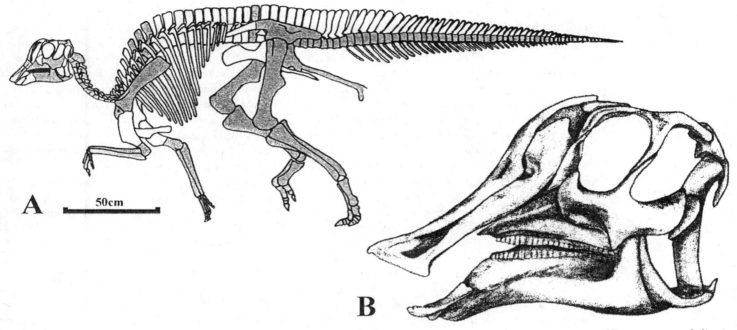

A

50cm

B

Nipponosaurus sachaliensis, UHR 6590, holotype (subadult), A. reconstruction of incomplete skeleton (gray elements are those preserved) based on Weishampel and Horner (1990), B. reconstruction of skull based in part on *Hypacrosaurus stebingeri* NSM-PV 20377. (After Suzuki, Weishampel and Minoura 2004.)

Nipponosaurus sachalinensis was based on poorly pre-served cranial and postcranial remains collected from the Kawakami colliery of the Mitsui Mining Company, in the Upper Cretaceous (late Santonian–early Campanian, based on correlated molluscs; see Matsumoto and Obata 1979, following Matsumoto 1942) "Upper Ammonites Bed" (now Upper Yezo Group), in "Toyohara County" (now Sinegorsk), "Japanese Sakhalin" (now South Sakhalin Russia).

As chronicled by Suzuki, Weishampel and Minoura (2004), the more than half complete holotype skeleton (UHR 6590) was found in late November 1934, during construction of a hospital in what was then Japanese Sakhalin Island. Three years later, Nagao organized a second expedition to Sakhalin which, in the summer of 1937, recovered additional remains belonging to the specimen, including fore-arms, right crus, and right and left pedes, which were described by that author in 1938. With these addi-tional remains, approximately 60 percent of the skele-ton of this dinosaur were then known. Despite the very eroded condition of the external surfaces of the material, UHR 6590 was one of the best Asian hadrosaurid available at the time. Contrary to earlier reports (see *D:TE*), there are no referred specimens pertaining to *Nipponosaurus sachalinensis*.

As Suzuki *et al.* pointed out, Nagao (1936) pri-marily based his new genus and species not on oste-ological characters, but rather "its occurrence at a place very far from North America where above re-ferred genera ... have been discovered, and moreover by the special importance from geological as well as paleontological points of view."

The first major revision of *Nipponosaurus* was that recently published by Suzuki *et al.*, in which these authors redescribed the holotype skeleton in detail, and also established its ontogenetic stage and system-atic position.

Suzuki *et al.* performed a phylogenetic analysis of *N. sachalinensis* utilizing 78 characters for seven in-group (*Lambeosaurus lambei*, *L. magnicristatus*, *Cory-thosaurus casuarius*, *Nipponosaurus sachalinensis*, *Hypa-crosaurus altispinus*, *L. stebingeri*, and *Parasaurolophus* [combination of *P. walkeri* and *P. cytocristatus*]) and six outgroup (a selection of basal hadrosaurids and non-hadrosaurid iguanodontians). This analysis confirmed that *Nipponosaurus* is nestled within the Lambeo-saurinae, based on various lambeosaurine characters cited in their description (*e.g.*, premaxilla with vesti-bule invading anterolateral process, presence of max-illary shelf, distance between ventral and dorsal mar-gin of coracoid greater than in hadrosaurines) of the holotype.

Suzuki *et al.*'s analysis indicated that, within Lambeosaurinae, *Nipponosaurus* shares a sister-taxon relationship with the type species *Hypacrosaurus al-tispinus*, both of these taxa having a jugal with an an-gular flange, a character unknown in any other hadrosaurid. According to their analysis, *Nippono-saurus* and *H. altispinus* thereby constitute a clade that is, in turn, the sister group to *Corythosaurus* and *Lam-beosaurus*. As this analysis did not indicate a sister-taxon relationship between *H. altispinus* and referred species *Hypacrosaurus stebingeri*, Suzuki *et al.* ques-tioned the monophyly of *Hypacrosaurus*, the only "synapomorphy" shared by the two species being vertebral neural spines that are four times greater than centrum height, a feature believed to have allometric significance. As two synapomorphies (*i.e.*, jugal with angular ventral flange; ischial expansion boot-shaped) are shared by *H. altispinus* and *Nipponosaurus* but not by *H. stebingeri*, the two species that have been referred to *Hypacrosaurus* have less in common than do *H. altispinus* and *Nipponosaurus*. Moreover, the authors pointed out, *Nipponosaurus* seems to be more closely related to *H. altispinus* than either of these taxa are to *H. stebingeri*, sharing with that species several apomorphies but lacking such salient cranial features relevant to their relationship as the diagnostic cranial crest possessed by *H. altispinus*, no evidence of which was preserved with UHR 6590. While presently unable to reject or support the possibility that *Nipponosaurus* and *Hypacrosaurus* are congeneric, Suzuki *et al.* found the systematic position of *H. stebingeri* to be undecided, the authors noting that "the genus *Hypacrosaurus* did not justify monophyly." Consequently, Suzuki *et al.* found it "best to retain the genus *Nipponosaurus* for the material from Sakhalin Island" (see also *Olorotitan* entry).

Originally, Nagao (1936) considered the *Nipponosaurus* type material to represent an adult animal, his interpretation based on the completely coossified sacral vertebrae. However, as Suzuki *et al.* pointed out, the sacrals in all presumably subadult hadrosaurid species (*e.g.*, *Lambeosaurus lambei*, AMNH 5340), which are approximately equivalent in size to *Nipponosaurus*, are also coosified. Contrary to Nagao (1936), Rozhdestvensky (1964) regarded the holotype of *Nipponosaurus* as representing a juvenile animal, an assessment accepted by most subsequent authors (*e.g.*, Brett-Surman 1989, who regarded this genus as a juvenile because it had a domed dorsal margin of the skull with open sutures, a character that had been noted as juvenile by Langston 1960). However, as Suzuki *et al.* pointed out, all of these discussions had been based upon the relatively small size of UHR 6590 and the suggestion by Nagao (1936) that "*Nipponosaurus* is similar to *Cheneosaurus* and *Tetragonosaurus*," taxa now known to be not valid adult genera, but juvenile forms of *Hypacrosaurus* and *Corythosaurus* or *Lambeosaurus*, respectively.

As indicated by the study of Suzuki *et al.*, however, the presence of open neurocentral sutures, a feature indicative of immaturity (see Horner and Currie 1994), suggests strongly the subadult nature of UHR 6590. Furthermore, their study showed that the presence of just two teeth per tooth position in the dentary of this specimen also points to its subadult status, a condition also found in other juvenile or subadult hadrosaur specimens (*e.g.*, Hall 1993). Other subadult features noted by Suzuki *et al.* in the *Nip-*

ponosaurus holotype include the comparatively small number of tooth positions, the incipient olecranon, the rounded tip of the ischial booth, and the prominent epiphyseal expansion of the metatarsals.

Until recently, *Nipponosaurus* was largely regarded as a *nomen dubium* (*e.g.*, see Norman and Sues 2000). As noted by Suzuki *et al.*, however, this genus, while one of the most poorly known lambeosaurines, still presents autapomorphies establishing it as a valid genus and reveals synapomorphies indicating its sister-taxon relationship with *A. altispinus*. Therefore, "*Nipponosaurus* can no longer be considered an 'enigmatic dinosaur.'"

Key references: Brett-Surman (1989); Hall (1993); Horner and Currie (1994); Langston (1960); Nagao (1936, 1938); Norman and Sues (2000); Rozhdestvensky (1964); Suzuki, Weishampel and Minoura (2004).

†NOASAURUS

Saurischia: Eusaurischia: Theropoda: Neotheropoda: Ceratosauria: Abelisauroidea: Noasauridae.

Comments: In 1980, José F. Bonaparte and Jaime Eduardo Powell named *Noasaurus leali*, a rather small abelisauroid theropod founded upon very incomplete cranial and postcranial material (PVL 4061) from the Upper Cretaceous (?late Campanian–Maastrichtian) Lecho Formation of Argentina. Among the elements described by those authors was a claimed dromaeosaur-like raptorial second pedal ungual (see *D:TE*).

More recently, as reported in a published abstract, Agnolin, Apesteguía and Chiarelli (2004) restudied this putative raptorial claw ("One of the most striking aspects of abelisaur anatomy"), observing in it the following features: Ungual claw strongly laterally compressed, abnormally curved in lateral aspect; articular medial keel and proximo-ventral process strongly developed; symmetrical lateral sulci.

As observed by Agnolin *et al.*, the above features strongly suggest that the putative foot claw is, in fact, a manual ungual. Consequently, *Noasaurus* possessed well-developed, sharp prehensile manual claws. Also supporting this new interpretation, the authors noted, is the lack of dicotomized lateral sulci and the lateral bump (rather than autapomorphic features). Moreover, the symmetry in the proximal articular facets suggest that this claw belongs to a nonlateral digit, possibly the second.

According to Agnolin *et al.*, the same above-observed features can be seen in a second undescribed claw of the same size, this new specimen lacking only the possibly pathological lateral sulcus.

Both sides of these claws are sub-parallel in dorsal aspect, the authors noted, this constituting a feature unique to *Noasaurus*.

As Agnolin *et al.* pointed out, the claws of abelisauroid dinosaurs have previously been described from their hind feet. Although the pedes of *Noasaurus* are unknown, they are probably nonraptorial but rather cursorial, as evidenced by the feet of "closely related velocisaurines (*e.g.*, *Velocisaurus*, *Masiakasaurus* [see entry; also Carrano, Sampson and Loewen 2004], *Santanaraptor*)."

Features observed by the authors in *Noasaurus* suggesting abelisauroid affinities include a deep excavation in the ventral side of the manual claws and the lack of a flexor tubercle. Finally, the features cited by Agnolin *et al.* "suggest that the claimed 'velocisaurid'-noasaurid lineage show a good development of the forelimbs whereas the lineage that drove to *Carnotaurus* shows the opposite trend."

Key references: Agnolin, Apesteguía and Chiarelli (2004); Bonaparte and Powell (1980); Carrano, Sampson and Loewen (2004).

†NODOCEPHALOSAURUS

Ornithischia: Predentata: Genasauria: Thyreophora: Thyreophoroidea: Eurypoda: Ankylosauria: Ankylosauridae: ?Ankylosaurinae.

Diagnosis: Cranial ornamentation closely resembling that of *Saichania* and *Tarchia* (including pyramidal squamosal bosses, deltoid quadratojugal flanges, bulbous nodelike pattern of cranial sculpturing) (Sullivan 1999); paranasal sinus cavity in maxilla (Vickaryous, Maryańska and Weishampel 2004).

Comment: Described by Robert M. Sullivan (1999) as a member of the Ankylosauridae, this genus was reassessed by Vickaryous, Maryańska and Weishampel (2004) in their review of the Ankylosauria. Vickaryous *et al.* tentatively referred *Nodocephalosaurus* to the subfamily Ankylosaurinae, noting that the skull ornamentation of this armored dinosaur is very similar to that seen in the ankylosaurines *Tarchia* and *Saichania*

Key references: Sullivan (1999); Vickaryous, Maryańska and Weishampel (2004).

†NOMINGIA

Saurischia: Eusaurischia: Theropoda: Neotheropoda: Tetanurae: Avetheropoda: Coelurosauria: Tyrannoraptora: Maniraptoriformes: Maniraptora: Metornithes: Oviraptorosauria: Caenagnathoidea: ?Caenagnathidae.

Comment: In their review of the Oviraptorosauria, Osmólska, Currie and Barsbold (2004) found

Nomingia gobiensis, GIN 100/119, holotype caudal vertebrae. The last five vertebrae in this series are fused into a pygostyle (see *S2* for photograph).

Courtesy Philip J. Currie.

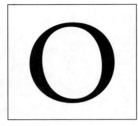

the type species *Nomingia gobiensis*— distinguished as the first dinosaur to be found possessing a pygostyle (see *S2*)— possibly to be closely related to the caenagnathid *Chirostenotes*.

Key reference: Osmólska, Currie and Barsbold (2004).

†NOTHRONYCHUS

Saurischia: Eusaurischia: Eusaurischia: Theropoda: Neotheropoda: Tetanurae: Avetheropoda: Coelurosauria: Tyrannoraptora: Maniraptoriformes: Maniraptora: Metornithes: Therizinosauroidea *incertae sedis*.

Diagnosis of genus (as for type species): Autapomorphies including the following: cheek teeth having denticles reaching to base of crown; manual unguals without dorsal lip proximally; humerus slender (as in *Alxasaurus*, but not in Therizinosauridae) (Clark, Maryańska and Barsbold 2004).

Comment: In their review of the Therizinosauroidea, Clark, Maryańska and Barsbold (2004) rediagnosed the type species *Nothronychus mckinleyi* (see *S3*), at the same time noting that the relationships within that clade are not clear due to lack of fossil material.

Key reference: Clark, Maryańska and Barsbold (2004).

†OHMDENOSAURUS

Saurischia: Eusaurischia: Sauropodomorpha: Sauropoda: ?Vulcanodontidae.

Diagnosis of genus (as for type species): Distinct cavity on ventral surface of astragalus (Upchurch, Barrett and Dodson 2004).

Comment: In their review of the Sauropoda, Upchurch, Barrett and Dodson (2004) rediagnosed the type species *Ohmdenosaurus liasicus* (see *D:TE*), commenting that "The status of this taxon as a valid genus and its placement outside Eusauropoda should be treated as provisional."

Key reference: Upchurch, Barrett and Dodson (2004).

OLOROTITAN   Godefroit, Bolotzky and Alifanov 2003

Ornithischia: Predentata: Genasauria: Cerapoda: Ornithopoda: Euornithopoda: Iguanodontia: Dryomorpha: Ankylopollexia: Styracosterna: Iguanodontoidea: Hadrosauroidea: Euhadrosauria: Hadrosauridae: Lambeosaurinae: Corythosaurini.

Name derivation: *Olor* [genus of swan] + Greek *Titan* [giant offspring of Uranus and Gaea] [for "giant swan"].

Type species: *O. arharensis* Godefroit, Bolotzky and Alifanov 2003.

Other species: [None.]

Occurrence: Tsagayan Formation, Far Eastern Russia.

Age: Late Cretaceous (middle or late Maastrichtian).

Known material/holotype: AENM 2/845, almost complete skeleton.

Diagnosis of genus (as for type species): Helmet-shaped hollow crest and lateral premaxillary process developed caudally far beyond level of occiput; caudodorsal portion of premaxillary process depressed along midline; postorbital process of jugal very high (height of postorbital process/length of jugal ratio of 0.9); rostral portion of jugal shorter than in other lambeosaurines, rostral margin perfectly straight; maxilla very asymmetrical in lateral aspect, ventral margin downward turned; predentary square in dorsal aspect; neck and sacrum very elongated, respectively having 18 cervical and 15 or 16 sacral vertebrae; additional articulation between adjacent neural spines on proximal third of tail (?pathological feature); scapula more elongated than in other hadrosaurids, length/width ratio of 6.2 (Godefroit, Bolotzky and Alifanov 2003).

Comments: The rather large lambeosaurine genus *Olorotitan* was founded upon a nearly complete skeleton with skull (AENM 2/845), collected during 1999 to 2001 field campaigns from the top of the basal or middle part of the Tsagayan Formation (*Wodehouseia spinata–Aquilapollenites subtillis* palynozone), at Kundur, Amur Region, in Far Eastern Russia. Based on preliminary palynological investigations, this locality—which also yielded disarticulated bones of hadrosaurines, lambeosaurines, theropods, ?nodosaurids, turtles, and crocodiles, plus one multituberculate mammal tooth—could be synchronous with the Blagoveschensk and Jiayin localities, which are also located in the Amur Region. To date the holotype of the type species *Olorotitan arharensis* is celebrated as the most complete dinosaur skeleton yet found in Russia and, considering its very well-preserved supracranial crest, the most complete lambeosaurine known outside of North America (Godefroit, Bolotzky and Alifanov 2003).

Performing a cladistic analysis of this genus, incorporating 36 characters and using *Bactrosaurus johnsoni* and Hadrosaurinae as successive outgroups, Godefroit *et al.* found *O. arharensis* to be clearly lambeosaurine based upon the following synapomorphies: Hollow supracranial crest; vertically developed prefrontal; external nares entirely surrounded by premaxillae; jugal having truncated rostral process; wide maxillary shelf; dentary teeth with sinuous median carinae; humerus with strongly developed deltopectoral crest. Additionally, the authors found *Olorotitan* to share one character (*i.e.*, caudal extension of lateral premaxillary process) with "the corythosaur clade"— essentially Brett-Surman's (1989) Corythosaurini "tribe"— comprising *Corythosaurus*, *Hypacrosaurus*, and *Lambeosaurus*. Moreover, *Olorotitan* shares a sister-taxon relationship with the North American genera *Corythosaurus* and *Hypacrosaurus* based upon one character (*i.e.*, nasal participating in supracranial crest) (see also *Nipponosaurus* entry).

This study by Godefroit *et al.* showed that the most basal members of the Lambeosaurinae occur in Asia, these successively including *Tsintaosaurus spinorhinus* (from the Campanian Wangshi Series of Shandong Province, eastern China), *Jaxartosaurus aralensis* (from the Santonian Syuksyuk Formation of Kazakhstan), and *Amurosaurus riabini* (from the Maastrichtian Tsagayan Formation, Amur Region). Consequently, lambeosaurines migrated towards western North America before or at the start of the late Campanian, probably across a land route, postulated to have opened during Aptian–Albian times and persisting into the Late Cretaceous times between Asia and western North America across the Berigian isthmus. According to Godefroit *et al.*, the development of very different kinds of dinosaur communities (*e.g.*, ceratopsians, "titanosaurid" sauropods) following the kinds not represented in Amur Region Maastrichtian localities, could reflect geographical isolation between eastern Asia and western North America during that time, or differences in climatic or paleoecological conditions, topics that require further investigation.

Key references: Brett-Surman (1989); Godefroit, Bolotzky and Alifanov (2003).

†OPISTHOCOELICAUDIA

Saurischia: Eusaurischia: Sauropodomorpha: Sauropoda: Eusauropoda: Neosauropoda: Macronaria: Titanosauriformes: Titanosauria: Lithostrotia: Saltasauridae: Opisthocoelicaudinae.

Diagnosis of genus (as for type species): Centra of dorsal and sacral vertebrae having concave bentral surfaces with ventral midline keel; centra of proximal caudal vertebrae opisthocoelous; pubes and ischia coossified throughout their lengths, closing opening normally present in ventral floor of pelvis (Upchurch, Barrett and Dodson 2004).

Comment: In their review of the Sauropoda, Upchurch, Barrett and Dodson (2004) rediagnosed the type species *Opisthocoelicaudia skarzynskii* (see *D:TE*).

Key reference: Upchurch, Barrett and Dodson (2004).

†OPLOSAURUS

Saurischia: Eusaurischia: Sauropodomorpha: Sauropoda:

Diagnosis of genus (as for type species): Labial

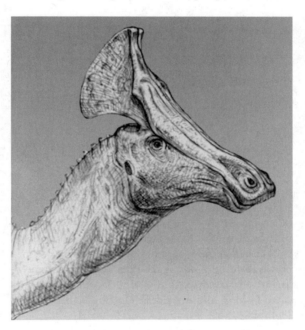

Life restoration by Berislav Krzic of *Olorotitan arharensis.*

Life restoration by Berislav Krzic of the opisthocoelicaudine titanosaur *Opisthocoelicaudia skarzynskii.*

Ornithomimoides

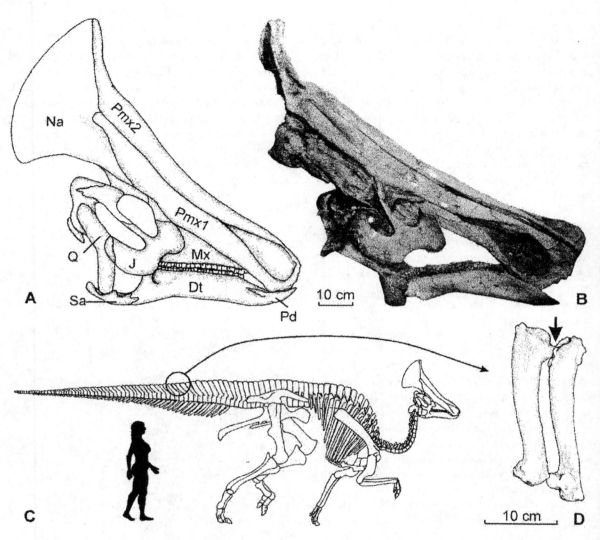

surface of tooth crown lacking grooves near mesial and distal margins; convexity of labial surface of tooth crown forming almost acute ridge extending up midline of surface to apex; lingual surface of crown concave, lacking midline ridge (Upchurch, Barrett and Dodson 2004).

Comment: In their review of the Sauropoda, Upchurch, Barrett and Dodson (2004) rediagnosed the type species *Oplosaurus armatus* (see *D:TE*).

Key reference: Upchurch, Barrett and Dodson (2004).

†ORNITHOMIMOIDES—(=?*Coeluroides*, ?*Dryptosauroides*, ?*Indosaurus*, ?*Indosuchus*, ?*Jubbulpuria*)
Saurischia: Eusaurischia: Theropoda: Neotheropoda: Ceratosauria: Abelisauroidea *incertae sedis*.
Type species: *O. mobilis* Huene 1932.
Other species: ?*O. barasimlensis* Huene 1932.

Comments: In 1932, Friedrich von Huene named and described *Ornithomimoides*, a theropod genus founded upon a number of vertebrae (presumed to be dorsals) collected from the Lameta Formation of India. Huene based the type species *O. mobilis* on five large and elongate specimens (GSI K20/610, K20/614B, K27/586, K27/597, and K27/600) and a second species ?*O. barasimlensis*, only tentatively referred to the new genus, on a suite of smaller specimens (GSI K27/531, K27/541, K27/604, and K27/682), These vertebrae were subsequently described again by Huene in Huene and Matley (1933), an extensive report on dinosaurs from India (see *D:TE*).

The genus *Ornithomimoides* and its species were recently reassessed by Novas, Agnolin and Bandyopadhyay (2004) in their extensive review of the theropods discussed in Huene and Matley. As the authors pointed out, the vertebrae referred by Huene to these taxa are not dorsals, but, in fact, caudal vertebrae having a morphology corresponding to vertebrae of the abelisaurid *Majungatholus* (Novas *et al.*, personal observation). As in *Majungatholus*, the vertebrae referred to *Ornithomimoides* display the following features: Prezygapophyses close to one another, lacking ventral projections in "neoceratosaurian" (see "Systematics" chapter, *S2* and this volume) dorsal vertebrae; prespinal depression deep, divided by tiny sagittal crest; neural spine craniocaudally extended; base of transverse process ventrally buttressed and excavated; apneumatic centrum longer than deep.

Recognizing no diagnostic features in the material referred to *Ornithomimoides*, while noting the close similarity between the caudal vertebrae of this taxon and those of other abelisauroids, Novas *et al.* followed previous authors (*e.g.*, Norman 1990) in regarding this genus as a *nomen dubium* and an indeterminate member of the Abelisauroidea.

According to Novas *et al.*, the bones referred to *Ornithomimoides*, *Compsosuchus*, *Dryptosauroides*, and *Jubbulpuria* (see entries) all pertain to different areas of the neck and tail, intimating that some or all of these taxa may be congeneric.

Key references: Huene (1932); Huene and Matley (1933); Molnar, Kurzanov and Dong (1990); Norman (1990).

†ORNITHOMIMUS — (=*Coelosaurus*, *Dromiceiomimus*)

Saurischia: Eusaurischia: Theropoda: Neotheropoda: Tetanurae: Avetheropoda: Coelurosauria: Tyrannoraptora: Maniraptoriformes: Ornithomimosauria: Ornithomimidae.

Diagnosis of genus (as for type species): Autapomorphies including the following: metacarpal I longer than other metacarpals; squamosal having bifid dorsal ramus (for reception of descending ramus of squamosal); well-defined incision in caudal border of quadratojugal (for quadrate foramen) (Makovicky, Kobayashi and Currie 2004).

Comments: In their review of the Ornithomimosauria, Makovicky, Kobayashi and Currie (2004), as had Nicholls and Russell (1981), found *Dromiceimimus* — a genus erected in 1972 by Dale A. Russell (see *D:TE*) — to be a junior synonym of the Canadian genus *Ornithomimus*, specifically the referred species *O. edmontonicus*.

As Makovicky *et al.* pointed out, Nicholls and Russell had questioned Russell's original diagnosis of *Dromiceimimus*, noting that it was based on minor differences in select ratios between certain bones. In reexamining Russell's ratios in a wide range of specimens, Makovicky *et al.* found no statistical support for his diagnosis. Based upon the diagnostic character of the bifid dorsal ramus of the quadratojugal, Makovicky *et al.* referred both species of *Dromiceiomimus* (*D. samueli* and *D. brevitertius*) to *O. edmontinicus*.

Makovicky *et al.* were unable to distinguish the fragmentary type species *Ornithomimus velox* from *O. edmontonicus*, noting the possibility that, pending the discovery of more complete material, these two taxa may proved to be conspecific.

Key references: Makovicky, Kobayashi and Currie (2004); Nicholls and Russell (1981)l Russell (1972).

†ORNITHOPSIS Seeley 1870 [*nomen dubium*]

Saurischia: Eusaurischia: Sauropodomorpha: Sauropoda: Eusauropoda: Neosauropoda: Macronaria: ?Titanosauriformes *incertae sedis*.

Name derivation: Greek *ornis* = "bird" + Greek *opsis* = "appearance."

Type species: *O. hulkei* Seeley 1870 [*nomen dubium*].

Other species: [None.]

Occurrence: Hastings Beds, East Sussex, England.

Age: Early Cretaceous ("Wealden").

Known material/holotype: BMNH R89, partial dorsal centrum.

Diagnosis of genus (as for type species): [None published.]

Comments: In 1870, Harry Govier Seeley described *Ornitopsis hulkei*, a new sauropod type species based upon two dorsal vertebrae (BMNH R89 and R90) recovered from Hastings Beds of Cuckfield, Tilgate, East Sussex, England. Seeley, who did not figure this material, interpreted these fossils as representing a gigantic pterosaur, while at the same time noting a possible relationship to dinosaurs.

As measured by Seeley, these specimens are, respectively, approximately 23 centimeters (nine inches) and 36 centimeters (14 inches) long.

Since the erection of this taxon, however, *O. hulkei* has largely been regarded as a junior synonym of the sauropod *Pelorosaurus* (see *D:TE*).

Over a century later following Seeley's description, Blows (1995), in a review of this taxon and also *Eucamerotus* (see entry), interpreted *Ornithopsis* as a valid brachiosaurid genus founded upon diagnosable material.

Later, in a review of the Sauropoda, Upchurch, Barrett and Dodson (2004) noted some unusual features exhibited by the *Ornithopsis* vertebrae (*e.g.*, centrum wider dorsoventrally than transversely, although possibly belonging to middle or caudal area of the presacral vertebral series; pleurocoel occupying caudal two-thirds of centrum, as opposed to the more cranial placement of most sauropods). Also, Upchurch *et al.* noted, while Blows referred these vertebrae to the Brachiosauridae, no synapomorphies are currently known in that clade from the middle and caudal dorsal centra.

Upchurch *et al.* regarded *Ornithopsis* as potentially

valid, probably referrable to the Titanosauriformes based upon "the coarse cancellar tissue structure within the body of the centrum."

Key references: Blows (1995); Seeley (1870); Upchurch, Barrett and Dodson (2004).

†ORODROMEUS

Ornithischia: Predentata: Genasauria: Cerapoda: Ornithopoda; Euronithopoda.

Comments: Wolff and Horner (2003), in a published abstract for a poster, briefly reported on the discovery of postcranial remains of the primitive ornithopod type species, *Orodromeus makelai*, collected from Upper Cretaceous (late Campanian) Judith River Formation of Phillips County, in eastern Montana, this constituting the first occurrence of the species reported from that formation. According to these authors, the report of *Orodromeus* teeth from the same formation is confirmed by examination of the proximal femur, tibia, and distal metatarsals of this newly recovered material, based upon morphological characters from earlier studies.

As noted by Wolff and Horner, this new specimen displays various characters (*e.g.*, constricted femoral neck, lateral disposition of lesser trochanter relative to greater trochanter, blunted aspect to cnemial crest, triangular midshaft of tibia, partially load-bearing first pedal digit) suggesting placing this genus between *Heterodontosaurus* and *Gasparinisaura*, with the added character of proximal tibial condyles indicating a relationship either with *Lesothosaurus*, *Hypsilophodon*, or *Orodromeus*. However, referral of the specimen to *Lesothosaurus* or *Hypsilophodon* was discouraged by the authors because of a lack of known occurrence of these genera in the Upper Cretaceous global record; moreover, the stratigraphic level of the Phillips County site is chronally equivalent to the Willow Creek Anticline type locality that yielded *O. makelai*. Therefore, Wolff and Horner found it most parsimonious to refer the Phillips County specimen to that species.

In a phylogenetic analysis of basal Ornithopoda, Norman, Sues, Witmer and Coria (2004) found *O. makelai* to be a member of Euronithopoda, closely related to *Othnielia rex*, the two of them less derived than *Hypsilophodon foxii* and *Zephyrosaurus schaffi*, all of these taxa sharing a suite of characters (see "Systematics" chapter).

Key references: Norman, Sues, Witmer and Coria (2004); Wolff and Horner (2003).

†OVIRAPTOR

Saurischia: Eusaurischia: Theropoda: Neotheropoda: Tetanurae: Avetheropoda: Coelurosauria: Tyrannoraptora: Maniraptoriformes: Maniraptora: Metornithes: Oviraptorosauria: Caenagnathoidea: Oviraptoridae: Oviraptorinae.

Comments: When Henry Fairfield Osborn first described the toothless type species *Oviraptor philoceratops* in 1924, its holotype (AMNH 6517) discovered in Mongolia in a presumed grasping posture near a nest of dinosaur eggs, he naturally assumed that the eggs belonged to the horned dinosaur *Protoceratops* and that the theropod was the predator of these eggs. More recent analyses, however, have shown that many of the fossil eggs originally believed to belong to *Protoceratops* are, in fact, those of theropods (see Sabath 1991). Additionally, a number of recently discovered

Life restoration of *Oviraptor philoceratops* by artist Todd Marshall.

Oviraptor skeletons (*e.g.*, Norell, Clark, Chiappe Dashveg (1995); Dong and Currie 1996), preserved in apparent brooding postures over their nests, have altered the image of this theropod from the traditional "egg thief" to "egg mother" (see *Oviraptor* entries, *D:TE, S1*; *Protoceratops* entry, *D:TE*), with jaws more suited to consuming molluscs (*e.g.*, Barsbold 1986) or vegetation (*e.g.*, Smith 1993) than eggs.

Headden (2003), however, in an abstract for a poster, noted that oviraptorid jaw anatomy illustrates the development of several features indicating "dietary specialization to crushing, including an expanded secondary body palate, enlargement of the temporal musculature, and a palatal design that enhances the holding, puncturing, pulverization, and swallowing of an egg or its contents." This indicated to Headden that oviraptorids may have consumed eggs "often enough to lead to selection favoring this food," with other kinds of food being secondary. Such an interpretation, however, neither contradicts the hypothesis that oviraptorids were good mothers, that author stated.

Key references: Barsbold (1986); Dong and Currie (1996); Headden (2003); Norell, Clark, Chiappe and Dashveg (1995); Osborn (1024); Ostrom (1973); Sabath (1991); Smith (1993).

†OZRAPTOR

Saurischia: Eusaurischia: Eusaurischia: Theropoda: Neotheropoda: Tetanurae: Avetheropoda *incertae sedis*.

Diagnosis of genus (as for type species): Angular oblong shape of astragalar condyles (Holtz, Molnar and Currie (2004).

Comment: Holtz, Molnar and Currie (1994), in their review of basal Tetanurae, rediagnosed the type species *Ozraptor subotaii* (see *S2*), identifying it as an avetheropod based upon one feature — *e.g.*, cranial rather than caudal orientation of astragal condyles.

Key reference: Holtz, Molnar and Currie (2004).

†PACHYRHINOSAURUS

Ornithischia: Predentata: Genusauria: Cerapoda: Chasmatopia: Marginocephalia: Ceratopsia: Neoceratopsia: Coronosauria: Ceratopsoidea: Ceratopsidae: Centrosaurinae.

Comments: Fiorillo and Gangloff (2003), in an abstract, published preliminary notes on the taphonomic and paleoecologic setting of a *Pachyrhinosaurus* bonebed at the Kikak-Tegoseak Quarry, located in mostly fluvial sediments, shed from the rising Brooks Range, in the Upper Cretaceous (Campanian–Maastrichtian) Prince Creek Formation, along the Colville River, in northern Alaska (for a recent survey report

on the record of northern Alaskan dinosaurs — including troodontids, tyrannosaurids, marginocephalians, and hadrosaurines — see Gangloff 2003).

As related by Fiorillo and Gangloff, excavation of a four meter by four meter pit within this bonebed has, to date of their writing, skeletal remains — as indicated by the number of recovered occipital condyles — of at least eight apparently subadult *Pachyrhinosaurus* individuals, the condyles ranging from five to eight centimeters in diameter. The authors interpreted this bonebed as having been formed by catastrophic capture of the animals, "suggesting that seasonal runoff from the rising Brooks Range may have been a substantial hazard to gregarious dinosaurs on the ancestral North Slope."

Other vertebrate taxa collected from this quarry, Fiorillo and Gangloff reported, include such dinosaurs as dromaeosaurs, tyrannosaurids, ornithomimids, and hadrosaurids, and also osteichthyan fishes. Recovered nonanimal fossils include the insect-pollinated *Aquillapollenites* and *Fibulapollis scabratus*, and small pieces of amber.

Note: Tanke (2004) published an informal yet detailed account of the 2003 Royal Tyrrell Museum of Palaeontology expedition to the Grande Prairie Region of northwestern Alberta, Canada. Included in this account was a report on the Pipestone Creek Pachyrhinosaur Bonebed, preserving a mass mortality event, and distinguished arguably as "currently the single most important dinosaur site in the Grande Prairie area" and "the best-known horned dinosaur bonebed in North America."

As chronicled by Tanke, the locality was discovered in 1975 by Al Lakusta, a science teacher at Crystal Park School (see Fleming 1975). Fossil bones from

Mounted composite skeleton (cast) of *Pachyrhinosaurus canadensis*.

Photograph by Darren Tanke.

Panoplosaurus

Head, restored by artist Katy Hargrove, of *Pachyrhinosaurus canadensis*). Originally published in *Alberta Paleontological Society Bulletin*.

eling exhibit — of five composite adult and juvenile pachyrhinosaurine skeletons.

As Tanke reported, 99 percent of the bones recovered from this site are ceratopsian. Other nonvertebrate remains yielded by the Pipestone Creek site include well-preserved insects in hard amber, permitting "the first opportunity to learn about truly contemporaneous dinosaur and insect faunas."

Tanke noted that a major research paper describing the skull osteology and ontogeny of the Pipestone Creek pachyrhinosaurine is in preparation by Wann Langston, Jr., Philip J. Currie and Darren H. Tanke.

Key references: Fiorillo and Gangloff (2003); Fleming (1975); Gangloff (2003); Skidnuk (1985); Tanke (2004).

†PACHYSAURISCUS — (See *Plateosaurus*.)

†PANOPLOSAURUS

Ornithischia: Predentata: Genasauria: Thyreophora: Thyreophoroidea: Eurypoda: Ankylosauria: Nodosauridae.

Diagnosis of genus (as for type species): Rostrum tapering in dorsal aspect; vomer with distended palatal margin; four sacral vertebrae; coracoid with rounded ventral margin; manus tridactyl; cervical osteoderm morphology unique (*i.e.*, ovoid and craniocaudally elongate in dorsal aspect) (Vickaryous, Maryańska and Weishampel 2004).

Comment: In their review of the Ankylosauria, Vickaryous, Maryańska and Weishampel (2004) rediagnosed the type species *Panoplosaurus mirus* (see *D:TE*).

Key reference: Vickaryous, Maryańska and Weishampel (2004).

†PARALITITAN

Saurischia: Eusaurischia: Sauropodomorpha: Sauropoda: Eusauropoda: Neosauropoda: Macronaria: Titanosauriformes: Titanosauria: Lithostrotia.

Diagnosis of genus (as for type species): Tabular process on caudoventral margin of scapula, distal to proximal expansion; humerus having ridge on proximocaudal face; humerus with rectangular radial condyle (Upchurch, Barrett and Dodson 2004).

Comment: In their review of the Sauropoda, Upchurch, Barrett and Dodson (2004) rediagnosed the type species *Paralititan stromeri* (see *S3*).

Key reference: Upchurch, Barrett and Dodson (2004).

this bonebed, collected by Lakusta over a several-years period, were stored at the then-named Grande Prairie Pioneer Museum. Ten years after the site's discovery, Lakusta identified the bones as those of *Pachyrhinosaurus*, at that time North America's most poorly known ceratopsian. In November 1985, this material was donated to the Royal Tyrrell Museum of Palaeontology (Skidnuk 1985).

Although originally believed to pertain to *Pachyrhinosaurus*, the identity of the Pipestone Creek ceratopsian bones was later questioned in lieu of relatively recent discoveries of quite similar genera (*e.g.*, *Achelosaurus*; see *D:TE*). For the present, therefore, the Pipestone Creek taxon is regarded simply as a "pachyrhinosaurine."

Subsequent excavations by the Royal Tyrrell Museum at the Pipestone Creek bonebed from 1986 to 1989 would yield numerous mostly disarticulated but well-preserved cranial and postcranial elements representing four size classes, and including a number of large, 50 to 75 percent complete adult skulls. The elements recovered were sufficient enough to allow the reconstruction — by Darren H. Tanke and other personnel assembled by the staff of the Ex Terra Foundation for the Alberta-Canada-China Dinosaur trav-

†PARANTHODON

Ornithischia: Predentata: Genasauria: Thyreophora: Thyreophoroidea: Eurypoda: Stegosauria *incertae sedis*.

Diagnosis of genus (as for type species): Snout region having uniquely long, broad caudal process to premaxilla (Galton and Upchurch 2004*b*).

Comment: In their review of the Stegosauria, Galton and Upchurch (2004*b*) rediagnosed the type species *Paranthodon africanus* (see *D:TE*).

Key reference: Galton and Upchurch (2004*b*).

†PATAGONYKUS

Saurischia: Eusaurischia: Theropoda: Neotheropoda: Tetanurae: Avetheropoda: Coelurosauria: Tyrannoraptora: Maniraptoriformes: Maniraptora: Paraves: Alvarezsauridae.

Comments: A new and fragmentary specimen apparently belonging to the small, very birdlike dinosaur *Patagonykus* was described by Chiappe and Coria (2003). The specimen (MCF-PVPH-102) consists of an articulated phalanx 1 and 2 (ungual) of the left manual digit I, collected from the northern shore of Los Barriales Lake, Plaza Huincul, in the Upper Cretaceous of Neuquén Province, Patagonia, Argentina.

As this specimen — referred by Chiappe and Coria to *Patagonykus* sp. cf. *P. puertai* — was collected by amateurs, precise stratigraphic information concerning was not available. However, as Chiappe and Coria pointed out, only the Late Cretaceous Neuquén Group outcrops in this area. Furthermore, the holotype of the type species *Patagonykus puertai* (see Novas 1997*a*) was discovered in beds then attributed to the Portezuelo Member of the Rio Neuquén Formation [now Portezuelo Formation, belonging to the Rio Neuquén Subgroup, dated as of middle Coniacian age; see Leanza, Apesteguía, Novas and Fuente 2004]; consequently, Chiappe and Coria provisionally referred the provenance of MCF-PVPH-102 to that unit.

In describing this specimen, Chiappe and Coria observed various differences between it (*e.g.*, more robust; deeper, more subcircular extensor fossa in dorsal view) and the similarly sized holotype (MCF-PVPH-37) of *P. puertai*. Nevertheless, the authors referred this specimen to *Patagonykys* due to "the

Reconstructed skeletal cast of *Patagonykus puertai* mounted under the direction of paleontologist Rodolfo A. Coria, on exhibit at the Museo Municipal Carmen Funes in Neuquén Province, Patagonia, Argentina.

Photograph by Luis M. Chiappe, courtesy Museo Municipal Carmen Funes.

quantitative nature of observed differences and because of the lack of information regarding morphological variation within alvarezsaurid species (including sexual dimorphism).

Chiappe and Coria pointed out that, despite its fragmentary nature, this new specimen is important in contributing anatomical data permitting the assessment of various character states. For example, the central keel in the proximoventral surface of the ungual of manual digit I demonstrates a condition shared by *Alvarezasaurus calvoi* and *P. puertai*, thereby casting doubts on Novas' (1997*a*) proposal that this is an autapomorphy of the former species. Not yet included in any published cladistic analysis, this derived character state "is likely to represent the plesiomorphic condition for basal alvarezsaurids (and hence an alvarezsaurid synapomorphy) rather than a synapomorphy of a clade formed by these two basal taxa," the latter hypothesis requiring the independent origin of several derived character states that have been proposed to unite all Alvarezsauridae excluding *Alvarezsaurus* (see Novas 1997*a*; Chiappe, Norell and Clark 1998), one apparently a pair of notches or foramina on the proximoventral surface of the ungual of manual digit I.

The phylogenetic relationships of the Alvarezsauridae with other theropod taxa have been controversial (see *D:TE*, *S1*, *S2*, and *S3*; see also "Systematics" chapter). However, as Chiappe and Coria noted, MCF-PVPH-102 sheds light on character states that Sereno (1999*a*, 2001) utilized to support a sister-group relationship between Alvarezsauridae and Ornithomimidae, one of these involving the ventral surface of the unguals (only manual digit I being known in alvarezsaurids when Sereno did his analyses). Sereno (1999, 2001) had proposed flattened and broad ventral surfaces of the manual digits, rather than the plesiomorphic narrow and rounded condition of these surfaces, as a synapomorphy of Alvarezsauridae and Ornithomimidae. More recently, Suzuki, Chiappe, Dyke, Watabe, Barsbold and Tsogtbaatar (2002) argued that this character state should be restricted to the first manual digit (see *Shuvuuia* entry, *S3*). Moreover, MCF-PVPH-102 shows that, while the ungual phalanx of the first manual digit of more advanced alvarezsaurids (*e.g.*, *Shuvuuia deserti* and *Mononykus olecranus*) has a broad and flattened surface, that of more basal forms (*P. puertai*) is closer to the plesiomorphic condition, this also suggested by the more fragmentary claw of MCF-PVPH-37.

Additionally, Chiappe and Coria noted that MCF-PVPH-102 casts doubts on the validity of another synapomorphy uniting Alvarezsauridae and Ornithomimidae, as proposed by Sereno (1999*a*, 2001), this interpreting the distal displacement of the flexor

ligaments shared by these clades as a derived character state. As Chiappe and Coria observed, however, the area for the attachment of the flexor ligaments is poorly developed in the ungual phalanges of the alvarezsaurid manus, while the flexor tubercles are bulbous and much better developed in ornithomimids. In the basal alvarezsaurid represented by MCF-PVPH-102, the flexor ligaments of the unguals of digit I "are attached to low keels flanked by deep depressions." Moreover, the authors pointed out, these areas are not displaced distally as are the flexor tubercles of the ungual phalanges in ornithomimids, which in some examples are "emplaced at the midpoint of the claw."

Key reference: Chiappe and Coria (2003); Chiappe, Norell and Clark (1998); Leanza, Apesteguía, Novas and Fuente (2004); Novas (1997*a*); Sereno (1999*a*, 2001); Suzuki, Chiappe, Dyke, Watabe, Barsbold and Tsogtbaatar (2002).

†PATAGOSAURUS

Saurischia: Eusaurischia: Sauropodomorpha: Sauropoda: Eusauropoda: Cetiosauridae.

Diagnosis of genus (as for type species): Maxillary ascending process projecting caurodorsally in lower half, turning abruptly to extend dorsally in its distal half; summits of neural spines of caudal vertebrae having well-developed dorsally directed process (Upchurch, Barrett and Dodson 2004).

Comments: Although sauropod dinosaurs constitute a significant component of Mesozoic terrestrial faunas, our knowledge of the early history of the Sauropoda is quite incomplete. Indeed, skull material belonging to this group of dinosaurs, particularly the more primitive forms, remains rare (see McIntosh 1990). Consequently, the recovery of any such material is significant.

Recently, Rauhut (2003*b*) described such a significant discovery—an isolated, incomplete, subadult right dentary (MPEF-PV 1670), referred to the primitive, Middle Jurassic sauropod *Patagosaurus*, collected from lacustrine sediments of the Cerro Cóndor locality in the Middle Jurassic (Callovian) Cañadón Asfalto Formation (*e.g.*, Rauhut and Puerta 2001; Rauhut, Puerta and Martin 2001; Rauhut, Martin, Ortiz-Jaureguizar and Puerta 2002) of Chubut province, in southern Argentina.

In describing this specimen, Rauhut noted that it is relatively short and high, its rostral portion medially curved. As preserved, the maxillary part of the dentary measures 148 millimeters in length; its length in lateral aspect, measured parallel to the mandibular symphysis and ignoring the curvature of the specimen, is 135 millimeters.

Patagosaurus is distinguished as the only Cañadón

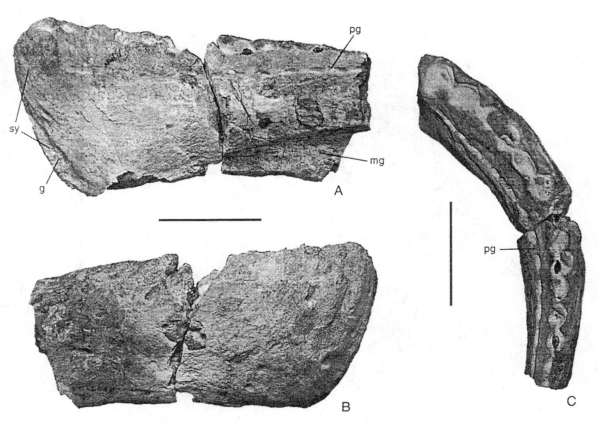

Asfalto Formation sauropod for which skull material had already been described. Almost two decades earlier, José F. Bonaparte (1986*a*) assigned three skull elements—a premaxilla (PVL 4076), right and left maxillae (MACN CH 934), and parial mandible (MACN CH 933; juvenile)—to the type species *Patagosaurus fariasi*. In comparing these specimens with MPEF-PV 1670, Rauhut found but minor differences, the two dentaries being quite similar in shape and many details (*e.g.*, probably apomorphic characters of structure of symphysis; lack of Meckelian groove in rostral half of bone). Noting that the holotype (PVL 4170; see *D:TE* for photograph) of *P. fariasi* does not preserve any cranial elements, a comparison by Rauhut of the associated postcranial remains of MACN CH 933 and PVL 4170 confirmed the referral of the former to that species.

Comparing the dentary teeth with those found in the maxillae of *P. fariasi* referred specimen MACN CH 934, however, revealed to Rauhut various differences. Most notably, all the replacement maxillary teeth of MACN CH 934 almost surely lack marginal denticles, although the carinae of all the teeth preserved in MPEF-PV 1670 and MACN CH 933 are serrated. Rauhut observed additional differences between MACN CH 934 and *P. fariasi* in the postcranial remains associated with the maxillae (*e.g.*, in MACN CH 934, neural arches of dorsal vertebrae

presenting differences in shape of neural canal, inclination of zygapophyses, short spinodiapopphyseal lamina; also, ilium relatively lower than in holotype, differing also in relative length of pubic peduncle and preacetabular blade). Thus, Rauhut found the Middle Jurassic, Cañadón Asfalto sauropod fauna to be more diverse than previously realized, with at least one additional taxon present. However, the formal description of this new taxon must "await a complete revision of *Patagosaurus*, which is currently being carried out by the author."

While Rauhut's description of the jaw of *Patagosaurus* was admittedly limited by the incomplete material, the articulated lower jaw allowed that author to estimate a tooth row of approximately 140 to 150 centimeters in length, while the very short and high dentary suggested a comparatively high and short skull. Therefore, Rauhut suggested, the skull of *Patagosaurus* apparently had a somewhat short and broad muzzle, as perhaps in most sauropods (Christiansen 1999*a*).

As MPEF-PV 1670 derives from "an old juvenile or subadult" animal, the differences between this specimen and the smaller dentary MACN CH 933 could, Rauhut explained, be ontogenetic. Most notable among these differences, MACN CH 933 is more slender, with a less pronounced rostral expansion of the bone. Other differences observed by Rauhut were

Patagosaurus fariasi, reconstructed skeleton including holotype (PVL 4170). (After Bonaparte 1986*a*.)

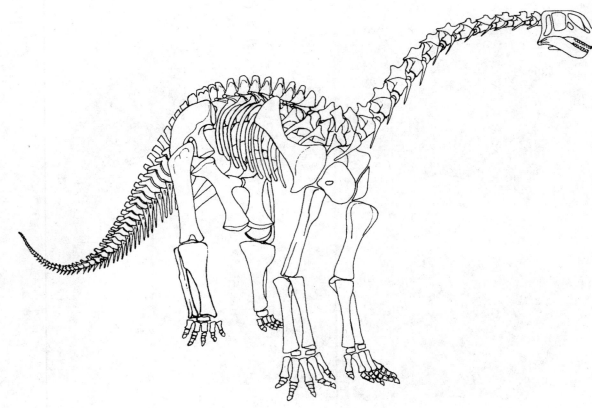

explained as proportional (*e.g.,* relatively larger teeth, alveolar part making up nearly half of height of bone). Therefore, that author noted, "it seems that the dentary of *Patagosaurus* exhibited a positive allometry in increase in dorsoventral height as compared to dentary length during ontogeny," the allometry being "mainly expressed as an increase in the height and massiveness of the subalveolar dentary body."

The number of teeth might be an additional ontogenetic change, Rauhut suggested. Given Bonaparte's estimate of 13 teeth in MACN CH 933, Rauhut's estimated 15 to 16 alveoli in MPEF-PV 1670 may suggest that the tooth count increased slightly during ontogeny, this in accordance with the pattern noted by Sereno (1990) in *Psittacosaurus.*

Rauhut considered the previous phylogenies of the Sauropod published by Wilson and Sereno (1998), and Upchurch (1998), the latter being the only such analysis thus far to include *Patagosaurus.* On the basis of dentary and dental characters included in those studies, while also taking into consideration data from sauropod taxa described subsequent to those studies (*e.g., Jobaria*), Rauhut found *Patagosaurus* to be "an advanced, nonneosauropodan eusauropodan" genus.

However, Rauhut also noted the following additional characters in the *Patagosaurus* material that might inevitably prove to be either autapomorphies of the genus or synapomorphies of some subset of the Sauropoda, or ontogenetically variable characters, once lower jaw material is known for more taxa: Lower part of dentary symphysis having pronounced longitudinal groove; Meckelian groove restricted to caudal half of dentary; caudal part of Meckelian groove not bordered ventrally by dentary; tooth denticles restricted to apicalmost third of crown.

In their review of the Sauropoda, Upchurch, Barrett and Dodson (2004) accepted *Patagosaurus* as a cetiosaurid having a sister-taxon relationship with *Cetiosaurus.*

Key references: Bonaparte (1986*a*); McIntosh (1990); Rauhut (2003*b*); Rauhut, Martin, Ortiz-Jaureguizar and Puerta (2002); Rauhut and Puerta (2001); Rauhut, Puerta and Martin (2001); Sereno (1990); Upchurch (1998); Upchurch, Barrett and Dodson (2004); Wilson and Sereno (1998).

†**PALAEOSAURISCUS**—(See *Efraasia.*)

†**PAWPAWSAURUS**

Ornithischia: Predentata: Genasauria: Thyreophora: Thyreophoroidea: Eurypoda: Ankylosauria: Nodosauridae.

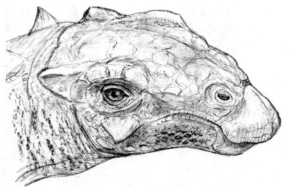

Life restoration by Berislav Krzic of *Pawpawsaurus campbelli*.

Diagnosis of genus (as for type species): Similar to *Silvisaurus*; osseous secondary plate limited to rostral end of palatal region; premaxilla with (four) teeth; osseous nasal septum not completely segregating (sagittaly) nasal cavities proper (unlike more deeply nested nodosaurids) (Vickaryous, Maryańska and Weishampel 2004).

Comment: In their review of the Ankylosauria, Vickaryous, Maryańska and Weishampel (2004) rediagnosed the type species *Pawpawsaurus campbelli* (see *D:TE*).

Key reference: Vickaryous, Maryańska and Weishampel (2004).

†PELECANIMIMUS

Saurischia: Eusaurischia: Theropoda: Neotheropoda: Tetanurae: Avetheropoda: Coelurosauria: Tyrannoraptora: Maniraptoriformes: Ornithomimosauria.

Diagnosis of genus (as for type species): Autapomorphies including the following: Large number of teeth; seven premaxillary teeth; possibly convergent evolution of elongate metacarpal I, independent of higher ornithomimosaurs (Makovicky, Kobayashi and Currie 2004).

Comment: In their review of the Ornithomimosauria, Makovicky, Kobayashi and Currie (2004) rediagnosed the type species *Pelecanimimus polyodon* (see *D:TE*).

Key reference: Makovicky, Kobayashi and Currie (2004).

†PELLEGRINISAURUS—(See *Epachthosaurus*)

†PELOROSAURUS

Saurischia: Eusaurischia: Sauropodomorpha: Sauropoda: Eusauropoda: Neosauropoda: Macronaria: Titanosauriformes *incertae sedis*.

Comment: In their review of the Sauropoda, Upchurch, Barrett and Dodson (2004) commented that the type species *Pelorosaurus conybeari*, while difficult to diagnose, "has a shallow olecranon fossa that is deeper in all other sauropods except *Lapparentosaurus* (Upchurch and Martin 2003)" (see *D:TE*).

Key references: Upchurch, Barrett and Dodson (2004); Upchurch and Martin (2003).

†PENTACERATOPS

Ornithischia: Predentata: Genusauria: Cerapoda: Chasmatopia: Marginocephalia: Ceratopsia: Neoceratopsia: Coronosauria: Ceratopsoidea: Ceratopsidae: Chasmosaurinae.

Comments: Reser, Heckert and Lucas (2003), in an abstract, reported on the most complete skull of the type species *Pentaceratops sternbergii* ever found in New Mexico, one that is also rare for this genus in preserving the lower jaws:

In 1978, a specimen (MNA Pl. 1747; see *S2* for photograph of the unprepared specimen in the Museum of Northern Arizona laboratory) comprising "a remarkably complete skull and jaws" (lacking only the nasal horn) was collected by the Museum of Northern Arizona in Flagstaff from the Fruitland Formation in northwestern New Mexico. For a decade, this specimen was displayed mostly as found, crushed and slightly disarticulated, in the Cretaceous Seacoast hall of the New Mexico Museum of Natural History (now New Mexico Museum of Natural History and Science) in Albuquerque. Eventually, the specimen was returned to the Arizona museum.

Before this return, however, Reser *et al.* made a mold of the specimen, casting the disatriculated bones and then assembling them in a new, three dimensional

Life restoration of *Pentaceratops sternbergii* by artist Berislav Krzic.

Left lower jaw of *Pentaceratops sternbergii*, part of a skull and postcranial skeleton (MNA Pl. 1747) collected in 1977 by the Museum of Northern Arizona from the upper part of the Fruitland Formation of San Juan County, New Mexico. The specimen was described in 1981 by Timothy Rowe, Edwin H. Colbert and J. Dale Nations.

resin mount currently on exhibit in the New Mexico museum's redone Cretaceous hall. Although again preserving the specimen as found, the new display is free standing, allowing the skull to be examined from all angles and without "correcting" deformation.

As Reser *et al.* noted, restoring this skull permitted a reevaluation of much of the cranial anatomy of *Pentaceratops*, including the following newly realized details: The marginal epoccipitals cannot confidently be placed on the frill, despite the fact that this is one of the best-preserved frills of this genus known. However, the well-preserved epoccipitals between the parietals confirm previous diagnoses of *Pentaceratops*. Also, the frill is about twice the length of the "face," *i.e.*, preorbital length of 740 millimeters on the cast comparing with a 1,480-millimeter "frill length" (from rostral margin of orbit to caudal edge of parietal), total length of skull almost 2.2 meters (more than seven feet). These measurements indicate that the incomplete *Pentaceratops* skull (OMNH 10165; see *S2*) from the San Juan Basin (see Sullivan and Lucas 2003a, for a brief report on vertebrate faunal succession in the San Juan Basin; also, see

Williamson and Weil 2003, for a brief report on the latest Cretaceous dinosaurs in the San Juan Basin), exhibited at the Sam Noble Museum of Natural History in Norman, Oklahoma, is correctly reconstructed with a length of about three meters (at least 10 feet).

The authors also made the following measurements on the skull cast: Diameter of occipital condyle 78 millimeters; length of squamosal 1,140 millimeters; sheared supratemporal fenestra on right 660 millimeters long and 600 millimeters wide, on left (better preserved) 376 millimeters long and 26 millimeters wide; length of left lower jaw (as preserved) 790 millimeters.

Notes: Sullivan and Lucas (2003b) introduced a new land-vertebrate age, the Kirtlandian, representing 2.9 million years of Campanian time spanning "a long-standing biochronologic gap between the Judithian and Edmontonian" land-vertebrate ages, this new age being characterized by the vertebrate fossil assemblages of the Fruitland Formation and Kirtland Formation, San Juan Basin, New Mexico, and with *Pentaceratops sternbergii* distinguished as the principal index fossil. These authors defined the Kirtlandian as the time interval "between the first appearance of *Pentaceratops sternbergii* (=end of the Judithian) and the first appearance of *Pachyrhinosaurus canadensis* (=beginning of the Edmontonian)." Characteristic vertebrate taxa of the Kirtlandian include the actinopterigian fish *Melvius chauliodous*, the "mesocuchian" crocodilian *Denazinosuchus kirtlandicus*, the hadrosaurine hadrosaurids *Kritosaurus navajovius*, "*Anasazisaurus horneri*," and "*Naashoibitosaurus ostromi*" (the latter two taxa regarded as junior synonyms of *K. navajovius*), the lambeosaurine hadrosaurids *Parasaurolophus tubicen* and *P. cyrtocristatus*, the nodosaurid ankylosaur *Nodocephalosaurus kirtlandensis*, and the pachycephalosaurine pachycephalosaur *Prenocephale goodwini*.

In a follow up abstract, Sullivan and Lucas (2004) gave the date as from 74.9 to 72 million years ago. At the same time, these authors stated that recognizing the Kirtlandian undermines the idea "of two paleogeographically distinct dinosaur paleocommunities in the Western Interior during the late Campanian," the earlier perceived endemism of dinosaurian fauna explained mostly as the result of temporal diachroneity rather than provinciality. According to Sullivan and Lucas (2004), the small geographic ranges of hadrosaurid and other dinosaurian taxa are actually "artifacts of a combination of limited stratigraphic exposures and temporal isolation." Moreover, the authors noted, the Judithian and Edmontonian land-vertebrate ages span more time than does that of the Kirtlandian; consequently, the former two show greater taxonomic diversity, both at the genus and species levels.

In an abstract, Sullivan, Lucas and Braman (2003) briefly reported on the problematic age of the upper part or Naashoibito Member of the Kirtland Formation, a member that has yielded numerous non-reworked dinosaur fossils, and that has sometimes been regarded as of Paleocene age (based upon palynmorph evidence), thereby constituting evidence supporting the hypothesis that some non-avian dinosaurs survived beyond the Late Cretaceous (see Fassett 1982).

According to Sullivan *et al.*, however, some dinosaurs (*e.g.*, *Pentaceratops*, *Parasaurolophus*), having been formerly cited from that member, are actually from the underlying De-na-zin Member, while the identifications of few diagnostic dinosaurian taxa (*e.g.*, *Torosaurus*, *Tyrannosaurus*) are questionable. Samplings by Sullivan *et al.* failed to produce any Paleocene-age palynomorphs. Instead, the authors found only palynomorphs of Campanian and Maastrichtian age, with the taxa *Pandaniidites typicus* and *Umoideipites krempi* further restricting their sample to the Maastrichtian. Although some palynomorph taxa spanning the Cretaceous–Tertiary boundary were recovered, none were found exclusive to the Paleocene, this leading to the conclusion that "there is no convincing evidence of Paleocene dinosaurs in the San Juan Basin."

Key references: Fassett (1982); Reser, Heckert and Lucas (2003); Rowe, Colbert and Nations (1987); Sullivan and Lucas (2003a, 2003b, 2004); Sullivan, Lucas and Braman (2003).

†PHUWIANGOSAURUS

Saurischia: Eusaurischia: Sauropodomorpha: Sauropoda: Eusauropoda: Neosauropoda: Macronaria: Titanosauriformes: Titanosauria.

Diagnosis of genus (as for type species): Cranial cervical vertebrae having low, wide neural arches; subequal transverse widths of proximal and distal ends of humerus (Upchurch, Barrett and Dodson 2004).

Comments: In their review of the Sauropoda, Upchurch, Barrett and Dodson (2004) rediagnosed the enigmatic type species, *Phuwiangosaurus sirindhornae* (see *S2*).

Originally described by Valérie Martin, Éric Buffetaut, and Varavudh Suteethorn in 1994 as a sauropod of uncertain affinities (see *D:TE*), *Phuwiangosaurus* was subsequently reinterpreted by Martin, Suteethorn and Buffetaut (1999) as a possible nemegtosaurid (see *S2*), and later, in subsequent cladistic analyses by Upchurch (1998) and Upchurch *et al.*, as the most basal know member of Titanosauria.

Key references: Martin, Buffetaut and Suteethorn (1994); Martin, Suteethorn and Buffetaut (1999); Upchurch (1998); Upchurch, Barrett and Dodson (2004).

†PIATNITZKYSAURUS

Saurischia: Eusaurischia: Theropoda: Neotheropoda: Tetanurae: Spinosauroidea: Megalosauridae: Eustreptospondylinae.

Comments: In 1986, José F. Bonaparte named and described *Piatnitzkysaurus*, a Middle Jurassic basal tetanuran based upon incomplete cranial and postcranial material collected from the Canadón Asfalto Formation of Chubut, Argentina (see *D:TE* for details and photographs of the composite reconstructed skeleton).

Recently, Rauhut (2004a) described in detail, for the first time, the rather well-preserved and undistorted, yet somewhat eroded braincase belonging to the holotype (PVL 4073) of the type species *Piatnitzkysaurus floresi*.

In this description, Rauhut noted such details as follows: Extremely shortened and narrow basipterygoid processes, parasphenoid recesses seemingly

Piatnitzkysaurus

Piatnitzkysaurus floresi, holotype braincase (PVL 4073) in (left) left lateral and (right) right lateral views. Scale = 5 cm. (After Rauhut 2004.)

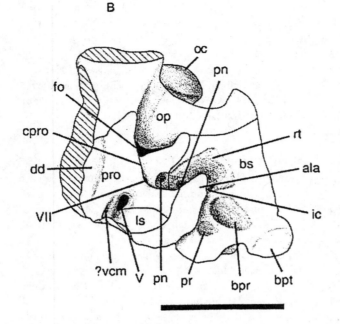

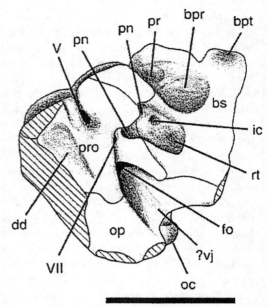

communicating with one another, and basipterygoid recesses approximately as long rostrocaudally as high (probably autapomorphic characters for this taxon); subrectangular pituitary fossa wider than high, and transverse span between basipterygoid processes smaller than width of basal tubera (possibly synapomorphies with European megalosaurine *Piveteau-*

saurus); subrectangular pituitary fossa wider than basal tubera width; higher number of accessory pneumatic recesses (suggesting presence of rostral and dorsal tympanic recesses and possibly also of subcondylar and basipterygoid recesses being plesiomorphic for Tetanurae; bones enclosing brain (*e.g.*, laterosphenoid, prootic, supraoccipital) very massive, lacking

Piatnitzkysaurus floresi, reconstructed composite skeleton (including holotype PVL 4073). (After Bonaparte 1986a.)

24 cm

Life restoration by Berislav Krzic of *Piatnitzkysaurus floresi*.

internal pneumatic chambers (present in later tetanurans).

According to Rauhut, the observed braincase morphology of *Piatnitzkysaurus*, considering the phylogenetic position of this genus, has important implications for understanding the distribution of braincase characters at the base of Tetanurae. Furthermore, the braincase of this genus allows for interesting insights into the braincase pneumatization in basal members (*e.g.*, *Syntarsus*, *Dilophosaurus*, *Ceratosaurus*, *Allosaurus*, *Majungatholus*, others) of this clade for which such pneumatization has been described (see Rauhut for details and references). However, Rauhut pointed out, while a high degree of pneumatization appears to have been present at the base of this clade, the pneumatic recesses found in *Piatnitzkysaurus* are only superficial, not pneumaticizing the interior of the bones of the braincase, contrary to the condition found often in more advanced members of Tetanurae (*e.g.*, see Clark, Perle and Norell 1994; Currie and Zhao 1994; Chure and Madsen 1996, 1998; Clark, Norell and Rowe 2002).

In their review of basal tetanuran theropods, Holtz, Molnar and Currie (2004), in performing a phylogenetic analysis, found *Piatnitzkysaurus floresi* to be a member of the megalosaurid subfamily Eustreptospondylinae, sharing with other members of this clade the following synapomorphies: Maxillary fenestra (not known in Spinosauridae or nontetanuran theropods, but present in Avetheropoda); distal ischial tubercle (see Hutchinson 2001; also found in allosauroid carnosaurs); reversion to lack of deep groove on medial side of proximal end of fibula.

Key references: Bonaparte (1986*a*); Chure and Madsen (1996, 1998); Clark, Norell and Rowe (2002); Clark, Perle and Norell (1994); Currie and Zhao (1994); Holtz, Molnar and Currie (2004); Hutchinson (2001); Rauhut (2004*a*).

†PINACOSAURUS

Ornithischia: Predentata: Genasauria: Thyreophora: Thyreophoroidea: Eurypoda: Ankylosauria: Ankylosauridae: Ankylosaurinae.

Diagnosis of genus: Medium-sized ankylosaurid, attaining length of approximately five meters, skull longer than wide (in adult); edge of premaxillary beak not covered by secondary dermal ossifications; large, rostrally facing nares roofed by osteoderms; premaxillary struts defining at least two additional openings in narial region, leading to extensive premaxillary sinus; prominent, hornlike protuberances above orbit, formed by lateralmost supraorbital bone; lacrimal incisure (marked pinching of snout in lacrimal area laterally beyond incisure); beak only slightly wider than distance between caudalmost maxillary teeth; quadrate not coossified with paroccipital process; quadrate cotyla directly below caudal margin of orbit (Hill, Witmer and Norell 2003).

Diagnosis of *P. grangeri*: *Pinacosaurus* having squamosal dermal ossifications present as weakly developed pyramids; spines not long as in *P. mephistocephalus* (Hill, Witmer and Norell 2003; but see below).

Comments: *Pinacosaurus* is the best known of all Asian ankylosaurs, represented by more than 15 specimens (see Coombs and Maryańska 1990). More ankylosaur material was recovered between 1990 and 1993 during the American Museum of Natural History's expeditions to the Gobi Desert in Mongolia. Several new Upper Cretaceous fossil localities were discovered during those expeditions, including the fossil-rich Ukhaa Tolgod (see Dashzeveg, Novacek, Norell, Clark, Chiappe, Davidson, McKenna, Dingus, Swisher and Perle 1995).

In 2003, Hill, Witmer and Norell described in detail the first diagnostic ankylosaur remains from Ukhaa Tolgod, a nearly complete juvenile skull (IGM 100/1014) with associated mandibles and osteoderms.

As observed by these authors, IGM 100/1014 displays the following synapomorphies of the Ankylosauridae: Two pairs of osteodermal "horns" projecting

Pinacosaurus grangeri, AMNH 6523, holotype skull in left lateral view.

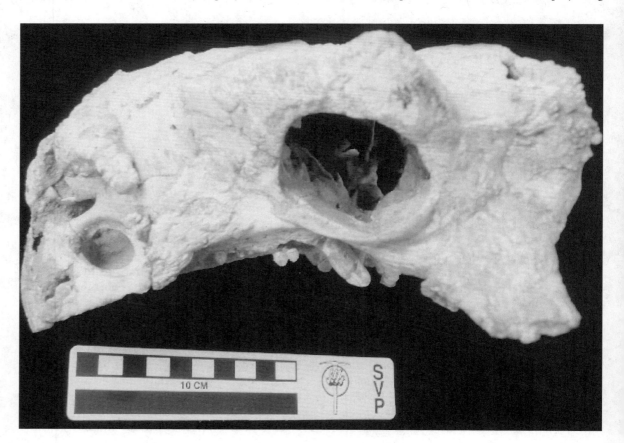

Courtesy Robert M. Sullivan.

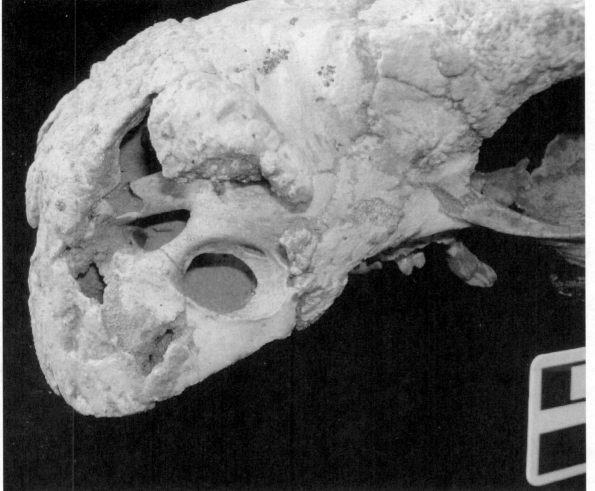

Pinacosaurus grangeri,
**AMNH 6523, holotype
skull, detail of snout in left
lateral view.**

from quadratojugals and squamosals; skull wide, triangular; edge of premaxillary beak not continuous with maxillary tooth row; and absence of premaxillary teeth.

Hill *et al.* referred this specimen to the type species *Pinacosaurus grangeri* based upon the following features: Large premaxillary sinus; quadrate not coossified with paroccipital process; and several pairs of accessory openings in narial region. However, IGM 100/1014 differs from the holotype (AMNH 6523) of *P. grangeri* and also other specimens of this species in having five pairs of openings (real or otherwise) per side in the narial region (apparently three in AMNH 6523 and the very well-preserved juvenile ZPAL MgD-II/1; four in IMM 96BM3/1, the holotype of referred species *P. mephistocephalus*; see *S2*, also below), thereby demonstrating the existence of extensive morphological variation in the narial region of this taxon.

Juvenile ankylosaur skulls, as Hill *et al.* pointed out, are rare. IGM 100/1014 was identified as belonging to a juvenile animal based on its small size and the incomplete fusion of secondary dermal osteoderms to the roof of the skull, exposing sutural boundaries. As the authors stated, the skulls of juvenile armored dinosaurs are important in "understanding the basic anatomy of the highly fused and apomorphic adult skull."

In order to determine diagnostic characters contributing to an attempted resolution of ankylosaurian relationships, Hill *et al.* added data from IGM 100/1014, as well as other specimens (see the authors' paper for complete list), to existing analyses of the Ankylosauria (see "Systematics" chapter). Hill *et al.*'s analysis found *Pinacosaurus*—contrary to earlier analyses (*e.g.,* Coombs and Maryańska; Kirkland 1998*a*; Carpenter 2001) that had found this genus to be a highly derived ankylosaurid — basal to a clade including *Shamosaurus* and *Tsagantegia*, taxa regarded as quite primitive among Ankylosauridae. "This may be," the authors suggested, "because the adult *Pinacosaurus* lacks many putatively derived character states that have previously been scored only from the juvenile skull of ZPAL MgD-II/1." As Hill *et al.* observed, the adult holotype skull of *P. grangeri* is plainly longer

Pinacosaurus grangeri, AMNH 6523, holotype skull in dorsal view.

than wide, but juvenile skulls (ZPAL MgD–II/1 and IGM 100/1014) are wider than long. Also, the adult skull has weakly developed squamosal protuberances and an occipital that remains visible in dorsal aspect, while lacking the elaborate ornamentation typical of more highly nested ankylosaurids.

IGM 100/1014, Hill *et al.* noted, offers important data concerning the ontogenetic sequence of secondary dermal ossification. As the authors observed, dermal ossifications cover just the narial region, quadratojugals, and squamosals of this skull, the mandibular osteoderms having been preserved *in situ*, remaining unfused to the underlying bones. This evidence supports the hypothesis that osteoderms in these areas appear early in the ontogeny of *Pinacosaurus*. In all previously studied adult ankylosaur specimens (*e.g.*, AMNH 6523), the mandible shows fusion of the elements to the underlying bones. Consequently, while the mandibular osteoderms appear relatively early during ontogeny, they do not become fused until much later.

As pointed out by Witmer (2003) in a published abstract, ankylosaurian narial regions are unusual and derived, this bony region in most taxa, corresponding to that of the nasal vestibule, being enlarged. However, this enlargement is not always externally apparent, due to overgrowth of the narial region by osteoderms.

According to Witmer, CT scans of skulls of juvenile *Pinacosaurus* individuals confirm that the bony nostril—defined by the margins of premaxilla and nasal—is quite large. Moreover, in most ankylosaurians including *Pinacosaurus*, "the apparent size and orientation of the nasal opening is dictated largely by the extent of osteoderm formation within the narial skin." Interpretation of these openings is made more difficult by the presence of osteoderms in the nasal area; at the same time, these osteoderms simplify interpretation by nature of their highly sculptured surfaces contrasting markedly with the smoothly surfaced bone of the nasal vestibule, permitting each to be assigned clearly to their respective anatomical domains.

In *Pinacosaurus*, Witmer noted, the external surfaces of the nasal osteoderms "bear ornamentation patterns characteristic of skin-covered bone, whereas their internal surfaces are smooth, reflecting their having been lined with most nasal epithelium." Witmer further pointed out that in many ankylosaurs there are apertures in the narial area in addition to the airway; and that, in almost all ankylosaurs, a caudolateral opening conducts large blood vessels into that region. Fossae rostral to that aperture "are consistent with the presence of a mass of erectile tissue," this mass aiding to "corroborate a position of the fleshy nostril at the rostroventral margin of the narial opening." According to Witmer, some ankylosaurids possess apertures opening into a large space within the premaxilla, their variability—"taken to an extreme in *Pinacosaurus*"—supporting their interpretation as pneumatic foramina.

Recently the species *P. mephistocephalus* was reassessed by Vickaryous, Maryańska and Weishampel (2004) in their review of the Ankylosauria. According to the analysis of these authors, the differences cited as separating this species from *P. grangeri* (*i.e.*, arrangement of paranasal apertures; shape of lacrimal; deltopectoral crest of humerus long in *P. mephistocephalus*, short in *P. grangeri*; see Godefroit, Pereda Suberbiola and Dong 1999) are unclear, possibly representing ontogenetic or taxonomic variation rather than specific differences within the same genus.

Key references: Carpenter (2001); Coombs and Maryańska (1990); Dashveg, Novacek, Norell, Clark, Chiappe, Davidson, McKenna, Dingus, Swisher Perle (1995); Godefroit, Pereda Suberbiola and Dong (1999); Hill, Witmer and Norell (2003); Kirkland (1998a); Vickaryous, Maryańska and Weishampel (2004); Witmer (2003).

†PISANOSAURUS

Ornithischia: ?Genasauria.

Diagnosis: Autapomorphies including recessing of tibia for reception of ascending prossess of astragalus (Norman, Witmer and Weishampel 2004a).

Comments: In a review of basal ornithischians, Norman, Witmer and Weishampel (2004a) reassessed *Pisanosaurus mertii*, a quite problematic type species that has generally been regarded in recent years as the basalmost member of Ornithischia (*e.g.*, see Weishampel and Witmer 1990; Sereno 1991a).

As these authors noted, however, interpretation of this taxon has been limited by the poor preservation of the original type material, and also due to loss of data concerning the association of this material. Further complicating an assessment of this dinosaur, it is now known from two specimens representing individuals of different size (and possibly different taxa) (see Sereno).

Norman *et al.* observed the following ornithischian synapomorphies in the jaws of *Pisanosaurus*: Separation of crown and root of teeth by neck; maximal tooth size close to middle of tooth row; rostral portion of coronoid process formed by dentary. The following features, the authors noted, are found in Cerapoda: Pronounced buccal emargination of maxillary and dentary tooth rows; development of extensive, apparently confluent wear facets between blades formed by maxillary and dentary teeth.

Based upon the above-cited skull features, Norman *et al.* found it possible that *Pisanosaurus* could be referrable to the Genasauria. However, other skeletal details required for a more precise placement of this genus within Ornithischia, such as those gleaned from impressions of the pelvis and vertebrae (Bonaparte 1976; Sereno; see *D:TE*), are difficult to interpret.

Furthermore, Norman *et al.* pointed out that one feature (*i.e.*, lack of flaring of the associated tibia) is plesiomorphic with respect to Ornithischia and also Dinosauria; moreover, another feature (*i.e.*, apex of ascending process of astragalus laterally located near articulation with calcaneum) is also seen in *Lesothosaurus*, basal Thyreophora, Prosauropoda, basal Theropoda, and basal Dinosauromorpha.

Considering this suite of features, Norman *et al.* suggested the following: If the jaws, ambiguous pelvic impression, tibia, and proximal tarsals of this genus pertain to a single individual, the most parsimonious character distribution places *Pisanosaurus* in the Genusauria, the narrowness of the distal tibia and position of the astragalar ascending process therefore constituting apomorphies of this genus; however, if the elements are considered individually, the jaw can unequivocally be regarded as cerapodan, and the hindlimb elements possibly nondinosaurian.

Key references: Bonaparte (1976); Norman, Witmer and Weishampel (2004a); Sereno (1991a); Weishampel and Witmer (1990).

†PLATEOSAURUS—(=*Dimodosaurus*, *Dinosaurus*, *Gresslyosaurus*, *Sellosaurus*)

Saurischia: Eusaurischia: Sauropodomorpha: Prosauropoda: Plateosauridae.

Name derivation: Greek *plate* = "broad area" or "broadway" + Greek *sauros* = "lizard."

New species: *P. gracilis* (Huene 1907–08).

Occurrence of *P. gracilis*: Löwenstein Formation, Heslach, Trossingen, Germany.

Age of *P. gracilis*: Late Triassic (lower Norian).

Lectotype of *P. engelhardti*: UEN 550, incomplete sacrum.

Known materials of *P. gracilis*: Two specimens including incomplete postcranial skeleton, skull.

Holotype of *P. gracilis*: SMNS 5157, incomplete postcranium comprising dorsal vertebrae, two primordial sacral vertebrae, proximal and middle caudal vertebrae, left pubis, conjoined proximal ischia, fragment of left fibula.

Diagnosis of genus: Five (rarely six) premaxillary teeth; broad antorbital fossa having greatly convex to straight rostral margin of antorbital fenestra (convergent in *Coloradisaurus*); sacrum comprising two primordial sacral vertebrae and caudosacral vertebra; proxial and middle caudal centra having median, ventral furrow; ischium with caudal notch between obturator plate and shaft (in lateral aspect), symphyseal fenestra (in ventral aspect) (Yates 2003a).

Diagnosis of *P. engelhardti*: Dorsal end of lacrimal having broad, weakly rugose, lateral sheet covering caudodorsal corner on antorbital fenestra; jugal

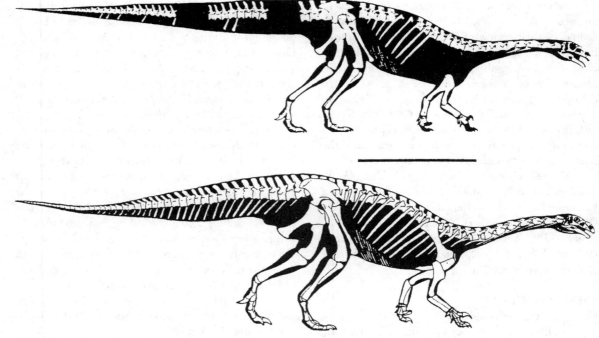

Top: Plateosaurus gracilis, reconstructed skeleton (composite based on SMNS 5175, GPIT 18392, and GPIT 18318a); *bottom: Plateosaurus engelhardti* (based on SMNS 13200). Scale = 1 m. (After Yates 2003.)

short, with dorsoventrally deep suborbital bar; palatine having centrally located, ventral peglike process; interbasipterygoid septum deep, filling entire space between basipterygoid processes, central processes paired; metacarpal V stout, with cervicals two through six forming elongate spikes that extend caudally from rim of postzygapophyses; (in specimens from overlying Trossingen Formation, *e.g.,* those from Halberstadt) epipophyses not overhanging caudal rim of postzygapophyses; first four or five caudal vertebrae bearing broad, rectangular neural spines, their proximodistal width at midheight greater than 40 percent of their height (Yates 2003*a*).

Diagnosis of *P. gracilis:* Possible metaspecies of *Plateosaurus,* differing from *P. engelhardti* in having proximodorsally narrow neural spines (width less than 40 percent of their height) on proximal caudal vertebrae, and by retaining larger, sharply defined brevis shelf on ilium (Yates 2003*a*).

Comments: Two major studies pertaining to the large European prosauropod *Plateosaurus,* and the species and specimens that have been referred to this genus, were published in 2003 (see *D:TE, S1, S2,* and *S3*):

Markus Moser (2003), in a monograph, focused upon on the type species *Plateosaurus engelhardti,* known from the Feuerletten (Upper Triassic, Middle Keuper) of Bavaria. That author described and discussed this taxon in detail from numerous perspectives, including the history of its discovery, the type and referred material belonging to this species, the

other taxa that have been referred to *P. engelhardti* over the years, variation among the specimens and referred taxa, related valid prosauropod and sauropod taxa, and the *Plateosaurus* locality at Ellingen, Germany, as well as other relevant topics.

As chronicled in detail by Moser, the original *Plateosaurus* discovery was made in the summer of 1834 by Professor Doctor Johann Friedrich Philipp Engelhart (a chemistry teacher based in Nuremberg), probably in a clay put at the Buchenbühl on the Haidberg, south of Heroldsberg, in northeastern Nuremberg, Middle Franconia, Bavaria. On September 19 of that year, Engelhart presented the fossil bones he had collected from that pit to a congress of German natural scientists in Stuttgart (*e.g.,* see Kielmeyer and Jager 1835). Christian Erich Hermann von Meyer (1837), one of the attendants at the congress, subsequently proposed the name *Plateosaurus engelhardti* for these remains, at the same time offering a preliminary description of them. Meyer did not select a holotype specimen to represent his new taxon, but did mention that the material included vertebrae and some long, heavy, and hollow limb bones. Subsequently, Meyer (1939) noted that these elements include a so-called "cross" or "holy bone" (sacrum; UEN 552) comprising three fused vertebrae, a feature to that date observed only in mammals.

Although Meyer did not explain the etyomology of *Plateosaurus,* the consensus of most subsequent authors has been that the name stemmed from the Greek word *platys,* meaning "flat." As pointed out by Moser,

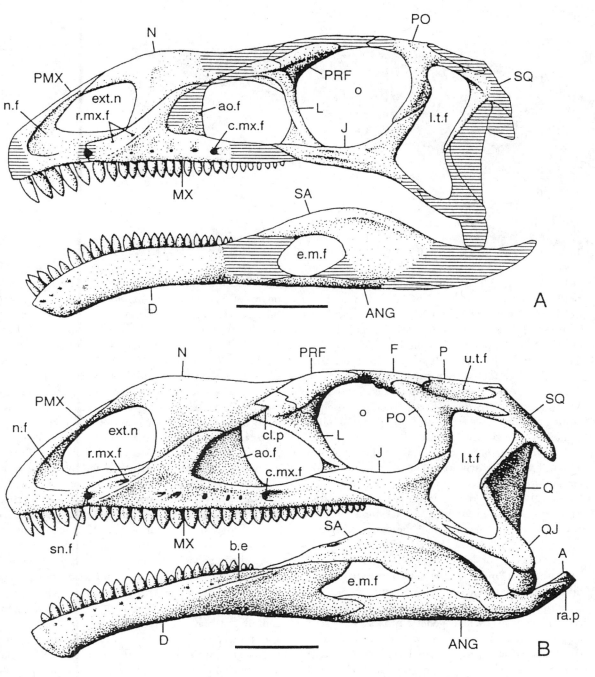

however, this interpretation contrasts sharply with the intentions of Meyer, who had compared this dinosaur "to large land mammals (not really flat) and proposed (MEYER 1845) for *Plateosaurus* and its relatives the name Pachypodes" (=Dinosauria), meaning "thick feet." Instead, according to Moser and as had already been noted by Schmidt (1938), the Old Greek dictionary gives the word *plate* for "broad area" or "broadway," which seems to be the correct word stem for the name *Plateosaurus*.

As Moser related, numerous unsatisfactory attempts had been made, over the past two decades, to select from the myriad remains referred to *Plateosaurus* an appropriate lectotype (*e.g.*, Galton 1984, 1990, 2000; Weishampel and Chapman 1990). According to Moser, however, only four of the original syntype specimens — a sacrum (UEN 552), first caudal vertebra, femur, and tibia — reported on by Meyer (1837, 1839) qualify for this distinction. Because the sacrum has received in taxonomic discussions the highest attention, Moser designated UEN 552 as the lectotype of *Plateosaurus engelhardti*.

Moser described most of the syntype specimens of *P. engelhardti*, these comprising the following: UEN

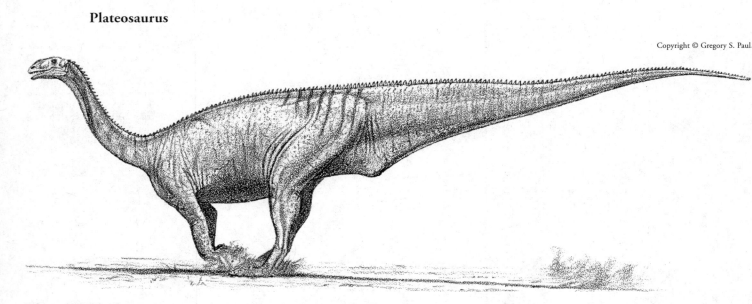

Life restoration by Gregory S. Paul of *Plateosaurus engelhardti* running.

561 and 562 middle dorsal vertebrae; UEN 557a–b, caudal dorsal vertebra; UEN 563a–c, middle dorsal rib; lectotype UEN 552; UEN 550, first caudal vertebra; UEN 558, neural arch of middle caudal vertebra; UEN 551, proximal chevron; UEN 554 and 555, femur; UEN 559, fragment of femoral head; UEN 556, tibia; (caudal vertebra lost and fragments of pubis lost). Also, that author described comparable elements referred to *Plateosaurus*, and also those pertaining to other sauropodomorph and nondinosaurian archosaurian taxa (see paper for details).

According to Moser's research, the taxonomy, variability, and distinctiveness of the many plateosaurid specimens collected from the German Knollenmergel and Feuerletten localities, especially from Ellingen, could be explained by diagenesis. In paleontology, Moser explained, morphological differences observed in different individuals of a single species are explained as biological variability, the latter distinguished by "individual genetic variability, sexual dimorphism, ontogenetic allometry, and pathologies." Consequently, appearance of fossils can be dramatically affected by such diagenetic processes as "scavenging, rottening, transport, weathering, pedogenesis, compaction, cementation, chemical alteration, techtonal deformation, and erosion," such alterations being capable of affecting morphology as well as color and chemistry of the fossils. Following an analysis of these various processes and their effects upon the prosauropod material from the above-mentioned localities (see paper for details), Moser concluded that all of the prosauropod remains from the Middle Keuper area of Germany pertain to but one species, *Plateosaurus engelhardti*, with the observed variations between these specimens explained as resulting from diagenetic influences on their morphology, rather than (*contra* Weishampel and Chapman) due to intraspecific biological variability.

The following taxa were accepted as junior synonyms of *Plateosaurus engelhardti*: *Dimodosaurus poligniensis*, *Gresslyosaurus robustus*, *G. torgeri*, *Pachysauriscus* ("*Pachysaurus*") *ajax*, *P.* ("*Pachysaurus*") *giganteus*, *P.* ("*Pachysaurus*") *magnus*, *P.* ("*Pachysaurus*") *wetzelianus*, *Plateosaurus erlenbergiensis*, *P. longiceps*, *P. plieningeri*, *P. reinigeri*, and *P. trossingensis*.

Also, Moser questioned the validity of *Sellosaurus* (see *D:TE*, *S2*, *S3*), noting that most finds referred to that genus from the Stubensandstein of Würtemberg, Germany, are indistinguishable from *Plateosaurus* (see below). Furthermore, Moser challenged Galton's (1999, 2001*b*) identification of a second type of sacrum (*i.e.*, having a dorsosacral vertebra) allegedly present in five *Sellosaurus* specimens (see *S2*, *S3*), noting that in all of Galton's cited cases this assumption had been based upon either indication (*i.e.*, the presence of an articulation facet for a more cranially located dorsosacral rib; an articulation facet for on the ilium for a dorsosacral rib; or the reassessment of an isolated caudosacral or dorsosacral vertebra). Moser further pointed out that a first caudosacral vertebra, when compressed, may approach a second sacral vertebra in appearance, particularly in the caudodorsally ascending sacral rib; moreover, a first caudosacral rib can have, when craniocaudally compressed, a more vertical orientation, thereby not conforming to the "typical" more or less horizontal orientation.

More extensive work on the nomenclature and taxonomy of *Plateosaurus engelhardti*, Moser ventured, will be forthcoming from both Galton (in manuscript) and Moser (in preparation).

In the second of the above-cited recent studies, Adam M. Yates (2003*a*) reassessed the taxonomy of the species of sauropodomorph dinosaurs from the Löwenstein Formation of Germany. As that author noted, previous work has generally grouped these forms into two taxa—*Plateosaurus engelhardti* (the type species of the genus *Plateosaurus*), from a single monotypic accumulation of materials from the Löwenstein Formation, near the town of Trossingen, Germany, and the type species *Sellosaurus gracilis*, represented at a number of German localities.

Until quite recently, *Sellosaurus* has been regarded as a valid genus encompassing a substantial amount of variation (*e.g.*, see Galton 1999, 2001*a*). Included in this variations are differences in the teeth, the structure of the skull, the composition of the sacrum, and the structure of the caudal vertebrae and pelvic girdle. Regarding the sacra, Galton (1999, 2001*b*; see also Moser 2003, above) had divided the hypodigm of *S. gracilis* into two groups—one in which the sacrum were interpreted as having three sacral vertebrae, the other having two sacrals. Galton (1999) first treated these two types of sacra as sexual dimorphs, and subsequently (Galton 2001*a*, 2001*b*) as specimens in which the extra sacral is a modified caudal and those in which it is a modified dorsosacral, this variation interpreted as intraspecific.

Yates, utilizing a specimen-based parsimony analysis of the Löwenstein sauropodomorphs, analyzed this variation, discovering that the current hypodigm of *Sellosaurus* consists of two discrete taxa.

One of these clades, which included the *Sellosaurus*-referred sauropodomorph materials collected at Pfaffenhofen and Ochsenbach (see also *S2, S3*), can be diagnosed by two unambiguous postcranial apomorphies—*i.e.*, hypertrophy of pubic tubercle, loss of craniocaudal swelling of distal pubic apron. This material Yates referred to the genus *Efraasia* (see entry).

The second clade can be diagnosed by the following apomorphies—five premaxillary teeth; broad rostral antorbital fenestra; enlarged caudal process of prefrontal; braincase floor strongly downstepped; and downturned dentary tip; (under ACCTRAN) sacrum comprising two primordial sacral vertebrae and a caudosacral; pedicillate postzygapophyses on proximal caudal vertebrae; ilium with caudally pointed postacetabular blade; and elongate interischial fenestra with notch at caudal end of obturator plate. As Yates noted, these features do not unambiguously diagnose this latter group, as most of the postcranium is missing in a basal member (GPIT 18318a, probably referrable to *S. gracilis*).

Yates found that, while there are no shared characters linking GPIT 18318a to SMNS 3715, the holotype of *Sellosaurus gracilis*, both of these specimens are more closely related to *Plateosaurus engelhardti* than they are to the specimens from Pfaffenhofen and Ochsenbach, although they lack some of the apomorphies of *P. engelhardti*.

That author further stated that, as both GPIT 1831a and SMNS 3715 represent small sauropodomorphs found high in the Löwenstein Formation, it is probable that they represent a single species. Yates referred this material, tentatively treated as such, to the genus *Plateosaurus* as the new species *P. gracilis*. As he pointed out, the holotype of *S. gracilis* shares a number of derived character states with specimens referred to *P. engelhardti*, the differences between them being only slight. Therefore, Yates proposed that "the continued separation of *Sellosaurus* from *Plateosaurus* is not warranted, and it is hereby returned to the synonymy of *Plateosaurus*, repeating the action of Huene (1926)."

Concerning the type species *P. engelhardti*, Yates cited Galton's (2000) observation that the syntype specimens of that species do not exhibit the diagnostic characters of the common species present at Trossingen generally regarded as *Plateosaurus*. It was the opinion of Yates that "if Galton's interpretation of the incomplete sacrum [*i.e.*, UEN 552, see above] is correct, the type of *Plateosaurus engelhardti* represents a different taxon from the one at Trossingen." However, as the excellent Trossingen skeleton (SMNS 13200) has formed the basis of the concept of this genus for almost a century (Huene 1926), Yates treated this specimen "as an unofficial holotype of *Plateosaurus engelhardti*, while recognizing that this decision will need to be ratified by the ICZN" [International Commission for Zoological Nomenclature] (see also Yates 2003*b*). (However, according to Galton, personal communication 2004, the original holotype sacrum described by Meyer in 1837 is indeed comparable to those found at Trossingen; see Galton 2001; Moser 2003, above; see also *S3*.)

Traditionally, most body reconstructions in the paleontological literature of *Plateosaurus* and also skeletons mounted in museums have depicted the hind feet in a digitigrade posture, with an almost 180-degree angle between crus and metatarsus, and a considerable expansion at the metatarsophalangeal joints. This stance was more recently challenged in a published abstract by Sullivan, Jenkins, Gatesy and Shubin (2003), who reassessed the pedal posture and function in this dinosaur based upon an almost complete skeleton (approximately 5.5 meters long) having well-preserved tarsal bones, collected from the Fleming Fjord Formation of East Greenland.

Sullivan *et al.*'s examination of this skeleton revealed that the configuration of the metatarsophalangeal joints allowed for just slight extension of the proximal phalanges, unlike the high degree of angulation generally seen in reconstructions, with digitigrade feet. The authors also observed that the plane of the metatarsus forms an angle of from 30 to 40 degrees during weight bearing. The convex distal articular surface of astragalus faces craniodorsally (not ventrally, as seen in most reconstructions), this orientation, along with the wedge-shaped third and fourth distal tarsals, accommodating "the required angulation between the distal foot in contact with the substrate and the upright crus." Also, while the crurotarsal, proximal and distal metatarsal, and interphalangeal joints are well ossified, the mesotarsal joint seems to have been greatly cartilaginous.

Sullivan *et al.* concluded that the kind of plantigrady seen in *Plateosaurus*, unlike the digitigrady observed in numerous other dinosaurian taxa, could be a synapomorphy of the Sauropoda and at least some members of Prosauropoda, or could alternatively be an example of convergence pertaining to large body mass.

Moser, citing in his 2003 monograph various previous authors and their hypotheses in regards the posture and gait of *Plateosaurus*, ascertained the following: 1. Hindlimbs positioned in almost straight orientation beneath the body (deduced from knee joint morphology, with the same-sized condylus lateralis of the femur, articular surface of the tibia perpendicular to its shaft; 2. ilium and, consequently, the verebral column in that area presumably horizontally orientated ("otherwise the processus articularis ossis ischii would prevent the femur from swinging backward beyond the vertical line or expell [*sic*] the femur from the acetabulum"). Moreover, Moser pointed out that in the classic skeletal reconstruction of *Plateosaurus* published by Huene in 1926—digitigrade, bipedal, upright vertebral column—"the femur is in its caudalmost position and cannot swing back," an arrangement that would force the animal to trip.

As Moser further recounted, Wellnhofer (1994) had observed, in the proximal caudal vertebrae of the Ellingen *Plateosaurus* material, articular surfaces that do not parallel each other, but instead converge ventrally or build an angle to each other, resulting in vertebrae that are wedge-shaped. This Wellnhofer interpreted as a specific difference between the *Plateosaurus* specimens from Ellingen and Trossingen, later prompting Galton (2000) to separate the Bavarian *P. engelhardti* (type and Ellingen specimens) from other *Plateosaurus* remains that he, consequently, referred to *P. longiceps* (see *S3*; also, see Galton and Upchurch 2003a, below, for a contrary opinion). This caudal series arrangement suggested to Wellnhofer that the tail of *Plateosaurus* was strongly bowed downward in its proximal part, and that the animal must have been an obligatory quadruped. An investigation by Moser of the Ellingen caudal material, however, led that author to reject Wellnhofer's postulation, attributing the differences observed by Wellnhofer between the vertebrae of *Plateosaurus* specimens largely to intraspecific

variation. Therefore, Moser rejected both the taxonomic separation of plateosaurs as proposed by Wellnhofer and Galton (2000), and also the obligatory quadrupedality hypothesized by Wellnhofer, as based upon the shape of the caudal vertebrae.

In their 2004 review of the Prosauropoda, Galton and Upchurch regarded "*Plateosaurus longipes*, the common species of *Plateosaurus*," as a valid taxon, which they diagnosed by the following autapomorphies: Nasal length greater than half length of skull roof; medially directed, peglike process from middle of palatine; transverse subvertical lamina of basisphenoid between basipterygoid processes.

Notes: Yates (2003a) also discussed the German taxa *Thecodontosaurus? hermannianus* Huene 1908 (see also *Thecodontosaurus* entry) and *Teratosaurus trossingensis* Huene 1908, regarded as *nomina dubia*, both of which had previously been referred to *Sellosaurus*, with the former species referred by Galton (2001a) to *Sellosaurus gracilis* (see *S3*).

Thecodontosaurus? hermannianus was based on a fragmentary right maxilla (SMNS 4388) from the Upper Triassic (lower Norian) ?lower Löwenstein Formation of Heslach, near Stuttgart, southwest Germany, deriving from the same quarry that yielded the holotype of *Plateosaurus gracilis*. While certain features (*i.e.*, unrecurved, leaf-shaped teeth with coarse serrations, enlarged, caudally-facing external neurovascular foramen) identify the specimen as a prosauropod, the dorsal process is too incomplete for Yates (2003a) to determine if it had the broad antorbital fossa diagnostic of *Plateosaurus*. This specimen could, therefore, belong to *Plateosaurus*, *Efraasia*, or any other early sauropod.

T. trossingensis was based on a fragmentary right fibula, a right astragalus, right distal tarsals I–III, plus a partial right foot including a complete metatarsal (GPIT 18064), collected from the Upper Triassic (middle Norian) middle Löwenstein Formation at Trossingen, Baden-Württemberg. Based upon the transversely expanded proximal end of the fifth metatarsal, this specimen belongs to a sauropodomorph; however, Yates (2003a) noted, it offers no characters distinguishing the specimen from *Plateosaurus*, *Efraasia*, or most other Triassic sauropodomorphs.

Key references: Galton (1984, 1990, 1999, 2000, 2001a, 2001b); Galton and Upchurch (2004a); Huene (1907–08, 1926); Kielmeyer and Jager (1835); Meyer (1837, 1839, 1845); Sullivan, Jenkins, Gatesy and Shubin (2003); Moser (2003); Schmidt (1938); Weishampel and Chapman (1990); Wellnhofer (1994); Yates (2003a, 2003b).

†**PRENOCEPHALE**—(=*Sphaerotholus*; =?*Tylocephale*)
Ornithischia: Predentata: Genusauria: Cerapoda:

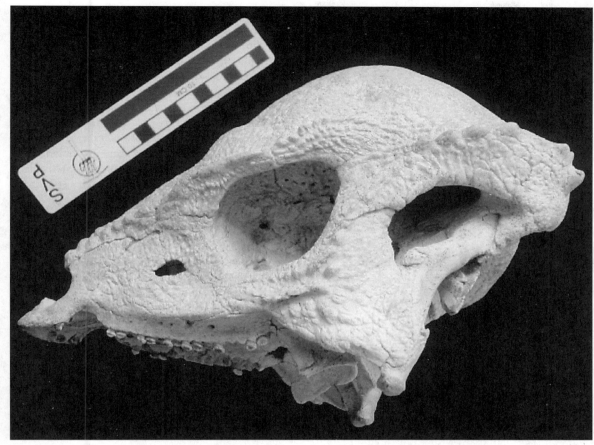

Prenocephale prenes, ZPAL MgD-I/104, holotype skull in left lateral view.

Chasmatopia: Marginocephalia: Pachycephalosauria: Goyocephala: Homalocephaloidea: Pachycephalosauridae: Pachycephalosaurinae.

Type species: *P. prenes* Maryańska and Osmólska 1974.

New species: *P. goodwini* (Williamson and Carr 2003).

Other species: (None.)

Occurrence of *P. goodwini*: Kirtland Formation, New Mexico, North America.

Age of *P. goodwini*: Late Cretaceous (Campanian).

Known material/holotype of *P. goodwini*: NMMNH P-27403, incomplete skull, lacking facial and palatal bones.

Comments: In a recent revision of the domeheaded genus *Stegoceras*, pachycephalosaur specialist Robert M. Sullivan also reassessed the genus *Prenocephale* and the various species that have been referred to it.

In 2003, Thomas E. Williamson and Thomas D. Carr erected the new genus *Sphaerotholus*, including in it two species, the type species *S. goodwini*, established on an incomplete skull (NMMNH P-27403) from the Kirtland Formation of New Mexico, and *S. buchholtzae*, a referred species founded upon a

Prenocephale prenes, ZPAL MgD-I/104, holotype frontoparietal dome in dorsal view.

Prenocephale edmontonensis, CMN 8831, holotype frontoparietal dome, dorsal view.

Life restoration of "Prenocephale brevis" by artist Berislav Krzic. This species has been referred back to the genus Stegoceras as the species S. breve.

ilar to that in the type species *Prenocephale prenes* Maryańska and Osmólska 1974 than to that of any other known pachycephalosaurian genus.

Williamson and Carr (2003*b*) considered the above taxon to be a *nomen dubium* (see *S3*). However, according to Sullivan (2003), the holotype of *S. buchholtzae* (also referred material previously discussed by Sullivan; 2000*a*), "is clearly the same taxon as the holotype of *Prenocephale edmontonensis*, based on strong morphological autapomorphies (downturned parietal coupled with medial-most nodes on the parietal) that distinguish it from other pachycephalosaur taxa." Consequently, Sullivan (2003) regarded *S. buchholtzae* as synonymous with *P. edmontonensis*.

Regarding *S. goodwini*, Sullivan (2003) criticized Williamson and Carr's diagnosis of this species, pointing out that it was based entirely upon having a (not greatly) downward reduced parietosquamosal bar. Also, Williamson and Carr had referred to this species an unassociated dentary, a fragment of squamosal, and some unidentified skull fragments (NMMNH P-30068) recovered from another locality and a lower (Farmington Member) stratigraphic level. Furthermore, these authors compared this species to "*Stegoceras*" specimens from the Judith River Group, but not to the holotype of *S. goodwini*, apparently due to lack of common elements, thereby failing to justify their reference of the referred specimens to this species.

According to Sullivan (2003), NMMNH P-27403 is referrable to the genus *Prenocephale* based upon skull ornamentation comprising a linear row of nodes on each squamosal, as the new combination *P. goodwini*. The species differs from other *Prenocephale* species and is distinguished by four prominent nodes on each squamosal, with a large inferior-positioned corner node.

Sullivan (2003) referred to *Prenocephale* sp. an incomplete frontoparietal dome (TMP 87.50.29) from the Dinosaur Park Formation, Steveville area, Alberta, Canada, "based on the strong down-turned, medial projection of the parietal." As described by Sullivan (2003), this specimen is larger than any specimens referred to *Prenocephale brevis*. It is slightly larger than the skull (TMP 87.113.3) of *P. edmontonensis* and distinguished from it by two salient features found in that specimen but not in TMP 87.50.29 — *i.e.*, distinct pair of nodes located largely on medial caudal extension of parietal; incipiently developed frontal (nasal) lobe with prefrontal and nasal regions fully inflated rostrally (distinct but rather incipient trilobate appearance of prefrontal/nasal region in TMP 87.50.29, the latter similar to that in *P. brevis*; see Sullivan 2000*a*). Sullivan (2003) found Williamson and Carr's suggestion that TMP 87.50.29 could

partial skull (TMP 87.113.3) from the Hell Creek Formation of Montana (see *S3* and below).

Earlier, Sullivan (2000*a*) had referred the species originally described by Brown and Schlaikjer (1943) as *Troodon* [=*Stegoceras*; see below] *edmontonensis* to *Prenocephale* as the new species *P. edmontonensis* (see *S2*), this assessment "based on the occurrence of three nodes on the squamosals, with a fourth lapping onto the medial extension of the strongly down-turned parietal" (Sullivan 2003), an arrangement more sim-

represent adult individuals of *P. brevis* unsupported. Possibly, that author stated, this specimen "may represent a new taxon, but until more complete specimens are recovered, only a generic identification is possible."

Williamson and Carr had rejected Sullivan's (2000*a*; see *S2*) referral of the species *Stegoceras breve* to the genus *Prenocephale*, as the new species *P. brevis* (see *S3*). Sullivan's (2000*a*) referral had been based upon the presence of distinct nodes on the medial extension of the parietal (strongly down-turned in adult individuals). Williamson and Carr's rejection of this referral was based on the "common position of grooves in the frontal above the orbit," giving it a "trilobate" appearance along the rostral border of the frontal region, this constituting one of Sullivan's (2000*a*) diagnostic characters for this species. However, as Sullivan (2003) pointed out, none of the small pachycephalosaurian specimens belonging to this species have open supratemporal fenestrae; consequently, they cannot be referred to *Stegoceras* and are interpreted as mature individuals. Furthermore, Williamson and Carr regarded this species as the most basal species of the genus *Stegoceras*, yet also interpreted these small specimens as belonging to subadults of that genus, an interpretation, Sullivan (2003) noted, "not only inconsistent, but also indefensible in the light of the data presented by Sullivan (2000*a*) and [in his 2003 paper]."

Regarding this species, Sullivan (2003) found one specimen — TMP 85.43.68, designated cf. *Prenocephale brevis*, comprising an isolated parietal having a slender, medial, caudally projecting extension with two small, sharply pointed nodes on each edge where it articulates with both squamosals — to be of particular interest. In lateral aspect, the infratemporal fossae of this specimen are elongate and shallow; the smooth (rather than rugose) upper margins suggest a dorsal supratemporal slit. Sullivan (2003) interpreted this specimen as representing an immature individual which, if that identification is correct, offers "evidence for an ontogenetic change in the morphology of the parietal from immature to adult."

In their review of the Pachycephalosauria, Maryańska, Chapman and Weishampel (2004) rejected both *P. edmontonensis* and *P. brevis* as valid species of *Prenocephale* because these taxa "are poorly documented and not supported in our phylogenetic analysis" (see "Systematics" chapter). Therefore, these taxa are herein, at least for the present, again regarded as species of the genus *Stegoceras*.

Key references: Brown and Schlaikjer (1943); Lambe (1918); Maryańska, Chapman and Weishampel (2004); Maryańska and Osmólska (1974); Sullivan (2000*a*, 2003, 2003); Williamson and Carr (2003*b*).

PRENOCERATOPS   Chinnery 2004

Ornithischia: Predentata: Genusauria: Cerapoda: Chasmatopia: Marginocephalia: Ceratopsia: Neoceratopsia: Ceratopsoidea: Leptoceratopsidae: Leptoceratopsinae.

Name derivation: Greek *preno* = "sloping" + Greek *ceratops* = "horn-face."

Type species: *P. pieganensis* Chinnery 2004.

Other species: [None.]

Occurrence: Two Medicine Formation, Montana, United States.

Age: Late Cretaceous (Campanian).

Known material: Incomplete skull material, partial skeletons, at least four individuals, subadult.

Holotype: TCM 2003.1.1, disarticulated surangular fused with angular.

Diagnosis of genus (as for type species): (For skull only) basal neoceratopsian having caudally oriented external naris; maxillary projection rather than maxillary shelf; rostral position of pterygoid-maxilla contact; caudal portion of nasal constricted; deep, sharp frontal depression demarcated by straight, transverse border; postorbital bar narrow in dorsal aspect (at contact between frontal and postorbital), tall in lateral aspect; jugal wide, triangular; ventral tip of jugal having rostral curvature; quadratojugal tall and compressed mediolaterally and dorsocaudally; surangular very gracile; reduced articular and corresponding inequality of quadrate condyles; dorsal border of articular entirely convex; caudal expansion of coronoid reduced (Chinnery 2004*a*).

Comments: The genus *Prenoceratops* was founded upon a surangular with fused angular (TCM 2003.1.1.), this specimen having been recently extracted from a monospecific bonebed — distinguished as the only currently known bonebed deposit of a basal neoceratopsian — located on privately owned and deeded land of the Blackfeet Indian Reservation, in the Two Medicine Formation of Pondera County, Montana. Referred to the type species *P. pieganensis*, collected from the same site, were a number of partial skeletons discovered together although not associated into distinct skeletons. All of these specimens had been privately collected, after which they were sold to the commercial company Canada Fossils, Inc., which permitted the study of the material prior to their mounting of two composite skeletons that were subsequently sold to the Mokpo Natural History and Culture Museum in Mokpo, Korea, and The Childrens Museum in Indianapolis, Indiana (Chinnery 2004*a*).

As detailed by Chinnery, the collected remains represent every element of the skull and postcrania. The material indicates the presence of at least four individuals at the site in various stages of ontogeny; all are immature, as evidenced by their bone texture and

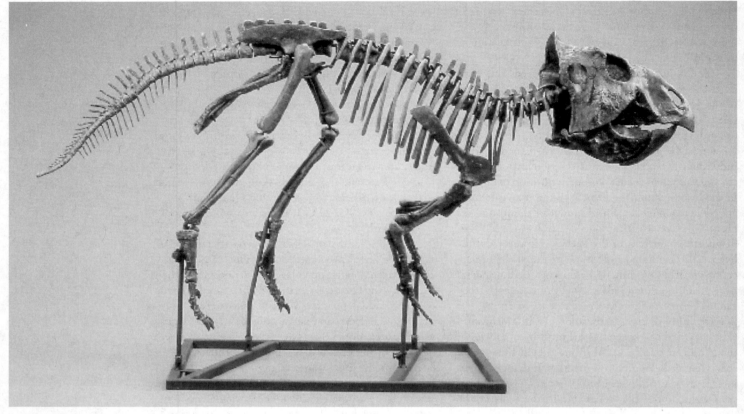

Prenoceratops pieganensis, original composite subadult skeleton (ICM collection) mounted by Canada Fossils, Inc. for The Children's Museum of Indianapolis, in Indianapolis, Indiana.

the lack of fusion of elements (see Sampson, Ryan and Tanke 1997). However, even though many of the recovered elements fit together, they — aside from partial skull and limb associations — cannot be jointed to form a single complete skeleton.

Chinnery described in detail the cranial material of *P. pieganensis* in her initial publication on this new taxon, a full description of the postcrania to appear elsewhere at some later date. Chinnery further noted that the nearly completely disarticulated state of the cranial material allows for a more complete understanding of the skull morphology of basal Neoceratopsia. The premaxillary of *Prenoceratops* contributes to the external naris, suggesting a more caudally oriented external naris, and the nasal is straight and quadrate caudodorsally angled, suggesting a longer and lower head than in the closely related genus *Leptoceratops*, this hypothesis supported, Chinnery noted, by "the short maxilla, more horizontally oriented antorbital fossa, and more upright, triangular jugal." Generally speaking, Chinnery observed that when the cranial elements of *Prenoceratops* are articulated into a composite skull, the result should remarkably resemble "a low version of the *Leptoceratops gracilis* paratype NMC 8887 (Sternberg, 1951: pl. XLIX)."

Although the postcranium of this taxon was not yet formally described, Chinnery noted that it does not differ significantly from the postcranium of *Leptoceratops*, although most of the limb elements of *Prenoceratops* are more gracile than their counterparts in that genus. Slight differences cited by Chinnery in her preliminary description of *P. pieganensis* include "a difference in orientation of the deltopectoral crest on the humerus," although distinctions between the taxonomic and developmental differences remain, for the present, unclear.

Chinnery performed a preliminary cladistic analysis of *Prenoceratops*, including 16 taxa and 102 cranial and postcranial characters, with the pachycephalosaur *Stegoceras* used as the outgroup, and the centrosaurine *Centrosaurus apertus* and chasmosaurine *Triceratops horridus* used as representing the two subfamilies belonging to Ceratopsidae. Included in this analysis were all presently recognized basal members of Neoceratopsia with the exception of *Breviceratops kozlowskii* (regarded by some workers as a junior synonym of *Bagaceratops rozhdestvenskii*; see Sereno 2000; Makovicky 2001) and *Turanoceratops tardabilis*, the latter not included for lack of material. The most parsimonious tree generated by Chinnery's analysis found (*contra* Makovicky; Xu, Makovicky, Wang, Norell and You 2002) *Chaöyangosaurus youngi* to be a basal member of Neoceratopsia, with the family Protoceratopsidae including only the Asian genera *Protoceratops* and *Graciliceratops*. Chinnery also found the family Leptoceratopsidae (see Makovicky), with the inclusion of *Prenoceratops*, to be supported and include all North American basal taxa as well as the Asian *Udanoceratops tschizhovi*. Agreeing with Makovicky and Xu *et al.*, Chinnery found the Ceratopsidae to be monophyletic, with *Zuniceratops christopheri* clustering as the sister taxon to that family. *Asiaceratops* and *Chaöyangosaurus* grouped as sister taxa within Neoceratopsia rather than within Leptoceratopsidae (see "Systematics" chapter).

As Chinnery noted, the above results support the hypothesis of multiple dispersal events of early horned dinosaurs from Asia to North America (see Chinnery and Weishampel 1998; Chinnery, Lipka, Kirkland, Parrish and Brett-Surman 1998; Makovicky). The analysis specifically supports the postulation of two such events — "one with the ancestor of Leptoceratopsidae and one with the ancestor of the Ceratopsidae lineage" — plus a dispersal event of an ancestor of *Udanoceratops* back to Asia.

Key references: Chinnery (2004*a*); Chinnery, Lipka, Kirkland, Parrish and Brett-Surman (1998); Chinnery and Weishampel (1998); Makovicky (2001); Sampson, Ryan and Tanke (1997); Sereno (2000); Sternberg (1951); Xu, Makovicky, Wang, Norell and You (2002).

†PROBACTROSAURUS

Ornithischia: Predentata: Genasauria: Cerapoda: Ornithopoda: Euornithopoda: Iguanodontia: Dryomorpha: Ankylopollexia: Styracosterna: Iguanodontoidea.

Age: Early Cretaceous (Barremian).

Comment: Numerous fossils pertaining to the genus *Probactrosaurus* have been recovered from the Dashuiguo Formation of Inner Mongolia, China. Because of the evolutionary position of *Probactrosaurus* — a dinosaur exhibiting both iguanodontid and hadrosaurid features — the dinosaur-bearing sediments of the Dashuiguo Formation have generally been considered to be of Early to Middle Cretaceous (Aptian–Albian) age.

According to a study by Van Itterbeeck, Narkevich and Horne (2004), however, new micropaleontological data based upon charophytes, ostracods, and palynomorphs indicate a substantially older age for the Dashuiguo Formation. As these authors noted, the presence of three charophyte species collected from that formation indicate a Barremian–Aptian age (*e.g.*, see Shu and Zhang 1985); nine genera and 13 species of nonmarine ostracods, allowing correlation of the formation with the Dzun Bayn suite of the

Gobi Basin and adjacent areas in China, suggest Barremian–Albian (*e.g.*, see Galeeva 1955); and the palynomorph assemblage is quite similar to that of the nearby Inner Mongolian Tebch site, the latter having an estimated age of Barremian–?early Aptian (see Eberth, Russell, Braman and Deino 1993).

Itterbeeck *et al.* concluded that, based upon the above three lines of evidence, the Dashuiguo Formation is of Barremian age. Moreover, the authors cautioned that "Age estimations of dinosaur sites based on dinosaur evidence ... need to be confirmed by independent age estimations."

Key references: Eberth, Russell, Braman and Deino (1993); Galeeva (1955); Van Itterbeeck, Markevich and Horne (2004).

†PROTARCHAEOPTERYX—(=*Incisivosaurus*)

Saurischia: Eusaurischia: Theropoda: Neotheropoda: Tetanurae: Avetheropoda: Coelurosauria: Tyrannoraptora: Maniraptoriformes: Maniraptora: Metornithes.

Type species: *P. robusta* Ji and Ji 1997.

Other species: *P. gauthieri* (Xu, Cheng, Wang and Chang 2002).

Comments: In 1997, Ji and Ji formally described the new type species *Protarchaeopteryx robusta*, based on a nearly complete skeleton with a crushed skull (NGMC 2125), collected from the ?Lower Cretaceous Chaomidianzi Formation of Liaoning Province, China (see *S1*). Five years later, Xu, Cheng, Wang and Chang (2002) introduced *Incisivosaurus gautieri*, a new species based on an almost complete skull and a partial vertebra (IVPP V13326) from the Lower Cretaceous Yixian Formation of Liaoning Province, and referred to those authors to the Oviraptorosauria (see *S3*).

More recently, Senter, Barsbold, Britt and Burnham (2004), in a paper presenting a phylogenetic revision of the Dromaeosauridae (see "Systematics" chapter), observed that, except for tooth count, the overlapping elements of both *P. robusta* and *I. gauthieri* are identical. As these authors observed, both *Protarchaeopteryx robusta* and *I. gauthieri* "uniquely share a very bizarre dentition," including the following attributes: Single pair of enlarged, rostrocaudally compressed teeth at rostral portion of premaxilla; very small, peglike teeth immediately prior to enlarged pair of teeth; very small, lanceolate distal teeth; and absence of teeth at tip of dentary (in NGMC 2125; see Xu *et al.*). Additionally, despite that the crushed state of the skull of NGMC 2125 does not allow identification of the teeth as either right or left, this specimen clearly shares with *P. gauthieri* the following features: Short, high skull; tall premaxilla; and strongly beveled dentary margin, dorsal margin terminating in 50- to 60-degree point.

In Senter *et al.*'s estimation, the above-noted similarities, particularly the dental characters, justify regarding both *P. robusta* and *I. gauthieri* as belonging to the same genus, *Protarchaeopteryx*; significant differences in tooth count (Ji and Ji; Xu *et al.*), however, warrant their separation into distinct taxa, *Protarchaeopteryx robusta* and *P. gauthieri*. Also, Senter *et al.* addressed the claim that the teeth of "*I.*" *gauthieri* lack serrations (Xu *et al.*), while those of *P. robusta* are serrated (Ji and Ji). Close-up observations of NGMC 2125 by one of the authors (Philip Senter), however, "revealed that the apparent serrations on the one preserved enlarged premaxillary tooth crown are places where the edges of the teeth are chipped," no serrations being seen on the distal teeth, nor in the photographs of these teeth published by Ji and Ji.

Key references: Ji and Ji (1997); Senter, Barsbold, Britt and Burnham (2004); Xu, Cheng, Wang and Chang (2002).

PROTECOVASAURUS   Heckert 2004

Ornithischia *incertae sedis*.

Name derivation: Greek *pro* = "first/primary" + Tecovas [Formation] + Greek *sauros* = "lizard."

Type species: *P. lucasi* Heckert 2004.

Other species: [None.]

Occurrence: Tecovas Formation, Texas, United States.

Age: Late Triassic (Carnian).

Known material: Teeth.

Holotype: NMMNH P-34196, complete tooth crown.

Diagnosis of genus (as for type species): Basal ornithischian distinguished by recurved teeth, apex of crown even with or overhanging distal margin of crown at base; apex of crown sharply acute (less than 45 degrees); mesial margin strongly convex; distal margin straight to slightly recurved or backswept (Heckert 2004).

Comments: Apparently the first documented carnivorous ornithischian, the genus *Protecovasaurus* (first mentioned by Heckert 2002*b*, but considered then to be a *nomen nudum*) was founded upon a nearly complete tooth crown (NMMNH P-34196) from the Upper Triassic (Carnian ["Otischalkian–Adamanian"]) lower Kalgary locality in the lowermost Tecovas Formation (Chinle Group) of Crosby County, west Texas. Dental specimens referred to the type species, *P. lucasi*, collected from the same locality (therefore designated as paratypes) include an almost complete crown (NMMNH P-34197), incomplete crown (NMMNH P-34321), worn tooth (NMMNH P-34322), nearly complete crown (NMMNH P-34392), and an incomplete crown (NMMNH P-

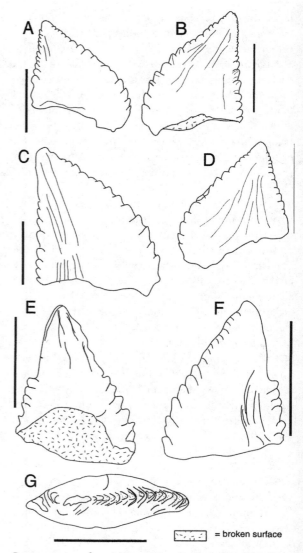

Protecovasaurus lucasi, interpretive sketches of teeth: A–B. NMMNH P-34196, holotype tooth in A. lingual and B. labial views; C–D. NMMNH P-34197, paratype tooth in C. labial and D. lingual views; E–G. NMMNH P-34221, referred tooth in E. labial, F. lingual, and G. occlusal views. Scales = 1 mm. (After Heckert 2004.)

41466); from other lowermost Tecovas Formation Crosby County localities, an almost complete crown (NMMNH P-34221), and a tooth (NMMNH P-26441); and from the upper Kalgary locality of the Tecovas Formation of Crosby County, a tentatively assigned tooth (NMMNH P-26441) (Heckert 2004).

Although these teeth meet the criteria for their referral to the Ornithischia (*e.g.*, see Sereno 1991*a*, 1998, 1999*b*; Heckert 2000), Heckert (2004) interpreted them as most likely not belonging to herbivorous animals. According to Heckert (2004), various features of these teeth (*e.g.*, sharply pointed crowns an denticles, recurved shape) suggest "a carnivorous diet," implying clearly "that at least some basal ornithischians retained the carnivorous habits of dinosaurian precursors" (see Heckert and Lucas 1999, 2001; Heckert 2000; Weishampel and Jianu 2000).

Heckert (2004) also described various teeth from the same locality as NMMNH P-31496 that, generally similar in form but having proportionally finer denticles, could pertain to *Protecovasaurus*. These include the almost complete, slightly larger NMMNH P-34198, and also NMMNH P-30807, the incomplete, moderately tall NMMNH P-34259, and the broken and worn NMMNH P-34323 and P-34324.

Key references: Heckert (2000, 2002*b*, 2004); Heckert and Lucas (1999, 2001); Sereno (1991*a*, 1998, 1999*a*); Weishampel and Jianu (2000).

†PSITTACOSAURUS

Ornithischia: Predentata: Genusauria: Cerapoda: Chasmatopia: Marginocephalia: Ceratopsia: Psittacosauridae.

Comments: In 1992, Éric Buffetaut and Varavudh Suteethorn described a new species of the primitive ceratopsian dinosaur *Psittacosaurus*, which they named *Psittacosaurus sattayaraki*. It was established on a fragmentary right dentary and an incomplete maxilla (TF 2449, first reported by Buffetaut, Sattayarak and Suteethorn 1989) collected from the Early to Middle Cretaceous (Aptian–Albian) Khok Kruat Formation at Ban Dong Bang Noi, Chiataphum Province, in northeastern Thailand.

Dodson (1996), in his book *The Horned Dinosaurs*, was reluctant to accept Buffetaut *et al.*'s referral of this material to the Psittacosauridae "on the basis of such an incomplete specimen." Later, Sereno (2000), in a review of Asian marginocephalians, questioned the Thai material's referral to *Psittacosaurus*, concluding that it should be referred to Ceratopsia *incertae sedis*.

However, in a subsequent paper by Buffetaut and Suteethorn (2002), the authors of *Psittacosaurus sattayaraki* stated that "Sereno's paper contains a number of inaccuracies." Furthermore, the purpose of Buffetaut and Suteethorn's (2002) "present note is to point them out and to reassert the validity of the description and conclusions given in our 1992 paper." These inaccuracies, the authors noted, and also Sereno's doubts and criticisms, apparently stem from "an insufficient acquaintance with the original material from Thailand."

Sereno regarded with suspicion the association of the dentary and maxilla because, according to that author, they had been "collected years apart." As corrected by Buffetaut and Suteethorn (2002), however, "only a few months elapsed between the initial discovery by Nares Sattayarak and our visit to the locality, during which the maxilla was found." Moreover, the Ban Dong Bang Noi locality is a small outcrop comprising an area of just a few square meters "of very hard red sandstone, which weathers and erodes very slowly"; also, the dentary and maxilla "were found close to each other in the same bed." As already noted by Buffetaut and Suteethorn (1992), it cannot be unambiguously shown that the two elements belong to a single individual. However, their similar sizes and compatible morphology suggest that they probably belong together. For that reason, Buffetaut and Suteethorn (1992) described these remains as possibly belonging to a single individual.

As Sereno stated, the type dentary of this species is poorly preserved, its rostral end appearing to be "unfinished and weathered." Contrarily, Buffetaut and Suteethorn (2002) posited that the acid-prepared dentary is exquisitely preserved and has not suffered from either weathering or wear induced by transport. Indeed, only the teeth are incompletely preserved, many of them having broken crowns.

Sereno doubted the validity of *P. sarrayaraki* because "all basal ceratopsians have short, deep dentary rami," and also because the primary ridge on the dentary teeth of TF 2449 "is not bulbous as in *Psittacosaurus*." While agreeing that a deep and short dentary cannot be used to identify this genus, Buffetaut and Suteethorn (2002) maintained "that the dentary teeth of the Thai specimen show the bulbous median ridge which Sereno considers to be a diagnostic feature of *Psittacosaurus*." Moreover, the authors noted that, while most of the crowns are broken, replacement teeth in the specimen's third and fifth tooth positions reveal enough crown to establish the presence of a very prominent and broader median ridge, therefore being bulbous and resembling the primary ridges on the dentary teeth of the type species *P. mongoliensis* and referred species *P. meileyingensis* (see Sereno, Chao, Cheng and Rao 1988 for figures).

Also, Sereno questioned Buffetaut and Suteethorn's description of the holotype dentary because "a dentary flange is developed only in some psittacosaurs (*P. mongoliensis* and *P. meileyingensis*) and extends vertically as a ridge across the posterior portion of the ramus [...], unlike the dentary from Thailand." While noting that a flange is developed only in some psittacosaurs (Buffetaut and Suteethorn 1992), the authors stated that such a flange can been seen in an incipient developmental state (*i.e.*, a small, lateral protrusion on the ventral side of the dentary) in TF 2449, thereby constituting a distinguishing feature of *P. sattayaraki*. Furthermore, this feature appears "in the same position as the flanges of other flange-bearing psittacosaurs." The flange in *P. sattayaraki* "does not extend vertically across the lateral face of the dentary,"

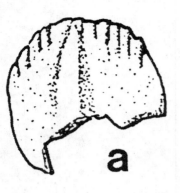

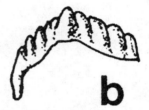

Dentary teeth (lingual view) of (a, b) ***Psittacosaurus sattayaraki*** (holotype TF 2449; crown of replacement tooth in fifth tooth position) and (c) *P. meileyingensis* (after Sereno, Chao, Cheng and Rao 1988). Scale = 5 mm (a, b) and 2 mm (c). (After Buffetaut and Suteethorn 2002.)

differing from the flanges in both *P. mongoliensis* and *P. meileyingensis*, supporting the former's identification as a distinct species of *Psittacosaurus*.

Furthermore, the dentary of *P. sattayaraki* displays a less markedly convex alveolar edge than in the type species, while the dentaries of other species of *Psittacosaurus* seem to have a somewhat straight dorsal edge. The condition in the Thai material, according to Buffetaut and Suteethorn (2002), "seems to be a valid feature of a distinct species."

Finally, Buffetaut and Suteethorn (2002) commented on two features of *P. sattayaraki* that Sereno found to be "unusual"—*e.g.*, the relatively "low position of the predentary attachment surface relative to the tooth row," and "the abrupt symphysial arching pf the symphysial region of the dentary." The first of these observations, according to the authors, "is largely due to the complexity of the alveolar edge." Regarding the second observation, Buffetaut and Suteethorn (2002) pointed out that on most described *Psittacosaurus* specimens the predentary bone, firmly attached to the rostral ends of the dentaries, obscures the shape of their symphysial region. Consequently, when not hidden, "the symphysial region of other *Psittacosaurus* species might show a condition similar to *Psittacosaurus sattayaraki*."

Until recently, *Psittacosaurus* has been reported only from Mongolia, China, and, if the above discussed species is valid, Thailand. Now the provenance

of this genus has been expanded to another country. In 2003, Averianov, Starkov and Skutschas identified and described remains representing six dinosaurian taxa—one of these referred to *Psittacosaurus* sp.—from a microvertebrate site discovered by Pavel Skutschas in Early or Middle Cretaceous (late Barremian to middle Aptian, *e.g.*, see Nessov and Starkov 1992; possibly early to middle Albian, *e.g.*, Averianov and Skutschas 2000) strata of the Murtoi Formation, at the Mogoito locality, on the west coast of Gusinoe Lake, at Buryatia, southwest of the city of Ulan-Ude, in western Transbaikalia, Russia.

The psittacosaur material, discovered via screen-washing during 1998–1999, consists of a ?right maxillary tooth (ZIN PH 6/13), a juvenile maxillary tooth (ZIN PH 12/13), and a dentary tooth (ZIN PH 13/13). In describing these teeth, Averianov *et al.* noted that they "are remarkably similar to the teeth of *Psittacosaurus*" and, consequently, were referred to that genus. The authors also observed that the dentary tooth lacks the bulbous median ridge dominating the crowns in the Aptian–Albian type species *P. mongoliensis* and referred species *P. meileyingensis* (see Sereno *et al.*), and also in the Barremian *Psittacosaurus* sp. (Xu and Wang 1988); is more similar in that respect to teeth of the apparently older species *P. xingiangensis*, yet differs from the latter in having a comparatively taller and more leaflike crown. However, Averianov *et al.* cautioned, "ontogenetic tooth variation in *Psittacosaurus* is poorly known, which limits use of tooth structure for systematic purposes."

Meng, Varricchio, Liu, Huang and Gao (2004*a*) reported on "a dramatic specimen" of *Psittacosaurus* sp. (Dalian Natural History Museum D2156) collected recently from a massively bedded unit in an outcrop of variegated mudstones of the Lower Cretaceous Yixian Formation, at Shangyuan, Lianoning Province, China. As the authors pointed out, small dinosaur skeletons (such as those included in D2156) are generally preserved in this unit completely articulated and in three-dimensional, near-life positions. Typically such specimens are discovered with the vertebral column resting dorsal-side up and with ribcage intact, and the limbs under the torso or to side (as opposed to the more common flattened, almost complete to complete skeletons with integument or body outlines, preserved in thin lacustrine laminae units).

The specimen reported on by Meng *et al.* comprises a tight aggregation of an adult plus 34 juvenile individuals that the authors referred to *Psittacosaurus* sp. Neither partial skeletons nor isolated elements are included in this specimen (other than "those damaged by recent, pre-discovery erosion or excavation error").

Meng *et al.* (2004*a*, 2004*b*) briefly described the

*Life restoration of Psitta-
cosaurus mongoliensis* by
artist Todd Marshall.

specimen as follows: Skeletons lying concentrated in
0.25-square meter area, individuals usually overlapping each other, skulls uncovered by other skeletons;
more peripheral individuals situated higher in substrate than those at center, suggesting original bowl-
shaped depression; adult skull measuring 115 millimeters in length, juvenile skulls approximately 40
millimeters; total juvenile body of about 21 centimeters; size and degree of ossification of juveniles indicating significantly older age than hatchlings; juveniles showing consistent pattern

As Meng *et al.* (2004*a*, 2004*b*) observed, these
skeletons had minimal exposure prior to burial, as evidenced by the absence of such disturbances as weathering, disarticulation, and scavenging; moreover, the
"life positions" of these skeletons preclude hydraulic
concentration, possibly also indicating that these dinosaurs were buried alive.

Meng *et al.* (2004*a*, 2004*b*) noted that the extant archosaurs of birds and crocodilian both exhibit
post-hatching care for their young; however, the radically different physiology, behavior, and ecology of
these groups question any homology of parental care
between them. Nevertheless, the above-described
close association of *Psittacosaurus* adult and young
most compellingly suggests that post-hatching prena-
tal care had occurred. Moreover, "Discovery of similar aggregations for other dinosaurs," Meng *et al.*
(2004*b*) noted, "would strengthen the idea that post-
hatching parental care is the ancestral condition in

Dinosauria and therefore a homologous character among crocodilians and birds."

Notes: Other dinosaurian remains from the Mogoito site described by Averianov include the following: A pedal ungual phalanx (ZIN PH 2/13), lacking its distal end, belonging to an indeterminate therizinosaurid theropod, resembling in some ways (e.g., more convex articular surface, sulci for claw extending far more caudally) the pedal unguals of *Erlikosaurus andrewsi*; a left femur (ZIN PH 1/13) with damaged distal epiphysis, representing the oldest known Asian ornithomimosaur; a rostral dentary or maxillar tooth (ZIN PH 10/13) and two dentary or maxillary teeth (ZIN PH3. 11/13), belonging to an indeterminate dromaeosaurid; a juvenile tooth (ZIN PH 9/13), adult tooth (ZIN PH 7/13), distal caudal vertebra (ZIN PH 8/13), and a thoracic rib (uncatalogued), referred by the authors to cf. *Chiayüsaurus* sp.; and a fragmentary tooth (ZIN PH 5/13) generally resembling the holotype tooth of *Mongolosaurus haplodon*, and therefore referred by Averianov *et al.* to cf. *Mongolosaurus* sp. Nondinosaurian materials recovered at the Mogoito site includes a scincomorph lizard (cf. *Paramacellodus* sp.) and the eutherian mammal *Murtoilestes abramovi*.

As Averianov *et al.* pointed out, this Russian vertebrate dinosaurian assemblage most closely resembles the Early Cretaceous assemblages of Khuren Dukh, in Mongolia, and Elesital, in Inner Mongolia, China.

In the past, Mesozoic mammals generally have been regarded as mainly insectivorous, probably nocturnal shrew- or rat-sized animals that "lived in the shadow of dinosaurs." Until recently, the largest Mesozoic mammal known from substantial remains has been the triconodont type species *Repenomamus robustus*, an adult of which attained the size of a Virginia opossum, from the lower Cretaceous of Liaoning Province, in northern China.

Recently, Hu, Meng, Wang and Li (2005) reported the discovery of a new species of *Repenomamus*, *R. giganticus*, represented by a postcranial skeleton (IVPP V14155) from the basal member of the Early Cretaceous Yixian Formation of China. The specimen represents an animal approximately 50 percent larger than *R. robustus*. Most remarkable about this discovery, fossilized stomach contents — including remains of a juvenile *Psittacosaurus* — were found associated with this specimen in the stomach area. The *Psittacosaurus* bones, some of which are still articulated, belong to a single individual.

This find, Hu *et al.* noted, is significant in showing that some triconodonts were meat-eaters and fed on small vertebrates (*e.g.*, young dinosaurs), and that Mesozoic mammals had a much greater range of body sizes than previously known. Moreover, this discovery "suggests that Mesozoic mammals occupied diverse niches and that some large mammals probably competed with dinosaurs for food and territory."

Key references: Averianov and Skutschas (2000); Averianov, Starkov and Skutschas (2003); Buffetaut, Sattayarak and Suteethorn (1989); Buffetaut and Suteethorn (1992); Dodson (1996); Hu, Meng, Wang and Li (2005); Meng, Varricchio, Liu, Huang and Gao (2004*a*, 2004*b*); Nessov and Starkov (1992); Sereno (2000); Sereno, Chao, Cheng and Rao (1988); Xu and Wang (1988).

PYCNONEOSAURUS   Kellner and Campos 2002

Saurischia: Eusaurischia: Eusaurischia: Theropoda: Neotheropoda: Ceratosauria: Abelisauroidea: ?Abelisauridae.

Name derivation: Greek *pycnós* = "thick" + Greek *nemos* = "forest" + Greek *sauros* = "lizard."

Type species: *P. nevesi* Kellner and Campos 2002.

Other species: [None.]

Occurrence: Baurú Group, Mato Grosso, Brazil.

Age: Late Cretaceous ("Senonian").

Known material/holotype: DGM 859-R, five incomplete teeth, parts of seven caudal vertebrae, right pubis lacking proximal part, right tibia, distal articulation of right fibula.

Diagnosis of genus (as for type species): Tibia with prominent, distally dorsoventrally expanded cnemial crest (length almost half that of tibia) (Kellner and Campos 2002).

Comments: The type species *Pycnonemosaurus nevesi* was founded upon teeth and various poorly preserved postcranial remains (DGM 859-R) associated with titanosaurian remains, found by Llewellyn Price in 1952–1953 in a red conglomerate sandstone at the Fazenda Concador locality, Baurú Group (Upper Cretaceous), state of Mato Grosso, Brazil (Kellner and Campos 2002).

In describing the type specimen, Kellner and Campos estimated the total length of this dinosaur, based on that of the tibia, to be approximately six to seven meters (about 21 to 24 feet).

Kellner and Campos referred *Pycnonemosaurus* to the "Abelisauria" based on one feature: Expanded distal end of transverse processes in some (not all) caudal vertebrae. However, this genus differs from all other known members of that group in the following: Small pubic foot; tibia having hatchet-shaped cnemial crest.

As the authors noted, this discovery confirms the presence of "abelisaurs" in Upper Cretaceous strata of continental Brazil.

Key reference: Kellner and Campos (2002).

RAJASAURUS Wilson, Sereno, Srivastava, Bhatt, Khosla and Sahni 2003

Saurischia: Eusaurischia: Theropoda: Neotheropoda: Abelisauroidea: Abelisauridae: Carnotaurinae.

Name derivation: Sanskritt *raja* = "prince or princely" + Greek *sauros* = "lizard."

Type species: *R. narmadensis* Wilson, Sereno, Srivastava, Bhatt, Khosla and Sahni 2003.

Other species: [None.]

Occurrence: Lameta Formation, Narmada, India.

Age: Late Cretaceous (Maastrichtian).

Known material: Partial skeleton, possibly other specimens.

Holotype: GSI 21141/1–33 (casts of several elements at the University of Michigan Museum of Paleontology, UMMP 9085), partial skeleton including braincase, cervical centrum, partial dorsal verte-brae, sacrum, partial caudal vertebrae, partial scapula, partial ilia, left proximal pubis, right femur, left distal femur, right distal tibia, right proximal fibula, right and left metatarsal II, right metatarsal IV.

Diagnosis of genus (as for type species): Characterized by following autapomorphies: median nasofrontal prominence, frontals forming only caudal rim of prominence; supratemporal fenestrae rostrocaudally elongate, with length about 150 percent transverse breadth of frontal; ilium robust, transverse ridge separating brevis fossa from acetabulum (Wilson, Sereno, Srivastava, Bhatt, Khosla and Sahni 2003).

Comments: The first Indian theropod preserving associated cranial and postcranial remains, the genus *Rajasaurus* was founded upon a partial skeleton (GSI 21141/1–33) representing a single individual, preserved

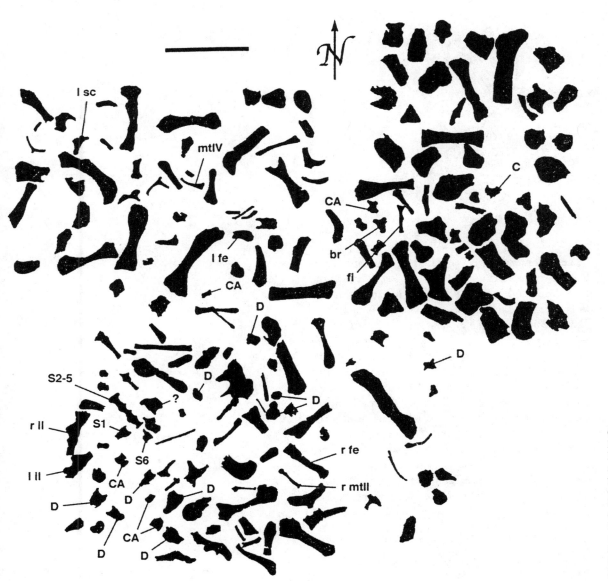

Quarry map of the Temple Hill locality, Gujarat State, India (after original quarry map, drawn by Suresh Srivastava in 1982–84), bones drawn in black representing holotype (GSI 21141/1–33) of *Rajasaurus narmadensis* (shaded bones pertaining to titanosaurian sauropods). Scale = 1 m. (After Wilson, Sereno, Srivastava, Bhatt, Khosla and Sahni 2003.)

Holotype (GSI 21141/1) braincase of *Rajasaurus narmadensis* in A. right lateral and B. dorsal views. Scale = 10 cm. (After Wilson, Sereno, Srivastava, Bhatt, Khosla and Sahni 2003.)

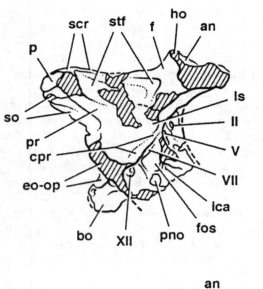

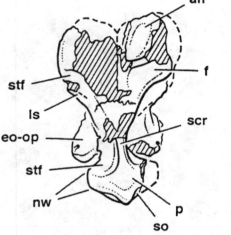

in a conglomerate layer lying under a dinosaur tooth-bearing calcareous sandstone (*e.g.*, see Mathur and Pant 1986), collected in 1983 from "infratraoean" sediments of the Lameta Formation (latest Cretaceous), Temple Hill locality, in Gujarat State, Kheda District, near the village of Rahioli (*e.g.*, see Dwivedi, Mohabey and Bandyopadhyay 1982), in western India. The specimen was found by Suresh Srivastava during the 1982–84 excavations of a series of quarries near Rahioli (see Sahni 2001). Possibly referrable to the type species, *Rajasaurus narmadensis*, are an ilia and sacrum (lost) from Bara Simla, described by Matley (1923) as *Lametasaurus indicus*, this material matching GSI 21141/1–33 "in its heavy construction and strongly divergent preacetabular process (Wilson, Sereno, Srivastava, Bhatt, Khosla and Sahni 2003).

In describing the holotype material, Wilson *et al.*

Holotype (GSI 21141/14-15) sacrum of *Rajasaurus narmadensis* in A. left lateral and B. ventral views. Scale = 20 cm. (After Wilson, Sereno, Srivastava, Bhatt, Khosla and Sahni 2003.)

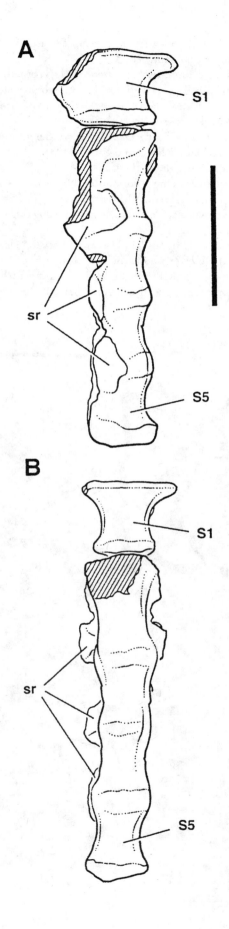

Photograph by Wendy Taylor, courtesy Paul C. Sereno and University of Chicago.

Reconstructed holotype skull (cast) of *Rajasaurus narmadensis* made by fossil preparator Tyler Keillor.

noted that the remains apparently represent "a heavy-bodied, stout-limbed abelisaurid." Furthermore, the authors suggested that much of the material (*e.g.*, the ilia and sacrum described by Matley) pertaining to large-bodied theropods recovered from latest Cretaceous rocks in central and western India could belong to *R. narmadensis*. However, the authors reserved formal referral of that material to *R. narmadensis* pending completion of a taxonomic review of the collection of remains from Bara Simla (Sereno and Wilson, in preparation).

A phylogenetic analysis by Sereno *et al.* (in review) found *Rajasaurus* to be a derived abelisaurid more closely allied to *Majungatholus* from Madagascar and *Carnotaurus* from Argentina than to related African genera. *Rajasaurus* was found to belong to the Ceratosauria based on the following ceratosaurian synapomorphies: Skull table having prominent parietal crest; cervical vertebrae with two pleurocoels; iliac peduncle oriented about 60 degrees from horizontal; peg-in socket iliopubic and ilioischial contacts; crescentic, cranially invaginated medial fibular fossa. Abelisaurid synapomorphies of *Rajasaurus* include: Thick parietal caudomedian process capping nuchal wedge, the latter tall, positioned caudal to occipital condyle; skull roof thickened; fused frontoparietal

Rapetosaurus

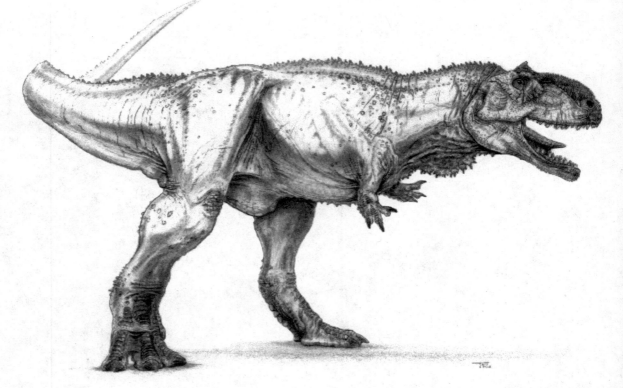

Life restoration of *Rajasaurus narmadensis* drawn by Todd Marshall under the direction of Paul C. Sereno.

suture; hypertrophied nuchal wedge; parietal alae. Carnotaurine synapomorphies present in this genus include: Positioning of caudal process of nasal dorsal to orbit; and presence of frontal excrescence.

With *Rajasaurus* closer to the genera from Madagascar and South America, carnotaurines appear to be restricted to those land masses, with their outgroups present in Africa. This postulation gives to support the hypothesis that Africa separated from other Gondwanan landmasses before land connections were severed between those areas. However, Wilson *et al.* cautioned, temporal sampling between these four landmasses is uneven, with only India, Madagascar, and South America thus far contributing adequately known Maastrichtian faunas, these sharing several tetrapod sister taxa (*e.g.*, see Sampson, Witmer, Forster, Krause, O'Connor, Dodson and Ravoavy 1998; Krause, Rogers, Forster, Hartman, Buckley and Sampson 1999); latest Cretaceous African horizons, on the contrary, are poorly known. Furthermore, pre–Maastrichtian Cretaceous vertebrates are very poorly known in India and Madagascar, while post–Cenomanian vertebrates are poorly sampled in Africa.

Note: As reported in various media accounts (*e.g.*, the *Chicago Sun-Times*) announcing *Rajasaurus narmadensis*, the discovery of this theropod was made by University of Chicago paleontologist Paul C. Sereno while doing field work in India in the spring of 2001. Sereno had been informed that the bones of

this dinosaur, collected from a river bed two decades earlier, were housed at the Geological Survey of India in Jaipur. Upon examining those remains, Sereno recognized them as representing a new genus and species. Following this discovery, Sereno brought the material to the University of Chicago, where research technician Tyler Keillor made a cast of the reconstructed skull. By Sereno's estimates, the animal was approximately 35 feet long, nine feet tall at the hips, and weighed about four tons, establishing it as "the biggest, heaviest predator from India," giving "the impression of a sabotage attacker."

Key references: Dwivedi, Mohabey and Bandyopadhyay (1982); Mathur and Pant 1986); Matley (1923); Sahni (2001); Wilson, Sereno, Srivastava, Bhatt, Khosla and Sahni (2003).

†RAPETOSAURUS

Saurischia: Eusaurischia: Sauropodomorpha: Sauropoda: Eusauropoda: Neosauropoda: Macronaria: Titanosauriformes: Titanosauria.

Diagnosis of genus (as for type species): Antorbital fenestra enlarged, extending over tooth row; preantorbital fenestra caudal to antorbital fenestra; rostrally located, dorsoventrally elongate subnarial foramen; narrow, caudodorsally elongate maxillary jugal process; median dome on frontal; "V"-shaped quadratojugal articulation on quadrate; supracoccipital

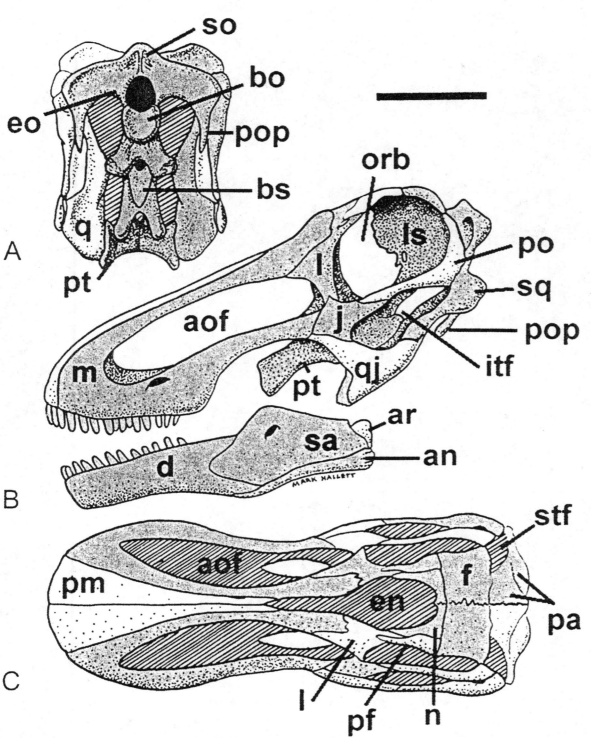

Rapetosaurus krausei, reconstructed skull based on holotype UA 8698 and referred specimens FMNH PR 2184–2192, 2194, and 2196–2197, in A. caudoventral, B. left lateral, and C. dorsal views. Scale = 10 cm. (After Curry Rogers and Forster 2004.)

with two rostrally directed median parietal processes; rostral process of pterygoid dorsoventrally expanded; basipterygoid articulation of pterygoid extremely shallow; basipterygoid processes only diverging near their distal ends; dentary having 11 alveoli, covering two-thirds of dentary length (Upchurch, Barrett and Dodson 2004).

Comments: In 2001, Kristina Curry Rogers and Catherine A. Forster described *Rapetosaurus krausei* (see *S3*), a new Late Cretaceous type species currently celebrated as the best-preserved and most complete skull material yet described for a titanosaur.

As Curry Rogers and Forster (2004) subsequently pointed out, the skull of *Rapetosaurus* is especially

Rapetosaurus

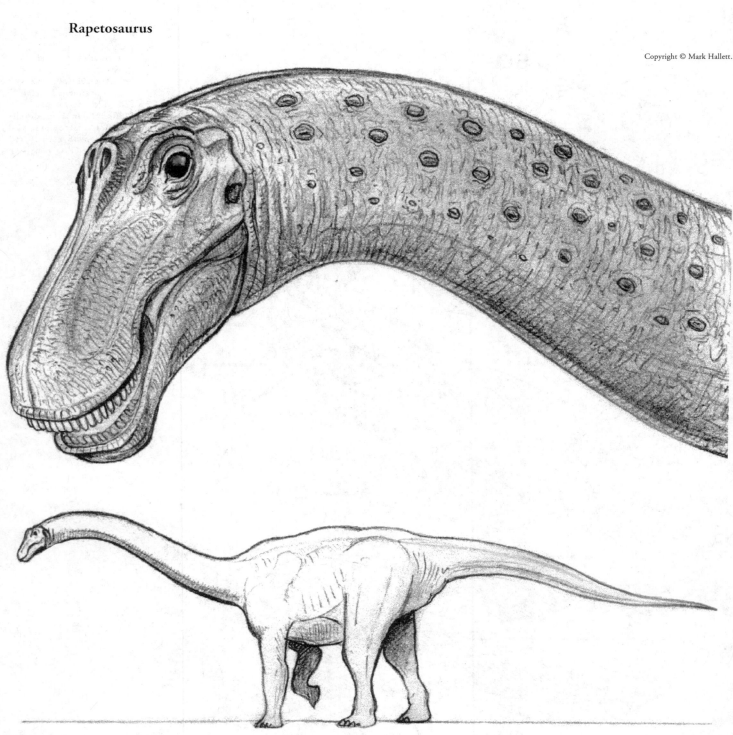

Life restoration of *Rapetosaurus krausei* by Mark Hallett.

important in that most members of the Titanosauria are diagnosed solely based upon fragmentary postcranial remains, with knowledge of the skull remaining incomplete.

In this later study, the authors described in detail the skull of *Rapetosaurus* based upon the following material collected from the Anembalemba Member of the Maevarano Formation (Maastrichtian), in the Mahajanga Basin of northwestern Madagascar (see Rogers, Hartman and Krause 2000): The adult holo-

type skull (UA 8698), including the right maxilla with teeth, the left maxilla, right lacrimal, left jugal, nasals, right quadrate, pterygoids, a partial basioccipital, a right paroccipital process, left dentary containing 11 teeth, angulars, right surangular, and five associated teeth; also, the following referred juvenile specimens: FMNH PR 2184 — right exoccipital/opisthotic, supraoccipital, and laterosphenoid; FMNH PR 2185 — right prefrontal, right and left frontals; FMNH PR 2186 — right prefrontal; FMNH PR 2187 — left surangular; FMNH PR 2188 — right parietal; FMNH PR 2189 — left squamosal; FMNH PR 2190 — right quadrate; FMNH PR 2191 — left pterygoid; FMNH PR 2192 — right exoccipital-opisthotic; FMNH PR 2194 — right angular; FMNH PR 2196 — three associated teeth; and FMNH PR 2197 — fused basioccipital, basisphenoid, and parasphenoid.

Curry Rogers and Forster (2004) observed that the skull of *Rapetosaurus* is similar in overall shape to the skulls of diplodocids, having an elongated snout and retracted external nares yet, the skull is more similar to those of macronarians (*e.g.*, *Camarasaurus*, *Brachiosaurus*) in that the teeth are distributed throughout the upper and lower jaws, and in the articulations of the bones comprising the margins of the external narial region and the orbit. Among the most diagnostic elements of the skull are the maxilla, basicranium, paroccipital process, pterygoid, enlarged antorbital fenestra, anteroventrally oriented braincase, and mandible (see *S3* for diagnosis).

Taking into account the paucity of cranial material known for other sauropods, Curry Rogers and Forster (2004) pointed out that the skull of this dinosaur "has great potential to clarify higher and lower level titanosaur phylogeny." Moreover, based upon their description of this skull, it seems that there "may not be a narrowly constrained baüplan for the skull of titanosaurs and that generalizations about evolution based on the previously known and fragmentary fossil data require reevaluation.

In their review of the Sauropoda, Upchurch, Barrett and Dodson (2004) pointed out that many of the characters of the tail and appendicular skeleton, listed by Curry Rogers and Forster in their original diagnosis of *Rapetosaurus krausei*, have a broader distribution among Titanosauria.

Key references: Curry Rogers and Forster (2001, 2004); Rogers, Hartman and Krause (2000); Upchurch, Barrett and Dodson (2004).

†RAYOSOSAURUS

Saurischia: Eusaurischia: Sauropodomorpha: Sauropoda: Eusauropoda: Neosauropoda: Diplodocoidea: Rebbachisauridae.

Type species: *A. agrioensis* Bonaparte 1996.

Other species: [None.]

Note: Second species *R. tessonei* was referred by Salgado, Garrido, Cocca and Cocca (2004) to the new genus *Limayasaurus* (see entry).

Erratum: In *S1*, the type species of *Raysosaurus* was incorrectly listed as *R. tessonei* rather than *R. agrioensis*.

Key reference: Salgado, Garrido, Cocca and Cocca (2004).

†REVUELTOSAURUS [*nomen dubium*]

New species: *R. hunti* Heckert 2002 ?[*nomen dubium*].

Occurrence of *R. hunti*: Santa Rosa Formation, New Mexico, Arizona, United States.

Age of *R. hunti*: Late Triassic (latest Carnian/"Adamanian").

Known material of *R. hunti*: Numerous isolated tooth crowns.

Holotype of *R. hunti*: NMMNH P-29358, almost complete tooth crown.

Diagnosis of genus: Moderately large, primitive ornithischian, distinguished from all other known ornithischians by combination of its size (tooth crowns approximately seven to 10 millimeters in height [*i.e.*, length of tooth crown from base to tip, measured perpendicular to base]); numerous small denticles (more than seven per carina); denticles proportionately short, often worn to enamel by precise occlusion; lacking true cingulum involved in mastication; differing from all other known ornithischians (except heterodontosaurids) by having premaxillary tooth crowns approximately twice as tall as maxillary and dentary tooth crowns (Heckert 2002*b*).

Diagnosis of *R. callenderi*: Distinguished by denticles extending equally far down rostral and caudal carinae; denticles very fine basally, coarser apically, fine again near tip; denticles often set lingually near base on both rostral and caudal margin, ranging from approximately 1.5 to 3.3 millimeters; tooth tips and denticles generally worn flat or perpendicular to height of tooth; premaxillary teeth often loss laterally compressed than maxillary and dentary teeth (Heckert 2002*b*).

Diagnosis of *R. hunti*: Distinguished by caudal denticles being slightly coarser, extending farther basally than rostral denticles; denticles generally coarser (1.5 per millimeter, often 1.0 per millimeter); denticles coarsening basally; pronounced bulge on lingual surface, resulting in lingually concave outline in medio-distal views; rostral denticles frequently offset near base lingually, occasionally with carinae bifurcating, resulting in basal denticles labial and lingual to split carina; apex of tooth worn oblique to vertical axis of tooth (down to labial side on lower teeth, down to lingual side on upper teeth [following Thulborn 1971]) (Heckert 2002*b*).

Comments: As noted by Andrew B. Heckert (2002*b*), body fossils belonging to Triassic age ornithischian dinosaurs are extremely rare throughout the world, and the most common Upper Triassic ornithischian is *Revueltosaurus*, a genus known from Chinle Group rocks in both New Mexico and Arizona. Indeed, all large (greater than one centimeter in height) and numerous small ornithischian teeth from the Chinle have been assigned to the type species of

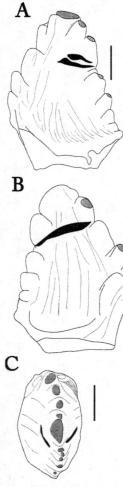

A

B

C

Revueltosaurus hunti,
NMMNH P-29356, holo-
type tooth, in A. labial, B.
lingual, and C. occlusal
views. Scale = 1 mm. (After
Heckert 2002*b*).

this genus, *Revueltosaurus callenderi*, which Adrian P. Hunt named and described in 1989 (see *D:TE*).

In more recent years, however, the validity of *Revueltosaurus* as a valid taxon has been challenged, based upon the proposition that dinosaurian teeth are almost never diagnostic at low taxonomic levels (see Dodson and Dawson 1991; Dodson 1997). Defending the taxonomic position of *Revueltosaurus*, Heckert pointed out the following:

1. Dinosaur teeth are regarded almost universally as diagnostic to family- and higher taxonomic levels, with, especially, all modern diagnoses of Ornithischia including multiple characters based upon teeth (see, for example, Sereno 1986, 1991, 1999*a*; Benton 1990, 1997); Sander 1997).

2. Theropods typically have simpler, more plesiomorphic teeth than do herbivorous dinosaurs in general and ornithischians in particular.

3. Detailed studies (*e.g.*, Currie, Rigby and Sloan 1990; Farlow, Brinkman, Abler and Currie (1991) have shown that at least several Cretaceous theropod species (several of them sympatric) can be identified by teeth, despite ongoing changes in our understanding of theropod phylogeny (*e.g.*, Sereno 1999*a*; Holtz 2000).

Accepting that isolated teeth can be identified as ornithischian and may sometimes be diagnostic to the level of species, Heckert further stated that isolated teeth referred to *Revueltosaurus* can be readily identified as ornithischian based on the following synapomorphies (*e.g.*, Sereno 1999*a*) of Ornithischia: Tooth crown low, triangular in lateral aspect (Sereno 1986); recurvature absent from maxillary and dentary teeth (Sereno 1986); well-developed neck separating tooth crown from root (Sereno 1986); denticles large, prominent, arranged at 45 degrees or greater to mesial and distal edges; premaxillary teeth distinct from dentary and maxillary teeth; maxillary and dentary teeth asymmetrical in mesial and distal aspects (Hunt and Lucas 1994).

In this current study, Heckert listed and fully described myriad teeth that have been referred to *R. callenderi* (see paper for complete details). Also, Heckert noted that a few ornithischian teeth from the Bull Canyon Formation of New Mexico and in the NMMNH collections may belong to *R. callenderi*, but are too incomplete to make a positive identification as such. These include NMMNH P-17362, two teeth, the best preserved of these specimens, resembling the maxillary and dentary teeth of *R. callenderi*; NMMNH P-17382, a single tooth, similar in size to *R. callenderi* teeth, but with finer (four plus per two millimeters) and shorter denticles; and NMMNH P-17187, an indeterminate specimen similar in size to teeth of *R. callenderi*.

In addition to retaining *Revueltosaurus callenderi* as a valid type species belonging to the Ornithischia, Heckert named and described a second and more derived, yet older (latest Carnian, based on such age-diagnostic taxa as the phytosaurs *Angistorhinus* and *Rutiodon*; see Hunt, Lucas and Bircheff 1993; Lucas and Hunt 1995) species, *R. hunti* (previously reported on briefly by Heckert 2002*a*, although neither named nor described at that time) established on a nearly complete tooth crown (NMMNH P-29357) from the Los Esteros Member of the Santa Rosa Formation (Chinle Group), Santa Fe County, New Mexico. Referred specimens collected from the Santa Rosa Formation in New Mexico and Arizona include the following: (Paratypes) NMMNH P-29358, nearly complete crown, and NMMNH P29359, incomplete crown; (topotypes) NMMNH P-29347–29354, UCMP V173839, V173840, and V173841, incomplete crowns (UCMP specimens from the Blue Hills, in east-central Arizona); and UCMP V139563–V139575, incomplete crowns (from the Blue Hills, Arizona). All of these specimens, Heckert (2002*b*) noted, had formerly been referred to the type species.

Other specimens cited by Heckert (2002*b*) as possibly belonging to *R. hunti*, but which are too poorly preserved for positive referral to that species, include the following: NMMNH P-29355, a badly broken and worn tooth apparently having the general shape as teeth of *R. hunti*, particularly the prominent lingual bulge; NMMNH P-29359, a small, broken recurved crown with deflected denticles; UCMP V139565, a badly eroded, broken tooth having an expanded base; and UCMP V139572, broken basally and caudally, matching other UCMP specimens in general shape.

As Heckert (2002*b*) pointed out, the occurrence of *R. callenderi* is limited to the lower part of Painted Desert Member of the Petrified Forest Formation and the Bull Canyon Formation, while being "conspicuously absent higher in the stratigraphic section," possibly suggests that the biochron of this species "is shorter than the Revueltian and may perhaps represent only an early Revueltian age." Therefore, *Revueltosaurus*—represented by teeth that are locally abundant, easy to identify, and have a restricted stratigraphic range—is an ideal index fossil (see, for example, Padian 1990; Hunt and Lucas 1994). As suggested by some authors (*e.g.*, Hunt 2001), the range of the species *R. callenderi* may subdivide "Revueltian" time; similarly, according to Heckert (2002*b*), *R. hunti* may correlate "Adamanian" strata.

In their review of basal ornithischians, Norman, Witmer and Weishampel (2004*a*)—presumably written before *R. hunti* was described—regarded *R. callendri* as a *nomen dubium* (see "Systematics" chapter).

Note: According to Heckert (2002*b*), numerous other ornithischian teeth that have been incorrectly referred to *Revueltosaurus*. Among these, Heckert (2002*b*) regarded specimens "possibly referrable" to *R. callenderi* by Kaye and Padian (1994) as not referrable to that species, including teeth of *Tecovasaurus* plus a new taxon included in Heckert's dissertation. Other teeth, Heckert (2002*b*) noted, bearing the same MNA catalog numbers, represent "indeterminate [possibly yet more basal] ornithischians and nondinosaurian archosaurs."

Key references: Benton (1990, 1997); Currie, Rigby and Sloan (1990); Dodson and Dawson (1991); Farlow, Brinkman, Abler and Currie (1991); Heckert (2002*a*, 2002*b*); Holtz (2000); Hunt (1989); Hunt and Lucas (1994, 1995); Hunt, Lucas and Bircheff (1993); Kaye and Padian (19940; Padian (1990); Norman, Witmer and Weishampel (2004*a*); Sander (1997); Sereno (1986, 1991, 1999*a*); Thulborn (1971).

†**RHABDODON**—(=*Oligosaurus*, *Ornithomerus*; =?*Mochlodon*, ?*Onychosaurus*)

Ornithischia: Predentata: Genasauria: Cerapoda: Ornithopoda: Euornithopoda: Iguanodontia: Rhabdodontidae.

Diagnosis of genus (as for type species): Two foramina on lateral surface of surangular; large, oblique shelf between alveolar row and lateral wall of dentary; nine dentary alveoli; dentary with parallel dorsal and ventral margins; maxillary teeth having parallel ridges, without prominent primary ridge; dentary teeth having prominent primary ridge shifted slightly distally from midline of tooth; enamel thicker on buccal side of maxillary teeth and lingual side of dentary teeth; cervical vertebrae having broad, well-developed neural spines with cranial orientation, centra opisthocoelous; dorsal vertebrae with very large neural spines (64 percent total height); amphicoelous to platycoelous centra; sacrum comprising six true fused sacral vertebrae and one unfused dorsosacral; fused sacral neural spines; scapula with strongly widened distal extremity; dorsal and ventral margins of scapula concave; dorsal process of scapula less developed than ventral process; well-developed acromial process; coracoid having prominent sternal process, coracoid foramen closed to glenoid cavity; prepubic blade long, straight, laterally flattened, obturator foramen closed; blade of ischium straight, laterally flattened, distal end wide; obturator process on proximal half of shaft of ischium; femur having prominent bulge on caudal surface of shaft; femur longer than

Copyright © Berislav Krzic.

Life restoration of *Rhabdodon priscus*, drawn by Berislav Krzic.

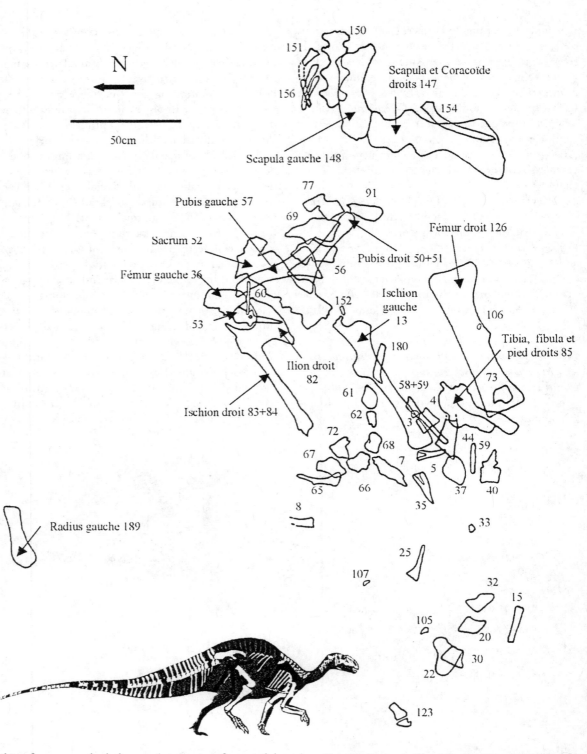

Excavation map of the Couperigne locality at Vitrolles, Bouches-du-Rhône, France, with bones (MHN-AIX collection, labels corresponding to references in the text) of partial skeleton of *Rhabdodon priscus*, and the partially reconstructed skeleton. Scale = 50 cm. (After Pincemaille-Quillevere 2002, modified after Garcia, Pincemaille, Vianey-Liaud, Marandat, Lorenz, Cheylan, Cappetta, Michaux and Sudre 1999.)

N

50cm

150
151
156
Scapula et Coracoïde droits 147
154
Scapula gauche 148

77
Pubis gauche 57
91
69
Sacrum 52
Fémur droit 126
Pubis droit 50+51
56
Fémur gauche 36
152
Ischion gauche 13
60
106
53
180
Tibia, fibula et pied droits 85
Ilion droit 82
73
58+59
Ischion droit 83+84
61
4
62
3
44
59
72
68
5
67
7
65
66
37
40
8
35
33
Radius gauche 189
25
107
32
15
105
20
22
30
123

tibia; four ungual phalanges (suggesting four pedal digits) (Pincemaille-Quillevere 2002).

In 2002, Pincemaille-Quillevere described an incomplete, partially articulated skeleton (MHN-AIX PV 1995, numbers 1–91, 99–107, 122–126, 133–142, 147–148, 150–152, 154–156, 158, 168–174, 180, 189, and 190) of the ornithopod type species *Rhabdodon priscus*, recovered from "Early Rognacian gray marls"

(see Garcia, Pincemaille, Vianey-Liaud, Marandat, Lorenz, Cheylan, Cappetta, Michaux and Sudre 1999) of the Lower Cretaceous (early Maastrichtian; see Westphal and Durand 1990) rocks at Couperigne, in the area of Vitrolles, Bouches-du-Rhône, France (see S2).

Pincemaille-Quillevere described this new specimen in detail and proposed a new diagnosis of the genus and type species, based primarily on the MHN-AIX material, but also including in her study the following specimens: (lectotype) MPLM 30, fragment of left dentary from the "Early Rogcacian gray marl," Tunnel de la Nerthe (Bouches-du-Rhône); and (paratypes) MPLM 31, fragment of right dentary, MPLM 32, fragment of indeterminate dentary, MPLM 34, caudal dorsal vertebra, MPLM 36, two fused sacral vertebrae, MPLM 51, left radius, MPLM 61, distal end of right femur, MPLM 59, proximal end of right femur, and MPLM 60, right tibia.

As observed by Pincemaille-Quillevere, the lectotype of *R. priscus*, although having deteriorated since being described by Matheron (1869), contains several incomplete crowns, each displaying a prominent primary ridge on the lingual surface. This, Pincemaille-Quillevere proposed, seems to be a diagnostic character for the genus. Consequently, the specimen from Couperigne is clearly referrable to *Rhabdodon*. Furthermore, the paratype proximal right femur exhibits a strong lateral bulge on the caudal surface of its end, although the cranial surface possesses a rather shallow median groove; these characters suggested to Pincemaille-Quillevere that the new partial skeletons can be referred to *R. priscus*.

Pincemaille-Quillevere noted that *R. priscus* shares a number of anatomical characters with *Tenontosaurus tilletti*, among these primarily the following: Dentary with parallel margins; dentary without diastema; ischial peduncle of ilium flat, rugose, cranial surface laterally oriented forming caudal surface of acetabulum; well-developed prepubic process, forming laterally flattened blade; cranial end of prepubic blade rounded, ventrally oriented; prepubic process with small process in middle of its ventral edge; obturator process on proximal third of total length of ischium, its distal end thickened; caudal end of ischial blade flaring gently in lateral view, curving ventrally; four pedal digits.

Additionally, Pincemaille-Quillevere found *R. priscus* to be "characterized by a series of peculiar characters"—i.e., absence of premaxillary teeth; parallel margins of dentary; strong primary ridge on lingual surface of dentary teeth; enamel thickened on lingual surface of dentary and buccal surface of maxillary teeth; proximally located obturator process of ischium; femur with broad, deep caudal intercondylar groove and not very deep cranial intercondylar groove; and prominent, nonpendant fourth trochanter. Such characters have been listed as diagnostic of the Iguanodontia (see Norman 1984a, 1986; Sereno 1986).

Consequently, Pincemaille-Quillevere concluded that, based mostly on the MHN-AIX partial skeleton, *Rhabdodon priscus* is a basal member of the Iguanodontia [as suggested by Weishampel, Jianu,

Csiki and Norman 1998] and is closely related to *T. tilletii*.

Weishampel, Jianu, Csiki and Norman (2003), in describing the new genus *Zalmoxes* (see entry) and introducing the new family Rhabdodontidae (see "Systematics" chapter) to include *Rhabdodon*, reassessed the small holotype material (including a dentary, isolated teeth, a femur, and other material) of the type species *Mocholodon suessi* (see *Mochlodon* entry).

Key reference: Bunzel (1871); Garcia, Pincemaille, Vianey-Liaud, Marandat, Lorenz, Cheylan, Cappetta, Michaux and Sudre (1999); Matheron 1869); Norman (1984a, 1986); Pincemaille-Quillevere (2002); Sereno (1986); Weishampel, Jianu, Csiki and Norman (1998, 2003); Westphal and Durand (1990).

RINCHENIA   Barsbold 1997
Saurischia: Eusaurischia: Theropoda: Neotheropoda: Tetanurae: Avetheropoda: Coelurosauria: Tyrannoraptora: Maniraptoriformes: Maniraptora: ?Metornithes: Oviraptorosauria: Oviraptoridae:
Name derivation: "Rinchen [Barsbold]."
Type species: *R. mongoliensis* (Barsbold 1986).
Occurrence: Nemegt Formation, Omnogov, Mongolia.
Age: Late Cretaceous (Campanian–Maastrichtian).
Known material/holotype: GIN 100/35, incomplete skull.

Diagnosis: Distinguished from *Oviraptor philoceratops* by thick, extremely tall, "cupola-shaped" crest extending along upper part of skull from premaxilla to parietals (Barsbold 1986).

Comments: The genus *Rinchenia* was founded upon a skull (GI 100/35) collected from the Nemegt Formation, Altan-Uul, Omnogov, Mongolia. This specimen was originally identified by Barsbold (1981) as pertaining to the genus *Ingenia*, after which Barsbold (1986) referred it to *Oviraptor* as a new species, *O. mongoliensis* (see *D:TE* for an illustration of the holotype). More than a decade later, Barsbold (1997), in a chapter on Oviraptorosauria in the book *Encyclopedia of Dinosaurs* (see Currie and Padian 1997), renamed this taxon *Rinchenia mongoliensis*.

Barsbold (1986) briefly described this type species as having a crest, the apex of which is above the orbit rather than at the front of the skull (unlike the condition in *Oviraptor*), and a skull measuring about 16 centimeters in length. Later, Barsbold (1997) added that this species compares in size with *Oviraptor*, differing from that genus in having a more lightly built postcranium, a skull with a higher, dome-shaped crest incorporating the parietals in addition to the premaxillae, nasals, and frontals, and in having comparatively rather low cervical vertebrae.

The crest of this species, as speculated by Bara-bold, Maryańska and Osmólska (1990), may have constituted a display structure or served to aid the dinosaur in passing through obstructions (*e.g.*, vegetation).

Osmólska, Currie and Barsbold (2004), in their review of the Oviraptorosauria, added the following details concerning *Rinchenia mongoliensis*: Six sacral and 32 caudal vertebrae; ilium deep, with convex, cranially rising dorsal margin, pointed cranioventral process on preacetabular portion, postacetabular process half as deep as preacetabular process; preacetabular and postacetabular processes of approximately same length.

To date of this writing, *Rinchenia* has not yet been formally described.

Key references: Barsbold (1981, 1986, 1997); Osmólska, Currie and Barsbold (2004).

RINCONSAURUS   Calvo and Riga 2003

Saurischia: Eusaurischia: Sauropodomorpha: Sauropoda: Eusauropoda: Neosauropoda: Macronaria: Titanosauriformes: Titanosauria.

Name derivation: "Rincón de los Sauces" + Greek *sauros* = "lizard."

Type species: *R. caudamirus* Calvo and González Riga 2003.

Other species: [None.]

Occurrence: Neuquén Subgroup, Neuquén Province, Argentina.

Age: Late Cretaceous (Turonian–Coniacian).

Known material: Miscellaneous associated cranial and postcranial bones, teeth, juvenile and adult.

Holotype: MRS-Pv 26, 13 articulated proximal-middle and middle-distal caudal vertebrae, ilia.

Diagnosis of genus (as for type species): Slender "titanosaurid" characterized by the following autapomorphies: neural spines in midcranial dorsal vertebrae inclined caudally more than 60 degrees with respect to vertical; middle caudal vertebrae having bony processes supporting articular facets of postzygapophyses; distal caudal vertentarae with procoelous centra, eventual intercalation of series of amphicoelous-biconvex or amphicoelous-opisthocoelous-biconvex centra (Calvo and González Riga 2003).

Comments: A slendor titanosaur, the genus *Rinconsaurus* was established upon 13 caudal vertebrae and two ilia (MRS-Pv 26), found by Gabriel Benítez in 1997, at the Cañadón Rio Seco site in the Upper Cretaceous (Turonian–Coniacian; see Leanza and Hugo 2001) Neuquén Subgroup (Neuquén Group), north of Rincón de los Sauces, Neuquén Province, northern Patagonia, Argentina. Paratype specimens of the type species *R. caudamirus*, recovered from the same locality, include a prefrontal (MRS-Pv 102), an angular and surangular (MRS-Pv 112), teeth (MRS-Pv 117 and 263), cervical vertebrae (MRS-Pv 2, 3, 4, 8, and 21), dorsal vertebrae (MRS-Pv 5 [three articulated craniomedial neural arches possibly associated

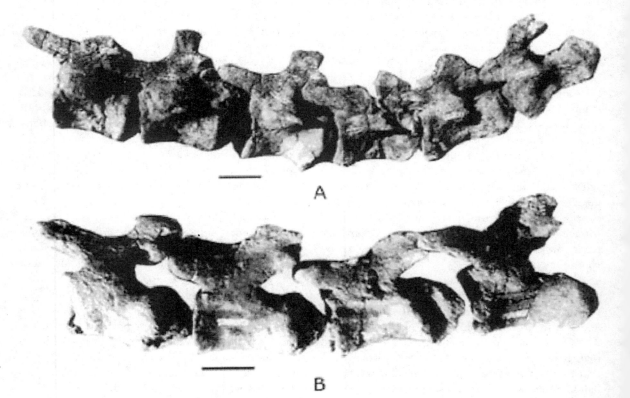

A

B

Rinconsaurus caudamirus, A. MRS-Pv 26, articulated series of proximal-middle caudal vertebrae, and B. MRS-Pv 27, paratype articulated series of middle caudal vertebrae (lateral views). Scale = 5 cm. (After Calvo and Riga 2003.)

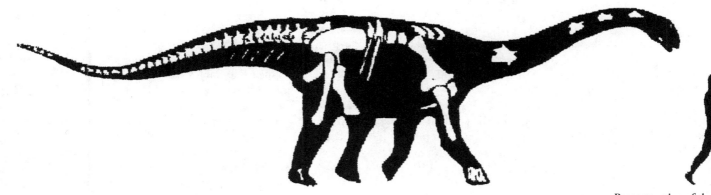

Reconstruction of the skeleton of *Rinconsaurus caudamirus*, based upon holotype and paratype specimens. (After Calvo and González Riga 2003.)

with the holotype], 6, 9, 11, 13, 16–19), proximal caudal vertebrae (MRS-Pv 22–25, and 27), middle caudals (MRS-Pv 27–28 and 31), distal caudals (MRS-Pv 29–30 and 32–40), hemal arches (MRS-Pv 20, 42, 93, 99, 109, and 113), a scapula and coracoid (MRS-Pv 43), sternal plates (MRS-Pv 46 and 103–104), a humerus (MRS-Pv 47), metacarpals (MRS-Pv 98), ischia (MRS-Pv 94 and 101), ilia (MRS-Pv 96), pubes (MRS-Pv 97 and 100), femora (MRS-Pv 49 and 92), and a metatarsal (MRS-Pv 111). All of the above specimens represent a total of three individuals, including one juvenile and two adults (Calvo and González Riga 2003).

Calvo and González Riga estimated the total length of an adult individual of *R. caudamirus* to be approximately 11 meters (about 37 feet).

In performing a phylogenetic analysis for *Rinconsaurus*, Calvo and González Riga basically followed the schemes proposed earlier by Salgado, Coria and Calvo (1997) and Wilson and Sereno (1999) while incorporating new data gleaned from *R. caudamirus*. This analysis was based on 46 characters, regarding as the outgroup *Camarasaurus grandis*, and as the ingroup *Brachiosaurus brancai*, *Andesaurus delgadoi*, *Malawisaurus dixeyi*, *Aeolosaurus rionegrinus*, *Lirainosaurus astibae*, *Alamosaurus sanjuanensis*, *Neuquensaurus australis*, *Isisaurus* [=*Titanosaurus* of their usage] *colberti*, *Opisthocoelicaudia skarzynskii*, *Saltasaurus loricatus*, and *R. caudamirus*.

Contrary to other recent analyses (see "Systematics" chapter, *e.g.*, Wilson and Upchurch 2003), Calvo and González Riga accepted the "Titanosauridae" as a valid family, defined as by Salgado *et al.* "as the clade including the most recent common ancestor of *Malawisaurus*, *Epachthosaurus*, *Argentinosaurus*, *Opisthocoelicaudia*, *Aeolosaurus*, *Alamosaurus*, Saltasaurinae and all its descendants," and diagnosed by five synapomorphies defined by delayed optimization (*i.e.*, teeth chisel-like; absence of cervical pleurocoels divided by septa; absence of hyposphene-hypantrum articulation in caudal dorsal vertebrae; centra of proximal caudal vertebrae strongly procoelous, distal condyles prominent; and semilunar sternal plates).

Calvo and González Riga excluded from their diagnosis of "Titanosauridae" two characters — middle and distal caudal centra strongly procoelous, condyles prominent; and six sacral vertebrae — proposed by Salgado *et al.* as synapomorphies of that group, pointing out that the first is not found in *Malawisaurus*, while the second is unknown in most of the taxa studied.

As Calvo and González Riga noted, the "Titanosauridae" have traditionally been diagnosed by the presence of strongly procoelous vertebrae throughout the caudal series (*e.g.*, see Huene 1929; McIntosh 1990). The discovery of *Rinconsaurus* as well as other "titanosaurid" specimens (see Powell 1986), however, have established that this was neither a uniform nor permanent character. In *Rinconsaurus*, the caudal sequence is typically strongly procoelous, discontinued by amphicoelous, opisthocoelous, and biconvex centra (this unusual morphology constituting the first such occurrence reported in the Sauropoda). However, in a new "titanosaurid" from Mendoza Province, the middle caudal centra are slightly procoelous with reduced distal condyles, associated with the more typically strongly procoelous distal caudals.

The authors' analysis further found a clade comprising *Aeolosaurus* plus *Rinconsaurus* to have a sister-group relationship with a clade (*Opisthocoelicaudia* plus (*Alamosaurus* plus (*Neuquensaurus* plus *Saltasaurus*))). These two genera, according to Calvo and González Riga, are united by the presence of relatively long prezygapophyses, a single nonexclusive character also found in *Titanosaurus* sp. (DMG "Series C" from Brazil; Powell 1987) and *Malawisaurus* (see Jacobs, Winkler, Downs and Gomani 1993).

Key references: Calvo and González Riga (2003); Jacobs, Winkler, Downs and Gomani (1993); Huene (1929); Mcintosh (1990); Powell (1986, 1987); Salgado, Coria and Calvo (1997); Wilson and Sereno (1998); Wilson and Upchurch (2003).

†RIOJASAURUS

Saurischia: Eusaurischia: Sauropodomorpha: Sauropoda: Prosauropoda: Anchisauria: Melanorosauridae.

Diagnosis of genus (as for type species): Autapomorphies including the following: Premaxilla having rostral prominence; rounded lacrimal-prefrontal crest; basipterygoid process with expanded distal end; coracoid having cranial process (Galton and Upchurch 2004*a*).

Comment: In their review of the Prosauropoda, Galton and Upchurch (2004*a*) *Riojasaurus incertus* (see *D:TE*), a type species referred by these authors to Prosauropoda *incertae sedis*.

Key reference: Galton and Upchurch (2004*a*).

†ROCASAURUS

Saurischia: Eusaurischia: Sauropodomorpha: Sauropoda: Eusauropoda: Neosauropoda: Macronaria: Titanosauriformes: Titanosauria: Lithostrotia.

Diagnosis of genus (as for type species): Deep cavity on ventral surface of caudal vertebrae, divided by longitudinal ridge (also in *Saltasaurus*); caudal articular condyle of caudal vertebrae depressed relative to centrum, oriented cranioventrally; distal expansion on lateral margin of pubis; ischium with prominent lamina (Upchurch, Barrett and Dodson 2004).

Comment: In their review of the Sauropoda, Upchurch, Barrett and Dodson (2004) rediagnosed the type species *Rocasaurus muniozi* (see *S2*).

Key reference: Upchurch, Barrett and Dodson (2004).

†RUEHLEIA

Saurischia: Eusaurischia: Sauropodomorpha: Sauropoda: Prosauropoda *incertae sedis*.

Diagnosis of genus (as for type species): Three-vertebrae sacrum having dorsosacral (caudosacral in *Plateosaurus*); manus with three large carpals with complex articular surfaces; ilium having large pubic peduncle, extremely short and small preacetabular process (plesiomorphic); length of articular surface of proximal end of pubis (for ilium) much longer than wide, articular process short (equal to approximately half width of iliac surface (Galton and Upchurch 2004*a*).

Comment: In their review of the Prosauropoda, Galton and Upchurch (2004*a*) rediagnosed the type species *Ruehleia bedheimensis* (see *S3*), which they regarded as Prosauropoda *incertae sedis*.

Key reference: Galton and Upchurch (2004*a*).

RUGOPS   Sereno, Wilson and Conrad 2004

Saurischia: Eusaurischia: Theropoda: Neotheropoda: Ceratosauria: Abelisauroidea: Abelisauridae.

Name derivation: Latin *ruga* = "wrinkle" + Greek *opsi* = "face."

Type species: *R. primus* Sereno, Wilson and Conrad 2004.

Other species: [None.]

Occurrence: Echkar Formation, near In Abangharit, Niger Republic.

Age: Middle Cretaceous (Cenomanian).

Known material/holotype: MNN IGU1, partial cranium lacking caudolateral portions of skull roof and palate.

Diagnosis of genus (as for type species): Characterized by small fenestra in skull roof between prefrontal, frontal, postorbital, and lacrimal, row of seven small invaginated depressions on dorsal surface of each nasal (Sereno, Wilson and Conrad 2004).

Comments: Documenting unequivocally the presence of basal abelisaurids in Africa, the hornless genus *Rugops* was established on a partial skull (MNN IGU1) recovered from the Ehkar Formation, near In Abangharit, Niger Republic (Sereno, Wilson and Conrad 2004).

In describing the type species *Rugops primius*, Sereno *et al.* observed a number of abelisaurid features, including the following: U-shaped dental arcade; broad maxillary-jugal contact; socket on maxilla for rostroventral process of nasal; subrectangular aleoli. Derived features of latest Cretaceous abelisaurids

Rugops primus life restoration by artist Todd Marshall reconstructed with medium crests, illustration prepared under the supervision of Paul C. Sereno.

not found in this species include a thickened skull roof, cranial horn(s), and robust orbital brows. As noted by Sereno *et al.*, "The incipient orbital brow in *Rugops* suggests that the fully formed lacrimal-post-orbital brown in later abelisaurid evolved independently from that in other theropod groups."

In 2002, Lamanna, Martinez and Smith described a maxilla from rocks of similar age in Patagonia. According to Sereno *et al.*, the remarkable similarity between this maxilla and that of *Rugops* (almost identical pattern of external ornamentation [an often diagnostic feature of Abelisauridae]; predominance of grooves over pits under antorbital fenestra; and, internally, relatively elevated position of dental lamina and fine striae marking surface) suggests a close relationship between the South American and Africa taxa.

In a brief article published in *National Geographic* magazine (see Moffet 2004), Sereno stated that the two rows of holes found on both sides of the snout "could have anchored ornamental crests — headgear that served to make an impression on potential mates or enemies." Sereno also noted in the article that the jaws of *Rugops* were not "designed for bone crushing, and that its short snout indicates it may have been a scavenger."

A reconstructed skull cast of *Rugops primus* as well as a fleshed-out sculpture of the head, both made by University of Chicago fossil preparator Tyler Keillor, went on display at Chicago's Garfield Park Conservatory in June, 2004, becoming part of the temporary "Giants: African Dinosaurs" exhibition.

Note: Until recently, abelisauroids have been documented almost exclusively in South America, Madagascar, and India, this distribution having been used as evidence supporting the "Africa-first" model for the fragmentation of Gondwana" (see Sampson, Witmer, Forster, Krause, O'Connor, Dodson, and Ravoavy 1998). However, fossils reported by Sereno *et al.* from three Cretaceous stratigraphic levels of Niger constitute unequivocal evidence that a hornless abelisaurid (*Rugops*, approximately 95 million years ago), early Abelisauroids (abelisaurids and noasaurids, about 110 million years ago; see *Deltadromeus* entry), and their immediate antecedents (about 130 to 110 million years ago; see *Spinostropheus* entry) have challenged that hypothesis. According to Sereno *et al.*, these reported materials collectively "fill in the early history of abelisauroid radiation and provide key

Rugops primus, MNN IGU1, holotype incomplete skull, a. invaginations 3–6 of right nasal, dorsal view; b. cranium, dorsal view; c. cranium, lateral view; d. third to fifth alveoli of left maxilla, ventral view; and e. comparison of left maxillae of (left) *R. primus* and (right) contemporaneous abelisaurid from Patagonia (Lamanna, Martinez and Smith 2002). Scale = (a, d) 2 cm., (e) 10 cm. (After Sereno, Wilson and Conrad 2004.)

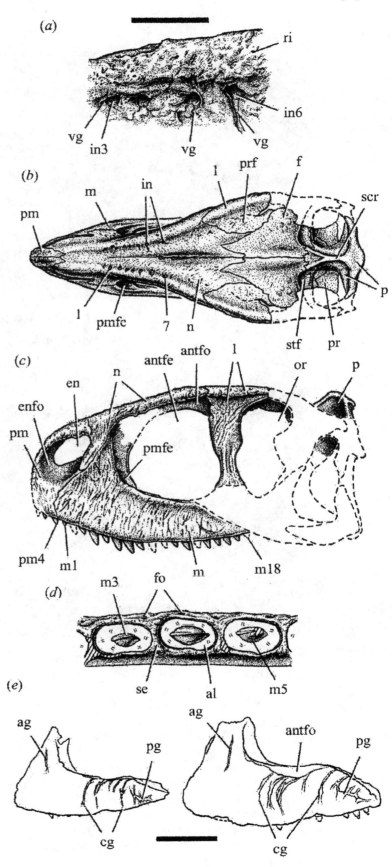

Photograph by Allen A. Debus.

Tyler Keillor's life restoration sculpture and cast of reconstructed holotype skull (MNN IGU1) of *Rugops primus*, as displayed in 2004 in "Giants: African Dinosaurs," an exhibit at Garfield Park Conservatory, Chicago.

evidence for continued faunal exchange among Gondwanan landmasses until the end of the Early Cretaceous (*ca.* 100 Myr ago)."

Sereno *et al.* proposed the following alternative "pan–Gondwanan" model (*e.g.*, Sereno, Beck, Dutheil, Iarochene, Larsson, Lyon, Magwene, Sidor, Varricchio and Wilson 1996; Scotese 2001): During the Early Cretaceous, three narrow, most likely intermittent, passages connected the major Gondwanan landmasses. These passages were severed during a relatively short interval of time (from the latest Albian/earliest Cenomanian to the Coniacian, *ca.* 100 to 90 million years ago). A trans–Atlantic land bridge present until the end of the Early Cretaceous distin-

guishes the model proposed by Sereno *et al.* (2004) from that of Sampson *et al.*, at the same time more closely matching recent palaeocoastline maps published by Scotese. No earlier than the end of the Albian or beginning of the Late Cretaceous, a significantly deep, permanent seaway was in place between Africa and South America. "The absence of a hierarchical biogeographic pattern among fossils or recent organisms from Gondwanan landmasses (Maisey 1993)," Sereno *et al.* (2004) concluded, "is consistent with a narrow time interval for their permanent separation."

Key references: Lamanna, Martinez and Smith (2002); Maisey (1993; Moffet (2004); Sampson,

Witmer, Forster, Krause, O'Connor, Dodson, and Ravoavy (1998); Scotese (2001); Sereno, Beck, Dutheil, Iarochene, Larsson, Lyon, Magwene, Sidor, Varricchio and Wilson (1996); Sereno, Wilson and Conrad (2004).

†SALTASAURUS — (=?*Loricosaurus*, ?*Microcoelus*)

Saurischia: Eusaurischia: Sauropodomorpha: Sauropoda: Eusauropoda: Neosauropoda: Macronaria: Titanosauriformes: Titanosauria: Lithostrotia: Saltasauridae: Saltasaurinae.

Diagnosis of genus (as for type species): Basal tubera fused; proximal caudal vertebrae about twice as wide (measured between tips of caudal ribs) as high; proximal caudal ribs robust, expanded dorsoventrally at distal ends; proximal and midcaudal centra with midline ridge on ventral surfaces within ventral fossae (Upchurch, Barrett and Dodson 2004).

Comments: Originally described by José F. Bonaparte and Jaime Eduardo Powell in 1980, the type species *Saltasaurus loricatus*—founded upon a number of specimens from the Upper Cretaceous ("Senonian," ?Campanian, or Maastrichtian) Lecho Formation, Balbuena Subgroup, Salta Group, El Brete (locality), Department of Candelaria, southern part of Salta Province, Argentina, and the first for which "armor" was unequivocally reported (see "Note," below, and *D:TE*) in a sauropod — was redescribed by Powell (2003) in his study of South American "titanosaurid" dinosaurs.

Powell listed the following material that has been referred to *S. loricatus* and which would figure into his description of that species: Specimens designated PVL 4017 and as CNS-V 10.023 and 10.024 representing at least five adult and subadult individuals, these including three distinct cranial fragments, one axis, vertebrae (14 cervicals, 20 dorsals, three sacrals, and 26 caudals), four scapulae, three coracoids, four sternal plates, 10 humeri, five ulnae, four radii, five metacarpals, five ilia, four pubes, two ischia, five femora, five tibiae, four fibulae, seven metatarsals, six dermal plates, plus four associated small dermal ossicles.

In redescribing this genus and type species, Powell found *Saltasaurus* to be closest, in its affinities, to *Neuquensaurus*, both genera being represented by relatively small to medium-sized forms, and exhibiting various morphological and proportional resemblances in their limb bones. Moreover, these taxa share depressed caudal centra having cancellous structures in at least one area of the sequence, differing in their degree of development. Other differences separating *Saltasaurus* from *Neuquensaurus* include the following—(in *Saltasaurus*) longer, more expanded preacetabular projections of iliac laminae; first caudal procoelous (rather than biconvex); ventral depression having sagittal lamina (very broad in *Neuquensaurus*, usually showing no trace of this lamina); all caudal centra cancellous (restricted to proximal caudals in *Neuquensaurus*); scapula broader, lamina fusing to proximal part, making greater angle with crest bounding supraglenoid depression.

As Powell pointed out, both the braincase and axial skeleton of *S. loricatus* display sets of derived characters indicative of an advanced "titanosaurid," this assessment being consistent with the dinosaur's late appearance in the late Senonian of South America. Previously reported differences in some of the material from El Brete were provisionally interpreted by Powell "as owing to individual or sexual variation."

Note: Salgado (2004) published a survey report of titanosaurian osseous plates — "armor" that has been referred to such taxa as *Saltasaurus*— collected from two localities, Lago Pellegrini-Cinco Saltos and Salitral

Saltasaurus loricatus, reconstructed skeleton based upon disarticulated remains of different individuals collected from the El Brete locality, Salta Province, Argentina. (After Powell 2003.)

Life restoration of *Saltasaurus loricatus* by E. Guanuco. (After Powell 2003.)

Moreno, in Río Negro Province, Argentina. Salgado reviewed the history of discoveries of such plates, described these ossifications in detail, reported histological observations, and cited various previously published speculations as to their possible functions (see paper for details).

In describing these ossifications, Salgado noted that most of the plates are symmetrical, these having been located at the midline of body above the neural spines; a relatively small number are asymmetrical and were positioned laterally on both sides of the body. Histologically, the plates consist ventrally of cancellous bone and externally by Haversian bone; Sharpey's fibers are present mainly in the periphery on the dorsal surface of these ossifications.

As Salgado stressed, although a number of postulations have been put forth over the years attempting to explain the functions of these dermal plates (*e.g.*, thermoregulation, calcium storage, protection, ornamentation), no researcher had yet offered a hy-

pothesis suggesting their primary function. It was Salgado's opinion that the rise in titanosaurs of bony plates and ossicles could "reflect the implementation of an evolutionary process involving changes in the distribution of the osseous matter during growth, or the consequence of a difference between the deposition rate of bony tissue and the growth rate of the animal." Other previously suggested functions for these ossifications, Salgado speculated, may have developed subsequently.

Key references: Bonaparte and Powell (1980); Powell (2003); Salgado (2004); Upchurch, Barrett and Dodson (2004).

†**SARCOSAURUS** [*nomen dubium*]
Saurischia: Eusaurischia: Eusaurischia: Theropoda:
   Neotheropoda: Ceratosauria: ?Coelophysoidea:
Type species: *S. woodi* Andrews 1921 [*nomen dubium*].
Other species: ?*S. andrewsi* Huene 1932 [*nomen dubium*].

Comments: In a review of the available materials pertaining to coelophysoid theropods from the Early Jurassic of Europe, Carrano and Sampson (2004) addressed the two species of the genus *Sarcosaurus*— the type species *S. woodi* Andrews 1921 and the tentatively referred species ?*S. andrewsi* Huene 1932, the former species founded on a vertebral centrum, partial pelvis, and femur (BMNH 4840/1) from the Lower Jurassic (Lower Lias) Barrow-on-Soar, Leicestershire, England, the latter on a right tibia (BMNH R.3542) from the Lower Jurassic (Lower Lias/Hettangian) Angulata Zone of Wilmcote, Warwickshire, England (see *D:TE*).

In examining BMNH 48401/1 of *S. woodi*, Carrano and Sampson (agreeing with Rowe 1989 and Rowe and Gauthier 1990) concluded that the holotype of the type species exhibits no autapomorphies; therefore, the authors regarded *Sarcosaurus woodi* as "a *nomen dubium* based strictly on its preserved morphology, but one that is also probably distinct from other known taxa based on its provenance."

Carrano and Sampson made the following comments regarding *S. woodi* based upon Andrews' original detailed description of the holotype: *Sarcosaurus woodi* resembling both coelophysoids *Liliensternus liliensterni* and *Dilophosaurus wetherilli*, but not referrable to either (*e.g.*, proximal femur strikingly similar to that of *L. liliensterna*, ilium more strongly resembling that of *D. wetherilli*); and *S. woodi* apparently an animal half the size of *D. wetherilli*, comparable in size to *L. liliensterni* (assuming fusion of pelvic structure is reliably indicative of sexual maturity, although *S. woodi* could have grown larger than indicated by the holotype).

In 1932, Huene referred to *Sarcosaurus woodi* a partial postcranial skeleton (Warwick Museum collection; including two dorsal centra, partial right pubis, both femora, right and partial left tibiae, distal fibula, distal left metatarsals II through IV, partial pedal phalanx) recovered from Lower Jurassic (Lower Lias/lower Sinemurian) *bucklandii* zone at Wilmcote, Warwickshire, England.

As Carrano and Sampson noted, this referred specimen— originating from the same stratigraphic level as BMNH 4840/1, but a different locality— seemingly represents a single individual. Unfortunately, there are but few overlapping elements between the referred specimen and the holotype. Furthermore, the dorsal vertebrae seem to belong to different parts of the verebral columns of both specimens, while the referred specimen does not preserve enough of the neural arch for direct comparison with the holotype dorsal. However, Carrano and Sampson stated, the relatively long centra of the Wilmcote specimen suggests affinities with Coelophysoidea, while the lack of

a distinct pleurocoelous foramen in the centrum shows that these vertebrae were most likely situated caudal to the fifth dorsal vertebra.

Comparing the reasonably complete femora of both specimens, Carrano and Sampson noted that, while their shared features are plesiomorphic for Theropoda (*e.g.*, see Holtz 2000; Carrano, Sampson and Forster 2002), "they do not display any features inconsistent with the two specimens belonging to the same genus."

Most importantly, Carrano and Sampson noted, the distal end of the nearly complete right tibia of the Wilmcote specimen displays, in distal aspect, the notched circular profile characteristic of Coelophysoidea (see Carrano *et al.*); and the distal end of the weathered and less complete left tibia has a profile resembling the tibiae of such colophysoids as *Liliensternus*, both bones showing a prominent fibular crest and long flat fibular contact facet (typical for Neotheropoda). None of the other elements preserved in this specimen "are particularly specialized above the basic neotheropod condition."

It was the conclusion of Carrano and Sampson that the Wilmcote specimen preserves enough morphology to identify it as a probable coelophysoid of approximately the same size as *S. woodi*; however, because the holotype of *S. woodi* does not display any apomorphic features, the two specimens cannot unequivocally be assigned to a single taxon. In lieu of finding more complete materials, Carrano and Sampson considered "it prudent to refer to the Wilmcote materials as cf. *Sarcosaurus woodi*."

Carrano and Sampson recounted the complicated taxonomic history of the referred species, ?*S. andrewsi*:

Originally, Woodward (1908) described this tibia as "megalosaurian," after which Huene (1926) referred it to *Megalosaurus*, Huene (1932) subsequently (and simultaneously) making this specimen the holotype of two new taxa, *Sarcosaurus andrewsi* and *Magnosaurus woodwardi*. Huene referred the first of these species to *Sarcosaurus* despite that *S. andrewsi* overlaps only— and is morphology distinct from— the Wilmcote specimen of *S. woodi*. He referred the second species to the genus *Magnosaurus* regardless of important morphological differences and also an at least 20 million-year temporal gap between BMNH R.3542 and the type species *Magnosaurus nethercombensis*. Later, not mentioning *M. woodwardi*, Huene (1956) referred all three specimens (BMNH 4840/1, the Wilmcote specimen, and BMNH R.3542) of *Sarcosaurus* to the two species belonging to this genus. Further complicating this history, Waldman (1974) later formally referred this material to *Megalosaurus*, although, as Carrano and Sampson pointed out, "there is little evidence to support such an assignment."

As with the two other specimens referred to *Sarcosaurus*, Carrano and Sampson found BMNH R.3542 not to display any discernible diagnostic features, with ?*S. andrewsi* thereby considered to be a *nomen dubium*. Moreover, while this species can be distinguished from *S. woodi* by its larger size, "it cannot be specifically allied with that form beyond the fact that both probably reside within the clade Coelophysoidea, and both are from the same geographic area and similar (but not identical) temporal horizons." Unequivocal synonymy of these species, the authors stated, remains impossible lacking more complete specimens.

In describing BMNH R.3542, Carrano and Sampson noted that its size is closer to *Liliensternus*, *Gojirasaurus*, and *Dilophosaurus* than to *Coelophysis*, *Syntarsus*, or *Procompsognathus* (the latter now regarded as nondinosaurian; see "Excluded Genus" chapter), although its proportions are rather slender.

Carrano and Sampson concluded that BMNH R.3542 clearly belongs to the Neotheropoda (based on prominent fibular facet; fibular crest) and apparently to the Coelophysoidea (based on rounded profile of distal end and condition of astragalar notch, these being intermediate between the conditions in *Herrerasaurus* and Tetanurae). While this specimen could pertain to *Sarcosaurus*, the authors found it best, in lieu of the recovery of more materials, to refer to BMNH R.3542 as an indeterminate member of the Coelophysoidea.

Key references: Andrews (1921); Carrano and Sampson (2004); Carrano, Sampson and Forster (2002); Holtz (2000); Huene (1926, 1932, 1956); Rowe (1989); Rowe and Gauthier (1990); Waldman (1974); Woodward (1908).

†SATURNALIA

Saurischia: Eusaurischia: ?Sauropodomorpha: ?Prosauropoda.

Comments: In 1999, Max Cardoso Langer, Fernando Abdala, Martha Richter, and Michael J. Benton, in a preliminary report, named and described the new genus and species *Saturnalia tupiniquim*, based on three partial skeletons (MCP 3844-PV, the holotype, plus paratypes MCP 3845-PV and 3846-PV) from the Upper Triassic (Carnian) Santa Maria Formation of Brazil. Langer *et al.* assessed this type species to be the most basal known sauropodomorph.

Although Galton and Upchurch (2000; 2003) considered *Saturnalia* to be a primitive prosauropod,

various other workers (*e.g.*, Kellner and Campos 2000*b*; Leal and Azevedo 2003; Yates 2003*b*) have agreed with the assessment of Langer *et al.* (see *S2*).

In a brief report published as an abstract, Langer (2002) subsequently questioned whether or not *Saturnalia* is, in fact, a prosauropod or even a sauropodomorph. Langer noted various features of *Saturnalia* indicating the primitiveness of this genus relative to all well-known sauropodomorphs, including the basal prosauropod *Thecodontosaurus*. These features include the following: Straight cranial portion of dentary; finer, more right-angled tooth serrations; femur having well-developed trochanteric shelf, proximally located fourth trochanter; less robust pes, metatarsal II with straight medioproximal margin, metatarsal III proximal articulation more than twice as broad as that of II, metatarsal II distal articulation narrower than that of III, and metatarsal V less proximally expanded.

According to Langer, various features (*i.e.*, short skull, lanceolate tooth crowns longer in mesial portion of series, broad distal humerus) suggest that *Saturnalia* belongs to the Sauropodomorpha (a clade including Prosauropoda plus Sauropoda). However, as *Saturnalia* seems to be basal to taxa including *Thecodontosaurus*, *Anchisaurus*, and *Plateosaurus* (forms regarded by most workers as prosauropods), Langer found it better to define this genus "as a dinosaur in the stem-lineage to Sauropodomorpha, but not as a sauropodomorph *sensu stricto*."

Later, Langer (2003) published a complete description of the pelvic and hindlimb anatomy of this dinosaur, based upon the three recovered skeletons. In this study, Langer reiterated that, as *Saturnalia* "is clearly more basal in the dinosaur phylogeny than any sauropod or 'prosauropod,' this genus "cannot be regarded as a sauropodomorph *sensu stricto*, and is better considered a taxon in the stem-lineage (Jeffries 1979) to that group."

As Langer (2003) pointed out, the three collected skeletons of *S. tupiniquim* allow an almost complete description of the sacrum, pelvic girdle, and hindlimb of this primitive dinosaur. Moreover, the information gleaned from these skeletons "improves our knowledge of the anatomy of basal dinosaurs, providing the basis for a reassessment of various morphological transformations that occurred in the early evolution of these reptiles."

Among these morphological transformations, Langer (2003) observed the following: Increase in the number of sacral vertebrae (*Saturnalia* having two main sacrals [the plesiomorphic archosaurian condition; *e.g.*, Romer 1956], with two "caudosacral" vertebrae located within the boundaries of the iliac postacetabular alae); development of a brevis fossa (see Novas 1996*a*) of the ilium (in *Saturnalia*, a ventrally

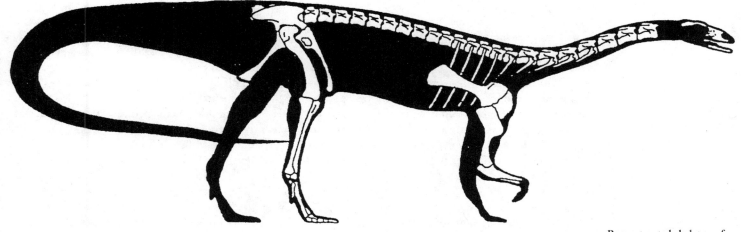

Reconstructed skeleton of *Saturnalia tupiniquim*, based on three partial skeletons (MCP 3844-PV, the holotype, and the paratypes MCP 3845-PV and 3846-PV). (After Langer 2003.)

concave surface defined by lateral and medial ridges at the cranial portion of the postacetabular ala, corresponding to the large origin area of the M. caudofem. brevis; Gatesy 1990); performation of the acetabulum of the ilium (the acetabulum almost closed in *Saturnalia*); in-turning of the femoral head (in *Saturnalia*, the femoral head is plesiomorphically bowed cranially and medially); plus various modifications in the insertion of the iliofemoral musculature and the tibio-tarsal articulation.

Following reconstruction of the pelvic musculature and study of its locomotion pattern (see Langer 2003 for details), Langer concluded that the hindlimb of *Saturnalia* as well as other early dinosaurs did not perform, as suggested by various authors (*e.g.*, Wade 1989; Padian and Olsen 1989; Carrano 2000), just a fore-and-aft stiff rotation of the parasagittal plane, but that lateral and medial leg movements (as suggested for *Plateosaurus*; see Christian, Koberg and Preuscoft 1996; also, see Van Heerden 1979) may also have been present and important.

As pointed out by Langer (2003), some of the inferences regarding movement of the limbs in *Saturnalia* are supported by evidence from fossil footprints. For example, the positive-inwards-rotation of the pes has been described in numerous dinosaur trackways, especially those made by bipedal trackmakers (*e.g.*, Padian and Olsen; Thulborn 1990), this showing "that the foot was inturned during the kick-off phase (see Thulborn and Wade 1989)." It is during this kick-off phase, Langer (2003) noted, that the leg of *Saturnalia* was rotated more medially and the pes more inturned.

Regarding posture and locomotion in *Saturnalia*, Langer (2003) cited various skeletal features (*e.g.*, long distal limb elements, short muscle lever arms in hind limb) as indicators that this dinosaur was more cursorial than any known typical sauropodomorph, save for possibly *Thecodontosaurus* (Benton, Juul, Storrs and Galton 2000). Moreover, *Saturnalia* posesses the hindlimb features elongation required for achieving bipedal locomotion (see Christian, Horn and Preuscoft 1994). As to whether or not *Saturnalia* was an obligatory biped or if this animal sometimes came down on all fours, Langer (2003) noted that the trunk to hindlimb ratio (*i.e.*, 1.0 to 1.1) in this genus is lower than that of obligatorily bipedal dinosaurs, higher than in most prosauropods (possibly excluding *Massospondylus*; see Galton 1976; Cooper 1981), and probably between that of fully bipedal forms such as *Coelophysis* and mostly quadrupedal forms like *Plateosaurus*, which seemingly became bipedal only during rapid locomotion (see Christian and Preuscoft 1996). In conclusion, Langer (2003) speculated that "*Saturnalia* would have used a bipedal gait more often than other 'prosauropods,' probably to escape from predators, but also for active hunting of small prey, when relatively fast locomotion was advantageous." While at rest or when walking at a slower pace, as in "when moving through areas with vegetation that could be eaten (Upchurch 1997)," *Saturnalia* probably walked on all four legs.

More recently, in a published abstract for a poster, Langer (2004) briefly reconstructed the humeral myology of *S. tupiniquim*, noting that it "was probably close to the plesiomorphic condition for both Saurischia in general and Sauropodomorph in particular." Utilizing the Extant Phylogenetic Bracket Method, Langer (2004) reconstructed the muscles of the pectoral girdle and forelimb, allowing for determination of the attachment sites to the humerus of the coracobrachialis, deltoides, pectoralis, scapulohumeralis, subscapularis, supracoracoideus, extensor, and flexor muscles. This method also suggested to Langer (2004) that some other muscles (*e.g.*, brachialis) found in extant reptile groups were most likely also present in *Saturnalia*, although, as their insertions and origins vary among living taxa, their locations in *Saturnalia* could not be reconstructed.

In a recent review of the Prosauropoda, Galton and Upchurch (2004a) reevaluated *Saturnalia tupiniquim*, concluding that "it is a basal prosauropod," placing "'above' *Thecodontosaurus*" in their cladogram (see "Systematics" chapter). Galton and Upchurch (2004a) criticized the assessment by Langer *et al.* as being supported by "overall morphology" as opposed to a suite of synapomorphies uniting Prosauropoda with Sauropoda. A cladistic analysis by Galton and Upchurch (2004a), however, placed *Saturnalia* within Prosauropoda based upon the following synapomorphies: Centra of dorsal vertebrae elongate (ratio of length to height greater than 1.0 (this character highly variable, possibly size-related); large pubic foramen.

Acknowledging that additional preparation and discoveries could reveal new information supporting the original assessment of Langer *et al.*, and noting that the above-cited character-state distributions are equivocal, Galton and Upchurch (2004a) suggested that "the proposed relationships of *Saturnalia* should be regarded as tentative," while it is presently "safer to regard *Saturnalia* as a basal prosauropod."

Key references: Benton, Juul, Storrs and Galton (2000); Carrano (2000); Christian, Horn and Preuscoft (1994); Christian, Koberg and Preuscoft (1996); Christian and Preuscoft (1996); Cooper (1981); Galton (1976); Galton and Upchurch (2000; 2003, 2004a); Jeffries (1979); Gatesy (1990); Kellner and Campos (2000b); Langer (2002, 2003, 2004); Langer, Abdala, Richter and Michael Benton (1999); Leal and Azevedo (2003); Novas (1996a); Padian and Olsen (1989); Romer (1956); Thulborn (1990); Thulborn and Wade (1989); Upchurch (1997); Van Heerden (1979); Wade (1989); Yates (2003b).

†SAUROPELTA

Ornithischia: Predentata: Genasauria: Thyreophora: Thyreophoroidea: Eurypoda: Ankylosauria: Nodosauridae.

Diagnosis of genus (as for type species [*S. edwardsorum*]): Cervical armor including three sets of coossified osteoderms, all having prominent points (Carpenter and Kirkland 1998); tail long, including at least 40 caudal vertebrae (Vickaryous, Maryańska and Weishampel 2004).

Comments: Warren and Carpenter (2004), in an abstract for a poster, reported recently collected fragmentary remains belonging to "a huge nodosaurid better matched to *Sauropelta* (previously recorded only in the Early to Middle Cretaceous [Aptian–Albian] Cloverly Formation of Montana and Wyoming; see *D:TE*, *S1*, *S2*, and *S3*) than any other ankylosaur," found weathered out of the Ruby Ranch Member of the Cedar Mountain Formation in eastern Utah.

As Warren and Carpenter reported, a very large right humerus and two very large cervical spikes constitute the most describable elements belonging to this specimen, with other identifiable elements including a fibula, centra of dorsal vertebrae, and two small dermal scutes. Based on the approximate 65-centimeter long humerus, the authors estimated the total length of this animal to have been about 6.8 meters (approximately 24 feet), distinguishing the taxon as one of the largest known members of the Nodosauridae.

Discovery of *Sauropelta* in the Ruby Ranch Member of the Cedar Mountain Formation supports earlier interpretations of the upper portions of this member being equivalent to parts of the Cloverly Formation (based on the occurrence of the iguanodontian *Tenontosaurus*). As Warren and Carpenter noted, this correlation further implies that the Ruby Ranch Member is, in part, Aptian–Albian in age.

Key reference: Carpenter and Kirkland (1998); Vickaryous, Maryańska and Weishampel (2004); Warren and Carpenter (2004);

†SAUROPHAGANAX—(=?*Allosaurus*, *Epanterias*)
Saurischia: Eusaurischia: Eusaurischia: Theropoda:

Life restoration by Berislav Krzic of *Sauropelta edwardsorum*.

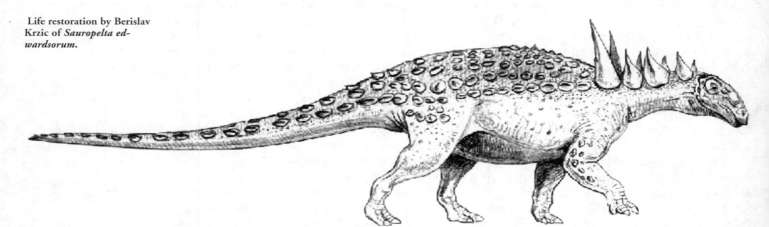

Paleontologist Robert A. Long with the right tibia (OMNH 4666) of *Saurophaganax maximus*.

Neotheropoda: Tetanurae: Avetheropoda: Carnosauria: Allosauroidea: Allosauridae.

Name derivation: Greek *saurophagus* = "reptile eater" + Greek *anax* = "master, ruler, king."

Type species: *S. maximus* (Ray 1941).

Other species: [None.]

Occurrence: Morrison Formation, Oklahoma, United States.

Age: Late Jurassic (Kimmeridgian–Tithonian).

Known material: Fragmentary cranial remains, postcranial elements (much unidentified and unpublished), representing at least four individuals.

Holotype: OMNH 01123, middorsal neural arch.

Diagnosis of genus (as for type species): Distinguished from *Allosaurus* by the following: horizontal lamina along base of each side of spinous process of cranial dorsal vertebrae; atlas lacking prezygapophyses for proatlas, not roofing neural canal; postorbital lacking postorbital boss; some cervicals having almost vertical postzygapophyses; pneumatic vertebral centrum foramina well developed into caudal dorsal vertebrae; laterally bowed femur; no astragalar buttress on craniodistal face of tibia; metatarsal IV less divergent distally than in other carnosaurs (Chure, in press, *see in* Holtz, Molnar and Currie 2004).

Comments: As chronicled by Daniel J. Chure (1995), G. R. Rays, in a popular article published in 1941, named and briefly described a new giant theropod that Ray named *Saurophagus maximus*, this type species based upon fossil remains — mostly postcranial

Mounted skeletal cast of *Saurophaganax maximus* displayed at Dinofest, held from December 8, 2000 through January 8, 2001, at Chicago's Navy Pier.

elements, and including a middorsal neural arch (OMNH 01123; see *D:TE* and *S2* for photographs of individual elements and composite mounted skeletons) — collected during the 1930s by the University of Oklahoma from Quarry 1 in the Brushy Basin Member of the Morrison Formation, on the Colorado Plateau, in Cimarron County, Oklahoma, United States. The material was mostly prepared by untrained Works Progress Authority (WPA) laborers who, in the process of their work, damaged much of the original material.

Although Ray did not figure the material, included in his article was a "staged" photograph of a very large theropod femur taken in Permian-age redbeds near Norman, Oklahoma (W. Langston, Jr., personal communication to Chure 1993).

Paleontologist J. Willis Stovall, in Ray's article, estimated the total length of this dinosaur — based upon the composite hindlimb — to have been approximately 14 meters (about 47 feet), comparable in size to or even larger than the celebrated *Tyrannosaurus rex*.

Over the years, the validity of Ray's type species

has come into question. In 1953, Camp, Welles and Green posited that the name *Saurophagus maximus* is both a *nomen nudum* and preoccupied (Swainson 1831). Decades later, Hunt and Lucas (1987) argued that Ray's taxon, although preoccupied, had been correctly established; at the same time, these authors designated a right tibia (OMNH 4666) to be the lectotype, but considered this taxon to be synonymous with *Allosaurus fragilis*.

Indeed, the Quarry 1 theropod has generally been regarded as representing a very large form of *Allosaurus fragilis* (e.g., see Paul 1988). In 1995, however, Chure identified the material referred to this theropod as belonging to a valid genus and species. Uncertain as to whether or not Ray's informal description of the material met the criteria of the International Code of Zoological Nomenclature, and also noting that OMNH 4666 is not distinctive, Chure proposed the emended name *Saurophaganax* (suggested by Benjamin J. Creisler) for the Quarry 1 theropod, designating a distinctive neural arch (OMNH 01123) as the holotype (see *Allosaurus* entry, *S2* for additional details).

Life restoration of
Saurophaganax maximus by
artist Todd Marshall.

Originally, Chure diagnosed *S. maximus* as follows: Allosauroid attaining extremely large size, differing from other allosauroids in presence of horizontal lamina along base of each side of neural spine, lamina arising from base of spine cranially, free caudally, roofing over craniocaudally elongated space floored by dorsal surface of transverse process; differing from other allosaurids in atlas lacking prezygapophyses for proatlas, not roofing over neural canal, chevrons craniocaudally expanded distally.

Chure, basing his calculations on the same composite hindlimb, corroborated Stoval's estimated size for *S. maximus*, further noting that this species was apparently more massive (*contra* Ray, Paul) than *T. rex*. Following Anderson, Hall-Martin and Russell's (1985) method of using long bone circumferences to calculate mass in some groups of animals, paleontologist John S. McIntosh found the probable weight of *S. maximus* to have been about 2720 kilograms (nearly three tons).

The validity of *S. maximus* was again contested in 1998. *Allosaurus* specialist David K. Smith performed studies of extensive material belonging to that genus, mostly specimens recovered from the Cleveland-Lloyd Dinosaur Quarry in Utah, representing different ontogenetic stages and a considerable degree of individual variation. It was Smith's conclusion that the material assigned to *S. maximus* in fact belonged to *Allosaurus*, although a particularly large species, which he renamed *Allosaurus maxima* (see *S2* for details).

More recently, Holtz, Molnar and Currie (2004), in their review of basal tetanurans, accepted Chure's original proposal that the Quarry 1 theropod material represents a valid genus and species.

Key references: Anderson, Hall-Martin and Russell (1985); Camp, Welles and Green (1953); Chure (1995, in press); Holtz, Molnar and Currie (2004); Hunt and Lucas (1987); Paul (1988); Ray (1941); Smith (1998).

†SAUROPOSEIDEN

Saurischia: Eusaurischia: Sauropodomorpha: Sauropoda: Eusauropoda: Neosauropoda: Macronaria: Titanosauriformes: Brachiosauridae.

Diagnosis of genus (as for type species): Prominent centroparapophyseal laminae on cervical vertebrae extending to caudal end of centrum; neural spines deeply excavated, perforate in central cervicals; hypertrophied pneumatic fossae extending to caudal end of centrum (Upchurch, Barrett and Dodson 2004).

Comment: In their review of the Sauropoda, Upchurch, Barrett and Dodson (2004) rediagnosed the type species *Sauroposeiden proteles* (see *S2*).

Key reference: Upchurch, Barrett and Dodson (2004).

†SAURORNITHOIDES

Saurischia: Eusaurischia: Theropoda: Neotheropoda: Tetanurae: Avetheropoda: Coelurosauria: Tyrannoraptora: Maniraptoriformes: Troodontidae.

Diagnosis of *S. mogoliensis*: Differs from *S. junior* in having exit for facial nerve (c.n. VII) outside lateral depression; proportionally slightly longer accessory anorbital fenestra and naris; comparatively smaller size (Makovicky and Norell 2004).

Diagnosis of *S. junior*: (Apparent autapomorphy) distinguished from *S. mongoliensis*, *Troodon formosus*, and *Byronosaurus jaffei* in having exit for facial nerve (c.n. VII) within lateral depression; snout longer than in *S. mongoliensis* and *B. jaffei* (Makovicky and Norell 2004).

Comments: Norell and Hwang (2004) described a very fragmentary troodontid specimen (IGM 100/1083) found as float at the Upper Cretaceous Grangers Flats sublocality of Ukhaa Tolgod (Dashveg, Novacek, Norell, Clark, Chiappe, Davidson, McKenna, Dingus, Swisher and Perle 1995), Mongolia. The specimen consists of a reasonably complete right quadrate and an associated maxillary fragment, plus fragments of the axial and appendicular skeleton. It was collected in 1993 during the Mongolian Academy of Sciences-American Museum of Natural History Paleontological Expedition.

The authors identified the specimen as belonging to the Troodontidae based upon the following features: Arctometatarsalian pes; closely packed mesial maxillary teeth; maxillary border to external nares; cervical vertebrae having sharp ventral keel and low neural spine (Makovicky and Norell 2004).

Norell and Kwang provisionally referred IGM 100/1083 to the Mongolian troodontid *Saurornithoides mongoliensis*, noting is close similarity of the holotype (AMNH 6516; see *D:TE* for photograph) from the approximately coeval Djadokhta beds at Bayn Dzak. Similarities noted by the authors between the two specimens include the following: Packing of teeth; pattern of sculpture on rostral maxillary fragment; conformation of preserved parts of metatarsal III. As Norell and Kwang observed, the only significant difference between IGM 100/1083 and AMNH 6516 is size, the former specimen representing a larger individual (ungual length of pedal digit II being 34.7 millimeters for IGM 100/1083 and 29.3 millimeters for AMNH 6516).

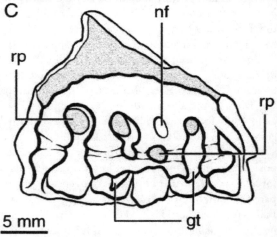

IGM 100/1083, left maxilla provisionally referred to *Saurornithoides mongoliensis*, in A. lateral and B. medial views, C. interpretive drawing of the medial surface. (After Norell and Hwang 2004.)

As Norell and Kwang pointed out, only one other specimen has previously been referred to *S. mongoliensis*—a hindlimb collected from the Chinese Djadokhta locality at Mandahum and identified by Currie and Peng (1993) as a juvenile of this species. However, the authors found the referral of that specimen to *S. mongoliensis* "somewhat questionable" (Norell, Clark, Makovicky, Barsbold and Rowe, manuscript).

In describing IGM 100/1083, Norell and Hwang observed that the putative interdental bone on the maxillary fragment consists of thin stalklike structures which are expanded distally into knobs, the latter to have fit into the roots and crowns of the adjacent teeth, an avian-like characteristic not found in most other theropods and also observed by Currie (1987) in troodontid specimen TMP 82.16.138. Norell and Hwang further noted that, as in avians, IGM 100/1083 possesses a vertical tooth row, with the germ teeth erupting vertically into the mature teeth, as in crocodilians and birds.

Martin and Stewart (1999) had previously argued that the lack of similarity between bird and theropod tooth morphology and replacement teeth precludes a theropod origin for birds, these authors positing that unserrated teeth, constrictions between crowns and expanded roots, vertical tooth replacement, and tooth replacement pits closed at their bases are features found only in birds. As Norell and Hwang pointed out, however, vertical tooth families and tooth replacement pits closed at their bases are found in IGM 100/1083. These authors further noted that constriction between crown and root can be seen in troodontids (see Currie), therizinosaurids (Clark, Perle and Norell 1994), alvarezsaurids (Perle, Norell, Chiappe and Clark 1993), and the microraptorian *Microraptor zhaoianus* (Xu, Zhou and Wang 2000; Hwang, Norell, Ji and Gao 2002), although these constrictions need not be homologous. Additionally, unserrated teeth are also found in the Mongolian troodontid *Byronosaurus jaffei* (see Norell, Makovicky and Clark 2000) and in the dromaeosaurid *Sinornithosaurus milleni* and microraptor *M. zhaoianus* (see Xu, Wang and Wu 1999; Xu *et al.* 2000; Hwang *et al.*). Therefore, Norell and Hwang concluded, those dental characters regarded by Martin and Stewart as limited to birds and crocodilians actually have a considerably broader distribution.

IGM 100/1093 is significant, Norell and Hwang noted, in documenting the occurrence of another member of the Troodontidae besides *B. jaffei* at Ukhaa Tolgod.

In their review of the Troodontidae, Makovicky and Norell found the material assigned to *S. mongoliensis* "insufficient to identify autapomorphies."

Key references: Clark, Perle and Norell (1994); Currie (1987); Currie and Peng (1993); Dashveg, Novacek, Norell, Clark, Chiappe, Davidson, McKenna, Dingus, Swisher and Perle (1995); Hwang, Norell, Ji and Gao (2002); Makovicky and Norell (2004); Martin and Stewart (1999); Norell, Clark, Makovicky,

Barsbold and Rowe, in press; Norell and Hwang (2004); Norell, Makovicky and Clark (2000); Perle, Norell, Chiappe and Clark (1993); Xu, Wang and Wu (1999); Xu, Zhou and Wang (2000).

†**SAURORNITHOLESTES** (=?*Bambiraptor*)
Saurischia: Eusaurischia: Theropoda: Neotheropoda: Tetanurae: Avetheropoda: Coelurosauria: Tyrannoraptora: Maniraptoriformes: Maniraptora: Metornithes: Paraves: Deinonychosauria: Dromaeosauridae: Dromaeosaurinae.

Notes: Kiernan and Schwimmer (2004) reported the discovery of the first specimen representing a dromaeosaurine [="velociraptorine" of their usage; see Senter, Barsbold, Britt and Burnham 2004, "Systematics" chapter] theropod from the eastern gulf coastal United States. The specimen—a single, well-preserved tooth (ALMNH 2001) collected from the Upper Cretaceous (latest Santonian–early Campanian) Moorville Chalk Formation (Selma Group) of Greene County, western Alabama—constitutes the first evidence documenting the presence of the Dromaeosauridae in southeastern North America during the Late Cretaceous. The tooth was found, the authors recounted, by Caitlin R. Kiernan while excavating the carapace and plastron of *Toxochelys moorevillensis*, a toxochelyid turtle.

In describing this tooth, Kiernan and Schwimmer noted such details as follows: Strongly recurved distally, laterally compressed; not D-shaped in basal cross section; minute mesial denticles present, denticular portion of mesial carina extending less than halfway from tip of crown; 23 denticles distally (approximately seven per millimeter), 19 to 22 denticles on mesial carina (about nine per millimeter); root and tip of tooth missing, preserved portion having length of 3.6 millimeters mesio-distally, apical-basal height of 4.9 millimeters.

Currie, Rigby and Sloan (1990) considered significant size disparity between mesial and distal denticles in dromaeosaurid teeth to be diagnostic for the Velociraptorine. Observing that same feature in ALMNH 2001, Kiernan and Schwimmer referred the tooth to that subfamily. At the same time, Kiernan and Schwimmer noted that ALMNH 2001 compares favorably with TMP 82.19.180, a tooth that Currie *et al.* had referred to the type species *Saurornitholestes langstoni*, a Late Cretaceous (late Campanian to Maastrichtian) dromaeosaurid (referred by Senter *et al.* to the Dromaeosaurinae) known from the western United States and Canada.

Therefore, Kiernan and Schwimmer identified ALMNH 2001 as "a small velociraptorine dromaeosaurid, possibly congeneric with *Saurornitholestes*,"

Saurornitholestes langston, (left) cast of holotype (PMAA P74.10.5) frontal region of skull in ventral view, (right) endocast.

that lived on the Appalachian subcontinent during early Campanian times. Moreover, the possible occurrence of *Saurornitholestes* on both sides of the Western Interior Seaway could offer "evidence that western and eastern dinosaur faunas were not completely isolated during the Late Cretaceous," or that "dromaeosaurid populations may have descended in parallel on either side of the Seaway from pre–Seaway (*i.e.*, Middle Cretaceous) common ancestors."

Key references: Currie, Rigby and Sloan (1990); Kiernan and Schwimmer (2004); Senter, Barsbold, Britt and Burnham (2004).

†SCIPIONYX

Saurischia: Eusaurischia: Theropoda: Neotheropoda: Tetanurae: Avetheropoda: Coelurosauria: Maniraptoriformes *incertae sedis*.

Comments: Distinguished as the first — and to date one of the only — Italian dinosaurs known from body fossils, the type species *Scipionyx samniticus* is also renowned for its excellently preserved soft tissues (see *S2*).

In a recent review of the dinosaurs of Italy, Dal Sasso (2003) presented additional historical information regarding the discovery and housing of this exceptional specimen. As chronicled by Dal Sasso, the find was made in 1980 by fossil collector Giovanni Todesco in the Pietraroria Plattenkalk (a Middle Cretaceous/Albian formation known since the 1700s for its excellently preserved fossil fishes) at the small village of Pietraroia, located approximately 80 kilometers northeast of Naples (Benevento Province).

The specimen remained, almost forgotten, in Todesco's basement for 13 years, when the collector requested that paleontologists from the Museo di Storia Naturale di Milano examine it. At last recognized for its scientific importance, the specimen, according to Italian law, was then given by Todesco to the Superintendenza Archaeologica di Salerno, where it was housed, prepared, and subjected to more critical examination.

As Dal Sasso pointed out, the amazing preservation of *S. samniticus* can be attributed to fine marly limestones "deposited in a shallow lagoon environment during cyclic anoxic periods," resulting in "very peculiar environmental conditions [that] allowed fossilisation of soft tissues in association with animal bony remains." Moreover, the association of fishes and marine invertebrates with the terrestrial fauna suggests that the skeleton of *Scipionyx* may have been "carried into the sea by rivers during violent storms," although, as that author noted, it is difficult to determine if this animal had drowned or perished for other reasons.

According to Dal Sasso, paleobiogeographical information (see Cati, Sartorio and Venturini 1987; Zappaterra 1990) supports the hypothesis that *Scipionyx* "evolved on isolated, emergent lands in the Cretaceous Central Tethys Sea." Isolation in the form of a small island within the peri–Adriatic Domain "could have led to biological consequences such as the evolution of endemic species (see Dal Sasso 2001).

Key references: Dal Sasso (2001, 2003); Cati, Sartorio and Venturini (1987); Zappaterra (1990).

†SEGNOSAURUS

Saurischia: Eusaurischia: Eusaurischia: Theropoda: Neotheropoda: Tetanurae: Avetheropoda: Coelurosauria: Tyrannoraptora: Maniraptoriformes: Maniraptora: Metornithes: Therizinosauroidea: Therizinosauridae.

Diagnosis of genus (as for type species): Features including the following: mesial mandibular teeth markedly flattened, slightly recurved; 24 dentary teeth; six sacral vertebrae (Clark, Maryańska and Barsbold 2004).

Comment: In their review of the Therizinosauroidea, Clark, Maryańska and Barsbold (2004) rediagnosed the type species *Segnosaurus galbinensis* (see *D:TE*).

Key reference: Clark, Maryańska and Barsbold (2004).

†SEISMOSAURUS

Saurischia: Eusaurischia: Sauropodomorpha: Sauropoda: Eusauropoda: Neosauropoda: Diplodocoidea: Diplodocidae.

Diagnosis of genus (as for type species): Distal end of ischial shaft curving strongly upward, forming hook shape in lateral aspect (Gillette 1991) (Upchurch, Barrett and Dodson 2004).

Comment: In their review of the Sauropoda, Upchurch, Barrett and Dodson (2004) rediagnosed *Seismosaurus halli*, at the same time noting that other characters listed by Gillette (1991) as diagnostic "are either subtle differences in proportion that could reflect the large size of *Seismosaurus* or [are] plesiomorphic characters that are widespread among other sauropods" (see *D:TE*).

Key references: Gillette (1991); Upchurch, Barrett and Dodson (2004).

†SELLOSAURUS—(See *Plateosaurus*.)

†SHANSHANOSAURUS—(See *Tarbosaurus*.)

SHENZHOUSAURUS Ji, Norell, Makovicky, Gao, Ji and Yuan 2003

Saurischia: Eusaurischia: Theropoda: Neotheropoda: Tetanurae: Avetheropoda: Coelurosauria: Tyrannoraptora: Maniraptoriformes: Ornithomimosauria.

Name derivation: "Shenzhou [ancient name of China]" + Greek *sauros* = "lizard."

Type species: *S. orientalis* Ji, Norell, Makovicky, Gao, Ji and Yuan 2003.

Other species: [None.]

Occurrence: Yixian Formation, Liaoning Province, China.

Age: Early Cretaceous (Hauterivian).

Known material/holotype: NGMC 97–4-002, partial skeleton with crushed skull, missing distal hindlimbs, forelimbs (except for part of right manus), and pectoral girdle.

Diagnosis of genus (as for type species): Ornithomimosaur differing from all others (except *Harpymimus*) in having teeth restricted to rostral dentary; primitive characters not found in advanced ornithomimosaurs including straight ischium and gently curved (rather than truncated) postacetabular process; distinguishable from *Pelecanimimus* by tooth distribution pattern and primitive configuration of manus, where digit I is shorter than II and III (Ji, Norell, Makovicky, Gao, Ji and Yuan 2003).

Comments: One of the only known toothed ornithomimosaurs, the genus *Shenzhousaurus* was based on a partial skeleton (NGMC 97–4-002) preserved in death pose on a sandstone block, collected by local farmers from the lowermost, fluvial part of the Lower Cretaceous (see Swisher, Wang, Zhou, Wang, Jin, Zhang, Xu, Zhang and Wang 2001) Yixian Formation, in beds near the Jurassic–Cretaceous boundary, in western Liaoning Province, China (Ji, Norell, Makovicky, Gao, Ji and Yuan 2003).

In describing the type species *S. orientalis*, Ji *et al.* noted that the thoracic cavity of the holotype contains numerous, unevenly distributed pebbles, with a concentration of these stones just cranial to the preserved part of the gastral basket. The pebbles are heterogenous in size, shape, composition. These stones the authors interpreted to be probably gastroliths. As Ji *et al.* pointed out, the presence of both teeth and gastroliths in this ornithomimosaur suggests a highly specialized diet.

A phylogenetic analysis by Ji *et al.* yielded the following results: *Shenzhousaurus* occupying a position near the base of Ornithomimosauria (Makovicky, Kobayashi and Currie 2004), being more advanced than *Pelecanimimus*; the monophyletic Ornithomimosauria being the sister group to a clade consisting of Maniraptora (including *Ornitholestes*); and

Shenzhousaurus orientalis, NGMC 97-4-002, holotype skeleton as preserved on main block, parts of counterblock having been reattached. (After Ji, Norell, Makovicky, Gao, Jiand Yuan 2003.)

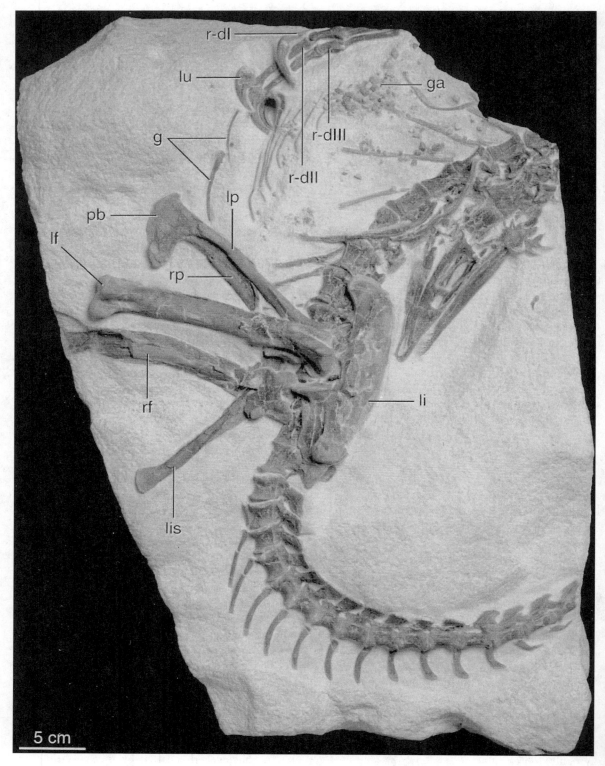

Alvarezsauridae as the sister group of all other maniraptorans except *Ornitholestes* (see "Systematics" chapter).

According to this analysis, "*Shenzhousaurus* and other ornithomimosaurs are more derived than *Pelecanimimus* in the progressive loss of teeth from the upper jaws and all but the tip of the dentary (*Shenzhousaurus, Harpymimus*) or complete loss of teeth (higher ornithomimosaurs)." As noted by these authors, *Shenzhousaurus* and *Harpymimus* both have primitive hand proportions, metacarpal I being shorter than II or III, although the latter genus shares one characters (*i.e.*, derived curvature of the ischium) with higher ornithomimids.

Key references: Ji, Norell, Makovicky, Gao, Ji and Yuan (2003); Makovicky, Kobayashi and Currie (2004).

SHUANGMIAOSAURUS   You, Ji, Li and Li 2003
Ornithischia: Predentata: Genasauria: Cerapoda: Ornithopoda: Euornithopoda: Iguanodontia: Dryomorpha: Ankylopollexia: Styracosterna: Iguanodontoidea: Hadrosauroidea.

Name derivation: Phinyin *Shuangmiao* = "twin temples [name of village]" + Greek *sauros* = "lizard."

Type species: *S. gilmorei* You, Ji, Li and Li 2003.

Other species: [None.]

Occurrence: Middle Cretaceous.

Age: Sunjiawan Formation, Liaoning Province, China.

Known material: Partian crania, complete left dentary.

Holotype: LPM0165, complete left maxilla, partial articulated premaxilla and lacrimal.

Diagnosis of genus (as for type species): Sister taxon to Hadrosauridae, distinguished from other known basal hadrosauroids by butt-jointed maxilla-jugul suture (You, Ji, Li and Li 2003).

Comments: The genus *Shuangmiaosaurus* was founded upon a complete left dentary, premaxilla, and lacrimal, recovered between 1999 and 2000 from fossiliferous horizons of the Upper Cretaceous (see below) Sunjiwan Formation, at Shuangmiao village, Beipiao, Liaoning, China. An isolated complete left dentary (LMP0166), collected from the same locality, was referred to the type species, *S. gilmoreis* (You, Ji, Li and Li 2003).

Performing a phylogenetic analysis (based on the data matrix of Norman 2002, incorporating 18 taxa and 67 characters), You *et al.* found *Shuangmiaosaurus* to be closer to "Hadrosauriformes" (defined as a node-based clade including *Iguanodon, Parasaurolophus*, their most recent common ancestor and all their descendants; see Sereno 1997, 1998, 1999*b*) than to *Camptosaurus*; within "Hadrosauriformes," more derived than *Iguanodon* and *Ouranosaurus* (having dorsally located maxillary process, laterally offset coronoid process with horizontal shelf, partially cemented tooth roots); more highly derived than *Altirhinus* and *Eolambia* (displaying narrow, parallel-sided alveolar trough grooves); and more derived than *Protohadros* (having straight dentary ramus, rugosely cemented tooth roots).

As the authors pointed out, one significant feature — the butt-jointed maxilla-jugal suture — is shared by this new genus and the Hadrosauridae, although it is not present in other known basal mem-

bers of Hadrosauroidea, *e.g.*, *Probactrosaurus, Telmatosaurus* (see Weishampel, Norman and Grigorescu 1993), and *Bactrosaurus*. *Shuangmiaosaurus* does not, however, exhibit other hadrosaurid synapomorphies (*e.g.*, diamond-shaped maxillary crowns having reduced primary ridges and reduced marginal denticals).

Considering the phylogenetic placement of this genus, You *et al.* dated the Sunjiawan Formation as of possibly early Late Cretaceous age, as all other known basal hadrosauroids (*e.g.*, *Bactrosaurus, Protohadros*, and *Eolambia*; see Godefroit, Dong, Bultynck, Li and Feng 1998, Head 1998, and Kirkland 1998*b*, respectively) are of that age, while all known members of the Hadrosauridae are typically of Late Cretaceous age.

Key references: Godefroit, Dong, Bultynck, Li and Feng (1998); Head (1998); Kirkland (1998*b*); Norman (2002); You, Ji, Li and Li (2003); Sereno (1997, 1998, 1999*b*); Weishampel, Norman and Grigorescu (1993).

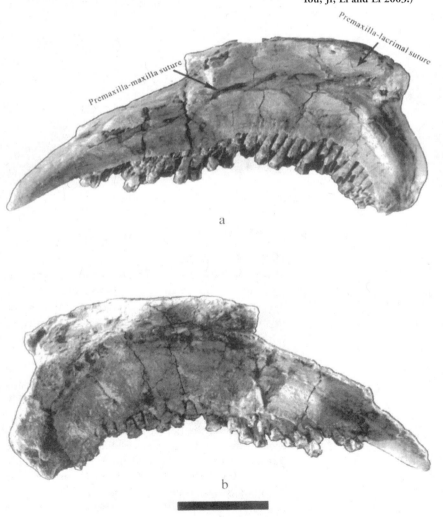

Shuangmiaosaurus gilmorei, LMP0165, holotype partial premaxilla and lacrimal, in a. lateral and b. medial views. Scale = 10 cm. (After You, Ji, Li and Li 2003.)

Shuangmiaosaurus gilmorei, LMP0166, referred left dentary, in a. lateral, b. medial, and c. dorsal views. Scale = 10 cm. (After You, Ji, Li and Li 2003.)

†SIAMOSAURUS

Saurischia: Eusaurischia: Theropoda: Neotheropoda: Tetanurae: Spinosauroidea: Spinosauridae.

Comments: In 1986, Éric Buffetaut and Rucha Ingavat named and described *Siamosaurus suteethorni*, founded upon a tooth collected from the Sao Kua Formation of Thailand (see *D:TE*).

More recently, Hasegawa, Buffetaut, Manabe and Takakuwa (2003) described an isolated tooth crown with a small portion of preserved root (GMNH-PV-999) possibly belonging to a spinosaurid theropod, recovered in 1994 by fossil collector Ryosuke Matsumoto from the Lower Cretaceous (uppermost Barremian to Aptian, based upon ammonites collected from the underlying Ishido Formation and overlying Sanyama Formation; see Matsukawa 1983; Matsukawa and Obata 1994) Sebayashi Formation

(Sanchu Group), near the Ichinose Bridge, Mamonozawa River, Nakazato Village, Gunma Prefecture, Japan.

Originally interpreted as pertaining to a marine reptile, this tooth was subsequently compared with other taxa and identified by Hasegawa *et al.* as possibly pertaining to a spinosaurid theropod. In describing the specimen, Hasegawa *et al.* noted that the crown is cone-shaped, slender, only slightly recurved (those features distinguishing the tooth from the teeth of crocodilians), slightly compressed labiolingually, and nearly oval in cross section. High magnification revealed that the enamel has a finely granular appearance resembling that described in the European spinosaurid *Baryonyx walkeri*, this texture of enamel lacking in both crocodilians and marine reptiles.

According to Hasegawa *et al.*, GMNH-PV-999, although slightly smaller, is otherwise almost identical morphologically (*e.g.*, straight crown and distinctive ornamentation) to the holotype tooth (DMR TF 2043a) of *Siamosaurus suteethorni*, from the Lower Cretaceous (possibly Valanginian to Barremian in age, not Jurassic, *contra* Buffetaut and Suteethorn 1998) Sao Khua Formation of northeastern Thailand (see *D:TE*). Moreover, Hasegawa *et al.* noted, GMNH-PV-999 and the *Siamosaurus* material from Japan are close in age.

In their original description of *Siamosaurus*, Buffetaut and Ingavat tentatively referred this genus to the Spinosauridae. While numerous teeth referred to *Siamosaurus* have been subsequently collected in Thailand, no jaw material had been recovered belonging to this genus, making positive assignment of this genus to the Spinosauridae difficult. However, the authors noted, "the resemblances between the teeth of *Siamosaurus* and those of African and European spinosauroids do suggest that *Siamosaurus* is related to them, and pending the discovery of more complete material, we refer it tentatively to that group of specialized theropods."

Because of its close similarities to the teeth of *Siamosaurus*, Hasegawa *et al.* classified the tooth from Japan as a possible spinosaurid (and possibly *Siamosaurus*, species unknown), an assignment, if correct, distinguishing GMNH-PV-999 as the second dinosaur species identified from the Sebayashi Formation and the second report of the Spinosauridae in Asia.

More recently, *S. suteethorni* was regarded by Holtz, Molnar and Currie (2004), in their review of basal tetanurans, as a *nomen dubium*.

That status was contradicted, however, by Buffetaut, Suteethorn and Tong (2004) who, in an abstract for a poster, reported the discovery of a partial skeleton (including several cervical and dorsal vertebrae,

a1 a2 a3 a4

b1 b2 b3 b4

Possible spinosaurid teeth: a. ?*Siamosaurus* (GMNH-PV-999) and b. *Siamosaurus suteethorni* (DMR TF 2043a, holotype tooth) in 1. lingual, 2. labial, 3. mesial, and 4. distal views. (Produced by Tomoyuki Ohashi, University of Tokyo, after Hasegawa, Buffetaut, Manabe and Takakuwa 2003.)

ribs, and a metapodial) representing a large theropod excavated from a new locality, near the city of Khon Kaen, in the Khok Kruat Formation of Thailand. (A tooth found with the specimen could belong to the same individual, or may pertain to a scavenger.)

Buffetaut *et al.* observed the following in this specimen: Cervical vertebrae resembling in some ways (*e.g.*, elongation of centrum; articular face of centrum not offset; epipophyses large; ligament scars prominent) those of the spinosaurid *Baryonyx walkeri*; dorsal vertebrae resembling those of *Spinosaurus aegyptiacus* (neural spines not as tall as in *S. aegyptiacus*, but much taller than in *B. walkeri*).

As Buffetaut *et al.* pointed out, this discovery "demonstrates that spinosaurid theropods were present in Asia during the Early Cretaceous," while at the same time supporting the identification of *Siamosaurus* as a member of the Spinosauridae, this family now known to have "clearly had a wider geographical distribution than previously assumed, including not only Africa, Europe and South America, but also eastern Asia."

Key references: Buffetaut and Ingavat (1986); Buffetaut and Suteethorn (1998); Buffetaut, Suteethorn and Tong (2004); Hasegawa, Buffetaut, Manabe and Takakuwa (2003); Holtz, Molnar and Currie (2004); Matsukawa (1983); Matsukawa and Obata (1994).

†SIAMOTYRANNUS

Saurischia: Eusaurischia: Eusaurischia: Theropoda: Neotheropoda: Tetanurae: Avetheropoda: ?Carnosauria *incertae sedis*.

Comments: In 1996, Éric Buffetaut, Varavudh Suteethorn, and Haiyan Tong described the type species *Siamotyrannus isanensis*, founded upon a partial skeleton (PW9–1) from the Sao Khua Formation of northeastern Thailand. In that original report, Buffetaut *et al.* referred *Siamotyrannus* to the Tyrannosauridae, distinguishing the genus as the oldest known member of that clade (see *D:TE*), a position subsequently supported provisionally by Holtz (2001). Among the criteria used by Buffetaut *et al.* for their referral of this genus to the Tyrannosauridae was an element interpreted by those authors as a median crest on the ilium dorsal to the acetabulum.

In a more recent review of basal Tetanurae, however, theropod specialists Holtz, Molnar and Currie (2004) noted that the presumed "median crest" is, in fact, a pair of crests, the supracetabular crest being larger than in Tyrannosauridae.

Additionally, Holtz *et al.* observed the following: Pubic boot resembling that in Tyrannosauridae and Ornithomimosauria, but more similar in propor-

tion to latter (*i.e.*, length less than one-third pubic vertical length); spinous processes of middle caudal vertebrae bearing short, cranially oriented spur and distinct kink (as in *Lourinhanosaurus* and more derived Carnosauria); obturator notch on pubis partially closed by cranially oriented hook (unlike condition in Coelurosauria, most reminiscent of partially closed condition in carnosaur *Sinraptor*).

Following the opinion of Rauhut (2003*a*), Holtz *et al.* assessed *Siamotyrannus* to be a primitive carnosaur rather than a basal tyrannosauroid.

Key references: Buffetaut, Suteethorn and Tong (1996, 2004); Holtz (2001); Holtz, Molnar and Currie (2004); Rauhut (2003*a*).

SINORNITHOMIMUS   Kobayashi and Lü 2003

Saurischia: Eusaurischia: Theropoda: Neotheropoda: Tetanurae: Avetheropoda: Coelurosauria: Tyrannoraptora: Maniraptoriformes: Ornithomimosauria: Ornithomimidae.

Name derivation: Latin *Sinae* = "China" + Greek *ornithos* = "bird" + Greek *sauros* = "lizard."

Type species: *S. dongi* Kobayashi and Lu" 2003.

Other species: [None.]

Occurrence: Ulansuhai Formation, Nei Mongol Autonomous Region, China.

Age: Early Late Cretaceous.

Known material: At least 14 skeletons, nine of them relatively compete and uncrushed, juvenile, subadult, gastroliths.

Holotype: IVPP-V11797-10, almost complete skeleton (femur 32 centimeters long) lacking distal caudal vertebrae, subadult.

Diagnosis of genus (as for type species): Ornithomimid distinguished by the following apomorphies: depression on dorsolateral surface of rostral process of parietal; fenestra within quadratic fossa divided into two by vertical lamina; low ridge on ventral surface of parasphenoid bulla; loss of caudolateral extension of proatlas (Kobayashi and Lü 2003).

Comments: The genus *Sinornithomimus* was founded upon a well-preserved, nearly complete subadult skeleton (IVPP-V11797-10) discovered by Dong Zhi-Ming in the summer of 1997, during the Mongol Highland International Dinosaur Project in a monospecific bonebed of the Ulansuhai Formation, near Ulan Suhai, in Alashanzuo Banner, Nei Mongol Autonomous Region of the northern part of China, near the boundary of China with Mongolia (Kobayashi and Lü 2003; first reported but unnamed by Kobayashi, Lü, Dong, Barsbold, Azuma and Tomida 1999), see "Introduction," *S2*).

Specimens from the same locality referred to the type species *S. dongi* include the following (11 juveniles

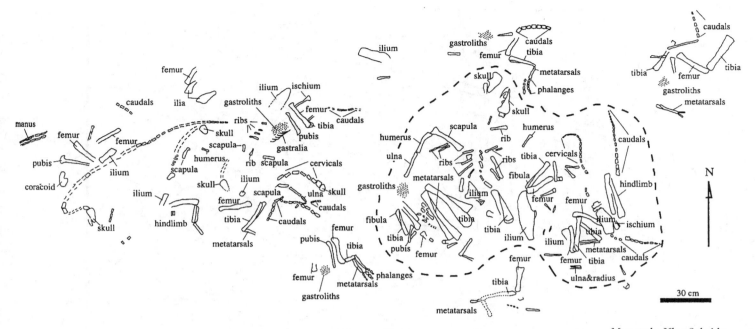

Map at the Ulan Suhai locality showing distribution of bones of *Sinornithomimus dongi*, dotted line indicating approximate area of large block containing specimens. (After Koboyashi and Lü 2003.)

and two subadults, not as well preserved as the holotype): IVPP-V11797–19 (larger than holotype, ulna 24.6 centimeters long); IVPP-V1797–29 (larger than holotype, femur 41 centimeters long); IVPP-V11797–1, IVPP-V11797–2, IVPP-V11797–3, IVPP-V11797–11, IVPP-V11797–12, IVPP-V11797–13, IVPP-V11797–14, and IVPP-V11797–15, all complete or nearly so skeletons; IVPP-V11797–9, missing the skull and distal caudal vertebrae; IVPP-V11797–16, including cervical vertebrae, pectoral girdle, forelimbs, and gastroliths; IVPP-V11797–17, rostral part of skull, cervical vertebrae; associated material including IVPP-V11797–18, right ulna, radius, metacarpals, manual phalanges, IVPP-V11797–19, left ulna, IVPP-V11797–20, coracoid, IVPP-V11797–21, sacral vertebrae, ischia, partial femur, IVPP-V11797–22, right femur, IVPP-V11797–23, left hindlimb, IVPP-V11797–24, left tibia, fibula, partial femur, IVPP-V11797–25, proximal right femur, IVPP-V11797–26, left metatarsals, pedal phalanges, partial astragalus and tiia, IVPP-V11797–27, caudal vertebra, IVPP-V11797–28, proximal caudal vertebra, IVPP-V11797–29, femur, tibia, fibula, metatarsals, phalanges, IVPP-V11797–30, three caudal vertebrae, IVPP-V11797–31, occipital region of skull, IVPP-V11797–32, caudal vertebra, IVPP-V11797–33, sacral vertebra, and IVPP-V11797–34, left ilium and sacral vertebrae. Because these specimens are fragile, intact, with larger elements articulated, Kobayashi and Lü deduced that the skeletons endured but little postmortem transportation.

Largest block containing eight complete and partial skeletons of *Sinornithomimus dongi*, gray areas indicating gastrolith masses. Scale = 30 centimeters. (After Koboyashi and Lü 2003.)

In performing a phylogenetic analysis, Kobayashi and Lü found *Sinornithomimus* to be positioned within Ornithomimidae (as suggested by Kobayashi *et al.*), a genus more derived than *Archaeornithomimus* and more basal to a clade of [(*Anserimimus* plus *Gallimimus*) plus [*Struthiomimus* plus ("*Dromicieomimus*" plus *Ornithomimus*)]] (see "Systematics" chapter for more details on this analysis). This assessment was primarily based on the ginglymoid distal condyles of metacarpal I in *Sinornithomimus*, a structure of the manus similar to that of *Archaeornithomimus*, thereby

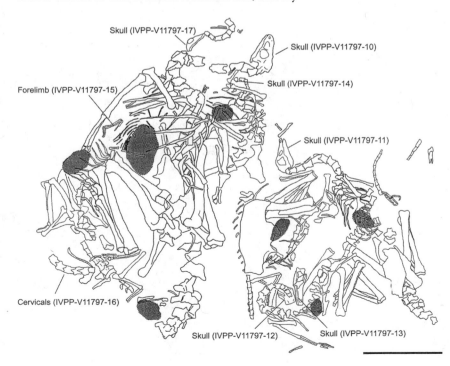

Skull (IVPP-V11797-17)

Skull (IVPP-V11797-10)

Forelimb (IVPP-V11797-15)

Skull (IVPP-V11797-14)

Skull (IVPP-V11797-11)

Cervicals (IVPP-V11797-16)

Skull (IVPP-V11797-12)

Skull (IVPP-V11797-13)

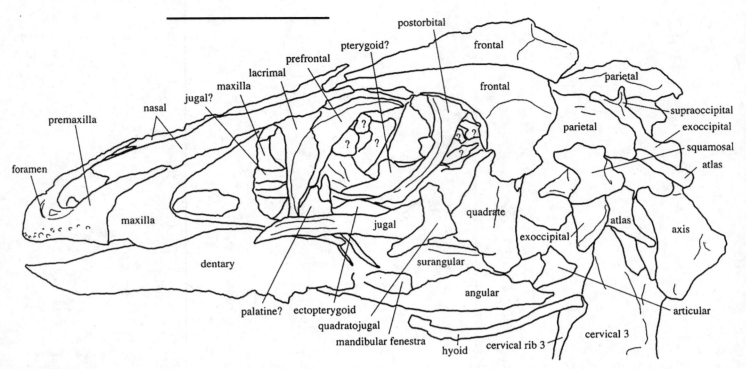

premaxilla · nasal · jugal? · maxilla · lacrimal · prefrontal · pterygoid? · postorbital · frontal · frontal · parietal · parietal · supraoccipital · exoccipital · squamosal · atlas · foramen · maxilla · dentary · palatine? · ectopterygoid · quadratojugal · mandibular fenestra · hyoid · jugal · surangular · angular · cervical rib 3 · quadrate · exoccipital · cervical 3 · atlas · axis · articular

Sinornithomimus dongi, IVPP-V11797-10, subadult holotype skull in left lateral view. Scale = 5 cm. (After Koboyashi and Lü 2003.)

representing an intermediate condition between the primitive (*e.g.*, *Harpymimus*) and derived (*e.g.*, *Anserimimus*, *Gallimimus*, *Struthiomimus*, "*Drocieomimus*" [=*Ornithomimus*] and *Ornithomimus*) conditions.

The skeletons of *S. dongi* are nearly complete and articulated and found in a single horizon as a monospecific bonebed. Moreover, their preservation is uniform, with the bone surfaces displaying no signs of weathering or scavenging. This suggested to Kobayashi and Lü that these dinosaurs suffered a single mass death event and were buried simultaneously and somewhat rapidly. Analysis of the specimens further revealed that the juvenile individuals were of similar age, suggesting "altricial (or selective) mortality for juveniles or a catastrophic (nonselective) mass mortality with a high proportion of juveniles in the living

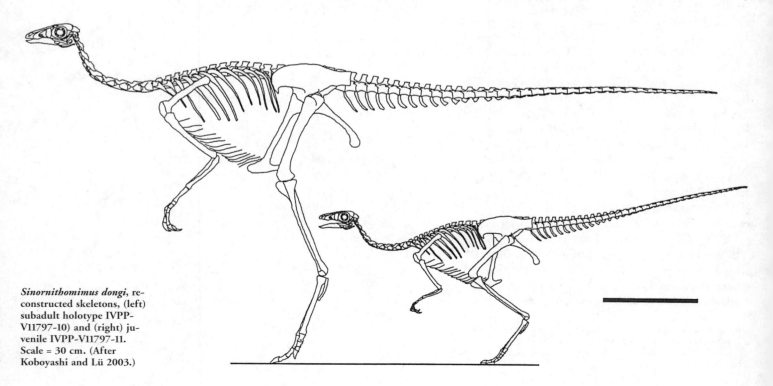

Sinornithomimus dongi, reconstructed skeletons, (left) subadult holotype IVPP-V11797-10) and (right) juvenile IVPP-V11797-11. Scale = 30 cm. (After Koboyashi and Lü 2003.)

Life restoration by artist Berislav Krzic of a subadult *Sinornithomimus dongi.*

population (Varricchio and Horner 1993)." As no evidence was found indicating that these dinosaurs perished in proximity to a nesting site, and because all the juveniles were mature enough (inferred from the well-formed articular surfaces of the limb bones) to have traveled with the adults, Kobayashi and Lü concluded that *S. dongi* engaged in gregarious behavior that included a large number of juvenile individuals. Furthermore, as *S. dongi* seems to have been an herbivore (based on the presence of gastroliths; see Kobayashi *et al.*), the authors found it possible that this species formed herds as a protection against predators.

Kobayashi and Lü found ontogenetic variation in *S. dongi* to be comparable to that observed in *Gallimimus bullatus* (see Osmólska, Roniewicz and Barsbold 1972), with a decrease in ratio of skull length to femur length, and increases in ratios of the antorbital region of the skull to skull length and radius length to femur length during ontogeny. While earlier studies (*e.g.*, Osmólska *et al.*; Russell 1972; Nicholls and Russell 1981) found little ontogenetic change in ornithomimid limb proportions, Kobayashi and Lü found significant changes in *S. dongi*. In larger *S. dongi* individuals, the humerus to femur length ratio is greater, the increases in the humerus and radius relative to femur length indicating a relative elongation of the forelimb during ontogeny. Also, this species demonstrates an increase in the relative tibia to femur ratio. Currie (1998), in comparing the lengths of tyrannosaurid limb bones with those of ornithomimids, had suggested that ornithomimids and juvenile tyrannosaurids were similarly proportioned,

thereby indicating greater cursoriality in the latter. Contrarily, the change in the ratio of tibia to femur in *S. dongi* suggested to Kobayashi and Lü "that adult ornithomimids may have been better adapted for fast running than juveniles."

Key references: Currie (1998); Kobayashi, Lü, Dong, Barsbold, Azuma and Tomida (1999); Kobayashi and Lü (2003); Nicholls and Russell (1981); Osmólska, Roniewicz and Barsbold (1972); Russell (1972); Varricchio and Horner (1993).

†SINORNITHOSAURUS

Saurischia: Eusaurischia: Theropoda: Neotheropoda: Tetanurae: Avetheropoda: Coelurosauria: Tyrannoraptora: Maniraptoriformes: Maniraptora: Metornithes: Paraves: Deinonychosauria: Dromaeosauridae: Dromaeosaurinae.

Diagnosis of genus (as for type species): Sternum large; most elongate forelimbs among known Dromaeosauridae; coracoid fenestra; rugosely textured antorbital fossa (Norell and Makovicky 2004).

Comment: Ji, Ji, Yuan and Ji (2002) restudied a small, subadult dromaeosaurid skeleton with extensive and well-distributed feather impressions (NGMC 91), previously described by Xu, Wang and Wu (1999), collected from the Lower Cretaceous (see Swisher, Wang, Zhou, Wang, Jin, Zhang, Xu, Zhang and Wang 2001) Yixian Formation of Liaoning Province, China (see *S3*).

As Ji *et al.* observed, some cranial and postcranial characteristics of this specimen identify it as belonging to the birdlike genus *Sinornithosaurus*. Differences between this specimen and the holotype of the type species *Sinornithosaurus milleni* might be attributed to ontogeny. Therefore, the authors could only identify NGMC 91 as representing an indeterminate species of *Sinornithosaurus*.

After briefly discussing the possible origin and early evolution of feathers, Ji *et al.* pointed out that numerous findings of flightless non-avian feathered theropods found in western Liaoning and have, via phylogenetic analysis, been shown to lie outside of Aves, offering "evidence that the origin of feathers is unrelated to the origin of flight in Avialae."

Lingham-Soliar (2003*b*) criticized the identification, by Xu *et al.* in their description of *Sinornithosaurus*, of two different forms of "integumental appendages" associated with this dromaeosaur, these coinciding with the latter authors' model for the evolution of feathers. Firstly, Lingham-Soliar (2003*b*) noted, Xu *et al.* described fibers seemingly joined in a basal tuft. Being an isolated occurrence and also a condition similar in some ways to that seen in ichthyosaurs, Lingham-Soliar (2003*b*) explained this

Sinornithosaurus

Skeleton with feather impressions (NGMC 91, slab A) belonging to a juvenile dromaeosaurid referred to *Sinornithosaurus*.

this evidence being tenuous; and towards the tip, three fibers of equal length lie parallel with the putative rachis and do not resemble branching barbs. It was the opinion of Lingham-Soliar (2003*b*), therefore, that "there is nothing to preclude the structures being modified, elongated scales, as in some modern reptiles," and also as described in the nontheropod dinosaur *Psittacosaurus* (see Mayr, Peters, Plodowski and Vogel (2002).

According to Lingham-Soliar (2003*b*), among the most convincing examples of feather impressions in a dromaeosaur are those reported by Ji, Norell, Gao, Ji and Ren (2001; see "Note," *Sinornithosaurus* entry, *S3*). However, a problem noted by Lingham-Soliar (2003*b*) in such reports is the lack of fundamental information concerning "dimensions (including those of alleged rachis and barbs) and concentrations of the filaments per unit area." Moreover, that author stated, "The short, knobby thick fibers ... are very similar to extensively preserved fibers, complete with tiny stubs along the pseudo-rachis" observed in a complete skeleton (SMF 457) of the ichthyosaur *Stenopterygius quadriscissus*, collected from Holzmaden in southern Germany. Lingham-Soliar (2003*b*) further pointed out that, in other areas of this skeleton, "fine fibers of one layer are compressed onto thick fibers of another, giving an uncanny resemblance to rachis and barbs."

As Lingham-Soliar (2003*b*) noted, the hypothesis of dromaeosaur feathers, as any theory, must take into account preservational aberrations that could explain fibers diverging or forming herringbone and barb-like patterns. One of the examples given by that author was the pressing, before fossilization, of overlying structures into the fibers below during compaction, possibly causing the paths of the fibers to diverge (see Lingham-Soliar (2001).

Lingham-Soliar (2003*b*) also regarded as speculative the assumption by Chen, Dong and Zhen (1998) that integumentary structures along the tail of the ?compsognathid theropod *Sinosauropteryx* are featherlike. According to Lingham-Soliar (2003*b*), the claim by Currie and Chen (2001; see *S3*) that fossilized integumentary structures in more recently studied material were "soft and pliable" is confusing, as the biological composition of these structures is unknown, and as fibers made of collagen have different forms, such as straight or bent, that are affected by various conditions during decomposition. Furthermore, Currie and Chen reported that magnification revealed the margins of the larger structures to be darker along the edges but light medially, this suggesting to those authors that the structures could have been hollow. Investigation by Lingham-Soliar (2003*b*) of ichthyosaur specimen SMF 457, however, showed that this

as possible representing "a taphonomic aberration." Additionally, Xu *et al.* "assertion that patches of multiple filaments represent a primary condition, *i.e.*, 'integumental appendages,' is speculative and unconvincing." Secondly, Xu *et al.* described some filaments as forming a pattern resembling the rachis and barbs of a pinnate feather." According to Lingham-Soliar (2003*b*), however, this interpretation raises two problems: Xu *et al.* figure only two places apparently showing signs of fibers diverging from putative feathers,

Life restoration by artist Todd Marshall of *Sinornithosaurus*, based on juvenile specimen NGMC 91.

Photograph by Mick Ellison, courtesy Mark A. Norell.

condition could more probably be explained as the result of different stages of mineralization. As alternative scenarios to explain the integumentary structures in the tail of *Sinosauropteryx*, Lingham-Soliar (2003*b*) suggested that tightly strung caudal ligaments separated from the vertebrae during postmortem decomposition, coming to lie alongside the caudal series of vertebrae, or that the skin of the animal "possessed masses of strengthening fibers or rays vertically oriented to the long axis of the body," the latter also found in icthyosaurs (see Owen 1840–1845).

Furthermore, Lingham-Soliar (2003*b*) pointed out that differing kinds of extant vertebrates (*e.g.*, sharks, snakes, turtles, dolphins) possess dermal collagen fibers grouped in various-sized bundles. In the case of dolphins, decomposed integument reveals "a breakdown of the fiber bundles and formation of myriad patterns of the disrupted fibers, many distinctly feather-like (unpublished data)."

In conclusion, Lingham-Soliar (2003*b*) found that it not possible to state that these Chinese dinosaurs were not feathered or that the structures associated with their skeletal remains are not collagen structures; moreover, the thesis of dinosaurian "protofeathers" necessitates more substantial support than currently exists.

Key references: Ji, Ji, Yuan and Ji (2002); Lingham-Soliar (2003*b*); Norell and Makovicky (2004); Swisher, Wang, Zhou, Wang, Jin, Zhang and Wang (2001); Xu, Wang and Wu (1999).

Skeleton with feather impressions (NGMC 91, slab B) belonging to a juvenile dromaeosaurid referred to *Sinornithosaurus*.

†SINOVENATOR

Saurischia: Eusaurischia: Theropoda: Neotheropoda: Tetanurae: Avetheropoda: Coelurosauria: Tyrannoraptora: Maniraptoriformes: Maniraptora: Metornithes: Paraves: ?Eumaniraptora: ?Deinonychosauria.

Diagnosis: diagnosed by the following characters — subotic recess on side of braincase ventral to middle ear; metatarsal IV deep oval in cross section (Makovicky and Norell 2004).

Comments: In performing a new phylogenetic analysis of the deinonychosaurian family Dromaeosauridae, Senter, Barsbold, Britt and Burnham (2004) found the genus *Sinovenator* — previously classified by Xu, Norell, Wang, Makovicky and Wu (2002) as a basal member of the Troodontidae (see *S3*; see also Makovicky and Norell 2004, "Systematics" chapter) — to be a basal member of Deinonychosauria with a close relationship with dromaeosaurids.

As Senter *et al.* noted, *Sinovenator* exhibits three unambiguous deinonychosaurian synapomorphies: Centra of cervical vertebrae having ventrally facing cranial articular surfaces; caudoventral "lip" on pedal phalanx II-2; and enlarged second pedal ungual. Although the latter two character states are found also in Troodontidae, *Sinovenator* also exhibits retropuby and a distally ginglymoid metatarsal III, synapomorphies shared by Paravis but not Troodontidae.

Key references: Senter, Barsbold, Britt and Burnham (2004); Makovicky and Norell (2004); Xu, Norell, Wang, Makovicky and Wu (2002).

SINUSONASUS   Xu and Wang 2004

Saurischia: Eusaurischia: Theropoda: Neotheropoda: Tetanurae: Avetheropoda: Coelurosauria: Tyrannoraptora: Maniraptoriformes: Maniraptora: Metornithes: Paraves: ?Deinonychosauria: Troodontidae *incertae sedis*.

Name derivation: "Sinusoid [nasal]."

Type species: *S. magnodens* Xu and Wang 2004.

Other species: [None.]

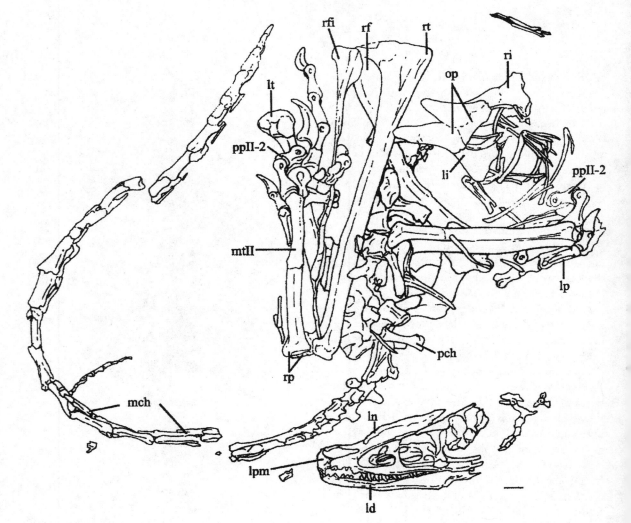

Sinusonasus magnodens, IVPP V11527, holotype skeleton. Scale = 1 cm. (After Xu and Wang 2004.)

Occurrence: Yixian Formation, Liaoning Province, China.

Age: Early Cretaceous (Hauterivian).

Known material/holotype: IVPP V11527, articulated skeleton missing presacral vertebrae, shoulder girdles, forelimbs.

Diagnosis of genus (as for type species): Small, differing from other known troodontids in the following apomorphies: nasal sinusoid in lateral aspect, absence of passage connecting antorbital and maxillary fenestrae, teeth relatively large, platelike chevrons forming bandlike structure along most length of tail, long neck between femoral head and shaft (Xu and Wang 2004).

Comments: The genus *Sinusonasus* was founded on a nearly complete articulated skeleton (IVPP V11527) collected from the Lower Cretaceous (see Swisher, Wang, Zhou, Wang, Jin, Zhang, Xu, Zhang and Wang 2001) Yixian Formation, Lujiatun locality, Beipiao, western Liaoning Province, China (Xu and Wang 2004).

Xu and Wang identified the type species *S. magnodens* as a member of the Troodontidae based upon the following derived features: Numerous tightly packed teeth; dentary roughly triangular in lateral aspect, mental foramina in groove (see Currie 1987); lacrimal T-shaped, cranial process long; distal caudal vertebrae having sagittal sulcus above neural canal, centrum significantly reduced; metatarsal II slender, shorter than IV (see Currie and Peng 1993; Norell, Makovicky and Clark 2000).

In comparing *S. magnodens* with other troodontids, Xu and Wang found the new genus and species probably to be more derived than either *Sinovenator changii* or *Sinornithoides youngi*, while sharing a number of features with geologically younger and more derived forms that are not found in *S. changii* (*e.g.*, anteroventrally oriented pubis; large triangular obturator process located at midshaft of ischium; fully arctometatarsalian metatarsus; highly abbreviated pedal phalanx II-2, proximoventral heel developed). Also, *S. magnodens* appears to be more derived than *S. youngi*, based upon various features on the caudal vertebrae and ischium (*e.g.*, ischium of *S. youngi* showing intermediate condition between *S. changii* and more derived taxa such as *S. magnodens*, having smaller, more distally located obturator process; distal caudal vertebrae of *S. youngi* lacking dorsal sulcus found in *S. magnodens* and other troodontids).

Xu and Wang noted that the small size, the unserrated mesial teeth, and relatively small denticles on the middle and distal teeth suggest that *Sinusonasus magnodens* could be a more primitive form than most Late Cretaceous members of the Troodontidae. However, the exact phylogenetic placement of this taxon must await a numerical cladistic analysis, which was beyond the scope of the authors' present study.

According to Xu and Wang, the coexistence of the relatively derived *S. magnodens* and the most basal known troodontid, *S. changii*, during Hauterivian time in western Liaoning, has implications concerning the early evolution of the Troodontidae. As these authors explained, the three main lineages of the clade Paraves are Aves, Dromaeosauridae, and Troodontidae. The oldest known member of Aves is from the Late Jurassic (Tithonian), while the oldest known dromaeosaurids and troodontids are of Hauterivian age. Considering that *S. changii* is very similar to the microraptorian *Microraptor*, that both *S. changii* and *S. magnodens* exhibit most features diagnostic of Troodontidae, and that *S. magnodens* exhibits various reversal features absent in *S. changii* but seen in later, highly derived troodontid forms, Xu and Wang deduced that "1) the basal deinonychosaur split might not be significantly earlier than Hauterivian, possibly in the earliest Cretaceous; and 2) the troodontids have rapidly acquired most of their autapomorphies and derived troodontid lineage have reversed to more primitive condition in many characters rapidly after the origin of troodontids." This scenario, the authors pointed out, conflicts with earlier studies (*e.g.*, Sereno 1999*a*; Xu, Zhao and Clark 2001) predicting an earlier fossil record for the Troodontidae and other derived coelurosaurian lineages. As Xu and Wang noted, the temporal constraints of the three major paravian lineages, combined with the character distribution among the earliest known members of Troodontidae and Microraptoria [=basalmost members of "Dromaeosauridae" of their usage; see *Microraptor* entry

and "Systematics" chapter], indicates that Troodontidae could be restricted to the Cretaceous, probably having "a rapid rate of character evolution at the base of the group."

Key references: Currie (1987); Currie and Peng (1993); Norell, Makovicky and Clark (2000); Sereno (1999*a*); Swisher, Wang, Zhou, Wang, Jin, Zhang, Xu, Zhang and Wang (2001); Xu and Wang (2004); Xu, Zhao and Clark (2001).

†**SPHAEROTHOLUS**—(See *Prenocephale*.)

SPINOSTROPHEUS Sereno, Wilson and Conrad 2004

Saurischia: Eusaurischia: Theropoda: Neotheropoda: Ceratosauria.

Name derivation: Greek *spinos* = "spine" + Greek *strophe* = "vertebra."

Type species: *S. gautieri* Sereno, Wilson and Conrad 2004.

Other species: [None.]

Occurrence: Tiouarén Formation, In Tedreft, also (southwest of Agadez), Niger Republic.

Age: Middle Cretaceous ("Neocomian" [=Hauterivian]).

Known material: Various postcranial remains, referred cervical and dorsal vertebrae overlapping with holotype.

Holotype: Musée National d'Histoire Naturelle collection, disarticulated vertebrae, partial left humerus, partial right tibia.

Diagnosis of genus (as for type species): Basal ceratosaurian characterized by midcervical vertebrae having strongly canted cranial articular face on centra (30-degree angle to caudal face of centrum), partitioned cranial pleurocoels, dorsoventrally flattened epipophyseal processes, broad subrectangular neural spines (Sereno, Wilson and Conrad 2004).

Comments: A small-bodied theropod, the genus *Spinostropheus* was founded upon a partial postcranial skeleton (Musée National d'Histoire Naturelle collection) discovered in 1959 by Albert F. de Lapparent in the Tiuouarén Formation, at In Tedreft, in the Niger Republic. Incorrectly, Lapparent referred these to the Late Jurassic theropod *Elaphrosaurus* (see *D:TE*) as the new species *Elaphrosaurus gautieri*. More recently, additional remains (MNN TIG6)—comprising an articulated axial column preserving the third cervical to the cranial sacral vertebrae, with complete cervical and more fragmentary dorsal ribs—were collected from the same formation, southwest of Agadez, Niger Republic, the cervical and dorsal vertebrae overlapping with the holotype (Sereno, Wilson and Conrad 2004).

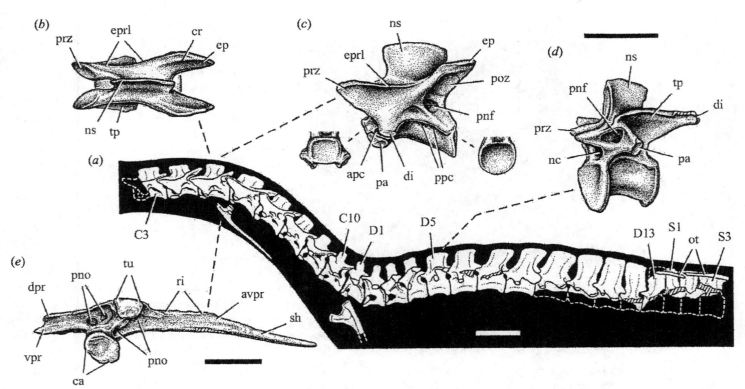

As noted by Sereno *et al.*, *Spinostropheus* is intermediate in age and phylogenetic position between *Elaphrosaurus* and the Late Cretaceous abelisauroids, sharing with the latter the following features: Cervical vertebrae having paired pleurocoels; middorsal vertebrae with prominent parapophyses; cervical ribs having broadened bifurcate spines interlocking with adjacent cervical ribs; and (most significantly), prominent ridge on cervical neural arches (this ridge further developed as lamina in Abelisauroidea).

Key references: Lapparent (1960); Sereno, Wilson and Conrad (2004).

†STAURIKOSAURUS

Saurischia: Herrerasauria: Herrerasauridae.

Comments: Since the original description in 1970 by Edwin H. Colbert of *Staurikosaurus*, the systematic position of this small to medium-sized, bipedal South American archosaur has been controversial. Indeed, this genus has been, at various times, classified as a basal dinosaur, basal saurischian, primitive theropod, carnivorous prosauropod, even a nondinosaurian archosaur (see *D:TE, S1, S2*, and *S3*).

Recently, as briefly reported in a published abstract, Bittencourt and Kellner (2004) attempted to resolve this problem of the phylogenetic position of *Staurikosaurus*. Bittencourt and Kellner's reassessment included preparation of additional parts of the holotype (MCZ 1669) partial skeleton of the type species *Staurikosaurus pricei*, exposing previously unknown anatomical data. A data matrix was then constructed including nine dinosaurian taxa and two outgroups, incorporating 113 characters, with the inclusion in Dinosauria of *S. pricei* assumed *a priori* based upon several dinosaurian synapomorphies (*e.g.*, femoral head set off more distinctly from bone shaft; reduction of tuberosity laterally bounding ligament of femoral head; caudal process of distal tibia ventrally projected [with ascending process of astragalus inserting beneath tibia]).

The analysis of Bittencourt and Kellner yielded the following conclusions: *S. pricei*—based upon reduction of iliac brevis fossa and shortening of caudal dorsal centra—clustering in Herrerasauridae along with *Herrerasaurus* plus *Chindesaurus*; short, distally rounded pre- and postacetabular processes of ilia supporting closer relationship between *Staurikosaurus* and *Herrerasaurus* than either with *Chindesaurus*; three characters uniting Herrerasauridae with Neotheropoda (*i.e.*, developed mandibular joint; neural spines of dorsal; vertebrae higher than long; prezygapophyses of distal caudal vertebrae elongated found in *Staurikosaurus*).

This suite of derived traits, the authors suggested, "allows classification of *Staurikosaurus pricei* as a theropod dinosaur." (For contrary views, however, see Langer 2004 and other authors, "Systematics" chapter.)

Key references: Bittencourt and Kellner (2004); Colbert (1970); Langer (2004).

Spinostropheus gautieri, MNN TIG6, referred a. articulated presacral vertebral column (reconstructed), left lateral view; b. fifth cervical vertebra, dorsal view; c. fifth cervical vertebra, lateral view, with cranial and caudal views of articular faces of centrum; d. fifth dorsal vertebra, craniolateral view; e. midcervical rib (reversed from left), dorsomedial view. Scale = (a) 10 cm., (b–d) 5 cm., and (e) 2 cm. (After Sereno, Wilson and Conrad 2004.)

Life restoration by artist Mark Hallett of *Staurikosaurus pricei*. The theropod status of this taxon was demonstrated in 2004 in a study by Jonathas de Souza Bittencourt and Alexander Kellner.

†STEGOCERAS—(=*Ornatotholus*)

Ornithischia: Predentata: Genusauria: Cerapoda: Chasmatopia: Marginocephalia: Pachycephalosauria: Goyocephhala: Homalocephaloidea: Pachycephalosauridae.

Type species: *S. validum* (Lambe 1902).

Other species: *S. breve* (Lambe 1918), *S. edmontonense* (Brown and Schlaikjer 1943).

Occurrence: Dinosaur Park Formation, Oldman Formation, Alberta, Canada.

Diagnosis (as for type species): Differing from all other pachycephalosaurs in having pronounced parietosquamosal shelf with incipient frontoparietal dome; nasals inflated; postorbital located caudolaterally on dome; ornamentation comprising numerous minute tubercles on lateral and caudal sides of squamosals, prominent dorsal row of up to six tubercles on each squamosal, as many as two nodes on median caudal projection of parietal (Sullivan 2003).

Comments: Over the years (and to the present), numerous species have been referred to the small to the North American pachycephalosaurid genus *Stegoceras*, in fact more than to any other named pachycephalosaur. As related by Robert M. Sullivan, a specialist in dome-headed dinosaurs, this genus has, consequently, "become (perhaps unintentionally) a 'wastebasket taxon' for any small-to-medium sized North American pachycephalosaurs."

As Sullivan pointed out, most of the species that had been referred to *Stegoceras* were later synonymized with the type species *S. validum*, while some were either referred to other genera (*i.e.*, *Gravitholus* and *Ornatotholus*; see below) or regarded as sexual dimorphs (see *D:TE*, *S2*, *S3*). According to Sullivan, however, most earlier studies have resulted in dubious conclusions, being not conducted within the bounds of a rigorous taxonomic framework. Indeed, many of the previously noted cranial differences observed by other workers can be interpreted as variation within a single taxon, *S. validum*. Indeed, some details formerly used to diagnose *S. validum* (see Sues and Galton 1987) can also be found in other pachycephalosaurs.

More recently, Sullivan, in his ongoing study (begun in the late 1980s) of *Stegoceras*, performed a new phylogenetic analysis, incorporating 49 characters including nine cranial characters based on pachycephalosaurian frontoparietal domes, allowing for a revision of this genus. Sullivan's study involved examination of all the pachycephalosaur specimens in the collections of the Royal Tyrrell Museum of Palaeontology (wherein most pachycephalosaur specimens are housed), the Canadian Museum of Nature, the Museum of the Rockies, the Royal Ontario Museum, and the University of Alberta. Additionally, Sullivan studied pachycephalosaur specimens housed at the American Museum of Natural History, the Carnegie Museum of Natural History, the Denver Museum of Nature and Science, the Natural History Museum of Los Angeles County, the New Mexico Museum of Natural History and Science, and the National Museum of Natural History; and also the holotypes of *Prenocephale prenes* and *Homalocephale calathocercos* included in the recently United States-touring Great Russian Dinosaur Exhibition. (See Appendix 1 in Sullivan's paper for a complete list of the specimens studied.)

As most of the examined specimens for his study consist of incomplete skull or frontoparietal material, Sullivan was able only to present diagnoses based upon cranial autapomorphies (*contra* Williamson and Carr 2003*b*) as the main criteria for differentiating pachycephalosaurian taxa.

Courtesy Robert M. Sullivan.

Stegoceras validum, CMN 515, lectotype frontoparietal, holotype of *S. validus*, dorsal view.

Sullivan proposed a newly revised diagnosis for the genus *Stegoceras* and type species *S. validum*. Again that author recognized the type species *Ornatotholus browni* as a junior synonym of *S. validum* (see *S2, S3*), representing an earlier growth stage of that species (as proposed by Goodwin, Buchholtz and Johnson 1998), and rejected the suggestion by Williamson and Carr that this species is a *nomen dubium*.

Formerly, Sullivan (2000*a*) transferred the small species *Stegoceras breve* to the genus *Prenocephale* (see *S2*), after which Williamson and Carr, rejecting Sullivan's referral, transferred it back to the genus *Stegoceras* (see *S3*). According to Sullivan (2003), however, Williamson and Carr's referral cannot be adequately defended; therefore, Sullivan (2003) referred this species back to *Prenocephale* (see *Prenocephale* entry). More recently, Maryańska, Chapman and Weishampel (2004), in reviewing the Pachycephalosauria, rejected Sullivan's (2000*a*) referral of the species *Stegoceras edmontonensis* and *S. brevis* (renamed *Stegoceras edmontonense* and *S. breve*, respectively, by Galton and

Sues) to the genus *Prenocephale* (see entry), noting that these taxa "are poorly documented and not supported" by these authors' phylogenetic analysis (see "Systematics" chapter). Therefore, for the present at least, these taxa are again considered to be species of *Stegoceras*.

Regarding some of the many specimens that had been referred to *S. validum*, Sullivan (2003) noted that UCMP 130048 and UCMP 130050, both identified as such by Goodwin (1990), lack any diagnostic characters that would warrant their referral to this taxon. Furthermore, Sullivan (2003) observed, these two specimens differ from each other "in that UCMP 130048 has a distinctive down-turned parietal as in *Colepiocephale lambei* [see *Colepiocephale* entry], whereas UCMP 130050 is characterized by a frontoparietal dome that's very high, nearly symmetrical (rostral to caudal), with sutures for lateral peripheral elements that are positioned low on the dome," the latter being "further distinguished by a well-developed medial (nasal) lobe." While very similar to *C. lambei*

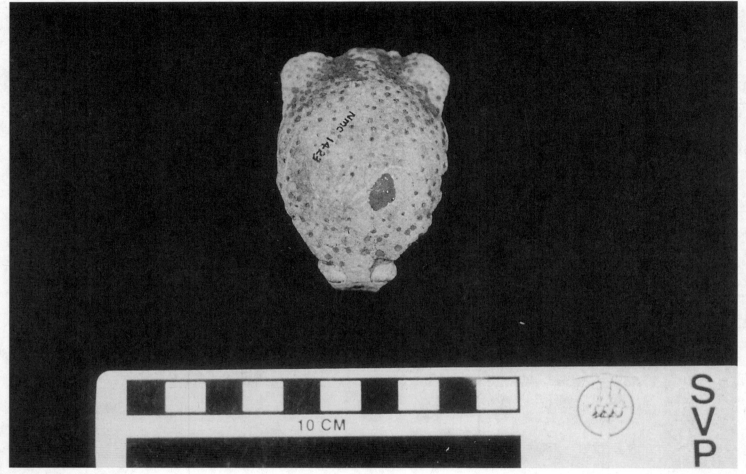

Stegoceras breve, CMN 1423, holotype frontoparietal dome, dorsal view.

referred specimen TMP 97.99.2, which shares these same features, Sullivan (2003) was not able to assign UCMP 130050 to any genus or species.

Further addressing the specimens referred to *Stegoceras validum*, Sullivan (2003) noted the following: Morphotypes of this species "run the spectrum of frontoparietals being flat (as in TMP 78.19.4), to intermediate (as in ROM 803), to more incipiently-domed forms (as in UALVP-2). The frontoparietal dome is never fully-inflated (as in other genera), and there is always a distinct lateral shelf on both sides of the skull made of the peripheral elements (postorbital and posterior supraorbital). Therefore, morphologic variation in frontoparietal dome development appears to be, in part, ontogenetic." Specimens having flat, paired frontals were interpreted by Sullivan (2003) as juveniles of *S. validum*.

Sullivan (2003) described the ornamentation in *Stegoceras* as generally made up of tiny tubercles on the caudal and caudolateral sides of the squamosals. Some specimens (*e.g.*, TMP 99.62.1) also have, on the caudalmost part of the parietal and (left) squamosal, a well-developed row of larger nodes with upwardly di-

rected apices. Below this row lie numerous randomly positioned, minute nodes. Sullivan (2003) noted that specimen CMN 38428 has well-developed nodes on the caudal margin of the squamosals, while TMP 2000.26.01, recently recovered from the Oldman Formation of Alberta, preserving the rostral portion of the left postorbital and greater caudal part of the left caudal supraorbital, conforms to UALVP-2. The left postorbital and left caudal supraorbital have irregular, incipient nodes with apices extending dorsolaterally to the dome. Sullivan (2003) noted that, as their suture traces can be seen both dorsally and laterally, these elements are not entirely incorporated into the dome.

Sullivan (2003) agreed in general with Sereno's (2000) suggestion that *S. validum* "bridges a morphological gap between flat-headed [pachycephalosaurs] and those with a fully developed dome," but cautioned that that statement "does not necessarily suggest, or demonstrate, that there is a linear progression from flat-headed, to incipiently domed, to fully-domed forms."

The lectotype (CMN [formerly GSC and then NMC] 515) of *S. validum* (formerly *S. validus*), an almost complete frontoparietal, was collected along the Red Deer River at a place where most of the fossiliferous exposures are in the Dinosaur Park Formation (formerly, in part, the "Belly River Beds"), the formation that has yielded the majority of *Stegoceras* specimens. However, as Sullivan (2003) pointed out, according to a 2000 personal communication from D. A. Eberth, "there is a remote possibility that the specimen came from the Oldman Formation (sensu Eberth and Hamblin, 1993)," which has also yielded material belonging to this genus. Furthermore, according to Eberth (personal communication to Sullivan, 2001), one *S. validum* specimen (CMN 38428), reported as from the Bearpaw Shale, is actually from the Dinosaur Park Formation. Sullivan (2003) further stated that no *Stegoceras* material is known from the Foremost Formation, the oldest Judith River Group unit (see Eberth and Hamblin).

In performing a phylogenetic analysis, Sullivan (2003) confirmed *Stegoceras validum* to be the sister taxon for two clades, one an unnamed clade uniting the recently named type species *Colepiocephale lambei* and *Hanssuesia sternbergi*, the other the new clade Pachycephalosaurini (see "Systematics" chapter), including *Stygimoloch* and *Pachycephalosaurus*.

More recently, in a published abstract, Goodwin, Colbert and Rowe (2004) reported on their use of "high resolution computed tomography (HRCT) to characterize and compare the micron scale structure of AMNH 5450 [holotype of *Ornatotholus browni*] with a juvenile skull of *Stegoceras* (TMP84.05.01) to determine the relative age of this putative "flat-headed" pachycephalosaurid," the data gleaned from this analysis then to be used to reassess the diagnosis of the genus *Ornatotholus* and also test the hypothesis that its holotype represents an early ontogenetic stage of *Stegoceras*. As Goodwin *et al.* (2004) pointed out, HRTC allows for the examination of the cranial histology of the above-mentioned specimens without destructive results.

HRCT examination of AMNH 5450 revealed to the authors "a highly vascular complex of fast-growing primary bone with open frontal-frontal and frontal-parietal sutural contacts, indicating a juvenile stage of ontogeny." These data compare favorably with cranial histology determined via HRCT of a juvenile *S. validum*. Furthermore, the holotype of *O. browni* shows various features (*e.g.*, smaller than domed *Stegoceras* specimens; frontals and parietal shelf thick but inflated, with large, open supratemporal fenestrae) "that do not appear to be valid diagnostic characters for *Ornatotholus* but instead reflect an early growth stage."

Key references: Brown and Schlaikjer (1943); Eberth and Hamblin (1993); Goodwin, Buchholtz and Johnson (1998); Goodwin, Colbert and Rowe (2004); Lambe (1902, 1918); Maryańska, Chapman and Weishampel (2004), Sereno (2000); Sues and Galton (1987); Sullivan (2000*a*, 2003); Williamson and Carr (2003*b*).

†STEGOSAURUS

Ornithischia: Predentata: Genasauria: Thyreophora: Thyreophoroidea: Eurypoda: Stegosauria: Stegosauridae: Stegosaurinae.

Diagnosis of genus: Skull characterized by ventral process of jugal; proximal caudal vertebrae with greatly expanded apex to neural spine, prominent dorsal process on transverse process; femur to humerus length ratio of at least 1.80; osteoderms consisting of series of thin, large plates, lengths equal to vertical height (Galton and Upchurch 2004*b*).

Comments: In 1919, paleontologist Charles Whitney Gilmore mounted for display at the United States National Museum (now National Museum of Natural History), Smithsonian Institution, a skeleton of the plated dinosaur *Stegosaurus stenops* (see *D:TE* for photograph). As chronicled by Young, Jabo, Kroehler and Carrano (2004), in an abstract for a poster, this skeleton as well as others on exhibit in the museum's Dinosaur Hall had been mounted using antiquated techniques (*e.g.*, "bones resting in direct contact with their metal armature, commonly attached by screws drilled directly into the elements"). That, the authors noted, combined with heat, humidity, and the high traffic flow of museum visitors to the hall has produced "an unstable environment for some of our intensely fragile specimens."

A survey of the hall identified the *Stegosaurus* as well as various other mounts to be requiring conservation (the National Museum's *Triceratops* mount was restored in 2002; see *S2, S3*). The *Stegosaurus* specimen, Young *et al.* reported, had begun to deteriorate, as evidenced by bone fragments found on the floor below the mount, some of the broken bones remained held together solely by the mount's metal armature;

Skull of *Stegosaurus stenops* ("Moritz") at the Sauriermuseum Aathal.

Photograph by Urs Möckli, copyright © and courtesy Sauriermusuem Aathal.

Above: Skeleton of *Stegosaurus stenops* mounted at the Sauriermuseum Aathal. This specimen, nicknamed "Moritz," was discovered in 1995 at Howe Ranch, in the Morrison Formation of northern Wyoming. Prepared by Ben Pabst, the skeleton measures 4.8 meters (approximately 16 feet) in length and 2.3 meters (more than 7.5 feet) in height. Original bones are lighter in color (see Ayer 1999).

Details of the plates of *Stegosaurus ungulatus* (CM 1134).

and numerous other broken bones had already been repaired during past years.

Conservation of this skeleton began with its dismantling and removal from the Dinosaur Hall, after which each element was repaired, restored, molded, and cast. Existing elements were replicated, while preparators sculpted, molded, and cast the nuchal ossicles that were missing from the original mount. In June, 2003, the authors reported, hollow hydrocal gypsum-cement casts, strengthened by fiberglass cloth, were filled with expanding foam and remounted over a new armature, the result being a more anatomically accurate skeleton of *S. stenops*, mounted from within and in a pose more responsive to its display environment (*i.e.*, a reactive stance before the hall's "attacking" *Allosaurus* skeleton).

The original bones of the old *Stegosaurus* mount now reside in the National Museum's collections, accessible both to researchers and visitors.

Key references: Galton and Upchurch (2004*b*); Young, Jabo, Kroehler and Carrano (2004).

†STRUTHIOMIMUS
Saurischia: Eusaurischia: Theropoda: Neotheropoda: Tetanurae: Avetheropoda: Coelurosauria: Tyrannoraptora: Maniraptoriformes: Ornithomimosauria: Ornithomimidae.

Diagnosis of genus (as for type species): Derived features including the following: extreme length of manus (longer than skull or humerus); extreme length of manual unguals (constituting more than one-fourth manual length) (Makovicky, Kobayashi and Currie 2004).

Comment: In their review of the Ornithomimosauria, Makovicky, Kobayashi and Currie (2004) rediagnosed the type species *S. altus* (see *D:TE*).

Key reference: Makovicky, Kobayashi and Currie (2004).

†STRUTHIOSAURUS (=*Craetomus, Danubiosaurus, Hoplosaurus, Leipsanosaurus, Pleuropeltus*; =?*Rhodanosaurus*)
Ornithischia: Predentata: Genasauria: Thyreophora: Thyreophoroide: Eurypoda: Ankylosauria: ?Nodosauridae.
New species: *S. languedocensis* Garcia and Pereda Suberbiola 2003.
Occurrence of *S. languedocensis*: Languedoc, France.
Age of *S. languedocensis*: Late Cretaceous (early Campanian).
Known material of *S. languedocensis*: Postcranial remains including vertebrae, cervical spine, pelvic girdle, dermal scutes, teeth.

Struthiosaurus

Photograph by the author, courtesy
North American Museum of Ancient
Life.

Skeleton (cast) of
Struthiomimus altus.

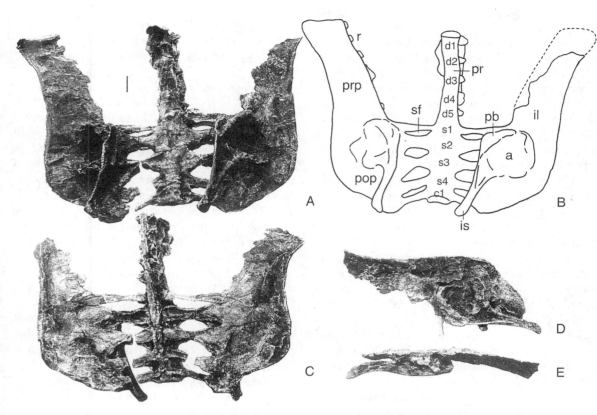

Struthiosaurus languedoensis, UM2 OLV-D50 A-C CV, holotype pelvic girdle and synsacrum in A. ventral and C. dorsal views, B. schematic drawing of same (ventral view), D. right pelvic girdle in ventral view, and E. left pelvic girdle in medial view. (After Garcia and Pereda Suberbiola 2003.)

Holotype of *S. languedocensis*: UM2 OLV-D50 A-G CV, partial postcranial skeleton including synsacrum, pelvic girdle, four dorsal vertebrae.

Diagnosis of *S. species*: Small nodosaurid (2.5 to 3.0 meters in length), ischium directed immediately caudal to acetabulum; distal dorsal centra very compressed laterally, "hourglass" shaped; shares almost straight to slightly curved ischium with type species *S. austriacus*; differs from *S. austriacus* in having robust, ischium oriented almost parallel to longitudinal axis of synsacrum, ending distally in blunt knob (Garcia and Pereda Suberbiola 2003).

Comments: A new species of *Struthiosaurus*, a "dwarf" nodosaurid ankylosaur known only from central and southwestern Europe, was described by Garcia and Pereda Suberbiola (2003).

As reported by these authors, the new species—distinguished as the first well-known armored dinosaur from the Upper Cretaceous of southern France—was founded on a complete synsacrum, pelvic girdle, and the four caudalmost dorsal vertebrae, collected by the Laboratoire de Paléontologie of the Université de Montpellier II and the field museum La Plaine des Dinosaures (Mèze, Hérault) from Upper Cretaceous (lower Campanian ["Fuvelian" continental local stage]) lignite-bearing gray clays in the L'Olivet Quarry, east of Montpellier in the Villeveyrac-Mèze Basin, in the Department of Hérault. The specimen was discovered lying dorsal-side up, unlike

the more common upside-down position in which most ankylosaurian skeletons are found (see Sternberg 1970; Carpenter 1984). Referred specimens from the same stratigraphic horizon include three isolated teeth (UM2 OLV-D18–20 CV), one distal caudal vertebra with fused chevron (UM2 OLV-D29 CV), one cervical spine (UM2 OLV-D27 CV), and two dermal scutes (UM2 OLV-D21–22 CV).

Reported nondinosaurian remains collected from the same quarry include those of lepisosteidid and sparid bony fish, anuran amphibians, and squamates, solemydid and bothremydid turtles, and eususchian crocodilians.

In describing this new species, Garcia and Pereda Suberbiola noted that the synsacrum comprises 10 coossified vertebrae (including five dorsals, four sacrals, and one caudal), a condition to date found only in *Polacanthus foxii* (see Hulke 1888; Pereda Suberbiola 1994) and *Struthiosaurus* sp. (Suberbiola 1999) among all ankylosaurs, the latter in other ankylosaurian taxa being generally fewer. However, the pelvic structures of *Struthiosaurus* and *Polacanthus* significantly differ (*e.g.*, postacetabular process of *S. languedocensis* diverging craniolaterally, and distal knoblike terminus of postacetabular process situated medially in *Struthiosaurus*, contrary to the condition in *Polacanthus*).

As Garcia and Pereda Suberbiola pointed out, the ischium of *S. languedocensis* has a gently curved shaft, a condition also found in an ischium referable to *S. austriacus* (see Pereda Suberbiola and Galton 2001). Coombs (1979) had characterized the ischium of nodosaurids as having a distinct flexion at midsection and that of ankylosaurids as being rectilinear or only slightly curved. However, as *S. languedocensis* exhibits a number of pelvic features regarded by Coombs (1978*a*, 1979) as typical of the nodosaurid condition (*e.g.*, preacetabular process of ilium relatively narrow [transversely broad in most ankylosaurids], postacetabular segment of ilium relatively long [abbreviated in ankylosaurids], body of pubis crescent-shaped [nubbin in ankylosaurids]), Garcia and Pereda Suberbiola suggested that such a form most likely constitutes an autapomorphy for *Struthiosaurus*.

Garcia and Pereda Suberbiola noted that, among the referred specimens, the teeth show distinct cingula and the osteoderms lack an excavation along the ventral surface, features usually considered to be characteristic of the Nodosauridae (see Coombs and Maryańska 1990). Additionally, an isolated dermal spine referred to this new species resembles closely one described by Pereda Suberbiola, Astibia and Buffetaut (1995) for the cervical half-rings of *Struthiosaurus*.

Although Garcia and Pereda Suberbiola referred the French material to a new species, these authors acknowledged that the differences between *Struthiosaurus languedocensis*, *S. austriacus*, and the referred species *S. transylvanicus* might also be attributed to individual variation or constitute a sexual dimorphism.

Note: For a survey review of the dinosaurs (including *Struthiosaurus*) of France, see Allain and Pereda Suberbiola (2003). As pointed out by these authors, the French record of dinosaurs "is one of the most extensive in Europe," stratigraphically ranging from the Late Triassic through latest Cretaceous, with all major clades (particularly Theropoda) represented except Marginocephalia, and including fossil footprints and eggs as well as skeletal remains.

Key references: Allain and Pereda Suberbiola (2003); Carpenter (1984); Coombs (1978*a*, 1979); Coombs and Maryańska (1990); Garcia and Pereda Suberbiola (2003); Hulke (1888); Pereda Suberbiola (1994, 1999); Pereda Suberbiola, Astibia and Buffetaut (1995); Pereda Suberbiola and Galton (2001); Sternberg (1970).

†STYGIMOLOCH

Ornithischia: Predentata: Genusauria: Cerapoda: Chasmatopia: Marginocephalia: Pachycepalosauria: Pachycephalosauridae: Pachycephalosaurinae: Pachycephalosaurini.

Diagnosis: Differing from all other known pachycephalosaurids in having relatively narrow, laterally compressed skull with vaulted frontoparietal dome; squamosals robust, with three or more clustered hypertrophied nodes; distinct frontals (Sullivan 2003).

Comments: In his revision of the genus *Stegoceras*, Sullivan (2003) also addressed the genus *Stygimoloch*, from the Hell Creek Formation of Montana and Wyoming, at the same time providing a revised diagnosis for the type species, *S. spinifer*, based on holotype UCMP 119433 (an incomplete left squamosal with a cluster of hypertrophied nodes) and referred specimens (see Galton and Sues 1983; Goodwin, Buchholtz and Johnson 1998).

Sullivan officially recognized the type species *Stenotholus kohleri* Giffin, Gabriel and Johnson 1987 as a junior synonym of *Stygimoloch spinifer*.

Note: Sullivan also mentioned a species informally named "*Stygimoloch garbanii*," which was found listed on an Internet website. This could actually be, Sullivan noted, the holotype of ?*Thescelosaurus garbanii*, comprising incomplete cervical and dorsal vertebrae and an incomplete left hindlimb. Galton (1995), who had reviewed this material, suggested that it could pertain to a new genus or perhaps be referred to *Stygimoloch*, although he tentatively assigned the holotype of that species to the "hypsilophodontid" *Bugenasaura infernalis*.

Key references: Galton (1995); Galton and Sues (1983); Giffin, Gabriel and Johnson (1987); Goodwin, Buchholtz and Johnson (1998); Sullivan (2003).

†STYRACOSAURUS

Ornithischia: Predentata: Genusauria: Cerapoda: Chasmatopia: Marginocephalia: Ceratopsia: Neoceratopsia: Ceratopsoidea: Ceratopsidae: Centrosaurinae.

Comments: A recently collected and studied, complete and entirely articulated pes possibly referrable to *Styeracosaurus*, from the Late Cretaceous (Campanian) Dinosaur Park Formation of southern Alberta, Canada, has provided new information regarding the phalangeal formula of the hind foot of centrosaurine ceratopsids.

As chronicled in an abstract by Noriega, Sumida, Eberth, Brinkman and Skrepnick (2003), this formula, for more than a century, has been listed as 2–3–4–5–0, originally based upon a reconstruction of a presumably complete yet partly scattered pes assigned to the centrosaurine *Brachyceratops*. Because of a lack of articulated centrosaurine hind feet, the formula was assumed to be correct and was, consequently, applied to other members of the Centrosaurinae. Thus, this formula has been accepted as the actual versus reconstructed one throughout the twentieth century.

Life restoration of *Styracosaurus albertensis*, drawn by Berislav Krzic.

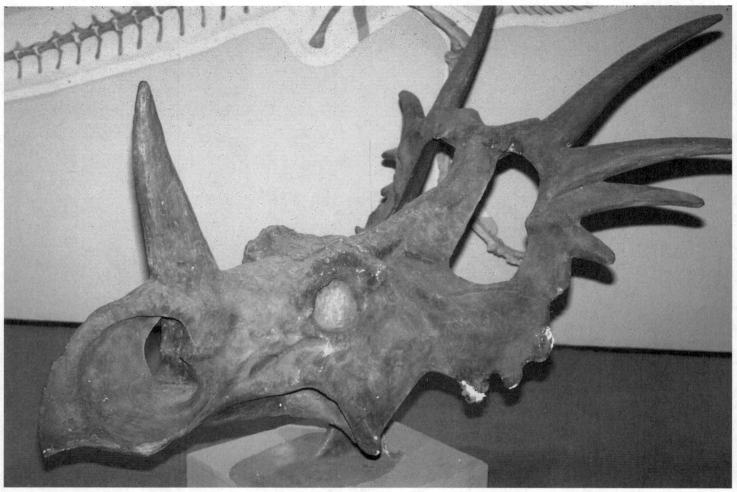

Styracosaurus albertensis, cast (LACM 53915) of ROM skull collected from the Oldman Formation of Red Deer Valley, Alberta, Canada.

As observed by Noriega *et al.*, the phalangeal formula of this new specimen—"intact and articulated down to the unguals of each digit—is 4-4-3-3-0, a drastic change from the old interpretation that could offer serious implications regarding both posture and locomotion among Centrosaurinae in particular and Neoceratopsia in general.

Key reference: Noriega, Sumida, Eberth, Brinkman and Skrepnick (2003).

†**SUPERSAURUS**

Saurischia: Eusaurischia: Sauropodomorpha: Sauropoda: Eusauropoda: Neosauropoda: Diplodocoidea: Flagellicaudata: Diplodocidae.

Comments: Lovelace, Wahl and Hartman (2003), in a published abstract for a poster, reported on the discovery of rib pleurocoels—structures previously known only in titanosauriforms—in a new specimen of the gigantic sauropod type species *Supersaurus vivianae*. The recovered material, comprising six pneumatic dorsal ribs, has been interpreted as belonging to a single individual.

As briefly described by Lovelace *et al.*, a pneumatic foramen is present on the cranial surface proximal to the juncture of the tuberculum and capitulum, this differing from the titanosauriform *Brachiosaurus*, in which the foramen is found below the head of the proximalmost portion of the shaft. The authors made the following measurements in the *S. vivianae* specimen: foramen 51 millimeters long, 18 millimeters at widest point of suboval opening, 360 millimeters from proximal end of tuberculum; pneumatocoel extending 320 distally, approximately 175 proximally from foramen, maximum width of cavity 720 millimeters, maximum thickness 30 millimeters. Lovelace *et al.* observed that both tuberculum and capitulum are pneumaticized.

This discovery in a derived diplodocid suggested to Lovelace *et al.* that pneumatization evolved at least twice within the Sauropodomorpha. However, as the widespread distribution of pneumatic pleurocoels within the Sauropoda implies "a developmental mechanism to account for this parallelism," the authors noted that caution should be used when including costal pneumaticity in phylogenetic studies.

Photograph by the author, Courtesy North American Museum of Ancient Life.

Reconstructed skeleton (cast by DINOLAB) of *Supersaurus viviane* displayed at the North American Museum of Ancient Life.

Upchurch, Barrett and Dodson (2004), in their review of the Sauropoda, interpreted the genus *Dystylosaurus* — referred by Curtice and Stadtman in 2001 to *Supersaurus* (see *S3*) — to be "a potentially valid brachiosaurid, although the incomplete nature of the material means that both its taxonomic status and supposed affinities should be treated with extreme caution."

Note: For a brief report on the taphonomy and paleoenvironment of a new Morrison Formation locality near Douglas, Wyoming, which has yielded remains assigned to cf. *Supersaurus vivianae*, see the abstract by Lovelace (2004).

Erratum: In *S3*, the photograph identified as the mounted skeleton of *Supersaurus vivianae* at the North American Museum of Ancient Life, is actually that of *Camarasaurus grandis*, mounted at the Gunma Museum of Natural History; also, the picture was taken by Clifford A. Miles and not the author.

Key references: Lovelace, Wahl and Hartman (2003); Upchurch, Barrett and Dodson (2004).

SUUWASSEA Harris and Dodson 2004

Saurischia: Eusaurischia: Sauropodomorpha: Sauropoda: Eusauropoda: Neosauropoda: Diplodocoidea: Flagellicaudata *incertae sedis*.

Name derivation: Crow (Native American) *suuwassa* = "first thunder heard in Spring."

Type species: *S. emilieae* Harris and Dodson 2004.

Other species: [None.]

Occurrence: Morrison Formation, Montana, United States.

Age: Late Jurassic (?Tithonian).

Known material/holotype: ANSP 21122, disarticulated but associated partial skeleton including dentigerous partial left premaxilla, dentigerous maxillary fragment, quadrate, complete braincase, atlas, axis, four cranial to middle cervical vertebrae and fragments, three cranial dorsal vertebrae, several ribs, numerous proximal, middle, and distal caudal centra, right scapula, coracoid, humerus, partial right tibia, complete right fibula, calcaneum, several metatarsals and pedal phalanges.

Diagnosis of genus (as for type species): Ventral end of supraoccipital drawn out into narrow, elongate

Suuwassea emilieae, ANSP 2122, holotype basicranium (dorsal view). (After Harris and Dodson 2004.)

process, contributing very little to dorsal margin of foramen magnum; basioccipital not contributing to dorsal side of occipital condylar neck; antotic processes of laterosphenoid separated from frontals by deep notches; cranial cervical neural spines restricted to caudal halves of their respective centra, compressed craniocaudally, expanded distally, concave on all sides, not bifurcate; distal caudal ("whiplash") centra amphiplatyan; humerus with well-developed dorsal tuberculum; proximal articular surface of tibia wider mediolaterally than long craniocaudally; calcaneum spheroidal; pedal phalanges longer proximodistally than wide mediolaterally (Harris and Dodson 2004).

Comments: A relatively small (length estimated at 14 to 15 meters, or approximately 47 to 50 feet) sauropod and the first nondiplodocid member of the Diplodocoidea reported from North America, the type species *Suuwassea emilieae* was founded on a partial skeleton including an incomplete skull (ANSP 21122), found in 1999 from the ?Brushy Basin Member equivalent of the Morrison Formation, in southern Carbon County, south-central Montana (Harris and Dodson 2004).

Performing a cladistic analysis, Harris and Dodson found *Suuwassea* to be a diplococoid more derived

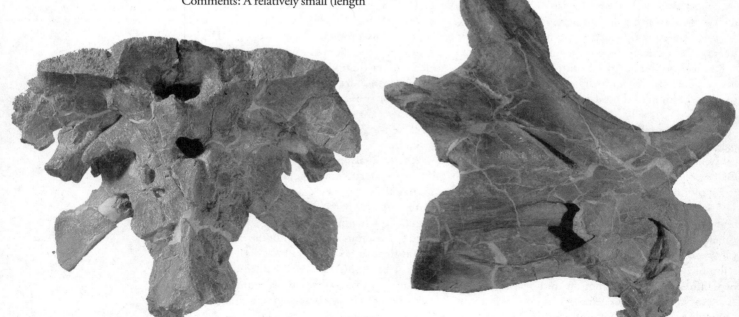

Left: Suuwassea emilieae, ANSP 2122, holotype basicranium (dorsal towards top view). (After Harris and Dodson 2004.) *Right: Suuwassea emilieae*, ANSP 2122, fifth cervical vertebra (right lateral view). (After Harris and Dodson 2004.)

than rebbachisaurids, but belonging to a trichotomy with the Diplodocidae and the Dicraeosauridae. To embrace the new genus plus these two families, the authors introduced the new clade Flagellcaudata (see "Systematics" chapter).

S. emiliea, as Harris and Dodson noted, presents a mosaic of diplodocid and dicraeosaurid character states, suggesting that many of the character states generally regarded as autapomorphic for either the Diplodocidae (currently known only from Gondwanan continents) or Dicraeosauridae (known from both Gondwana and Laurasia) could actually be plesiomorphies either lost or retained in each terminal clade. Furthermore, the presence of a diplodocid with seemingly dicraeosaurid features on a Laurasian landmass questions whether the ancestral member of Flagellicaudata had a Laurasian or Gondwana distribution or both (see Bonaparte 1986a; Salgado and Bonaparte 1991; Upchurch, Hunn and Norman 2002). If the primitive nature of *Suuwassea* indicates a Laurasian origin for Flagellicaudata followed by a later migration Gondwana (as suggested by *Cetiosauriscus sterwarti* from the Late Jurassic of England), dicraeosaurids might also have been present in Laurasia

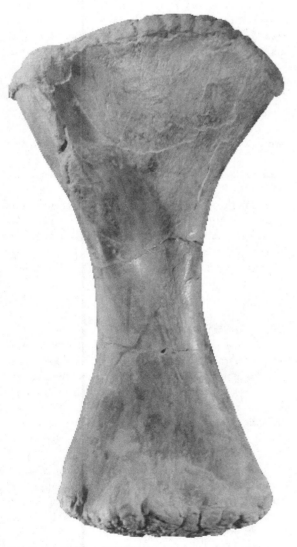

Suuwassea emilieae, ANSP 2122, right humerus (cranial view). (After Harris and Dodson 2004.)

Suuwassea emilieae, ANSP 2122, holotype calcaneum (?proximal view). (After Harris and Dodson 2004.)

Suuwassea emilieae, ANSP 2122, holotype pedal unguals I (top) and ?III (lateral view). (After Harris and Dodson 2004.)

before eventually migrating and becoming restricted to Gondwana. Alternatively, Harris and Dodson noted, basal members of Flagellicaudata had a more worldwide distribution, yet "only after the breakup of Pangaea did a Gondwanan population give rise to dicraeosaurids."

The discovery of the comparatively small genus *Suuwassea* in the Morrison Formation of Montana is in accord with other relatively recent reports of reported "small" sauropods from northern reaches of the Morrison depositional basin, Harris and Dodson noted (Horner 1989; Curry 1994; Turner and Peterson 1999; Storrs and Garcia 2001). The Morrison Formation can be considered to be "time-transgressive," following the northward retreat of the Middle Jurassic Sundance Sea; possibly, the authors speculated, the environs nearest to the regressing shoreline may have supported "a somewhat different fauna than is currently known from deposits in the more expansive southern portion of the basin."

Key references: Bonaparte (1986*b*); Curry (1994); Harris and Dodson (2004); Horner (1989); Salgado and Bonaparte (1991); Storrs and Garcia (2001); Turner and Peterson (1999); Upchurch, Hunn and Norman (2002).

†**SYNGONOSAURUS** Seeley 1879 [*nomen dubium*]

Ornithischia: Predentata: Genasauria: Cerapoda: Ornithopoda *incertae sedis*.

Name derivation: Greek *syggonos* = "of the same parent" or "kindred" + Greek *sauros* = "lizard."

Type species: *S. macrocercus* (Seeley 1869) [*nomen dubium*].

Other species: [None.]

Occurrence: Cambridge Greensand, Cambridge, England.

Age: Middle Cretaceous (late Albian–Cenomanian).

Known material: vertebrae, fragmentary humerus and tibia, four metatarsals, two phalanges, 11 osteoderms, unidentified elements.

Holotype: SMC B55571–55579, B55582–55586, vertebrae (lost).

Diagnosis of genus (as for type species): [None published.]

Comments: In 1879, Harry Govier Seeley erected the new genus and species *Syngonosaurus macrocercus* upon composite remains (SMC B55570–55609) — including vertebrae (one cervical, nine dorsals, four sacral, and five caudals), fore- and hindlimb elements, and almost a dozen osteoderms — recovered from the Cambridge Greensand, near Cambridge, Cambridgeshire, England. Seeley (1869) originally, because the dermal plates had been found in apparent association with the vertebrae, referred these remains to the ankylosaurian genus *Acanthopholis* as the new species, *A. macrocercus*.

As later pointed out by other workers (Pereda Suberbiola and Barrett 1999; see *S2*), some of the vertebrae (SMC B55571–55579, B55582–55586) included in the above material belongs to an ornithopod rather than an armored dinosaur. The armor, however, is referrable to the Ankylosauria, Pereda Suberbiola and Barrett noted.

Key references: Seeley (1869, 1879); Pereda Suberbiola and Barrett (1999).

†**SYNTARSUS**—(=*Megapnosaurus*; =?*Coelophysis*)

Saurischia: Eusaurischia: Theropoda: Neotheropoda: Ceratosauria: Coelophysoidea: Coelophysidae.

Diagnosis of genus: Small pit below basae of nasal process of premaxilla; nasal fenestrae in skull roof; rostrally directed spur of basioccipital roofing basisphenoidal recess; large pneumatic foramen in lateral surface of basisphenoid, laterally overlapped by crista prootica (Tykoski and Rowe 2004).

Diagnosis of *S. kayentakatae*: Caudal margin of frontals separated on midline by short rostral projection of parietals; faint groove across cranial surface of astragalus (as in *Dilophosaurus wetherilli*; see Welles 1983, 1984); low nasal crests and premaxillary fenestra (both reportedly not present in *S. rhodesiensis* and *Coelophysis*) (Tykoski and Rower 2004).

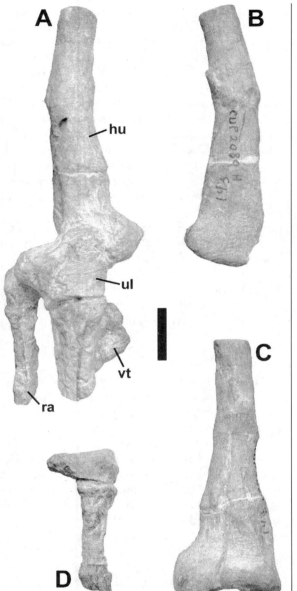

Elements (FMNH CUP 2089) from the Lufeng Formation of China referred to *Syntarsus* sp: A. left humerus (medial view) and left ulna (lateral view); B. left humerus (lateral view); C. left humerus (cranial view); and D. left radius (medial view). Scale = 1 cm. (After Irmis 2004.)

Elements (FMNH CUP 2089) from the Lufeng Formation of China referred to *Syntarsus* sp: A. right distal tarsal (proximal view); B. distal tarsals and metatarsals II and III (cranial view); and C. distal tarsals and metatarsals II and III (caudal view). Scale = 1 cm. (After Irmis 2004.)

Comments: In 2001, entomologists Ivie, Slipinski and Wegrzynowicz, noting that the name *Syntarsus* has long been preoccupied by a genus of beetle named by Fairmaire in 1869, proposed the new name *Megapnosaurus* for this small and primitive carnivorous dinosaur (see *S3*). This replacement name, however, has not been adopted, as most authors continue to use the name *Syntarsus* (*e.g.*, Arcucci and Coria 2003; Maisch and Matzke 2003; Rauhut 2004; Carrano and Sampson 2004; Tykoski and Rowe; others), leaving open the potential of the name *Megapnosaurus* being eventually regarded as a *nomen oblitum*. The final decision on which name will be declared correct may be the decision of the International Commission for Zoological Nomenclature.

At least for the present, then, the original name of *Syntarsus* is reinstated in this document.

Tykoski and Rowe (2004), in their review of the Ceratosauria, noted that the holotype skull of *Syntarsus rhodesiensis* was originally reconstructed incorrectly by Raath (1977), with the lacrimal reversed. When corrected, "the lacrimal abuts the maxilla and jugal ventrally, and it also has the effect of shortening the preorbital length of the skull." Once corrected, Tykoski and Rowe observed, the type species "lacks unambiguous apomorphies beyond those of *Syntarsus* ancestrally."

Irmis (2004) identified the first remains pertaining to *Syntarsus* [=*Megapnosaurus* of his usage] found in China and also in the whole of Asia. The specimens — collected from the Zhangiawa Member of the Lufeng Formation, Ta Ti, Yunnan Province, China — comprise a distal humerus, proximal radius and ulna, and fragments of metacarpals and phalanges (FMNH CUP [The Field Museum, Catholic University of Peking collection] 2089), and right distal tarsals II and III, and proximal metatarsals II and III (FMNH CUP 2090). This material was originally described by Simmons (1965) and referred by that author to the now abandoned family Podokesauridae. However, as Irmis pointed out, "Simmons's description misidentified elements and lacked good Early Jurassic theropod material for comparison." Moreover, these specimens have been mostly overlooked since the publication of Simmons' paper.

In redescribing these specimens in detail, Irmis noted that FMNH CUP 2090 can unequivocally be referred to the Ceratosauria (see Holtz 2000) based upon the fusion of the second and third distal tarsals to their respective metatarsals (see Rowe 1989; Rowe and Gauthier 1990; Tykoski 1998; Holtz); that it does not pertain to a member of the more advanced group Tetanurae, as "the proximal end of metatarsal III is not hourglass shaped" (see Carrano, Sampson and Forster 2002); and fusion of metatarsals II and III constitutes an unambiguous synapomorphy of the genus *Syntarsus* [=*Megapnosaurus* of his usage] (see Raath 1969; Rowe; Rowe and Gauthier; Tykoski). Given the poor preservation and preparation of this specimen, however, Irmis identified FMNH CUP 2090 as cf. "*Megapnosaurus*" sp. [=*yntarsus* cf. sp.], with no characters observed allowing referral of the material to either existing species or a new species of this genus.

Alone, Irmis stated, FMNH CUP 2089 cannot be referred to *Syntarsus* [=*Megapnosaurus* of his usage]; however, the association of this specimen "with FMNH CUP 2090 strongly suggests that both specimens came from the same individual." Additionally, the curved humeral shaft is consistent with the S-shaped profile diagnostic of the Coelophysoidea (see Holtz), while the lack of flattened distal humeral condyles is reflected by the condition in tetanurans (Carrano *et al.*). Moreover, while FMNH CUP 2089 can only be unequivocally assigned to the Coelophysoidea, it is most "unlikely that two coelophysoid specimens with nonduplicating elements that are found together would represent two different individuals or taxa."

As Irmis pointed out, the discovery of this material in China not only represents the first record of the genus from China, it also increases the known diversity of the fauna of the Lufeng Formation. Known currently from the Early Jurassic of three continents (Africa, North America, and Asia), the wide geographic range of this well-understood genus "makes it a possible index taxon for Early Jurassic age for the Lufeng Formation, and strengthens the evidence for an Early Jurassic age for the Lufeng Formation." Moreover, the fact that such Early Jurassic terrestrial tetrapods as *Syntarsus* [=*Megapnosaurus* of his usage] were pancontinental "suggests that the breakup of Pangaea did not present serious barriers for dispersal of terrestrial vertebrates."

Key references: Arcucci and Coria (2003); Carrano and Sampson (2004); Carrano, Sampson and Forster (2002); Holtz (2000); Irmis (2004); Ivie, Slipinski and Wegrzynowicz (2001); Maisch and Matzke (2003); Raath (1969, 1977); Rauhut (2004); Rowe (1989); Rowe and Gauthier (1990); Simmons (1965); Tykoski (1998); Tykoski and Rowe (2004); Welles (1983, 1984).

†SZECHUANOSAURUS

Saurischia: Eusaurischia: Eusaurischia: Theropoda: Neotheropoda: Tetanurae: Avetheropoda: Carnosauria: Allosauroidea: ?Allosauridae.

Note: In 1942, Zhungjian Yang (then spelled Young Chung-Chien) based the new genus and species *Szechuanosaurus campi* upon broken theropod teeth from the Upper Shaximiao Formation of northern Sichuan, China. Four decades later, Dong, Zhou and Zhang (1983) referred to this type species a reasonably complete postcranial skeleton from the Shangshaximiao Formation of Zigong, China (see *D:TE*).

Subsequently, Gao (1993) erected the new species *Szechuanosaurus zigongensis* for a skeleton recovered from the Dashanpu Quarry, in the Middle Jurassic Lower Shaximiao Formation, Zigong. As noted by Holtz, Molnar and Currie (2004), however, in their review of basal tetanurans, neither of these skeletons can be confidently referred to the tooth-based genus *Szechuanosaurus* (Chure, in press). Moreover, as pointed out by Holtz *et al.*, the skeleton described by Gao clearly shows the presence metacarpal IV, comparable to the element suggested to be the fourth metacarpal in the sinraptorid allosauroid *Sinraptor dongi* (see Currie and Zhao 1993).

Holtz *et al.* interpreted "*Szechuanosaurus*" zigongensis as the most basal of known tetanurans, diagnosed based upon the following features: Cervical vertebrae two through six opisthocoelous (other cervicals and all dorsals amphiplatyan); ischium having cranially directed boot without caudal expansion.

Key references: Currie and Zhao (1993); Dong, Zhou and Zhang (1983); Gao (1993); Holtz, Molnar and Currie (2004); Yang (1942).

TALENKAUEN Novas, Cambiasco and Ambrosio 2004

Ornithischia: Predentata: Genasauria: Cerapoda: Ornithopoda: Euornithopoda: Iguanodontia: Dryomorpha *incertae sedis*.

Name derivation: Aonikenk Indian *talenk* = "small" + Aonikenk Indian *kauen* = "skull."

Type species: *T. santacrucensis* Novas, Cambiasco and Ambrosio 2004.

Other species: [None.]

Occurrence: Pari Aike Formation, Santa Cruz Province, Argentina.

Age: Late Cretaceous (Maastrichtian).

Known material/holotype: MPM-10001, almost complete skeleton comprising skull (including rostrum, jaws, and teeth), precaudal vertebral column, ribs, pectoral and pelvic girdles, fore- and hindlimb elements, partially articulated.

Diagnosis of genus (as for type species): Autapomorphies including well-developed epipophysis on third cervical vertebra, and platelike uncinate process on rib cage; (from cladistic analysis) lacrimal and premaxilla not contacting; dentaries convergent rostrally (Novas, Cambiasco and Ambrosio 2004).

Comments: The type species *Talenkauen santacrucensis* was founded upon a partially articulated skeleton (MP-10001) collected in February, 2000, from medium-grained sandstone beds (interpreted as a fluvial channel) at the Los Hornos Hill locality in

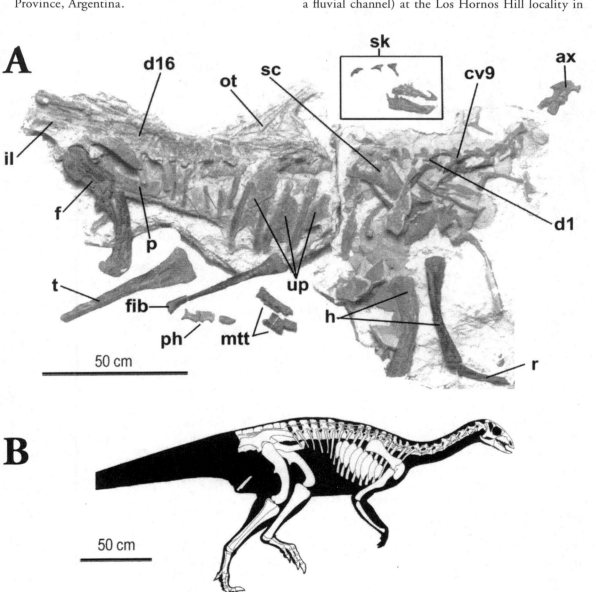

Talenkauen santacrucensis, MPM-10001, A. holotype incomplete skeleton, B. reconstruction (right lateral view). (After Novas, Cambiasco and Ambrosio 2004.)

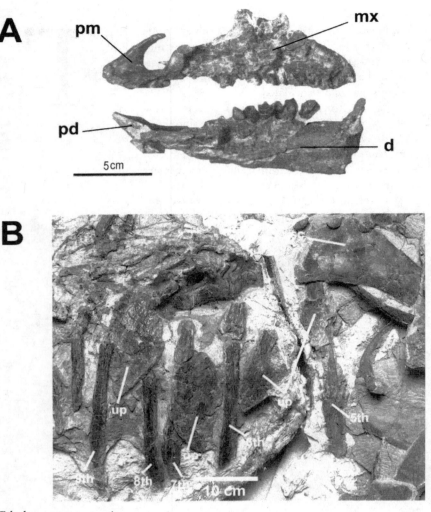

A

pm

mx

pd

d

5cm

B

up

5th

9th 8th 7th 10 cm

Talenkauen santacrucensis, holotype MPM-10001, A. rostrum (left lateral view), and B. detail of uncinate processes on ribs corresponding to fifth through ninth vertebrae. (After Novas, Cambiasco and Ambrosio 2004.)

the Upper Cretaceous (Maastrichtian; *e.g.*, see Kraemer and Riccardi 1997) Pari Aike Formation, on the southern coast of Viedma Lake, Santa Cruz Province, Argentina (Novas, Cambiasco and Ambrosio 2004).

In describing MPM-10001, Novas *et al.* noted that "the presence of polygonal plates on both sides of the thorax is outstanding," this derived character being shared by the North American, Maastrichtian thescleosaurid [="hypsilophodontid" of their usage] *Thescelosaurus neglectus,* these taxa being the only known ornithopods for which such plates have been documented. However, as no other derived characters have been recognized to unite these two species, the presence of these platelike structures in them "implies that such plates may have been independently acquired." Moreover, as ossification depends upon maturity, size, and sex, the presence of such plates among Ornithopoda could be more widespread than believed, the authors stated.

Novas *et al.* rejected the interpretation of the platelike structures in *Talenkauen* as defensive devices,

pointing out their fragility and arrangement in a restricted area of the thorax, this contrasting with the thick, profusely ornamented dermal ossifications found in dinosaurs bearing armor (*i.e.*, titanosaurids and thyreophorans). Rather, the interpretation of these structures as uncinate processes — present in extant and extinct diapsids, including *Sphenodon,* crocodilians, basal maniraptorans, and most birds (see Heilmann 1926; Paul 2002) — is supported by a number of features, including their nearness to the caudal margin of the ribs, and their serial arrangement on the thorax. However, the uncinate processes in *Talenkauen* and *Thescelosaurus* are much expanded and widely overlap one another, a condition not yet reported in any other diapsids (wherein these processes are modest, striplike projections). If these processes in *Talenkauen* participated in thoracic movements for lung ventilation as they do in birds (see Fedde 1987), wherein uncinate process length is directly proportional to external intercostal muscle-effectiveness to set the ribs into motion, then a well-developed musculature would be expected in this dinosaur. This suggests, Novas *et al.* noted, "an important participation in rib cage dynamics through well-developed intercostal muscles."

Novas *et al.* noted various derived features uniting *Talenkauen* with other Gondwanan ornithopods — *e.g.*, greatly reduced deltopectoral crest of the humerus shared with *Anabisetia* and the Argentinian *Notohypsilophodon* (see, respectively, Coria and Calvo 2002; Martínez 1998); transversely compressed metatarsal II shared with the Patagonian *Anabisetia* and *Gasparinisaura* (Salgado, Coria and Heredia 1997), the South African *Kangnasaurus* (Cooper 1985), and an unnamed iguanodontian from the Upper Cretaceous Antarctic Peninsula (Novas, Cambiasco, Lirio and Núñez 2002). However, the authors found this collective evidence to support insufficiently any iguanodontian clade endemic from the Southern Hemisphere. Rather, Novas *et al.* (2004) interpreted the South American *Anabisetia, Talenkauen,* and *Gasparinisaura* as constituting successively more distant outgroups of a globally distributed Dryomorpha.

Key references: Cooper (1985); Coria and Calvo (2002); Fedde (1987); Heilmann (1926); Kraemer and Riccardi (1997); Martínez (1998); Novas, Cambiasco and Ambrosio (2004); Novas, Cambiasco, Lirio and Núñez (2002); Paul (2002); (Salgado, Coria and Heredia 1997)

†TARASCOSAURUS

Saurischia: Eusaurischia: Eusaurischia: Theropoda: Neotheropoda: Ceratosauria: Abelisauroidea *incertae sedis.*

Comment: In a review of the Ceratosauria, Tykoski and Rowe (2004) readdressed the phylogenetic standing of the type species *Tarascosaurus salluvicus*, which was named and described in 1991 by Jean Le Loeuff and Éric Buffetaut, based on two specimens (see below) from southern France (see *D:TE*). Le Loeuff and Buffetaut had referred this material to the abelisauroid family Abelisauridae.

More recently, as observed by Tykoski and Rowe, the incomplete dorsal vertebra (FSL 330203) referred to this taxon "has numerous pneumatic foramina in the neural arch reminiscent of those in abelisaurids." While little definitive information could be gleaned from the holotype femur (FSL 330201) of this species, Tykoski and Rowe tentatively classified *Tarascosaurus* as Abelisauroidea *incertae sedis*.

Key references: Le Loeuff and Buffetaut (1991); Tykoski and Rowe (2004).

†**TARBOSAURUS** (=*Jenghizkhan*, *Maleevosaurus*, *Shanshanosaurus*; =?*Alioramus*)

Saurischia: Eusaurischia: Theropoda: Neotheropoda: Tetanurae: Avetheropoda: Coelurosauria: Tyrannoraptora: Maniraptoriformes: Tyrannoraptora: Tyrannosauroidea: Tyrannosauridae: Tyrannosaurinae.

Diagnosis of genus (as in type species): Nasal lacking caudally oriented lacrimal process (also in *Alioramus*, unlike North American tyrannosaurids; caudodorsal process of maxilla more massive than in *Tyrannosaurus rex*; caudal surangular foramen reduced compared to that of other tyrannosaurids; articulation of intramandibular joint producing locking mechanism unique among known tyrannosaurids (Hurum and Currie 2000); forelimb more reduced than in other known tyrannosaurids (Holtz 2001; Currie 2000, 2003*a*); femur to humerus ratio greater than 3.5, metacarpal I greater than half length of II due to reduction of I (general theropod reduction in digital and metacarpal elements from digit V toward I more so in this species than in other tyrannosaurids [Wagner and Gauthier 1999] and in most nonalvarezsaurid theropods); comparable in size to *T. rex* (adults with skull length of over 139 centimeters) (Holtz 2004).

Comments: Again the Asian species *Tarbosaurus bataar* is recognized as belonging to a genus distinct from the North American *Tyrannosaurus* (see *S3, contra* Carr 2003). Until recently, however, no bone-by-bone comparison of the skulls of these two gigantic theropods had ever been published. In 2003, Hurum and Sabath offered such a comprehensive study in which they compared the skulls of the type species *Tarbosaurus bataar* and *Tyrannosaurus rex*.

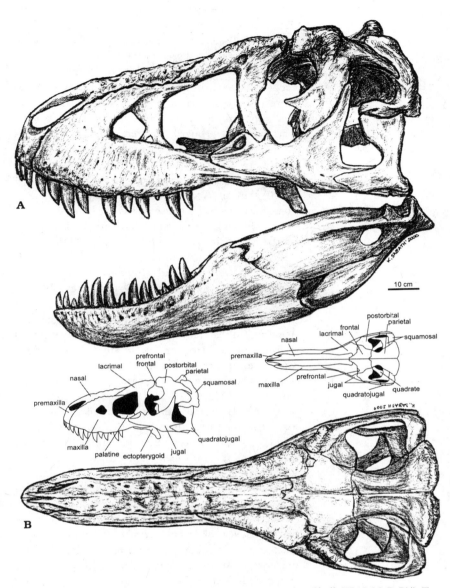

Skull (ZPAL MgD-I/4) *Tarbosaurus bataar* in A. left lateral and B. dorsal views. (After Hurum and Sabath 2003.)

Regarding *T. bataar*, Hurum and Sabath primarily based their study on the skull of this species on ZPAL MgD-I/4, a previously undescribed, incomplete "large skeleton," discovered during the Polish-Mongolian Palaeontological Expeditions (1963–1971) in the Nemegt Formation, Nemegt Basin, Mongolia (see Kielan-Jaworowska and Dovchin 1968/1969; Kielan-Jaworowska and Barsbold 1972). As the skull of this specimen was partly eroded with only the left side preserved, the authors were able—for the first time—to take the skull apart bone by bone and examine each bone in three dimensions. Only recently has this skull been fully prepared. Also figuring into Hurum and Sabath's study of *T. bataar* were various observations made decades earlier by Evgeny [Eugene] Alexandrovich Maleev (*e.g.*, 1974)—who named and first described this genus (see Maleev 1955*a*, 1955*b*,

1955c) — based upon specimens available to him during the 1950s, and also examination by the authors of new *Tarbosaurus* material in the Warsaw (these specimens previously undescribed) and Ulaanbataar collections (see Hurum and Sabath for list and descriptions of these specimens).

Concerning *T. rex*, Hurum and Sabath's comparative study primarily focused upon a cast of BHI-3033, the specimen nicknamed "Stan" (see *S3* and also *Tyrannosaurus* entry, this volume, for additional photographs of casts); and a cast of the holotype (CM 9380) skull of *Tyrannosaurus rex* housed at the Geological Museum, University of Oslo, Norway.

Following their detailed descriptions of the skulls of these two dinosaurs, Hurum and Sabath listed the following anatomical differences between the skulls of *Tarbosaurus bataar* and *Tyrannosaurus rex* (character states applying to *T. rex* in parentheses): Maxilla with massive, caudodorsal process, rostral end of lacrimal sheath around its caudal end (thin, platelike); nasal lacking lateral expansion and caudally oriented lacrimal process (see below), articulation to lacrimal only smooth groove (lacrimal process); horizontal ramus of lacrimal narrowing gradually towards rostral end, there divided by short mediolateral cleft, cleft process fitting into robust caudal end of maxilla, caudal surface of apex forming suture to frontal, prefrontal divided vertically by rugose ridge (rostral end of horizontal ramus clearly bifurcated, fitting into nasal); lateral side of prefrontal with several ridges for attachment of lacrimal, supporting most of caudomedial side of bone (smaller contact area); dorsoposterior jugal-lacrimal process of palatine in contact with most ventral part of lacrimal, visible in lateral aspect (not visible); caudoventral part of dentary having abrupt, square end, concave medially in transverse section where it meets angular, this caudal end articulating with perfectly matched vertical ridge on lateral surface of angular (thin caudoventral end having no abrupt end); angular with vertical ridge on lateral surface for articulation with dentary (angular with smooth groove, no abutting ridge; splenial with abrupt lip for supradentary (tip not very pronounced); 12–13 maxillary and 14–15 dentary teeth (11–12 maxillary, 12–14 dentary).

As Currie (2003b) noted, at least two characters — the locking mechanism of the jaws (Hurum and Currie 2000) and the extreme shortness of the forelimbs (see Holtz 2001; Currie 2003a) — suggest that *Tarbosaurus* is a more derived form than *Daspletosaurus* or *Tyrannosaurus*, and therefore cannot be ancestral to either genus.

Based upon their study of the new material of *T. bataar*, Hurum and Sabath speculated that the Tyrannosaurinae (see "Systematics" chapter) might further

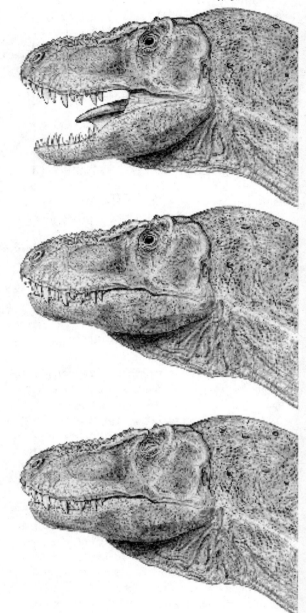

Head study of *Tarbosaurus bataar* by artist Berislav Krzic.

be subdivided into North American and Asiatic groups based upon the different ways by which the skull handled stress forces related to biting. (The authors stressed that "This is not a formal division, and more of a working hypothesis that needs to be addressed more thoroughly in a biomechanical analysis, which" was beyond the scope of their present study.) Hurum and Sabath noted that North American tyrannosaurids "show a consistent pattern of cranial joints with minor differences" (*e.g.*, see Russell 1970; Bakker, Williams and Currie 1988; Molnar 1991; Carr 1999), the exception being *Daspletosaurus*, which may constitute a link between the Asiatic and North American groups (see also Currie 2003b).

As Hurum and Sabath explained (see also Currie, Hurum and Sabath 2003), the nasal bone in diverse theropod taxa (e.g., Allosaurus, Carnotaurus, Ceratosaurus, Sinraptor, Albertosaurinae, and Tyrannosaurus) possesses the plesiomorphic feature of a lacrimal process in its caudal end for articulating with the cranial end of the lacrimal, this process being present in all North American tyrannosaurines except a large specimen of Daspletosaurus (see Currie 2003b). As stated above, however, the nasal in Asiatic tyrannosaurines is excluded from the major series of bones participating that deflect during biting the impact in the upper jaw. This anatomical feature — possibly a synapomorphy of the Asiatic tyrannosaurines — results in a less kinetic upper jaw in the Asian tyrannosaurines and also a more rigid lower jaw.

Speculating further, Hurum and Sabath cited the different kinds of prey available to the North American tyrannosaurids and Asiatic forms such as Tarbosaurus, these constituting the largest carnivorous animals in their respective ecosystems. While T. rex, capable of a higher crushing force, "probably specialized in bringing down large horned dinosaurs, like Triceratops," meat eaters such as Tarbosaurus "were forced to feed on [less well-armed] sauropods, hadrosaurs (also true for NATs [North American Tyrannosaurines], see Carpenter 2000), and perhaps ankylosaurs," and consequently did not require so great a crushing force. Such differences in typical prey items, according to Hurum and Sabath, therefore, "might have exerted different selective pressures, concerning hunting strategy and mechanical requirements maximizing their success rate as predators."

The authors further pointed out that tyrannosaurines probably passed through several ecological niches during their growth from hatchling to adult, specializing in different categories of prey at subsequent allometric stages. Interestingly, the adult Tyrannosaurus attained a stage never reached by the largest Tarbosaurus, the skull of the latter also exhibiting a "paedomorphic" appearance when compared with the North American genus.

With Tarbosaurus reinstated as a valid taxon, other taxa have been referred to this genus. In a recent study on the allometric growth in Asian and North American tyrannosaurids, Currie (2003a), following Currie and Dong (2001) (see Shanshanosaurus entry, S3, for details), regarded the genus Shanshanosaurus — a taxon originally described by Dong Zhiming in 1977, based upon a partial skull with associated postcranial remains (IVPP V4878) from the Subashi Formation of China — as a juvenile of the type species Tarbosaurus bataar.

Key references: Bakker, Williams and Currie (1988); Carpenter (2000); Carr (1999, 2003a); Currie (2003a, 2003b); Currie and Dong (2001); Currie, Hurum and Sabath (2003); Dong (1977); Holtz (2001, 2004); Hurum and Currie (2000); Hurum and Sabath (2003); Kielan-Jaworowska and Dovchin (1968/1969); Kielan-Jaworowska and Barsbold (1972); Maleev (1955a, 1955b, 1955c, 1974); Molnar (1991); Russell (1970); Wagner and Gauthier (1999).

†TARCHIA

Ornithischia: Predentata: Genasauria: Thyreophora: Thyreophoroidea: Eurypoda: Ankylosauria: Ankylosauridae: Ankylosaurinae.

Diagnosis of genus (as for type species): Cranial sculpturing pattern resembling that of Saichania (series of bulbous polygons), but distinguished from that genus by the following: larger basicranium; premaxillary rostrum having width greater than maximum distance between maxillary tooth rows; unfused paroccipital process-quadrate contact (Vickaryous, Maryańska and Weishampel 2004).

Comment: In their review of the Ankylosauria, Vickaryous, Maryańska and Weishampel (2004) rediagnosed the type species Tarchia gigantea (see D:TE), the geologically "youngest of the Asian ankylosaurs."

Key reference: Vickaryous, Maryańska and Weishampel (2004).

TAZOUDASAURUS   Allain, Aquesbi, Dejax, Meyer, Monbaron, Montenat, Richir, Rochdy, Russell and Taquet 2004

Saurischia: Eusaurischia: Sauropodomorpha: Sauropoda: Vulcanodontidae

Name derivation: "Tazouda" [locality] + Greek sauros = "lizard."

Type species: T. naimi Allain, Aquesbi, Dejax, Meyer, Monbaron, Montenat, Richir, Rochdy, Russell and Taquet 2004.

Other species: [None.]

Occurrence: Douar of Tazouda, Province of Quarzazate, Morocco.

Age: Early Jurassic (Toarcian).

Known material: Two incomplete skeletons, adult and juvenile.

Holotype: Musée des Sciencesde la Terre, Rabat, Morocco, To 2000–1, partially articulated skeleton and skull material, including complete left mandible with teeth, quadrate, jugal, postorbital, parietal, frontal, exoccipital, adult.

Diagnosis of genus (as for type species): Primitive sauropod exhibiting the following autapomorphies:

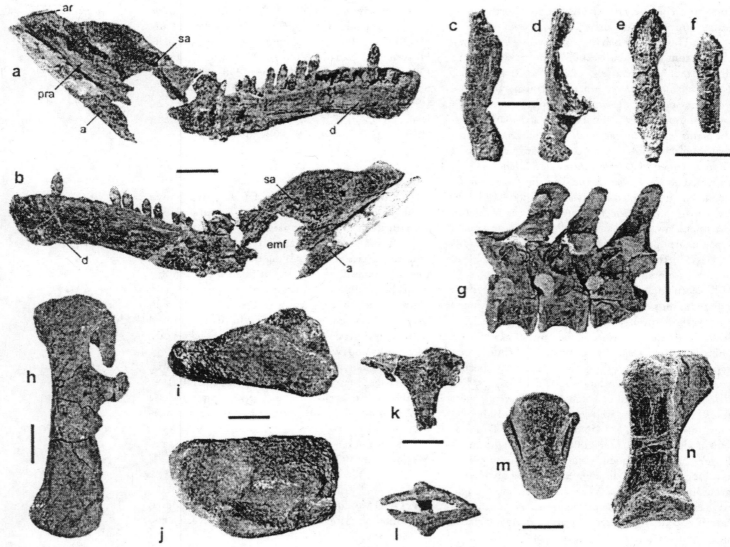

Tazoudasaurus naimi, Musée des Sciences de la Terre, To 2000-1, holotype a–b. left mandible (medial and lateral views, respectively), c–d. right quadrate (caudal and lateral views, respectively), e–f. teeth (lateral and medial views, respectively), g. dorsal vertebrae (left lateral view), h. right pubis (cranial view), i–j. right astragalus (ventral and caudal views, respectively), l. distal chevron (ventral view), m. ungual phalanx of pedal digit II (dorsal view), and n. left metatarsal II (dorsal view). Scale = 4 cm (a–b, i–j, l, n), 10 cm. (g–h), 3 cm. (c–d, k), and 1 cm. (e–f). (After Allain, Aquesbi, Dejax, Meyer, Monbaron, Montenat, Richir, Rochdy, Russell and Taquet 2004.)

thin, bony plate extending from caudodorsal margin of postorbital; chevrons of distal caudal vertebrae forked, proximal and distal processes unfused; prominent crest on lateral surface of proximal end of fibula; unique combination of sauropod synapomorphies and symplesiomorphies, including 20 dentary teeth having denticulate crown margins; rostral end of dentary only slightly expanded relative to depth of dentary at midlength; dentaries meeting in V-shaped symphysis; caudal fossa absent from quadrate; lesser trochanter present laterally on femur; pubic apron flat; plantar surface of pedal unguals II–III flattened (Allain, Aquesbi, Dejax, Meyer, Monbaron, Montenat, Richir, Rochdy, Russell and Taquet 2004).

Comments: Distinguished as the "most primitive and relatively completely known" basal sauropod, the genus *Tazoudasaurus* was established on a partially articulated incomplete skeleton with partial skull (To 2000-1) collected recently at Douar of Tazouda, near Toudoute Village, in the Province of Quarzazate, High Atlas of Morocco. Associated remains (Musée des Sciencesde la Terre, To 2000–2) of a juvenile individual, recovered from the same site, were referred to the type species *Tazoudasaurus naimi*. Associated with these remains were isolated elements belonging to indeterminate medium-sized and large theropods and also fossil plant material, including evidence of ferns, cycads, and conifers (Allain, Aquesbi, Dejax, Meyer, Monbaron, Montenat, Richir, Rochdy, Russell and Taquet 2004).

Conducting a phylogenetic analysis (see "Systematics" chapter), incorporating 29 ingroup taxa including *Tazoudasaurus* and the Moroccan genus *Atlasaurus*, using Wilson's (2002a) database of 235 characters but adding one character (*i.e.,* pedal digits II and III significantly broader than deep proximally, previously considered to be an autapomorphy of *Vulcanodon* by Wilson and Carrano 1999), Allain *et al.*

found *Tazoudasaurus* to place outside the Eusauropoda as the sister taxon of the chronally contemporaneous *Vulcanodon*. Moreover, the authors noted that *Tazoudasaurus* exhibits the following sauropod plesiomorphic characters: Flat pubic apron; femur with lesser trochanter; nonungual pedal phalanges longer than broad; flat plantar surface on pedal unguals II and III. Allain *et al.* referred both *Tazoudasaurus* and *Vulcanodon* to the Vulcanodontidae, defined by these authors as "all sauropods closer to *Vulcanodon* than to eusauropods (*i.e.*, *Vulcanodon* and *Tazoudasaurus*)," excluding from that family other primitive forms such as *Barapasaurus*, *Kotasaurus*, and *Shunosaurus*.

Derived characters shared by *Tazoudasaurus* with other sauropods, Allain *et al.* noted, include the following: Dorsoventrally expanded prearticular; crown-to-crown teeth occlusion; D-shaped tooth crowns; wrinkled tooth enamel surfaces; centra of cervical vertebrae opisthocoelous; dorsal vertebrae having broad neural spines; obligatory quadrupedal posture; deltopectoral crest of humerus reduced to ridge; humerus to femur ratio greater than 0.60; femoral fourth trochanter reduced; midshaft of femur elliptical in cross section; foramina absent near base of ascending process of astragalus; pedal digit I 25 percent longer than II; pedal ungual I sickle-shaped.

Key references: Allain, Aquesbi, Dejax, Meyer, Monbaron, Montenat, Richir, Rochdy, Russell and Taquet (2004); Wilson (2002*a*); Wilson and Carrano (1999).

†TECOVASAURUS

Diagnosis: Teeth moderately low to low, asymmetrical in labial and lingual aspects as well as in occlusal aspect; mesial margin convex, bearing up to twice as many denticles as does concave distal margin (Heckert 2004).

Comments: In 1994, Adrian P. Hunt and Spencer G. Lucas described *Tecovasaurus murryi*, a new genus and species of basal ornithischian established on teeth recovered from the Tecovas Member of the Dockum Formation (Chinle Group) of Crosby County, west Texas, with teeth referred to this taxon from Blue Mesa Member of the Petrified Forest Formation (Chinle Group) of Arizona (see *D:TE*).

In their review of basal Ornithischia, Norman, Witmer and Weishampel (2004*a*) regarded *T. murryi* as a *nomen dubium* on the grounds that this species exhibits ornithischian synapomorphies but lacks autapomorphies.

However, Heckert (2004), in a monograph on Late Cretaceous microvertebrates from the lower Chinle Group ("Otischalkian–Adamanian": Carnian)

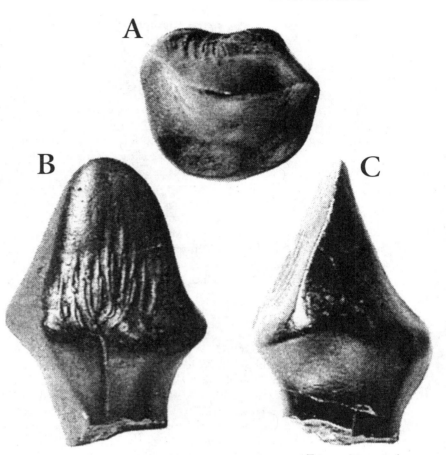

Tecovasaurus murryi, NMMNH P-18192, holotype tooth in A. labial, B. lingual, and C. occlusal views. Scale = 1 mm. (After Heckert 2004.)

of the southwestern United States, described additional teeth belonging to this primitive dinosaur collected from an upper Kalgary locality of the Tecovas Formation (Chinle Group), Crosby County. These specimens — much better preserved than the holotype (NMMNH P-18192), and described in detail by Heckert — consist of three new topotypes (NMMNH P-26417 and P-41715).

Heckert proposed a revised diagnosis of the type species.

Key references: Heckert (2004); Hunt and Lucas (1994); Norman, Witmer and Weishampel (2004*a*).

†TEHUELCHESAURUS

Saurischia: Eusaurischia: Sauropodomorpha: Sauropoda: Eusauropoda: "Euhelopodidae": Euhelopodinae.

Diagnosis of genus (as for type species): Distal end of humerus with craniolateral width just slightly less than transverse width (craniocaudally compressed in other Sauropoda) (Upchurch, Barrett and Dodson 2004).

Comment: In their review of the Sauropoda, Upchurch, Barrett and Dodson (2004) rediagnosed the type species *Tehuelchesaurus benitezii* (see *S2*).

Key reference: Upchurch, Barrett and Dodson (2004).

†TENDAGURIA

Saurischia: Eusaurischia: Sauropodomorpha: Sauropoda *incertae sedis*.

Diagnosis of genus (as for type species): Neural spines of dorsal vertebrae extremely reduced; dorsal depression lateral to each prezygapophysis; deep cavities on cranial surface of transverse processes, shallower cavities on reverse side; extremely robust epipophyses (Upchurch, Barrett and Dodson 2004).

Comment: In their review of the Sauropoda, Upchurch, Barrett and Dodson (2004) rediagnosed the type species *T. tanzaniensis* (see *S2*).

Key reference: Upchurch, Barrett and Dodson (2004).

†TENONTOSAURUS

Ornithischia: Predentata: Genasauria: Cerapoda: Ornithopoda: Euornithopoda: Iguanodontia.

Diagnosis of genus: External naris enlarged; dentary ramus having parallel dorsal and ventral margins; caudal dorsal vertebrae elevated neural spines; loss of phalanx from manual digit III (Norman 2004).

Comments: Werning, in an abstract for a poster, briefly reported on an osteological study of the type species *Tenontosaurus tilletii*. Her study was based upon a number of specimens collected by personnel of the Sam Noble Oklahoma Museum of Natural History from both the Antlers Formation of northern Texas and Oklahoma and from the Cloverly Formation of northern Wyoming and southern Montana, these representing two seeming populations separated by about 10 longitudinal degrees.

Werning studied osteohistological samples of this taxon representing multiple ontogenetic stages from each population, the samples then undergoing comparisons to determine differences in bone histology between the various growth stages and also between the populations. That author also analyzed these samples in order to determine relative growth rates between different bones belonging to a single individual.

As Werning stated, preliminary conclusions from this study suggest that the northern and southern *T. tilletti* populations show differences in bone histology, these possibly explained by differences in environment or latitude, perhaps also indicating the existence of two subspecies of *Tenontosaurus*. Additionally, Werning's study revealed different relative ontogenetic rates among the various bones of a single

individual (details of which will presumably be published at a later date).

Key references: Norman (2004); Werning (2004).

†THECODONTOSAURUS

Saurischia: Eusaurischia: Sauropodomorpha: ?Prosauropoda: Thecodontosauridae.

New species: *T. caducus* Yates 2003.

Occurrence of *T. caducus*: Pant-y-ffynnon Quarry, South Wales, United Kingdom.

Age of *T. caducus*: Late Triassic.

Known material: Skull, various postcranial specimens, cranial material, juvenile.

Holotype of *P. caducus*: BMNH P24, almost complete, disarticulated skull, including both mandibular rami, complete series of cervical vertebrae, proximal ends of humeri, proximal right scapula, coracoids, juvenile.

Diagnosis of genus: Small, gracile sauropodomorph with the following apomorphies: basipterygoid elongate, slender, length of process, measured from tip to dorsal margin of parabasisphenoid, equal to height of braincase, measured from dorsal margin of parabasisphenoid to top of supraoccipital (convergent in "*Efraasia diagnostica*" [=*E. minor*]; dentary short, deep, occupying less than 40 percent of total mandibular length, maximum dorsoventral depth more than 20 percent of its length (converging with *Saturnalia tupiniquim*); epipophyses of cranial cervical vertebrae flat plates overhanging caudal margins of postzygapophyseal facets, not forming raised ridges on dorsal surface of postzygapophysis; proximal and midcaudal neural spines at extreme distal end of their neural arches, filling interpostzygapophyseal space (convergent with "*E. diagnostica*"); ventral furrowing of caudal centra reduced, only weakly present in proximal caudal vertebrae, absent from mid- and distal caudals (Yates 2003*b*).

Diagnosis of *T. caducus*: Distinguished by the following apomorphies: pleurocoel-like pits on neurocentral sutures of sixth through eighth cervical vertebrae; plesiomorphic states including medial tubercle of proximal end of humerus that does not project strongly (strongly projecting in *T. antiquus*), preacetabular process of ilium projecting cranially (preacetabular process downcurved in *T. antiquus*) (Yates 2003*b*).

Comments: In 2003, Adam M. Yates formally described a new species of the primitive dinosaur *Thecodontosaurus*, which he named *Thecodontosaurus caducus* (for a preliminary report on this species, then still unnamed, see Yates 2001, *S2*; for a report on the specimens, see Kermack 1984), founded on a skull and partial postcrania (BMNH P24) representing a single individual collected from the Pant-y-ffynnon

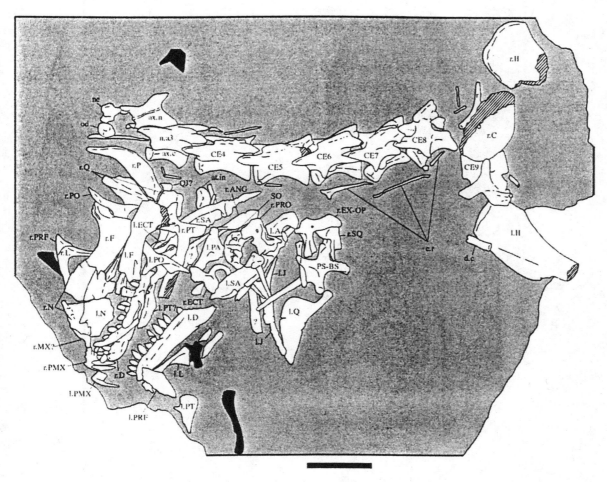

Quarry, near Bonvilston, South Wales. Paratype specimens from the same locality include the following: BMNH P24/3, right ischium; BMNH P39/2, left coracoid; BMNH P59/5, right quadrate; BMNH P641/1, right ectopterygoid; BMNH P77/1, series of distal caudal vertebrae, right ilium, femur, tibia, fibula, pes; BMNH P126/1, ?proximal pubis; and BMNH P141/1, basioccipital (Yates 2003*b*).

In addition to describing this new species, Yates (2003*b*) also proposed a newly revised diagnosis of the type species, *Thecodontosaurus antiquus*.

Yates (2003*b*) produced a new and revised skeletal reconstruction of *T. caducus*. An earlier reconstruction of this (as yet unnamed) species published by Kermack (see *S2*) combined holotype BMNH P24 with paratype BMNH P77/1. In this reconstruction, Yates (2003*b*) observed, the pelvic, hindlimb, and caudal elements of BMNH P77/1 were scaled up, resulting in a femur that was nearly twice the length of the humerus of BMNH P24 so as to bring "the humero-femoral ratio into line with that of other Triassic sauropodomorphs." Additionally, Yates (2003*b*) noted, Kermack believed "that if BMNH P77/1 were not scaled up relative to BMNH P24 then the ilium

would appear unrealistically small in comparison to the skull."

Regarding Kermack's approach to his reconstruction, Yates (2003*b*) stated the following observations:

1. In a large sample of postcranial bones (uncatalogued BRSUG collection) from Thytherington, referred to *T. antiquus*, the largest humeri and largest femora are of similar length (about 200 millimeters), suggesting that, at least in the type species, the humero-femoral ratio was substantially higher than in other basal sauropodomorphs.

2. The skull of *Mussasaurus patagonicus*, a basal sauropodomorph known only from juvenile remains, is probably longer and taller than its ilium (see Bonaparte and Vince 1979), intimating a similar ratio in the juvenile *T. caducus*.

Yates' (2003*b*) reconstruction treated BMNH P24, P65/1, and P77/1 as representing different parts of a single specimen. According to that author, all three of the above "were found in the same spoil heap on the same day (Kermack 1984) and contain no overlapping parts." Moreover, a small, displaced ischium (BMNH P23/4)—found in the slab containing the

Thecodontosaurus caducus, reconstructed skull of holotype BMNH P24, in A right lateral, B. ventral, and C. dorsal views, D. mandibular ramus in ventral view. Scale = 10 mm. (After Yates 2003*b*.)

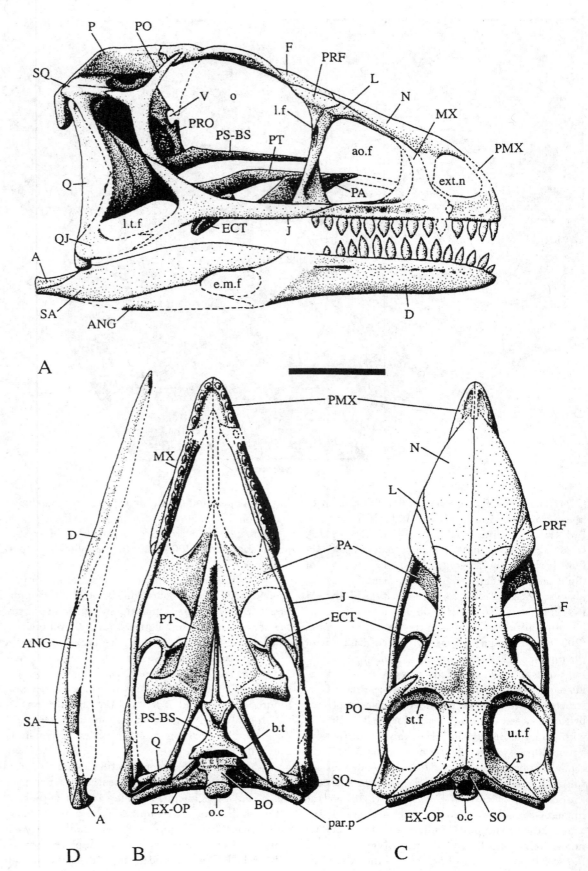

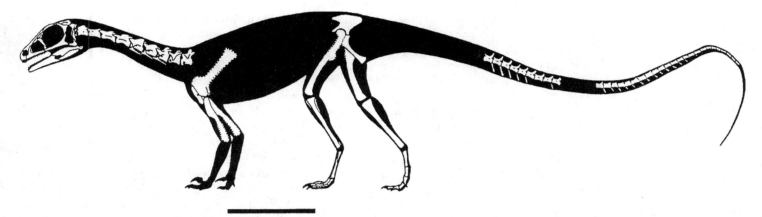

Skeletal reconstruction of *Thecodontosaurus caducus*, based upon holotype BMNH P24 and paratypes BMNH P64/1 and P77/1. Scale = 100 mm. (After Yates 2003*b*.)

skull, neck, and pectoral skeleton (BMNH P24)—would fit with the ilium of BMNH P77/1.

The forearms in Yates' (2003*b*) reconstruction are comparatively longer than in the reconstruction by Kermack, while the hindlimbs are shorter relative to the length of the trunk. If correct, these proportions indicating to Yates (2003*b*) that *Thecodontosaurus* was not an obligate biped, as generally assumed (*e.g.*, Kermack; Galton 1990, 2000; Van Heerden 1997), but could have sometimes progressed walking on all fours. Noting that the proportions of *Saturnalia tupiniquim* indicate faculative rather than obligate bipedalism (see Langer, Abdala, Richter and Benton 1999), Yates (2003*b*) proposed the possibility that some degree of bipedalism could be a basal condition among sauropodomorphs.

In performing various cladistic analyses, Yates (2003*b*) found both *Thecodontosaurus* and *Saturnalia tupiniquim* to be basal members of the Sauropodomorpha lying outside — contrary to most earlier studies — of Prosauropoda (*e.g.*, Schouten 2000; see "Systematics" chapter for that author's analysis of this latter group).

Conflicting with the conclusions of Yates (2003*b*), however, Galton and Upchurch (2004*a*) performed their own analysis of *Thecodontosaurus* in their review of the Prosauropoda (see "Systematics" chapter). These authors found *Thecodontosaurus* to occupy its more traditional phylogenetic position as a fully bipedal basal prosauropod.

Key references: Bonaparte and Vince (1979); Galton (1990, 2000); Galton and Upchurch (2004*a*); Kermack (1984); Langer, Abdala, Richter and Benton, (1999); Schouten (2000); Van Heerden (1997); Yates (2001, 2003*b*).

†THERIZINOSAURUS

Saurischia: Eusaurischia: Eusaurischia: Theropoda: Neotheropoda: Tetanurae: Avetheropoda: Coelurosauria: Tyrannoraptora: Maniraptoriformes: Maniraptora: Metornithes: Therizinosauroidea: Therizinosauridae.

Life restoration by Todd Marshall of the therizinosaurid *Therizinosaurus cheloniformis*.

Diagnosis of genus (as for type species): Humerus having long deltopectoral crest (more than half humeral length); distal carpals partially fused to metacarpals I and II; manual unguals elongate, only slightly curved (Clark, Maryańska and Barsbold 2004).

Comment: In their review of the Therizinosauroidea, Clark, Maryańska and Barsbold (2004) rediagnosed the type species *Therizinosaurus cheloniformes* (see *D:TE*).

Key reference: Clark, Maryańska and Barsbold (2004).

†**TIANZHENOSAURUS**   Pang and Cheng 1998
Ornithischia: Predentata: Genasauria: Thyreophora: Thyreophoroidea: Eurypoda: Ankylosauria: Ankylosauridae: Ankylosaurinae.

Name derivation: "Tianzhen [County]" + Greek *sauros* = "lizard."

Type species: *T. youngi* Pang and Cheng 1998.

Other species: [None.]

Occurrence: Huiquanpu Formation, Shanxi, China.

Age: Late Cretaceous.

Known material: Remains including three skulls, partial mandible, nearly complete disarticulated postcranial skeleton, numerous dermal scutes, tail club.

Holotype: HBV-10001, almost complete skull.

Diagnosis of genus (as for type species): Skull low, flat, medium-sized, having shape of isoceles triangle [in dorsal aspect]; skull roof covered with irregular dermal bony tubercles; premaxilla relatively long; orbit small, surrounded by dermal bony ring; narial opening horizontally elongate, septomaxilla not separate narial openings; maxillary tooth rows almost parallel, slightly convergent caudally; basicranial part short; maxiloturbinal situated laterally in middle part of palatal vault; occipital region almost vertical, with narrow, high occipital condyle not extending beyond caudal margin of skull roof; opisthotic extended lateroventrally as curved process; mandible deep, having convex ventral border and no dermal covering on lateral surface; tooth crowns having basal cingulum labially, swollen base, and well-developed middle ridge lingually; cervical centrum short, amphicoelous; centrum of dorsal vertebrae forming presacral rod, succeeded by fusion of four true sacral vertebrae and first caudal vertebra; anterior caudal vertebrae short, thick, posterior caudals narrow and elongate, ending with tail club; scapula roughly triangular and platelike; both ends of humerus moderately expanded (not twisted); femur thick, without fourth trochanter; tarso-metatarsal and digital bones ankylosaur-type (Pang and Cheng 1998).

Comments: In 1998, Pang Qiqing, and Cheng Zhengwu described *Tianzhenosaurus youngi*, a new type species of armored dinosaur founded upon remains representing several individuals, collected from the Upper Cretaceous (age based on associated hadrosaurid, ?"titanosaurid," and various other nondinosaurian Late Cretaceous fossils from the same locality) Huiquanpu Formation at Kangdailian, near Zhaojiagou Village, Tianzhen County, Shanxi. The first of these specimens, a dozen articulated vertebrae, were found by Pang and Cheng in 1983. A series of excavations at this site yielded more than 3,300 fossil specimens (see Pang, Cheng, Yang, Xie, Zhu and Luo (1996) representing a fauna comprising the new ankylosaurid, a sauropod, a theropod, and a hadrosaurid (see Cheng and Pang 1996).

Of the recovered ankylosasaurid material, Pang and Cheng designated a well-preserved, nearly complete skull (HBV-10001) as the holotype of *T. youngi*, and an incomplete right mandible (HBV-10002) and almost entire postcranial skeleton (HBV-1003) the paratypes.

Pang and Cheng referred *Tianzhenosaurus* to the Ankylosauridae, based on the following: Skull short, wider than long; skull roof covered with dermal scutes and nodes; occipital region wider than high; orbit small. In comparing *Tianzhenosaurus* with other ankylosaurids (including *Pinacosaurus* and *Ankylosaurus*), Pang and those authors found the genus to be closest in morphology to *Saichania*. In both taxa, the following features were observed: Skulls having general shape of isosceles triangle; orbit located at midcaudal part of skull; occipital condyle not extending beyond caudal edge of skull roof; skull roof covered with dermal plates and bony nobs. However, the two genera differ in the shapes of their skulls: *Tianzhenosaurus* having longer premaxilla, therefore long snout, *Saichania* with short snout; *Tianzhenosaurus* skull 275 millimeters long, with maximum width 294 millimeters, *Saichania* 455 millimeters in length, maximum width 480 millimeters; *Tianzhenosaurus* having maxillary tooth rows almost parallel, slightly narrower rostral width than snout width, "vertical postemporal region having narrow and vertically expanded occipital condyle"; in *Tianzhenosaurus*, cranial dermal tubercles differing in shape, irregularly arranged, in *Saichania*, polygonal in shape, symmetrically arranged.

Recently, some authors have regarded *Tianzhenosaurus* as a junior synonym of *Shanxia tianzhensis*, a Chinese taxon founded upon very incomplete material (*e.g.*, Sullivan 1999; Upchurch and Barrett 2000) (see *S2* for additional details on the above).

More recently, in their review of the Ankylosauria, Vickaryous, Maryańska and Weishampel (2004) interpreted *Tianzhenosaurus* to be a valid genus "based upon a unique combination of primitive and derived character states" (see also Vickaryous, Russell and Currie 2001), with *Shanxia* regarded by those authors a *nomen dubium*. Moreover, the analysis of Vickaryous *et al.* (2004) found *Tianzhenosaurus* plus *Pinacosaurus mephistocephalus* (see *Pinacosaurus* entry) be the sister group to *P. grangeri*.

Key references: Cheng and Pang (1996); Pang and Cheng (1998); Pang, Cheng, Yang, Xie, Zhu and Luo (1996); Sullivan (1999); Upchurch and Barrett (2000); Vickaryous, Maryańska and Weishampel (2004); Vickaryous, Russell and Currie (2001).

†**TITANOSAURUS** [*nomen dubium*]
Saurischia: Eusaurischia: Sauropodomorpha: Sauropoda: Eusauropoda: Neosauropoda: Macronaria: Titanosauriformes: Titanosauria *incertae sedis.*
Type species: *T. indicus* Lydekker 1877 [*nomen dubium*].
Other species: ?*T. madagascariensis* Depéret 1896 [*nomen dubium*] ?*T. nanus* Lydekker 1893 [*nomen dubium*].
Occurrence: Lameta Formation, Bara Simla Hill, Jabalpur, India; ?Río Colorado Formation, Neuquén Province, ?Cinco Saltos, Río Negro Province, Argentina; ?Upper Cretaceous near Mahajanga, Madagascar; ?Upper Cretaceous of Saint-Chinian, France.
Age: Late Cretaceous (Maastrichtian).
Known material: Postcranial remains including vertebrae, ?partial humerus, ?dermal ossification.
Holotype: IM K20/310, two distal caudal vertebrae.

Comments: For more than a century, *Titanosaurus* (see *D:TE, S1, S3*) has been a poorly understood genus; and recently the validity of this genus and its type species, *Titanosaurus indicus* has again been addressed (*e.g.*, Wilson 2002*b*; see also below).

In his long awaited revision of the "titanosaurid" dinosaurs of South America, Jaime Eduardo Powell (2003) recounted how *Titanosaurus indicus* was founded upon a pair of caudal vertebrae collected from "the lower level of the 'Sandy Limestone Formation,' at the western foothills of the Bara Simla Hills, Jabalpur, India." These remains were first reported by Hugh Falconer in 1868, after which they were named and described formally by Lydekker in 1877, and then redescribed by that author in 1879 (see below). Much later, Swinton (1947) referred to *T. indicus* material recovered from the Chota Simla, near Jabalpur, including an incomplete left humerus, proximal part of a right humerus, a right tibia, right fibula, plus a series of caudal vertebrae, although with just two elements represented in the type specimen, Powell noted, this reference should be verified based upon new findings (see below).

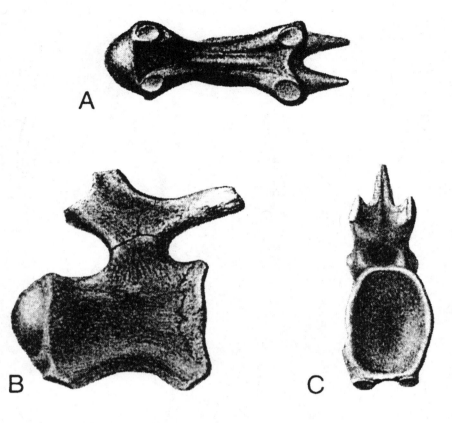

Titanosaurus indicus, IM K20/310, holotype distal caudal vertebra in A. ventral, B. right lateral, and C. proximal views. Scale = 15 cm. (After Falconer 1868, reproduced by Wilson and Upchurch 2003.)

Powell accepted both the genus *Titanosaurus* and its type species *T. indicus* as valid, proposing the following new diagnosis for these taxa: Medium to large size, with slender limb bones, fibula with lateral prominent crest located perpendicular over lateral tuberosity; proximal and middle caudal vertebrae laterally compressed, much taller than wide; caudal centra lacking cancellous structure.

Specimens recovered from other localities and different stratigraphic levels — Bajo La Carpa Member of the Neuquén-Río Colorado Formation, Anacleto Member of the General Roca-Río Colorado Formation, and Rancho de Avila-Neuquén Group — were referred by Powell to *Titanosaurus* sp.

Powell also commented on the species *Titanosaurus? nanus* (see below), based on an incomplete, poorly preserved cervical vertebra and dorsal vertebra (MLP.Ly. 18/19) collected from the ?Bajo de La Carpa Member of the Río Colorado Formation (Neuquén Group), on the right bank of Río Neuquén, near the city of Neuquén. Lydekker (1893) distinguished this material from "*T.*" *australis* [=*Neuquensaurus australis*] by its comparatively small size, for which reason he considered referring it to a different genus. Powell found this material, although apparently belonging to a "titanosaurid" (*e.g.*, neural canal

Titanosaurus

?Titanosaurus robustus [now *Neuquensaurus robustus*], MPL 26-259, lectotype left femur in A. distal, B. medial, and C. proximal views. Scale = 10 cm. (After Huene 1929, reproduced by Wilson and Upchurch 2003.)

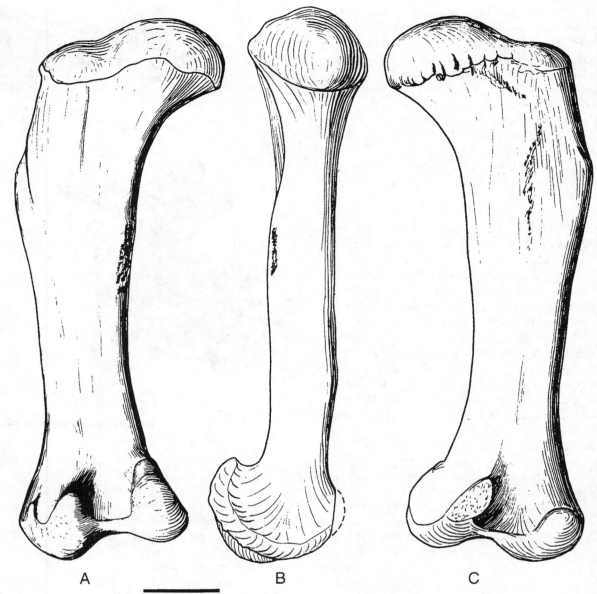

A   B   C

of dorsal vertebra relatively large, pleurocoel reduced, as generally seen in "titanosaurids"), to present no morphological details allowing clear identification at either the generic or species level. Moreover, "the morphology and proportions as well as its geographic and stratigraphic origin suggest that these specimens may eventually be referred to *Neuquensaurus* sp."

To cf. *Titanosaurus* sp. (see below), Powell referred a final sacral vertebra and a series of 18 articulated caudal vertebrae (DGM "Series C"), collected from Upper Cretaceous (Santonian) lower and middle levels of the Baurú Formation, at Peirópolis, State of Minas Gerais, Brazil, and obtained by Dr. Llellwyn I Price. In describing this material, Powell observed that caudal vertebrae 13 through 15 resemble closely those of the type specimen of *T. indicus*, although the

centrum in the type species is more compressed. As in other specimens referred to *Titanosaurus*, the ventral faces of the caudals are relatively narrow and the lateral walls are longitudinally concave.

However, most of Powell's study had been adapted from his previously unpublished Ph.D dissertation of 1986 (see "Systematics" chapter; also *Laplatasaurus* entry). A more recent comprehensive work on *Titanosaurus* was published in 2003 by sauropod specialists Jeffrey A. Wilson and Paul Upchurch. In the latter work, the validity of *Titanosaurus* and its species were subject to rigorous challenging. To date, Wilson and Upchurch noted, 14 species have been referred to *Titanosaurus*, "which, if valid, give the genus a geographical distribution covering Argentina, Europe, Madagascar, India and Laos, and a temporal

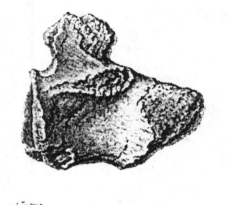

distribution spanning 60 million years of the Cretaceous."

Wilson and Upchurch, as had Powell, reviewed the early history of *Titanosaurus* discoveries, but underscored early taxonomic choices that had influenced later studies. Wilson and Upchurch's review, however, began somewhat earlier than Powell's (see paper for full details). As recounted by the former authors, the recorded history of Indian sauropod discoveries commences as early as 1828, with the collection by Captain Sleeman, a British army officer, of two fossil caudal vertebrae from Bara Simla Hill. These remains were then entrusted to a Mr. Spilsbury, who, in 1832, sent them on to the Indian Museum in Calcutta (now Kolkata). Decades later, in 1862, the fossils were given over to Falconer, then Superintendent of the new Geological Survey of India. In 1968, Falconer described and provided basic measurements of these vertebrae (from the middle third of the tail, according to Wilson and Upchurch, "based on the absence of transverse processes and the presence of neural arches"), also recognizing their reptilian character. Falconer observed three diagnostic features in these caudals — strong procoely with greatest convexity at axis of centrum; chevron facets at both ends of centrum; lack of prezygapophyseal facets.

These vertebrae — plus a fragmentary femur collected by Medlicott in 1871 from the same locality — were subsequently named and described by Lydekker, who recognized the bones as belonging to a dinosaur. As Lydekker failed to designate any of these remains as the type specimen, all of them comprised the type series of *T. indicus*. (In 1921, Matley showed that, while originating from the same locality, the vertebrae and femur came from different stratigraphic levels, the vertebrae having been yielded by the "Sauropod bed" above the "Main Lameta Limestone," the femur from the "Green sand" below the "Main Lameta Limestone"; consequently in 1933, Huene and Matley removed the femur from the type series of *T. indicus*, referring it to the South American genus *Antarctosaurus*.)

At the same time, Lydekker referred to *T. indicus* a series of caudal vertebrae collected by W. T. Blandord and some vertebrae and a femur (mentioned by Hislop 1864), all recovered from Pisdura, a locality 300 kilometers south of Bara Simla, in central India. Later, noting differences between the Jabalpur and Pisdura caudal vertebrae, Lydekker (1879) used two of the latter as a basis for the first of many referred species of *Titanosaurus*, which he named *Titanosaurus blandfordi*.

As recounted by Wilson and Upchurch, additional, disarticulated and damaged sauropod materials was collected between 1917 and 1919 from several localities on the western slope of Bara Simla, most of it recovered about 1.2 meters above the "Main Lameta Limestone" in the "Sauropod bed" that had yielded the original *T. indicus* material (see Huene and Matley 1933). At first, Matley believed that all of these remains represented a single individual. Subsequently, Huene and Matley, observing morphological differences in the sampling, determined the presence of at least three individuals representing two taxa (*T. indicus* and "*Antarctosaurus*" [renamed *Jainosaurus*; see SI; also, see below] *septentrionalis*). Later, following the collection at Pisdura by Matley in 1920 of more sauropod material, five taxa were recognized — *T. indicus*, *T. blandfordi*, ?*Antarctosaurus* sp., "*Laplatasaurus*" *madagascariensis*, plus an indeterminate form.

Regarding the remains from Chota Simla described by Swinton (see above), Wilson and Upchurch pointed out that the caudal vertebrae — "the only elements that overlap the type series of *T. indicus*" — were not described or figured, nor can they presently be located in the BMNH collections (P. Upchurch, personal observation). Moreover, Swinton's referral of this "material to *T. indicus* was based on overall similarities seen in the available femora combined with the geographical and stratigraphical proximity of the Bara Simla and Chota Simla remains."

Wilson and Upchurch discussed the possibility of there being but one titanosaur represented at Bara Simla, noting that the precise associations of the sauropod material collected there will always be confused and controversial in lieu of the absence of detailed field records and the poor preservation of the elements. As these authors pointed out, there is no duplication of the postcranial elements described by Huene and Matley from the "Sauropod bed" at Bara Simla. Among the differences cited by Huene and Matley between "*A.*" *septentrionalis* and *T. indicus* was the relatively more slender limb proportions of the former, this assessment having been made when the only limb bones referred to the latter taxon were a tibia and fibula from the Bara Simla "Sauropod bed," and with the type material of *T. indicus* comprising only two caudal vertebrae. Moreover, Wilson and Upchurch noted, comparisons with the proportions of limb elements belonging to other sauropods indicates that those elements referred to "*A.*" *septentrionalis* and *T. indicus* could, in fact, potentially pertain to the same individual. In conclusion, the authors found Huene and Matley's separation of the "Sauropod bed" remains into two taxa and several individuals to be unsupported by the currently available evidence. Possibly, as originally suggested by Matley in 1921, only a single individual is represented by these remains; nor can two or more taxa be reliably distinguished even if more than one individual is present. "However," the author stated, "although morphological and geological data do not argue against the presence of a single species at Bara Simla, there is simply no positive evidence supporting this hypothesis."

Regarding the validity of *Titanosaurus indicus*, Wilson and Upchurch noted that Lydekker (1877) originally listed five features to distinguish this taxon from *Cetiosaurus* — procoelous caudal vertebrae with neural arches on distal half of centrum; double chevron facets; centrum having longitudinal ventral furrow bounded by chevron ridges; squared centrum cross section; cylindrical, elongate prezygapophyses. Subsequently, Lydekker (1879) added a sixth feature to his diagnosis of this species — pair of ridges running from near middle of bone to four angles of ventral surface, in each case running from near center of periphery of this surface.

All six of the above features, however, are now known to be broadly distributed within Titanosauria, some of these unique to this clade (*e.g.*, procoely extending into middle third of tail), others also found in other sauropod lineages (*e.g.*, double chevron facets, found also in diplodocids). The genus *Titanosaurus* and its type species, therefore, is invalid, having been diagnosed in the past by "obsolete" characters that have acquired "a broader taxonomic distribution over time," in effect becoming synapomorphies of taxa of higher levels (*e.g.*, Titanosauria). Consequently, with no diagnostic characters to identify *T. indicus*, this taxon must remain a *nomen dubium*.

Wilson and Upchurch reassessed in detail the taxonomic histories and validity of all the species that have been referred to *Titanosaurus*, concluding the following:

T. blandfordi Lydekker 1879: The transverse and dorsoventral diameters of the proximal centrum face of the holotype (IM K27/506) are subequal, as opposed to the taller proportions of the type species; the proportions and morphology caudal vertebra resemble closely those but are not identical to those other titanosaurs (*e.g.*, "*Pellegrinosaurus*" [=*Epachthosaurus*], "*T. australis*" [=*Neuquensaurus*], "*Gondwanatitan*" [=*Aeolosaurus*]); the differences between this species and other titanosaurs are within the variation range in the caudal series of a single individual; and there are no displayed autapomorphies. Therefore, "*T.*" *blandfordi* is an invalid species:

(?) *T. rahioliensis* Mathur and Srivastava 1987: This tentatively named species was based on several narrow-crowned teeth (GSI 19,997–20,007) collected near the village of Rahioli, in Gujarat, India. Similar also to teeth of the diplodocoid *Nigersaurus* and lacking any postcranial elements for comparison, this taxon is regarded as an indeterminate neosauropod based upon the slender crowns lacking denticles.

T. colberti Mathur and Bandyopadhyay 1997 (see *S1*): This is a valid taxon with its associated remains overlapping the type vertebrae of *T. indicus*. However, Mathur and Bandyopadhyay, while demonstrating the differences between *T. colberti* and the type species, offered no explanation for their regarding them as congeneric. As this species cannot be referred to *Titanosaurus* (see also the review of Sauropoda by Upchurch, Barrett and Dodson 2004) Wilson and Upchurch placed it in the new genus *Isisaurus* (see entry).

T. australis Lydekker 1893: Wilson and Upchurch accepted Powell's (1986) referral of this South American species to the new genus *Neuquensaurus* (see *S2*), but cautioned that additional studies will determine whether or not the material from Cinco Saltos can be referred with confidence to that genus (see entry).

? *T. nanus* Lydekker 1893: The authors accepted Powell's (1986) assessment that, other than their small size, these vertebrae exhibit no distinguishing features, and that this species should be regarded as a *nomen dubium*.

T. robustus Huene 1929: Although McIntosh (1990) referred this species to *Saltasaurus* (as the new species *S. robustus*; see *D:TE*), Wilson and Upchurch tentatively agreed with Powell (1992) that this species is a *nomen dubium* in need of further study.

T. araukanicus (Huene 1929): Powell (1986) had referred Huene's (1929) type species *Laplatasaurus araukanicus*, referring it to *Titanosaurus* as a new species of that genus. As noted by Wilson and Upchurch, however, these remains cannot be reliably referred to *Titanosaurus*; therefore, the authors preferred retaining this species in the genus *Laplatasaurus* (see entry).

Titanosaurus sp. (see above): Although this material from Minas Girais State, described by Powell (1987), is diagnostic and worthy of additional study, is cannot be referred to *Titanosaurus*.

T. madagascariensis Depéret 1896: This species (see *D:TE*) was based upon two fragmentary caudal vertebrae, a partial humerus, and a dermal ossification from the Upper Cretaceous of Madagascar. Although Huene referred this material to *Laplatasaurus* (as the new species *L. madagascariensis*), Wilson and Upchurch pointed out that the lectotype of the type species *L. araukanicus* comprises a tibia and fibula (see Bonaparte and Bossi 1967). Therefore, as comparisons of these elements are limited, *T. madagascariensis* was regarded as a *nomen dubium* in need of further study.

T. falloti Hoffet 1942: Founded upon a femur from Muong Phalane, Laos, the specimen has a deflected shaft diagnostic of the Titanoformes. Although Allain, Taquet, Battail, Dejax, Richir, Véran, Limon-Duparcmeur, Vacant, Mateus, Sayarath, Khenthavong and Phouyavong (1999) referred this specimen to their new genus and species *Tangvayosaurus hoffeti* (see *S2*), Wilson and Upchurch found Hoffet's material to be nondiagnostic, referred to Titanosauria *incertae sedis* based upon its short ischium (Wilson 2002*a*; Upchurch *et al.* 2004).

T. valdensis Lydekker 1887: This species, based on caudal vertebrae (BMNH R146a and R151) from the Wessex Formation, Isle of Wight, was referred by Le Loeuff (1993) to the new genus *Iuticosaurus* (see *D:TE*). As noted by Wilson and Upchurch, the type material for this species offer no diagnostic features identifying it as anything but an indeterminate sauropod, these authors agreeing with Naish and Martill (2001) that *I. valdensis* should be regarded as a *nomen dubium*.

T. lydekkeri Huene 1929: Based on a proximal caudal centrum and partial neural arch (BMNH 32390) from the Upper Greensand (Cenomanian), Isle of Wight, originally described by Lydekker (1888), this bone was subsequently used by Huene to establish yet another new species of *Titanosaurus*. Later, Le Loeuff referred this specimen to *Iuticosaurus* (see entry) but labeled it a *nomen dubium*, the latter opinion shared by Naish and Martill and also Wilson and Upchurch.

T. dacus Nopcsa 1915: Established on two procoelous vertebrae from the Upper Cretaceous (Maastrichtian) of Romania, this material and later additional remains were referred to the new genus *Magyarosaurus* by Huene (1932), who distributed the fossil among three species. McIntosh and Le Loeuff accepted Huene's referral to the new genus, but considered the three species to be conspecific. According to Wilson and Upchurch, "it is not yet clear whether all are appropriately assigned."

Cf. *Titanosaurus* sp.: These limb bones and procoelous vertebrae from the Maastrichtian of Saint-Chinian, in southeastern France, were first briefly mentioned and referred to *Titanosaurus* by Depéret (1899). According to Le Loeuff, the holotype material includes as yet undescribed and not figured caudal vertebrae (five centimeters long; see Lapparent 1947), a humerus, and a femur (one meter long; Huene 1929) now in the collection of the Université de Lyon. However, this material has not yet been compared with the caudal vertebrae of *Titanosaurus indicus*.

Cf. *Titanosaurus indicus*: Among material from the ?Upper Cretaceous of Fox-Amphous, Provence, France, described by Lapparent (1947), is an amphicoelous proximal caudal vertebra bearing "the special form of the neurapophysis, forked anteriorly with two very divergent branches that rise posteriorly as single and broad blade, which characterize *T. indicus*." According to Wilson and Upchurch, this feature is broadly distributed among the Sauropoda and is not restricted to any titanosaurian genus, the caudal vertebrae do not share general or specific features with *I. indicus*, and the limb elements do not preserve any titanosaurian features; consequently and pending revision, this material should now be regarded as representing an indeterminate sauropod.

Traditionally, Gondwana faunas (*e.g.*, *Titanosaurus* and other titanosaurs) were believed to have been produced by the Late Jurassic separation of the northern and southern landmasses (*e.g.*, see Bonaparte 1999). According to Wilson and Upchurch, this vicariant scenario can be rejected for two reasons:

First, this proposed scenario requires that Titanosauria diverge from their sister groups due to the Late Jurassic separation of Pangaea into Laurasia and Gondwana (see Smith, Smith and Funnell 1994). Both titanosaurian body fossils and ichnofossils appear by the Middle Jurassic. However, Wilson and Upchurch noted, "This does not exclude the possibility of a vicariant signal at lower levels, which may be expected based on titanosaur distributions on southern continents during the Cretaceous, when Gondwana separated into individual continental landmasses."

Second, as shown by subsequent discoveries, the titanosaurian clade is not restricted to the southern landmasses (see Wilson and Upchurch for references).

Paleobiogeographically, titanosaurian taxa from northern landmasses have generally been explained away by the so-called "austral immigrant" hypothesis (*e.g.*, see Lucas and Hunt 1989; Le Loeuff; Sullivan and Lucas 2000), *i.e.*, "exceptions that evidenced independent dispersal events from south to north sometime during the Cretaceous." This idea has been challenged, however, in lieu of recent discoveries of Early Cretaceous North American titanosaurs and cladistic reassessments of other earlier described taxa (see Wilson and Upchurch for references; also see Upchurch *et al.*, in press, for an opposing view). Wilson and Upchurch stated that, based on the currently available data, distributions of Titanosauria and the predicted origin of that group before the breakup of Pangaea (see Wilson and Sereno 1998; Hunn, Upchurch and Norman 2002) "support the hypothesis that soon after their origin, titanosaurs dispersed across the substantial continental connections that still existed."

Notes: Powell also described a number of indeterminate "titanosaurid specimens," these including the following: DGM, "Series A"([2]), a complete series of cervical vertebrae (including axis but not atlas, and 11 cervicals), three cranial dorsal vertebrae, and DGM "Series B"([1]), five cervicals, 10 dorsals (the last cervical and all dorsals articulated), a sacrum with ilium articulated, and 10 partially articulated caudals, from the Upper Cretaceous ("Senonian") of Peirópolis, near Uberaba, State of Minas Gerais, Brazil; DGM collection, a sacrum articulated with the right ilium, and two dorsals, from the lower part of the Upper Cretaceous ("Senonian"; Huene 1939 *ee in* Oliveira and Leonardos 1978) Baurú Formation (Baurú Member or Facies), Peirópolis, the most striking feature of this large specimen being the ossified supra-spinal ligament (a feature otherwise known only in *Epachthosaurus sciuttoi*); fragmentary specimens from several localities in the Upper Cretaceous ("Senonian," possibly pre–Maastrichtian) Asencio Formation (see Bossi, Fernando, Elizalde, Morales, Ledesma, Carballo, Medina and Ford 1975) of Uruguay, including a proximal caudal vertebra (MMAB 4073) from the lands of Moxie and Corti, near Mercedes, Soriano Department, a proximal caudal vertebra, fragment of proximal end of left tibia, unidentifiable fragments (MMAB 250) from a site near the village of Bemúdez, among the arroyas La Lancha and Maceil, Soriano Department, lands of José Gallow, medial caudal vertebrae (MMAB 697) from Arroyo Piedra Sola, near San Jacinto, Canelones Department, distal caudals (MMAB 3143) from "Estancia Las Rosas," in the Ineguay country, a right humerus, portions of tibia, and long bone fragments (MMAB 4069) from, and also fragments of distal end of humerus (MMAB 207) from Molles, Durazno Department, the centra of these specimens similar in some respects to those of "*T.*" [=*Laplatasaurus] araukensis* and "*T.*" *blandfordi*; and finally, specimens from the Upper Cretaceous (pre–Maastrichtian) upper section of the Los Blanquitos Formation (Pirgua Subgroup, see Reyes and Salfity 1973; Salta Group, see Powell 1987*b*), at Arroyo Morterito, western foothills of the Sierra de Candelaria or Castillejo, Candelaria Department, Salta Province, Argentina, belonging to "a tall, medium to large dinosaur, such as *Antarctosaurus* and *Titanosaurus.*"

Ghosh, Bhattacharya, Sahni, Kar, Mohabey and Ambwani (2003) reported on a large number of titanosaur coprolites collected from a single locality of the Lameta Formation at Pisdura. As described by these authors, the coprolites are dark gray internally. They contain abundant plant tissues (mostly of gymnospermous origin, but also pollen, spores, cuticles, woody tissues of cycads and conifers, fungal spores, and algae) as well as other matter (*e.g.*, sponge spicules). Thus, the producers of these coprolites "were mainly herbivorous animals capable of cropping trees, a suggestion that was verified independently by the carbon and nitrogen isotopic composition of the organic matter preserved in the Type-A [large, having smooth surfaces lacking ornamentation] coprolite samples." In comparing the nitrogen content of these specimens with fecal matter of extant herbivores and carnivores, Ghosh *et al.* found carbon and nitrogen levels suggesting that, contrary to suggestions made in earlier studies on sauropod dinosaurs, "gut fermentation may not have been an active mechanism in the digestion process of titanosaurs" (see Ghosh *et al.* for further details).

Key references: Allain, Taquet, Battail, Dejax, Richir, Véran, Limon-Duparcmeur, Vacant, Mateus, Sayarath, Khenthavong and Phouyavong (1999); Bonaparte (1999); Bonaparte and Bossi (1967); Bossi, Fernando, Elizalde, Morales, Ledesma, Carballo, Medina and Ford (1975); Depéret (1896, 1899); Falconer (1868); Ghosh, Bhattacharya, Sahni, Kar, Mohabey and Ambwani (2003); Hislop (1864); Hoffet (1942); Huene (1929, 1932); Huene and Matley (1933); Hunn, Upchurch and Norman (2002); Jain and Bandyopadhyay (1997); Lapparent (1947); Le Loeuff (1993); Lucas and Hunt (1989); Lydekker (1877, 1879, 1887, 1893); Lydekker (1888); Mathur and Srivastava (1987); Matley (1921); McIntosh (1990); Naish and Martill (2001); Nopcsa (1915); Oliveira and Leonardos (1978); Powell (1978*b*, 1986, 1987, 1992, 2003); Reyes and Salfity (1973); Smith, Smith and Funnell (1994); Sullivan and Lucas (2000); Swinton (1947); Upchurch, Barrett and Dodson (2004); Wilson (2002*a*, 2002*b*); Wilson and Sereno (1998); Wilson and Upchurch (2003).

†TOCHISAURUS

Saurischia: Eusaurischia: Eusaurischia: Theropoda: Neotheropoda: Tetanurae: Avetheropoda: Coelurosauria: Tyrannoraptora: Maniraporiformes: Troodontidae.

Diagnosis of genus (as for type species): Metatarsus more derived than *Sinornithoides youngi* in metatarsal III being obscured from caudal view by metatarsals II and IV for part of its length (Makovicky and Norell 2004).

Comment: In their review of the Troodontidae, Makovicky and Norell (2004) rediagnosed the type species *Tochisaurus nemegtensis* (see *D:TE*).

Key reference: Makovicky and Norell (2004).

†TORNIERIA

Saurischia: Eusaurischia: Sauropodomorpha: Sauropoda: Eusauropoda: Neosauropoda: Diplodocoidea: Flagellicaudata: Diplodocidae.

Name derivation: "[Gustav] Tornier."

Type species: *T. africana* (Fraas 1908).

Other species: [None.]

Occurrence: Tendaguru Formation, Mtwara, Tanzania.

Age: Late Jurassic (Tithonian).

Known material: More than three partial skeletons, skull elements, numerous postcranial elements.

Diagnosis of genus (as for type species): Rostral end of dentary displaying little dorsoventral expansion; "post-parietal" fenestra (also in Dicraeosauridae); short, cylindrical basipterygoid processes (Upchurch, Barrett and Dodson 2004).

Comments: In 1908, Eberhard Fraas described a new sauropod which he named *Gigantosaurus africanus*, based on several incomplete specimens from the Upper Jurassic (Tithonian) upper Tendaguru beds of Mtwara, Tanzania. Fraas originally "diagnosed" this species as being of very massive construction, with quite strong hindlimbs. As the name *Gigantosaurus* proved to be preoccupied (Seeley 1869), Sternfield (1911) subsequently referred this material to the new genus and species *Tornieria africana*, after which Janensch (1922) referred it to the North American genus *Barosaurus*.

In his review of the Sauropoda, McIntosh regarded this referral as only tentative (see *D:TE*).

More recently, the validity of ?*Barosaurus africana* was addressed by Remes (2004) in an abstract for a poster. Remes found the presumed African existence of *Barosaurus* to be surprising, pointing out that "terrestrial faunal exchange between Laurasia and Gondwana during the Late Jurassic is considered improbable due to marine barriers."

Reviewing the material referred to "*Barosaurus*"

Tornieria

Photograph taken during the 1920s of a cast of the right humerus of *Tornieria africana*, as once displayed in the Fossil Reptile Gallery of the formerly named British Museum (Natural History). The girl is holding a yardstick.

africana, Remes — in order to test whether or not he African species can, in fact be referred to *Barosaurus*, and also if it is a diplodocid or some basal diplodocoid — made a number of observations. According to Remes, the skull and proximal caudal vertebrae of this taxon "demonstrate unambiguously that the type material and referable specimens belong to the diplodocid subfamily Diplodocinae." However, various "significant differences to the North American diplodocines" preclude referral of this material to *Barosaurus* or to any other known North American genus.

Considering the above, Remes proposed that the available name *Tornieria africana* be used for this taxon (the original *Gigantosaurus* being undiagnostic; see Upchurch 1993).

A preliminary cladistic analysis by Remes placed this species as the probable "sister taxon to a clade comprising the North American diplodocines *Diplodocus* and *Barosaurus*"; consequently, diplodocids, although poorly represented in the fossil record, were present in Gondwanan terrestrial ecosystems during Late Jurassic times.

Upchurch, Barrett and Dodson (2004), in their review of the Sauropoda, also regarded *Tornieria africana* as a valid genus and species. Furthermore, the authors noted that this taxon displays various derived features (*e.g.*, small rugosities on dorsolateral margins of metatarsals I–III near their distal ends) suggesting its placement with the Diplodocoidea or Diplodocidae (see Upchurch 1995).

Note: A continuing series of histological experiments have been performed in recent years by Stempniewicz and Pyzalla (*e.g.*, 2003, 2004; see also Pyzalla and Stempniewicz 2002*a*, 2002*b*) to assess the diagenetic changes and also the orientation distribution of associated bone mineral occurring during 150 million years of fossilization in sauropod bones excavated from 1909–1913 during Werner Janensch's Tendaguru Expedition to Tanzania, East Africa. Included in these studies was material mainly pertaining to *Tornieria africana* [=*Barosaurus africanus* of Stempniewicz and Pyzalla's usage] and also *Brachiosaurus brancai*, including a midshaft sample of a right humerus belonging to *T. africana* (the largest humerus known for this taxon).

Data gleaned from these studies include the following: Mineral orientation in midshaft of long bones following direction of bone axis; some rather insignificant chemical changes taking place (*e.g.*, incorporation of strontium into bone mineral), with manganese present only in pores and not infiltrating bone cortex, bone mineral particles having not fully recrystalized, with further analyses of these crystalites interpreted in an ontogenetic context; long bones of *T. africana* individuals showing two different kinds of

growth, *i.e.*, 1. very rapid continuous growth having very limited remodeling, producing type "A histology" (*i.e.*, "mostly fibrolamellar bone with irregularly oriented lumina and sparse secondary osteons in the inner cortex"), and slower interrupted growth that is at least partially cyclical and accompanied by much remodelling, producing type "B histology" (*i.e.*, "isolated secondary osteons in outer cortex and dense Haversian bone [in] inner cortex"), existence of both histology types in single species suggesting possible dimorphism; and apatite crystallites preferentially oriented along bone axis, this orientation in slow-growing bone being almost constant going from outside to inside of bone, this kind of orientation distribution found only in remodeled part of fast-growing bone.

Key references: Fraas (1908); Janensch (1922); McIntosh (1990); Pyzalla and Stempniewicz 2002*a*, 2002*b*); Remes (2004); Seeley (1869); Stempniewicz and Pyzalla (2003, 2004); Sternfield (1911); Upchurch (1993, 1995); Upchurch, Barrett and Dodson (2004).

†**TORVOSAURUS**—(=*Edmarka*)

Comment: Tykoski and Rowe (2004), in their review of basal tetanurans, referred to the type species *Torvosaurus tanneri* the type species *Edmarka rex*, the latter having been established upon incomplete cranial and postcranial remains (CPS 1005, 1004, and 1002) from the Morrison Formation of Wyoming, originally described in 1992 by Robert T. Bakker, Donald Kralis, James Siegwarth and James Filla as a gigantic new theropod taxon (see *D:TE*).

Reconstructed skeleton (cast) of *Torvosaurus taneri*, prepared by DINOLAB for the North American Museum of Ancient Life. The smaller skeletons (casts) are of the ornithopod *Othnielia rex*.

Photograph by the author, courtesy North American Museum of Ancient Life.

Key references: Bakker, Kralis, Siegwarth and Filla (1992); Tykoski and Rowe (2004).

†TRICERATOPS

Ornithischia: Predentata: Genusauria: Cerapoda: Chasmatopia: Marginocephalia: Ceratopsia: Neoceratopsia: Coronosauria: Ceratopsoidea: Ceratopsidae: Chasmosaurinae.

Comments: New information pertaining to the appearance, and possible stance and gait of this giant three-horned dinosaur has been gleaned from a skeleton (TCMI 2001.93.1) of the type species *Triceratops horridus* from the Upper Cretaceous (Maastrichtian) Lance Formation of Niobrara County, Wyoming. As reported by Larson, Evans and Ott (2004), in an abstract for a poster, previously unrealized details of the axial and appendicular skeleton of this taxon surfaced during the preparation and mounting of this specimen.

As Larson *et al.* observed, the almost complete, relatively undistorted sacrum and presacral vertebral column and rib cage of this specimen reveal "a much broader and rotund belly region than previous mounts imply."

The authors also made the following observations: Rib cage narrowing cranially, necessitating articulation of coracoids; first six dorsal ribs showing clear depression to accommodate scapulae, displaying incontrovertible positioning of pectoral girdle and new insight into forelimb locomotion; complete pelvis, articulated with dorsal vertebrae and ribs, showing widely diverging pubes; double articular femoral facets on ilia, with wide rib cage and arched femora, clearly indicating broad divergence of femora away from midline, giving distinct bow-legged appearance (see also the recent study by Chinnery 2004, "Introduction").

As noted by Larson *et al.*, the awkward gait reflected by TCMI 2001.93.1 indicates "that *Triceratops* was a trotter, not a galloper." Centra of proximal caudal vertebrae are longer dorsally than ventrally, the centra having a near-wedge shape in lateral aspect; furthermore, as no specimen of this genus preserves more than five or six vertebrae of the caudal series, it is possible that the tail of *Triceratops* "is much

Triceratops horridus (TCM 2001.93.1) being collected by the Black Hills Institute of Geological Research from the Lance Formation, Niobrara County, Wyoming.

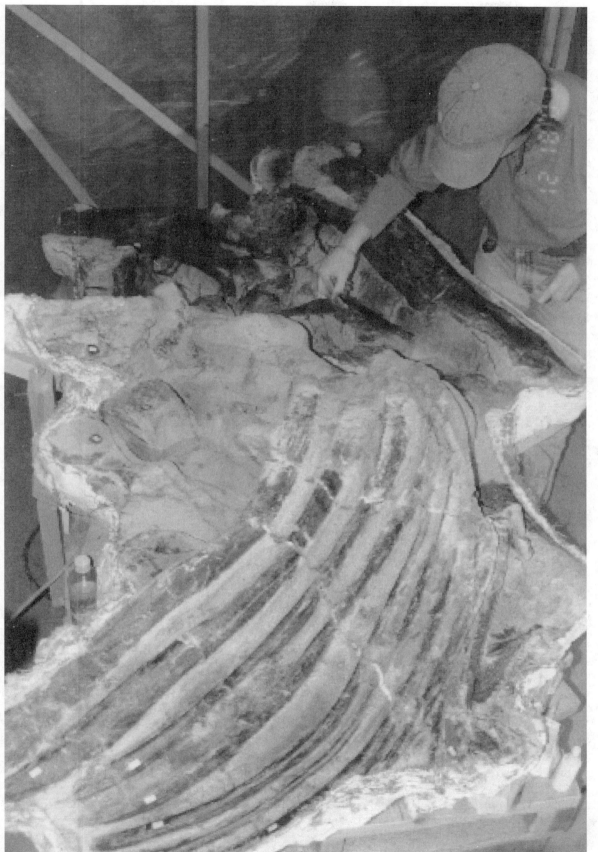

Skeleton of *Triceratops horridus* (TCM 2001.93.1) undergoing preparation at the Black Hills Institute of Geological Research.

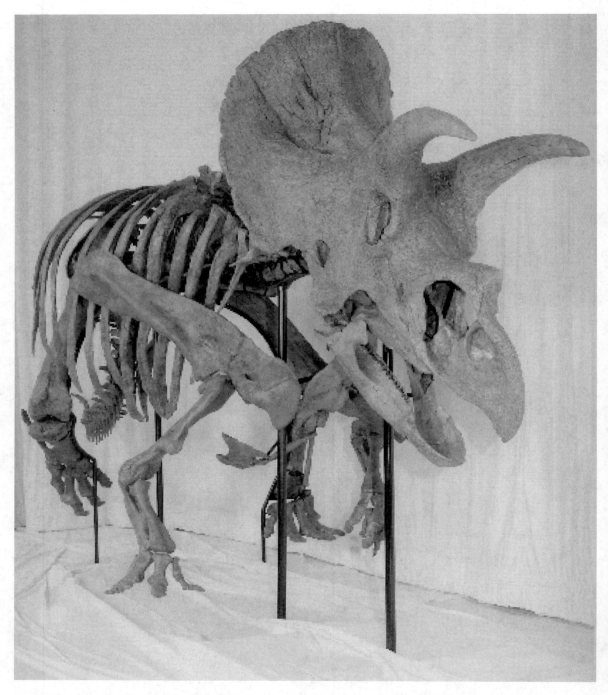

Triceratops skeleton (TCM 2001.93.1), nicknamed "Kelsey," mounted by the Black Hills Institute of Geological Research at The Children's Museum of Indianapolis.

shorter than assumed, directed ventrally and curved somewhat anteriorly."

Happ (2003), in an abstract for a poster, analyzed injuries in a mature skull (SUP-9713) of the giant three-horned dinosaur *Triceratops*, collected from the Upper Cretaceous (Maastrichtian) Hell Creek Formation near Jordan, Montana.

The following observations were made by Happ regarding this specimen: Comparing the left and right supraorbital bones, the left brow horn is missing over a third (24 centimeters) of its complete length (about 60 centimeters), with damage apparent at the remaining end. Two opposing conical depressions are on the edge of this damaged area, on opposite sides of the horns, these being consistent with the shape of the teeth of a tyrannosaurid or large crocodilian. As the point of injury consists of thick layers of compact bone, the damage seems to have been caused by a considerably powerful bite. Cancellous bone, from the internal portion of the horn, has been exposed by the injury. On this bone were anomalous patches of compact bone not ordinarily observed, these overgrowths

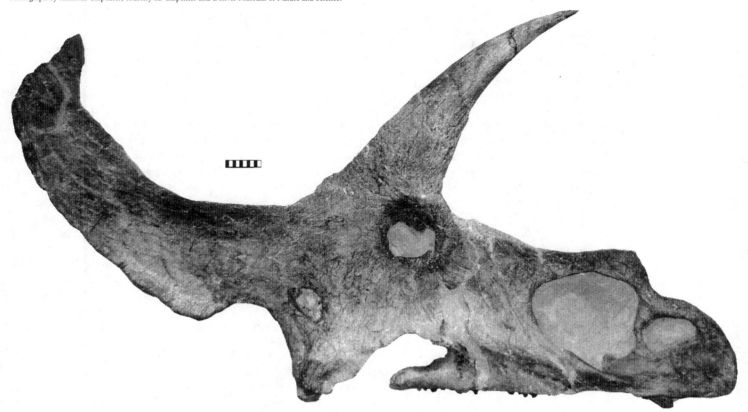

possessing multidirectional bone fibers interpreted by Happ as periosteal reaction to the injury.

As Happ further observed, the left squamosal of SUP-9713 shows three parallel marks — the first, very prominent mark measuring 60 millimeters long and 22 millimeters wide, being 65 millimeters from the second mark; the second, more superficial mark 95 millimeters long, six millimeters wide, and 63 millimeters from the third; the third, more faint mark 90 millimeters long, six millimeters wide.

Happ noted that the distance between these marks corresponds to the inter-tooth distance seen in the teeth of tyrannosaurids, *Tyrannosaurus rex* being the only known Hell Creek Formation theropod having an inter-tooth distance of the magnitude of SUP-9713. Furthermore, the first of these marks exhibits signs of periosteal reaction to the injury, the bone at that mark having grown four millimeters above the regular surface, the length of the mark interlaced with expanded bone fibers. X-ray analysis by Happ offered additional evidence for periosteal reaction to the injury.

From the above evidence, Happ concluded that

the *Triceratops* individual represented by SUP-9713 seems to have survived injuries apparently inflicted by an attacking *T. rex*.

Note: Young (2004), in the publication *Fossil*

Above: Triceratops horridus skull (DMNH 48617) recovered in 2003 from a Lennar Homes subdivision of the Denver Formation, Colorado.

Life restoration by Gregory S. Paul of *Triceratops horridus*. A recent study by Peter L., Dallas Evans, and Christopher Ott (2004) refutes the hypothesis that this giant horned dinosaur could gallop.

News, reported on a new *Triceratops* specimen discovered on November 9, 2003 on a hill slope of a Lennar Homes subdivision in the Denver Formation, Denver Basin, Colorado. The adult specimen (now catalogued as DMNH 48617)—including the right face, horn, and partial frill, and measuring seven feet in length and 4.5 feet wide (horn across to interior quadrate)—was collected by and is being prepared at the Denver Museum of Nature and Science. With *Triceratops* specimens rare in the Denver Basin, this find is important for the state, being the second *Triceratops* known from the Front Range of Colorado (the first having been discovered and collected during the early 1980s by Kenneth Carpenter). The skull is currently displayed at the Denver Museum.

Key reference: Chinnery (2004); Happ (2003); Larson, Evans and Ott (2004); Young (2004).

†TROODON

Saurischia: Eusaurischia: Theropoda: Neotheropoda: Tetanurae: Avetheropoda: Coelurosauria: Tyrannoraptora: Maniraptoriformes: Troodontidae:

Diagnosis of genus (as for type species): Potential autapomorphies including the following: teeth having denticles on mesial and distal carinae; basal tubera stout, wide; temporal arcade short (Barsbold and Osmólska 1990*a*); expanded pubic boot (only slightly developed in other taxa preserving pubis); larger than other troodontids (except *Saurornithodes junior*) (Makovicky and Norell 2004).

Comments: Numerous studies have already been published describing in detail the eggs, embryos, and nests, and proposing possible egg-laying behavior, of the type species *Troodon formosus* (see *S1*, *S2* for information and references). More recently, Varricchio and Jackson (2004) speculated on the reproductive physiology of this very birdlike, relatively large-brained dinosaur, based upon their interpretation of nests, egg clutches, and embryos yielded by the Two Medicine Formation of Montana.

However, Varricchio and Jackson cautioned that two levels of inference are involved in such speculations—interpretations of behavior based upon body and trace fossil evidence; and, following, physiology inferred from behavior—this tiering of interpretation, the authors pointed out, offering a greater opportunity for error (see Witmer 1995).

That stated, Varricchio and Jackson considered such speculations regarding *Troodon* to merit consideration for a number of reasons:

1. Direct evaluation of metabolism, body temperature, and rate of oxygen consumption are currently impossible to determine in extinct vertebrates, any physiologic interpretations thereby relying on inference.

2. *Troodon* specimens represent direct products of reproductive behavior or physiology; specimens such as eggs are the direct output of breeding females; and features such as egg position, clutch arrangement, and nest structure reproductive are trace fossils, the product of adult behavior.

3. Reproductive behavior in extant vertebrates is inherently linked to physiology; consequently, hypothesized reproductive behavior in *Troodon* will include physiological implications.

4. The proposed hypotheses for *Troodon* seem to be robust, incorporating a wide range of specimens and concurring with established phylogenies.

As described by Varricchio and Jackson, as well as various previous authors (see paper for references), *Troodon* eggs—belonging to the oospecies *Prismatoolithus levis* (see "Appendix," *S3*—are elongate and symmetrical, ranging in length from 12 to 16 centimeters and having a volume of about 440 cubic centimeters, with exterior surfaces varying from smooth to faintly striated. The clutches are oval, containing as many as 24 eggs. The eggs in bottom view are generally arranged in pairs, while in top view they seem to be tightly packed. One clutch includes embryos.

Based upon these specimens, Varricchio and Jackson deduced the following scenario: "*Troodon* had monoautochronic ovulation and lacked egg retention, producing two eggs at daily or greater intervals," with eggs placed in the ground subvertically to vertically, upper portions exposed, remaining unincubated until the clutch was completed. Upon incubation the eggs were gathered into a tighter configuration, obscuring the original paired pattern in top view. Probably the adult directly incubated the eggs with body heat, the precocial young hatching synchronously.

Varricchio and Jackson stated that the above described behavior differs little from the behavior seen among most extant birds, particularly such groups as Paleognathes, Galliformes, and Anseriformes. In modern birds, the authors pointed out, such features as iterative egg-laying, delayed incubation by brooding, and synchronous hatching of precocial young "are inherently linked with and dependent upon the avian endothermic physiology." The implication follows that that, if the reproductive behaviors postulated for *Troodon* are correct, this non-avian dinosaur "maintained an elevated metabolism and body temperature, as in these living birds."

As Varricchio and Jackson noted, their above interpretation is consistent with a variety of morphological data, including upright stance (see Bakker 1972), high encephalization quotient or EQ (Hopson 1980), bone histology (Varricchio 1993), and the high probability of feathers within the Troodontidae (Xu, Tang and Wang 1999).

Life restoration of *Troodon formosus* by artist Todd Marshall.

According to Varricchio and Jackson, the most significant preservable physical attributes for extrapolating the possible reproductive behavior of *Troodon* include the relatively large size of the eggs, their asymmetrical shape, the fact that the eggs were laid in pairs, and the partially exposed clutches. Excepting increased egg size in the reptilian lineage leading to dinosaurs and in the Lambeosaurinae, these characteristics appear only in Coelurosauria or perhaps Maniraptora; consequently, such reproductive features as iterative egg-laying, delayed incubation by brooding, and synchronous hatching, generally considered to be typically avian, may have originated within either of these non-avian theropod clades.

Note: In a published abstract for a poster, Difley, Brooks and Policelli (2004) briefly reported on a nest of 13 troodontid eggs found in the uppermost Cretaceous (Maastrichtian) North Horn Formation, in Black Dragon Canyon, Emory County, central Utah. Difley *et al.* reported that nest was found "in a stacked series of paleosols in a motled grey horizon just below a rooted oxidized horizon," the paleosols representing "weakly developed soils on a vegetated floodplain." As eggs of this kind occur both in sandstone and mudstone, both substrates were seemingly utilized in the nesting.

In describing this discovery, Difley *et al.* noted the dimensions of the nest to be 61 centimeters by 31 centimeters. The eggs are elongate and ovoid, about 76 millimeters in diameter with shell 1.06 millimeters thick, with an estimated restored length of approximately 170 millimeters. They are arranged upright on rounded bases and, having been slightly disordered before burial, clustered from 10 to 58 millimeters apart.

Key references: Bakker (1972); Barsbold and Osmólska (1990*a*); Difley, Brooks and Policelli (2004); Hopson (1980); Makovicky and Norell (2004); Varricchio (1993); Varricchio and Jackson (2004); Witmer (1995); Xu, Tang and Wang (1999).

†TSAGANTEGIA

Ornithischia: Predentata: Genasauria: Thyreophora: Thyreophoroidea: Eurypoda: Ankylosauria: Ankylosauridae: Ankylosaurinae.

Diagnosis of genus (as for type species): Unique among known ankylosaurines in having amorphous cranial armor (not subdivided into mosaic of polygons); squamosal and quadratojugal bosses weakly developed (unlike condition in other known ankylosaurids (Vickaryous, Maryańska and Weishampel 2004).

Comment: In their review of the Ankylosauria, Vickaryous, Maryańska and Weishampel (2004) rediagnosed the type species *Tsagantegia longicranialis* (see *D:TE*).

Key reference: Vickaryous, Maryańska and Weishampel (2004).

†TUOJIANGOSAURUS

Ornithischia: Predentata: Genasauria: Thyreophora: Thyreophoroidea: Eurypoda: Stegosauria: Stegosauridae: Stegosaurinae.

Diagnosis of genus (as for type species): Proximal caudal vertebrae unique in having neural spines with craniolaterally oriented sheets; osteoderms comprising 17 pairs of symmetrical bony plates and spines, some nuchal plate spherical, large high spines in lumbar and sacral regions (Galton and Upchurch 2004*b*).

Comment: In their review of the Stegosauria, Galton and Upchurch (2004*b*) rediagnosed the type species *Tuojiangosaurus multispinus* (see *D:TE*).

Key reference: Galton and Upchurch (2004*b*).

†TYRANNOSAURUS (=*Aublysodon*, *Dinotyrannus*, *Dynamosaurus*, *Manospondylus*, *Nanotyrannus*, *Stygivenator*)

Saurischia: Eusaurischia: Theropoda: Neotheropoda: Tetanurae: Avetheropoda: Coelurosauria: Tyrannoraptora: Maniraptoriformes: Tyrannoraptora:

Photograph by the author, courtesy National Museum of Wales.

Skeleton (CV 209) of *Tuojiangosaurus multispinus*, detail of dermal plates, on temporary exhibit in 1985 at the National Museum of Wales.

Tyrannosauroidea: Tyrannosauridae: Tyrannosaurinae.

Diagnosis of genus (as for type species): Greatest constriction of nasals between lacrimals (less than one-sixth maximum nasal thickness); rostralmost point of quadratojugal ventral process rostral to infratemporal fenestra; distal margin of metatarsal III sigmoid, concavity in distolateral margin in cranial aspect (also in *Daspletosaurus*); scapula caudally expanded (also in *Albertosaurus*); greatest lateral expansion of skull among known tyrannosaurids (Holtz 2001, Currie 2003*a*), transverse width of rostrum at caudal end of maxillary tooth row about three times maximum width of nasals, maximum postorbital skull width more than two-thirds premaxilla-occipital condyle length; orbits facing more rostrally than laterally (Molnar 1991) (Holtz 2004).

Comments: Formerly a quite rare type species, *Tyrannosaurus rex* is now known from numerous specimens (more than 30 recorded skeletons, making this species "the most commonly found North American Late Cretaceous theropod"; see Horner and Padian 2004, below), with additional materials currently being discovered, collected, prepared, and described (see *D:TS*, *S1*, *S2*, *S3*, and "Notes," below).

Photograph by John Weinstein, courtesy The Field Museum, negative number GN88735_17.

Attention has recently focused upon a *T. rex* specimen that was recovered almost two decades ago. As related by Williamson and Carr (2003*a*) in an abstract, the New Mexico Museum of Natural History (now New Mexico Museum of Natural History and Science), during the spring of 1984, collected a portion of a *T. rex* skull and postcranial skeleton (NMMNH P-3698) from the Hall Lake Member of the McRae Formation, near the Elephant Butte Reservoir, in Elephant Butte, New Mexico. The specimen includes a left dentary, a few loose teeth, and a hemal arch, with additional reported elements remaining *in situ*, the locality subsequently having been drowned by rising lake levels, those elements remaining inaccessible for almost 19 years.

In September 2000, following a drop in lake level, the museum collected additional disarticulated parts of the specimen, found clustered in a conglomerate, these remains including a partial right splenial, angular, articular, and squamosal, a right postorbital, portions of several teeth, and a few more hemal arches. The authors referred these remains to *T. rex* based upon diagnostic characters of the palatine and postorbital.

As Williamson and Carr pointed out, NMNH P-3698 is significant as 1. representing "the only specifically diagnostic dinosaur to be collected from the McRae Formation," thereby supporting that the Hall Lake Member of this formation is of late Maastrichtian age; 2. confirming the earlier identification of this specimen as *Tyrannosaurus rex*, consequently verifying the presence of this taxon in the southern Rocky Mountain region; and 3. being the most complete specimen of this species yet collected from New Mexico and the southern United States.

Paleontologist William F. Simpson with the skull (FMNH PR2081) of *Tyrannosaurus rex* nicknamed "Sue."

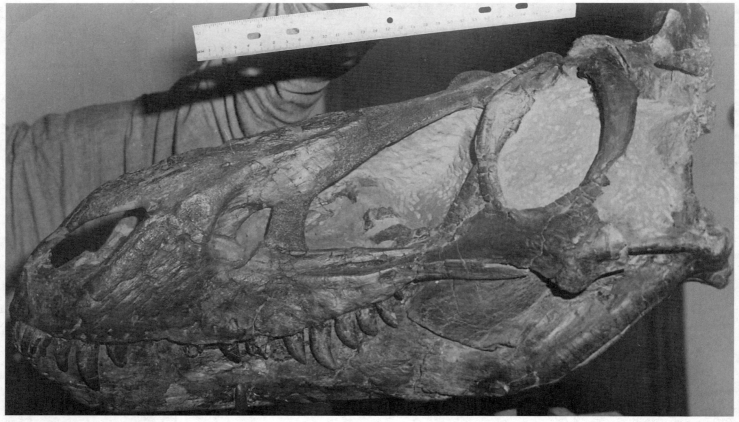

Holotype skull (CM 7541) of *Gorgosaurus lancensis*, a species subsequently named *Nanotyrannus lancensis*, but regarded by some tyrannosaurid specialists as a juvenile *Tyrannosaurus rex*.

Williamson and Carr noted that *Tyrannosaurus rex*— currently also known from the Hell Creek Formation of Montana, the Denver Formation of Colorado, and also upper Maastrichtian deposits of Wyoming, North Dakota, South Dakota, Alberta, Saskatchewan, and possibly the Kirtland Formation of New Mexico — represents "the most widespread Mesozoic dinosaur species." As these authors also regarded the Asian genus *Tarbosaurus* as synonymous with *Tyrannosaurus*, they also found *Tyrannosaurus* to be "one of the most widespread as relatively complete and diagnostic remains are present in both Asia and western North America."

As Williamson and Carr noted, the pattern of diversity of the Tyrannosauridae during the Late Cretaceous (see Carr and Williamson 2004, below) is similar to that of other North American dinosaurs in general "in that there is a decline in generic diversity approaching the end of the Cretaceous," this phenomenon "due, in part, to a decrease in provinciality as faunas in western North America become increasingly more homogenous." However, according to Williamson and Carr, this decrease constitutes an unusual component of the late Maastrichtian fauna, as it "does not reflect the general biogeographic division between north and south Laramidia as seen in other Late Cretaceous dinosaurian clades."

The taxonomy of *Tyrannosaurus rex* continues to elicit opinions, some of them accepting the taxa *Aublysodon mirandus*, *Nanotyrannus lancensis*, *Stygivenator molnari*, and *Dynotyrannus megagraciilis* as valid type species or as junior synonyms of *T. rex* (see *D:TE* and previous supplements).

For example, theropod specialist Philip J. Currie (2003*a*), in a study on the allometric growth in North American and Asian tyrannosaurids, regarded *Aublysodon*— a genus established by Joseph Leidy (1868) upon three teeth (ANSP 9535) collected from the Judith River Formation of Montana — as a juvenile *Tyrannosaurus rex* (see "Notes," below).

Most tyrannosaurid specialists (*e.g.*, Rozhdestvensky 1965; Carpenter 1992*a*; Carr 1999; Carr and Williamson, below) now interpret the holotype skull (CMNH 7541) of the type species *Nanotyrannus lancensis* (originally *Gorgosaurus lancensis* Gilmore 1946*b*) to be a juvenile *T. rex* (see *S1, S2*). However, Currie (2003*b*), one of the coauthors of the original paper proposing *Nanotyrannus* as a distinct genus (see Bakker, Williams and Currie 1988), recently criticized such assessments, pointing out that, while CMNH 7541 "is almost certainly an immature tyrannosaurid that is closely related to *Tyrannosaurus*," most of the 13 characters used to demonstrate the synonymy of

Life restoration by Todd Marshall based upon a skull (CMNH 7541) currently regarded by most tyrannosaurid specialists as a juvenile *Tyrannosaurus rex*. In 1988, Robert T. Bakker, Michael Williams, and Philip J. Currie described this specimen as a "pygmy" tyrannosaurid which they named *Nanotyrannus lancensis* (see *D:TE*).

"*Nanotyrannus*" and *Tyrannosaurus* are found also in *Tarbosaurus* and *Daspletosaurus*.

Currie (2003*b*) commented upon all 13 characters (see paper for details) individually, concluding in short that nearly all of them "define a broader taxonomic unit than just *Tyrannosaurus* and *Nanotyrannus*," and that "*Nanotyrannus lancensis* is closer to *Tyrannosaurus rex* than to any other tyrannosaurid in that it is relatively broader (compared to the snout width) behind the orbit than albertosaurines." According to Currie (2003*b*), *Nanotyrannus lancensis* differs from *Tyrannosaurus* in at least one way — at least 14 maxillary teeth (see Gilmore), or possibly 15 (see Bakker *et al.*), in the holotype of *N. lancensis*, as opposed to 11 or 12 in *Tyrannosaurus*. According to Carr, the number of teeth might be reduced ontogentically, although Currie (2003*a*) found the evidence for this to be only weakly supported. Moreover, according to Currie (2003*b*), "There is no indication that any other theropod did this, and the counts always vary within one or two teeth."

Considering that it is difficult to distinguish *Nanotyrannus* from an immature *Daspletosaurus* (a tyrannosaurid that survived into the early Maastrichtian), while tooth counts between *Daspletosaurus* and *Tyrannosaurus* are intermediate, Currie (2003*b*) found it "more conservative to retain *Nanotyrannus* as a distinct genus at this time." In the future, however,

pending the recovery of additional specimens for study, "tooth counts and stratigraphic position may turn out to be a valid way to distinguish *N. lancensis* from *T. rex* at the generic or species level."

Recently, Holtz (2004), in a review of the Tyrannosauroidea, citing the conflicting opinions regarding this taxon, tentatively retained "*Nanotyrannus*" as a valid genus. At the same time, that author noted that this taxon "either represents a juvenile *Tyrannosaurus rex* or the juvenile of another tyrannosaurine sympatric with *T. rex*, closer to *T. rex* than to all other tyrannosaurids but not yet recognized from adult material." Moreover, Holtz stated, the potential "discovery of either an adult *Nanotyrannus* that can be clearly distinguished from *Tyrannosaurus rex* or a juvenile *T. rex* of the same skull length and/or ontogenetic stage as, but morphologically distinct from, *Nanotyrannus* would resolve this taxomonic situation."

This volume (at least for the present and pending the possible discovery of material as mentioned by Holtz, above) subscribes to the opinion that CMNH 7541 represents a juvenile individual of *Tyrannosaurus rex*.

In 2004, Carr and Williamson, in a major study on the diversity of late Maastrichtian tyrannosaurids from North America, addressed this issue of taxonomy, reviewing in detail the taxonomic histories of the above-mentioned type species and redescribing the specimens assigned to them:

Photograph by the author, courtesy Natural History Museum of Los Angeles County.

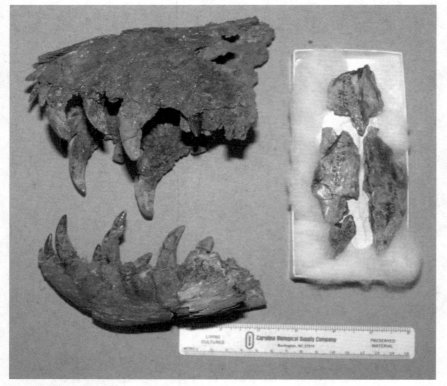

Partial skull and fragments (LACM 28471) of a juvenile *Tyrannosaurus rex* (the "Jordan theropod"), formerly referred to the new genus and species *Stygivenator molnari* (see *S3*).

Aublysodon mirandus was founded upon three partial incisiform tooth crowns, two of them having denticulate carinae, and (ANSP 9539, the lectotype) a smaller crown with nondenticulate carinae, this feature of the latter leading some workers (*e.g.*, Carpenter 1992a) to regard this species as valid (see *D:TE*). Other material was subsequently referred to *A. mirandus*, including a partial skeleton described by Lehman and Carpenter (1990; see *D:TE*) possibly referrable, according to Carr and Williamson, to a new genus of basal tyrannosauroid; and LACM 28471, the so-called "Jordan theropod," based on material including a partial juvenile skull from the Hell Creek Formation of Montana, originally described but not named by Molnar (1978; see *D:TE*). Later, Paul (1988) referred this skull to *Aublysodon* as a new species *A. molnaris* (see *D:TE*), after which Olshevsky, Ford and Yamamoto (1995a, 1995b) referred it to the new genus and species *Stygivenator molnari* (see *S2*).

As reported by Carr and Williamson, the lectotype tooth of *A. mirandus* was recently lost (T. Daeschler, personal communication to Carr and Williamson 2001). As the specimen is no longer available for study, the name *A. mirandus*, according to ICZN rules, no longer has its international standard of reference for providing objectivity in zoological nomenclature, and may therefore be considered a *nomen dubium*. Casts, however, exist of ANSP 9535; consequently, "a neo-

type could be designated based on one of these, if found to differ from other taxa."

Regarding LACM 28471, Carr and Williamson noted that this specimen displays numerous typically tyrannosaurid characters, including the following: Separate joint surfaces of lateral and medial frontal processes of nasal; short orbital rim; expanded frontopostorbital suture having buttress (undeveloped in this specimen); caudolateral suture; frontals separated on midline by parietals; frontals flat between orbits; dorsotemporal fossa covering much of dorsal surface of frontals; first maxillary tooth small, incisiform; first dentary tooth subconical, smallest member of tooth row. No characters preclude referral of this specimen to the Tyrannosauridae, the authors noted.

Also, Carr and Williamson observed that LACM 28471 shares the following characters with *T. rex*: Dorsal and lateral surfaces of rostral third of nasals set at abrupt angles to each other, the bones angular in cross section (as in *T. rex* juveniles); nasals not separating distal ends of nasal processes of premaxillae by pair of median ridges (indicating processes were appressed through their complete length, as seen in *T. rex* specimens AMNH 5027 and CMNH 7541). Based on these shared features, Carr and Williamson regarded LACM 28471 as referrable to *T. rex*.

Among the general features identified by Carr and Williamson in LACM 28471 typical of juvenile tyrannosaurids (*sensu* Carr 1999) are the following: Small size (estimated skull length of about 450.0 millimeters); teeth labiolingually narrow or "bladelike"; cranial remains lightly constructed, particularly those of dorsal skull roof (*e.g.*, nasals, frontals, parietals). According to Carr and Molnar, LACM 28471 represents an ontogenetic stage preceding that of "small Stage 1" previously described by Carr for *Gorgosaurus* [=*Albertosaurus* of Carr's usage] *libratus* (see *S2*).

Carr and Williamson also detailed various other features of LACM 28471 found in juvenile tyrannosaurids, including the following: Smooth state of joint surface for maxilla on nasal; frontal process of nasal not constricted between nasals; nasals not rugose (as in juvenile *T. rex* specimen CMNH 7541); maxilla dorsoventrally shallow, transversely narrow (see Carr); rostral margin maxillary fenestra not approaching rostral margin of external antorbital fenestra (comparable to CMNH 7541 and other tyrannosaurid specimens); dorsotemporal fossa of frontal present, dorsal margin of its depression indistinct (Carr); joint surface of lacrimal rostrocaudally elongate and transversely narrow in dorsal aspect (Carr); muscle attachment area on lateral surface of surangular, ventral to glenoid fossa, shallow groove.

Carr and Williamson stated that two features regarded by Molnar as unique for LACM 28471—*i.e.*,

Life restorations of male (left) and female (right) *Tyrannosaurus rex* individuals by artist Todd Marshall.

shallow angle of symphysis and slope of alveolar margin, in lateral aspect—are, in their view, typical of Tyrannosauridae.

Furthermore, the authors noted that characters (*i.e.*, nasals low; triangular profile of maxilla; nondenticulate front teeth) used by Paul to refer LACM 28471 to *Aublysodon molnari* are vague and nondiagnostic, that the nasals are, in fact, dorsoventrally crushed, and that the condition of the front teeth seem to reflect immaturity, as observed in other theropods (*e.g.*, Norell, Clark, Dashveg, Barsbold, Chiappe, Davidson, McKenna, Perle and Novacek 1994); and that the criteria (*i.e.*, long maxillary teeth; mesiodistally narrow, smaller "premaxillary" tooth; convex ros-

tral end of alveolar margin of dentary; procumbent rostral three dentary teeth) by which Olshevsky *et al.* referred LACM 28471 to *Stygivenator molnari* can also be observed in other juvenile, subadult, and small tyrannosaurids.

Carr and Williamson concluded, therefore, that "LACM 28471 exemplifies a juvenile *T. rex.*"

LACM 23845, originally described by Molnar (1980), comprises the partial skull and skeleton of a medium-sized tyrannosaurid collected from the Hell Creek Formation of Montana in a quarry adjacent to one containing an adult specimen (LACM 23844) of *T. rex*. Molnar first referred LACM 23845 to *Albertosaurus* cf. *lancensis*, after which Paul declared it to

Peter L. Larson, of the Black Hills Institute of Geological Research, with the discovery of the furcula of the *Tyrannosaurus rex* specimen (TCM 2001.90.1) nicknamed "Bucky," at the Wade Derflinger Ranch site in the Hell Creek Formation of Perkins County, South Dakota.

be the holotype of a new species, *Albertosaurus megagracilis* (see *D:TE*), and then Olshevsky *et al.* made the specimen the holotype of a new genus, *Dinotyrannus* (see *S2*).

As noted by Carr and Williamson, LACM 23845 shares the following features with *Tyrannosaurus* and *Daspletosaurus*: External surface of frontal process of nasals constricted between lacrimals, in dorsal aspect; dorsoventral notched between constriction and rostral extent of joint surface for lacrimal, to receive stout process from dorsomedial edge of lacrimal; frontals transversely wide in dorsal aspect, frontolacrimal and frontoprefrontal sutures widened; sagittal crest divided on frontals, deep midline cleft separating paired crests (as in subadult and adult *Tyrannosaurus* and *Daspletosaurus* specimens); large foramen piercing sagittal crest on midline, crest diminishing rostrolateral or rostroventral to opening (as in other tyrannosaurids and juvenile *T. rex*, *e.g.*, CMNH 7541 and LACM 28471); dorsotemporal fossa deep, dorsal surface rostral to fossa rostrocaudally short; frontoparietal suture transversely oriented except on midline; lingual ridge and groove in associated crown (probably mesial maxillary tooth).

Also, Carr and Williamson noted, LACM 23845 exhibits the following characters of *Tyrannosaurus*: Long caudolateral process of nasal (short or absent in *Daspletosaurus* and *Tarbosaurus bataar*); lacrimal without cornual process, dorsal surface instead wide, flat, accessory pneumatic fossa distal to lacrimal recess; sagittal crest extending rostrally on frontals, midline cleft separating paired crests (as in subadult and adult *Tyrannosaurus* specimens); also, postcranial characters are consistent with other *T. rex* specimens: in scapula in ventral aspect, caudal margin of joint surface of humerus narrower than cranial margin, acromion elongate in lateral view (as in FMNH PR2081).

Carr and Williamson further noted that the criteria (*e.g.*, "extremely atrophied forelimbs, down-bent nasals, very long snout ... long hind limbs," plus "overall large size and gracile build") utilized by Paul to refer LACM 23845 to the new species *Albertosaurus megacracilis* are difficult to interpret allometrically lacking an independent estimate of body size, this undermining their usefulness as evidence of taxonomic difference; and suggested that characters new characters (*e.g.*, wide caudal region of frontals suggesting rostrally facing orbits; wide gap between lacrimal and postorbital joint surfaces) used by Olshevsky *et al.* to diagnose *Dinotyrannus* are incorrect, the caudal region the frontal lying within the dorsotemporal fossa, independent of orbit orientation, and the joint surface of the postorbital being missing on both sides, the presumed wide gap not occurring in subadult and adult tyrannosaurids (*e.g.*, AMNH 5336, AMNH 5664, CMN 2120, ROM 1247).

Based upon the above observations, Carr and Williamson also found LACM 23845 to represent "a subadult *T. rex*.

Consequently, Carr and Williamson, based upon current evidence and the above findings, concluded that there is but one tyrannosaurid species—*Tyrannosaurus rex*—represented in the late Maastrichtian of western North America. Additionally, the authors stressed that they based their referral of LACM 28471 and LACM 23845 to *Tyrannosaurus rex* on diagnostic characters, while the stratigraphical position and geographical location of these specimens are consistent with their identifications; that the documented juvenile characters in these specimens are taxonomically neutral and, therefore, "must be removed from the diagnoses of *Aublysodon*, *Stygivenator* and *Dinotyrannus*"; and that, apart from these diagnostic characters, these specimens would be regarded as indeterminate small tyrannosaurids, displaying several juvenile characters (*e.g.*, dorsoventrally shallow dentaries) typical of most adult small theropods.

Performing a quantitative analysis incorporating 84 morphological characters among five *T. rex* individuals and a hypothetical embryo, Carr and Williamson reconstructed the following a five-stage growth series in this species:

First growth stage (small juvenile, *e.g.*, LACM 238471): Rostroventral margin of antorbital fossa grading into lateral surface of maxilla; first maxillary tooth nondenticulate; joint surface for internasal septum wide in ventral aspect, indicating proportionately wide septum; relatively wide sagittal ridge overlying closed internasal suture, occupying nearly one-third width of paired bones; interparietal suture closed in dorsal and ventral aspects, traceable rostrally in ventral aspect; nuchal crest only moderately indented on midline in caudal aspect.

Second growth stage (large juvenile, *e.g.*, CMNH 7451; greatest morphological development occurring between this and third stage, partly due to lack of juvenile and subadult specimens in Carr and Williamson's analysis): Sagittal crest present, deep on frontal; frontoparietal suture transverse; dentary deep.

Third growth stage (subadult, *e.g.*, LACM 23845): Elaborate cranial ornamentation (*e.g.*, gnarled nasals); intracranial buttressing (*e.g.*, columnar, thick

Skeleton (TCM 2001.90.1) of *Tyrannosaurus rex* ("Bucky") being mounted at the Hills Institute of Geological Research for display at The Children's Museum of Indianapolis.

nasals; deep frontal and parietal; required for mechanically optimal large skull); constricted frontal process of nasals between lacrimals, short and wide frontal (reflecting inflation of bones by antorbital air sac); deep dorsotemporal fossa on frontal, low and wide sagittal crest of parietal, lateroventral orientation of surangular shelf, deep surangular and prearticular, rostrally positioned dorsal margin of prearticular, caniniform teeth (indicating increase in mass of temporal musculature); thick nuchal crest (reflecting hypertrophied cervical musculature); enlarged marginal alveolar foramina of maxilla; nasal with elongate, laterally concave premaxillary process; deep, rugose scar lateroventral to glenoid fossa of surangular.

Completed skeletal (TCM 2001.90.1) mount of *Tyrannosaurus rex* ("Bucky").

Fourth growth stage (young adult, *e.g.*, AMNH 5027): Obliteration of ridge encircling rostroventral margin of antorbital fossa by thickened nature of maxilla; rostral ramus of lacrimal grossly inflated, ramus deeper than pneumatic recess, surangular shelf horizontally oriented.

Fifth growth stage (old adult, *e.g.*, LACM 23844): Additional pneumatic bone destruction in antorbital fossa, principally in interfenestral strut.

In a published abstract for a poster, Buckley (2003), in part of an ongoing investigation into the kinetic possibilities of the *T. rex* skull (see *S2*), addressed the issue of possible cranial kinesis (the movement of skull elements relative to each other) in *Tyrannosaurus*, pointing out that much of the discussion on this topic has been speculative, without comparisons to extant animals having kinetic skulls (*e.g.*, lizards and birds). Buckley examined the possibility of kinesis in the skull of *T. rex* by way of the articulations of the palate bones, the palate being involved in many forms of skull kinesis. Buckley directly compared the individual palate bones of a *T. rex* skull (BHI-3033; the specimen nicknamed "Stan") and their articulation points with the corresponding elements in the monitor lizard *Varanus*, the latter displaying a high degree of cranial kinesis. Preliminary observations of certain

features of BHI-3033 — *e.g.*, loose articulations of vomer, palatine, ectopterygoid, and ectopterygoid to pterygoid — plus their similarity to *Varanus*, suggested to Buckley that kinesis might also exist in the skull of *T. rex*. (However, the joints between the elements of the dermocranium do not match expectations derived from the joints of the palate, nor the distribution of the joints in varanids; R. E. Molnar, personal communication 2004, noting that his study on this topic will be published at a later date).

If the skull of *T. rex* was indeed kinetic, Buckley speculated that "Kinesis may have been used for shock absorption to compensate for the large bite force in *T. rex*." The degree of this kinesis as of yet unknown, "the question remains whether kinesis was used in feeding, as in extant taxa."

Snively (2003), in a published abstract, briefly presented a theoretical model of neck musculoskeletal function in *T. rex*, pointing out the importance of neck functional morphology as related to feeding amniotes. Snively's reconstruction of major cervical and craniocervical muscles in this species indicated a combination of traits closer to the conditions of both birds and crocodilians than to other amniote taxa. This inferred morphology, that author pointed out, "forms the basis for a theoretical model of neck function,

Skull and cervical vertebrae (cast from BHI-3033) of *Tyrannosaurus rex*, part of the specimen popularly known as "Stan."

incorporating musculoskeletal geometry and aspects of muscle force generating capacity," this model predicting "aspects of craniocervical feeding function in terms of a summation of muscle torques," and facilitating testing of various hypotheses.

Snively offered the following examples: The strong, upward beveling of caudal cervical vertebrae indicating a favorable moment arm for dorsiflexion of the neck by the M. longus colli dorsalis; in smaller tyrannosaurids, a proportionally greater horizontal component of the muscle pull possibly compensating for shorter dorsiflexive moment arms; and bilateral contraction of the M. longissimus perhaps having affected powerful action of the head in cutting out flesh.

Although Snively's modeling approach suggested constraints on tyrannosaurid feeding capabilities, it is less adequate, that author noted, for addressing issues of behavioral plasticity (*e.g.*, tyrannosaurids possibly paralleling extant archosaurs in the modulation of inertial feeding).

Lipkin and Sereno (2004), in an abstract, briefly described the furcula ("the only indisputable evidence for the presence, shape, and articulation" of this element in *T. rex*) in an articulated postcranial specimen (UCPC V1) found in 2001 in a sandstone concretion of the Lance Formation (Maastrichtian) in eastern Wyoming. Preserved in articulation, with a modicum of transverse or dorsoventral distortion, are bones of the midsection including dorsal vertebrae with associated ribs, gastralia, furcula, pectoral girdles, and forelimbs. Lipkin and Sereno reported the following: Furcula positioned between pectoral girdles in articulation with acromial processes of scapulae; clavicular rami broken off at edge of concretion; right ramus more complete, ventral margin and distalmost tip preserved in concretion *in situ* (left ramus broken at midlength).

Lipkin and Sereno described the furcula in this specimen as follows: U-shaped or (more accurately) lyre-shaped in cranial aspect, with rounded dorsal and ventral margins; transverse depression or trough on cranial side of central body; no development of hypocleideal process or rugosity at ventral apex, no

Skeletons of *Tyrannosaurus rex* (left, TCM 2001.90.1 ["Bucky"], right cast of BHI-3033 ["Stan"], middle *Triceratops horridus*, TCM 2001.93.1 ["Kelsey"], now part of the "Dinosphere" exhibit at The Children's Museum of Indianapolis.

median line of fusion; caudal side of central body flat or very slightly concave; intrafucular angle of approximately 45 degrees (measured from ventral half of clavicular rami); most closely resembling furcula of *Gorgosaurus*.

As Lipkin and Sereno pointed out, UCPC VI unambiguously documents "that the furcula in *Tyrannosaurus rex* is a symmetrical lyre-shaped bone readily distinguishable from gastralia or posteriormost dorsal ribs."

As Hutchinson, Anderson and Delp (2003) explained in an abstract, the ability to locomote is dependent upon "generating adequate vertical ground reaction forces (VGRF)," or the passive resistance of a skeleton to gravity. Hutchinson *et al.* produced detailed three-dimensional dynamic models of various bipedal taxa (*e.g.*, *Tyrannosaurus*, the dromaeosaurid *Velociraptor*, a chicken, ostrich, and human) to quantify their capacity to generate these forces. Each model was actuated by numerous muscle groups and included the trunk, femur, tibia, metatarsal, and toe segments connected by joints, with musculoskeletal geometry based upon phylogenetically constrained re-

constructions and dissections (the *T. rex* model including "10 degrees of joint freedom [hip to toe] and 33 main muscle groups crossing the hip, knee, ankle, and toe joints of the right hindlimb"; see Hutchinson, Anderson, Blemker and Delp 2004). The authors then used these "models to compute the amount of support that is passively provided by the skeleton and actively generated by muscles," and also to evaluate "how limb orientation and musculoskeletal geometry affect the capacity of muscles to generate support."

Hutchinson *et al.*'s analysis found the chicken, ostrich, and human models to produce results commensurate with experimental date, and having striking similarities to the models of *Tyrannosaurus* and *Velociraptor*.

This analysis showed that for *Tyrannosaurus*, in upright and the most straight-legged poses, the skeleton's passive resistance to gravity supported up to 85 percent of body weight. For even slightly crouching poses, however, this dropped to under 15 percent. Among the muscles found to be most influential in contributing support were the M. gastrocnemius pars medialis, M. ambiens, and M. iliotibialis 3, which could, respectively, have generated as much as 1.5, 1.2, and 0.92 Newtons of VGRF per Newton of muscle. A uniarticular ankle, followed by multiarticular muscles, produced the most VGRF; proximal hip and knee extensor muscles (*e.g.*, M. caudofemoralis, M. femorotibialis) generated less VGRF, respectively, 0.27 and 0.69 Newtons per Newton of muscle force.

Results (these and other details presumably to be published at a later date) of this analysis showed how the muscles and the skeleton are more effective in giving support when the limbs are "in upright orientations," the authors to discuss this conclusion in light of previously reported evidence supporting "a more crouched pose."

Paul (2004), in an abstract for a poster, presented data relating to the possible speed of giant tyrannosaurs such as *Tyrannosaurus*, his study based upon anatomical and scaling comparisons of the running potential of extant animals (*e.g.*, elephants and bulls), and also computer-generated simulations (for details of this simulation, based on a reconstruction of CM 9380, the holotype of *Tyrannosaurus rex*, and a calculated body weight of 5,700 kilograms, see the abstract by Sellers and Paul 2004). As Paul stated, "All giant tyrannosaurs were speed adapted, small bellied predators with weight reducing pneumatics, shortened distal tails, and hypotrophic arms, propelled by long, bird like legs powered by muscles anchored on expansive pelvic plates, prominent cnemial crests, and stout tail bases," with leg muscles comprising 20 to 30 percent of the animal's total mass.

Although no giant animals live today that are comparable to *Tyrannosaurus*, Paul explained that a heavily bellied, multi-tonne rhinoceros, with short, moderately muscled legs possessing but minimal running power, can attain full gallops of up to about 13 meters per second; moreover, massively bellied elephants, having weakly muscled legs devoid of speed adaptations, can achieve speed in excess of six meters per second. According to Paul's study, such similar-sized yet longer striding and better muscled tyrannosaurids such as "albertosaurs and daspletosaurs" could probably achieve running speeds of from 14 to 18 meters per second. Paul concluded that *Tyrannosaurus*—having "flexed jointed, running legs operated by muscles two to three times larger and more powerful"—must have been at least as swift, perhaps more so, than its smaller relatives.

In a related study to determine the possible maximum running speed of large theropods such as *Tyrannosaurus*, but one producing rather different results than Paul's, Hutchinson (2004) utilized "a simple mathematical model of the inverse dynamics of locomotion to estimate the minimum muscle masses required to maintain quasi-static equilibrium about the four main limb joints at mid-stance of fast running." That author's study (see paper for additional details) incorporated an analysis of 10 extant taxa—human, kangaroo, two lizards (iguana and basilisc), alligator, and five birds (tinamou, chicken, turkey, emu, and ostrich)—in a number of "bipedal poses to examine how anatomy, size, limb orientation, and other model parameters influence running ability." In order to observe how support ability varies across the limb, Hutchinson compared the muscles needed for fast running to the muscle masses actually capable of exerting moments about the joints of the hips, knees, ankles, and toes. Hutchinson calculated extant animals known to be bipedal runners as able to preserve quasistatic equilibrium about the joints of their hindlimbs at midstance; that author recognized nonbipedal runners (*e.g.*, alligators, iguanas), however, as having not enough muscle mass to run on their hind legs quickly. This approach to modeling, Hutchinson proposed, "should be reliable for reconstructing running ability in extinct bipeds such as non-avian dinosaurs." Additionally, these models illustrated how various key features (*e.g.*, limb orientation, muscle moment arms, muscle fascicle lengths, body size) are important for the capacity to run bipedally.

Hutchinson criticized various methods of evidence largely based upon inferences and assumptions, used in earlier studies (see, for example, Coombs 1978*b*; Bakker 1986; Paul 1988, 1998; Horner and Lessem 1993; Garland and Janis 1993; Holtz 1994; Witmer 1995; Carrano 1999; Christainsen 1999*b*, 2002) to create reconstructions of the running ability of *Tyrannosaurus* as being only rarely explicit or directly testable, the genus being "intuitively concluded to 'look fast.'" Noting that both scientific and popular writings of such dinosaurs have traditionally "had a certain fervor, evoking hyperbolic functional inferences," Hutchinson quoted Henry Fairfield Osborn (1917), the American Museum of Natural History paleontologist who named and described *Tyrannosaurus rex* in 1905, thusly: "*Tyrannosaurus* is the most superb carnivorous mechanism among the terrestrial Vertebrata, in which raptorial destructive power and speed are combined."

Hutchinson's biomechanical approach showed that the ability to run in theropod dinosaurs probably declined with large body size, the larger bipedal animals having to reduce their range of locomotor performance with increasing size, the largest taxa (*e.g.*, *Tyrannosaurus*) possibly also reducing their absolute maximum performance. More specifically, Hutchinson found *Tyrannosaurus* not to have been a fast runner "because its hip and ankle extensors were not large enough to exert the necessary moments" (although medium-sized theropods—*e.g.*, *Allosaurus*, *Dilopho-*

Bones of the *Tyrannosaurus rex* specimen popularly known as "Wyrex," *in situ* at a locality in the Hell Creek Formation of Montana. The specimen will eventually be collected and prepared by the Black Hills Institute of Geological Research of South Dakota.

saurus— could have been rather good runners). While finding the some of the proposed higher running speeds for *Tyrannosaurus* "dubious" and even "outrageous," Hutchinson did not advocate a particular posture or maximum speed for *T. rex* in his present study, finding no rigorous conclusion yet possible.

Sampson, Loewen, Farlow and Carrano (2003), in a published abstract, explained that studies of extant and recently extinct vertebrates show "that body size is correlated with a variety of ecological parameters, often with resultant evolutionary consequences." The largest known terrestrial carnivorous animals occur with the Theropoda, and the best known of the giant theropods is *Tyrannosaurus rex*.

As Sampson *et al.* noted, recent phylogenetic analysis shows that, within Theropoda, gigantism (*i.e.*, femur length greater than 1.2 meters) evolved independently during the Mesozoic at least four times, all representative taxa seemingly having achieved biologically equivalent body size (from about five to seven metric tonnes). This similarity suggested strongly to the authors that the evolution of gigantism in the Theropoda could have been subjected both to eco-

logical and mechanical constraints. According to Sampson *et al.*, ecological correlates among extant terrestrial carnivorous animals suggest that the largest members of the Theropoda were ectothermic, having low mass-specific metabolic rates nevertheless necessitating extensive, continent-sized geographic ranges. Supporting that hypothesis, the authors correlated known occurrences of gigantic carnivorous dinosaurs with continent-sized landmasses.

Sampson *et al.* based their study upon a recently found specimen of *T. rex* from the North Horn Formation of Utah, documenting the co-occurrence of this theropod in an upland, intermontane setting with the titanosaur *Alamosaurus*. New data based upon this specimen, combined with information gleaned from earlier finds, indicated "that *T. rex* was an ecological generalist, spanning a broad geographic area that included diverse habitats and a range of prey species." Also, while tyrannosaurids were in isolation for at least 25 million years in both western and eastern North America, the earlier forms significantly had smaller bodies (*i.e.*, femur length less than 1.1 meter). It was Sampson *et al.*'s conclusion that the evolution of

Courtesy Natural History Museum of Los Angeles County.

gigantism in *Tyrannosaurus rex* is "casually linked to the doubling of habitat area associated with retreat of the Western Interior Seaway."

Horner and Padian (2004) addressed the question, regarding the recovered skeletons of *T. rex*, "how old they were at maturity or death." Using histological evidence from seven *T. rex* individuals, Horner and Padian, for the first time, were able to assess whether those specimens represented fully grown animals and to predict the longevity of each individual. A substantial age range of from 15 to 20 years was projected for the specimens, with the species apparently having attained full size well before the age of 20.

Not all of the specimens examined by Horner and Padian seem to have reached full size before death. The authors determined the following: Three specimens apparently effectively ceased active growth two or three years before death, while their cortical radius continued increasing annually by 0.5 to 0.7 percent; and four specimens seemingly were still growing, although interval decreases in lines of arrested growth (LAGs) suggest each specimen would have effectively achieved full size in from one to three years. Moreover, evidence from femora and tibiae suggest that reached full adult size by slightly over 16 years, although the studied sample was small, with individual variation perhaps affecting age at maturity.

Horner and Padian's study concluded "that *T. rex* grew quickly to adult size, and that its growth dynamics are similar to large mammals and would appear to indicate high basal metabolic rates to sustain that growth." Further samples, the authors noted, could reveal if these theropods generally lived much beyond their attainment of adult size.

Various studies have been published over the years attempting to identify sexual dimorphism in different kinds of dinosaurs, including *Tyrannosaurus*.

Paleontologist Luis M. Chiappe (right) and field assistant with the jacketed right femur (LACM 150167) of *Tyrannosaurus rex*, during the Natural History Museum of Los Angeles County's expedition to the Hell Creek Formation of Montana in 2003.

Fossilized skin impressions
found with the *Tyran-
nosaurus rex* specimen
nicknamed "Wyrex."

Schweitzer, Wittmeyer and Horner (2004), in an abstract with implications relating to this topic, reported
on "novel dinosaurian skin tissue" found in a femur
of the oldest yet recorded specimen of *T. rex*, elements
of which were collected in the summer of 2003 from
the Hell Creek Formation in eastern Montana. Never
before recorded in a dinosaur bone, this thin tissue
layer "is completely distinct from the cortical and endosteal bone external to it."

Briefly, Schweitzer *et al.* described this tissue as
follows: Highly vascular; bone matrix surrounding the
vessels exhibiting random structure; (as confirmed by
ground thin sections) sharp demarcation between
laminar endosteal bone and new tissue, with "con-
current dramatic increase in vascularity."

It was Schweitzer *et al.*'s hypothesis that this observed tissue could "be the functional analogue of
avian medullary bone," a specialized kind of bone (not
produced by extant reptiles and mammals) that serves
to store, for a short term, calcium produced by ovu-
lating female birds in response to increased estrogen
levels, utilized by them in the formation of eggshells.
Moreover, the authors pointed out, the discovery of
medullary bone in *T. rex* "provides the first objective
means of assigning gender to a dinosaur, and additionally, demonstrates that the animal was in reproductive phase" when it died.

The debate over whether *Tyrannosaurus rex* was
an active predator or a scavenger has persisted without resolution for nearly a century. Most studies on

this topic have focused upon the former interpretation
of this giant carnivore, and many of the arguments
have been based on jaw morphology and teeth (*e.g.*,
see Erickson, Van Kirk, Su, Levenston, Caler and
Carter 1996).

More recently, Ruxton and Houston (2003)
tackled this question from a novel approach — utilizing energetic arguments to calculate the minimum
productivity that would be required for an ecosystem
to support an obligate scavenger of the size (approximately six metric tonnes) of *Tyrannosaurus rex*.

Ruxton and Houston's hypothesis was "that the
key constraint for scavengers is generally their ability
to find food items," this being "in contrast to predators, where capturing rather than discovering prey is
the key constraint, and herbivores, where processing
consumed food is often the key restriction on energy
gain rate." Their study argued that an ecosystem as
productive as the current Serengeti could offer enough
carrion to sustain an animal the size of *T. rex* (see Ruxton and Houston's paper for details regarding the
mathematical equations employed in this study).

Ruxton and Houston concluded that *Tyrannosaurus rex* would indeed be capable of surviving
strictly as a scavenging animal providing various conditions are met, these including the following:

1. The Late Cretaceous ecosystem in which
Tyrannosaurus rex lived yields the same carrion density as does the present-day Serengeti. Although
widely varying, estimates of primary productivity at

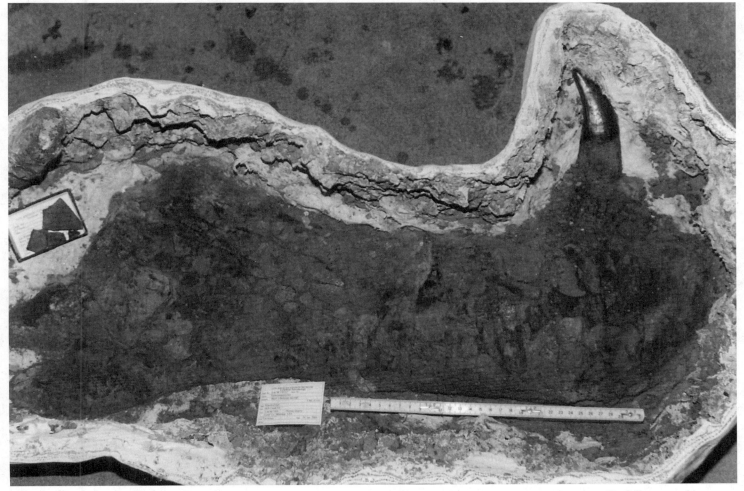

Partially prepared incomplete maxilla of the *Tyrannosaurus rex* specimen LACM 150167) nicknamed "Thomas" in the vertebrate paleontology laboratory of the Natural History Museum of Los Angeles County.

the time and place corresponding to *T. rex* encompass values similar to those of today's Serengeti (see Beerling and Woodward 2001). Moreover, any given primary productivity could have supported a greater biomass of ectothermic dinosaurs compared to the endothermic mammals dominating the Serengeti (see Farlow 1990), the higher biomass more than compensating "for the lower turnover rate per unit biomass that one would predict if dinosaurian herbivores had longer lifespans than the [Serengeti] mammalian herbivores ... [because of] their larger size and probably lower specific metabolic rates."

2. *Tyrannosaurus rex* can detect carcasses at a distance of 80 meters. Based on computed tomographic (CT) analysis of the skull of the *T. rex* specimen (FMNH PR2081) called "Sue," Brochu (2000; see also Brochu 2003*a* for an essay regarding popular misconceptions — *e.g.*, regarding alleged bite marks, healed fractures, *etc.*, about this specimen promoted by the media) argued that this species seems to have possessed greatly enlarged olfactory bulbs indicative of a keen sense of smell. Farlow (1994) further speculated

that the elevated stance of this theropod could have enhanced the location of carrion, both by visual and olfactory means.

3. Presumably the carcass was only detectable to a *Tyrannosaurus rex* for an approximately 24-hour period. Although little is known regarding the length of time a carcass is accessible to vertebrate scavenger, the assumption that prey remains available for just one day — before being consumed by other carrion eaters, *e.g.*, maggots, other vertebrate species, other *T. rex* individuals, and so forth — seemed reasonable to Ruxton and Houston, perhaps even on the low side. Assuming that their "focal individual" was able to access but 25 percent of the carrion density of the Serengeti, the authors calculated that *T. rex* would have had to be able to detect prey at a distance of 330 meters in order to balance its energy budget, this, although challenging, still in the bounds of possibility.

Although Ruxton and Houston did not state that *T. rex* made its living strictly as a scavenger, their energy budget analysis suggested "that a reptile as large as *T. rex* could have survived using a purely scavenging lifestyle, providing that competition for carrion was low."

Ruxton and Houston's conclusion led to an obvious question: Why is there no scavenger like *Tyrannosaurus rex* on the Serengeti today; or, more generally, why are vultures the only extant vertebrates having a predominantly scavenging lifestyle? An avian scavenger, the authors explained, can outcompete a terrestrial one because, as mentioned above, a scavenger's main requirement "is to minimize energy expenditure while searching." Even powered flight is faster and much less energetically expensive per distance covered compared to terrestrial locomotion (see Schmidt-Nielson 1984). Soaring birds, such as vultures, have considerably lower energy expenditure than do any terrestrial scavenger. Therefore, if *Tyrannosaurus rex* were indeed a scavenger, then this was most likely "possible because avian radiation had yet to have a substantial effect on ecosystems."

Notes: The holotype skeleton of *Tyrannosaurus rex*, mounted at the Carnegie Museum of Natural History since 1942 (McGinnis 1982; also see *D:TE* and "Introduction," this volume, for photographs), is being precisely measured in micron level accuracies, using two networked Coherent Laser Radar systems, as reported briefly by Hand, Clark, Beard and McDaniel (2004) in an abstract for a poster. As these authors reported, "The generation of four and a half million point measurements into a point cloud is the first step in digitizing and 3D modeling the full size exhibit and its individual components." The generated models can then be utilized "for dimensional analysis, animation ... and replication in any scale (either direct or inverse) for solid free-form or mold generation using 3D printing technology." Results of these measurements are to be published in detail at a later date.

As stated above, some theropod specialists (*e.g.*, Carr and Williamson 2001; 2004) consider *Tyrannosaurus rex* to be the only valid tyrannosaurid taxon occurring in the Hell Creek Formation. However, another opinion was offered by Larson, Nellermoe and Gould (2003) in a published abstract for a poster following a study of theropod teeth collected from a low-species-density hadrosaur bonebed in the lower Hell Creek Formation of Corson County, South Dakota. As reported by these authors, 95 theropod teeth from this site, which has also yielded more than 5,500 bones tentatively referred to the duckbilled ornithopod *Edmontosaurus* (see entry). Four of these teeth were identified as pertaining to troodontids, the remaining 91 to tyrannosaurids (basal lengths of the latter ranging from 4.2 to 22.5 millimeters, the exceptions being two larger teeth having basal lengths of 33 and 34 millimeters).

It was Larson *et al.*'s intent "to define the apparent differences in the teeth (related primarily to shape and size) and to determine if those differences represented various juveniles of a typical tyrannosaur, or were differences enough to indicate the possibility of another species of small tyrannosaurid." All specimens to be studied were photographed with a macro lens in lateral aspect, then enlarged to produce a standard fore-aft 51-millimeter basal length, after which shape and size comparisons were made utilizing these photographs.

Larson *et al.* found two groups of tyrannosaurid teeth based upon both size and curvature, the latter possibly indicating placement in the jaws. Also, one group of teeth is laterally compressed and the other more robust. According to the authors, this might suggest that not all of these tyrannosaurid teeth are scaled-down versions of adult teeth, becoming more robust during ontogeny. This hypothesis would not, however, explain the presence of both small robust and larger laterally compressed teeth. Larson *et al.*, therefore, concluded "that two species of tyrannosaur are present in the bonebed, one most likely *T. rex*, the other a smaller tyrannosaurid" (*i.e.*, perhaps "*Nanotyrannus*"; R. E. Molnar, personal communication 2004).

Averianov and Yarkov (2004) described some isolated theropod remains from the Upper Cretaceous (Maastrichtian) Bereslavka (sometimes referred to as Karpovka) water reservoir (Volgograd Region), Volga-Don Interfluve, Russia. The material includes a fragmentary braincase (VGI 231/1), represented by the basioccipital and basisphenoid fused together, and possible exoccipitals, resembling the braincase in megalosaurids; a short, thick tooth crown (VGI 231/2) with lingual development of the mesial carina, characteristic of dromaeosaurids; and a relatively short and stout metacarpal ?I (VGI 231/3) possibly referrable to a ceratosaur or megalosaurid. This latter specimen had been identified by Yarkov (2000) as a "large digital phalanx" belonging to *Tyrannosaurus*. According to Averianov and Yarkov, the relatively sudden emergence of these primitive theropods, as well as other kinds of primitive dinosaurs, in the Maastrichtian of both the Lower Volga Region and Romania, might be explained by a general climatic cooling of those regions.

As already stated, *Tyrannosaurus rex* was once a quite rare dinosaurian species, known from a relatively small number of specimens. In recent years, however, a wealth of new fossil material pertaining to this theropod has been collected, and specimens continue to be found, some of them having not yet been described:

In 1997, Lou Trembley found a very large *T. rex*

Photograph by the author, courtesy Natural History Museum of Los Angeles County.

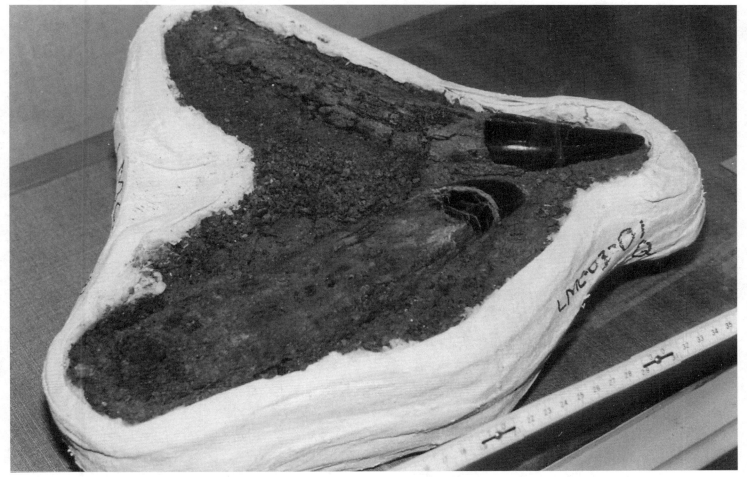

Two teeth of the *Tyrannosaurus rex* specimen (LACM 150167) nicknamed "Thomas" on display at the Natural History Museum of Los Angeles County.

skeleton on a ranch in the Hell Creek Formation at Fort Peck, McCone County, Montana. The specimen—estimated to be approximately 65 percent complete—was collected later that year by University of Notre Dame paleontologist J. Keith Rigby, Jr. and a team from Fort Peck Paleontology Inc., the nonprofit partner of the Fort Peck Interpretive Center. Given the trademarked nickname of "Peck's Rex," the specimen was prepared by Fort Peck Paleontology and then mounted for display at the Interpretive Center.

Although not yet formally described, various press and internet articles on this specimen have reported that a vestigial metacarpal III (about the size of a human's little finger, possibly an individual variant; R. E. Molnar, personal communication 2004) is preserved with the manus. *Tyrannosaurus*, as well as other tyrannosaurids, are usually described as possessing but two fingers on each manus (a comparatively slightly larger vestigial third finger had already been known in the older and smaller tyrannosaurid *Gorgosaurus libratus*).

A cast of the skull of this specimen went on display at the University of Notre Dame's Eck Visitor Center in 2003.

"Bucky" (reported on in a 2004 press release written by Neal L. Larson) is the nickname given to a subadult *T. rex* skeleton (TCM 2001.90.1) discovered in 1998 by Bucky Derflinger on the Wade Derflinger Ranch in the Hell Creek Formation of Perkins County, South Dakota (eight miles west of the site where "Sue" was found). The specimen was excavated from 2001–2002 by the Black Hills Institute of Geological Research, Inc., which recovered approximately 39 percent of the skeleton (including nearly complete vertebral column to end of sacrum, cervical ribs, most of gastralia basket, most complete series of caudal vertebrae next to the specimens called "Sue" and "Stan" [also collected by the Black Hills Institute] pelvis, feet, almost complete rib cage, scapulae, coracoid, ulna, two finger bones, and five shed or broken teeth).

The specimen showed no signs of scavenging. However, associated with this skeleton was a partial skeleton of the duckbilled dinosaur *Edmontosaurus annectens* showing "some large gouges in the sacral vertebrae that can only be attributed to *T. rex* bites."

Photograph by Mindy McNaugher, courtesy Carnegie Museum of Natural History.

Partially prepared skull of *Tyrannosaurus rex*, specimen popularly known as "Samson," on display in 2004 at the Carnegie Museum of Natural History.

A robust morphotype, the specimen seems to represent a young female animal (see Larson 1997).

Other fossils discovered at this site include remains of *Triceratops*, *Pachycephalosaurus*, and *Thescelosaurus*, also unidentified ankylosaur, theropod, mammal, crocodile, turtle, fish, and plant material.

In June 2004, a reconstructed skeletal cast of "Bucky" went on display at The Children's Museum of Indianapolis, its missing skull molded from elements of "Stan," "Duffy" (a *T. rex* specimen collected by the Black Hills Institute in 1993–1994 near the "Stan" site), and other specimens, with lengths of the limb calculations taken from the similarly sized AMNH 5027 and others.

In 2004, the Black Hills Institute began excavation of "Wyrex," another *T. rex* specimen, this one found by Don Wyrick in the Hell Creek Formation of Montana.

The discovery of another recently collected *T. rex* specimen was announced in the August, 2003, issue of *Docent Doings*, an in-house newsletter of the Natural History Museum of Los Angeles County. In that report, an anonymous author announced the collection in July of that year of a new specimen of *T. rex*

from the Thomas Quarry in the Hell Creek Formation of Carter County, Montana.

The specimen (LACM 150167), an almost complete skeleton, was found by American history school teacher Bob Curry in Baker, Montana, and was nicknamed "Thomas" after Curry's brother. The skeleton was collected for the Natural History Museum by a field team, sponsored by Andrew Getty and led by Luis M. Chiappe, that museum's Curator of Vertebrate Paleontology, and comprising museum staff members, university students, and Montana State University (Bozeman) paleontologists. It was excavated at the end of three seasons of field work by the Los Angeles museum in Wyoming and Montana (the previous year having resulted in the collection in Wyoming of a partial *Triceratops* skeleton).

This *Tyrannosaurus* skeleton is distinguished as "the best preserved, most complete, specimen [of that species] currently in any collection on the West Coast." With the arrival of the specimen on July 24, two of "Thomas'" very long teeth — measuring 13 inches in length including the root — went on exhibit in the Los Angeles' museum's Director's Gallery.

U

As noted in the article, the remaining parts of the specimen may be recovered in 2004. "We don't known what else we'll find," Dr. Chiappe was quoted. "But we do know, based on what we've already uncovered, that we have the most complete adult specimen excavated by the Museum in a very long time."

Another tyrannosaurid specimen, apparently a juvenile *Tyrannosaurus rex* ("*Nanotyrannus*"), was reported on in the November 11, 2003 edition of the *Chicago Tribune*, in an article written by Richard Wronski. According to this report, the juvenile skeleton — first announced in 2002 — was discovered in the Montana Badlands by a largely amateur fossil-collecting group from the Burpee Museum of Natural History in Rockford, Illinois. The specimen has been nicknamed "Jane," in honor of Burpee Museum of Natural History benefactor Jane Solem. Collected material belonging to this specimen [BMRP 2002.4.1] includes more than half the skeleton.

Two *Tyrannosaurus* skeletons were reported in newspapers (*e.g.*, the *Chicago Sun-Times*) in May, 2004.

The May 14 edition of that newspaper announced the collection by the Carnegie Museum of Natural History of what promises to be the most complete skull (nicknamed "Samson") of *T. rex* yet discovered. Carnegie Museum paleontologist Christopher K. Beard was quoted in the article as stating, "Samson could be the most important T. rex skull ever collected. There is a tremendous amount of scientifically important information to be garnered."

The newspaper's May 17 edition announced that a partial skeleton (apparently approximately 20-percent complete) of *T. rex* (nicknamed "Barnum," for Barnum Brown, the discoverer of *Tyrannosaurus*; see *D:TE*), had been sold for $93,250 to a consortium of South Dakota investors by Bonhams & Butterfields auction house in Los Angeles. The specimen — including teeth and portions of the forearms and feet — was found in 1995 in Wyoming, in the same area where Barnum Brown made his famous discovery. Casts of the bones apparently match remains (presumably BMNH 7994 [originally AMNH 5866], the holotype of "*Dynamosaurus imperiosus*") of *T. rex* housed at The Natural History Museum, London, and may possibly belong to the same specimen.

In the 67th issue (August/September 2004) issue of the magazine *Prehistoric Times*, in an interview with paleontologist John R. Horner conducted by Vincent JJ Curley (2004), Horner reported eight new *T. rex* specimens discovered by the Museum of the Rockies in the lower third of the Hell Creek Formation of Montana. Varying in completeness, they "represent some of the most interesting specimens found in the last two decades."

These specimens include the following: "L-rex" and "J-rex," not collected due to poor preservation and inaccessible terrain, the latter specimen representing a small individual (including a disarticulated braincase that "will provide important data concerning the relationship between *Daspletosaurus* and *Tyrannosaurus*"); "F-rex" and "G-rex," providing mostly histological data; "N-rex," an articulated leg (excavated and displayed by the National Museum of Natural History); "C-rex," the largest of these specimens, including a poorly preserved partial jaw, dorsal vertebrae, pubii, ischia, partial ilia, complete ribcage, and numerous gastralia, indicating an animal the size of the *Tyrannosaurus* specimen called "Sue"; and "B-rex," the best preserved and relatively small specimen, including a disarticulated skull having a total length of less than 130 centimeters (48 inches), "providing important information about the pneumaticity of T-rex's skull" and also "interesting information about biomolecules."

Key references: Averianov and Yarkov (2004); Bakker (1986); Bakker, Williams and Currie (1988); Beerling and Woodward (2001); Brochu (2000, 2003*a*); Buckley (2003); Carpenter (1992*a*); Carr (1999); Carr and Williamson (2001, 2004); Carrano (1999); Christainsen (1999*b*, 2002); Coombs (1978*b*); Curley (2004); Currie (2003*a*); Erickson, Van Kirk, Su, Levenston, Caler and Carter (1996); Farlow (1990, 1994); Garland and Janis (1993); Gilmore (1946*b*); Hand, Clark, Beard and McDaniel (2004); Holtz (1994, 2001, 2004); Horner and Lessem (1993); Horner and Padian (2004); Hutchinson (2004); Hutchison, Anderson and Delp (2003); Larson (1997); Larson, Nellermoe and Gould (2003); Lehman and Carpenter (1990); Leidy (1868); Lipkin and Sereno (2004); McGinnis (1942); Paul (1988, 1998, 2004); Molnar (1978, 1980, 1991); Norell, Clark, Dashveg, Barsbold, Chiappe, Davidson, McKenna, Perle and Novacek (1994); Olshevsky, Ford and Yamamoto (1995*a*, 1995*b*); Osborn (1905, 1917); Rozhdestvensky (1965); Ruxton and Houston (2003); Sampson, Loewen, Farlow and Carrano (2003); Schmidt-Nielson (1984); Schweitzer, Wittmeyer and Horner (2004); Sellers and Paul (2004); Snively (2003); Williamson and Carr (2003*a*); Witmer (1995); Yarkov (2000).

UNENLAGIA Novas and Puerta 1997
Saurischia: Eusaurischia: Theropoda: Neotheropoda: Tetanurae: Avetheropoda: Coelurosauria: Tyrannoraptora: Maniraptoriformes: Maniraptora: Metornithes: Paraves: Deinonychosauria.
Name derivation: Latinized from local Mapuche Indian names *uñen* = "half" + *lag* = "bird."
Type species: *U. comahuensis* Novas and Puerta 1997.
Occurrence: Neuquén Group, Sierra del Portezuelo,

Unenlagia comahuensis, MCF PVPH 78, holotype left scapula in a. dorsal and b. lateral views, c. pelvis in right lateral view, d. pubes in d. cranial view, and e. 13th dorsal vertebra in left lateral view. (After Novas and Puerta 1997.)

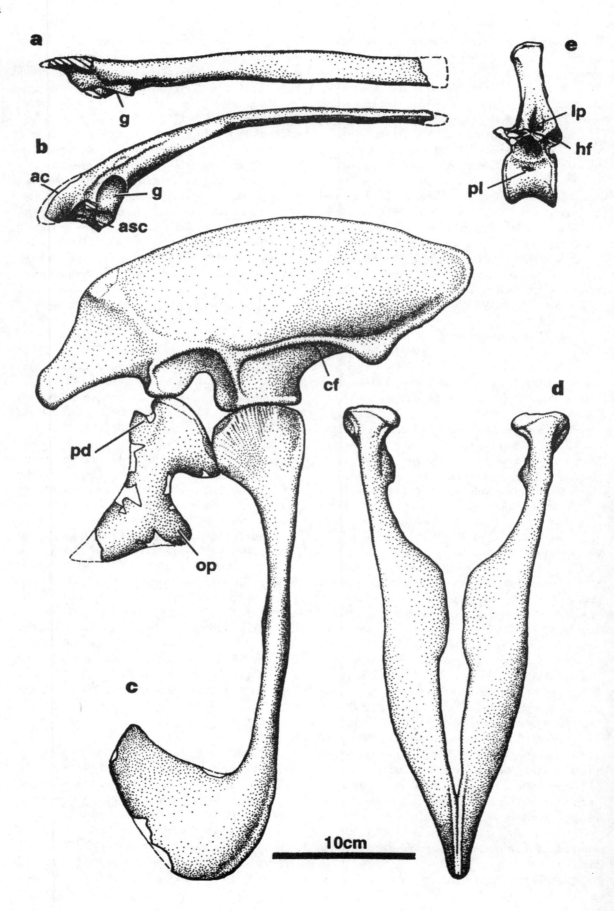

Reconstructed skeletal cast of *Unenlagia comahuensis* mounted under the direction of Rodolfo A. Coria, at the Museo Municipal Carmen Funes in Neuquén Province, Patagonia, Argentina.

Neuquén Province, Neuquén Province, North-West Patagonia, Argentina.

Age: Late Cretaceous (Turonian–Coniacian).

Known material/holotype: MCF PVPH 78, partial postcranial skeleton, including almost complete left scapula, almost complete pelvis, 13th dorsal vertebra.

Diagnosis of genus (as for type species): Caudal dorsal and cranial sacral vertebrae having tall neural spines, almost twice height of centra; lateral pits deep in base of those neural spines; shaft of scapula twisted; dorsal margin of postacetabular iliac blade inflected (Novas and Puerta 1997).

Comments: In 1997, Fernando E. Novas and Pablo F. Puerta described the so-called "half bird" *Unenlagia comahuensis*, based on partial postcrania (MCF PVPH 78) collected from the Upper Cretaceous Río Neuquén Formation (Neuquén Group) of Sierra del Portezuelo, Argentina.

The authors originally diagnosed this type species as follows: Neural spines of caudal dorsal vertebrae and cranial sacral vertebrae tall, nearly twice height of centrum; lateral pits deep in base of those neural spines; scapular shaft twisted; dorsal margin of postacetabular iliac blade inflected.

In describing this taxon, Novas and Puerta noted that the skeleton is that of a medium-sized maniraptoran which, if complete, would measure nearly two meters (seven feet) in length, about two-thirds the size of the dromaeosaurid *Deinonychus*.

At that time, Novas and Puerta identified *Unenlagia* as a non-avian theropod possessing both dinosaurian and avian features, perhaps bridging the morphological gap between the Dromaeosauridae and the bird *Archaeopteryx lithographica*. Moreover, the authors referred *Unenlagia* to the clade Deinonychosauria, envisioning the animal to be a relic descendant of a theropod lineage that existed before the line leading directly to *Archaeopteryx* and true birds.

Novas and Puerta cited the following non-avian dinosaurian and avian features in the *Unenlagia* holotype: Scapula straplike in dorsal aspect, curved in lateral aspect (very similar to *Archaeopteryx*); acromion process triangular in lateral aspect, projected sharply cranioventrally (as in *Archaeopteryx*); humeral articulation oriented laterally (as in birds); ischium with triangular obturator process (as in most advanced Coelurosauria); dorsal edge of ischium exhibiting prominent proximodorsal process, separated from ischiadic antitrochanter by deep notch (previously found only in *Archaeopteryx* and other birds); ilium with well-developed fossa for m. cuppedicus (in Coelurosauria including basal birds), narrow extensive inner wall to hip socket (as in *Archaeopteryx* and other birds); pubic distal expansion or "boot" large (as in Coelurosauria), primitive forward "toe" of boot lost (as in birds).

Additionally, Novas and Puerta noted the lateral orientation of the glenoid cavity of the scapula of

Unenlagia, a derived feature found also in *Archaeopteryx* and other birds, although not previously known in non-avian dinosaurs. This suggested to the authors that the forelimbs of this animal could be raised to produce an avian-like full upstroke in anticipation of the down and forward flight stroke. While *Unenlagia* was clearly a flightless creature, as evidenced by its relatively large size and short forelimbs, and one not derived from a volant form, it had already acquired the near-avian forelimb movements not found in more remote coelurosaurian outgroups. Possessing "a prerequisite for powered, flapping flight, offering necessary thrust to lift winged theropods from the ground," the morphology of *Unenlagia* offers new evidence, Novas and Puerta suggested, to strengthen the postulation "that a bipedal, cursorial theropod was ancestral to birds, and used its arms not only in predation, but probably also in maintenance of balance and to control its body attitude while running and leaping" (also see Ostrom 1976*b*, 1986*b*).

The non-avian status of *Unenlagia* was, however, challenged just one year after the issuance of Novas and Puerta's publication. Forster, Sampson, Chiappe, and Krause (1998) argued that, rather than being a very birdlike non-avian theropod as Novas and Puerta had envisioned their new taxon, *Unenlagia* is actually a bird exhibiting various non-avian features (see *S1* for additional information relating to the above, plus a drawing of the reconstructed skeleton).

For more than half a decade, *Unenlagia* has been regarded as a bird rather than a non-avian theropod (*e.g.*, see Chiappe and Witmer 2002 and various papers within). In fact, Novas (2004) subsequently pointed out various derived traits observed in the ilium of *U. comahuensis* and also the ilia of birds, features otherwise not found in dromaeosaurids or less derived theropods (*e.g.*, lobe-shaped preacetabular wing, prominent supratrochanteric process, reduced brevis fossa).

More recently, Norell and Makovicky (1999; see also 2004) noted many similarities between *Unenlagia* and dromaeosaurids, these including the following: Stalked parapophyses; expanded distal neural spine on dorsal vertebrae, forming spine table.

Later, Senter, Barsbold, Britt and Burnham (2004), in performing cladistic analyses of the Coelurosauria with an emphasis on the Dromaeosauridae (see "Systematics" chapter), confirmed the non-avian deinonychosaurian status of *Unenlagia comahuensis*, as well as of the presumed dromaeosaurid *Hulsanpes perlei* and *Pyroraptor olympius*. Furthermore, *Unenlagia* was found by Senter *et al.* be the sister taxon of both Dromaeosauridae and Aves.

Note: Fossil teeth of "medium size," recently collected from the Futalognko quarry in Neuquén Province and described in an abstract by Poblete and Calvo (2004), may belong either to *Unenlagia* or an unknown dromaeosaurid. Some of the details in these teeth noted by the authors follow: Unique character of crest starting at root of labial side, continuing upward to apical portion, reaching tip on mesial side; resembling dromaeosaurids in absence of mesial carina, mesial convex crown, and high-angled caudal inclination of crown.

Key references: Chiappe and Witmer (2003); Forster, Sampson, Chiappe, and Krause (1998); Norell and Makovicky (1999, 2004); Novas (2004); Novas and Puertas (1997); Ostrom (1976*b*, 1986*b*); Poblete and Calvo (2004); Senter, Barsbold, Britt and Burnham (2004).

†UNQUILLOSAURUS

Saurischia: Eusaurischia: Theropoda: Neotheropoda: Tetanurae: Avetheropoda: Coelurosauria: Tyrannoraptora: Maniraptoriformes: Maniraptora: Metornithes.

Diagnosis: Pubis large (51.4 centimeters in length) compared with those of other basal maniraptorans, proportionally long and slender; proximal end presenting thick edge defining deep groove (regarded as diagnostic by Powell 1979, but is morphologically abnormal, not recorded in other theropods, better explained as broken pubic pedecile of ilium adhered to external surface of pubis) (Novas and Agnolin 2004).

Comments: In 1979, Jaime Eduardo Powell named and described *Unquillosaurus ceibalii*, a large theropod type species of uncertain, possibly tetanuran affinities, based only upon an isolated left pubis (PVL 3670–11) from the Los Blanquitos Formation of Salta Province, in northwestern Argentina (see *D:TE*).

More recently, the type material of *U. ceibali* was redescribed and its phylogentic relationships reassessed by Novas and Agnolin (2004). As these authors observed, the pubic anatomy of *Unquillosaurus* excludes it from both the Abelisauroidea and Carnosauria. In Abelosauroidea, Novas and Agnolin pointed out, the pubis retains various plesiomorphic features (*e.g.*, obturator foramen enclosed by bone; ischiadic facet proximodistally deep; extended pubic symphysis; pubic boot enlarged, dorsoventrally depressed; see, for example, Carrano, Sampson and Forster 2002) not seen in *Unquillosaurus*; in Carnosauria, the pubis has retained a symphysis and developed a large "boot" (Padian, Hutchinson and Holtz 1999), conditions not present in *Unquillosaurus*.

Rather, Novas and Agnolin found the pubis of *Unquillosaurus* to resemble more that seen in Coelurosauria. Moreover, the authors identified an apomorphic trait supporting the inclusion of this genus

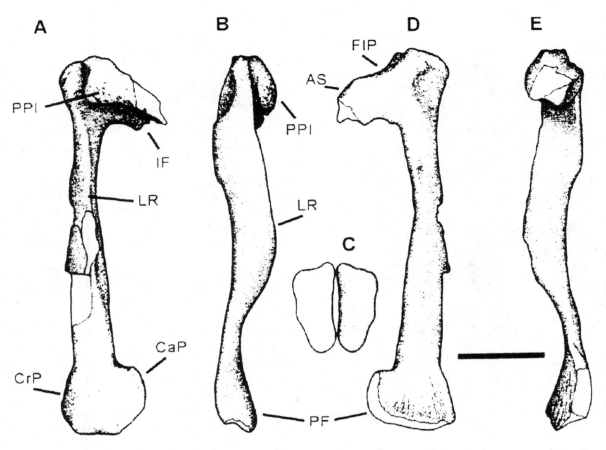

Unquillosaurus ceibali, PVL 3670-11, holotype left pubis in A. lateral, B. cranial, C. distal (reconstructed), D. medial, and E. caudal views. Scale = 10 cm. (After Novas and Agnolin 2004.)

in the coelurosaurian clade Metornithes, *i.e.*, pelvis opisthopubic (for an alternative interpretation of this character, see Chiappe 2001). Additionally, Novas and Agnolin noted, the following features found in *Unquillosaurus* can also been seen in Paraves: Pubic peduncle of ilium craniocaudally wide; ventral margin of pubic peduncle strongly concave; cranial process of pubic foot short; pubic foot less than 30 percent total length of pubis. Also, *Unquillosaurus* notably shares with basal birds (*e.g.*, *Rahonavis* and *Archaeopteryx*) a proximodistally tall, craniocaudally short pubic foot (shorter than in the dromaeosaurids *Deinonychus*, *Velociraptor*, and *Unenlagia*), while its highly reduced pubic symphysis resembles that in Alvarezsauridae and birds more derived than *Archaeopteryx* (see Chiappe).

Unquillosaurus is one of the largest known members of Maniraptora, constituting a giant member of this group of birdlike theropods. As Novas and Agnolin suggested, a radiation of large-sized maniraptorans seems to have taken place in South America during the Late Cretaceous, perhaps including various other recent discoveries (*e.g.*, Coria, Currie Eberth, Garrido and Koppelhus 2001; Novas, Canale and Isasi 2003). Moreover, the unique features of the pubis of this genus "prompt to the conclusion that *Unquillosaurus* was part of a lineage of predatory dinosaurs endemic to South America."

Key references: Carrano, Sampson and Forster (2002); Chiappe (2001); Coria, Currie, Eberth, Garrido and Koppelhus (2001); Novas and Agnolin (2004); Novas, Canale and Isasi (2003); Padian, Hutchinson and Holtz (1999); Powell (1979).

†UTAHRAPTOR

Saurischia: Eusaurischia: Eusaurischia: Theropoda: Neotheropoda: Tetanurae: Avetheropoda: Coelurosauria: Tyrannoraptora: Maniraptoriformes: Maniraptora: Metornithes: Paraves: Deinonychosauria: Dromaeosauridae: Dromaeosaurinae.

Comment: In their review of the Dromaeosauridae, Norell and Makovicky (2004) referred the type species *Utahraptor ostrommaysi* to the Dromaeosauridae based upon the following: Modified raptorial pedal digit II; elongate prezygapophyses on distal caudal vertebrae; in premaxilla, interdental plate apparent, fused to one another; premaxillary teeth "D"-shaped in cross section (similar to those in *Dromaeosaurus albertensis*).

Key reference: Norell and Makovicky (2004).

†VELOCIRAPTOR

Saurischia: Eusaurischia: Theropoda: Neotheropoda: Tetanurae: Avetheropoda: Coelurosauria: Tyran-

Velociraptor

Velociraptor mongoliensis life restoration drawn by artist Todd Marshall. Although *Velociraptor* was probably feathered, no feather-like structures have yet been found pertaining to specimens of this nonavian dinosaur.

noraptora: Maniraptoriformes: Maniraptora: Metornithes: Paraves: Deinonychosauria: Dromaeosauridae: Velociraptorinae.

Diagnosis of genus (as for type species): Premaxilla having process thin, elongate subnarial process; muzzle long, low, profile dorsally concave; three pneumatic recesses surrounding middle ear (Norell and Makovicky 2004).

Comments: Norell, Makovicky and Clark (2004) described in detail the braincase of *Velociraptor mongoliensis*, primarily based upon two adult specimens — GIN 100/976 (preserved as a single piece, broken off from the remainder of the skull) and GIN 100/982 (missing dorsal and lateral regions) — collected recently in Mongolia by field parties of the Mongolian Academy of Sciences and the American Museum of Natural History. This new description, the authors noted, supplements an earlier description of the braincase of this type species offered by Barsbold and Osmólska (1999; see S2); moreover, Norell *et al.* examined GIN 100/25, the specimen described by the previous authors.

Norell *et al.* observed that the braincase superficially resembles that of the dromaeosaurine *Dromaeosaurus albertensis*, although it differs from that type species in the following significant features: Basal

tubera shallower (also present in the microraptorian *Bambiraptor*), divergent, bearing depressions (presumably for rectus capitus rostral muscles); basipterygoid processes short, extending ventrolaterally (rostroventrally in *Dromaeosaurus*); basipterygoid processes curved, tapering (tablike in *Dromaeosaurus*); hypoglossal and vagus foramina exiting within fossa on occiput (present in *Deinonychus*, not in *Dromaeosaurus* and *Bambiraptor*); dorsal tympanic recess well developed (as in *Deinonychus*, not *Dromaeosaurus*); much shallower basisphenoidal recess (also in *Bambiraptor*); prootic recess rostral to otic recess (as in many other coelurosaurs, not in *Dromaeosaurus*); more pronounced swelling around vertical semicircular canal; foramen seemingly present on occipital surface of paroccipital process.

The authors found the above-mentioned differences between the velociraptorine *Velociraptor* and dromaeosaurine *Dromaeosaurus* to be "surprising given the supposed close relationship of these two genera," similarities between these genera (also *Itemirus*; see Kurzanov 1976a) including "the relative positions of the cranial nerve exits within the acoustic fossa, when compared to ornithomimids and troodontids (Makovicky and Norell 1998)."

In a related report published as an abstract, Kundrát (2004a) briefly described two braincases (IGM 100/982 and IGM 100/976) that have been referred to *V. mongoliensis*, noting that both specimens differ from each other in morphologies that seem to have either ontogenetic or phylogenetic significance.

Kundrát observed that, in contrast to the first specimen, IGM 100/976 is characterized by the following details: Auricular foss triangle-shaped; ultriculo-saccular and rostral semicircular canal prominence not extruding too far medially; absence of hollowed area behind caudal internal acoustic fossa; cerebral impressions indicating minor expansion of medulla oblongata, either rostrally between roots of III–IV and VII, ventrolaterally below metotic fissure; endoneurocranial base not clearly corrugated longitudinally; absence of transversal convexity of endoneurocranial base at rostralmost point of metotic fissure; superior tympanic recess less expanded rostrally; absence of crista intertuberalis; shallow parabasisphenoid recess separated by low median ridge; basiexoccipital recess encompassing passages for jugular vein and IX–XII nerves projecting ventrally; foramen magnum considerably compressed dorsoventrally.

As concluded by Kundrát, the above details show IGM 100/976 to be a more primitive morphotype than IGM 100/982, the former possibly referrable, therefore, to a new velociraptorine taxon.

Key references: Barsbold and Osmólska (1999); Kundrát (2004a); Kurzanov (1976a); Makovicky and

Norell (1998); Norell and Makovicky (2004); Norell, Makovicky and Clark (2004).

†VENENOSAURUS

Saurischia: Eusaurischia: Sauropodomorpha: Sauropoda: Eusauropoda: Neosauropoda: Macronaria: Titanosauriformes: Titanosauria *incertae sedis*.

Diagnosis of genus (as for type species): Centra of proximal caudal vertebrae with mildly convex cranial articular surface; spines of midcaudal vertebrae directed craniocaudally (also in *Cedarosaurus* and *Aeolosaurus*) (Upchurch, Barrett and Dodson 2004).

Comment: In their review of the Sauropoda, Upchurch, Barrett and Dodson (2004) rediagnosed the type species *Venenosaurus ricrocei* (see *S3*).

Key reference: Upchurch, Barrett and Dodson (2004).

†VOLKHEIMERIA

Saurischia: Eusaurischia: Sauropodomorpha: Sauropoda *incertae sedis*.

Diagnosis of genus (as for type species): Neural canal of caudal vertebrae cutting deeply into top of centra (Upchurch, Barrett and Dodson 2004).

Comment: In their review of the Sauropoda, Upchurch, Barrett and Dodson (2004) rediagnosed the type species *Volkheimeria chubutensis* (see *D:TE*).

Key reference: Upchurch, Barrett and Dodson (2004).

†WALKERIA—(See *Alwalkeria*.)

†WUERHOSAURUS

Ornithischia: Predentata: Genasauria: Thyreophora: Thyreophoroidea: Eurypoda: Stegosauria: Stegosauridae: Stegosaurinae.

Diagnosis of genus (as for type species): Autapomorphies including the following: Proximal caudal vertebrae having elongated neural spines; distal end of ischium dorsally expanded (Dong and Milner 1998; Galton and Upchurch 2004*b*).

Comment: In their review of the Stegosauria, Galton and Upchurch (2004*b*) rediagnosed the type species *Wuerhosaurus homheni* (see *D:TE*).

Key references: Dong and Milner (1998); Galton and Upchurch (2004*b*).

†XUANHANOSAURUS

Saurischia: Eusaurischia: Eusaurischia: Theropoda: Neotheropoda: Tetanurae.

Diagnosis of genus (as for type species): Forelimb robust; manus retaining four metacarpals; scapula with prominent acromial projection; cervical vertebrae opisthocoelous (Holtz, Molnar and Currie 2004).

Comments: In 1984, Dong Zhi-Ming described *Xuanhanosaurus qilixiaensis*, a type species founded upon two cervical vertebrae, four dorsal vertebrae, and a forelimb with shoulder girdle (IVP AS V6729) collected from the Lower Shaximiao Formation of Sichuan, China. Dong originally referred this taxon to the Megalosauridae (see *D:TE*).

More recently, Holtz, Molnar and Currie (2004), in a review of basal Tetenurae, observed the following concerning this species: Forelimb robust; manus retaining four metacarpals; scapula with prominent acromial projection; putative sternum (reported by Dong) correctly identified by Rauhut (2003*a*) as large coracoid; cervical vertebrae opisthocoelous.

While Dong had suggested that *Xuanhanosaurus* was a quadruped, Holtz *et al.* pointed out that other bipedal basal tetanuran taxa (*e.g.*, *Torvosaurus*, *Poekilopleuron*, spinosaurids) possess massive forelimbs. It was the conclusion of Holtz *et al.* that *Xuanhanosaurus* is "a basal tetanuran not included among the spinosauroids, carnosaurs, or coelurosaurs."

Key references: Dong (1984); Holtz, Molnar and Currie (2004); Rauhut (2003*a*).

†YANDUSAURUS

Ornithischia: Predentata: Genasauria: Cerapoda: Ornithopoda: Euronithopoda *incertae sedis*.

Comments: In 1983, He Xinlu, and Cai Kaiji described a new primitive ornithopod species which they referred to the genus *Yandusaurus*. This species, which the authors named *Yandusaurus multidens*, was founded upon an almost complete skeleton (ZDM T6001), missing the rostral end of the skull, most of the mandibles, and distal end of the tail, collected from the Lower Shaximiao Formation (Late Jurassic: ?Bajocian) of Dashanpu, Sichuan Province, China. In 1992, Peng referred this species to the genus *Agilisaurus*, as the new species *Agilisaurus multidens* (see *Yandusaurus* and *Agilisaurus* entries, *D:TE*). Carpenter (1994) subsequently regarded the type species *Y. hongheensis* (from the Upper Shaximiao Formation; Middle Jurassic: ?Oxfordian) and the smaller *Y. multidens* as synonymous, the latter taxon interpreted by that author as representing a juvenile stage.

Recently, Knoll and Barrett (2003), in a published abstract for a poster, reassessed "*Y.*" *multidens*, pointing out a number of significant differences between that and the type species *Yandusaurus, hongheensis* including the following: Coracoid of "*Y. multidens* lacking ridge on lateral surface and ventral

Life restoration of ?"*Yandusaurus*" *multidens* by Berislav Krzic. (This species could also be referrable to *Agilisaurus*.)

embayment (present in *Y. hongeensis*); scapula shorter than humerus in "*Y.*" *multidens* (equal length in *Y. hongeensis*); also, unexplained differences in morphology of maxillary teeth, thickness of enamel, and degree of tooth wear. According to these authors, the more numerous teeth of "*Y.*" *multidens* contradicts the idea that this species represents juvenile *Y. hongeensis* individuals. These differences, therefore, "appear to be sufficient to warrant a generic distinction between these two species." Knoll and Barrett added that the validity of both the species *Y. hongeensis* and the genus *Yandusaurus* are likewise questionable.

Based upon recent cladistic analyses, Knoll and Barrett found "*Y.*" *multidens* to be more primitive than *Dryosaurus*, although its exact phylogenetic position is currently problematic. Moreover, the type species *Agilisaurus louderbacki* and *Othnelia rex* could be sister taxa to "*Y.*" *multidens*.

More recently, Norman, Sues, Witmer and Coria (2004), in a review of basal ornithopods, cited Barrett (personal communication), who suggested that significant differences in cranial structure between *A. louderbacki* and "*Y.*" *multidens* could merit generic separation between these taxa. Norman *et al.* noted the following anatomical changes between these forms (*e.g.*, reduction in size of external antorbital fenestra; loss of contact between lacrimal and premaxilla; reduction in length of palpebral; development of distinct cingulum on tooth crowns; angular deltopectoral crest). For these reasons, Norman *et al.* preferred referring to this species as "*Agilisaurus*" *multidens*.

Key references: Carpenter (1994); He and Cai (1983); Knoll and Barrett (2003); Norman, Sues, Witmer and Coria (2004); Peng (1992).

†YAVERLANDIA

Dinosauria *incertae sedis*.

Comments: In 1971, Peter M. Galton, a paleontologist specializing in pachycephalosaurian as well as other groups of dinosaurs, described the new type species *Yaverlandia bitholus*, based upon a single specimen — a small "skull cap" (MIWG 1530), comprising two frontals — collected the Lower Cretaceous (Barremian) Wealden Marls of the Isle of Wight, England. Galton interpreted this specimen as belonging to the most primitive known pachycephalosaur, celebrated at the time of its description as the earliest known member of the Pachycephalosauridae and the first member of that clade found outside North America (see *D:TE*).

More recently, Robert M. Sullivan (2000*a*, 2003*a*), also a specialist in pachycephalosaurs, in reexamining the holotype of this species and also reassessing other well-known "bone-headed" dinosaurs, found *Yaverlandia* not to be a member of the Pachycephalosauria for two reasons: First, *Yaverlandia* occurs too early in the fossil record, predating Asian and North American members of this group by 44 to 50 million years; second, Galton's diagnosis of this genus shows that it lacks any traits allowing for its inclusion in Pachycephalosauria, that author having noted the following: 1. Skull cap thickened, possessing two small domes, one per frontal; 2. dorsal surface pitted; 3. frontal excluded from edge of orbit by prefrontal; and 4. supratemporal fenestra not constricted to any extent by postorbital.

However, as Sullivan (2000*a*) observed, all members of Pachycephalosauria possess domes comprising fused frontoparietals, a feature, according to Galton's description, not seen in *Yaverlandia*. In pachycephalosaurian dinosaurs, supratemporal fenestrae are always associated with the parietal area of the dome, not with the frontals as implied by Galton. Also, the frontals of *Yaverlandia* are not individually domed and do not contribute to the edge of the orbits; rather, they contact the nasals rostrally and the supraorbitals laterally. Finally, Sullivan (2000*a*) pointed out that all pachycephalosaurian supratemporal openings are flanked by the postorbitals, their lack of constriction implying that they are well-developed, this being a primitive feature having no phylogenetic significance.

Finding no synapomorphies of the Pachycephalosauria (see also Sereno 2000) in MIWG 1530, Sullivan (2000*a*) concluded that the specimen was originally misidentified as a member of that clade.

Naish (2004*a*), in an abstract for a poster in which he referred to *Y. bitholus* as "Britain's most controversial dinosaur," more recently reexamined the type specimen, noting that (when viewed from the perspective of pachycephalosaurian phylogeny) it

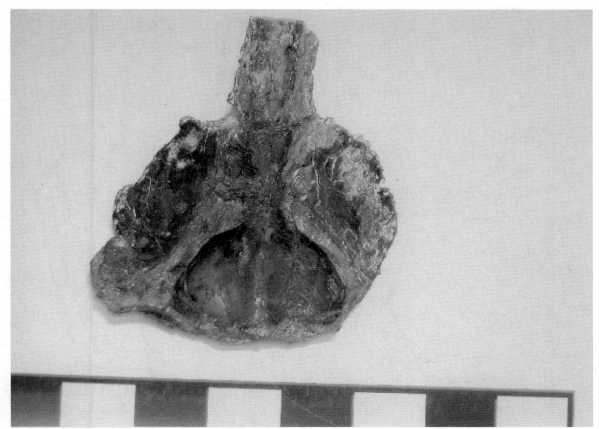

Holotype (MIWG 1539) rostral part of cranium (dorsal view) of *Yaverlandia bitholus*, formerly classified as a primitive pachycephalosaur, but now regarded by Robert M. Sullivan (2000*a*) as nonpachycephalosaurian.

offers a number of previously not highlighted unusual features, thereby constituting a paradox bringing together "an unusual combination of both basal and highly derived characters." Questioning whether *Yaverlandia* is a pachycephalosaur, Naish pointed out that this genus even differs in some salient respects from all other known ornithischians. "Overlooked thus far," that author stated, "is the fact that *Yaverlandia* exhibits derived characters of a clade with which it has not previously been linked." Naish will disclose his evidence and conclusions regarding the phylogenetic status of *Yaverlandia* in his forthcoming PhD dissertation (D. Naish, personal communication 2004).

Key references: Galton (1971); Naish (2004*a*); Sereno (2000); Sullivan (2000*a*, 2003*a*)

†YIMENOSAURUS

Saurischia: Eusaurischia: Sauropodomorpha: Sauropoda: Prosauropoda *incertae sedis*.

Diagnosis of genus (as for type species): Autapomorphies including the following: Elongate ascending process of maxilla (approximately 50 percent of length); club-shaped distal ends of chevrons of caudal vertebrae; distal end of pubis with large inflated crest (Galton and Upchurch 2004*a*).

Comment: In their review of the Prosauropoda,

Galton and Upchurch (2004*a*) rediagnosed *Yimenosaurus youngi*, a type species that they regarded as Prosauropoda *incertae sedis*.

Key reference: Galton and Upchurch (2004*a*).

YIXIANOSAURUS Xu and Wang 2003

Saurischia: Eusaurischia: Theropoda: Neotheropoda: Tetanurae: Avetheropoda: Coelurosauria: Tyrannoraptora: Maniraptoriformes: Maniraptora:

Name derivation: "Yixian [County]" + Greek *sauros* = "lizard."

Type species: *Y. longimanus* Xu and Wang 2003.

Other species: [None.]

Occurrence: Yixian Formation, Wangiagou, Liaoning Province, China.

Age: Early Cretaceous (middle Berrimian).

Known material/holotype: IVPP V 12638, articulated nearly complete shoulder girdles (right and incomplete left scapulae, coracoids) and forearms (humeri, ulnae, carpus with four metacarpals), ribs, feather impressions.

Diagnosis of genus (as for type species): Small, distinguished from all other known maniraptoran species except *Scansoriopteryx* (=*Epidendrosaurus* of the authors' usage) by unusually long manual phalanx II-2 (longer than metacarpal II); differs from all known

Yixianosaurus longimanus, IVPP V 12638, holotype partial skeleton. Scale = 2 cm. (After Xu and Wang 2003.)

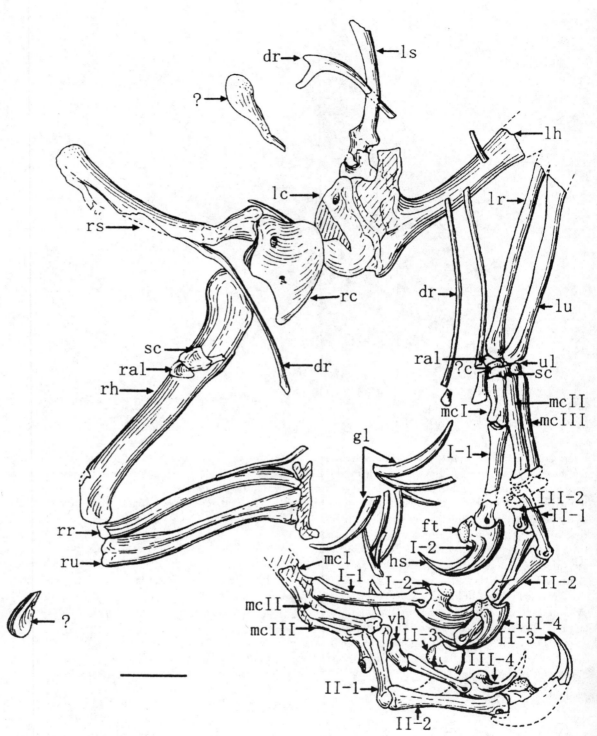

maniraptorans in having proportionately much longer manual phalanx III-3 (244 percent as long as III-1 in *Yixianosaurus*, 86 percent in *Scansoriopteryx*; manus longer, 1.4 manus/humerus length ratio) than in other maniraptorans except *Confuciusornis, Protarchaeopteryx*, and *Scansoriopteryx*, proximoventral heel on manual phalanx III-2 (feature shared with basal dromaeosaurs) (Xu and Wang 2003).

Comments: *Yixianosaurus longimanus* is celebrated as the 11th theropod species and the ninth feathered non-avian dinosaur species reported from western Liaoning Province, China, increasing the known diversity of the Jehol fauna. This type species was founded upon almost complete shoulder girdles and forearms plus some ribs (IVPP V 12638) from the lower part of the Lower Cretaceous (see Swisher,

Wang, Zhou, Wang, Jin, Zhang, Xu, Zhang and Wang 2001) Yixian Formation, Jehol Group, Wangiagou, Yixian County, western Liaoning (Xu and Wang 2003).

The humerus, as measured by Xu and Wang, is only 89 millimeters long, establishing the holotype of *Yixianosaurus* as representing one of the smallest non-avian theropod dinosaurs to date reported. However, the authors pointed out, the carpals are well ossified, while all of the preserved bones lack the fine striations characteristic of juvenile specimens, suggesting that IVPP V 12638 does not represent a juvenile animal. Moreover, lack of fusion of the scapula and coracoid could be indicative of a subadult.

Xu and Wang referred *Yixianosaurus* to the Maniraptora based upon the following synapomorphic features (*e.g.*, see Gauthier 1986; Makovicky and Sues 1998; Sereno 1999*a*; Norell, Clark and Makovicky 2001; Xu, Norell, Wang, Makovicky and Wu 2002; Xu 2001): Scapula short; coracoidal portion of glenoid fossa relatively small; large subquadratic coracoid; ulna bowed; radius thin.

As Xu and Wang pointed out, elongation of the manus constitutes an evolutionary trend from non-avian theropods to birds. In primitive theropods, the manus is shorter than the humerus, while that in maniraptorans is much longer than the humerus. The penultimate manual phalanges of *Y. longimanus* are elongated (phalanx II-2 longer than metacarpal II), comparatively longer than in any other known non-avian maniraptoran with the exception of *Protarchaeopteryx* and *Scansoriopteryx*, this feature apparently constituting a derived feature among Theropoda and in *Y. longimanus*.

Xu and Wang interpreted this elongated phalanx, also the elongation of the distal phalanges and strongly curved condition of the manual unguals, as suggesting a strong grasping capability, possibly indicative of an arboreal habit. Moreover, this feature seems to support the hypothesis that the forelimb could have been utilized in the climbing of trees during the evolutionary transition from non-avian theropods to birds (*e.g.*, see Chiappe 1997).

Key references: Chiappe (1997); Gauthier (1986); Makovicky and Sues (1998); Norell, Clark and Makovicky (2001); Sereno (1999*a*); Xu (2002); Xu, Norell, Wang, Makovicky and Wu (2002); Xu and Wang (2003).

†YUNNNANOSAURUS

Saurischia: Eusaurischia: Sauropodomorpha: Sauropoda: Prosauropoda: Plateosauria: Yunnanosauridae.

Diagnosis of genus (as for type species): Au-

tapomorphy of maxillary and dentary teeth weakly spatulate, apices directed slightly labially, only few coarse apically directed marginal denticles (Galton and Upchurch 2004*a*).

Comment: In their review of the Prosauropoda, Galton and Upchurch (2004*a*) rediagnosed the type species *Yunnanosaurus huangi* (see *D:TE*).

Key references: Galton and Upchurch (2004*a*).

ZALMOXES Weishampel, Jianu, Csiki and Norman 2003 —(=?*Mochlodon*)

Ornithischia: Predentata: Genasauria: Cerapoda: Ornithopoda: Euornithopoda: Iguanodontia: Rhabdodontidae.

Name derivation: "Zalmoxes [also spelled "Zalmoxis," said to have been the slave of Pythagoras, eventually deified]."

Type species: *Z. robustus* Weishampel, Jianu, Csiki and Norman 2003.

Other species: *Z. shqiperorum* Weishampel, Jianu, Csiki and Norman 2003.

Occurrence: Sânpetru and Densus-Ciula formations, Sânpetru, Valioara, Tustea, Pui, Hunedoara County, unnamed formation, Vurpar, Vintu de Jos, Alba County, Hateg Basin, Transylvania, western Romania.

Age: Late Cretaceous (early to middle Maastrichtian; see "Note," below).

Known material: Numerous cranial and postcranial specimens representing most skeletal elements, including associated skeleton (juvenile), representing adult and juvenile individuals.

Holotype: BMNH R.3392, right dentary.

Diagnosis of genus: Rhabdodontid differing from *Rhabdodon* in having extensive, complex squamose suture between quadratojugal and quadrate; posttemporal foramen transmitted through body of squamosal; absence of scar for M. adductor mandibulae externus superficialis on squamosal; curved shelf (?muscular scar) on external surface of postorbital; rostromedial rim of supratemporal fenestra, formed by postorbital; frontal having complex transverse sutural surface extensively overlapping parietal; transverse frontal crest (?sexual dimorphism); quadrates splaying laterally, giving triangular aspect to occiput; quadratojugal large, disc-shaped; predentary massive, with paired triangular ventral processes; reduced external mandibular fenestra, located along upper rostral border of surangular, overlapped by dentary; secondary surangular foramen; surangular "spike"; ilium having long, dorsoventrally narrow, twisted acetabular process, narrow acetabular margin; absence of supra-acetabular rim; ischium without obturator; ischial shaft arched (Weishampel, Jianu, Csiki and Norman 2003).

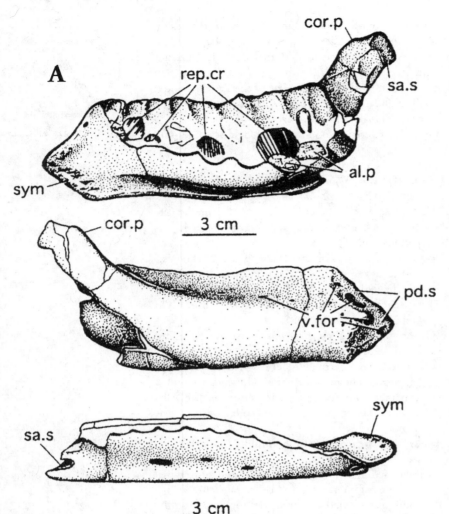

A

cor.p

rep.cr

sa.s

sym

al.p

cor.p

3 cm

pd.s

v.for

sym

sa.s

3 cm

Zalmoxes robustus, BMNH R.3392, holotype right dentary of *Mocholodon robustum*, in (top) medial, (middle) lateral, and (bottom) dorsal views. (After Weishampel, Jianu, Csiki and Norman 2003.)

Diagnosis of *Z. robustus*: Ilium having supra-acetabular process; (other features listed as diagnostic of genus may be determined to be synapomorphic of this species, pending discovery of additional, better material of *Rhabdodon priscus* and *Z. shqiperorum*; Weishampel, Jianu, Csiki and Norman 2003).

Diagnosis of *Z. shqiperorum*: Dentary with wide, angular buccal emargination forming horizontal platform that extends for full length of dentition behind and medial to coronoid process; scapular blade narrow, straplike proximally, expanding sharply caudodistally; expansion of region adjacent to coracoid suture and acromial process, latter forming prominent flange; ischium having bootlike distal expansion of its distal end (Weishampel, Jianu, Csiki and Norman 2003).

Comments: As recounted by Weishampel, Jianu, Csiki and Norman (2003), the genus now known as *Zalmoxes* has had a lengthy taxonomic history:

In 1871, Emanuel Bunzel referred a new species to the ornithopod genus *Iguanodon*, which he named

Iguanodon suessi, founded upon a right dentary with teeth (plus associated additional teeth possibly belonging to the same individual, and a parietal and proximal scapula) recovered from a coal mine in the Upper Cretaceous Gosau Formation of Niederösterreich, Neu Welt, in eastern Austria. Nearly two decades later, Harry Govier Seeley (1881) removed this species from *Iguanodon*, referring it to the new genus *Mochlodon* (see entry), as the new combination *M. suessi*.

Later, Baron Franz Nopcsa (1902) described a second species of *Mochlodon*, which he named *M. robustum* (later amended to *M. robustus*), the latter founded upon skull elements and much postcrania recovered from localities in the Hateg Basin in Transylvania, Hungary (now in Romania). In 1915, that author synonymized *Mochlodon* with *Rhabdodon*, a genus from southern France, his opinion being that the differences between these two forms constituted sexual dimorphism. Until relatively recently, most workers have accepted Nopcsa's assessment of these taxa, with *Mochlodon* generally regarded as a junior synonym of *Rhabdodon* (*e.g.*, Romer 1933, 1956; Kuhn 1936, 1964; Steel 1969; see *Rhabdodon* entry, *D:TE*), with that genus classified either with the Camptosauridae or Iguanodontidae.

With renewed interest in European dinosaurs during the latter twentieth century, various authors (*e.g.*, Weishampel and Weishampel 1983; Norman 1984*a*, 1984*b*; Milner and Norman 1984) used the name *Mochlodon* for material referred to *Rhabdodon* due to nomenclatural confusion (the named *Rhabdodon* had been erected earlier by Fleischmann 1831 for a colubrid snake), these authors also regarding *Mochlodon* as either a dryosaurid or hyspilophodontid ornithopod rather than a camptosaurid or iguanodontid. Sereno (1986), who also retained the name *Mochlodon* for the Transylvanian material, considered the genus to be a basal iguanodontian.

The issue of the validity of the generic name was resolved by the International Commission for Zoological Nomenclature (see Brinkman 1986), which accepted *Rhabdodon* over *Mochlodon*. Subsequent studies (*e.g.*, Norman and Weishampel 1990; Weishapel, Grigorescu and Norman 1991; Jianu 1994) suggested that this taxon is an euornithopod of uncertain position.

More recently, following the recovery of new material, Weishampel *et al.* 2003 recognized that material referred to *Mochlodon robustus*, in fact, represents a distinct genus, which those authors named *Zalmoxes*, encompassing two species, *Z. robustus* and *Z. shiqiperorum*. The new genus was based upon an extensive accumulation of cranial and postcranial specimens (AMNH, BMNH, CCG, CM, CPSP, CMV, FGGUB,

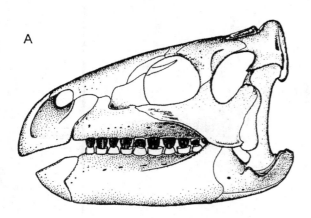

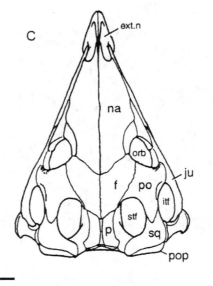

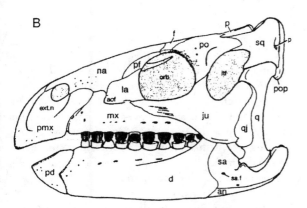

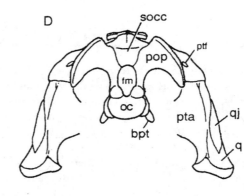

10 cm

Zalmoxes robustus, reconstructed skull in A. left lateral view, B. outline with features labeled, C. skull reconstruction in dorsal and D. occipital views. (After Weishampel, Jianu, Csiki and Norman 2003.)

FWMSH, HMN, IRSNB, MAFI, MCDRD, MCNA, MCZ, MDE, MHNA, MNHM, MNHN, MOR, MUC, PIUW, ROM, SMNH, SNOMNH, UBB, UMNH, USNM, UT, YPM, YPM-BB [Buffalo Bill], and YPM-PU [Princeton University] collections; see Weishampel *et al.* 2003 for a detailed list of this material). Of this material, Weishampel *et al.* (2003) designated BMNH R.3392, a right dentary (originally part of the material upon which Nopcsa 1902 founded *Mochlodon robustum*), as the holotype of *Zalmoxes robustus*. The authors designated BMNH R.4900 as the holotype of second species *Z. shqiperorum*, consisting of a left dentary, sacrum, right scapula, right coracoid, partial ?left ilium, a partial right ilium, right ischium, left distal ischium, and a left femur — the left femoral midshaft also catalogued with BMNH R.4900 being too small to belong to this individual — (material also referred by Nopcsa 1902a, 1915 to *M. robustum*).

To resolve the phylogenetic position of *Zalmoxes*, Weishampel *et al.* undertook a cladistic analysis of nonhadrosaurid Euornithopoda, including 15 terminal species known from well-preserved or well docu-

mented skeletal remains; using *Iguanodon bernissartensis*, *I. atherfieldensis*, and *Camptosaurus dispar* as basal Ankulopollexia; and polarizing a matrix of 75 cranial, dental, and postcranial characters by successive out-group comparisons with *Heterodontosaurus tucki* and Marginocephalia (see "Systematics" chapter for additional results of this analysis).

Both species of *Zalmoxes* were confirmed as sister-taxa united by eight characters: Coranoid having long, narrow sternal process; ilium with strongly twisted preacetabular process; acetabulum very narrow; absence of obturator process; ischial shaft distinctly downwardly curved; ischial shaft ovoid to subcylindrical in cross section; prepubic process rod-shaped; fourth trochanter at midshaft or on distal half of femur.

Based upon its close relationship with *Rhabdodon priscus*, Weishampel *et al.* (2003) referred *Zalmoxes* to the new node-based family Rhabdodontidae (see "Systematics" chapter).

In describing *Zalmoxes*, Weishampel *et al.* (2003) noted that *Z. robustus* was a medium-sized, somewhat rotund ornithopod most likely measuring some three

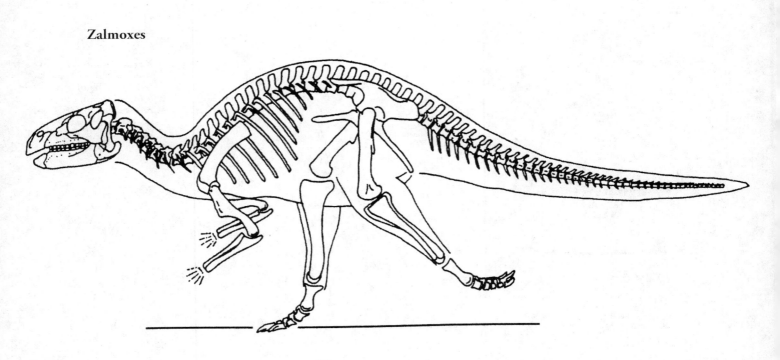

40 cm

Zalmoxes robustus, skeletal reconstruction with presacral and caudal vertebral count based upon *Hypsilophodon*. (After Weishampel, Jianu, Csiki and Norman 2003.)

meters (slightly more than 10 feet) in length, while *Z. shqiperorum* was much closer in size (from about 4.0 to 4.5 meters long) to ornithopods like *Camptosaurus* and *Tenontosaurus*. Like other known adult dinosaurs from Upper Cretaceous sites in Transylvania, *Zalmoxes* was comparatively smaller (though only modestly so) than related adult forms elsewhere in the world, an apparent example of dwarfism in dinosaurs caused by "insulatory evolution," according to Nopcsa (1914, 1915, 1923); see *Magyarosaurus* entry, *S2*). However, Weishampel *et al.* (2003) found evidence for such dwarfing only modestly supported in *Zalmoxes*, noting that this condition does not occur apomorphically in the Rhabodontidae, and suggesting instead that this genus, along with *Magyarosaurus* and *Telmatosaurus*, may be regarded as dwarfs within the Hateg Basin ecosystem. (See Dalla Vecchia 2001*b*, 2002, and 2003*a* for somewhat related studies pertaining to Cretaceous insular dwarfism, particularly among sauropods; and the replacement in Transylvania of sauropods by primitive hadrosaurs, immigrants from central-southern Asia via the Adriatic-Dinaric Carbonate Platform of Italy and Croatia, as the primary dinosaurian plant consumers.)

In comparing *Zalmoxes* to related taxa, Weishampel *et al.* observed that this genus differs little in proportions from its closest euornithopod relatives, but noted the following ontogenetic changes: Number of dentary tooth families increasing ontogenetically from eight to 10, as the dentary changes from being markedly convex ventrally (small individuals) to rather parallel-sided (adults); with lengthening of the humerus, the deltopectoral crest lengthening, becoming more angular (also reported in *Tenontosaurus tilletti*; see Forster 1985); femur exhibiting a more prominent cranial trochanter and slight distal shift in the position of the fourth trochanter; tibia becoming more robust, with a larger cnemial crest with increasing size; femor relatively shorter in younger individuals, in adults it is equivalent in length to, or longer than, the tibia (as demonstrated by Dodson 1980 in *Tenontosaurus*).

Regarding the possibility of sexual dimorphism in *Zalmoxes*, Weishampel *et al.* (2003) related that Nopcsa (1915, 1929) had identified what he believed represented sexual dimorphism in this ornithopod, mostly in differences in the structure of the ischium — males characterized by an expanded, bootlike distal ischium; females by a lack of this expansion — this expansion being correlated with the location and attachment of penile musculature. However, Weishampel *et al.* (2003) found it unlikely that this distal ischial expansion played "a role in sexual dimorphism in view of the presence (and absence) of ischial expansion in other ornithopod taxa." Indeed, these authors found more likely candidates for sexual dimorphism the transverse crest on the rostral end of the frontal, seen in only one specimen (MAFI v.13528), and the development of the ischial shaft, where both a robust (BMNH R.3814) and a gracile (BMNH R.3810) morph were recognized.

As described by Weishampel *et al.*, the jaw of *Zalmoxes* is strong and robust, with an elevated coronoid process and a large jaw adductor muscle chamber, these features indicating that closure of the jaw was powerful, with the motion of the lower jaw

Life restoration of *Zalmoxes robustus* by artist Berislav Krzic.

restricted by a complex jaw joint and a tight predentary-dentary suture. Possibly the absence of a scar for the M. adductor mandibulae externus superficialis on the external surface of the squamosal was compensated for by what seems to be a scar for this muscle on the outer surface of the postorbital. In interpreted correctly, the authors speculated, "this alteration in the area of origin of superficial jaw adductors should reflect the altered geometry of the skull caused by the splayed cheek and suspensorium and its effect on the unusual jaw mechanics of this animal."

As Weishampel *et al.* (2003) pointed out, euornithopods primitively have a pleurokinetic jaw mechanism, by which the upper jaw and associated bones are capable of slight rotational movement during mastication (*e.g.*, see Norman 1984*a*; Weishampel 1984; Norman and Weishampel 1985). Such a system may also have been present in *Zalmoxes*, as suggested by several features (*i.e.*, potentially mobile premaxilla-maxilla articulation; tooth wear indicating transverse jaw motion during chewing; synovial squamosal-quadrate joint). Other features (*e.g.*, unusually strong predentary-dentary suture; strong divergence of jaw rami; oblique orientation of suspensorium), however, argue against such intracranial mobility. This combination of features apparently "represents the transformation of the mobile pleurokinetic framework to a system related to the subdivision of relatively more resistant food items."

Weishampel *et al.* found it curious that, regardless of its relatively large skull of *Zalmoxes*, the premaxillae and predentary are narrow, retaining a simple, nondenticulate oral margin, this condition suggesting to the authors that this dinosaur was potentially a selective feeder — "using its narrow beak to selectively obtain preferred food items, perhaps selecting frutifications or soft shoots" (see Norman and Weishampel 1991).

Considering possible locomotion in *Zalmoxes*, Weishampel *et al.* (2003) noted the following: Postcranially, the skeleton of this genus is robust, with even juvenile stages more massive than other, similar-sized adult ornithopods (*e.g.*, *Hypsilophodon foxii*). Also, the rib cage is more rounded, suggesting a comparatively large fermentation chamber, this condition perhaps correlated with anatomical alterations seen in the pelvis (*e.g.*, ilium with thick, twisted acetabular process, narrow acetabulum, reduced dorsal portion of acetabulum, main iliac blade ventrolaterally oriented, dorsal margin of ilium everted, ischium lacking obturator process) and hindlimb (*e.g.*, femur and tibia laterally bowed). Such features indicated to the authors that *Zalmoxes* employed hindlimb kinematics very different from those of other basal ornithopods, the reorientation of the ilium, narrowing of the

Zalmoxes shqiperorum, BMNH R.4900, holotype right dentary in A. medial, B. lateral, and C. dorsal views. (After Weishampel, Jianu, Csiki and Norman 2003.)

50 mm

Zalmoxes shqiperorum, UBB collection, articulated sacrum, ilia, ischia, and left pubis, in A. dorsal and B. ventral views. (After Weishampel, Jianu, Csiki and Norman 2003.)

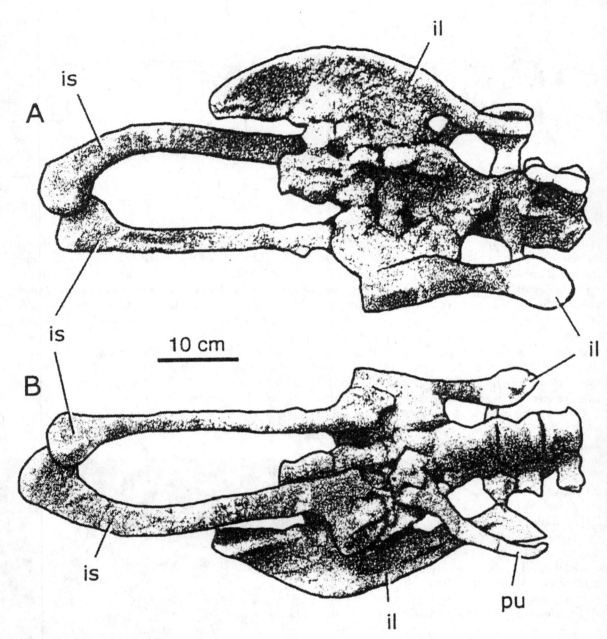

acetabulum, and bowed nature of the femur and tibia suggesting "that *Zalmoxes* may have walked and run with an especially wide gait."

Note: The Sânpetru Formation of Romania's Hateg Basin, mainly because of its lack of dinosaurian remains in the uppermost 200 meters of this formation, has long been thought to span the Cretaceous–Tertiary boundary. Recently, Therrien (2004), in an abstract, addressed the age of the Sânpetru Formation, subjecting samples collected from a 1,000-meter thick composite stratigraphic section of the formation to paleopedologic and magnetostratigraphic analyses. Therrien's study (see abstract for details) found the Sânpetru Formation to be probably of early-to-middle Maastrichtian rather than late Maastrichtian age. Consequently, the paleoenvironmental changes and coincident seeming disappearance of these dinosaurs did not occur at the K-T boundary, but considerably earlier. In conclusion, Therrien proposed that the results of this study, combined with the recent discovery of dinosaur fossils in distinctive dry floodplain facies stratigraphically equivalent or superior to the highest wetland Sânpetru deposits, "suggest that the apparent disappearance of dinosaurs in the Sânpetru Formation is not associated with the terminal Cretaceous extinction but rather reflect a preservational artifact, due to taphonomic and/or paleoecological causes" (see "Introduction," section on dinosaur extinctions).

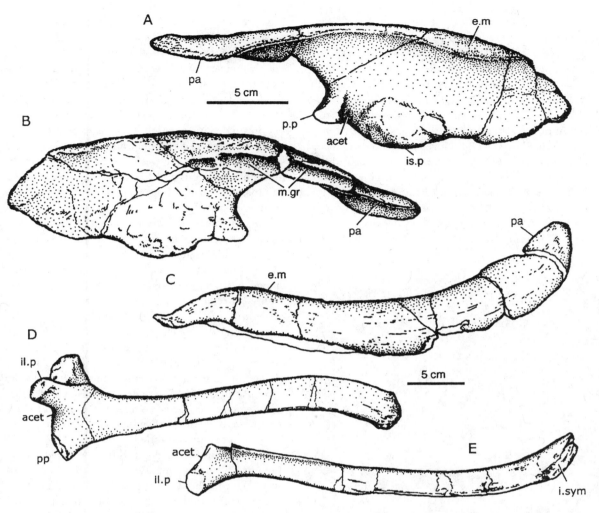

Zalmoxes shqiperorum, BMNH R.3810, left ilium in A. lateral and B. medial, and C. dorsal views, D. left ischium (BMNH R.3814) in lateral view, and E. left ischium (BMNH R.3810) in medial view. (After Weishampel, Jianu, Csiki and Norman 2003.)

Key references: Brinkman (1986); Bunzel (1871); Dodson (1980); Forster 1985); Jianu (1994); Kuhn (1936, 1964); Milner and Norman (1984*a*, 1984*b*); Nopcsa (1902, 1914, 1915, 1923, 1929); Norman (1984*a*, 1984*b*); Norman and Weishampel (1985, 1990, 1991); Romer (1933, 1956); Seeley (1881); Sereno (1986); Steel (1969); Weishampel (1984); Weishampel, Grigorescu and Norman (1991); Weishampel, Jianu, Csiki and Norman (2003); Weishampel and Weishampel (1983).

†ZEPHYROSAURUS

Ornithischia: Predentata: Genasauria: Cerapoda: Ornithopoda.

Comments: Kutter (2003), in a published abstract, briefly reported on new material referred to the primitive ornithopod *Zephyrosaurus schaffi* recently collected by the Sam Noble Oklahoma Museum of Natural History and the University of the Pacific from the Early to Middle Cretaceous (Aptian–Albian) Cloverly Formation of south-central Montana. The

material represents at least seven individuals, most of them recovered from variegated mudstones representing overbank deposits laid down during an early Albian fluvial phase. The material includes two premaxillae, one maxilla, three frontals, three dentaries, and at least one example of every appendicular bone (except the pubis and several manual and pedal elements), including two scapulae, a coracoid, two humeri, an ischium, ilium, three femora, a tibia and fibula.

As Kutter stated, "The results of a morphological and phylogenetic analysis of *Zephyrosaurus* will be presented," presumably in a future publication.

Note: On January 7, 2005, newspapers and other news media services reported amateur paleontologist Robert E. Weems' discovery at College Park, Maryland of Middle Cretaceous fossil footprints belonging to an approximately 1.75-meter (six-foot) long ornithischian dinosaur. Presumably the trackmaker resembled or was *Zephyrosaurus schaffi*.

Key reference: Kutter (2003).

†ZUNICERATOPS

Ornithischia: Predentata: Genusauria: Cerapoda: Chasmatopia: Marginocephalia: Ceratopsia: Neoceratopsia: Coronosauria: Ceratopsoidea.

Note: In a published abstract, Wolfe, Beekman, McGuiness, Robira and Denton (2004) reported briefly on the taphonomic characterization of a minimum of least seven partial skeletons of *Zuniceratops* (represented by several hundred mostly disarticulated elements) and also one of the therizinosaurid theropod *Nothronychus*, found amongst specimens of carbonized logs, in the Haystack Butte bonebed, located in a limited interval of the Late Cretaceous (Turonian) Moreno Hill Formation, New Mexico.

As interpreted by Wolfe *et al.*, some partly articulated and associated elements preserve delicate

Life restoration of *Zuniceratops christopheri* by artist Todd Marshall.

processes and teeth, indicating that the carcasses had been reduced to a skeletal state before burial, and that transport of the elements was local.

Moreover, Wolfe *et al.* deduced the following from the taphonomic evidence at this site: Fine grain size, coal deposits, and freshwater aquatic taxa within Morena Hill strata suggesting relatively stagnant floodplain deposition; high-angle cross-beds sets, clay, bone and charcoal clasts, bone and log "stacking," and specimen orientation suggesting rapid deposition from higher energy floods or debris flow; fossil wood, *in situ* stumps, and charcoal suggesting nearby seasonally emergent conditions.

As the authors pointed out, the *Zuniceratops* skeletal elements found at this site are not equally represented. Skull elements comprise seven left dentaries and four left brow horns, and distal appendicular elements are rare. (By contrast, *Northonychus* is more evenly represented by bones from throughout the skeleton.)

Among the conclusions reached by Wolfe *et al.* (see paper for more details) was that the depositional history of the Moreno Hill bonebed could be explained by seasonal or extreme drought, followed by flood. Additionally, The paucity of distal and right-side elements may be explained as the result of "Secondary mobilization and winnowing of several *Zuniceratop* skeletons stranded together, foundered in mud, partly buried by flood, or accumulated due to drought." Such elements, Wolfe *et al.* concluded, possibly "lagged behind the exposed skull and dorsal elements transported into the bonebed/log jam."

Key reference: Wolfe, Beekman, McGuiness, Robira and Denton (2004).

ZUPAYSAURUS Arcucci and Coria 2003

Saurischia: Eusaurischia: Theropoda: Neotheropoda: Tetanurae *incertae sedis*.

Name derivation: Quechua native language *zupay* = "devil" + Greek *sauros* = "lizard."

Type species: *Z. rougieri* Arcucci and Coria 2003.

Other species: [None.]

Occurrence: Los Colorados Formation, La Rioja Province, Argentina.

Age: Late Triassic.

Known material/holotype: PULR-076, skull (missing premaxillae), articulated caudal cervical and cranial dorsal vertebrae, two incomplete fused sacral vertebrae, proximal end of right scapula and coracoid, distal ends of right tibia and fibula, fused right astragalus and calcaneum, proximal portions of two pedal unguals.

Diagnosis of genus (as for type species): Antorbital fenestra oval, rostroventrally oriented; nasals forming two parasagittal crests on snout; rostral process of lacrimal longer than ventral; main body of maxilla having parallel dorsal and ventral borders; tibial-astragalar articulation locked mediocaudally by astragalar process in caudally open tibial notch (Arcucci and Coria 2003).

Comments: Distinguished as the earliest known tetanuran theropod, the genus *Zupaysaurus* was established on an incomplete skull and postcrania (PULR-076) discovered and collected under the direction of Guillermo Rougier, at Quebrada de los Jachaleros, in middle part of the upper levels of the Upper Triassic (see Caselli, Marsicano and Arucci 2001) Los Colorados Formation (upper part of the Agua de la Peña Group), Ischigualasto-Villa Union Basin, La Rioja Province, western Argentina. Found associated with the holotype, belonging to a smaller animal of uncertain affinities, were a fused left scapulocoracoid, a left ilium, and the distal end of a right femur (Arcucci and Coria 2003).

As measured by Arcucci and Coria, the skull of the type species *Zupaysaurus rougieri* has an estimated complete length of 45 centimeters (about 17.5 inches), establishing this theropod as larger than such other Triassic carnivorous forms as *Coelophysis*, *Liliensternus*, *Eoraptor*, and *Herrerasaurus*, but similar in size to *Gojirasaurus*.

To determine the relationships of *Zupaysaurus* within the theropod clade Neotheropoda, Arcucci and Coria performed a cladistic analysis including the taxa *Dilophosaurus*, *Coelophysis*, *Syntarsus*, *Ceratosaurus*, *Carnotaurus*, *Zupaysaurus*, Allosauridae, *Giganotosaurus*, and Coelurosauria, with *Herrarasaurus* and Sauropodomorpha as more distant successive outgroups. The authors found *Zupaysaurus* to be "the closest theropod to the more derived allosaurids, tyrannosaurs and other tetanuran theropods," therefore nestled within Tetanurae, with ceratosaurs and *Herrerasaurus* more plesiomorphic successive sister groups. Derived tetanuran characters found in *Zupaysaurus* include the following — promaxillary and maxillary openings in antorbital fossa; reduced, keyhole-shaped lateral temporal fenestra; maxillary tooth row ending rostral to orbit; lacrimal pneumatic recess; lacrimal horn developed as low crest or ridge; distal end of tibia transversely expanded; fibula with distal end expanded almost double shaft width; astragalus with cranially positioned ascending process.

Arcucci and Coria noted that *Zupaysaurus* has a coossified astragalus and calcaneum; however, these elements are not fused to the tibia. More inclusively,

Zupaysaurus rougieri, PULR-076, holotype skull in A. right lateral, B. left lateral, and C. dorsal views, and reconstructed D. dorsal and E. right lateral views. (After Arcucci and Coria 2003.)

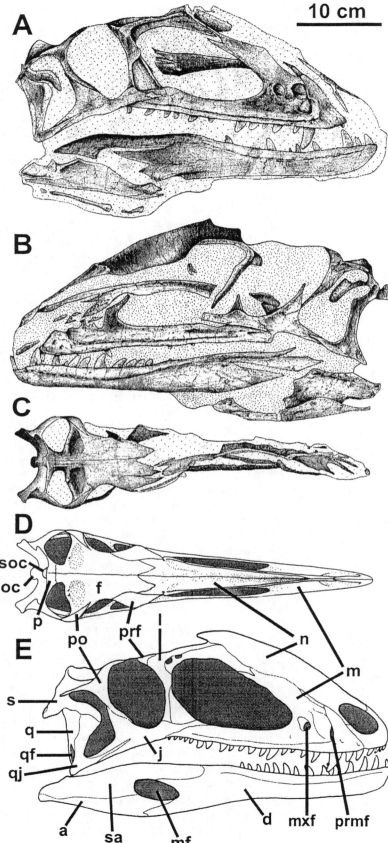

10 cm

this genus shares with coelophysids a maxilla having an alveolar ridge. Furthermore, this genus displays the apomorphic condition of an antorbital fossa that is greater than 25 percent of the length of the skull, the latter diagnosing the node-based clade proposed by Rowe (1989) for *Coelophysis* and *Syntarsus*. The maxilla alveolar ridge (a subnarial gap inferred by a fang-like dentary tooth) and the lateral process of the coracoid were regarded by Arcucci and Coria as primitive theropod features retained in *Zupaysaurus*.

As noted by Arcucci and Coria, the tarsus of *Zupaysaurus* has a morphology that is intermediate between basal theropods (*i.e.*, *Herrerasaurus* [*contra* Langer 2004; see "Systematics" chapter] and Ceratosauria) and more derived members of Tetanurae (see Coria and Arcucci 1999), this condition permitting a proposed sequence of evolutionary changes, as inferred from the authors' proposed phylogenetic hypothesis.

Regarding the lateral expansion of the distal end of the tibia as related to the position of the fibula: The fibula in basal theropods (*e.g.*, *Herrerasaurus*) is positioned lateral to the tibia; in *Zupaysaurus* the tibia slightly overlaps the distal end of the fibula in caudal aspect; in more derived tetanurans (*e.g.*, *Allosaurus*) the distal end of the fibula is entirely cranial to the lateral maleolous of the tibia.

Regarding the facet of the tibia for the ascending process of the astragalus: This facet in primitive theropods is robust and larger than the caudal process of the tibia, with subequal transverse and craniocaudal axes; in *Zupaysaurus*, both facet and process are approximately the same size, the profile broader in distal aspect; in more derived tetanurans (*e.g.*, *Allosaurus*) this facet is reduced, the transverse width nearly twice the anteroposterior length.

Regarding the ascending process of the astragalus: The astragalus in primitive forms is pyramidal, dorsocaudally oriented, having no contact with the fibula; in *Zupaysaurus*, the ascending process has parallel cranial and caudal sides, with a dorsal articular surface for the tibial facet on the cranial side of the astragalus having contact with the fibula; in more derived tetanurans, the ascending process is thin and platelike, slightly overlapper by the fibula.

Arcucci and Coria's interpretation of *Zupaysaurus* as the most primitive tetanuran suggests that the divergence of the two major theropod clades, Ceratosauria and Tetanurae, took place not long after the basal split of the Dinosauria, during the Carnian (see Sereno 1997), into the Ornithischia and Saurischia.

Key references: Arcucci and Coria (2003); Caselli, Marsicano and Arucci (2003); Coria and Arucci (1999); Langer (2004); Sereno (1997).

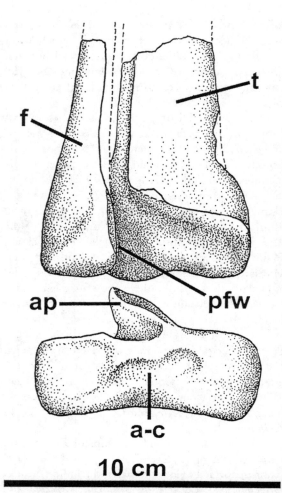

Zupaysaurus rougieri, PULR-076, holotype right tibio-tarsal joint, in cranial view. (After Arcucci and Coria 2003.)

FINAL NOTE

Much time can pass between a book's completion, its going "to press" and actual publication. Consequently, a number of new genera and species were named and described in the paleontological literature too late for inclusion in this volume. These include the following (although there may be more):

Appalachiosaurus montgomeriensis (tyrannosauroid from the Late Cretaceous [Middle Campanian] Demopolis Formation of Alabama, North America).

Brachytrachelopan mesai (short-necked dicraeosaurid sauropod from the Late Jurassic [Tithonian] Cañadón Formation, near Cerro Cóndor, Patagonia, Argentina).

Buitreraptor gonzalezorum (earliest South American dromaeosaurid, from the Upper Cretaceous Candeleros Formation, Río Negro Province, Argentina).

Changchunsaurus parvus (small, primitive ornithopod from the Early Cretaceous Quantou Formation of central Jilin Province, China).

Falcarius utahensis (primitive therizinosauroid from the Early Cretaceous Cedar Mountain Formation, Grand County, Utah, United States).

Hungarosaurus tormai (nodosaurid ankylosaur from the Late Cretaceous [Santonian] Csehbánya Formation, Iharkút, Veszprém County, Bakony Mountains, Transdanubian Range, western Hungary).

Karongasaurus gittelmani (titanosaurian sauropod from the Early Cretaceous of Malawi, Africa, apparently having a long, low skull).

Nemegtia barsboldia (oviraptorid with a well-developed naso-premaxillary crest, from the Late Cretaceous (middle Maastrichtian) Nemegt Formation, Nemegt Basin, Mongolia).

Neuquenraptor argentinus (probable dromaeosaurid deinonychosaurian theropod from the Late Cretaceous of Patagonia).

Pedopenna daohugouensis (long-feathered eumaniraptoran theropod from the Middle to Late Jurassic of Nei Mongol, China, apparently near the dinosaur-bird transition).

Shixinggia oblita (oviraptorid from the Upper Cretaceous [Maastrichtian] Pingling Formation, Nanxiong Basin, Guangdong, China).

Stormbergia dangershocki (comparatively large fabrosaurid from the Lower Jurassic [Hettangian–Sinemurian] Upper Elliot Formation of Cape Province, South Africa.

Tanycolagreus topwilsoni (genus formerly a *nomen nudum* [see *S4*], a maniraptoran theropod similar to *Coelophysis*, from the Upper Jurassic Morrison Formation at Bone Cabin Quarry West, Wyoming).

Tyrannotitan chubutensis (basal carcharodontosaurid theropod from the Middle Cretaceous [Aptian] Cerro Barcino Formation of Chubut Province, Patagonia, Argentina).

Unayasaurus tolentinoi (Brazilian prosauropod).

Xingiangovenator parvus (maniraptoran theropod from the Early to Middle Cretaceous [?Valanginian–Albian] Lianmugin Formation of Xinjiang, China).

IV: Excluded Genera

Previous volumes in this encyclopedia series included lists of genera that were, at one time or more, classified as dinosaurs, but are, at present, generally regarded as belonging to other nondinosaurian groups. The following listing supplements those lists.

Note: Lamanna, Smith, Dodson and Attia (2004) removed from the Dinosauria an unnamed left humerus and associated cranial and dorsal rib fragments (CGM 30975) — originally identified by Awad and Ghobrial (1966) as belonging to a dryosaurid ornithischian — from the Upper Cretaceous (Santonian–Campanian) Quseir Formation, Kharha Oasis, Western Desert of Egypt, reinterpreting it as representing instead a dyrosaurid member of the Crocodyliformes. This reclassification by Lamanna *et al.* effectively removes the only supposed record of post–Cenomanian (Late Cretaceous) Ornithischia from Africa.

PROCOMPSOGNATHUS Fraas 1913
Nondinosaurian ornithodiran.
Comment: Previously assigned to various theropod and also nondinosaurian groups (see *D:TE, S1, S3*); recent restudy of the well-preserved type material by Allen (2004; results published as an abstract for a poster), combining a detailed description with cladistic methology, incomporating cranial and postcranial characters and comparing the material with "a broad range of dinosaurian, ornithodiran, sphenosuchian, basal archosaurian and nonarchosaurian taxa," demonstrating that the type species *Procompsognathus triassicus* represents a nondinosaurian member of Ornithodira.

SHUVOSAURUS Chatterjee 1993
Nondinosaurian.
Comment: Originally described by Chatterjee (1933) as the most primitive known ornithomimid theropod (see *D:TE*), later interpreted by Murry and Long (1997) as a possible rauischuan reptile (see *S1*), subsequently interpreted by Rauhut (1997) as a nontetanuran theropod (see *S3*); considered to be nondinosaurian by Makovicky, Kobayashi and Currie (2004) in their review of Ornithomimosauria.

A List of Abbreviations

The following abbreviations, which are used in this book, refer to museums and other institutions in which fossil specimens are housed:

AENM Amur Natural History Museum, Amur Complex Integrated Research Institute, Far Eastern Branch, Russian Academy of Sciences, Blagoveschensk, Russia

ALMNH Alabama Museum of Natural History, Tuscaloosa, Alabama, United States

AMNH American Museum of Natural History, New York, New York, United States

ANSP The Academy of Natural Sciences of Philadelphia, Philadelphia, Pennsylvania, United States

ASDM Arizona Sonora Desert Museum, Tucson, Arizona, United States

BHI Black Hills Institute of Geological Research, Rapid City, South Dakota, United States

BMNH The Natural History Museum, London (formerly British Museum [Natural History]), London, England

BMRP Burpee Museum of Natural History, Rockford, Illinois, United States

BP Bernard Price Institute for Palaeontological Research, University of Witwatersand, Johannesburg, South Africa

BPM Beipiao Paleontological Museum, Beipiao City, Liaoning Province, China

BPV Beijing Natural History Museum, Beijing, China

BSP [also BSPM] Bayerische Staatssammiung für Paläontologie und Historische Geologie, Munich, Germany

BYU [also BYUVP] Brigham Young University Vertebrate Paleontology, Provo, Utah, United States

CAGS China Academy of Geological Sciences, Beijing, China

CAMSM Sedgwick Museum, Cambridge University, Cambridge, England

CCG Chengdu College of Geology, Chengdu, Sichuan, China

CCM Carter County Museum, Ekalaka, Montana, United States

CD *Desirée Collection* of Rainer Alexander von Blittersdorff, Rio de Janeiro, Brazil

CEUM College of Eastern Utah Prehistoric Museum (also known as Prehistoric Museum), Price, Utah, United States

CGM Egyptian Geological Museum, Cairo, Egypt

CM Carnegie Museum of Natural History, Pittsburgh, Pennsylvania, United States

CMN Canadian Museum of Nature (formerly National Museum of Canada

CMNH Cleveland Museum of Natural History, Cleveland, Ohio, United States

CMV Collection Méchin, Vitrolles, France

CNRST Centre Nationale de la Recherche Scientifique et Technologique, Bamako, Mali

CPS Wyoming-Colorado Paleontological Society

CTES Laboratorio de Paleozoologia, Departamento de Biologia de la Facultad de Ciencias Exactas y Naturales y Agrimensura de la Univeridad Nacional del Nordeste, Corrientes, Argentina

CV Municipal Museum of Chungking, Chunking, China

DGM Divisao de Geologia y Minerologia, Direccion Nacional of Producao Minerologia, Rio de Janeiro, Brazil

DINO Dinosaur National Monument, Utah, United States

DM Dinosaur Museum, Blanding, Utah, United States

DMNH Denver Museum of Nature and Science (formerly Denver Museum of Natural History), Denver, Colorado, United States

DMR Department of Mineral Resources, Palaeontological Collection, Bangkok, Thailand

D2K Discovery 2000, Birmingham, Alabama, United States

FC-DPV Fossil Vertebrate Collection, Departamento de Paleontologia, INGEPA, Facultad de Ciencias, Montevideo, Uruguay

FFCL Faculdade de Filosofia, Ciencias e Letras de Sao do Rio Preto, Brazil

FGGUB Facultatea de Geologie si Geofizies, Universitatea din Bucuresti, Romania

FHSM Sternberg Museum of Natural History, Fort Hays University, Hays, Kansas, United States

FMNH The Field Museum (formerly Field Museum of Natural History; Chicago Natural History Museum), Chicago, Illinois, United States

FPMN Fukui Prefectural Dinosaur Museum, Vertebrates, Fukui Prefecture, Japan

FSL Collections de la Faculté des Sciences de Lyon, Lyon, France

FWMSH Fort Worth Museum of Science and History, Fort Worth, Texas, United States

GIN Mongolian Geological Institute (formerly Geological Institute Section of Palaeontology and Stratigraphy), Ulan-Bataar, Mongolian People's Republic

GM Geological Museum of China, Beijing, China

GMNH-PV Gunma Museum of Natural History, Paleo-Vertebrate Collection, Tomioka, Gunma, Japan

GMV National Geological Museum of China, Beijing, China

GPIT Geological Museum, Universität Tübingen, Tübingen, Germany

GSC Geological Survey of Canada (see also CMN)

GSI Geological Survey of India, Kolkata (Calcutta), India

HASMG Hastings Museum and Art Gallery, Hastings, East Sussex, England

HBV Hebei College, Chinese Academy of Geological Sciences, Beijing, China

HMN Museum für Naturkunde der Humboldt-Universität zu Berlin, Berlin, Germany

IANIGLA-PV Laboratory of Paleovertebrates, Paleontology Unit, Instituto Argentino de Nivologia, Glaciologia y Ciencias Ambientales, Argentina

ICM Indianapolis Children's Museum, Indianapolis, Indiana, United States

IGO Museo Mario Sánchez Roid, Instituto de Geología y Paleontología, Havana, Cuba

IMCF Iwaki Museum of Coal and Fossil, Fukushima, Japan

IGM [also GI] Mongolian Museum of Natural History (formerly Geological Institute Section of Palaeontology and Stratigraphy), The Academy of Sciences of the Mongolian People's Republic Geological Institute, Ulan Bataar

IMM Inner Mongolia Museum, Hohhot, Inner Mongolia, China

IPFUB Institut für Geologische Wissenschaften, Fachrichtung Paläontologie, Freie Universität Berlin, Berlin, Germany

IRSN [also IRSNB] Institut Royal des Sciences Naturelle de Belgique, Brussels, Belgium

ISI Indian Statistical Institute, Kolkata, India

IVP [also IVPP] Institute of Vertebrate Paleontology and Paleoanthropology, Academia Sinica, Beijing, China

JZMP Jinzhou Paleontological Museum, Liaoning Province, China

KUVP Kansas University, Vertebrate Paleontology, Lawrence, Kansas, United States

LH Las Hoyas collection, Universidad de Paleontología, Universidad Autónoma de Madrid, Spain

LHV Department of Land and Resources of Liaoning Province, China

LINH Long Island Natural History Museum, Levittown, New York, United States

LPM Liaoning Paleontological Museum, Beipiao, Liaoning Province, China

MACN Museo Argentino de Ciencias Naturales, Buenos Aires, Argentina

MAFI Magyar Állami Földtani Intézet, Budapest, Hungary

MB Museum für Naturkunde, Berlin, Germany

MCDRD Muzeul Civilzatiel Dacice si Romane Deva, Deva, Romania

MCF Museo Municipal Carmen Funes, Paleontología de Vertebrados, Plaza Huincul, Argentina

MCN Museo de Ciências Naturais da Fundacão Zoobotânica do Rio Grande do Sul, Brazil

MCNA Museo de Ciencias Naturalles de Alva, Vitoria, Spain

MCSNB Museo Civico di Scienze Naturali, Bergamo, Italy

MCZ Museum of Comparative Zoology, Harvard University, Cambridge Massachusetts, United States

MDE Musée des Dinosaures, Espéraza, France

MFSN Museo Friulano di Storia Naturale, Udine, Italy

MGCT Museo de Geociencias de Tacuarembo, Tacuarembo, Uruguay

MGUH Geological Museum, Copenhagen, Denmark

MHIN Museo de Historia Natural, Universidad Nacional de San Luis, San Luis, Argentina

MHN-AIX [also MHNA] Musée d'Historie Naturelle d'Aix-en-Provence, Aix-en-Provence, France

MHNM Musée d'Histoire Naturelle, Marseilles, France

MIGM Museu Geológico do Instituto Geológico e Mineiro, Portugal

MIWG Museum of Isle of Wight Geology, Sandown, Isle of Wight, England

MLP Museo de La Plata, La Plata, Argentina

MMAB Museo Municipal "Alejandro Berro," Mercedes, Uruguay

MN Museu Nacional, Universidade Federal do Rio de Janeiro, Brazil

MND Museum Natura Docet, Denekamp, The Netherlands

MNHN Museum National d'Histoire Naturelle, Paris, France

MNN Musée National d'Histoire Naturelle, Luxembourg

MOR Museum of the

	Rockies, Bozeman, Montana, United States	
MPCA	Museo de Ciencias Naturales, Universidad Nacional del Comahue, Buenos Aires, Neuquén, Argentina	
MPEF	Museo Argentino Paleontológico Egidio Feruglio, Trelew, Argentina	
MPLM	Musée Longchamp of Marsaille, Bouches-du-Rhône, France	
MPM	Museo Padre Molina, Rio Gallegos, Santa Cruz, Argentina	
MRS	Laboratory of Rincón de los Sauces Museum, Neuquén Province, Patagonia, Argentina	
MSNM	Museo di Storia Naturale di Milano, Milan, Italy	
MTCO	Muzeul Tarii Crisurilor, Oradea, Romania	
MU	University of Missouri, Columbia, Missouri, United States	
MUCPv [also MUC]	Museo de Ciencias Naturales, Universidad Nacional del Comahue, Buenos Aires, Argentina	
NAMAL	North American Museum of Ancient Life, Thanksgiving Point, Lehi, Utah, United States	
NGMC	National Geological Museum of China, Xisi, Beijing, China	
NHMM	Natuurhistorisch Museum Maastricht, The Netherlands	
NJSM	New Jersey State Museum, Trenton, New Jersey, United States	
NMC	National Museums of Canada (see also CMN)	
NMMNH	New Mexico Museum of Natural History and Science, Albuquerque, New Mexico, United States	
NSM	National Science Museum, Tokyo, Japan	
OCP	Office Chérifien des Phosphates, Service Géologique, Khourbga, Morocco	

OGP	Oertijdmuseum de Groene Poort, Boxtel, The Netherlands	
OMNH [also SMOMNH]	Sam Noble Oklahoma Museum of Natural History, University of Oklahoma, Norman, Oklahoma, United States	
OUM [also OUMNH]	Oxford University Museum of Natural History, Oxford, England	
PEFO	Petrified Forest Natural Park, Arizona, United States	
PIN	Paleontological Institute Nauk, Academy of Sciences, Moscow, Russia	
PIUW	Paläontologisches Institut, Universität Wien, Vienna, Austria see TMP	
PMA	see TMP	
PMAA	Palaeontological Collections, Provincial Museum of Alberta, Canada	
PO	Collection of Zoological Institute, Russian Academy of Sciences, Moscow, Russia	
PULR	Paleontología, Universidad de La Rioja, Argentina	
PVL	Paleontología de Vertebrados, Instituto Lillo, Tucamán, Argentina	
Pv-MOZ	Museum "Professor Dr. Juan Olsacher," Zapala, Neuquén Province, Argentina	
PVSJ	Museo do Ciencia Naturales, Universidad Nacional de San Juan, San Juan, Argentina	
PW	Paleontological collection, Department of Mineral Resources, Bangkok, Thailand	
ROM	Royal Ontario Museum, Toronto, Canada	
RTMP	see TMP	
SAM	South African Museum, Cape Town, South Africa	
SGM	Ministère de l'Energie et des Mines, Rabat, Morocco	
SMC	The Sedgwick Museum, University of Cambridge, England	
SMF	Forschunginstitut und	

	Natur-Museum Senckenberg, Frankfurt-am-Main, Germany	
SMNH	Saskatchewan Museum of Natural History, Regina, Saskatchewan, Canada	
SMNK	Staatliches Museum für Naturkunde Karlsruhe, Karlsruhe, Germany	
SMNS	Staatliches Museum für Naturkunde, Stuttgart, Germany	
SNOMNH	see OMNH	
SUNY	Stony Brook University, Stony Brook, New York, United States	
SUP	Shenandoah University, Winchester, Virginia, United States	
TATE [also TM]	Tate Geological Museum, Casper Community College, Casper, Wyoming, United States	
TCM [also TCMI]	Children's Museum of Indianapolis, Indianapolis, Indiana, United States	
TF	Thai Department of Mineral Resources, Sahat Sakhan, Thailand	
TM	Tate Museum, Casper, Wyoming, United States	
TMM	Texas Memorial Museum, The University of Texas, Austin, Texas, United States	
TMP	Royal Tyrrell Museum of Palaeontology, Drumheller, Alberta, Canada	
TTU	Museum of Texas Tech University, paleontology collection, Lubbock, Texas, United States	
UA	Université d'Antananarivo, Antananrivo, Madagascar	
UALVP	University of Alberta, Laboratory of Vertebrate Paleontology, Edmonton, Canada	
UAMNH	Alabama Museum of Natural History, Tuscaloosa, Alabama, United States	
UBB	Facultatea de Biologie si Geologie, Universitatea din Babes-Bolyai, Cluj, Romania	

A List of Abbreviations

UCMP University of California Museum of Paleontology, Berkeley, California, United States

UCPC University of Chicago Paleontological Collection, Chicago, Illinois, United States

UEN Institut für Paläontologie der Universität Erlangen-Nürnberg, Erlangen, Bayern, Germany

UFRJ-DG Universidade Federal do Rio de Janeiro, Department de Geologia, Brazil

UHR Hokkaido University Museum, Hokkaido University, Sapporo, Japan

UMMP University of Michigan Museum of Paleontology, Ann Arbor, Michigan, United States

UMNH Utah Museum of Natural History, University of Utah, Salt Lake City, Utah, United States

UM2 Université des Sciences et Techniques du Languedoc, Montpellier, France

UMR Museum National d'Histoire Naturelle, Department Histoire de la Terre, Paris, France

UMZC University Museum of Zoology, Cambridge University, Cambridge, England

UNPSJB-PV Universidad Nacional de la Patagonia "San Juan Bosco," Paleovertebrados, Comodoro Rivadavia, Argentina

USNM National Museum of Natural History (formerly United States National Museum), Smithsonian Institution, Washington, D.C., United States

UT Universität Tübingen, Germany

UUVP University of Utah, Vertebrate Paleontology Collection, Salt Lake City, Utah, United States

VGI Volga Humanitarian Institute, Volzhsk, Volgograd Region, Russia

VRD Sierra College, Rocklin, California, United States

WDC-RTA Wyoming Dinosaur Center, Thermopolis, Wyoming, United States

WL Wann Langston, Jr., Texas Memorial Museum, Austin, Texas, United States

ZDM [also ZG] Zigong Dinosaur Museum, Zigong, China

ZIN Zoological Institute, Russian Academy of Sciences, Saint Petersburg, Russia

ZISP-PO Paleornithological Collection, Zoological Institute of the Russian Academy of Sciences, St. Petersburg, Russia

ZNM Natural History Museum of Zhejiang (also Zhejiang Natural Museum), Zhejiang, China

ZPAL Instytut Paleobiologii (also known as Institute of Paleobiology), Polish Academy of Sciences, Warsaw, Poland

Appendix One: Pterosaurs

During most of the Mesozoic Era, the skies were the domain of a group of flying archosaurs called pterosaurs (name meaning "wing or flight lizards"). Not dinosaurs (although related to dinosaurs and being contemporaneous with them, and sometimes erroneously referred to in the popular press as "flying" or "winged dinosaurs"), the Pterosauria comprise a unique and amazing group of winged reptiles that thrived from the Late (Norian) and possibly Middle Triassic through the Late Cretaceous (Maastrichtian) periods.

Pterosaurian remains have been known (although not at first recognized for what they truly represented) since 1764, when historian and naturalist Cosimo Alessandro Collini first examined a fossil in the collection of Karl Theodori, the Elector Palatine, housed in the latter's castle in Mannheim. The fossil had been recovered from the limestone quarries in Eichstätt, Bavaria. In 1809, the Parisian anatomist George Cuvier — having recognized the fossil as belonging to an ancient winged reptile — gave it the name *Pterodactyle* (now *Pterodactylus*).

Pterosaurs appeared in many diverse forms and ranged in size from genera such as the small *Eudimorphodon* to the gigantic *Quetzalcoatlus* (wingspan of at least 36 feet). To date, pterosaurian fossil remains have been found on all continents with the exception of Antarctica.

Following the phylogeny proposed by Paul C. Sereno

Life restoration by Todd Marshall of an as yet unnamed Late Jurassic pterosaur from Niger. Known from a specimen including a partial wing and naillike teeth. The flying reptile will presumably be named and described by Paul C. Sereno.

(1991*b*), the Pterosauria belong to the much larger archosaurian clade Ornithodira, which also includes Dinosauromorpha, the latter group including "lagosuchids," Dinosauria, and Aves (see "Appendix One"), the latter two taxa possibly sharing a sister-group relationship (this relationship not accepted by all pterosaur specialist, *e.g.*, S. Christopher Bennett). According to Sereno's scheme, possibly ancestral to the Pterosauria is a small (approximately 23 centimeters, or about nine inches) reptile named *Sclermochlus taylori*, known from the Upper Triassic Elgin sandstone of Lossiemouth, Scotland (for a dramatically different and controversial view, see the article by Peters 2004, published in the magazine *Prehistoric Times*).

Members of the Pterosauria are distinguished by a suite of diagnostic characters. In general, all pterosaurs have relatively large skulls, usually large eye sockets, rostrally set nasal openings, relatively large brain cavities, strongly developed cervical vertebrae, hollow long bones, relatively small trunks, disproportionately large pectoral girdles and forelimbs, and small, weakly developed hind legs.

The most striking feature of the pterosaur skeleton is the construction of the wings. Unlike the conditions in birds and bats, the first three digits of the pterosaur manus are developed normally, the fifth digit having regressed and being completely missing. The fourth finger, however, has been extended — via each phalanx increasing in length, with each element in very tight atriculation — to an extreme degree. A membrane stretched, reinforced by strong fibers (called "actinofibrils") between this finger and the body and upper part of the hind leg, thereby constituting the wing.

In the past pterosaurs were believed to have been gliders or soarers (*e.g.*, Hankin and Watson 1914; Kripp 1943) rather than fliers that propelled themselves through the air by movement of their wings, the animals seemingly not possessing the musculature required for active flight. However, considering the large areas on the scapulocoracoid and humerus for the origin and attachment the required muscles, pterosaurs are now believed to have been capable of flight powered by flapping wings (*e.g.*, see Lawson 1975*b*; Bennett 2003*c*; Frey, Buchy and Martill 2003). Also, the bodies of some, if not all, pterosaurs seem to have been covered by a coat of short hairs, seeming evidence of insulation. The facts that the pterosaur skeleton is designed for the active flapping of wings, the body was insulated, that some bones are pneumatic (*e.g.*, see Seeley 1870*b*; Bonde and Christainsen 2003*b*) — a feature also found in birds and some dinosaurs — and that most specimens have been found with nothing in the stomach area (suggesting high food requirements) constitute additional evidence that these animals were endothermic.

Pterosauria is generally considered to be the sister taxon of Dinosauromorpha (the clade including all dinosaurs and birds, as well as various other related archosaurian taxa, *e.g.*, Lagosuchidae), both of these clades belonging to the more encompassing group Ornithodira. Over the past two centuries, various phylogenies have been proposed to explain pterosaurian relationships. Traditionally, the Pterosauria was thought to comprise two major groups — the more primitive grade "Rhamphorhynchoidea," made up of small, crestless, long-tailed forms (see below), and, descending from that group, the clade Pterodactyloidea, comprising small to giant, crestless to crested, short-tailed forms. In view of more modern cladistic approaches to classification, however, that rather simplified division of the group is no longer regarded as correct.

The most recent and thorough cladistic analyses have been those published back to back in 2003 by pterosaur specialists Alexander W. A. Kellner and David M. Unwin, respectively. As these phylogenies differ in certain substantial ways, both are herein presented.

Kellner's study (see paper for cladogram), based on 39 terminal taxa and 74 characters, suggested the following: Anurognathidae as the most primitive pterosaurian taxon, followed by *Sordes* plus all remaining pterosaurs; *Dendrorhynchoides* an anurognathid closely related to *Batrachognathus*; *Preondactylus* a more derived form than *Sordes*, casting doubt upon its previous assessment as the most primitive known pterosaur; "Rhamphorhynchoidea" being polyphyletic (as had been suggested by other workers, *e.g.*, Carpenter, Unwin, Cloward, Miles and Miles 2003), with Rhamphorhynchidae more closely related to Pterodactyloidea than to more basal pterosaurs; Pterodactyloidea showing a basal dichotomy — Archaeopterodactyloidea plus Dsungaripteroidea; Archaeopterodactyloidea formed by *Pterodactylus* plus *Germanodactylus* and a clade comprising Gallodactylidae plus Ctenochasmatidae; Nyctosauridae occupying the basal position within Dsungaripteroidea, followed by Pteranodontoidea and Tapejaroidea; Pteranodontoidea with *Pteranodon* at the base, succeeded stepwise by *Istiodactylus*, *Ornithocheirus*, and Anhangueridae; Tapejaroidea comprising Dsungaripteridae at the base, succeeded by Tapejaridae and Azhdarchidae. Kellner's phylogeny includes a number of unnamed taxa at various nodes, and also introduced the new clades Asiaticognathidae and Novialoidea (see Kellner's paper for further information).

The present document follows the more conservative phylogeny proposed by Unwin, based on 20 terminal taxa and 60 characters (see paper for further details and discussion). Unwin's study, which introduced a number of new and converted clades (see below), breaks down in simplified form as shown on the following page.

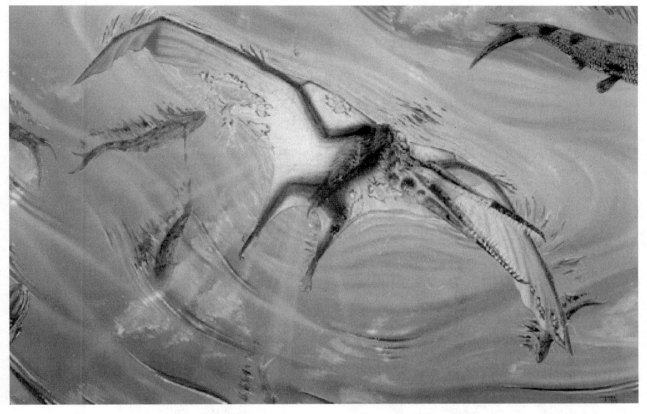

Dead *Pterodactylus antiquus* individual afloat in waters of Late Jurassic Germany, as restored by artist Todd Marshall.

PTEROSAURIA
    MACRONYCHOPTERA
        DIMORPHODONTIDAE
        CAELIDRACONES
           ANUROGNATHIDAE
          LONCHOGNATHA
             CAMPYLOGNATHOIDIDAE
            BREVIQUARTOSSA
               RHAMPHORHYNCHIDAE
                  RHAMPHORHYNCHINAE
               SCAPHOGNATHINAE
           PTERODACTYLOIDEA
             ORNITHOCHEIROIDEA
               EUORNITHOCHEIRA
                  ORNITHOCHEIRIDAE
                  PTERANODONTIA
                     PTERANODONTIDAE
                  NYCTOSAURIDAE
             LOPHOCRATIA
               CTENOCHASMATOIDEA
                 EUCTENOCHASMATIA
                  PTERODACTYLIDAE
                  LONCHODECTIDAE
                  CTENOCHASMATIDAE
                     CTENOCHASMATINAE
                     GNATHOSAURINAE

GNATHOSAURINAE (cont.)
DSUNGARIPTEROIDEA
DSUNGARIPTERIDAE
AZHDARCHOIDEA
TAPEJARIDAE
NEOAZHDARCHIA
AZHDARCHIA

Peters (2000) offered the following node-based definition of the Pterosauria: *Preondactylus buffarinii*, *Quetzalcoatlus northropi*, their most common ancestor, and all its descendants.

Unwin defined and diagnosed (synapomorphies based largely on earlier studies) the above clades within Pterosauria as follows:

Macronychoptera: *Dimorphodon macronyx*, *Quetzalcoatlus northropi*, their most recent common ancestor, and all its descendants. Dentary forming more than 75 percent of length of mandible (see Unwin 1995); coracoid at least 66 percent of scapular length; wing phalanges relatively robust compared to pedal phalanges; forelimb length more than 2.5 times hindlimb length (Unwin 1995; Unwin *et al.*); humerus longer than femur (Unwin 1995).

Caelidracones: *Anurognathus ammoni*, *Quetzalcoatlus northropi*, their most recent common ancestor and all its descendants. Quadrate inclined anteriorly; ulna longer than tibia; fibula less than 80 percent of tibial length.

Lonchognatha: *Eudimorphodon ranzii*, *Rhamphorhynchus muensteri*, their most recent common ancestor and all its descendants. Rostrum low, with straight or concave dorsal outline (Unwin 1995); caudal process of maxillae interfingers between frontals (Unwin 1995); external narial opening low, elongate; nasal process of maxilla inclined backwards; broad maxilla-nasal contact; orbit larger than antorbital fenestra (Unwin 1995).

Breviquartossa: *Rhamphorhynchus muensteri*, *Quetzalcoatlus northropi*, their most recent common ancestor and all its descendants. Ventral margin of skull downwardly curved (Unwin 1995); loss of coronoic eminence on caudal end of mandible; development of bony mandibular symphysis (Unwin 1995); mandibular symphysis forming more than 30 percent of mandibular length (Unwin 1995); loss of heterodonty in mandibular teeth (1995); metacarpals I, II, and III of equivalent length; short metatarsal IV; short metatarsal IV (Unwin 1995; Unwin *et al.*).

Rhamphorhynchidae: *Sordes pilosus*, *Rhamphorhynchus muensteri*, their most recent common ancestor, and all its descendants. Fewer than 11 pairs of teeth in rostrum; deltopectoral crest tongue-shaped, with necked base.

Pterodactyloidea: *Pteranodon longiceps*, *Quetzalcoatlus northropi*, their most recent common ancestor, and all its descendants. Narial and antorbital fenestrae confluent (Unwin 1995); basipterygoids united, forming median bar of bone (Unwin 1995); reduction of cervical ribs (Howse 1986; Bennett 1994; Unwin 1995); caudal vertebral series shorter than dorsal series (Unwin 1995; Unwin *et al.*); pteroid long, slender (Unwin 1995; Unwin *et al.*); wing metacarpal (IV) at least 80 percent length of humerus (Unwin *et al.*); pedal digit V having single phalanx or absence of phalanx (Bennett 1994; Unwin 1995; Unwin *et al.*)

Ornithocheiroidea: *Istiodactylus latidens*, *Pteranodon longiceps*, their most recent common ancestor, and all its descendants. Notarium developed (Bennett 1989, 1994; Unwin and Lü 1997); coracoid longer than scapula (Bennett 1994; Unwin 1995; Unwin and Lü); humerus with warped deltopectoral crest (Padian 1984*a*; Bennett 1989, 1994; Unwin 1995; Unwin and Lü); pneumatopore piercing anconal surface of proximal portion of humerus (Bennett 1989, 1994; Unwin 1995; Unwin and Lü); distal end of humerus with triangular outline; ornithocheiroid carpus (Unwin 1995; Unwin and Lü); proximal ends of metacarpals I–III reduced (Bennett 1989; 1994); femur having stout neck, steeply directed caput (Unwin 1995; Unwin and Lü 1997).

Euornithocheira: *Criorhynchus mesembrinus*, *Pteranodon longiceps*, their most recent common ancestor, and all its descendants. Nasoantorbital fenestra having concave caudal margin (Unwin 1995; Unwin and Lü 1997); infilled basal region of orbit (Unwin 1995; Unwin and Lü 1997); coracoid facets on sternum lateral to each other (Bennett 1994).

Pteranodontia: *Nyctosaurus gracilis*, *Pteranodon longiceps*, their most recent common ancestor, and all its descendants. Frontal crest tall, narrow (Bennett 1994); edentulous (Bennett 1994; Unwin 1995; Unwin and Lü 1997); mandibular rami elevated well above level of lower jaw symphysis; pneumatic opening in palmar surface of proximal portion of humerus; hyperelongation of wing-metacarpal (Bennett 1994; Unwin and Lü 1997).

Lophocratia: *Pterodaustro guinazui*, *Quetzalcoatlus northropi*, their most recent common ancestor, and all its descendants. Humerus having elongate, rectangular delopectoral crest; extensive sagittal cranial crest (Unwin and Lü 1997).

Ctenochasmatoidea: *Cycnorhamphus suevicus*, *Pterodaustro guinazui* their most recent common ancestor, and all its descendants. Quadrate oriented in subhorizontal position (Unwin 1995; Unwin and Lü 1997; Kellner cited in Chiappe, Kellner, Rivarola, Davila and Fox 2000); squamosal level with or below base of lacrimal process of jugal (Unwin 1995; Unwin and Lü 1997; Chiappe *et al.*); occipital facing ventrally (Unwin 1995; Unwin and Lü 1997).

Skeleton (cast) of the Late Cretaceous pterosaur *Pteranodon longipes* on display with Triebold Paleontology's "Savage Ancient World: The Last American Dinosaurs" traveling exhibit.

Euctenochasmatia: *Pterodactylus kochi*, *Pterodaustro guinazul*, their most recent common ancestor, and all its descendants. Neural arch of midseries cervical vertebrae depressed, neural spine low (Howse 1986; Bennett 1989, 1994; Unwin 1995; Unwin and Lü 1997); elongate midseries cervicals (Howse 1986; Bennett 1989, 1994; Unwin 1995; Unwin and Lü 1997).

Dsungaripteroidea: *Germanodactylus cristatus*, *G. rhamphastinus*, *Dsungaripterus weii*, and all of its descendants (Maisch, Matzke and Sun 2004, *sensu* Unwin and Lü 1997; Unwin 2003). Tips of jaws edentulous (except for *G. rhamphastinus*); maxillary teeth almost as broad as tall; largest teeth towards end of tooth row; distal ends of paroccipital process strongly expanded, forming distinct bulge in lateral profile of occiput (Unwin and Lü 1997); also, at least slight ringlike bony wall surrounding alveoli (convergent in Lonchodectidae); at least low sagittal crest (convergent with Ctenochasmatoidea); limb bones thick walled; femur strongly bowed; wing-phalanx I having strongly bowed cranially (Maisch, *et al.*).

Azhdarchoidea: *Tapejara wellnhoferi*, *Quetzalcoatlus northropi*, their most recent common ancestor, and all its descendants. Orbit well below level of dorsal margin of nasoantorbital fenestra (Kellner 1995*b*; Unwin 1995; Kellner and Langston 1995; Unwin and Lü 1997).

Neoazhdarchia (clade originally proposed by Unwin and Lü 1997): *Tupuxuara longicristatus*, *Quetzalcoatlus northropi*, their most recent common ancestor, and all its descendants. Notarium present (Buffetaut 1999; Unwin, personal observation); loss of contact between metacarpals I–III and distal syncarpal.

Recently collected pterosaur material including exceptionally well-preserved soft parts, described by Frey, Tischlinger, Buchy and Martill (2003), have cast new light upon the life appearances of these animals, with implications concerning locomotion. These remarkable specimens — recovered from the Solnhofen Lithographic Limestone in southern Germany, the Karatau Formation in Kazakhstan, and the Santana Formation and Crato Formation in northeastern Brazil — have revealed a number of previously unknown details including the following: Bristles covered the dermis of the pterosaur body, neck bristles having only been found in Solnhofen pterodactyloid specimens (*e.g.*, Frey and Martill 1998). The new *Pterodactylus* (see entry) specimen reveals this genus (and likely other kinds of pterosaurs) possessed a keratinous beak, and also a soft-tissue crest (similar in structure to the wing membrane described by Martill and Unwin 1989), the latter possibly having served as a rudder during flight. The internal anatomy of the brachiopatagium, found in the Solnhofen *Rhamphorhynchus* and a Santana specimen, include blood vessels suggestive of a thermoregulatory function. Webbing on the feet of the new *Pterodactylus*, co-inciding with fossil footprint evidence from France (see Mazin, Hanzpergue, LaFaurie and Vignaud 1995), may also have had aerodynamic functions.

Following is a list of named pterosaurian genera with selected basic pertinent information, including collection numbers for holotypes. For more complete details and additional illustrations, consult the papers cited; also see the semipopular book *The Illustrated Encyclopedia of Pterosaurs*, by Peter Wellnhofer, published in 1991), and the volumes of technical papers, *Handbuch der Paläoherpetologie (Encyclopedia of Paleoherpetology*, written and edited by Wellnhofer (1978; note that much of the information contained in this latter publication is now dated, *e.g.*, the very long diagnosis of *Dimorphodon*, but has not yet been emended), and the more recent *Evolution and Palaeobiology of Pterosaurs*, edited by Éric Buffetaut and J.-M. Mazin (2003).

Pterosaurian Genera

AMBLYDECTES   Hooley 1914—(See *Coloborhynchus*.)
Name derivation: Greek *amblys* = "blunt" + Greek *dektes* = "biter."
Type species: *A. eurygnathus* (Seeley 1869).

ANGUSTINARIPTERUS   He, Yan and Su 1983
Rhamphorhynchinae.
Name derivation: Latin *angustus* = "narrow" + Latin *nares* = "nostrils" + Greek *pteron* = "wing."
Type species: *A. longicephalus* He, Yan and Su 1983.
Occurrence: Dashanpu Quarry, Lower Shaximiao Formation, near Zigong, Sichuan Province, China.
Age: Middle Jurassic.
Holotype: SMNS 56342, almost complete articulated skeleton with skull.

"Narrow-nostriled," teeth large, interlocking (similar to those of *Dorygnathus*).

ANHANGUERA   Campos and Kellner 1985
Ornithocheiridae.
Name derivation: Tupi *anhanga* = "what was, old" + Tupi *nera* = "devil" [name of Tupi Indian malignant spirit].
Type species: *A. blittersdorffi* Campos and Kellner 1985.
Other species: *A. santanae* (Wellnhofer 1985).
Occurrence: Romualdo Member, Santana Formation, Barra do Jardim, Chapada do Araripe (Araripe Plateau), Province of Ceara, northeastern Brazil.
Age: Middle to Early Cretaceous (Aptian–Albian).
Holotype: Private *Collection Desirée*, complete skull missing mandible.

Diagnosis of genus (as for type species): Large sagittal crest on rostral part of skull, located on premaxillae, extending almost at beginning of external naris; small parietal sagittal crest on caudal part of skull; dentition from caudal part of skull on to middle region of naris preorbital opening, corresponding to beginning of internal naris; enlargement of caudal part of skull, where are found premaxillary teeth (largest in dentition) (Campos and Kellner 1985).

Diagnosis of *A. santanae*: Large; skull small, long, upper edge of jaws curving; jaw end straight in ventral aspect; toothed, teeth probably more curved towards rostral end of jaws; nasal process jutting down into nasoparietal opening; pterygoid with basipterygoid process of basisphenoid and quadrate joined; only upper end of premaxilla before nasoparietal opening; fossa depression of lower jaw very large and deep, retroarticular process flat downwardly directed; radius more weakly developed than ulna; proximal row of carpus with two carpals, distal row with three carpals, one distal carpal continuing laterally (Wellnhofer 1985).

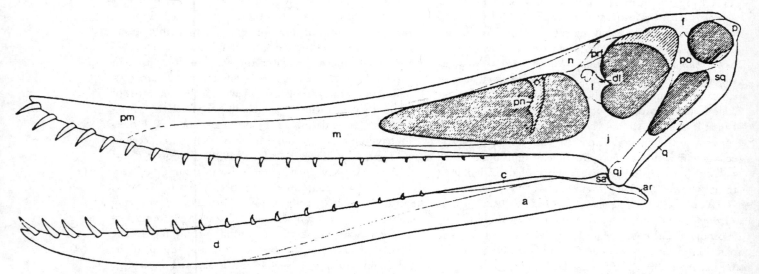

Anhanguera santanae, reconstructed holotype skull (BSP 1982 90) of *Araripesaurus santanae*, in left lateral view. (After Wellnhofer 1985).

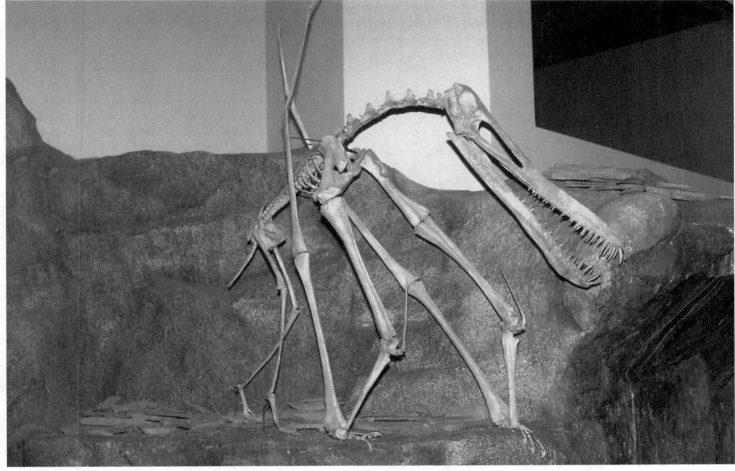

Mounted skeletal cast of *Anhanguera santanae* on display at the North American Museum of Ancient Life.

Life restoration of *Anhanguera santanae* by Berislav Krzic.

Large pterosaur with a slender skull having a rounded crest above the snout, skull twice as long as the body, wingspan of 4.15 meters (more than 13 feet).

Note: As pointed out by Wellnhofer (1991*a*), the *A. santanae* type specimen AMNH 22555 "is the most complete pterosaur skeleton of this size range known."

ANUROGNATHUS   Döderlein 1923

Anurognathidae.

Name derivation: Greek *a* = "without" + Greek *oura* = "tail" + Greek *gnathos* = "jaw."

Type species: *A. ammoni* Döderlein 1923.

Occurrence: Solnhofen Lithographic Limestone, Unteres Untertithon, Eichstätt, Bavaria, southern Germany.

Age: Late Jurassic (early Kimmeridgian–Tithonian).

Known material/holotype: BSP 1922.I.42, impression of almost complete skeleton.

Diagnosis of genus (as for type species): Small, naris high, triangular, large preorbital fenestra, quadrate inclined at high angle; three premaxillary, five maxillary, and seven dentary teeth; teeth vertically oriented, sharply pointed, barely curved; maxilla with vertically ascending prolongation, nasal and preorbital fenestrae divided; eight cervical, 12 dorsal, five sacral, and 11 caudal vertebrae; 10 dorsal vertebrae with ribs; caudal vertebrae short, doubled ventrally; wing-arms and hind legs very long; bones long, slender, delicate; pedal phalangeal formula (2, 3, 4, 5, 4) (Wellnhofer 1978).

ARAMBOURGIANA Nessov and Yarkov 1989—(=*Titanopteryx*)
Azhdarchia.
Name derivation: "[C. M.] Arambourg [paleontologist]."
Type species: *A. philadelphiae* (Arambourg 1959).
Occurrence: Senegal, Rosita bei Amman, Jordan.
Age: Late Cretaceous.
Holotype: Cervical vertebra.

Giant-sized, neck very long (cervical vertebra almost .06 meter or about two feet); holotype originally interpreted as a metacarpal.

ARARIPEDACTYLUS Wellnhofer 1997
Pterodactyloidea *incertae sedis*.
Name derivation: "Araripe [Plateau]" + Greek *dactylos* = "finger."
Type species: *A. dehmi* Wellnhofer 1997.
Occurrence: Santana Formation, Araripe Plateau, Providence of Ceará, Brazil.
Age: Early Cretaceous (Aptian).
Holotype: BSP 1975.I.166, phalanx of right flight digit.

Diagnosis of genus (as for type species): Large, wing with elongated first phalanx; shaft rounded triangle in cross section, dorsal side flat; proximal prolongation short; proximal articulation with deep, long pit on distal and ventral sides, terminating in pneumatic foramen; bone walls rather thick; distal articulation stronger at tip of wing membrane; estimated wingspan of 5 meters (approximately 17 feet) (Wellnhofer 1978).

Very large pterosaur.

ARARIPESAURUS Price 1971
?Ornithocheroidea *incertae sedis*.
Name derivation: "Araripe [Plateau]" + Greek *sauros* = "lizard."
Type species: *A. castilhoi* Price 1971.
Occurrence: Santana Formation, Araripe Plateau, Brazil.
Age: Early Cretaceous (Aptian).
Holotype: Lower arm, carpals, metacarpals, upper end of wing.

First pterosaur found on the Araripe Plateau; rather large, with an estimated wing span of about 2.2 meters (7.2 feet), robust squamosal, its descending process the entire caudal edge of skull to quadrate.

ARTHURDACTYLUS Frey and Martill 1994
Ornithocheiroidea.

Name derivation: "Arthur [Conan Doyle, author of novel *The Lost World*] + Greek *dactylos* = "finger."
Type species: *A. conandoylei* Frey and Martill 1994.
Occurrence: Nova Olinda Member, Crato Formation, Chapado do Aripe, northeastern Brazil.
Age: Early Cretaceous (Aptian).
Holotype: SMNK 11332 PAL, crushed, slightly disarticulated skeleton (lacking skull, neck, and sternum).

Diagnosis of genus (as for type species): Large pterosaur, adjacent sacral ribs unfused with each other distally, probably even centra and articulares processes unfused; probably six unfused sacral vertebrae; ischium and pubis unfused caudally, leaving open wide oval recessus puboischiadicus; processus postacetabularis short, pointed; notarium comprising three vertebrae, at least dorsal part of neural spines fused; fourth phalanx of digit IV curved distally (Frey and Martill 1994).

First pterosaur described from the Crato Formation, wings longest of any known pterosaur (wingspan of 4.60 meters).

AUSTRIADACTYLUS Dalla Vecchia, Wild, Hopf and Reitner 2002
Campylognathoidea.
Name derivation: "Austria" + Greek *dactylos* = "finger."
Type species: *A. cristatus* Dalla Vecchia, Wild, Hopf and Reitner 2002.
Occurrence: Abandoned mine near Ankerschlag, Seefelder Schichten, Tyrol, northwestern Austria.
Age: Late Triassic (middle–late Norian).
Holotype: SMNS 56342, almost complete, poorly preserved, articulated skeleton, slab and counterslab.

Diagnosis of genus (as for type species): Sagittal cranial crest extending from tip of snout back to at least middle of orbit, deepest rostral to naris; teeth heterodont; premaxillary teeth tall, slender, conical; one to two very large, finely denticulated, bladelike teeth in middle maxilla opposite ascending process; triangular multicusped teeth having up to 12 denticles along each cutting edge in caudal part of maxilla; mesial mandibular teeth similar to premaxillary teeth, subsequent (about 25) teeth small, leaf-shaped, with four to six cusps on each cutting edge; mesial multicusped teeth taller than long, with small side cusps, distal multicusped teeth longer than tall, cusps larger, tooth size decreasing slightly distally; tail very long without bony sheath formed by enormously elongated pre- and post-zygapophyses and hemal arches of caudal vertebrae in other long-tailed pterosaurs (shared with *Eudimorphodon*) (Dalla Vecchia, Wild, Hopf and Reitner 2002).

Comparatively large for a Triassic pterosaur, wingspan approximately 20 centimeters (more than 7.5 inches), cranial crest from snout to back of head (as in derived pterodactyloids), tail without the stiffening found in the well-known Jurassic flying reptiles.

AZHDARCHO   Nessov 1984

Azhdarchia.

Name derivation: Uzbek *Azhdarkho* = "[name for mythical dragon]."

Type species: *A. lancicollis* Nessov 1984.

Occurrence: Dzharakhuduk, Navoi District, Bakhura Region, Uzbekistan; Laño, Condado de Treviño, Spain, Ebegistan, ?Hungary; Dinosaur Park Formation, Alberta, Canada.

Age: Late Cretaceous (upper Turonian).

Holotype: TsNIGR 1/11915, cranial portion of cervical vertebra.

   Diagnosis of genus (as for type species): [No English translation available.]

   Large pterosaur, neck very long, long cervical vertebrae similar to those of *Quetzalcoatlus*.

BATRACHOGNATHUS   Riabinin 1948

Anurognathidae.

Name derivation: Greek *batrachos* = "frog" + Greek *gnathos* = "jaw."

Type species: *B. volans* Riabinin 1948.

Occurrence: Karatau Mountains, Tien-shan, Kazakhstan.

Age: Late Jurassic.

Holotype: PIN 52-2, incomplete, disarticulated skeleton including fragments of skull and jaw, vertebrae, ribs, fore- and hindlimbs.

   Diagnosis of genus (as for type species): Teeth conical with thin points, curved backwardly; minimum of 11 teeth in upper jaw; skull approximately 48 millimeters long; scapula narrow, caudal end in form of trapezoid; sternum high, narrow, in form of trapezoid, caudal portion rounded with lateral cut; humerus robust, femur weaker (Wellnhofer 1978).

   Skull apparently high and short (about 48 millimeters or 1.9 inches long), 24 peglike teeth in upper jaw, probably insectivorous, possibly similar to *Anurognathus*.

BEIPIAOPTERUS   Lü 2003

Ctenochasmatidae.

Name derivation: "Beipiao [City] + Greek *pteron* = "wing."

Type species: *B. chenianus* Lü 2003.

Occurrence: Yixian Formation, Sihetun, Beipiao City, western Liaoning Province, China.

Age: Early Cretaceous (Hauterivian; see Swisher, Wang, Zhou, Wang, Jin, Zhang, Xu, Zhang and Wang 2001).

Holotype: BPM 0002, partial skeleton with well-preserved soft tissues.

   Diagnosis of genus (as for type species): Three sacral vertebrae; length of wing-metacarpal IV about equal to that of ulna; first wing phalanx highly elongated, reaching 53 percent length of total wing finger; ratio of second wing phalanx to first wing phalanx of digit IV approximately 0.46; ratio of femur to tibia 0.41 (Lü 2003).

Life restoration by Todd Marshall of *Batrachognathus volans* flying above the primitive crocodile *Protosuchus*.

BENNETTAZHIA   Nessov 1991 [*nomen dubium*]

Azhdarchoidea *incertae sedis*.

Name derivation: "[S. Christopher] Bennett."

Type species: *B. oregonensis* (Gilmore 1928) [*nomen dubium*].

Occurrence: Oregon, United States.

Age: Early Cretaceous.

Holotype: USNM 11925, dorsal vertebra.

BOGOLUBOVIA   Nessov and Yarkov 1989 [*nomen dubium*]

Azhdarchoidea.

Name derivation: "[Nikolai Nikolaevich] Bogolubov."

Type species: *B. orientalis* (Bogoloubov 1914) [*nomen dubium*].

Occurrence: Upper Cretaceous of Saratoff, Petrovsk District, Russia.

Age: Late Cretaceous.

Holotype: Fragment of cervical vertebra.

Originally described by Bogolubov (1914) as *Ornithostoma orientalis*; large.

BOREOPTERUS   Lü and Ji 2005
Ornithocheridae.

Name derivation: Greek *bore* = "north" + Greek *pteron* = "wing."

Type species: *B. cuiae* Lü and Ji 2005.

Occurrence: Yixian Formation, Liaoning Province, Yixian County, China.

Age: Early Cretaceous.

Holotype: JZMP-04-07-3, almost complete skeleton with skull.

Diagnosis of genus (as for type species): At least 17 pairs of teeth in upper and lower jaws respectively; first nine pairs of teeth lager than others; third and fourth pairs of teeth largest; ratio of length of mandibular symphysis to lower jaw length about 65 percent; femur and tibia of equal length, humerus slightly shorter than femur (Lü and Ji 2005).

BRACHYTRACHELUS   Giebel 1852 [*nomen oblitum*]—
(See *Scaphognathus*.)

Name derivation: Greek *brachy* = "short" + Greek *trachelos* = "neck."

Type species: *B. crassirostris* (Goldfuss 1831).

BRASILEODACTYLUS   Kellner 1984
Ornithocheiridae.

Name derivation: "Brazil" + Greek *dactylos* = "finger."

Type species: *B. araripensis* Kellner 1984.

Occurrence: Santana Formation (Romualdo Member; Albian), Province of Ceará, Piaui, and Perbambuco, Brazil.

Age: Middle Cretaceous (Albian).

Holotype: MN 4804-V, cranial portion of mandible.

Diagnosis of genus (as for type species): Apomorphies including the following: rostral end of mandible expanded from third aveoli, forming flat surface; medial groove on dorsal part of symphysis, beginning on rostral tip, widening caudally (Kellner and Tomida 2000).

Distinguished by upwardly bent snout.

CACIBUPTERX   Gasparini, Fernández and Fuentes Vidarte 2004
Rhamphorhynchidae.

Name derivation: Taino *Cacibu* ("lord of the sky" of aboriginal Cubans) + Greek *pteron* = "wing."

Type species: *C. caribensis* Gasparini, Fernández and Fuentes Vidarte 2004.

Occurrence: Jagua Formation, Mogote Jágua Vieja, Viñales Valley, Pinar del Rio Province, western Cuba.

Age: Late Jurassic (middle–upper Oxfordian).

Holotype: IGO-V 208, incomplete, three-dimensional, uncrushed skull missing mandibles, distal end of left ulna, fragments of left radius, left first phalanx of wing-finger, phalanx ?4 of wing-finger (forelimb bones found against palate, indicating one individual).

Diagnosis of genus (as for type species): Skull roof (mainly frontals and parietals) broadly expanded; orbit subcircular, ventral half more compressed; ventral margin of orbit level with dental border; section of jugal forming caudo-ventral border of orbit bearing well-developed pocketlike recess; small fenestra in caudal part of pterygoid (Gasparini, Fernández and Fuentes Vidarte 2004).

One of the largest known Jurassic pterosaurs.

Note: Among the few Jurassic pterosaurs well preserved in three dimensions, one of the most complete middle to late Oxfordian pterosaur taxa.

CAMPYLOGNATHOIDES   Strand 1928
Campylognathoididae.

Name derivation: Greek *kampylos* = "curved" + Greek *gnathos* = "jaw."

Type species: *C. zitteli* (Plieninger 1895).

Other species: ?*C. indicus* Jain 1974, *C. liasicus* (Quenstedt 1858).

Occurrence: Lower Toarcian, Holzmaden, Wittberg bei Metzingen, Erzingen bei Balingen, Württemberg, northern Germany; ?Kota Formation, Chanda District, Deccan, India.

Age: Middle Jurassic (lower Toracian).

Holotype: SMNK collection, almost complete skeleton.

Diagnosis of genus: Skull relatively short, high; orbit round, largest cranial opening; naris larger than preorbital fenestra; quadrate positioned relatively high; rostral end of jaws pointed, bearing teeth; tip of lower jaw short, edentulous, slightly bowed rostrally; teeth short, conical, inserted vertically in jaw, backwardly directed, diminishing in size distally; four premaxillary, 10 maxillary, and 12–17 dentary teeth in lower jaw; fourth premaxillary tooth most robust; vomers long, barlike, slender, with divided choana extending throughout; tail relatively long; fused scapulocoracoid; sternal plate broad, rectangular, with short forwardly projecting crest; humerus robust, deltopectoral process broad, angular; wing-finger long in comparison with short forearm; second wing phalanx largest; pelvis with relatively short ilium, ischium and pubis uniform, broad, prepubis fan-shaped; four sacral vertebrae; five short pedal digits, last phalanx short diagonally (Wellnhofer 1978).

Diagnosis of *C. zitelli*: Large species; 17 teeth in lower jaw; wings very large; hind legs relatively longer than in *C. liasicus*; tibia longer than ulna; first wing phalanx more than twice length of ulna (Wellnhofer 1974).

Diagnosis of ?*C. indicus*: ?Four premaxillary teeth;

Flying Reptiles
Birds were not the first vertebrates to take to the air. Before them, winged reptiles, or **pterodactyls**, evolved the ability to fly. Although most were small, agile fliers, some later forms had wingspans of 17 meters, making them the largest airborne creatures ever.

Campylognathoides
Many pterodactyls were highly specialized for catching fish. They skimmed across the water, or dived beneath the surface, spearing fish with their long beaks or fine forward-pointing teeth. Campylognathoides was a small, active flier.

Campylognathoides zitteli

West Germany

Cast of the so-called "Pittsburgh specimen" of *Campylognathoides liasicus*, original specimen now in the collections of the Carnegie Museum of Natural History. The postcranial remains were found in 1897 by paleontologist Bernhard Hauff in Holzmaden, Germany; the skull was discovered by Hauff the following year (see Wellnhofer 1974).

first three maxillary teeth small, equal in size, tips arched distally; fourth maxillary tooth possibly larger; front teeth with fine tips; nasal process of premaxilla not much enlarged (Jain 1974).

Diagnosis of *C. liasicus*: Small species; only 12 teeth in lower jaw, ends shorter than in *C. zitteli*; tibia shorter than ulna; first wing phalanx half length of ulna (Wellnhofer 1978).

First pterosaur found in the Württemberg Lias; head shorter and teeth smaller than in the contemporaneous *Dorygnathus*, eyes large, wingspan of type species approximately one meter (3.3 feet), *C. zitteli* larger (wingspan of about 1.75 meters or 5.7 feet).

Note: Flight arm bones, now comprising the holotype of *C. liasicus*, were originally described by Quenstedt (1858) as *Pterodactylus liasicus*

CEARADACTYLUS   Leonardi and Borgomanero 1985
Gnathosaurinae.

Name derivation: "Ceará [Brazillian province] + Greek *dactylos* = "finger."

Type species: *C. atrox* Leonardi and Borgomanero 1985.

Other species: ?*C. ligabuei* Dalla Vecchia 1993.

Occurrence: [Precise locality unknown], Santana Formation, Araripe Group, Chapada do Araripe, Province of Ceará, northeastern Brazil.

Age: Middle Cretaceous (middle to upper Aptian, possibly younger; see Martill and Wilby 1993).

Holotype: F-PV-93, incomplete skull with mandibles partially enclosed in concretions, lacking tabular region and braincase.

Diagnosis of genus (as for type species): Expanded, spatulate rostral end of mandibular symphysis considerably wider than corresponding expansion of rostrum (see Kellner and Tomida 2000); basal diameter of third rostral tooth more than three times basal diameter of fifth tooth (Unwin 2002).

Diagnosis of ?*C. ligabuei*: Large, estimated maximum wingspan of approximately six meters; rostral part of skull

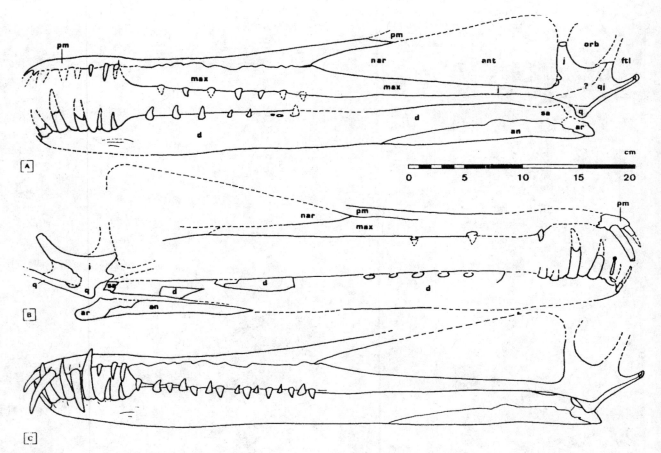

Cearadactylus atrox, F-PV-93, holotype skull in A. left lateral, B. right lateral, and C. reconstruction employing elements preserved from both sides. (After Leonardi and Borgomanero 1985.)

elongate, low, laterally compressed, snout with spatulate tip; lack of well-developed premaxillar sagittal crest; concavity in alveolar margin of rostralmost portion of maxilla; premaxilla bearing four (largest) teeth; 22 teeth between tip of snout and rostral tip of nasoantorbital fenestra; teeth having longitudinal ridges; premaxillae with sharp, gibbous dorsal margin in middle-rostral part of snout; palate with longitudinal ridge, most evident rostrally, in correspondence with maxillar concavity, where palate is inclined in V-shape; rostralmost part of upper margin of nasoantorbital fenestra bordered by maxilla; postorbital process of jugal less steep than in type species and other known pterosaurs; maxillary and lacrimal processes of jugal not forming lower caudal margin of nasoantorbital fenestra (Dalla Vecchia 1993).

Very large pterosaur, with long and slender skull, teeth in rostral part of the mouth large, estimated wingspan about 5.5 meters (18 feet).

CHAOYANGOPTERUS Wang and Zhou 2003
Nyctosauridae.
Name derivation: "Chaoyang [locality]" + Greek *pteron* = "wing."

Type species: *C. zhangi* Wang and Zhou 2003.
Occurrence: Jiufotang Formation, Jehol Group, Gongaggao, Dapingfang, Chaoyang, western Liaoning Province, China.
Age: Early Cretaceous (Aptian).
Holotype: IVPP V13397, incomplete skeleton including rostral part of skull, almost complete lower jaw, most cervical vertebrae, pectoral girdle, forelimb, pelvis, hindlimb.

Diagnosis of genus (as for type species): Medium- to large-sized pterodactyloid; wingspan approximately 1.85 meters; skull long, low, rostrum pointed; edentulous; manual digits I–III robust, wing claws large, curved; wing digit comprising four phalanges, progressively shorter toward distal end; wing metacarpal and first phalanx of wing digit relatively short compared to *Nyctosaurus gracilis*; ratios of tibia to femur and tibia to humerus 1.5 and 2.2, respectively (0.5 and 1.5 in *N. gracilis*); ratio of forelimb (humerus plus ulna plus wing metacarpal) to hindlimb (femur plus tibia plus metacarpal III) 1.1 (1.5 in *N. gracilis*) (Wang and Zhou 2003).

Second edentulous pterosaur from the Jehol Biota, probably piscivorous based on the long, pointed snout.

CIMOLIORNIS   Owen 1846 — (See *Ornithocheirus*).
Name derivation: Greek *kimolios* = "white chalky earth [=Cretaceous]" + Greek *ornis* = "bird."
Type species: *C. diomedius* (Owen 1846).

COLOBORHYNCHUS   Owen 1874 — (=*Amblydectes*, *Tropeognathus*)
Ornithocheiridae.
Name derivation: Greek *kolobos* = "stunted" + Greek *rhynkhos* = "snout."
Type species: *C. clavirostris* Owen 1874.
Other species: *C. capito* (Seeley 1869), *C. crassidens* (Seeley 1869), *C. robustus* (Wellnhofer 1987), *C. spielbergi* Veldmeijer 2003, ?*C. sedgwicki* (Owen 1859), *C. wadleghi* Lee 1994.
Occurrence: Middle Chalk, Kent, Upper Greensand, near Cambridge, England; [unknown type locality] Santana Formation (Romualdo Member; Albian), Chapada do Araripe, Araripe Basin, northeast Brazil; Paw Paw Formation, Texas, United States.
Age: Middle Cretaceous (Albian).
Holotype: BMNH R1822, jaw fragment.

Diagnosis of genus (as for type species): Medial depression on rostral margin of upper jaw; flattened rostral margin of premaxilla triangular; pair of teeth projecting rostrally from blunt rostral margin of upper jaw at significant elevation above palate relative to subsequent teeth; medial crest on upper jaw rising from tip of snout; upper jaw expanded laterally in spoon shape in dorsal aspect from second to fourth pair of alveoli; lower jaw having medial crest rising from rostral end; lower jaw expanded laterally in spoon shape from first to third pair of alveoli; second and third pair of alveoli of upper and lower jaws enlarged to other alveoli (Veldemeijer 2003a).

Life restoration by Todd Marshall of *Coloborhynchus robustus*.

Diagnosis of *C. spielbergi*: Ill-defined, almost absent (lowest, shallowest of all *Coloborhynchus* species) palatial ridge and corresponding mandibular groove; mandibular groove not extending onto spoon-shaped expansion; slight, almost absent, ventrolaterally extending tooth-bearing maxillae; large premaxillary sagittal crest, in ratio length-total skull length, extending dorsally from rostral aspect until rostral border of nasoantorbital fenestra; strongly medial bended rami; sternum having rounded triangular posterior plate, length of latter equal to width (Veldmeijer 2003*a*).

Very large form, head long with rounded crests above snout and under lower jaw, 26 upper and 22 lower teeth, wingspan of about 6.2 meters (20 feet), probably piscivorous.

COMODACTYLUS   Galton 1981
Pterosauria *incertae sedis*.
Name derivation: "Como [Bluff]" + Greek *dactylos* = "finger."
Type species: *C. ostromi* Galton 1981.
Occurrence: Mammal Quarry (Quarry 9), Morrison Formation, Como Bluff, Wyoming, United States.
Age: Late Jurassic (Tithonian).
Holotype: YPM 9150, right metacarpal IV.

Diagnosis of genus (as for type species): Fourth metacarpal large, proximal end transversely expanded, width to height ratio 2.4:1, distal end transversely expanded so that maximum width is greater than craniocaudal width of lateral condyle (Galton 1981).

Among the largest known Jurassic pterosaurs, specimen suggesting a possible wingspan of about 2.5 meters (8.2 feet).

CRETORNIS   Fritsch 1881 [*nomen dubium*] — (See *Ornithocheirus*.)
Name derivation: Greek *krete* = "Cretan, chalk earth [=Cretaceous]" + Greek *ornis* = "bird."
    [No species designated.]

CRIORHYNCHUS   Owen 1874 [*nomen dubium*]
Pterodactyloidea *incertae sedis*.
Name derivation: Greek *krios* = "battering ram" + Greek *rhynkhos* = "snout."
Type species: *C. simus* (Owen 1861) [*nomen dubium*].
Other species: *C. mesembrinus* (Wellnhofer 1987).
Occurrence: Wealden, Hastings Sand, St. Leonard's-on-Sea, Sussex, Cambridge Greensand, Cambridge, Isle of Wight, England; Santana Formation, Araripe Plateau, Brazil.
Age: Early to Late Cretaceous.
Holotype: CAMSM, fragment of premaxilla with tooth and five alveolae.

Diagnosis of genus: Lower jaw having mandibular crest on symphysis; lower jaw not expanded rostrally (Fastnacht 2001).

Diagnosis of *C. mesembrinus*: Symphysis with high, rounded mandibular crest, smaller [than crista premaxillaris; see Veldmeijer 2002] (Wellnhofer 1987).

Type species originally described as a new species of *Pterodactylus*; crested, possibly similar to *Coloborhynchus*; *C. mesembrinus* originally described by Wellnhofer (1987) as a referred species of "*Tropeognathus*."

CTENOCHASMA   Meyer 1852
Ctenochasminae.
Name derivation: Greek *kteis* = "comb" + Greek *chasma* = "opening." Type species: *C. roemeri* Meyer 1852.
Other species: *C. elegans* (Wagner 1861), *C. gracile* Oppel 1862; *C. porocristatum* Buisonje 1981.
Occurrence: Norddeutschland, Solnhofen Lithographic Limestone, Unteres Untertithon, Eichstätt, Solnhofen, Deister, Hanover area (Lower Saxony), Malm, Bavaria, southern Germany; Purbeck, "Calcaires táchetés, France.
Age: Late Jurassic (early Tithonian).
Holotype: Institute of Geology and Paleontology, Technical University of Clausthal collection, rostral part of lower jaw with teeth.

Diagnosis of genus (as for type species): Straining apparatus comprising approximately 200 to 400 long, delicate teeth, placed regularly and closely together along jaws; teeth near alveoli directed laterally, slightly rostrally; distally teeth bending more gradually shorter; distances between successive teeth almost equal near their bases to diameter of teeth; postcranial skeleton identical in general build with *Pterodactylus*, but with relatively longer radius-ulna and wingfinger elements (Buisonje 1981).

Diagnosis of *C. elegans*: Numerous (more than 400 in adult) close-spaced, very long, extremely slender teeth, laterally directed forming basket; more distal teeth reaching level of rostral margin of nasoantorbital fenestra; snout very slender, extremely elongate, nasoantorbital fenestra short; mandibular tooth row ending at level of symphysis; neck moderately long, metacarpal IV short, wing phalanx 1 long, femur short (Jouve 2004).

First pterosaur found having "filter feeding" jaws, long slender jaws having numerous long, tightly packed teeth, jaws bent slightly upwards rostrally, low crest on skull, wingspan approximately 70 centimeters (about 2.3 feet); referred species *C. elegans* (this species originally described by Buisonjé 1981 as *C. porocristata*; referred to *Ctenochasma elegans* by Jouve 2004), with *Gnathosaurus subulatus*, largest pterodactyloids from the Solnhofen Limestone (skull of the former estimated at 24 centimeters, wingspan at about 1.60 meter) (Buisonje 1981).

Note: *Pterodactylus elegans*, described by Wagner (1861*a*), was formally referred by Jouve to *Ctenochasma* as

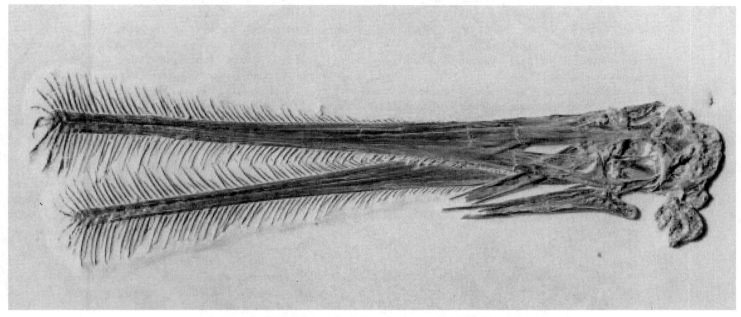

Referred skull (SMNS 81803) of *Ctenochasma gracile* in left lateral view.

the senior synonym of Busisonje's *C. porocristata*. Also, Jouve's study of UMR 5143, a skull and associate mandible (from "Calcaires táchetés, near Saint-Dizier, early Tithonian of eastern France) referred by that author to *Ctenochasma* sp., revealed that all teeth are not present in pterosaur hatchlings, their number increasing progressively during ontogeny.

CYCNORHAMPHUS   Seeley 1870—(=*Gallodactylus*)
Ctenochasmatoidea.

Name derivation: Greek *kyknos* = "swan" + Greek *rhamphos* = "beak."

Type species: *C. suevicus* (Quenstedt 1855).

Other species: *C. canjuersensis* (Fabre 1974).

Occurrence: Canjuers, France; Unteres Untertithon, Nusplingen, Württemberg, Eichstätt, Bavaria, southern Germany; Canjuers, France.

Age: Late Jurassic (Portlandian).

Holotype: GPIT collection, skeleton with skull.

Diagnosis of genus: Lacking sagittal crest, occipital region considerably larger than that of *Pterodactylus* [note: other features listed as diagnostic compared this genus to *Gallodactylus*, now generally regarded as a junior synonym of *Cycnorhamphus* (Fabre 1974).

Diagnosis of *C. suevicus*: Large; teeth fine, long, pointed, limited to beak (probably absent in *C. canjuersensis*); sternum round; wing phalanges reduced in length, first phalange of fourth digit vestigial; cervical vertebrae short; metacarpus much longer than forearm; scapula and coracoid fused, not deformed (Fabre 1974).

Diagnosis of *C. canjuersensis*: Nasopreorbital fenestra

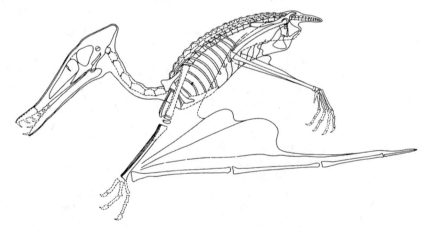

Cycnorhamphus canjuersensis, reconstructed holotype skeleton of *Gallodactylus canjuersensis*. (After Fabre 1974).

more than twice diameter of orbit; length of fourth wing phalanx reduced relative to third; open obturator foramen on pubis/ischium suture; slightly larger species, humerus and tibia smaller than in *C. suevicus* (Fabre 1974).

Type species originally named *Pterodactylus wurttembergicus* by Quenstedt (1854); skull long, narrow, beak flat (swanlike), no cranial crest.

DENDRORHYNCHOIDES   Ji, Ji and Padian 1999—
   (=*Dendrorhynchus*)
Anurognathidae.

Name derivation: Greek *dendron* = "tree" + Greek *rhynkos* = "snout" + Greek *oides* = "like, form."

Type species: *D. curvidentatus* (Ji and Ji 1998).

Occurrence: Zhangjiagou locality, Yixian Formation,

Chaomidianzi, Sihetun region, south of Beipiao city, western Liaoning Province, northeastern China.

Age: Early Cretaceous (Hauterivian; see Swisher, Wang, Zhou, Wang, Jin, Zhang, Xu, Zhang and Wang 2001).

Holotype: GMV 2128, almost complete skeleton with disarticulated skull.

Diagnosis of genus (as for type species): Skull very short, broad, lightly constructed, cranial openings large; tail short, slightly tapering, comprising six to eight small caudal vertebrae forming pygostyle-like structure (Ji and Ji 1998; Unwin, Lü and Bukhurina 2000).

Small pterosaur, wingspan of 40 to 50 centimeters (about 16 to 18 inches); originally described as a long-tailed "rhamphorhynchoid," thus the holotype was used to date the lower Liaoning beds as Late Jurassic, the specimen apparently having been doctored (Unwin, Lü and Bakhurina 2000); second pterosaur reported from the Yixian Formation.

DENDRORHYNCHUS   Ji and Ji 1998 — (Preoccupied Keilin 1920; see *Dendrorhynchoides*.)

Name derivation: Greek *dendros* = "tree" + Greek *rhynkos* = "snout."

Type species: *D. curvidentatus* Ji and Ji 1998.

DERMODACTYLUS   Marsh 1881 [*nomen dubium*]

Pterodactyloidea *incertae sedis*.

Name derivation: Greek *derma* = "skin" + Greek *dactylos* = "finger."

Type species: *D. montanus* (Marsh 1878) [*nomen duium*].

Occurrence: Morrison Formation, Como Bluff, Wyoming, United States.

Age: Late Jurassic (Tithonian).

Holotype: YPM 2000, distal end of right wing metacarpal.

Originally described by Marsh (1878) as *Pterodatylus montanus*, the first record of pterosaurs in the New World as early as the Late Jurassic; thickness of bone wall greater than in other known pterodactyloids; scapula and coracoid seemingly not fused; estimated wingspan of almost 1.5 to about 1.75 meters (five to six feet).

DIMORPHODON   Owen 1859

Dimorphodontidae.

Name derivation: Greek *dis* = "twice" + Greek *morphe* = "form" + Greek *odous* = "tooth."

Type species: *D. macronyx* (Buckland 1829).

Other species: *D. weintraubi* Clark, Hopson, Hernandez, Fastovsky and Montellano 1998.

Occurrence: Lower Lias, Lyme Regis, Dorset, England; lower part of La Boca Formation, Huizachal Canyon, Tamaulipus, Mexico.

Age: Early to ?Middle Jurassic (Hettangian–?Aalenian).

Holotype: BMNH R 1034, incomplete postcranial skeleton including most wrist elements.

Diagnosis of genus (as for type species): Skull very large relative to postcranium (22 centimeters), rostral end high, with large openings separated by thin areas of bone; nasal largest cranial opening, preorbital fenestra next largest, orbit smaller, in form of inverted triangle; quadrate vertically oriented; upper jaw toothed up to rostralmost end; premaxilla with four large teeth, sharp-pointed, laterally compressed, forwardly curved, with ample separations between teeth; fourth premaxillary tooth larger than others; in maxilla, nine notably smaller teeth, amply separated from each other, sharp-pointed, forwardly curved; third maxillary tooth largest, succeeding teeth grading down in size; three distalmost teeth much smaller; teeth of upper jaw continue to just beyond middle of preorbital fenestra; lower jaw with four or five larger teeth at rostralmost end, inclined forwardly, amply separated; behind those, continuing series of 30–40 much smaller teeth of same form, sharp-pointed, densely distributed, straight; ?intramandibular fenestra; seven robust cervical vertebrae, cervical ribs short, ?13 presacral dorsal vertebrae, 12 of these bearing ribs, at least four sacral vertebrae, more than 30 caudal vertebrae; first five to six caudal vertebrae short,

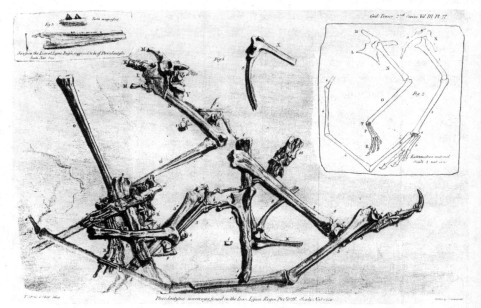

Dimorphodon macronyx, BMNH R 1034, holotype incomplete skeleton of *Pterodactylus macronyx*. (After Buckland 1835).

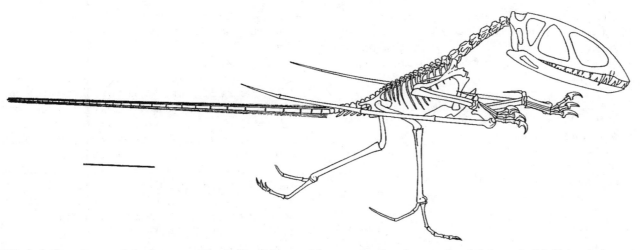

Dimorphodon macronyx, skeletal reconstruction in bipedial terrestrial progression, based upon referred skeletons in Yale University's Peabody Museum of Natural History. Scale = 10 cm. (After Padian 1985.)

movable, becoming progressively more extended and rigid with long ossified tendons; complete fusion of scapula and coracoid, suture visible; pelvis with wide ischiopubic shelf, cranial portion of pubis reinforced; ilium having strong postacetabular projection, preacetabular portion approximately same size; prepubis relatively short with wide, short ends, not grown together; humerus relatively long, slender, curved, deltopectoral crest developed; radius and ulna in intimate contact, only slightly longer than humerus; metacarpus shorter than middle forearm; wing-finger relatively short; first wing phalanx only slightly longer than forearm; wing-finger phalanges increasing in length from first to third, fourth longest; claws of first three fingers relatively large, laterally curved; hindlimbs very strongly developed; femur and humerus approximately equally long

and robust; tibia one-seventh longer than forearm; first four metatarsals of almost equal length; metatarsal V short, pedal digits I–IV laterally curved; fifth toe longer, with straight phalanges of approximately same length; total length of animal, from snout to end of tail, 100 centimeters, maximum wingspan 140 centimeters (Wellnhofer 1978).

Diagnosis of *D. weintraubi*: Differs from *D. macronyx* in first wing phalanx being not significantly shorter than ulna; sesamoid at base of pedal claws (reported in *D. macronyx*) not seen; holotype larger than largest *D. macronyx* specimen; largest known nonpterodactyloid pterosaur; 60.5-millimeter-long metacarpal IV longest yet reported (Clark, Hopson, Hernandez, Fastovsky and Montellano 1998).

Life restoration by J. Kevin Ramos of *Dimorphodon macronyx*, with wing configuration inferred from *Rhamphorhynchus*, furry covering from *Sordes pilosus*, and rostral horny covering after an inference by Wellnhofer (1974–1975) for *Rhamphorhynchus*. Scale = 10 cm. (After Padian 1985.)

Among the oldest known Jurassic pterosaurs and the first described from Lyme Regis, with a relatively large head and deep snout, short wings (wingspan approximately 1.4 meters or 4.6 feet), long hindlimbs, long and stiff tail, possibly a fish-eater.

DIOPECEPHALUS   Seeley 1871
Pterodactyloidea *incertae sedis.*
Name derivation: Greek *di* = "two" + Greek *ope* = "opening" + Greek *kephale* = "head."
Type species: *D. longicollum* (Meyer 1854).
Occurrence: Solnhofen Lithographic Limestone, Eichstätt, Bavaria, southern Germany.
Age: Late Jurassic (Kimmeridgian).
Neotype: Eberhard Fraas collection, skeleton with skull.

Diagnosis of genus (as for type species): Lacking sagittal crest, occipital region considerably larger than in *Pterodactylus*; temporal fenestrae larger than in "*Gallodactylus*" [=*Cycnorhamphus*]; cervical vertebrae very elongate, neck longer than skull (Fabre 1974).

Originally tentatively referred by Muenster (1836) to *Pterodactylus*; no cranial crest, neck relatively long.

DOLICHORHAMPHUS   Seeley 1880 [*nomen dubium*]—
(See *Rhamphocephalus.*)
Name derivation: Greek *dolichos* = "long" + Greek *rhamphos* = "beak."
Type species: *D. prestwichi* (Seeley 1880) [*nomen dubium*].

DOMEYKODACTYLUS   Martill, Frey, Chong-Diaz and Bell 2000
Dsungaripteridae.
Name derivation: "[Cordillera de] Domeyko" + Greek *dactylos* = "finger."
Type species: *D. celiae* Martill, Frey, Chong-Diaz and Bell 2000.

Occurrence: Quebrada de la Cerreta, Cordillera de Domeyko [mountain range in Chilean Andes], Antofagasta, northern Chile.
Age: Early Cretaceous.
Holotype: Departmento de Ciencias Geologicas, Universidad Catolica del Norte, Antogafasa, Chile, collection, number 250973, fragmentary specimen including partial mandible with portions of both rami and symphysis.

Diagnosis of genus (as for type species): Crested; each mandible bearing at least 16 low, narrow, protuberant dental alveoli decreasing in size and spacing from caudal to rostral (Martill, Frey, Chong-Diaz and Bell 2000).

Sagittal crest along top of premaxilla, wingspan of approximately one meter (3.3 feet); first confirmed dsungaripterid found in South America; holotype originally referred to *Pterodaustro.*

DORATORHYNCHUS   Seeley 1875 [*nomen vanum*]
Pterodactyloidea *incertae sedis.*
Name derivation: Greek *dory* = "spear" + Greek *rhynkhos* = "snout."
Type species: *D. validus* (Owen 1870) [*nomen vanum*].
Occurrence: "Swanage," ?Langton Matravers quarry, "Middle Purbeck Beds," Purbeck Limestone Formation, Dorset, England.
Age: Late Jurassic (Tithonian) or Early Cretaceous (Berriasian).
Holotype: BMNH 40653, first or second phalanx of digit IV or right manus.

Large, long-tailed, with extremely long neck; possibly related to *Quetzalcoatlus.*

DORYGNATHUS   Wagner 1860
Rhamphorhynchinae.
Name derivation: Greek *dory* = "spear" + Greek *gnathos* = "jaw."

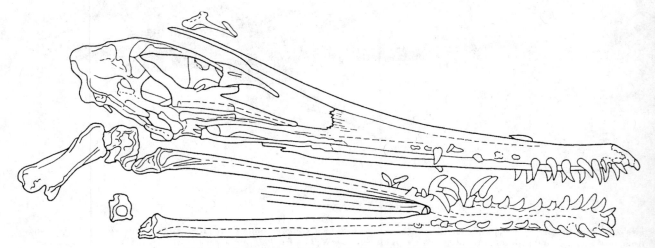

Holotype skull of *Diocephalus longicollum.* (After Fabres 1978.)

Life restoration by Todd Marshall of *Dorygnathus banthensis* about to snatch the fish *Dapedium pholidotum*. Overhead are two individuals of *Campylognathoides zitteli*.

Type species: *D. banthensis* (Theodori 1830).

Other species: *D. mistelgauensis* Wild 1971.

Occurrence: Upper Liassic, Banz, Holzmaden (Württemberg), Ohmden (Württemberg), Flechtorf (Niedersachsen), Monotisbank, Bayreuth, Bavaria, Germany.

Age: Middle Jurassic (Toarcian).

Holotype: Schloss Banz collection, bones representing more than one individual.

Diagnosis of genus (as for type species): Skull shorter, relatively smaller than that of *Rhamphorhynchus*, nearly twice as small as that of *Campylognathoides*; maxilla relatively high, narial opening small, preorbital fenestra larger, both openings smaller than orbit; quadrate relatively high, in inclined position; four large predentary teeth, seven smaller maxillary teeth; tip of lower jaw sharp ventrally, with three very long teeth, slanting forwards, rostralmost tooth almost horizontally oriented, these teeth followed by eight smaller teeth, jaw edge straight; sternum small, weakly constructed, with triangular outline; scapula and coracoid not fused together; pelvis with broad ischio-pubic shelf; obturator foramen; prepubis short, shovel-like in form; sacrum not fused with ilia; wing-finger short; first phalanx shortest, second distinctly longer, fourth as long as or longer than first; femur shorter than humerus, relatively longer than in *Rhamphorhynchus*; second phalanx of fifth pedal digit long, thick (Wellnhofer 1978).

Diagnosis of *D. mistelgauensis*: Very large, with strong, extended forearm and metacarpus; tibia relatively short, fused with fibula; fibula without proximal end joint; skeleton otherwise having proportions as in *D. banthensis* (Wellnhofer 1978).

Mesial upper and lower teeth long and forwardly directed, wingspan relatively small, hindlimbs long, fifth toe of foot long with bent phalanx (suggesting webbing), probably piscivorous.

DSUNGARIPTERUS   Yang 1964

Dsungaripteridae.

Name derivation: Chinese *Dsungar* = "Junggar [Basin]" + Greek *pteron* = "wing."

Type species: *D. weii* Yang 1964.

Other species: ?*D. brancai* (Reck 1931).

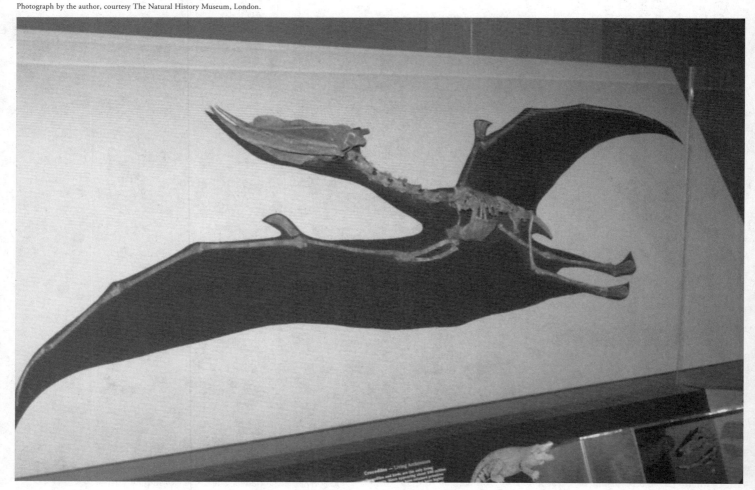

Skeleton of the Chinese pterosaur *Dsungaripterus weii*.

Occurrence: Tugulu Group, Urho, Dsungari Basin, near Wuerho, Xinjiang, China; ?Tendaguru, Tanzania, East Africa.

Age: ?Late Jurassic to Early Cretaceous.

Holotype: IVPP V.2776, incomplete skeleton including anterior part of skull and lower jaws, two cervical vertebrae, 13 consecutive vertebrae (including three caudal "Notarium," three caudal dorsals, seven sacrals, seven consecutive caudals, two isolated distal caudals), proximal end of left humerus, ?left ulna, distal ends of both wing-metacarpals, both first digits of fourth finger and three consecutive digits of left side of same; almost complete pelvic girdle with ilia attached to sacrum; proximal portion of tibia.

Diagnosis of genus (as for type species): Rather large; rostral part of skull laterally compressed, sharply pointed, bending upwards; well-developed median crest above nasal and preorbital openings, both openings apparently entirely confluent; lower jaws firmly connected by symphysis; lower jaws sharply pointed, part of symphysis bending upwards; teeth with points bending backwards; teeth well separated except few most caudal upper teeth; probably 12 upper teeth, 11 lower teeth; rostral lower teeth small, tending towards reduction; "notarium"; sacrum comprising seven vertebrae; fourth metacarpal very long; four very long wing fingers; total width of wings presumably between three and 3.5 meters, almost four times length of animal; pelvic girdle of typical pterodactyloid construction; femur comparatively long, longer than half of first wing finger; femur craniocaudally curved; tibia straight, apparently longer than femur (Yang 1964).

Rostral part of jaws edentulous, jaws bent upwards at tip, long crest running along midline of upper part of skull, shorter crest at back of head, eyes relatively small, set rather high on skull.

EOSIPTERUS   Ji and Ji 1997
Ctenochasmatinae.

Name derivation: Greek *eos* = "dawn" + Greek *pteron* = "wing."

Type species: *E. yangi* Ji and Ji 1997.

Occurrence: Tuanshangou locality, upper part of Hengdaozi Member, Yixian Formation, Sihetun region, south of Beipiao City, western Liaoning Province, China.

Age: Early Cretaceous (Hauterivian; see Swisher, Wang, Zhou, Wang, Jin, Zhang, Xu, Zhang and Wang 2001).

Holotype: GMV 2117, partial articulated postcranial skeleton (lacking cervical vertebrae, lost caudal vertebrae, hindlimbs, and wing-fingers) including wing membranes, uropatagia, subadult.

Diagnosis of genus (as for type species): Medium-sized, total width approximately 1.2 meters across two ends of distal wing-fingers; tail short; gastralia narrow, weak; forelimb strong, radius and ulna 1.3 times length of wing-metacarpal; joints of wing-finger extensible transversely;

femur slightly straight, occupying two-thirds length of tibia; radius, first wing-finger as long as tibia; metatarsals I–IV long, narrow; phalanx V of pes degenerated, small (Ji and Ji 1997).

Relatively small pterosaur, wingspan of about 1.25 meters (almost 4.5 feet), skull resembling that of *Germanodactylus rhamphastinus*, apparently lived along the coast of a freshwater lake; first pterosaur reported from the Yixian Formation (Jehol Fauna).

EUDIMORPHODON   Zambelli 1973
Campylognathoididae.

Name derivation: Greek *eu* = "good/true" + *Dimorphodon*.

Type species: *E. ranzii* Zambelli 1973.

Other species: *E. cromptonellus* Jenkens, Shubin, Gatesy and Padian 2001, "*E.*" *rosenfeldi* Dalla Vecchia 1994.

Occurrence: Zorzino limestones (middle to late Norian),

Life restoration by Todd Marshall of the pterosaurs (left) *Eudimorphodon ranzii* and (right) *Austriadactylus cristatus*.

Eudimorphodon ranzii, holotype skeleton at the Civico Museo di Scienze Naturali di Bergamo.

near Bergamo, lower part of Dolomia di Forni (middle Norian), Udine Province, Cene, (Norian) northern Friuli, Italy; lower part of Carlsberg Fjord beds, Fleming Fjord Formation, Ørsted Dal Member, Scoresby Land Group, Jameson Land, East Greenland; northern Calcareous Alps, Karwendel Mountains, Tyrol, Austria. Age: Late Triassic (middle to late Norian). Holotype: MCSNB 2888, almost complete skeleton.

Diagnosis of genus (as for type species): Dentition multicuspid, upper and lower jaws having small, close-set tricuspid and pentacuspid teeth of similar size (Wild 1973; Dalla Vecchia 2003*b*).

Diagnosis of *E. cromptonellus*: Very small, sharing with the type species heterodont dentition consisting of uni-, tri-, and quinticuspid teeth (unknown in other pterosaurian taxa); some teeth quadricuspid; tooth count estimated at 11 or 12 postmaxillary teeth (14 or 15 fewer than in the type species); tibia relatively shorter than in most other known pterosaurs; no evidence of two enlarged, fanglike maxillary teeth beneath ascending process characteristic of type species; differing from juvenile specimen (MCSNB 8950) referred to *E. ranzii* (Wild 1994) in that

metatarsals are about 25 percent longer, while all other limb bones are substantially shorter; differing from "*E.*" *rosenfeldi* in humerus being shorter than femur (Jenkens, Shubin, Gatesy and Padian 2001).

Diagnosis of "*E.*" *rosenfeldi*: Wingspan of approximately 65–70 centimeters; quinticuspid teeth having smooth surface; pterygoid lacking teeth; caudal part of lower jaw very deep at coronoid process; apparently long diastema between distalmost tooth and tip of coronoid process; shaft of coronoid short, wide; humeral shaft proportionally longer, slenderer than in type species, deltopectoral crest narrow, with rectangular profile slightly different from that of type species; pteroid rodlike, with characteristic angled shape; ?five carpals; first wing phalanx longest, slightly longer than third; hindlimbs proportionally longer than in type species; tibia very long (almost length of ulna, considerably longer than humerus); probably two tarsals; sesamoid bone on proximal portion of first phalanx of pedal digit V; pedal phalangeal formula (2, 3, 4, 5, 2) (Dalla Vecchia 1994).

Among the smallest (wingspan one meter) known pterosaurs, big eyes, larger mesial fangs, more distal teeth smaller, pointed, possibly insectivorous; presumably subadult skeletal fragments (BSP 1994.I.51) from Austria referred by Wellnhofer (2003) to *Eudimorphodon* cf. *ranzii*, differing slightly from the holotype of *E. ranzii*, referred to that genus based upon comparable dentition.

GALLODACTYLUS Fabre 1974 — (See *Cycnorhamphus*.)
Name derivation: Latin *gallus* = "chicken" + Greek *dactylos* = "finger."
Type species: *G. canjuersensis* Fabre 1974.

GEOSTERNBERGIA Miller 1978 — (See *Pteranodon*.)
Name derivation: "Geo[rge F.] Sternberg."
Type species: *G. sternbergi* (Harksen 1966).

GERMANODACTYLUS Yang [Young] 1964 — (=?*Pterodactylus*)
Dsungaripteridae.
Name derivation: "Germany" + Greek *dactylos* = "finger."
Type species: *G. cristatus* (Wiman 1925).
Other species: *G. rhamphastinus* (Wagner 1851).
Occurrence: Solnhofen and Mörnsheimer Limestone, Unteres Untertithon, Eichstätt, Daiting, Bavaria, southern Germany; Kimmeridge Clay, Kimmeridge Bay, Dorset, England.
Age: Late Jurassic (early Kimmeridgian–Tithonian).
Holotype: BSP 1982.IV.1, mostly disarticulated incomplete skeleton.
Diagnosis of genus: Skull having broad sagittal crest above naris and orbit; jugal extending vertically toward lower border of maxilla; quadrate relatively vertical; rostral end of jaw edentulous or toothed; average of 13–16 teeth per jaw; five premaxillary teeth, conical, robust, sharply pointed, with oval cross section; nasopreorbital opening more than double size of orbit; bones of pelvic girdle as well as shoulder girdle fused; neck two-thirds length of skull; metacarpus shorter than forearm; prepubis flat, broad, bladelike (Wellnhofer 1978).

Diagnosis of *G. cristatus*: Skull with serrated bony crest, extending from rostral border of naris to caudal border of orbit; rostral end of jaw pointed, rostral part edentulous; upper jaw with five premaxillary and approximately eight maxillary teeth; teeth short, flat, conical, forwardly inclined, curved, oval in cross section (Wellnhofer 1978).

Diagnosis of *G. rhamphastinus*: Skull relatively larger than in type species; sagittal crest lower, extending from beginning of naris but not extending as far back of skull as in type species; five forwardly positioned and curved premaxillary teeth, 11 vertically oriented, consistently large; teeth sharply pointed, conical, oval in cross section, edges rounded; quadrate rather more highly positioned than in *G. cristatus*; ischium having obturator foramen (Wellnhofer 1978).

Superficially resembling *Pterodactylus* and possibly an adult form of that genus (see Bennett 1996), short medial crest at caudal part of head, teeth restricted to rostral area of jaws, distinguished as first pterosaur (specimen MCZ 1886) known to have "a soft tissue crest extending upward from the bony premaxillary crest," the former more than doubling the height of the latter, probably consisting of cornified epidermis" (see Bennett 2002); according to Bennett (2003*b*), *G. cristatus* and *G. rhamphastinus* are distinct species, the former lacking edentulous jaw tips, although they are seemingly congeneric based on similar dentition and proportions.

GNATHOSAURUS Meyer 1834
Gnatosaurinae.
Name derivation: Greek *gnathos* = "jaw" + Greek *sauros* = "lizard."

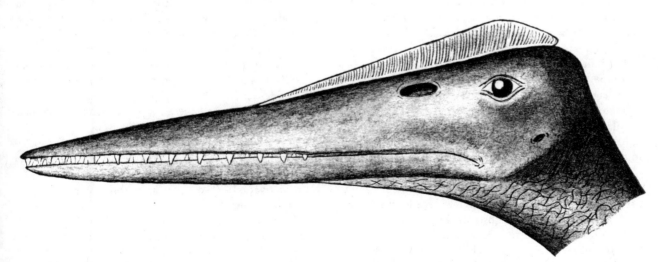

Life restoration of the head of a subadult *Germanodactylus rhamphastinus*, based upon MCZ 1886, a specimen showing traces of the soft tissue crest. This crest may have been larger in fully adult animals. (After Bennett 2002.)

Life restoration by Todd Marshall of *Gnathosaurus subulatus*. In the background, the theropod *Compsognathus longipes* is depicted hunting crabs.

Type species: *G. subulatus* Meyer 1834.

Other species: *G. macrurus* (Seeley 1869).

Occurrence: Solnhofen Lithographic Limestone, Unteres Untertithon, Solnhofen, Eichstätt, Bavaria, southern Germany; quarry (precise location unknown) near Langton Matravers, Purbeck, Dorset, England.

Age: Late Jurassic (early Tithonian) to ?Early Cretaceous (Berriasian).

Holotype: BSP AS.VII.369, isolated portion of dentary.

Diagnosis of genus (as for type species): Relatively large ctenochasmatid, with long, slender skull, jaw tips spatulate and rostrally rounded; premaxillae with low sagittal crest extending from one third of skull length behind snout tip to level of orbit; dentition prominent (30 to 32 teeth), extending back to level of rostral edge of nasoantorbital fenestra; rostral spatula teeth short, rostrally directed, caudal spatula teeth longer; teeth, from fifth tooth back on each side, substantially lengthening, rostrodorsally directed so that each tooth overlaps outside tooth in front (caudal teeth much shorter); teeth arranged to give food-grabbing, "fish-basket" dentition, with teeth inserted on lateral edge of jaw margin, tips directed in-

wardly (Wellnhofer 1978; points in parentheses, Howse and Milner 1995).

Diagnosis of *G. macrurus*: Spatula on lower jaw with 10 teeth (14 in type species); main series of post-spatula teeth almost laterally directed (rostro-laterally in type species) (Howse and Milner 1995)

Large pterosaur (skull of type species 28 centimeters, or 11 inches in length), low crest on skull, teeth more powerful and less densely arranged than in *Ctenochasma*, possibly a filter feeder. The British species *G. macrurus*, based on a portion of large lower jaw, was originally described by Seeley (1869) as *Pterodactylus macrurus*.

HAOPTERUS   Wang and Lü 2001

Ornithocheiridae.

Name derivation: "Hao [Chinese paleontologist]" + Greek *pteron* = "wing."

Type species: *H. gracilis*. Wang and Lü 2001.

Occurrence: Jianshangou Bed, Lower Yixian Formation, western Liaoning Province, China.

Age: Early Cretaceous (see Swisher, Wang, Zhou, Wang, Jin, Zhang, Xu, Zhang and Wang 2001) (?Barremian).

Holotype: IVPP V11726, partial skeleton, including complete skull, pectoral girdle, forelimbs, sternum, cervical and dorsal vertebrae, metatarsals and digits, subadult.

Diagnosis of genus (as for type species): Skull low, long, without bony crest, rostrum pointed; upper and lower jaws with 12 relatively short, sharply pointed teeth on either side, most teeth distally inclined; caudal part of jaws edentulous; sternum fan shaped; length of metacarpals almost equal to that of metatarsals; tarsals and pedal digits very reduced in size (Wang and Lu 2001).

Medium-sized, wingspan estimated at approximately 1.35 meters (4.5 feet), skull 14.5 centimeters (six inches) in length; slender feet suggesting a piscivorous diet, small hindfeet suggesting quadrupedal locomotion.

HARPACTOGNATHUS Carpenter, Unwin, Cloward, Miles and Miles 2003
Scaphognathinae.
Name derivation: Greek *harpact* = "seize/grasp" + Greek *gnathos* = "jaws."
Type species: *H. gentryi* Carpenter, Unwin, Cloward, Miles and Miles 2003.
Occurrence: Bone Cabin Quarry Extension, Lower half of Dinosaur Zone 2 (equivalent to Upper Salt Water Wash member of Colorado Plateau), Morrison Formation, Albany County, Wyoming, United States.
Age: Late Jurassic (Kimmeridgian).
Holotype: NAMAL 101, rostral portion of rostrum.

Diagnosis of genus (as for type species): Thin median crest extending from tip of rostrum caudally above external nares; antorbital fenestra bounded rostrally by shallow triangular antorbital fossa; lateral surface of premaxilla and maxilla scalloped between widely spaced alveoli; ventral profile of dental margin undulating, deeply emarginated below external nares (Carpenter, Unwin, Cloward, Miles and Miles 2003).

Oldest known Morrison Formation pterosaur, wingspan estimated to be at least 2.5 meters.

HATZEGOPTERYX Buffetaut, Grigorescu and Ciski 2002
Azhdarchoidea *incertae sedis*.
Name derivation: "Hatzeg [Basin]" + Greek *pteron* = "wing."
Type species: *H. thambema* Bufferaut, Grigorescu and Ciski 2002.
Occurrence: Densus-Ciula Formation, northwestern Hatzeg Basin, Valiora, Hunedoara county, Transylvania, Tustea, western Romania.
Age: Late Cretaceous (late Maastrichtian).
Holotype: FGGUB R1083, skull fragments, incomplete left humerus, other bone fragments.

Diagnosis of genus (as for type species): Skull very robust, caudally broad, possibly up to three meters (about 10 feet) in length; internal structure of skull unique among

Pterosauria, comprising dense network of very thin trabeculae enclosing small alveolae; jaw articulation having smoothly rounded helical condyles on quadrate; humerus with large, wing-shaped deltopectoral crest (similar to *Quetzalcoatlus*) (Buffetaut, Grigorescu and Csiski 2002).

Giant pterosaur, unique construction of the skull presumably lessened the weight while offering strength; possibly lived in inland freshwater environments; wingspan estimated as close to that of *Quetzalcoatlus northropi*, but with comparatively longer and robust skull, skull bones comprising "a very thin outer cortex enclosing an inner meshwork of extremely thin trabeculae surrounding very numerous small alveoli, an unusual structure reminiscent of expanded polystyrene," this "peculiar structure, combining strength with lightness [probably interpreted to be] an adaptation to flight in a very large animal, through reduction of skull weight" (Buffetaut *et al.* 2003).

HERBSTOSAURUS Casamiquela 1974
Dsungaripteroidea.
Name derivation: "[R.] Herbst [collector of the type specimen]" + Greek *sauros* = "lizard."
Type species: *H. pigmaeus* Casamiquela 1974.
Occurrence: Lotena Formation, Patagonia, Argentina.
Age: Middle Jurassic (Callovian).
Holotype: CTES-PZ 1711, partly articulated postcrania including sacral vertebrae, pelvis, femora, other elements.

Diagnosis of genus (as for type species): Distinguished by pelvis, ilium relatively long, ischium short (Casamiquela 1974).

Diagnosis of type species: Distinguished by small size (Casamiquela 1974).

Very small, originally diagnosed and described as a compsognathid theropod dinosaur.

HUANHEPTERUS Dong 1982
Gnathosaurinae.
Name derivation: "Huane [river]" + Greek *pteron* = "wing."
Type species: *H. quingyangensis* Dong 1982.
Occurrence: Ordos, Gansu Province, China; Tendaguru, Tanzania, East Africa.
Age: Late Jurassic.
Holotype: Skeleton.

Diagnosis of genus (as for type species): Rather large; skull lower, longer, well-developed median crest above nasal, teeth slender, pointed; premaxillary teeth larger than maxillary teeth, trend towards reduction caudally; neck long with seven centra, "notarium" absent; sacrum with seven vertebrae (Dong 1982).

Relatively large (wingspan approximately 2.5 meters or 8.2 feet), jaws fringed with long and slender teeth, those rostral in jaws tightly packed, skull with low sagittal crest, neck long with elongate cervical vertebrae.

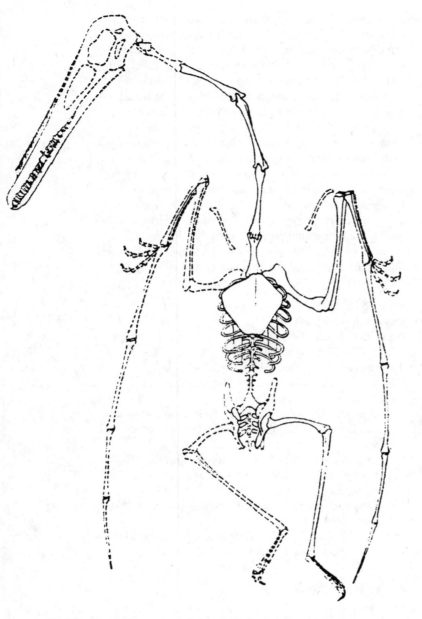

Huanhepterus quingyangensis, holotype skeleton. (After Dong 1982.)

ISTIODACTYLUS   Howse, Milner and Martill 2001
Ornithocheiroidea.

Name derivation: Greek *istion* = "sail" + Greek *dactylos* = "finger."

Type species: *I. latidens* (Seeley 1901).

Occurrence: Vectis Formation, Isle of Wight, England.

Age: Early Cretaceous (Barremian–Aptian).

Holotype: BMNH R176, poorly preserved incomplete skeleton including caudal part of skull, sternum, sacrum, right humerus.

Diagnosis of genus (as for type species): Skull (approximately 56 centimeters in length) unique among known pterosaurs in following features: beak section elongated, short section rostral to nostrils forming heavily built blunt tip; very long combined nasal opening and antorbital fenestra; orbit connecting downward, with long, narrow opening; teeth petal-shaped, restricted to rostral part of jaws beyond nostrils, teeth wide and compressed, with sharp crowns that interlock when upper- and lower-jaw tips shut together; 24 upper and 25 lower teeth (preserved); also, sternum primitive in appearance, with saddle-shaped facets for coracoid (Howse, Milner and Martill 2001).

Very Large, wingspan estimated at five meters (about 17 feet), head long; unusual interlocking teeth and blunt jaw tips possibly suggesting this pterosaur could remove chunks of meat using "cookie-cutter" style bites, or by biting while twisting its head.

JEHOLOPTERUS   Wang, Zhou, Zhang and Xu 2002
Anurognathidae.

Name derivation: "Jehol [Group]" + Greek *pteron* = "wing."

Type species: *J. ningchengensis* Wang, Zhou, Zhang and Xu 2002.

Occurrence: Lower Yixian Formation, Jehol Group, lake deposits at Daohugou, Nincheng County, Inner Mongolia, northeastern China.

Age: Early Cretaceous (see Swisher, Wang, Zhou, Wang, Jin, Zhang, Xu, Zhang and Wang 2001) (?Barremian).

Holotype: IVPP V12705, almost completely articulated skeleton, wing membrane and "hair" impressions.

Diagnosis of genus (as for type species): Distinguished from *Dendrorhynchoides* and other anurognathid taxa by its almost twice body size (wingspan 90 centimeters in length), much more robust and longer first phalanx of pedal digit V (first phalanx of pedal digit V robust, as long as metatarsals I–IV), and straight second phalanx of pedal digit V; skull wider than long; wing metacarpal less than one fourth length of lower arm; among four phalanges of wing digit, first is longer than radius, second close to radius, third and fourth remarkably shorter; wing claws extremely long, about 1.5 times length of pedal claws; pedal digit V long, about 1.5 times length of digit III (Wang, Zhou, Zhang and Xu 2002).

Moderate-sized (wingspan of 90 centimeters or about three feet) pterosaur, but largest known anurognathid; probably piscivorous; Peters (2003), in a controversial abstract, proposed this genus to have been a possible "vampire," as indicated by a suite of characters presumably supporting this hypothesis.

JIDAPTERUS   Dong, Sun and Wu 2003
Pterodactyloidea *incertae sedis*.

Name derivation: "Jilin [University, China]" + Greek *pteron* = "wing."

Type species: *J. edentus* Dong, Sun and Wu 2003.

Occurrence: Jiufotang Formation, Jehol Group, Liaoning Province, China.

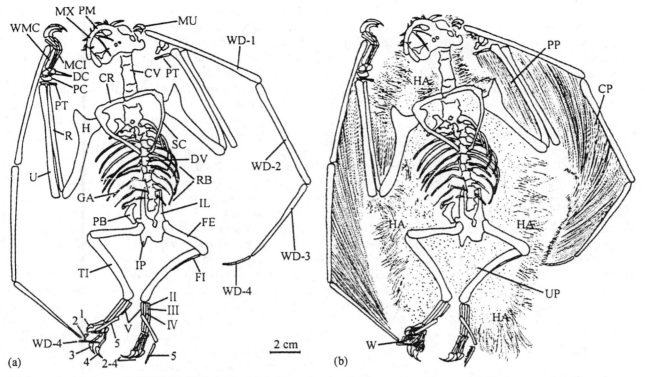

Jeholopterus ningchengensis, IVPP V12705, holotype (a) skeleton of part and counterpart specimens, and (b) reconstruction of attachment of various parts of wing membrane to the skeleton, and distribution of "hairs." (After Wang, Zhou, Zhang and Xu 2002.)

Age: Early Cretaceous.

Holotype: Almost complete skeleton with incomplete skull.

Second record of toothless pterosaur from the Jehol Group; medium-sized, skull relatively long with straight, pointed beak, large nasoantorbital fenestra (occupying one-tenth length of skull), small orbit, absence of sagittal crest on rostral lower margins of mandible.

KEPODACTYLUS   Harris and Carpenter 1996
Dsungaripteroidea.
Name derivation: Greek *kepos* = "garden [for Garden Park]" + Greek *dactylos* = "finger."
Type species: *K. insperatus* Harris and Carpenter 1996.
Occurrence: Small *Stegosaurus* Quarry, Morrison Formation, Garden Park, Colorado, United States.
Age: Late Jurassic.
Known material/holotype: DMNH 21684, cervical vertebrae, left humerus, left proximal phalanx of wing finger, distal end of right proximal wing-finger phalanx, proximal end of left second wing-finger phalanx, metatarsal.

Diagnosis of genus (as for type species): Large, with estimated wingspan of 2.5 meters; cervical centrum elongated as in *Pterodactylus*, but with postzygapophyses extended beyond centrum; cervical centrum lacking diapophyses of "rhamphorhynchoids" and accessory exapophyses of azhdarchids; pneumatic foramen caudally lo-

cated, elongated oval on centrum rather than on neural arch as in "rhamphorhynchoids"; first wing phalanx without longitudinal groove of "rhamphorhynchoids," ovoid in cross section; deltopectoral crest large, rectangular, not hatchet-shaped (as in "rhamphorhynchoids" and nyctosaurids), not warped (as in "pteranodontids") (Harris and Carpenter 1996).

Large form, among the largest of known Jurassic pterosaurs (comparable in size to the German contemporary *Pterodactylus grandis*, wingspan of about 2.5 meters (almost 8.5 feet).

LAOPTERYX   Marsh 1881 [*nomen dubium*]
Pterosauria *incertae sedis*.
Name derivation: Greek *laos* = "stone" + Greek *pteron* = "wing."
Type species: *L. priscus* Marsh 1881 [*nomen dubium*].
Occurrence: Morrison Formation, Como Bluff, Wyoming, United States.
Age: Late Jurassic (Tithonian–Kimmeridgian).
Holotype: YPM collection, caudal part of skull including braincase.

Originally described by Marsh (1888) as avian, later identified by Ostrom (1986a) as a pterosaur; skull width across occiput 24 millimeters, possibly toothed as evidenced by a single tooth preserved in matrix attached to the skull.

LIAONINGOPTERUS   Wang and Zhou 2003
?Ornithocheiridae.
Name derivation: "Liaoning [Province]" + Greek *pteron* = "wing."
Type species: *L. gui* Wang and Zhou 2003.
Occurrence: Jiufotang Formation, Xiaoyugou, Lianhe, Chaoyang, Liaoning Province, China.
Age: Early Cretaceous (Aptian).
Holotype: IVPP V13291, incomplete skull including premaxilla, maxilla, jugal, quadrate, lower jaw, most teeth, postcrania including cervical vertebrae, digit of wing.

    Diagnosis of genus (as for type species): Large pterodactyloid; estimated skull length 610 millimeters, wingspan approximately five meters; skull long, low; premaxilla and dentary having sagittal crest; teeth restricted to rostral part of upper and lower jaws; toothed portion of jaws not extending distally to one third of nasopreorbital; toothed portion of jaws about half length of skull; teeth near rostral end of jaws huge; fourth premaxillary tooth largest, first and third premaxillary teeth much smaller than second and fourth (Wang and Zhou 2003).

    Probably piscivorous, as shown by the long, pointed snout.

LIAOXIPTERUS   Dong and Lü 2005
Ctenochasmatidae.
Name derivation: "Liaoxi [fossil locality]" + Greek *pteron* = "wing."
Type species: *L. brachypgnathus* Dong and Lü 2005.
Occurrence: Liaoxi locality, Jiufotang Formation, Chaoyang City, western Liaoning Province, China.
Age: Early Cretaceous.
Holotype: CAR-0018 (Jilin University collection), almost complete lower jaw.
Diagnosis of genus (as for type species): Differs from all other known ctenochasmatids in having fewer tooth count in mandible (11), relatively shorter teeth (Dong and Lü 2005).

LITHOSTEORNIS   Gervais 1844 [*nomen nudum*]— (See *Ornithocheirus.*)
Name derivation: Greek *lithos* = "stone" + Greek *ornis* = "bird."
Type species: *L. ardeaceus* (Gervais 1844) [*nomen nudum*].

LONCHODECTES   Hooley 1914 —(See *Ornithocheirus.*)
Name derivation: Greek *logkhos* = "lance" + Greek *dektes* = "fighter."
Type species: *L. compressirostris* (Owen 1851).

LONCHOGNATHOSAURUS   Maisch, Matzke and Sun 2004
Dsungaripteroidea.
Name derivation: Greek *logkhos* = "lance" + Greek *gnathos* = "jaw" + Greek *sauros* = "lizard."
Type species: *L. acutirostris* Maisch, Matzke and Sun 2004
Occurrence: Lower part of Lianmuxin Formation (Upper Tugulu Group), Liuhonggiy, southwest of Urumqi, Xinjiang Autonomous Region, China.
Age: ?Early to ?Middle Cretaceous (?Aptian–?Albian).
Holotype: SGP 2001/19, rostral part of skull.

    Diagnosis of genus (as for type species): Large, estimated skull length (assuming skull proportions similar to *Dsungaripterus* and "*Phobetor*") probably about 400 millimeters; alveolar margin of upper jaw entirely straight; rostrum of premaxilla very delicate and slender, ending in needle-like tip; sagittal crest well developed, striated, grooved, with concave rostral margin; only eight maxillary teeth; tip of upper jaw edentulous; tooth row starting far mesial to sagittal crest, ending rostral to nasopreorbital opening; teeth widely spaced (distance between individual tooth positions more than distomesial length of tooth); alveoli not bulbously expanded, but surrounded by low ring of bone (Maisch, Matzke and Sun 2004).

    Snout delicate, needlelike; large dsungaripteroid, sister taxon of *Dsungaripterus.*

LUDODACTYLUS   Frey, Martill and Buchy 2003
Ornithocheiridae.
Name derivation: Latin *ludus* = "game, play" + Greek *dactylos* = "finger."
Type species: *L. sibbicki* Frey, Martill and Buchy 2003.
Occurrence: Nova Olinda Member, Crato Formation, Chapada do Araripe region, Province of Ceará, northeastern Brazil.
Age: Early Cretaceous (Aptian).
Holotype: SMNK PAL 3828, very well-preserved skull (with associated fish and plant remains).

    Diagnosis of genus (as for type species): Differing from all other known ornithocheirids in the following: caudally directed, laterally compressed parieto-occipital crest; dorsoventrally compressed lacrimal spine (*spina lacrimalis*) protruding caudally into orbit; lacrimal foramen rounded triangular in outline, one corner facing ventrally; maxillary teeth present caudally as far as midpoint of nasoantorbital fenestra; dorsal surface of rostrum rounded, no trace of any crest; tooth row of mandible extending distally to rostral fourth of nasoantorbital fenestra; specimen coincident with *Ornithocheirus* in almost perpendicular orientation of mesialmost four pairs of teeth to long axis of jaws, at least in lateral aspect (diagnostic for that genus; see Unwin 2001); differs from all other known ornithocheirids lack of premaxillary crest; dorsal surface of rostrum rounded; bladelike crest (not reported in any other known ornithocheirid) (Frey, Martill and Buchy 2003*a*).

First ornithocheirid specimen found possessing a parieto-occipital crest, individual represented by the holotype apparently killed by a lanceolate leaf preserved lodged the mandibular rami.

MACROTRACHELUS Giebel 1852 — (See *Pterodactylus*.)

Name derivation: Greek *makros* = "long" + Greek *trachelos* = "neck."

Type species: *M. longirostris* (Cuvier 1819)

MESADACTYLUS Jensen and Padian 1989

Pterodactyloidea *incertae sedis*.

Name derivation: "[Dry] Mesa" + Greek *dactylos* = "finger."

Type species: *M. ornithosphyos* Jensen and Padian 1989.

Occurrence: Dry Mesa Quarry, Brushy Basin Member, Morrison Formation, western Colorado, United States.

Age: Late Jurassic (?Tithonian).

Holotype: BYU 2024, synsacrum.

Diagnosis of genus (as for type species): Seven fused sacral vertebrae, having strongly procoelous, laterally ellipsoidal cranial facet to first sacral centrum; neural arches of first five sacral vertebrae ankylosed into synsacral plate, which decreases in height caudally (Jensen and Padian 1989).

Unique among all other known pterosaurs in its synsacrum, having seven fused sacral vertebrae, the first five of which form a neural blade via fusion of the upper neural spines; upper arm bones resembling those of Solnhofen pterodactyloids.

MONTANAZHDARCHO Padian, Ricqlés and Horner 1995

Azhdarchia.

Name derivation: "Montana" + "azhdarchid."

Type species: *M. minor* Padian, Ricqlés and Horner 1995.

Occurrence: Upper Two Medicine Formation, Glacier County, Blackfeet Indian Nation, Montana, United States.

Age: Late Cretaceous (Campanian).

Holotype: MOR 691, most of left wing, including humerus, ulna, partial radius, proximal and partial medial carpals, wing metacarpal, and partial first wing phalanx, also right and partial left scapulocoracoids, partial mandible, crushed cervical vertebra, natural impression of another wing phalanx.

Diagnosis of genus: Pterodactyloid having small, subcircular orbit located below midline of nasal-orbital fenestra; ventrally directed occiput; elongate cervical vertebrae having reduced or absent neural spines; brachial flange on coracoid more than half total length of shaft; wing phalanges II and III T-shaped in cross section; elongate humeral deltopectoral crest without distal expansion (McGowen, Padian, de Sosa and Harmon 2002).

Diagnosis of *M. minor*: Small adult size (wingspan approximately 2.5 meters) relative to other azhdarchids; ulna of equal or greater length than wing metacarpal (McGowen, Padian, de Sosa and Harmon 2002).

Adult small compared to related forms, *e.g.*, the gigantic *Quetzalcoatlus*.

NESODACTYLUS Colbert 1969 — (=*Nesodon*)

Pterosauria *incertae sedis*.

Name derivation: Greek *nesos* = "island" + Greek *dactylos* = "finger."

Type species: *N. hesperius* Colbert 1969.

Occurrence: Viñales, north of Pina del Rio, western Cuba.

Age: Late Jurassic (Oxfordian).

Holotype: AMNH 2000, incomplete skeleton including skull fragment, ?right postorbital squamosal bar, quadrates, ?other skull elements, isolated vertebrae (at least five or six cervicals, several dorsals, one sacral, caudals), long and ossified caudal tendons (indicating long tail), scapulae, coracoids, sternum, humeri, radii, ulnae, left and right carpi, metacarpals I–IV, left and right proximal phalanges of digit IV, miscellaneous left and right prepubes, head of left femur, distal end of right femur, at least one metatarsal, ribs.

Diagnosis of genus (as for type species): Comparable in size with *Rhamphorhynchus*; sternum very strongly keeled, posterior border pointed (rather than transversely straight); forelimb relatively large, humerus proportionally larger than in *Rhamphorhynchus*; humerus and first wing phalanx extremely long; prepubis expanded, platelike; hindlimbs apparently comparatively robust, long (Wellnhofer 1978, based in part on Colbert 1969).

First pterosaur found in Cuba, apparently with longer, more heavily constructed wings and hindlimbs than *Rhamphorhynchus*.

NESODON Jensen and Ostrom 1977 — (See *Nesodactylus*.)

Name derivation: Greek *nesos* = "island" + Greek *odous* = "tooth."

Type species: *N. hesperius* Jensen and Ostrom 1977.

NORIPTERUS Yang 1973

Dsungaripteridae.

Name derivation: Mongolian *nuur* = "lake" + Greek *pteron* = "wing."

Type species: *N. complicidens* Yang 1973.

Occurrence: Upper part of Lower Cretaceous of Junggar Basin, Xinjiang Uygur Autonomous Region, northwestern China.

Age: Early Cretaceous.

Holotype: IVPP 64041, rostral part of skull, lower jaw, postcrania including numerous vertebrae, parts of limbs, partial pelvis, wing fragments.

Diagnosis of genus (as for type species): Small, about one third smaller than *Dsungaripterus*; rostral part of lower jaw edentulous (as in *Dsungaripterus*), present teeth spaced apart from one another; cervical vertebra narrow, long; angle between scapula and coracoid not great; distal end of coracoid seemingly not connected to sternum; shaft of humerus rather long; ratio of ulna to metacarpal 0.7; manual phalangeal formula (2, 3, 4, 4); xpedal phalangeal formula (2, 4, 4, 5, 0) (Wellnhofer 1978, after Yang 1973).

Lower jaws edentulous rostrally, teeth strong, set rather far apart, neck vertebrae long, closely related to the slightly larger *Dsungaripterus*.

NORMANNOGNATHUS   Buffetaut, LePage and LePage 1998 — (=?*Pterodactylus*)

Dsungaripteroidea.

Name derivation: Latin *Normannia* = "Normandy [Medieval Latin spelling]" + Greek *gnathos* = "jaw."

Type species: *N. wellnhoferi* Buffetaut, LePage and LePage 1998.

Occurrence: Cliffs of Ecqueville, Octeville, Seine-Maritime, Haute-Normandie, France.

Age: Late Jurassic (Kimmeridgian).

Holotype: Musée Géologique Cantonal de Lausanne 59'583, rostral parts of upper jaw, associated mandible.

Diagnosis of genus (as for type species): Premaxilla having five teeth, maxilla with at least nine teeth, dentary with at least 14 teeth; teeth not markedly elongate, extending to tip of jaws; presence of tall, dorsally located sagittal crest with concave rostral edge, crest formed by premaxillae and beginning rostral to nasopreorbital fenestra (Buffetaut, LePage and LePage 1998).

Crest similar to that of *Dsungaripterus*, much higher than in the apparently closely related *Germanodactylus*.

NYCTODACTYLUS   Marsh 1881— (See *Nyctosaurus*.)

Name derivation: Greek *nykt* = "night" + Greek *dactylos* = "finger."

Type species: *N. gracilis* (Marsh 1876).

Note: Unnecessary renaming, Marsh incorrectly believing the name *Nyctosaurus* to be preoccupied.

NYCTOSAURUS   Marsh 1876 — (=*Nyctodactylus*)

Nyctosauridae.

Name derivation: Greek *nykt* = "night" + Greek *sauros* = "lizard."

Type species: *N. gracilis* Marsh 1876.

Other species: ?*N. bonneri* (Miller 1972), *N. lamegoi* Price 1953, *N. nanus* (Marsh 1881).

Occurrence: Niobrara Chalk Formation, upper and lower Smoky Hill Chalk Member, western Kansas, United States; Gramame Formation, Paraiba, Brazil.

Age: Late Cretaceous (Coniacian–early Campanian)

Holotype: YPM 1178, postcranial skeleton.

Diagnosis of genus (as for type species): Autapomorphies including the following: jaw edentulous; hyperelongate metacarpal IV, metacarpals I–III reduced, not reaching

Holotype skeleton (FHSM VP-11311) of the tentative species ?*Nyctosaurus bonneri*, collected from Logan County, Kansas.

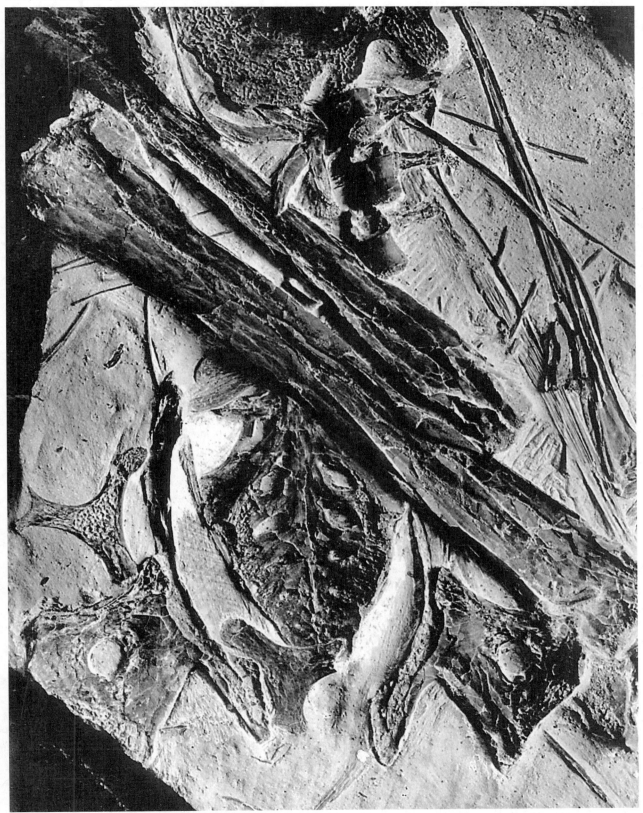

Nearly complete skeleton (FMNH collection) of *Nyctosaurus gracilis* collected by H. T. Martin from the Upper Cretaceous of western Kansas, and described by Samuel Wendel Williston in 1903.

Life restoration by Gregory S. Paul of the unusually crested pterosaur *Nyctosaurus gracilis.*

carpus (convergent with *Pteranodon* and *Quetzalcoatlus*); wing finger having only three digits (see Brown 1986); neural spines of midnotarial vertebrae T-shaped in cranial view; centra of dorsal vertebrae crescentic in cross section (Bennett 1994).

Diagnosis of *N. nanus*: Small; humerus with small head, enormous, downward-curving radial crest; scapula and coracoid strongly ankylosed; some trunk vertebrae with very long transverse processes, or ankylosed backward curved ribs (Marsh 1881).

Medium size (wingspan approximately 2.35 to 2.9 meters, or eight to 10 feet), closely related to *Pteranodon*; some (fully mature) specimens crested, the crest (apparently used primarily for display) being extremely long and very thin with superior ramus and caudal ramus, other (immature) specimens crestless, suggesting either sexual dimorphism, or, more likely, ontogenetic stages (see Bennett 2003); *N. gracilis* and ?*N. bonneri* possibly conspecific (Bennett 1994); referred species *N. lamegoi* distinguished as the first pterosaur named from South America.

Note: For photograph of crestless skeleton FMNH 25026 on exhibit, see *D:TE.*

ODONTORHYNCHUS   Stolley 1936 [*nomen dubium*] (preoccupied, Pelzeln 1868)

Pterosauria *incertae sedis.*

Name derivation: Greek *odous* = "tooth" + Greek *rhynkhos* = "snout."

Type species: *O. aculeoatus* Stolley 1936 [*nomen dubium*].

Occurrence: Solnhofen Lithographic Limestone, Unteres Unterithon, Solnhofen, Bavaria, southern Germany.

Age: Late Jurassic (early Tithonian).

Holotype: [Formerly geological collection of Hochschulsammlung Braunschweig, lost] skull with lower jaw.

Skull very delicately constructed; toothed upper jaw resembling that of *Rhamphorhynchus*; toothed lower jaw typical; front teeth long, slender, forwardly directed; pair of front teeth united together, extending beyond tip of dentary; joined premaxillary teeth and tip of upper jaw without teeth constituting excellent apparatus for prey capture (Wellnhofer 1978).

Small form, skull at best 6.5 to 7.0 centimeters long, length of jaws approximately five centimeters, lower jaws having long, narrow teeth.

ORNITHOCEPHALUS Soemmering 1812 [*nomen oblitum*]—(See *Pterodactylus.*)
Name derivation: Greek *ornis* = "bird" + Greek *kephale* = "head."
Type species: *O. antiquus* Soemmering 1812 [*nomen oblitum*].

ORNITHOCHEIRUS Seeley 1869—(=*Cimoliornis, Cretornis, Lithosteornis, Lonchodectes, Osteornis, Palaeornis*)
Ornithocheiridae.
Name derivation: Greek *ornis* = "bird" + Greek *cheir* = "hand."
Type species: *O. compressirostris* (Owen 1851).
Other species: *O. bunzeli* Seeley 1881, ?*O. clifti* (Mantell 1835), *O. daviesi* (Owen 1874), ?*O. diomedius* (Owen 1846), *O. wiedenrothi* Wild 1990.
Occurrence: Cambridge Greensand, Cambridge, Wealden, Tilgate Forest near Cuckfield, Hastings Beds, Sussex, Burnham chalk, Galt, Folkestone, Kent, ("*Ornithocheirus*" sp. A; Howse and Milner 1995) see "Near Swanage," "Middle Purbeck Beds," Purbeck Limestone Formation, Dorset, England; Gosau Formation, Austria; Turonian of Bohemia, Slovakia; Neocomian of Hanover, Germany; Albian of Gault, Le Meuse, Hauterivian of Haute-Marne, Albian of Aube, France; ?Toolebuc Formation, Queensland; ?Rio Belgrano Formation, Santa Cruz, Argentina; ?Campanian–Maastrichtian of New Zealand; ?Cenomianian–Turonian of Zaire, Africa.
Age: Late Jurassic (Tithonian) to Middle or Late Cretaceous (Cenomanian–?Maastrichtian).
Holotype: BMNH 39410, two jaw and other fragments.

Diagnosis of genus: Skull long, very slender, snout laterally compressed, tip of snout more or less blunt or pointed; teeth short, robust, of same size from tip to rear of snout; separation between teeth equal to width of tooth, teeth oval to flat in cross section, surface finely serrated longitudinally; palate roof with median keel, corresponding to channel at symphysis of lower jaw bordered by two protuberances; borders of toothed jaws parallel; jaw triangular in cross section; nasopreorbital opening much larger than orbit, situated high; scapula broadened distally, articulating with notarium; proximal tarsal fused with tibia; fibula generally no longer independent (Wellnhofer 1978).

Diagnosis of *O. compressirostris*: Rather large species; front part of skull with long, very narrow rostrum; numerous small teeth; total length of skull (calculated by Owen 1851) approximately 45 centimeters (Wellnhofer 1978).

Diagnosis of *O. wiedenrothi*: Lower jaw about 40 centimeters long; rostrum narrow at tip; tip of rostrum bifurcated ventrally, alveoli indicating 20–22 teeth slanting in rostral, dorsal, and lateral directions; teeth with long oval cross section; alveolar border increased; dorsal rostrum with very narrow median groove between raised symphysis borders, originating from rostral tip; joint end of lower jaws with retroarticular process, although without fenestra-like fossa depression as in *O. bunzeli*; distal caudal end of radius having pneumatic foramen; distal end of ulna with pneumatic foramen at rostral and caudal ends and articular surface; latter with oval carpal fovea and keellike tuberculum (Wild 1990).

Originally described as a species of *Pterodactylus*; large (upper jaw measuring 18 centimeters or seven inches in length), skull crestless with long, slender jaws, numerous small, sharp teeth extending to rostral tip of upper and lower jaws, apparently piscivorous; among the most common of known Cretaceous pterosaurs.

ORNITHOCHIRUS Cope 1872 [*nomen dubium*]—(See *Pteranodon.*)
Name derivation: Greek *ornis* = "bird" + Greek *cheir* = "hand."
Type species: *O. umbrosus* Cope 1872 [*nomen dubium*].

ORNITHOPTERUS Meyer 1846 [*nomen dubium*]—(See *Rhamphorhynchus*)
Name derivation: Greek *ornis* = "bird" + Greek *pteron* = "wing."
Type species: *O. lavateri* (Meyer 1838) [*nomen dubium*].

ORNITHOSTOMA Seeley 1871 [*nomen dubium*]
Pteranodontidae.
Name derivation: Greek *ornis* = "bird" + Greek *stoma* = "mouth."
Type species: *O. sedgwicki* Seeley 1871 [*nomen dubium*].
Occurrence: Cambridge Greensand, eastern England.
Age: Late Cretaceous.
Holotype: CAMSM B54.485, fragment of edentulous jaw.

Apparently similar to *Pteranodon*; referred fragmentary vertebra apparently large when complete, width of exapophysis 50 millimeters, centrum strongly dorsoventally compressed caudally.

OSTEORNIS Gervais 1844 [*nomen nudum*]—(See *Ornithocheirus.*)
Name derivation: Greek *osteon* = "bird" + Greek *ornis* = "bird."
Type species: [No species designated.]

PACHYRHAMPHUS Fitzinger 1843 [*nomen obli-tum*] — (See *Scaphognathus*)
Name derivation: Greek *pachys* = "thick" + Greek *rham-phos* = "beak."
Type species: *P. crassirostris* (Goldfuss 1831).

PALAEORNIS Mantell 1835 — (See *Ornithocheirus*.)
Name derivation: Greek *palaios* = "ancient" + Greek *ornis* = "bird."
Type species: *P. clifti* Mantell 1835.

PARAPSICEPHALUS Arthaber 1919
Scaphognathinae.
Name derivation: Greek *para* = "beside" + Greek *hapsis* = "arch" + Greek *kephale* = "head."
Type species: *P. purdoni* (Newton 1888).
Occurrence: Alum Shale, Loftus, Whitby, Yorkshire, England.
Age: Middle Jurassic (early Toarcian).
Holotype: Geological Survey of London collection, incomplete skull (missing approximately 30 percent of rostral part).

Diagnosis of genus (as for type species): Skull long, slender; orbit situated high, rounded-triangular; naris long, large; preorbital fenestra largest opening in skull; quadrate positioned high; postorbital fenestra large, rounded; palate with one wide interpterygoid opening; vomers long, narrow; toothed (Wellnhofer 1978).

Type specimen rare (among Pterosauria) in having endocast preserved.

PETEINOSAURUS Wild 1978; Dimorphodontidae.
Name derivation: Greek *peteinos* = winged" + Greek *sauros* = "lizard."
Type species: *P. zambellii* Wild 1978.
Occurrence: Calcare di Zorzino, Val Seriana, Alpine foothills, near Bergamo, Lombardy, northern Italy.
Age: Late Triassic (middle–late Norian).
Holotype: MCSNB 2886, disarticulated very incomplete skeleton (originally preserved in two slabs) including caudal part of mandibular ramus missing both extremities, several disarticulated skull bones, right (Dalla Vecchia 2003*b*) tibia plus fibula, wing phalanges, wing metacarpals, ?sternal plate, subadult (see Dalla Vecchia 1998; 2003*b*).

Diagnosis of genus (as for type species): Teeth trimorphodont; tip of mandible bearing couple of moderately long, narrow, recurved teeth, these followed by small, monocuspid teeth slightly curved backwards, higher than long, with mesial and distal sharp cutting margins, set in crater-like alveoli; most distal teeth corresponding with labial side of mandible being higher than lingual side; most

distal teeth no smaller than preceding teeth, triangular, longer than high, not recurved backwards, bearing at least two or three small cuspules along each cutting margin; fibula not reduced in length, slightly expanded distally, fused to upper part of lateral tibiotarsal condyle without distal condyle (Dalla Vecchia 2003*b*).

Among the earliest known pterosaurs, more primitive than *Eudimorphodon*, teeth single-cusped, flattened, with sharp mesial and distal cutting edges, wings relatively short (about twice length of hindlimbs, wingspan of about 60 centimeters or 24 inches), possibly insectivorous.

"PHOBETOR" Bakhurina 1986 (preoccupied, Kreyer 1844) [*nomen nudum*]
Dsungaripteridae.
Name derivation: Greek *phobetor* = "the frightening one."
Type species: "*P.*" *parvus* (Bakhurina 1982) [*nomen nudum*]
Occurrence: Zagan Zabsk Formation, West Mongolia.
Age: Early Cretaceous.

To be described formally by Natalie N. Bakhurina, originally described by Bakhurina (1982) as a new species of *Dsungaripterus*; medium-sized (wingspan approximately 1.5 meters or 4.9 feet), crested, possessing pointed teeth, rostral area of jaws toothless.

Life restoration by Todd Marshall of "*Phobetor*" *parvus*.

PHOSPHATODRACO Pereda Suberbiola, Bardet, Jouve, Iarochéne, Bouya and Amaghzaz 2003
Azhdarchoidea *incertae sedis.*
Name derivation: "Phosphate:" + Latin *draco* = "dragon."
Type species: *P. maurinaticus* Pereda Suberbiola, Bardet, Jouve, Iarochéne, Bouya and Amaghzaz 2003.
Occurrence: Sidi Daouri, northern Grand Doui, near Khouribga, upper "couche III," Qualad Abdoun Phosphatic Basin, Morocco.
Age: Late Cretaceous (late Maastrichtian).
Holotype: OCP DEK/GE 111, five cervical vertebrae, indeterminate bone.

Diagnosis of genus (as for type species): Large (estimated wingspan of 5 meters or approximately 17 feet); differs from other known azhdarchids in having very elongated caudal (eighth) cervical vertebra, length more than 50 percent that of fifth cervical vertebra, prominent neural spine almost height of centrum, neural spine squarely truncated at top, very caudally located; maximum vertebral length/cranial width between prezygapophyses ratio of midseries cervical vertebrae about 4.3 (fifth cervical), 4.1 (sixth cervical) (Pereda Suberbiola, Bardet, Jouve, Iarochéne, Bouya and Amaghzaz 2003).

Described as an "azhdarchid"; large, one of the few "azhdarchids" known from a relatively complete neck, one of the latest known pterosaurs, its discovery documenting the first occurrence of Late Cretaceous "Azhdarchidae" in northern Africa.

PLATALEORHYNCHUS Howse and Milner 1995
Gnathosaurinae.
Name derivation: Latin *Platalea* [genus of modern spoonbill bird]" + Greek *rhynkhos* = "snout."
Type species: *P. streptorophorodon* Howse and Milner 1995.
Occurrence: Quarry near Langton Matravers, "Middle Purbeck Beds," Purbeck Limestone Formation, Dorset, England.
Age: Late Jurassic or Early Cretaceous (Tithonian or Berriasian).
Holotype: BMNH R.11957 (previously, Corfe Castle Museum and Dorset County Museum collections), incomplete rostrum bearing terminal spatula with teeth.

Diagnosis of genus (as for type species): Large ctenochasmatid, skull at least 400 millimeters in length (assuming *Gnathosaurus*-like proportions); spatula roughly circular, relatively sharply demarcated from narrow rostrum caudal to it; spatula with 22 teeth having shallow roots not reaching to center of spatula; rostral tip of palatines forming slender point wedged between two premaxillaries; palatal face of spatula and anterior rostrum partly covered in rugose bone, indicative of presence of keratinous pad; no ridge on midline of palate; entire rostrum bearing more than 62 (perhaps up to 76) teeth (Howse and Milner 1995).

Restoration by paleontologist Stafford C. B. Howse of the head of *Plataleorhynchus streptophorodon*, based on *Gnathosaurus* and *Ctenochasma*, showing the relationship of the spatula to the head. (After Howse and Milner 1995.)

Various features (*e.g.*, more differentiated terminal spatula, relatively smaller teeth [based on alveoli size], palatal surface apparently covered by horny surface) suggesting a slightly different method of feeding than that employed by other large ctenochasmatids, this pterosaur possibly having "used its spatula and anterior dentition to rake through mud or weed to disturb animals in the water or substratum with the horny spatula as they were disturbed."

PREONDACTYLUS Wild 1984
Pterosauria *incertae sedis.*
Name derivation: Italian *Preone* [Preone valley]" + Greek *dactylos* = "finger."
Type species: *P. buffarinii* Wild 1984.
Occurrence: Dolomia di Formi, Udine, Preone valley, Alps of the Veneto, Nando Buffarini, Seazza Creek, "dolomia di Formi" (lower Norian), Rio Seazza Valley, Preone, province of Udine, Italy.
Age: Late Triassic (?early–late Norian).
Holotype: MFSN 1770, negative print of skeleton (bones destroyed), subadult (see Dalla Vecchia 2003*b*).

Diagnosis of genus (as for type species): Heterodonty between upper and lower jaws; premaxillary and mesial mandibular teeth relatively narrow, elongated, recurved backwards; one to ?three very enlarged, triangular maxillary teeth below ascending process of maxilla, followed distally by triangular teeth that decrease regularly in size; maxillary teeth serrated; numerous small teeth in lower jaw distal to first larger teeth; large, elliptical and rostrocaudally very elongated narial opening; tip of snout made of short, dorsally convex premaxilla; dentary less than half length of complete lower jaw (Dalla Vecchia 2003*b*).

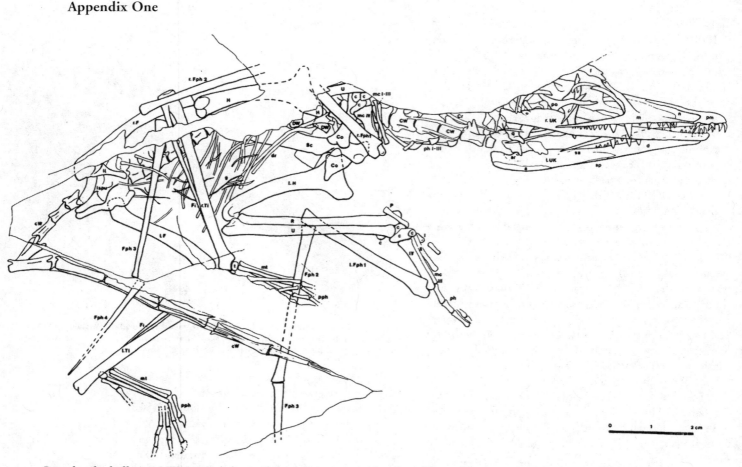

Preondactylus buffarinii, MFSN 1770, holotype skeleton (reconstruction based on silicon-rubber impression). Scale = 2 cm. (After Wild 1984.)

Among the earliest known pterosaurs; small, wings relatively short (estimated wingspan from 45 to less than 50 centimeters; see Wellnhofer 1991*b* and Dalla Vecchia 1998, respectively), legs long, possibly insectivorous or piscivorous, ?ancestral to the similar (in body proportions) *Dorygnathus*; basal member of Pterosauria (Unwin 2003); disarticulated skeleton (MFSN 1891) designated cf. *P. buffarinii*, from Rio Seazza Valley, found in gastric pellet (Dalla Vecchia, Muscio and Wild 1989).

PRICESAURUS   Martins Neto 1986 [*nomen dubium*]
Pterosauria *incertae sedis*.
Name derivation: "[Llellwyn I.] Price" + Greek *sauros* = "lizard."
Type species: *P. megalodon* Martins Neto 1986 [*nomen dubium*].
Occurrence: Santana Formation. Araripe Plateau, Brazil.
Age: Early Cretaceous (Aptian).

PTENODACTYLUS   Seeley 1869 — (preoccupied, Gray 1845; see *Pterodactylus*.)
Name derivation: Greek *ptenos* = "wing" + Greek *dactylos* = "finger."

PTENODRACON   Lydekker 1888 — (See *Pterodactylus*.)
Name derivation: Greek *ptenos* = "wing" + Greek *drakos* = "dragon."
Type species: *P. brevirostris* (Soemmering 1817).

PTERANODON   Marsh 1876 — (=*Geosternbergia*, *Ornithochirus*)
Pteranodontidae.
Name derivation: Greek *pteron* = "wing" + Greek *an* = "without" + Greek *odous* = "tooth."
Type species: *P. longiceps* Marsh (1876).
Other species: *P. harpyia* (Cope 1872) [*nomen dubium*], *P. ingens* (Marsh 1872) [*nomen dubium*], *P. occidentalis* (Marsh 1872) [*nomen dubium*], *P. sternbergi* Harksen 1966, *P. umbrosus* (Cope 1872) [*nomen dubium*], *P. velox* (Marsh 1872) [*nomen dubium*].
Occurrence: Smoky Hill Chalk Member, Niobrara Chalk Formation, western Kansas and South Dakota, Sharon Springs Member, Pierre Shale Formation, western Kansas, South Dakota, Wyoming, ?Mooreville Chalk Member, ?Selma Formation, Alabama, ?Merchantville Formation, Delaware, United States.
Age: Late Cretaceous (Coniacian–early Campanian).
Holotype: YPM 1177, almost complete skull (lacking most of cranial crest).

Skeleton of the giant pterosaur *Pteranodon longipes*.

Diagnosis of genus: Cranial crest formed by frontals, directed upward or backward from skull; premaxillary crest having relatively straight dorsal margin, not rounded in profile; jaws edentulous, marginal ridges raised; beak long, slender, premaxillae and dentaries tapering to points; premaxillae extending beyond end of mandible; mandibular symphysis about two thirds length of mandible; ceratobranchials of hyoid appartus greatly reduced or unossified; nasal process reduced; neural spines of dorsal and sacral vertebrae narrow craniocaudally; notarial and synsacral supraneural plates formed of ossified interspinous ligaments; postacetabular process of ilium contacting neural spines of caudal synsacral vertebrae, fused with them in mature adults; proximal caudal vertebrae having duplex centra; distal caudal vertebrae reduced, coossified to form caudal rod; proximal pneumatic foramen of humerus on ventral surface near proximal end of deltopectoral crest; nutrient foramen on dorsal surface of humerus; distal pneumatic foramen of humerus on ventral surface, just proximal to and between condyles; metacarpus length equal to or greater than 1.5 times length of antebrachium; proximal ends of metacarpals I to III not reaching distal

Skeleton (cast) of the giant pterosaur *Pteranodon longipes* mounted in quadrupedal walking position.

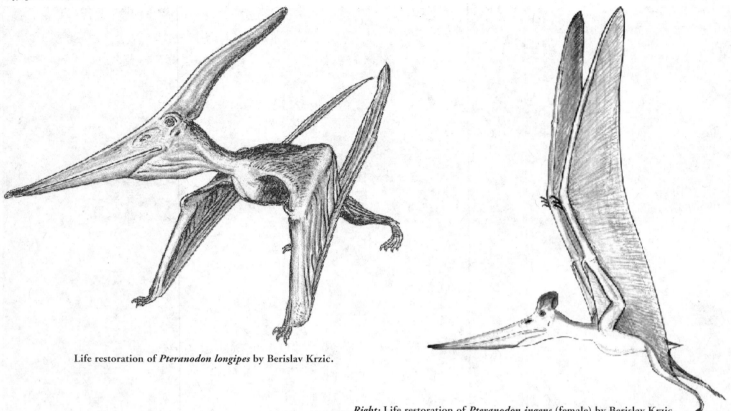

Life restoration of *Pteranodon longipes* by Berislav Krzic.

Right: Life restoration of *Pteranodon ingens* (female) by Berislav Krzic.

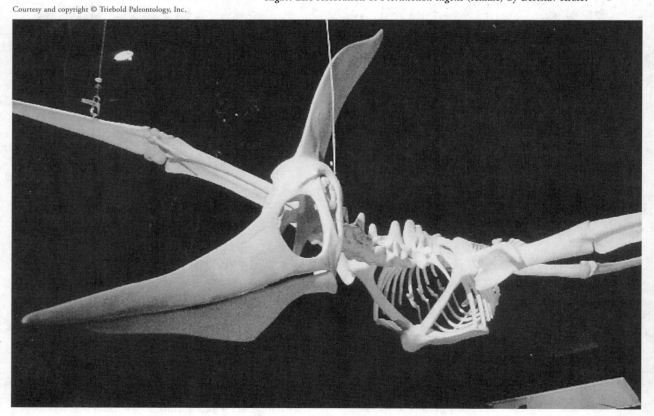

Skeletal cast of *Pteranodon ingens*.

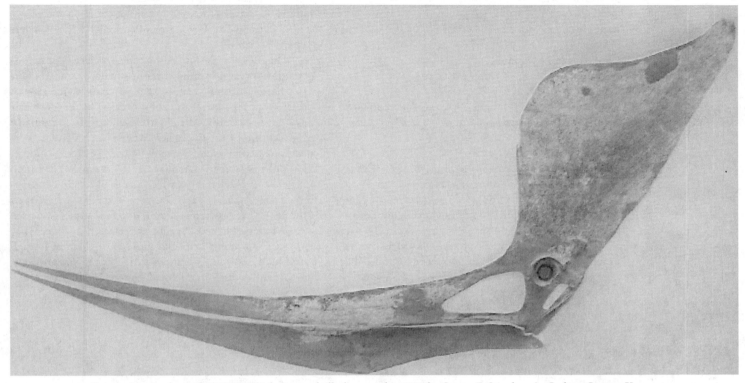

Pteranodon sternbergi, FHSM VP-339, holotype skull, discovered in 1952 by George F. Sternberg in Graham County, Kansas.

syncarpal; distal syncarpal lacking facets for meta-carpals I to III; distal end of wing metacarpal without elevation between condyles (some characters may not be synapomorphies of *Pteranodon*, although none are shared with other known pteranodontids) (Bennett 1994).

Diagnosis of *P. longiceps*: Cranial crest blade-like, caudally directed; differing from *P. sternbergi* in caudal direction of crest, crest in males being arcuate and tapering evenly from base to end, and occiput being possibly more reclined (Bennett 1994).

Diagnosis of *P. sternbergi*: Crest directed upward, bulbous in profile and broader above base in males; premaxillae extending moderate distance up front of crest; apparently having median process formed by palatines or vomers extending caudally into confluent choanae (Bennett 1994).

Cranial crest extending dorsoventrally from back of head, toothless, tail extremely short, among the largest of pterosaur genera (wingspan of *P. ingens* approximately seven meters or 23 feet, that of *P. sternbergi* greater); this genus accounting for the majority of pterosaur specimens from the Niobrara Formation; apparently piscivorous, with a life style similar to that of extant seabirds.

Note: For a photograph of a skeletal cast of *Pteranodon* specimen USNM 5472 on exhibit at the National Museum of Natural History, see *D:TE*.

Life restoration by Gregory S. Paul of *Pteranodon sternbergi*.

PTERODACTYLE Cuvier 1809 [*nomen oblitum*]—(See *Pterodactylus*.)

Name derivation: Greek *pteron* = "wing" + Greek *dactylos* = "finger."

[No species designated.]

PTERODACTYLUS Cuvier 1809—(=*Macrotrachelus, Ornithocephalus, Ptenodracon, Pterodactyle, Pterotherium;* =?*Normannognathus*)

Pterodactylidae.

Type species: *P. antiquus* (Soemmering 1812).

Other species: *P. grandis* Rafinesque 1815.

Occurrence: Solnhofen Lithographic Limestone, Unteres Untertithon, Solnhofen, Eichstätt, Mörnsheim, Bavaria, Kelheim, Bavaria, southern Germany; Cerin, Department Ain, Purbeckian, Boulogne-sur-Mer, France; Kimmeridge Clay, Weymouth, Dorset, England; Obere Saurier-Mergel, Tendaguru, Tanzania.

Age: Late Jurassic (Kimmeridgian–early Tithonian).

Holotype: Bayerische Staatssammlung für Paläontologie und Historische Geologie collection, AS.I.739, complete skeleton.

Diagnosis of genus (as for type species): Skull elongate, dorsal margin straight; snout slender, elongate; fenestra nasoantorbital length approximately twice that of orbit; about 90 conical and robust teeth; upper tooth row reaching or extending distally to level of rostral margin of nasoantorbital fenestra; nasal process very slender, perpendicular to maxilla (Jouve 2004).

First described pterodactyloid; the most common species, *P. kochi*, having a wingspan of about 18 centimeters (seven inches); based on recent studies by Bennett (2003*b*) of Solnhofen material, *P. antiquus* adults possessed a premaxilla crest; most specimens referred to *P. kochi* belong in *P. antiquus*; and *P. longicollum* is distinct from *P. antiquus* based on differences in teeth and proportions, the former representing a distinct genus [=Gnathosaurus].

Photograph by Ron Testa, courtesy The Field Museum, negative number GEO83954.

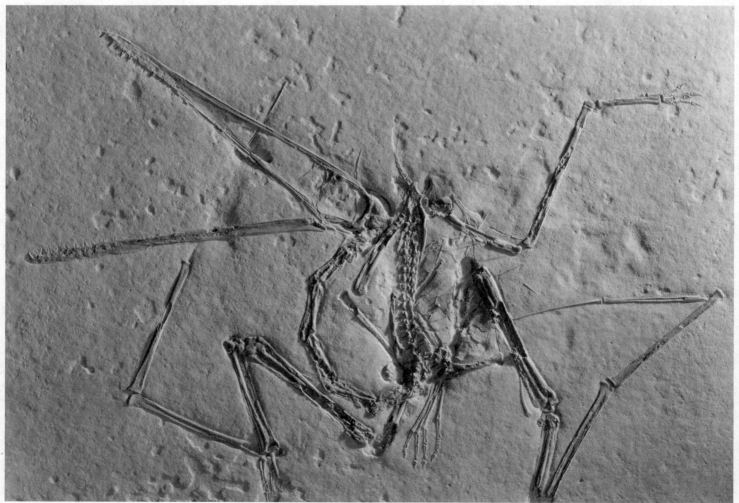

Cast (FMNH PR424) of the holotype skeleton (Bayerische Staatssammlung für Paläontologie und Historische Geologie collection, AS.I.739) of *Pterodactylus antiquus*.

Skeleton referred to *Pterodactylus antiquus*.

Largest species *P. grandis* had a wingspan of over eight feet.

Note: Phylogenetic analysis by Andres and Ji (2003) found the genus *Pterodactylus* to be paraphyletic, with the referred species *P. elegans* Wagner 1861 and *P. micronyx* Meyer 1856 belonging to the Ctenochasmatidae, and *P. longicollom*, and a sister group of *P. antiquus* plus *P. kochi* constituting successive sister taxa to a clade comprising "Cycnorhamphidae" and Ctenochasmatidae. This implies "that the distribution of cranial crests in pterosaurs has a wider distribution than is preserved in the fossil record." Bennett (1996) found no substantial evidence to show that *P. antiquus* and *P. kochi* are not conspecific, but stated that "further work is needed to resolve the problem." Subsequently, Jouve (2004) referred *P. elegans* to the genus *Ctenochasma* (see entry) and found *P. kochi* to be a junior synonym of *P. antiquus*. That author could not determine if *P. micronyx*, known only from juvenile material, is synonymous with *Ctenochasma roemeri*, *Ctenochasma* sp., or *Gnathosaurus subulatus*.

PTERODAUSTRO Bonaparte 1970—(=*Puntanipterus*) Ctenochasmatinae.
Name derivation: Greek *pteron* = "wing" + Latin *de austro* = "from the south."
Type species: *P. guinazui* Bonaparte 1970.
Occurrence: Loma del *Pterodaustro* site, lower member of Lagarcito Formation, Parque Nacional Sierra de las Quijadas, La Cruz Formation, province of San Luis, Argentina.
Age: Upper Jurassic–Early Cretaceous.
Holotype: PLV 2572, skull fragment, vertebrae, elements of appendicular skeleton including almost complete right humerus.

Diagnosis of genus (as for type species): Autapomorphies including the following: skull characterized by remarkably long, slender, upwardly curved preorbital region, comprising more than 85 percent of skull length; spatulate teeth dentary differing from those of all other known pterosaurs; maxillary teeth not set in alveoli, associated with row of ossicles (Bonaparte 1971); postorbital separated from frontal; quadratojugal apparently forming ventral margin of infratemporal fenestra (Sanchez 1973)

Life restoration of *Pterodactylus antiquus* including recently acquired information regarding preserved pterosaurian soft tissues. (After Frey, Tischlinger, Buchy and Martill 2003.)

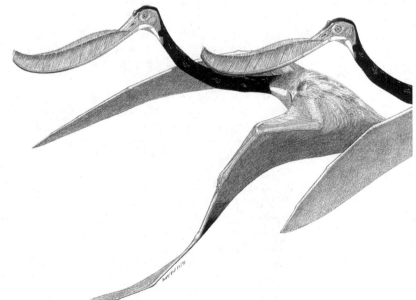

Life restoration by Gregory S. Paul of the "filter feeding" pterosaur *Pterodaustro guinazui*.

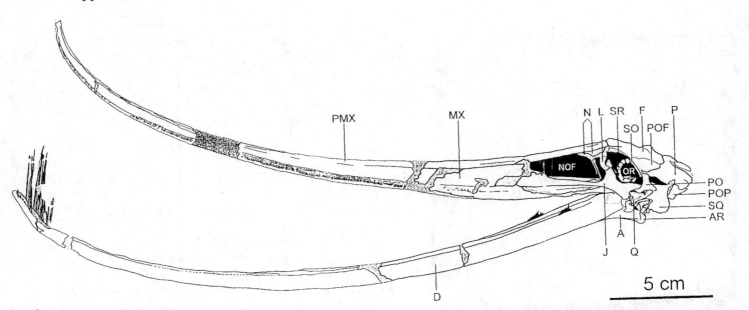

Pterodaustro guinazui, MHIN-UNSI-GEO-V-57, referred skull and jaws (left lateral view) from the Lagarcito Formation of Argentina. (After Chiappe, Kellner, Rivarola, Davila and Fox 2000.)

(mostly formed by quadrate in other pterosaurs; see Wellnhofer 1978); four jugal processes [possibly autapomorphic]; mandible having large number of teeth (almost 500 per ramus), filamentlike (unique among known pterosaurs); mandible extremely long, following extension of preorbital region of skull (lower jaw considerably shorter than preorbital region in other known pterosaurs; see Bennett 1991) (Chiappe, Kellner, Rivarola, Davila and Fox 2000).

First pterosaur found in Argentina, the second in South America, first to offer strong evidence that pterosaurs evolved a filter-feeding morphology atypical for tetrapods, probably a plankton eater; among the most specialized of pterosaurs, with hundreds of filament-like mandibular teeth and other skull features, its cranial morphology corroborating a sister-taxon relationship with *Ctenochasma*, as suggested by previous authors (Chiappe *et al.*).

Note: The genus *Puntanipterus*, based by Bonaparte and Sanchez (1975) on several postcranial bones (PVL 3869) from the La Cruz Formation, should be regarded as a junior synonym of *Pterodaustro* (L. Codorniú and L. M. Chiappe, personal communication 2004).

PTEROMONODACTYLUS Teriaev 1967 —(See *Rhamphocephalus*.)
Name derivation: Greek *pteron* = "wing" + Greek *monos* = "alone" + Greek *dactylos* = "finger."
Type species: *P. phyllurus* (Marsh 1882).

PTERORHYNCHUS Czerkas and Ji 2002
Rhamphorhynchidae *incertae sedis*.

Name derivation: Greek *pteron* = "wing" + Greek *rhynchus* = "snout."
Type species: *P. wellnhoferi* Czerkas and Ji 2002.
Occurrence: Haifangou Formation, Daofugou Village, Chefeng County, Inner Mongolia (east part), Autonomous Region, China.
Age: ?Middle to ?Late Jurassic.
Holotype: CAGS02-IG-gausa-2/DM 608, almost complete and articulated skeleton, missing last two distal phalanges of [manual] digit IV, integumentary impressions of wing and headcrest, wing membranes with altinofibrils, multi-filamentous integumentary structures, slab and counterslab.

Diagnosis of genus (as for type species): Sagittal headcrest (presumably made of keratinous material) unique among known "rhamphorhynchoids"; crest having low ridge having vertical striae, located beneath leading edge of remaining crest, extending well above and across caudal two-thirds of skull; tail and wing about equal in length; tail membrane apparently long, low, extending more than distal two-thirds of tail (Czerkas and Ji 2002*a*).

"Hair-like" integumentary structures possibly offering "evidence on the origin of feathers and the possibility of a remarkably early ancestral relationship between pterosaurs and birds."

PTEROTHERIUM Fischer 1813 [*nomen oblitum*] —(See *Pterodactylus*.)
Name derivation: Greek *pteron* = "wing" + Greek *therion* = "beast."
[No species designated.]

PUNTANIPTERUS Bonaparte and Sanchez 1975 —
(See *Pterodaustro*.)

Name derivation: Spanish *Puntano* [native of San Luis] + Greek *pteron* = "wing."

Type species: *P. globosus* Bonaparte and Sanchez 1975.

QUETZALCOATLUS   Lawson 1975

Azhdarchia.

Name derivation: "Quetzalcoatlus [feathered serpent god of the Aztecs]."

Type species: *Q. northropi* Langston 1978.

Occurrence: Javelina Formation, Big Bend National Park, Brewster County, West Texas, United States; ?Oldman Formation, Alberta, Canada.

Age: Late Cretaceous (Maastrichtian).

Holotype: TMM 41450-3, left humerus, partial radius, ulna, proximal and distal carpals, metacarpals, phalanges of manual digit IV.

Diagnosis of genus (as for type species): Humerus larger than in any other known pterosaur; mandibles long, slender; dentary edentulous, apparently expanding rostrally, becoming triangular toward tip; cervical vertebrae slender, caudal end of cervical overhanging bulbous end of centrum, the latter giving rise ventrolaterally to short posthypapophyses; rostral end of cervical vertebrae having stout prezygapophyses extending far beyond recessed procoelous centrum and weakly developed prehypapophyses (Lawson 1975*b*).

First described (with neither naming the genus and species nor designating a type specimen) by Lawson (1975*a*); largest known flying creature (wingspan more than 11 meters [approximately 36 to 39 feet]), head with short crest, neck very long; possibly piscivorous, possibly an eater of carrion, soaring ability probably similar to that of vultures (Lawson 1975*a*).

RHAMPHINION   Padian 1984

Pterosauria *incertae sedis*.

Name derivation: Greek *rhamphos* = "beak" + Greek *inion* = "back of head."

Type species: *R. jenkinsi* Padian 1984.

Life restoration by Gregory S. Paul of *Quetzalcoatlus northropi*, the largest known pterosaur.

Occurrence: Foxtrot Mesa locality, Middle Kayenta Formation, Little Colorado River Valley, northeastern Arizona.

Age: Early Jurassic.

Holotype: MNA V 4500, skull material comprising occipital region, fragment of left jugal, ?mandibular fragment with two associated teeth and impression of third tooth, unidentifiable bone fragment.

Diagnosis of genus (as for type species): Nearly rounded antorbital and orbital margins next to ascending process of jugal; apparent suture between maxilla and jugal having long, low sloping contact, orbit located at approximately same height above tooth row as antorbital opening (Padian 1984*b*).

Earliest record of pterosaurs in the Western Hemisphere; skull measuring 4.0 by 3.5 centimeters; shape of jugal not similar to pterodactyloids, suggesting referral to "Rhamphorhynchoidea" (Padian 1984*b*).

RHAMPHOCEPHALUS   Seeley 1880 [*nomen dubium*]
(=*Dolichoramphus, Ornithopterus, Pteromonodactylus*)

Pterosauria *incertae sedis*.

Name derivation: Greek *rhamphos* = "beak" + Greek *kephale* = "head."

Type species: *R. bucklandii* (Meyer 1832) [*nomen dubium*].

Other species: ?*R. depressirostris* (Huxley 1859) [*nomen dubium*], *R. prestwichi* (Seeley 1880) [*nomen dubium*].

Occurrence: Stonesfield Slate, Stonesfield, Oxfordshire, ?Sarsden near Chipping Norton, Oxfordshire, Kineton near Stow-on-the-Wold, Oxfordshire, England.

Age: Middle Jurassic (Bathonian).

Holotype: Professor Queketts collection, mandible.

Diagnosis of genus (as for type species): Mesial teeth of lower jaw larger than distal teeth, almost vertically oriented; interorbital space very narrow; scapula and coracoid fused; five sacral vertebrae (Wellnhofer 1978).

?*R. depressirostris* very large species; lower jaw with five teeth; *R. prestwichi* with postorbital part of skull very long; strong compression of facial region between orbits (Wellnhofer 1978).

Originally described as a new species of *Pterodactylus*; presumed wingspan of about 0.9 to 1.2 meters (from about three to four feet), possibly related to *Rhamphorhynchus*.

RHAMPHORHYNCHUS   Meyer 1846

Rhamphorhynchinae.

Name derivation: Greek *rhamphos* = "beak" + Greek *rhynkhos* = "snout."

Type species: *R. muensteri* (Goldfuss 1831).

Occurrence: Oberjura, Unteres Untertithon, Nusplingen (Württemberg), Solnhofen Lithographic Limestone,

Cast of an excellently preserved, articulated skeleton of *Rhamphorhynhus muenstri* at the Ulster Museum, original specimen at the Jura-Museum in Eichstatt.

Solnhofen, Langenaltheim, Eichstätt, Schernfeld, Wintershof, Workerszell Bavaria, Zandt, Bavaria, southern Germany; Oxford Clay, Peterborough, Huntingdonshire, St. Ives, Huntingdonshire, Kimmeridge Clay, Weymouth, England; Oberjura, Obere Saurier-Mergel, Tendaguru-Schichten, Tanzania; ?Kota Formation, Unterjura, India; Pedróga, Guimarota, near Leiria, Portugal.

Age: Middle to Late Jurassic (Callovian–early Tithonian).

Holotype: Teyler-Museum collection, number 6924, skeleton.

Diagnosis of genus (as for type species): Skull elongate with long snout; lower jaw convex upwards; rostral-most part of jaw edentulous; 10 teeth in upper jaw (four premaxillary, six maxillary), seven teeth in each lower jaw;

CYCNORHAMPHUS
This pterosaur, with a 10-inch wingspread, had a duck-like head and neck, although its jaws have small teeth.
JURASSIC   NEAR SOLNHOFEN, BAVARIA   C. M. 11,428

RHAMPHORHYNCHUS GEMMINGI
This beautifully preserved pterosaur has a wingspread of 42 inches (1065 mm.). It was a small-headed, large-eyed species, with teeth pointing forward in dagger-shaped jaws which terminate in a toothless spear. (Part of one wing and half of the tail missing).
JURASSIC   SOLENHOFEN, BAVARIA   C. M. 11,427

Skeleton of *Rhamphorhynchus muenstri* (specimen originally referred to *R. gemmingi*).

large teeth in rostral area of jaw, inclining forwardly and outwards, shorter teeth farther back in jaw; fourth tooth up upper jaw vertical, inserted more laterally in premaxilla; quadrate inclined rostally and outwardly; preorbital fenestra generally rather larger than nasal, both smaller than orbit; infratemporal fenestra narrow, supratemporal opening larger, rounder; first phalanx of wing-finger longer, approximately length of skull; femur shorter than humerus; prepubis slender, resembling clothespin, continuing laterally; second phalanx of fifth pedal digit curved, shorter than first (Wellnhofer 1978).

Originally described as a species of *Pterodactylus*; small (wingspan ranging from about three centimeters or 1.18 inches to 1.75 meters or 5.7 feet, apparently piscivorous, apparently sexually dimorphic (putative males having relatively longer skull and flight digit).

Note: Bennett (1996) regarded all Solnhofen referred

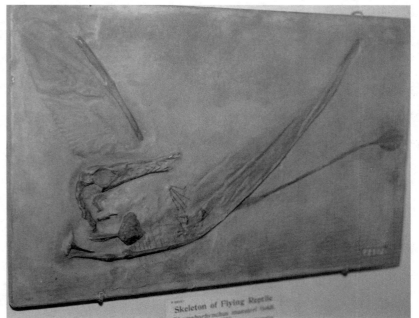

Skeleton of Flying Reptile

Rhamphorynchus muensteri, cast of holotype skeleton of *R. phyllurus*, a "new species" that Othniel Charles Marsh named and described in 1882. The original Solnhofen specimen is distinguished as the first to be found preserving flight membranes.

Life restoration by Gregory S. Paul of *Rhamphorhynchus muensteri*.

species (see Wellnhofer 1978) of *Rhamphorhynchus* as growth stages of the type species.

SANTANADACTYLUS   Buisonje 1980

?Ornithocheiroidea.

Name derivation: "Santana [Formation]" + Greek *dactylos* = "finger."

Type species: *S. brasilensis* Buisonje 1980.

Other species: *S. araripensis* Wellnhofer 1985, *S. pricei* Wellnhofer 1985, *S. spixi* Wellnhofer 1985.

Occurrence: Romualdo Member of Santana Formation, Barra do Jardim, Araripe Plateau, Province of Ceara, northeastern Brazil.

Age: Early Cretaceous (Aptian).

Holotype: Geological Institute of the University of Amsterdam number 4894, proximal portion of right humerus, ankylosed glenoidal parts of right scapulocoracoid.

Diagnosis of genus (as for type species): Large sized, with ankylosed area swollen cranially, having large, vertically positioned longitudinal foramen in less bulbous ankylosed area; original suture between scapula and coracoid completely obliterated except in glenoidal cavity; rather low acromion developed parallel to exterior side of scapula near glenoidal cavity; coracoid with cranial process, sharply protruding from shaft near glenoidal cavity, separated from coracoidal part of this cavity by deep fossa; fossa having wide foramen, divided into two deep cavities by small bony bridge; glenoidal cavity with vertically placed long axis consisting of two surfaces, set at obtuse angle; smaller, upper articular surface of scapula, slightly concave vertically and horizontally; larger, lower articular surface of coracoid, slightly concave vertically, convex horizontally; humerus with broad, crescent-shaped proximal articular surface, divided along oblique line into two areas with slightly different convexity; from proximal articular surface, gradually broadening deltopectoral radial crest starting at opposite side of crescent-shaped proximal surface, extending distally over almost same length as radial crest; humerus, in proximal part of its palmar side, slightly concave lengthwise, deeply concave perpendicular to shaft; more distally palmar, shaft becoming convex in both directions, almost circular in cross section where distal part of radial crest meets shaft; humerus possessing wide foramen pneumaticum, two-fifths down ulnar crest on convex anconal side; preserved proximal portion of humerus measuring 90 millimeters, total humeral length estimated at between 210 and 270 millimeters; thickness of compact outer bone layer in humeral shaft less than 0.5 millimeters; large, extremely elongated midcervical vertebrae, having relatively low neural crest over total length of neural arch; two ventrolateral distal apophyses projecting slightly beyond reniform hinder ball of centrum; one single, centrally placed proximal apophysis; apophyses nonarticular; neural canal constricted, five millimeters wide, flanked by lateral openings or pneumatic foramina of same size; two elongated foramina in each side of centrum, about halfway its length, placed slightly obliquely; thickness of compact outer bone layer in cervical vertebrae less than 0.3 millimeters (Buisonje 1980).

Diagnosis of *S. araripensis*: Large species distinguished by the following: skull without nasal process; quadrate with pterygoid and basisphenoid firmly joined; jaws gently curved ventrally; jaws probably narrowing to tips; dorsal edge of premaxilla with upper nasoparietal opening sharply keeled; fossa depression of lower jaw ascending slightly, retroarticular process steep caudally; creased upper edge of lateral process of humerus; proximal and distal carpals ascending; proximal carpals with pronounced tuberculum for carpal fovea of unla (Wellnhofer 1985).

Diagnosis of *S. pricei*: Smaller than *S. araripensis* and *S. brasilensis*; humerus without epiphysis of trochlea, upper edge of processus lateralis with bend (Wellnhofer 1985).

Diagnosis of *S. spixi*: Smaller than type species and *S. araripensis*; radius relatively strongly developed, two-thirds as robust as ulna; carpus with three carpals; proximal carpal squarish in outline; ulna small, ulnare tuburculum for carpal fovea; distal carpal with sharp, rectangular flat part dorsally; no joint facets for small metacarpals that are probably reduced proximally (Wellnhofer 1985).

Very large, relatively long-necked pterosaur, snout relatively short, laterally compressed, teeth in snout, wingspan up to about 5.7 meters (18.7 feet), wing extremely adapted for gliding rather than flapping flight.

SCAPHOGNATHUS Wagner 1861—(=*Brachytrachelus*, *Pachyrhamphus*)

Scaphognathinae.

Name derivation: Greek *scaphe* = "boat" + Greek *gnathos* = "jaw."

Type species: *S. crassirostris* (Goldfuss 1831).

Occurrence: Solnhofen Lithographic Limestone, Unteres Untertithon, Eichstätt, Mühlheim, Bavaria, southern Germany.

Age: Early Jurassic (early Tithonian).

Holotype: Universität Bonn collection, number 1304, almost complete skeleton.

Diagnosis of genus (as for type species): Skull with short snout, large openings; preorbital fenestra larger than nasal opening; quadrate situated in high position; teeth at tip of upper jaw, teeth [nine long teeth on each side was included in this diagnosis; but see Bennett 2004 and "Notes," below] inserted vertically in jaw; distalmost teeth very small; tip of lower jaw short diagonally, like prow of boat; except for front teeth of upper jaw, teeth are separated from each other; sternum heart-shaped; scapula and coracoid not fused; prepubis with only weak lateral process; first wing phalanx notably shorter than forearm, shorter than second and third wing phalanges; femur relatively long, about length of humerus; fifth pedal digit long (Wellnhofer 1978).

Originally described as a species of *Pterodactylus*; Medium-sized (wingspan of about 90 centimeters (3 feet); superficially resembling *Rhamphorhynchus*, with relatively shorter head, teeth long and in upright position, tips of jaws blunted, possibly insectivorous or piscivorous.

Notes: The "mane" of long fibers reported by Meyer (1846, 1859) in a specimen of *Scaphognathus*, an interpretation rejected by subsequent workers, was confirmed by Tischlinger (2002) via investigation under ultraviolet light.

A third (juvenile) complete and articulated specimen of *S. crassirostris* from the Solnhofen Limestone, briefly described in an abstract by Bennett (2004), reveals—along with reexamination of the holotype—the following new details: Snout broader than previously thought; only two premaxillary teeth, six maxillary teeth, and five mandibular teeth, additional teeth being replacement teeth; skull

bone having dense, convoluted grain pattern suggesting bone was thicker and heavier than in other known Solnhofen pterosaurs of similar size; combination of skull shape, dentition, and robust bone suggesting adaptations for preying upon larger fishes than other Solnhofen pterosaurs; nine cervical vertebrae in this specimen (if first vertebra bearing large rib that articulates with sternum is interpreted as first dorsal vertebra, suggesting (if this interpretation is correct) that this genus as well as other rhamphorhynchoids and pterodactyloids possessed nine cervicals (not eight and seven, respectively, as traditionally believed), the number of cervicals thereby remaining constant throughout pterosaurian evolution.

SINOPTERUS Wang and Zhou 2002

Tapejaridae.

Name derivation: Greek *Sinai* = "China" + Greek *pteron* = "wing."

Type species: *S. dongi* Wang and Zhou 2002.

Other species: *S. gui* Li, Lü and Zhang 2002.

Occurrence: Jiufotang Formation, Jehol Group, western Liaoning Province, northeastern China.

Age: Early Cretaceous (Aptian.

Holotype: Well-preserved, almost complete skeleton.

Diagnosis of genus (as for type species): Small to medium size, skull large, toothless, wingspan approximately 1.2 meters (more than 3.75 feet); skull having bird-like pointed, horny beak; large bony crest extending from premaxilla to caudal margin of skull (Wang and Zhou 2002).

Diagnosis of *S. gui*: Small; 11 dorsal vertebrae fused into notarium, nearly equal in length; at least four sacral vertebrae; humerus longer than scapula; wing-metacarpal slightly shorter than first wing-phalanx; distal end of deltopectoral process not expanded; ratio of femur to tibia length approximately 0.49 (Li, Lü and Zhang 2002).

Possibly omnivorous, with diet of fish and plants; representing the first record of the Tapejaridae outside of Brazil and the earliest occurrence and most complete skeleton belonging to this family, suggests Jehol pterosaur fauna having links to Late Cretaceous South American forms; referred species *S. gui*, founded on an almost complete skeleton (BPV-077), the smallest toothless pterosaur yet found in the Jiufutang Formation (see Li *et al.*).

SIROCCOPTERYX Mader and Kellner 1999

?Ornithocheiridae.

Name derivation: "Sirocco [hot, dry North African wind] + Greek *pteron* = "wing."

Type species: *S. moroccoensis* Mader and Kellner 1999.

Occurrence: Near Beg'aa, southwest of Taouz, Province of Ksar es Souk, southern Morocco.

Age: Middle Cretaceous (Albian or Cenomanian).

Holotype: LINHM 016, fragmentary, rostral part of upper jaw with teeth.

Diagnosis of genus (as for type species): Snout relatively broad and massive, rostral tip straight, higher than in *Anhanguera*, lower than in "*Tropeognathus*" [=*Coloborhynchus*] (Mader and Kellner 1999).

Only pterosaur species yet named from Morocco; rugose, pitted bone surface possibly evidence of disease.

SORDES   Sharov 1971
Scaphognathinae.
Name derivation: Latin *sordes* = "filth [referring to evil spirit of Russian folklore]."
Type species: *S. pilosus* 1971.
Occurrence: Oberjura, Karatau mountains, Kazakhstan.
Age: Late Jurassic.
Holotype: Nearly complete skeleton including skin and hair impressions.

Diagnosis of genus (as for type species): Skull relatively short, length 3.5 times height; toothed down to tip of jaw; six or seven teeth in each dentary; teeth of lower jaw (with exception of first pair) inclined slightly distally; teeth of upper jaw vertical; (compared with *Rhamphorhynchus*) humerus and forearm long, metacarpus short, wing-finger quite shorter, notably shorter than tail; second and third wing phalanges of equal length, much shorter than first; fifth rudimentary wing phalanx; ?claw phalanx; prepubis slender, with lateral prolongation; tail lightly constructed, widened at distal end, but without rhomboid membrane; fifth pedal digit having three long phalanges; pedal phalangeal formula (2, 3, 4, 5, 3); wing membrane apparently very wide; brachiopatagium extending over tibia, possibly independent of tail (Wellnhofer 1978).

First pterosaur found preserving traces of "hair" (longest strand six millimeters or .24 inches in length) that covered the flight membrane with a thick coat of fine "fur" apparently covering the neck and body; head and teeth similar to those in *Scaphognathus*; membrane (*i.e.,* uropatagium) apparently stretched between hind legs, free of the tail, attached to separated fifth pedal digit and used as an active control surface for flight or landing (see Bakhurina and Unwin 1992).

TAPEJARA   Kellner 1989
Tapejaridae.
Name derivation: Tupi *tapejara* = "[in mythology of Tupi Indians] old being."

Life restoration by Todd Marshall of *Sordes pilosus* fishing.

Type species: *T. wellnhoferi* Kellner 1989.

Other species: *T. imperator* Campos and Kellner 1997, *T. navigans* Frey, Martill and Buchy 2003.

Occurrence: Crato Member, Santana Formation, Nova Olinda Member Konservat Lagerstätt, Crato Formation, Araripe Basin, northeastern Brazil.

Age: Early Cretaceous (Aptian).

Holotype: CD-R-080, incomplete skull including rostral part of both sides until part of nasopreorbital fenestra, lower part with lower margin of orbit and lower temporal fenestra, left lacrimal, unidentified bones.

Diagnosis of genus (as for type species): Large, very high sagittal crest on rostral part of skull, extended backwards; rostrum very inclined downwards; absence of mesial ridge on palate; orbit below level of upper margin of nasopreorbital fenestra (Kellner 1989).

Diagnosis of *T. navigans*: Tapejarid having bones of premaxillomaxillary crest striated rostrally and dorsally; processus caudalis of jugal twice as broad as in other *Tapejara* species; dorsal soft tissue of cranial crest preceded by vertical spinelike suprapremaxillary ossification; processus caudalis of premaxillae fused to cranium roof (Frey, Martill and Buchy 2003*b*).

Skull having long crest along the midline, eyes relatively small, in type species rostral end of jaws downwardly directed like an avian beak (possibly suggesting frugivorous diet); holotype (SMNK PAL 2344) of referred species *T. navigans* preserving bladelike rostral soft-tissue extension in association with sagittal cranial crest, this feature possibly also present in other tapejarids (see Frey, Martill and Buchy 2003*b*; Frey, Tischlinger, Buchy and Martill 2003).

TENDAGURIPTERUS   Unwin and Heinrich 1999
Dsungaripteroidea.

Name derivation: "Tendaguru [Tanzania]" + Greek *pteron* = "wing."

Type species: *T. recki* Unwin and Heinrich 1999.

Occurrence: Middle Saurian Beds (exact stratigraphic position unknown), Tendaguru, Tanzania.

Age: Late Jurassic (Kimmeridgian–Tithonian).

Holotype: MB.R.1290, incomplete section of mandibular symphysis.

Diagnosis of genus (as for type species): Deeply concave ventral profile of caudal section of mandibular symphysis; teeth in caudal section of mandibular symphysis caudodorsally inclined (Unwin and Heinrich 1999).

Small, estimated complete skull length of less than 200 millimeters, wingspan approaching 1,000 millimeters; first pterosaur cranial material reported from the Upper Jurassic of Tendaguru.

THALASSODROMEUS   Kellner and Campos 2002
Tapejaridae.

Name derivation: Greek *thalassa* = "sea" + Greek *dromeus* = "rummer."

Type species: *T. sethi* Kellner and Campos 2002.

Occurrence: Romualdo Member, Santana Formation, Araripe Basin, near town of Santana do Cariri, state of Cariri, northeastern Brazil.

Age: Middle Cretaceous (Albian).

Holotype: DGM 1476-D, well-preserved skull and lower jaw.

Diagnosis of genus (as for type species): Developed cranial crest comprising maxillae, frontal, parietal, and supraoccipital, starting at tip of skull, extended caudally, well behind occipital region; caudal end of cranial crest V-shaped; suture between premaxillae and frontoparietal portion of crest rectilinear; rostral portion of premaxillae and dentary having sharp dorsal and ventral edges; palatines before palatal crest strongly concave; caudal (occipital) region broader than in other tapejarids (width over quadrates 20 percent of squamosal to premaxilla length) (Kellner and Campos 2002).

Large, wingspan of approximately 1.8 meters (six feet), head 1.42 meters (more than 4.75 feet) including the crest; crest large, thin, knifelike or spearhead-like crest comprising about three-fourths of the head (largest cranial crest of all known pterosaurs); flattened jaws and scissors-like beak suggesting that this pterosaur may have skimmed over the water's surface, lower jaw slightly submerged, in catching fish.

TITANOPTERYX   Arambourg 1959 — (Preoccupied; see *Arambourgiania*.)

Name derivation: Greek *Titan* [offspring of Uranus and Gaea, symbolizing strength and size]" + Greek *pteron* = "wing."

Type species: *T. philadelphiae* Arambourg 1959.

TROPEOGNATHUS   Wellnhofer 1987 — (See *Coloborhynchus*.)

Name derivation: Greek *tropeos* = "keel" + Greek *gnathos* = "jaw."

Type species: *T. robustus* Wellnhofer 1987.

TUPUXUARA   Kellner and Campos 1989
Neoazhdarchia.

Name derivation: Tupi *tupuxuara* [familiar spirit in Tupi Brazillian Indian culture].

Type species: *T. longicristatus* Kellner and Campos 1989.

Other species: *T. leonardii* Kellner and Campos 1994.

Occurrence: Romualdo Member, Santana Formation, Araripe Plateau, northeastern Brazil.

Age: Early Cretaceous (Aptian).

Holotype: CD-R-003, rostral part of skull, distal portion

of metacarpals I to IV, proximal portion of first phalanx of digit IV of right manus, distal portion of metacarpal IV, proximal portion of first phalanx of digit IV of left manus, ungual.

Diagnosis of genus (as for type species): Edentulous, medium sized, large sagittal crest at rostral part of premaxillae extending backwards; medial ridge at ventral part of palate; first wing-phalanx and metacarpal IV comparatively slender and long; proximal articulation of first wing-phalanx having two pneumatic foramina, one at superior part of articulation with metacarpal IV (Kellner and Campos 1989).

Diagnosis of *T. leonardii*: Strong mesial ridge on palate, ridge not extending to rostral part of skull (Kellner and Campos 1994).

Medium-sized pterosaur having medial crest on rostral area of skull, edges of jaw toothless.

UTAHDACTYLUS   Czerkas and Mickleson 2002
Pterosauria *incertae sedis*.
Name derivation: "Utah" + Greek *dactylos* = "finger."
Type species: *U. kateae* Czerkas and Mickleson 2002.
Occurrence: Tidwell Member, Morrison Formation, Utah, United States.
Age: Late Jurassic (Kimmeridgian–Tithonian).
Holotype: DM 002/CEUM 32588, incomplete skeleton including caudal fragment of cranium, cervical vertebra, three dorsal vertebrae, fragment of caudal vertebra preserved as natural mold with elongated zygapophyses, several isolated ribs, uncrushed scapulocoracoid, limb bones (mostly partial portions or natural molds).

Diagnosis of genus (as for type species): Cervical vertebra comparatively large, not elongate; no indications of inset groove (typical of manual digit IV of "rhamphorhynchoids") in forelimb bones (Czerkas and Mickleson 2002).

Moderate size, with wingspan of about 120 centimeters, tail typically long.

"WYOMINGOPTERYX"   Bakker 1995 [*nomen dubium*]
Name derivation: "Wyoming" + Greek *pteron* = "wing."
[No species designated.]
Not yet described.

ZHEJIANGOPTERUS   Cai and Wei 1994
Azhdarchia.
Name derivation: "Zhengian [Province, China]" + Greek *pteron* = "wing."
Type species: *Z. linhaiensis* Cai and Wei 1994.
Occurrence: Tangshang Formation, Aolicun Village, Linhai, Zhejiang Province, southeastern China.
Age: Late Cretaceous (?Santonian).
Holotype: ZNM M1330, almost complete skull impres-

sion, crushed, articulated cranial and postcranial material, preserved wing membranes.

Diagnosis of genus (as for type species): Apparently crestless, skull with long, pointed, lightly constructed rostrum, edentulous; nasal opening and antorbital fenestra combining in simple large opening extending to half skull length; seven long, lightly constructed cervical vertebrae; humerus short, robust, with well-developed deltopectoral crest; metacarpal of wing finger longer than radius and ulna; femur long, gracile, nearly 50 percent longer than humerus (Cai and Wei 1994).

Very large pterosaur, with very large and thin head, long neck, long legs, short wings, and apparently no cranial crest; estimated skull length of 43 centimeters (over 1.6 inches), wingspan of five meters (almost 17 feet).

Pterosaur Ichnogenera

Once rare, tracks of flying reptiles are now known from over 30 sites. Pterosaur tracks that have been given generic and specific names are listed as follows:

AGADIRICHNUS   Ambroggi and Lapparent 1954 — (=?*Pteraichnus*)
Name derivation: "Agadir [Morocco]" + Greek *ichnos* "track."
Type species: *A. elegans* Ambroggi and Lapparent 1954.
Occurrence: Upper Cretaceous, Morocco.
Age: Late Cretaceous (Maastrichtian).

Pes prints, elongated, plantigrade, with four slender digits of subequal length, first interpreted as lacertilian; possibly a senior synonym of *Pteraichnus* (see Billon-Bruyat and Mazin 2003).

HAENAMICHNUS   Hwang, Huh, Lockley, Unwin and Wright 2002
Name derivation: "Haenam [County]" + Greek *ichnos* = "track."
Type species: Hwang, Huh, Lockley, Unwin and Wright 2002.
Occurrence: Uhangri Formation, Haenam County, southwestern coastline of Korea.
Age: Late Cretaceous.

First pterosaur tracks reported from Asia and currently the largest pterosaur ichnites known; digitigrade tridactyl manus impressions, pes impressions not showing individual digits, toes rounded or triangular without distinct claw impressions, indicate quadrupedal locomotion; possibly belonging to the Azhdarchia.

PTERAICHNUS   Stokes 1957 — (=?*Agadirichnus*)
Pterodactyloidea.

Name derivation: Greek *pteron* = "wing" + Greek *ichnos* "track."

Type species: *P. saltwashensis* Stokes 1957.

Occurrence: Morrison Formation, Arizona, Blackhawk Formation, Mesaverde Group, Utah, Sundance Formation, Wyoming, Summerville Formation, Colorado, Utah, United States; Oncala Group, Soria, Spain.

Age: Late Jurassic–Late Cretaceous (Oxfordian–Campanian).

Once thought to be crocodilian, a notion now rejected (*e.g.*, Lockley, Logue, Moratella, Hunt, Schultz and Robinson 1995; Mazin, Billon-Bruyat, Hantzpergue and LaFaurie 2003); type trackway showing quadrupedal locomotion, with a digitigrade manus and plantigrade pes, suggesting low-velocity locomotion in an erect (see Bennett 1997) or semierect (Mazin *et al.*) posture; trackmakers possibly members of Azhdarchia; some tracks referred to cf. *Pteraichnus*, from the Summerville and Sundance formations, indicating swimming or floating behavior resembling that of certain seabirds (Lockley and Wright 2003).

PURBECKOPUS   Delair 1963

Name derivation: "[Isle of] Purbeck" + Greek *pous* = "foot."

Type species: *P. pentadactylus* Delair 1963.

Occurrence: Isle of Purbeck, Dorset, England.

Age: Early Cretaceous.

?Pterosaurian (see Billon-Bruyat and Mazin 2003); large, five-toed, originally thought to be manus prints of the dinosaur *Iguanodon*.

Appendix Two: Mesozoic Birds

While pterosaurs were the dominant flying vertebrates during the Mesozoic Era, birds were also appearing during this time in significant numbers and varieties.

The close anatomical similarities between birds and dinosaurs have been recognized for almost one and a half centuries. In 1868, British paleontologist Thomas Henry Huxley—then the most ardent and vocal defender of Charles Darwin and the latter's theory of evolution through natural selection—noted the striking resemblances in the recently collected skeletons of *Archaeopteryx*, celebrated as the first discovered and earliest known fossil bird, and the tiny theropod dinosaur *Compsognathus*, both specimens having been wonderfully preserved in the most exquisite detail in Bavaria's famed Solnhofen Lithographic Limestone. "Surely," Huxley wrote, "there is nothing very wild or illegitimate in the hypothesis that the phylum of the Class of Aves has its foot in the Dinosaurian Reptiles" (for details, see Feduccia 1980).

Even before Huxley, a connection had been recognized between birds and theropod dinosaurs. In 1841, Professor Edward Hitchcock of Amherst College acquired a stone slab marked by five small, three-toed fossil footprints, dug up some 30 years earlier by Pliny Moody on his father's farm in South Hadley, Massachusetts.

After studying these impressions, Professor Hitchcock concluded that they were made by some ancient bird. Because of their resemblance to the American coot (*Fulica americana*), he named them *Ornithoidichnites fulicoides* (for details, see Thulborn 1990; see also *S1*, "Introduction," section on dinosaurs and birds, *S3*, "Appendix").

Clearly, birds and theropod dinosaurs share a close phylogenetic relationship. In more recent years—largely stemming from the work initiated by John H. Ostrom (1969), who pointed out the numerous avian features in his newly described dromaeosaurid theropod *Deinonychus* (see *D:TE*)—the majority of workers have accepted the hypothesis that (as boldly suggested so long ago by Huxley) that birds descended directly from a theropod dinosaurian ancestor. More recently, in fact, numerous paleontologists (*e.g.*, Luis M. Chiappe, a specialist in fossil birds) have declared that "birds are dinosaurs," distinguishing the vast majority of forms generally regarded as dinosaurs by the adjective "non-avian" (for pro and con arguments on this issue, see *D:TE* and all previous supplements).

Currently, true birds are known unequivocally in the fossil record as early as the Late Jurassic period, although there have been reports (*e.g.*, Chatterjee (1991, 1995, 1997*a*, 1998, 1999; see *Protoavis* entries, *D:TE*, *S1*, and *S2*) of putative birds dating back to the Late Triassic (Norian).

Until relatively recently, all birds—extinct and extant—had been classified as members of the amniote group Aves, introduced in 1758 by Carolus Linnaeus. Much later, the group also embraced *Archaeopteryx*, a fossil bird discovered during the latter half of the eighteenth century. More recently, Jacques Gauthier, in his landmark paper published in 1986, introduced the term Aviale to embrace both *Archaeopteryx* and living birds, at the same time limiting the term Aves to crown group or extant birds. Since Gauthier's introduction of the clade Aviale, some workers have opted to use the terms Aviale and Aves interchangeably, while others have applied the term Neornithes to crown group birds (see below).

In the past, the present writer had followed Weishampel, Dodson and Osmólska (1990), in the original edition of *The Dinosauria*, in excluding avian taxa from the entries in the "Dinosaurian Genera" chapter of *D:TE* and its sequels. While Weishampel *et al.* then acquiesced to the hypothesis "that birds are present-day dinosaurian descendants," they did not offer "discussion of avian taxonomy, phylogeny, and biology," reserving such discussion for taxa traditionally regarded as dinosaurs, while urging instead "readers seeking information on birds to look elsewhere." Following the accumulation of a vast amount of data linking birds with theropod dinosaurs, Weishampel *et al.* (2004) included a chapter on "Basal Avialae" (see Padian 2004*b*) in the second edition of *The Dinosauria*.

In Linnean systematics, the clade Aves was given the designation of "class." The group was formerly diagnosed with the presence of feathers included as an avian synapomorphy. However, the mere possession of feathers or feather-like integumentary structures can no longer be regarded as a major diagnostic criterion for Aves, in lieu of recent discoveries of various non-avian dinosaur fossils preserving impressions of feathers and primitive feather-like structures (*e.g.*, *Caudipteryx*, *Sinosauropteryx Beipiaosaurus*, and others).

Following Padian and Chiappe (1997), Aves has the

Life restoration by artist Mark Hallett of ***Archaeopteryx lithographica***, the first Mesozoic bird known from fossil remains. In the background are a pair of brachiosaurid sauropod individuals.

node-based definition of *Archaeopteryx* plus living birds and all descendants of their most recent common ancestor, extinct and extant. As Padian (2004*b*) noted however, some workers, in order to eschew confusion over the term Aves, have opted to use a stem-based definition of Avialae, *i.e.*, living birds and all maniraptoran theropods closer to them than to the dromaeosaurid *Deinonychus*, with the informal term "birds" applicable to *Archaeopteryx* and all more derived members of Avialae (with Aves/Neornithes regarded as the crown group).

Aves is herein considered to be the immediate sister group of the non-avian coelurosaurian theropod clade Deinonychosauria (see Senter, Barsbold, Britt and Burnham 2004, "Systematics" chapter).

Padian (2004*b*) diagnosed Aves [=Avialae of his usage] as follows: Premaxillae long, narrow, pointed, with long nasal processes; double-condyled quadrate articulating with prootic; teeth reduced in size and number, not serrated; scapula having pronounced acromion process, scapula at least nine times as long as broad maximally; coracoid with pronounced sternal process; forelimbs nearly as long as, or longer than, hindlimbs; forearm approximately as long as, or longer than, humerus; second (major) metacarpal almost half length of humerus; metatarsal I attached to distal quarter of II, its digit "reversed" in orientation; also (in skull), quadratojugal joined to quadrate by ligament; no contact between quadratojugal and squamosal; (in pelvis) cranial process of ischium reduced or absent (*e.g.*, see Chiappe 1995*b*); also, caudal marhin of naris almost reaching or overlapping rostral border of antorbital fossa; postacetabular process of ilium shallow, pointed, depth less than 50 percent that of preacetabular wing at acetabulum (see Chiappe 2001); feathers long and large enough to allow powered flight, with complex, interlocking barbules making their airworthy.

With both sister-taxa Deinonychosauria and Aves nestled within the encompassing dinosaurian clade Thero-

poda, it then follows that all extinct and living birds, as the above-cited claim above so boldly states, must be classified as dinosaurs.

The following simplified breakdown of Aves is based upon various cladograms proposed by Chiappe (*e.g.*, 1993, 2002*a*, 2002*b*; also L. M. Chiappe, personal communication 2003):

DEINONYCHOSAURIA
AVES (=AVIALAE of some workers)
    ARCHAEOPTERYGIFORMES
        Rahonavis
        ARCHAEOPTERYGIDAE
    PYGOSTYLIA
        CONFUCIUSORNITHIDAE
        ORNITHOTHORACES
            ENANTIORNITHES
                Iberomesornis
                Noguerornis
                EUENANTIONRNITHES
                    Lectavis
                    Yungavolucris
                    Neuquenornis
                    LONGIPTERYGIDAE
                    CATHAYORNITHIDAE
                    AVISAURIDAE
                    ALEXORNITHIDAE
                    CUSPIROSTRISORNITHIDAE
                    ENANTIORNITHIDAE
        ORNITHUROMORPHA
            ?*Vorona*]
            ORNITHURAE
               BAPTORNITHIDAE
               HESPERORNITHITHES
                   HESPERORNITHIDAE
                   ENALIORNITHIDAE
            Apsaravis
            ZHYRAORNITHIDAE
        CARINATAE
            ICHTHYORNITHES
            NEORNITHES (=AVES *sensu* Gauthier 1986)
               PALAEOGNATHAE
               NEOGNATHAE
                   ANSERIFORME
                     ANATOIDEA
                       ANSERANATIDAE
                       PRESBYORNITHIDAE
                   ?*Vegavis*
               GALLIFORMES
               PANGALLIFORMES
                GAVIIFORMES
                 GAVIIDAE
               PROCELLARIIFORMES
               CHARADIFORMES

CHARADIFORMES (cont.)
GRACULAVIDAE
TYTTHOSTONYCHIDAE
[All other avian taxa not present in the Mesozoic]

Archaeopterygiformes (to which the Late Cretaceous yet basal genus *Rahonavis* belongs [see *S1*], and the Late Jurassic family Archaeopterygidae belong) comprises the most primitive unequivocally known, Late Jurassic to Late Cretaceous birds, having varying flight capabilities. This clade has not yet been formally defined or diagnosed.

Sister clade to the Archaeopterygiformes, the Pygostylia (Early to Late Cretaceous forms having a pygostyle) is characterized by caudal vertebrae fused into a single element (Chatterjee 1997*a*). Within this clade are the subgroups Confuciusornithidae (small, Early Cretaceous forms) and Ornithothoraces (primitive Early to Late Cretaceous birds).

Chiappe, Ji, Ji and Norell (1999) offered the following node-based definition of the family Confuciusornithidae: The common ancestor of *Confuciusornis sanctus* and *Changchengornis hengdaoziensis* plus all of its descendants. These authors diagnosed the Confuciusornithidae as follows: Jaws edentulous; rostral end of mandibular symphysis forked; distinct, round foramen (presumably maxillary fenestra) pneumatizing ascending ramus of maxilla within antorbital cavity; prominent, subquadrangular deltopectoral crest of humerus; metacarpal I not coossified to semilunate-metacarpal II and III complex; proximal phalanx of manual digit III much shorter than remaining nonungual phalanges; claw of manual digit II much smaller than claws of I and III; caudal end of sternum V-shaped.

The Ornithothoraces, a monophyletic clade including the groups Enantiornithes and Ornithuromorpha, was defined by Sereno (1998) as all taxa phylogenetically bracketed by *Sinornis* and Neornithes. Senter *et al.* 2004 diagnosed this taxon by the following synapomorphies: Craniomandibular joint suborbital; ischium greater than 0.7 times pubic length; fibula not reaching tarsus (also see Chiappe 2002*b*).

Enantiornithes (a group of Early to Late Cretaceous small to large, so-called "opposite birds," including the genera *Iberomesornis* and *Noguerornis*, and the clades Euenantiornithes and Ornithuromorpha) is diagnosed by the following four synapomorphies: Hypocleidium well developed; ulna almost same length or longer than humerus; minor metacarpal (III) projecting distally more than major metacarpal (II); round proximal articular surface of tibiotarsus (Chiappe 2002*b*).

The Ornithuromorpha (a large clade of Early Cretaceous to present-day flying and flightless birds, including possibly the genus *Vorona*, plus the clades Ornithurae and Carinatae) is diagnosed by the following eight synapo-

morphies: Presence of caudal vertebra prezygapophyses; shaft of scapula sagitally curved; distal end of metacarpals partially or completely fused; intermetacarpal space at least as wide as maximum width of minor metacarpal (III) shaft; absence of postacetabular process; metatarsals II to IV completely (or nearly so) fused to each other; tarsometatarsal vascular distal foramen completely enclosed by metatarsals III and IV; absence of tubercle on dorsal face of metatarsal II (Chiappe 2002*b*).

Within Enantiornithes, the clade Euenantiornithes (small to large Early to Late Cretaceous forms capable of flight, including the genera *Lectavis*, *Yungavolucris*, and *Neuquenornis*, plus various families) is diagnosed by unambiguous synapomorphies including the following: parapophyses (costal foveae) in central part of bodies of dorsal vertebrae; distinctly convex lateral margin of coracoid; supracoracoid nerve foramen opening into elongate furrow medially, separated from medial margin of coracoid by thick, bony bar; broad, deep fossa on dorsal surface of scapular blade, with prominent, longitudinal furrow; ventral margin of furcula distinctly wider than dorsal margin; hypocleidium well developed; dorsal (superior) margin of humeral head concave in central position, rising ventrally and dorsally; humerus with prominent bicipital crest; ventral face of humeral bicipital crest having small fossa for muscular attachment; dorsal cotyla of ulna strongly convex, separated from olecranon by groove; shaft of radius having long axial groove on interosseous surface; minor metacarpal projecting distally more than major metacarpal; hypertrophied femoral caudal trochanter; very narrow, deep intercondylar sulcus on tibiotarsus, proximally undercutting condyles; metatarsal IV significantly thinner than II and III; other diagnostic characters including lateral and medial processes of sternum, and very cranocaudally compressed distal end of humerus (Chiappe 2002*b*).

Within Ornithuromorpha, the Ornithurae (Early to Late Cretaceous forms, primitive although more closely resembling modern birds, including the families Baptornithidae and Zhyraornithidae, the genus *Apsaravis*, and the clade Hesperornithes). Clarke (2004, in a paper revising the avian genera *Ichthyornis* and *Apatornis*) defined Ornithurae as an apomorphy-based clade (following de Queiroz and Gauthier 1992) "stemming from the first panavian with a 'bird tail,' namely, a tail that is shorter than the femur (subequal to or shorter than the tibiotarsus) with a pygostyle of avian aspect ... that is homologous (synapomorphic) with that of Aves (*Vultur gryphus*; Linnaeus, 1758)" (Gauthier and de Queiroz 2001). Clarke followed Gauthier's (1986) more restrictive definition of

Aves, which includes the last common ancestor of all extant birds and all of its descendants.

Hope (2002) diagnosed (limited) the Ornithurae as follows: Derived features including premaxilla fused with maxilla; maxilla very reduced, almost entirely restricted to palatal region; mandibular symphysis fused; dentary fused with surangular; absence of teeth; coracoidal humeral facet not extended sternally beyond scapular facet of coracoid; coracoid humeral facet oriented laterally or craniolaterally; humeral head large; distinct sulcus for transverse ligament of humerus; deltopectoral crest inflected cranially;

pneomotricipital fossa of humerus having pneumatic foramen. (For an alternate diagnosis, see Senter *et al.*, "Systematics" chapter.)

Within Ornithurae, the Hesperornithes (a group of Late Cretaceous, small to large flightless and aquatic birds) was defined by Clarke as a stem-based clade (converted by Clarke following de Queiroz) including all taxa or specimens more closely related to *Hesperornis regalis* than to Aves (*sensu* Gauthier). Galton and Martin (2002) diagnosed this clade as follows: Fusion of cranial bones caudal to frontoparietal suture; palate with short, broad pterygoids,

Photograph by Mick Ellison, courtesy Mark A. Norell and American Museum of Natural History.

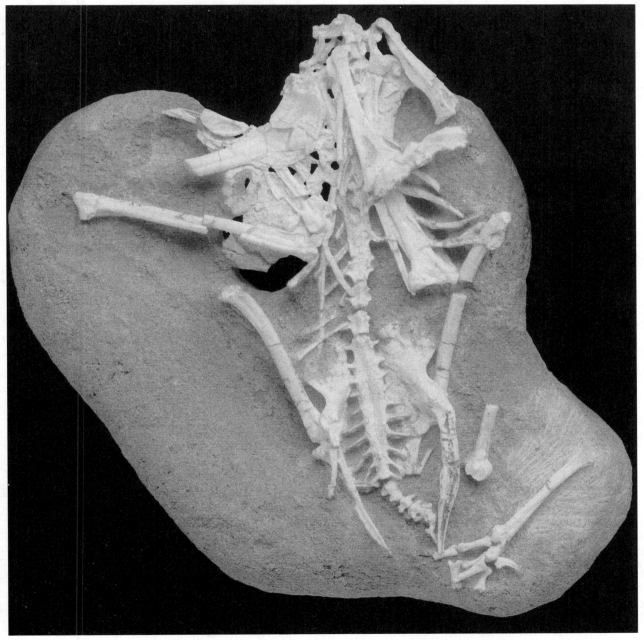

Apsaravus ukhaana, IGM 100/1017, holotype almost complete skeleton.

long, narrow palatines; quadrate pneumaticity reduced or absent; small predentary bone; intramandibular articulation between angular and spenial; all thoracic vertebrae heterocoelous; sternum unkeeled; long bones pneumatic; wing reduced; humerous lacking distinct distal condyles; acetabulum partly closed; postacetabular pelvis greatly elongated; femur relatively short, broad; tibiotarsus with large cnemial crest shaped like isosceles triangle in cranial view; large, triangular patella with foramen for ambiens tendon; tarsometatarsus transversely compressed, distinct craniolateral ridge leading to lateral trochlea (IV); lateral trochlea at least as large and distally extending as middle trochlea (III); fourth toe longest.

The Carinatae (Late Cretaceous to present day, divided into the two subgroups Ichthyornithes and Neornites, and including all modern birds) is distinguished by a humerus having a shaped, convex head, and by the complete fusion of the bones of the outer arm and lower leg.

The Ichthyornithes (Late Cretaceous) is a clade of swimming birds that were also capable of flight. Clarke defined (but did not diagnose) Icthyornithithes as a stem-based clade including taxa and specimens more closely related to *Ichthyornis dispar* than to Aves (*sensu* Gauthier).

The Neornithes (Late Cretaceous to present day, this clade embracing all modern birds) is diagnosed as follows: Maxilla with reduced ascending process; absence of lacrimal/jugal contact; contralateral dorsal tympanium diverticula participating with skull roof; contralateral dorsal tympanium diverticula participating with cranium; participation of ipsilateral dorsal and caudal tympanium diverticula; long bones pneumatic (Gauthier 1986).

Within Neornithes are two major clades, the Palaeognathae and the Neognathae. The Palaeognathae includes ratites and tinamous birds. The Neognathae includes the following clades, not all of which are known from the Mesozoic: Anseriformes (ducks, geese, screamses, and swans), Galliformes (grouse, turkeys, pheasants, quails, peafowl, and related birds), Pangalliformes (name proposed by Clarke 2004 for taxa similar to galliforms but outside of that clade), Gaviiformes (loons), Ciconiiformes (herons, storks, bitterns, spoonbills, egrets, and ibises), Pelecaniformes (pelicanes, gannets, frigate birds, darters, cormorants, and anhingas), Procellariiformes (albatrosses, shearwaters, and petrels), Sphenisciformes (penguins), Charadriiformes (phalaropes, avocets, woodcocks, plovers, sandpipers, oystercatchers, gulls, terns, auks, and puffins), Columbiformes (pigeons, dodo, and doves), Psittaciformes (parrots and cocatoos), Falconiformes (falcons and caracaras), Cucculiformes (cuckoos, anis, and coucals), Pandionidae (ospreys), Acciptriformes (hawks, Old World vultures, and eagles), and Neoaves (a node-based clade including the last common ancestor of all extant neognaths closer to *Passer domesticus* than to Galloanserae; see Clarke).

(Within the above Mesozoic clades are various additional families and subfamilies — some of them redundantly including but a single taxon — the diagnoses for which are beyond the scope of this book.)

Following is a list of named Mesozoic avian genera including selected basic information. For this compilation, only the catalogue numbers for holotypes of type species are noted. For more details and illustrations, consult the papers cited. See also the books *Fossil Birds*, by W. E. Swinton (1965), and *The Age of Birds*, by Alan Feduccia (1980). On a technical level, see the best and most up to date reference book of the subject, *Mesozoic Birds: Above the Heads of Dinosaurs*, edited by Luis M. Chiappe and Lawrence M. Witmer (2002).

Mesozoic Avian Genera

ABAVORNIS   Panteleev 1998
Enantiornithes *incertae sedis*.
Name derivation: Latin *abavus* = "great-great-grandfather" + Greek *ornis* = "bird."
Type species: *A. bonaparti* Panteleev 1998.
Occurrence: Bissekty Formation, Uzbekistan, Central Kyzylkum.
Age: Late Cretaceous (Coniacian).
Holotype: TsNIGRI 56/11915, middle portion of shaft of coracoid, lacking head.

Lateral edge of coracoid convex, presence of dorsal fossa, suggesting that this genus is an enantiornithine (Panteleev 1998).

ABERRATIODONTUS   Gong, Hou and Wang 2004
Enantiornithes *insertae sedis*.
Name derivation: Latin *aberrare* = "to stray" + Greek *odous* = "tooth."
Type species: *A. wui* Gong, Hou and Wang 2004.
Occurrence: Jiufutang Formation, Shangheshou, Chaoyang County, Liaoning Province, China.
Age: Early Cretaceous (Aptian).
Holotype: LHV0001a and LHV0001b, almost complete articulated skeleton on main part and counterpart slabs with feather impressions.

Diagnosis of genus (as for type species): Primitive enantiornithine, twice as large as *Longipteryx*; skull low, postorbital well developed; quadrate pillarlike at lower region, expanded at upper region; furcula differing from that of other known enantiornithines, having long furcular process and short, V-shaped clavicle branches, the latter longer than in other known enantiornithines; well-developed lateral process of coracoids at distal end; largest number of teeth (up to 21 on each lower jaw) of any known early bird; teeth showing pseudoheterodont characteristics, unlike teeth of other known early birds; teeth on rostral side thin, fine, front teeth very large, like "dentes canini";

(as in *Eoenantiornis*) middle cheek becoming smaller, largest teeth distally; new teeth growing out of insides of tooth rows (as in *Archaeopteryx* (Gong, Hou and Wang 2004).

Largest known member of Enantiornithes; primitive, with numerous pseudoheterodont teeth (some showing different stages of development, development pattern similar to that of *Archaeopteryx* and crocodilians, but not of dinosaurs); referred by Gong, Hou and Wang to new enantiornithine order Aberratiodontuiformes and family Aberratiodonthidae, which the authors did not define or diagnose, nor did they specify the placement of these taxa within Enantiornithies.

ALEXORNIS   Brodkorb 1976
Alexornithidae.
Name derivation: "Alex[ander Wetmore, paleornithologist]" + Greek *ornis* = "bird."
Type species: *A. antecedens* Brodkorb 1976.
Occurrence: Bocana Roja Formation, near El Rosario, Baja California, Mexico.
Age: Late Cretaceous (Campanian).
Holotype: LACM 33213, distal end of right humerus.

Diagnosis of genus (as for type species): Autapomorphies including (for humerus) deep olecranal fossa; external condyle oriented transversely at approximately 60-degree angle to shaft; transverse ridge across anconal surface proximal to its base; (ulna) olecranon having pit in tip; external cotyla large, strongly convex, separated from olecranon by deep groove; internal cotyla having flat surface; proximal radial depression deeply undercutting entire width of rim of internal cotyla; (scapula) acromion somewhat short; glenoid facet flat; (coracoid) brachial tuberosity having recurved hook, directed toward area where procoracoid process (if preserved) would be; scapular facet very broad; (femur) external condyle quite long, extending proximally and distally beyond internal and fibular condyles; shallow rotular groove; (tibiotarsus) fibular crest wide; cranial and caudal surfaces of fibular crest concave, cranial and caudal groove running along junction with shaft; proximal internal articular surface without caudal overhang (Brodkorb 1976).

Sparrow-sized land bird, apparently ancestral to Coraciformes and Piciformes.

AMBIORTUS   Kurochkin 1982
Neornithes.
Name derivation: Latin *ambiguus* = "uncertain, ambiguous" + Latin *ortus* = "beginning, origin."
Type species: *A. dementjevi* Kurochkin 1982.
Occurrence: Khurilt Ulaan Bulag locality, Altai Mountains, Bayankhongor Aimag, Bööntsagaan, Central Mongolia.
Age: Early Cretaceous (Berriasian–Valanginian).
Holotype: PIN 3790+, 3790-, and 3790-272, portion of

articulated left shoulder girdle, left forelimb, cervical and thoracic vertebrae.

Diagnosis of genus (as for type species): Procoracoid process wide, long; scapular acromion long, dorsoventrally compressed; deep groove along lateral side of scapula; scapular blade narrow; short, fossa-like groove cranial to tubercle on projecting ventral edge of proximal end of humerus; metacarpals fused at proximal end; intermediate phalanx of major digit dorsoventrally compressed (Kurochkin 2000).

Earliest known stage in evolution of Neornithes; similar to *Otogornis* and to the flying palaeognath *Lithornis*, wing feathers having tightly bonded barbs.

ANATALAVIS   Olson and Parris 1987
?Anseranatidae.
Name derivation: Latin *anas* = "duck" + Latin *ala* = "wing" + Latin *avis* = "bird."
Type species: *A. rex* (Shufeldt 1915).
Other species: *A. oxfordi* Olson and Parris 1987.
Occurrence: Navesink Formation, Hornerstown Formation, New Jersey, Hell Creek Formation, Dog Creek, Montana, United States; London Clay, Walton-on-the-Naze, Essex, England.
Age: ?Late Cretaceous–early Eocene (?latest Maastrichtian–Ypresian).
Holotype: YPM 902, two humeri.

Diagnosis of genus (as for type species): Differing from *Telmatornis* and [Paleocene bird] *Presbyornis* in having very short, stout, much more curved humeral shaft in both dorsoventral and lateromedial aspects; differing from *Telmatornis* and agreeing with *Presbyornis* in having distal end of humerus deeper in distal aspect, and narrower, much deeper olecranal fossa; also, brachial depression smaller, narrower than in *Telmatornis*, neither as deep nor proximally located as in *Presbyornis* (Olson and Parris 1987).

Apparently a strong, swift flier; earliest waterfowl of the clade Anseriformes, closely related to the modern magpie goose.

ANGELINORNIS   Kashin 1972 — (See *Ichthyornis*.)
Name derivation: "Angelina [Mikhaylovna Sudilovskaya, ornithologist]" + Greek *ornis* = "bird."
Type species: *A. antecessor* (Wetmore 1962).

APATORNIS   Marsh 1873
?Neognathae.
Name derivation: Greek *apatao* = "deceptive" + Greek *ornis* = "bird."
Type species: *A. celer* (Marsh 1873).
Occurrence: Smoky Hill Member, Niobrara Chalk Formation, along Smoky Hill River, "yellow chalk of the *Pteranodon* Beds," western Kansas, United States.

Age: Late Cretaceous (Coniacian–early Campanian).

Holotype: YPM 1451, synsacrum lacking caudal end.

Diagnosis of genus (as for type species): Four or more midseries sacral vertebrae having diminutive, dorsally projected transverse processes (Clarke 2004).

Ternlike, very small, apparently part of an early radiation of Neognathae, maybe closely related to Amseriformes (see Hope 2002); probably web-footed (see Lim, Martin, Zhou, Baek and Yang 2002).

Note: Originally described by Marsh 1873 as the referred species *Ichthyornis celer*.

APSARAVIS   Norell and Clarke 2001

Ornithurae.

Name derivation: "Apsara [mythical female winged creature in Buddhist and Hindu art]" + Latin *avis* = "bird."

Type species: *A. ukhaana* Norell and Clarke 2001.

Occurrence: Camel's Humps sublocality, Ukhaa Tolgod locality, Omnogov Aimag, Southern Mongolia.

Age: Late Cretaceous (?Campanian).

Holotype: IGM 100/1017, almost complete, partially articulated skeleton, including crushed skull with ring of scleral ossicles in ?left orbit, incomplete left quadrate, partia left jugal, partial mandible, postcrania including (vertebrae) 12 cervicals, seven thoracic, 10 ankylosed sacrals, five free caudals), pygostyle, fragmentary thoracic ribs, fragment of cranial portion of sternum, scapulae, coracoids, humeri, ulnae, radii, radiale, right ulnare, partial metacarpi, right first phalanx of manual digit II, ilia, ischia (right ischium missing distal end), pubes (right pubis fragmentary), proximal ends of femora, distal tibiotarsi, tarsometatarsi (coossified metatarsals II–IV), incomplete series of pedal phalanges of digits II–IV from both feet.

Diagnosis of genus (as for type species): Distinct from other birds based on unique presence of tubercle on proximocaudal humerus, hypertrophied trochanteric crest on femur, and well-projected wings of caudal trochlear surface of tibiotarsus (see Norell and Clarke 2001); trochlea cartilanginis tibialis (Baumel and Witmer 1993); following 10 characters optimizing as autapomorphies: ossified mandibular symphysis; dentary strongly forked caudally; scapula with hooked acromion process; dorsal condyle of humerus highly angled; humeral condyles weakly defined; distal edge of humerus angling strongly ventrally; humerus flared dorsoventrally at its distal terminus; lateral condyle of tibiotarsus wider than medial; neither condyle of tibiotarsus tapering toward midline; trochlea metatarsal II rounded (not ginglymoid) (Clarke and Norell 2002).

Small, volant, most basal known bird with extensor process; remains from a continental deposit establish ornithurines as living in other than marine or near-shore environments.

ARCHAEOPTERYX   Meyer 1861—(=*Archaeornis, Griphosaurus, Jurapteryx*)

Archaeopteryigidae.

Name derivation: Greek *archaio* = "ancient" + Greek *pteron* = "wing."

Type species: *A. lithographica* Meyer 1861.

Occurrence: Upper Solnhofen Lithographic Limestone, Langenaltheimer (near Solnhofen), Blumenberg (near Eichstätt), Solnhofen, southern Germany; ?Haarlem, Netherlands.

Age: Late Jurassic (early Tithonian).

Holotype: BMNH 37001 (the "London specimen"), almost complete skeleton, with feathers, slab and counterslab.

Diagnosis of genus: Manual digit I having ungual approximately half length of basal phalanx; manual digit

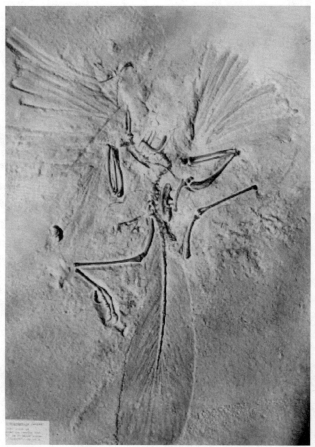

The "London specimen" (BMNH 37001) of *Archaeopteryx lithographica*, the so-called "reptile bird." Found in 1861 in a lithographic limestone quarry near the Bavarian village of Solnhofen, this specimen (including feather impressions) is celebrated as the first complete skeleton collected of this species. The discovery of this specimen — originally preserved in the Humboldt Museum für Naturkunde in Berlin, now at The Natural History Museum, London — offered compelling information supporting Charles Darwin's then still-new theory of evolution through natural selection (published as *The Origin of Species* in 1959), demonstrating a link between reptiles and birds.

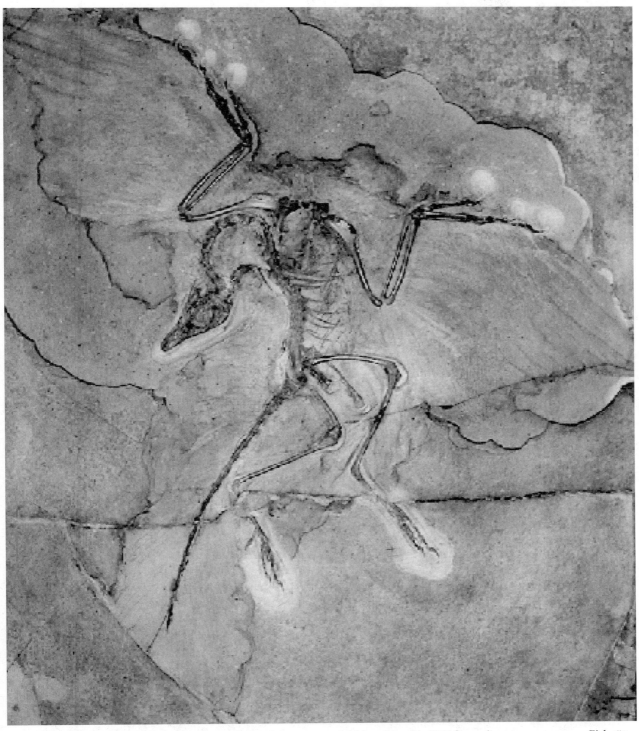

Cast of the exquisitely preserved "Berlin specimen" of *Archaeopteryx,* main slab, collected in 1877 from a limestone quarry near Eichstätt, a town in Bavaria, housed at the Humboldt Museum für Naturkunde. The original specimen has been hailed as possibly "the most important natural history specimen in existence, perhaps comparable in value to the Rosetta Stone" (Feduccia 1980).

III having unfused (even though tightly connected) first and second phalanges; metatarsal II not tapered proximally; pedal digit IV with five phalanges, about 99 percent (more than 80 percent) length of digit III); flexor tubercles of pedal claws incompletely differentiated or absent; pedal digit IV having ungual shorter than or subequal to basal phalanx (Elźanowski 2002).

The so-called first true bird, jaws with teeth, specimens constituting the first body fossils to indicate an evolutionary link between reptiles and birds; apparently "an

Life restoration by artist Mark Hallett of the primitive bird *Archaeopteryx lithographica*.

occasional or opportunistic flier that maintained an essentially dinosaurian life style on the shore but took to the air when circumstances were favourable" (Thulborn 2003); lacking powerful flight muscles and complex wing movements required for takeoff from the ground, possibly launched itself from a perch, a more efficient and cost-effective means of flight, making "short flights between trees, utilizing a novel method of phugoid gliding" (Chatterjee and Templin 2003).

Notes: Senter and Robins (2003) recently recommended that all referred species of *Archaeopteryx*—i.e., *A. bavarica* Wellnhofer 1993 and *A. siemensii* (Dames 1897)—be synonymized with *A. lithographica*, the proportional and dental differences between then attributed to ontogeny.

Although sometimes considered to be a feathered non-avian theropod, Wellnhofer (2004) confirmed the avian pedigree of this genus, noting that in all *Archaeopteryx* specimens "the flight feathers are uniform in structure, pattern, and arrangement and, except for the feathered tail, the plumage was definitely modern and adapted for active, powered flight," implying that the feathers are already highly evolved, advanced avian structures with an evolutionary history dating before the Late Jurassic.

ARCHAEORNIS   Peteronievics *see in* Peteronievics and Woodward 1917 —(See *Archaeopteryx*.)
Name derivation: Greek *archaio* = "ancient" + Greek *ornis* = "bird."
Type species: *A. siemensii* (Dames 1897).

ARCHAEOVOLANS   Czerkas and Xu 2002 —(See *Yanornis*.)
Name derivation: Greek *archaio* = "ancient" + Latin *volans* = "flyer."
Type species: *A. repatriatus* Czerkas and Xu 2002.

ASIAHESPERORNIS   Nessov and Prizemlin 1991
Herperornithiformes *incertae sedis*.
Name derivation: "Asia" + *Hesperornis*.
Type species: *A. bazhanovi* Nessov and Prizemlin 1991.
Occurrence: Priozernyi Quarry, Kushmurun locality, near settlement of Kushmurun, Eginsai Svita, Turgai Strait, Kustanaiskaya Province, North Kazakhstan.
Age: Late Cretaceous (latest Santonian–early Campanian).
Holotype: IZASK 5/287/86a, shaft of tarsometatarsal, vertebrae.

Diagnosis of genus (as for type species): Medial condyle of tibiotarsus markedly mediolaterally compressed, cranial intercondylar furrow relatively deep; tarsometatarsus comparatively gracile, with parallel lateral and medial sides; lateral and medial crests on plantar side of tarsometatarsus with sharp plantar margin, flexor groove shallow; dorsal facet in middle of tarsometatarsal shaft deep, narrow, covered by high dorsolateral crest, separate medial facet developed on distal portion of shaft; base of trochlea of digit IV much larger than base of trochlea of digit III, fossa for metacarpal I very small and short (Kurochkin 2000).Large flightless bird; first record of the Hesperornithiformes in the former USSR.

AUSTINORNIS   Clarke 2004 [?*nomen dubium*]
Pangalliformes.
Name derivation: "Austin [Chalk" + Greek *ornis* = "bird."
Type species: *A. lentus* (Marsh 1880) [?*nomen dubium*].
Occurrence: Austin Chalk, Collin County, near Fort McKinney, Texas, United States.
Age: Late Cretaceous.
Holotype: YPM 1796, well-preserved, incomplete distal left tarsometatarsus.

Differing from *Ichthyornis dispar* in almost all comparable anatomical features —*e.g.*, slight groove extending proximally from juncture of metatarsals II and III on dorsal surface of metatarsus; distinct groove on metatarsus, extending proximally from distal vascular foramen (distal enclosure much more solid in *I. dispar*); metatarsal II approaching IV in distal extent (rather than much shorter than IV); trochlea of metatarsal II strongly rounded (rather than glymoid); fossa of metatarsal I slightly more proximally located; intermuscular lines well developed on distal plantar surface (not marked in *I. dispar*); trochlear surface on metatarsal III asymmetrically (rather than symmetrically) developed, lateral edge extending distinctively proximal to medial) pending further studies, possibly a *nomen dubium* based on an undiagnostic type specimen (Clarke 2004).

Note: Originally published by Marsh (1880) as the referred species *Graculavus lentus.*

AVISAURUS   Brett-Surman and Paul 1985
Avisauridae.
Name derivation: Latin *avis* = "bird" + Greek *sauros* = "lizard."
A. archibaldi Brett-Surman and Paul 1985
A. gloriae Varricchio and Chiappe 1995
Occurrence: Hell Creek Formation, Garfield County, Two Medicine Formation, Montana, United States; Lecho Formation, Argentina.
Age: Late Cretaceous (Campanian–Maastrichtian).
Holotype: UCMP 117600, left metatarsus.

Diagnosis of genus: Metatarsal III visible in anterior aspect over its entire length, broadest element proximally; metatarsals II and IV of equal length, having large, medial, concave articular facets proximally; trochlea of fourth metatarsal vestigial, highly divergent, spoon shaped, asymmetrical; knob on second metatarsal (for insertian of m. tibialis anticus?) relatively larger that in any other theropod; metatarsus very strongly lunate in cross section, caudally concave; shaft of metatarsal IV flat strap; metatarsal III triangular in cross section; metatarsal II most robust; tendency for metatarsus to be coosified into pseudo-tarsometatarsus; fusion at proximal end only (Brett-Surman and Paul 1985).

Diagnosis of *A. archibaldi*: Trochlea of fourth metatarsal remarkably concave medially, resulting in crescent shape in distal aspect (Varricchio and Chiappe 1995).

Diagnosis of *A. gloriae*: Small avisaurid; midlength cross section of tarsometatarsus relatively straight (*i.e.*, nonlunate); tubercle of second metatarsal distal to midpoint of shaft; small medially curving ridge on dorsal portion distal of metatarsal II; distal fusion between metatarsals III and IV (Varricchio and Chiappe 1995).

Type species originally described by Brett-Surman and Paul as a non-avian theropod, first occurrence of the same genus from both Laurasia and Gondwana.

BAPTORNIS   Marsh 1877
Baptornithidae.
Name derivation: Greek *bapto* = "dive" + Greek *ornis* = "bird."
Type species: *B. advenus* Marsh 1877.
Occurrence: Smoky Hill Member, Niobrara Chalk Formation, Wallace County, Kansas, United States.
Age: Late Cretaceous (?Santonian).

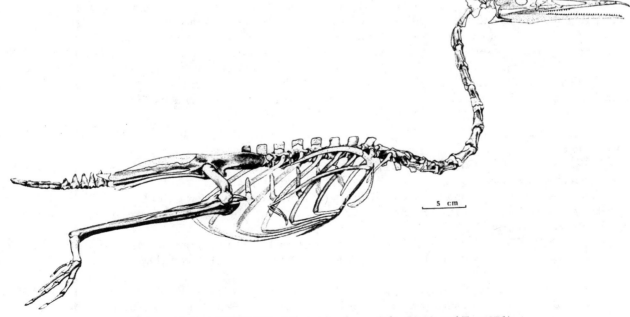

5 cm

Holotype skeleton (YPM 1465) of *Baptornis advenus*. (After Martin and Tate 1976.)

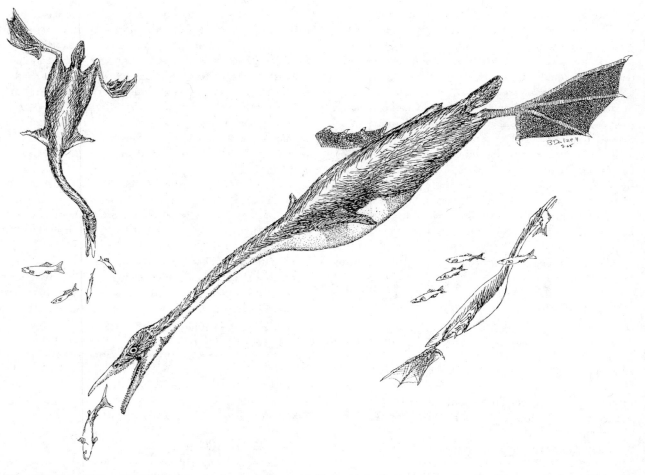

Life restoration of the aquatic bird *Baptornis advenus*, the feet probably not totipalmate as depicted in this illustration. (After Martin and Tate 1976.)

Lectotype: YPM 1465, distal end of tarsometatarsus.

Diagnosis of genus (as for type species): Foot-propelled diving bird approximately size of yellow-billed loon (*Gavia adamsii*); neck elongate; wing greatly reduced, radius and ulna present; tarsometatarsus less compressed than in *Neogaeornis* (Martin and Tate 1976).

Flightless, foot-propelled swimming bird, toothed but lacking teeth in predentary.

BOLUOCHIA   Zhou 1995
Enantiornithes.

Name derivation: "Boluochi [China]."

Type species: *B. zhengi* Zhou 1995.

Occurrence: Jiufotang Formation, Xidagou, Boluchi, Chaoying, Liaoning Province, northeastern China.

Age: Early Cretaceous (Aptian).

Holotype: IVPP V9770, incomplete skull, almost complete pelvic limbs, pygostyle, sternum, vertebrae, pelvic girdle.

Diagnosis of genus (as for type species): Premaxillary teeth absent, dentary teeth present; premaxilla hook-shaped; sternum caudally notched, with low keel distrib-

uted caudally; pygostyle longer than tarsometatarsus; pubis retroverted, strongly curved; intercondylar groove narrow at distal tibiotarsus; medial condyle of tibiotarsus almost as wide as lateral condyle, cranial margin of medial condyle flat in distal view; metatarsals II–IV almost equal in length; trochlea of metatarsal II wider than those of III and IV; trochlea of metatarsals II–IV on about same plane; pedal claws long, curved (Zhou and Hou 2002).

CANADAGA   Hou 1999
Hesperornithiformes.

Name derivation: "Canada" + Latin *ago* = "having characteristics of."

Type species: *C. arctica* Hou 1999.

Occurrence: Bylot Island, Arctic region of Northwest Territories of Canada.

Age: Late Cretaceous (middle Maastrichtian).

Holotype: CMN [formerly NMC] 41050, three cervical vertebrae, juvenile.

Diagnosis of genus (as for type species): Caudal part of cervical vertebrae laterally expanded, centrum wider than width of zygapophysis; concavitas lateralis large, deep, large process ventralis occupying crano-middle part of ventral side of centrum; dorsal process of vertebral arch short, robust; well-developed area for elastic ligament (Hou 1999).

Very large (1.5 meters or more than five feet in length) hesperornithiform (largest known member of this group) and the latest known occurrence of the Hesperornithiformes; referred juvenile bones suggesting colony breeding.

CATENOLEIMUS   Panteleev 1998
?Enantiornithes *incertae sedis.*
Name derivation: Latin *catena* = "lineage/chain" + Latin *leimma* = "remainder."
Type species: *C. anachoretus* Panteleev 1998.
Occurrence: Bissekty Formation, Uzbekistan, Central Kyzylkum.
Age: Late Cretaceous (Coniacian).
Holotype: PO 4606, shaft of ?coracoid.

Head of putative coracoid "oriented differently" than in other enantiornithies (Panteleev 1998).

CATHAYORNIS   Zhou, Jin and Zhang 1992 — (See *Sinornis*); Cathayornithidae.
Name derivation: "Cathay [old poetic name for China]" + Greek *ornis* = "bird."
Type species: *C. yandica* Zhou, Jin and Zhang 1992.

CERAMORNIS   Brodkorb 1963
Neornithes *incertae sedis.*
Name derivation: Greek *keramos* = "pottery clay" + Greek *ornis* = "bird."
Type species: *C. major* Brodkorb 1963.
Occurrence: Lance Formation, near Lance Creek, Wyoming, United States.
Age: Late Cretaceous (Maastrichtian).
Holotype: UCMP 53959, shoulder end of right coracoid.

Diagnosis of genus: Coracoid similar to that of *Cimolopteryx*, glenoid facet comparatively shorter; scapular cup somewhat less deep; procoracoid foramen high, approaching level of scapular cup (Brodkorb 1963).

Diagnosis of *C. major*: Smaller than *Cimolopteryx maxima*, larger than other species of *Cimolopteryx* (Brodkorb 1963).

Almost as big as a large gull.

CHANGCHENGORNIS   Ji, Chiappe and Ji 1999
Confuciusornithidae.
Name derivation: Chinese *Chang Cheng* = "Great Wall" + Greek *ornis* = "bird."
Type species: *C. hengdaoziensis* Ji, Chiappe and Ji 1999.
Occurrence: Hengdaozi Member of the Chaomidianzi Formation (formerly considered to be the lower part of the Yixian Formation), Jianshangou village, western Liaoning Province, northeastern China.
Age: Early Cretaceous (see Swisher, Wang, Zhou, Wang, Jin, Zhang, Xu, Zhang and Wang 2001).
Holotype: GMV2129-a/b, nearly complete skeleton including most feathers, slab and counterslab.

Diagnosis of genus (as for type species): Beak strongly curved; mandible very high caudally, much shorter than skull; deltopectoral crest of humerus not perforated by large foramen (as in *Confuciusornis*); metacarpal I almost half length of II; hallux proportionally longer than in *Confuciusornis* (Ji, Chiappe and Ji 1999).

Bluejay-sized, very similar to *Confuciusornis*, but with curved beak and much shorter lower jaw, these and other morphological differences (*e.g.*, more advanced perching foot) possibly attributed to feeding and ecological differences; large curved digits on wings possibly used in climbing.

CHAOYANGIA   Hou and Zhang 1993 — (=*Songlingornis*; =?*Yanornis*)
Ornithurae.
Name derivation: "Chaoyang [China]."
Type species: *C. beishanensis* Hou and Zhang 1993.
Occurrence: Jiufotang Formation, Xidagou, Boluochi, Chaoyang, Liaoning Province, northeast China.
Age: Early Cretaceous (Aptian).
Holotype: IVPP V9934, pelvis, femora, tibiotarsus, vertebrae, ribs with uncinate processes.

Diagnosis of genus (as for type species): Premaxillary and dentary teeth; sternum elongated, keel extending along its full length; craniolateral process, costal process, and deep facet for articulation with coracoid developed on sternum; pair of small medial fenestrae and short, expanded lateral trabecula on sternum caudally; coracoid with procoracoidal process and deep, round scapular facets developed; furcula U-shaped, lacking hypocleidium; synsacrum comprising more than eight vertebrae; uncinate processes on ribs long, slender, ventrally distributed; caudal process of ilium slightly rounded; pubic symphysis about one-third length of pubis; crest of trochanter high on femur; cnemial crest on proximal tibiotarsus; tarsometatarsus partially fused distally; well-developed external rim of trochlea of pedal digit IV; ungual phalanx of pedal digit I smaller than others on foot (Zhou and Hou 2002).

Referred specimen IVPP V10913 sold as holotype of *Songlingornis linghensis* (see Hou 1997*b*).

More modern in appearance than other known birds from this site.

CIMOLOPTERYX   Marsh 1892
?Charadriiformes.
Name derivation: Greek *kilolia* = "chalk [Cretaceous]" + Greek *pteron* = "wing."
Type species: *C. rara* Marsh 1892.

Other species: *C. maxima* Brodkorb 1963, *C. minima* Brodkorb 1963, *C. petra* Hope 2002.

Occurrence: Lance Formation, Laramie Deposits, Ceratops Beds, Niobrara [formerly Converse] County, Wyoming, United States; Shaunavon, Saskatchewan, Dinosaur Park Formation, Alberta, Canada.

Age: Late Cretaceous (Middle Campanian–late Maastrichtian).

Holotype: YPM 1805, left coracoid.

Diagnosis of genus (as for type species): Derived features including the following: coracoid robust; neck of coracoid stout, subtriangular in cross section; scapular cotyla of coracoid slightly elongated transverse to long axis of coracoid; small lateral process of coracoid (Hope 2002).

Diagnosis of *C. maxima*: About twice size of *C. rara*; neck of shaft flatter, broader; foramen for N. surpacoracoideus less recessed from scapular facet, much less steeply angled in its course than in *C. rara* (Hope 2002).

Diagnosis of *C. minima*: Agreeing with *C. rarus* in having scapular facet a deep cup and caudal opening of procoracoid foramen well below level of scapular facet, differing in much smaller size (Brodkorb 1963).

Diagnosis of *C. petra*: As for *C. rara*, but approximately one-third smaller (Hope 2002).

Very small to moderately large, about gull-sized.

COLONOSAURUS   Marsh 1872 — (See *Ichthyornis*.)
Name derivation: Greek *kylos* = "stunted" + Greek *sauros* = "lizard."
Type species: *C. mudgei* Marsh 1872

CONCORNIS   Sanz and Buscalioni 1992 — (=?*Sinornis*)
Euornithoformes.
Name derivation: Latin *concha* = "shell" plus Greek *ornis* = "bird."
Type species: *C. lacustris* Sanz and Buscalioni 1992.
Occurrence: Calizas de la Huérguina Formation, Las Hoyas fossil site, La Cierva township, province of Cuenca, Spain.
Age: Early Cretaceous (late Barremian).
Holotype: LH-2814, incomplete skeleton, most postcranial elements articulated including right forelimb and thoracic girdle, sternum, some dorsal, synsacral, and caudal vertebrae, pubis, ischium, hindlimbs, feathers, preserved in slab and smaller counterslab.

Diagnosis of genus (as for type species): Enantiornithine having the following autapomorphies: ischium ribbon-like; transverse ginglymoid articulation of trochlea of metatarsal I; strongly curved, laterally excavated distal end of metatarsal IV (latter two features differentiating this taxon from all others for which tarsometatarsus is known); differing from *Enantiornis leali* (latter very robust and large, humerus having large, shallow transverse ligamental groove); differing from *Neuquenornis volans* by furcula

having long hypocleidium, sternal carina developed only in caudal half of sternum, straight metatarsal I, much stronger lateral grooves on centra of dorsal vertebrae, major metacarpal more robust than minor metacarpal, much broader intermetacarpal space (distinguishing taxon from "*Cathayornis yandica*" [=*Sinornis santensis*], latter having extremely narrow intermetacarpal space; *C. lacustris* also differing from "*C. yandica*" in having larger claws in forelimb and by dorsal centra not excavated by two (cranial and caudal) small depressions (Sanz, Chiappe and Buscalioni 1995).

Oldest enantiornithine bird yet found in the Western Hemisphere.

CONFUCIUSORNIS   Hou, Zhou, Gu and Zhang 1995
Confuciusornithidae.
Name derivation: "Confucius [Chinese teacher and philosopher, 551–479 B.C.]" + Greek *ornis* = "bird."

Photograph by Mick Ellison, courtesy Luis M. Chiappe.

Confuciusornis sanctus (GMV-2132), referred specimen from the Chamidianzi Formation of northeastern China.

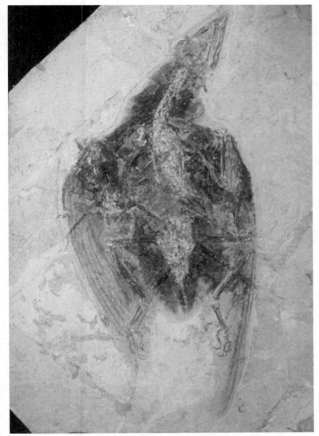

One of the numerous referred specimens of *Confuciusornis sanctus* from the Early Cretaceous of northeastern China.

Type species: *C. sanctus* Hou, Zhou, Gu and Zhang 1995.

Other species: *C. dui* Hou, Martin, Zhou, Feduccia and Zhang 1995.

Occurrence: Yixian Formation, Huanghuagou and Sihetun, Shangyuan, Beipiao, Liaoning Province, northeast China.

Age: Early Cretaceous (Hauterivian; see Swisher, Wang, Zhou, Wang, Jin, Zhang, Xu, Zhang and Wang 2001).

Holotype: IVPP V10918, skull, humerus, radius, manus.

Diagnosis of genus (as for type species): Teeth completely lost; horny beak; postorbital robust, Y-shaped, with slender ascending process; quadrate high, no orbital process developed; dentary branched caudally; large rostral mandibular fenestra, small, rounded caudal mandibular fenestra; centrum of dorsal vertebrae having deep lateral depressions; synsacrum comprising seven vertebrae; pygostyle comprising eight or nine vertebrae; sternum without keel; gastralia; coracoid short, fused with scapula; furcula robust, lacking hypocleidium; humerus large at proximal end, with developed deltopectoral crest, elliptical fenestra or depression; humerus slightly longer than ulna; semilunate bone fused with major metacarpal; ulnare slender; major and minor metacarpals nearly equal in length; minor metacarpal reduced, proximally narrow; manual phalangeal formula of 2-3-4-x-x; short first phalanx of minor digit; ungual phalanges large, curved in alular and minor digits, small in major digit; major and minor digits of almost equal length; ischium having high, strut-like proximodorsal process; fibula about three-fourths length of tibiotarsus; metatarsal V approximately one-third length of III (Zhou and Hou 2002).

Known from several hundred specimens, many with feather impressions.

CONIORNIS Marsh 1893 — (=?*Hesperornis*)

Hesperornithiformes.

Name derivation: Greek *konis* = "chalk [Cretaceous]" + Greek *ornis* = "bird."

Type species: *C. altus* Marsh 1893.

Occurrence: Judith River deposits, Dog Creek, Montana, United States.

Age: Late Cretaceous (Campanian).

Holotype: YPM collection, right tibia.

Diagnosis of genus (as for type species): Differs from *Hesperornis* having lower outer condyle of tibia, inner condyle almost on line with inner margin of shaft (Marsh 1893).

About two-thirds the size of *Hesperornis regalis*; deposits where this bird was collected indicate that hesperoriforms also lived in freshwater environments.

Life restoration by artist Gregory S. Paul of *Confuciusornis sanctus*.

CRETAAVICULUS   Bazhanov 1969
Aves *incertae sedis.*
Name derivation: "Cretaceous" + Latin *avis* = "bird"
Type species: *C. sarysuensis* Bazhanov 1969.
Occurrence: Taldysai, Dzhezkazgan Province, Kazakhstan.
Age: Late Cretaceous.
Holotype: Feather impressions.

CUSPIROSTRISORNIS   Hou 1997
Cuspirostrisornithidae.
Name derivation: Latin *cuspirostris* = "having pointed rostrum" + Greek *ornis* = "bird."
Type species: *C. houi* Hou 1997.
Occurrence: Jiufotang Formation, Boluchi, Chaoyang, Liaoning Province, northeastern China.
Age: Early Cretaceous (?Barremian).
Holotype: IVPP V 10897, mostly articulated skeleton with skull.

Diagnosis of genus (as for type species): Rostrum slender; premaxilla having long, slender nasal process, short maxillary process; five premaxillary and five dentary teeth; lower jaw straight, slender; humerus slightly shorter than ulna and radius; moderately developed pneumatic fossa and capital groove of humerus, tuberculum vetrale and tuburculum dorsale conspicuous; humeral shaft curved (as in modern birds); sternum with manubium, with short cranial lateral process; keel relatively developed; cranial process approximately same length as caudal process; femur with large internal condyle; cnemial crest of tibiotarsus clearly present; pedal claw curved (Hou, Zhou, Zhang and Gu 2002).

Approximately size of a large sparrow.

ENALIORNIS   Seeley 1876 —(=*Palaeocolymbus, Pelagornis*)
Enaliornithiodae.
Name derivation: Greek *enalios* = "belonging to the sea" + Greek *ornis* = "bird."
Type species: *E. barretti* Seeley 1876.
Other species: *E. sedgwicki* Seeley 1876.
Occurrence: Cambridge Greensand of Upper Gault, neighborhood of Coldham Common or at Granchester, Cambridgeshire, England.
Age: Middle Cretaceous (late Albian).
Lectotype: BMNH A477 (original bone for cast BMNH A112; see Galton and Martin 2002), distal end of left tarsometatarsus.

Diagnosis of genus: Antitrochanter on ilium (not strongly produced laterally); femur proximally lacking distinct neck; proximal end of tarsometatarsus having small medial cotyla, distal end arched in distal view with dorsal edge of lateral trochlea (IV) plantar to prominent dorsal edge of subequal middle trochlea (III) (Galton and Martin 2002*a*).

Diagnosis of *E. barretti*: Large; femoral trochanter large, rugose; proximal tibiotarsus proportionally deep, narrow, with massive lateral and medial condyles cranially, slope of lateral condyle continuous with intercondylar sulcus meeting medial condyle at obtuse angle (outline of deep sulcus roughly L-shaped), small angular condylesc caudally having intercondylar angle slightly lateral in position; medial cotylus (II) proximal end of tibiotarsus almost square in outline (Galton and Martin 2002*b*).

Diagnosis of *E. sedgwicki*: Small; distal tibiorarsus having small lateral and medial condyles that are almost equal in size, with broad shallo cranial intercondylar fossa, caudally intercondylar angle slightly lateral in position (Galton and Martin 2002*b*).

Basal hesperornithiform, earliest known foot-propelled diving bird, larger than the common pidgeon, *E. sedgwicki* the less common species.

ENANTIORNIS   Walker 1981
Enantiornithies.
Name derivation: Greek *enantios* = "opposite" + Greek *ornis* = "bird."
Type species: *E. leali* Walker 1981.
Other species: *E. martini* Nessov and Panteleev 1993, *E. walkeri* Nessov and Panteleev 1993.
Occurrence: Dzharakhuduk locality, Bissekty Svita, Navoi District, Bukhara Province, Uzbekistan.
Age: Late Cretaceous (Coniacian).
Holotype: PO 4825, dorsal fragment of left coracoid.

Diagnosis of genus: Deep fossa on cranial surface of scapula; scapular facet and scapular glenoid separated; ischium wide; tibiotarsus having straight, robust shaft; metatarsal III having strongly convex transversely dorsal surface; medial ridge of trochlea on metatarsal III projecting markedly on planar side (Kurochkin 2000).

Diagnosis of *E. leali*: Shoulder end of coracoid short, robust; acrocoracoid and coracoidal process stout; scapular acromion broad, top obtuse; fossa or foramen on cranial surface of shoulder end of scapula; scapular facet and glenoid facet of scapula separated; dorsal portion of humeral head longer than ventral portion; distinct cranial fossa in cranial surface of proximal end of humerus; deltopectoral crest having thin proximal base; distinct depression in caudal surface of proximal end of humerus (Kurochkin 2000).

Diagnosis of *E. martini*: Coracoidal process stout; proximal portion of coracoidal shaft gracile (Kurochkin 2000).

Diagnosis of *E. walkeri*: Coracoidal process narrow lateromedially; proximal portion of coracoidal shaft stout (Kurochkin 2000).

EOALULAVIS   Sanz, Chiappe, Perez-Moreno, Buscalioni, Moratalla, Ortega and Poyato-Ariza 1996
Enantiornithes.

Name derivation: Greek *eos* = "dawn" plus Latin *alula* = "bastard wing" plus Latin *avis* = "bird."

Type species: *E. hoyasi* Sanz, Chiappe, Perez-Moreno, Buscalioni, Moratalla, Ortega and Poyato-Ariza 1996.

Occurrence: Calizas de la Huérguina Formation, Las Hoyas fossil site, La Cierva township, province of Cuenca, Spain.

Age: Early Cretaceous (late Barremian).

Holotype: LH 13500, skeleton including (slab, 13500*a*) 15 vertebrae (including five cervicals), scapulae, left coracoid, proximal half of right coracoid, furcula and its hypocleidium, several ribs, almost complete left wing, right wing excluding manus, portions of left ilium, proximal end of left femur, sacrum, (counterslab, 13500*b*) seven vertebrae (including five cervicals), coracoids, proximal end of left scapula, furcula, sternum, several ribs, left wing, right humerus, right ulna-radius, (both slabs) feathers, digestive contents (crustacean).

Diagnosis of genus (as for type species): Autapomorphies including the following: laminar, keellike cervical and dorsal centra; furcula with undulating ventral surface; distal end of humerus having thick, caudally projected ventral margin; several small tubercles on distal, caudal surface of minor metacarpal; sternum depressed, spear-shaped, with footlike caudal expansion and faint carina; sternum with deep, rostral cleft (Sanz, Pérez-Moreno, Chiappe and Buscalioni 2002).

Oldest known bird showing evidence of alula, or "bastard wing," suggesting "that as early as 115 million years ago birds had evolved a sophisticated structural system that enabled them to fly at low speeds and to attain high maneuverability."

EOCATHAYORNIS   Zhou 2002

Cathayornithidae.

Name derivation: Greek *Eo* = "dawn" + *Cathay* [old poetic name for China] + Greek *ornithos* = "bird."

Type species: *E. walkeri* Zhou 2002.

Occurrence: Jiufotang Formation, Boluochi, Chaoyang County, Liaoning Province, northeast China.

Age: Early Cretaceous (Aptian).

Holotype: IVPP V10916, skeleton including skull, complete forelimbs and coracoids, scapulae, sternum, rib fragments.

Diagnosis of genus (as for type species): Cranial cervical vertebrae heterocoelous; length of coracoid approximately twice width; sternum having pair of posterolateral processes; length of ulna about 100 percent that of humerus; radius approximately three-fourths as wide as ulna; manus slightly shorter than forearm (Zhou 2002).

Small, more primitive than "*Cathyornis* [=*Sinornis*], jaws with teeth, advanced features of scapula and wing suggesting powerful flapping flight capability.

EOENANTIORNIS   Hou, Martin, Zhou and Feduccia 1999

Enantiornithes.

Name derivation: Greek *eo* = "dawn" + *Enantiornis*.

Type species: *E. buhleri* Hou, Martin, Zhou and Feduccia 1999.

Occurrence: Yixian Formation, Shihetun, Beipiao, Liaoning Province, China.

Age: Early Cretaceous (Hauterivian; see Swisher, Wang, Zhou, Wang, Jin, Zhang, Xu, Zhang and Wang 2001).

Holotype: IVPP V11537, almost complete skeleton (lacking right wing).

Diagnosis of genus (as for type species): Moderate-sized, toothed, with short rostrum; skull deep; dorsal maxillary process forming entire posterior margin of narial opening; neck long, 11 cervical vertebrae; furcula "V" shaped, with long hypocleidium; coracoids broad at base, relatively short; sternum with single, short caudolateral process; claws on wings, less reduced than in *Sinornis*; carpometacarpus short, outer metacarpal (IV) extending past but not fused to distal end of middle metacarpal (III); manual digit II long, slender; pygostyle long; sternum not strongly emarginate caudally; ?gastralia (Hou, Martin, Zhou and Feduccia 1999).

Holotype preserving alula (bastard wing) and offering best preserved example of avian teeth after *Archaeopteryx*, "demonstrating that all birds share a uniform-tooth morphology presently unknown in adult or juvenile dinosaurs"; smaller than *Archaeopteryx* and *Confuciusornis*, larger than Early Cretaceous enantiornithines (see Martin 1995).

EUROLIMNORNIS   Kessler and Jurcsák 1986

Ornithurae *incertae sedis*.

Name derivation: Latin *Euro* = "European" + "*Limnornis* [Greek *limne* = 'swamp' + Greek *ornis* = 'bird']."

Type species: *E. corneii* Kessler and Jurcsák 1985.

Occurrence: Wealden, Bihor County, Cornet, Romania.

Age: Early Cretaceous.

Holotype: MTCO 7896, poorly preserved distal end of right humerus with small part of shaft, fragment of shaft of ulna, distal end of carpometacarpus.

Distinct brachial fossa, rounded condyles on humerus, shown on figure published by Kessler and Jurcsák (1984), suggesting possible referral to Neornithes; however, evidence is insufficient to refer with confidence so ancient a bird to any clade beyond Ornithurae (Hope 2002).

EXPLORORNIS   Panteleyev 1998

Enantiornithes *incertae sedis*.

Name derivation: Latin *explorare* = "to explore" + Greek *ornis* = "bird."

Type species: *E. nessovi* Panteleyev 1998.

Other species: ?*E. walkeri* (Nessov and Panteleyev 1993).

Occurrence: Bissekty Formation, Uzbekistan, Central Kyzylkum.

Age: Late Cretaceous (Coniacian).

Holotype: PO 4819, distally incomplete coracoid.

Diagnosis of genus (as for type species): Coracoid process less prominent than in other known enantiornithines (possibly due to wear) (Panteleev 1998).

Diagnosis of ?*E. walkeri*: Coracoid head ventrally convex (distinguishing this species from most taxa, except ?*Neuquenornis*) (Panteleyev 1998).

GALLORNIS   Lambrecht 1931

?Neornithines.

Name derivation: Latin *Gallus* [ancient inhabitant of France] + Greek *ornis* = "bird."

Type species: *G. straeleni* Lambrecht 1931.

Occurrence: Auxerre, France.

Age: Early Cretaceous (Hauterivian).

Holotype: Proximal end of femur, fragment of humerus.

Material too poor for precise evaluation.

GANSUS   Hou and Liu 1984

Neornithes *incertae sedis*.

Name derivation: "Gansu [Province]."

Type species: *G. yumanensis* Hou and Liu 1984.

Occurrence: Xiagou Formation, Shenjiawan, Changma, Yumen, Gansu Province, northwest China.

Age: Early Cretaceous.

Holotype: IVPP V6862, distal tibiotarsus, complete left tarsometatarsus and foot.

Diagnosis of genus (as for type species): Lateral condyle of tibiotarsus larger than medial condyle; trochlea of metatarsal II remarkably higher and projected plantarly than those of III and IV; tarsometatarsus almost completely fused; pedal digit IV longer than III, both longer than tarsometatarsus; pedal phalanges long, ungual phalanges relatively short; ungual phalanges slightly curved; ungual phalanges with well-developed extensor tubercles (Zhou and Hou 2002).

First Mesozoic bird discovered in China, probably ornithurine, foot seemingly convergently similar to foot of neornithine diving birds.

GARGANTUAVIS   Buffetaut and Le Loeuff 1998

Name derivation: "Gargantua [giant from French medieval folk literature" + Latin *avis* = "bird."

Type species: *G. philoinos* Buffetaut and Le Loeuff 1988.

Occurrence: Bellevue site, Campagne-sur-Aude (department Aude), base of Marnes de la Maurine Formation, Combebelle site, (department Herault), southern France.

Age: Late Cretaceous (late Campanian–early Maastrichtian).

Holotype: MDE-C3-525, synsacrum with parts of pelvis.

Diagnosis of genus (as for type species): Very large, pelvis broad, acetabulum in very cranial position (at level of third and fourth synsacral transverse processes); synsacrum robust, relatively short, comprising 10 completely fused vertebrae; ilia not meeting each other dorsally; antitrochanter well developed, caudodoral to relatively large acetabulum (Buffetaut and Le Loeuff 1988).

Largest (pelvis heavy, 20 by 18 centimeters; femur stout, about 15 centimeters in circumference) known Mesozoic bird, flightless.

GOBIPTERYX   Elźanowski 1974 — (=?*Nanantius*)

?Enantiornithes.

Name derivation: "Gobi [Desert]" + Greek *pteron* = "wing."

Type species: *G. minuta* Elźanowski 1974.

Occurrence: Khulsan locality, Barun Goyot (Baruungoyot) Formation, Nemegt Basin, South Gobi Desert, Mongolian People's Republic.

Age: Late Cretaceous (late Campanian).

Holotype: ZPAL MgR-I/12, rostral portion of skull.

Diagnosis of genus (as for type species): Culmen straight and very thin above nasal openings; rostral ends of premaxilla and mandible flattened, tips rounded; mandibula having low, short symphysis on ventral margin of premaxilla and maxilla, dorsal margin of mandible flat; no distinct grooves on lateral surface of rostral portions of premaxilla and mandible; dorsal mandibular margin distinctly elevated above level of lateral mandibular process; large choanal fenestra in rostral area of palatal shelf (Kurochkin 2000).

Skull unique among birds in the unusual shape of the quadrate; only circumstantial evidence associating *Gobipteryx* with Enantiornithes, *e.g.*, lack of advanced characters common among that group, possession of primitive characters of the quadrate, pterygoid, and palate unknown in other enantiornithines.

GRACULAVUS   Marsh 1872 — (=*Limosavis*)

Graculavidae.

Name derivation: Latin *graculus* = "cormorant" + Latin *avus* = "ancestor, grandfather."

Type species: *G. velox* Marsh 1872.

Other species: *G. augustus* Hope 1999.

Occurrence: Navesink Formation or basal part of Hornerstown Formation, Monmouth County, New Jersey, Lance Formation, Niobrara County, Wyoming, United States.

Age: ?Late Cretaceous (?latest Maastrichian–?earliest Paleocene).

Holotype: YPM 855, proximal end of left humerus.

Diagnosis of genus: Derived features including the following: head of humerus small compared with that of extant charadriiforms; dorsal tubercle very far from humeral head; dorsal tubercle projected well away from shaft; broad, flat surface between ventral tubercle and dorsal tubercle of humerus; capital incisure of humerus terminated caudally by shallow sulcus; humeral head undercut by transversely oriented suclus; deep impressions for fascicles of M. humerotriceps within pneumotricipital fossa and raised scar near base of ventral tubercle (probably site for attachment of central tendon of muscle (Hope 2002, following Olson and Parris 1987, Hope 1999).

Diagnosis of *G. augustus*: Distinguished from *G. velox* by dorsal tubercle being positioned much farther from humeral head (Hope 2002).

Fairly large, about the size of [Paleocene bird] *Presbyornis* cf. *pervetus*, somewhat larger than the extant *Esacus magnirostris* (Olson and Parris 1987); resembles cormorants in some features, moderately large, "well-flying, probably far-ranging shorebirds" (Hope 2002).

GRIPHOSAURUS   Wagner 1861—(See *Archaeopteryx*.)
Name derivation: Greek *gryphos* = "enigma" + Greek *sauros* = "lizard."
Type species: *G. problematicus* Wagner 1861.

GUILDAVIS   Clarke 2004
?Neognathae.
Name derivation: "[E. W.] Guild [discoverer and collector of the holotype] + Latin *avis* = "bird."
Type species: *G. tener* (Marsh 1880).
Occurrence: Niobrara Chalk Formation, Wallace County, Kansas, United States.
Age: Late Cretaceous (Coniacian–early Campanian).
Holotype: YPM 1760, two fragments of sacrum; fragment from cranial end preserving cranial articular surface and three cranialmost ankylosed vertebrae; second fragment crushed, from middle of sacral series.

Diagnosis of genus (as for type species): Ilium overlapping at least one set of ribs (indicated by parapophyses visible on first sacral vertebra) (Clarke 2004).

Differing from holotype of *Ichthyornis dispar* in the following: Smaller size, diameter of cranial articular surface of first sacral vertebra being less by about one third; parapophysis on left side of completely fused first sacral vertebra; widths of iliosacral sulci seemingly greater.

Note: Originally described by Marsh (1880) as the referred species *Ichthyornis tener*.

GURILYNIA   Kurochkin 1999
Enantiornithes *incertae sedis*.
Enantiornithes.
Name derivation: "Gurilyn [Tsav locality]."
Type species: *G. nessovi* Kurochkin 1999.

Occurrence: Nemegt Formation, Gurilyn Tsav, South Gobi Aimak, Mongolia.
Age: Late Cretaceous (Maastrichtian).
Holotype: PIN 4499-12, distal end of left humerus, PIN 4499-13, shoulder end of left coracoid.

Diagnosis of genus (as for type species): Distinguished from all other known enantiornithines for which the processes of the shoulder bones and the dorsal head of the coracoid are known by the following: both branches of humeral head approximately same size; top of coracoidal process acute, dorsal portion of coracoidal shaft very thin (Kurochkin 1999).

Documents the presence of relatively large enantiornithines in Central Asia during the Maastrichtian.

HALIMORNIS   Chiappe, Lamb and Ericson 2002
Enantiornithes.
Name derivation: Greek *halimos* = "belonging to the sea" + Greek *ornis* = "bird."
Type species: *H. thompsoni* Chiappe, Lamb and Ericson 2002.
Occurrence: Mooreville Chalk Formation (unnamed lower member), west of Clinton, Greene county, western Alabama, United States.
Age: Late Cretaceous (early–middle Campanian).
Holotype: D2K 035 (formerly Red Mountain Museum collection), proximal end of right humerus, distal end of right femur, two trunk vertebrae, caudal vertebra, pygostyle; and (UAMNH PV996.1.1), shoulder half of left scapula, thoracic vertebral column, thoracic neural arch.

Diagnosis of genus (as for type species): Enantiornithine; autapomorphies comprising the following: bicipital crest of humerus approaching level of humeral head, thus more proximally located than in any other known enantiornithine; inflated area projecting laterally in distal end of femur (Chiappe, Lamb and Ericson 2002).

The "first enantiornithine bird to be discovered in deposits formed on the eastern margin of the Western Interior Seaway."

HARGERIA   Lucas 1903—(See *Hesperornis*.)
Name derivation: "[Oskar] Harger [assistant to Othniel Charles Marsh]."
Type species: *H. gracilis* (Marsh 1876).

HESPERORNIS   Marsh 1873—(=*Hargeria*, *Lestornis*; =?*Coniornis*)
Hesperornithithidae.
Name derivation: Greek *hesperos* = "western" + Greek *ornis* = "bird."

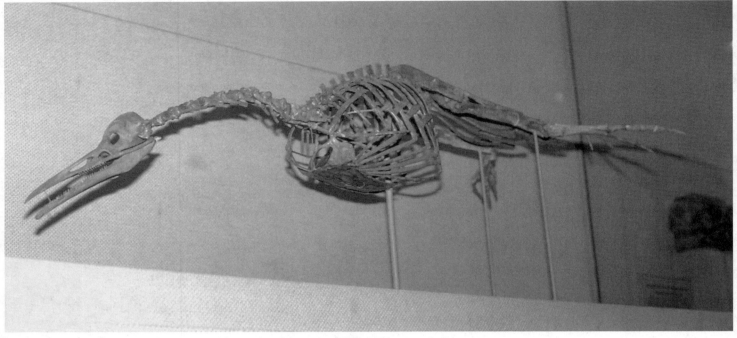

Skeleton of *Hesperornis regalis*.

Life-sized model of *Hesperornis regalis*.

Type species: *H. regalis* Marsh 1873.

Other species: *H. bairdi* Martin and Lim 2002, *H. chowi* Martin and Lim 2002, *H. crassipes* Marsh 1876, *H. gracilis* Marsh 1876, *H. macdonaldi* Martin and Lim 2002, *H. mengeli* Martin and Lim 2002, *H. rossicus* Nessov and Jarkov [Yarkov] 1993.

Occurrence: Niobrara Chalk Formation, Kansas, Pierre Shale Formation, Sharon Springs (lower Member), Pennington County, South Dakota, Buffalo Gap, southwestern South Dakota, United States, Bentonite quarries near Morden, southern Manitoba, Pierre Shale, Saskatchewan, Canada; Early Campanian of Volgograd Province, Russia.

Age: Late Cretaceous (Campanian).

Lectotype: YPM 1200, almost complete skeleton, including almost entire hindlimbs from femur to terminal phalanges, parts of pelvis, several cervical and caudal vertebrae, numerous ribs.

Diagnosis of genus (as for type species): Teeth in grooves; sternum without keel; rudimentary wings; hindlimbs closely resembling those of modern birds (Marsh 1873).

Diagnosis of *H. chowi*: Approximately the size of *H. regalis*, differing in having more elongate tarsometatarsus, with slender shaft, less enlarged outer trochlea, more slender caudal metatarsal ridge, inner metatarsal ridge shorter, less prominent (Martin and Lim 2002).

Diagnosis of *H. bairdi*: Smaller than *H. gracilis*, differing from *Parahesperornis* in having outer trochlea more enlarged and distal to middle trochlea (Martin and Lim 2002).

Diagnosis of *H. gracilis*: Smaller, more slender than *H. regalis*; tarsometatarsal very similar to but much less robust than in *H. regalis* (Marsh 1876c).

Diagnosis of *H. mengeli*: Smaller than *H. bairdi*, tarsometatarsus more slender than in other *Hesperornis* species; trochlea for digit III relatively smaller than in other species; distal end more compressed, trochlea for digit II completely behind that of III (Martin and Lim 2002).

Diagnosis of *H. macdonaldi*: Smallest known "hesperornithid," having C-shaped lateral margin of femur (characteristic of *Hesperornis* (Martin and Lim 2002).

Diagnosis of *H. rossicus*: Proximal articular surface of tarsometatarsus having very large transverse width, small dorsoplantar depth, diagonal slant strongly expressed, lateral edge of cotyla exceeding intercondylar prominence proximally, medial cotyla located more distal relative to lateral cotyla (Kurochkin 2000).

Large (type species about 1.8 meters long), with diminutive wings and very large feet, a foot-propelled diving bird.

HOREZMAVIS   Nessov and Borkin 1983

Aves incertae sedis.

Name derivation: "Horezm [oasis]" + Latin *avis* = "bird."

Type species: *H. eocretacea* Nessov and Borkin 1983.

Occurrence: Khodzhakul locality, middle member of Khodzhakul Svita, Karakalpuk Autonomous Region, near northwestern end of Sultan-Uvais mountain ridge, Karakalpakia, Uzbekistan.

Age: Middle Cretaceous (late Albian).

Holotype: PO 3390, proximal part of shaft of tarsometatarsus.

Diagnosis of genus (as for type species): Medial cotyla of tarsometatarsus inclined dorsally, located markedly more proximal than lateral cotyla; intercotylar prominence low; dorsal infracotylar fossa deep, elongate; dorsomedial margin sharpened; tuberosity for insertion of M. tibialis cranialis short, high, situated in proximal region of fossa; large vascular foramen on lateral side and impression for ligamental attachment on medial side being almost symmetrical relative to tuberosity; retinacula attachment proximal to ligamental attachment (mentioned above), close to dorsomedial margin; plantar crest relatively weak (Nessov and Borkin 1983).

IACEORNIS   Clarke 2004

?Neognathae.

Name derivation: Latin *Iaceo* = "to be neglected" + Greek *ornis* = "bird."

Type species: *I. marshi* Clarke 2004.

Occurrence: Niobrara Chalk Formation, Kansas, United States.

Age: Late Cretaceous (Coniacian–early Campanian).

Holotype: YPM 1734, postrania including pelvis, coracoids, scapulae, proximal left clavicle, proximal left radius, left ulnare and radiale, right carpometacarpus, first and second right phalanges on manual digit II, proximal and distal fragments of left femur, distal right tibiotarsus, rib, miscellaneous indeterminate elements.

Diagnosis of genus (as for type species): Autapomorphies of strongly tapering or pointed omal tip of furcula, hooked scapular acromion process (Clarke 2004).

Note: Holotype originally referred by Marsh (1880) to *Aptornis celer*.

IBEROMESORNIS   Sanz and Bonaparte 1992 —(=?*Sinornis*)

Enantiornithes.

Name derivation: "Iberian [Peninsula]" + Greek *ornis* = "bird."

Type species: *I. romerali* Sanz and Bonaparte 1992.

Occurrence: Las Hoyas site, Calizas de la Huérguina Formation, province of Cuenca, Spain.

Age: Early Cretaceous (late Barremian).

Holotype: LH-22 (provisionally housed in Unidad de Paleontologia of the Universidad Autónoma de Madrid, Spain), almost complete articulated skeleton lacking skull, cranial portion of neck, most of hands.

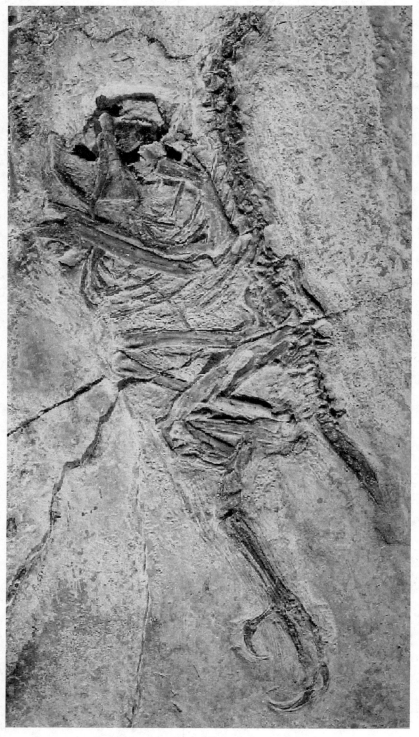

Iberomesornis romerali, LH-22, holotype skeleton.

Diagnosis of genus (as for type species): Autapomorphies including the following: cervical vertebrae having lateral shelf linking cranial and caudal zygapophyses; high vertebral arches of dorsal vertebrae, neural arches and laminar spines relatively high; very large laminar pygostyle;

tibiotarsus without cnemial crest (Sanz, Pérez-Moreno, Chiappe and Buscalioni 2002).

Primitive bird significant in regards early avian diversification; flight capability close to that of modern birds.

ICHTHYORNIS Marsh 1872 — (=*Angelinornis, Colonosaurus*); Ichthyornithiformes.

Name derivation: Greek *ikhthys* = "fish" + Greek *ornis* = "bird."

Type species: *I. dispar* Marsh 1872.

Occurrence: Smoky Hill Chalk Member of the Niobrara Formation, Kansas, Austin Chalk, Texas, Selma Chalk, Alabama, United States; ?Asia.

Age: Cretaceous (?Santonian).

Holotype: YPM 1450, incomplete skeleton.

Diagnosis of genus (as for type species): Quadrate having single, large pneumatic foramen on craniomedial surface of corpus, close to pterygoid articulation; cervical vertebrae amphicoelous or "biconcave"; proximal free caudal vertebrae having well-developed prezygapophyses clasping dorsal surface of preceding vertebra; scapula with extremely diminutive acromion process; bicipital crest of humerus with pit-shaped fossa for muscular attachment located directly at distal end of crest; dimensions of dorsal condyle of ulna such that length of trochlear surface along caudal surface of distal ulna is about equal to trochlear surface taken across its distal end; caudoventral surface

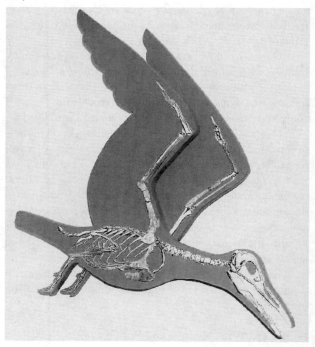

Ichthyornis dispar, FHSM VP-2503, referred skeleton discovered in 1970 in Graham County, Kansas, by paleontologist J. D. Stewart.

The aquatic bird *Ichthyornis dispar* as depicted in a detail from a mural at the Sternberg Museum of Natural History.

of distal radius having oval scar in center of depression (depressio ligamentosa in Aves [*sensu* Gauthier 1986]; see Baumel and Witmer 1993); carpometacarpus with large tubercle developed close to articular surface for first phalanx of second digit, where deep tendinal groove for m. extensor digitorum communis ends as this tendon passes distally to insert of first phalanx in crown clade (Stegmann 1978); phalanx II with internal index process (see Stegmann) (Clarke 2004).

Toothed, pigeon-sized (about 21 centimeters or eight inches tall), aquatic bird, basically modern in appearance (ternlike), probably web-footed (see Lim, Martin, Zhou, Baek and Yang 2002), vertebrae biconcave (unlike saddle-shaped vertebrae of extant birds), wings proportionally large; based on recent studies of the numerous specimens belonging to this genus, of eight species referred to this genus, only *I. dispar* is valid, variations in size and morphology explained by ontogeny, sexual dimorphism, and individual variation (see Clarke's 2004 major revision of this genus).

INCOLORNIS Panteleev 1998

Enantiornithes *incertae sedis*.

Name derivation: Latin *incola* = "inhabitant" + Greek *ornis* = "bird."

Type species: *I. silvae* Panteleev 1998.

Other species: *I. martini* Panteleev 1998.

Occurrence: Bissekty Formation, Uzbekistan, Central Kyzylkum.

Age: Late Cretaceous (Coniacian).

Holotype: PO 4604, proximal end of coracoid.

Diagnosis of genus: Coracoid shaft very deep (more than 40 percent length of proximodistal head); proximodorsal corcacoid bump (Panteleev 1998).

Diagnosis of *I. silvae*: Proximodorsal coracoid bump more distally located (Panteleev 1998).

Diagnosis of *I. martini*: Proximodorsal coracoid bump more proximally located (Panteleev 1998).

JEHOLORNIS Zhou and Zhang 2002 — (See *Shenzhouraptor.*)

Name derivation: "Jehol [Group]" +
Greek *ornis* = "bird."
Type species: *J. prima* Zhou and Zhang
2002

JIBEINIA Hou 2000
Pygostyla *incertae sedis*.
Name derivation: Chinese *Jibei niao* =
"Jibei [old name for Hebei Province]
bird."
Type species: *J. luanhera* Hou 2000.
Occurrence: Dongtuyao Quarry, Yixian
Formation, Tuyao village, Luanjitu
township, Fengning County, Hebei
Province, near Luan River (Luan
Hei), northern China.
Age: Early Cretaceous (Hauterivian; see
Swisher, Wang, Zhou, Wang, Jin,
Zhang, Xu, Zhang and Wang 2001).
Holotype: [No catalogue number given],
almost complete skeleton missing ros-
tral part of skull, preserved with
feather outlines.

   Diagnosis of genus (as for type
species): Skull 2.6 centimeters long, jaws
with numerous unserrated teeth; ?11 cervical vertebrae, centra nonhetero-
coelous; sternum wide, median process
long, lateral processes not expanded;
humerus 2.33 centimeters long; radius
2.42 centimeters long; ulna 2.4 centimeters long; carpometatarsus bones
close to each other but not fused; all
three manual digits with small claws; ?13
thoracic vertebrae; eight sacral vertebrae; tips of pubic bones fused, not expanded; femur 2.22 centimeters long;
tibiotarsus 2.8 centimeters long; tarsometatarsus 1.63 centimeters long;
metatarsal bones not completely fused
at proximal ends, distal ends not fused;
second metatarsal shorter than third and
fourth; 10 to 12 caudal vertebrae; pygostyle (Hou 1997*c*).

   Relatively primitive, sparrow-sized; first described by
Hou (1997*c*) as the unnamed "Jibei bird."

JINFENGOPTERYX Ji, Ji, Lü, You, Chen, Liu and Liu
2005
Archaeopteryigidae.
Name derivation: Chinese *Jinfeng* = "golden phoenix
[queen of birds in Chinese folklore]" + Greek *pteron* =
"wing."
Type species: *J. elegans* Ji, Ji, Lü, You, Chen, Liu and Liu
2005.

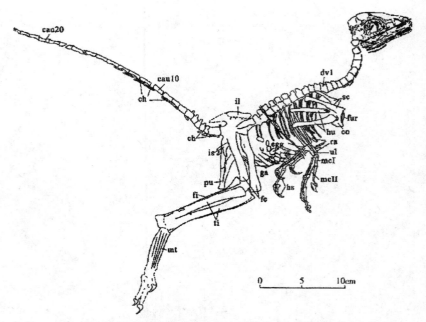

Jinfengopteryx elegans, CAGS-IG-04-0801, holotype skeleton. (After Ji, Ji, Lü, You,
Chen, Liu and Liu 2005.)

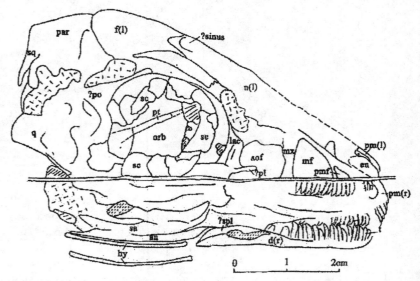

Jinfengopteryx elegans, CAGS-IG-04-0801, holotype skull. (After Ji, Ji, Lü, You, Chen,
Liu and Liu 2005.)

Occurrence: Northern part of Qiatou Formation, Hebei
Province, Fenging County, China.
Age: ?Late Jurassic or Early Cretaceous.
Holotype: CAGS-IG-0801, nearly complete skeleton with
skull, associated feather impressions.

   Diagnosis of genus (as for type species): Large [54.8
centimeters from rostrum to end of tail]; differing from *Archaeopteryx* in having more and closely packed teeth (18 in
upper and lower jaws, respectively), relatively shorter and
higher preorbital area of skull, relatively shorter metatarsal
II (in comparison with I), comparatively large, more robust hindlimb (forelimb to hindlimb ratio of 0.62); mainly

differing from *Shenzouraptor* and *Jixiangornis* in having much more teeth, much shorter forelimb compared to hindlimb; differing from troodontids in having fewer and unserrated teeth; differing from dromaeosaurids in lacking extremely long extension of prezygapophyses of caudal vertebrae (Ji, Ji, Hü, You, Chen, Liu and Liu 2005).

First "avalian" bird described from China, sister taxon of *Archaeopteryx*; strong hindlimbs indicative of a cursorial forager (Jin *et al.*).

JINZHOUORNIS   Hou, Zhou, Zhang and Gu 2001
Confuciusornithidae.
Name derivation: "Jinzhou [City] + Greek *ornis* = "bird.""
Type species: *J. yixianensis* Hou, Zhou, Zhang and Gu 2001.
Other species: *J. zhangjiyangia* Hou, Zhou, Zhang and Gu 2001.
Occurrence: Yixian Formation, Jinzhou City, Wutun Yi County, Liaoning Province, China.
Age: Early Cretaceous (Hauterivian; see Swisher, Wang, Zhou, Wang, Jin, Zhang, Xu, Zhang and Wang 2001).
Holotype: Skeleton.

Diagnosis of genus (as for type species): Medium-sized confuciusornithid; skull long, low; rostrum long, robust; braincase small; orbit of moderate size; length of rostrum before orbit more than half total length or skull; cervical vertebrae shorter than in *Confuciusornis*; more than 12 thoracic vertebrae; manual claws extremely curved; digits of metacarpal II nor much expanded; scapula approximately length of humerus; humerus slender; middle of metatarsal II with triangular process; metatarsal III with small process (Hou, Zhou, Zhang and Gu 2001).

Diagnosis of *J. zhangjiyingia*: Skull large, long; premaxilla protruding caudally, extending to caudal margin of orbit, located ventral to frontal; lower temporal fenestra particularly well developed; quadratojugal forming part of caudal margin of orbit; orbit of moderate size; furcula more slender than in *Confuciusornis*; clavicles widely separated distally; humeral shaft more robust than in the type species (Hou, Zhou, Zhang and Gu 2001).

JIXIANGORNIS   Ji, Ji, Zhang, You, Zhang, Wang, Yuan and Ji 2002
Aves *incertae sedis*.
Name derivation: "Jixiang" + Greek *ornis* = "bird."
Type species: *J. orientalis* Ji, Ji, Zhang, You, Zhang, Wang, Yuan and Ji 2002.
Occurrence: Lower Yixian Formation, Shihetun area, Beipiao City, northeastern Liaoning, China.
Age: Early Cretaceous (see Swisher, Wang, Zhou, Wang, Jin, Zhang, Xu, Zhang and Wang 2001).
Holotype: Skeleton including complete skull.

Diagnosis of genus (as for type species): Beak; sternum large with weak keel; furcula typically U-shaped;

forelimbs much longer than hindlimbs (ratio approximately 131:100); tail long, comprising about 27 caudal vertebrae (Ji, Ji, Zhang, You, Zhang, Wang, Yuan and Ji 2002).

Seemingly more capable of flight than *Shenzouraptor* and *Archaeopteryx*.

JUDINORNIS   Nessov and Borkin 1983
Baptornithidae.
Name derivation: "[ornithologist Konstantin Alexkseyevich] Yudin" + Greek *ornis* = "bird."
Type species: *J. nogontsovenis* Nessov and Borkin 1983.
Occurrence: Nogoon Tsav locality, Nemegt Formation, western area of Trans-Altai Gobi, Bayankhongor Aimag, southern Mongolia. Age: Late Cretaceous.
Holotype: PO 3389, incomplete thoracic vertebra.

Diagnosis of genus (as for type species): Articular surfaces of centrum of thoracic vertebra trapezoidal, extending transversely; ventral side of centrum distinctly narrowed in middle, very broad caudally, cranial zygapophyses close together on midline (Kurochkin 2000).

Small, foot-propelled seabird.

JURAPTERYX   Howgate 1985 — (See *Archaeopteryx*.)
Name derivation: "Jurassic" + Greek *pteron* = "wing."
Type species: *J. recurva* (Howgate 1984).

KIZYLKUMAVIS   Nessov 1984 — (=? *Sazavis*)
Alexornithidae.
Name derivation: "Kizylkum [Desert]" + Latin *avis* = "bird."
Type species: *K. cretacea* Nessov 1984.
Occurrence: Dzharakhuduk locality, Bissekty Svita, Navoi District, Bukhara Province, Uzbekistan.
Age: Late Cretaceous (Campanian–Maastrichtian).
Holotype: TsNIGR 51/11915, distal fragment of right humerus.

Diagnosis of genus (as for type species): Distal end of humerus very wide dorsoventrally; ventral portion of distal end of humerus remarkably enlarged; dorsal condyle broad; intercondylar furrow narrow; flexor process strongly projected distally (Kurochkin 2000, emended after Nessov 1984).

First member of the Enantiornithes described from the Old World; very small bird enantiornithine, maximum width of distal end of humerus just 5.1 millimeters.

KUSZHOLIA   Nessov 1992
Aves *incertae sedis*.
Name derivation: Kazakh *Kazakh kus zholi* = "bird's road," or "Milky Way."
Type species: *K. mengi* Nessov 1992.

Occurrence: Dzhyrakuduk locality, upper member of Bissekty Svita, Navoi District, Bukhara Province, Uzbekistan.

Age: Late Cretaceous (Coniacian).

Holotype: PO 4602, caudal portion of synsacrum.

Diagnosis of genus (as for type species): Synsacrum wide; transverse process of penultimate vertebra on synsacrum strongly developed, stout; caudal pleurocoels small but deep; caudal articular surface large, wide, dorsoventrally compressed; postzygapophyses of last vertebra on synsacrum very large; ventral groove particularly deep in articulated areas of centra; centrum of third vertebra from caudal end heavily compressed dorsoventrally (Nessov 1992).

Chicken-sized bird, flightless or nearly so; synsacra of this genus and that of *Patagopteryx* are similar in having an enlarged pair of transverse processes, although "*Patagopteryx* lacks the pleurocoels, a concave caudal articular surface, and a ventrally convex synsacrum" (present in *Kuszholia*) (Kurochkin 2000).

LAORNIS   Marsh 1870

Graculavidae.

Name derivation: Greek *laos* = "stone" + Greek *ornis* = "bird."

Type species: *L. edvardsiamus* Marsh 1870.

Occurrence: Pemberton Marl Company, "upper marl bed," Greensand, Birmingham, New Jersey, United States.

Age: Late Cretaceous (Maastrichtian).

Holotype: YPM collection, portion of shaft and distal end of left tibia.

Almost swan-sized wading bird; specimen showing "that the tibia, when entire, was of medium length, and quite robust" (Marsh 1870*b*).

LARGIROSTRISORNIS   Hou 1997

Cuspirostrisornithidae.

Name derivation: Latin *largus* = "large" + Latin *rostrum* = "rostrum" + Greek *ornis* = "bird."

Type species: *L. sexdentornis* Hou 1997.

Occurrence: Jiufotang Formation, near Boluochi, Chaoyang County, Liaoning Province, northeastern China.

Age: Early Cretaceous (Aptian).

Holotype: IVPP V 10531, almost complete, articulated skeleton with skull.

Diagnosis of genus (as for type species): Skull long; rostrum large, long; braincase shorter than rostral part of skull; nasal long; frontal wide; parietal round caudally; sex dentary teeth, teeth inclined distally; vertebrae amphicoelous; spinal crest especially high; sacrum basically fused; lateral process of sternum long; humerus S-shaped; capital groove on humerus; carpometacarpus basically fused; claws on distal manual phalanges (Hou, Zhou, Zhang and Gu 2002).

Sparrow-sized bird with large rostrum, six teeth in both sides of rostral area of upper jaw.

LECTAVIS   Chiappe 1993

Euenantiornithines *incertae sedis*.

Name derivation: Latin *lectus* = "bed [for Lecho Formation]" + Latin *avis* = "bird."

Type species: *L. bretincola* Chiappe 1993.

Occurrence: Lecho Formation, Estancia El Brete, Department of Candelaria, Province of Salta, northwestern Argentina.

Age: Late Cretaceous (Maastrichtian).

Holotype: PVL-4021-1, left tibiotarsus, incomplete tarsometatarsus (missing distal end of latter, most of metatarsal IV).

Diagnosis of genus (as for type species): Enantiornithine having long, slender tibiotarsus and tarsometatarsus having these autapomorphies: suboval articular surface of proximal end of tibiotarsus; distal tibiotarsal condyles strongly projected cranially; plantar surface of proximal half of metatarsal II forming prominent edge; subcircular knob on proximal end of metatarsal II; hypotarsus developed mostly over metatarsal II (Chiappe 1993).

LENESORNIS   Kurochkin 1996

Alexornithidae.

Name derivation: "Le[v]" + "Nes[spv, for 'Alexandrovich Nessov']" + Greek *ornis* = "bird."

Type species: *L. matlschevskyi* Kurochkin 1996.

Occurrence: Dzhyrakuduk locality, Bissektinskaya Svita, Navoi District, Bukhara Province, Uzbekistan.

Age: Late Cretaceous (Coniacian).

Holotype: PO 3434, cranial half of synsacrum.

Diagnosis of genus (as for type species): Cranial portion of synsacrum just slightly convex dorsally, cranial articular surface of synsacrum transversely elongated; third and fourth vertebrae of synsacrum having largest costal processes; central costal processes at right angle to sagittal plane; ventral groove wide, shallow (Kurochkin 2000).

Similar to *Nanantius valifanovi* (see Kurochkin 2000).

LESTORNIS   Marsh 1876 — (See *Hesperornis*.)

Name derivation: Greek *lestes* = "robber, thief" + Greek *ornis* = "bird."

Type species: *L. crassipes* (Marsh 1876).

LIAONINGORNIS   Hou 1997

Ornithurae.

Name derivation: "Liaoning [Province]" + Greek *ornis* = "bird."

Type species: *L. longidigiris* Hou 1997.

Occurrence: Yixian Formation, Shihetun, Shangyuan, Beipiao, Liaoning Province, northeast China.

Age: Early Cretaceous (Hauterivian; see Swisher, Wang, Zhou, Wang, Jin, Zhang, Xu, Zhang and Wang 2001).

Holotype: IVPP V11303, incomplete right forelimb, sternum, coracoid, complete right hindlimb, left tarsometatarsus, pedal phalanges.

Diagnosis of genus (as for type species): Smaller than "*Cathayornis*" [=*Sinornis*]; sternum elongated, keel extending along its full length; craniolateral process of sternum long; xiphoid end of sternum expanded laterally; sternum broad cranially, progressively narrow caudally, pair of large, deep notches on both sides; tarsometatarsus short, about half length of tibiotarsus; tarsometatarsus fused at both ends, but not along most of shaft; claws curved (Zhou and Hou 2002).

LIAOXIORNIS Hou and Chen 1999 —(=*Lingyuanornis*)

Aves *incertae sedis*.

Name derivation: Chinese *Liaoxi* [*liao* = "distant" + *xi* = "west," for western part of Liaoning Province] + Greek *ornis* = "bird."

Type species: *L. delicatus* Hou and Chen 1999.

Occurrence: Yixian Formation, Liaoxi, Liaoning Province, China.

Age: Early Cretaceous (Hauterivian; see Swisher, Wang, Zhou, Wang, Jin, Zhang, Xu, Zhang and Wang 2001).

Holotype: IVPP 130723, almost complete skeleton, some bones preserved as impressions.

Diagnosis of genus (as for type species): Rostral portion of premaxilla very narrow; external naris caudally located, extending nearly to caudal border of antorbitale fenestra; ?antorbital fenestra very small; retroarticular process very elongate; pygostyle very thin, spikelike; pygostyle longer than femur; ?no proximal ischial process (Hou and Chen 1999).

Smallest known adult Mesozoic bird, length approximately 8.5 centimeters (3.3 inches), with long bony tail (longest next to *Archaeopteryx*), manus with reduced number of phalanges and apparently lacking claws; resembling the primitive *Archaeopteryx* in some details, enantiornithines in other, possibly an evolutionary link between them.

LIMENAVIS Clark and Chiappe 2001

Carinatae *incertae sedis*.

Name derivation: Latin *limen* = "threshold" + Latin *avis* = "bird."

Type species: *L. patagonica* Clark and Chiappe 2001.

Occurrence: Allen Formation, Salitral Moreno, Río Negro Province, Patagonia, south-central Argentina.

Age: Late Cretaceous (late Campanian–early Maastrichtian).

Holotype: PVL 4731, parts of right wing, including end portions of humerus, ulna, carpometacarpus, digit II.

Diagnosis of genus (as for type species): Carinate bird with the following autapomorphies: attachment of pars ulnaris of trochlea humeroulnaris on proximal ulna developed as pit-shaped fossa, location of pisiform process with its proximal surface at approximately same level as proximal surface of metacarpal I, and scar of ligamentum collaterale, ventrale of ulna proximodistally elongate, extending down caudal margin of brachial impression; other characters including well-developed infratrochlear groove on ulnare; deep infratrochlear fossa of carpometacarpus; three fossae on proximal surface of dorsal supracondylar process of humerus (Clarke and Chiappe 2001).

Closer to modern birds than is *Ichthyornis*, yet outside avian crown group.

LIMNORNIS Jurcsák and Kessler 1983 —(Preoccupied, Gould 1839; see *Palaeocursornis*.)

Name derivation: Greek *limne* = "swamp, marsh" + Greek *ornis* = "bird."

LIMOSAVIS Shufeldt 1915 —(See *Graculavus*.)

Name derivation: Latin *limosus* = "muddy" + Latin *avis* = "bird" [for "godwit"].

Type species: *L. velox* (Marsh 1872).

LINGYUANORNIS Ji and Ji 1999 —(See *Liaoxiornis*.)

Name derivation: Chinese *Lingyuan* [city in Liaoning Province, China] + Greek *ornis* = "bird."

Type species: *L. parvus* Ji and Ji 1999.

LONCHODYTES Brodkorb 1963

?Procellariiformes.

Name derivation: Greek *logkhos* = "lance" + Greek *dytes* = "diver."

Type species: *L. estesi* Brodkorb 1963.

Other species: *L. pterygius* Brodkorb 1963.

Occurrence: Lance Formation, near Lance Creek, Wyoming, United States.

Age: Late Cretaceous (late Maastrichtian).

Holotype: UCMP 53954, distal end of right tarsometatarsus.

Diagnosis of genus (as for type species): Differing from *Gavia* in having less-compressed shaft of tarsometatarsus, with rounded edges, tendinal grooves less sharp; wide intertrochlear space; middle trochlea without swollen area on medial face; outer trochlea shorter, falling decidedly short of middle trochlea, its planter face shorter, its shaft with deep, wide groove leading from distal foramen; inner trochlea less deflected, wider, extending farther medial, with distinct intertrochlear space, its shaft and acrotarsial face rounded; no separate infratendinal shelf extending from below opening for extensor brevis digit quarti; depression on plantar surface of shaft at base of inner trochlea located proximo-mediad (rather than slightly disto-mediad) to distal foramen; more distinct facet for metatarsal I (Brodkorb 1963).

Diagnosis of *L. pterygius*: Differs from *Gavia* in having less fused metacarpals, metacarpal II longer (rather than shorter) than III, pit (rather than convex scar) near tip of metacarpal II, facet for digit III large, subtriangular sloping centromedially (rather than narrow, transverse, and horizontal) (Brodkorb 1963).

Possibly related to petrels; a large bird about twice the size of the petrel *Puffinus griseus*, less modified to a diving foot form than procellariidids and loons (see Hope 2002).

LONGCHENGORNIS   Hou 1997

Cathayornithidae.

Name derivation: Chinese *Longcheng* = "Longcheng 'Dragon Town,' ancient name for modern city of Chaoyang]" + Greek *ornis* = "bird."

Type species: *L. sanyanensis* Hou 1997.

Occurrence: Jiufotang Formation, Boluochi, Chaoyang County, Liaoning Province, northeastern China.

Age: Early Cretaceous (?Barremian).

Holotype: IVPP V. 10530, incomplete skeleton, skull fragments.

Diagnosis of genus (as for type species): Frontal narrow, expanded caudally; cervical vertebra with ventral crest; thoracic vertebra long, amphiplatyan; Concavitas lateralis large; caudal vertebrae free, long; proximal end of humerus larger than in *Sinornis*, expanding to two lateral portions; large, round depression at center of proximal end of humerus; humeral shaft straight; coracoid small, narrow, distally straight; furcula fin; furcular process long; tibiotarsus slim; pedal claw large, curved (Hou, Zhou, Zhang and Gu 2002).

LONGIPTERYX   Zhang, Zhang, Hou and Gu 2001

Longipterygidae.

Name derivation: Latin *longus* = "long" + Greek *pteron* = "wing."

Type species: *L. chaoyangensis* Zhang, Zhang, Hou and Gu 2001.

Occurrence: Jiufotang Formation, near Chaoyang City, Liaoning Province, China.

Age: Early Cretaceous (?Barremian).

Holotype: IVPP V 12325, complete skeleton, feather impressions.

Diagnosis of genus (as for type species): beak elongate, forming more than 60 percent skull length; forelimb long relative to hindlimb, humerofemoral ratio over 1.6; metatarsal IV longer than III (Zhang, Zhang, Hou and Gu 2001).

Resembles small (approximately 20 centimeters or eight inched in length) kingfisher; apparently a better flier than other primitive birds, but with claws on three wing fingers.

LONGIROSTRAVIS   Hou, Chiappe, Zhang and Chuong 2004

Euenanthiornithes.

Name derivation: Latin *longus* = "long" + Latin *rostrum* = "rostrum/beak."

Type species: *L. hani* Hou, Chiappe, Zhang and Chuong 2004.

Occurrence: Middle to upper Yixian Formation, Yixian County, Liaoning Province, northeastern China.

Age: Early Cretaceous (see Swisher, Wang, Zhou, Wang, Jin, Zhang, Xu, Zhang and Wang 2001)..

Holotype: IVPP V 11309, almost complete articulated skeleton with feather impressions.

Diagnosis of genus (as for type species): Small euenantionithine with the following autapomorphies: rostrum and mandible long, tapering, slightly curved; dentition restricted to rostral tip of rostrum and mandible; lateral process of sternum having three-branched, "moose-horn"-like distal expansion (Hou, Chiappe, Zhang and Chuong 2004).

Quail-sized; skull morphology suggesting probing feeding behavior, a specialization only known previously for Enantiornithes, this discovery offering "the first evidence of such a foraging behavior among basal lineages of Mesozoic birds."

NANANTIUS   Molnar 1986 — (=?*Gobipteryx*)

?Enantiornithes.

Name derivation: Greek *nanos* = "dwarf.

Type species: *N. valifanovi* Kurochkin 1996.

Other species: *N. eos* Molnar 1986.

Occurrence: Hermiin Tsav locality (northern slope), Barun Goyot (Baruungoyot) Formation, Trans-Altai Gobi Desert, South Gobi Aimag, Mongolia.

Age: Late Cretaceous (late Campanian).

Holotype: PIN 4492-1, partial skeleton including portions of skull, vertebrae, synsacrum, all bones of shoulder girdle, pelvis, most forelimb and hindlimb bones.

Diagnosis of genus: Maxilla and mandible short, high, stout; culmen very straight and thick above nasal opening; humerus with curved shaft having thin midportion; shaft of radius bowed; proximal phalanx of major digit with rectangular top; tibiotarsus with long, remarkably thin shaft, shaft bowed laterally; conspicuous intercondylar prominence on caudal area of proximal articular surface of tibiotarsus; lateral area of proximal articular surface of tibiotarsus sloping distally; well-developed fibular crest reaching margin of proximal articular surface; fibular crest situated along craniolateral edge of shaft of tibiotarsus;

proximal origin of fibular crest and top of cranial cnemial crest united together; elongate depressions running along cranial and caudal base of fibular crest; medial condyle of tibiotarsus transversely elliptical (not circular) in cranial aspect; fibula very short, flat, thin; metatarsals II to IV of similar thickness (Kurochkin 2000).

Diagnosis of *N. valifanovi*: Shallow longitudinal groove on ventral side of mandible; shallow, broad axial groove on ventral side of synsacrum; short fibular crest on tibiorsus measuring approximately five times transverse width of proximal articular surface; nutrient foramen on cranial side of tibiotarsus, close to tibial extremity of fibular crest; proximal shaft of tibiotarsus having subtriangular cross section and sharpened caudal edge; transversely compressed lateral condyle of tibiotarsus, projecting markedly craniad in distal aspect; metatarsal IV shorter than II (Kurochkin 2000).

Diagnosis of *N. eos*: Distinguished from *N. valifanovi* in having relatively shorter fibular crest, lesser transverse width of proximal articular surface of tibiotarsus, absence of nutrient formanen near end of fibular crest (present in the type species), rounded caudal side of proximal shaft (sharpened in the type species), more proximally located turbercle of ascending process (centrally placed in the type species), smaller cranial protrudence of lateral condyle, more circular medial condyle (slightly compressed proximodistally in the type species), shallower and narrower cranial intercondylar fossa, and smaller size (tibiotarsus of the type species approximately 30 percent longer) (Kurochkin 2000).

Short tarsometatarsus and relatively short, powerful pedal digits II and III of *N. valifanovi*, with strong, slightly curved claws indicative of arboreal behavior; although sometimes regarded as synonymous with *Gobipteryx minuta* (from the same formation of the South Gobi, sharing some common features with that taxon, *e.g.*, configuration of maxillary segment, conspicuous rows of nutrient foramina in maxilla and mandible), *N. valifanovi* differs from *G. minuta* in various ways, *e.g.*, rostral portions of upper jaw and mandible more robust; rostral ends of upper jaw and mandible sharper; thin, acute contact surfaces of maxilla and mandible; deep grooves with nutrient foramina in both upper jaw and mandible; nutrient foramina restricted to rostral half of maxillary rostrum; nutrient foramina becoming larger caudally; axial groove on ventral side of mandible (Kurochkin 2000).

NEOGAEORNIS   Lambrecht 1929
Baptornithidae.
Name derivation: Greek *neos* = "new" + Greek *gaia* = "earth" + Greek *ornis* = "bird."
Type species: *N. wetzeli* Lambrecht 1929.
Occurrence: Quiriquina Formation, Arauco Group, west end of Bahia San Vicente, southern point of Peninsula Tumbers, Province of Concepción, Chile.

Age: Late Cretaceous (Campanian but probably largely Maastrichtian; see Riccardi 1988).
Holotype: GPMK 123, right tarsometatarsus lacking proximal articular surface and inner trochlea, subadult.

First Cretaceous bird known from the southern hemisphere; foot-propelled diving bird, earliest known loon (not a hesperorniform, as previously described; see Olson 1992).

NEUQUENORNIS   Chiappe and Calvo 1994
Avisauridae.
Name derivation: "Neuquén" + Greek *ornis* = "bird."
Type species: *N. volans* Chiappe and Calvo 1994.
Occurrence: Bajo de la Carpa Formation, area of Universidad Nacional del Comahue, city of Neuquén, Province of Neuquén, Argentina.
Age: Late Cretaceous (Coniacian–early Santonia).
Holotype: MUCPv-142, fairly complete and articulated skeleton including caudal part of skull, incomplete humeri, ulnae, and radii, most of right carpometacarpus, cranial portion of sternum, furcula, incomplete coracoids and left scapula, five fragmentary thoracic vertebrae, incomplete femora, tibiotarsi, and tarsometatarsi, several predal phalanges, indeterminate fragments.

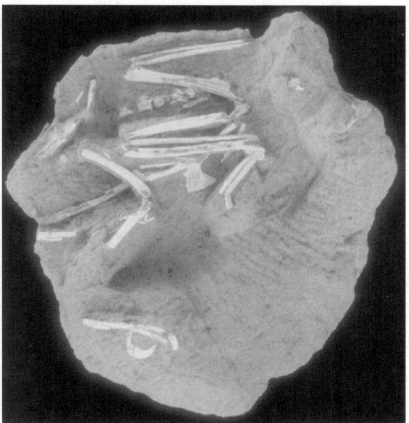

Neuquenornis volans, MUCPv-142, holotype skeleton.

Diagnosis of genus (as for type species): Differs from all other known avisaurids in having much more gracile tarsometatarsus; differs from all known enantiornithines in having femur with wide, winglike caudal trochanter; lateral border of distal end of femur less projected caudally; furcula laminar, laterally compressed, cranial border projecting outwards; major and minor metacarpals subequal; much less prominent lateral grooves on thoracic vertebral bodies (Chiappe and Calvo 1994).

Active flyer, as indicated by the structures of the wing and pectoral girdle.

NOGUERORNIS   La Casa-Ruiz 1989
Enantiornithes.

Name derivation: "[Riu (River)] Noguera" + Greek *ornis* = "bird."

Type species: *N. gonzalezi* La Casa-Ruiz 1989.

Occurrence: La Pedrera de Rúbies Lithographic Limestones,

Meiá, La Pedrera de Meiá, Sierra del Montsec, province of Lleida, Spain.

Age: Early Cretaceous (upper Berriasian–lower Barremian).

Holotype: LP.1702 P ("La Pedrera" collection, Institut d'Estudis Ilerdencs, Lleida, Spain), fragmentary skeleton including portions of humeri, radii, and carpometacarpi, left ulna, furcula, tibia, three trunk vertebrae, pelvis, other osseous remains, feathers.

Diagnosis of genus (as for type species): Autapomorphy of strongly curved humerus (Chiappe and Lacasa-Ruiz 2002).

While not the most basal bird exhibiting a protpatagium (a feathered skinfold essential for flight, not found in *Archaeopteryx*), one of the earliest known birds after *Archaeopteryx*.

NOVACAESAREALA   Parris and Hope 2002
Neornithes *incertae sedis*.

Name derivation: Latin "Nova Casesar [conventional usage for New Jersey]" + Latin *ala* = "wing."

Type species: *N. hungerfordorum* Parris and Hope 2002.

Occurrence: Inversand Company marl pit, basal part (Main Fossiliferous Layer) of Hornerstorn Formation, near Sewell, Mantua Township, Gloucester County, New Jersey, United States.

Age: ?Late Cretaceous–early Tertiary (?latest Maastrichtian–Danian).

Holotype: NJSM 11302, left forelimb elements all associated *in situ*, including distal end and another midshaft section of humerus, midshaft section of ulna, proximal end and midshaft segments of radius, other unidentified bone splinters.

Diagnosis of genus: Unique combination of derived features of the humerus, including the following: very large, deep, well-defined, distinctly tripartite brachial depression, divided by pronounced crests into more proximal brachial fossa proper and ventral and dorsal supracondylar fossa; flexor process broad, very short (Parris and Hope 2002).

Diagnosis of *N. hungerfordi*: As for genus; also, shaft of humerus slightly flattened caudocranially; brachial fossa proper divided indistinctly into shallow proximal shelf and much deeper distal pit; ventral rim of brachial depression very narrow; small attachment for ventral collateral ligament (Parris and Hope 2002).

Apparently robustly built, resembling in some ways (*e.g.*, absence of feather papullae on abraded ulna) pelecaniforms; part of an aquatic neornithine assemblage "closely related to charadriforms, procellariiforms, pelecaniforms, and others."

OMNIVOROPTERYX   Czerkas and Ji 2002
Aves *incertae sedis*.

Name derivation: Latin *omni* = "all or multi-" + Latin *vor* = "eating (for 'omnivorous')" + Greek *pteron* = "wing."

Type species: *O. sinousaorum* Czerkas and Ji 2002.

Occurrence: Upper Jiufotang Formation, Shangheshou, Chaoyang City, Liaoning Province, China.

Age: Early Cretaceous.

Holotype: CAGS02-IG-gausa-3/DM 609, almost complete skeleton, only missing portions of cervical vertebrae, coracoids, sternum, cranial portion of one scapula, parts of one wing including manus.

Diagnosis (preliminary) of genus (as for type species): Moderate size, differing from all other known volant Mesozoic birds (except *Eoenantiornis*) in having rather short skull, with area rostral to orbits comprising less than half skull length; skull resembling that of *Caudipteryx* in having procumbent premaxillary teeth, large nasal openings, dentaries curved ventrally resulting in concave profile of lower jaws; humeri and ulnae longest bones of skeleton; wings longer than hindlimbs (humerus plus ulna plus metacarpal II to femur plus tibia plus metatarsals ratio no less than 1.5); hind legs short, tibiotarsus only slightly longer than femur; metatarsals not fused; manual digit III absent except for phalanx III-1, latter apparently reduced to narrow splint; hallux large, first phalanx of pedal digit I longer than other pedal phakabges (Czerkas and Ji 2002*b*).

Apparently herbivorous, having "adapted to a different dietary ecological niche from that of predaceous birds."

OTOGORNIS   Hou 1994
Neornithes.

Name derivation: "Otog-qi [China]" + Greek *ornis* = "bird."

Type species: *O. genghisi* Hou 1994.

Occurrence: Yijingholuo Formation, Chaibu-Sumi, Otog-qi, Yikezhaomeng, Inner Mongolia, China.

Age: Early Cretaceous.

Holotype: IVPP V9607, pair of scapulae and coracoids, forelimb, feather impressions.

Diagnosis of genus (as for type species): Ulna approximately 120 percent length of humerus; ulna almost twice as wide as radius; medial margin of scapula straight; coracoid having long neck (Zhou and Hou 2002).

Possibly closely related to the palaeognathid bird *Ambiortus dementjevi* (see Kurochkin 2000), wing feathers not tightly arranged, suggesting the lack of barbules and that this genus was incapable of flight.

PALAELIMNORNIS Kessler and Jurcsák 1986 — (Preoccupied, Gould 1839; see *Palaeocursornis*.)

Name derivation: Greek *palaios* = "ancient" + Greek *ornis* = "bird."

Type species: *P. corneti.*

PALAEOCOLYMBUS Seeley 1869 —(See *Enaliornis*.)

Name derivation: Greek *palaios* = "ancient" + *Colymbus* [genus of colymbine bird].

Type species: *P barrettii* Seeley 1869

PALAEOCURSORNIS Kessler and Jurcsák 1986 [*nomen dubium*]

Ornithurae *incertae sedis.*

Name derivation: Greek *palaios* = "ancient" Latin *cursor* = "running" + Greek *ornis* = "bird."

Type species: *P. corneti* (Kessler and Jurcsák 1986) [*nomen dubium*].

Occurrence: Wealden, Padurea Craiului Mountain, Astileu village, Bihor County, Romania.

Age: Early Cretaceous.

Holotype: MTCO 1637, badly worn distal end of femur.

Diagnosis of genus (as for type species): Small running bird; femur conspicuously differing from that of *Archaeopteryx* and all known carinates by following characters: external condyle prominent, longer than internal condyle; rounded tibio–fibular crest and internal condyle; narrow intercondylar fossa; deep fossa for attachment of ligamentum cruciatum under external condyle; fibular crest laterally oriented at right angle (similar to Ratitae), not obliquely (as in *Archaeopteryx* and all other known carinates) (Kessler and Jurcsák 1986).

Small, ?earliest known ratite; only identifiable as an ornithurine (Hope 2002), based on possession of patellar sulcus and large tibiofibular crest (see Chiappe 1995*a*).

PALAEOTRINGA Marsh 1870

Graculavidae.

Name derivation: Greek *palaios* = "ancient" + Greek *tryggas* = "shore bird [mentioned by Aristotle]."

Type species: *P. littoralis* Marsh 1870.

Other species: *P. vagans* Marsh 1872.

Occurrence: "Middle marl beds," ?basal Hornerstown Formation or ?Navesink Formation, near Hornerstown, New Jersey, United States.

Age: Late Cretaceous (Maastrichtian).

Holotype: YPM 830, distal portion of left tibiotarsus (lacking most of inner condyle).

P. vagans smaller than *P. littoralis*, with tibia distinguished from that of type species by proportionally more narrow and shallow tendinal canal on cranial face of distal end; trochlear surface on caudal side contracting more rapidly, at its upper margin passing directly (not abruptly) into shaft (Marsh 1872*b*); genus small wading bird, similar to [Paleocene bird] *Presbyornis*, larger than *Telmatornis priscus* (Olson and Parris 1987); holotype tibia of type species resembling "in size and general form that of the European Curlew (*Numenius arquata* Linn.)" (Marsh 1870*b*).

PALINTROPUS Brodkorb 1970

Neornithes.

Name derivation: Greek *palin* = "backwards" + Greek *tropo* = "bend."

Type species: *P. retusus* Brodkorb 1970.

Other species: [To be named.]

Occurrence: Lance Formation, Niobrara [formerly Converse] County, Wyoming, United States; Dinosaur Park Formation, Foremost Formation, Alberta, Canada.

Age: Late Cretaceous (Campanian–Maastrichtian).

Holotype: YPM 513, shoulder end and part of shaft of left coracoid.

Diagnosis of genus (as for type species): Derived features including complete absence of procoracoid process of coracoid; very large size of foramen for N. supracoracoideus; latter's central position on coracoidal shaft well distal to scapular facet (Hope 2002).

Small, possibly similar to extant galliforms.

PARAHESPERORNIS Martin 1984

Hesperornithiformes.

Name derivation: Greek *para* = "near" + *Hesperornis*.

Type species: *P. alexi* Martin 1984.

Occurrence: Smoky Hill Member, Niobrara Chalk Formation, Graham County, Kansas, United States.

Age: Late Cretaceous (Campanian–Maastrichtian).

Holotype: KUVP 2287, almost complete skeleton.

Diagnosis of genus (as for type species): Skull mesokinetic; lacrimal more elongated dorsoventrally than in *Hesperornis*; nasal process of lacrimal more extended rostrally than in *Hesperornis*; orbital process of quadrate very elongate; coracoid more elongate than in *Hesperornis*; femur more elongate, proximal end less laterally extended, than in *Hesperornis*, tibiotarsus less compressed; tarsometatarsus having outer trochlea only about one-fourth larger than middle trochlea, both at about same level distally (outer trochlea almost twice size of inner trochlea, more distally located, in *Hesperornis*); crescent and peg articulations developed on phalanges of pedal digit IV (as in other herperornithids; absent in baptornithids) (Martin 1983).

Loonlike, foot-propelled diving bird, feathers fine; about 30 percent smaller than *Hesperornis gracilis*, larger than *Baptornis advenus*.

PARASCANIORNIS Lambrecht 1933 [*nomen dubium*] Hesperornithiformes.
Name derivation: Greek *para* = "near" + *Scaniornis* [Latin name for Scandanavia] + Greek *ornis* = "bird."
Type species: *P. stensoi* Lambrecht 1933 [*nomen dubium*].
Occurrence: Ivö Klack locality, southern Sweden. Age: Late Cretaceous (Campanian).
Holotype: MGUH collection, vertebra.

Based upon heterocoelous vertebra representing a small hesperornithiform (see Nessov and Prizemlin 1991), possibly resembling the Paleocene bird *Scaniornis*.

PASQUIAORNIS Tokaryk, Cumbaa and Storer 1997
Baptornithidae.
Name derivation: *Pasquia* = "Pasquia [Hills region} + Greek *ornis* = "bird."
Type species: *P. hardiei* Tokaryk, Cumbaa and Storer 1997.
Other species: *P. tankei* Tokaryk, Cumbaa and Storer 1997.
Occurrence: Along Carrot River, near the Pasquilla Hills, Saskatchewan, Canada.
Age: Early Late Cretaceous (Cenomanian).
Holotype: SMNH P2077.117, left tarsometatarsus.

Diagnosis of genus: Differs from the baptornithid *Baptornis* in the following: trochanteric ridge of femur closer to shaft; proximal end relatively less expanded lateromedially; cranial intercotylar prominence of tarsometatarsus, overhangs shaft; and trochlea for pedal digit II caudal, close to base pf trochlea for III (Tokaryk, Cumbaa and Storer 1997).

Diagnosis of *P. hardiei*: Internal cotyle of tarsometatarsi deflected toward shaft; neck of third trochlea higher cranially than fourth; femur small, distal rim of femoral head perpendicular to shaft (Tokaryk, Cumbaa and Storer 1997).

Diagnosis of *P. tankei*: Internal cotyla of tarsometatarsi almost cranio-caudal; neck of fourth trochlea higher cranially than third; femur large, distal rim of head slanted toward shaft (Tokaryk, Cumbaa and Storer 1997).

Foot-propelled diving bird, more primitive than *Baptornis*, femur resembling that of flying birds.

PATAGOPTERYX Alvarenga and Bonaparte 1992
Ornithothoraces.
Name derivation: "Patagonia" + Greek *pteron* = "wing."

Type species: *P. deferrarissi* Alvarenga and Bonaparte 1992.
Occurrence: Bajo de la Carpa Formation, Boca del Sapo, Neuquén, Argentina.
Age: Late Cretaceous (Campanian–early Santonian).
Holotype: MACN-N-03, partial skeleton including five cervical vertebrae, 11 thoracic vertebrae, complete synsacrum, two caudal vertebrae, humeri, proximal portions of radius and ulna, shoulder ends of scapulae and coracoids, acetabular and postacetabular portions of ilia, portions of femora and tibiotarsus.

Diagnosis of genus (as for type species): Autapomorphies including the following: quadrate fused to pterygoid; quadrate pneumatic foramen laterally located; fifth thoracic vertebrae biconvex; thoracic vertebrae six to 11 procoelous, centra wide, kidney-shaped; synsacrum procoelous; shoulder end of coracoid formed by broad, tonguelike caudolateral surface including humeral articular facet and area of scapular articulation; acromium of scapula dorsoventrally expanded, keyhole-shaped in proximal view; strong muscular lines in humeral shaft; distal half of ulnar shaft strongly compressed craniocaudally; minor metacarpal more robust than major metacarpal; major metacarpal having cranioventral, laminar projection; ilium having prominent iliac crest and well-developed caudolateral spine; pubis craniocaudally compressed, straplike, caudal third cranioventrally curved; ischium paddle-shaped; prominent M. iliofibularis tubercle on fibula; fibular spine distally fused to cranial surface of tibiotarsus; tarsometatarsus transversely wide; pamprodactyl foot (Chiappe 2002*a*).

Hen-sized flightless bird, important for documenting "a distinct lineage of basal birds" and also constituting "the best represented Mesozoic avian from the Southern Hemisphere, being known from several specimens" (Chiappe 2002*a*).

PELAGORNIS Seeley 1866 — (Preoccupied, Lartet 1857; see *Enaliornis.*)
Name derivation: Greek *pelagos* = "sea" + Greek *ornis* = "bird."
Type species: *P. sedgwicki* Seeley 1866.

PIKSI Varricchio 2002
Ornithothoraces *incertae sedis*
Name derivation: Blackfoot *piksi* = "bird or chicken."
Type species: *P. barbarulna* Varricchio 2002.
Occurrence: Two Medicine Formation, Blackfeet Nation, Glacier County, Montana, United States.
Age: Late Cretaceous (Campanian).
Holotype: MOR 1113, partial right humerus, ulna, radius.

Diagnosis of genus (as for type species): Medium-size, humerus with large dorsal epicondyle, subequal to dorsal condyle; flexor process of humerus having proximodistally angled wall; large dorsal cotyla on ulna, twice as broad as ventral cotyla; dorsal cotyla on ulna, outline elongate; shaft of ulna lacking quill knobs (papillae remigalis ventralis) (Varricchio 2002).

Heavy-bodied ground bird, resembling galliforms.

Medium-sized (about the size of the modern ringnecked pheasant, *Phasianus colchicus*), heavy-bodied, ground-feeding bird.

PLATANAVIS   Nessov 1992 [*nomen dubium*]
Aves *incertae sedis*.
Name derivation: Latin *Platanus* [genus name for sycamore tree] + Latin *avis* = "bird."
Type species: *P. nana* Nessov 1992 [*nomen dubium*]
Occurrence: Dzhyrakuduk locality, Bissekty Svita, Navoi District, Bukhara Province, Uzbekistan.
Age: Late Cretaceous (Coniacian).
Holotype: PO 4601, fragment of synsacrum comprising two or three vertebrae.

Diagnosis of genus (as for type species): Middle vertebrae of synsacrum strongly compressed dorsoventrally; pleurocoels very deep; double ridge along ventral side of synsacrum (Kurochkin 2000).

Small bird; regarded by Padian (2004*b*) as a *nomen dubium*.

POLARORNIS   Chatterjee 2002
Gaviidae.
Name derivation: *Polar* [referring to Antarctica] + Greek *ornis* = "bird."
Type species: *P. gregori* Chatterjee 2002.
Occurrence: Sandwich Bluff Member, Lopez de Bertodano Formation, central valley of Seymour Island, near coast of Lopez de Bertodano Bay, Antarctica.
Age: Late Cretaceous (Maastrichtian).
Holotype: TTU P9265, associated skull, four cervical vertebrae, complete left femur, proximal half of left tibiotarsus, proximal portion of right femur, sternal fragment.

Diagnosis of genus (as for type species): External naris small; frontals narrow across orbit, salt gland depressions narrow; orbital process of quadrate thick, short, horizontally directed; pterygoid condyle of quadrate bordered by dorsal groove; caudal tympanic recess in same plane with fenestra ovalis and fenestra pseudorotunda, not bounded caudally by overhanging wall; lateral wall of rostral tympanic recess flat (not bulbous); vomers fused, rounded rostrally; neck of femur long; distal condyles of femur subequal, projecting caudally (not twisted sidewise); intercnemial sulcus perforate by nutrient foramen (Chatterjee 2002).

Loon closely related to the extant *Gavia*, more derived than *Hesperornis*.

POTAMORNIS   Elźanowski, Paul and Stidham 2001
?Hesperornithiformes.
Name derivation: Greek *potamos* = "stream, river" + Greek *ornis* = "bird."
Type species: *P. skutchi* Elźanowski, Paul and Stidham 2001.
Occurrence: Lance Formation, near Lance Creek, Niobrara County, Wyoming, United States.
Age: Late Cretaceous (Maastrichtian).
Holotype: UCMP 73103, quadrate.

Diagnosis of genus (as for type species): Head of quadrate strongly asymmetrical, beak-shaped medial part overhanging otic process; rostrally open pit near medial apex of head; caudomedial depression shallow but distinct; orbital process small; lateral process having quadratojugal buttress; medial and lateral mandubular condyles meeting at about 115-degree angle, both smoothly connecting to caudal condyle (Elźanowski, Paul and Stidham 2001).

Small, apparently flightless, foot-propelled diver.

PRAEORNIS   Rautian 1978
Avis *incertae sedis*.
Name derivation: Latin *praes* = "surety" + Greek *ornis* = "bird."
Type species: *P. sharovi* Rautian 1978.
Occurrence: Aulie (Mikhailovka) locality, Balabansai Svita, Chimkent Province, Kazakhstan.
Age: Late Jurassic.
Holotype: PIN 2585/32, flight feather impression.

Diagnosis of genus (as for type species): Relatively large bird (crow-sized); edges of barbs absolutely flat (not breaking up into barbules); barbs having pulp caps; outer and inner sides of barbs flattened, broadened, thereby showing some similarity to vanes; vanes near dorsal side of barb shaft, the latter filled by pulp caps; barbs forming complete vane; no more than four barbs percentimeter; plane of vane twisted; outer vane narrower than inner vane; distal portion of shaft noticeably flexed in horizontal plane; pulp caps large; pulp caps in shaft larger than those in barbs; ends of barbs clearly pointed (Kurochkin 2000).

Perhaps the earliest known record of a feather.

PROORNIS   Lim *see in* Pak and Kim 1996
Pygostylia *incertae sedis*.
Name derivation: Greek *pro* = "before" + Greek *ornis* = "bird."
Type species: *P. coreae* Lim *see in* Pak and Kim 1996.
Occurrence: Sinuiju Series, North Korea.
Age: Early Cretaceous (?Barremian).
Holotype: Skull, cervical vertebrae, forelimb, feather impressions.

Diagnosis of genus (as for type species): Metacarpal I longer than in *Confuciusornis*, shorter than in *Changchengornis* (Lim *see in* Pak and Kim 1996).

Possibly intermediate between *Archaeopteryx* and *Protopteryx*.

PROTOPTERYX   Zhang and Zhou 2000

Enantiornithines *incertae sedis*.

Name derivation: Greek *proto* = "first" + Greek *pteron* = "wing."

Type species: *P. fengningensis* Zhang and Zhou 2000.

Occurrence: Fengning County, Heibei Province, China.

Age: Early Cretaceous (?Barremian).

Holotype: IVPP V 11665, almost complete skeleton, feather impressions, slab and counterslab.

Diagnosis of genus (as for type species): One tooth per premaxilla; procoracoid process (Zhang and Zhou 2000).

Large bird, skeleton exhibiting mixture or primitive and derived features, orbit large, manus longer than forearm, flight and down feathers present, tail feathers long, primitive, resembling unbranched scales; apparently well adapted to flight.

RAHONA   Forster, Sampson, Chiappe and Krause 1998 — (Preoccupied, Griveaud 1975; see *Rahonavis*.)

Name derivation: Malagasy *rahona* = "cloud, menace."

Type species: *R. ostromi* Forster, Sampson, Chiappe and Krause 1998.

RAHONAVIS   Forster, Sampson, Chiappe and Krause 1998

Archaeopterygiformes.

Name derivation: Malagasy *rahona* = "menace/threat" or "cloud" + Latin *avis* = "bird."

Life restoration of *Rahonavis ostromi* by artist Todd Marshall.

Type species: *R. ostromi* Forster, Sampson, Chiappe and Krause 1998.

Occurrence: Sandstone of northwestern Madagascar.

Age: Late Cretaceous.

Holotype: UA 8656, partial skeleton, including dorsal and caudal vertebrae, synsacrum, radius, ulna, shoulder and pelvic girdles, femur, tibia, fibula, calcaneum, astragalus, tarsals, metatarsals, phalanges.

Diagnosis of genus (as for type species): Distinguished from all other avians by retention of robust, hyperextendible, pedal digit II; from all other avians (and non-avian theropods except *Patagonykus*) by dorsal vertebrae having hyposphene-hypantra articulations; from *Archaeopteryx* by six fused sacral vertebrae and greatly reduced fibula lacking contact with calcaneum; from non-avian theropods, *Archaeopteryx*, and alvarezsaurids [now generally regarded as non-avian theropods; see *S2*] by relatively elongate ulna with ulnar papillae and mobile scapulocoracoid articulation; from all other birds except *Archaeopteryx* and alvarezsaurids by retention of long tail lacking pygostyle; from non-avian theropods by neural canals at least 40 percent of height of dorsal vertebral centra, proximal tibia of equal width and length, lack of medial fossa on fibula, and reversed pedal digit I (Forster, Sampson, Chiappe and Krause 1998*a*).

Raven-sized bird, slightly larger than *Archaeopteryx*, apparently ground-dwelling, second toe of foot terminating in "killer claw"; displaying both theropod (*e.g.*, pubic foot) and avian (*e.g.*, reversed hallux, splintlike fibula, ulnar papillae) features; regarded by some a small number of workers as a chimera comprising theropod and avian elements (see *S1*).

SAPEORNIS Zhou and Zhang 2003

Aves *incertae sedis*.

Name "SAPE [acronym for Society of Avian Paleontology and Evolution]" + Greek *ornis* = "bird."

Type species: *S. chaoyangensis* Zhou and Zhang 2002.

Occurrence: Jiufutang Formation, Shangheshou and Dapingfang areas, Chaoyang City, Liaoning Province, China.

Age: Early Cretaceous (Aptian).

Holotype: IVPP V13275, postcranial skeleton including some vertebrae, pygostyle, pectoral girdle, furcula, forelimbs, pelvic girdle, hind limb.

Diagnosis of genus (as for type species): Furcula robust, having slender hypocleidium, two furcula rami forming approximately 105-degree angle (robust furcula in other basal birds lacking hypocleidium); forelimb extremely elongated; forelimb about half length of hind limb; proximal end of humerus having elliptical fenestra; manual digit III comprising two slender phalanges (Zhou and Zhang 2003*a*).

Primitive (exhibiting mosaic of primitive and derived features), largest known Early Cretaceous bird, one referred specimen including gastroliths suggesting herbivorous feeding habits.

SAZAVIS Nessov 1989 *see in* Nessov and Jarkov 1989 — (=?*Kizylkumavis*)

Alexornithidae.

Name derivation: Kazakh *saz* = "clay" + Latin *avis* = "bird."

Type species: *S. prisca* Nessov 1989 *see in* Nessov and Jarkov 1989.

Occurrence: Dzharakhuduk locality, Central Kizikum Desert, Bissekty Svita, Navoi District, Bukhara Province, Uzbekistan.

Age: Late Cretaceous (Coniacian).

Holotype: PO 3472, distal fragment of right tibiotarsus.

Diagnosis of genus (as for type species): Small bird; distal end of tibiotarsus wide, its large medial condyle with rounded dorsal margin in cranial aspect; intercondylar furrow laterally displaced, lateral condyle thereby narrow; diameter of tibia strongly reduced dorsal to distal end of tibiotarsus; ligamental tubercle on cranial surface of tibiotarsus weak, situated relatively distal (Kurochkin 2000).

Very small, width of distal end of tibiotarsus only 4.5 millimeters, comparable in size and possibly congeneric or conspecific with *Kizylkumavis cretacea*, although the respective material is not comparable (Kurochkin 2000).

SHENZHOURAPTOR Ji, Ji, You, Zhang, Yuan, Ji, Li and Li 2002 — (=*Jeholornis*)

Aves *incertae sedis*.

Name derivation: Chinese Pinyin *Shenzou* [ancient name for China] + Latin *raptor* = "robber" or "thief."

Type species: *S. sinensis* Ji, Ji, You, Zhang, Yuan, Ji, Li and Li 2002,

Occurrence: Jiufotang Formation, Baitaigou Village, Toutai Township, Yixian County, Dapingfang area, Chaoyang, Liaoning Province, western China.

Age: Early Cretaceous (Aptian).

Holotype: LPM0193, complete skeleton including skull, feathers on forelimbs and tail.

Diagnosis of genus (as for type species): Small, distinguished by the following characters: beaked mouth lacking teeth; mandibles robust, symphysis ossified; furcula typically U-shaped; lacrimal having two vertical, elongated pneumatic fossae; ratio of forelimbs to hindlimbs approximately 1.2 to 1.27; humerus with long deltopectoral crest; first phalanx of manual digit II very wide, first phalanx of manual digit III twice as long as II; flight feathers (remiges) distinctly longer than total length of both ulna and manus; tail long, comprising at least 23 caudal vertebrae (up to 27 in "*Jeholornis*"; Zhou and Zhang 2003*b*), length of each vertebra three to four times width (Ji, Ji, You, Zhang, Yuan, Ji, Li and Li 2002).

Earliest known fossil bird except for *Archaeopteryx*; different from other known Late Jurassic–Early Cretaceous birds having a beaked mouth without teeth, forelimbs much longer than hindlimbs, and flight feathers that are much longer than its body; ["*Jeholornis*"] tail much longer than that of *Archaeopteryx*, suggesting the common ancestor of birds had a more primitive tail than did *Archaeopteryx* and "confirming the side branch position of *Archaeopteryx* in the early avian evolution," tail feathers shaped more like those of dromaeosaurs, synsacrum with six sacral vertebrae, representing transitional stage between *Archaeopteryx* and more advanced birds (see Zhou and Zhang 2003*b*).

SINORNIS Sereno and Rao 1992 —(=*Cathayornis*; =?*Concornis*, ?*Iberomesornis*)
Cathayornithidae.
Name derivation: Greek *Sinai* = China + Greek *ornis* = "bird."
Type species: *S. santensis* Sereno and Rao 1992.
Occurrence: Jiufotang Formation, Huanghuagou, Shengli, Chaoyang, Liaoning Province, northeast China.
Age: Early Cretaceous (Aptian).

Holotype: BPV 538A (part) and 538B (counterpart), nearly complete skeleton.

Diagnosis of genus (as for type species): Skull relatively short; cross sections of manual digit II and ulna twice width of manual digit I and radius, respectively; manual digit I reduced; manual digits I and II with small, curved claws; metatarsals distally fused; pygostyle (Hou, Zhou, Zhang and Gu 2002).

Sparrow-sized, second Mesozoic bird found in China, currently the most completely known enantiornithine, morphologically very similar to *Iberomesornis romerli*, *Concornis lacustris*, and *Eoalulavus hoyasi*; design of foot suggesting "that *Sinornis* and other similar-sized enantiornithines were arboreal birds that had achieved a level of performance in flight and perching that would be indistinguishable from sparrow-sized birds living today" (Sereno and Gao 2002).

Photograph by Mick Ellison, courtesy Luis M. Chiappe.

Holotype skeleton (IVPP V9769) of *Cathayornis yandica*, currently regarded as a junior synonym of *Sinornis santensis*.

Note: Junior synonym (see Sereno and Gao 2002) *Cathayornis yandica* established on almost complete skeleton (IVPP V9769A and B, part and counterpart) from same locality as holotype of *S. santensis* (Zhou, Jin and Zhang 1992).

SONGLINGORNIS   Hou 1997 — (See *Chaoyangia*.)
Name derivation: "Songling [Mountains]" + Greek *ornis* = "bird."
   S. linghensis Hou 1997

SOROAVISAURUS   Chiappe 1993
Avisauridae.
Name derivation: Latin *soror* = "sister" + *Avisaurus*.
Type species: *S. australis* Chiappe 1993.
Occurrence: Lecho Formation, Esancia El Brete, Department of Candelaria, Province of Salta, Argentina.
Age: Late Cretaceous (Maastrichtian).
Holotype: PVL-4690, left tarsometatarsus.
   Diagnosis of genus (as for type species): Enantiornithine with following autapomorphies: plantar surface of proximal half of metatarsal II forming sharp edge (convergent with *Lectavis bretincola*); long, narrow fenestra open between proximal halves of metatarsals III and IV; dorsally projected edge on trochlea for metatarsal IV (Chiappe 1993).
   Holotype previously referred by Brett-Surman and Paul (1985) to *Avisaurus* sp.

TELMATORNIS   Marsh 1870
?Charadriiformes.
Name derivation: Greek *telma* = "marsh, swamp" + Greek *ornis* = "bird."
Type species: *T. priscus* Marsh 1870.
Occurrence: Cream Ridge Marl Company pits, "middle marl bed," Navesink Formation, near Hornerstown, New Jersey, United States.
Age: ?Late Cretaceous (?latest Maastrichtian).
Holotype: YPM 840, distal end of left humerus.
   Most abundant Cretaceous New Jersey bird; smaller than *Graculavus*, similar in size and robustness to *Cimolopteryx rara*; "In general appearance it resembles the humerus of some of the Rail family, and the species it represents is probably related to this group of birds," as evidence by "the unusual flattening of the lower part of the shaft and distal extremity; in the small articular condyles; in the diminutive protuberance for the attachment of the extensor muscle of the hand; and in the oval impression of the anterior brachial muscle" (Marsh 1870*b*).

TEVIORNIS   Kurochkin, Dyke and Karhu 2002
Presbyornithidae.
Name derivation: "Victor Tereschenko [finder of the specimen]" + Greek *ornis* = "bird."
Type species: *T. gobiensis* Kurochkin, Dyke and Karhu 2002.

Skeletal reconstruction and life restoration by artist Mark Hallett of *Sinornis santensis*.

Occurrence: Gurilyn Tsav locality, Nemegt Basin, north of Atlan Ula ridge, east of Bugeen Tsav, northwest corner of Umnogobid Aimak, Nemegt Formation, lower Nemegt Horizon, southern Mongolia.
Age: Late Cretaceous (Maastrichtian).
Holotype: PIN 44991-1, partially crushed associated remains of right forelimb, including fragment of distal humerus, radiale and ulnare, complete carpometacarpus, first phalanx of major digit, phalanx of minor digit.
   Diagnosis of genus (as for type species): Distinguished from other know presbyornithids based on the following characters: tuburculum supracondylare dorsale of humerus extended far proximally; fossa infratrochlearis of carpometacarpus stretched markedly craniocaudally; proximal portion of branch of os metacarpale minus widened dorsoventrally and craniocaudally with respect to its distal continuation; facies articularis digitis minoris on os metacarpale minus divided by craniocaudal groove into two distinct facets; distal extension of facies articularis digitalis major widened distally; ventral portion of facies articularis digitalis major elevated in direction of tubercle for insertion of m. abductor digit majoris (Kurochkin, Dyke and Karhu 2002).
   Large swimming bird, confirming the presence of the Anseriformes in the Late Cretaceous.

TOROTIX   Bordkorb 1963
?Pelecaniformes.
Name derivation: Greek *torotix* [imitation of flamingo cry, attributed to ancient Greek playwright Aristophanes].
Type species: *T. clemensi* Brodkorb 1963.

Occurrence: Lance Formation, near Lance Creek, Wyoming, United States.

Age: Late Cretaceous (late Maastrichtian).

Holotype: UCMP 53958, distal end and partial shaft of right humerus.

Diagnosis of genus (as for type species): Humerus similar to that of "Phoenicopteridae," but with unhooked external condyle; origin of anconal branch of extensor metacarpi radialis a rounded pit on ectepicondylar process palmar to origin of tensor patagii brevis; pit of anconal brance of flexor carpi ulnaris restricted to side of bone, barely visible in palmar aspect (Brodkorb 1963).

Small, type specimen resembling the humerus (inflated appearance, contours rounded) of more volant pelecaniforms than that (contours finely sculpted) of diving birds (see Hope 2002).

TYTTHOSTONYX   Olson and Parris 1987

Tytthostonychidae.

Name derivation: Greek *tytthos* = "little" + Greek *stonyx* = "small point."

Type species: *T. glauconiticus* Olson and Parris 1987.

Occurrence: Inversand Company marl pit, basal portion of Hornerstown Formation, Sewell, Gloucester County, New Jersey, United States.

Age: Late Cretaceous to Early Paleocene (late Maastrichtian–early Danian).

Holotype: NJSM 11341, right humerus (lacking ventral tubercle, portions of pectoral crest, and other parts of proximal end).

Diagnosis of genus (as for type species and Tytthostonychidae): Differing from Lari and other Charaadriformes in 1. low, narrow head; 2. very large, long pectoral crest; 3. virtual absence of incisura capitis or any excavation for M. coracobrachialis crabialis; and 4. shallow, indistinct tricipital grooves; agrees with Procellariiformes and differs from [Eocene pelecaniforms] *Phaethon* and *Limnofregata* in above characters 2 and 4, and in large, deeply excavated brachial depression; ectepicondylar spur better developed than in any known Pelecaniformes, not as developed as in Procellariiformes; pector crest apparently very broad, extending much farther distally than in Procellariiformes and *Limnofregata*; differing from other known taxa in having very rounded ventral condyle, extending distally well past dorsal condyle (Olson and Parris 1987).

Possibly related to Procellariiformes.

VEGAVIS   Clarke, Tambussi, Noriega, Erickson and Ketcham 2005

Anatoidea.

Name derivation: "Vega [Island]" + Latin *avis* = "bird."

Type species: *A. iaai* Clarke, Tambussi, Noriega, Erickson and Ketcha 2005.

Occurrence: Cape Lamb, Vega Island, western Antarctica.

Age: Late Cretaceous (middle–late Maastrichtian).

Holotype: MLP 93-I-3-1, disarticulated partial postcranial skeleton preserved in two halves of concretion, including (elements revealed to date of writing) five thoracic and two cervical vertebrae, more than six dorsal ribs, sacrum, left scapula, right coracoid, proximal left humerus, distal right radius, right ulna, all pelvic bones, femora, fibulae, left tibiotarsus, ?left tarsometatarsal shaft, left tibiotarsus, distal right radius.

Diagnosis of genus (as for type species): Unique in having low ridge on medial edge of proximal tibiotarsus (autapomorphy) (Clarke, Tambussi, Noriega, Erickson and Ketcham 2005).

First record of the extant Anatoidea (an anseriform subclade including true ducks) avian radiation during the Cretaceous period.

VESCORNIS   Zhang, Ericson and Zhou 2004

Euenantiornithes.

Name derivation: Latin *vesc* = "thin, attenuated" + Greek *ornis* = "bird."

Type species: *V. hebeiensis* Zhang, Ericson and Zhou 2004.

Occurrence: Yixian Formation, Senjitu, Fengning County, Hebei Province, northern China.

Age: Early Cretaceous.

Holotype: Nanjing Institute of Geology and Paleontology, Chinese Academy of Sciences, 130722, almost complete, articulated skeleton impression split in slab (counterslab location unknown).

Diagnosis of genus (as for type species): First phalanx of manual digit I reduced, slender, less than half length and diameter of major metacarpal; ungual phalanges of manual digits I and II small and vestigial; coracoid slender, length to width ratio approaching three, distinguishing it from all other known Early Cretaceous enantiornithines (Zhang, Ericson and Zhou 2004).

Adapted towards improved flight capability, climbing ability reduced compared with that of many other enantiornithines.

VOLGAVIS   Nessov and Jarkov 1989

?Charadriiformes.

Name derivation: "Volga [Basin]" + Latin *avis* = "bird."

Type species: *V. marina* Nessov and Karov 1989.

Occurrence: Malaja Ivanovka locality, Krasnaja Derevnja Spring, Belly Jar Valley, Volga Basin, Dubovsky Region, Volgograd District, Russia.

Age: Late Cretaceous (late Maastrichtian).

Holotype: ZISP-PO 3638, rostral part of lower jaw including both rami, fragment of surangular.

Diagnosis of genus (as for type species): Tip of mandible strongly deflected ventrally (Kurochkin 2000).

Frigate-like in downward orientation of the hooked tip of the mandible, about the size of a modern marine gull.

VORONA Forster, Chiappe, Krause and Sampson 1996; ?Ornithuromorpha.

Name derivation: Malagasy *vorona* = "bird."

Type species: *V. berivotrensis* Forster, Chiappe, Krause and Sampson 1996.

Occurrence: Maevarona Formation, Mahajanga Basin, near village of Berivotra, northwestern Madagascar.

Age: Late Cretaceous (Maastrichtian).

Holotype: UA 8651, distal left tibiotarsus articulated with complete tarsometatarsus.

Diagnosis of genus (as for type species): Tibiotarsus with short, blunt cnemial crest; irregular low ridge on mesial surface of proximal tibiotarsus; narrow, deep notch on proximodorsal tarsometatarsus between metatarsals II and III; expanded vascular groove proximal to distal foramen on tarsometatarsus (Foster, Chiappe, Krause and Sampson 2002).

Primitive bird, marking first record of avian skeletal remains found in part of Gondwana including Africa, Madagascar, Indian subcontinent, and mainland Antarctica.

WELLNHOFERIA Elźanowski 2001

Archaeopterygidae.

Name derivation: "[Peter] Wellnhofer."

Type species: *W. grandis* Elźanowski 2001.

Occurrence: Langenaltheimer Haardt quarry, upper Solnhofen Lithographic Limestone, Solnhofen, southern Germany.

Age: Late Jurassic (early Tithonian).

Holotype: Bürgermeister Müller Museum [currently] ("sixth specimen"), skeleton, feather impressions.

Diagnosis of genus (as for type species): Larger than *Archaeopteryx*; manual digit I having ungual of about one-third length of basal phalanx; first and second phalanges of manual digit III fused; metatarsal II tapering proximally; pedal digit IV having four phalanges, about 75 percent (less than 80 percent) length of digit III; pedal digit IV having ungual as longest phalanx; pedal claws having well-developed flexor tubercles (Elźanowski 2002).

Holotype originally interpreted to be the largest specimen of *Archaeopteryx*.

YANDANGORNIS Cai and Zhao 1999

Aves *incertae sedis*.

Name derivation: Chinese *Yandang* ["Yandang Mountains"] + Greek *ornis* = "bird."

Type species: *Y. longicaudus* Cai and Zhao 1999.

Occurrence: Tangshang Group, near Aoli Village, Yandang Mountains, Zhejiang Province, eastern China.

Age: Late Cretaceous (?Santonian).

Holotype: ZMN M1326, almost complete skeleton, including skull with lower jaws, nine cervical vertebrae, four dorsal vertebrae, dorsal ribs, gastralia, 19 caudal vertebrae, sternum, sternal ribs, distal scapula, partial coracoid, partial furcula, humeri, proximal radii, proximal ulnae, distal phalanx II-1, phalanx II-2, manual ungual II, distal phalanx III-2, phalanx III-3, manual ungual III, pubis, femora, tibiae, fibula, tarsometatarsus, pedal phalanges, pedal unguals.

Diagnosis of genus (as for type species): Premaxillae very large (ventral edge equalling 40 percent skull length); premaxillae, maxillae, and dentaries edentulous, lower jaw less than three-fourths length of skull; last cervical vertebra longer than others; ?no cervical ribs; fewer than six caudal vertebrae having transverse processes; ?no chevrons; sternal ribs subequal to sternum in length; sternum concave caudally; distal femoral condyles over twice width of shaft; phalanx III-1 shortest in pedal digit III (Cai and Zhao 1999).

Approximately crow- or *Archaeopteryx*-sized, flightless, ground-dwelling bird, with toothless, *Confuciusornis*-like skull, short hallux, uncurved claws, and heavy, bony *Archaeopteryx*-like tail; very non-avian theropod-like.

YANORNIS Zhou and Zhang 2001—(=*Archaeovolans*; =?*Chaoyangia*)

Ornithurae *incertae sedis*.

Name derivation: Chinese *Yan* [former "Yan" Dynasty] + Greek *ornis* = "bird."

Type species: *Y. martini* Zhou and Zhang 2001.

Occurrence: Jiufotang Formation, Chaoyang City, Yixian County, Liaoning Province, China.

Age: Early Cretaceous (?Barremian).

Holotype: IVPP V12558, almost complete skeleton without feather impressions.

Diagnosis of genus (as for type species): Dentary straight, about two-thirds skull length, with approximately 20 teeth; cervical vertebrae long, heterocoelous; synsacrum with nine sacral vertebrae; pygostyle short, less than one-third length of tarsometatarsus; sternum having pair of caudal fenestrae; distal end of lateral process of sternum semicircular; ratio of forelimb to hindlimb length about 1.1; manus shorter than ulna and radius; tarsometatarsus entirely fused; ratio of third pedal digit to length of tarsometatarsus 1.1; proximal pedal phalanges longer, more robust than distal ones (Zhou and Zhang 2001).

Crow-sized; long, narrow tooth jaws and relatively long neck suggesting it ate fish and other aquatic animals (specimen IVPP V13259 containing fish remains); long toes, short claws, and reduced hallux suggesting a largely terrestrial animal; distinguished from *Yixianornis* by the following: longer skull; relatively longer cervical vertebrae; furcula craniocaudally compressed (as opposed to latero-medially); more robust limb bones; forelimbs comparatively longer, manus and pedal digits relatively shorter, pubic symphysis longer, metacarpal III more robust.

YIXIANORNIS   Zhou and Zhang 2001
Ornithurae *incertae sedis*.
Name derivation: Chinese *Yixian* [County] + Greek *ornis* = "bird."
Type species: *Y. grabaui* Zhou and Zhang 2001.
Occurrence: Jiutotang Formation, Qianyang, Yixian County, Liaoning Province, China.
Age: Early Cretaceous (?Barremian).
Holotype: IVPP V12631, nearly complete skeleton including feather impressions.

   Diagnosis of genus (as for type species): Ratio of skull length to width approximately 1.5; postcranial long bones slender; humeral head protruding, elliptical; metacarpal III less than one third width of II; pubic symphysis about one fifth pubis length; ratio of femur to tarsometatarsus length 1.6; ratio of pedal digit III to length of tarsometatarsus 1.3 (Zhou and Zhang 2001).

   Larger and with less elongated skull than *Laornis*; strong flight capability.

YUNGAVOLUCRIS   Chiappe 1993
Euenantiornithes *incertae sedis*.
Name derivation: "Yunga [phytogeographic region wherein El Brete is located]" + Latin *volucris* = "bird."
Type species: *Y. brevipedalis* Chiappe 1993.
Occurrence: Lecho Formation, Estancia El Brete, Department of Candelaria, Province of Salta, Argentina.
Age: Late Cretaceous (Maastrichtian).
Holotype: PVL-4053, almost complete right tarsometatarsus (lacking craniolateral border of lateral cotyla, cranial portion of trochlea of metatarsal IV).

   Diagnosis of genus (as for type species): Enantiornithine having short, broad tarsometatarsus with these autapomorphies: distal end much broader than proximal end; broad, dorsoplantarly compressed, pully-like trochlea of metatarsal II; distal end of metatarsal III laterally curved; metatarsal IV equal in length to III; prominent dorsal ridge between distal halves of metatarsals II and III (Chiappe 1993).

ZHYRAORNIS   Nessov 1984
Zhyraornithidae.
Name derivation: *Zhyra* [=Dzhyra waterwell] + Greek *ornis* = "bird."
Type species: *Z. kashkarovi* Nessov 1984.
Other species: *Z. longunovi* Nessov 1992.
Occurrence: Bissekty Svita, Navoi District, Bukhara Province, Uzbekistan.
Age: Late Cretaceous (Coniacian).
Holotype: TsNIGR 42/11915, incomplete cranial synsacrum including more than seven vertebrae, lacking caudalmost portion.

   Diagnosis of genus: Cranial portion of synsacrum noticeably convex dorsally; cranial end of synsacrum remarkably broad; synsacrum only slightly broadened across both sacral vertebrae; just one thoracic vertebra preceding two sacral vertebrae; caudal half of synsacrum long, narrow; two largest costal processes inclined caudally; no longitudinal groove on ventral side of synsacrum (Kurochkin 2000).

   Diagnosis of *Z. kashkarovi*: First vertebra of synsacrum expanding gradually cranially; transverse processes on second sacral vertebra slightly marked on dorsal surface; two pairs of largest costal processes slender, distinctly inclined lengthwise; synsacrum generally extended and narrow (Kurochkin 2000).

   Diagnosis of *Z. longunovi*: First vertebra of synsacrum expanding abruptly cranially; transverse processes of second sacral vertebra prominently marked on dorsal surface; two pairs of largest costal processes thick; costal processes of second sacral vertebra perpendicular to sagittal plane; synsacrum generally expanded and broadened (Kurochkin 2000).

Avia Ichnogenera

   Mesozoic birds are also known by their fossil tracks, or inchnites. Those Mesozoic avian tracks that have been given generic and specific names are listed below (for a list of dinosaurian tracks, some of which were first described as avian, see *S3*):

AQUATILAVIPES   Azuma, Arakawa, Tomida and Currie 1981.
Name derivation: Latin *aqua* = "water" + Latin *avis* = "bird" + Latin *pes* = "foot."
Type species: *A. izumiensis*
Other species: *A. curriei* McCrae and Sarjeant 2001, *A. sinensis* Zhen, Zhang, Chen and Zhu 1987, *A. swiboldae* Currie 1981.
Occurrence: Itoshiro Formation, Tetori Group, Itoshiro River, Central Japan; Gates Formation, Alberta, Gething Formation, northeastern British Columbia, Canada; Jiaguan Formation, Emei County, Sichuan Province, China.
Age: Early to Middle Cretaceous (Berriasian–Albian).

   Type species distinguished as the oldest bird track known from eastern Asia, type species prints measuring, on the average, 37.7 millimeters long and 44.5 millimeters wide.

ARCHAEORNITHIPUS   Fuentes Vidarte 1996
Name derivation: Name derivation: Greek *archaio* = "ancient" + Greek *ornis* = "bird" + Greek *pous* = "foot."
Type species: *A. meijidei* Fuentes Vidarte 1996.
Occurrence: Weald, Oncala Group, Spain.

Age: Early Cretaceous (Berrisian).

Digit II with cranially concave bend; oldest confirmed avian tracks reported to date, larger than any other Cretaceous bird tracks (maximum length of 16.6 centimeters, mean length of 12 centimeters); only parallel Mesozoic bird tracks, suggesting gregarious behavior.

HWANGSANIPES   Yang, Lockley, Greben, Erickson and Lim 1995

Name derivation: "Hwangsan [Tuff, just below strata in which these tracks occur]" + Latin *pes* = "foot."

Type species: *H. choughi* Yang, Lockley, Greben, Erickson and Lim 1995.

Occurrence: Uhangri Formation, Hwangsan Basin, Haenam, South Korea.

Age: Late Cretaceous (?Campanian).

Large, tetradactyl, rare among Mesozoic ichnites in showing evidence for full webbing between digits II and IV, prominent caudally directed digit I impressions; relatively large, single trackway suggesting "that this bird was not a gregarious species" (see Lim, Martin, Zhou, Baek and Yang 2002).

IGNOTORNIS   Mehl 1931

Name derivation: Latin *ingorare* = "we do not know" + Greek *ornis* = "bird."

Type species: *I. mcconelli* Mehl 1931.

Occurrence: Dakota Sandstone, Dakota Group, Golden, Colorado, United States.

Age: Middle Cretaceous (earliest Cenomanian).

Prominent hallux showing in most instances, distinguished as the first Mesozoic bird ichnites ever reported.

JINDONGORNIPES   Lockley, Logue, Moratella, Hunt, Schultz and Robinson 1995.

Name derivation: "Jindong [Formation]" + Greek *ornis* = "bird" + Latin *pes* = "foot."

Type species: *J. kimi* Lockley, Logue, Moratella, Hunt, Schultz and Robinson 1995.

Occurrence: Jindong Formation, Tetori Group, Goseong-Hai, Goseong-Donghae, South Korea; Dunvegan Formation, western Canada (A. G. Plint, personal communication to M. G. Lockley, 1997).

Age: ?Lower to ?Middle Cretaceous (?Aptian–Albian).

Digit II with cranially concave bend; among the largest known Lower Cretaceous bird footprints.

KOREANAORNIS   Kim 1969

Name derivation: "Korea" + Greek *ornis* = "bird."

Type species: *K. hamenensis* Kim 1969.

Occurrence: Haman Formation, Haman, South Korea.

Age: Early Cretaceous (?Aptian).

First Mesozoic avian footprints reported from Asia, oldest bird impressions showing webbed feet.

LAIYANGPUS   Yang [Young] 1960

Name derivation: "Laiyang [city]" + Greek *pous* = "foot."

Type species: *L. liui* Yang [Young] 1960.

Occurrence: Shandong Province, China.

Age: Cretaceous.

Tracks resembling those of modern shorebirds, probably non-avian theropod but possibly avian (see also "Appendix," *S3*).

MAGNOAVIPES   Lee 1997

Name derivation: Latin *magnus* = "great" + Latin *avis* = "bird" + Latin *pes* = "foot."

Type species: *M. lowei* Lee 1997.

Occurrence: Woodbine Formation, Texas, United States.

Age: Middle Cretaceous (lower to middle Cenomanian).

Large tracks lacking hallux impressions, step long, trackmaker possibly a cranelike bird; according to Lockley and Rainforth (2002), possibly non-avian.

PATAGONICHORNIS   Leonardi 1987

Name derivation: "Patagonia" + Greek *ornis* = "bird."

Type species: *P. venetiorum* Leonardi 1987.

Occurrence: Rio Negro Province, Patagonia, Argentina.

Age: Late Cretaceous (late Maastrichtian).

Medium-sized, either bird or non-avian theropod (see also "Appendix," *S3*).

Note: This taxon was never formally described, the name having been found by Giuseppe Leonardi in a typewritten note in the house of Rodolfo Casamequela and subsequently published by Leonardi in 1987 and other authors, *e.g.*, Lockley and Rainforth (2002); Leonardi does not regard this taxon as valid (G. Leonardi, personal communication 2003).

UHANGRICHNUS   Yang, Lockley, Greben, Erickson and Lim 1995

Name derivation: "Uhungri [Formation]" + Greek *icnhos* = "track."

Type species: *U. chuni* Yang, Lockley, Greben, Erickson and Lim 1995.

Occurrence: Uhangri Formation, Hwangsan Basin, Haenam, South Korea.

Age: Late Cretaceous (?Campanian).

Small, tridactyl lacking digit I (hallux) impressions, rare among Mesozoic ichnites in showing evidence for webbed feet; high density of these tracks suggesting "flocking or some form of social behavior" (see Lim, Martin, Zhou, Baek and Yang 2002).

YACORAITHICHNUS   Alonso and Marquillas 1986
Name derivation: "Yacoraite [Formation]" + Greek *ichnos* = "track."

Type species: *Y. avis* Alonso and Marquillas 1986.
Occurrence: Yacoraite Formation, northern Argentina.
Age: Late Cretaceous (Maastrichtian).
   Digit II with cranially concave bend.

Glossary

Included herein are technical and some nontechnical terms that appear in this volume, but which are generally not defined anywhere else in the text. Definitions of terms were based in part upon those published in a number of earlier sources, these including various dictionaries of the English language, and also the following texts: A Dictionary of Scientific Terms *(Kenneth 1960 seventh edition),* The Penguin Dictionary of Geology *(Whitten and Brooks 1972),* The Illustrated Encyclopedia of Dinosaurs *(Norman 1985),* The Dinosauria *(Weishampel, Dodson and Osmólska 1990),* Encyclopedia of Dinosaurs *(Currie and Padian 1997),* The Complete Dinosaur *(Farlow and Brett-Surman 1998), and "Ceratosaurus (Dinosauria, Theropoda), a Revised Osteology" (Madsen and Welles 2000).*

A PRIORI— Conclusion reached about a specific instance based upon something generally known.

ABDUCTOR— Muscle that brings one boney part away from another.

ABERRANT— Out of the ordinary; outside the normal range of variation.

ABRADED— Worn.

ABSTRACT— Relatively brief, concise summary of information that is presented (or is intended for presentation) in detail in a formal paper.

ACCTRAN— Character states present at a node under accelerated transformation.

ACETABULUM— Cup-shaped socket in the pelvic girdle for the head of the femur.

ACROMIAL— Artery, process, or ligament pertaining to the acromion.

ACROMION— Ventral prolongation of the scapular spine.

ACUMINATE— Tapering to a point.

ADAPTATION— Ability of a species or population of organisms to undergo change in response to its environment.

ADDUCTION— Movement of part of a body toward the midline of the axis of the body (opposite of abduction).

ADDUCTOR— Muscle that brings one bony part towards another.

AEROBIC— Thriving only in the presence of free oxygen.

AEROSOL— Gaseous suspension of fine solid or liquid particles.

ALAE— Winglike projections or structures.

ALIFORM— Wing-shaped.

ALLOMETRY— Study of relative growth; change of proportions relating to growth.

ALLUVIAL— Deposits having been formed by finely divided minerals laid down by running water.

ALTRICIAL BEHAVIOR— Behavior in which a parent or parents care for the newly born.

ALULA— In birds, a spurious or bastard wing.

ALVEOLI— Pits or sockets on the surface of an organ or a bone.

AMBIENS— Thigh muscle.

AMMONITE— Any of various invertebrate organisms of the Mesozoic, belonging to the Cephalopoda, having a flat, coiled, chambered shell.

AMNIOTE— Animal characterized by possession of amnion during fetal life.

AMPHIBIAN— Tetrapod adapted to live on both land and in water.

AMPHICOELOUS— Concave on both surfaces of a vertebral centra.

AMPHYPLATYAN— Flat on both ends of vertebral centra.

AN— Prefix meaning "not" or "without."

ANAGENTIC— Evolving progressively.

ANALAGOUS— Describing structures in different kinds of organisms which serve the same function, without being derived from the same ancestral structure.

ANGIOSPERM— Seed plant in which its seed is enveloped by a seed vessel fruit; the flowering plants.

ANKYLOSIS— Complete fusion of bone to bone (or other hard parts, as in tooth to bone) to form a single part.

ANGULAR— In most vertebrates, a dermal bone in the lower jaw, upon which rest the dentary and splenial bones.

ANLAGEN— First structure or cell group showing development of part of an organ.

ANOXIC— Lacking oxygen.

ANTEBRACHIUM— Forearm or corresponding portion of a forelimb.

ANTERIOR— Toward the front end, also referred to as "cranial."

ANTITROCHANTER— Articular surface of the ilium of birds, against which the trochanter of the femur plays.

ANTORBITAL— In front of the orbits of a skull, sometimes referred to as "preorbital."

ANTORBITAL FENESTRA— Opening in the skull, behind the external nares and in front of the orbit.

ANTORBITAL FOSSA— Depression surrounding the antorbital fenestra.

ANTRUM— Sinus or cavity.

APICAL— At the summit or tip.

APOPHYSIS— Process from a bone, usually serving as a place for muscle attachment.

APOMORPHIC— In cladistics, the derived state occurring only within members of an ingroup, when a character exhibits two states within that ingroup.

APOMORPHY— In cladistics, a derived character.

APPENDICULAR SKELETON— That part of the skeleton including the pectoral girdles, forelimbs, pelvic girdles and hindlimbs.

APRISMATIC— Regarding eggs, the condition in which the shell unit is visible in the first layer, but is concealed in successive layers due to differences in crystallographic orientation of the layers.

ARBOREAL— Living mostly or exclusively in trees, bushes, or shrubs.

AQUATIC— Living in the water.

ARCADE— In anatomy, a bony bridge.

ARCHOSAURIA— Diapsid group of reptiles (archosaurs) including dinosaurs, pterosaurs, "thecodontians," and crocodiles, defined primarily by the possession of an antorbital fenestra.

ARCHOSAUROMORPH— One of a group of diapsids including dinosaurs, birds, pterosaurs, crocodilians, and their close relatives.

ARCTOMETATARSALIAN CONDITION— Central metatarsal (III) pinched proximally, therefore obscured from view cranially, reduced or excluded from contact with the tibiotarsus.

ARMOR— Bony scutes, plates, shields, horns, spikes and clubs possessed by some dinosaurs.

ARTICULAR— In dinosaurs, the bone toward the rear of the mandible by which the lower jaw articulates with the quadrate bone.

ARTICULATED— Jointed or joined together.

ASPIRATION— Act of expelling breath.

ASSEMBLAGE— Large group of fossils and other items found at the same location, considered to originate from the same time period.

ASTRAGALOCALCANEUM— The astragalus fused to the calcaneum.

ASTRAGALUS— Larger tarsal bone which mostly articulates with the tibia dorsally and metatarsus ventrally.

ATLANTAL— Pertaining to the atlas bone.

ATLAS— First cervical vertebra.

ATTRITIONAL— Bone or dental accumulations resulting from recurring "normal" death events of numerous individual animals over a long span of time (as opposed to a catastrophic, short-term mass mortality event).

AUTAPOMORPHY— In cladistics, a character state unique to one taxon.

AVES— Clade comprising extinct and extant birds.

AVIALE—(See AVES.)

AVIAN— Pertaining to birds.

AXIAL SKELETON— That part of the skeleton including the vertebral column and ribs.

AXIS— Second cervical vertebra.

BADLANDS— Area of barren land heavily roughly eroded by water and wind into ridges, mesas, and peaks.

BARB— Delicate threadlike structure that extends obliquely from a feather rachis, forming the vane.

BARBULE— Small hooked process fringing the barbs of a feather.

BASAL— Placed at or near the base; in cladistics, placed at or neat the base or "trunk" or a phylogenetic tree; a

group outside a more derived clade; the earliest form of a lineage.

BASI— Prefix meaning "basis."

BASICRANIUM— Base of the skull.

BASIOCCIPITAL— Median bone in the occipital region of the skull, forming at least part of the occipital condyle.

BASIPTERYGOID— Process of the basisphenoid contacting the pterygoid.

BASISPHENOID— Cranial bone between the basioccipital and presphenoid.

BATTERY— Distinctive tooth pattern wherein a number of small, slender teeth are tightly wedged together along the length of the jaw, with multiple teeth stacked in a single tooth position (as in hadrosaurs), forming a grinding or cutting surface.

BAUPLAN— General body plan for a group of organisms; literally, a German word meaning an architect's or a building plan.

BED— In geology, distinct layers of sedimentary rock.

BERINGIA— Northeastern Asia and northwestern North America, plus the land ridge connecting them, during the Cretaceous period.

BICIPITAL— Groove on the upper part of the humerus; crests of the greater and lesser tubercles of the humerus; also, divided into two parts at one end.

BICONCAVE— Concave on both ends.

BIFURCATED— Forked; having two prongs or branches.

BILOBATE— Having two lobes.

BINOCULAR— Having vision in two eyes, able to see in three dimensions.)

BIOCHRON— Short interval of geologic time defined on the basis of fossil evidence.

BIOGEOGRAPHIC— Relating to biogeography, the study of the location and distribution of life on Earth.

BIOLOGICAL— Pertaining to biology, the science of life.

BIOLOGY— Science of life.

BIOMASS— Total estimated body mass or weight of all the animals of a population combined; also, the total mass or weight of a single individual.

BIOMECHANICS— Study of the motion of a body of a given organism in the context of mechanical laws and principles.

BIOMOLECULE— Molecule relating to life.

BIOSTRATIGRAPHY— Study of the distribution of fossils in distinct strata.

BIOTA— Flora and fauna of a region.

BIOTURBATION— Turning around of parts of a plant or animal during fossilization.

BIPED— Animal that habitually walks on two feet.

BIPEDAL— Habitually walking on two feet.

BIPEDALITY— State of habitually walking on two feet.

BIVALVE— Invertebrate organism consisting of two valves or plates, such as a mussel shell.

BIVARIATE— Variable condition occurring simultaneously with another variable.

BODY FOSSIL— Fossil consisting of an actual part of the organism.

BONEBED (also **BONE BED** and **BONE-BED**)— Sedimentary layer having a large concentration of fossil remains.

BOSS— Raised ridge or rounded body part, such as the bony mass on the snout of some ceratopsians; in "polacanthid" ankylosaurs, an elongate or rounded keeled element incorporated into a pelvic shield.

BRAINCASE— Part of the skull enclosing the brain.

BRANCH— On a cladogram, a line connecting a taxon to a node that joins it to another taxon, representing the divergence of a taxon from its nearest relatives.

BREVIS SHELF— Median shelf on the postacetabular section of the ilium for the origin of some of the caudifumoralis brevis muscle.

BROWSER— Animal that feeds on high foliage (*e.g.*, bushes, not grasses).

BUCCAL— Pertaining to the cheek; the surface of a tooth toward the cheek or lip.

BUTTRESS— Bony structure for reinforcement.

CALCANEUM— Smaller tarsal bone, lateral to the astragalus and distal to the fibula.

CALCAREOUS— Composed of, containing, or characteristic of calceum carbonate, calcium, or limestone.

CALLUS— Bone growth.

CAMELLAE— Pneumatic cavities in vertebrae.

CAMELLATE— Vertebrae in which the internal structure is composed entirely of camellae, the neural arch laminae is not reduced, and with large external fossae also possibly present.

CAMERA— A large chamber in a vertebra.

CAMERATE— Vertebrae having large and enclosed camerae having a regular branching pattern, cameral generations usually being at least three, and with more branches at each generation.

CANCELLOUS— Made up of lamillae and slender fibres, joining to form a network-like structure.

CANCELLOUS BONE— Spongy bone, having tissues that are not closely packed.

CANINIFORM— Teeth of "canine" form.

CAPITULUM— Knoblike swelling at the end of a bone.

CARAPACE— Hard outer covering to the body, like the shell of a turtle.

CARCASS— Dead body of an animal.

CARINA— On some bones and teeth, a keellike ridge or edge.

CARNIVORE— Flesh-eater.

CARNOSAUR— In the original (and abandoned) usage, an informal term generally referring to any large theropod; in the modern sense, a member of the Carnosauria, a restricted group of large theropods.

CARPAL— Pertaining to the wrist; also, a bone of the wrist.

CARTILAGE— Translucent firm and elastic tissue usually found in connection with bones and on the articular ends of limb bones.

CAT SCAN (See CT SCAN.)

CATASTROPHIC— Pertaining to theories and beliefs that mass extinctions were the result of cataclysmic events.

CAUDAL— Pertaining to the tail; toward the tail; more recently, used in place of "posterior."

CENTRUM— Main body of the vertebra (ventral to the neural chord) from which rise the neural and hemal arches.

CERATOBRANCHIAL— Hornlike element of the bronchial arch.

CERVICAL— Pertaining to the neck.

CERVICAL RING (See RING.)

CF.— Abbreviation from the Latin confere, meaning "to confer," informally used as "compares favorably within."

CHARACTER— Distinctive feature or trait of an organism, or any difference among organisms, that can be used in classification or in estimating phylogeny.

CHARACTER STATE— Range of expressions or conditions of a character.

CHAROPHYTE— Green algae belonging to the class Charophyceae.

CHELONIAN— Member of the Chelonia, a reptilian group including turtles and tortoises.

CHEVRON— Bone that hangs below a caudal vertebra.

CHOANA— Funnel-shaped internal nasal opening.

CHONDROCYTES— Cells that produce and maintain the plate, producing a mineralized matrix around themselves.

CINGULUM— Girdle-like structure on teeth.

CLADE— Monophyletic taxon as diagnosed by synapomorphies.

CLADISTICS— Scientific approach in taxonomy to classify groups of organisms in terms of the recency of their last common ancestor.

CLADOGRAM— Diagram representing the distribution of shared-derived characters for groupings of organisms.

CLASSIFICATION— Process of organizing clades into groups related by common descent.

CLAST— Made up of fragments.

CLAVICLE— Collar-bone forming the cranial portion of the shoulder-girdle.

CNEMIAL CREST— Crest along the cranial dorsal margin of the tibia.

COCHLEA— Part of the labyrinth of the ear.

COLD-BLOODED— Informal term for "ectothermic."

COEL— A hollow or excavation in a bone.

COELUROSAUR— In the original (and abandoned) usage, an informal term generally referring to all small theropods; in the modern sense, a large group of theropods including both small and gigantic forms.

COEVAL— Originating or living during the same time period.

COLLAGEN— Gelatinous protein present in all multicellular organisms, particularly in connective tissue.

COMMON ANCESTOR— In cladistics, a taxon exhibiting all synapomorphies of that taxon but neither autapomorphies nor the synapomorphies at higher levels within that taxon.

COMMUNITY— Ecological relationships between a local environment and all its fauna and flora.

COMPETITION— Simultaneous use of a limited resource by more than one species, resulting in conflicting efforts by them for continued survival.

CONDYLE— Process on a bone utilized in articulation.

CONGENERIC— Belonging to the same genus.

CONIFER— One of a group of gymnosperms including pines, spruces, larches, firs, and related plants.

CONSERVATIVE— Tending to remain unchanged, as in being similar to an ancestral group.

CONSPECIFIC— Belonging to the same species.

CONVERGENCE (also CONVERGENT EVOLUTION)— Organisms evolving similar appearances due to responses to similar lifestyle demands, though not sharing direct common ancestors.

COOSSIFIED— Bones fused together.

COPROLITE— Fossilized dung.

CORACOID— Bone between the scapula and the sternum, participates in the shoulder joint.

CORONOID PROCESS— In reptiles, prong-shaped bony process on the lower jaw for the attachment of jaw-closing muscles.

CORTICAL BONE— Bone tissue on the outer surface.

COSTAL— Involving the ribs.

COTYLE— Cuplike cavity in a bone.

COTYLUS— Ball-shaped structure.

COTYPE— Additional type specimen, usually collected at the same time and from the same locality as the holotype, or a specimen, along with others, from which the type is defined.

CRANIA (also CRANIAL SKELETON)— Bones of the skull, excluding those of the lower jaws.

CRANIAL— Toward the head; more recently, used in place of "anterior."

CRANIUM— Skull, particularly the braincase, but excluding bones of the lower jaw.

CREST— Ridge or rounded area of bone; in hadrosaurids, a rounded area of bone on the upper part of the skull, sometimes containing hollow passages.

CRETACEOUS PERIOD— Third and latest division of the Mesozoic Era, 145.5 to 65.5 million years ago.

CRISTA— Crest or ridge.

CROCODILIAN— Member of the Crocodilia, a successful group of Mesozoic and extant archosaurs related to dinosaurs.

CROWN— Exposed part of the tooth.

CROWN GROUP— All descendants of the closest common ancestor of living forms.

CRUS— Shank.

CRUSTACEAN— A member of the Crustacea, a group of mostly aquatic invertebrates having segmented bodies, chitinous skeletons, and paired, jointed limbs.

CT SCAN (also CAT SCAN)— Process by which a computer is used to process data from a tomograph in order to display a reconstructed cross section of an organism's body without physically cutting into it.

CULTRIFORM— Sharp-edged and pointed.

CURSORIAL— Running.

CYCAD— Flowering gymnosperm prevalent from the Triassic to Early Cretaceous.

DELTOID— Thick, triangular muscle covering the shoulder joint.

DELTOPECTORAL CREST— Bony flange of the humerus for attachment of the deltoid and pectoralis muscles.

DELTRAN— Character states present at a node under delayed transformation.

DENTARY— Largest bone of the lower jaw, usually bearing teeth.

Glossary

DENTICLE— Small bumplike processes along the edges of teeth.

DENTICULATE— Having denticles.

DENTIGEROUS— Tooth-bearing.

DENTITION— Teeth.

DEPOSIT— Accumulation of a substance (*e.g.*, sediment, bones).

DERIVED CHARACTER— More specialized character evolved from a simpler, more primitive condition.

DERM or **DERMAL**— Pertaining to the skin.

DERMAL ARMOR— Platelets or small plates of bone that grew in the flesh but were not connected to the skeleton.

DERMAL PLATE— (See Plate.)

DESCRIPTION— In paleontology, a detailed verbal representation of material.

DETRITIVORE— Animal that eats food in the form of particles or grains.

DIAGENESIS— Processes affecting a sediment while it is at or near the Earth's surface.

DIAGNOSIS— Concise statement enumerating the distinctive characters of a particular organism.

DIAPOPHYSIS— Lateral or transverse process of the neural arch.

DIAPSID— Reptiles with a skull having a pair of openings behind the orbit, belonging to the group Diapsida.

DIASTEMA— Toothless space in a jaw, generally between two different kinds of teeth (such as the canine and postcanines in mammals).

DIDACTYLOUS— Having two digits.

DIGIT— Toe or finger.

DIGITIGRADE— Walking with only the digits touching ground.

DIMORPHISM— State of having two different forms, usually according to sex.

DINOSAUR— One of a diverse group (Dinosauria) of terrestrial archosaurian reptiles that flourished from the Late Triassic through the Late Cretaceous periods of the Mesozoic Era, with an erect gait, closely related to other archosaurian groups such as crocodilians and pterosaurs, one lineage (maniraptoran theropods) seemingly the direct ancestors of birds.

DINOSAUROMORPHA— Ornithodiran clade including "lagosuchids," dinosaurs, and birds.

DISARTICULATED— Pulled apart.

DISPERSAL— In biogeography, spreading out.

DISTAL— End of any structure farthest from the midline of an organism, or from the point of attachment; away from the mass of the body; segments of a limb or of elements within a limb; the edge of a tooth away from

the symphysis along the tooth row; part of the tail farthest from the hips.

DIURNAL— Active only in the daytime.

DIVERGENCE— In evolution, moving away from a central group or changing in form.

DIVERTICULUM— Sac or tube, "blind" at the distal end, that branches off from a cavity or canal.

DORSAL— Relating to the back; toward the back.

DORSI- (also **DORSO**)— Prefix meaning "back."

DORSIFLEXION— Upwards and backwards pulling.

DORSUM— Back or upper surface.

ECOMORPH— Predictable ecological role performed by an organism with a fixed set of characters.

ECOSYSTEM— Ecological system formed by interaction of organisms and their environment.

ECOLOGY— Biological study of the relationship between organisms and their environment.

ECTEPICONDYLE— Lateral projection of the distal end of the humerus.

ECTO— Prefix meaning "outer" or "outside."

ECTOPTERYGOID— Ventral membrane bone behind the palatine, extending to the quadrate.

ECTOTHERMIC— Relying on external sources of heat to maintain body temperature; popularly, "cold-blooded."

EDENTULOUS— Toothless.

EMBAYMENT— A baylike shape or depression in a bone.

EMBRYO— Young organism in pre-birth stages of development.

ENAMEL— Form of calceum phosphate forming the hard outer covering on teeth.

ENANTIOTHORNES— Group of Mesozoic birds.

ENDEMIC— Relating to an indigenous species or population occurring in a specific geographic range.

ENDO— Suffix meaning "within."

ENDOCAST— Fill-in of the brain cavity by sediment, revealing the shape of the brain.

ENDOCHONDRAL— Forming or beginning within the cartilage.

ENDOCRANIAL— Pertaining to the brain cavity.

ENDOCRANIUM— Brain cavity.

ENDOSTEAL— Internal bone, or that lining the cavities of bones.

ENDOTHERMIC— Able to generate body heat internally by means of chemical reactions; popularly, "warm-blooded."

ENVIRONMENT— Surroundings in which organisms live.

EPAXIAL— Above the axis; dorsal.

EPEIRIC— Sea in which the basin is formed by deformation of the earth's crust.

EPICONDYLE— Medial/inner projection at the distal end of the humerus and femur.

EPIDEMIOLOGY— Study of epidemic diseases and epidemics.

EPIDERMIS— Outer, nonvascular, and protective layer of the skin.

EPIJUGAL— Hornlike projection off the jugal in ceratopsians.

EPIPHYSEAL— Pertaining to the part or process of a bone formed from a separate center of ossification, later fusing with the bone.

EPIPHYSIS— Part or process of a bone formed from a separate center of ossification, later fusing with the bone.

EPIPOPHYSIS— In theropods and some primitive birds, a dorsally directed additional process on the postzygapophysis of a cervical vertebra.

EPITHELIAL— Pertaining to epithelium (*i.e.*, cellular tissue covering a free surface or lining a cavity or tube).

EPITHELIUM— Cellular tissue covering a free surface or lining a cavity or tube.

EPOCH— Lesser division of geologic time, part of a period.

EPOCCIPITAL— Small bone located on the edge of the ceratopsian frill.

ERA— Largest division of geologic time.

ERODED— Worn away by abrasion, dissolution, or transportation.

EROSION— Result of weathering on exposed rocks.

ETIOLOGY— Science of causation; origin of causes.

EUTHERIAN— Member of a large group of placental mammals.

EVOLUTION— Change in the characteristics of a population of organisms, caused by natural selection over time.

EXOCCIPITAL— Bone of the skull on each side of the foramen magnum.

EXPOSURE— In geology, where rock is exposed due to weathering.

EXTENSOR— Muscle that extends a limb or part of a limb; also used to designate surfaces of a limb, manus, or pes.

EXTINCTION— Termination of a species.

FACIES— In geology, one of different types of contemporaneous deposits in a lateral series of deposits; also, the paleontological and lithological makeup of a sedimentary deposit.

FACULTATIVE— Having the ability to live and adapt to certain conditions, while not being restricted to those conditions.

FAMILY— In Linnaean classification, a grouping of similar genera.

FASCICLE— Small bundle.

FAUNA— All the animals of a particular place and time.

FEMUR— Thigh-bone.

FENESTRA— Opening in a bone or between bones.

FIBRO-LAMELLAR BONE— Somewhat open hard tissue, filled with blood vessels, indicative of fast-growing bone.

FIBULA— Smaller, outer shin bone.

FLEXOR— Muscle which bends a joint; also used to designate surfaces of a limb, manus, or pes.

FLOAT— Fossil material collected on the surface, rather than being excavated.

FLORA— All the plants of a particular place and time.

FONTANELLE— Opening on the frill in some ceratopsians.

FORAMEN— Opening through a bone or membraneous structure.

FORAMEN MAGNUM— Opening in the occipital area of the skull through which the spinal cord passes.

FORMATION— In geology, a formally defined and mappable unit of sedimentary rock.

FOSSA— Pit or trenchlike depression.

FOSSIL— Preserved remains of an animal or plant at least 10,000 years old, usually formed through burial and possibly involving a chemical change; evidence of life in the geologic past.

FOSSILIZED— Having become a fossil.

FOVEA— Small pit, fossa or depression.

FRACTURE— Break in a bone.

FRONTAL— Bone of the skull roof in front of the parietal.

FRONTOPARIETAL— Frontal and parietal bones, usually referring to suture or fusion of both bones.

FRUGIVOROUS— fruit-eating.

FUNCTIONAL MORPHOLOGY— Study of the movements and patterns of locomotion of an organism, mostly relative to its form or structure.

FUSION— In anatomy, the firm joining together of bones, either naturally or abnormally.

FUSED— Firmly jointed together, usually when bones grow together; coossified.

GASTRALIA (singular: **GASTRALIUM**)— Belly ribs that help to support the viscera in some dinosaurs.

GASTROLITH— Small "stomach" stone or "gizzard" stone that is swallowed for ballast or to grind up already consumed food.

GENESIS— Suffix meaning "descent" or "formation."

GENUS— Group of closely related species.

GEOLOGIC TIME— Period of time spanning the formation of the Earth to the beginning of recorded history.

GEOLOGY— Science of the study of the Earth.

GHOST LINEAGE— Missing sections of a clade, unknown from the fossil record, but implied by phylogeny; theorized geological extension of the range of a taxon before its earliest known occurrence.

GINGLYMOID— Hinge joint, or constructed like one.

GIRDLE— Curved or circular structure, particularly one that encircles another.

GIZZARD— Muscular portion of the stomach utilized in grinding up food.

GIZZARD STONE— (See Gastrolith).

GLENOID— Socket in the pectoral girdle to which the head of the humerus attaches.

GONDWANA— Southern continent including South America, Africa, India, Madagascar, Australia, and Antarctica.

GRACILE— Having a graceful or slim build of form.

GRADE— In cladistics, a paraphyletic taxon as diagnosed by the absence and presence of synapomorphies, delineated based upon morphologic distance; also, in a series of bones, the gradual changing of shape of those bones.

GRAVIPORTAL— Slow-moving or lumbering.

GREGARIOUS— Animals of the same species living in groups rather than in isolation.

GUILD— Group of animals having a characteristic mode of existence.

GYMNOSPERM— Seed plant in which the seed is not enveloped by a fruit, including cycadophytes, seed ferns, conifers, and related plants.

HABITAT— Place in which an organism or population of organisms normally lives or occurs.

HAEMAL— (See **HEMAL**.)

HALF-RING— In ankylosaurs, the unification of the first and second transverse rows of keeled plates to form a pair of yokes around the neck.

HALLUX— First digit of the pes.

HATCHLING— Organism newly hatched from an egg.

HAVERSIAN BONE— Kind of secondary bone that replaces primary bone, forming a series of vascular canals called "Haversian canals."

HEAD-BUTTING— Behavior in which two (usually male) individuals of the same species compete for dominance of their group by repeatedly colliding head to head.

HEMAL (or **HAEMAL**)— Pertaining to blood or blood vessels.

HERBIVORE— Plant-eater.

HERD— Large group of (usually herbivorous) animals of the same species.

HETERO— Prefix meaning "other" or "different."

HETEROCHRONY— Condition of having a different beginning and ending of growth, or a different growth rate for a different feature, relative to the beginning and end, or the rate of development, of the same feature in an ancestor; a kind of evolutionary mechanism.

HETEROGENEOUS— Having dissimilar elements.

HISTO— Prefix meaning "pertaining to tissue."

HISTOLOGY— Study of the fine structure of body tissues.

HOLOTYPE— Single specimen chosen to designate a new species.

HOMEOTHERMY— Maintaining a fairly constant body temperature regardless of environmental temperature changes.

HOMEOTIC— Having to do with the assumption of one part of likeness to another (*e.g.*, modification of a dorsal vertebra into a sacral vertebra).

HOMO— Prefix meaning "same" or "alike."

HOMOLOGOUS— Similar because of common ancestry; similarity.

HOMOPLASY— In cladistics, a shared similarity between taxa explained by character reversal, convergence, or chance, and not a result of common ancestry.

HORIZON— Soil layer formed at a definite time and characterized by definite fossil species.

HUMERUS— Upper arm bone.

HYALINE— Clear, transparent; free of inclusions.

HYOID— Pertaining to a bone or series of bones lying at the base of the tongue.

HYPANTRUM— In some reptiles, a notch on a vertebra for articulation with the hyposphene.

HYPAXIAL— Below the vertebral column; ventral.

HYPER— Prefix meaning "more than," "greater than," etc.

HYPEREXTENSIBLE— Capable of being atypically extended.

HYPERTROPHY— Atypical enlargement or expansion of a body part.

HYPHAE— In fungus, threadlike elements or filaments of vegetative mycelium.

HYPOCLEIDEUM— Interclavicle bone.

HYPOGLOSSAL— Relating to a cranial nerve distributed to the base of the tongue.

HYPOSPHENE— In some reptiles, a

wedge-shaped process on the neural arch of a vertebra, fitting into the hypantrum.

IBERIAN PENINSULA— Region of southwestern Europe, consisting of Spain and Portugal, separated from France by the Pyrenees mountains.

ICHNITE— Fossil footprint.

ICHNO— Prefix meaning "track" or "footprint."

ICHNOGENUS— Genus name for a trackmaker.

ICHTHYOSAURS— Mesozoic marine reptiles with streamlined, somewhat dolphin-shaped bodies (not dinosaurs).

ILIUM— Dorsal bone of the pelvic arch; hipbone.

IN OVO— Referring to specimens preserved within fossil eggs.

IN SITU— Referring to specimens in place in the ground where they are discovered.

INCISIFORM— Incisor-shaped.

INCISOR— Teeth at the very front of the mouth.

INCISURE— Notch, depression, interdentation.

INCRASSATE— Thickened or becoming thicker.

INDETERMINATE— Incapable of being defined or classified.

INDEX FOSSIL— Fossil restricted to a particular span of geologic time which can, therefore, be reliably utilized to date rocks in which other fossils are found.

INFRA— Prefix meaning "below."

INFRAORDER— In Linnaean classification, category between family and suborder.

INFRAPREZYGAPOPHYSAL— Below the prezygapophysis.

INGROUP— In cladistics, a monophyletic grouping of taxa.

INSECTIVOROUS— Insect-eating.

INSPIRATION— Act of drawing air into the lungs.

INTEGUMENT— Outer covering, usually pertaining to skin.

INTERCENTRUM— Second central ring in a vertebra having two vertical rings in each centrum.

INTERDIGITATE— Coming between one another (as applying to teeth).

INTERMEDIUM— Small bone of the carpus and tarsus.

INTERMONTANE— Between mountains.

INTERORBITAL— Between the orbits.

INTRA— Prefix meaning "within."

INTRASPECIFIC— Within the same species.

INVAGINATED— Enclosed, as if in a sheath.

INVERTEBRATE— Animal without a backbone.

ISCHIUM— Ventral and caudal bone of each half of the pelvic girdle.

ISOGNATHOUS— Having both jaws alike.

ISOLATED— Set apart from similar items.

ISOMETRIC— Exhibiting equality in measurements or dimensions.

ISOTOPE— Atom that differs in atomic weight from another atom of the same element.

JUGAL— Skull bone between the maxilla and quadrate.

JUNIOR SYNONYM— Taxon suppressed because another name, pertaining to the same fossil materials, was published previously.

JURASSIC PERIOD— Second and middle division of the Mesozoic Era, 199.6 to 145.5 million years ago.

JUVENILE— Young or immature animal.

KERATINOUS— Pertaining to keratin, *i.e.*, matter composed of fibrous protein, the main constituent in vertebrates of such epidermal structures as hair, nails, and horn.

KINETIC— In zoology, bones joined together but capable of movement.

K-T BOUNDARY (also KT and K/T BOUNDARY)— In geologic time, the transition from the end of the Cretaceous (K) period to the beginning of the Tertiary (T), approximately 65 million years ago.

LABIAL— Near the lip.

LABYRINTH— Complex internal ear, either bony or membranous.

LACERTILIAN— Member of Lacertiliia, a reptilian suborder comprising lizards.

LACRIMAL (also LACRIMAL BONE, LACHRIMAL)— Skull bone contributing to the rostral border of the orbit.

LACUNAE— Cavities in bones; also, spaces between cells.

LACUSTRINE— Living in or beside a lake.

LAGS—(See Lines of Arrested Growth.)

LAMELLAR— Referring to lamella, *i.e.*, a thin, scale- or platelike tissue structure.

LAMINA—Thin sheet or layer.

LANDMARK—(Morphologically) certain homologous features that are recognizable between animals (*e.g.*, orbit, teeth, etc.).

LATERAL— At the side externally; away from the midline.

LATEROSPHENOID— One of the bones of the braincase.

LAURASIA— Hypothetical northern super-continent including North America, Europe, and parts of Asia.

LECTOTYPE— Specimen chosen from syntypes to redesignate the type of a species.

LEPIDOSAUR— Reptilians including lizards, snakes and their close relatives.

LIGAMENT— Strong fibrous band of tissue that support joints between bones and joins muscles to bones.

LINEAGE— Continuous line of descent, over an evolutionary span of time, from a particular ancestor.

LINEAR— In a line.

LINES OF ARRESTED GROWTH (also LAGs)— Pattern of development wherein there are pauses in the deposition of bone and a related slower growth rate.

LINGUAL— Pertaining to the tongue; the surface of a tooth toward the tongue.

LOCALITY— In geology, a named place where specimens have been found.

LOCOMOTION— An organism's ability to move from place to place; also, the manner in which an organism moves.

LONG BONE— Limb bone.

LUMBAR— Pertaining to the region of the loins.

LUMINA— Cavities in an organ.

LUNATE— Crescent-shaped.

M.— Abbreviation identifying a muscle, preceding the formal name for that muscle.

MAMMALIA— Group of vertebrate animals distinguished by self-regulating body temperature, hair, and in females, milk-producing mammae, almost all species giving live birth.

MAMMILATION— Condition of being studded with small protuberances.

MANDIBLE— Lower jaw.

MANDIBULAR— Relating to the mandible.

MANUS— Part of the forelimb corresponding to the hand, comprising metacarpals and phalanges.

MARINE— Pertaining to the sea.

MARL— Muddy limestone.

MARLY— Relating to marl (muddy limestone).

MASS EXTINCTION— Death of all members of a number of diverse animal groups apparently due to a common cause.

MATRIX— Fossil-embedded rock.

MAXILLA— Usually tooth-bearing principal bone in the upper jaw.

MAXILLARY— Relating to the maxilla.

MEDIAL— From the inside or inner; toward the midline.

MEDULLA— Central part of a bone or organ.

MEGA— Prefix meaning "large."

MESIAL— In a middle longitudinal or vertical plane; the edge of a tooth toward the symphysis or premaxillary midline; more recently, used in place of "anterior" in regards teeth.

MESOZOIC ERA— Geologic time span during which non-avian dinosaurs flourished, 248 to 65 million years ago.

METABOLISM— Constructive and destructive chemical changes in the body for maintenance, growth, and repair of an organism.

METACARPAL— Relating to the metacarpus; also, a bone of the metacarpus, generally one per digit.

METACARPUS— Bones of the manus between the wrist and fingers.

METAPHYSEAL— Having to do with growing bone.

METAPODIALS— In tetrapods, bones of the metacarpus and metatarsus.

METAPODIUM— In tetrapods, the metacarpus and metatarsus.

METATARSAL— Relating to the metatarsus; also, a bone of the metatarsus, generally one per digit.

METATARSUS— Part of the foot between the tarsus and toes.

MICACEOUS— Containing mica, any of a group of physically and chemically related mineral silicates.

MICRO— Prefix meaning "very small."

MICROBE— Minute organism.

MIDLINE— Imaginary line extending dorsally along the length of an animal.

MIGRATION— Behavior pattern whereby a group of animals of the same species move from one location to another on a regular or recurring basis.

MODERN— Living now or recently.

MOLLUSC (also MOLLUSK)— Member of the Mollusca, a group of bilaterally symmetrical invertebrates, such as snails, clams, cephalopods, and other forms.

MONAUTOCHRONIC— Eggs being laid at daily intervals.

MONOPHYLETIC— Group of taxa including a common ancestor and all of its descendants; derived from a single origin; having the condition of "monophyly."

MORPH— Shape; also used as a suffix to denote a general shape, as for a group of organisms, in "archosauromorph" or "dinosauromorph."

MORPHOGENESIS— Development of shape.

MORPHOLOGY— Science of form.

MORPHOMETRIC— Regarding the analysis or measurement of an organism's shape or form.

MORPHOTYPE— Type specimen of one form of a polymorphic species.

MOSASAURS— Large Cretaceous marine lizards related to the modern monitor (not dinosaurs).

MULTI— Prefix meaning "many."

MULTITUBURCULATE— Member of the Multituberculata, a successful group of early mammals that may have been the first herbivorous members of the Mammalia.

MUMMIFIED— A state in which parts of a dead animal (*e.g.*, soft tissues), which would normally not be preserved over time, are preserved.

MUMMY— A dead body having some of its soft tissues preserved.

MUSCULATURE— Arrangement of muscles.

MUZZLE— Anterior part of the head containing the nostrils and jaws.

MYA— Abbreviation for "million years ago."

MYCELIA— Networks of filamentous cells (hyphae) forming the typical vegetative structures of fungi.

MYOLOGY— Study of muscles.

NARIAL— Pertaining to the nostrils.

NARIS— Nostril opening.

NASAL— Bone near the front of the skull, between the premaxilla and the frontal; also, that which pertains to the nostrils or nose.

NEO— Prefix meaning "new."

NEOCOMIAN— Old term used to designate a subdivision of the Early Cretaceous period, equivalent to Hauterivian.

NEOGNATHOUS— More advanced palate of modern birds (excluding ratites).

NEORNITHES— Avian crown group including modern birds.

NEURAL— Closely connected with nerves or nervous tissues.

NEURAL ARCH— Bony bridge over the passage of the spinal cord.

NEURAL CANAL— Canal formed by the neural arch and centrum.

NEURAL SPINE— Spine rising up from the neural arch.

NEUROCENTRAL— Having to do with a neurocentrum, a type of centrum in primitive vertebrates.

NEUROCRANIUM— Bony or cartilaginous case containing the brain and capsules of specials sense organs.

NICHE— Unique place occupied by a particular species within a larger ecological community.

NODE—(In cladistic classification) point on a cladogram where two or more lines meet, this constituting a taxon including all descendant taxa that will meet at that point; (morphologically) a knob or swelling.

NODE-BASED— Defining a taxonomic group as the descendants of the most recent common ancestor of two other groups and all descendants of that ancestor.

NOMEN DUBIUM— Taxon founded upon material of questionable diagnostic value; plural, nomina dubia.

NOMEN NUDUM— Taxon improperly founded without published material, diagnosis, type designation, and figure; plural, *nomina nuda.*

NOMENCLATURE— Official naming or system of naming of taxa.

NON-AVIAN (also NONAVIAN)— Pertaining to dinosaurs other than birds; also, not pertaining to birds in general.

NUCHAL— Pertaining to the neck.

OBLIGATE— Limited or restricted to a particular mode of behavior or environmental condition.

OBTURATOR— Pertaining to any structure in the area of the obturator foramen.

OBTURATOR FORAMEN— Oval foramen within the ischium for the passage of the obturator nerve/vessels.

OCCIPUT— Back part of the skull.

OCCIPITAL CONDYLE— Condyle with which the skull moves on the atlas and axis.

OCCLUSAL— Where surfaces of upper and lower teeth touch when the jaws are closed.

OCCLUSION— Surfaces of the upper and lower teeth making contact with each other when the jaws are closed in a bite.

OCULAR— Of or pertaining to the eye.

OLECRANON— Process for insertion of the triceps muscle at the proximal end of the ulna.

OLFACTORY— Pertaining to the sense of smell.

OMAL— In birds, the glenoid region of the shoulder girdle.

OMNIVORE— Animal that eats both plant and animal food.

ONTOGENY— Growth and development of an individual.

OOSPECIES— Specific name given to a genus of fossil egg.

OPHTHALMIC— Pertaining to the eye, a division of the trigeminal nerve; superior and inferior veins of the orbit.

OPISTHOCOELOUS— Having the centrum concave caudally.

OPISTHOPUBIC— Pubis that is directed rearward.

OPISTHOTIC— Inferior caudal bony element of the otic capsule.

OPTIC LOBE— Part of the brain connected with vision.

ORBIT— Bony cavity in which the eye is housed.

ORBITOSPHENOID— Paired elements in the skull located between the presphenoid and frontal.

ORDER— In Linnaean classification, a category including related families within a class.

ORGANIC— Relating to things alive.

ORGANISM— Any individual living being.

ORNAMENTATION— Visible external body feature (*e.g.*, horn, frill, etc.) that primarily functions in social behavior.

ORNITH— Prefix meaning "bird" or "birdlike."

ORNITHODIRA— Group including, among other taxa, pterosaurs and dinosauromorphs.

ORNITHOLOGIST— Scientist who specializes in ornithology (*i.e.*) the study of birds.

ORNITHOTHORACES— Avian group including all birds except Archaeopteryx.

ORNITHURAE— Group of modern birds.

OROPHARYNGEAL— Pertaining to the cavity of the mouth and pharynx.

ORTHAL— Jaw movement that is straight up and down.

OSSEOUS— Resembling or composed of bone.

OSSICLE— Bony platelets set under the skin, serving as secondary armor, often round, oval, or subtriangular.

OSSIFICATION— The process by which bone forms.

OSSIFIED TENDONS— Strandlike calcified tissues that connect and strengthen the vertebrae.

OSSIFY— To change into bone.

OSTEO— Prefix meaning "bone" or "relating to bones."

OSTEOBLAST— Bone-forming cell.

OSTEOBLASTIC RESPONSE— Response to a condition involving osteoblasts (*i.e.*, bone-forming cells)

OSTEODERM— Bony plates or scutes in the skin.

OSTEOLOGY— Part of zoology dealing with the structure and development of bones.

OSTEON— Haversian bone growth.

OSTRACOD— Microscopic crustacean consisting of a hinged, bivalved shell.

OTIC— Pertaining to the ear.

OTO— Prefix meaning "ear."

OUTGROUP— In cladistics, the character state occurring in the nearest relatives of an ingroup.

OTOSPHENOIDAL CREST— Bony crest formed by fusion of the opisthotic and spendoid bones.

PACHYOSTOTIC— Thickened bone.

PALATE— Roof of the mouth.

PALATINE— One of the bones of the palate, located near the front of the skull and to the side of the vomer; also, pertaining to the palate.

PALEO- (also **PALAEO-**)— Prefix meaning "ancient" or "past," pertaining to something very old or prehistoric.

PALEOBIOLOGY— Study of ancient extinct organisms.

PALEOECOLOGICAL— Pertaining to paleoecology, the study of the relationships between extinct organisms and their paleoenvironments.

PALEOECOLOGY— Study of the relationships between extinct organisms and their paleo-environments.

PALEOENVIRONMENT— Environmental conditions in the geologic past.

PALEOGEOGRAPHIC— Pertaining to paleogeography, the study of the geographic distribution of life forms in the geologic past.

PALEOGNATHOUS BIRDS— Primitive birds (including ratites).

PALEONTOLOGY— Scientific study of past life, based on the study of fossil and fossil traces.

PALEOPEDOLOGIC— Having to do with paleopedology, the study of ancient soils.

PALEOSOL— Ancient soil that has become fossilized.

PALEOVERTISOL— Ancient geologic process that operated on some soils, caused by cycles of wetting and drying, having caused an expansion and contraction on the soil.

PALMAR— Surface of the manus in contact with the ground.

PALPEBRAL— Small bone located on the rim of the eye socket, often forming a bony eyelid.

PALYNOLOGY— Study of fossil pollen grains and spores.

PALYNOMORPH— Spores, pollen, and cysts of certain algae.

PANGAEA (also **PANGEA**)— Deduced huge super-continent formed by the collision of all Earth's continents during the Permian period.

PAPILLA— Conical dermal structure constituting the beginning of a feather.

PARA— Prefix meaning "beside."

PARALLELISM—(See Convergence.)

PARAPHYLETIC— In cladistics, relating to a taxonomic group including a hypothetical common ancestor and only some of that ancestor's descendants.

PARASAGITTAL— Parallel to the midline of an animal.

PARASPHENOID— Membrane bone forming the floor of the braincase.

PARATYPE— Specimen used along with the holotype in defining a new species.

PARIETAL— Bone of the skull roof behind the frontal.

PAROCCIPITAL PROCESS— Bony process at the back of the skull.

PARSIMONY— In cladistic analysis, a subjective criterion for selecting taxa, usually that which proposes the least number of homoplasies.

PATHOLOGY— The study of disease.

PATHOLOGIC— Diseased.

PECTORAL— Pertaining to the chest area of the skeleton.

PECTORAL GIRDLE— Bones of the shoulder, including scapula, corocoid, sternum, and clavicle.

PEDAL— Pertaining to the foot.

PEDOGENESIS— Formation of soil.

PEDUNCLE— Stalk- or stemlike process of a bone.

PELVIC GIRDLE— Hip area of the skeleton, composed of the ilium, ischium, and pubis.

PENNACEOUS FEATHER— A visible plumage feather (as opposed to down).

PENTADACTYL— Having five digits.

PERAMORPHOSIS— Evolutionary change wherein juveniles of a descendant species exhibit some adult characteristics of the ancestral species.

PERIOD— Division of geologic time, a subdivision of an Era.

PES— Foot.

PETRIFY— Minerals replacing a fossilized organism's hard tissues so that it becomes stonelike.

PHALANGEAL FORMULA— Formula giving the number of phalanges in the digits of the manus and pes.

PHALANX— Segment of the digits, a bone of the fingers or toes.

PHENETIC— Resemblancing in form.

PHYLOGENETIC— Concerning the evolutionary relationships within and among groups of organisms.

PHYLOGENY— Evolutionary treelike diagram or "tree" showing the relationships between ancestors and descendants.

PHYLUM— A group of closely related classes within a kingdom, sharing a basic body plan.

PHYSIOLOGY— Biological study dealing with the functions and activities of organisms.

PHYTOSAUR— crocodile-like, semi-aquatic "thecodontians" of the Triassic (not dinosaurs).

PISCIVOROUS— Fish-eating.

PISIFORM— Tiny bone in the carpus.

PLANKTON— Generally microscopic plant and animal organisms that drift or float in large masses in fresh or salt water.

PLANTAR— Pertaining to the sole of the foot.

PLANTIGRADE— Walking with the entire sole of the foot touching the ground.

PLASTRON— Ventral portion of a turtle shell.

PLATE (also **DERMAL PLATE**)— In paleobiology, a piece of bone embedded in the skin; in thyreophorans, a dermal bone consisting of a tall dorsal keel with rounded or sharp points.

PLATYCOELOUS— Condition in which the caudal articular end of a vertebral centrum is flat.

PLESIOMORPHIC— In cladistics, the more primitive character state of two that are exhibited within members of an ingroup while also occurring in the nearest outgroup; a primitive feature.

PLEUROCOEL— Cavity in the side of a vertebral centrum.

PLEUROKINETIC— Skull bones adapted to move to the side.

PLUMULACEOUS— Downy feathers.

PNEUMATIC— Bones penetrated by canals and air spaces.

PNEUMATOPORE— Minute air cavity.

POLLEX— In the manus, the thumb or innermost digit of the normal five.

POLYCAMERATE— Vertebrae with large and enclosed camerae having a regular branching pattern, cameral generations usually numbering at least three, with more branches at each generation.

POLYPHYLETIC— Associated groups that do not share a single common ancestor.

POLYTOMY— In cladistics, more than two branchings of a tree.

PORE— Minute opening.

POST— Prefix meaning "after"; in anatomy, meaning "closer to the rear."

POSTACETABULAR PROCESS— Portion of the ilium caudal to the acetabulum.

POSTCRANIA (or POSTCRANIAL SKELETON)— Skeleton excluding the skull.

POSTER— Presentation of data at a technical gathering (*e.g.*, a symposium or annual meeting of the Society of Vertebrate Paleontology) in the form of a poster, generally including drawings, photographs, charts, cladograms, graphs, etc.

POSTERIOR— Toward or at the rear end, more recently generally referred to as "caudal."

POSTMORTEM— Following the death of an organism.

POSTURE— Walking or standing position.

POSTZYGAPOPHYSIS— Process on the caudal face of the neural arch, for articulation with the vertebra behind it.

POSTURE— Walking or standing position.

PRE— Prefix meaning "before."

PREACETABULAR PROCESS— Por-

tion of the ilium cranial to the acetabulum.

PREARTICULAR— Bone in the lower jaw of primitive tetrapods.

PRECOCIAL— Species in which the young are relatively advanced upon hatching.

PROCUMBENT— Forwardly directed.

PRECURSOR— Earlier form of life from which a later form is descended.

PREDATOR— Organism that hunts and eats other organisms.

PREDENTARY— In ornithischians, a small crescent-shaped bone located at the tip of the lower jaw.

PREMAXILLA— A usually paired bone at the front of the upper jaw.

PREOCCUPIED— In zoological nomenclature, a taxonomic name identical to one published previously by another author.

PREORBITAL— Anterior to the orbit, sometimes referred to as "antorbital."

PREPARATION— One or more procedures applied to a fossil specimen so that the specimen can be strengthened, handled, preserved, studied, displayed, etc.

PREPARATOR— Person who prepares fossils for study or display.

PRESERVATION— General condition of a fossil specimen, referring to its quality and completeness.

PREY— Creature hunted and caught for food.

PREZYGAPOPHYSIS— Process on the cranial face of the neural arch, for articulation with the vertebra in front of it.

PRIMARY BONE— Bone that is formed as an organism grows.

PRIMITIVE— Characters or features found in the common ancestor of a taxonomic group, which are also found in all members of that group, also referred to as "plesiomorphic"; also (more generally), less developed, earlier.

PRIORITY— Rule in scientific nomenclature stating that, in the case of different taxonomic names given to the same form or groupings of forms, the name published first is valid.

PRISMATIC— Regarding eggs, the condition by which the shell unit originating at the membrana testacea can be seen throughout the thickness of the eggshell.

PRO— Prefix meaning "for."

PROCAMERATE— Vertebrae in which deep fossae penetrate the median septum, are not enclosed by ostial margins.

PROCESS— Outgrowth or projection of bone.

PROCOELOUS— Condition in which the cranial articular end of a vertebral

centrum is concave and the caudal end strongly convex.

PROKINESIS— Primitive avian kind of cranial kinesis derived from either akinetic or mesokinetic archosaurian skulls.

PRONATION— Act by which the palm of the manus is turned downwards by pronator muscles.

PROOTIC— Anterior bone of the otic capsule.

PROTO— Prefix signifying "first" or "earliest."

PROTOFEATHER— Incipient feather including branching barbs, but lacking the aerodynamic quality of the true avian feather.

PROVENANCE— Place of origin.

PROXIMAL— Nearest to the center of the body; toward the mass of the body; segment of a limb or of elements within a limb.

"PSEUDOSUCHIAN"— Usually bipedal Upper Triassic "thecodontian."

PTEROSAUR— One of a group of flying reptile of the Mesozoic, related to (but not) dinosaurs, with somewhat batlike wings consisting of membrane stretched from an elongated finger to the area of the hips, one group generally having teeth and long tails, the other toothless and possessing short tails.

PTERYGOID— Winglike caudal bone of the palate.

PUBIC— Relating to the pubis.

PUBIS— Antero-ventral bone of the pelvic girdle.

PUBOISCHIAL— Place where the pubis and ischium meet.

PULMONARY— Pertaining to the lungs.

PYGOSTYLE— In birds and some theropods, a structure at the tail end of the vertebral column consisting of fused vertebrae.

QUADRATE— In birds, reptiles and amphibians, the bone with which the lower jaw articulates.

QUADRATOJUGAL— Bone connecting or overlying the quadrate and jugal.

QUADRUPED— Animal that walks on all four feet.

QUADRUPEDALITY— Habitually walking on four legs.

RACHIS (also RHACHIS)— Shaft of a feather.

RADIALE— Carpal bone aligned with the radius.

RADIATION— Process by which a group of species diverge from a common ancestor, thereby producing an increased biological diversity, usually over a relatively short span of time.

RADIOMETRIC DATING— Dating

method involving the measurement of decay, at a constant known rate, in various naturally occurring radioactive isotopes.

RADIUS—Smaller forelimb bone between the humerus and carpals, lying next to the ulna.

RAMUS—Branchlike structure.

RANK—In classification, the position of a given level relative to levels above and below it.

RAPTOR—One of various modern birds of prey, including falcons and hawks; also, a suffix used in the names of a number of sometimes rather diverse theropods; more recently, a popular term inaccurately used to designate any dromaeosaur.

RAPTORIAL—Subsisting by or adapted for the seizure of prey.

RATITE—One of a group of flightless birds having an unkeeled sternum; also, an eggshell morphotype in which the shell structure is discrete only in the inner one-sixth to one half of the shell thickness (mammillary layer); most of the eggshell formed of a single, continuous layer.

RECONSTRUCTION—Drawn or modeled skeleton or partial skeleton, based upon the original fossil remains, often incorporating extrapolation or knowledge of the more complete remains of other taxa (sometimes used to mean "restoration").

RECTRICES—Stiff tail feathers of a bird or some non-avian theropods, used in steering.

RECTUS CAPITUS—A neck muscle.

RECURVED—Curved backward.

RED BEDS—Sedimentary beds that are reddish in color.

RELICT—Not functional, although originally adaptive.

REMIGES—Large feathers or quills on a bird's wing, consisting of primaries and secondaries.

REMODELING—Resorption and reprecipitation of bone for the purpose of maintaining its physiological and mechanical competence.

RENIFORM—Kidney-shaped.

RESPIRATION—Breathing process, accomplished by an exchange of gases between an organism and its surrounding atmosphere.

RESPIRATORY TURBINATE (also RT)—Thin, complex structure consisting of cartilage or bone in the nasal airway.

RESTORATION—In paleontology, a drawn, sculpted, or other representation of a fossil organism as it may have appeared in life (sometimes used as synonymous with "reconstruction").

REVERSAL—(In cladistic classification) transformation of a character in an advanced lineage back to its ancestral state.

"REVULETIAN"—Infrequently used term, often employed by authors in the New Mexico area, referring to the early to middle Norian stage of the Late Triassic period.

"RHAETIAN"—Mostly obsolete term referring to a stage of the Upper Triassic of England.

RHAMPHOTHECA—Horny sheath of a bird's beak.

RIB—Elongate and sometimes curved bone of the trunk articulating with vertebrae.

RING (also CERVICAL RING)—In ankylosaurs, curved group of from two to six elements surrounding the dorsal and lateral areas of the neck.

ROBUST—Strongly formed or built; also, a method of study or analysis, verified by past results, which will probably result in a correct inference.

ROSTRAL (also ROSTRUM)—In ceratopsians, median unpaired bone located at the tip of the upper jaw; also (rostral), toward the rostrum or tip of the head (term replacing "anterior").

RUGOSE—Possessing a rough surface (or "rugosity").

SACRAL—Pertaining to the sacrum.

SACRAL RIB—Rib that connects the sacral vertebrae to the pelvis.

SACRUM—Structure formed by the sacral vertebrae and pelvic girdle.

SAGITTAL—Pertaining to the midline on the dorsal aspect of the cranium.

SAURIURAE—Group of Mesozoic birds comprising Archaeopteryx plus the enantiornithines.

SCANSORIAL—Adapted to climbing.

SCAPULA—Shoulder blade.

SCAVENGER—Animal that feeds on dead animal flesh or other decomposing organic matter.

SCLEROTIC RING—Ring of a series of overlapping bones around the outside of the eyeball.

SCUTE—Low ridged, keeled, oval-shaped, horny or bony element embedded in the skin.

SECONDARY OSTEONS—Osteons formed during internal reconstruction following the dissolution and reconstitution of preexisting bone.

SEDIMENT—Deposit of inorganic or organic particles.

SEDIMENTARY ROCKS (also SEDIMENTS)—Rocks formed from sediment.

SELECTION—Principle that organisms having a certain hereditary characteristic will have a tendency to reproduce at a more successful rate than those of the same population not hav-

ing this characteristic, consequently increasing their numbers in later generations.

SEMILUNATE—Having the approximate shape of a half-crescent.

SENIOR SYNONYM—Taxon having priority over another identically named taxon and regarded as the valid name, because of the former's earlier publication.

SENONIAN—Term (generally used by European and South American paleontologists) for an epoch including the Late Cretaceous "ages" Conician, Santonian, Campanian and Maastrichtian.

SEPTUM—Partition separating spaces.

SERRATED—Having a notched cutting edge.

SESAMOID—Bone developed inside a tendon and near a joint.

SEXUAL DIMORPHISM—Marked differences in shape, shape, color, structure, etc. between the male and female of the same species.

SHARPEY'S FIBERS—Calcified bundles of fibers perforating and holding together periosteal lamellae.

SHIELD—In polacanthid ankylosaurs, a flat, broad layer of bone that covers the pelvis and sacrum (including the presacral rod).

SIGMOID—S-shaped.

SINUS—Space within a body.

SINUSOID—Small space for blood.

SISTER GROUP (or SISTER TAXON, SISTER CLADE)—Group of organisms descended from the same common ancestor as its closest group.

SOCIAL BEHAVIOR—Association of two or more individuals of a single species over a period of time other than the usual interaction of males and females for the purpose of reproduction.

SOMATIC—Pertaining to the body.

SPALLING—Chipping, flaking, as if from a tooth or stone.

SPATULATE—Spatula-shaped.

SPECIALIZATION—Modification in a particular way.

SPECIALIZED—Modified in a particular way in response to certain environmental conditions.

SPECIES—In paleontology, a group of animals with a unique shared morphology; in zoology, a group of naturally interbreeding organisms that do not naturally interbreed with another such group.

SPECIMEN—Sample for study.

SPHENOID—Large, wedge-shaped bone at the base of the skull.

SPINE—In thyreophorans, a tall, pointed element having a solid, rounded base, its diameter less than the total height.

SPINAL— Having to do with the backbone or tail.

SPLENIAL— Dermal bone in the lower jaw, covering much of Meckel's groove.

SPONGIOSA— Bone having a spongy texture; bone full of small cavities.

SQUAMATE— One of a group (Squamata) of lepidosaurian reptiles including lizards and snakes.

SQUAMOSAL— In the vertebrate skull, a bone that forms part of the caudal side wall.

STEM-BASED— Pertaining to a taxonomic group defined as all those entities that share a more recent common ancestor with one group than with another.

STERNAL— Pertaining to the breastbone or chest.

STERNUM— Breastbone.

STRATIGRAPHY— Study of the pattern of deposition.

STRATA— Layers of sediment.

SUB— Prefix meaning "under."

SUBFAMILY— In Linnaean classification, a category smaller than a family, including genus one or more.

SUBGENUS— Subtle classification between a genus and a species; a group of related species within a genus.

SUBORDER— In Linnaean classification, a category smaller than an order, larger than an infraorder, including one or more families.

SUITE— Group of characters associated with a particular organism or species.

SULCUS— Groove in a bone.

SUPER— Prefix meaning "greater" or "above."

SUPERORDER— In Linnaean classification, a grouping smaller than a class, including one or more order.

SUPRA— Prefix meaning "above" or "over."

SUPRAORBITAL— Small bone along the upper rim of the orbit of the skull; in ceratopsians, a horn above the eye or brow.

SUPRATEMPORAL FENESTRA— Opening in the top of the skull, caudal to the orbit.

SURANGULAR— Bone of the upper rear area of the lower jaw, contacting (and caudal to) the dentary, the angular, and the articular.

SUTURE— Line where bones contact each other.

SYMPHYSIS— Line of junction of two pieces of bone.

SYMPLESIOMORPY— In cladistics, a character state shared by a member of one higher-level taxon with a member of a more primitive higher-level taxon.

SYN— Prefix meaning both "together" and "with"; also "united" or "fused."

SYNAPOMORPHY— Shared/derived feature defining a monophyletic group; unique character shared by two or more taxa.

SYNONYM— Different names for the same taxon.

SYNSACRUM— Single-unit structure formed by the fusion of several vertebrae.

SYNTYPE— When a holotype and paratypes have not been selected, one of a series of specimens used to designate a species.

SYSTEMATICS— Scientific study that involves the classification and naming of organisms according to specific principles.

TABLE— Top of the skull.

TAPHONOMY— Study of the processes of burial and fossilization of organisms.

TARSAL— Ankle bone.

TARSOMETATARSUS— In birds and some dinosaurs, a bone formed by the fusion of the distal row of tarsals with the second to fourth metatarsals.

TARSUS— Region where the leg and foot join; ankle bones.

TAXON— Definite unite in the classification of animals and plants.

TAXONOMIC— Pertaining to or according to the principles of taxonomy.

TAXONOMY— Science of naming and classifying biological organisms.

TEMPORAL— Bone on either side of the skull that forms part of its lateral surface; also, pertaining to that area of the skull.

TERRESTRIAL— Land-dwelling.

TETHYSIAN SEA [also **SEAWAY**]— Seaway that existed between Laurasia and Gondwana during the early Cretaceous.

TETRADACTYL— Having four digits.

TETRAPOD— Vertebrate with four limbs.

THERMOREGULATION— One of various processes by which the body of an organism maintains internal temperature.

THORACIC— Pertaining to the thorax; in the chest region.

THORAX— Part of the body between the neck and abdomen.

TIBIA— Shin bone.

TIBIOTARSUS— In birds and some dinosaurs, the tibial bone to which are fused the proximal tarsals.

TOMIAL— Sharp [edge].

TOMOGRAPHY— Recording internal images in a body via X-rays; a CT (or CAT) scan.

TOOTH BATTERY—(See Battery.)

TOPOTYPE— Specimen from the locality of the type specimen.

TORSION— Act of turning or twisting.

TOTIPALMATE— Feet being completely webbed.

TRABECULAE— Small sheets of bone.

TRABECULAR— Bone consisting of small sheets.

TRACE FOSSIL— Not the actual remains of an extinct organism, but rather the fossilized record of something left behind by that organism; the fossil record of a living animal.

TRACKWAY— Series of at least three successive footprints made by a moving animal.

TRANSGRESSION— In geology, in the intrusion of a body of water onto a land mass.

TRANSVERSE PROCESS— Laterally directed process of the vertebral centrum, for attachment of intervertebral muscles.

TRI— Prefix meaning "three."

TRIASSIC PERIOD— First and earliest division of the Mesozoic Era, 251.0 to 199.6 million years ago.

TRICIPITAL— Having three "heads" or insertions.

TRIDACTYL— Having three digits.

TRIGEMINAL— Consisting of or pertaining to three structures.

TRIGEMINAL FORAMEN— Opening for the fifth cranial nerve.

TRIGEMINAL NERVE— Fifth cranial nerve.

TRIPODAL— Upright stance incorporating the hind feet and tail.

TROCHANTER— Prominence or process on the femur to which muscles are attached.

TROCHLEAR— Pulley-shaped.

TROPHIC— Pertaining to food or the feeding process.

TROPICAL— Hot and humid area with lush vegetation.

TUBERA— Rounded protuberances; cranial projections of the tibia.

TUBERCLE— Small, rounded protuberance; in polacanthid ankylosaurs, a raised knob of bone, groups of which are clustered and packed between the bosses of the sacral shields.

TUBULE— Small, hollow, cylindrical structure.

TYMPANIC— Pertaining to the ear or eardrum.

TYPE LOCALITY— Geographic site at which a type specimen or type species was found and collected.

TYPE SPECIMEN— Specimen used to diagnose a new species.

ULNA— In the forearm, the larger long bone on the medial side, parallel with the radius.

ULNARE— In the proximal row of carpals, the bone at the distal end of the ulna.

UNCINATE PROCESS— In birds and some reptiles, a process on the ribs which overlaps other ribs.

UNGUAL— Phalanx bearing a nail or claw.

UTRICULUS— Membraneous sac of the ear-labyrinth.

VACUITY— Open space.

VAGUS— Tenth cranial nerve.

VARIATION— Range of appearance within a group of organisms.

VASCULAR— Of or pertaining to the circulatory system.

VASCULARIZED— Possessing blood vessels.

VASCULARIZATION— Formation or development of blood vessels.

VENTRAL— From beneath, relating to the belly or venter [abdomen or lower abdominal surface]; toward the belly.

VENTRI- (also **VENTRO**)— Prefix meaning "belly."

VERTEBRA— Bony segment of the backbone.

VERTEBRATE— Animal with a backbone.

VERTEBRATE PALEONTOLOGY— Scientific study of fossil animals having backbones.

VICARIANCE— Branching pattern of faunal distribution.

VISCERA— Internal organs of the body, particularly those of the digestive tract.

VOLANT— Flying or capable of flying.

VOLCANIC— Pertaining to volcanoes or to volcanic activity or force.

VOMER— Bone at the front of the palate.

ZIPHODONT— Kind of tooth having an inwardly curved, serrated shape.

ZOOLOGY— Science dealing with the structure, behavior, functions, classification, evolution and distribution of animals.

ZYGAPOPHYSIS— Bony, usually peg-like process on the neural arch of a vertebra, by which it articulates with other vertebrae.

Bibliography

[Anonymous], 1848, *Proceedings of the Ashmolean Society*, 25, pp. 191–194.

Adams, Jason, and Chris Organ, 2003, Ontogenetic development of ossified tendons in hadrosaurian dinosaurs: *Journal of Vertebrate Paleontology*, 23 (Supplement to Number 3), Abstracts of Papers, Sixtythird Annual Meeting, p. 29A.

Agnolin, Federico, Sebastián Apesteguía, and Pablo Chiarelli, 2004, The end of a myth: the mysterious ungual claw of *Noasaurus leali*: *Journal of Vertebrate Paleontology*, 24 (Supplement to Number 3), Abstracts of Papers, Sixty-fourth Annual Meeting, p. 33A.

Alexander, R. McNeill, 1983, On the massive legs of a moa (*Pachyornis elephantophus*, Dinornithes): *Journal of Zoology, London*, 201, pp. 363–376.

_____, 1989, *Dynamics of Dinosaurs and Other Extinct Giants*. New York: Columbia University Press, 167 pages.

_____, 1997, Engineering a dinosaur, *in*: James O. Farlow and Michael K. Brett-Surman, editors, *The Complete Dinosaur*. Bloomington and Indianapolis: Indiana University Press, pp. 414–423.

Alexander, R. McNeill, G. M. O. Maloiy, R. Njau, and A. S. Jayes, 1979, Mechanics of running of the ostrich (*Struthio camelus*): *Journal of Zoology, London*, 187, pp. 169–178.

Alifavov, Vladimir R., and Alexander O. Averianov, 2003, *Ferganasaurus verzilini* gen. et sp. nov., a new neosauropod (Dinosauria, Saurischia, Sauropoda) from the Middle Jurassic of Fergana Valley, Kirghizia: *Journal of Vertebrate Paleontology*, 23 (2), pp. 358–372.

Allain, Ronan, Najat Aquesbi, Jean Dejax, Christian Meyer, Michael Monbaron, Christian Montenat, Philippe Richir, Mohammed Rochdy, Dale A. Russell, and Philippe Taquet, 2004, A basal sauropod dinosaur from the Early Jurassic of Morocco: *Comptes Rendus Palevol*, 3, pp. 199–208.

Allain, Ronan, and Daniel J. Chure, 2002, *Poekilopleuron bucklandii*, the theropod dinosaur from the Middle Jurassic (Bathonian) of Normandy: *Palaeontology*, 45 (6), pp. 1107–1121.

Allain, Ronan, and Xabier Pereda Suberbiola, 2003, Dinosaurs of France (Dinosaures de France): *Comptes Rendus Palevol*, 2, pp. 27–44.

Allain, Ronan, Philippe Taquet, Bernard Battail, Jean Dejax, Philippe Richir, Monette Véran, Franck Limon-Duparcmeur, Renaud Vacant, Octávio Mateus, Phouvong Sayarath, Bounxou Khenthavong, and Sitha Phouyavong, 1999, Un nouveau genre de dinosaure sauropode de la formation des Grès supérieurs (Aptien–Albien) du Laos: *Comtes Rendu des Séances de l'Académie des Sciences, Paris, de la Terre et des Planètes*, 329, pp. 609–616.

Allen, David, 2004, The phylogenetic status of *Procompsognathus* revisited: *Journal of Vertebrate Paleontology*, 24 (Supplement to Number 3), Abstracts of Papers, Sixty-fourth Annual Meeting, p. 34A.

Allman, John M., 1999, *Evolving Brains*. New York: Scientific American Library, 256 pages.

Alonso, R. N., and R. A. Marquillas, 1985, Nueva localidad con huellas de dinosaurios y primer hallazgo de huellas de Aves en la Formación Yacorite (Maastrichtiano) del Norte Argentino: *Actas, IV Congreso Argentino de Paleontologiá y Biostratigrafiá, Mendoza*, 2, pp. 33–41.

Alverenga, Herculano M. F., and José F. Bonaparte, 1992, A new flightless land bird from the Cretaceous of Patagonia, *in*: Kenneth E. Campbell, editor, *Papers in Avian Paleontology, Honoring Pierce Brodkorb*, Science Series 36. Los Angeles: Natural History Museum of Los Angeles County, pp. 51–64.

Ambroggi, R., and Albert F. de Lapparent, 1954, Les empreintes de pas fossiles du Maestrichtian d'Agadir: *Notes du Service Géologique du Maroc*, 10 (122), pp. 43–66.

Ameghino, Florentino, 1889, Sinopsis Geológico-paleontológica. Segundo Censo de República Argentina: *Folia, Buenos Aires*, 1, pp. 112–255.

Anderson, J. F., A. Hall-Martin, and Dale A. Russell, 1985, Longbone circumferences and weight in mammals, birds and dinosaurs: *Journal of the Zoological Society of London*, 207, pp. 53–61.

Andres, Brian, and Ji, Chiang, 2003, Two new pterosaur species from Liaoning, China, and the relationships of the Pterodactyloidea: *Journal of Vertebrate Paleontology*, 23 (Supplement to Number 3), Abstracts of Papers, Sixty-third Annual Meeting, p. 29A.

Andrews, Charles W., 1913, On some bird remains from the Upper Cretaceous of Transylvania: *Geological Magazine*, 5 (10), pp. 193–196.

_____, 1921, On some remains of a theropodous dinosaur from the Lower Lias of Barrow-on-Soar: *The Annals and Magazine of Natural History*, Series 9 (8), pp. 570–576.

Antunes, Miguel Telles, and Octávio Mateus, 2003, Dinosaurs of Portugal (Dinosaures du Portugal): *Comptes Rendus Palevol*, 2, pp. 77–95.

Apesteguía, Sebastián, 2004, *Bonitasaura salgadoi* gen. et sp. nov.: a beaked sauropod from the Late Cretaceous of Patagonia: *Naturwissenschaften*, September (published online), 7 pages.

Apesteguía, Sebastián, and P. A. Gallina, 2004, A new titanosaur from "Rancho de Avila" (Río Negro) in the upper levels of the Bajo de la Carpa Formation: *Ameghiana*, 40 (4), Suplemento, p. 51R.

Apesteguía, Sebastián, and Leonardo Salgado, 2004, Remarks on titanosaur pelvic girdle: *Ameghiana*, 40 (4), Suplemento, p. 51R.

Arambourg, C. M., 1959, *Titanopteryx philadelphiae* nov. gen., nov. sp., ptérosaurien géant: *Notes et Mémoires du Moyen Orient*, 7, pp. 229–234.

Archangelsky, S. E. S., S. Bellosi, G. A. Jalfin, and C. Perrot, 1994, Palynology and alluvial facies from the mid–Cretaceous of Patagonia, subsurface of San Jorge Basin, Argentina: *Cretaceous Research*, 15, pp. 127–142.

Arcucci, Andrea B., and Rodolfo A. Coria, 2003, A new Triassic carnivorous dinosaur from Argentina: *Ameghiniana*, 40 (2), pp. 217–228.

Arid, F. M., and L. D. Vizotto, 1971, *Antarctosaurus brasiliensis*, um novo sauropode do Cretáceo superior do Sul do Brasil: *Anais do XXV Congresso Brasileiro de Geologia*, pp. 297–305.

Arribas, C. Pasquel, and E. Sanz Perez, 2000, Huellas de pterosaurios en l grupo Oncala (Soria, España): *Estudio Geológicos*, 56, pp. 73–100.

Arthaber, G. von, 1919, Studien uber Flugsaurier auf Grund der Bearbeitung des Wiener exemplares von *Dorygnathus Banthensis* Theod Sp.: *Denkschriften der königlichen Akademie der Wissenschaften. Mathematisch-Naturwissenschaftlichen Klasse*, 97, pp. 391–464.

Attila, Ösi, 2002, A new nodosaurid (Ankylosauria) from the Upper Cretaceous (Santonian) Csehbánya Formation, Bakony Mts, Hungary: *The 7th European Workshop of Vertebrate Paleontology, Sibu, Romania, 2–7 July 2002, Abstracts Volume and Excursions Field Guide*, p. 28.

Averianov, Alexander O., Thomas Martin, and Aizek A. Bakirov, 2005, Pterosaur and dinosaur remains from the Middle Jurassic Balabansai Svita in the northern Fergana Depression, Kyrgyzstan (Central Asia): *Palaeontology*, 48 (1), pp. 135–155.

Averianov, Alexander O., Alexei Starkov, and Pavel Skutschas, 2003, Dinosaurs from the Early Cretaceous Murtoi Formation in Buryatia, eastern Russia: *Journal of Vertebrate Paleontology*, 23 (3), pp. 586–594.

Bibliography

Averianov, Alexander O., and A. A. Yarkov [Jarkov], 2004, Carnivorous dinosaurs (Saurischia, Theropoda) from the Maastrichtian of the Volga-Don Interfluve, Russia: *Paleontological Journal*, 38 (1), pp. 78–82 (translated from *Paleontologicheskii Zhurnal*, 1, 2004, pp. 73–77).

Awad, G. H., and M. G. Ghobrial, 1966, Zonal stratigraphy of the Kharga Oasis: *General Egyptian Organization for Geological Research and Mining*, Paper 34, 77 pages.

Ayer, Jacques von, 1999, *The Howe Ranch Dinosaurs (Die Howe Ranch Dinosaurier)*, foreword by Hans Jakob Siber. Zurich: Saurier museum Aathal, 95 pages.

Azuma, Yoichi, Yohei Arakawa, Yukimitsu Tomida, and Philip J. Currie, 1981, Early Cretaceous bird tracks from the Tetori Group, Fukui Prefecture, Japan: *Memoirs of the Fukui Prefecture Dinosaur Museum*, 1, pp. 1–6.

Azuma, Yoichi, and Philip J. Currie, 2000. A new carnosaur (Dinosauria: Theropoda) from the Lower Cretaceous of Japan: *Canadian Journal of Earth Sciences*, 37 (12), pp. 1735–1753.

Azuma, Yoichi, and Yukimitsu Tomida, 1997, Japanese dinosaurs, *in*: Philip J. Currie and Kevin Padian, editors, *Encyclopedia of Dinosaurs*. San Diego: Academic Press, pp. 375–379.

Bader, Kenneth, 2003, The local flora and fauna of a site in the upper Morrison Formation (Upper Jurassic) of northeastern Wyoming: *Journal of Vertebrate Paleontology*, 23 (Supplement to Number 3), Abstracts of Papers, Sixty-third Annual Meeting, p. 30A.

Bakker, Robert T., 1972, Anatomical and ecological evidence of endothermy in dinosaurs: *Nature*, 238, pp. 81–85.

_____, 1986, *The Dinosaur Heresies: New Theories Unlocking the Mystery of the Dinosaurs and Their Extinction*. New York: William Morrow, 481 pages.

_____, 1995, Pterodactyls —flying marvels of the Mesozoic *in*: *Science Year 1996*. Chicago, London, Sydney, and Toronto: World Book, 1995, pp. 60–73.

Bakker, Robert T., and Gary Bir, 2004, Dinosaur crime scene investigations: theropod behavior at Como Bluff, Wyoming, and the evolution of birdness, *in*: Philip J. Currie, Eva B. Kopelhus, Martin A. Shugar, and Joanna L. Wright, 2004, editors, *Feathered Dragons: Studies on the Transition from Dinosaurs to Birds*. Bloomington and Indianapolis: Indiana University Press, pp. 301–342.

Bakker, Robert T., Donald Kralis, James Siegwarth, and James Filla, 1992, *Edmarka rex*, a new, gigantic theropod dinosaur from the middle Morrison Formation, Late Jurassic of the Como Bluff outcrop region: *Hunteria*, 2 (9), pp. 1–24.

Bakker, Robert T., Michael Williams, and Philip J. Currie, 1988, *Nanotyrannus*, a new genus of pygmy tyrannosaur, from the Latest Cretaceous of Montana: *Hunteria*, 1 (5), pp. 1–30.

Bakhurina, Natalia N., 1982, [Pterodactyl from the Lower Cretaceous of Mongolia: *Palae-*

ontological Journal], 4, pp. 104–108, Moscow.

_____, 1986: *Priroda*, Akademia Nauk SSR, Moscow.

Bakhurina, Natalia N., and David M. Unwin, 1993, *Sordes pilosus* and the function of the fifth toe in pterosaurs: *Journal of Paleontology*, 12 (Supplement to Number 3), Abstracts of Papers, Fifty-second Annual Meeting, p. 18A.

Bandyopadhyay, Saswati, Dhurjati Saswati, and David D. Gillette, 2003, Dentition of *Barapasaurus tagorei* from the Kota Formation (Upper Jurassic) of India: *Journal of Vertebrate Paleontology*, 23 (Supplement to Number 3), Abstracts of Papers, Sixty-third Annual Meeting, pp. 31A–32A.

Barker, F. K., A. Chibois, P. Shickler, J. Feinstein, and J. Cracraft, 2004, Phylogeny and diversification of the larger avian radiation: *Proceedings of the National Academy of Sciences*, 101, pp. 11040–11045.

Barrett, Paul M., 1999, A sauropod dinosaur from the Lower Lufeng Formation (Lower Jurassic) of Yunnan Province, People's Republic of China: *Journal of Vertebrate Paleontology*, 19 (4), pp. 785–787.

_____, 2000, Paradigms, prosauropods and iguanas: speculation on the diets of extinct reptiles, *in*: Hans-Dieter Sues, editor, *Evolution of Terrestrial Herbivory, Perspectives from the Fossil Record*. New York: Cambridge University Press, pp. 48–72.

Barrett, Paul M., and Paul Upchurch, 2001, Feeding mechanisms and changes in sauropod paleoecology through time: *Journal of Vertebrate Paleontology*, 21 (Supplement to Number 3), Abstracts of Papers, Sixty-first Annual Meeting, p. 32A.

Barrett, Paul M., Xiao-Dan Zhou, and Xiao-Lin Wang, 2003, Prosauropod dinosaurs from the Lower Lufeng Formation (Lower Jurassic) of China: *Journal of Vertebrate Paleontology*, 23 (Supplement to Number 3), Abstracts of Papers, Sixty-third Annual Meeting, p. 32A.

Barsbold, Rinchen, 1974, [The duel of the dinosaurs]: *Prioda*, 2, pp. 81–83.

_____, 1981, Predatory toothless dinosaurs from Mongolia: *Trudy, Sovmestnaâ Sovetsko-Mongolskaâ Paleontologiceskaâ Ekspediciâya* [*The Joint Soviet-Mongolian Paleontological Expedition: Transactions*], 15. pp. 28–39.

_____, 1983, Carnivorous dinosaurs from the Cretaceous of Mongolia: *Ibid.*, 19, 117 pages.

_____, 1986, Raubdinosaurier Oviraptoren, *in*: E. I. Vorobyeva, editor, *Herpetologische Untersuchungen in der Mongolischen Volksrepublik*. Moscow: Akademia Nauk SSSR Institut Evolyucionnoy Morfologii i Ekologii Zhivotnikhim, A. M. Severtsova, pp. 210–223.

_____, 1997, Oviraptorosauria, *in*: Philip J. Currie and Kevin Padian, editors, *Encyclopedia of Dinosaurs*. San Diego: Academic Press, pp. 505–509.

Barsbold, Rinchen, and Halszka Osmólska, 1990a, Ornithomimosauria, *in*: David B. Weishampel, Peter Dodson, and Halszka Osmólska, editors, *The Dinosauria*. Berkeley and Los Angeles: University of California Press, pp. 225–244.

_____, 1990b, Segnosauria, *Ibid.*, pp. 408–415.

_____, 1999, The skull of *Velociraptor* (Theropoda) from the Late Cretaceous of Mongolia: *Acta Palaeontologica Polonica*, 44 (2), pp. 189–219.

Barsbold, Rinchen, and Altangerel Perle, 1984, O pervoy nakhodke primirivnogo ornithomimozavra iz mela MNR: *Palaeontologicheskii Zhurnal*, 2, pp. 121–123 (The first record of a primitive ornithomimosaur from the Cretaceous of Mongolia: *Palaeontological Journal*, pp. 118–120).

Baumel, Julian J., and Lawrence M. Witmer, 1993, Osteologia, *in*: J. J. Baumel, A. S. King, J. E. Breazile, H. E. Evans, and J. C. Vanden Berge, editors, *Handbook of Avian Anatomy: Nomina Anatomica Avium*, 2nd edition, Publications of the Nuttall Ornithological Club, 23, pp. 45–132.

Bazhanov, V. S., 1969, [On the record of a bird remain living in the Cretaceous of the U.S.S.R.]: *Tezisy Dokladov XV Sessii Vsesoyuznogo Paleontologicheskogo Obshchestva*, pp. 5–6, Leningrad.

Baziak, Brian, and Mark Loewen, 2004, Intraspecific variation and ontogeny in cranial elements of *Allosaurus fragilis* from the Late Jurassic Cleveland-Lloyd Dinosaur Quarry of central Utah: *Journal of Vertebrate Paleontology*, 24 (Supplement to Number 3), Abstracts of Papers, Sixty-fourth Annual Meeting, p. 37A.

Beerling, David J., and F. Ian Woodward, 2001, *Vegetation and the Terrestrial Carbon Cycle: The First 400 Million Years*. Cambridge, England: Cambridge University Press, 405 pages.

Bennett, S. Christopher, 1989, A pteranodontid pterosaur from the Early Cretaceous of Peru, with comments on the relationships of Cretaceous pterosaurs: *Journal of Paleontology*, 63, pp. 669–677.

_____, 1991, Morphology of the Late Cretaceous pterosaur *Pteranodon* and systematics of the Pterodactyloidea. Doctoral dissertation, University of Kansas, 680 pages.

_____, 1994, Taxonomy and systematics of the Late Cretaceous pterosaur *Pteranodon* (Pterosauria, Pterodactyloidea): *Occasional Papers of the Natural History Museum, The University of Kansas, Lawrence, Kansas*, 169, pp. 1–70.

_____, 1995, A statistical study of *Rhamphorhynchus* from the Solnhofen Limestone of Germany — year-classes of a single large species: *Journal of Paleontology*, 69, pp. 569–580.

_____, 1996, Year-classes of pterosaurs from the Solnhofen Limestone of Germany: taxonomic and systematic implications: *Journal of Vertebrate Paleontology*, 16 (3), pp. 432–444.

_____, 1997, Terrestrial locomotion of pterosaurs: a reconstruction based on *Pteraichnus* trackways: *Journal of Vertebrate Paleontology*, 17 (1), pp. 104–113.

_____, 2002, Soft tissue preservation of the cranial crest of the pterosaur *Germanodactylus* from Solhhofen: *Ibid.*, 22 (1), pp. 43–48.

_____, 2003a, New crested specimens of the Late Cretaceous pterosaur *Nyctosaurus*:

Paläontologische Zeitschrift, 77 (1), pp. 61–75.

———, 2003*b*, New information on the genera *Pterodactylus* and *Germanodactylus* from the Solnhofen Limestone of southern Germany: *Journal of Vertebrate Paleontology*, 23 (Supplement to Number 3), Abstracts of Papers, Sixty-third Annual Meeting, p. 33A.

———, 2003*c*, Morphological evolution of the pectoral girdle of pterosaurs: *in*: Éric Buffetaut and Jean-Michel Mazin, editors, *Evolution and Palaeobiology of Pterosaurs*. London: The Geological Society, Special Publications, 217, pp. 191–215.

———, 2004, New information on the pterosaur *Scaphognathus crassirostris* and the pterosaurian cervical series: *Journal of Vertebrate Paleontology*, 24 (Supplement to Number 3), Abstracts of Papers, Sixty-fourth Annual Meeting, p. 38A.

Benton, Michael J., 1986, The Late Triassic reptile *Teratosaurus*—a rauisuchian, not a dinosaur: *Palaeontology*, 29, pp. 293–301.

———, 1990, Origin and Interrelationships of Dinosaurs, *in*: David B. Weishampel, Peter Dodson, and Halszka Osmólska, editors, *The Dinosauria*. Berkeley and Los Angeles: University of California Press, pp. 11–30.

———, 1997, Origin and early evolution of dinosaurs *in*: James O. Farlow and Michael K. Brett-Surman, editors, *The Complete Dinosaur*. Bloomington and Indianapolis: Indiana University Press, pp. 204–215.

———, 2004, Origin and relationships of Dinosauria, *in*: David B. Weishampel, Peter Dodson, and Halszka Osmólska, editors, *The Dinosauria* (second edition). Berkeley and Los Angeles: University of California Press, pp. 1–20.

Benton, Michael J., Lars Juul, Glenn W. Storrs, and Peter M. Galton, 2000, Anatomy and systematics of the prosauropod dinosaur *Thecodontosaurus antiquus* from the upper Triassic of southwest England: *Journal of Vertebrate Paleontology*, 20 (1), pp. 77–108.

Benton, Michael J., and P. S. Spencer, 1995, *Fossil Reptiles of Great Britain*. London: Chapman and Hall, 386 pages.

Bergeron, Melody, and Mary H. Schweitzer, 2003, The extent of preservation of brachylophosaur bones from the Judith River Formation, Malta, MT: *Journal of Vertebrate Paleontology*, 23 (Supplement to Number 3), Abstracts of Papers, Sixty-third Annual Meeting, p. 33A.

Berman, David S, and John S. McIntosh, 1978, Skull and relationships of the Upper Jurassic sauropod *Apatosaurus* (Reptilia, Saurischia): *Bulletin of Carnegie Museum of Natural History*, 8, 35 pages.

Bertrand, C. E., 1903, Les Coprolithes des Bernissart, I. partie: Les Coprolithes qui ont ete attributes aux Iguanodons: *Mémoire du Musée royal d'historie naturalle de Belgique, Brussels*, 1, pp. 1–194.

Bidar, Alain, Louis Demay, and Gérard Thomel, 1972, *Compsognathus corralestris*, nouvelle espèce de Dinosaurien Théropode du Portlandien de Canjuers (Sud-Est de la France): *Annales du Muséum d'Historie Naturelle de Nice*, 1 (1), pp. 1–34.

Billon-Bruyat, Jean-Paul, and Jean-Michel Mazin, 2003, The systematic problem of tetrapod ichnotaxa: the case study of *Pteraichnus* Stokes, 1957 (Pterosauria, Pterodactyloidea): *in*: Éric Buffetaut and Jean-Michel Mazin, editors, *Evolution and Palaeobiology of Pterosaurs*. London: The Geological Society, Special Publications, 217, pp. 315–324.

Bittencourt, Jonathas de Souza, and Alexander Wilhelm Armin, 2002, Abelisauria (Theropoda, Dinosauria) teeth from Brazil: *Boletim do Museu Nacional*, 63, pp. 1–8.

Bittencourt, Jonathas de Souza, and Alexander Kellner, 2004, The phylogenetic position of *Staurikosaurus pricei* from the Triassic of Brazil: *Journal of Vertebrate Paleontology*, 24 (Supplement to Number 3), Abstracts of Papers, Sixty-fourth Annual Meeting, p. 39A.

Blows, William T., 1995, The Early Cretaceous brachiosaurid dinosaurs *Ornithopsis* and *Eucamerotus* from the Isle of Wight, England: *Palaeontology*, 38 (1), pp. 187–197.

Boas, J. E. V., 1929, Biologisch-anatomische Studien über den Hals der Vögel: *Die Kongelige Danske Videnskabernes Selskabs Skrifter, Naturvidenskabelig og Mathematisk Afdeling*, Ser. 9, 1, pp. 105–222.

Bock, Walter, 1985, The arboreal theory for the origin of birds, *in*: Max K. Hecht, John H. Ostrom, G. Viohl and Peter Wellnhoffer, editors, *The Beginnings of Birds*. Eichstätt: Freunde des Jura-Museums, pp. 199–208.

———, 1986, The arboreal origin of avian flight, *in*: Kevin Padian, editor, *The Origin of Birds and the Evolution of Flight*. San Francisco: California Academy of Sciences, pp. 57–72.

———, 2000, Explanatory history of the origin of feathers: *American Zoologist*, 40, pp. 478–485.

Bogolubov, Nikolai Nikolaevich, 1914, A propos d'une vertebre de pterodactyle des depots cretaces superieurs du gouvernement de Saratoff: *Ann. Geol. Min. Russie*, 16 (1), pp. 1–7.

Bolotsky, Yuri L., and Pascal Godefroit, 2004, A new hadrosaurine dinosaur from the Late Cretaceous of far eastern Russia: *Journal of Vertebrate Paleontology*, 24 (2), pp. 351–365.

Bolotsky, Yuri L., and V. G. Moiseyenko, 1988, Dinosaurs from Priamur: *Academia Nauk SSSR, Amur KNII, Blagoveschensk*, 40 pages.

Bonaparte, José F., 1970, *Pterodaustro guinazui* gen. et sp. nov. pterosaurio de la formación Lagarcito, provincia de San Luis, Argentina: *Acta Geologica Lilloana*, 10 (10), pp. 207–226, Tucuman.

———, 1971, Descripcion del craneo y mandibulas de *Pterodaustro guiñazui* (Pterodactyloidea — Pterodaustridae nov.), de la Formacion Lagarcito, San Luis, Argentina: *Publicaciones del Museo Municipal de Ciencias Naturales de Mar del Plata*, 1 (9), pp. 263–272.

———, 1976, *Pisanosaurus mertii* Casamiquela and the origin of the Ornithischia: *Journal of Paleontology*, 50, pp. 808–820.

———, 1986*a*, Les dinosaures (carnosaures, allosaur idés, sauropodes, cétiosauridés) de Jurassic moyen de cerro cóndor (Chubut, Argentine): *Annales de Paléontologie (Vert. Invert.)*, 72 (3), pp. 247–289.

———, 1986*b*, Hystory [*sic*] of the terrestrial Cretaceous vertebrates of Gondwana: *IV Congreso Argentino de Paleontología y Bioestratigrafía*, Revista del Museo Argentina de Ciencias Naturales "B. Rivadavia," Paleontología, 4, pp. 17–123.

———, 1987, Late Cretaceous dinosaurs of Laurasia and Gondwana, *in*: José F. Bonaparte and Zophia Kielan-Jaworowska, editors, *4th Symposium on Mesozoic Terrestrial Ecosystems*, pp. 24–29.

———, 1996, Cretaceous tetrapods of Argentina: *Müncher Geowissenschaftliche Abhandlung*, A (30), pp. 73–130.

———, 1997, *Rayososaurus agrioensis* Bonaparte 1995: *Ameghiniana*, 34 (1), pp. 1–16.

———, 1999, Tetrapod faunas from South America and India: a palaeobiogeographic interpretation: *Proceedings of the Indian National Academy*, 65A, pp. 25–44.

Bonaparte, José F., and J. Bossi, 1967, Sobre la presencia de dinosaurios en la Formación Pirgua del Grupo Salta y su significado cronológico: *Acta Geológica Lilloana*, 9, pp. 24–44.

Bonaparte, José F., and Rodolfo Anibal Coria, 1993, Un nuevo y gigantesco saurópodo titanosaurio de la Formacion Rio Limay (Albiano–Cenomaniano) de la Provincia del Neuquén, Argentina: *Ameghiniana*, 30 (3), pp. 271–282, Buenos Aires.

Bonaparte, José F., Jorge Ferigolo, and Ana Maria Ribeiro, 1999, A new early Late Triassic saurischian dinosaur from Rio Grande do Sul State, Brazil: *in*: Yukimitsu Tomida, Rich, and Vickers-Rich, editors, *Proceedings of the Second Gondwanan Dinosaur Symposium*, National Science Museum Monographs, 15, Tokyo, pp. 89–109.

Bonaparte, José F., M. R. Franchi, Jaime Eduardo Powell, and E. G. Sepúlveda, 1984, La Formación Los Alamitos (Campanio–Maastrichtiano) del sudeste de Río Negro, con descripcion de *Kritosaurus australis* n. sp. (Hadrosauridae). Significado paleogeografico de los vertebrados: *Actas V del Congreso Geológica Argentino, Neuquén*, 2, pp. 393–406.

Bonaparte, José F., and Zulma B. Gasparini, 1979, Los saurópodos de los grupos Neuquén y Chubut, y sus relaciones cronológicas: *Actas V del Congreso Geológica Argentino, Neuquén*, 2, pp. 393–406.

Bonaparte, José F., Wolf-Dieter Heinrich, and Rupert Wild, 2000, Review of *Janenschia* Wild, with the description of a new sauropod from the Tendaguru beds of Tanznia and a discussion on the systematic value of procoelous caudal vertebrae in sauropods: *Palaeontographica*, Abt. A, 256 (1–3), pp. 25–76, Stuttgart.

Bonaparte, José F., and Fernando E. Novas, 1985, *Abelisaurus comahuensis*, N.G., N.SP., carnosauria del Cretacio tardo de Patagonia: *Ameghiniana*, 21 (2–4), pp. 259–265.

Bonaparte, José F., Fernando E. Novas, and

Bibliography

Rodolfo A. Coria, 1990, *Carnotaurus sastrei* Bonaparte, the horned, lightly built carnosaur from the Middle Cretaceous of Patagonia: *Natural History Museum of Los Angeles County Contributions in Science*, 416, pp. 1–42.

Bonaparte, José F., and Jaime E. Powell, 1980, A continental assemblage of tetrapods from the Upper Cretaceous beds of El Brete, northwestern Argentina (Sauropoda–Coelurosauria–Carnosauria–Aves): *Memoires de la Société Géologique de France, Nouvelle Serie*, pp. 19–28.

Bonaparte, José F., and Teresa M. Sanchez, 1975, Restos de un pterosaurio *Puntanipterus globosus* de la formación La Cruz, provincia San Luis, Argentina: *Acta Primo Congresso Argentino de Paleontologia e Biostratigraphica*, 2, pp. 105–113, Tucuman.

Bonaparte, José F., and M. Vince, 1979, El hallazgo del primer nido de Dinosaurios triásicos (Saurischia, Prosauropoda), Triásico Superior de Patagonia, Argentina: *Ameghiniana*, 16, pp. 173–182.

Bonde, Niels, and Per Christiansen, 2003a, New dinosaurs from Denmark (Nouveau dinosaures du Danemark): *Comptes Rendus Palevol*, 2, pp. 13–26.

——, 2003b, The detailed anatomy of *Rhamphorhynchus*: axial pneumaticity and its implications: *in*: Éric Buffetaut and Jean-Michel Mazin, editors, *Evolution and Palaeobiology of Pterosaurs*. London: The Geological Society, Special Publications, 217, pp. 217–232.

Bonnan, Matthew F., 2003, The evolution of manus shape in sauropod dinosaurs: implications for functional morphology: *Journal of Vertebrate Paleontology*, 23 (3), pp. 595–613.

——, 2004a, Morphometric analysis of humerus and femur shape in Morrison sauropods: implications for functional morphology and paleobiology: *Paleobiology*, 30 (3), pp. 444–470.

——, 2004b, Inherit the limbs: did near-isometric growth in sauropod dinosaur humeri and femora exapt them for gigantism?: *Journal of Morphology*, 260 (3), 7th International Congress of Vertebrate Morphology, p. 280.

Bonnan, Matthew F., and Mathew J. Wedel, 2004, First occurrence of *Brachiosaurus* (Dinosauria: Sauropoda) from the Upper Jurassic Morrison Formation of Oklahoma: *PaleoBios*, 24 (2), pp. 13–21.

Borkhvardt, V. G., 1982, *Morphologies and Evolution of the Axial Skeleton: The Theory of the Skeletal Segment*. Leningrad: Leningrad Gos. Univ. [in Russian].

Borsuk-Bialyicka, M., 1977, a new camarasaurid sauropod *Opisthocoelicaudia skarzynskii*, gen. n., sp. n. from the Upper Cretaceous of Mongolia: *Acta Palaeontologica Polonica*, 37, pp. 1–64.

Bossi, J., L. A. Fernando, G. Elizalde, H. Morales, J. J. Ledesma, E. Carballo, E. Medina, and I. Ford, 1975, Carta geológica del Uruguay: *Dir. Suelos y Fertilizantes*, 22 pages.

Boyd, Clint, and Adam Darwin Bahmaier Behlke, 2003, The hole truth: investigating the presence of obturator foramina in

the ischia of *Edmontosaurus annectens*: *Journal of Vertebrate Paleontology*, 23 (Supplement to Number 3), Abstracts of Papers, Sixty-third Annual Meeting, pp. 35A–36A.

Brett-Surman, Michael K. [Keith], 1975, The appendicular anatomy of hadrosaurian dinosaurs: M.A. thesis, University of California (Berkeley), 70 pages (unpublished).

——, 1979, Phylogeny and paleobiogeography of hadrosaurian dinosaurs: *Nature*, 277, pp. 560–562.

——, 1989, A revision of the Hadrosauriae (Reptilia: Ornithischia) and their evolution during the Campanian and Maastrichtian: PhD dissertation, Graduate School of Arts and Sciences of The George Washington University, Washington, D.C., 272 pages (unpublished).

Brett-Surman, Michael K., and Gregory S. Paul, 1985, A new family of birdlike dinosaurs linking Laurasia and Gondwanaland: *Journal of Vertebrate Paleontology*, 5 (2), pp. 133–138.

Brill, Kathleen, and Kenneth Carpenter, 2004, Articulated dermal armor of the ankylosaur *Gastonia*: *Journal of Vertebrate Paleontology*, 24 (Supplement to Number 3), Abstracts of Papers, Sixty-fourth Annual Meeting, p. 41A.

Brinkman, W., 1986, *Rhabdodon* Matheron, 1869 (Reptilia, Ornithischia): proposed conservation by suppression of *Rhabdodon* Fleishmann, 1831 (Reptilia, Serpentes): *Bulletin of Zoological Nomenclature*, 43, pp. 269–272.

Britt, Brooks B., 1993, Pneumatic postcranial bones in dinosaurs and other archosaurs, Ph.D dissertation, University of Calvary (unpublished).

——, 1997, Postcranial pneumaticity, *in*: Philip J. Currie and Kevin Padian, editors, *Encyclopedia of Dinosaurs*. San Diego: Academic Press, pp. 590–593.

Britt, Brooks B., David Eberth, Rodney D. Scheetz, and Brent Greenlagh, 2004, Taphonomy of the Dalton Wells Dinosaur Quarry (Cedar Mountain Formation, Lower Cretaceous, Utah): *Journal of Vertebrate Paleontology*, 24 (Supplement to Number 3), Abstracts of Papers, Sixty-fourth Annual Meeting, p. 41A.

Britt, Brooks B., Rodney D. Scheetz, John S. McIntosh, and Kenneth L. Stadtman, 1998, Osteological characters of an Early Cretaceous titanosaurid sauropod from the Cedar Mountain Formation of Utah: *Journal of Vertebrate Paleontology*, 18 (Supplement to Number 3), Abstracts of Papers, Fifty-eighth Annual Meeting, p. 29A.

Britt, Brooks B., Kenneth L. Stadtman, Rod D. Scheetz, and John S. McIntosh, 1997, Camarasaurid and titanosaurid sauropods from the Early Cretaceous Dalton Wells Quarry (Cedar Mountain Formation), Utah: *Journal of Vertebrate Paleontology*, 17 (Supplement to Number 3), Abstracts of Papers, Fifty-seventh Annual Meeting, p. 34A.

Britt, Brooks B., Rod D. Scheetz, Kenneth L. Stadtman, and Daniel J. Chure, 2003, Relicts of soft tissue and osteophagous

fungi in partially ossified tendons of *Ceratosaurus* (Theropoda, Dinosauria): *Journal of Vertebrate Paleontology*, 23 (Supplement to Number 3), Abstracts of Papers, Sixty-third Annual Meeting, p. 36A.

Brochu, Christopher A., 1996, Closure of neurocentral sutures during crocodilian ontogeny: implications for maturity assessment in fossil archosaurs: *Journal of Vertebrate Paleontology*, 16 (1), pp. 49–62.

——, 2000, A digitally-rendered endocast for *Tyrannosaurus rex*: *Journal of Vertebrate Paleontology*, 20 (1), pp. 1–6.

——, 2003a, Lessons from a tyrannosaur: the ambassadorial role of paleontology: *Palaios*, 18 (6), pp. 475–476.

——, 2003b, Osteology of *Tyrannosaurus rex*: insights from a nearly complete skeleton and high-resolution computed tomographic analysis of the skull: *Society of Vertebrate Paleontology Memoir*, 7, *Journal of Vertebrate Paleontology*, Volume 22, Supplement to Number 4, 138 pages.

Brodkorb, Pierce, 1963, Birds from the Upper Cretaceous of Wyoming, *in*: C. G. Sibley, editor, *Proceedings of the 13th International Ornithological Congress*. Baton Rouge: American Ornithologists' Union, pp. 50–70.

——, 1970, The generic position of a Cretaceous bird: *Quarterly Journal of the Florida Academy of Sciences*, 32 (3), pp. 239–240.

——, 1976, Discovery of a Cretaceous bird, apparently ancestral to the orders Coraciiformes and Piciformes (Aves: Carinatae): *Smithsonian Institution Contributions to Paleobiolog*, 27, pp. 67–73.

——, 1978, Catalogue of fossil birds, part 5 (Passeriformes): *Bulletin of the Florida State Museum, Biological Sciences*, 23 (3), pp. 139–228.

Brown, Barnum, 1908, The Ankylosauridae, a new family of armored dinosaurs from the Upper Cretaceous: *Bulletin of the American Museum of Natural History*, 24, pp. 187–201.

——, 1914, *Leptoceratops*, a new genus of Ceratopsia from the Edmonton Cretaceous of Alberta: *Bulletin of the American Museum of Natural History*, 33, pp. 576–580.

——, 1938, The mystery dinosaur: *American History*, 41, pp. 190–202, 235.

Brown, Barnum, and Erich Maren Schlaikjer, 1940, The structure and relationships of *Protoceratops*: *Annals of the New York Academy of Sciences*, 40, pp. 133–66.

——, 1942, The skeleton of *Leptoceratops* with the description of a new species: *American Museum Novitates*, 955, pp. 1–12.

——, 1943, A study of the troödont dinosaurs with the description of a new genus and four new species: *Bulletin of the American Museum of Natural History*, 82, pp. 1–149.

Brown, Gregory W., 1986, Recostruction of *Nyctosaurus*: new wings for an old pterosaur (abstract): *Proceedings of the Nebraska Academy of Sciences*, p. 47.

Brush, A. H., 2000, Evolving a protofeather and feather diversity: *American Zoologist*, 40, pp. 631–639.

Bryant, H. N., and Anthony P. Russell, 1992, The role of phylogenetic analysis in the inference of unpreserved attributes of extinct taxa: *Philosophical Transactions of the Royal Society of London*, B, 337, pp. 405–418.

Buchholz, Peter W., 2002, Phylogeny and biogeography of basal Ornithischia, *in: The Mesozoic in Wyoming, Tate 2002*. Casper, WY: The Geological Museum, Casper College, pp. 18–34.

Buck, Brenda J., Andrew D. Hanson, Richard A. Hengst, and Hu Shusheng, 2004, "Tertiary dinosaurs" in the Nanxiong Basin, southern China, are reworked from the Cretaceous: *The Journal of Geology*, 112, pp. 111–118.

Buckland, William, 1824: Notice on the *Megalosaurus* or great fossil lizard of Stonesfield: *Transactions of the Geological Society of London*, 2, pp. 390–396.

_____, 1829: *Proceedings of the Geological Society*, 1, p. 127.

_____, 1835, On the discovery of a new species of Pterodactyl in the Lias at Lyme Regis: *Transactions of the Geological Society of London, Series 2*, 3, pp. 217–222.

Buckley, Lisa, 2003, Addressing the potential for cranial kinesis in *Tyrannosaurus rex*: a comparison of the palate complexes of *Tyrannosaurus rex* to *Varanus*: *Journal of Vertebrate Paleontology*, 23 (Supplement to Number 3), Abstracts of Papers, Sixty-third Annual Meeting, p. 37A.

Buffetaut, Éric, 1999, Pterosauria from the Upper Cretaceous of Laño (Iberian Peninsula): a preliminary comparative study: *Estudios Museo Ciencias Naturales Alava*, 14, 1 (special), pp. 289–294.

_____, 2002, New data from old finds: the dinosaurs from the Early Cretaceous Greensand ("Sables verts") of the eastern Paris Basin: *The 7th European Workshop of Vertebrate Paleontology, Sibu, Romania, 2–7 July 2002, Abstracts Volume and Excursions Field Guide*, p. 5.

_____, 2003, A sauropod with prosauropod teeth from the Jurassic of Madagascar: *1st Meeting of the EAVP, Abstracts with Program, Thursday 15th of July to Saturday 19th of July*, p. 14.

Buffetaut, Éric, Dan Grigorescu, and Zoltan Ciski, 2002, A new giant pterosaur with a robust skull from the latest Cretaceous of Romania: *Naturwissenschaften*, 89, pp. 180–184.

_____, 2003, Giant azhdarchid pterosaurs from the terminal Cretaceous of Transylvania (western Romania): *in:* Éric Buffetaut and Jean-Michel Mazin, editors, *Evolution and Palaeobiology of Pterosaurs*. London: The Geological Society, Special Publications, 217, pp. 92–104.

Buffetaut, Éric, and Rucha Ingavat, 1986, Unusual theropod dinosaur teeth from the Upper Jurassic of Phu Wiang, northeastern Thailand: *Revue de Paléobiologie*, 5 (2), pp. 217–220.

Buffetaut, Éric, and Jean Le Loeuff, 1998, A new giant ground bird from the Upper Cretaceous of southern France: *Quarterly Journal of the Geological Society of London*, 155, pp. 1–4.

Buffetaut, Éric, Jean-Jacques Lepage, and Gilles Lepage, 1998, A new pterodactyloid pterosaur from the Kimmeridgian of the Cap de la Heve (Normandy, France): *Geological Magazine*, 135 (5), pp. 719–722.

Buffetaut, Éric, and Jean-Michel Mazin, 2003, editors, *Evolution and Palaeobiology of Pterosaurs*. London: The Geological Society, Geological Society Special Publication No. 217, 346 pages.

Buffetaut, Éric, and Varavudh Suteethorn, 1998, The biogeographical significance of the Mesozoic vertebrates from Thailand, *in:* R. Hall and J. D. Holloway, editors, *Biogeography and Geological Evolution of SE Asia*. Leiden, Netherlands: Backhuys, pp. 83–90.

_____, 2002, Remarks on *Psittacosaurus sattayaraki* Buffetaut & Suteethorn, 1992, a ceratopsian dinosaur from the Lower Cretaceous of Thailand: *Oryctos*, 4, pp. 71–73.

Buffetaut, Éric, Varavudh Suteethorn, Gilles Cuny, Haiyan Tong, Jean Le Loeuff, Sasidhorn Khansubha, and Sutee Jongautchariyakul, 2000, The earliest known sauropod dinosaur: *Nature*, 407 (7), pp. 72–74.

Buffetaut, Éric, Varavudh Suteethorn, and Haiyan Tong, 1996, The earliest known tyrannosaur from the Lower Cretaceous of Thailand: *Nature*, 381, pp. 689–691.

_____, 2004, Asian spinosaur confirmed: *13th Symposium on Vertebrate Palaeontology and Comparative Anatomy, Papers*, pp. 8–9.

Buisonje, P. H., de, 1980, *Santanadactylus brasiliensis* nov. gen., nov. sp., a long-necked, large pterosaur from the Aptian of Brazil: *Proceedings of the Koninklijke Nederlandse Akademie van Wetenschappen*, B, 83 (2), pp. 145–172, Amsterdam.

_____, 1981, *Ctenochasma porocristata* nov. sp. from the Solnhofen Limestone, with some remarks on other Ctenochasmatidae: *Ibid.*, B, 84 (4).

Bundle, Matthew W., and Kenneth P. Dial, 2003, Mechanics of wing-assisted incline running (WAIR): *The Journal of Evolutionary Biology*, 206, pp. 4553–4564.

Bunzel, Emanuel, 1871, Die Reptilfauna der Gosauformation in der neuen Welt bei Wiener-Neustadt: *Abhandlungen der Kaiserlich-Königlichen Geologischen Reichsanstalt Wien*, 5, pp. 1–18.

Burnham, David A., 2004, New information on *Bambiraptor feinbergi* (Theropoda: Dromaeosauridae) from the Late Cretaceous of Montana: *in:* Philip J. Currie, Eva B. Kopelhus, Martin A. Shugar, and Joanna L. Wright, 2004, editors, *Feathered Dragons: Studies on the Transition from Dinosaurs to Birds*. Bloomington and Indianapolis: Indiana University Press, pp. 67–111.

Burnham, David A., Philip J. Currie, Robert T. Bakker, Zhonghe Zhou, and John H. Ostrom, 2000, Remarkable new birdlike dinosaur (Theropoda: Maniraptora) from the Upper Cretaceous of Montana: *The University of Kansas Paleontological Contributions*, New Series, 13, pp. 1–14.

Bush, L. P., 1903, Note on the dates of publication of certain genera of fossil vertebrates: *American Journal of Science*, series 4, 16, pp. 96–97.

Cai, Zhengquan, and Wei Feng, 1994, On a new pterosaur (*Zhejiangopterus linhaiensis* gen. et sp. nov.) from Upper Cretaceous in Linhai, Zhejiang, China: *Vertebrata PalAsiatica*, 32 (3), pp. 181–194.

Cai, Zhengquan, and Zhao L., 1999, A long tailed bird from the Late Cretaceous of Zhejiang: *Science in China*, 42 (4), pp. 434–441.

Calvo, Jorge Orlando, 1991, Huellas de dinosaurios en la Formación Río Limay (Albiano–Cenomaniano?), Picún Leufú, Provincia del Nequen, República Argentina (Ornithischia–Saurischia: Sauropoda–Theropoda): *Ameghiniana*, 28, pp. 241–258.

_____, 1994, Jaw mechanics in sauropod dinosaurs: *GAIA*, 10, 183–193.

_____, 1999, Dinosaurs and other vertebrates of the Lake Ezequiel Ramos Mexia Area, Neuquén-Patagonia, Argentina: *Proceedings of the Second Gondwana Dinosaur Symposium, Natural Science Museum, Tokyo*, 15, pp. 13–45.

Calvo, Jorge Orlando, and Bernardo J. González Riga, 2003, *Rinconsaurus caudamirus* gen. et sp. nov., a new titanosaurid (Dinosauria: Sauropoda) from the Late Cretaceous of Patagonia, Argentina: *Revista Geológica de Chile*, 30 (2), pp. 1–25.

Calvo, Jorge Orlando, and D. Grill, 2004, Titanosaurid sauropod teeth from Futalognko quarry, Barreales Lake, Neuquén, Patagonia, Argentina: *Ameghiana*, 40 (4), Suplemento, pp. 52R–53R.

Calvo, Jorge Orlando, and Juan Domingo Porfiri, 2004, More evidence of basal Iguanodontians from Barreales Lake (Upper Turonian–Lower Coniancian), Neuquén, Patagonia, Argentina: *Ameghiana*, 40 (4), Suplemento, p. 53R.

Calvo, Jorge Orlando, Juan Domingo Porfiri, Claudio Darmo J. Veralli, and Fernando E. Novas, 2002, *Megaraptor namunhuaiquii* (Novas, 1998), a new light about its phylogenetic relationships: *I Congreso Latinoamericano de Paleontologia de Vertebrados, Octubre de 2002, Santiago de Chile, en calidad de Expositor*, abstract.

Calvo, Jorge Orlando, and Leonardo Salgado, 1995, *Rebbachisaurus tessonei* sp. nov. a new Sauropoda from the Albian–Cenomanian of Argentina; new evidence on the origin of the Diplodocidae: *Gaia*, 11, pp. 13–33.

Camp, Charles L., Samuel P. Welles, Jr., and M. Green, 1953, Bibliography of fossil vertebrates 1944–1948: *Geological Society of America, Memoirs*, 57, 456 pages.

Campos, Diogenenes de Almeida, and Alexander W. A. Kellner, 1985, Panorama of the flying reptiles study in Brazil and South America: *Anais da Academia Brasileira Ciencias*, 1985, 57 (4), pp. 453–466, Rio de Janeiro.

_____, 1997, Short note on the first occurrence of Tapejaridae in the Crato Member (Aptian), Santana Formation, Araripe Basin, northeast Brazil: *Ibid.*, 69 (1), pp. 83–87.

_____, 1999, On sauropod (Titanosauridae) pelves from the continental Cretaceous of Brazil, *in:* Yukimitsu Tomida, Thomas R. Rich, and Patricia Vickers-Rich, editors, *Second Symposium Gondwana Dinosaur, 12–13 July, 1998, National Science Museum,*

Bibliography

Tokyo, Abstracts with Program, pp. 143–166.

Cappetta, H., 1987, Chondrichthyes II, *in*, H. P. Schultze, editor: *Handbook of Palaeoichthyology*. Stuttgart and New York: Gustav Fischer Verlag, pp. 1–193.

Caravajal, A. Paulina, Rodolfo A. Coria, and Philip J. Currie, 2004, Primer hallazgo de Abelisauria en la Formación Lisandro (Cretácico Superior), Neuquén: *Ameghiana*, 40 (4), Suplemento, p. 65R.

Carney, Ryan, 2003, Phylogenetically testing the hypothesis of secondary flightlessness in maniraptoriformes: *Journal of Vertebrate Paleontology*, 23 (Supplement to Number 3), Abstracts of Papers, Sixty-third Annual Meeting, p. 38A.

Carpenter, Kenneth, 1984, Skeletal reconstruction and life restoration of *Sauropelta* (Ankylosauria: Nodosauridae) from the Cretaceous of North America: *Canadian Journal of Earth Sciences*, 21, pp. 1491–1498.

_____, 1992a, Tyrannosaurids (Dinosauria) of Asia and North America, *in*: Niall J. Mateer and Chen Pei-Ji, editors: *International Symposium on Non-marine Cretaceous Correlation*. Beijing: China Ocean Press, pp. 250–268.

_____, 1992b, Behavior of hadrosaurs as interpreted from footprints in the "Mesaverde" Group (Campanian) of Colorado, Utah, and Wyoming: *Contributions to Geology, University of Wyoming*, 29, pp. 81–96.

_____, 1994, Baby *Dryosaurus* from the Upper Jurassic Morrison Formation of Dinosaur National Monument, *in*: Kenneth Carpenter, Karl F. Hirsch, and John R. Horner, editors, *Dinosaur Eggs and Babies*. Cambridge: Cambridge University Press, pp. 288–297.

_____, 2000, Evidence of predatory behavior by carnivorous dinosaurs, *in* B. P. Pérez-Moreno, Thomas R. Holtz, Jr., José Luis Sanz, and José J. Moratalla, editors, Aspects of theropod paleobiology: *Gaia*, 15 (December 1998), pp. 135–144.

_____, 2001a, Phylogenetic analysis of the Ankylosauria, *in*: Kenneth Carpenter, editor, *The Armored Dinosaurs*. Bloomington and Indianapolis: Indiana University Press, pp. 455–483.

_____, 2001b, Skull of the polacanthid ankylosaur *Hylaeosaurus armatus* Mantell, 1833, from the Lower Cretaceous of England, *in*: Kenneth Carpenter, editor, *The Armored Dinosaurs*. Bloomington and Indianapolis: Indiana University Press, pp. 169–172.

_____, 2004, Redescription of *Ankylosaurus magniventris* Brown 1908 (Ankylosauridae) from the Upper Cretaceous of the Western Interior of North America: *Canadian Journal of Earth Sciences*, 41, pp. 961–986.

Carpenter, Kenneth, David Dilkes, and David B. Weishampel, 1995, The dinosaurs of the Niobrara Chalk Formation (Upper Cretaceous, Kansas): *Journal of Vertebrate Paleontology*, 15 (2), pp. 275–297.

Carpenter, Kenneth, and James I. Kirkland, 1998, Review of Lower and Middle Cretaceous ankylosaurs from North America, *in*: Spencer G. Lucas, Kirkland, and J. W.

Estep, editors, *Lower and Middle Cretaceous Terrestrial Ecosystems*. Albuquerque: New Mexico Museum of Natural History and Science, Bulletin No. 14, pp. 249–270.

Carpenter, Kenneth, James I. Kirkland, Donald Burge, D., and John H. Bird, J., 2001, Disarticulated skull of a new primitive ankylosaurid from the Lower Cretaceous of Eastern Utah, *in*: Kenneth Carpenter, editor, *The Armored Dinosaurs*. Bloomington and Indiana: Indiana University Press, pp. 211–238.

Carpenter, Kenneth, and John H. McIntosh, 1994, Upper Jurassic sauropod babies from the Morrison, *in*: Kenneth Carpenter, Karl F. Hirsch, and John R. Horner, editors, *Dinosaur Eggs and Babies*. New York: Cambridge University Press, pp. 265–278.

Carpenter, Kenneth, Clifford A. Miles, and Karen C. Cloward, 1998, Skull of a Jurassic ankylosaur (Dinosauria): *Nature*, 393, pp. 782–783.

Carpenter, Kenneth, David M. Unwin, Karen Cloward, Clifford A. Miles, and Clark Miles, 2003, A new scaphognathine pterosaur from the Upper Jurassic Morrison Formation of Wyoming, USA, *in*: Éric Buffetaut and Jean-Michel Mazin, editors, *Evolution and Palaeobiology of Pterosaurs*. London: The Geological Society, Special Publications, 217, pp. 45–54.

Carr, Thomas D., 1999, Craniofacial ontogeny in Tyrannosauridae (Dinosauria: Coelurosauria): *Journal of Vertebrate Paleontology*, 19 (3), pp. 497–520.

_____, 2003, New insight into the evolution of tyrannosauroid theropods: "event pair cracking" and the integration of ontogenetic and phylogenetic data in paleontology: *Journal of Vertebrate Paleontology*, 23 (Supplement to Number 3), Abstracts of Papers, Sixty-third Annual Meeting, p. 38A.

Carr, Thomas D., and Thomas E. Williamson, 2000, A review of Tyrannosauridae (Dinosauria, Coelurosauria) from New Mexico, *in*: Spencer G. Lucas and Andrew B. Heckert, editors, *Dinosaurs of New Mexico*. Albuquerque: New Mexico Museum of Natural History and Science, Bulletin 17, pp. 113–145.

_____, 2001, Resolving tyrannosaurid diversity: skeletal remains referred to *Aublysodon* belong to *Tyrannosaurus rex* and *Daspletosaurus*: *Journal of Vertebrate Paleontology*, 21 (Supplement to Number 3), Abstracts of Papers, Sixty-first Annual Meeting, p. 38A.

_____, 2004, Diversity of late Maastrichtian Tyrannosauridae (Dinosauria: Theropoda) from western North America: *Zoological Journal of the Linnean Society*, 142, pp. 479–523.

Carr, Thomas D., Thomas D. Williamson, and David R. Schwimmer, in press, A new genus and species of tyrannosauroid from the Late Cretaceous (middle Campanian) Dermopolis Formation of Alabama: *Journal of Vertebrate Paleontology*.

Carrano, Matthew T., 1998, Locomotion in nonavian dinosaurs: integrating data from

hindlimb kinematics, in vivo strains, and bone morphology: *Paleobiology*, 24, pp. 450–469.

_____, 1999, What, if anything, is a cursor? Categories versus continua for determining locomotor habit in mammals and dinosaurs: *Journal of the Zoological Society of London*, 247, pp. 29–42.

_____, 2000, Homoplasy and the evolution of dinosaur locomotion: *Paleobiology*, 26 (3), pp. 489–512.

Carrano, Matthew T., and Scott D. Sampson, 1999, Evidence for a paraphyletic "Ceratosauria" and its implications for theropod dinosaur evolution: *Journal of Vertebrate Paleontology*, 19 (Supplement to Number 3), Abstracts of Papers, Fifth-ninth Annual Meeting, p. 36A.

_____, 2003, The evolutionary history of basal theropod dinosaurs: *Journal of Vertebrate Paleontology*, 23 (Supplement to Number 3), Abstracts of Papers, Sixty-third Annual Meeting, pp. 38A–39A.

_____, 2004, A review of coelophysoids (Dinosauria: Theropoda) from the Early Jurassic of Europe, with comments on the late history of the Coelophysoidea: *Neus Jahrbuch für Geologie und Paläontologie, Monatshefte*, 9, pp. 537–558.

Carrano, Matthew T., Scott D. Sampson, and Catherine R. Forster, 2002, The osteology of *Masiakasaurus knopfleri*, a small abelisauroid (Dinosauria: Theropoda) from the Late Cretaceous of Madagascar: *Journal of Vertebrate Paleontology*, 22 (3), pp. 510–534.

Carrano, Matthew T., Scott D. Sampson, and Mark Loewen, 2004, New discoveries of *Masiakasaurus knopfleri* and the morphology of the Noasauridae (Dinosauria: Theropoda): *Journal of Vertebrate Paleontology*, 24 (Supplement to Number 3), Abstracts of Papers, Sixty-fourth Annual Meeting, p. 44A.

Carrier, D. R., and C. G. Farmer, 2000, The evolution of pelvic aspiration in archosaurs: *Paleobiology*, 26, pp. 271–293.

Casamiquela, Rodolfo M., 1975, *Herbstosaurus pigmaeus* (Coeluria, Compsognathidae) n. gen. sp. des Jurasico medio del Neuguen (Patagonia septentrional). Uno de los mas pequenos dinosaurios: *Acta primero Congreso Argentino Paleontologia et Bioestragrafía*, 2, pp. 87–102.

Casamiquela, Rodolfo M., J. Corbalan, and F. Franquesa, 1969, Hallazgo de dinosaurios en el Cretácio Superior de Chile: *Instituto de Investigaciones Geológicas, Boletín*, 25, pp. 1–31.

Caselli, A. T., C. A. Marsicano, and A. B. Arucci, 2001, Sedimentologia y Paleontologia de la Formación Los Colorados, Triásico Superior (Provincias de La Rioja y San Juan, Argentina): *Revisa de la Asociación Geológica Argentina*, 56, pp. 173–188.

Cati, A., D. Sartorio, and S. Venturini, 1987, Carbonate platforms in the subsurface of the northern Adriatic Area: *Memoirs of the Geological Society of Italy*, 40, pp. 295–308.

Chapman, Ralph E., and Michael K. Brett-Surman, 1990, *in*: Kenneth Carpenter and Philip J. Currie, editors, *Dinosaur*

Systematics: Approaches and Perspectives. Cambridge and New York: Cambridge University Press, p. 163–177.

Chapman, Ralph E., Peter M. Galton, John Sepkowski, Jr., and William P. Wall, 1981, A morphometric study of the cranium of the pachycephalosaurid dinosaur *Stegoceras: Journal of Paleontology*, 55 (3), pp. 608–618.

Chapman, Sandra D., and David Gray, 2004, The history and preparation of the enigmatic dinosaur *Hylaeosaurus armatus* BMNH R 3375: *13th Symposium on Vertebrate Palaeontology and Comparative Anatomy, Papers*, p. 4.

Charig, Alan J., and Angela C. Milner, 1997, *Baryonyx walkeri*, a fish-eating dinosaur from the Wealden of Surrey: *Bulletin of The Natural History Museum, London*, (Geology) 53 (1), pp. 11–70.

Chatterjee, Sankar, 1978, *Indosuchus* and *Indosaurus*, Cretaceous carnosaurs from India: *Journal of Paleontology*, 52 (3), pp. 570–580.

_____, 1987, A new theropod dinosaur from India with remarks on the Gondwana-Laurasia connection in the Late Triassic, *in*: Garry D. McKenzie, editor, *Gondwana Six: Stratigraphy, Sedimentology, and Paleontology*, Geophysical Monograph, 41, American Geophysical Union, Washington, D.C., pp. 183–189.

_____, 1991, Cranial anatomy and relationships of a new Triassic bird from Texas: *Philosophical Transactions of the Royal Society of London*, B, 332, pp. 277–346.

_____, 1993, *Shuvosaurus*, a new theropod: *Natural Geographic Research Exploration*, 9 (3), pp. 274–285.

_____, 1995, The Triassic Bird *Protoavis*: *Archaeopteryx*, 13, pp. 15–31, Eichstätt.

_____, 1997a, The beginnings of avian flight, *in*: Donald L. Wolberg, Edmund Stump, and Gary Rosenberg, editors, *Dinofest International: Proceedings of a Symposium Held at Arizona State University*. Philadelphia: Academy of Natural Sciences, pp. 311–335.

_____, 1997b, *The Rise of Birds*. Baltimore: Johns Hopkins University Press.

_____, 1998, The avian status of *Protoavis*: *Archaeopteryx*, 16, pp. 99–122, Eichstätt.

_____, 1999, *Protoavis* and the early evolution of birds: *Palaeontographica*, Abt. A, 254, pp. 1–100.

_____, 2002, The morphology of *Polarornis*, a Cretaceous loon (Aves: Gaviidae) from Antarctica, *in*: Zonghe Zhou and Fucheng Zhang, editors, *Proceedings of the 5th Symposium of the Society of Avian Paleontology and Evolution*. Beijing: Science Press, pp. 125–155.

Chatterjee, Sankar, and Benjamin S. Creisler, 1994, *Alwalkeria* (Theropoda) and *Morturneria* (Plesiosauria), new names for preoccupied *Walkeria* Chatterjee 1987 and *Turneria* Chatterjee and Small 1989: *Journal of Vertebrate Paleontology*, 14 (1), p. 142.

Chatterjee, Sankar, and D. K. Rudra, 1996, KT events in India: impact, rifting, volcanism and dinosaur extinction: *Proceedings of the Gondwanan Dinosaur Symposium: Memoirs of the Queensland Museum*, 39 (part 3), pp. 489–532.

Chatterjee, Sanka, and R. Jack Templin, 2003, The flight of *Archaeopteryx*: *Naturwissenschaften*, 90, pp. 27–32.

_____, 2004, Feathered coelurosaurs from China: new light on the arboreal origin of avian flight: *in*: Philip J. Currie, Eva B. Kopelhus, Martin A. Shugar, and Joanna L. Wright, 2004, editors, *Feathered Dragons: Studies on the Transition from Dinosaurs to Birds*. Bloomington and Indianapolis: Indiana University Press, pp. 251–281.

Chen, Pei-Ji, Zhi-ming Dong, and Shuo-nan Zhen, 1998, An exceptionally well-preserved theropod dinosaur from the Yixian Formation of China: *Nature*, 391, pp. 147–152.

Cheng Zhengwu and Pang Qiqing, 1996, A new dinosaurian fauna from Tianzhen, Shanxi Province with its stratigraphical significance: *Acta Geoscientia Sinica*, 17, p. 135.

Chiappe, Luis M., 1993, Enantiornithine (Aves) tarsometatarsi from the Cretaceous Lecho Formation of northwestern Argentina: *American Museum Novitates*, 3083, pp. 1–27.

_____, 1995a, The phylogenetic position of the Cretaceous birds of Argentina: Enantiornithes and *Patagopteryx deferrariisi*, *in*: D. S. Peters, editor, *Proceedings of the 3rd Symposium of the Society of Avian Paleontology and Evolution, Courier Forschungsinstitut Senckenberg*, 181, Frankfurt am Main, pp. 55–63.

_____, 1995b, The first 85 million years of avian evolution: *Nature*, 378, pp. 349–355.

_____, 1997, Aves, *in*: Philip J. Currie and Kevin Padian, editors, *Encyclopedia of Dinosaurs*. San Diego: Academic Press, pp. 32–38.

_____, 2001, Phylogentic relationships among basal birds, *in*: Jacques Gauthier and I. F. Gall, editors, *New Prospectives on the origin and early evolution of birds: proceedings of the International Symposium in Honor of John H. Ostrom*. New Haven, CT: Peabody Museum of Natural History, pp. 125–139.

_____, 2002a, Osteology of the flightless *Patagopteryx deferrariisi* from the Late Cretaceous of Patagonia (Argentina), *in*: Luis M. Chiappe and Lawrence M. Witmer, editors, *Mesozoic Birds: Above the Heads of Dinosaurs*. Berkeley and Los Angeles: University of California Press, pp. 281–316.

_____, 2002b, Basal bird phylogeny, *Ibid.*, pp. 449–472.

Chiappe, Luis M., and Jorge O. Calvo, 1994, *Neuquenornis volans*, a new Late Cretaceous bird (Enantiornithines: Avisauridae) from Patagonia, Argentina: *Journal of Vertebrate Paleontology*, 14 (2), pp. 230–246.

Chiappe, Luis M., and Rodolfo A. Coria, 2003, A new specimen of *Patagonykus puertai* (Theropoda: Alvarezsauridae) from the Late Cretaceous of Patagonia: *Ameghiniana*, 40 (1), pp. 119–122.

Chiappe, Luis M., and Lowell Dingus, 2000, *Walking on Eggs: The Astonishing Discovery of Dinosaur Eggs in the Badlands of Patagonia*. New York: Scribner, 219 pages.

Chiappe, Luis M., Shúan Ji, Qiang Ji, and Mark A. Norell, 1999, Anatomy and systematics of the Confuciusornithidae (Theropoda: Aves) from the Late Mesozoic of northeastern China: *Bulletin of the American Museum of Natural History*, 242, pp. 1–89.

Chiappe, Luis M., Alexander W. A. Kellner, David Rivarola, Sergio Davila, and Marilyn Fox, 2000, Cranial morphology of *Pterodaustro guinazui* (Pterosauria: Pterodactyloidea) from the Lower Cretaceous of Argentina: *Contributions in Science*, 483, pp. 1–19.

Chiappe, Luis M., and Antonio Lacasa-Ruiz, 2002, *Noguerornis gonzalezi* (Aves: Ornithothoraces) from the Early Cretaceous of Spain, *in*: Luis M. Chiappe and Lawrence M. Witmer, editors, *Mesozoic Birds: Above the Heads of Dinosaurs*. Berkeley and Los Angeles: University of California Press, pp. 230–239.

Chiappe, Luis M., James P. Lamb, Jr., and Per G. P. Ericson, 2002, New enantiornithine bird from the marine Upper Cretaceous of Alabama: *Journal of Vertebrate Paleontology*, 22 (1), pp. 170–174.

Chiappe, Luis M., Mark A. Norell, and James M. Clark, 1998, The skull of a relative of the stem-group bird *Mononykus*: *Nature*, 392, pp. 275–278.

Chiappe, Luis M., Leonardo Salgado, and Rodolfo A. Coria, 2001, Embryonic skulls of titanosaur sauropod dinosaurs: *Science*, 293, pp. 2444–2446.

Chiappe, Luis M., James C. Schmitt, Frankie D. Jackson, Alberto Garrido, Lowell Dingus, Gerald Grellet-Tinner, 2004, Nest structure for sauropods: sedimentary criteria for recognition of dinosaur nesting traces: *Palaios*, 19, pp. 89–95.

Chiappe, Luis M., and Lawrence M. Witmer, 2002, *Mesozoic Birds: Above the Heads of Dinosaurs*. Berkeley and Los Angeles: University of California Press, xii, 520 pages.

Chin, Karen, David A. Eberth, Mary H. Schweitzer, Thomas A. Rando, Wendy J. Sloboda, and John R. Horner, 2003, Remarkable preservation of undigested muscle tissue within a Late Cretaceous tyrannosaurid coprolite from Alberta, Canada: *Palaios*, 18, pp. 286–294.

Chinnery, Brenda J., 2004a, Description of *Prenoceratops pieganen sis* gen. et sp. nov. (Dinosauria: Neoceratopsia) from the Two Medicine Formation of Montana: *Journal of Vertebrate Paleontology*, 24 (3), pp. 572–590.

_____, 2004b, Morphometric analysis of evolutionary trends in the ceratopsian postcranial skeleton: *Journal of Vertebrate Paleontology*, 24 (3), pp. 591–609.

Chinnery, Brenda J., and Jack [John R.] Horner, 2003, New basal neoceratopsian from the lower Two Medicine Formation of Montana provides a link between Asian and North American taxa: *Journal of Vertebrate Paleontology*, 23 (Supplement to Number 3), Abstracts of Papers, Sixty-third Annual Meeting, p. 40A.

Chinnery, Brenda J., Thomas R. Lipka, James I. Kirkland, J. Michael Parrish, and

Bibliography

Michael K. Brett-Surman, 1998, Neoceratopsian teeth from the Lower to Middle Cretaceous of North America, *in*: Spencer G. Lucas, James I. Kirkland, and John W. Estep, editors, *Lower and Middle Cretaceous Terrestrial Ecosystems*. Albuquerque: New Mexico Museum of Natural History and Science, Bulletin 14, pp. 297–292.

Chinnery, Brenda J., and David B. Weishampel, 1998, *Montanoceratops cerorhynchus* (Dinosauria: Ceratopsia) and relationships among basal neoceratopsians: *Journal of Vertebrate Paleontology*, 18 (3), pp. 569–585.

Chinsamy, Anusuya, 1994, Dinosaur bone histology: implications and inferences, *in*: Gary D. Rosenberg and Donald L. Wolberg, editors, DinoFest: *Paleontological Society Special Papers*, 7, pp. 213–227.

Chinsamy, Anusuya, and Peter Dodson, 1995, Inside a dinosaur bone: *American Scientist*, 83, pp. 174–180.

Christian, Andreas, 2004, Reconstruction of the neck posture in sauropods: *13th Symposium on Vertebrate Palaeontology and Comparative Anatomy, Papers*, p. 9.

Christian, Andreas, H.-G. Horn, and H. Preuscoft, 1994, Biomechanical reasons for bipedalism in reptiles: *Amphibia-Reptilia*, 15, pp. 275–284.

Christian, Andreas, D. Koberg, and H. Preuscoft, 1996, Shape of the pelvis and posture of the hindlimbs in *Plateosaurus*: *Paläontologische Zeitschrift*, 52, pp. 138–159.

Christian, Andreas, and H. Preuscoft, 1996, Deducing the body posture of extinct large vertebrates from the shape of the vertebral column: *Paläontologische Zeitschrift*, 52, pp. 138–159.

Christiansen, Per, 1998, Strength indicator values of theropod long bones, with comments on limb proportions and cursorial potential, *in*: B. P. Perez-Moreno, T. R. Holtz, Jr., J. L. Sanz, and J. Moratalla, editors., *Aspects of Theropoda Paleobiology*, Gaia, 15, pp. 241–255 [cover dated 1998, published in 2000].

———, 1999a, On the head size of sauropodomorph dinosaurs: implications for ecology and physiology: *Historical Biology*, pp. 269–297.

———, 1999b, Long bone scaling and limb posture in nonavian theropods: evidence for differential allometry: *Journal of Vertebrate Paleontology*, 19 (4), pp. 666–680.

———, 2002, Locomotion in terrestrial mammals: the influence of body mass, limb length and bone proportions on speed: *Zoological Journal of the Linnean Society*, 136, pp. 685–714.

Christainsen, Per, and Niels Bonde, 2002, Limb proportions and avian terrestrial locomotion: *Journal für Ornithologie*, 143, pp. 356–371.

———, 2003, The first dinosaur from Denmark: *Neus Jahrbuch für Geologie und Paläontologie, Abhandlungen*, 227 (2), pp. 287–299.

Chuong, Cheng-Ming, 1998, editor, *Molecular Basis of Epithelial Appendage Morphogenesis*. Austin, TX: R. G. Landes Bioscience, 449 pages.

Chuong, Cheng-Ming, Ping Wu, Fu-Cheng Zhang, Xing Xu, Minke Yu, Randall B. Widelitz, Ting-Xin Jiang, and Lianhai Hou, 2003, Adaptation to the sky: defining the feather with integument fossils from Mesozoic China and experimental evidence from molecular laboratories: *Journal of Experimental Zoology (Mol Dev Evol)*, 298B, pp. 42–56.

Chure, Daniel J., 1995, A reassessment of the gigantic theropod *Saurophagus maximus* from the Morrison Formation (Upper Jurassic) of Oklahoma, USA, *in*: A. Sun and Y. Wang, editors, *Sixth Symposium on Mesozoic Terrestrial Ecosystems and Biota, Short Papers*. Bejing: China Ocean Press, pp. 103–106.

———, The second record of the African theropod *Elaphrosaurus* (Dinosauria, Ceratosauria) from the Western Hemisphere: *Neus Jahrbuch für Geologie und Paläontologie, Monatshefte*, 9, pp. 565–576.

Chure, Daniel J., and James H. Madsen, Jr., 1996, On the presence of furculae in some nonmaniraptoran Theropoda: *Journal of Vertebrate Paleontology*, 16 (3), pp. 573–577.

———, 1998, An unusual braincase (?*Stokesosaurus clevelandi*) from the Cleveland-Lloyd Dinosaur Quarry, Utah (Morrison Formation: Late Jurassic): *Ibid.*, 18 (1), pp. 115–125.

Chure, Daniel J., and John S. McIntosh, 1989, *A Bibliography of the Dinosauria (Exclusive of the Aves), 1677–1986*. Grand Junction, CO: Museum of Western Colorado, Paleontology Series 1, 226 pages.

Claessens, Leon P. A. M., 2001, The function of the gastralia in theropod lung ventilation: *The Paleobiology and Phylogenetics of Large Theropods*, A. Watson Armour III Symposium, The Field Museum, 12 May 2001, unpaginated.

———, 2004, Dinosaur gastralia: origin, morphology, and function: *Journal of Vertebrate Paleontology*, 24 (1), pp. 89–106.

Clara, Mario, 2000, Aves: *Facultad de Ciencias Sección Zoologia Vertebrados, Curso de Biologia Animal*, 28 pages.

Clark, James M., James A. Hopson, Rene Hernandez, David E. Fastovsky, and M. Montellano, 1998, Foot posture in a primitive pterosaur: *Nature*, 391, 886–889.

Clark, James M., Teresa Maryańska, and Richnen Barsbold, 2004, Therizinosauroidea, *in*: David B. Weishampel, Peter Dodson, and Halszka Osmólska, editors, *The Dinosauria* (second edition). Berkeley and Los Angeles: University of California Press, pp. 151–164.

Clark, James M., Mark A. Norell, and Rinchen Barsbold, 2001, Two new oviraptorids (Theropoda: Oviraptorosauria), Upper Cretaceous Djadokhta Formation, Ukhaa Tolgod, Mongolia: *Journal of Vertebrate Paleontology*, 21 (2), pp. 209–213.

Clark, James M., Mark A. Norell, and Luis M. Chiappe, 1999, An oviraptorid skeleton from the Late Cretaceous of Ukhaa Tolgod, Mongolia, preserved in an avian-like brooding position over an oviraptorid nest: *American Museum Novitates*, 3265, pp. 1–36.

Clark, James M., Mark A. Norell, and Timothy Rowe, 2002, Cranial anatomy of *Citipati osmolskae* (Theropoda, Oviraptorosauria), and a reinterpretation of the holotype of *Oviraptor philoceratops*: *American Museum Novitates*, 3364, 24 pages.

Clark, James M., Altangerel Perle, and Mark A. Norell, 1994, The skull of *Erlikosaurus andrewsi*, a Late Cretaceous "segnosaur" (Theropoda: Therizinosauridae) from Mongolia: *American Museum Novitates*, 3115, pp. 1–39.

Clarke, Julia A., 2004, Morphology, phylogenetic taxonomy, and systematics of *Ichthyornis* and *Apatornis* (Avialae: Ornithurae): *Bulletin of the American Museum of Natural History*, 286, 179 pages.

Clarke, Julia A., and Luis M. Chiappe, 2001, A new carinate bird from the Late Cretaceous of Patagonia (Argentina): *American Museum Novitates*, 3323, pp. 1–23.

Clarke, Julia A., and Mark A. Norell, 2002, The morphology and phylogenetic position of *Apsaravis ukhaana* from the Late Cretaceous of Mongolia: *American Museum Novitates*, 3387, 46 pages.

Clarke, Julia A., Claudia P. Tambussi, Jorge I. Noriega, Gregory M. Erickson, and Richard A. Ketchum, 2005, Definitive fossil evidence for the extant avian radiation in the Cretaceous: *Nature*, 433, pp. 305–308.

Colbert, Edwin H. [Harris], 1955, *Evolution of the Vertebrates*. New York: John Wiley & Sons, 479 pages.

———, 1969, A Jurassic pterosaur from Cuba: *American Museum Novitates*, 2370, pp. 1–26.

———, 1970, A saurischian dinosaur from the Triassic of Brazil: *Ibid.*, 2405, pp. 1–39.

———, 1989, The Triassic dinosaur *Coelophysis*: *Museum of Northern Arizona Bulletin*, 57, xv, 160 pages.

———, 1995, *The Little Dinosaurs of Ghost Ranch*. New York: Columbia University Press, 250 pages.

Coombs, Walter P., 1978a, The families of the ornithischian dinosaur order Ankylosauria: *Paleontology*, 21, part 1, pp. 143–170.

———, 1978b, Theoretical aspects of cursorial adaptations in dinosaurs: *Revisions in Biology*, 53 (4), pp. 393–410.

———, 1979, Osteology and myology of the hindlimb in the Ankylosauria (Reptilia: Ornithischia): *Journal of Paleontology*, 53, pp. 666–684.

———, 1982, Juvenile specimens of the ornithischian dinosaur *Psittacosaurus*: *Palaeontology*, 25, part 1, pp. 89–107.

———, 1995, Ankylosaurian tail clubs of middle Campanian to early Maastrichtian age from western North America, with descriptions of a tiny tail club from Alberta and discussion of tail orientation and tail club function: *Canadian Journal of Earth Sciences*, 32, pp. 902–912.

Coombs, Walter P., Jr., and Teresa Maryańska, 1990, Ankylosauria, *in*: David B. Weishampel, Peter Dodson, and Halszka Osmólska, editors, *The Dinosauria*. Berkeley and Los Angeles: University of California Press, pp. 456–483.

Cooper, Michael R., 1981, The prosauropod

dinosaur *Massospondylus carinatus* Owen from Zimbabwe: its biology, mode of life and phylogenetic significance: *Occasional Papers of the National Museums of Rhodesia, Natural Science*, 6, pp. 689–840, Bulawayo.

_____, 1984, A reassessment of *Vulcanodon karibaensis* Raath (Dinosauria: Saurischia) and the origin of the Sauropoda: *Paleontologica Africana*, 25, pp. 203–231.

_____, 1985, A revision of the ornithischian dinosaur *Kangnasaurus coetzeei* Haugton, with a classification of the Ornithischia: *Annals of the South African Museum*, 95 (6), pp. 281–317.

Cope, Edward Drinker, 1872, Two new ornithosaurians from Kansas: *Proceedings of the American Philosophical Society*, 12, pp. 420–422.

_____, 1877, On a gigantic saurian from the Dakota epoch of Colorado: *Paleontology Bulletin*, 27, pp. 5–10.

_____, 1878, A new species of *Amphicoelias*: *American Naturalist*, 12, pp. 563–565.

Cope, L. C. W., K. L. Duff, C. E. Parsons, H. S. Torrens, W. A. Wimbledon, and J. K. Wright, 1980, Pt. 2, Jurassic: *Geological Society of London, Special Report*, 15, pp. 1–109.

Coria, Rodolfo A., and Andrea B. Arcucci, 1999, Nuevos aportes sobre la evolución del tarso en dinosaurios terópodos: *Ameghiniana*, 36, p. 98.

Coria, Rodolfo A., and Jorge O. Calvo, 2002, A new iguanodontian ornithopod from Neuquen Basin, Patagonia, Argentina: *Journal of Vertebrate Paleontology*, 22 (3), pp. 503–509.

Coria, Rodolfo A., Philip J. Currie, David A. Eberth, Alberto C. Garrido, and Eva Koppelhus, 2001, Nuevos vertebrados fósiles del Cretacico Superior de Neuquén: *Ameghiana*, 38 (4), Suplemento, p. 6R.

Coria, Rodolfo A., and Leonardo Salgado, 1996, A basal iguanodontian (Ornithischia: Ornithopoda) from the Late Cretaceous of South America: *Journal of Vertebrate Paleontology*, 16 (3), pp. 445–457.

Coulson, Alan, Reese Barrick, William Straight, Sara Decherd, and John Bird, 2004, Description of the new brachiosaurid (Dinosauria: Sauropod) from the Ruby Ranch Member (Cretaceous: Albian) of the Cedar Mountain Formation, Utah: *Journal of Vertebrate Paleontology*, 24 (Supplement to Number 3), Abstracts of Papers, Sixty-fourth Annual Meeting, p. 48A.

Cracraft, Joel, 1981, The use of functional and adaptive criteria in phylogenetic systematics: *American Zoologist*, 21, pp. 21–36.

Csiki, Zoltan, and Dan Grigorescu, 1998, Small theropods from the Late Cretaceous of the Hateg Basin (western Romania)—an unexpected diversity at the top of the food chain: *Oryctos*, 1, pp. 87–104.

Cuny, Gilles, and Peter M. Galton, 1993, Revision of the Airel theropod dinosaur from the Triassic-Jurassic boundary (Normandy, France): *Neus Jahrbuch für Geologie und Paläontologie, Abhandlungen*, 187 (3), pp. 261–288.

Curley, Vincent JJ, 2004, The PT interview: Dr. Jack Horner from the Museum of the Rockies: *Prehistoric Times*, 67, pp. 49–51.

Currie, Philip J., 1978, The orthometric linear unit: *Journal of Paleontology*, 52, pp. 964–971.

_____, 1981, Birds footprints from the Gething Formation (Aptian, Lower Cretaceous) of northeaster British Columbia, Canada: *Journal of Vertebrate Paleontology*, 1 (3–4), pp. 257–264.

_____, 1987, Birdlike characteristics of the jaws and teeth of troodontid theropods (Dinosauria: Saurischia): *Ibid.*, 7 (1), pp. 72–81.

_____, 1995, New information on the anatomy and relationships of *Dromaeosaurus albertensis* (Dinosauria: Theropoda): *Journal of Vertebrate Paleontology*, 15 (3), pp. 237–249.

_____, 1998, Possible evidence of gregarious behavior in tyrannosaurids: *GAIA*, 15, pp. 271–277.

_____, 2003*a*, Allometric growth in tyrannosaurids (Dinosauria: Theropoda) from the Upper Cretaceous of North America and Asia: *Canadian Journal of Earth Sciences*, 40, pp. 651–665.

_____, 2003*b*, Cranial anatomy of tyrannosaurid dinosaurs from the Late Cretaceous of Alberta, Canada: *Acta Palaeontologica Polonica*, 48 (2), pp. 191–226.

Currie, Philip J., and Kenneth Carpenter, 2000, A new specimen of *Acrocanthosaurus atokensis* (Theropoda, Dinosauria) from the Lower Cretaceous Antlers Formation (Lower Cretaceous, Aptian) of Oklahoma, USA: *Geodiversitas*, 22 (2), pp. 207–246.

Currie, Philip J., and Pei-ji Chen, 2001, Anatomy of *Sinosauropteryx prima* from Liaoning, northeastern China: *Canadian Journal of Earth Sciences*, 38 (12), pp. 1705–1727.

Currie, Philip J., and Dong Zhiming, 2001, New information on *Shanshanosaurus huoyanshanensis*, a juvenile tyrannosaurid (Theropoda, Dinosauria) from the Late Cretaceous of China: *Canadian Journal of Earth Sciences*, 38 (12), pp. 1729–1737.

Currie, Philip J., and David A. Eberth, 1993, Palaontology, sedimentology and palaeoecology of the Iren Dabasu Formation (Upper Cretaceous), Inner Mongolia, People's Republic of China: *Cretaceous Research*, 14, pp. 127–144.

Currie, Philip J., Jørn H. Hurum, and Karol Sabath, 2003, Skull structure and evolution in tyrannosaurid dinosaurs: *Acta Palaeontologica Polonica*, 48 (2), pp. 227–234.

Currie, Philip J., Eva B. Kopelhus, Martin A. Shugar, and Joanna L. Wright, 2004, editors, *Feathered Dragons: Studies on the Transition from Dinosaurs to Birds*. Bloomington and Indianapolis: Indiana University Press, xiii, 361 pages.

Currie, Philip J., Mark Norell, and Shuan Ji, 1998, The anatomy of two feathered dinosaurs from Liaoning, China: *Journal of Vertebrate Paleontology*, 18 (Supplement to Number 3), Abstracts of Papers, Fifty-eighth Annual Meeting, p. 36A.

Currie, Philip J., and J.-H. Peng, 1993, A juvenile specimen of *Saurornithoides mongoliensis* from the Upper Cretaceous of northern China: *Canadian Journal of Earth Sciences*, 30, pp. 2037–2081.

Currie, Philip J., J. Keith Rigby, Jr., and Robert E. Sloan, 1990, *in*: Kenneth Carpenter and Currie, editors, *Dinosaur Systematics: Approaches and Perspectives*. Cambridge, NY and Melbourne: Cambridge University Press, pp. 107–125.

Currie, Philip J., and David J. Varricchio, 2004, A new dromaeosaurid from the Horseshoe Canyon Formation (Upper Cretaceous) of Alberta, Canada: *in*: Philip J. Currie, Eva B. Kopelhus, Martin A. Shugar, and Joanna L. Wright, 2004, editors, *Feathered Dragons: Studies on the Transition from Dinosaurs to Birds*. Bloomington and Indianapolis: Indiana University Press, pp. 112–132.

Currie, Philip J., and Xi-Jin Zhao, 1993, A new carnosaur (Dinosauria, Theropoda) from the Jurassic of Xinjiang, People's Republic of China: *Canadian Journal of Earth Sciences*, 30 (10–11), pp. 2037–2081.

_____, 1994, A new troodontid (Dinosauria, Theropoda) braincase from the Dinosaur Park Formation (Campanian) of Alberta: *Canadian Journal of Earth Sciences*, 30, pp. 2231–2247.

Curry, Kristina, 1994, Juvenile sauropods of the Morrison Formation of Montana: *Journal of Vertebrate Paleontology*, 14 (Supplement to Number 3), Abstracts of Papers, Fifty-fourth Annual Meeting, p. 21A.

Curry Rogers, Kristina, Gregory Erickson, and Mark A. Norell, 2003, Dinosaurian life history strategies, growth rates, and character evolution: new insights garnered from bone histology and developmental mass extrapolation: *Journal of Vertebrate Paleontology*, 23 (Supplement to Number 3), Abstracts of Papers, Sixty-third Annual Meeting, p. 90A.

Curry Rogers, Kristina, and Catherine A. Forster, 2001, The last of the dinosaur titans: a new sauropod from Madagascar: *Nature*, 412, pp. 530–534.

_____, 2004, The skull of *Rapetosaurus krausei* (Sauropoda: Titanosauria) from the Late Cretaceous of Madagascar: *Journal of Vertebrate Paleontology*, 24 (1), pp. 121–144.

Curtice, Brian D., and Kenneth L. Stadtman, 2001, The demise of *Dystylosaurus edwini* and a revision of *Supersaurus vivianae*: *Western Association of Vertebrate Paleontologists and Mesa Southwest Museum and Southwest Paleontological Symposium, Bulletin*, 8, pp. 33–40.

Cuvier, Baron Georges, 1809, Memoire sur le squelette fossile d'un Reptil Volant des environs d'Aichstedt, que quelues naturalists ont pris pour unoiseau, et donc nous formons un genre de Sauriens, sous le nom de Ptero-Dactyle: *Ann. Mus. Hist. Nat.*, 13, p. 424.

_____, 1819: *Isis von Oken* [*Oken's Isis*], pp. 1788–1795.

Czerkas, Stephen A., and Qiang Ji, 2002*a*, A new rhamphorhynchoid with a headcrest

Bibliography

and complex integumentary structures, *in*: Czerkas, Sylvia J., editor, 2002, *Feathered Dinosaurs and the Origin of Flight*. Blanding, UT: The Dinosaur Museum, pp. 15–41.

———, 2002*b*, A preliminary report on an omnivorous volant bird from northeastern China, *in*: Czerkas, Sylvia J., editor, 2002, *Feathered Dinosaurs and the Origin of Flight*. Blanding, UT: The Dinosaur Museum, pp. 127–135.

Czerkas, Stephen A., and Debral L. Mickelson, 2002, The first occurrence of skeletal pterosaur remains in Utah, *in*: Czerkas, Sylvia J., editor, 2002, *Feathered Dinosaurs and the Origin of Flight*. Blanding, UT: The Dinosaur Museum, pp. 5–13.

Czerkas, Stephen A., and Xing Xu, 2002, A new toothed bird from China, *in*: Czerkas, Sylvia J., editor, 2002, *Feathered Dinosaurs*. Blanding, UT: The Dinosaur Museum, pp. 43–61.

Czerkas, Stephen A., Dianshuang Zhang, Jinglu Li, and Yinxian Li, 2002, Flying dromaeosaurs, *in*: Sylvia J. Czerkas, editor, 2002, *Feathered Dinosaurs*. Blanding, UT: The Dinosaur Museum, pp. 97–126.

Czerkas, Sylvia J., editor, 2002, *Feathered Dinosaurs and the Origin of Flight*. Blanding, UT: The Dinosaur Museum, vi, 136 pages.

Czerkas, Sylvia Massey, and Donald F. Glut, 1982, *Dinosaurs, Mammoths and Cavemen: The Art of Charles R. Knight*. New York: E. P. Dutton, vii, 120 pages.

Czerkas, Sylvia J., and Everett C. Olson, editors, *Dinosaurs Past and Present*, two volumes. Los Angeles: Natural History Museum of Los Angeles County, xvi, 161 pages, and xiii, 149 pages, respectively.

Dal Sasso, Cristiano, 2001, *Dinosauri italiani*. Venezia: Marsilio Editori, 260 pages.

———, 2003, Dinosaurs of Italy (Dinosaures d'Italie, Dinosauri d'Italia): *Comptes Rendus Palevol*, 2, pp. 45–66.

Dalla Vecchia, Fabio Marco, 1993, *Cearodactylus? ligabuei* nov. sp., a new Early Cretaceous (Aptian) pterosaur from Chapada do Araripe (northeastern Brazil): *Bollettino Societa Paleontologia Italiana*, 32 (3), pp. 401–409.

———, 1994, A new pterosaur (Reptilia, Pterosauria) from the Norian (Late Triassic) of Friuli (northeastern Italy). Preliminary note: *Gortania*, 16, pp. 59–66.

———, 1995, A new pterosaur (Reptilia, Pterosauria) from the Norian (Late Triassic) of Friuli (Northeastern Italy), preliminary note: *Gortania*, 16, pp. 59–66.

———, 1998, New observations on the osteology and taxonomic status of *Preondactylus buffarinii* Wild, 1984 (Reptilia, Pterosauria): *Bollettino della Società Paleontologica Italiana*, 36,pp. 355–366.

———, 2001*a*, A new theropod dinosaur from the Lower Jurassic of Italy: *Dino Press*, 3, pp. 81–87.

———, 2001*b*, Terrestrial ecosystems on the Mesozoic peri–Adriatic carbonate platforms: the vertebrate evidence: *Asociación Paleontológica Argentina*, Publicación Especial 7, VII I International Symposium on Mesozoic Terrestrial Ecosystems, Buenos Aires, pp. 77–83.

———, 2002, Cretaceous dinosaur in the Adriatic-Dinaric carbonate platform (Italy and Croatia): paleoenvironmental implications and paleogeographical hypotheses: *Memoirs of the Geological Society of Italy*, 57, pp. 89–100.

———, 2003*a*, Observations on the presence of plant-eating dinosaurs in an oceanic carbonate platform: *Natura Nascosta*, 27, pp. 14–27.

———, 2003*b*, New morphological observations on Triassic pterosaurs: *in*: Éric Buffetaut and Jean-Michel Mazin, editors, *Evolution and Palaeobiology of Pterosaurs*. London: The Geological Society, Special Publications, 217, pp. 23–44.

Dalla Vecchia, Fabio Marco, Rupert Wild, H. Hopf and J. Reitner 2002, A crested rhamphorhynchoid pterosaur from the Late Triassic of Austria: *Journal of Vertebrate Paleontology*, 22 (1), pp. 196–199.

Dalla Vecchia, G. Muscio, and Rupert Wild, 1989, Pterosaur remains in a gastric pellet from the Upper Triassic (Norian) Rio Seazza Valley (Udine, Italy): *Gortania*, 10, pp. 121–132.

Dames, W., 1897, Ueber Brustbein, Schulter- und Beckengurtel der *Archaeopteryx*. Berlin: S. B. Preuss. Akad. Wiss, 1, pp. 127–135.

Dashveg, Demberelynin, Michael J. Novacek, Mark A. Norell, James M. Clark, Luis M. Chiappe, Amy Davidson, Malcolm C. McKenna, Lowell Dingus, C. C. Swisher, III, and Altangerel Perle, 1995, Unusual preservation in a new vertebrate assemblage from the Late Cretaceous of Mongolia: *Nature*, 374, pp. 446–449.

Day, Julia J., and Paul M. Barrett, 2004, Material referred to *Megalosaurus* (Dinosauria: Theropoda) from the Middle Jurassic of Stonesfield, Oxfordshire, England: one taxon or two?: *Proceedings of the Geological Association*, 115, pp. 359–366.

de Queiroz, Kevin, and Jacques A. Gauthier, 1992, Phylogenetic taxonomy: *Annual Review of Ecology and Systematics*, 23, pp. 449–480.

de Souza Carvalho, Ismar, Leonardo dos Santos Avilla, and Leonardo Salgado, 2003, *Amazonsaurus maranhensis* gen. et sp. nov. (Sauropoda, Diplodocoidea) from the Lower Cretaceous (Aptian–Albian) of Brazil: *Cretaceous Research*, 00 (2003), pp. 1–17.

Debus, Allen A., 2003, Versus: Ancient nemeses as perceived in the "Prehistoric World" [parts 1 and 2]: *Fossil News*, 9 (5), pp. 14–16, and 9 (6), pp. 15–17. Jose, CA: Authors Choice Press, xxviii, pp. 608 pages.

Delair, Justin B., 1963, Notes on Purbeck fossil footprints, with descriptions of two hitherto unknown forms from Dorset: *Proceedings of the Dorset Natural History and Archaeological Society*, 84, pp. 92–100.

Dementiev, F. V., 1940, *Handbook on Zoology: Vertebrates, Birds*, Volume 6. Leningrad: Akademii Nauk SSSR [in Russian].

Depéret, Charles, 1896, Note sur les dinosauriens sauropodes et théropodes du Crétacé supérieur de Madagascar: *Bulletin de la Société Géologique de France*, 17, pp. 686–709.

———, 1899, Apercu sur la géologie du Chainon de Saint-Chinian: *Ibid.*, 27, pp. 686–709.

Derstler, Kraig, 2003, Comparison of hadrosaur skin preservation in the Lance and Judith River Formation (Upper Cretaceous; western North America): *Journal of Vertebrate Paleontology*, 23 (Supplement to Number 3), Abstracts of Papers, Sixty-third Annual Meeting, p. 45A.

Dial, Kenneth P., 2003, Wing-assisted incline running and the evolution of flight: *Science*, 299, pp. 402–404.

———, 2004, What use is half a wing and WAIR?: *Journal of Vertebrate Paleontology*, 24 (Supplement to Number 3), Abstracts of Papers, Sixty-fourth Annual Meeting, p. 52A.

Difley, Rose, Brooks B. Britt, and Philip Policelli, 2004, A troodontid nest in the North Horn Formation, central Utah: *Journal of Vertebrate Paleontology*, 24 (Supplement to Number 3), Abstracts of Papers, Sixty-fourth Annual Meeting, p. 52A.

Dingus, Lowell, and Timothy Rowe, 1998, *The Mistaken Extinction*. New York: W. H. Freeman, 332 pages.

Döderlein, Z., 1923, *Anurognathus ammoni*, ein neuer Flugsaurier: *SB. Ak. Wiss. Muchen*, pp. 117–164.

Dodson, Peter, 1975, Taxonomic implications of relative growth in lambeosaurine hadrosaurs: *Systematic Zoology*, 24, pp. 37–54.

———, 1976, Quantitative aspects of relative growth and sexual dimorphism in *Protoceratops*: *Journal of Paleontology*, 50 (5), pp. 929–940.

———, 1980, Comparative osteology of the American ornithopods *Camptosaurus* and *Tenontosaurus*: *Mémoires de la Société Géologique de France*, 139, pp. 81–85.

———, 1990, Ceratopsia, *in*: David B. Weishampel, Peter Dodson, and Halszka Osmólska, editors, *The Dinosauria*. Berkeley and Los Angeles: University of California Press, p. 578.

———, 1996, *The Horned Dinosaurs*. Princeton: Princeton University Press, 346 pages.

———, 1997, Distribution and diversity, *in*: Philip J. Currie and Kevin Padian, editors, *Encyclopedia of Dinosaurs*. San Diego: Academic Press, pp. 186–188.

Dodson, Peter, and Philip J. Currie, 1990, Neoceratopsia, *in*: David B. Weishampel, Peter Dodson, and Halszka Osmólska, editors, *The Dinosauria*. Berkeley and Los Angeles: University of California Press, pp. 593–618.

Dodson, Peter, and Susan D. Dawson, 1991, Making the fossil record of dinosaurs: *Modern Geology*, 16, pp. 3–15.

Dodson, Peter, Catherine A. Forster, and Scott D. Sampson, 2004, Ceratopsidae, *in*: David B. Weishampel, Peter Dodson, and Halszka Osmólska, editors, *The Dinosauria* (second edition). Berkeley and Los Angeles: University of California Press, pp. 494–516.

Doering, A., 1882, Expedición al Río Negro (Patagonia) 3ra. parte: Geología, pp. 299–530.

Dong Zhiming [also Zhi-Ming], 1977, On the

dinosaurian remains from Turpan, Xinjiang: *Vertebrata PalAsiatica*, 15 (1), pp. 59–66.

_____, 1982, On a new Pterosauria (*Huanhepterus quingyangensis* gen. et sp. nov.) from Ordos, China: *Vertebrata PalAsiatica*, 20 (2), pp. 115–121.

_____, 1990, Stegosaurs in Asia, *in*: Kenneth Carpenter and Philip J. Currie, editors, *Dinosaur Systematics: Approaches and Perspectives*. Cambridge and New York: Cambridge University Press, pp. 255–268.

_____, 1992, *Dinosaurian Faunas of China*. Beijing: China Ocean Press, 188 pages.

_____, 1997, A gigantic sauropod (*Hudiesaurus sinojapanorum*, gen. et sp. nov.) from the Turpan Basin, China: *Sino-Japanese Silk Road Dinosaur Expedition*. Beijing: China Ocean Press, pp. 102–110.

_____, 2001, Primitive armored dinosaur from the Lufeng Basin, China, *in*: Darren Tanke and Kenneth Carpenter, editors, 2001, *Mesozoic Vertebrate Life: New Research Inspired by the Paleontology of Philip J. Currie*. Bloomington and Indianapolis: Indiana University Press, pp. 237–242.

_____, 2002, A new armored dinosaur (Ankylosauria) from Beipiao Basin, Liaoning Province, northeastern China: *Vertebrata PalAsiatica* 40 (3), pp. 276–283.

Dong Zhi-Ming [formerly Zhiming], and Yoichi Azuma, 1997, On a primitive neoceratopsian from the Early Cretaceous of China, *in*: Dong Zhi-Ming, editor, *Sino-Japanese Silk Road Dinosaur Expedition*. Beijing: China Ocean Press, pp. 68–89.

Dong Zhi-Ming, and Philip J. Currie, 1996, On the discovery of an oviraptorid skeleton on a nest of eggs at Bayan Mandahu, Inner Mongolia, People's Republic of China: *Canadian Journal of Earth Sciences*, 33, pp. 631–636.

Dong Zhi-Ming, and Lü Junchang, 2005, A new ctenochasmatid pterosaur from the Early Cretaceous of Liaoning Province: *Acta Geologica Sinica*, 79 (2), pp. 164–167.

Dong Zhi-Ming, and Angela C. Milner, 1998, *Dinosaurs from China*. London: British Museum of Natural History, 114 pages.

Dong Zhi-ming, Sun Yue-wu, and Wu Shaoyuan, 2003, On a new pterosaur from the Lower Cretaceous of Chaoyang Basin, Western Liaoning, China: *Global Geology*, 22 (1), pp. 1–5.

Dong, Zhi-Ming, Zhou Shiwu, and Zhang Zicheng, 1983, The dinosaurian remains from Sichuan Basin, China: *Paleontologia Sinica*, whole number 162, New Series C, 23, pp. 1–145.

Drent, R., 1972, The natural history of incubation, *in*: D. S. Farmer, editor, *Breeding Biology of Birds*. Washington, D.C., National Academy of Sciences, pp. 262–311.

Dwivedi, G. N., D. M. Mohabey, and S. Bandyopadhyay, 1982, On the discovery of vertebrate fossils from infratrappean Lameta Beds, Kheda District, Gujarat: *Current Trends in Geology*, 7, pp. 79–87.

Dyke, Gareth J., and Mark A. Norell, 2005, *Caudipteryx* as a non-avian theropod rather than a flightless bird: *Acta Palaeontologica Polonica*, 50 (1), pp. 101–116.

Dzerzhinsky, F. Ya., 1998, *Comparative Anatomy of Vertebrates*: Moscow: Mosk. Gos. Univ. [in Russian].

Eberth, David A., 1990, Stratigraphy and sedimentology of vertebrate microfossil sites in the uppermost Judith River Formation (Campanian), Dinosaur Provincial Park, Alberta, Canada: *Palaeogeography, Palaeoclimatology, Palaeoecology*, 78, pp. 1–36.

Eberth, David A., Philip J. Currie, Donald B. Brinkman, Michael J. Ryan, Dennis R. Braman, James D. Gardner, V. D. Lam, D. N. Spivak, and A. G. Newman, 2001, Alberta's dinosaurs and other fossil vertebrates: Judith River and Edmonton Groups (Campanian–Maastrichtian), *in*: C. I. Hill, editor, *Mesozoic and Cenozoic Paleontology in the Western Plains and Rocky Mountains: Museum of the Rockies, Occasional Paper*, 3, pp. 47–75.

Eberth, David A., and A. P. Hamblin, 1993, Tectonic, stratigraphic, and sedimentological significance of a regional discontinuity in the upper Judith River Group (Belly River wedge) of southern Alberta, Saskatchewan, and southern Montana: *Canadian Journal of Earth Science*, 30, pp. 174–200.

Eberth, David A., Dale A. Russell, Dennis R. Braman, and A. L. Deino, 1993, The age of dinosaur-bearing sediments at Tebch, Inner Mongolia, People's Republic of China: *Canadian Journal of Earth Sciences*, 30, pp. 2101–2106.

Efremov, Ivan A., 1962, *Doroga vetrov (gobiskie zametki) (Highway of Winds: Gobi Travel Notes)*. Moscow: Geograf. Lit. Elżanowski, Andrzej, 1974, Preliminary note on the paleognathous bird from the Upper Cretaceous of Mongolia: *Palaeontologia Polonica*, 30, pp. 103–109.

_____, 1999, A comparison of the jaw skeleton in theropods and birds, with a description of the palate in the Oviraptoridae: *Smithsonian Contributions to Paleobiology*, 89, pp. 311–323.

_____, 2001, A new genus and species for the largest specimen of *Archaeopteryx*: *Acta Palaeontological Polonica*, 46 (4), pp. 519–532.

_____, 2002, Archaeopterygidae (Upper Jurassic of Germany), *in*: Luis M. Chiappe and Lawrence M. Witmer, editors, *Mesozoic Birds: Above the Heads of Dinosaurs*. Berkeley and Los Angeles: University of California Press, pp. 129–159.

Elżanowski, Andrzej, Gregory S. Paul, and Thomas A. Stidham, 2001, An avian quadrate from the Late Cretaceous Lance Formation of Wyoming: *Journal of Vertebrate Paleontology*, 20 (4), pp. 712–719.

Engelmann, George F., Daniel J. Chure, and Anthony R. Fiorillo, 2004, The implications of a dry climate for the paleoecology of the fauna of the Upper Jurassic Morrison Formation: *Sedimentary Geology*, 167, pp. 297–308.

Erickson, Gregory M., S. D. Van Kirk, J. Su, M. E. Levenston, W. E. Caler, and D. R. Carter, 1996, Bite-force estimation for *Tyrannosaurus rex* from tooth-marked bones: *Nature*, 382, pp. 706–708.

Erickson, Gregory M., Kristina Curry Rogers, and Scott A. Yerby, 2001, Dinosaurian growth patterns and rapid avian growth rates: *Nature*, 412, pp. 429–433.

Erickson, Gregory M., Peter J. Makovicky, Philip J. Currie, Mark A. Norell, Scott Yerby, and Christopher A. Brochu, 2004, Gigantism and comparative life-history of tyrannosaurid dinosaurs: *Nature*, 430, 772–775.

Evans, Dallas, and Peter L. Larson, 2003, Tumors, tears, fusion, decalcification, fractures and infection — tough times for a tyrannosaur: *Journal of Vertebrate Paleontology*, 23 (Supplement to Number 3), Abstracts of Papers, Sixty-third Annual Meeting, p. 48A.

Evans, David C. 2003, Cranial osteology and ontogeny of *Corythosaurus* (Ornithischia: Hadrosauridae): *Journal of Vertebrate Paleontology*, 23 (Supplement to Number 3), Abstracts of Papers, Sixty-third Annual Meeting, p. 48A–49A.

_____, 2004, Cranial crests of lambeosaurine Hadrosauridae: function and evolution of nasal passages: *Journal of Morphology*, 260 (3), 7th International Congress of Vertebrate Morphology, p. 289.

Evans, David C., and Robert Reisz, 2004, Anatomy of *Lambeosaurus magnicristatus* (Ornithischia: Hadrosauridae): *Journal of Vertebrate Paleontology*, 24 (Supplement to Number 3), Abstracts of Papers, Sixty-fourth Annual Meeting, p. 55A.

Everhart, Michael J., 2004, Notice of the transfer of the holotype specimen of *Niobrarasaurus coleii* (Ankylosauria: Nodosauridae) to the Sternberg Museum of Natural History: *Transactions of the Kansas Academy of Science*, 107 (34), pp. 173–174.

Fabre, Jacques, 1974, Un nouveau Pterodactylidae du gisement de Canjures (Var) *Gallodactylus canjuersensis* nov. gen. nov. sp.: *Ann. Pal.*, 62 (1), pp. 35–70.

_____, 1981, *Les Rhynchocephales et les Ptérosauriens à Crête Pariétale du Kimméridgien Supérieur-Berriasien d'Europe Occidentale: Le Gisement de Canjuers (Var-France) et ses Abords*. Paris: Editions de la Fondation Singer-Polignac, 188 pages.

Falconer, Hugh, 1868, Memorandum of two remarkable vertebrae sent by Dr Oldham from Jubbelpoor-Soilsbury bed, *in*: M. D. Murchison, editor, *Palaeontological Memoirs and Notes of the Late Hugh Falconer, Fauna antiqua sivalensis*, 1, pp. 418–419.

Fang, Pang, Lu, Zhang, Pan, Wang, Li and Cheng, 2000: The definition of Lower, Middle and Upper Jurassic Series in Lufeng, Yunnan: *Proceedings of the Third National Stratigraphical Conference of China*. Beijing: Geological Publishing House, pp. 208–214.

Farke, Andrew, 2003, Ceratopsid dinosaur cranial morphology and behavior reinterpreted: evaluating the bovid paradigm: *Journal of Vertebrate Paleontology*, 23 (Supplement to Number 3), Abstracts of Papers, Sixty-third Annual Meeting, p. 49A.

_____, 2004, Ceratopsid dinosaurs from the Upper Cretaceous Almond Formation of southwestern Wyoming: *Rocky Mountain Geology*, 39 (1), pp. 1–5.

Farlow, James O., 1987, Speculations about the diet and digestive physiology of herbivo-

Bibliography

rous dinosaurs: *Paleobiology*, 13 (1), pp. 60–72.

_____, 1990, Dinosaur energetics and thermal biology, *in*: David B. Weishampel, Peter Dodson and Halszka Osmólska, editors, *The Dinosauria*. Berkeley and Los Angeles: University of California Press, pp. 43–55.

_____, 1992, Sauropod tracks and trackmakers: integrating the ichnological and skeletal records: *Zubia*, 5, pp. 89–138.

_____, 1994, Speculations about the carrion-locating ability of tyrannosaurs: *Historical Biology*, 7, pp. 159–165.

Farlow, James O., and David L. Brinkman, 1994, Wear surfaces on the teeth of tyrannosaurs: *Paleontological Society*, special publication 7, pp. 165–175.

Farlow, James O., David L. Brinkman, William L. Abler, and Philip J. Currie, 1991, Size, shape and serration density of theropod dinosaur lateral teeth: *Modern Geology*, 16, pp. 161–197.

Farlow, James O., Stephen M. Gatesy, and Thomas R. Holtz, Jr., John R. Hutchinson, and John M. Robinson, 2000, Theropod locomotion: *American Zoologist*, 40, pp. 640–663.

Farlow, James O., Jeffrey G. Pittman, and J. Michael Hawthorne, 1989, *Brontopodus birdi*, Lower Cretaceous sauropod footprints from the U.S. Gulf Coastal Plain, *in*: David D. Gillette and Martin G. Lockley, editors, *Dinosaur Tracks and Traces*. Cambridge, New York, and Melbourne: Cambridge University Press, pp. 371–394.

Fassett, James E., 1982, Dinosaurs of the San Juan Basin, New Mexico, may have survived the event that resulted in creation of an iridium-enriched zone near the Cretaceous–Tertiary boundary: *Geological Society of America, Special Paper*, 190, pp. 435–447.

Fastnacht, Michael, 2001, First record of *Coloborhynchus* (Pterosauria) from the Santana Formation (Lower Cretaceous) of the Chapada do Aripe of Brazil: *Paläontologische Zeitschrift*, 75 (1), pp. 23–36.

Fastovsky, David, Yifan Huang, Jason Hsu, Jamie Martin-McNaughton, Peter M. Sheehan, and David B. Weishampel, 2004, Shape of Mesozoic dinosaur richness: *Geology*, 32 (10), pp. 877–2004.

Fedak, Tim, 2003, A new interpretation and description of the *Anchisaurus polyzelus* (Saurischia: Sauropodomorpha) braincase and its implications for prosauropod systematics: *Journal of Vertebrate Paleontology*, 23 (Supplement to Number 3), Abstracts of Papers, Sixty-third Annual Meeting, p. 49A.

_____, 2004, Ontogeny issues among sauropodomorph dinosaurs and new specimens from the earliest Jurassic sandstones of Nova Scotia: *13th Symposium on Vertebrate Palaeontology and Comparative Anatomy, Papers*, pp. 14.

Fedde, M. R., 1987, Respiratory muscles, *in*: T. J. Seller, editor, *Bird Respiration*. Bocca Ratón, FL: CRC Press, pp. 3–37.

Feduccia, Alan, 1980, *The Age of Birds*. Cambridge, MA, and London: Harvard University Press, ix, 196 pages.

_____, 1999, *The Origin and Evolution of Birds*, second edition. New Haven, CT: Yale University Press, 466 pages.

Feduccia, Alan, and Rupert Wild, 1993, Bird-like characters in the Triassic archosaur *Megalancosaurus*: *Naturwissenschaften*, 80, pp. 564–566.

Filla, James B., and Pat D. Redman, 1994, *Apatosaurus yahnapin*, a preliminary description of a new species of diplodocid dinosaur from the Late Jurassic Morrison Formation of southern Wyoming, the first sauropod dinosaur found with a complete set of "belly ribs": *Forty-fourth Annual Field Conference, Wyoming Geological Association Guidebook*, pp. 159–178.

Fiorillo, Anthony R., 1998, Dental microwear patterns from the sauropod dinosaurs *Camptosaurus* and *Diplodocus*: evidence for resource partitioning in the Late Jurassic of North America: *Historical Biology*, 13, pp. 1–16.

_____, 2004, Dinosaurs of Alaska and the assembling of Beringia: *Journal of Vertebrate Paleontology*, 24 (Supplement to Number 3), Abstracts of Papers, Sixty-fourth Annual Meeting, p. 57A.

Fiorillo, Anthony R., and Roland Gangloff, 2003, Preliminary notes on the taphonomic and paleoecologic setting of a *Pachyrhinosaurus* bonebed in northern Alaska: *Journal of Vertebrate Paleontology*, 23 (Supplement to Number 3), Abstracts of Papers, Sixty-third Annual Meeting, p. 50A.

Fleishmann, F. L., 1831, *Dalmatiae Nova Serpentum Genera*. Erlangen: Heyder, 35 pages.

Fleming, J., 1823, Observations on the *Setularia cuscuta* Ellis: *Memoirs of the Wernerian Natural History Society*, 4, pp. 485–491.

Fleming, S., 1975, Local man finds area rich in dinosaur fossils: *Grand Prairie Herald-Tribune*, April 24, p. 1.

Ford, Tracy L., 2002, A new look at the armor of *Ankylosaurus*, just how did it look?, *in*: *The Mesozoic in Wyoming, Tate 2002*. Casper, WY: The Geological Museum, Casper College, pp. 48–69.

Ford, Tracy L., and Daniel J. Chure, 2001, Ghost lineages and the paleogeographic and temporal distribution of tyrannosaurids: *Journal of Vertebrate Paleontology*, 21 (Supplement to Number 3), Abstracts of Papers, Sixty-first Annual Meeting, pp. 50A–51A.

Forster, Catherine A., 1985, The postcranial skeleton of the Early Cretaceous ornithopod dinosaur *Tenontosaurus tilletti*, Cloverly Formation, Montana and Wyoming. Unpublished MSc Thesis, University of Pennsylvania, 128 pages.

Forster, Catherine A., Luis M. Chiappe, David W. Krause, and Scott D. Sampson, 1996, The first Cretaceous bird from Madagascar: *Nature*, 382, pp. 532–534.

_____, 2002, *Vorona berivotrensis*, a primitive bird from the Late Cretaceous of Madagascar, *in*: Luis M. Chiappe and Lawrence M. Witmer, editors, *Mesozoic Birds: Above the Heads of Dinosaurs*. Berkeley and Los Angeles: University of California Press, pp. 268–280.

Forster, Catherine A., Scott D. Sampson, Luis M. Chiappe, and David W. Krause, 1998a, The theropod ancestry of birds: new evidence from the Late Cretaceous of Madagascar: *Science*, 279, pp. 1915–1919.

_____, 1998b, Genus correction: *Ibid.*, p. 185.

Foster, John R., 2003, *Allosaurus* as a generalized predator in the Morrison Formation paleoecosystem (Late Jurassic; North America): *Journal of Vertebrate Paleontology*, 23 (Supplement to Number 3), Abstracts of Papers, Sixty-third Annual Meeting, p. 51A.

Foster, John R., and Daniel J. Chure, 2000, An ilium of a juvenile *Stokesosaurus* (Dinosauria, Theropoda) from the Morrison Formation (Upper Jurassic: Kimmeridgian), Meade County, SD: *Brigham Young University Geology Studies*, 45, pp. 5–9.

Fowler, Denver, Keith Simmonds, Mick Green, and Kent A. Stevens, 2003, The taphonomic setting of two mired sauropods (Wessex Fm, Isle of Wight, UK), palaeoecological implications and taxon preservation bias in a Lower Cretaceous wetland: *Journal of Vertebrate Paleontology*, 23 (Supplement to Number 3), Abstracts of Papers, Sixty-third Annual Meeting, p. 51A.

Fraas, Eberhard, 1908, Ostafrikanische Dinosaurier: *Palaeontographica*, 55, pp. 105–144.

_____, 1913, Die neuesten Dinosaurierfunde in der Schwäbischen Trias: *Naturwissenschaften*, 45, pp. 1097–1100, Stuttgart.

Frey, Eberhard, Marie-Céline Buchy, and David M. Martill, 1995, A possible oviraptorosaurid theropod from the Santana Formation (Lower Cretaceous, Albian) of Brazil: *Neus Jahrnuch für Geologie und Paläontologie, Monatschefte*, pp. 397–412.

_____, 2003, Middle- and bottom-decker Cretaceous pterosaurs: unique designs in active flying vertebrates: *in*: Éric Buffetaut and Jean-Michel Mazin, editors, *Evolution and Palaeobiology of Pterosaurs*. London: The Geological Society, Special Publications, 217, pp. 268–274.

Frey, Eberhard, and David M. Martill, 1994, A new pterosaur from the Crato Formation (Lower Cretaceous, Aptian) of Brazil: *Neus Jahrbuch für Geologie und Paläontologie, Abhandlungen*, 194 (2/3), pp. 379–412.

_____, 1998, Soft tissue preservation in a specimen of *Pterodactylus kochi* (WAGNER) from the Upper Jurassic of Germany: *Ibid.*, 210, pp. 421–441.

Frey, Eberhard, David M. Martill, and Marie-Céline Buchy, 2003a, A new crested ornithocheirid from the Lower Cretaceous of northeastern Brazil and the unusual death of an unusual pterosaur: *in*: Éric Buffetaut and Jean-Michel Mazin, editors, *Evolution and Palaeobiology of Pterosaurs*. London: The Geological Society, Special Publications, 217, pp. 55–63.

_____, 2003b, A new species of tapejarid pterosaur with soft-tissue crest: *Ibid.*, pp. 65–72.

Frey, Eberhard, Helmut Tischlinger, Marie-Céline Buchy, and David M. Martill, 2003, New specimens of Pterosauria (Reptilia) with soft parts with implications for pterosaurian anatomy and locomotion: *in*: Éric Buffetaut and Jean-Michel Mazin, editors, *Evolution and Palaeobiology of Pterosaurs*. London: The Geological Society, Special Publications, 217, pp. 233–266.

Fricke, Henry, 2003, Elucidating the nature of dinosaur ecology and behavior using carbon isotope ratios of tooth enamel and associated sedimentary organic matter: *Journal of Vertebrate Paleontology*, 23 (Supplement to Number 3), Abstracts of Papers, Sixty-third Annual Meeting, p. 52A.

Fritsch, A., 1881. Über die Entdeckung von Vogelresten in der bömischen Kreideformation. Prague: *Sitzungsberichte der königlich-bömischen Gesellschaft der Wissenschaften*, 1885, 85 pages.

Fuentes Vidarte, C. F., 1996, Primeras huellas de Aves en el Weald de Soria (Espana). Neovo icnogenero, *Archaeornithipus* y neuva icnoespecie *A. meijidei*: *Estudios Geologicos*, 52, pp. 63–75.

Gabriel, Stefan N., and Max C. Langer, 2004, A reconstruction of the humeral myology of the basal sauropodomorph *Saturnalia tupiniquim*: *13th Symposium on Vertebrate Palaeontology and Comparative Anatomy, Papers*, p. 32.

Galeeva, L. I., 1955, Ostracoda from the Cretaceous deposits of Mongolian People's Republic: *Gostoptekhizdat*, Moscow, 98 pages.

Galton, Peter M., 1970, Pachycephalosaurids: dinosaurian battering rams: *Discovery*, 6, pp. 22–32.

———, 1971, A primitive dome-headed dinosaur (Ornithischia: Pachycephalosauridae) from the Lower Cretaceous of England and the function of the dome of pachycephalosaurids: *Journal of Paleontology*, 45, pp. 40–47.

———, 1973a, Redescription of the skull and mandible of *Parksosaurus* from the Late Cretaceous, with comments on the family Hypsilophodontidae (Ornithischia): *Life Science Contributions, Royal Ontario Museum, Life Sciences*, 89, pp. 1–21.

———, 1973b, On the anatomy and relationships of *Efraasia diagnostica* (Huene), n. gen., a prosauropod dinosaur (Reptilia: Saurischia) from the Upper Triassic of Germany: *Paläontographica Zeitschrift*, 47 (5), pp. 229–255.

———, 1976, Prosauropod dinosaurs (Reptilia: Saurischia) of North America: *Postilla*, 169, pp. 1–98.

———, 1980, Avian-like tibiotarsi of the pterodactyloids (Reptilia: Pterosauria) from the Upper Jurassic of East Africa: *Paläontologische Zeitschrift*, 54, pp. 331–342, Stuttgart.

———, 1981, A rhamphorhyncoid pterosaur from the Upper Jurassic of North America: *Journal of Paleontology*, 55 (5), pp. 1117–1122.

———, 1984, Cranial anatomy of the prosauropod dinosaur *Plateosaurus*, from the Knollenmergel (Middle Keuper, Upper Triassic) of Germany. 1. Two complete skulls from Trossingen/Württ with comments on the diet: *Geologica et Palaeontologica*, 18, pp. 139–171.

———, 1985a, the poposaurid thecodontian

Teratosaurus suevicus v. Meyer, plus referred specimens mostly based on prosauropod dinosaurs, from the Middle Stubensandstein (Upper Triassic of Nordwürttemberg: *Stutgarter Beitruäge zur Naturkunde*, Serie B (Geologie und Paläontologie), 116, pp. 105–123, Oslo.

———, 1985b, Cranial anatomy of the prosauropod dinosaur *Plateosaurus* from the Knollenmergel (Middle Keuper) of Germany, II. all the cranial material and details of soft-part anatomy: *Geologica et Palaeontologica*, 19, pp. 119–159.

———, 1985c, Cranial anatomy of the prosauropod dinosaur *Sellosaurus gracilis* from the Middle Stubensandstein (Upper Triassic) of Nordwürttemberg: *Ibid.*, (B), 118, pp. 1–39, Stuttgart.

———, 1990, Basal Sauropodomorpha — Prosauropoda, *in*: David B. Weishampel, Peter Dodson and Halszka Osmólska, editors, *The Dinosauria*. Berkeley and Los Angeles: University of California Press, pp. 320–344.

———, 1995, The species of the basal hypsilophodontid dinosaur *Thescelosaurus* Gilmore (Ornithischia: Ornithopoda) from the Upper Cretaceous of North America: *Neus Jahrbuch für Geologie und Paläontologie, Abhandlungen*, 198 (3), pp. 297–311.

———, 1999, Sex, sacra and *Sellosaurus gracilis* (Saurischia, Sauropodomorpha, Upper Triassic, Germany) — or why the character "two sacral vertebrae" is plesiomorphic for Dino sauria: *Ibid.*, 213 (1), pp. 19–55.

———, 2000, The prosauropod dinosaur *Plateosaurus* Meyer 1837 (Saurischia: Sauropodomorpha). 1. the syntypes of *P. engelhardti* Meyer 1837 (Upper Triassic, Germany), with notes on other European prosauropods with "distally straight" femora: *Revue Paléobiologie, Genève*, 216 (2), pp. 233–275.

———, 2001a, Prosauropod dinosaurs from the Upper Triassic of Germany, *in*: Colectivo Arqueologico-Paleontologico de Salas, C.A.S., editors, *Actas de las I Jornadas Internacionales sobre Paleontologia de Dinosaurus y su Entorno (Proceedings of the Ist International Symposium on Paleontology of Dinosaurs and their Environment)*. Burgos, Spain, pp. 25–92.

———, 2001b, Prosauropod dinosaur *Sellosaurus gracilis* (Upper Triassic, Germany): third sacral vertebra as either a dorsosacral or a caudosacral: *Neus Jahrbuch für Geologie und Paläontologie, Montashefte*, 11, pp. 688–704.

Galton, Peter M., and Larry D. Martin, 2002a, *Enaliornis*, an Early Cretaceous hesperornithiform bird from England, with comments on other hesperornithiformes: *in*: Luis M. Chiappe and Lawrence M. Witmer, editors, *Mesozoic Birds: Above the Heads of Dinosaurs*. Berkeley and Los Angeles: University of California Press, pp. 317–338.

———, 2002b, Postcranial anatomy and systematics of *Enaliornis*, a foot-propelled diving bird (Aves: Hesperornithiformes) from the Early Cretaceous of England: *Revue de Paléobiologie*, 21 (2), pp. 489–538.

Galton, Peter M., and Hans-Dieter Sues, 1983, New data on pachycephalosaurid dinosaurs (Reptilia: Ornithischia) from North America: *Canadian Journal of Earth Sciences*, 20, pp. 462–472.

Galton, Peter M., and Paul Upchurch, 2000, Prosauropod dinosaurs: homeotic transformations ("frame shifts") with third sacral as a caudosacral or a dorsosacral: *Journal of Vertebrate Paleontology*, 20 (Supplement to Number 3), Abstracts of Papers, Sixtieth Annual Meeting, p. 43A.

———, 2004a, Prosauropoda, *in*: David B. Weishampel, Peter Dodson, and Halszka Osmólska, editors, *The Dinosauria*, second edition. Berkeley: University of California Press, pp. 232–258.

———, 2004b, Stegosauria, *Ibid.*, pp. 343–362.

Gangloff, Roland, 2003, The record of Arctic dinosaurs from northern Alaska, paleogeographic and paleoecologic implications: *Journal of Vertebrate Paleontology*, 23 (Supplement to Number 3), Abstracts of Papers, Sixty-third Annual Meeting, p. 53A.

Gao, Keqin, 1993, [A new species of *Szechuanosaurus* from the Middle Jurassic of Danshapu, Zigong, Sichuan]: *Vertebrata PalAsiatica*, 31, pp. 156–165.

Garcia, Géaldine, and Xabier Pereda Suberbiola, 2003, A new species of *Struthiosaurus* (Dinosauria: Ankylosauria) from the Upper Cretaceous of Villeveyrac (southern France): *Journal of Vertebrate Paleontology*, 23 (1), pp. 156–165.

Garcia, Géraldine, Marie Pincemaille, Monique Vianey-Liaud, Bernard Marandat, Edgar Lorenz, Gilles Cheylan, Henri Cappetta, Jacques Michaux, and Jean Sudre, 1999, Découverte du premier squelette presque complet de *Rhabdodon priscus* (Dinosauria, Ornithopoda) du Maastrichtian inférieur de Provence (Discovery of an almost complete skeleton of *Rhabdodon priscus* [Dinosauria, Ornithopoda] in the early Maastrichtian of Provence (southern France): *Comtes Renddes Séances de l'Académie des Sciences, Paris, de la Terre et des Planètes*, 328, pp. 415–421 (in French with English abridgement).

Garcia, Rodolfo, Leonardo Salgado, and Rodolfo A. Coria, 2003, Primeros restos de dinosaurios saurópodos en el Jurásico de la Cuenca Neuquina, Patagonia, Argentina: *Ameghiniana*, 49 (1), pp. 123–126.

Garland, T., Jr., and C. M. Janis, 1993, Does metatarsal/femur ratio predict maximum running speed in cursorial mammals?: *Journal of Zoology*, 229, pp. 133–151.

Garner, Thomas, 2004, A brief review of origins of ankylosaur skull "armor": *Journal of Vertebrate Paleontology*, 24 (Supplement to Number 3), Abstracts of Papers, Sixty-fourth Annual Meeting, p. 62A.

Gasparini, Zulma, Marta Fernández, and Marcelo de la Fuente, 2004, A new pterosaur from the Jurassic of Cuba: *Palaeontology*, 47 (4), pp. 919–927.

Gatesy, Stephen M., 1990, Caudofemoral musculature and the evolution of theropod locomotion: *Paleobiology*, 16 (2), pp. 170–186.

———, 1991, Hindlimb scaling in birds and other theropods: implications for terrestrial locomotion: *Journal of Morphology*, 209 (1), pp. 83–96.

_____, 1995, Functional evolution of the hindlimb and tail from basal theropods to birds, *in*: J. J. Thomason, editor. *Functional Morphology in Vertebrate Paleontology*. Cambridge, United Kingdom: Cambridge University Press, pp. 219–234.

Gauthier, Jacques A., 1986, Saurischian monophyly and the origin of birds, *in*: Kevin Padian, editor, The Origin of Birds and the Evolution of Flight. *Memoirs of the California Academy of Sciences*, 8, pp. 1–55.

Gauthier, Jacques A., and Kevin de Queiroz, 2001, Feathered dinosaurs, flying dinosaurs, crown dinosaurs and the name "Aves," *in*: Jacques Gauthier and I. F. Gall, editors, *New Prospectives on the origin and early evolution of birds: proceedings of the International Symposium in Honor of John H. Ostrom*. New Haven, CT: Peabody Museum of Natural History, pp. 7–41.

Geist, Nicholas R., and Alan Feduccia, 2000, Gravity-defying behaviors: identifying models for protoaves: *American Zoologist*, 40 (4), pp. 664–675.

Gervais, P., 1844, These sur les oiseaux: *L'Inst.*, p. 12.

Getty, Mike, Eric Roberts, and Mark Loewen, 2003, Taphonomy of a chasmosaurine ceratopsian skeleton from the Campanian Kaiparowits Formation, Grand Staircase-Escalante National Monument, UT: *Journal of Vertebrate Paleontology*, 23 (Supplement to Number 3), Abstracts of Papers, Sixty-third Annual Meeting, pp. 55A–56A.

Ghosh, Prosenjit, S. K. Bhattacharya, Ashok Sahni, R. K. Kar, D. M. Mohabey, and K. Ambwani, 2003, Dinosaur coprolites from the Late Cretaceous (Maastrichtian) Lameta Formation of India: isotopic and other markers suggesting a C_3 plant diet: *Cretaceous Research*, 24, pp. 743–750.

Giebel, C. G., 1852, *Allgemeine Palaeontologie*, viii, 413 pages.

Giffin, Emily B., Diane L. Gabriel, and Rolfe E. Johnson, 1987, a new pachycephalosaurid skull (Ornithischia) from the Cretaceous Hell Creek Formation of Montana: *Journal of Vertebrate Paleontology*, 7 (4), pp. 398–407.

Gill, Frank B., 1994, *Ornithology*, 2nd edition. New York: W. H. Freeman, 763 pages.

Gillette, David D., 1991, *Seismosaurus halli*, gen. et sp. nov., a new sauropod dinosaur from the Morrison Formation (Upper Jurassic/Lower Cretaceous) of New Mexico, USA: *Journal of Vertebrate Paleontology*, 11 (4), pp. 417–433.

_____, 1996a, Origin and early evolution of the sauropod dinosaurs of North America: the type locality and stratigraphic position of *Dystrophaeus viaemalae* Cope 1877, *in*: A. C. Huffman, W. R. Lund, and L. H. Godwin, editors, *Geology and Resources of the Paradox Basin*. Utah Geological Association Guidebook, 25, pp. 313–324.

_____, 1996b, Stratigraphic position of the sauropod *Dystrophaeus viaemalae* Cope and implications: International conference on continental Jurassic of the world, *in*: Michael Morales, editor, *The Conti-nental Jurassic, Museum of Northern Arizona Bulletin*, 60, pp. 59–68.

_____, 2003, The geographic and phylogenetic position of sauropod dinosaurs from the Kota Formation (Early Jurassic) of India: *Journal of Asian Earth Sciences*, 21, pp. 683–689.

Gilmore, Charles Whitney, 1920, Osteology of the carnivorous dinosauria in the United States National Museum, with special reference to the genera *Antrodemus* (*Allosaurus*) and *Ceratosaurus*: *Bulletin of the United States National Museum*, 110, pp. 1–154.

_____, 1922, A new sauropod dinosaur from the Ojo Alamo Formation of New Mexico: *Smithsonian Miscellaneous Collections*, 72 (2), pp. 1–9.

_____, 1923, A new species of *Corythosaurus* with notes on other Billy River dinosaurs: *Canadian Field Naturalist*, 37, pp. 46–52.

_____, 1925, A nearly complete articulated skeleton of *Camarasaurus*, a saurischian dinosaur from the Dinosaur National Monument: *Bulletin of the United States National Museum*, 81 (18), pp. 1–21.

_____, 1928, A new pterosaurian reptile from the marine Cretaceous of Oregon: *Proceedings of the United States National Museum*, 73 (24), pp. 1–5.

_____, 1936a, Osteology of *Apatosaurus*, with special reference of specimens in the Carnegie Museum: *Memoirs of the Carnegie Museum*, 11, pp. 175–300.

_____, 1936b, Remarks on the skull cap of the genus *Troödon*: *Annals of the Carnegie Museum*, 25, pp. 109–112.

_____, 1946a, A new carnivorous dinosaur from the Lance Formation of Montana: *Smithsonian Miscellaneous Collections*, 106 (13), 19 pages.

_____, 1946b, Reptilian fauna of the North Horn Formation of Central Utah: *United States Geological Survey Professional Paper*, 210-C, pp. 29–53.

Giménez, Olga, 1992, Estudio preliminar del miembro anterior de los sauropodos titanosauridos: *Ameghiniana*, 30, p. 154.

Gishlick, Alan, and Ryan Carney, 2003, Using digital scanning and modeling to reconstruct and test the forelimb function of *Deinonychus antirrhopus*: *Journal of Vertebrate Paleontology*, 23 (Supplement to Number 3), Abstracts of Papers, Sixty-third Annual Meeting, p. 55A.

Glut, Donald F., 1980, *The Dinosaur Scrapbook*: Secaucus, NJ: The Citadel Press, 320 pages.

Godefroit, Pascal, and Yuri L. Bolotsky, 2002, A remarkable new hollow-crested hadrosaurid dinosaur from Far Eastern Russia: *The 7th European Workshop of Vertebrate Paleontology, Sibu, Romania, 2–7 July 2002, Abstracts Volume and Excursions Field Guide*, p. 15.

Godefroit, Pascal, Yuri L. Bolotsky, and Vladimir Alifanov, 2003, A remarkable hollow-crested hadrosaur from Russia: an Asian origin for lambeosaurines: *Comptes Rendus Palevol*, 2, pp. 143–151.

Godefroit, Pascal, Yuri L. Bolotsky, and Jimmy Van Itterbeeck, 2004, The lambeosaurine dinosaur *Amurosaurus riabinini*, from the Maastrichtian of Far Eastern Russia: *Acta Palaeontologica Polonica*, 49 (4), pp. 585–618.

Godefroit, Pascal, and Gilles Cuny, 1997, Archosauriform teeth from the Upper Triassic of Saint-Nicolas-de-Port (northeastern France): *Palaeovertebrata*, 26, pp. 1–34.

Godefroit, Pascal, Dong Zhi-Ming, Pierre Bultynck, Li Hong, and Feng Lu ["with the collaboration in the field of Shang Chang-Yong, Guo Dian-Yong, Dong Yu-Long, Sun Yan, Zhang Zhe-Min, Hugo De Potter, Georges Lenglet, Thierry Smith, and Eric Dermience"], 1998, Sino-Belgian Cooperation Program, "Cretaceous dinosaurs and mammals from Inner Mongolia," Part 1: New *Bactrosaurus* (Dinosauria: Euhadrosauria) material from Iren Dabasu (Inner Mongolia, P. R. China): *The Sino-Belgian Dinosaur Expedition in Inner Mongolia, Bulletin, Institut Royal des Sciences Naturelle de Belgique*, Suppl. 68, pp. 1–70.

Godefroit, Pascal, and Fabien Knoll, 2003, Late Triassic dinosaur teeth from southern Belgium (Dents de dinosaures du Trias supérieur de Lorraine belge): *Comptes Rendus Palevol*, 2, pp. 3–11.

Godefroit, Pascal, Xabier Pereda Suberbiola, Li Hong, and Dong Zhi-Ming, 1999, A new species of the ankylosaurid dinosaur *Pinacosaurus* from the Late Cretaceous of Inner Mongolia (P.R. China): *Bulletin van het Koninkluk Belgisch Instituut voor Natuurwetenschappen, Aardwetenschappen*, 69-Supp, B, pp. 17–36.

Godefroit, Pascal, Shuqin Zan, and Liyong Jin, 2000, *Charonosaurus jiayiensis*, n.g., n.sp., a lambeosaurine dinosaur from the Late Maastrichtian of northeastern China: *Comptes rendus de l'Académie des Sciences de Paris, Sciences de la Terre et des Planètes*, 330, pp. 875–882.

_____, 2001, The Maastrichtian (Late Cretaceous) lambeosaurine dinosaur *Charonosaurus jiayinensis* from north-eastern China: *Bulletin de l'Institut Royal des Sciences Naturelle de Belgique, Sciences de la Terre*, 71, pp. 119–168.

Godfrey, Stephen J., and Philip J. Currie, 2004, A theropod (Dromaeosauridae, Dinosauria) sternal plate from the Dinosaur Park Formation (Campanian, Upper Cretaceous) of Alberta, Canada: *in*: Philip J. Currie, Eva B. Kopelhus, Martin A. Shugar, and Joanna L. Wright, 2004, editors, *Feathered Dragons: Studies on the Transition from Dinosaurs to Birds*. Bloomington and Indianapolis: Indiana University Press, pp. 144–149.

Godfrey, Stephen J., and Robert B. Holmes, 1995, Cranial morphology and systematics of *Chasmosaurus* (Dinosauria: Ceratopsidae) from the Upper Cretaceous of western Canada: *Journal of Vertebrate Paleontology*, 15, pp. 726–742.

Goldfuss, Georg August, 1831, Beitrage zur Kenntnis verschiedener Reptilien der Vorwelt: *Nova Acta Acad. Leop. Carol*, 15, pp. 61–128.

Gomani, Elizabeth M., Louis Jacobs, and David Winkler, 1999, Comparison of the African titanosaurian, *Malawisaurus*, with a North American Early Cretaceous sauropod, *in*: Yukimitsu Tomida, Thomas R. Rich, and Patricia Vickers-Rich, editors, *Proceedings of the Second Gondwanan Dinosaur Symposium*. Japan: National Science Museum Monographs, p. 15.

Gong Enpu, Hou Lianhai, and Wang Lixia, 2004, Enantiornithine bird with diapsidian skull and its dental development in the Early Cretaceous in Liaoning, China: *Acta Geologica Sinica*, 78 (1), pp. 1–7.

González Riga, Bernardo J., 2003, A new titanosaur (Dinosauria, Sauropoda) from the Upper Cretaceous of Mendoza Province, Argentina: *Ameghiana*, 40 (2), pp. 155–172.

González Riga, Bernardo J., and S. Casadio, 2000, Primeer registro de Dinosauria (Ornithischia, Hadrosauridae) en la provincia de La Pampa (Argentina) y sus implicacias paleobiogeograficas: *Ameghiniana*, 37 (3), pp. 341–351.

Goodchild, Drake, 2004, A new specimen of *Allosaurus* from north-central Wyoming: *Journal of Vertebrate Paleontology*, 24 (Supplement to Number 3), Abstracts of Papers, Sixty-fourth Annual Meeting, p. 65A.

Goodwin, Mark B., 1990, Morphometric landmarks of pachycephalosaurid cranial material from the Judith River Formation of northcentral Montana, *in*: Kenneth Carpenter and Philip J. Currie, editors, *Dinosaur Systematics: Approaches and Perspectives*. Cambridge and New York: Cambridge University Press, pp. 189–201.

Goodwin, Mark B., Emily A. Buchholtz, and Rolfe E. Johnson, 1998, Cranial anatomy and diagnosis of *Stygimoloch spinifer* (Ornithischia: Pachycephalosauria) with comments on cranial display structures in agonistic behavior: *Journal of Vertebrate Paleontology*, 18 (2), pp. 363–375.

Goodwin, Mark B., Matthew Colbert, and Timothy Rowe, 2004, High-resolution computed tomography of the type *Ornatotholus browni* (Ornithischia: Pachycephalosauria) confirms its early ontogenetic stage and synonymy with *Stegoceras*: *Journal of Vertebrate Paleontology*, 24 (Supplement to Number 3), Abstracts of Papers, Sixty-fourth Annual Meeting, p. 65A.

Goodwin, Mark B., and John R. Horner, 2004, Cranial morphology of pachycephalosaurs (Ornithischia: Marginocephalia) reveals transitory structures inconsistent with head-butting behavior: *Paleobiology*, 30 (2), pp. 253–267.

Gould, Rebecca, Robb Larson, and Ron Nellermoe, 2003, An allometric study comparing metatarsal II's in *Edmontosaurus* from a low-diversity hadrosaur bone bed in Corson Co., SD: *Journal of Vertebrate Paleontology*, 23 (Supplement to Number 3), Abstracts of Papers, Sixty-third Annual Meeting, pp. 56A–57A.

Gradstein, Felix M., James Ogg, Alan Smith, *et al.*, 2004, *A Geologic Time Scale 2004*. Cambridge: Cambridge University Press.

Gradziński, R., Zofia Kielan-Jaworowska, and Teresa Maryańska, 1977, Upper Cretaceous Djadokhta, Barun Goyot and Ne-

megt formations of Mongolia, including remarks on previous subdivisions: *Acta Palaeontologica Polonica*, 27, pp. 281–318.

Gray, David, and Sandra D. Chapman, 2004, The history and preparation of the enigmatic dinosaur *Hylaeosaurus armatus* BMNH R 3375: *13th Symposium on Vertebrate Palaeontology and Comparative Anatomy, Papers*, pp. 2.

Greengalgh, Brent, Mark Nolte, Jeanette Lyman, and Brooks B. Britt (2004), Integration of digital maps and data tables to facilitate taphonomic evaluation of the Dalton Wells Dinosaur Quarry (Lower Cretaceous, Cedar Mountain Fm), UT: *Journal of Vertebrate Paleontology*, 24 (Supplement to Number 3), Abstracts of Papers, Sixty-fourth Annual Meeting, p. 66A.

Grellet-Tinner, Gerald, and Luis M. Chiappe, 2004, Dinosaur eggs and nesting: implications for understanding the origin of birds: *in*: Philip J. Currie, Eva B. Kopelhus, Martin A. Shugar, and Joanna L. Wright, 2004, editors, *Feathered Dragons: Studies on the Transition from Dinosaurs to Birds*. Bloomington and Indianapolis: Indiana University Press, pp. 185–214.

Grenard, Steve, *Handbook of Alligators and Crocodiles*. Malabar, FL: Krieger, 236 pages.

Hall, Jean P., 1993, A juvenile hadrosaurid from New Mexico: *Journal of Vertebrate Paleontology*, 13 (3), pp. 367–369.

Hamley, Timothy, 1990, Functions of the tail in bipedal locomotion in lizards, dinosaurs, and pterosaurs: *Memoirs of the Queensland Museum*, 28 (1), pp. 153–158.

Hamm, Shawn A., and Michael J. Everhart, 2001, Notes on the occurrence of nodosaurs (Upper Cretaceous) of western Kansas: *Journal of Vertebrate Paleontology*, 21 (Supplement to Number 3), Abstracts of Papers, Sixty-first Annual Meeting, p. 58A.

Hand, Steven, James Clark, Christopher Beard, and Jeffrey McDaniel, 2004, Measurement of the holotype skeleton of *Tyrannosaurus rex* using coherent laser radar achieving sub-millimeter results: *Journal of Vertebrate Paleontology*, 24 (Supplement to Number 3), Abstracts of Papers, Sixty-fourth Annual Meeting, p. 68A.

Hankin, E. H., and D. M. S. Watson, 1914, On the flight of pterodactyls: *The Aeronautical Journal*, 72, pp. 1–12.

Happ, John, 2003, Periosteal reaction to injuries of the supraorbital horn and squamosal of an adult *Triceratops* (Dinosauria: Ceratopsidae): *Journal of Vertebrate Paleontology*, 23 (Supplement to Number 3), Abstracts of Papers, Sixty-third Annual Meeting, p. 59A.

Harksen, J. C., 1966, *Pteranodon sternbergi*, a new pterodactyl from the Niobrara Cretaceous of Kansas: *Proceedings of the South Dakota Academy of Sciences*, 45, pp. 74–77.

Harris, Jerald D. [David], and Kenneth Carpenter, 1996, A large pterodactyloid from the Niobrara Cretaceous of Kansas: *Neus Jahrbuch für Geologie und Paläontologie, Abhandlungen*, 8, pp. 473–484.

Harris, Jerald D., and Peter Dodson, 2004, A new diplodocoid sauropod from the Upper Jurassic Morrison Formation of Montana, USA: *Acta Palaeontologica Polonica*, 49 (2), pp. 197–210.

Harris, Susan K., Andrew B. Heckert, Spencer G. Lucas, and Adrian P. Hunt, 2002, The oldest North American prosauropod, from the Upper Triassic Tecovas Formation of the Chinle Group (Adamanian: latest Carnian), West Texas, *in*: Andrew B. Heckert and Spencer G. Lucas, editors, *Upper Triassic Stratigraphy and Palaeontology, New Mexico Museum of Natural History and Science Bulletin*, 21, pp. 249–252.

Harrison, C. J. O., and Cyril A. Walker, 1975, The Bradycnemidae, a new family of owls from the Upper Cretaceous of Romania: *Palaeontology*, 18 (3), pp. 563–570.

Hartman, Scott, 2004, Stance and carriage in *Brachylophosaurus*: evidence from articulated specimens: *Journal of Vertebrate Paleontology*, 24 (Supplement to Number 3), Abstracts of Papers, Sixty-fourth Annual Meeting, p. 68A.

Hasegawa Yoshikazu, Éric Buffetaut, Manabe Makoto, and Takakuwa Yuji, 2003, A possible spinosaurid tooth from the Sebayashi Formation (Lower Cretaceous), Gunma, Japan: *Bulletin of the Gunma Museum of Natural History*, 7, pp. 1–5.

Hatcher, John Bell, 1901, *Diplodocus* (Marsh): its osteology, taxonomy, and probable habits, with a restoration of the skeleton: *Memoirs of the Carnegie Museum*, 1 (1), pp. 1–61.

He Xinlu, and Cai Kaiji, 1983, A new species of *Yandusaurus* (hypsilophodont dinosaur) from the Middle Jurassic of Dasahanpu, Zigong, Sichuan: *Journal of Chengdu College of Geology 1983, Supplement 1*, pp. 5–14.

Head, Jason J., 1998, A new species of basal hadrosaurid (Dinosauria, Ornithischia) from the Cenomanian of Texas: *Journal of Vertebrate Paleontology*, 18 (4), pp. 718–738.

_____, 2001, A reanalysis of the phylogenetic position of *Eolambia caroljonesa* (Dinosauria, Iguanodontia): *Journal of Vertebrate Paleontology*, 21 (2), pp. 392–396.

Head, Jason J., and Yoshitsugu Kobayashi, 2001, Biogeographic histories and chronologies of derived iguanodontians: *Asociacion Paleontológical Argentina*, Publicatión Especial 7, VII International Symposium on Mesozoic Terrestrial Ecosystems, Buenos Aires, 30-6-2001, pp. 107–111.

Headden, Jaime, 2003, Henry Fairfield Osborn and revising the *Oviraptor* myth: *Journal of Vertebrate Paleontology*, 24 (Supplement to Number 3), Abstracts of Papers, Sixtythird Annual Meeting, pp. 59A–60A.

Heathcote, Julia, and Paul Upchurch, 2003, The relationships of *Cetiosauriscus stewarti* (Dinosauria; Sauropoda): implications for sauropod phylogeny: *Journal of Vertebrate Paleontology*, 23 (Supplement to Number 3), Abstracts of Papers, Sixtythird Annual Meeting, p. 60A.

Heckert, Andrew B., 2000, Triassic dinosaur

evolution: tempo and trends: *Geological Society of America Abstracts with Programs*, 32 (7), p. 497.

_____, 2002*a*, Taxonomy and biostratigraphic significance of the ornithischian dinosaur *Revueltosaurus* from the Chinle Group (Upper Triassic), Arizona and New Mexico: *New Mexico Geology*, 24 (2), pp. 65–66.

_____, 2002*b*, A revision of the Upper Triassic ornithischian dinosaur *Revueltosaurus*, with a description of a new species: *in*: Andrew B. Heckert and Spencer G. Lucas, editors, *Upper Triassic Stratigraphy and Palaeontology, New Mexico Museum of Natural History and Science Bulletin*, 21, pp. 253–268.

_____, 2004, Late Triassic microvertebrates from the lower Chinle Group (Otischalkian-Adamanian: Carnian), southwestern U.S.A.: *New Mexico Museum of Natural History and Science*, Bulletin 27, v, 170 pages.

Heckert, Andrew B., and Spencer G. Lucas, 1999, Late Triassic ornithischian dinosaur evolution: *Journal of Vertebrate Paleontology*, 19 (Supplement to Number 3), Abstracts of Papers, Fifty-ninth Annual Meeting, p. 50A.

_____, 2001, North America's oldest herbivorous dinosaurs: *Paleontology, Stratigraphy, and Sedimentology: GSA Rocky Mountain Section and South-Central Section Meeting*, abstracts, p. A-21.

Heckert, Andrew B., Spencer G. Lucas, and Stan E. Krzyzanowski, 2003, Vertebrate fauna of the late Campanian (Judithian) Fort Crittenden Formation, and the age of Cretaceous vertebrate faunas of southeastern Arizona (U.S.A.): *Neus Jahrbuch für Geologie und Paläontologie, Abhandlungen*, 227 (3), pp. 343–364.

Heilmann, Gerhard, 1926, *The Origin of Birds*. London: H. F. G. Witherby, 208 pages.

Henderson, Donald M., 1999, Estimating the masses and centers of mass of extinct animals by mathematical slicing: *Palaeobiology*, 25 (1), pp. 88–106.

_____, 2003*a*, Sauropod body shapes and narrow- and wide-guage trackways: *Alberta Palaeontological Society, Seventh Annual Symposium, "Fossils in Motion," Abstracts*, pp. 29–32.

_____, 2003*b*, Footprints, trackways, and hip heights of bipedal dinosaurs — testing hip height predictions and computer models: *Ibid.*, pp. 33–37.

_____, 2003*c*, Sauropod dinosaurs were the colossal corks of the Mesozoic: *Journal of Vertebrate Paleontology*, 23 (Supplement to Number 3), Abstracts of Papers, Sixty-third Annual Meeting, p. 60A.

Henderson, J. H., 1960, *A Dictionary of Scientific Terms* (seventh edition). Edinburgh and London: Oliver and Boyd, xiv, 595 pages.

Hengst, Richard A., 2004, Gravity and the *T. rex* backbone: *Journal of Vertebrate Paleontology*, 24 (Supplement to Number 3), Abstracts of Papers, Sixty-fourth Annual Meeting, pp. 67A–68A.

Hernandez, Rene, James I. Kirkland, Gregory S. Paul, Claudia B. Serrano, Juan Pablo Garcia, and Sabinas Pasac, 2003, A large hadrosaurine from the Sabinas Basin, Coahuila, Mexico: *Journal of Vertebrate Paleontology*, 23 (Supplement to Number 3), Abstracts of Papers, Sixty-third Annual Meeting, p. 61A.

Herrmann, Karin R., 2003, The phylogenetic interrelationships of thyreophoran dinosaur species (Stegosauria, Ankylosauria, and basal Thyreophora): *Journal of Vertebrate Paleontology*, 23 (Supplement to Number 3), Abstracts of Papers, Sixty-third Annual Meeting, p. 61A.

Hildebrand, Milton, 1995, *Analysis of Vertebrate Structure*, 4th edition. New York: John Wiley, 672 pages.

Hill, Robert V., 1999, Phylogenetic relationships among Ankylosauria: an analysis of cranial characters: *Journal of Vertebrate Paleontology*, 19 (Supplement to Number 3), Abstracts of Papers, Fifty-ninth Annual Meeting, p. 51A.

Hill, Robert V., Lawrence M. Witmer, and Mark A. Norell, 2003, A new specimen of *Pinacosaurus grangeri* (Dinosauria: Ornithischia) from the Late Cretaceous of Mongolia: ontogeny and phylogeny of ankylosaurs: *American Museum Novitates*, 3395, 29 pages.

Hinic, Sanja, 2002, The cranial anatomy of *Massospondylus carinatus* Owen, 1854 and its implications for prosauropod phylogeny: *Journal of Vertebrate Paleontology*, 23 (Supplement to Number 3), Abstracts of Papers, Sixty-second Annual Meeting, p. 65A.

Hislop, S., 1864, Extracts from letters relating to further discovery of fossil teeth of reptiles in central India: *Quarterly Journal of the Geological Survey of London*, 20, pp. 280–282.

Hitchcock, Edward, 1841, *Final Report on the Geology of Massachusetts*, 2, Northampton, Massachusetts, 1841, pp. 301–831.

Hitchcock, Edward, Jr., 1865, *A Supplement to the Ichnology of New England*. Boston: Wright and Potter, 96 pages.

Hoffet, Josué-Heilmann, 1942, Description de quelques ossements de Titanosauriens du Sénonien du Bas-Laos: *Comtes Rendu des Seances Conseil Recherches des Sciences, Indochina*, pp. 51–57.

Hogg, D. A., 1984, The development of pneumatisation in the postcranial skeleton of the domestic fowl: *Journal of Anatomy*, 139, pp. 105–113.

Holtz, Thomas R., Jr., 1994, The arctometatarsalian pes, an unusual structure of the metatarsus of Cretaceous Theropoda (Dinosauria: Saurischia): *Journal of Vertebrate Paleontology*, 14 (4), pp. 480–519.

_____, 1996, Phylogenetic taxonomy of the Coelurosauria (Dinosauria: Theropoda): *Ibid.*, 70, pp. 536–538.

_____, 1998, Spinosaurids as crocodile mimics: *Science*, 282, pp. 276–1277.

_____, 2000, A new phylogeny of the carnivorous dinosaurs, *in* B. P. Pérez-Moreno, Thomas R. Holtz, Jr., José Luis Sanz, and José J. Moratalla, editors, Aspects of theropod paleobiology: *Gaia*, 15 (December 1998), pp. 5–61.

_____, 2001, The phylogeny and taxonomy of the Tyrannosauridae, *in*: Darren Tanke and Kenneth Carpenter, editors, *Mesozoic Vertebrate Life: New Research Inspired by the Paleontology of Philip J. Currie*. Bloomington and Indianapolis: Indiana University Press, pp. 64–83.

_____, 2003*a*, Dinosaur predation, *in*: Patricia H. Kelley, Michal Kowalewski, and Thor A. Hansen, editors, *Predator-Prey Indications in the Fossil Record*. New York: Kluwer Academic/Plenum, pp. 325–340.

_____, 2003*b*, Evidence for the evolution of wing-assisted incline running in non-avialian theropods: *Journal of Vertebrate Paleontology*, 23 (Supplement to Number 3), Abstracts of Papers, Sixty-third Annual Meeting, p. 62A.

_____, 2004, Tyrannosauroidea, *in*: David B. Weishampel, Peter Dodson, and Halszka Osmólska, editors, *The Dinosauria* (second edition). Berkeley and Los Angeles: University of California Press, pp. 111–136.

Holtz, Thomas R., Jr., and Michael K. Brett-Surman, 1997, The osteology of the dinosaurs, *in*: James O. Farlow and Michael K. Brett-Surman, editors, *The Complete Dinosaur*. Bloomington and Indianapolis, Indiana University Press, pp. 78–91.

Holtz, Thomas R., Jr., Ralph E. Molnar, and Philip J. Currie, 2004, Basal Tetanurae, *in*: David B. Weishampel, Peter Dodson, and Halszka Osmólska, editors, *The Dinosauria* (second edition). Berkeley and Los Angeles: University of California Press, pp. 71–110.

Holtz, Thomas R., and Halszka Osmólska, 2004, Saurischia, *in*: David B. Weishampel, Peter Dodson, and Halszka Osmólska, editors, *The Dinosauria* (second edition). Berkeley and Los Angeles: University of California Press, pp. 21–24.

Hooley, F. G. S., 1914, On the ornithosaurian genus *Ornithocheirus*, with a review of the specimens from the Cambridge Greensand in the Sedgwick Museums, Cambridge: *Annals and Magazine of Natural History*, Eighth Series, 78, pp. 529–557.

Hope, Sylvia, 1999, A new species of *Graculavus* from the Cretaceous of Wyoming (Aves: Charadriiformes), *in*: Storrs L. Olson, editor, Peter Wellnhofer, Cecile Mourer-Chauvire, David W. Steadman, and Larry D. Martin, associate editors, *Avian Paleontology at the Close of the 20th Century: Proceedings of the 4th International Meeting of the Society of Avian Paleontology and Evolution, Washington, D.C., 4–7 June 1996, Smithsonian Contributions to Paleobiology*, 89, pp. 231–243.

_____, 2002, The Mesozoic radiation of Neornithies: *in*: Luis M. Chiappe and Lawrence M. Witmer, editors, *Mesozoic Birds: Above the Heads of Dinosaurs*. Berkeley and Los Angeles: University of California Press, pp. 339–388.

Hopp, Thomas P., and Mark J. Orsen, 2001, Dinosaur brooding and the origin of avian flight: *Journal of Vertebrate Paleontology*, 21 (Supplement to Number 3), Abstracts of Papers, Sixty-first Annual Meeting, p. 63A.

_____, 2004, Dinosaur brooding behavior and the origin of flight feathers: *in*: Philip J.

Currie, Eva B. Kopelhus, Martin A. Shugar, and Joanna L. Wright, 2004, editors, *Feathered Dragons: Studies on the Transition from Dinosaurs to Birds*. Bloomington and Indianapolis: Indiana University Press, pp. 234–250.

Hopson, James A., 1975, The evolution of cranial display structures in hadrosaurian dinosaurs: *Paleobiology*, 1, pp. 21–43.

———, 1979, Paleoneurology, *in*: C. Gans, R. G. Northcutt, and P. Ulinski, editors, *Biology of the Reptilia*, Vol. 9. New York: Academic Press, pp. 39–146.

———, 1980, Relative brain size in dinosaurs: implications for endothermy, *in*: Roger D. K. Thomas and Everett C. Olson, editors. *A Cold Look at the Warm-Blooded Dinosaurs*. Boulder, CO: AAAS Selected Symposium, 28, Westview Press, pp. 287–300.

Horner, John R., 1984, The nesting behavior of dinosaurs: *Scientific American*, 250 (4), pp. 130–137.

———, 1989, The Mesozoic terrestrial ecosystems of Montana, *in*: D. E. French and R. F. Grabb, editors, *Geologic Resources of Montana, Vol. I. Montana Geological Society 1989 Field Conference Guidebook: Montana Centennial Edition*. Billings: Montana Geological Society, pp. 153–162.

Horner, John R., and Philip J. Currie, 1994, Embryonic and neonatal morphology and ontogeny of a new species of *Hypacrosaurus* (Ornithischia: Lambeosauridae) from Montana and Alberta, *in*: Kenneth Carpenter, Karl F. Hirsch, and John R. Horner, editors, *Dinosaur Eggs and Babies*. New York: Cambridge University Press, pp. 312–336.

Horner, John R., and Mark B. Goodwin, 1998, Did pachycephalosaurs really head-butt? An osteohistogenic cranial analysis: *Journal of Vertebrate Paleontology*, 18 (Supplement to Number 3), Abstracts of Papers, Fifty-eighth Annual Meeting, p. 52A.

Horner, John R., and Don Lessem, 1993, *The Complete T. rex*. New York: Simon and Schuster, 239 pages.

Horner, John R., and Kevin Padian, 2004, Age and longevity of *Tyrannosaurus rex*: *Journal of Vertebrate Paleontology*, 24 (Supplement to Number 3), Abstracts of Papers, Sixty-fourth Annual Meeting, p. 72A.

Horner, John R., Kevin Padian, and Armand de Ricqlès, 1999, Osteohistology of some embryonic and perinatal archosaurs: phylogenetic and behavioral implications for dinosaurs: *Journal of Vertebrate Paleontology*, 19 (Supplement to Number 3), Abstracts of Papers, Fifty-ninth Annual Meeting, p. 51A.

———, 2001, Comparative osteohistology of some embryonic and perinatal archosaurs: developmental and behavioral implications for dinosaurs: *Paleobiology*, 27 (1), pp. 39–58.

Horner, John R., David J. Varricchio, and Mark B. Goodwin, 1992, Marine transgressions and the evolution of Cretaceous dinosaurs: *Nature*, 358, pp. 59–61.

Horner, John R., David B. Weishampel, and Catherine A. Forster, 2004, Hadrosauridae, *in*: David B. Weishampel, Peter Dodson, and Halszka Osmólska, editors, *The Dinosauria* (second edition). Berkeley and Los Angeles: University of California Press, pp. 438–463.

Hou Lianhai, 1994, A late Mesozoic bird from Inner Mongolia: *Vertebrata PalAsiatica*, 32 (4), pp. 258–266.

———, 1997*a*, A carinate bird from the Upper Jurassic of western Liaoning, China: *Chinese Science Bulletin*, 42 (5), pp. 413–416.

———, 1997*b*, *Mesozoic Birds of China*. Nan Tou, Taiwan: Taiwan Provincial Feng Huang Ku Bird Park, 228 pages.

———, 1997*c*, *Mesozoic Birds of China*. 228 pages.

———, 1999, A new hesperornithid (Aves) from the Canadian Arctic: *Vertebrata PalAsiatica*, 37 (7), pp. 228–233.

———, 2000, *Picture Book of Chinese Fossil Birds*.

Hou Lianhai, and Chen P., 1999, *Liaoxiornis delicatus* gen. et sp. nov., the smallest Mesozoic bird: *Chinese Science Bulletin*, 44 (9), pp. 834–838.

Hou, Lianhai, Luis M. Chiappe, Fucheng Zhang, and Cheng-Ming Chuong, 2004, New Early Cretaceous fossil from China documents a novel trophic specialization for Mesozoic birds: *Naturwissenschaften*, 91, pp. 22–25.

Hou Lianhai, and Liu Z., 1984, A new fossil bird from Lower Cretaceous of Gansu and early evolution of birds: *Sientific Sinica* (Series B), 27 (12), pp. 1296–1302.

Hou Lianhai, and J. Y. Zhang, 1993, A new fossil bird from Lower Cretaceous of China: *Vertebrata PalAsiatica*, 31 (3), pp. 217–224.

Hou Lianhai, Zhou Zhonghe, Zhang Fucheng, and Gu Yucai, 2001, Mesozoic birds from western Liaoning in China: *Liaoning Science and Technology Publishing House*, 120 pages.

Howgate, M. E., 1985, Problems of the osteology of *Archaeopteryx*: Is the Eichstatt specimen a distinct genus?, *in*: *The Beginnings of Birds, Proceedings of the International* Archaeopteryx *Conference, Eichstatt, 1984*, pp. 105–112.

Howse, Standford C. B., 1986, On the cervical vertebrae of the Pterodactyloidea (Reptilia, Archosauria): *Zoological Journal of the Linnean Society, London*, 88, pp. 307–328.

Howse, Standford C. B., and Andrew R. Milner, 1995, The pterodactyloids from the Purbeck Limestone Formation of Dorset: *Bulletin of The Natural History Museum, London (Geology)*, 51 (1), pp. 73–88.

Howse, Standford C. B., Andrew R. Milner, and David M. Martill, 2001, Pterosaurs, *in*: David M. Martill and Darren Naish, editors, *Dinosaurs of the Isle of Wight*. London: The Palaeontological Association, 10, pp. 324–335.

Hu, Yaoming, Jin Meng, Yuanqing Wang, and Chuankui Li, 2005, Large Mesozoic mammals fed on young dinosaurs: *Nature*, 433, pp. 149–152.

Huene, Friederich von, 1907–08, Die Dinosaurier der europäischen Triasformation mit Berucksichtigung der europaischen Vorkom misse: *Geologische und Paläontologische Abhandlungen*, Supplement 1, 419 pages.

———, 1923, Carnivorous Saurischia in Europe since the Triassic: *Bulletin of the Geological Society of America*, 34, pp. 449–458.

———, 1926, Volstaph"ndige Osteologie eines Plateosauriden aus der schwäbischen Trias: *Neus Jahrbuch Fuer Geologie und Paläontologie, Abhandlungen*, 15, pp. 129–179, Berlin.

———, 1929, Los Saurisquios y Ornitisquios del Cretaceo Argentina: *Annales Museo de La Plata*, 3, Serie 2a., 196 pages.

———, 1932, Die fossile Reptil-Ordnung Saurischia, ihre Entwicklung und Geschichte: *Monographien zur Geologie und Palaeontologie*, series 1, 4, 361 pages.

———, 1934, Ein neuer Coelurosaurier in der thüringischen Trias: *Paläontologische Zeitschrift*, 1935, 16, pp. 10–170.

———, 1956, *Paläontologie und Phylogenie der Niederen Tetrapoden*. Jena, Germany: Gustav Fisher, xii, pp. 103–253.

Huene, Friedrich von, and Charles Alfred Matley, 1933, The Cretaceous Saurischia and Ornithischia of the Central Provinces of India: *Paleontologica Indica*, 21 (1), pp. 1–74.

Hugo, Carlos A., and Héctor Leanza, 1999, Hoja Geológica 3969-IV, General Roca, provincias del Neuquén y Río Negro: *Inst. Geol. Rec. Nat. SEGEMAR 3969-IV*, pp. 1–95.

Hulke, James A., 1872, Appendix to a "Note on a new and undescribed Wealden vertebra," read 9th February 1870, and published in the *Quarterly Journal* for August in the same year: *Quarterly Journal of the Geological Society of London*, 28, pp. 36–37.

———, 1874, Note on a very large saurian limbbone adapted for progression upon land from the Kimmeridge Clay if Weymouth, Dorset: *Ibid.*, 30, pp. 16–17.

———, 1888, Supplemental note on *Polacanthus foxii*, describing the dorsal shield and some parts of the endoskeleton, imperfectly known in 1881: *Philosophical Transactions of the Royal Society of London*, 178, pp. 169–172.

Hungerbüler, A., 1998, Taphonomy of the prosauropod dinosaur *Sellosaurus*, and its implications for carnivore faunas and feeding habits in the Late Triassic: *Palaeogeography, Palaeoclimatology, Palaeoecology*, 143, pp. 1–29.

Hunn, Craig Andrew, Paul Upchurch, and David B. Norman, 2002, An analysis of dinosaurian biogeography: evidence for the existence of vicariance and dispersal patterns caused by geographical events: *Proceedings of the Royal Society of London, Series B*, 269, pp. 613–622.

Hunt, Adrian P., 1989, A new ?ornithischian dinosaur from the Bull Canyon Formation (Upper Triassic) of east-central New Mexico, *in*: Spencer G. Lucas and Adrian P. Hunt, editors, *The Dawn of the Age of Dinosaurs in the American Southwest*. Albuquerque: New Mexico Museum of Natural History, pp. 355–358.

———, 1996, A new clade of herrerasaur-like theropods from the Late Triassic of western North America: *Journal of Vertebrate Paleontology*, 16 (Supplement to Number 3), Abstracts of Papers, Fifty-sixth Annual Meeting, p. 43A.

Bibliography

_____, 2001, The vertebrate fauna, biostratigraphy and biochronology of the type Revueltian faunochron, Bull Canyon Formation (Upper Triassic), east-central New Mexico: *New Mexico Geological Society, Guidebook*, 52, pp. 123–152.

Hunt, Adrian P., and Spencer G. Lucas, 1987, J. W. Stovall and the Mesozoic of the Cimmaron Valley, Oklahoma, and New Mexico, *in*: Spencer G. Lucas and Adrian P. Hunt, editors, *New Mexico Geological Society Guidebook, 38th Field Conference, Northwestern New Mexico*, pp. 139–151.

_____, 1994, Ornithischian dinosaurs from the Upper Triassic of the United States, *in*: Nicholas C. Fraser and Hans-Dieter Sues, editors, *In the Shadow of the Dinosaurs: Early Mesozoic Tetrapods*. Cambridge: University of Cambridge Press, pp. 225–241.

_____, 1995, Vertebrate paleontology and biochronology of the lower Chinle Group (Upper Triassic), Santa Fe County, north-central New Mexico: *New Mexico Geological Society, Guidebook*, 46, pp. 243–246.

Hunt, Adrian P., Spencer G. Lucas, and P. Bircheff, 1993, Biochronological significance of the co-occurrence of the phytosaurs (Reptilia: Archosauria) *Angistorhinus* and *Rutiodon* in the Los Esteros Member of the Santa Rosa Formation, Santa Fe County, New Mexico, U.S.A.: *New Mexico Museum of Natural History, Bulletin*, 3, pp. 203–204.

Hunt, Rebecca, and Daniel J. Chure, 2003, An Early Cretaceous theropod from southwestern Arkansas: *Journal of Vertebrate Paleontology*, 23 (Supplement to Number 3), Abstracts of Papers, Sixty-third Annual Meeting, p. 64A.

Hurum, Jørn H., and Philip J. Currie, 2000, The crushing bite of tyrannosaurids: *Journal of Vertebrate Paleontology*, 20 (3), pp. 619–621.

Hurum, Jørn H., and Karol Sabath, 2003, Giant theropod dinosaurs from Asia and North America: skulls of *Tarbosaurus bataar* and *Tyrannosaurus rex* compared: *Acta Palaeontological Polonica*, 48 (2), pp. 161–190.

Hutchinson, John R., 2001, The evolution of pelvic osteology and soft tissues on the line to extant birds (Neornithes): *Zoological Journal of the Linnean Society of London*, 131, pp. 123–197.

_____, Biomechanical modeling and sensitivity analysis of bipedal running ability. 1. Extant taxa: *Journal of Morphology*, 262, pp. 421–440.

Hutchinson, John R., F. Clay Anderson, and Scott L. Delp, 2003, A 3-D analysis of musculoskeletal contributions to body support during bipedal locomotion: *Journal of Vertebrate Paleontology*, 23 (Supplement to Number 3), Abstracts of Papers, Sixty-third Annual Meeting, p. 61A.

Hutchinson, John R., F. Clay Anderson, Silvia S. Blemker, and Scott L. Delp, 2004, Analysis of hindlimb moment arms in *Tyrannosaurus rex* using a three-dimensional musculoskeletal computer model: *13th Symposium on Vertebrate Palaeontology and Comparative Anatomy, Papers*, 33.

Hutchinson, John R., and M. Garcia, 2001, *Tyrannosaurus* was not a fast runner: *Nature*, 415, pp. 1018–1021.

Hutchinson, John R., and Stephen M. Gatesy, 2000, Adductors, abductors, and the evolution of archosaur locomotion: *Paleobiology*, 26 (4), pp. 734–751.

Hutt, Stephen, and Penny Newbery, 2004, A new look at *Baryonyx walkeri* (Charig and Milner, 1986) based upon a recent fossil find from the Wealden of the Isle of Wight: *13th Symposium on Vertebrate Palaeontology and Comparative Anatomy, Papers*, p. 18.

Hutt, Stephen, Darren Naish, David M. Martill, Michael J. Barker, and Penny Newbery, 2001. A preliminary account of a new tyrannosauroid theropod from the Wessex Formation (Early Cretaceous) of southern England: *Cretaceous Research*, 22 (2), pp. 227–242.

Huxley, Thomas Henry, 1859, On *Rhamphorhynchus Bucklandii*, a pterosaurian from the Stonesfield Slate: *Quarterly Journal of the Geological Society*, 15, pp. 658–570.

_____, 1868, On the animals which are most nearly intermediate between the birds and reptiles: *Annals and Magazine of Natural History*, 2, pp. 66–75.

_____, 1870, Further evidence of the affinity between the Dinosaurian reptiles and birds: *Quarterly Journal of the Geological Society*, 26, pp. 12–31.

Hwang, Koo-Geun, Min Huh, Martin G. Lockley, David M. Unwin, and Joanna L. Wright, 2002, New pterosaur tracks (Pteraichnidae) from the Late Cretaceous Uhangri Formation, SW Korea: *Geological Magazine*, 139 (4), pp. 421–435.

Hwang, Sunny H., 2003, Patterns of enamel microstructure in dinosaurs: *Journal of Vertebrate Paleontology*, 23 (Supplement to Number 3), Abstracts of Papers, Sixty-third Annual Meeting, p. 64A.

Hwang, Sunny H., Mark A. Norell, Keqin Gao, and Ji Qiang, 2002, A large primitive coelurosaur from the Yixian Formation of northeastern China: *Journal of Vertebrate Paleontology*, 23 (Supplement to Number 3), Abstracts of Papers, Sixty-second Annual Meeting, p. 69A.

Hwang, Sunny H., Mark A. Norell, Ji Qiang, and Gao Keqin, 2002, New specimens of *Microraptor zhaoianus* (Theropoda: Dromaeosauridae) from northeastern China: *American Museum Novitates*, 3381, 44 pages.

_____, 2004a, A large compsognathid from the Early Cretaceous Yixian Formation of China: *Journal of Systematic Palaeontology*, 2 (1), pp. 13–30.

_____, 2004b, A new troodontid from the lower Yixian Formation of China and its affinities to Mongolian troodontids: *Journal of Vertebrate Paleontology*, 24 (Supplement to Number 3), Abstracts of Papers, Sixty-fourth Annual Meeting, pp. 73A–74A.

Ikejiri, Takehito, 2003, Sequence of closure of neurocentral sutures in *Camarasaurus* (Sauropoda) and implications for phylogeny in Reptilia: *Journal of Vertebrate Paleontology*, 23 (Supplement to Number 3), Abstracts of Papers, Sixty-third Annual Meeting, p. 65A.

_____, 2004, Relative growth and timing of ontogenetic changes in *Camarasaurus* (Dinosauria, Sauropoda): *Journal of Vertebrate Paleontology*, 24 (Supplement to Number 3), Abstracts of Papers, Sixty-fourth Annual Meeting, p. 74A.

Imhof, Margaret, and L. Barry Albright, 2003, Preliminary magnetostratigraphic analysis of the Upper Cretaceous Kaiparowits Formation, southern Utah: *Journal of Vertebrate Paleontology*, 23 (Supplement to Number 3), Abstracts of Papers, Sixty-third Annual Meeting, p. 65A.

Irmis, Randall B., 2004, First report of *Megapnosaurus* (Theropoda, Coelophysoidea) from China: *PaleoBios*, 24 (3), pp. 11–18.

Ishigaki, Shinobu, Mahito Watabe, Kishigjaw Tsogtbaatar, and Rinchen Barsbold, 2004, Footprint evidence of gregarious theropod dinosaurs from the Upper Cretaceous of Shar Tsav, South Gobi, Aimag, Mongolia: *Journal of Vertebrate Paleontology*, 24 (Supplement to Number 3), Abstracts of Papers, Sixty-fourth Annual Meeting, p. 74A.

Ivie, M. A., S. A. Slipinski, and P. Wegrzynowicz, 2001, Generic homonyms in the Colydiinae (Coleoptera: Zopheridae): *Insecta Mundi*, 15, pp. 63–64.

Jacobs, Louis L., Dale A. Winkler, William R. Downs, and Elizabeth M. Gomani, 1993, New material of an Early Cretaceous titanosaurid sauropod dinosaur from Malawi: *Palaeontology*, 36 (3), pp. 523–534.

Jagt, John W. M., Eric W. A. Mulder, Anne S. Schulp, Rudi W. Dortangs, and René H. B. Fraaije, 2003, Dinosaurs from the Maastrichtian-type area (southeastern Netherlands, northeastern Belgium) (Dinosaures de la région-type maastrichtienne [Sud-Est des Pays-Bas, Nord-Est de la Belgique]): *Comptes Rendus Palevol*, 2, pp. 67–76.

Jain, Sohan L., 1974, Jurassic pterosaur from India: *Journal of the Geological Society of India*, 15 (3), pp. 330–335.

Jain, Sohan L., and Saswati Bandyopadhyay, 1997, New titanosaurid (Dinosauria: Sauropoda) from the Late Cretaceous of central India: *Journal of Vertebrate Paleontology*, 17 (1), pp. 114–136.

Jain, Sohan L., T. S. Kutty, Tapan Row-Chowdbury, and Sankar Chatterjee, 1979, Some characteristics of *Barapasaurus tagorei*, a sauropod dinosaur from the Lower Jurassic of Deccan, India: *Proceedings of the IV International Gondwana Symposium, Calcutta*, 1, pp. 204–216.

Janensch, Werner, 1922, Das Handskellt von *Gigantosaurus robustus* und *Brachiosaurus brancai* aud den Tendaguru-Schichten Deutsch-Ostafrika: *Centralblatt fur Mineralogie, Geologie und Paläontologie*, 1922, pp. 225–235.

_____, 1947, Pneumatizitat bei Wirbein von Sauropoden und anderen Saurischien: *Palaeontographica*, Supplement 7 (3), pp. 1–25.

_____, 1950, Die Skelettrekonstruktion von *Brachiosaurus brancai*: *Ibid.*, 1, teil 3, lieferung 2, pp. 95–103.

Jeffries, A. S. P., 1979, The origins of the chordates — A methodological essay, *in*: M. R. House, editor, *The Origins of Major Invertebrate Groups, Systematic Association Special Volume*, 12, pp. 443–477.

Jenkins, Farish A., Jr., Neil A. Shubin, Stephen M. Gatesy, and Kevin Padian, 2001, A diminutive pterosaur (Pterosauria: Eudimorphodontidae) from the Greenlandic Triassic, *in*: Farish A. Jenkins, Jr., Michael D. Shapiro, and Tomas Owerkowicz, editors, "Studies in Organismic and Evolutionary Biology in honor of A. W. Crompton": *Bulletin of the Museum of Comparative Zoology*, 156 (1), pp. 151–170.

Jennings, Debra, 2004, Paleoenvironmental and taphonomic applications of geospacial technology at a new dinosaur quarry on the Warm Spring Ranch, Thermopolis, Wyoming: *Journal of Vertebrate Paleontology*, 24 (Supplement to Number 3), Abstracts of Papers, Sixty-fourth Annual Meeting, p. 75A.

Jensen, James A., 1987, New brachiosaur material from the Late Jurassic of Utah and Colorado: *Great Basin Naturalist*, 47 (4), pp. 592–608.

Jensen, James A., and John H. Ostrom, 1977, A second Jurassic pterosaur from North America: *Journal of Paleontology*, 51 (4), pp. 867–870.

Jensen, James A., and Kevin Padian, 1989, Small pterosaurs and dinosaurs from the Uncomphagre fauna (Brushy Basin Member, Morrison Formation (?Tithonian), Late Jurassic, Western Colorado: *Journal of Paleontology*, 63 (3), pp. 364–373.

Jerzykiewicz, T., 2000, Lithostratigraphy and sedimentary settings of the Cretaceous dinosaur beds of Mongolia, *in*: M. J. Benton, M. A. Shishkin, D. M. Unwin, and E. N. Kurochkin, editors, *The Age of Dinosaurs in Russia and Mongolia*. Cambridge: Cambridge University Press, pp. 279–296.

Jerzykiewicz, T., Philip J. Currie, David A. Eberth, P. A. Johnson, E. H. Koster and J. J. Zheng, 1993, Djadokhta Formation correlative strata in Chinese Inner Mongolia: an overview of the stratigraphy, sedimentary geology, and paleontology and comparisons with the type locality in the pre–Altai Gobi: *Canadian Journal of Earth Sciences*, 30, pp. 2180–2195.

Jerzykiewicz, T., and Dale A. Russell, 1991, Late Mesozoic stratigraphy and vertebrates of the Gobi Basin: *Cretaceous Research*, 12, pp. 345–377.

Ji Qiang, Luis M. Chiappe, and Ji Shúan, 1999, A new late Mesozoic confuciusornithid bird from China: *Journal of Vertebrate Paleontology*, 19 (1), pp. 1–7.

Ji Qiang, Philip J. Currie, Mark A. Norell, and Ji Shu-An, 1998, Two feathered dinosaurs from northeastern China: *Nature*, 393, pp. 753–761.

Ji Qiang, and Ji S., 1997, A protarchaeopterygid bird (*Protarchaeopteryx* gen. nov.) — fossil remains of archaeopterygids from China: *Chinese Geology*, 238, pp. 38–41.

Ji Qiang, Ji Shúan, Lü, You Hailu, Chen Wein, Liu Yongqing and Liu Yanxue, 2005, First avalian bird from China: *Geological Bulletin of China*, 24 (3), pp. 197–210.

Ji Qiang, Mark A. Norell, Ke-Qin Gao, Shu-An Ji, and Dong Ren, 2001, The distribution of integumentary structures in a feathered dinosaur: *Nature*, 410, pp. 1084–1088.

Ji Qiang, Mark A. Norell, Peter J. Makovicky, Ke-Qin Gao, Shúan Ji, and Chongxi Yuan, 2003, An early ostrich dinosaur and implications for ornithomimosaur phylogeny: *American Museum Novitates*, 3420, pp. 1–19.

Ji Qiang, Ji Shu-an, Yuan Chong-xi, and Ji Xin-xin, 2002, Restudy on a small dromaeosaurid dinosaur with feathers over its entire body: *Earth Science Frontiers*, 9 (3), pp. 57–63.

Ji Shúan, and Ji Qiang, 1997, Discovery of a new pterosaur from western Liaoning, China: *Acta Geologica Sineca*, 4, pp. 199–206.

_____, 1998, A new fossil pterosaur (Rhamphorhynchoidea) from Liaoning: *Jiangsu Geology*, 4, pp. 199–206.

Ji, Shuan, Qiang Ji, and Kevin Padian, 1999, Biostratigraphy of new pterosaurs from China: *Nature*, 398, pp. 573–574.

Ji Qiang, Ji Shuan, Zhang Hongbin, You Hailu, Zhang Jianping, Wang Lixia, Yuan Congxi, and Ji Xinxin, 2002, A new avialian bird *Jixiangornis orientalis* gen. et sp. nov. — from the Lower Cretaceous of Western Liaoning: *Journal of Nanjing University (Natural Sciences)*, 38 (6), pp. 723–736.

Jianu, Coralia-Maria, 1994, A right dentary of *Rhabdodon priscus* Matheron, 1869 (Reptilia: Ornithischia) from the Maastrichtian of the Hateg Basin: *Sargetia*, 16, pp. 29–15.

Jones, Terry D., James O. Farlow, John A. Ruben, Donald M. Henderson, and William J. Hillenius, 2000, Cursoriality in bipedal dinosaurs: *Nature*, 406, pp. 716–718.

Jouve, Stephane, 2004, Description of the skull of *Ctenochasma* (Pterosauria) from the latest Jurassic of eastern France, with a taxonomic revision of European Tithonian Pterodactyloidea: *Journal of Vertebrate Paleontology*, 24 (3), pp. 542–554.

Jurcsák, Tiberiu, and Eugen Kessler, 1985, La Paleofauna de Cornet — implications phylogenetiques et ecologiques: *Evolution et Adaptation*, 2, pp. 137–147.

Karhu, A. A., and A. S. Rautian, 1996, A new family of Maniraptora (Dinosauria: Saurischia) from the Late Cretaceous of Mongolia: *Paleontological Journal*, 30 (5), pp. 583–592.

Kaye, Fran Tannenbaum, and Kevian Padian, 1994, Microvertebrates from the *Placerias* quarry: a window on Late Triassic vertebrate diversity in the American Southwest, *in*: Nicholas C. Fraser and Hans-Dieter Sues, editors, *In the Shadow of the Dinosaurs: Early Mesozoic Tetrapods*. Cambridge: University of Cambridge Press, pp. 171–196.

Keiran, Monique, 1999, Albertosaurus, *Death*

of a Predator. Vancouver: Raincoast Books, 56 pages.

Kellner, Alexander W. A. [Wilhelm Armin], 1984, Occoréncia de uma mandibula de Pterosauria (*Brasileodactylus araripensis* nov. gen; nov. sp.) na formacão Santana, Cretáceo de Chapada do Araripe, Ceara-Brasil: *Anais Do XXXIIII Congresso Brasileiro de Geologia, Rio de Janeiro*, pp. 578–590.

_____, 1989, A new edentate pterosaur of the Lower Cretaceous from the Araripe Basin, northeast Brazil: *Anais da Academia Brasileira Ciencias*, 61 (4), pp. 1–7, Rio de Janeiro.

_____, 1994, A new species of *Tupuxuara* (Pterosauria, Tapejaridae) from the Early Cretaceous of Brazil: *Ibid.*, 66 (4), pp. 467–473.

_____, 1995a, Theropod teeth from the Late Cretaceous Bauru Group near Peirópolis, Minas Gerais, Brazil, *in*: Alexander W. A. Kellner and C. F. Viana, editors, *Congresso Brasileiro de Paleontologia*, 14. Rio de Janeiro: Atas, pp. 66–67.

_____, 1995b, The relationships of the Tapejaridae (Pterodactyloidea) with comments of pterosaur phylogeny: *Sixth Symposium on Mesozoic Terrestrial Ecosystems and Biota, short papers*. Beijing: China Ocean Press, pp. 73–77.

_____, 1996, Remarks on Brazilian dinosaurs: *Memoirs of the Queensland Museum*, 39 (3), pp. 611–626.

_____, 1999, Short note on a new dinosaur (Theropoda, Coelurosauria) from the Santana Formation (Romualdo Member, Albian), northeastern Brazil: *Boletim do Museu Nacional*, Nova Série, 49, pp. 1–8, Rio de Janeiro.

_____, 2003, Pterosaur phylogeny and comments on the evolutionary history of the group: *in*: Éric Buffetaut and Jean-Michel Mazin, editors, *Evolution and Palaeobiology of Pterosaurs*. London: The Geological Society, Special Publications, 217, pp. 106–137.

Kellner, Alexander W. A., and Diogenese de Almeida Campos, 1989, Sobre um novo pterosaurio com Crista Sagittal da Bacia do Araripe, Cretácio Inferior do Nordeste do Brasil: *Anais Academia Brasileira Ciencias (1988)*, 60 (4), pp. 459–469, Rio de Janeiro.

_____, 1994, A new species of *Tupuxuara* (Pterosauria, Tupejaridae) from the Early Cretaceous of Brazil: *Ibid.*, 66 (4), pp. 467–473.

_____, 1996, First early Cretaceous theropod dinosaur from Brazil: *Neus Jahsbuch für Geologie und Paläontologie, Abhandlungen*, Stuttgart, 199 (2), pp. 151–166.

_____, 2000a, New theropod dinosaur from the continental Cretaceous of Mato Grosso, Brasil, *in*: *Simposio Brasileiro de Paleontologia de Vertebrados*, 2, Boletim de Resumos. Rio de Janeiro: Museu Nacional, p. 30.

_____, 2000b, Brief review of dinosaur studies and perspectives in Brazil: *Anais de Academia Brasileira de Ciências*, Rio de Janeiro, 72 (4), pp. 509–538.

_____, 2002, The function of the cranial crest

and jaws of a unique pterosaur from the Early Cretaceous of Brazil: *Science*, 297, pp. 389–392.

Kellner, Alexander W. A., Sergio Azevedo, Luciana Carvalho, Deise Henriques, Terezinha Costa, and Diogenese Campos, 2004, Bones out of the jungle: on a dinosaur locality from Mato Grosso, Brazil: *Journal of Vertebrate Paleontology*, 24 (Supplement to Number 3), Abstracts of Papers, Sixty-fourth Annual Meeting, p. 78A.

Kellner, Alexander W. A., and Wann Langston, Jr., 1996, Cranial remains of *Quetzalcoatlus* (Pterosauria, Azhdarchidae) from Late Cretaceous sediments of Big Bend National Park, Texas: *Journal of Vertebrate Paleontology*, 16 (2), pp. 222–231.

Kellner, Alexander W. A., and Yukimitsu Tomida, 2000, Description of a new species of Anhangueridae (Pterodactyloidea) with comments on the pterosaur fauna from the Santana Formation (Aptian–Albian), northeastern Brazil: *Natural Science Museum of Tokyo Monograph*, 17, pp. 1–135.

Kermack, D., 1984, New prosauropod material from South Wales: *Zoological Journal of the Linnean Society*, 82, pp. 101–117.

Kessler, Eugen, and Tiberiu Jurcsák, 1984, Fossil bird remains in the bauxite from Cornet (Romania, Bihor County): *Travaus du Muséum National d'Histoire Naturelle "Grigore Antipa" (Bucharest)*, 25, pp. 393–401.

_____, 1986, New contributions to the knowledge of the Lower Cretaceous bird remains from Cornet (Romania): *Ibid.*, 28, pp. 289–295.

Kielan-Jaworowska, Zofia, and Rinchen Barsbold, 1972, Narrative of the Polish-Mongolian Palaeontological Expeditions 1967–1971: *Acta Palaeontologica Polonica*, 42, pp. 201–242.

Kielan-Jaworowska, Zofia, and N. Dovchin, 1968/1969, Narrative of the Polish-Mongolian Palaeontological Expeditions 1963–1965, *in*: Kielan-Jaworowska, Zofia, editor, Results of the Polish-Mongolian Palaeontological Expeditions: *Palaeontologica Polonica*, 19, pp. 7–30.

Kielmeyer, C. von, and G. Jager, 1835, Amtlicher Bericht über die [12.] Versammlung deutscher Naturforscher und Ärzte zu Stuttgart im September 1834: *1 Abb.*, p. 133.

Kiernan, Caitlin R., and David R. Schwimmer, 2004, First record of a velociraptorine theropod (Tetanurae, Dromaeosauridae) from the eastern gulf coastal United States: *The Mosasaur*, 7, pp. 89–93.

Kim, B. K., 1969, A study of several sole marks in the Haman Formation: *Journal of the Geological Society of Korea*, 5 (4), pp. 243–258.

Kirkland, James I. [Ian], 1998*a*, A polacanthine ankylosaur (Ornithischia: Dinosauria) from the Early Cretaceous (Barremian) of eastern Utah, *in*: Spencer G. Lucas, James I. Kirkland, and John W. Estep, editors, *Lower and Middle Cretaceous Terrestrial Ecosystems*. Albuquerque: New Mexico Museum of Natural History and Science, Bulletin 14, pp. 271–282.

_____, 1998*b*, A new hadrosaurid from the Upper Cedar Mountain Formation (Albian–Cenomanian: Cretaceous) of eastern Utah — the oldest known hadrosaurid (lambeosaurine?): *Ibid.*, pp. 283–296.

Kirkland, James I., and J. Michael Parrish, 1995, Theropod teeth from the Lower Cretaceous of Utah: *Journal of Vertebrate Paleontology*, 15 (Supplement to Number 3), Abstracts of Papers, Fifty-fifth Annual Meeting, p. 39A.

Kirkland, James I., Lindsay E. Zanno, Donald Deblieux, David K. Smith, and Scott D. Sampson, 2004: A new basal therizinosauroid (Theropoda: Maniraptora) from Utah demonstrates a pan–Laurasian distribution for Early Cretaceous (Barremian therizinosauroids: *Journal of Vertebrate Paleontology*, 24 (Supplement to Number 3), Abstracts of Papers, Sixty-fourth Annual Meeting, p. 78A.

Kitching, James W., and Michael A. Raath, 1984, Fossils from the Elliot and Clarens Formations (Karoo Sequence) of the northeastern Cape, Orange Free State and Lesotho, and a suggested biozonation based on tetrapods: *Palaeontol. Afr.*, 25, pp. 111–125.

Knoll, Fabien, 2004, Review of the tetrapod fauna of the "Lower Stormberg Group" of the main Karoo Basin (southern Africa): implication for the age of the Lower Elliot Formation: *Bulletin de la Société Géologique de France*, 175 (1), pp. 73–83.

Knoll, Fabien, and Paul M. Barrett, 2003, Systematic revision of "*Yandusaurus*" multidens, a Middle Jurassic ornithopod from China: *Journal of Vertebrate Paleontology*, 23 (Supplement to Number 3), Abstracts of Papers, Sixty-third Annual Meeting, p. 68A.

Kobayashi, Yoshitsugu, and Yoichi Azuma, 1999, Cranial material of a new iguanodontian dinosaur from the Early Cretaceous Kitadani Formation of Japan: *Journal of Vertebrate Paleontology*, 19 (Supplement to Number 3), Abstracts of Papers, Fifty-ninth Annual Meeting, p. 57A.

_____, 2003, A new iguanodontian (Dinosauria: Ornithopoda) from the Lower Cretaceous Kitadani Formation of Fukui Prefecture, Japan: *Journal of Vertebrate Paleontology*, 23 (1), pp. 166–175.

Kobayashi, Yoshitsugu, and Rinchen Barsbold, 2003, Re-examination of *Harpymimus okladnikovi* (Dinosauria: Theropoda) of Mongolia and phylogeny of Ornithomimosauria: *Journal of Vertebrate Paleontology*, 23 (Supplement to Number 3), Abstracts of Papers, Sixty-third Annual Meeting, p. 68A.

_____, 2004, Re-examination of a primitive toothless ornithomimosaur, *Garudimimus brevipes*, from the Late Cretaceous of Mongolia: *Journal of Vertebrate Paleontology*, 24 (Supplement to Number 3), Abstracts of Papers, Sixty-fourth Annual Meeting, p. 79A.

Kobayashi, Yoshitsugu, and Jun-Chang Lü, 2003, A new ornithomimid dinosaur with gregarious habits from the Late Cretaceous of China: *Acta Palaeontologica Polonica*, 48 (2), pp. 235–259.

Kobayashi, Yoshitsugu, Jun-Chang Lü, Dong Zhi-Ming, Rinchen Barsbold, Yoichi Azuma, and Yukimitsu Tomida, 1999, Herbivorous diet in an ornithomimid dinosaur: *Nature*, 402, pp. 480–481.

Konishi, Takuya, 2004, Redescription of UALVP 40, a small chasmosaur dinosaur, with additional material, and its implications to Canadian chasmosaur systematics: *Journal of Vertebrate Paleontology*, 24 (Supplement to Number 3), Abstracts of Papers, Sixty-fourth Annual Meeting, p. 80A.

Kozisek, Jacqueline, 2003, New implications for the Cretaceous–Tertiary asteroid impact theory based upon the persistence of extant tropical honeybees (Hymenoptera: Apidae): *Journal of Vertebrate Paleontology*, 23 (Supplement to Number 3), Abstracts of Papers, Sixty-third Annual Meeting, p. 69A.

Kozisek, Jacqueline, and Kraig Derstler, 2004, Scapular facets of the dorsal ribs of sauropod and neoceratopsian dinosaurs: *Journal of Vertebrate Paleontology*, 24 (Supplement to Number 3), Abstracts of Papers, Sixty-fourth Annual Meeting, p. 80A.

Kraemer, P., and A. Riccardi, 1997, Estratigrafía de la region comprendida entre los lagos Argentino y Viedma (49°, 40'–50° 10' 1st. S), Provincia de Santa Cruz: *Revista de la Asociación Geológica Leopoldensia*, 21, pp. 119–135.

Krantz, Peter M., 1996, Notes on the sedimentary iron ores of Maryland and their dinosaurian fauna: *Maryland Geological Survey Special Publication*, 3, pp. 87–115.

_____, 1998, *Astrodon* rediscovered: America's first sauropod, *in*: Donald L. Wolberg, K. Gittis, S. Miller, and A. Raynor, editors, *The Dinofest Symposium* [abstracts], Presented by The Academy of Natural Sciences of Philadelphia, Pennsylvania, pp. 33–34.

_____, 2004, *Astrodon* rediscovered: America's first sauropod: *The Mosasaur*, 7, pp. 95–103.

Krause, David W., Raymond Robert Rogers, Catherine A. Forster, Joseph H. Hartman, G. A. Buckley, and Scott D. Sampson, 1999, The Late Cretaceous vertebrate fauna of Madagascar: implications for Gondwanan paleobiogeography: *GSA Today*, 9 (8), pp. 1–7.

Kripp, D. von, 1943, Ein Lebenshild von *Pteranodon ingens* auf flugtechnischer Grubdlage: *Nova Acta Leopoldina*, 12 (82), pp. 217–246, Halle.

Ksepka, Daniel T., and Mark A. Norell, 2004, Ornithomimosaur cranial material from Ukhaa Tolgod (Omnogov, Mongolia): *American Museum Novitates*, 3448, pp. 1–4.

Kuban, Glen J., 1989, Color distinctions and other curious features of dinosaur tracks near Glen Rose, Texas, *in*: David D. Gillette and Martin G. Lockley, editors, *Dinosaur Tracks and Traces*. Cambridge: Cambridge University Press, pp. 426–440.

Kuhn, Oskar, 1936, Ornithischia (Stegosauria excludes), *in*: W. Quendstedt, editor, *Fossilium Catalogus, I. Animalia, 78. Junk: 's-Gravenhage, 81 pages.

_____, 1959, Ein neuer Microsaurier aus dem deutschen Rotliegenden: Neus Jahrbuch für Geologie und Paläontologie, Monatshefte, 1959, pp. 424–426.

_____, 1961, Die Familien der rezenten und fossilen Amphibien und Reptilien. Bamberg, Germany: Verlaghaus Meisenbach KG, 79 pages.

_____, 1964, Ornithischia (Supplementum I), in: F. Westpal, editor, Fossilium Catalogus I: Animalia Pars 105. Uitgeverij, 80 pages.

Kukhareva, L. V., and R. K. Ileragimov, 1981, The young mammoth from Magadan, Nauka, Leningrad.

Kundrát, Martin, 2004a, Two morphotypes of the Velociraptor neurocranium: Journal of Morphology, 260 (3), 7th International Congress of Vertebrate Morphology, p. 305.

_____, 2004b, When did theropods become feathered?—evidence for pre-Archaeopteryx feathery appendages: Journal of Experimental Zoology (Mol Dev Evol), 302B, pp. 355–364.

Kundrát, Martin, Arthur R. I. Cruickshank, Terry W. Manning, John Nudds, Kenneth A. Joysey, and Ji Qiang, 2004, Skeletal and dental development of therizinosauroid embryos from China: Journal of Morphology, 260 (3), 7th International Congress of Vertebrate Morphology, p. 305.

Kundrát, Martin, Teresa Maryańska, and Halska Osmólska, 2004, Oviraptorid neurocranium from Mongolia: Journal of Morphology, 260 (3), 7th International Congress of Vertebrate Morphology, p. 305.

Kurochkin, Evgeny N., 1982, Novi otrjad ptizt iz nizhnego mela Mongolii: Dokladi Akademii Nauk SSSR 262. Moscow: Nauka, pp. 452–455.

_____, 1985, A true carnate bird from Lower Cretaceous deposits in Mongolia and other evidence of Early Cretaceous birds in Asia: Cretaceous Research, 6, pp. 271–278.

_____, 1996a, Morphological differences of palaeognathous and neognathous birds, in: D. S. Peters, editor, Proceedings of the 3rd Symposium of the Society of Avian Paleontology and Evolution, Courier Forschungsinstitut Senckenberg, 181, Frankfurt am Main, pp. 79–88.

_____, 1996b, A new enantiornithid of the Mongolian Late Cretaceous and a general appraisal of the infraclass Enantiornithes (Aves): Special Issue. Moscow: Palaeontological Institute, 50 pages.

_____, 1999, The relationships of the Early Cretaceous Ambiortus and Otogornis (Aves: Ambiortiformes), in: Storrs L. Olson, editor, Peter Wellnhofer, Cecile Mourer-Chauvire, David W. Steadman, and Larry D. Martin, associate editors, Avian Paleontology at the Close of the 20th Century: Proceedings of the 4th International Meeting of the Society of Avian Paleontology and Evolution, Washington, D.C., 4–7 June 1996, Smithsonian Contributions to Paleobiology, 89, pp. 275–284.

_____, 2000, Mesozoic birds of Mongolia and the former USSR, in: M. J. Benton, M. A. Shishkin, D. M. Unwin, and E. N. Kurochkin, editors, The Age of Dinosaurs in Russia and Mongolia. Cambridge: Cambridge University Press, pp. 533–559.

Kurochkin, Evgeny N., Gareth J. Dyke, and Alexandr A. Karhu, 2002, A new prebyosornithid bird (Aves, Anseriformes) from the Late Cretaceous of Southern Mongolia: American Museum Novitates, 3386, 11 pages.

Kurzanov, Sergei M. [Mikhailovich], 1972, O polovum dimorphizme protoseratopsov: Palaeontoloicheski Zhurnal, 1, pp. 104–112 (translation, On the sexual dimorphism of protoceratopsians: Paleontological Journal, 1, pp. 91–97, 1972).

_____, 1976a, [Braincase structure of the carnosaur Itemirus gen. nov. and some problems of cranial anatomy of dinosaurs]: Ibid., 3, pp. 127–137 (translation, Ibid., 10, pp. 361–379).

_____, 1976b, A new Late Cretaceous carnosaur from Nogon-Tsav, Mongolia: Soviet-Mongolian Paleontological Expedition, Transactions, 20, pp. 93–104.

Kutter, Martha Middlebrooks, 2003, New material of Zephyrosaurus schaffi (Dinosauria: Ornithischia) from the Cloverly Formation (Aptian–Albian) of Montana: Journal of Vertebrate Paleontology, 23 (Supplement to Number 3), Abstracts of Papers, Sixtythird Annual Meeting, p. 69A.

Lacasa-Ruiz, Antonio, 1985, Nota sobre las plumas fosiles del yacimiento eocretacico de "La Pedrera-Cabrua" en la Sierra del Montsec (Prov. Lerida, España): Lierda, 47, pp. 227–238.

_____, 1989, An Early Cretaceous bird from Montsec Mountain (Leida, Spain): Terra Nova, 1 (1), pp. 45–46.

Lacovara, Kenneth, Jerald Harris, Matthew C. Lamanna, Fernando E. Novas, Rúben Martinez, and Alfredo Ambrosio, 2004, An enormous sauropod from the Maastrichtian Pari Aike Formation of southernmost Patagonia: Journal of Vertebrate Paleontology, 24 (Supplement to Number 3), Abstracts of Papers, Sixty-fourth Annual Meeting, p. 81A.

Lamanna, Matthew C., Rubén D. Martinez, Marcelo Luna, Gabriel Casal, Lucio Ibiricu, and Edmondo Ivany, 2004, New specimens of the problematic large theropod dinosaur Megaraptor from the Late Cretaceous of central Patagonia: Journal of Vertebrate Paleontology, 24 (Supplement to Number 3), Abstracts of Papers, Sixtyfourth Annual Meeting, pp. 81A–82A.

Lamanna, Matthew C., Rubén D. Martinez, and Joshua B. Smith, 2002, A definitive abelisaurid theropod dinosaur from the early Late Cretaceous of Patagonia: Journal of Vertebrate Paleontology, 22 (1), pp. 58–69.

Lamanna, Matthew C., Joshua B. Smith, Peter Dodson, and Youry S. Attia, 2004, From dinosaurs to dyrosaurids (Crocodyliformes): removal of the post-Cenomanian (Late Cretaceous) record of Ornithischia from Africa: Journal of Vertebrate Paleontology, 24 (3), pp. 764–768.

Lambrecht, Kàlmàn, 1929, Neogaeornis wetzeli, n. g., n. s., der Kreidevogel der Südilchen Hemisphäre: Palaeontologische Zeitschrift, 11, pp. 121–129.

_____, 1931, Gallornis straeleni, n. g. n. sp., ein Kreidevogel aus Frankreich: Bulletin du Musée Royal d'Histories Naturelle de Belgique, 7, pp. 1–6.

_____, 1933, Handbuch der Palaeornithologie, 19, 1024 pages.

Lambe, Lawrence M., 1902, On vertebra of the Mid-Cretaceous of the North West Territory. 2. New genera and species from the Belly River Series (Mid-Cretaceous): Geological Survey of Canada, Contributions to Canadian Paleontology, 3, part 2, pp. 23–81.

_____, 1917, The Cretaceous theropodous dinosaur Gorgosaurus: Geological Series, Canada Department of Mines, Geological Survey Memoir, 100 (83), pp. 1–84.

_____, 1918, The Cretaceous genus Stegoceras, typifying a new family referred provisionally to the Stegosauria: Transactions of the Royal Society of Canada, series 3, 12, pp. 23–36.

Langer, Max Cardoso, 2002, Is Saturnalia tupinquim really a sauropodomorph?, in: Sociedad Paleontologica de Chile, SPACH (ed.), Resumenes del Primer Congreso Lationoamericano de Paleontologia de Vertebrados, pp. 38–39, Santiago de Chile.

_____, 2003, The pelvic and hind limb anatomy of the stem-sauropodomorph Saturnalia tupiniquim (Late Triassic, Brazil): PaleoBios, 23 (2), pp. 1–40.

_____, 2004, Basal Saurischia, in: David B. Weishampel, Peter Dodson, and Halszka Osmólska, editors, The Dinosauria (second edition). Berkeley and Los Angeles: University of California Press, pp. 25–46.

Langer, Max C. [Cardoso], Fernando Abdala, Martha Richter, and Michael J. Benton, 1999, A sauropodomorph dinosaur from the Upper Triassic (Carnian) of southern Brazil: Comtes Rendu des Séances de l'Académie des Sciences, Paris, de la Terre et des Planètes, 329, pp. 511–517.

Langston, Wann, Jr., 1960, The vertebrate fauna of the Selma Formation of Alabama, Part VI, The dinosaurs: Fieldiana: Geological Memoirs, 3 (6), pp. 313–363.

_____, 1974, Non-mammalian Comamchean tetrapods: Geoscience and Man, 8, pp. 77–102.

Lapparent, Albert F. de, 1947, Les dinosauriens du Crétace supérieur du Midi de France: Mémoires de la Société Géologique de France (Nat. Sci.), 56, pp. 1–54.

_____, 1955, Etude paléontologique des vertébrés du Jurassique d'El Mers (Moyen Atlas): Notes et Mémoires du Service Géologique du Maroc, 124, pp. 1–36.

_____, 1960, De les dinosauriens du "Continental intercalaire" du Sahara central: Mémoires de la Société Géologique de France (Nouvelle Série), 88A, pp. 1–57.

Lapparent, Albert F. de, and Georges Zbyszewski, 1957, Les dinosauriens du Portugal: Memoires des Services géologiques du Portugal, 2, pp. 1–63.

Larson, Peter L., 2007, Tyrannosaurus sex, in: Peter L. Larson, editor, The Rex Files. Hill

Bibliography

City, SD: Black Hills Institute of Geological Research, unpaginated.

Larson, Peter L., Dallas Evans, and Christopher Ott, 2004, Triceresies — a bold new look at *Triceratops*: *Journal of Vertebrate Paleontology*, 24 (Supplement to Number 3), Abstracts of Papers, Sixty-fourth Annual Meeting, p. 82A.

Larson, Robert, Ron Nellermoe, and Rebecca Gould, 2003, A study of theropod teeth from a low-species-density hadrosaur bone bed in the lower Hell Creek Formation in Corson Co., S.D.: *Journal of Vertebrate Paleontology*, 23 (Supplement to Number 3), Abstracts of Papers, Sixty-third Annual Meeting, pp. 70A–71A.

Larsonneur, C., and Albert F. de Lapparent, 1966, Un dinosaurien carnivore, *Halticosaurus*, dans le Rhétien d'Airel (Manche): *Bulletin of the Linnean Society, Normandie*, 10 (70), pp. 108–117.

Lavocat, René, 1954, Sur les dinosauriens du Continental Intercalaire des Kem-Kem de la Daoura: *Comptes Dendus de la Dix-Neuvième Session, Congrès Géologique International 21, Paris*.

Lawson, Douglas A., 1975a, Pterosaur from the latest Cretaceous of West Texas: discovery of the largest flying creature: *Science*, 187, pp. 947–948.

_____, 1975b, "Could pterosaurs fly?," response to author Crawford H. Greenwalt: *Ibid.*, 188, pp. 676–677.

Le Loeuff, Jean, 1993, European titanosaurids: *Revue de Paléo biolie, Vol. Spéc*, 7, pp. 105–117.

_____, 1995, *Ampelosaurus atacis* (nov. gen., nov. sp.), un nouveau Titanosauridae (Dinosauria, Sauropoda) du Crétacé supérieur de la Haute Vallée de l'Aude (France): *Académie des Sciences de Paris*, 321 (série II a), pp. 693–699.

Le Loeuff, Jean, and Éric Buffetaut, 1991, *Tarascosaurus salluvicus* nov. gen., nov. spéc., dinosaure théropode du Crétacé supéreur du sud de la France: *Géobios*, 25 (5), pp. 585–594.

Le Loeuff, Jean, Éric Buffetaut, L. Cavin, M. Martin, Valérie Martin, and H. Tong 1994, An armoured titanosaurid sauropod from the Late Cretaceous of Southern France and the occurrence of osteoderms in the Titanosauroidea: *Gaia*, 10, pp. 155–159.

Le Loeuff, Jean, Éric Buffetaut, E. Mechin, and A. Mechin-Salessy, 1992, The first record of dromaeosaurid dinosaurs (Saurischia, Theropoda) in the Maastrichtian of southern Europe: palaeobiogeographical implications: *Bulletin de la Société Géologique de France*, 163, pp. 337–343.

Leal, Luciano Artemio, and Sergio Alex Kugland Azevedo, 2003, A preliminary Prosauropoda phylogeny with comments on Brazilian Sauropodomorpha: *Journal of Vertebrate Paleontology*, 23 (Supplement to Number 3), Abstracts of Papers, Sixty-third Annual Meeting, p. 71A.

Leanza, Héctor, Sebastián Apesteguia, Fernando E. Novas, and Marcelo S. de la Fuente, 2004, Cretaceous terrestrial beds from the Neuquén Basin (Argentina) and their tetrapod assemblages: *Cretaceous Research*, 25, pp. 61–87.

Leanza, Héctor, and Carlos A. Hugo, 2001, Cretaceous red beds from southern Neuquén Basin (Argentina): age, distribution and stratigraphic discontinuities: *Asociación Paleontológical Argentina*, Publicatión Especial 7, VII International Symposium on Mesozoic Terrestrial Ecosystems, Buenos Aires, 30-6-2001, pp. 117–122.

Lee, Andrew, 2004, Ontogenetic histology of *Centrosaurus*: testing the relationship between limb bone form and function: *Journal of Vertebrate Paleontology*, 24 (Supplement to Number 3), Abstracts of Papers, Sixty-fourth Annual Meeting, p. 82A.

Lee, M. S. Y., 1996, Correlated progression and the origin of turtles: *Nature*, 379, pp. 811–815.

Lee, Yuong-Nam, 1994, The Early Cretaceous pterodactyloid pterosaur *Coloborhynchus* from North America: *Paleontology*, 37 (4), pp. 755–763.

_____, 1997, Bird and dinosaur footprints in the Woodbine Formation (Cenomanian), Texas: *Cretaceous Research*, 18, pp. 849–864.

Lehman, Thomas M., 1989, *Chasmosaurus mariscalensis*, sp. nov., a new ceratopsian dinosaur from Texas: *Journal of Vertebrate Paleontology*, 9 (2), pp. 137–162.

_____, 1990, The ceratopsian subfamily Chasmosaurinae: sexual dimorphism and systematics, *in*: Kenneth Carpenter and Philip J. Currie, editors, *Dinosaur Systematics: Approaches and Perspectives*. Cambridge and New York: Cambridge University Press, pp. 211–229.

Lehman, Thomas M., and Kenneth Carpenter, 1990, A partial skeleton of the tyrannosaurid dinosaur *Aublysodon* from the Upper Cretaceous of New Mexico: *Journal of Paleontology*, 64, pp. 1026–1032.

Leidy, Joseph, 1859, *Hadrosaurus foulkii*, a new saurian from the Cretaceous of New Jersey, related to the *Iguanodon*: *Proceedings of the Academy of Natural Sciences of Philadelphia*, 10, pp. 213–218.

_____, 1865, Memoir on the extinct reptiles of the Cretaceous Formations of the United States: *Smithsonian Contributions to Knowledge*, 14 (6), pp. 1–135.

_____, 1868, Remarks on a jaw fragment of *Megalosaurus*: *Proceedings of the Academy of Natural Sciences of Philadelphia*, 20, pp. 197–200.

Leonardi, Giuseppe, 1987, *Glossary and Manual of Tetrapod Footprint Paleoichnology*. Brazil: Departmento Nacional da Prodaucão Mineral, 75 pages.

Leonardi, Giuseppe, and G. Borgomanero, 1985, *Cearodactylus atrox* nov. gen., nov. sp.: Novo Pterosauria (Pterodactyloidea) da Chapado do Araripe, Brasil: *D.N.P.M., Coletana de trabalhos Paleontologicos, Séria Geológica*, 27, pp. 75–80, Brazil.

Lim, Jong-Deock, Larry D. Martin, Zonghe Zhou, Kwang-Seok Baek, and Seong-Young Yang, 2002, The significance of Early Cretaceous bird tracks, *in*: Zonghe Zhou and Fucheng Zhang, editors, *Proceedings of the 5th Symposium of the Society of Avian Paleontology and Evolution*. Beijing: Science Press, pp. 157–163.

Lingham-Soliar, Theagarten, 2001, The icthyosaur integument: skin fibers, a means for a strong, flexible and smooth skin: *Lethaia*, 34, pp. 287–302.

_____, 2003a, A functional and biomechanical perspective of locomotion in sauropod dinosaurs — or why sauropods did not waddle: *Neus Jahrbuch für Geologie und Paläontologie, Abhandlungen*, 229 (1), pp. 19–30.

_____, 2003b, Evolution of birds: icthyosaur integumental fibers conform to dromaeosaur protofeathers: *Naturwissechaften*, 90, pp. 428–432.

Lipkin, Christine, and Paul C. Sereno, 2004, The furcula in *Tyrannosaurus rex*: *Journal of Vertebrate Paleontology*, 24 (Supplement to Number 3), Abstracts of Papers, Sixty-fourth Annual Meeting, pp. 83A–84A.

Lisak, Francis J., 1980, *Allosaurus fragilis* from the Late Jurassic of southeastern Utah: MS thesis, Brigham Young University, Department of Geology, Provo, Utah.

Liu, Jun, 2004, Phylogeny of Ornithischia: *Journal of Vertebrate Paleontology*, 24 (Supplement to Number 3), Abstracts of Papers, Sixty-fourth Annual Meeting, p. 84A.

Liu, Y., and Wang Z., 1990, Uppermost Cretaceous and lowest Tertiary strata in the Nanxiong basin of Guangdong with reference to their petrographic characters and sedimentary environment: *Palaeontologia Cathayana*, 5, pp. 529–310.

Lockley, Martin G., 1986, A guide to dinosaur tracksites of the Colorado Plateau and American southwest: *University of Colorado Denver Geological Department Magazines Special Issue*, 1, pp. 1–56.

Lockley, Martin G., T. J. Logue, José J. Moratella, Adrian P. Hunt, Schultz and Robinson, 1995, The fossil trackway *Pteraichnus* is pterosaurian, not crocodilian: implications for the global distribution of pterosaur tracks: *Ichnos*, 4, pp. 7–20.

Lockley, Martin G., and Emma C. Rainforth, 2002, the Track Record of Mesozoic birds and pterosaurs, *in*: Luis M. Chiappe and Lawrence M. Witmer, editors, *Mesozoic Birds: Above the Heads of Dinosaurs*. Berkeley and Los Angeles: University of California Press, pp. 405–418.

Lockley, Martin G., and Joanna L. Wright, 2003, Pterosaur swim tracks and other ichnological evidence of behavior and ecology: *in*: Éric Buffetaut and Jean-Michel Mazin, editors, *Evolution and Palaeobiology of Pterosaurs*. London: The Geological Society, Special Publications, 217, pp. 297–213.

Loewen, Mark, Scott D. Sampson, Matthew T. Carrano, and Daniel J. Chure, 2003, Morphology, taxonomy, and stratigraphy of *Allosaurus* from the Upper Jurassic Morrison Formation: *Journal of Vertebrate Paleontology*, 23 (Supplement to Number 3), Abstracts of Papers, Sixty-third Annual Meeting, p. 72A.

Longman, Heber A., 1933, A new dinosaur from the Queensland Cretaceous: *Memoirs of the Queensland Museum*, 10, pp. 131–141.

Lovelace, David, 2004, Taphonomy and pale-oenvironment of a Late Jurassic dinosaur locality in the Morrison Formation of east-central Wyoming: *Journal of Vertebrate Paleontology*, 24 (Supplement to Number 3), Abstracts of Papers, Sixty-fourth Annual Meeting, p. 85A.

Lovelace, David, William R. Wahl, and Scott A. Hartman, 2003, Evidence for costal pneumaticity in a diplodocid dinosaur (*Supersaurus vivianae*): *Journal of Vertebrate Paleontology*, 23 (Supplement to Number 3), Abstracts of Papers, Sixty-third Annual Meeting, p. 73A.

Lü, Jun-Chang, 2003, A new pterosaur: *Beipiaopterus chenianus*, gen. et sp. nov. (Reptilia: Pterosauria) from western Liaoning Province of China: *Memoir of the Fukui Prefectural Museum*, 2, pp. 153–160.

Lü, Jun-Chang, and Bookun Zhang, 2003, A new oviraptorid dinosaur from the Late Cretaceous of Shixin, Nanxiong Basin of Guangdong Province, southern China: *Journal of Vertebrate Paleontology*, 23 (Supplement to Number 3), Abstracts of Papers, Sixty-third Annual Meeting, p. 73A.

Lü Junchang and Ji Qiang, 2005, A new ornithocheirid from the Early Cretaceous of Liaoning Province, China: *Acta Geologica Sinica*, 79 (2), pp. 157–163.

Lucas, A. M., and P. R. Stettenheim, 1972, *Avian Anatomy: Integument*, Agricultural Handbook 362. Washington, D.C.: U.S. Government Printing Office.

Lucas, F. A., 1903, A skeleton of *Hesperornis*: *Smithsonian Miscellaneous Collections*, 45, p. 95.

Lucas, Spencer G., 1996, The thyreophoran dinosaur *Scelidosaurus* from the Lower Jurassic Lufeng Formation, Yinnan, China, *in*: Michael Morales, editor, *Museum of Northern Arizona Bulletin*, 60, pp. 81–85.

_____, 1998, Global Triassic tetrapod diversity and biochronology: *Palaeogeography, Palaeoclimatology, Palaeoecology*, 143, pp. 347–384.

Lucas, Spencer G., and Adrian P. Hunt, 1989, *Alamosaurus* and the sauropod hiatus in the Cretaceous of the North American western interior: *Geological Society of America Special Paper*, 238, pp. 75–78.

Lull, Richard Swann, 1933, A revision of the Ceratopsia or horned dinosaurs: *Peabody Museum of Natural History Memoirs*, 3 (3), pp. 1–175.

Lull, Richard Swann, and Nelda E. Wright, 1942, The hadrosaurian dinosaurs of North America: *Geological Society of America Special Paper* 40, xii, 242 pages.

Lydekker, Richard, 1877, Notices of new and other Vertebrata from Indian Tertiary and Secondary rocks: *Records of the Geological Society of India*, 10, pp. 30–43.

_____, 1879, Indian pre–Tertiary Vertebrata part 3, fossil Reptilia and Batrachia: *Paleontologica Indica*, series 4, 1 (3), pp. 1–36.

_____, 1887, On certain dinosaurian vertebrae from the Cretaceous of India and the Isle of Wight: *Quarterly Journal of the Geological Society of London*, 43, pp. 157–160.

_____, 1888, *Catalogue of Fossil Reptilia and Amphibia in the British Museum (Natural History), Part I, Containing the orders Ornithosauria, Crocodilia, Dinosauria, Squamata, Rhynchocephalia, and Proterosauria*. London: British Museum (Natural History), 309 pages.

_____, 1890, _____, *Pt. IV*. London: Taylor and Francis, xxiii, 295 pages.

_____, 1893, The dinosaurs of Patagonia: *Museo de la Plata; Anales*, 2.

Lyell, Charles, 1838, *Elements of Geology*. London: John Murray, 543 pages.

Lyson, Tyler, H. Douglas Hanks, and Emily Tremain, 2003, New skin structures from a juvenile *Edmontosaurus* from the Late Cretaceous of North Dakota: *Journal of Vertebrate Paleontology*, 23 (Supplement to Number 3), Abstracts of Papers, Sixty-third Annual Meeting, p. 74A.

Mader, Bryn J., and Robert L. Bradley, 1989, A redescription and revised diagnosis of the syntypes of the Mongolian tyrannosaur *Alectrosaurus olseni*: *Journal of Vertebrate Paleontology*, 9 (1), pp. 41–55.

Mader, Bryn J., and Alexander W. A. Kellner, 1999, A new anhanguerid pterosaur from the Cretaceous of Morocco: *Boletim do Museum Nacional, Geologia*, 45, pp. 1–11.

Madsen, James J., Jr., 1974, A new theropod dinosaur from the Upper Jurassic of Utah: *Journal of Paleontology*, 48 (1), pp. 27–31.

_____, 1976, *Allosaurus fragilis*: a revised Osteology: *Utah Geological and Mineral Survey, a division of the Utah Department of Natural Resources*, Bulletin 109, xii, 163 pages.

Main, Derek, and Anthony Fiorillo, 2003, Report of new Cenomanian hadrosaur (Dinosauria: Ornithischia) postcrania from the Woodbine Formation of north central Texas: *Journal of Vertebrate Paleontology*, 23 (Supplement to Number 3), Abstracts of Papers, Sixty-third Annual Meeting, p. 75A.

Maisch, Michael W., and Andreas T. Matzke, 2003, Theropods (Dinosauria, Saurischia) from the Middle Jurassic Toutunhe Formation of the Southern Junggar Basin, NW China: *Paläontologische Zeitschrift*, 77 (2), pp. 281–292.

Maisey, J. G., 1993, Tectonics, the Santana Lagerstatten, and the implications for late Gondwanan biogeography, *in*: P. Galdblatt, editor, *Biological Relationships between Africa and South America*. New Haven, CT: Yale University Press, pp. 435–454.

Maisch, Michael W., Andreas T. Matzke, and Ge Sun, 2004, A new dsungaripteroid pterosaur from the Lower Cretaceous of the southern Junggar Basin, north-west China: *Cretaceous Research*, 25, pp. 625–634.

Makovicky, Peter J., 1995, Phylogenetic aspects of the vertebral morphology of Coelurosauria (Dinosauria: Theropoda). MSc thesis, University of Cambridge.

_____, 1997, Postcranial axial skeleton, comparative anatomy, *in*: Philip J. Currie and Kevin Padian, editors, *Encyclopedia of Dinosaurs*. San Diego: Academic Press, pp. 579–590.

_____, 2001, A *Montanoceratops cerorhynchus* (Dinosauria: Ceratopsia) braincase from the Horseshoe Canyon Formation of Alberta: *in*: Darren Tanke and Kenneth Carpenter, editors, *Mesozoic Vertebrate Life: New Research Inspired by the Paleontology of Philip J. Currie*. Bloomington and Indianapolis: Indiana University Press, pp. 243–262.

_____, 2004, Basal ceratopsians from China and Mongolia with a reappraisal of basal ceratopsian relationships: *Journal of Vertebrate Paleontology*, 24 (Supplement to Number 3), Abstracts of Papers, Sixty-fourth Annual Meeting, p. 88A.

Makovicky, Peter J., Yoshitsugu Kobayashi, and Philip J. Currie, 2004, Ornithomimosauria, *in*: David B. Weishampel, Peter Dodson, and Halszka Osmólska, editors, *The Dinosauria*, second edition. Berkeley: University of California Press, pp. 137–150.

Makovicky, Peter J., and Mark A. Norell, 1998, A partial ornithomimid braincase from Ukhaa Tolgod (Upper Cretaceous, Mongolia): *American Museum Novitates*, p. 60A.

_____, 2004, Troodontidae, *in*: David B. Weishampel, Peter Dodson, and Halszka Osmólska, editors, *The Dinosauria*, second edition. Berkeley: University of California Press, pp. 184–195.

Makovicky, Peter J., Mark A. Norell, James M. Clark, and Timothy Rowe, 2003, Osteology and relationships of *Byronosaurus jaffei* (Theropoda: Troodontidae): *American Museum Novitates*, 3402, 32 pages.

Makovicky, Peter J., and Hans-Dieter Sues, 1998, Anatomy and phylogenic relationships of the theropod dinosaur *Microvenator celer* from the Lower Cretaceous of Montana: *American Museum Novitates*, 3240, pp. 1–26.

Maleev, Evgeny [Eugene] Alexandrovich, 1955*a*, Gigantskiye Khishchnye Dinosavri Mongoll [Giant carnivorous dinosaurs from the Upper Cretaceous of Mongolia]: *Dokladi Akademii Nauk S.S.S.R.*, 104 (4), 104 (4), pp. 779–782.

_____, 1955*b*, [New carnivorous dinosaurs from the Upper Cretaceous of Mongolia: *Ibid.*, 104 (5), pp. 779–782.

_____, 1955*c*, [Carnivorous dinosaurs Mongolia]: *Piroda*, June, pp. 112–115.

_____, 1974, [Gigantic carnosaurs of the family Tyrannosauridae]: *Trudy Somestnaya Sovetsko-Mongol'skaya Paleontologischeskaya Ekspeditsiya* [*Transactions of the Joint Soviet-Mongolian Paleontological Expedition*], 1: pp. 32–191.

Manabe, Makoto, 1999, The early evolution of the Tyrannosauridae in Asia: *Journal of Paleontology*, 73 (6), pp. 1176–1178.

Manabe Makoto, Hasegawa Yoshikazu, and Takahashi Toshinobu, 2003, A hadrosaurid vertebra from the Ashizawa Formation, Futaba Group, Fukushima, Japan: *Bulletin of the Gunma Museum of Natural History*, 7, pp. 7–10.

Mantell, Gideon Algernon, 1833, *Geology of the South East of England*. London, 19, 415 pages.

_____, 1850, On the *Pelorosaurus*: an undescribed gigantic terrestrial reptile whose remains are associated with those of the *Iguanodon* and other saurians in the strata of Tilgate Forest, in Sussex: *Philosophical Transactions of the Royal Society of London*, 104, pp. 379–390.

Markevich, V. S., and Y. V. Bugdaeva, 1997, Flora and correlation of layers with dinosaur fossil remains in Russia's Far East: *Tikhookeanskaya Geologia*, 16, pp. 114–124.

_____, 2001, The Maastrichtian flora and dinosaurs of the Russian Far East, *in*: D. K. Goodman and R. T. Clarke, editors, *Proceedings of the IX International Palynological Congress, Houston, Texas, U.S.A., 1996*. American Association of Stratigraphic Palynologists Foundation, pp. 139–148.

Marsh, Othniel Charles, 1870a, Remarks on *Laornis edvadsianus, Palaeotringa littoralis, P. vertus, Telmatornis priscus, T. affinis, Grus haydeni*, and *Puffinus conradii*: *Proceedings of the Academy of Natural Sciences of Philadelphia*, 1070, pp. 5–6.

_____, 1870b, Notice of some fossil birds, from the Cretaceous and Tertiary Formations of the United States: *American Journal of Science*, Series 3, 49, pp. 205–217.

_____, 1872a, Discovery of additional remains of Pterosauria, with descriptions of two new species: *Ibid.*, Series 3, 3, pp. 241–248.

_____, 1872b, Preliminary description of *Hesperornis regalis*, with notices of four other new species of Cretaceous birds: *Ibid.*, Series 3, 3, pp. 360–365.

_____, 1872c, Notice of a new and remarkable fossil bird: *Ibid.*, Series 3, 4.

_____, 1873a, Notice of a new species of *Ichthyornis*: *Ibid.*, Series 3, p. 74.

_____, 1873b, On a new subclass of fossil birds (Odontornithes): *Ibid.*, Series 3, 5, pp. 161–167.

_____, 1876a, Principal characters of American pterodactyls: *Ibid.*, series 3, 12, pp. 479–480.

_____, 1876b, Notice of a new sub-order of Pterosauria: *Ibid.*, Series 3, 11, pp. 507–509.

_____, 1876c, Notice of new Odontornithes: *Ibid.*, Series 3, 11 (66), pp. 509–511.

_____, 1877a, Characters of the Odontornithes, with notice of a new allied genus: *Ibid.*, Series 3, 14, pp. 85–86.

_____, 1877b, Notice on new dinosaurian reptiles from the Jurassic formation: *Ibid.*, Series 3, 14 (53), pp. 514–516.

_____, 1878, Notes on American pterodactyls: *Ibid.*, Series 3, 21, pp. 342–343.

_____, 1880, Odontornithes: a monograph on the extinct toothed birds of North America: *Report of the United States Geological Exploration of the Fortieth Parallel*, 7, pp. 1–201.

_____, 1881, Note on American pterodactyls: *American Journal of Earth Science*, Series 3, 21, pp. 342–343.

_____, 1882b, Classification of the Dinosauria: *Ibid.*, Series 3, 23, pp. 81–86.

_____, 1882b, The wings of pterodactyls: *Ibid.*, Series 3, 23, pp. 251–256.

_____, 1883, Principal characters of American Jurassic dinosaurs. VI. Restoration of *Brontosaurus*: *Ibid.*, Series 3, 26, pp. 81–85.

_____, 1885, Names of extinct reptiles: *Ibid.*, 29, p. 169.

_____, 1888a, Notice of a new genus of Sauropoda and other dinosaurs from the Patomac Formation: *Ibid.*, Third Series, 35, pp. 89–94.

_____, 1888b, Comparison of the principal forms of Dinosaurs of Europe and America: *Reports of the British Association for the Advancement of Science*, 63, pp. 323–336.

_____, 1889, Notice on new American Dinosauria: *American Journal of Science*, Series 3, 38, pp. 501–506.

_____, 1891, Notice of new vertebrate fossils: *Ibid.*, 42, pp. 265–269.

_____, 1892, Notes on Mesozoic vertebrate fossils: *Ibid.*, 55, pp. 171–175.

_____, 1893, A new Cretaceous bird allied to *Hesperornis*: *Ibid.*, Series 3, 45 (265), pp, 81–82.

_____, 1896, The Dinosaurs of North America: *Sixteenth Annual Report of the U.S. Geological Survey*, 1, pp. 133–415.

Martill, David M., Eberhard Frey, G. Chong-Diaz, and M. Bell, 2000, Reinterpretation of a Chilean pterosaur and the occurrence of Dsungaripteridae in South America: *Geological Magazine*, 137 (1), pp. 19–25.

Martill, David M., Eberhard Frey, Hans-Dieter Sues, and Arthur R. I. Cruickshank, 2000, Skeletal remains of a small theropod dinosaur with associated soft structures from the Lower Cretaceous Santana Formation of northeastern Brazil: *Canadian Journal of Earth Sciences*, 37, pp. 891–900.

Martill, David M., and Darren Naish, 2001, editors, Dinosaurs of the Isle of Wight, *in*: *Field Guide to Fossils*, 10, The Palaeontological Association, London, 433 pages.

Martill, David M., and David M. Unwin, 1989, Exceptionally well preserved pterosaur wing membrane from the Cretaceous of Brazil: *Nature*, 340, pp. 138–140.

Martill, David M., and Philip Wilby, 1993, *in*: David M. Martill, editor, *Fossils of the Santana and Crato Formations, Brazil*. London: The Palaeontological Association Field Guides to Fossils, 5, pp. 20–50.

Martin, Larry D., 1983, The origin and radiation of birds, *in*: Alan H. Brush and George A. Clark, Jr., *Perspectives in Ornithology*. Cambridge, England: Cambridge University Press, pp. 291–338.

_____, 1984, A new hesperornithid and the relationships of the Mesozoic birds: *Transactions of the Kansas Academy of Science*, 87 (3–4), pp. 141–150.

_____, 1995, The Enantiornithes: terrestrial birds of Cretaceous in avian evolution: *in*: D. S. Peters, editor, *Proceedings of the 3rd Symposium of the Society of Avian Paleontology and Evolution, Courier Forschungsinstitut Senckenberg*, 181, Frankfurt am Main, pp. 23–36.

Martin, Larry D, and Stephen A. Czerkas, 2000, The fossil record of feather evolution in the Mesozoic: *American Zoologist*, 40, pp. 687–694.

Martin, Larry D., and Jong-Deock Lim, 2002, New information on the hesperornithiform radiation, *in*: Zonghe Zhou and Fucheng Zhang, editors, *Proceedings of the 5th Symposium of the Society of Avian Paleontology and Evolution*. Beijing: Science Press, pp. 165–174.

Martin, Larry D., and J. D. Stewart, 1999, Implantation and replacement of bird teeth, *in*: Storrs L. Olson, editor, Peter Wellnhofer, Cecile Mourer-Chauvire, David W. Steadman, and Larry D. Martin, associate editors, *Avian Paleontology at the Close of the 20th Century: Proceedings of the 4th International Meeting of the Society of Avian Paleontology and Evolution, Washington, D.C., 4–7 June 1996, Smithsonian Contributions to Paleobiology*, 89, pp. 295–300.

Martin, Larry D., J. D. Stewart, and K. N. Whetstone, 1980, The origin of birds: structure of the tarsus and the teeth: *The Auk*, 97, pp. 86–93.

Martin, Larry D., and James Tate, Jr., 1976, The skeleton of *Baptornis advenus* (Aves: Hesperornithiformes): *Smithsonian Contributions to Paleontology*, 27, pp. 35–73.

Martin, Valerie, Éric Buffetaut, and Varavudh Suteethorn, 1994, A new genus of sauropod dinosaur from the Sao Khua Formation (Late Jurassic to Early Cretaceous) of northeastern Thailand: *Comptes Rendus de l'Académie des Sciences de Paris*, 319 (II), pp. 125–132.

Martin, Valérie, Varavudh Suteethorn, and Éric Buffetaut, 1999, Description of the type and referred material of *Phuwiangosaurus sirindhornae* Martin, Buffetaut and Suteethorn, 1994, a sauropod from the Lower Cretaceous of Thailand: *Oryctos*, 2, pp. 39–91.

Martinez, Ricardo, Oscar Alcober, Eliana Fernandez, Maria Trotteyn, Carina Colombi, and Guillermo Heredia, 2004, A new prosauropod dinosaur from the Quebrada del Barro Formation (Upper Triassic?), Marayes Basin, northwestern Argentina: *Journal of Vertebrate Paleontology*, 24 (Supplement to Number 3), Abstracts of Papers, Sixty-fourth Annual Meeting, p. 89A.

Martínez, Rubén D., 1998, An articulated skull and neck of Sauropoda (Dinosauria: Saurischia) from the Upper Cretaceous of Central Patagonia, Argentina: *Journal of Vertebrate Paleontology*, 18 (Supplement to Number 3), Abstracts of Papers, Fifty-eighth Annual Meeting, p. 61A.

_____, 1998b, *Notohypsilophodon comodorensis* gen. et sp. nov. un Hypsilophodontidae (Ornithischia: Ornithopoda) del Cretaceo Superior de Chubut, Patagonia Central, Argentina: *Acta Geologica Leopoldensia*, 21 (46/47), pp. 119–135.

Martinez, Rúben, Gabriel Casal, Marcelo Luna, Lucio Ibiricu, Sonia Cardozo, and Matthew C. Lamanna, 2004, Last of an ancient lineage: remains of the youngest and most austral indisputable diplodocoid (Dinosauria: Sauropoda) ever recorded, from the Upper Cretaceous Bajo Barreal Formation of central Patagonia: *Journal of Vertebrate Paleontology*, 24 (Supplement to Number 3), Abstracts of Papers, Sixty-fourth Annual Meeting, p. 89A.

Martínez, Rubén D., Olga Giménez, Jorge

Rodríguez, and Marcelo Luna, 1988, A Patagonian discovery: *Archosaurian Articulations*, 3, pp. 23–24.

_____, 1989, Un titanosaurio articulado del genero *Epachthosaurus*, de la Formacíon Bajo Barreal, Cretacico del Chubut: *Ameghinana*, 25, p. 246.

Martínez, Rubén D., Olga Giménez, Jorge Rodríguez, Marcelo Luna, and Matthew C. Lamanna, 2004, An articulated specimen of the basal titanosaurian (Dinosauria: Sauropoda) *Epachthosaurus sciuttoi* from the early Late Cretaceous Bajo Barreal Formation of Chubut Province, Argentina: *Journal of Vertebrate Paleontology*, 24 (1), pp. 107–120.

Martins Neto, R. G., 1986, *Pricesaurus megalodon* nov. gen. nov. sp. (Pterosauria, Pterodactyloidea), Cretaceo Inferior, chapada do Araripe (NE-Brasil): *Suplem. Soced. Brasil. para o Progresso da Ciên e Cultura*, 38, p. 757.

Maryańska, Teresa, 1977, Ankylosauridae (Dinosauria) from Mongolia: *Palaeontologica Polonica*, 37, pp. 85–151.

_____, 1990, Pachycephalosauria, *in*: Philip J. Currie and Kevin Padian, editors, *Encyclopedia of Dinosaurs*. San Diego: Academic Press, pp. 564–577.

Maryańska, Teresa, Ralph E. Chapman, and David B. Weishampel, 2004, Pachycephalosauria, *in*: David B. Weishampel, Peter Dodson, and Halszka Osmólska, editors, *The Dinosauria* (second edition). Berkeley and Los Angeles: University of California Press, pp. 464–477.

Maryańska, Teresa, and Halszka Osmólska, 1974, Results of the Polish-Mongolian Palaeontological Expedition. Part V. Pachycephalosauria, a new suborder of ornithischian dinosaurs: *Acta Palaeontologia Polonica*, 30, pp. 45–102.

_____, 1975, Results of the Polish-Mongolian Palaeontological Expedition. Part VI. Protoceratopsidae (Dinosauria) of Asia: *Ibid.*, 33, pp. 133–182.

_____, 1981, Cranial anatomy of *Saurolophus angustirostris* with comments on the Asian Hadrosauridae (Dinosauria): *Ibid.*, 42, pp. 5–24.

Maryańska, Teresa, Halszka Osmólska, and Mieczyslaw Wolson, 2002, Avialan status for Oviraptorosauria: *Acta Palaeontologica Polonica*, 47 (1), pp. 97–116.

Mateus, Octávio, Thomas Laven, and Nils Knotschke, 2004, A dwarf between giants? A new Late Jurassic sauropod from Germany: *Journal of Vertebrate Paleontology*, 24 (Supplement to Number 3), Abstracts of Papers, Sixty-fourth Annual Meeting, p. 90A.

Matheron, Philippe, 1869, Notice sur les reptiles fossiles des dépôts fluvio-lacustres crétacés du bassin à lignite de Fuveau: *Mémoires de l'Académie des sciences, belles-lettres et arts de Marseille*, pp. 345–379.

Mathur, U. B., and S. C. Pant, 1986, Sauropod dinosaur humeri from Lameta Group (Upper Cretaceous) of Kheda district, Gujarat: *Journal of the Geological Society of India*, 29, pp. 554–566.

Mathur, U. B., and S. Srivastava, 1987, Dinosaur teeth from Lameta Group (Upper Cretaceous) of Kheda District, Gujarat: *Journal of the Geological Society of India*, 29, pp. 554–566.

Matley, Charles Alfred, On the stratigraphy, fossils and geological relationships of the Lameta Beds of Jubbulpore: *Records of the Geological Society of India*, 53, pp. 142–169.

_____, 1923, Note on an armoured dinosaur from the Lameta beds of Jubbulpore: *Records of the Geological Survey of India*, 55, pp. 105–109.

Matsukawa, M., 1983, Stratigraphy and sedimentary environments of the Sanchu Cretaceous, Japan: *Memoirs of Ehime University, Natural Sciences*, Series D, 4 (4), pp. 1–50.

Matsukawa, M., and I. Obata, 1994, Dinosaurs and sedimentary environments in the Japanese Cretaceous: a contribution to dinosaur facies in Asia based on molluscan palaeontology and stratigraphy: *Cretaceous Research*, 15, pp. 101–125.

Matsumoto, Tatsuro, 1942, Fundamental in the Cretaceous stratigraphy of Japan: *Memoirs of the Faculty of Science, Kyushu Imperial University*, Series D, Geology, 1, pp. 129–280.

Matsumoto, Tatsuro, and I. Obata, 1979, *in*: Obata, 1979, [The ages of the fossil reptiles of Japan]: *Kaseki*, 29, p. 5,358 (in Japanese).

Matthew, William Diller, 1920, Canadian dinosaurs: *Natural History*, 20 (5), pp. 1–162.

Mayr, Georg, David S. Peters, Gerhard Plodowsky, and Olaf Vogel, 2002, Bristle-like integumentary structures in the tail of the horned dinosaur *Psittacosaurus*: *Naturwissenschaften*, 89, pp. 361–365.

Mazin, Jean-Michel, Jean-Paul Billon-Bruyat, Pierre Hantzpergue, and Gérard LaFaurie, 2003. Ichnological evidence for quadrupedal locomotion in pterodactyloid pterosaurs: trackways from the Late Jurassic of Crayssac (southwestern France): *in*: Éric Buffetaut and Jean-Michel Mazin, editors, *Evolution and Palaeobiology of Pterosaurs*. London: The Geological Society, Special Publications, 217, pp. 283–296.

Mazin, Jean-Michel, P. Hanzpergue, G. LaFaurie, and P. Vignaud, 1995, Des pistes de ptérosaures dans le Tithonien de Crayssac (Quercy, France: *Comptes Rendus des Séances de l'Académie des Sciences, Paris, Series IIa*, 325, pp. 733–739.

McCrae, Richard T., and William A. S. Sarjeant, 2001, New ichnotaxa of bird and mammal footprints from the Lower Cretaceous (Albian) Gates Formation of Alberta, *in*: Darren Tanke and Kenneth Carpenter, editors, *Mesozoic Vertebrate Life: New Research Inspired by the Paleontology of Philip J. Currie*. Bloomington and Indianapolis: Indiana University Press, pp. 453–478.

McGinnis, Helen J., 1982, *Carnegie's Dinosaurs*. Pittsburgh: The Board of Trustees, Carnegie Institute, 119 pages.

McGowan, Christopher, 1991, *Dinosaurs, Spitfires, and Sea Dragons*. Cambridge: Harvard University Press, 384 pages.

_____, 1994, *Diatoms to Dinosaurs: The Size and Scale of Living Things*. Washington, D.C.: Island Press, 301 pages.

McGowen, Michael R., Kevin Padian, Michael A. de Sosa, and Robert J. Harmon, 2002, Description of *Montanazhdarcho minor*, an azhdarchic pterosaur from the Two Medicine Formation (Campanian) of Montana: *PaleoBios*, 22 (1).

McIntosh, John S., 1981, Annotated catalogue of the dinosaurs (Reptilia, Archosauria) in the collections of the Carnegie Museum of Natural History: *Bulletin of the Carnegie Museum of Natural History*, 18, pp. 1–67.

_____, 1990, Sauropoda, *in*: David B. Weishampel, Peter Dodson, and Halszka Osmólska, editors, *The Dinosauria*. Berkeley and Los Angeles: University of California Press, pp. 345–401.

_____, 1997, Sauropoda, *in*: Philip J. Currie and Kevin Padian, editors, *Encyclopedia of Dinosaurs*. San Diego: Academic Press, pp. 654–658.

McIntosh, John S., Michael K. Brett-Surman, and James O. Farlow, 1997, Sauropods, *in*: Farlow and Brett-Surman, editors, *The Complete Dinosaur*. Bloomington and Indianapolis: Indiana University Press, pp. 264–290.

McIntosh, John S., Walter P. Coombs, Jr., and Dale A. Russell, 1992, A new diplodocid sauropod (Dinosauria) from Wyoming, U.S.A.: *Journal of Vertebrate Paleontology*, 12 (2), pp. 158–167.

McKinney, M. L., and K. J. McNamara, 1991, *Heterochrony, The Evolution of Ontogeny*. New York: Plenum, 437 pages.

McNab, Brian K., and Walter A. Auffenberg, 1976, The effect of large body size on temperature regulation of the Komodo dragon, *Varanus komodoensis*: *Comparativ Biochemistry and Physiology*, 55A, pp. 345–350.

McWhinney, Lorrie, Angela Matthias, and Kenneth Carpenter, 2004, Corticated pressure erosions, or "pitting," in osteodermal ankylosaur armor: *Journal of Vertebrate Paleontology*, 24 (Supplement to Number 3), Abstracts of Papers, Sixty-fourth Annual Meeting, p. 92A.

Mehl, M. G., 1931, Additions to the vertebrate record of the Dakota Sandstone: *American Journal of Science*, 5 (21), pp. 441–452.

Melville, A. G., 1849, Notes on the vertebral column of *Iguanodon*: *Philosophical Transactions of the Royal Society of London*: 139, pp. 285–300.

Meng, Qingjin, David J. Varricchio, Jinyuan Liu, Timothy Huang, and Chunling Gao, An unusual *Psittacosaurus* specimen from the Lower Cretaceous Yixian Formation (Liaoning Province, China) as evidence for parental care: *Journal of Vertebrate Paleontology*, 24 (Supplement to Number 3), Abstracts of Papers, Sixty-fourth Annual Meeting, p. 93A.

_____, 2004b, Parental care in an ornithischian dinosaur: *Nature*, 431, pp. 145–146.

Meyer, Christain Erich Hermann von Meyer, 1832, *Palaeologica zur Geschichte der Erde*, 560 pages.

_____, 1834, *Gnathosaurus subulatus*, ein

Saurus aus dem lithographischen Schiefer von Solnhofen: *Museum Senkenbergianum*, 1, p. 3.

_____, 1837, Mitteilung an Prof. Bronn (*Plateosaurus engelhardti*): *Neus Jarbuch für Mineralogie, Geologie, und Paläontologie*, 1837, p. 817, Stuttgart.

_____, 1838: Briefl. Mitteilung, *Ibid.*, p. 415.

_____, 1839, [Brief an Prof. BRONN vom 1. Dezember 1838]: *Ibid.*, pp. 76–79.

_____, 1845, System der fossilen Saurier: *Ibid.*, pp. 278–285.

_____, 1846, *Pterodactylus (Rhamphorhynchus) Gemmingi* aus dem Kalschiefer von Solenhofne: *Palaeontographica*, 1, pp. 1–20.

_____, 1852: *Briefl. Mitteilung, Neus Jarbuch für Mineralogie, Geologie, und Paläontologie*, 1852, pp. 326–337.

_____, 1854: *Ibid.*, 1854, pp. 47–58.

_____, 1856: *Ibid.*, 1856, p. 826.

_____, 1859, Zur Fauna der Vorwelt, vierte Abt.: Reptilien aus dem lithographischen Schiefer des Jura in Deutschland und Frankreich. 1. Lief., pp. 1–84, Frankfurt.

_____, 1861, Vogul-Federn und *Palpipes priscus* von Solnhofen: *Ibid.*, 1861, p. 561.

Miller, H. W., 1964, Cretaceous dinosaurian remains from southern Arizona: *Journal of Paleontology*, 38, pp. 378–384.

_____, 1972, The taxonomy of *Pteranodon* species from Kansas: *Transactions of the Kansas Academy of Science*, 74, pp. 1–19.

Milner, Angela C., 2002, Theropod dinosaurs of the Purbeck Limestone Group, southern England: *Special Papers in Paleontology*, 68, pp. 191–201.

Milner, Angela C., and David B. Norman, 1984, The biogeography of advanced ornithopod dinosaurs (Archosauria: Ornithischia)—a cladistic-vicariance model, *in*: W.-E. Reif and F. Westphal, editors, *Third Symposium on Mesozoic Terrestrial Ecosystems*. Tubingen, Germany: Attempto Verlag, pp. 145–150.

Moffet, Barbara S., 2004, NHS research: Fossil links southern landmasses: *National Geographic*, 206 (1).

Molnar, Ralph E., 1977, Analogies in the evolution of combat and display structures in ornithopods and ungulates: *Evolutionary Theory*, 3, pp. 165–190.

_____, 1978, A new theropod dinosaur from the Upper Cretaceous of central Montana: *Journal of Paleontology*, 52 (1), pp. 73–82.

_____, 1980, An albertosaur from the Hell Creek Formation of Montana: *Journal of Paleontology*, 54 (1), pp. 102–108.

_____, 1986, An eantiornithine bird from the Lower Cretaceous of Queensland, Australia: *Nature*, 322 (6081), pp. 736–738.

_____, 1990, Problematic theropods: "Carnosaurs," *in*: David B. Weishampel, Peter Dodson, and Osmólska, editors, *The Dinosauria*. Berkeley and Los Angeles: University of California Press, pp. 306–317.

_____, 1991, The cranial morphology of *Tyrannosaurus rex*: *Paleontographica*, 217, pp. 137–176, Stuttgart.

_____, 1998, Mechanical factors in the design of the skull of *Tyrannosaurus rex* (Osborn, 1905): *Gaia*, 15, pp. 193–218.

Molnar, Ralph E., and Kenneth Carpenter, 1989, The Jordan theropod (Maastricht-

ian, Montana, U.S.A.) referred to the genus *Aublysodon*: *Geobios*, 22 (4), pp. 445–454.

Molnar, Ralph E., Seriozha M. Kurzanov, and Dong Zhi-Ming [Zhiming], 1990, Carnosauria, *in*: David B. Weishampel, Peter Dodson, and Halszka Osmólska, editors, *The Dinosauria*. Berkeley and Los Angeles: University of California Press, pp. 169–209.

Molnar, Ralph E., and N. S. Pledge, 1980, A new theropod dinosaur from South Australia: *Acheringa*, 4, pp. 281–287.

Monbaron, Michel, Dale A. Russell, and Philippe Taquet, 1999, *Atlasaurus imelakei* n.g., n.s., a brachiosaurid-like sauropod from the Middle Jurassic of Morocco: *Comtes Rendu des Séances de l'Académie des Sciences, Paris, de la Terre et des Planètes*, 329, pp. 519–526.

Morris, William J., 1973, A review of Pacific Coast hadrosaurs: *Journal of Paleontology*, 47 (3), pp. 551–556.

Moser, Markus, 2003, *Plateosaurus engelhardti* Meyer, 1837 (Dinosauria: Sauropodomorpha) aus dem Feuerletten (Mittelkeuper; Obertrias) von Bayern: *Zitteliana*, B 24 (40), pp. 3–188.

Muenster, Georg Graf zu, 1839a, Uber einige neu Versteinerungen in den lithographischen Schiefern von Baiern: *Briefl. Mitteilung, Neus Jarbuch für Mineralogie, Geologie, und Paläontologie*, pp. 676–682.

_____, 1839b, *Pterodactylus longipes*. Beitrage zur Petrefacten-Knude mit XVIII. Nach der natur gezeichneten tafein, unter Mitwirkkung: *Palaeontographica*, p. 83.

Muñoz, M. A. V., F. M. Gulisano, and A. T. M. Conti Persino, 1984, El origen eólico de la Formación Tordillo (miembro verde), en el yacimento Loma de la Lata, Provincia del Neuquén. 9° *Congreso Geológico Argentino* (S. C. de Bariloche, 1984), *Actas*: pp. 315–323.

Murry, Philip A., and Robert A. Long, 1997 Dockum Group, *in*: Philip J. Currie and Kevin Padian, editors, *Encyclopedia of Dinosaurs*, San Diego: Academic Press, pp. 191–193.

Myers, Timothy, 2003, Catastrophic mass mortality of a herd of young diplodocid sauropods from the Morrison Formation of Montana: *Journal of Vertebrate Paleontology*, 23 (Supplement to Number 3), Abstracts of Papers, Sixty-third Annual Meeting, p. 81A.

_____, 2004, Evidence for age segregation in a herd of diplodocid sauropods: *Ibid.*, 24 (Supplement to Number 3), Abstracts of Papers, Sixty-fourth Annual Meeting, p. 97A.

Nagao, Takumi, 1936, *Nipponosaurus sachalinensis*, a new genus and species of trachodont dinosaur from Japanese Saghalien: *Journal of the Faculty Science, University Hokkaido, Geology and Minerology*, 3 (2), pp. 185–220.

_____, 1938, On the limb-bones of *Nipponosaurus sachalinensis* Nagao, a Japanese hadrosaurian dinosaur: *Annotationes Zoologicae Japaneses*, 17, pp. 311–317.

Naish, Darren, 2002, Thecocoelurians, calamosaurs and Europe's largest sauropod: the

latest on the Isle of Wight's dinosaurs: *Dino Press*, 7, pp. 85–95 (translation pp. 21–25).

_____, 2003, A definitive allosauroid (Dinosauria: Theropoda) from the Lower Cretaceous of East Sussex: *Proceedings of the Geologists' Association*, 114, pp. 319–326.

_____, 2004a, So ... what is *Yaverlandia*?: *13th Symposium on Vertebrate Palaeontology and Comparative Anatomy, Papers*, pp. 21–22.

_____, 2004b, *Heptasteornis* was no ornithomimid, troodontid, dromaeosaurid or owl: the first alvarezsaurid (Dinosauria: Theropoda) from Europe: *Neus Jahrbuch für Geologie und Paläontologie, Mh.*, 7, pp. 385–401.

Naish, Darren, and David M. Martill, 2001, Saurischian dinosaurs I: Sauropods, *in*: David M. Martill and Darren Naish, editors, *Dinosaurs of the Isle of Wight*. London: The Palaeontological Association, 10, pp. 182–241.

Naish, Darren, David M. Martill, David Cooper, and Kent A. Stevens, 2004, Europe's largest dinosaur? A giant brachiosaurid cervical vertebra from the Wessex Formation (Early Cretaceous) of southern England: *Cretaceous Research*, (article in press), pp. 1–9.

Naish, Darren, David M. Martill, and Eberhard Frew, 2004, Ecology, systematics and biogeographical relationships of dinosaurs, including a new theropod, from the Santana Formation (?Albian, Early Cretaceous) of Brazil: *Historical Biology*, pp. 1–4.

Néraudeau, Didier, Ronan Allain, Vincent Perrichot, Blaise Videt, France de Lapparent de Broin, Francois Guillocheau, Marc Philippe, Jean-Claude Rage, and Romain Vullo, 2003, Découverte d'un dépôt paralique à bois fossiles, ambre insectifère et restes d'Iguanodontidae (Dinosauria, Ornithopoda) dans le Cénomanien inférieur de Fouras (Charente-Maritime, Sud-Quest de la France): *Comptes Rendus Palevol*, 2, pp. 221–230.

Nessov [also spelled Nesov], Lev A., 1984, Upper Cretaceous pterosaurs and birds from central Asia: *Pterozavry i ptitsy pozdniego mela Sredney Azii, Paleontologichesky Zhurnal 1984*, pp. 47–57 (reprinted in *Paleontological Journal 1984*, pp. 38–49).

_____, 1986, The first find of the Late Cretaceous bird *Ichthyornis* in the old world and some other bird bones from the Cretaceous and Paleogene of Soviet Middle Asia, *in*: R. L. Potapov, editor, *Ecological and Faunistic Investigations of Birds, USSR Academy of Sciences, Proceedings of the Zoological Institute*, 147, pp. 31–38.

_____, 1991, Giant flying reptiles of the family Azhdarchidae—1. morphology, systematics: *Newsletter of the Leningrad University*, Series 7 (Geology, Geography), 2 (14), pp. 14–23.

_____, 1992, Review of localities and remains of Mesozoic and Paleogene birds of the USSR and the description of new findings: *Russian Journal of Ornithology*, 1 (1), pp. 7–10.

Nessov, Lev A., and L. J. Borkin, 1983, New records of bird bones from the Cretaceous of Mongolia and Soviet Middle Asia: *Proceedings of the Zoological Institute, Leningrad*, 116, pp. 108–110.

Nessov, Lev A., and A. A. Jarkov, 1989, New Cretaceous Paleogene birds from the USSR and some remarks on the origin and evolution of the class Aves: *Proceedings of the Zoological Institute, Leningrad*, 239, pp. 78–97.

Nessov, Lev A., and B. V. Panteleev, 1993, *Russian Academy of Sciences, Proceedings of the Zoological Institute, St. Petersburg*, 252, pp. 84–92.

Nessov, Lev A., and B. V. Prizemlin, 1991, A large advanced flightless marine bird of the order Hesperornithiformes of the Late Senonian of Turgai Strait—the first finding of the group in the USSR: *USSR Academy of Sciences, Proceedings of the Zoological Institute*, 239, pp. 85–107.

Nessov, Lev A., and A. I. Starkov, 1992, [Cretaceous vertebrates of the Gusinoe Lake Depression in Transbaikalia and their contribution into dating and determination of sedimentation conditions]: *Geophysica*, 6, pp. 10–19.

Nicholls, Elizabeth L., and Anthony P. Russell, 1981, A new specimen of *Struthiomimus altus* from Alberta, with comments on the classicatory characters of Upper Cretaceous ornithomimids: *Canadian Journal of Earth Sciences*, 18, pp. 518–526.

Noè, Leslie, and Sarah Finney, 2004, The dismantling and cleaning of the Sedgwick Museum's *Iguanodon*: *13th Symposium on Vertebrate Palaeontology and Comparative Anatomy, Papers*, pp. 3.

Nopcsa, Baron Franz [also Ferencz, Francis] (von Felsö-Szilvás), 1902, Dinosaurierreste aus Siebenbürgen II. (Schädelreste von *Mochlodon*). Mit einem Anhange: zur Phylogenie der Ornithopodiden: *Denkschriften der königlichen Akademie der Wissenschaften. Mathematisch-Naturwissenschaftlichen Klasse*, 72, pp. 149–175.

———, 1914, Über das Vorkommen der Dinosaurier in Siebenbürgen: *Verhandlungen der königlich-kaiserlichen zoologisch-botanischen Gesellschaft*, 54, pp. 12–14.

———, 1915, Die Dinosaurier des siebenbürgen Landesteile Ungarns: *Mitteilungen aus dem Jahrbuche der königlich ungarischen geologischen Reichsanstalt, Budapest*, 23, pp. 3–24.

———, 1923, On the geological importance of the primitive reptilian fauna in the uppermost Cretaceous of Hungary; with a description of a new tortoise (*Kallokibotion*). *Quarterly Journal of the Geological Society of London*, 79, pp. 100–116.

———, 1928, The genera of reptiles: *Palaeobiologica*, 1, pp. 163–188.

———, 1929, Sexual differences in ornithopodous dinosaurs: *Palaeobiologica*, 2, pp. 187–200.

Norberg, Ulla Lindhe, 1990, *Vertebrate Flight: Mechanics, Physiology, Morphology, Ecology, and Evolution*. Zoophysiology Series, Vol. 27. Berlin: Springer-Verlag, 298 pages.

Norell, Mark A., and James M. Clark, 1996, Dinosaurs and their youth: *Science*, 273, pp. 165–168.

Norell, Mark A., James M. Clark, Luis M. Chiappe, and Demberely nin Dashveg, 1995, A nesting dinosaur: *Science*, 378, pp. 774–776.

Norell, Mark A., James M. Clark, Demberelynin Dashveg, Rinchen Barsbold, Luis M. Chiappe, Amy R. Davidson, Malcolm C. McKenna, Altangerel Perle, and Michael J. Novacek, 1994, A theropod dinosaur embryo and the affinities of the Flaming Cliffs dinosaur eggs: *Science*, 266, pp. 779–882.

Norell, Mark A., James M. Clark, and Peter J. Makovicky, 2001, Phylogenetic relationships among coelurosaurian theropods, *in*: Jacques Gauthier and I. F. Gall, editors, *New Prospectives on the origin and early evolution of birds: proceedings of the International Symposium in Honor of John H. Ostrom*. New Haven, CT: Peabody Museum of Natural History, pp. 49–67.

Norell, Mark A., James M. Clark, Peter J. Makovicky, Rinchen Barsbold, and Timothy Rowe, manuscript, A revision of *Saurornithoides*: *American Museum Novitates*.

Norell, Mark A., and Julia A. Clarke, 2001, Fossil that fills a critical gap in avian evolution: *Nature*, 409, pp. 181–184.

Norell, Mark A., and Sunny H. Hwang, 2004, A troodontid dinosaur from Ukhaa Tolgod (Late Cretaceous Mongolia): *American Museum Novitates*, 3446, pp. 1–9.

Norell, Mark A., and Peter J. Makovicky, 1997, Important features of the dromaeosaur skeleton: information from a new specimen: *American Museum Novitates*, 3215, 28 pages.

———, 1999, Important features of the dromaeosaurid skeleton II: information from newly collected specimens of *Velociraptor mongoliensis*: *Ibid.*, 3282, pp. 1–45.

———, 2004, Dromaeosauridae, *in*: David B. Weishampel, Peter Dodson, and Halszka Osmólska, editors, *The Dinosauria* (second edition). Berkeley and Los Angeles: University of California Press, pp. 196–209.

Norell, Mark A., Peter J. Makovicky, and James M. Clark, 2000, A new troodontid theropod from Ukhaa Tolgod, Mongolia: *Journal of Vertebrate Paleontology*, 20 (1), pp. 7–11.

———, 2004, The braincase of *Velociraptor*, *in*: Philip J. Currie, Eva B. Kopelhus, Martin A. Shugar, and Joanna L. Wright, 2004, editors, *Feathered Dragons: Studies on the Transition from Dinosaurs to Birds*. Bloomington and Indianapolis: Indiana University Press, pp. 133–143.

Noriega, Ken C., 2003, New information on the pes of centrosaurine ceratopsid dinosaurs: *PaleoBios, 2003 California Paleontology Conference, Abstracts, April 25–26, 2003*, p. 6.

Noriega, Ken C., Stuart S. Sumida, David A. Eberth, Donald Brinkman, and Michael W. Skrepnick, 2003, The pes of centrosaurine ceratopsid dinosaurs: new information from a completely articulated specimen: *Journal of Vertebrate Paleontology*, 23 (Supplement to Number 3), Abstracts of Papers, Sixty-third Annual Meeting, p. 83A.

Norman, David B. [Bruce], 1984a, On the cranial morphology and evolution of ornithopod dinosaurs: *Symposium of the Zoological Society of London*, 1984, pp. 521–547.

———, 1984b, A systematic reappraisal of the reptile order Ornithischia, *in*: W. Reif and F. Westphal, editors, *Third Symposium on Mesozoic Terrestrial Ecosystems, Short Papers*, Attempto Verlag, Tübingen University Press, pp. 157–162.

———, 1986, On the anatomy of *Iguanodon atherfieldensis* (Ornithischia: Ornithopoda): *Bulletin de l'Institut Royal d'Histoire Naturelle de Belgique*, 56, pp. 281–372.

———, 1990, Problematic Theropoda: "Coelurosaurs," *in*: David B. Weishampel, Peter Dodson, and Osmólska, editors, *The Dinosauria*. Berkeley and Los Angeles: University of California Press, pp. 280–305.

———, 1998, On Asian ornithopods (Dinosauria: Ornithischia). 3. A new species of iguanodontid dinosaur: *Zoological Journal of the Linnean Society*, 122, pp. 291–348.

———, 2004, Basal Iguanodontia, *in*: David B. Weishampel, Peter Dodson, and Halszka Osmólska, editors, *The Dinosauria* (second edition). Berkeley and Los Angeles: University of California Press, pp. 413–437.

Norman, David B., and Hans-Dieter Sues, 2000, Ornithopods from Kazakhstan, Mongolia and Siberia, *in*: M. J. Benton, M. A. Shishkin, D. M. Unwin and E. N. Kurochkin, editors, *The Age of Dinosaurs in Russia and Mongolia*. Cambridge: Cambridge University Press, pp. 462–479.

Norman, David N., Hans-Dieter Sues, Lawrence M. Witmer, and Rodolfo A. Coria, 2004, Basal Ornithopoda, *in*: David B. Weishampel, Peter Dodson, and Halszka Osmólska, editors, *The Dinosauria* (second edition). Berkeley and Los Angeles: University of California Press, pp. 393–412.

Norman, David B., and David B. Weishampel, 1985, Ornithopod feeding mechanisms: their bearing on the evolution of herbivory: *American Naturalist*, 126, pp. 151–164.

———, 1990, Iguanodontidae and related Ornithopoda, *in*: David B. Weishampel, Peter Dodson, and Osmólska, editors, *The Dinosauria*. Berkeley and Los Angeles: University of California Press, pp. 510–533.

———, 1991, Feeding mechanisms in some small herbivorous dinosaurs: processes and patterns, *in*: J. M. V. Rayner and R. J. Wootton, editors, *Biomechanics in Evolution*. Cambridge: Cambridge University Press, pp. 161–181.

Norman, David B., Lawrence M. Witmer, and David B. Weishampel, 2004a, Basal Ornithischia, *in*: David B. Weishampel, Peter Dodson, and Halszka Osmólska, editors, *The Dinosauria* (second edition). Berkeley and Los Angeles: University of California Press, pp. 325–334.

_____, 2004b, Basal Thyreophora, *Ibid.*, pp. 335–342.

Novas, Fernando E., 1992, Phylogenetic relationships of the basal dinosaurs, the Herrerasauridae: *Palaeontology*, 35, pp. 51–62, London.

_____, 1993, New information on the systematics and postcranial skeleton of *Herrerasaurus ischigualastensis* (Theropoda: Herrerasauridae) from the Ischigualasto Formation (Upper Triassic) of Argentina: *Journal of Vertebrate Paleontology*, 13 (4), pp. 400–423.

_____, 1996a, Dinosaur monophyly: *Journal of Vertebrate Paleontology*, 16 (4), pp. 723–741.

_____, 1996b, Alvarezsauridae, Cretaceous basal birds from Patagonia and Mongolia, *in*: Fernando S. Novas and Ralph E. Molnar, editors, *Proceedings of the Gondwanan Dinosaur Symposium*: *Memoirs of the Queensland Museum*, 39 (part 3), pp. 675–702.

_____, 1997a, Anatomy of *Patagonykus puertai* (Theropoda, Alvialae, Alvarezsauridae), from the Late Cretaceous of Patagonia: *Ibid.*, 17 (1), pp. 137–166.

_____, 1997b, Herrerasauridae, *in*: Philip J. Currie and Kevin Padian, editors, *Encyclopedia of Dinosaurs*. San Diego: Academic Press, pp. 303–311.

_____, 1997c, South American dinosaurs, *Ibid.* Pp. 678–689.

_____, 2002, On Asian ornithopods (Dinosauria: Ornithischia). 4. *Probactrosaurus* Rozhdestvensky, 1966, *in*: David B. Norman and David J. Gower, editors, *Archosaurian Anatomy and Palaeontology. Essays in Memory of Alick D. Walker. Zoological Journal of the Linnean Society*, 136, pp. 113–144.

_____, 2004, Avian traits in the ilium of *Unenlagia comahuensis* (Maniraptora, Avialae): *in*: Philip J. Currie, Eva B. Kopelhus, Martin A. Shugar, and Joanna L. Wright, 2004, editors, *Feathered Dragons: Studies on the Transition from Dinosaurs to Birds*. Bloomington and Indianapolis: Indiana University Press, pp. 150–166.

Novas, Fernando E., and Federico L. Agnolin, 2004, *Unquillosaurus ceibali* Powell, a giant maniraptoran (Dinosauria, Theropoda) from the Late Cretaceous of Argentina: *Revista del Museo Argentino de Ciencias Naturales*, n.s. 6 (1), pp. 61–66.

Novas, Fernando E., Federico L. Agnolin, and Saswati Bandyopadhyay, 2004, Cretaceous theropods from India: a review of specimens described by Huene and Matley (1933): *Revista del Museo Argentino de Ciencias Naturales*, n.s. 6 (1), pp. 67–103.

Novas, Fernando E., Andrea V. Cambiasco, and Alfredo Ambrosio, 2004, A new basal iguanodontian (Dinosauria, Ornithischia) from the Upper Cretaceous of Patagonia: *Ameghiniana*, 41 (1), pp. 75–82.

Novas, Fernando E., Andrea V. Cambiasco, J. Lirio, and H. Núñez, 2002, Paleobiogeografía de los dinosaurios cretácicos polares de Gondwana: *Ameghiniana (Resúmenes)*, 39 (4), p. 15R.

Novas, Fernando E., and Juan I. Canale, 2004, Un neuvo terópodo basal de la Formación Ischigualasto (Carniano) de la provincia de San Juan, Argentina: *Ameghiana*, 40 (4), Suplemento, p. 63R.

Novas, Fernando E., Juan I. Canale, and Marcelo Isasi, 2003, Un tetrópodo maniraptor del Campaniano-Maastrichtiano del norte patagónico: *Ameghiniana*, 40 (4), Supplemento, p. 63R.

_____, 2004, Giant deinonychosaurian theropod from the Late Cretaceous of Patagonia: *Journal of Vertebrate Paleontology*, 24 (Supplement to Number 3), Abstracts of Papers, Sixty-fourth Annual Meeting, p. 98A.

Novas, Fernando E., and Pablo F. Puerta, 1997, New evidence concerning avian origins from the Late Cretaceous of Patagonia: *Nature*, 387, pp. 390–92.

O'Connor, Patrick, 2004, Postcranial pneumaticity and pulmonary heterogeneity in archosaurs: evolution of the flow-through lung in non-avialan theropod dinosaurs and birds: *Journal of Vertebrate Paleontology*, 24 (Supplement to Number 3), Abstracts of Papers, Sixty-fourth Annual Meeting, p. 99A.

Ohashi, Tomoyuki, 2004, Pleurokinesis in a new ornithopod (Dinosauria) from the Lower Cretaceous Kuwajima Formation (Tetori Group), Japan: *Journal of Vertebrate Paleontology*, 24 (Supplement to Number 3), Abstracts of Papers, Sixty-fourth Annual Meeting, p. 99A.

O'Leary, Maureen A., Eric M. Roberts, Jason J. Head, Famory Sissoko, and Mamadou L. Bouare, 2004, Titanosaurian (Dinosauria: Sauropoda) remains from the "Continental Intercalaire" of Mali: *Journal of Vertebrate Paleontology*, 24 (4), pp. 923–930.

Oliveira, A. I., and O. H. Leonardos, 1978, Geologia do Brasil: *Escola Superior Agricultura de* Mossoró, series: Colecáo Mossoroense, 73, 813 pages.

Olshevsky, George, 1991, *A Revision of the Parainfraclass Archosauria Cope 1869, Excluding the Advanced Crocodylia*. Buffalo, NY: Publications Requiring Research, iv, 196 pages.

Olshevsky, George, Tracy L. Ford, and S. Yamamoto, 1995a, [The origin and evolution of the tyrannosaurids, (part 1): *Kyoryugaku Saizensen* [*Dino-Frontline*], 9, pp. 92–119.

_____, 1995b, (part 2): *Ibid.*, 10, pp. 75–99.

Olson, Storrs L., 1975, *Ichthyornis* in the Cretaceous of Alabama: *Wilson Bulletin*, 87, pp. 103–105.

_____, 1992, *Neogaeornis wetzeli* Lambrecht, a Cretaceous loon from Chile (Aves: Gaviidae): *Journal of Vertebrate Paleontology*, 12 (1), pp. 122–124.

Olson, Storrs L., and David C. Parris, 1987, The Cretaceous birds of New Jersey: *Smithsonian Contributions to Paleobiology*, 63, pp. 1–22.

Oppel, Albert, 1862, Über Fährten im lithographischen Schiefer: *Palaeontologische Mitteilungen des Museums des kgl. bayerischen Staates*, 1, pp. 121–125.

Osborn, Henry Fairfield, 1899, A skeleton of *Diplodocus*: *Memoirs of the American Museum of Natural History*, 1, pp. 191–214.

_____, 1905, *Tyrannosaurus* and other Cretaceous carnivorous dinosaurs: *Bulletin of the American Museum of Natural History*, 21, pp. 259–265.

_____, 1917, Skeletal adaptations of *Ornitholestes*, *Struthiomimus* and *Tyrannosaurus*: *Ibid.*, 35, pp. 733–771.

Osborn, Henry Fairfield, and Charles Craig Mook, 1921, *Camarasaurus*, *Amphicoelias* and other sauropods of Cope: *Memoirs of the American Museum of Natural History*, (new series), 3, pp. 247–287.

Osmólska, Halszka, 1993, Were the Mongolian "fighting dinosaurs" really fighting?: *Rev. Paléobiol. Spec, Vol.*, 7, pp. 161–162.

_____, 1996, An unusual theropod dinosaur from the Late Cretaceous Nemegt Formation of Mongolia: *Acta Palaeontologica Polonica*, 41 (1), pp. 1–38.

_____, 2003, Some aspects of the oviraptorosaur (Dinosauria, Theropoda) braincase: *1st Meeting of the EAVP, Abstracts with Program, Thursday 15th of July to Saturday 19th of July*, p. 32.

_____, 2004, Evidence on relation of brain to endocranial cavity in oviraptorid dinosaurs: *Acta Palaeontologica Polonica*, 49 (2), pp. 321–324.

Osmólska, Halszka, Philip J. Currie, and Rinchen Barsbold, 2004, Oviraptorosauria, *in*: David B. Weishampel, Peter Dodson, and Halszka Osmólska, editors, *The Dinosauria* (second edition). Berkeley and Los Angeles: University of California Press, pp. 165–183.

Osmólska, Halszka, Ewa Roniewicz, and Rinchen Barsbold, 1972, A new dinosaur, *Gallimimus bullatus* n. gen., n. sp. (Ornithomimidae) from the Upper Cretaceous of Mongolia: *Paleontologica Polonica*, 27, pp. 103–143.

Ostrom, John H., 1969a, A new theropod dinosaur from the Lower Cretaceous of Montana: *Postilla, Peabody Museum of Natural History*, 128, pp. 1–17.

_____, 1969b, Osteology of *Deinonychus antirrhopus*, an unusual theropod from the Lower Cretaceous of Montana: *Bulletin of the Peabody Museum of Natural History*, 30, pp. 1–165.

_____, 1973, The ancestry of birds: *Nature*, 242, p. 136.

_____, 1976a, *Archaeopteryx* and the origin of birds: *Biological Journal of the Linnean Society*, 8, pp. 91–182.

_____, 1976b, Some hypothetical anatomical stages in the evolution of avian flight: *Smithsonian Contributions to Paleontology*, 27, pp. 1–21.

_____, 1978, The osteology of *Compsognathus longipes*: *Zitteliana Abhandlungen der Bayerischen taatssammlung für Paläontologie und historische Geologie (München)*, 4, pp. 73–118.

_____, 1986a, The Jurassic "bird" *Laopteryx priscus* re-examined: *Contributions to Geology, University of Wyoming, Special Paper*, 3, pp. 11–19.

_____, 1986b, The cursorial origin of avian flight: *Memoirs of the California Academy of Sciences*, 8, pp. 73–81.

_____, 1990, The Dromaeosaurdae, *in*: David B. Weishampel, Peter Dodson, and Osmólska, editors, *The Dinosauria*. Berkeley and Los Angeles: University of California Press, pp. 269–279.

_____, 1997, How bird flight might have come about, *in*: Donald L. Wolberg, Edmund Stump, and Gary Rosenberg, editors. *Dinofest International: Proceedings of a Symposium Held at Arizona State University*. Philadelphia: Academy of Natural Sciences, pp. 301–310.

Ostrom, John H., S. O. Poore, and G. E. Goslow, Jr., 1999, Humeral rotation and wrist supination: important functional complex for the evolution of powered flight in birds?: *Smithsonian Contributions to Paleobiology*, 89, pp. 301–309.

Owen, Richard, 1840–1845, *Odontography* (two volumes), 655 pages, London.

_____, 1841, A description of a portion of the skeleton of the *Cetiosaurus*, a gigantic extinct saurian reptile occurring in the oolitic formations of different portions of England: *Proceedings of the Geological Society of London*, 3 (2), 80, pp. 457–462.

_____, 1842a, Deuxième rapport sur les reptiles fossiles de la Grande Bretagne. L'Institut, 10, pp. 11–14.

_____, 1842b, Report on British fossil reptiles. Part II. *Report of the British Association for the Advancement of Science 1842 (1841)*, pp. 60–204.

_____, 1844, Odontography, Pt. III: *Hippolyte Baillière*. London, 655 pages.

_____, 1846, On supposed fossil bones of birds: *Quarterly Journal of the Geological Society of London*, 2, p. 96.

_____, 1851, Monograph of the fossil reptilia of the Cretaceous Formations: *Palaeontographical Society*, 5 (11), pp. 1–118.

_____, 1857, Monograph on the Fossil Reptilia of the Wealden and Purbeck Formations. Part III. *Megalosaurus: Ibid.*, 34, pp. 1–26.

_____, 1859a, On a new genus (*Dimorphodon*) of pterodactyle, with remarks on the geological distribution of flying reptiles: *Report on the Twenty-eighth Meeting of the British Association for the Advancement of Science, 1859 (for 1858)*, pp. 97–98.

_____, 1859b, On remains of new and gigantic species of pterodactyle (*Pter. Fittoni* and *Pter. Sedgwickii*) from the Upper Greensand, near Cambridge: *Report on the Twenty-Eighth Meeting of the British Association for the Advancement of Science, 1859 (for 1858)*, pp. 98–103.

_____, 1874, Monograph of fossil Reptilia of the Mesozoic formations. 1. Pterosauria: *Palaeontological Society Monograph*, 27, pp. 1–14.

_____, 1875, Monographs of the fossil Reptilia of the Mesozoic formations (Pt. II) (genera *Bothriospondylus, Cetiosaurus, Omosaurus*): *Ibid.*, 11, pp. 20–44.

Padian, Kevin, 1983, Osteology and functional morphology of *Dimorphodon macronyx* (Buckland) (Pterosauria: Rhamphorhynchoidea) based on new material in the Yale Peabody Museum: *Postilla*, 189, pp. 1–44.

_____, 1984a, A large pterodactyloid pterosaur from the Two Medicine Formation (Campanian) of Montana: *Journal of Vertebrate Paleontology*, 4 (4), pp. 516–524.

_____, 1984b, Pterosaur remains from the Kayenta Formation (?Early Jurassic) of Arizona: *Palaeontology*, 27 (2), pp. 407–413.

_____, 1986a, A taxonomic note on two pterodactyloid families: *Ibid.*, 6 (3), p. 289.

_____, 1986b, On the type material of *Coelophysis* Cope (Saurischia: Theropoda) and a new specimen from the Petrified Forest of Arizona (Late Triassic: Chinle Formation), *in*: Kevin Padian, editor, *The Beginning of the Age of Dinosaurs: Faunal Change Across the Triassic–Jurassic Boundary*. Cambridge and New York: Cambridge University Press, pp. 45–60.

_____, 2003, Four-winged dinosaurs, bird precursors, or neither?: *BioScience*, 53 (5), pp. 450–452.

_____, 2004a, Origin of the avian body plan: *Journal of Morphology*, 260 (3), 7th International Congress of Vertebrate Morphology, p. 319.

_____, 2004b, Basal Avialae, *in*: David B. Weishampel, Peter Dodson, and Halszka Osmólska, editors, *The Dinosauria* (second edition). Berkeley and Los Angeles: University of California Press, pp. 210–231.

Padian, Kevin, and Luis M. Chiappe, 1997, Bird origins, *in*: Philip J. Currie and Kevin Padian, editors, *Encyclopedia of Dinosaurs*. San Diego: Academic Press, pp. 71–79.

Padian, Kevin, John R. Horner, and Jasmeet Dhaliwal, 2004, Species recognition as the principal cause of bizarre structures in dinosaurs: *Journal of Vertebrate Paleontology*, 24 (Supplement to Number 3), Abstracts of Papers, Sixty-fourth Annual Meeting, p. 100A.

Padian, Kevin, John R. Horner, and Armand Ricqlès, 2004, Growth in small dinosaurs and pterosaurs: the evolution of archosaurian growth strategies: *Journal of Vertebrate Paleontology*, 24 (3), pp. 555–571.

Padian, Kevin, John R. Hutchinson, and Thomas R. Holtz, Jr., 1999, Phylogenetic definitions and nomenclature of the major taxonomic categories of the carnivorous Dinosauria (Theropoda): *Journal of Vertebrate Paleontology*, 19 (1), pp. 69–80.

Padian, Kevin, and Paul E. Olsen, 1989, Ratite footprints and the stance and gait of Mesozoic theropods, *in*: David D. Gillette and Martin G. Lockley, editors, *Dinosaur Tracks and Traces*. Cambridge: Cambridge University Press, pp. 231–241.

Padian, Kevin, Armand J. De Ricqlès, and John R. Horner, 1995, Bone histology determines identification of a new fossil taxon of pterosaur (Reptilia: Archosauria): *Comtes Rendu des Séances de l'Académie des Sciences, Paris, de la Terre et des Planètes*, (320), Series II, pp. 77–84.

_____, 2001, Dinosaurian growth rates and bird origins: *Nature*, 412, pp. 405–408.

Pak, and Kim, 1996, Mesozoic Era, *in*, *Geology of Korea*.

Pal'fy, J., P. L. Smith, and J. K. Mortensen, 2000, A U-Pb and $^{40/30}$ Ar. A time scale for the Jurassic: *Canadian Journal of Earth Sciences*, 37, pp. 923–944.

Pang Qiqing, and Cheng Zhengwu, 1998, A new ankylosaur of Late Cretaceous from Tianzhen, Shanxi: *Progress in Natural Science*, 8 (3), pp. 326–334.

Pang Qiqing, Cheng Zhengwu, Yang Jianping, Xie Manze, Zhu Caifa, and Luo Junlin, 1996, The preliminary report on Late Cretaceous dinosaur fauna expedition, Tianzhen, Shanxi: *Journal of Hebei College Geology*, 19 (3–4), p. 227.

Panteleev, B. V., 1998, New species of enantiornithines (Aves, Enantiornithes) from the Upper Cretaceous of Central Kyzylkum: *Russkii Ornithologicheskii Zhurnal*. Exsoress-vy.pvsk 35, pp. 3–15.

Parish, Jolyon, 2003, Evolutionary history of the Ankylosauria (Dinosauria: Ornithischia): *Journal of Vertebrate Paleontology*, 23 (Supplement to Number 3), Abstracts of Papers, Sixty-third Annual Meeting, p. 85A.

Parker, W. K., 1891, On the morphology of a reptilian bird *Opisthocomus cristatus*: *Transactions of the Zoological Society of London*, 13, pp. 43–85.

Parks, William A., 1926, *Thescelosaurus warreni*, a new species of ornithopodous dinosaur from the Edmonton Formation of Alberta: *University of Toronto Studies (Geological Series)*, 21, pp. 1–42.

_____, 1928, *Albertosaurus arctungu*, a new species of theropodous dinosaur from the Edmonton Formation of Alberta: *Ibid.*, 25, pp. 1–42.

_____, 1931, A new genus and two new species of trachodont dinosaurs from the Belly River Formation of Alberta: *Ibid.*, 31, pp. 1–11.

Parris, David C., and Sylvia Hope, 2002, New interpretations of the birds from the Navesink and Hornerstown Formations, New Jersey, USA (Aves: Neornithes), *in*: Zonghe Zhou and Fucheng Zhang, editors, *Proceedings of the 5th Symposium of the Society of Avian Paleontology and Evolution*. Beijing: Science Press, pp. 113–124.

Parrish, J. Michael, 2003, Mapping ecomorphs onto sauropod phylogeny: *Journal of Vertebrate Paleontology*, 23 (Supplement to Number 3), Abstracts of Papers, Sixty-third Annual Meeting, pp. 85A–86A.

Parsons, William, and Kristen Parsons, 2003, Description of a new immature specimen of *Deinonychus antirrhopus*, (Saurischia, Theropoda): *Journal of Vertebrate Paleontology*, 23 (Supplement to Number 3), Abstracts of Papers, Sixty-third Annual Meeting, p. 86A.

Pascual, R., P. Bondesio, G. J. Schillaro Yane, M. G. Vucetich, and Z. B. Gasparini 1978, Vertebrados, *in*: *Geología y Recursos Naturales del Neuquén*. Relatorio del VII Congreso Geológico Argentino, pp. 177–185.

Paul, Gregory S., 1987, The science and art of restoring the life appearance of dinosaurs and their relatives, *in*: Sylvia J. Czerkas and Everett C. Olson, editors, *Dinosaurs Past and Present*, Volume II. Los Angeles: Natural History Museum of Los Angeles County, pp. 5–49.

_____, 1988, *Predatory Dinosaurs of the World: A Complete Illustrated Guide*. New York: Simon and Schuster, 403 pages.

_____, 1998, Limb design, function and running performance in ostrich-mimics and tyrannosaurs: *Gaia*, 15, pp. 257–270.

_____, 2002, *Dinosaur of the Air: The Evolution and Loss of Flight in Dinosaurs and Birds*. Baltimore and London: The Johns Hopkins University Press, 460 pages.

_____, 2003, Who says dromaeosaurs couldn't fly?: *Journal of Vertebrate Paleontology*, 23 (Supplement to Number 3), Abstracts of Papers, Sixty-third Annual Meeting, p. 86A.

_____, 2004, Speed in giant tyrannosaurs: anatomical and scaling comparison of running potential with living animals: *Ibid.*, 24 (Supplement to Number 3), Abstracts of Papers, Sixty-fourth Annual Meeting, p. 101A.

Peng Guangzhao, 1992, Jurassic ornithopod *Agilisaurus louderbacki* (Ornithopoda: Fabrosauridae) from Zigong, Sichuan, China: *Vertebrata PalAsiatica*, 30 (1), pp. 39–53.

Pereda-Suberbiola, Xabier [Javier, Xavier], 1994, *Polacanthus* (Ornithischia, Ankylosauria), a Transatlantic armoured dinosaur from the Early Cretaceous of Europe and North America: *Palaeontographica*, A, 323, pp. 133–159.

_____, 1999, Ankylosaurian dinosaur remains from the Upper Cretaceous of Laño (Iberian Peninsula), *in*: H. Astibia, J. C. Corral, X. Murelaga, X. Orue-Etxebarria, and X. Pereda Suberbiola, editors, *Geology and Palaeontology of the Upper Cretaceous Vertebrate-bearing Beds of the Laño Quarry (Basque-Cantabrian Region, Iberian Peninsula)*. Estudios del Museo de Ciencias Naturales de Alava 14 (número especial 1), pp. 273–288.

Pereda-Suberbiola, Xabier [Javier, Xavier], H. Astibia, and Éric Buffetaut, 1995, New remains of the armoured dinosaur *Struthiosaurus* from the Late Cretaceous of the Iberian peninsula (Laño locality, Basque-Cantabric basin): *Bulletin de la Sociéte Géologique de France*, 166, pp. 207–211.

Pereda-Suberbiola, Xabier [Javier, Xavier], Nathalie Bardet, Mohamed Iarochéne, Baâdo Bouya, and Mbarek Amaghzaz, 2004, The first record of a sauropod dinosaur from the Late Cretaceous phosphates of Morocco: *Journal of African Earth Sciences*, 40, pp. 81–88.

Pereda Suberbiola, Xabier, Nathalie Bardet, Stephane Jouve, Mohamed Iarochéne, Baâdi Bouya, and Mbarek Amaghzaz, 2003, 2003, A new azhdarchid pterosaur from the Late Cretaceous phosphates of Morocco: *in*: Éric Buffetaut and Jean-Michel Mazin, editors, *Evolution and Palaeobiology of Pterosaurs*. London: The Geological Society, Special Publications, 217, pp. 80–90.

Pereda Suberbiola, Xabier [Javier, Xavier] Pereda, and Paul M. Barrett, 1999, A systematic review of ankylosaurian dinosaur remains from the Albian of England: *Special Papers in Palaeontology*, 60, pp. 177–208.

Pereda Suberbiola, Xabier, and Peter M. Galton, 2001, Reappraisel of the nodosaurid ankylosaur *Struthiosaurus austriacus* Bunzel from the Upper Cretaceous Gosau Beds of Austria, *in*: Kenneth Carpenter, editor, *The Armored Dinosaurs*. Bloomington and Indianapolis: Indiana University Press, pp. 173–210.

Pérez-Moreno, Bernardo, Fernando E. novas, Angela D. Buscalloni, J. Moratalla, Francisco Ortéga, and Diego Rasskin-Gutman 1994, A unique multitoothed ornithomimosaur dinosaur from the Lower Cretaceous of Spain: *Nature*, 370, pp. 365–367.

Perle, Altangerel, 1977, On the first discovery of *Alectrosaurus* (Tyrannosauridae, Theropoda) from the Late Cretaceous of Mongolia: *Problems of Mongolian Geology*, 3, pp. 104–113.

_____, 1979, [Segnosauridae a new family of theropods from the Late Cretaceous of Mongolia]: [*Soviet-Mongolian Palaeontological Expedition, Transactions*], 8, pp. 45–55.

Perle, Altangerel, Luis M. Chiappe, Rinchen Barsbold, James M. Clark, and Mark A. Norell, 1994, Skeletal morphology of *Mononykus olecrans* (Theropoda: Aviale) from the Late Cretaceous of Mongolia: *American Museum Novitates*, 3105, pp. 1–29.

Perle, Altangerel, Mark A. Norell, Luis M. Chiappe, and James M. Clark, 1993, Flightless bird from the Cretaceous of Mongolia: *Nature*, 362, pp. 623–626.

Perry, S. F., 1983, Reptilian lungs, functional anatomy and evolution: *Advances in Anatomy, Embryology, and Cell Biology*, 79, pp. 1–81.

Peteronievics, B., and Arthur Smith Woodward, 1917, On the pectoral and pelvic arches of the British Museum specimen of *Archaeopteryx*: *Proceedings of the Zoological Society of London*, 1, pp. 1–6.

Peters, David, 2000, A redescription of four prolaceriform genera and implications for pterosaur phylogenesis: *Revista Italiana di Paleontologia e Stratigrafia*, 106, pp. 293–336.

_____, 2003, The Chinese vampire and other overlooked pterosaur ptreasures: *Journal of Vertebrate Paleontology*, 23 (Supplement to Number 3), Abstracts of Papers, Sixty-third Annual Meeting, p. 87A.

_____, 2004, Pterosaurs from another angle: *Prehistoric Times*, 64, pp. 36–40.

Peyer, Karin, 2003, A complete redescription of the French *Compsognathus* with special consideration of the anatomy of the hand: *Journal of Vertebrate Paleontology*, 23 (Supplement to Number 3), Abstracts of Papers, Sixty-third Annual Meeting, p. 87A.

_____, 2004, The phylogentic relationship of the French *Compsognathus* within the Compsognathidae and coelurosaurs: *Ibid.*, 24 (Supplement to Number 3), Abstracts of Papers, Sixty-fourth Annual Meeting, p. 101A.

Phillips, John, 1871, *Geology of Oxford and the Valley of the Thames*. Oxford, England: Clarendon Press, 529 pages.

Pierce, Michael, Larry F. Rinehart, Andrew B. Heckert, Spencer G. Lucas, and Adrian P. Hunt, 2004, Rotation of an Upper Triassic Ghost Ranch, New Mexico Whitaker (*Coelophysis*) Quarry block: turning over a fragile 12,000 lb rock: *Journal of Vertebrate Paleontology*, 24 (Supplement to Number 3), Abstracts of Papers, Sixty-fourth Annual Meeting, pp. 101A–102A.

Pincemaille-Quillevere, Marie, 2002, Description d'un quellette partiel de *Rhabdodon priscus* (Euronithopoda) du Cretace Superieur de vitrolles (Bouches du Rhône, France): *Oryctos*, 4, pp. 39–70.

Pinegar, Richard Tyler, Mark A. Loewen, Karen C. Cloward, Rick J. Hunter, and Christopher J. Weege, 2003, A juvenile allosaur with preserved integument from the basal Morrison Formation of central Wyoming: *Journal of Vertebrate Paleontology*, 23 (Supplement to Number 3), Abstracts of Papers, Sixty–third Annual Meeting, pp. 87A–88A.

Pisani, Davide, Adam M. Yates, and Max C. Langer, 2001, The first supertree for the Dinosauria: *Journal of Vertebrate Paleontology*, 21 (Supplement to Number 3), Abstracts of Papers, Sixty-first Annual Meeting, p. 89A.

Plieninger, Felix, 1895, *Campylognathus Zitelli*. Ein neuer Flugsaurier aus dem Oberen Lias Schwabens: *Palaeontographica*, 41, pp. 193–222.

Poblete, F., and Jorge O. Calvo, 2004, Upper Turonian dromaeosaurid teeth from Futalognko quarry, Barreales Lake, Neuquén, Patagonia, Argentina: *Ameghiana*, 40 (4), Suplemento, p. 66B.

Pons, D., P.-Y. Berthou, and D. de A. Campos, 1990, Quelques observations sur la palynologie de l'Aptien supérieur et de l'Albien du Bassin d'Araripe, *in*: D. de A. Campos, M.S.S. Viana, P.M. Brito, and G. Beurlen, editors, *Alas do simposio sobre a Bacia do Araripe e Bacias Interiores do Nordeste, Crato. 14–16 de Junio de 1990*, Crato, pp. 241–252.

Powell, Jaime Eduardo, 1978*a*, Morfologia del esqueleto axial de los dinosaurios titanosáuridos (Saurischia–Sauropoda) del Estado de Minas Gerais, Brasil: *Anain X Congreso Brasileiro de Paleontologia*, pp. 155–171, Rio de Janeiro.

_____, 1978*b*, Contribución al conocimiento geológico del extremo sur de la Candelaria, provincia de Salta, República Argentina: *Acta Geologiá Lilloana*, 15, pp. 50–58.

_____, 1980, Sobre la presencia de una armadura dérmica en algunos dinosaurios titanosáuridos: *Ibid.*, 15, pp. 41–47.

_____, 1986, Revisión de los Titanosauridos de América del Sur. Tésis Doctoral inédita Fac. de Ciencias Exactas y Naturales, Universidad Nacional de Tucumán, Argentina, 472 pages (unpublished).

_____, 1987, Morfologia del esqueleto axial de los dinosaurios titanosáuridos (Saurischia–Sauropoda) del Estado de Minas Gerais, Brasil: *Anain X Congreso Brasileiro de Paleontologia*, pp. 155–171, Rio de Janeiro.

_____, 1992, Osteologia de *Saltasaurus loricatus* (Sauropoda–Titanosauridae) del Cretácico Superior del Noroeste Argentino, *in*: José Luis Sanz and Ang'gela D. Buscalioni, editors, *Actas 2o Curso de Paleontología en Cuenca, Instituto "Juan de Valdés," Ayuntamiento de Cuenca, pp. 165–230.

———, 2003, Revision of South American titanosaurid dinosaurs: palaeobiological, palaeobiogeographical and phylogenetic aspects: *Records of the Queen Victoria Museum, Launceston*, 111, pp. 1–173.

Price, Llellwyn I., 1953, A presenca de Pterosauria no Cretaceo ineferior de Chapada do Araripe, Brasil: *Anais Acadademie Brasileira Ciencias*, 43 (Suppl.), pp. 451–461.

Prieto-Marquez, Albert, David B. Weishampel, and John R. Horner, 2003, Taxonomy and systematics of the holotype of *Hadrosaurus foulkii* (Dinosauria, Ornithopoda) from the Late Cretaceous of eastern North America: *Journal of Vertebrate Paleontology*, 23 (Supplement to Number 3), Abstracts of Papers, Sixtythird Annual Meeting, p. 88A.

Prum, Richard O., 1999, Development and evolutionary origin and diversification of feathers: *Journal of Experimental Zoology (Mol Dev Evol)*, 285, pp. 291–306.

Prum, Richard O., and Jan Dyck, 2003, A hierarchical model of plumage: morphology, development, and evolution: *Journal of Experimental Zoology (Mol Dev Evol)*, 298B, pp. 73–90.

Pyzalla, Anke, and Magda Stempniewicz, 2002a, SANS studies of fossil dinosaur bone: *GeNF Experimental Report 2002*, 2003/1, pp. 79–80.

———, 2002b, Texture of bone mineral in sauropod bones: *Ibid.*, pp. 151–152.

Qiang Ji, Ji Shúan, You Hailu, Zhang Jianping, Yuan Chongxi, Ji Xinxin, Li Jinglu, and Li Yinxian, 2002, Discovery of an avialae bird—*Shenzouraptor sinensis* gen. et sp. nov.—from China: *Geological Bulletin of China*, 21 (7), pp. 363–369.

Quenstedt, Friedrich August, 1855, Über *Pterodactylus suevicus* im lithographischen schiefer Württembergs: doctoral thesis, Universität Tübingen.

———, 1858, Uber *Pterodactylus liasicus*: *Jahreshect des Vereins für Vaterländische Naturkunde in Württemberg*, 14, pp. 299–336.

Raath, Michael R., 1969, A new coelurosaurian dinosaur from the Forest Sandstone of Rhodesia: *Arnoldia (Rhodesia)*, 4 (28), pp. 1–25.

———, 1977, The anatomy of the Triassic theropod *Syntarsus rhodesiensis* (Saurischia: Podokesauridae) and a consideration of its biology, Ph.D thesis, Rhodes University, Grahamstown (unpublished).

———, 1990, Morphological variation in small theropods and its meaning in systematics: evidence from *Syntarsus rhodesiensis*, *in*: Kenneth Carpenter and Philip J. Currie, editors, *Dinosaur Systematics: Approaches and Perspectives*. Cambridge and New York: Cambridge University Press, pp. 91–105.

Radinsky, Len, 1974, Fossil evidence on anthropoid brain evolution: *American Journal of Physical Anthropology*, 41, pp. 15–27.

Ratkevitch, Ronald P., 1998, New Cretaceous brachiosaurid dinosaur, *Sonorasaurus thompsoni* gen. et sp. nov, from Arizona: *Journal of the Arizona-Nevada Academy of Science*, 31 (1), pp. 71–82.

Rauhut, Oliver W. M., 1997, Zur Schädelanatomie von *Shuvosaurus inexpectatus* (Dinosauria; Theropoda), in S. Sachs, O. W. M. Rauhut, and A. Wright, editors, *Treffender deutschsprachigen Palaeoherpetologen, Düsseldorf*, extended abstracts, pp. 21–23 (on the cranial anatomy of *Shuvosaurus inexpectus* [Dinosauria; Theropoda], translated by Rauhut).

———, 2000, The dinosaur fauna from the Guimarota mine, *in*: T. Martin and B. Krebs, editors, *Guimarota. A Jurassic Ecosystem*. Munich: Verlag Dr. Friedrich Pfeil, pp. 75–82.

———, 2003a, A tyrannosauroid dinosaur from the Upper Jurassic of Portugal: *Palaeontology*, 46 (5), pp. 903–910.

———, 2003b, A dentary of *Patagosaurus* (Sauropoda) from the Middle Jurassic of Patagonia: *Ameghiana*, 40 (3), pp. 425–432.

———, 2003c, The interrelationships and evolution of basal theropod dinosaurs: *Special Papers in Paleontology*, 69, pp. 1–213.

———, 2004a, Braincase structure of the Middle Jurassic theropod dinosaur *Piatnitzkysaurus*: *Canadian Journal of Earth Sciences*, 41, pp. 1109–1122.

———, 2004b, Provenance and anatomy of *Genyodectes serus*, large-toothed ceratosaur (Dinosauria: Theropoda) from Patagonia: *Journal of Vertebrate Paleontology*, 24 (4), pp. 894–902.

———, 2005, Osteology and relationships of a new theropod dinosaur from the Middle Jurassic of Patagonia: *Palaeontology*, 48 (1), pp. 87–110.

Rauhut, Oliver W. M., G. Cladera, Patricia Vickers-Rich, and Thomas H. V. Rich, 2003, Dinosaur remains from the Lower Cretaceous of the Chubut Group, Argentina: *Cretaceous Research*, 24, pp. 487–497.

Rauhut, Oliver W. M., T. Martin, E. Ortiz-Jaureguizar, and P. Puerta, 2002, A Jurassic mammal from South America: *Nature*, 416, pp. 165–168.

Rauhut, Oliver W. M., and P. Puerta, 2001, New vertebrate fossils from the Middle–Late Jurassic, Cañadón Asfalto Formation of Chubut, Argentina: *Ameghiana, Suplemento Resúmenes*, 38, p. 168.

Rauhut, Oliver W. M., P. Puerta, and T. Martin, 2001, Jurassic vertebrates from Patagonia: *Journal of Vertebrate Paleontology*, 21 (Supplement to Number 3), Abstracts of Papers, Sixty-first Annual Meeting, p. 91A.

Rauhut, Oliver W. M., and C. Werner, 1995, First record of the family Dromaeosauridae (Dinosauria: Theropoda) in the Cretaceous of Gondwana (Wadi Milk Formation, northern Sudan): *Paläontologische Zeitschrift*, 69, pp. 475–489.

Rautian, A. S., 1978, A unique bird feather from Jurassic lake deposits in the Karatau: *Paleontological Journal*, 12 (4), pp. 520–526.

Rawson, P. F., D. Curry, F. C. Dilley, J. M. Hancock, W. J. Kenedy, J. W. Neale, C. J. Wood, and B. C. Worssam, 1978, Cretaceous: *Geological Society of London Special Report*, 9, pp. 1–70.

Ray, G. R., 1941, Big for his day: *Natural History*, 48 (1), pp. 36–39.

Rayfield, Emily J., 2004, Using finite element analysis to investigate intracranial mobility: a case study using large, carnivorous dinosaurs: *Journal of Morphology*, 260 (3), 7th International Congress of Vertebrate Morphology, p. 320.

Rayfield, Emily J., David B. Norman, Celeste C. Horner, John R. Horner, P. M. Smith, Jeff J. Thomason, and Paul Upchurch, 2001, Cranial design and function in a large theropod dinosaur: *Nature*, 409, pp. 1033–1037.

Rayner, J. M. V., 1991, Avian flight and the problem of *Archaeopteryx*, *in*: J. M. V. Rayner and R. J. Wooton, editors, *Biomechanics and Evolution*. New York: Cambridge University Press, pp. 183–212.

Reck, H., 1931, Die deutschostafrikanischen Flugsaurier: *Centralblatt f. Mineral. Geol. Paläont.*, Abt. B, 7, pp. 321–336.

Rees, P. McAllister, Christopher R. Noto, J. Michael Parrish, and Judith T. Parrish, 2004, Late Jurassic climates, vegetation, and dinosaur distributions: *The Journal of Geology*, 112, pp. 643–653.

Regal, P. J., 1975, The evolutionary origin of feathers: *Quarterly Review of Biology*, 50, pp. 35–66.

Reid, Robin E. H., 1996, Bone histology of the Cleveland-Lloyd dinosaurs and of dinosaurs in general, part 1: Introduction: *Introduction to Bone Tissues*, Brigham Young University Geology Studies, 41, pp. 25–71.

———, 1997, How dinosaurs grew, *in*: James O. Farlow and Michael K. Brett-Surman, editors, *The Complete Dinosaur*. Bloomington and Indianapolis: Indiana University Press, pp. 403–423.

Remes, Kristian, 2004, The Tendaguru sauropod "*Barosaurus*" *africanus* and the paleobiogeography of diplodocid sauropods: *13th Symposium on Vertebrate Palaeontology and Comparative Anatomy, Papers*, pp. 23–24.

Reser, P. K., Andrew B. Heckert, and Spencer G. Lucas, 2003, New Mexico's most complete skull of the Cretaceous dinosaur *Pentaceratops* (Ornithischia: Ceratopsidae)—insights into the cranial anatomy of the genus: *New Mexico Geology*, 25 (2), p. 54.

Retallack, Gregory J., 2004, End-Cretaceous acid rain as a selective extinction mechanism between birds and dinosaurs, *in*: Philip J. Currie, Eva B. Kopelhus, Martin A. Shugar, and Joanna L. Wright, editors, *Feathered Dragons: Studies on the Transition from Dinosaurs to Birds*. Bloomington and Indianapolis: Indiana University Press, pp. 35–63.

Reyes, F. C., and J. Salfity, 1973, Consideraciones sobre la estratigrafía del Cretácico (Subgrupo Pirgua) del Noroeste argentino: *Actas V Congresso Geológico Argentino*, 3, pp. 355–385.

Riabinin, Anatoly Nikolaenvice N., 1939, The Upper Cretaceous vertebrate fauna of south Kazakhstan. I. Pt. 1, Ornithischia: *Centralnyi Naucno-issledovatelnyi geologiceskij Instituta, Trudy*, 118, pp. 1–40.

Bibliography

_____, 1948, Bemerkung uber ein Flugreptil aus dem Jura des Kara-Tau: *Trudy Paleozoologicheskogo Instituta, Akademiya Nauk USSR*, 15 (1), pp. 86–93.

Riccardi, A. C., 1988, The Cretaceous system of southern South America: *Geological Society of America Memoir*, 168, pp. 1–161.

Ricqlès, Armand J. de, 1980, Tissue structure of dinosaur bone: functional significance and possible relation of dinosaur physiology, *in*: Roger D. K. Thomas and Everett C. Olson, editors. *A Cold Look at the Warm-Blooded Dinosaurs*. Boulder, CO: AAAS Selected Symposium, 28, Westview Press, pp. 103–139.

_____, 2003, Benissart's *Iguanodon*: the case for "fresh" versus "old" dinosaur bone: *Journal of Vertebrate Paleontology*, 23 (Supplement to Number 3), Abstracts of Papers, Sixty-third Annual Meeting, p. 45A.

Ricqlès, Armand de, F. J. Meunier, J. Castanet, and H. Francillon-Viellot, 1991, *in*: B. K. Hall, editor, *Bone*. Boca Raton, FL: CRC, pp. 1–78.

Ricqlès, Armand de, Kevin Padian, and John R. Horner, 2003, On the bone histology of some Triassic pseudosuchian archosaurs and related taxa: *Annales de Paléontologie*, 89, pp. 67–101.

Ridgely, Ryan, and Lawrence Witmer, 2004, New application of CT scanning and 3D modeling for dinosaur visualization: *Journal of Vertebrate Paleontology*, 24 (Supplement to Number 3), Abstracts of Papers, Sixty-fourth Annual Meeting, pp. 103A–104A.

Rigby, J. Keith, A. Rice, and Philip J. Currie, 1987, Dinosaur thermoregulatory Cretaceous/Tertiary survival strategies: *Geological Society of America Abstracts with Programs*, 19 (7), p. 820.

Rigby, J. Keith, Jr., L. W. Sneel, D. M. Unruh, S. S. Harlan, J. Guan, F. Li, J. Keith Rigby, and B. J. Kowalis, 1993, $^{40}Ar/^{39}$ and U-Pb dates for dinosaur extinction, Nanxiong Basin, Guangdong Province, People's Republic of China: *Geological Society of America Conference, Boston, Abstract Program*, 25, p. A296.

Riley, H., and S. Stutchbury, 1836, A description of various fossil remains of three distinct saurian animals discovered in the autumn of 1834, in the Magnesian Conglomerate on Durdham Down, near Bristol: *Proclamations of the Geological Society of London*, 2, pp. 397–399.

Rinehart, Larry F., Andrew B. Heckert, Spencer G. Lucas, and Adrian P. Hunt, 2004, The sclerotic ring of the Late Triassic theropod dinosaur *Coelophysis*: *New Mexico Geology*, 26 (2), p. 64.

Rinehart, Larry F., Spencer G. Lucas, Andrew B. Heckert, and Adrian P. Hunt, 2004, Vision characteristics of *Coelophysis bauri* based on sclerotic ring, orbit, and skull morphology: *Journal of Vertebrate Paleontology*, 24 (Supplement to Number 3), Abstracts of Papers, Sixty-fourth Annual Meeting, p. 104A.

Rogers, Raymond R., Joseph H. Hartman, and David W. Krause, 2000, Stratigraphic analysis of Upper Cretaceous rocks in the Mahajanga Basin, northwestern Madagascar: implications for ancient and modern faunas: *Journal of Geology*, 108, pp. 275–301.

Rogers, Raymond R., David W. Krause, and Kristina Curry Rogers, 2003, Cannibalism in the Madagascan dinosaur *Majungatholus atopus*: *Nature*, 422, pp. 515–518.

Romer, Alfred S. [Sherwood], 1933, *Vertebrate Paleontology*. Chicago: University of Chicago Press, 491 pages.

_____, 1956, *Osteology of the Reptiles*. Chicago: University of Chicago Press, xxi, 772 pages.

Rose, Peter, 2004, A titanosauriform sauropod (Dinosauria, Saurischia) from the Early Cretaceous of central Texas: *Journal of Vertebrate Paleontology*, 24 (Supplement to Number 3), Abstracts of Papers, Sixty-fourth Annual Meeting, p. 105A.

Rosenbaum, Jason N., and Kevin Padian, 2000, New material of the basal thyreophoran *Scutellosaurus lawleri* from the Kayenta Formation (Lower Jurassic) of Arizona: *PaleoBios*, 20 (1), pp. 13–23.

Rossetti, D., A. M. Goés, and W. Truckenbrodt, 2001, *O Cretáceo na Bacia de São Luis-Grajaú*. Belém, Pará: Museu Paraense Emilio Goeldi/Coleção Friedrich Katzer, 264 pages.

Rothschild, Bruce M., Ralph E. Molnar, and Mark Helbling, II, 2003, Behavioral implications of sauropod stress fractures: *Journal of Vertebrate Paleontology*, 23 (Supplement to Number 3), Abstracts of Papers, Sixty-third Annual Meeting, p. 90A.

Rothschild, Bruce M., and Robin Panza, 2004, The pivotal ankle determinant of dinosaur and bird osteoarthritis: *Journal of Vertebrate Paleontology*, 24 (Supplement to Number 3), Abstracts of Papers, Sixty-fourth Annual Meeting, p. 106A.

Rothschild, Bruce M., and Darren H. Tanke, 1997, Thunder in the Cretaceous: interspecies conflict as evidence for ceratopsian migration?, *in*: Donald L. Wolberg, Edmund Stump, and Gary Rosenberg, editors. *Dinofest International: Proceedings of a Symposium Held at Arizona State University*. Philadelphia: Academy of Natural Sciences, pp. 77–81.

_____, 1968, The finding of a giant dinosaur: *Priroda*, 2, pp. 115–116.

Rothschild, Bruce M., Darren H. Tanke, Mark Helbing, and Larry D. Martin, 2003, Epidemiologic study of tumors in dinosaurs: *Naturwissenschaften*, 90, pp. 495–500.

Rowe, Timothy, 1989, A new species of theropod dinosaur *Syntarsus* from the Early Jurassic Kayenta Formation of Arizona: *Journal of Vertebrate Paleontology*, 9 (2), pp. 125–136.

Rowe, Timothy, Edwin H. Colbert, and J. Dale Nations, 1981, The occurrence of *Pentaceratops* with a description of its frill, *in*: Spencer G. Lucas, J. Keith Rigby, Jr., and Barry S. Kues, editors, *Advances in San Juan Basin Paleontology*. Albuquerque: University of New Mexico Press, pp. 29–48.

Rowe, Timothy, and Jacques A. Gauthier, 1990, Ceratosauria, *in*: David B. Weis-hampel, Peter Dodson, and Halszka Osmólska, editors, *The Dinosauria*. Berkeley and Los Angeles: University of California Press, pp. 151–168.

Rozhestvensky, Anatoly Konstantinovich, 1952, Discovery of iguanodonts in Mongolia: *Doklady Akademii Nauk CCCP*, 84, pp. 1243–1246.

_____, 1964, Family Hadrosauridae, *in*: Y. A. Orlov, editor, *Osnovy Paleontologii, Izdatelstvo Nauka*. Moscow, pp. 559–572.

_____, 1965, Growth changes in Asian dinosaurs and some problems of their taxonomy: *Palaeontologicheskii Zhurnal*, 3, pp. 95–109.

_____, 1967, New iguanodonts from Central Asia: *International Geology Review*, 9, pp. 556–566.

_____, 1968, [Hadrosaurs of Kazakhstan], *in*: *Upper Paleozoic and Mesozoic Amphibians and Reptiles of the USSR*. Moscow: Nauka, pp. 97–141.

_____, 1993, The role of Central Asia in dinosaurian biogeography: *Canadian Journal of Earth Sciences*, 20, pp. 2002–2012.

Ruben, John A., and Terry D. Jones, 2000, Contrasting locomotory styles in bipedal dinosaurs and cursorial birds: *Publications in Paleontology* [The Florida Symposium on Dinosaur Bird Evolution, abstracts of papers], 2, p. 23–24.

Ruben, John A., Terry D. Jones, and Nicholas R. Geist, 2003, Respiratory and reproductive paleophysiology of dinosaurs and early birds: *Physiological and Biochemical Zoology*, 76 (2), pp. 141–164.

Russell, Dale A., 1969, A new specimen of *Stenonychosaurus* from the Oldman Formation (Cretaceous) of Alberta: *Canadian Journal of Earth Sciences*, 6, pp. 595–612.

_____, 1970, Tyrannosaurs from the Late Cretaceous of western Canada: *National Museum of Natural Sciences, Publications in Paleontology*, 1, viii, 34 pages.

_____, 1972, Ostrich dinosaurs from the Late Cretaceous of western Canada: *Canadian Journal of Earth Sciences*, 9, pp. 375–402.

_____, 1993, The role of Central Asia in dinosaurian biogeography: *Ibid.*, 20, pp. 2002–2012.

_____, 1996, Isolated dinosaur bones from the Middle Cretaceous of the Tafilalt, Morocco: *Bulletin du Museum national d'Histoire naturelle, Paris*, sér. 4 (18), Section C, nos. 2–3, pp. 3409–402.

Russell, Dale A., and Peter Dodson, 1997, The extinction of the dinosaurs: a dialogue between a catastrophist and a gradualist, *in*: James O. Farlow and Michael K. Brett-Surman, editors, *The Complete Dinosaur*. Bloomington and Indianapolis, Indiana University Press, pp. 78–91.

Russell, Dale A., and Dong Zhi-Ming, 1993, The affinities of a new theropod from the Alxa Desert, Inner Mongolia, People's Republic of China: *Canadian Journal of Earth Sciences*, 30 (10–11), pp. 2107–2127.

_____, 1994, A nearly complete skeleton of a new troodontid dinosaur from the Early Cretaceous of the Ordos Basin, Inner Mongolia, People's Republic of China: *Ibid.*, 30 (10–11), pp. 2163–2173.

Russell, Dale A., and Zhao Xijin, 1996, New

psittacosaur occurrences in Inner Mongolia: *Canadian Journal of Earth Sciences*, 33, pp. 637–648.

Russell, Dale A., and Zhong Zheng, 1993, A large mamenchisaurid from the Junggar Basin, Xinjiang, People's Republic of China: *Canadian Journal of Earth Sciences*, 30 (10–11), pp. 2082–2095.

Ruxton, Graeme D., and David C. Houston, 2003, Could *Tyrannosaurus rex* have been a scavenger rather than a predator? An energetics approach: *Proceedings of the Royal Society of London*, B270, pp. 731–733.

Ryan, Michael, and Anthony P. Russell, 2003, New centrosaurine ceratopsids from the Late Campanian of Alberta and Montana and a review of contemporaneous and regional patterns of centrosaurine evolution: *Journal of Vertebrate Paleontology*, 23 (Supplement to Number 3), Abstracts of Papers, Sixty-third Annual Meeting, p. 91A.

Sabath, Karol, 1991, Upper Cretaceous amniotic eggs from the Gobi Desert: *Paleontological Polonica*, 36, pp. 151–192.

Sacchi Vialli, G., 1964, Revisione della fauna di Saltrio: *Atti Ist. Geol. Unività di Pavia*, 15, pp. 146–161.

Sadleir, Rudyard, Paul M. Barrett, and Philip Powell, 2004, Anatomy and systematics of *Eustreptospondylus oxoniensis* (Dinosauria: Theropoda): evolutionary implication: *Journal of Vertebrate Paleontology*, 24 (Supplement to Number 3), Abstracts of Papers, Sixty-fourth Annual Meeting, p. 107A.

Sahni, A., 2001, *Dinosaurs of India*. New Delhi: National Book Trust, 110 pages.

Salgado, Leonardo, 1996, *Pellegrinisaurus powelli* nov. gen. et sp. (Sauropoda, Titanosauridae) from the upper Cretaceous of Lago Pellegrini, North-western Patagonia, Argentina: *Ameghiniana*, 33 (4), pp. 355–365.

_____, 2001, Los Saurópodos de Patagonia: sistermática, evolución y paleobiologia, *in*: Colectivo Arqueologico-Paleontologico de Salas, C.A.S., editors, *Actas de las I Jornadas Internacionales sobre Paleontologia de Dinosaurios y su Entorno (Proceedings of the 1st International Symposium on Paleontology of Dinosaurs and their Environment)*. Burgos, Spain, pp. 139–168.

_____, 2003, Los saurópodos de Patagonia: sistemática, evolución y paleobiología, *in*: *Actas de las II Journadas Internacionales sobre Paleontológia de Dinosaurios y su Entorno, Salas de Los Infantes, España*, pp. 139–168.

_____, 2004, Considerations on the bony plates assigned to titanosaurs (Dinosauria, Sauropoda): *Ameghiniana*, 40 (3), pp. 441–456.

Salgado, Leonardo, and José F. Bonaparte, 1991, Un nuevo sauropodo Dicraeosauridae, *Amargasaurus cazui* gen. et sp. nov., de la Formacion la Amarga, Neocomiano de la Provincia del Neuquen, Argentina: *Ameghiniana*, 28 (3–4), pp. 333–346, Buenos Aires.

Salgado, Leonardo, and Jorge Orlando Calvo, 1997, Evolution of titanosaurid sauropods. II. The cranial evidence: *Ameghiniana*, 34 (1), pp. 33–48.

Salgado, Leonardo, and Rodolfo A. Coria, 1993a, Consideraciones sobre las relaciones filogenticas de *Opisthocoelicaudia skarynskii* (Sauropoda) del Cretácico superior de Mongolia: *Ameghiniana*, 30, p. 339.

_____, 1993b, Un nuevo titanosaurino (Sauropoda–Titanosauridae) de la Fm. Allen (Campaniano–Maastrichtiano) de la Provincio de Río Negro, Argentina: *Ibid.*, 33, pp. 367–371.

Salgado, Leonardo, Rodolfo Aníbal Coria, and Jorge Orlando Calvo, 1997, Evolution of titanosaurid sauropods. I: Phylogenetic analysis based on the postcranial evidence: *Ameghiniana*, 34 (1), pp. 3–32.

Salgado, Leonardo, Rodolfo Aníbal Coria, and Susana E. Heredia, 1997, New materials of *Gasparinisaura cincosaltensis* (Ornithischia, Ornithopoda) from the Upper Cretaceous of Argentina: *Journal of Paleontology*, 71 (5), pp. 933–940.

Salgado, Leonardo, Rodolfo A. Coria, and Luis M. Chiappe, 2005, Osteology of the sauropod embryos from the Upper Cretaeous of Patagonia: *Acta Palaeontological Polonica*, 50 (1), pp. 79–92.

Salgado, Leonardo, Alberto Garrido, Sergio E. Cocca, and Juan R. Cocca, 2004, Lower Cretaceous rebbachisaurid sauropods from Cerro Aguada del León (Lohan Cura Formation), Neuquen Province, Northwestern Patagonia, Argentina: *Journal of Vertebrate Paleontology*, 24 (4), pp. 903–912.

Salgado, Leonardo, and Rubén D. Martínez, 1993, Relaciones filogeneticas de los titanosauridos basales *Andesaurus delgadoi* y *Epachthosaurus* sp.: *Ameghiniana*, 30, pp. 339–340.

Sampson, Scott D., and Catherine A. Forster, 2001, Parallel evolution in hadrosaurid and ceratopsid dinosaurs: *Journal of Vertebrate Paleontology*, 21 (Supplement to Number 3), Abstracts of Papers, Sixty-first Annual Meeting, p. 96A.

Sampson, Scott D., Mark A. Loewen, James O. Farlow, and Matthew T. Carrano, 2003, Ecological and evolutionary implications of gigantism in theropod dinosaurs: *Journal of Vertebrate Paleontology*, 23 (Supplement to Number 3), Abstracts of Papers, Sixty-third Annual Meeting, p. 92A.

Sampson, Scott D., Michal J. Ryan, and Darren H. Tanke, 1997, Craniofacial ontogeny in centrosaurine dinosaurs (Ornithischia: Ceratopsidae): taphonomic and behavioral phylogenetic implications: *Zoological Journal of the Linnean Society*, 121, pp. 293–337.

Sampson, Scott D., Lawrence M. Witmer, Catherine A. Forster, David W. Krause, M. P. O'Connor, Peter Dodson, and Florent Ravoavy, 1998, Predatory dinosaur remains from Madagascar: implications for the Cretaceous biogeography of Gondwana: *Science*, 280, pp. 1048–1051.

Sanchez, Teresa M., 1973, Redescripción del craneo y mandibulas de *Pterodaustro guinazui* Bonaparte (Pterodactyloidea, Pterodaustriidae): *Ameghiniana*, 10, pp. 313–325.

Sander, P. Martin, 1997, Teeth and jaws, *in*:

Philip J. Currie and Kevin Padian, editors, *Encyclopedia of Dinosaurs*. San Diego: Academic Press, pp. 717–725.

_____, 2003, Long and girdle bone histology in sauropod dinosaurs: methods of study and implications for growth, life history, taxonomy, and evolution: *Journal of Vertebrate Paleontology*, 23 (Supplement to Number 3), Abstracts of Papers, Sixty-third Annual Meeting, p. 93A.

Sander, P. Martin, Thomas Laven, Octávio Mateus, and Niels Knoetschke, 2004, Insular dwarfism in a brachiosaurid sauropod from the Upper Jurassic of Germany: *Journal of Vertebrate Paleontology*, 24 (Supplement to Number 3), Abstracts of Papers, Sixty-fourth Annual Meeting, p. 108A.

Sanz, José Luis, Bernardino P. Pérez-Moreno, Luis M. Chiappe, and Angela D. Buscalioni, 2002, The birds from the Lower Cretaceous of Las Hoyas (Province of Cuenca, Spain), *in*: Luis M. Chiappe and Lawrence M. Witmer, editors, *Mesozoic Birds: Above the Heads of Dinosaurs*. Berkeley and Los Angeles: University of California Press, pp. 209–229.

Sanz, José Luis, and José F. Bonaparte, 1992, A new order of birds (Class Aves) from the Lower Cretaceous of Spain, *in*: Kenneth E. Campbell, editor, *Papers in Avian Paleontology, Honoring Pierce Brodkorb*, Science Series 36. Los Angeles: Natural History Museum of Los Angeles County, pp. 39–49.

Sanz, José Luis, and Angela D. Buscalioni, 1992, A new bird from the Early Cretaceous of Las Hoyas, Spain, and the Early radiation of birds: *Paleontology*, 35 (4), pp. 829–845.

Sanz, José Luis, Luis M. Chiappe, Bernardino P. Pérez-Moreno, Angela D. Buscalioni, José J. Moratalla, Fracisco Ortega, and Francisco J. Poyata-Ariza, 1996, An Early Cretaceous bird from Spain and its implications for the evolution of avian flight: *Nature*, 382, pp. 442–445.

Sanz, José Luis, Jaime E. Powell, Jean Le Loeuff, Rubén Martinez, and Xabier Pereda-Suberbiola, 1999, Sauropod remains from the Upper Cretaceous of Laño (northcentral Spain), Titanosaur phylogenetic relationships: *Est. Museo de Ciencias Naturales de Alava*, 14 (1), pp. 235–255.

Sauer, E. G. F., and E. M. Sauer, 1966, The behavior and ecology of the South African ostrich: *Living Bird*, 5, pp. 45–75.

Sauvage, H. E., 1882, Recherches sur les reptiles trouvés dans le Gault de l'est du basin de Paris: *Mémoires de la Société géologique de France*, 2 (4), pp. 1–41.

Sawyer, Robert H., and Loren W. Knapp, 2003, Avian skin development and the evolutionary origin of feathers: *Journal of Experimental Zoology (Mol Dev Evol)*, 298B, pp. 1023–1026.

Scheyer, Torsten M., and P. Martin Sander, 2004, Histology of ankylosaur osteoderms: implications for systematics and function: *Journal of Vertebrate Paleontology*, 24 (4), pp. 874–893.

Schmidt, M., 1938, *Die Lebewelt unserer Trias: Natchtrag 1938*. Oehringen, Germany:

Bibliography

Hohenlohésche Buchhandlung F. Rau, 143 pages.

Schmidt-Nielson, Knut, 1984, *Scaling: Why Is Animal Size So Important?* Cambridge, England: Cambridge University Press, 241 pages.

Schouten, Remmert, 2000, The Tyherington *Thecodontosaurus*, a prosauropod dinosaur: *5th European Workshop on Vertebrate Palaeontology, Karlsruhe,* 27.06 – 01.07. 2000, p. 73.

Schubert, Blaine W., and Peter S. Ungar, 2005, Wear facets and enamel spalling in tyrannosaurid dinosaurs: *Acta Palaeontologica Polonica,* 50 (1), pp. 93–99.

Schudack, Michael E., Geological setting and dating of the Guimarota beds, *in:* T. Martin and B. Krebs, editors, *Guimarota. A Jurassic Ecosystem.* Munich: Verlag Dr. Friedrich Pfeil, pp. 21–26.

Schwarz, Daniela, 2004, Reconstructions of air-sac systems and musculature in the neck of *Diplodocus* (Sauropodomorpha): *13th Symposium on Vertebrate Palaeontology and Comparative Anatomy, Papers,* pp. 25–26.

Schweitzer, Mary H. [Higby], Jennifer Wittmeyer, and John R. Horner, 2004, A novel dinosaurian tissue exhibiting unusual preservation: *Journal of Vertebrate Paleontology,* 24 (Supplement to Number 3), Abstracts of Papers, Sixty-fourth Annual Meeting, p. 111A.

Scotese, Christopher R., 2001, *Atlast of Earth History.* Arlington, TX: PALEOMAP Project.

Seeley, Harry Govier, 1864, On the fossil birds of the Upper Greensand, *Palaeocolyntus barretti* and *Pekargonis sedgwicki: Proceedings of the Cambridge Philosophical Society,* 1, 228 pages.

_____, 1869, *Index to the fossil remains of Aves, Ornithosauria, and Reptilia, from the secondary system of strata arranged in the Woodwardian Museum of the University of Cambridge.* Cambridge, England: Deighton, Bell, 143 pages.

_____, Seeley, 1870a, *The Ornithosauria: An Elementary Study of the Bones of Pterodactyles.* Cambridge, 130 pages.

_____, 1870b, Remarks on Professor Owen's monograph on *Dimorphodon: Annals and Magazine of Natural History,* 4, pp. 129–152.

_____, 1870c, On *Ornithopsis,* a gigantic animal of the Pterodactyl kind from the Wealden: *Ibid.,* 4 (5), 283 pages.

_____, 1871, Additional evidence of the structure of the head in ornithosaurs from the Cambridge Upper Greensand; being a supplement to "The Ornithosauria": *Ibid.,* 7 (37), pp. 20–36.

_____, 1875, On an ornithosaurian (*Doratorhynchus validus*) from the Purbeck Limestone of Langton near Swanage: *Quarterly Journal of the Geological Society of London,* 31, pp. 465–468.

_____, 1876, On the British fossil Cretaceous birds: *Quarterly Journal of the Geological Society of London,* 32, pp. 496–512.

_____, 1879, On the Dinosauria of the Cambridge Greensand: *Ibid.,* 35, pp. 591–636.

_____, 1880, On *Rhamphorhynchus Prestwichi,*

Seeley, an Ornithosaurian from the Stonesfield Slate of Kineton: *Ibid.,* 36, pp. 27–30.

_____, 1881, On the reptile fauna of the Gosau Formation preserved in the Geological Museum on the University of Vienna: *Ibid.,* 37, pp. 619–707.

Sellers, William, and Gregory S. Paul, 2004, Speed in giant tyrannosaurs: evolutionary computer simulation: *Journal of Vertebrate Paleontology,* 24 (Supplement to Number 3), Abstracts of Papers, Sixty-fourth Annual Meeting, pp. 111A–112A.

Senter, Philip, 2004, Range of motion in the forelimbs of *Mononykus,* and functional implication: *Journal of Vertebrate Paleontology,* 24 (Supplement to Number 3), Abstracts of Papers, Sixty-fourth Annual Meeting, p. 112A.

Senter, Philip, Rinchen Barsbold, Brooks B. Britt, and David A. Burnham, 2004, Systematics and evolution of Dromaeosauridae (Dinosauria, Theropoda): *Bulletin of Gunma Museum of Natural History,* 8, pp. 1–20.

Senter, Philip, and James H. Robins, 2003, Taxonomic status of the specimens of *Archaeopteryx: Journal of Vertebrate Paleontology,* 23 (4), pp. 961–965.

Sereno, Paul C., 1986, Phylogeny of the bird-hipped dinosaurs (order Ornithischia): *National Geographic Research,* 2, pp. 234–256.

_____, 1990, New data on parrot-beaked dinosaurs (*Psittacosaurus*), *in:* Kenneth Carpenter and Philip J. Currie, editors, *Dinosaur Systematics: Approaches and Perspectives.* Cambridge and New York: Cambridge University Press, pp. 203–310.

_____, 1991a, *Lesothosaurus,* "fabrosaurids," and the early evolution of Ornithischia: *Journal of Vertebrate Paleontology,* 11 (2), pp. 168–197.

_____, 1991b, Basal archosaurs: phylogenetic relationships and functional implications: *Ibid.,* Supplement to Number 4, 31 December 1991, Society of Vertebrate Paleontology Memoir 2, ii, 53 pages.

_____, 1993, The pectoral girdle and forelimb of the basal theropod *Herrerasaurus ischigualastensis: Ibid.,* 13 (4), pp. 425–450.

_____, 1997, The origin and evolution of dinosaurs: *Annual Review of Earth and Planetary Sciences,* 25, pp. 435–490.

_____, 1998, A rationale for phylogenetic definitions, with application to the higher-level taxonomy of Dinosauria: *Neus Jahrbuch für Geologie und Paläontologie, Abhandlungen,* 1998 (189).

_____, 1999a, The evolution of dinosaurs: *Science,* 284, pp. 2137–2147.

_____, 1999b, A rationale for dinosaurian taxonomy: *Journal of Vertebrate Paleontology,* 19 (4), pp. 788–790.

_____, 2000, The fossil record, systematics and evolution of pachycephalosaurs and ceratopsians from Asia, *in:* M. J. Benton, M. A. Shishkin, D. M. Unwin, and E. N. Kurochkin, editors, *The Age of Dinosaurs in Russia and Mongolia.* Cambridge: Cambridge University Press, pp. 480–516.

_____, 2001, Alvarezsauridae: birds or ornithomimisaurs?, *in:* Jacques Gauthier and I. F. Gall, editors, *New Prospectives on*

the origin and early evolution of birds: proceedings of the International Symposium in Honor of John H. Ostrom. New Haven, CT: Peabody Museum of Natural History, pp. 69–98.

Sereno, Paul C., Allison L. Beck, Didier B. Dutheil, Boubacar Gado, Hans C. E. Larsson, Gabrielle H. Lyon, Jonathan D. Marcot, Oliver W. M. Rauhut, Rudyard W. Sadleir, Christian A. Sidor, David D. Varricchio, Gregory P. Wilson, and Jeffrey A. Wilson, 1998, A long-snouted predatory dinosaur from Africa and the evolution of spinosaurids: *Science,* 282 (5392), pp. 1298–1302.

Sereno, Paul C., Allison L. Beck, Didier B. Dutheil, Hans C. E. Larsson, Gabrielle H. Lyon, Bourahima Moussa, Rudyard W. Sadleir, Christian A. Sidor, David J. Varricchio, Gregory P. Wilson, and Jeffrey A. Wilson, 1999, Cretaceous sauropods from the Sahara and the uneven rate of skeletal evolution among dinosaurs: *Science,* 286, pp. 1342–1347.

Sereno, Paul C., Allison L. Beck, Didier B. Dutheil, M. Iarochene, Hans C. E. Larsson, Gabrielle H. Lyon, Paul M. Magwene, Christian A. Sidor, David J. Varricchio, and Jeffrey A. Wilson, 1996, Predatory dinosaurs from the Sahara and Late Cretaceous faunal differentiation: *Science,* 272, pp. 996–990.

Sereno, Paul C., and Dong Zhi-Ming, 1992, The skull of the basal stegosaur *Huayangosaurus taibaii* and a cladistic diagnosis of Stegosauria: *Journal of Vertebrate Paleontology,* 12 (3), pp. 318–343.

Sereno, Paul C., Catherine A. Forster, Raymond R. Rogers, and Alfredo M. Monetta, 1993, Primitive dinosaur skeleton from Argentina and the early evolution of Dinosauria: *Nature,* 361, pp. 64–66.

Sereno, Paul C., Chao Shichin [Zhao Xijin], and Rao Chenggang, 1988, *Psittacosaurus meileyingensis* (Ornithischia: Ceratopsia), a new psittacosaur from the Lower Cretaceous of Northeastern China: *Journal of Vertebrate Paleontology,* 8 (4), pp. 366–377.

Sereno, Paul C., Sichin Chao [Zhao Xijin], Zhengwu Cheng, and Rao Chenggang, 1988, *Psittacosaurus meileyingensis* (Ornithischia, Ceratopsia), a new psittacosaur from the Lower Cretaceous of northeastern China: *Journal of Vertebrate Paleontology,* 8 (4), pp. 366–377.

Sereno, Paul C., and Rao Chenggang, 1992, Early evolution of avian flight and perching: new evidence from the Lower Cretaceous of China: *Science,* pp. 845–848.

Sereno, Paul C., Rao Chenggang, and Li Jianjun, 2002, *Sinornis santensis* (Aves: Enantiornithes) from the Early Cretaceous of Northeastern China, *in:* Luis M. Chiappe and Lawrence M. Witmer, editors, *Mesozoic Birds: Above the Heads of Dinosaurs.* Berkeley and Los Angeles: University of California Press, pp. 184–208.

Sereno, Paul C., Jeffrey A. Wilson, and Jack L. Conrad, 2004, New dinosaurs link southern landmasses in the Mid-Cretaceous: *Proceedings of the Royal Society of London,* FirstCite E-Publishing, B, 6 pages.

Seymour, R. S., 1979, Dinosaur eggs: gas

conductance through the shell, water loss during incubation and clutch size: *Paleobiology*, 5, pp. 1–11.

Sharov, A. G., 1971, Nouveletayushche reptilli iz Mesozoy a Kazakhstanai i Kirgizii [New flying reptiles from the Mesozoic of Kazakhstan and Kirgizia]: *Trudy Paleozoologicheskogo Instituta, Akademiya Nauk USSR*, 130, pp. 104–113.

Shu Ziqing, and Zhang Zerun, 1985, Early Cretaceous charophytes from the Hetao area of Inner Mongolia: *Selected Papers of the First National Fossil Algae Symposium, Beijing*, pp. 63–74.

Shufeldt, R. W., 1915, The fossil remains of a species of *Hesperornis* found in Montana: *The Auk*, 32, pp. 290–294.

Sikes, Sylvia K., 1971, *The Natural History of the African Elephant*. New York: American Elsevier, 397 pages.

Simmons, David J., 1965, The non-theropod reptiles of the Lufeng Basin, Yunnan, China: *Fieldiana, Geology*, 15, pp. 1–93.

Sipla, Justin, Justin Georgi, and Catherine Forster, 2004, The semicircular canals of dinosaurs: tracking major transitions in locomotion: *Journal of Vertebrate Paleontology*, 24 (Supplement to Number 3), Abstracts of Papers, Sixty-fourth Annual Meeting, p. 113A.

Skidnuk, D., 1985, Make no bones about it: dinosaur find important: *Grand Prairie Daily Herald-Tribune*, November 6, p. 1.

Sloan, Robert E., 1987, Paleocene and latest Cretaceous mammal ages, biozones, magnetozones, rates of sedimentation and evolution, *in*: James E. Fassett and J. Keith Rigby, editors, *The Cretaceous-Tertiary Boundary in the San Juan and Raton Basins, New Mexico and Colorado*. Boulder, CO: Geological Society of America, Special Paper, 209, pp. 165–200.

Smith, Alan G., David G. Smith, and Brian M. Funnell, 1994, *Atlas of Mesozoic and Cenozoic Coastlines*. Cambridge: Cambridge University Press, p. 99.

Smith, David K., 1993, The type specimen of *Oviraptor philoceratops*, a theropod dinosaur from the Upper Cretaceous of Mongolia: *Neus Jahrbuch für Geologie und Paläontologie, Abhandlungen*, 186 (3), pp. 365–388.

_____, 1998, A morphometric analysis of *Allosaurus*: *Journal of Vertebrate Paleontology*, 18 (1), pp. 126–142.

_____, 2003, Cranial variation within *Allosaurus fragilis*: *Journal of Vertebrate Paleontology*, 23 (Supplement to Number 3), Abstracts of Papers, Sixty-third Annual Meeting, p. 98A.

Smith, David K., James I. Kirkland, Kent Sanders, Lindsay E. Zanno, and Donald Deblieux, 2004, A comparison of North American therizinosaur (Theropoda: Dinosauria) braincases: *Journal of Vertebrate Paleontology*, 24 (Supplement to Number 3), Abstracts of Papers, Sixty-fourth Annual Meeting, p. 114A.

Smith, David K., and Francis J. Lisak, 2001, An unusual specimen of *Allosaurus* from southeastern Utah: *BYU Geology Studies*, 46, pp. 93–98.

Smith, Joshua B., and Peter Dodson, 2003, A proposal for standard terminology of anatomical notation and orientation in fossil vertebrate dentition: *Journal of Vertebrate Paleontology*, 23 (11), pp. 1–12.

Smith, Joshua B., Jerald D. Harris, Gomaa I. Omar, Peter Dodson, and You Hailu, 2001, Biostratigraphy and avian origins in northeastern China, *in*: J. Gauthier and L. F. Gall, editors, *New Perspectives on the Origin and Early Evolution of Birds: Proceedings of the International Symposium in Honor of John H. Ostrom*. New Haven: Peabody Museum of Natural History, Yale University, pp. 549–589.

Smith, Joshua B., and David W. Krause, 2003, On the occurrence of *Majungatholus atopus* in India: implications for abelisauroid paleobiogeography: *Journal of Vertebrate Paleontology*, 23 (Supplement to Number 3), Abstracts of Papers, Sixty-third Annual Meeting, pp. 98A–99A.

Smith, Joshua B., Scott D. Sampson, Eric Roberts, Michael Getty, and Mark Loewen, 2004, A new chasmosaurine ceratopsian from the Upper Cretaceous Kaiparowits Formation, Grand Staircase-Escalante National Monument, UT: *Journal of Vertebrate Paleontology*, 24 (Supplement to Number 3), Abstracts of Papers, Sixty-fourth Annual Meeting, p. 114A.

Smith, Nathan, 2003, Implications of a pentadactyl ground state for the avian hand on the homology of the theropod manus: should the frame-shift hypothesis be shifted?: *Journal of Vertebrate Paleontology*, 23 (Supplement to Number 3), Abstracts of Papers, Sixty-third Annual Meeting, p. 99A.

Snively, Eric, 2003, A theoretical model of neck musculoskeletal function in the Tyrannosauridae: *Journal of Vertebrate Paleontology*, 23 (Supplement to Number 3), Abstracts of Papers, Sixty-third Annual Meeting, p. 99A.

Snively, Eric, and Donald Henderson, 2004, Nasal fusion reinforced: the rostrum of tyrannosauroids: *Journal of Vertebrate Paleontology*, 24 (Supplement to Number 3), Abstracts of Papers, Sixty-fourth Annual Meeting, p. 116A.

Snively, Eric, and Anthony P. Russell, 2003, A kinetic model of tyrannosaurid arctometatarsus function (Dinosauria: Theropoda): *Journal of Morphology*, 255, pp. 215–227.

Snively, Eric, Anthony P. Russell, and G. Lawrence Powell, 2004, Evolutionary morphology of the coelurosaurian arctometatarsus: descriptive, morphometric and phylogenetic approaches: *Zoological Journal of the Linnean Society*, 142, pp. 525–553.

Soemmering, Samuel Thomas von, 1912, Uber einin *Ornithocephalus*: *Denkschriften königlichen Bayerischen Akademie der Wissenschaften Mathematisch-phys.*, CI, 3, pp. 89–158.

Spamer, Earle E., 2004, The Great Extinct Lizard: *Hadrosaurus foulkii*, "first dinosaur" of film and stage: *The Mosaur*, 7, pp. 109–125.

Spinage, Clive A., 1994, *Elephants*. London: T. & A. D. Poyser, 319 pages.

Starck, J. M., 1996, Comparative morphology and cytokinetics of skeletal growth in hatchlings of altricial and precocial birds: *Zoologische Anzeiger.*, 235, pp. 53–75.

Steel, Rodney, 1969, Ornithischia, *in*, Oskar Kuhn, editor, *Handbuch der Palaeoherpetologie*, part 15. Stuttgart: Gustav Fischer Verlag, 87 pages.

_____, 1970, Saurischia, *in*, Oskar Kuhn, editor, *Handbuch der Palaeoherpetologie*, part 16. Stuttgart: Gustav Fischer Verlag, 87 pages.

Steele, Erin, Henry Fricke, and Raymond Rogers, 2003, Carbon isotope evidence for ecological niche partitioning among herbivorous dinosaurs of the Judith River Formation, Montana: *Journal of Vertebrate Paleontology*, 23 (Supplement to Number 3), Abstracts of Papers, Sixty-third Annual Meeting, p. 100A.

Stegmann, B. C., 1978, Relationships of the superorders Alectoromorphae and Charadriomorphae (Aves): a comparative study of the avian hand: *Publications of the Nuttall Ornithological Club*, 17, pp. 1–199.

Stempniewicz, Magdalena, and Anke Pyzalla, 2003, Tendaguru sauropod dinosaurs — characterization of diagenetic alterations in fossil bone: *Annual Report 2003 Selected Results*, pp. 42–43.

_____, 2004, Growth strategy of sauropod dinosaurs studied by pole figure analysis: *GeNF—Experimental Report 2003*, pp. 189–191.

Sternberg, Charles M., 1935, Hooded hadrosaurs of the Belly River Series of the Upper Cretaceous: *Bulletin of the National Museums of Canada*, 77, pp. 1–37.

_____, 1945, Pachycephalosauridae proposed for dome-headed dinosaurs, *Stegoceras lambei*, n. sp., described: *Journal of Paleontology*, 19, pp. 534–538.

_____, 1951, Complete skeleton of *Leptoceratops gracilis* Brown from the Upper Edmonton Formation on Red Deer River, Alberta: *Annual Report of the National Museum for the Fiscal Year 1948–1949*, Bulletin 123, pp. 225–255.

_____, 1970, Comments on dinosaurian preservation in the Cretaceous of Alberta and Wyoming: *National Museums of Canada, Publications in Natural History*, 4, pp. 1–9.

Sternfield, R., 1911, Zur Nomenklatur der Gattung *Gigantosaurus* Fraas: *Sitzungberichte der Gesellischafti Naturfürschender Freunde zu Berlin*, 398 pages.

Stevens, Kent A., and J. Michael Parrish, 1999, Neck posture and feeding of two Jurassic sauropod dinosaurs: *Science*, 284, pp. 798–800.

Stokes, William L., 1957, Pterodactyl tracks from the Morrison Formation: *Journal of Paleontology*, 31 (5), pp. 952–954.

Stolley, E., 1936, *Odontorhynchus aculeatus*, n. g. n. sp., ein neuer Rhamphorhynchidae von Solnhofen: *Neus Jarbuch für Mineralogie, Geologie, und Paläontologie*, Beil-Bd., 75, pp. 543–564.

Storrs, Glenn W., and W. J. Garcia, 2001, Preliminary analysis of a monospecific sauropod locality from Carbon County, Montana: *Journal of Vertebrate Paleontology*, 21

Bibliography

(Supplement to Number 3), Abstracts of Papers, Sixty-first Annual Meeting, p. 105A.

Stovall, J. Willis, and Wann Langston, Jr., 1950, *Acrocanthosaurus atokensis*, a new genus and species of Lower Cretaceous Theropoda from Oklahoma: *The American Midland Naturalist*, 43 (3), pp. 696–728.

Stoyanow, A. A., 1949, Lower Cretaceous stratigraphy in southeastern Arizona: *Geological Survey of America, Memoirs*, 38, pp. 1–169.

Strand, E., 1928, Miscellanea nomenclatorica Zoologies et Palaeontologica: *Arch. Naturgesch*, 92, pp. 30–75.

Suarez, Celina A., 2004, Taphonomy and rare earth element geochemistry of the *Stegosaurus* sp. at the Cleveland-Lloyd Dinosaur Quarry: *2004 GSA Northeastern and Southeastern Sections Meeting*, 95, p. 39.

Suarez, Celina A., and Marina Suarez, 2004, Use of facies and rare earth element geochemistry at the Cleveland-Lloyd Dinosaur Quarry: tools for bone bed interpretations: *Journal of Vertebrate Paleontology*, 24 (Supplement to Number 3), Abstracts of Papers, Sixty-fourth Annual Meeting, p. 119A.

Suarez, Marina, Celina A. Suarez, David Grandstaff, Dennis Terry, Jr., and James I. Kirkland, 2004, Sedimentological, taphonomic, and rare earth geochemical analyses of the Early Cretaceous (Barremian) Crystal Geyser Dinosaur Quarrt, east-central Utah: *Journal of Vertebrate Paleontology*, 24 (Supplement to Number 3), Abstracts of Papers, Sixty-fourth Annual Meeting, p. 119A.

Sues, Hans-Dieter, 1978, A new small theropod dinosaur from the Judith River Formation (Campanian) of Alberta, Canada: *Zoological Journal of the Linnean Society*, 62, pp. 381–400.

Sues, Hans-Dieter, Eberhard Frey, David M. Martill, and Diane M. Scott, 2002, *Irritator challengeri*, a spinosaurid (Dinosauria: Theropoda) from the Lower Cretaceous of Brazil: *Journal of Vertebrate Paleontology*, 22 (3), pp. 535–547.

Sues, Hans-Dieter, and Peter M. Galton, 1987, Anatomy and classification of the North American Pachycephalosauria (Dinosauria: Ornithischia): *Palaeontografica*, Abstract A, 198, pp. 1–40.

Sues, Hans-Dieter, and Philippe Taquet, 1979, A pachycephalosaurid dinosaur from Madagascar and a Laurasian-Gondwanaland connection in the Cretaceous: *Nature*, 279, pp. 633–635.

Sullivan, Corwin, Farish A. Jenkins, Stephen M. Gatesy, and Neil H. Shubin, 2003, A functional assessment of hind foot posture in the prosauropod dinosaur *Plateosaurus*: *Journal of Vertebrate Paleontology*, 23 (Supplement to Number 3), Abstracts of Papers, Sixty-third Annual Meeting, p. 102A.

Sullivan, Robert M., 1999, *Nodocephalosaurus kirtlandensis*, gen. et sp. nov., a new ankylosaurid dinosaur (Ornithischia: Ankylosauria) from the Upper Cretaceous Kirtland Formation (Upper Campanian), San Juan Basin, NM: *Journal of Vertebrate Paleontology*, 19 (1), pp. 126–139.

_____, 2000a, *Prenocephale edmontonensis* (Brown and Schlaikjer) new comb. and *P. brevis* new comb. (Dinosauria: Ornithischia: Pachycephalosauria) from the Upper Cretaceous of North America, *in*: Spencer G. Lucas and Andrew B. Heckert, editors, *Dinosaurs of New Mexico*. Albuquerque: New Mexico Museum of Natural History and Science, Bulletin 17, pp. 177–190.

_____, 2000b, *Stegoceras* revisited: *Journal of Vertebrate Paleontology*, 20 (Supplement to Number 3), Abstracts of Papers, Sixtieth Annual Meeting, p. 72A.

_____, 2003a, Revision of the dinosaur *Stegoceras* Lambe (Ornithischia, Pachycephalosauridae): *Ibid.*, 23 (1), pp. 181–207.

_____, 2003b, *Hanssuesia*, the correct generic name for "*Hanssussia*" Sullivan, 2003: *Ibid.*, 23 (3), p. 714.

Sullivan, Robert M., and Spencer G. Lucas, 2000, *Alamosaurus* (Dinosauria: Sauropoda) from the late Campanian of New Mexico and its significance: *Journal of Vertebrate Paleontology*, 20 (2), pp. 400–403.

_____, 2003a, Vertebrate faunal succession in the Upper Cretaceous, San Juan Basin, New Mexico, with implications for correlations within the North American Western Interior: *Ibid.*, 23 (Supplement to Number 3), Abstracts of Papers, Sixty-third Annual Meeting, p. 102A.

_____, 2003b, The Kirtlandian, a new land-vertebrate "age" for the Late Cretaceous of Western North America: *New Mexico Geological Society Guidebook, Geology of the Zuni Plateau, 2003*, pp. 369–377.

_____, 2004, The Kirtlandian land-vertebrate "age" and the end of Late Cretaceous dinosaur provincialism in the North American Western Interior as we know it: *Journal of Vertebrate Paleontology*, 24 (Supplement to Number 3), Abstracts of Papers, Sixty-fourth Annual Meeting, p. 120A.

Sullivan, Robert M., Spencer G. Lucas, and Dennis Braman, 2003, No Paleocene dinosaurs in the San Juan Basin, New Mexico: *2003 GSA Rocky Mountain Section, 55th Annual Meeting, 2003 Abstracts with Programs*, p. 15.

Suzuki, Daisuke, David B. Weishampel, and Nachio Minoura, 2004, *Nipponosaurus sachalinensis* (Dinosauria; Ornithopoda): anatomy and systematic position within Hadrosauridae: *Journal of Vertebrate Paleontology*, 24 (1), pp. 145–164.

Suzuki, Shigeru, Luis M. Chiappe, Gareth J. Dyke, Mahito Watabe, Rinchen Barsbold, and Khisigjaw Tsogtbaatar, 2002, A new specimen of *Shuvuuia deserti* Chiappe et al., 1998 from the Mongolian Late Cretaceous with a discussion of the relationships of Alvarezsaurids to other theropod dinosaurs: *Contributions to Science*, 494, pp. 1–8.

Sweetman, Steven C., 2004, The first record of velociraptorine dinosaurs (Saurischia, Theropoda) from the Wealden (Early Cretaceous, Barremian) of southern England: *Cretaceous Research*, 25, pp. 353–364.

Swinton, W. E., 1947, New discoveries of *Titanosaurus indicus* Lyd.: *Annals and Magazine of Natural History*, ser. 1, 14, pp. 112–123.

_____, 1965, *Fossil Birds*. London: Trustees of the British Museum (Natural History), vi, pages.

Swisher, C. C., III, Wang Xiaolin, Zhou Zhonghe, Wang Yuanqing, Jin Fan, Zhang Jiangyong, Xu Xing, Zhang Fucheng, and Wang Yuan, 2001, Further support for a Cretaceous age for the feathered-dinosaur beds of Liaoning, China: New ^{40}Ar/^{39}Ar dating of the Yixoan and Tuchengzi Formation: *Chinese Science Bulletin*, 47 (2), pp. 135–138.

Tang, Feng, Z.-X. Lou, Luo, Z.-H. Zhou, H.-L. You, A. Georgi, Z.-L. Tang, and X.-Z. Wang, 2001, Biostratigraphy and palaeoenvironment of the dinosaur-bearing sediments in Lower Cretaceous of Mazongshan area, Gansu Province, China: *Cretaceous Research*, 22, pp. 115–129.

Tanke, Darren H., 2004, Mosquitoes and mud: the 2003 Royal Tyrrell Museum of Palaeontology expedition to the Grande Prairie Region (northwestern Alberta, Canada): *Alberta Palaeontological Society Bulletin*, 19 (2), pp. 3–30.

Tanke, Darren H., and Andrew Farke, 2002, Bone resorption, bone lesions, and extra fenestrae in ceratopsid dinosaurs: *Journal of Vertebrate Paleontology*, 23 (Supplement to Number 3), Abstracts of Papers, Sixty-second Annual Meeting, p. 133A.

_____, Cranial abnormalities in horned dinosaurs: disease and normal biological processes — not combat wounds: *Alberta Palaeontological Society, Seventh Annual Symposium, "Fossils in Motion," Abstracts*, pp. 78–81.

Taquet, Philippe, 1976, Géologie et Paléontologie du Gisement de Gadoufaoua (Aptien du Niger): Cahiers de Paléontologie. Paris: *Editions du Centre National de la Recherche Scientifique*, pp. 1–191.

Taquet, Philippe, and Dale A. Russell, 1998, New data on spinosaurid dinosaurs from the Early Cretaceous of the Sahara: *Comptes Rendus des Séances de l'Académie des Sciences*, 327, pp. 347–353.

Tarsitano, S. F., A. P. Russell, F. Horne, C. Plummer, and K. Millerchip, 2000, On the evolution of feathers from an aerodynamic and constructional view point: *American Zoologist*, 40, pp. 676–686.

Tashiro, M., and K. Okuhira, 1993, Occurrence of *Trigonoides* from the Lower Cretaceous of Shikoku, and its significance: *Geological Reports of Shimane University*, 12, p. 109.

Taylor, P., 1992, Doctors try to diagnose dinosaur cancer: *Toronto Globe and Mail*, January 5, pp. A1–A2.

Tereschenko, Victor S., 1991, On the reconstruction of the protoceratopsian vertebral column: *Palaeontoloicheski Zhurnal*, 1, pp. 85–97.

_____, 1997, Sexual dimorphism of the postcranial skeleton in a primitive ceratopsian dinosaur, *Protoceratops andrewsi*: *Third World Congress of Hepetology, August 2–20, 1997*, Prague, p. 207.

_____, 2001, Sexual dimorphism in the postcranial skeleton of horned dinosaurs

(Neoceratopsia, Protoceratopsidae) from Mongolia: *Palaeontoloicheski Zhurnal*, 4, pp. 84–95.

_____, 2004, On the heterocelous vertebrae in horned dinosaurs (Protoceratopsidae, Neoceratopsia): *Ibid.*, 38 (2), pp. 200–205 (translated from *Ibid.*, 2, pp. 81–86).

Tereschenko, V. S., and V. R. Alifanov, 2003, *Bainoceratops efremovi*, a new protoceratopsid dinosaur (Protoceratopsidae, Neoceratopsia) from the Bain-Dzak locality (South Mongolia): *Paleontological Journal*, 37 (3), pp. 293–302.

Theodor, Karl, 1830, Knochen vom *Pterodactylus* aus der Liasformation von Banz: *Frorips Notizen für Natur-und Heilkunde*, 632, 101 pages.

Therrien, Francois, 2004, Paleoenvironments and magnetostratigraphy of the Maastrichtian Sanpetru Formation (Romania): is the disappearance of dinosaurs indicative of the K/T Boundary?: *Journal of Vertebrate Paleontology*, 24 (Supplement to Number 3), Abstracts of Papers, Sixty-fourth Annual Meeting, p. 121A.

Therrien, Francois, Donald M. Henderson, and Christopher B. Ruff, 2003, Biomechanical models of theropod mandibles and implications for feeding behavior: *Journal of Vertebrate Paleontology*, 23 (Supplement to Number 3), Abstracts of Papers, Sixty-third Annual Meeting, p. 103A.

Thulborn, Richard A., 1971, Tooth wear and jaw action in the Triassic ornithischian dinosaur *Fabrosaurus*: *Journal of Zoology*, 164, pp. 165–179.

_____, 1973, Teeth of ornithischian dinosaurs from the Upper Jurassic of Portugal with description of a hypsilophodontid (*Phyllodon henkeli* gen. et sp. nov.) from the Guimarota Lignite: *Memoria Servicos Geologicos de Portugal (new series)*, 22, pp. 89–134.

_____, 1990, *Dinosaur Tracks*. London and New York: Chapman and Hall, xvii, 410 pages.

_____, 1993, Mimicry in ankylosaurid dinosaurs: *Record of the South Australian Museum*, 27, pp. 151–158.

_____, 2003, Wind-assisted flight of *Archaeopteryx*: *Neus Jahrbuch für Geologie und Paläontologie, Abhandlungen*, 229 (1), pp. 61–74.

Thulborn, Richard A., and Mary Wade, 1989, A footprint as a history of movement, *in*: David D. Gillette and Martin G. Lockley, editors, *Dinosaur Tracks and Traces*. Cambridge, New York, and Melbourne: Cambridge University Press, pp. 51–56.

Tidwell, Virginia, and Kenneth Carpenter, 2003, Braincase of an Early Cretaeous titanosauriform sauropod from Texas: *Journal of Vertebrate Paleontology*, 23 (1), pp. 176–180.

Tidwell, Virginia, Kenneth Carpenter, and William Brooks, 1999, New sauropod from the Lower Cretaceous of Utah, USA: *Oryctos*, 2, pp. 21–37.

Tischlinger, Helmut, 2003, Der Eichstätter *Archaeopteryx* im langwelligen UV-Licht: *Archaeopteryx*, 20, pp. 21–38.

Tokaryk, Tim T., Stephen L. Cumbaa, and John E. Storer, 1997, Early Late Cretaceous birds from Saskatchewan, Canada: the oldest diverse avifauna known from North America: *Journal of Vertebrate Paleontology*, 17 (1), pp. 172–176.

Tornier, Gustav, 1913, Reptilia (Palaontologie): *Handworterb. Naturwiss.*, 8, pp. 337–376.

Trotta, Marcelo N. F., Diogenes de Almeida Campos, and Alexander W. A. Kellner, 2002, Unusual caudal vertebral centra of a titanosaurid (Dinosauria, Sauropod) from the continental Upper Cretaceous of Brazil: *Boletim do Museu Nacional*, 64, pp. 1–11.

Tsuihiji, Takanobu, 2003, Evolutionary changes in attachments of the axial musculature in the occipital region in Marginocephalia (Dinosauria): *Journal of Vertebrate Paleontology*, 23 (Supplement to Number 3), Abstracts of Papers, Sixty-third Annual Meeting, p. 105A.

_____, 2004a, The ligament system in the neck of *Rhea americana* and its implications for the bifurcated neural spines of sauropod dinosaurs: *Ibid.*, 24 (1), pp. 165–172.

_____, 2004b, The neck of non-avian maniraptorans: how bird-like was the cervical musculature of the "bird-like" theropods?: *Journal of Vertebrate Paleontology*, 24 (Supplement to Number 3), Abstracts of Papers, Sixty-fourth Annual Meeting, p. 122A.

Tumanova, Tat'yana A., Yu L. Bolotsky, and Vladimir R. Alifanov, 2004, The first finds of armored dinosaurs in the Upper Cretaceous of Russia (Amur Region): *Paleontological Journal*, 38 (1), pp. 73–33 (translated from *Paleontologicheskii Zhurnal*, 1, 2004, pp. 68–72).

Tumarkin, Allison, and Peter Dodson, 1998, A heterochronic analysis of enigmatic ceratopsids: *Journal of Vertebrate Paleontology*, 18 (Supplement to Number 3), Abstracts of Papers, Fifty-eighth Annual Meeting, p. 83A.

Turner, C. E., and F. Peterson, 1999, Biostratigraphy of dinosaurs in the Upper Jurassic Morrison Formation of the Western Interior, U.S.A., *in*: David D. Gillette, editor, *Vertebrate Paleontology in Utah*, Utah Geological Survey, Miscellaneous Publication, 99–1, pp. 76–114.

Tykoski, Ronald, 2004, Ontogenetic stage assessment and the position of Coelophysoidea within basal Theropoda: *Journal of Vertebrate Paleontology*, 24 (Supplement to Number 3), Abstracts of Papers, Sixty-fourth Annual Meeting, p. 124A.

Tykoski, Ronald, and Timothy Rowe, 2004, Ceratosauria, *in*: David B. Weishampel, Peter Dodson, and Halszka Osmólska, editors, *The Dinosauria* (second edition). Berkeley and Los Angeles: University of California Press, pp. 47–70.

Tykoski, Ronald S., 1998, The osteology of *Syntarsus kayentakatae* and its implications for ceratosaurid phylogeny, M.S. thesis, University of Texas, Austin.

Ubilla, D. Perea M., and A. Rojas, 2003, First report of theropods from the Tacuarembó Formation (Late Jurassic–Early Cretaceous), Uruguay: *Alcheringa*, 27, pp. 79–83.

Uliana, M., and D. Dellapa, 1981, Estratigrafia y evolución paleoambiental de la sucesión Maestrichtiano-Eoterciaria del Engolfamiento Neuquino (Patagonia Septentrional): *Actas VIII Congreso Geologico Argentino*, 3, pp. 673–711.

Unwin, David M., 1995, Preliminary results of a phylogenetic analysis of the Pterosauria (Diapsida: Archosauria), *in*: Ailung Sun and Yuanqing Wang, editors, *Sixth Symposium on Mesozoic Terrestrial Ecosystems and Biota, short papers*. Beijing: China Ocean Press, pp. 175–177.

_____, 2001, An overview of the pterosaur assemblage from the Cambridge Greensand (Cretaceous) of Eastern England: *Mitteilungen Museum für Naturkunde der Humboldt-Universität zu Berlin, Geowissenschaftliche Reihe*, 4, pp. 189–221.

_____, 2002, On the systematic relationships of *Cearadactylus atrox*, an enigmatic Early Cretaceous pterosaur from the Santana Formation of Brazil: *Ibid.*, 5, pp. 239–263.

_____, 2003, On the phylogeny and evolutionary history of pterosaurs, *in*: Éric Buffetaut and Jean-Michel Mazin, editors, *Evolution and Palaeobiology of Pterosaurs*. London: The Geological Society, Special Publications, 217, pp. 140–190.

Unwin, David M., and Natalie N. Bakhurina, 2000, Pterosaurs from Russia, Middle Asia and Mongolia, *in*: M. J. Benton, M. A. Shishkin, D. M. Unwin, and E. N. Kurochkin, editors, *The Age of Dinosaurs in Russia and Mongolia*. Cambridge: Cambridge University Press, pp. 420–433.

Unwin, David M., and Junchang Lü, 1997, On *Zhejiangopterus* and the relationships of pterodactyloid pterosaurs: *Historical Biology*, 12, pp. 199–210.

Unwin, David M., Junchang Lü, and Natalie N. Bakhurina, 2000, On the systematic and stratigraphic significance of pterosaurs from the Lower Cretaceous Yixian Formation (Jehol Group) of Liaoning, China: *Mitteilungen Museum für Naturkunde der Humboldt-Universität zu Berlin, Geowissenschaftliche Reihe*, 3, pp. 181–206.

Unwin, David M., and Wolf-Dieter Heinrich, 1999, On a pterosaur jaw from the Upper Jurassic of Tendaguru (Tanzania): *Mitteilungen Museum für Naturkunde der Humboldt-Universität zu Berlin, Geowissenschaftliche Reihe*, 2, pp. 121–134.

Upchurch, Paul, 1993, The anatomy, phylogeny, and systematics of the sauropod dinosaurs, PhD dissertation, University of Cambridge, 489 pages (unpublished).

_____, 1995, The evolutionary history of sauropod dinosaurs: *Philosophical Transactions of the Royal Society of London*, Series B 349, pp. 365–390.

_____, 1997, Prosauropoda, *in*: Philip J. Currie and Kevin Padian, editors, *Encyclopedia of Dinosaurs*. San Diego: Academic Press, pp. 599–607.

_____, 1998, The phylogenetic relationships of sauropod dinosaurs: *Zoological Journal of the Linnean Society of London*, 124, pp. 43–103.

_____, 1999, The phylogenetic relationships of the Nemegtosauridae (Saurischia, Sauropoda): *Journal of Vertebrate Paleontology*, 19 (1), pp. 106–125.

Upchurch, Paul, and Paul M. Barrett, 2000, The taxonomic status of *Shanxia tianzhenensis* (Ornithischia, Ankylosauridae); a response to Sullivan: *Journal of Vertebrate Paleontology*, 20 (1), pp. 216–217.

Upchurch, Paul, Paul M. Barrett, and Peter Dodson, 2004, Sauropoda, *in*: David B. Weishampel, Peter Dodson and Halszka Osmólska, editors, *The Dinosauria*, second edition. Berkeley and Los Angeles: University of California Press, pp. 232–258.

Upchurch, Paul, Craig A. Hunn, and David B. Norman, 2002, An analysis of dinosaurian biogeography: evidence for the existence of vicariance and dispersal patterns caused by geological events: *Proceedings of the Royal Society of London*, 269, pp. 613–621.

Upchurch, Paul, and John Martin, 2002, The Rutland *Cetiosaurus*: the anatomy and relationships of the Middle Jurassic British sauropod dinosaur: *Palaeontology*, 45 (6), pp. 1049–1074.

———, 2003, The anatomy and taxonomy of *Cetiosaurus* (Saurischia, Sauropoda) from the Middle Jurassic of England: *Journal of Vertebrate Paleontology*, 23 (1), pp. 208–231.

Van Heerden, Jacques, 1979, The morphology and taxonomy of *Euskelosaurus* (Reptilia: Saurischia; Late Triassic) from South Africa: *Navors-Res. Nasl. Mus. Bloemfontein*, 4 (2), pp. 21–84, Bloemfontein.

———, Prosauropoda, *in*: James O. Farlow and Michael K. Brett-Surman, editors, *The Complete Dinosaur*. Bloomington and Indianapolis, Indiana University Press, pp. 242–263.

Van Itterbeeck, Jimmy, Valentina S. Markevich, and David J. Horne, 2004, The age of the dinosaur-bearing Cretaceous sediments at Dashuiguo, Inner Mongolia, P. R. China based on charophytes, ostracods and palynomorphs: *Cretaceous Research*, 25, pp. 391–409.

Van Valen, Leigh, 1969, What was the largest dinosaur?: *Copeia*, 3, pp. 624–626.

Varriale, Frank, 2004, Dental microwear in *Triceratops* and *Chasmosaurus* and its implication for jaw mechanics in Ceratopsidae: *Journal of Vertebrate Paleontology*, 24 (Supplement to Number 3), Abstracts of Papers, Sixty-fourth Annual Meeting, pp. 124A–125A.

Varriccho, David D., 1993, Bone microstructure of the Upper Cretaceous theropod dinosaur *Troodon formosus*: *Journal of Vertebrate Paleontology*, 13 (1), pp. 99–104.

———, 2002, A new bird from the Upper Cretaceous Two Medicine Formation of Montana: *Canadian Journal of Earth Sciences*, 39, pp. 19–26.

Varriccho, David J., and Luis M. Chiappe, 1995, A new enantiornithine bird from the Upper Cretaceous Two Medicine Formation of Montana: *Journal of Vertebrate Paleontology*, 15 (1), pp. 201–204.

Varriccho, David J., and Frankie D. Jackson, 2004, Two eggs sunny-side up: reproductive physiology in the dinosaur *Troodon formosus*, *in*: Philip J. Currie, Eva B. Kopelhus, Martin A. Shugar, and Joanna

L. Wright, 2004, editors, *Feathered Dragons: Studies on the Transition from Dinosaurs to Birds*. Bloomington and Indianapolis: Indiana University Press, pp. 215–233.

Varricchio, David J., Frankie Jackson, J. J. Borkowski, and John R. Horner, 1997, Nest and egg clutches of the dinosaur *Troodon formosus* and the evolution of avian reproductive traits: *Nature*, 385, pp. 247–250.

Varricchio, David J., and John R. Horner, 1993, Hadrosaurid and lambeosaurid bone beds from the Upper Cretaceous Two Medicine Formation of Montana: taphonomic and biologic implications: *Canadian Journal of Earth Sciences*, 30, pp. 997–1006.

Veldmeijer, André, 2002, Pterosaurs from the Lower Cretaceous of Brazil in the Stuttgart Collection: *Stuttgarter Beiträge zur Naturkunde, Serie B (Geologie und Paläontologie)*, 327, 27 pages.

———, 2003a, Description of *Coloborhynchus spielbergi* sp. nov. (Pterodactyloidea) from the Albian (Lower Cretaceous) of Brazil: *Scripta Geology*, 125, pp. 35–135.

———, 2003b, Preliminary description of a skull and wing of a Brazillian Cretaceous (Santana Formation; Aptian–Albian) pterosaur (Pterodactyloidea) in the collection of the AMNH: *PalArch. nl.*, vertebrate paleontology, 0 (0), pp. 1–12.

Veralli, C., and Jorge O. Calvo, 2004, New findings of carcharodontosaurid teeth on Futalognko quarry (Upper Turonian), north Barreales Lake, Neuquén, Argentina: *Ameghiana*, 40 (4), Suplemento, p. 74R.

Vickaryous, Matthew K., Teresa Maryańska, and David B. Weishampel, 2004, Ankylosauria, *in*: David B. Weishampel, Peter Dodson, and Halszka Osmólska, editors, *The Dinosauria* (second edition). Berkeley and Los Angeles: University of California Press, pp. 363–392.

Vickaryous, Matthew K., and Anthony P. Russell, 1993, A redescription of the skull of *Euoplocephalus tutus* (Archosauria: Ornithischia): a foundation for comparative and systematic studies of ankylosaurian dinosaurs: *Zoological Journal of the Linnean Society, London*, 137, pp. 157–186.

Vickaryous, Matthew K., Anthony P. Russell, and Philip J. Currie, 2001, Cranial ornamentation of ankylosaurs (Ornithischia: Thyreophora): reappraisal of developmental hypotheses, *in*: Kenneth Carpenter, editor, *The Armored Dinosaurs*. Bloomington and Indianapolis: Indiana University Press, pp. 318–340.

Vietti, Laura, and Scott Hartman, 2004, A new diplodocid braincase (Dinosauria: Sauropoda) from the Morrison Formation of north-western Wyoming: *Journal of Vertebrate Paleontology*, 24 (Supplement to Number 3), Abstracts of Papers, Sixty-fourth Annual Meeting, p. 125A.

Wade, Mary, 1989, The stance of dinosaurs and the Cossack Dancer syndrome, *in*: David D. Gillette and Martin G. Lockley, editors, *Dinosaur Tracks and Traces*. Cambridge: Cambridge University Press, pp. 73–82.

Wagner, Günter P., and Jacques A. Gauthier, 1999, 1,2,3 = 2,3,4: a solution to the problem of the homology of the digits of the avian hand: *Proceedings of the National Academy of Sciences*, 96, pp. 5111–5116.

Wagner, J. A. [Johann Andreas], 1851, Beschreinung eines Art von *Ornithocephalus* nebst kritischer Vergleichung der in der K. palaeontologischen Sammlung zur Munchen aufgestellten Arten aus dieser Gattung: *Abhandlungen der Bayerischen Akaddemie der Wissenschaften, math. pphysik. Kl*, 6, 64 pages.

———, 1860, Bemerkungen uber die Arten von Fischen und Saurien, Welche im untern wie im obern Lias zugleich vorkommen sollen: *Sitzungsberichte der Königl Bayerischen Akademie der Wissenschaften Mathematisch-Physikalische Klasse*, 1860, pp. 36–52.

———, 1861a, Charakteristik einer neuen Flugeidesche *Pterodactylus elegans*: *Sitzungsberichte Bayerischen Akademie der Wissenschaften Mathematisch-naturwissenschaftliche*, Abteilung 1, pp. 363–365.

———, 1861b, Uber ein neues, angeblich mit Vogelfedern versehenes Reptil aus dem Solnhofener lithographischen Schiefer: *Ibid.*, 2, pp. 146–154.

———, 1861c, Neue Beitrage zur Kenntniss der urweltlichen der urweltlichen Fauna des lithographischen Schiefers. II. Schildkroten und Saurier: *Ibid.*, 9, pp. 65–124.

Wagner, Jonathan A., 2004, Hard-tissue homologies and their consequences for interpretation of the cranial crests of lambeosaurine dinosaurs (Dinosauria: Hadrosauria): *Journal of Vertebrate Paleontology*, 24 (Supplement to Number 3), Abstracts of Papers, Sixty-fourth Annual Meeting, pp. 125A–126A.

Waldman, M., 1974, Megalosaurid from the Bajocian (Middle Jurassic) of Dorset: *Palaeontology*, 17 (2), pp. 325–339.

Wall, William P., and Peter M. Galton, 1979, Notes on pachycephalosaurid dinosaurs (Reptilia: Ornithischia) from North America, with comments on their status as ornithopods: *Canadian Journal of Earth Sciences*, 16 (6), pp. 1176–1186.

Wang Xiaolin, and Lü Jun-Chang, 2001, Discovery of a pterodactyloid pterosaur from the Yixian Formation of western Liaoning, China: *Chinese Science Bulletin*, 46 (13), pp. 1112–1117.

Wang Xiaolin, and Xu Xing, 2001a, A new genus and species of iguanodont from the Yixian Formation in Liaoxi: Yang's Jinzhou dragon [Jinzhousaurus yangi]: *Chinese Science Bulletin* 46 (5), pp. 419–423.

Wang Xiao-Lin, and Zhou Zhong-He, 2002 [English translation, 2003], A new pterosaur (Pterodactyloidea, Tapejaridae) from the Early Cretaceous Jiufotang Formation of western Liaoning, China and its implications for biostratigraphy: *Chinese Science Bulletin*, 48 (1), pp. 16–23.

———, 2003, Two new pterodactyloid pterosaurs from the Early Cretaceous Jiufotang Formation of western Liaoning, China: *Vertebrata PalAsiatica*, 41 (1), pp. 34–41.

Wang Xiao-Lin, Zhou Zhong-He, Zhang Fucheng, and Xu Xing, 2002, A nearly completely articulated rhamphorhynchoid pterosaur with exceptionally well-preserved wing membranes and "hairs" from Inner Mongolia, northeast China: *Chinese Science Bulletin*, 47 (3), pp. 226–230.

Warren, David, and Kenneth Carpenter, 2004, A large nodosaurid ankylosaur from the Cedar Mountain Formation of Utah: *Journal of Vertebrate Paleontology*, 24 (Supplement to Number 3), Abstracts of Papers, Sixty-fourth Annual Meeting, p. 126A.

Wedel, Mathew J., 2001, The evolution of vertebral pneumaticity in the Sauropoda: *Journal of Vertebrate Paleontology*, 21 (Supplement to Number 3), Abstracts of Papers, Sixty-first Annual Meeting, p. 111A.

_____, 2003a, Vertebral pneumaticity, air sacs, and the physiology of sauropod dinosaurs: *Paleobiology*, 29 (2), pp. 243–255.

_____, 2003b, The evolution of vertebral pneumaticity in sauropod dinosaurs: *Journal of Vertebrate Paleontology*, 23 (2), pp. 344–357.

_____, 2004, Skeletal pneumatics in saurischian dinosaurs and implications for mass estimates: *Ibid.*, 24 (Supplement to Number 3), Abstracts of Papers, Sixty-fourth Annual Meeting, p. 127A.

Wedel, Mathew J., Richard L. Cifelli, and R. Kent Sanders, 2000a, *Sauroposeidon proteles*, a new sauropod from the early Cretaceous of Oklahoma: *Journal of Vertebrate Paleontology*, 20 (1), pp. 109–114.

_____, 2000b, Osteology, paleobiology, and relationships of the sauropod dinosaur Sauroposeidon: *Acta Paleontologica Polonica*, 45 (4), pp. 343–390.

Wegweiser, Marilyn, Brent Breithaupt, Loren E. Babcock, and Ethan Skinner, 2003, Dinosaur fossils from This Side of Hell, Wyoming; paleoenvironmental implications of an Upper Cretaceous Konservat-Lagerstätt in the Lance Formation: *Journal of Vertebrate Paleontology*, 23 (Supplement to Number 3), Abstracts of Papers, Sixty-third Annual Meeting, p. 108A.

Wegweiser, Marilyn, Brent Breithaupt, and Ralph Chapman, 2004, Attack behavior of tyrannosaurid dinosaur(s): Cretaceous crime scenes, really old evidence, & "smoking guns": *Journal of Vertebrate Paleontology*, 24 (Supplement to Number 3), Abstracts of Papers, Sixty-fourth Annual Meeting, p. 127A.

Weishampel, David B., 1984, Evolution of jaw mechanisms in ornithopod dinosaurs: *Advances in Anatomy, Embryology, and Cell Biology*, 87, pp. 1–110.

_____, 1986, The hadrosaurid dinosaurs from the Iren Dabasu Fauna (People's Republic of China, Late Cretaceous): *Journal of Vertebrate Paleontology*, 6 (1), pp. 38–45.

_____, 1990, Dinosaurian distribution, *in*: David B. Weishampel, Peter Dodson and Halszka Osmólska, editors, *The Dinosauria*. Berkeley and Los Angeles: University of California Press, pp. 63–139.

_____, 2004, Ornithischia, *in*: David B. Weishampel, Peter Dodson, and Halszka Osmólska, editors, *The Dinosauria* (second edition). Berkeley and Los Angeles: University of California Press, pp. 323–324.

Weishampel, David B., Paul M. Barrett, Rodolfo A. Coria, Jean Le Loeuff, Xu Xing, Xijin Zhao, Ashok Sahni, Elizabeth M. P. Gomani, and C. R. Noto, 2004, Dinosaur distribution, *in*: David B. Weishampel, Peter Dodson, and Halszka Osmólska, editors, *The Dinosauria* (second edition). Berkeley and Los Angeles: University of California Press, pp. 517–606.

Weishampel, David B., and Ralph Chapman, 1990, Morphometric study of *Plateosaurus* from Trössingen (Baden-Wurttemberg, Federal Republic of Germany), *in*: Kenneth Carpenter and Philip J. Currie, editors, *Dinosaur Systematic: Approaches and Perspectives*. New York: Cambridge University Press, pp. 43–52.

David Weishampel B., David B., Peter Dodson, and Halszka Osmólska, 2004, editors, *The Dinosauria*. Berkeley and Los Angeles: University of California Press, pp. xvi, 733 pages.

_____, *Ibid.* (second edition). Berkeley and Los Angeles: University of California Press, viii, pp. 861 pages.

Weishampel, David B., Dan Grigorescu, and David B. Norman, 1991, The dinosaurs of Transylvania: island biogeography in the Late Cretaceous of western Romania: *National Geographic Research and Exploration*, 7, pp. 196–215.

Weishampel, David B., and John R. Horner, 1990, Hadrosauridae, *in*: David B. Weishampel, Peter Dodson, and Halszka Osmólska, editors, *The Dinosauria*. Berkeley and Los Angeles: University of California Press, pp. 534–561.

Weishampel, David B., Coralia-Maria Jianu, Z. Csiki, and David B. Norman, 1998, *Rhabdodon*, an unusual euornithopod dinosaur from the Late Cretaceous of western Romania: *Journal of Vertebrate Paleontology*, 18 (Supplement to Number 3), Abstracts of Papers, Fifty-eighth Annual Meeting, p. 85A.

Weishampel, David B., and Coralia-Maria Jianu, 2000, Plant-eaters and ghost lineages: dinosaurian herbivory revisited, *in*: Hans-Dieter Sues, editor, *Evolution of Herbivory in Terrestrial Vertebrates: Perspectives from the Fossil Record*. Cambridge: Cambridge University Press, pp. 123–143.

_____, 2003, Osteology and phylogeny of *Zalmoxes* (N. G.), an unusual euornithopod dinosaur from the latest Cretaceous of Romania: *Journal of Systematic Palaeontology*, 1 (2), pp. 65–123.

Weishampel, David B., David B. Norman, and Dan Grigorescu, 1993, *Telmatosaurus transsylvanicus* from the Late Cretaceous of Romania: the most basal hadrosaurid dinosaur: *Palaeontology*, 36, pp. 361–385.

Weishampel, David B., Francois Therrien, Donald M. Henderson, and Christopher Ruff, 2004, Bite force estimates for non-avian theropods: *Journal of Vertebrate Paleontology*, 24 (Supplement to Number 3), Abstracts of Papers, Sixty-fourth Annual Meeting, pp. 127A–128A.

Weishampel, David B., and Judith B. Weishampel, 1983, Annotated localities of ornithopod dinosaurs: implications to

Mesozoic paleobiogeography: *The Mosasaur*, 1, pp. 43–87.

Weishampel, David B., and Lawrence M. Witmer, 1990, Heterodontosauridae, *in*: David B. Weishampel, Peter Dodson, and Halszka Osmólska, editors, *The Dinosauria*. Berkeley and Los Angeles: University of California Press, pp. 486–497.

Wellnhofer, Peter, 1970, Die Pterodactyloidea (Pterosauria) der Oberjura-Plattenkalke Süddeutschlands). *Bayerische Akademie der Wissenschaften, Mathematisch-Wissenchaftlichen Klasse, Abhandlungen*, 141, 133 pages.

_____, 1974, *Campylognathoides liassicus* (Quenstedt), an Upper Liassic pterosaur from Holzmaden — the Pittsburgh specimen: *Annals of the Carnegie Museum of Natural History*, 45 (2), pp. 5–34.

_____, 1974–1975, Die Rhamphorhynchoidea (Pterosauria) der Oberjura Plattenkalke Süddeutschlands. I. Allgemeine Skelettmorphologie: *Palaeontographica* A 148, pp. 1–33; II. System atische Beschreibung *Paläontographica* A 148, pp. 132–86; III. Palökologie und stammesgeschichte *Paläontographica* A 149, pp. 1–30.

_____, 1977, *Arapedactylus debmi* nov. gen., nov. sp., ein neur Flugsaurier aus der Unterkreide von Brasilien: *Mittelungen der Bayerischen Staatssammlung für Paläontologie und historische Geologie*, 17, pp. 157–167, Munich.

_____, 1978, Pterosauria, *in*: Peter Wellnhofer, editor, *Handbuch der Paläoherpetologie*, 19. Stuttgart: Gustav Ficsher Verlag, 82 pages.

_____, 1985, Neue pterosaurier aus der Santana Formation (Apt) der Chapada do Araripe Brasilien: *Palaeontographica*, A, 187, pp. 105–182, Stuttgart.

_____, 1987, New crested pterosaurs from the Lower Cretaceous of Brazil: *Mittelungen der Bayerischen Staatssammlung für Paläontologie und historische Geologie*, 27, pp. 175–186.

_____, 1991a, Weitere pterosaurierfunde aus der Santana-Formation (Apt) der Chapada do Araripe, Brasilien: *Palaeontographica*, Abt. A, 215, pp. 43–101, Stuttgart.

_____, 1991b, *The Illustrated Encyclopedia of Pterosaurs*. New York: Crescent Books, 192 pages.

_____, 1993, Das siebte Exemplar von *Archaeopteryx* aus den Solnhofer Schichten: *Archaeopteryx*, 11, pp. 1–47.

_____, 1994, Prosauropod dinosaurs from the Feuerletten (Middle Norian) of Ellingen near Weissenberg in Bavaria: *Revue de Paléobiologie*, 7, pp. 263–271.

_____, 2003, A Late Triassic pterosaur from the northern Calcareous Alps (Tyrol, Austria): *in*: Éric Buffetaut and Jean-Michel Mazin, editors, *Evolution and Palaeobiology of Pterosaurs*. London: The Geological Society, Special Publications, 217, pp. 5–22.

_____, 2004, The plumage of *Archaeopteryx*: feathers of a dinosaur?, *in*: Philip J. Currie, Eva B. Kopelhus, Martin A. Shugar, and Joanna L. Wright, 2004, editors, *Feathered Dragons: Studies on the Transi-*

tion from Dinosaurs to Birds. Bloomington and Indianapolis: Indiana University Press, pp. 282–300.

Welles, Samuel P., 1983, Allosaurus (Saurischia, Theropoda) not yet in Australia: Journal of Paleontology, 57 (2), pp. 196–197.

_____, 1984, Dilophosaurus wetherilli (Dinosauria, Theropoda) — osteology and comparisons: Palaeontographica, Abteilung A, 185, pp. 88–180.

Welles, Samuel P., and Robert A. Long, 1974, The tarsus of theropod dinosaurs: Annals of the South African Museum, 64, pp. 191–218.

Welman, J., 1999, The basicranium of a basal prosauropod from the Euskelosaurus range zone and thoughts on the origin of dinosaurs: Journal of African Earth Sciences, 29, pp. 227–232.

Welty, Joel Carl, and Luis Baptista, 1988, The Life of Birds. Fort Worth, TX: Saunders College, 698 pages.

Werning, Sarah, 2004, Osteohistology of Tenontosaurus (Early Cretaceous, North America): Journal of Vertebrate Paleontology, 24 (Supplement to Number 3), Abstracts of Papers, Sixty-fourth Annual Meeting, p. 128A.

Westphal, F., and J. P. Durand, 1990, Magnétostratigraphie des séries continentales fluvio-lacustres du Crétacé supérieur dans le synclinal de l'Arc (région d'Aix-en-Provence, France): Bulletin, Societé Géologique de France, (8), VI, 4, pp. 609–620.

Wetmore, Alexander, 1962, Notes on fossil and subfossil birds: Smithsonian Miscellaneous Collection, 145 (2), pp. 1–17.

Whitten, D. G. A., and J. R. V. Brooks, editors, 1972, The Penguin Dictionary of Geology. London: Penguin Books, 520 pages.

Wichmann, R., 1916, Las capas con dinosaurios en la costa sur del Río Negro, Frente a General Roca: Revisto de la Sociedad Argentina de Ciencias Naturales, 2, pp. 258–262.

Wild, Rupert, 1971, Dorygnathus mistelgauensis n. sp., ein neur Flugsaurier aus dem Lias Epsilon von Mistelgau (Frankischer Jura): Geol. Blatter NO-Bayern, 21 (4), pp. 178–195.

_____, 1978, Die Flugsaurier (Reptilia, Pterosauria) aus der Oberen Trias von Cene Bei Bergamo, Italien: Bollettino Della Societa Paleontologica Italiana, 17 (2), pp. 176–256.

_____, 1984, A new pterosaur (Reptilia, Pterosauria) from the Upper Triassic (Norian) of Friuli, Italy: Gortania-Atti Museo Friul. Storia Nat, 5, pp. 45–62.

_____, 1990, Ein Flugsaurierest (Reptilia, Pterosauria) aus der Unterkreide (Hauterivian) von Hannover (Niedersachen): Neus Jahrbuch für Geologie und Paläontologie, Abhandlungen, 181 (1–3), pp. 241–245.

_____, 1994, A juvenile specimen of Eudimorphodon ranzii Zambelli (Reptilia, Pterosauria) from the Upper Triassic (Norian) of Bergamo: Rivista Museo civico di Scienze Naturali "E." Caffi, 16, pp. 95–120.

Wilhite, Ray, 2002, Tales tails can tell: form, function, and distribution of diplodocid chevrons within the Dinosauria, in: The Mesozoic in Wyoming, Tate 2002. Casper,

WY: The Geological Museum, Casper College, pp. 132–154.

Wilkinson, M., 1994, Common cladistic information and its consensus representation: reduced Adams and cladistic consensus trees and profiles: Systematic Biology, 43, pp. 343–368.

Williams, Daniel, and Marilyn Wegweiser, 2003, Phenetic distinctions of lambeosaurine ribs from This Side of Hell, Wyoming: Journal of Vertebrate Paleontology, 23 (Supplement to Number 3), Abstracts of Papers, Sixty-third Annual Meeting, p. 110A.

Williamson, Thomas E., and Thomas D. Carr, 2003a, The Elephant Butte Tyrannosaurus rex: New Mexico Geology, 25 (2).

_____, 2003b, A new genus of derived pachycephalosaurian from western North America: Journal of Vertebrate Paleontology, 22 (4), pp. 799–801.

Williamson, Thomas E., and Anne Weil, 2003, Latest Cretaceous dinosaurs in the San Juan Basin, New Mexico: Journal of Vertebrate Paleontology, 23 (Supplement to Number 3), Abstracts of Papers, Sixty-third Annual Meeting, p. 110A.

Williston, Samuel Wendell, 1903, On the osteology of Nyctosaurus (Nyctodactylys) with notes on American pterosaurs: Field Columbian Museum, Geological Series, Publication 78, 2 (3), pp. 125–163.

Wilson, Jeffrey A., 1998, Evolution and phylogeny of sauropod dinosaurs: Journal of Vertebrate Paleontology, 18 (Supplement to Number 3), Abstracts of Papers, Fifty-eighth Annual Meeting, pp. 86A–87A.

_____, 1999a, The evolution and phylogeny of sauropod dinosaurs: PhD dissertation. University of Chicago, 384 pages.

_____, 1999b, A nomenclature for vertebral laminae in sauropods and other saurischian dinosaurs: Journal of Vertebrate Paleontology, 19 (4), pp. 639–653.

_____, 2002a, Sauropod dinosaur phylogeny: critique and cladistic analysis: Zoological Journal of the Linnean Society, 136, pp. 217–276.

_____, 2002b, A revision of the genus Titanosaurus (Dinosauria: Sauropoda) and its implications for titanosaur systematics: Journal of Vertebrate Paleontology, 23 (Supplement to Number 3), Abstracts of Papers, Sixty-second Annual Meeting, p. 120A.

_____, 2004, A redescription of the Mongolian sauropod Nemegtosaurus mongoliensis Nowinski (Dinosauria: Saurischia) and comments on Late Cretaceous sauropod diversity: Ibid., 24 (Supplement to Number 3), Abstracts of Papers, Sixty-fourth Annual Meeting, p. 130A.

Wilson, Jeffrey A., and Matthew T. Carrano, 1999, Titanosaurs and the origin of "wide-guage" trackways: a biomechanical and systematic perspective on sauropod locomotion: Paleobiology, 25, pp. 252–267.

Wilson, Jeffrey A., and Daniel Fisher, 2003, Are manus-only sauropod trackways evidence of swimming, sinking, or wading?: Journal of Vertebrate Paleontology, 23 (Supplement to Number 3), Abstracts of Papers, Sixty-third Annual Meeting, p. 111A.

Wilson, Jeffrey A., Ricardo N. Martinez, and Oscar Alcober, 1999, Distal tail segment of a titanosaur (Dinosauria: Sauropoda) from the Upper Cretaceous of Mendoza, Argentina: Journal of Vertebrate Paleontology, 19 (3), pp. 591–594.

Wilson, Jeffrey A., and Paul C. Sereno, 1998, Early evolution and higher-level phylogeny of sauropod dinosaurs: Journal of Vertebrate Paleontology, 15 (Supplement to Number 2), Society of Vertebrate Paleontology Memoir 5, 68 pages.

Wilson, Jeffrey A., Paul C. Sereno, Suresh Srivastava, Devendre K. Bhatt, Ashu Khosla, and Ashok Sahni, 2003, A new abelisaurid (Dinosauria, Theropoda) from the Lameta Formation (Cretaceous, Maastrichtian) of India: Contributions from the Museum of Paleontology, The University of Michigan, 31 (1), pp. 1–42.

Wilson, Jeffrey A., and M. B. Smith, 1996, New remains of Amphicoelias Cope (Dinosauria: Sauropoda) from the Upper Jurassic of Montana and diplodocid phylogeny): Journal of Vertebrate Paleontology, 16 (Supplement to Number 3), Abstracts of Papers, Fifty-sixth Annual Meeting, p. 73A.

Wilson, Jeffrey A., and Paul Upchurch, 2003, A revision of Titanosaurus Lydekker (Dinosauria — Sauropoda), the first dinosaur genus with a "Gondwanan" distribution: Journal of Systematic Palaeontology, 1 (3), pp. 125–160.

Wiman, Carl, 1925, Über Pterodactylus Westmani und andere Flug saurier: Bull. Geol. Inst. Univ. Upsalla, 20, pp. 1–38.

_____, 1929, Die Kreide-Dinosaurier aus Shantung: Palaeontologia Sinica, Series C, 6 (1), pp. 1–67.

Wings, Oliver, 2003, The function of gastroliths in dinosaurs — new considerations following studies on extant birds: Journal of Vertebrate Paleontology, 23 (Supplement to Number 3), Abstracts of Papers, Sixty-third Annual Meeting, p. 111A.

_____, 2004, The distribution of gastroliths in dinosaurs, including birds, and the implications for gastrolith function: 13th Symposium on Vertebrate Palaeontology and Comparative Anatomy, Papers, p. 28.

Winkler, Dale A., Louis Jacobs, Y. Lee, and Phillip A. Murry, 1995, Sea level fluctuation and terrestrial faunal change in North-Central Texas, in: Ailung Sun and Yuanqing Wang, editors, Sixth Symposium on Mesozoic Terrestrial Ecosystems and Biota, short papers. Beijing: China Ocean Press, pp. 175–177.

Winkler, Dale A., Louis L. Jacobs, and Phillip A. Murry, 1997, Jones Ranch: An Early Cretaceous sauropod bone-bed in Texas: Journal of Vertebrate Paleontology, 17 (Supplement to Number 3), Abstracts of Papers, Fifty-seventh Annual Meeting, p. 85A.

Witmer, Lawrence M., 1995, The extant phylogenetic bracket and the importance of reconstructing soft tissue in fossils: in: J. J. Thomason, editor, Functional Morphology in Vertebrate Paleontology. Cambridge: Cambridge University Press, pp. 19–33.

_____, 2003, Narial anatomy of ankylosaurian

dinosaurs: osteology and soft-tissue reconstruction: *Journal of Vertebrate Paleontology*, 23 (Supplement to Number 3), Abstracts of Papers, Sixty-third Annual Meeting, pp. 111A–112A.

———, 2004, The ear region, cerebral endocast, and cephalic sinuses of the abelisaurid theropod dinosaur *Majungatholus*: *Ibid.*, 24 (Supplement to Number 3), Abstracts of Papers, Sixty-fourth Annual Meeting, p. 131A.

Witzke, Brian, 2003, Interpretations of North American Cretaceous dinosaur diversity trends: *Journal of Vertebrate Paleontology*, 23 (Supplement to Number 3), Abstracts of Papers, Sixty-third Annual Meeting, p. 112A.

Wolfe, Douglas, Steve Beekman, Dan McGuiness, Tom Robira, and Robert Denton, 2004, Taphonomic characterization of a *Zuniceratops* bone bed from the Middle Cretaceous (Turonian) Moreno Hill Formation: *Journal of Vertebrate Paleontology*, 24 (Supplement to Number 3), Abstracts of Papers, Sixty-fourth Annual Meeting, p. 131A.

Wolff, Ewan, and John R. Horner, 2003, The first occurrence of *Orodromeus makelai* postcrania from the late–Campanian Judith River Formation of eastern Montana: *Journal of Vertebrate Paleontology*, 23 (Supplement to Number 3), Abstracts of Papers, Sixty-third Annual Meeting, p. 112A.

Woodward, Arthur Smith, 1901, On some extinct reptiles from Patagonia, of the genera *Miolania*, *Dinilysia*, and *Genyodectes*: *Proceedings of the Zoological Society of London, 1901*, pp. 169–184.

———, 1902, On two skulls of the ornithosaurian *Rhamphorhynchus*: *The Annals and Magazine of Natural History*, Seventh Series, 49, pp. 1–5.

———, 1908, Note on a megalosaurian tibia from the Lower Lias of Wilmcote, Warwickshire: *Ibid.*, 8 (1), pp. 257–259.

Woodward, John, 1905, On parts of the skeleton of *Cetiosaurus leedsi*, a sauropodous dinosaur from the Oxford clay of Peterborough: *Proceedings of the Zoological Society of London*, 1905, pp. 232–243.

Xu Xing, 2002, Deinonychosaurian fossils from the Jehol Group of western Liaoning and the coelurosaurian evolution. PhD dissertation, Chinese Academy of Sciences.

Xu Xing, Yen-Nien [Yennien] Cheng, Xio-Lin [Xiaolin] Wang, and Chun-Hsiang [Chunshian] Chang, 2002, An unusual oviraptorosaurian dinosaur from China: *Nature*, 419, pp. 291–293.

———, 2003, Pygostyle-like structure from *Beipiaosaurus* (Theropoda, Therizinosauridae) from the Lower Cretaceous Yixian Formation of Liaoning, China: *Acta Geologica Sinica*, 77 (3), pp. 294–298.

Xu Xing, Peter J. Makovicky, Xiao-lin Wang, Mark A. Norell, and Hai-lu You, 2002, A ceratopsian dinosaur from China and the early evolution of Ceratopsia: *Nature*, 416, pp. 314–317.

Xu, Xing, and Mark A. Norell, 2004, A new troodontid dinosaur from China with avian-like sleeping posture: *Nature*, 431, pp. 838–841.

Xu, Xing, Mark A. Norell, Xuewen Kuang, Xiaolin Wang, Qi Zhao, and Chengkai Jia, 2004, Basal tyrannosauroids from China and evidence for protofeathers in tyrannosauroids: *Nature*, 431, pp. 680–684.

Xu, Xing, Mark A. Norell, X.-L. Wang, Peter J. Makovicky, and X.-C. Wu, 2002, A basal troodontid from the Early Cretaceous of China: *Nature*, 415, pp. 780–784.

Xu Xing, Zhi-lu Tang, and Xiao-lin [Xiaolin] Wang, 1999, A new therizinosauroid dinosaur with integumentary structures from China: *Nature*, 399, pp. 350–354.

———, 2004, A new troodontid (Theropoda: Troodontidae) from the Lower Cretaceous Yixian Formation of western Liaoning, China: *Acta Geologica Sinica*, 78 (1), pp. 22–26.

Xu, Xing, and Xiaolin Wang, 1988, New psittacosaur (Ornithischia, Ceratopsia) occurrence from the Yixian Formation of Liaoning, China and its stratigraphical significance: *Vertebrata PalAsiatica*, 36, pp. 147–158.

———, 2003, A new maniraptoran dinosaur from the Early Cretaceous Yixian Formation of western Liaoning: *Ibid.*, 41 (3), pp. 195–202.

———, 2004, A new dromaeosaur (Dinosauria: Theropoda) from the Early Cretaceous Yixian Formation of western Liaoning: *Ibid.*, 42 (2), pp. 111–119.

———, in submission, A new troodontid (Theropoda: Troodontidae) from the Lower Cretaceous Yixian Formation of western Liaoning, China: *Acta Geologica Sineca* (English edition).

Xu, Xing, Xiao-Lin Wang, and Xiao-Chun Wu, 1999, A dromaeosaurid dinosaur with a filamentous integument from the Yixian Formation of China: *Nature*, 401 (16), pp. 262–265.

Xu, Xing, Xiao-Lin Wang, and Xiao-Chun Wu, 1999, A dromaeosaurid dinosaur with a filamentous integument from the Yixian Formation of China: *Nature*, 401 (16), pp. 262–265.

Xu, Xing, Zhonghe Zhou, and Xiaolin Wang, 2000, The smallest known non-avian theropod dinosaur: *Nature*, 408, pp. 705–708.

Xu, Xing, Zhonghe Zhou, Xiaolin Wang, Xuewen Kuwang, Fucheng Zhang, and Xiangke Du, 2003, Four-winged dinosaurs from China: *Nature*, 421, pp. 335–340.

Xu, Xing, Xiao-Lin Wang, and Xiao-Chun Wu, 1999, A dromaeosaurid dinosaur with a filamentous integument from the Yixian Formation of China: *Nature*, 401 (16), pp. 262–265.

Xu, Xing, Xijin Zhao, and James M. Clark, 2001, A new therizinosaur from the Lower Jurassic (Lufeng Formation) of Yunnan, China: *Journal of Vertebrate Paleontology*, 21 (3), pp. 477–483.

Xu, Xing, Zhong-he Zhou, and Richard O. Prum, 2001, Branched integumental structures in *Sinornithosaurus* and the origin of feathers: *Nature*, 410, pp. 200–204.

Xu, Xing, Zhonghe Zhou, Fucheng Zhang, Xiaolin Wang, and Xuewen Kuang, 2004, Functional hind-wings conform to the hip-structure in dromaeosaurids: *Journal of Vertebrate Paleontology*, 24 (Supplement to Number 3), Abstracts of Papers, Sixty-fourth Annual Meeting, p. 133A.

Yadagiri, P., 2001, The osteology of *Kotasaurus yamanpalliensis*, a sauropod dinosaur from the Early Jurassic Kota Formation of India: *Journal of Vertebrate Paleontology*, 21 (2), pp. 242–252.

Yadagiri, P., and K. Ayyasami, 1979, A new stegosaurian dinosaur from the Upper Cretaceous sediments of south India: *Journal of the Geological Society of India*, 20, pp. 521–530.

Yang Seong-Young, Martin G. Lockley, R. Greben, Bruce R. Erickson, and Lim S. Y., 1995, Flamingo and ducklike bird tracks from the Late Cretaceous and Early Tertiary: evidence and implications: *Ichnos*, 4, pp. 21–34.

Yang, Zhungjian [formerly Young Chung-Chien], 1942, Fossil vertebrates from Kuangyuan, N. Szechuan, China: *Bulletin of the Geological Society of China*, 22 (3–4), pp. 293–309.

———, 1958, The dinosaurian remains of Laiyang, Shantung: *Palaeontologica Sinica*, series C., 16, pp. 1–138.

———, 1960, Fossil footprints in China: *Vertebrata PalAsiatica*, 4 (2), pp. 53–66.

———, 1964, On a new pterosaurian from Sinkiang, China: *Vertebrata PalAsiatica*, 8 (3), pp. 221–255.

———, 1973, Pterosaurs from Wuerho. Reports of paleontological expedition to Sinkian (II), pterosaurian fauna from Wuerho, Sinkiang: *Memoirs of the Institute of Vertebrate Paleontology and Paleoanthropology Academia Sinica*, 11, pp. 18–36.

Yang, Zhungjian [Young Chung-Chien], and X.-J. Zhao, 1964, On a new pterosaurian from Sinkiang, China: *Vertebrata PalAsiatica*, 8 (3), pp. 221–255.

———, 1972, *Mamenchisaurus hochuanensis* sp. nov.: *Institute of Vertebrate Paleontology and Paleoanthropology Monographs*, A (8), pp. 1–30.

———, 1973, Pterosaurs from Wuerho. Reports of Paleontological Expedition to Sinkiang (II), pterosaurian fauna from Wuerho, Sinkiang: *Memoirs of the Institute of Vertebrate Paleontology and Paleoanthropology Academia Sinica*, 11, pp. 18–36.

Yarkov, A. A., 2000, Candidate's Dissertation in Geography: Volgogr. Gos. Ped. Inst., Volgograd.

Yates, Adam M., 2001, A new look at *Thecodontosaurus* and the origin of sauropod dinosaurs: *Journal of Vertebrate Paleontology*, 21 (Supplement to Number 3), Abstracts of Papers, Sixty-first Annual Meeting, p. 116A.

———, 2003a, The species taxonomy of the sauropodomorph dinosaurs from the Löwenstein Formation (Norian: Late Triassic) of Germany: *Palaeontology*, 46 (2), pp. 317–337.

———, 2003b, A new species of the primitive dinosaur *Thecodontosaurus* (Saurischia: Sauropodomorpha) and its implications for the systematics of early dinosaurs: *Journal of Systematic Palaeontology*, 1 (1), pp. 1–42.

Bibliography

_____, 2004, *Anchisaurus polizelus* Hitchcock: the smallest known sauropod dinosaur and the evolution of gigantism amongst sauropodomorph dinosaurs: *Postilla*, 230, pp. 1–58.

Yates, Adam M., and James W. Kitching, 2003, The earliest known sauropod dinosaur and the first steps towards sauropod locomotion: *Proceedings of the Royal Society of London*, 270, pp. 1753–1758.

You, Hai-Lu, 2002, Mazongsham dinosaur assemblage from late Early Cretaceous of Northwest China: PhD dissertation, University of Pennsylvania, 171 pages.

You, Hai-Lu, and Peter Dodson, 2003, Redescription of neoceratopsian dinosaur *Archaeoceratops* and early evolution of Neoceratopsia: *Acta Palaeontological Polonica*, 46 (2), pp. 261–272.

_____, 2004, Basal Ceratopsia, 2004, *in*: David B. Weishampel, Peter Dodson, and Halszka Osmólska, editors, *The Dinosauria* (second edition). Berkeley and Los Angeles: University of California Press, pp. 478–493.

You Hailu, and Dong Zhiming, 2003, A new protoceratopsid (Dinosauria: Neoceratopsia) from the Late Cretaceous of Inner Mongolia, China: *Acta Geologica Sinica*, 77 (3), pp. 299–303.

Hou Hailu, Tang Feng, and Luo Zhexi, 2003, A new basal titanosaur (Dinosauria: Sauropoda) from the Early Cretaceous of China: *Acta Geologica Sineca*, 77 (4), pp. 424–429.

You Hailu, Ji Qiang, Li Jinglu, and Li Yinxian, 2003, A new hadrosauroid from the Mid-Cretaceous of Liaoning, China: *Acta Geologica Sinica*, 77 (2), pp. 148–154.

You Hailu, Ji Qiang, Matthew C. Lamanna, Li Jinglu, and Li Yinxian, 2004, A titanosaurian sauropod dinosaur with opisthocoelous caudal vertebrae from the Early Cretaceous of Liaoning Province, China: *Acta Geological Sinica*, 78 (4), pp. 907–911.

You, Hai-lu, Zhe-xi Luo, Neil H. Shubin, Lawrence M. Witmer, Zhi-lu Tang, and Feng Tang, 2003, The earliest-known duck-billed dinosaur from deposits of late Early Cretaceous age in northwest China and hadrosaur evolution: *Cretaceous Research*, 24, pp. 347–355.

You Hailu, Xu Xing, and Wang Xiaolin, 2003,

A new genus of Psittacosauridae (Dinosauria: Ornithopoda) and the origin and early evolution of marginocephalian dinosaurs: *Acta Geological Sinica*, 77 (1), pp. 15–20.

Young, D. Bruce, 2004, A significant *Triceratops* find in the Denver Basin: *Fossil News*, 10 (1), pp. 15–17.

Young, Jennifer, Steven Jabo, Peter Kroehler, and Matthew T. Carrano, 2004, Conservation and remounting of the Smithsonian's *Stegosaurus stenops* exhibit, USNM 8612: *Journal of Vertebrate Paleontology*, 24 (Supplement to Number 3), Abstracts of Papers, Sixty-fourth Annual Meeting, p. 133A.

Zambelli, Rocco, 1973, *Eudimorphodon ranzii* Gen. Nov., Sp. Nov., uno pterosauro Triassico: *Instituto Lombardo (Rend. Sc.)*, B, 107, pp. 27–32.

Zanno, Lindsay E., 2004, The pectoral girdle and forelimb of a primitive therizinosauroid (Theropoda: Maniraptora): new information on the phylogenetics and evolution of therizinosaurs: *Journal of Vertebrate Paleontology*, 24 (Supplement to Number 3), Abstracts of Papers, Sixty-fourth Annual Meeting, p. 134A.

Zanno, Lindsay E., and Scott D. Sampson, 2003, A new caenagnathid specimen from the Kaiparowits Formation (Late Campanian) of Utah: *Journal of Vertebrate Paleontology*, 23 (Supplement to Number 3), Abstracts of Papers, Sixty-third Annual Meeting, p. 113A.

Zappaterra, E., 1990, Carbonate paleogeographic sequences of the periadriatic region: *Boll. Soc. Geol. Ital.*, 109, pp. 5–20.

Zhang Fucheng, Per G. P. Ericson, and Zhonghe Zhou, 2004, Description of a new enantiornithine bird from the Early Cretaceous of Hebei, northern China: *Canadian Journal of Earth Sciences*, 41, pp. 1097–1107.

Zhang Fucheng, and Zhou Zhonghe, 2000, A primitive enantiornithine bird and the origin of feathers: *Science* 290, pp. 1955–1959.

Zhang Fucheng, Zhou Zhonghe, Hou Lianhi, and Gu Y., 2001, Early diversification of birds: evidence of a new opposite bird: *Chinese Science Bulletin*, 46 (11), pp. 945–950.

Zhao Zi-Kui, 2003, The nesting behavior of

troodontid dinosaurs: *Vertebrata PalAsiatica*, 41 (2), pp. 157–168.

Zhen Shuonan, and Chen W. Z. S., 1994, Dinosaur and bird foot prints from the Lower Cretaceous of Emei County, Sichuan, China: *Memoirs of the Beijing Natural History Museum*, 54, pp. 108–120.

Zhen, Shuonan, Zhang B., Chen W., and Zhu S., 1987, Bird and dinosaur footprints from the Lower Cretaceous of Emei County, Sichuan, *in*: *First International Symposium, Nonmarine Cretaceous Correlations*. Urumqi, Xiangiang, China.

Zhou, Zhonghe, 1995, Discovery of a new enantiornithine bird from the Early Cretaceous of Liaoning, China: *Vertebrata PalAsiatica*, 33 (2), pp. 99–113.

_____, 2002, A new and primitive enantiornithine bird from the Early Cretaceous of China: *Journal of Vertebrate Paleontology*, 22 (1), pp. 49–57.

Zhou Zhonghe, and Hou Lianhai, 2002, The discovery and study of Mesozoic birds in China, *in*: Luis M. Chiappe and Lawrence M. Witmer, editors, *Mesozoic Birds: Above the Heads of Dinosaurs*. Berkeley and Los Angeles: University of California Press, pp. 160–183.

Zhou, Zhonghe, Jin Fan, and Zhang Jianping, 1992, Preliminary report on a Mesozoic bird from Lianong, China: *Chinese Science Bulletin*, 37 (16), pp. 1,365–1,368.

Zhou, Zhonghe, and Fucheng Zhang, 2001, (Two new genera of ornithurine birds from the Early Cretaceous of Liaoxi involved in the origin of modern birds.]: *Kexue Tongbao*, 46 (5), pp. 371–377.

_____, 2002, Largest bird from the Early Cretaceous and its implications for the earliest avian ecological diversification: *Naturwissenschaften*, 89, pp. 34–38.

_____, 2003a, Anatomy of the primitive bird *Sapeornis chaoyangensis* from the Early Cretaceous of Liaoning, China: *Canadian Journal of Earth Sciences*, 40, pp. 731–747.

_____, 2003b, *Jeholornis* compared to *Archaeopteryx*, with a new understanding of the earliest avian evolution: *Naturwissenschaften*, 90, pp. 220–225.

Zinke, J., 1998, Small theropod teeth from the Upper Jurassic coal mine of Guimarota (Portugal): *Paläontologische Zeitschrift*, 72, pp. 179–189.

Index

Indexed below are genera and species; the names of selected authors, discoverers, and other persons; selected institutions, organizations, localities, sites, events, and miscellaneous places; and also relevant general topics that are discussed or appear in the text as well as in picture captions. Junior synonyms are cross-referenced to the currently most widely accepted senior synonym. Page numbers printed in **bold italics** indicate subjects shown or implied in illustrations, or names and topics mentioned or implied in picture captions or credits. Not indexed are dinosaurian taxa above the level of genus (e.g., Theropoda), and institutions referred to only as abbreviations used to designate catalogue numbers for fossil specimens (e.g., AMNH).

Index

Index

Index

Index

Index